The Window XP/2000 Answer Book

The Windows XP/2000 Answer Book

A Complete Resource from the Desktop to the Enterprise

John Savill

Addison-Wesley

Boston • San Francisco • New York • Toronto • Montreal
London • Munich • Paris • Madrid
Capetown • Sydney • Tokyo • Singapore • Mexico City

The publisher offers discounts on this book when ordered in quantity for special sales. For more information, please contact:

Pearson Education Corporate Sales Division
201 W. 103rd Street
Indianapolis, IN 46290
(800) 428-5331
corpsales@pearsoned.com

Visit AW on the Web: www.awprofessional.com

Library of Congress Cataloging-in-Publication Data

Savill, John, 1975—
The Windows XP/2000 answer book : a complete resource from the Desktop to the Enterprise / John Savill.
p. cm.
ISBN 0-321-11357-8 (alk. paper)
1. Microsoft Windows (Computer file) 2. Operating systems (Computers)
I. Title.
QA76.76.063 S3566 2003
005.4'4769—dc21 2002074445

ISBN 0-321-11357-8
Text printed on recycled paper
1 2 3 4 5 6 7 8 9 10—CRS—0605040302
First printing, October, 2002

Contents

For my wife Emmaline and son Kevin,
who are my whole life and
without whose learning to sleep through the night
this book would not have been possible (Kevin I mean! ;-)).

Introduction

Windows NT was inaugurated in 1993. Six versions later (3.1, 3.5, 3.51, 4.0, 2000, and XP), we are waiting for the release of Windows .NET, the server equivalent of the Windows XP workstation product. Windows .NET has the .NET framework built into the product (hence its name), but it's important to realize Windows .NET is just the next version of Windows 2000 Server (which includes Windows NT 5.0). When inspecting the version number of Windows XP, we see it as 5.1, which demonstrates it's actually quite a minor upgrade that does, however, include some useful changes.

As a result of Windows' ease of use and large feature set (and the Microsoft name), Windows is the corporate desktop of choice. Windows 9x and NT have finally merged with the release of Windows XP, meaning XP will also become the home desktop of choice. The server market remains Microsoft's goal, and while it has a good percentage of the market, Microsoft continues its assault. When .NET is released, 64-bit processor support will be added as well as a full Web Services implementation. With Windows here to stay, learning how to get the most out of it is critical. In the corporate setting in particular, Windows system administrators must deal with many common challenges and tasks, but until now, no one resource addresses all of them.

The goal of this book is to provide Windows users and system administrators with valuable skills for handling these day-to-day tasks and to provide proven solutions to the many common challenges. Just as the administrator is task driven, this book is focused on tasks. How do I execute RDISK in Windows 2000? How do I configure Remote Assistance? Hundreds of such frequently asked questions (FAQs) and their answers are provided in this book!

The tasks and challenges cover all facets of Windows, from the simple to the complex, and should appeal to both experienced and inexperienced administrators and users. When first using Windows, everyone has the same challenges (or issues, to use Microsoftspeak), such as

- How do I convert FAT to NTFS?
- What operating systems can be upgraded to Windows XP?
- How do I copy Group Policy Objects between domains?

Every answer is structured in a step-by-step format with examples and a complete description of the procedure.

You may know some of the answers in this book, but it is designed to appeal to everyone from the beginning user to an experienced system administrator. I hope that every reader will find something helpful and informative within the hundreds of answers to common questions.

How It Began

I've been using Windows NT since its first version, Windows 3.1; however, when I first used it, I had no idea! I realized I wasn't in Kansas when the system hung (which I know seems impossible ☺). So I pressed Ctrl+Alt+Del and instead of rebooting, a strange dialog was displayed. From this point, I was hooked and have been ever since, learning all I can and participating in the Windows NT beta programs since Windows NT 4.0. I'm currently on Windows .NET beta.

When I first started learning, I found the best way to find answers to my many questions was via the NT newsgroups. I saw many other users posting exactly the same questions, and so to help, I put together a list of FAQs and posted this list on my Logica Web page (where I worked at the time). I quickly began to get requests and suggestions from many other NT users, and over the past five years, I've expanded the FAQs and added details about various other components such as Internet Information Server (IIS), Internet security, Acceleration server, and Exchange server, which are all topics in this book. The Web version of the FAQ (http://www.windows2000faq.com) now gets millions of hits a month and is used as a vital resource by many large companies including U.S. government agencies and many large computer and financial institutions. It is due in part to the creation and up-to-date maintenance of this Web-based FAQ that I was awarded the Microsoft Most Valuable Professional Award (MVP) from 1997 through to 2000.

Turning the Web-based FAQ into a book seemed to be a natural and worthwhile progression, and the first edition was received very well. As I'd hoped, readers found the printed edition to be very useful, and in the book, they found information they had never seen on the Web.

Who Should Read This Book?

If you are using Windows NT, 2000, or XP and have questions or simply wish to increase your understanding, this book will contain something for you. This book is aimed at beginners and advanced administrators.

Ideally people will read this book from start to finish; however, many people who deal with a specific area of technology will want to read only those particular chapters.

Gaining an understanding of elements that you don't currently use will open up the true power of Windows and potentially give you new and more efficient ways to achieve your day-to-day tasks. I hope this book can serve as the one Windows reference guide that helps you succeed as a user and system administrator.

Organization of the Book

So you can get to the solutions quickly, I've structured the book so each entry is self-contained—that is, you don't have to read other FAQs to understand any one FAQ. The book starts off with the core chapters describing the basic concepts of Windows, including an explanation of how to install Windows, and then moves on to customization and descriptions of domain concepts and optional components.

Each chapter starts off with the basics. The subject of the chapter is discussed, where applicable installation issues are addressed, and then we move on to the more advanced configuration options and actions.

This book is a technical book; the answers are to the point and do not include extra narrative—when you need a solution, you need a solution. You are not interested in an amusing story about my cat (of which I have many)! When a description is useful, I provide one, and in all cases, the information provided is consistent with that needed to achieve your goal and where appropriate to solve your problem.

What Version of Windows Is Covered in This Book?

This book covers mainly Windows 2000 and XP, and thanks to their common core functionality, most FAQs apply to both operating systems. However, to be able to bring you information about the new features of XP, for example, some FAQs do not apply to Windows 2000. In addition, some functionally has changed so some FAQs that apply exclusively to Windows 2000 do not apply to XP. The book also contains some NT 4.0 FAQs that may not apply to other operating systems, and these FAQs are distinguished by the bold text "NT Only".

A Big Thanks to . . .

Most importantly, I'd like to thank my wife Emmaline who has always given me unconditional love and support. I want to thank her also for putting up with me "always being on that computer."

I'd like to thank the technical reviewer of this book, Goga Kukira, for her great work, for spotting all my mistakes, and providing exceptional feedback. I want to extend a big thanks to Stephane Thomas for keeping the whole thing together and everyone else at Addison-Wesley. Their patience and professionalism helped transform my rough draft manuscript into this masterpiece ☺. Also thanks to Mark Smith, Eric Shanfelt, Warren Pickett, Michele Crockett, Kristi Forren, and everyone else at Penton who has helped develop the Web version of the site.

Finally I'd like to thank my eight-month-old son Kevin for putting everything into perspective and bringing me so much joy.

Let's go. . . .

John Savill
Petts Wood, England
June 2002

1 CORE

Windows NT (both the Workstation and Server) is a 32-bit operating system. It is a preemptive, multitasking operating system, which means that the operating system controls allocation of CPU time, stopping one application from hanging the OS. NT supports multiple CPUs, providing true multitasking, using symmetrical multiprocessing, meaning the processors share all tasks, as opposed to asymmetrical multiprocessing, where the OS uses one CPU and the applications another. NT is also a fault-tolerant operating system, with each 32-bit application operating in its own virtual memory address space (4GB), which means one application cannot interfere with another's memory space.

Unlike earlier versions of Windows (such as Windows for Workgroups and Windows 95), NT is a complete operating system and not an addition to DOS.

NT supports different CPUs: Intel x86 and the new 64-bit chip IA64.

NT's other main plus is its security feature with a special NT filesystem (NTFS) that enables permissions to be set on files and directories.

FAQ 1.1 What does NT stand for?

NT actually stands for Northern Telecom, but Microsoft licensed it, and in the Windows sense, it stands for New Technology. It's also interesting to note its heritage:

RSX -> VMS -> ELN -> NT all major designs of David Cutler

Also VMS +1 letter = WNT (Windows NT) ☺ (aka HAL and IBM in 2001)

Another theory is that NT originally came from the engineers working on it. The abbreviation stands for "N-Ten," the code name for the i860 chip that NT was being tested on.

FAQ 1.2 What is the history of NT?

In the late 1980s, the Windows environment was created to run on the Microsoft DOS operating system. Microsoft and IBM joined forces to create a DOS replacement that would run on the Intel platform that led to the creation of OS/2, and at the same time, Microsoft was working on a more powerful operating system that would run on other processor platforms. The idea was that the new OS would be written in a high-level language (such as C) so it would be more portable.

Microsoft hired Dave Cutler (who also designed Digital's VMS) to head the team for the New Technology Operating System (NT ☺). Originally the new OS was to be called OS/2 NT.

In the early 1990s, Microsoft released version 3.0 of its Windows OS, which gained a large user base, and at this point, Microsoft and IBM disagreed on the future of their operating systems. IBM viewed Windows as a stepping stone to the superior OS/2, whereas Microsoft wanted to expand Windows to compete with OS/2, so they split. IBM kept OS/2, and Microsoft changed OS/2 NT to Windows NT.

NT was once called OS/3, and OS/2 V3, which I learned from an alpha tester for IBM Microsoft.

The first version of Windows NT (3.1) was released in 1993 and had the same GUI as the normal Windows operating system; however, it was a pure 32-bit OS but provided the ability to also run older DOS and Windows applications, as well as character-mode OS/2 1.3 programs.

For a detailed history of Windows NT, have a look at http://windowsnt.miningco.com.

FAQ 1.3 What is the NT boot process?

First, the files required for NT to boot are the following:

- NTLDR—This is a hidden, read-only system file that loads the operating system.
- BOOT.INI—This is read-only system file, used to build the boot loader operating system selection menu on Intel x86-based computers.
- BOOTSECT.DOS—This is a hidden file loaded by NTLDR if another operating system is selected.
- NTDETECT.COM—This is a hidden, read-only system file used to examine the hardware available and to build a hardware list.
- NTBOOTDD.SYS—This file is used only by systems that boot from a SCSI disk.

The common boot sequence files are the following:

- NTOSKRNL.EXE—This file is the Windows NT kernel.
- SYSTEM—This file is a collection of system configuration settings.

- Device drivers—These are files that support various device drivers.
- HAL.DLL—This file contains the hardware abstraction layer software.

The boot sequence is as follows:

1. Power-on self test (POST) routines are run.
2. The master boot record is loaded into memory and the program is run.
3. The boot sector from active partition is loaded into memory.
4. NTLDR is loaded and initialized from the boot sector.
5. The processor is changed from real mode to 32-bit flat memory mode.
6. NTLDR starts the appropriate minifile system drivers. Minifile system drivers are built into NTLDR and can read FAT or NTFS.
7. NTLDR reads the BOOT.INI file. NTLDR loads the operating system selected; one of two things happen:
   - If Windows NT is selected, NTLDR runs NTDETECT.COM.
   - If an operating system other than NT is selected, NTLDR loads and runs BOOTSECT.DOS and passes control to it. The Windows NT process ends here.
8. NTDETECT.COM scans the computer hardware and sends the list to NTLDR for inclusion in HKEY_LOCAL_MACHINE\HARDWARE.
9. NTLDR then loads NTOSKRNL.EXE, HAL.DLL, and the system hive.
10. NTLDR scans the system hive and loads the device drivers configured to start at boot time.
11. NTLDR passes control to NTOSKRNL.EXE, at which point the boot process ends and the load phases begin.

FAQ 1.4 What is the NT kernel?

Most operating systems (OSs) require a way to separate user applications from the OS's core services. To achieve this, Windows 2000 has two modes, user and kernel. A user mode program can't read or write directly to the OS memory; instead, it can access its own virtual 4GB memory (2GB for applications, 2GB for OS), which a kernel process—the Virtual Memory Manager—controls. The Virtual Memory Manager then writes directly to the OS memory.

Basically, the system uses the kernel for critical OS services, which are kept separate from user programs to prevent the user programs from crashing the OS. The main parts of Win2K that run in kernel mode are the hardware abstraction layer (HAL—applications can't talk directly to hardware), NT kernel, and NT Executive.

1.5 What is virtual memory?

Virtual memory makes up for the lack of RAM in computers by using space on the hard disk as memory, virtual memory. When the actual RAM fills up (actually before the RAM fills), virtual memory is created on the hard disk. When physical memory runs out, the Virtual Memory Manager chooses sections of memory that have not been recently used and are of low priority and writes them to the swap file. This process is hidden from applications, and applications view both virtual and actual memory as the same.

Each application that runs under Windows NT is given its own virtual address space of 4GB (2GB for the application, 2GB for the operating system).

The problem with virtual memory is that as it writes and reads to the hard disk, it does so **much** slower than actual RAM, which is why if an NT system does not have enough memory, it will run very slowly as pages will be constantly written and read from the physical disk.

2 WINDOWS 2000

Windows 2000 was the major release after NT 4.0. It included the following new features:

- New X.500-style directory services called Active Directory. In the Active Directory, domain controllers store the entire directory database for their domain. This directory information can be structured to create a hierarchical directory system.
- Active Directory uses Domain Name Service (DNS) as a locator service and supports Lightweight Directory Access Protocol (LDAP) queries.
- Distributed File System. Dfs, which was an add-on for NT4, enables multiple volumes on different machines (not even Windows NT!) to appear as a single logical volume.
- Support for more than one monitor using new API commands (note that not all video cards are supported).
- Kerberos-style security, which is an MIT-developed security protocol and is used for distributed security within a domain tree. Kerberos-style security is based on passwords and private-key encryption.

  Windows 2000 security is not pure Kerberos because it implements a "data authorization field," which is normally left blank. Microsoft is using it but not documenting its use, making its Kerberos implementation incompatible with other implementations.
- Support for plug-and-play based on Advanced Configuration and Power Interface(ACPI).
- Common device driver model, so new drivers can work on both Windows NT and Windows 98.
- Built-in disk quota software—Per-user/per-volume only.
- Encrypted File System (EFS)—File encryption on a per-file or per-folder basis.

FAQ 2.1 What is Windows 2000?

Microsoft has renamed NT 5.0 to Windows 2000 in an attempt to simplify the product lines. The following is an extract from a Microsoft press release:

Four products to make up initial Windows 2000 offerings, all "Built on NT Technology.

The company has decided to rename the next release of the Windows NT® line of operating systems—formerly known as Windows NT 5.0—as Windows 2000. Now that millions of people use the Windows NT operating systems every day, Microsoft has decided to rename its next releases to reflect their shift into the mainstream market and to help customers understand their products. All currently released operating systems will retain their names.

The company has also expanded the Windows server line to meet customer demand for solutions that are more powerful than Windows NT Server Enterprise Edition and for lower cost clustering alternatives for branch-office servers.

"Windows NT was first released five years ago as a specialized operating system for technical and business needs. Today it has proven its value as the preferred technology for all users who want industry-leading cost-effectiveness, rich security features and demonstrated scalability," said Jim Allchin, senior vice president at Microsoft. "The Windows NT kernel will be the basis for all of Microsoft's PC operating systems from consumer products to the highest-performance servers."

The Windows 2000 line, which Microsoft began to roll out in 1999, included four products. Windows 2000 Professional is a desktop operating system aimed at businesses of all sizes. Microsoft designed Windows 2000 Professional as the easiest Windows yet, with high-level security and significant enhancements for mobile users. The operating system is also designed to provide industrial-strength reliability and to help companies lower their total cost of ownership with improved manageability.

Microsoft offers Windows 2000 Server as the ideal solution for small- to medium-sized enterprise application deployments, Web servers, workgroups, and branch offices. Windows 2000 Server can support new systems with up to two-way SMP; existing Windows NT Server 4.0 systems with up to four-way SMP can be upgraded to this product.

Windows 2000 Advanced Server is a more powerful departmental and application server that provides network operating system and Internet services. Supporting new systems with up to four-way SMP and large physical memories, this product is ideal for database-intensive work. In addition, Windows 2000 Server integrates clustering and load-balancing support to provide excellent system and application availability. Organizations with existing Windows NT 4.0 Enterprise Edition servers with up to eight-way SMP can install this product.

The Windows 2000 line will also include the new Windows 2000 Datacenter Server, which is the most powerful server operating system ever offered by Microsoft. Windows 2000 Datacenter Server supports up to 16-way SMP and up to 64GB of physical memory, depending on system architecture. Like Windows 2000 Advanced

> Server, it provides both clustering and load-balancing services as standard features. Microsoft designed this product especially for large data warehouses, econometric analysis, large-scale simulations in science and engineering, online transaction processing, and server-consolidation projects.
>
> Microsoft believes its new Windows 2000 name will help both its partners and customers. "The new name also serves our goal of making it simpler for customers to choose the right Windows products for their needs," said Brad Chase, vice president at Microsoft. "The new naming system eliminates customer confusion about whether 'NT' refers to client or server technology. Also, with our across-the-board improvements in ease of use, mobile support and total cost of ownership that provide benefits to so many users, 'NT' technology is no longer just for high-end workstations." Microsoft will use the tagline "Built on NT Technology" to help its customers through the naming transition.

The company believes that the Windows 2000 name and NT tagline will help people to identify which operating system will work best in their environment. And—as the name implies—Windows 2000 is ready for the next millennium.

FAQ 2.2 What hardware is needed to run Windows 2000?

The following is a list of the minimum hardware needed to install Windows 2000:

- 32-bit, Intel-based microprocessor computer (such as Pentium-compatible 166 MHz or higher) for both Windows 2000 Professional and Windows 2000 Server.
- VGA or higher resolution monitor.
- Keyboard.
- 32MB of RAM minimum (Windows NT Server: 64MB of RAM).
- Hard disk space with a minimum of 300MB of free disk space for Windows 2000 Professional. (Server: a minimum of 400MB of free disk space on the partition that will contain the Windows NT system files). Several factors affect free disk space required by Windows 2000 Setup, including disk cluster size, amount of RAM in the system, the filesystem used (for example, NTFS uses a smaller disk cluster size than FAT filesystems), and whether the computer will be part of a network or will be a local installation (which requires less free space). Setup determines if you have sufficient disk space to successfully complete the installation with the optional components you have selected.
- For CD-only installation, a bootable CD-ROM drive (so you can start Setup without using a floppy disk drive).
- For floppy disk and CD installation, a high-density 3.5-inch disk drive as drive A and a CD-ROM drive.

- For network installation, one or more network adapters installed on your computer and access to the network share containing the Setup files.
- A mouse or other pointing device.

The minimum memory **is** the minimum memory, and Setup performs a test to check whether you have that amount. If you don't, the installation will not proceed (which I found to be very annoying when I tried to install Windows 2000 Server on my portable that at that time only had 32MB of RAM). You can hack the TXTSETUP.SIF files, however, to install either Server or Workstation on systems with less memory. There is no check on CPU type.

The 64-bit Alpha processor is not supported in Windows 2000.

Hardware information is also in the file SETUP.TXT on the Windows 2000 CD-ROM.

FAQ 2.3 Where is the Hardware Compatibility List for Windows 2000?

The HCL for Windows 2000 is supplied on the CD in both text and HTML Help format. It can also be found at http://www.microsoft.com/hcl/.

FAQ 2.4 When does Windows 2000 need rebooting?

Microsoft has reduced the number of functions that require a reboot from about 50 in NT 4.0 to 7 in Windows 2000.

The following items used to require rebooting:

- Changing an IP address
- Changing the mouse
- Adding a new page file or changing its size
- Adding plug-and-play devices
- Adding new disks

Now the only items that require a reboot are the following:

- Changing the ISA adapter configuration
- Changing the system font (the USER and Graphics Device Interface have to be recreated)
- Adding and removing communication ports (due to possible jumper changes)
- Changing the default system locale

- Changing the computer/domain name
- Installing service packs or hotfixes

In Windows 2000 Server reboots are also needed for the following:

- Running DCPROMO
- Changing the DNS suffix name
- Switching language in a multilanguage edition
- Installing Terminal Services
- Removing Gateway Services for NetWare
- Changing the DNS server's IP address

FAQ 2.5 Is build 2195 the final version of Windows 2000?

Yes, the last build is 2195, which was released to manufacturing. You can check this with WinInfo (http://www.savilltech.com/wininfo.html).

Microsoft has changed its mind about the Microsoft Developer Network (MSDN) version, however, and the Windows 2000 build 2195 shipping with MSDN will be the FULL, no expiry version. In an effort to stop pirating, the CD has a hologram visible on front side of the CD covering the entire surface!

FAQ 2.6 Where do I get updates for Windows 2000?

Normal service packs for Windows 2000 will be released, but Microsoft is committed to providing more timely updates in the form of the Windows Update Web site, which can be accessed from the Start menu (see Figure 2-1).

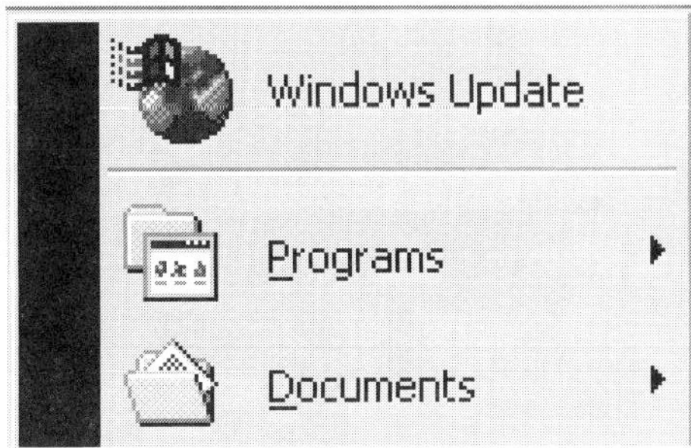

Figure 2-1 The Windows Update link

When the Windows Update shortcut is selected, Internet Explorer is started, and you connect to http://windowsupdate.microsoft.com/. At the Windows Update site, select the Product Updates link. Select the system description that corresponds to your system, and a list of fixes needed for your system will be displayed.

Select the Updates that are needed for your installation and click Download (see Figure 2-2).

A summary of what will be downloaded is shown; click the Start Download button to begin. Click Yes to the displayed agreement.

Depending on the downloaded fixes, a reboot may be required, and if so, a dialog will prompt you.

If you would like the updates in a non-WindowsUpdate form, go to http://www.microsoft.com/windows2000/downloads/default.asp. Also have a look at http://www.microsoft.com/windows2000/downloads/tools/appcompat/default.asp, which has an update to enable compatibility with a number of games and applications.

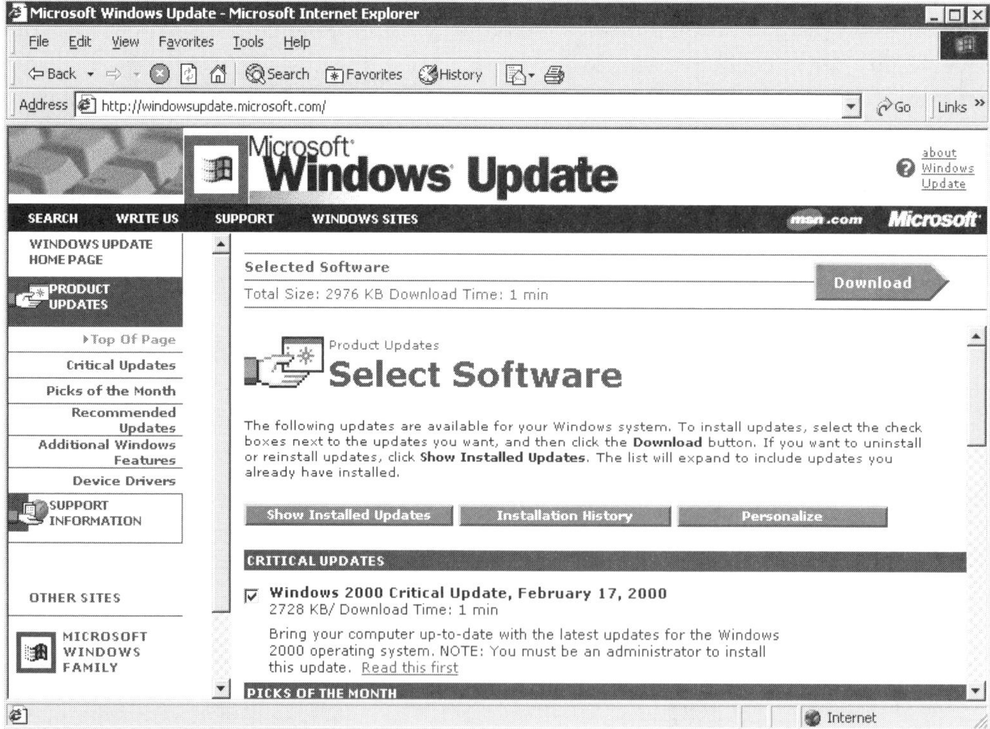

Figure 2-2 The Windows Update site for Windows 2000

FAQ 2.7 How can I check whether software x is compatible with Windows 2000?

Microsoft introduced a Windows 2000 logo certified program, and now many programs written for 2000 and above are certified ensuring 2000 compatibility.

There are other levels, the most useful is the Windows 2000 Ready application level, which means the software has been tested with Windows 2000 and the manufacturer provides 2000 support.

To search for the Windows 2000 compatibility of an application, enter the details at http://www.microsoft.com/windows2000/professional/howtobuy/upgrading/compat/search/software.asp (see Figure 2-3).

Any software company can have its software listed on this Web site and can apply at http://msdnisv.microsoft.com/msdnisv/win2000/.

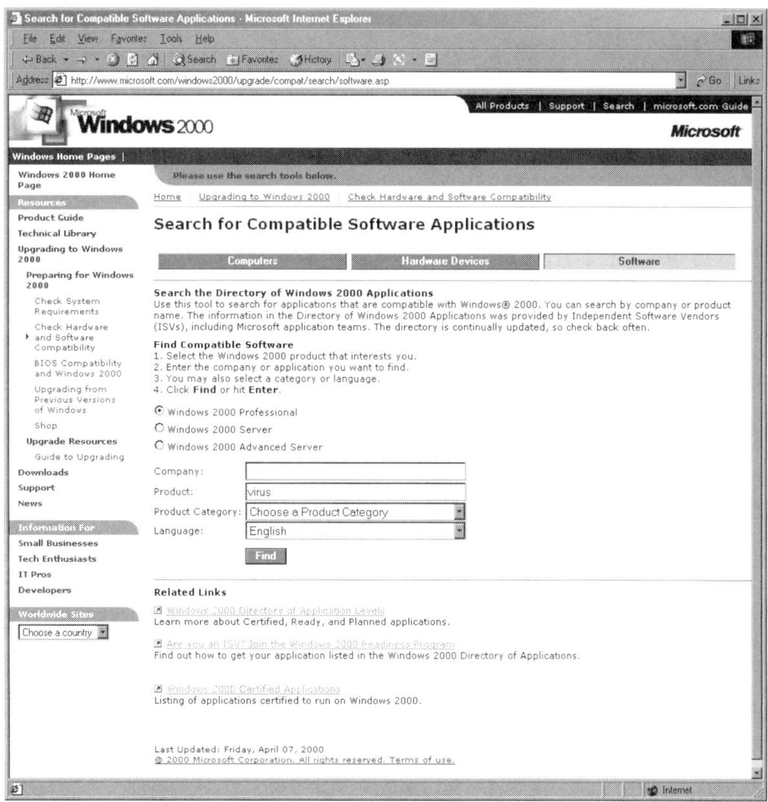

Figure 2-3 Windows 2000 search for compatible programs

3 WINDOWS XP

Windows eXPerience (Windows XP) is the name for the next version of Windows 2000 (formerly known as "Whistler"). Technically, Windows XP isn't the huge jump that Win2K was from Windows NT 4.0, but Windows XP does realize Microsoft's long-term plan of one code base. Starting with Windows XP, there will be no more Windows Millennium Edition (Windows Me) or Windows 9x.

This merging of the code bases brings the stability and security from Windows NT/2000 and the ease of use and hardware support from Windows 9x/Me.

The next-generation Windows family currently comprises the following products:

- Windows XP Home Edition (the Win9x replacement)
- Windows XP Professional (Win2K Professional)
- Windows .Net Web Server
- Windows .Net Standard Server
- Windows .Net Enterprise Server
- Windows .Net DataCenter

The differences between Windows XP Home Edition and Windows XP Professional are minor. Windows XP Home Edition supports only one processor; Windows XP Pro supports two. In addition, Windows XP Home Edition doesn't support Remote Desktop Protocol (RDP), but Windows XP Pro does. In fact, with Windows XP Pro, even local sessions use RDP, which means that you can log off your machine, someone else can log on to your machine then log off, and you can log on again with all your programs still running! Windows XP also adds support for the 64-bit processor, Itanium, which will ship in Windows XP Pro and Windows .Net Server.

Microsoft is adding some of the neat Windows Me features to Windows XP, including the Video Editor software. Windows XP also has an updated user interface, although the older style UI is still available for those who prefer it. Windows XP beta 1 (build 2296) shipped October 31, 2000. The final version of Windows XP shipped October 25, 2001 with a build number of 2600.

FAQ 3.1 What is the difference between Windows XP Professional Edition and Windows XP Home Edition?

With Windows XP, the two Windows OS lines merge, so we'll no longer have Windows 2000/Windows NT and Windows Me/Windows 98—just Windows XP. However, we still have two different types of users: the office user and the basic home user with one machine. Hence the two versions of Windows XP: Windows XP Professional, for those accustomed to Win2K Professional/NT Workstation, and Windows XP Home Edition, for those accustomed to Windows Me/Win98.

Although the XP Pro and Home Editions share the same common core code, they don't have the same features. The right version for you depends on the functionality you need. Think of XP Pro as a superset of XP Home. The following is a short list of supported features:

- **Backup**—XP Pro has the standard Win2K backup program available as default; XP Home has no backup program available by default (but one can be installed from the CD).
- **Dynamic disks**—XP Pro supports dynamic disks; XP Home doesn't.
- **Internet Information Server (IIS)**—XP Pro includes IIS; XP Home doesn't.
- **Encrypted File System (EFS)**—EFS debuted in Win2K, and it enables you to encrypt files on an NTFS partition, a very useful feature for mobile machines. XP Pro includes EFS; XP Home doesn't.
- **Multiple monitors**—XP Pro supports up to ten monitors; XP Home supports only one monitor (Windows Me/Win98 supported multiple monitors).
- **Multiprocessing**—XP Pro supports up to two processors; XP Home supports only one (as did Windows Me/Win98).
- **Remote Assistance**—Both editions support Remote Assistance, which lets someone from a Help desk connect to the client desktop to troubleshoot problems.
- **Remote desktop**—XP Pro adds to Remote Assistance by letting any machine running a Terminal Services client run one Terminal Services session against an XP Pro machine.
- **Domain membership**—XP Pro systems can be domain members; XP Home systems can't, but they can access domain resources.
- **Group Policy**—XP Pro supports Group Policies; XP Home doesn't.
- **IntelliMirror**—XP Pro supports IntelliMirror, which includes Microsoft Remote Installation Services (RIS), software deployment, and user setting management; XP Home doesn't support IntelliMirror.
- **Upgrade from Windows Me/Win98**—Both XP Pro and XP Home support this upgrade.

- **Upgrade from Win2K/NT**—Only XP Pro supports this upgrade.
- **64-bit support**—Only XP Pro has a 64-bit version that supports the Itanium systems.
- **Network support**—XP Pro includes support for Network Monitor, Simple Network Management Protocol (SNMP), IP Security (IPSec), and Client Services for NetWare (CSNW); XP Home doesn't.

For the best list of supported features, see the Feature Guide document (FEATGUID.DOC) on the root of the XP CD-ROM.

FAQ 3.2 With Windows XP, the system doesn't display the Security dialog box when I press Ctrl+Alt+Del. Where did the dialog box go?

You can get the Security dialog box back by disabling the welcome screen. Select Control Panel > User accounts > Change the way users log on or off, and then clear the Use the Welcome screen checkbox.

If you want only the Lock Computer option on the Task Manager Shut Down menu, you can disable fast user switching. Select Control Panel > User accounts > Change the way users log on or off, and then clear the Fast User Switching checkbox.

If the welcome screen and fast user switching are both enabled, Switch User (Winkey+L) returns you to the welcome screen (essentially locking the computer). Someone else can log on to his or her session, but your session remains safely locked.

FAQ 3.3 How do I control the welcome screen display and also whether fast user switching is allowed?

Under Control Panel > User Accounts > Change the way users log on or off is a simple dialog box that gives you two options (if you're in a domain, the Change the way users log on or off option is not available):

- **Use the welcome screen**—With this option enabled, when you first boot the machine, log off, or switch users, the system displays a screen that lists the local accounts and displays user pictures (if you configured the picture option). Also new to the welcome screen is the ability to have a user password hint.
- **Use fast user switching**—Fast user switching (see Figure 3-1), which works similarly to Terminal Services sessions, lets you log on as another user without having to log off the current session first.

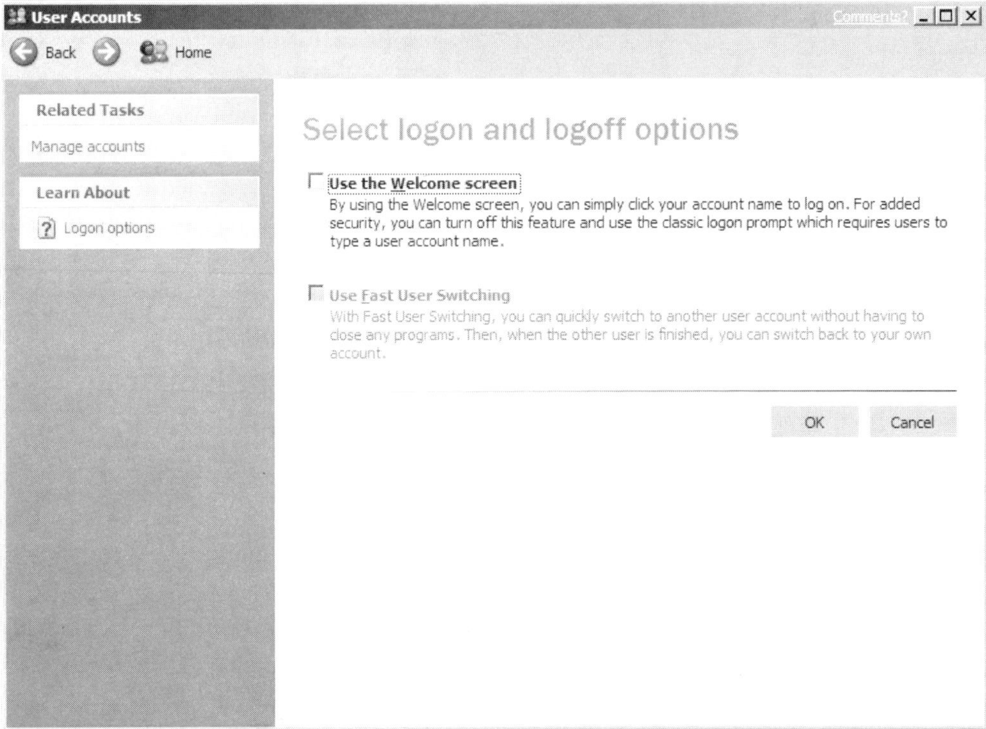

Figure 3-1 Option to use the new Windows XP logon screen

You can also set these two options from the Registry under the HKEY_LOCAL_MACHINE\SOFTWARE\Microsoft\Windows NT\CurrentVersion\Winlogon key:

- LogonType—Set to 0 to display the Security dialog box; set to 1 to display the new welcome screen.
- AllowMultipleTSSessions—Set to 0 to prohibit fast user switching; set to 1 to allow switching.

If you're in a domain, changing either of these two Registry keys has no effect.

3.4 How do I use the new Windows XP welcome screen?

The new XP welcome screen is actually as simple as it looks. When you first boot the machine, log off, or use fast user switching, the system displays a screen with the computer's local accounts. To log on as one of these accounts, click the appropriate

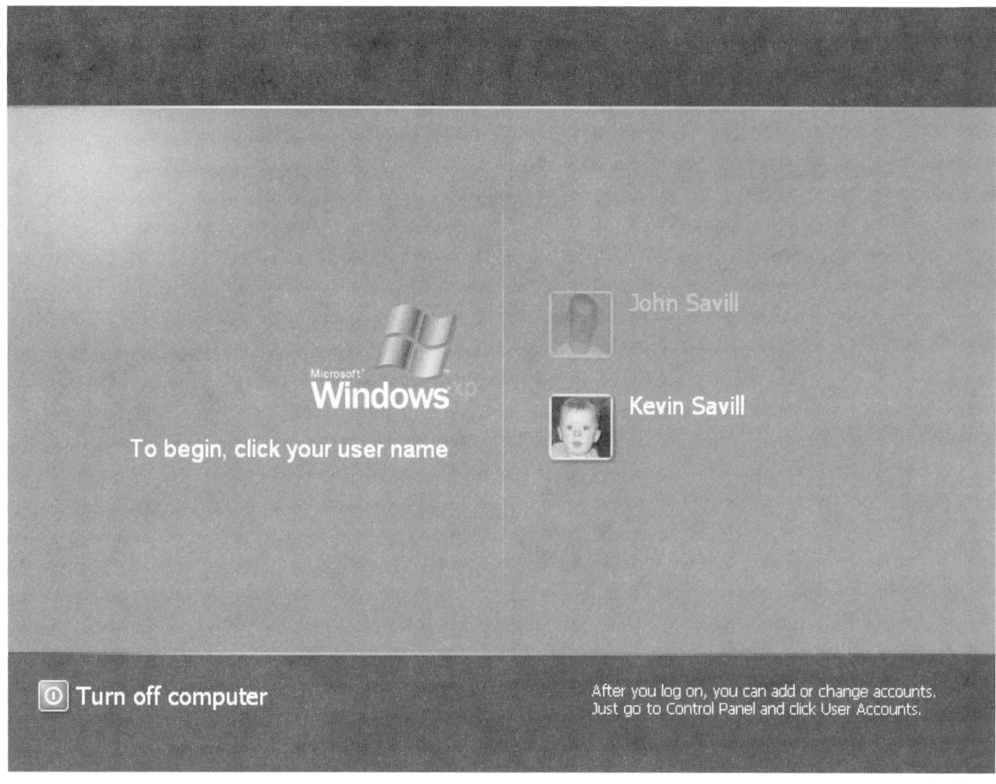

Figure 3-2 The new Windows XP "friendly" workgroup logon screen

user name or picture. If you have a password, the system will display an area for your password (if you don't need a password, you'll be logged on). See Figure 3-2.

Type your password and click the right arrow or press Enter. If you forget your password and you have configured a password hint, you can click the question mark (?) next to the right arrow to display your hint. Note that these password hints **aren't** secure; anyone can see them by clicking the question mark, so don't make them too obvious.

3.5 How do I change my picture for the welcome screen?

If you don't enjoy appearing as a cat, an astronaut, or a fish (the default picture choices for the welcome screen), you can configure your own picture by performing the following steps:

1. Start the User Accounts Control Panel applet (Start > Control Panel > User Accounts).
2. Select the account of the picture you want to change.
3. Click Change my picture (see Figure 3-3).
4. The system will display a list of default pictures. Click Browse for More Pictures.
5. By default, the system will open your My Pictures folder. Browse to your picture. (It should be 48 pixels x 48 pixels—if it's a different size, the system will force it into a 48x48 format—and it can be a BMP, JPG, or GIF file.) Select the picture you want and click Open.
6. The system will display all the pictures again, highlighting the one you added. Click Change Picture (see Figure 3-4).

This picture selection is actually stored in the Registry under the HKEY_LOCAL_MACHINE\SOFTWARE\Microsoft\Windows\CurrentVersion\Hints\[username]\

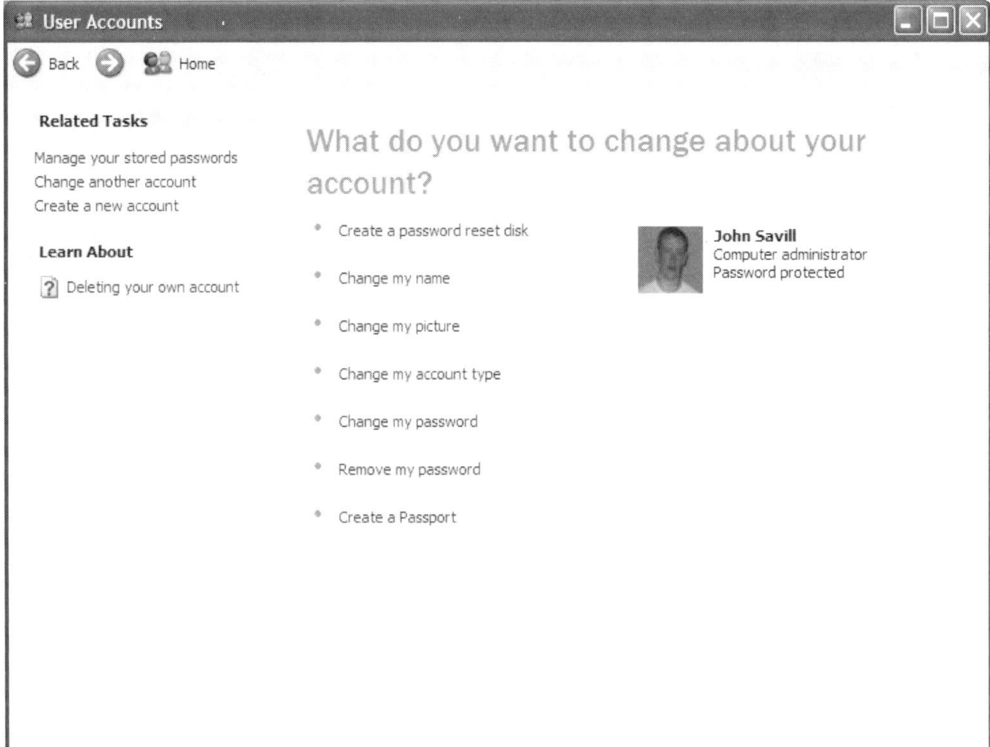

Figure 3-3 Modifying user accounts

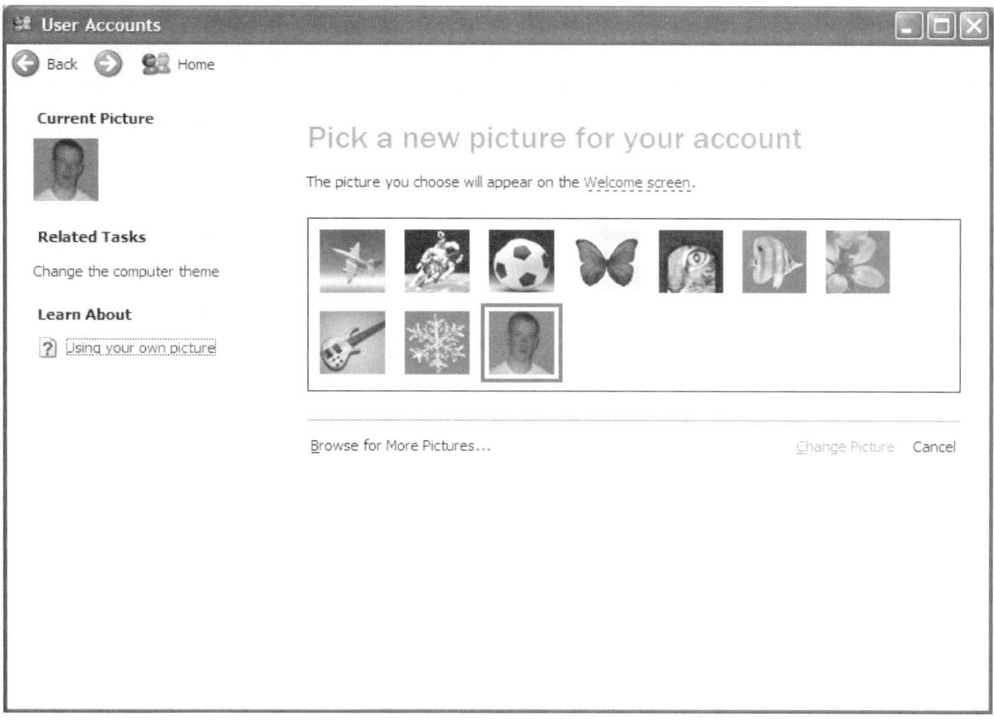

Figure 3-4 Selecting a new picture to be displayed for the welcome screen

PictureSource key, and you can change it there. By default, the pictures are stored in %systemdrive%:\Documents and Settings\All UsersApplication Data\Microsoft\User Account Pictures\Default Pictures.

FAQ 3.6 With Windows XP, how do I set a password hint?

XP introduced the option to have a password hint, which is useful in a workgroup (this option isn't available in a domain). To set a password hint, perform the following steps:

1. Start the User Accounts Control Panel applet (Start > Control Panel > User Accounts).
2. Select the account for which you want to add a password hint.
3. Click Change the password.
4. Enter your password in the two locations; in the bottom area, type your password hint (see Figure 3-5).
5. Click Change Password.

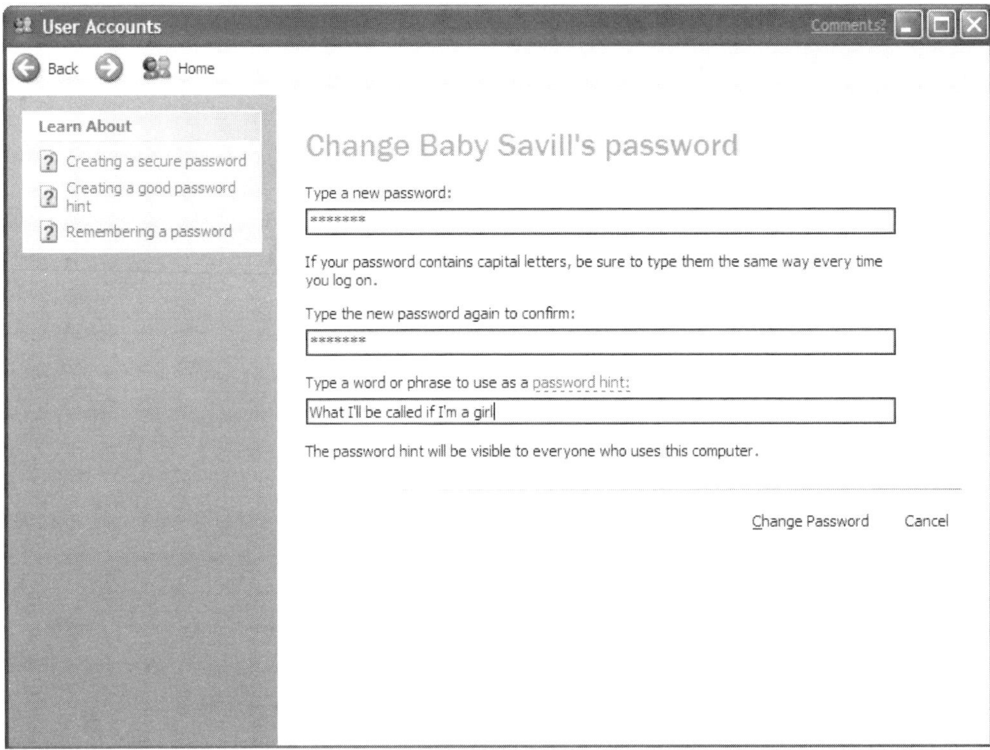

Figure 3-5 Modifying a user's password and setting a password hint

These hints are stored in the Registry under the HKEY_LOCAL_MACHINE\SOFTWARE\Microsoft\Windows\CurrentVersion\Hints\[username]\(Default) key, and you can change them there as well.

FAQ 3.7 In Windows XP, how do I use the password reset disk?

With XP, if you're in a workgroup, you have the option under your profile to create a password reset disk using a wizard. Click Start > Control Panel > User Accounts > [account name] > Create a Password Reset Disk > Create Disk.

1. When the wizard starts, click Next.
2. Select the drive that contains the media you want to create the information on (you can use a diskette or a Zip disk) and click Next.

3. Type your current password and click Next (see Figure 3-6).
4. Click Finish.

The password reset disk contains only one file, USERKEY.PSW, which is an encrypted version of your password. If you change your password, the password reset disk is useless; you must repeat this procedure.

To use the password reset disk, at the logon screen, leave the password field blank and press Enter or click the right arrow. The system will display a dialog box that offers the option to use your password reset disk as shown in Figure 3-7.

When you select this option, a wizard starts:

1. Click Next.
2. Select the drive to read the password reset disk from and click Next.
3. Enter a new password twice and click Next.
4. Click Finish.

Figure 3-6 The Forgotten Password Wizard

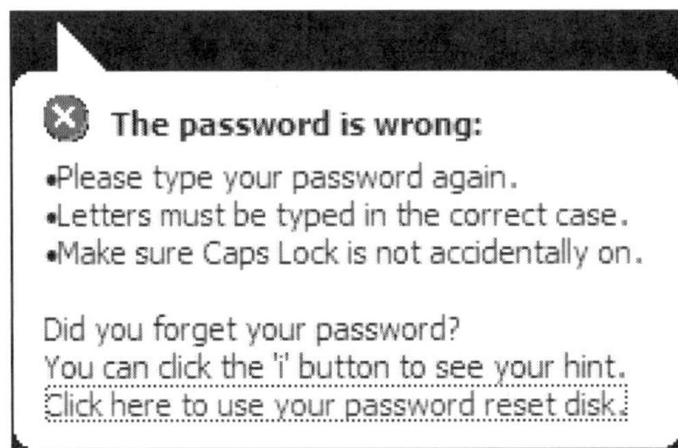

Figure 3-7 Windows XP incorrect password dialog with password reset disk options

5. Type your new password to log on. Note that the password reset disk is now useless, and you must create a new one.

3.8 What is Bootcfg?

Bootcfg is a new addition to the Windows XP Recovery Console. You use this command to modify the BOOT.INI file, which contains the choices at system startup. (In a multiboot environment, BOOT.INI contains the list of all the OSs and lets you choose one.)

The Bootcfg command recognizes Windows XP, Windows 2000, and Windows NT. It doesn't recognize Windows 9x. Bootcfg has the following options:

- /default—Sets the default OS (modifies the default= line in BOOT.INI).
- /add—Scans the computer for OSs and lets you add located installations. You can also specify optional boot switches.
- /rebuild—Same as /add except /rebuild automatically recreates BOOT.INI with all found installations if the user confirms.
- /scan—Identifies current installations but doesn't modify BOOT.INI.
- /list—Scans the BOOT.INI files and displays each entry.
- /redirect—Enables redirection of the boot loaded to a specific port and baud rate (this option is useful for the Headless Administration options).
- /disableredirect—Disables the redirection configured with /redirect.

Bootcfg is simply an extra tool. You can still modify BOOT.INI directly with Notepad (after removing read-only, system, and hidden attributes—entering **`attrib`** `c:\boot.ini -r -s -h` at the command line). Or you can use the System Control Panel applet or Msconfig.

FAQ 3.9 Under Windows XP in a workgroup, why don't I see the Security tab for a file/folder?

To view the Security tab for a file or folder in XP, hold down the Ctrl key while right-clicking the file or folder, and select Properties. If you are in a domain instead of a workgroup, this approach is unnecessary.

FAQ 3.10 What is Windows 2002?

Windows 2002 is the brand name for the Windows 2000 follow-on server and desktop line of OSs. The beta name for the server line was Whistler; however, the final name scheme is Windows .Net server, and for the desktop, Windows XP.

Within Windows XP, you will still see the Windows 2002 name used if you keep your eyes peeled!

FAQ 3.11 How do I enable Windows 2000-like file sharing and security in Windows XP workgroups?

In FAQ 3.9, we saw that to bring up the Security dialog box for files/folders/shares, you had to hold down the Ctrl key. To eliminate this requirement, perform the following steps:

1. Start the Microsoft Management Console (MMC) Local Security Policy snap-in (Start > Settings > Control Panel > Administrative Tools > Local Security Policy).
2. Expand the Local Policies branch.
3. Select Security Options.
4. Double-click Network access: Sharing and security model for local accounts.
5. Select Classic and click OK (see Figure 3-8).
6. Close the snap-in.
7. Reboot the system for the change to take effect.

Another method is do this is via Windows Explorer: Tools > Folder Options > View and then uncheck Use simple file sharing (Recommended).

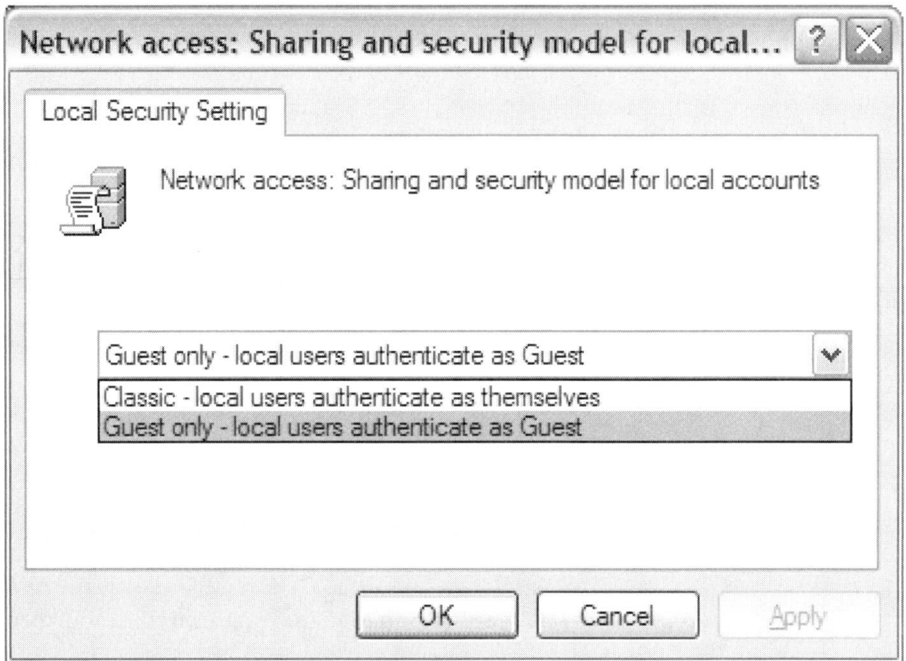

Figure 3-8 Guest-only local access

Now you have share permissions and file security on NTFS volumes. On FAT volumes, the Security menu will remain unavailable.

FAQ 3.12 How do I activate Windows XP from the command line?

Windows XP will typically remind you to activate the product (most users will have 30 days to activate XP after installation). To activate XP manually, you can use the Start menu shortcut in the System Tools Accessories folder. At the command prompt, type

```
oobe/msoobe /a
```

In case you're wondering, "msoobe" stands for "Microsoft Out of Box Experience."

FAQ 3.13 What is the Windows XP task switcher?

Microsoft is releasing XP with a host of new PowerToys (extra utilities that are great add-ons, although Microsoft doesn't support them). One PowerToy is an improved task switcher (i.e., the screen that's displayed when you press Alt+Tab to cycle through open programs).

The new task switcher shows an image of the application window so that you can see what each application is doing before you switch to a different application (see Figure 3-9).

To install the task switcher, you will need to download TASKINSTALL.EXE from Microsoft's Web site. Run the downloaded TASKINSTALL.EXE. After you complete the installation, you must log off and log on again for the change to take effect.

> **Be warned:** *When using this utility, I have seen severe performance degradation on certain types of machines. If you encounter problems, simply uninstall task switcher using the Add/Remove Programs Control Panel applet.*

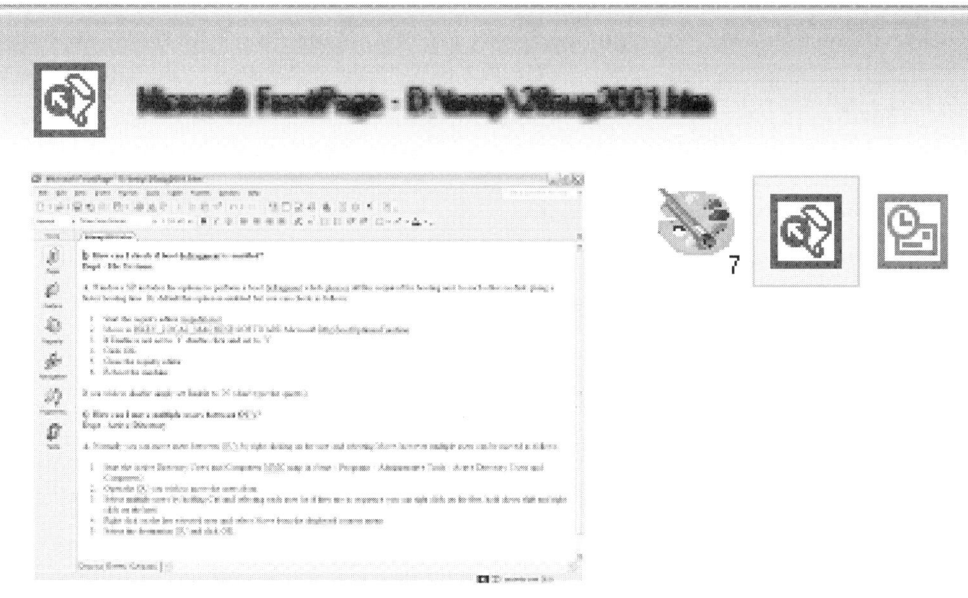

Figure 3-9 The enhanced Alt+Tab PowerToy

FAQ 3.14 Why can't I upgrade to the final version of Windows XP from an interim build?

Although you can technically upgrade from an interim build of XP to the final version, Microsoft has restricted the upgrade path for certain builds. However, I know of two methods for circumventing these restrictions.

Method 1

This method is the more complicated of the two. It involves modifying a file in your boot partition before you reboot.

1. Run Setup from the final XP image. If you receive a message stating that you can't upgrade this version of Windows, you need to perform a fresh install by selecting Fresh Install.
2. Continue with the installation and choose the same Windows directory for the installation that you want to upgrade.
3. When Setup prompts you to reboot, press Escape to manually reboot later, and Setup will return you to the Windows shell.
4. The directory win_nt.bt in the root of your boot partition (which is typically C) should contain a file named WINNT.SIF. Open this file in Notepad.
5. Look for the line that reads winntupgrade=no and change the winntupgrade value to yes.
6. Save the file and reboot your system.

Method 2

XP contains a Program Compatibility Wizard that you typically use to set up a virtual environment that mimics another version of Windows for programs that won't run under XP. Using this wizard, you can fool the final installation into thinking that you're running Windows 2000.

1. Start the Program Compatibility Wizard (go to Start > Programs > Accessories and click Program Compatibility Wizard).
2. Select I want to use the program in the CD-ROM drive and click Next.
3. Select Microsoft Windows 2000 and click Next.
4. Continue to click Next as appropriate to complete the wizard.

FAQ 3.15 How can I determine which product key I used to activate Windows XP?

You can't because XP converts the product key to the system's product ID. Exposing this product ID opens security concerns around the product ID generation process and the security of the product key. Therefore, make sure you keep track of all product keys you use.

FAQ 3.16 When must I activate the final version of Windows XP?

The final version of XP requires that you activate the product within 30 days of installation. Because the product activation doesn't grant an extra 30 days for users who previously installed the evaluation version, those users must activate the OS immediately after they complete the upgrade.

FAQ 3.17 What ports does Windows XP use during product activation?

XP uses the standard Hypertext Transfer Protocol (HTTP) port (port 80) and HTTP over Secure Socket Layer (HTTPS) port (port 443) for product activation. To confirm that these ports are available, try connecting to both ports by entering the following addresses in your Web browser:

- http://www.microsoft.com:80
- https://www.microsoft.com:443

If you receive an error, check with your administrator to determine whether your organization has blocked either port and whether you need to change your firewall client configuration.

FAQ 3.18 How do I correct a Windows XP installation that has become deactivated?

XP contains a new feature, System Restore, that restores the system to a previous configuration point. Should you restore your system to a point before you activated XP on your computer, the OS will forget that you activated it, and you'll need to reactivate XP. If the system restore point is past the 30-day grace period that Microsoft allows for activation, you'll have to activate XP immediately.

The only work around to reactivating your system is to perform the following steps:

1. Start your Windows installation in Minimal Safe mode.
2. Move to the \%systemroot%\system32 folder.
3. Rename WPA.DBL to WPA.NOACT.
4. Rename WPA.BAK to WPA.DBL.
5. Reboot your system as normal.

The preceding procedure will work only if you've made no significant hardware changes.

FAQ 3.19 Does Windows XP contain any Easter eggs?

To supply certain government agencies with software, Microsoft can't include undocumented features, including Easter eggs, in its software. As a result, no Easter eggs exist in XP.

FAQ 3.20 Where can I get Microsoft's extra Windows XP screensaver?

To highlight XP's and DirectX 8.0's features, Microsoft developed an extra screensaver for XP that consists of a 3D flag. You can download the screensaver for free from Microsoft's Web site at http://www.microsoft.com/windowsxp/pro/downloads/xpscreensaver.asp.

FAQ 3.21 Where can I find Microsoft PowerToys for Windows XP?

As with previous versions of Windows, Microsoft has released a set of great utilities to enhance the Windows experience. You can download Microsoft PowerToys for XP from Microsoft's Web site at http://www.microsoft.com/windowsxp/pro/downloads/powertoys.asp.

PowerToys for XP consists of the following:

- **Open Command Window Here:** Open a command window that points to a particular folder just by right-clicking that folder.
- **TweakUI:** Make many modifications to internal XP settings that aren't accessible in the default UI.
- **Power Calculator:** Graph and evaluate functions as well as perform unit conversions.
- **Image Resizer:** Easily resize multiple images into a target size with a right-click.
- **CD Slide Show Generator:** View images as a slide show.
- **Virtual Desktop Manager:** Have up to four virtual desktops.
- **Taskbar Magnifier:** Magnify part of the screen from the taskbar.
- **HTML Slide Show Wizard:** Create HTML slide shows of your digital pictures, ready to place on a Web site.
- **Webcam Timershot:** Take pictures at specified time intervals from a Webcam connected to your computer and save them to a location that you designate.

FAQ 3.22 What upgrade paths does Windows XP support?

XP Home Edition and XP Professional are available in full and upgrade versions. If you're upgrading from a qualifying OS, you can purchase the less-expensive upgrade version; otherwise, you need to purchase the full version. However, even if you purchase the full version, XP doesn't support all upgrade paths. Review the following table to determine whether XP supports your upgrade path:

Current Version	Windows XP Home	Windows XP Pro
Windows 3.1 or Windows 95	No	No
Any server version of Windows	No	No
Windows 98/98 SE	Yes	Yes
Windows Me	Yes	Yes
Windows NT 3.51	No	No (you need to upgrade to NT 4.0 orWin2K first)

(*continued*)

Current Version	Windows XP Home	Windows XP Pro
Windows NT 4.0	No	Yes
Windows 2000 Professional	No	Yes
Windows XP Home Edition		Yes
Windows XP Professional	No	

4 INSTALLATION

Before we can perform any of our neat system tweaks, we must first install the operating system, which is now very simple and wizard driven. With Windows XP, the installation (known as *dynamic update*) connects to the Web and downloads recent fixes and drivers without any user intervention.

NT4 ONLY

FAQ

4.1 Why does my installation hang when detecting the hardware?

The program being called is NTDETECT.COM. The best course of action is to use the DEBUG version of NTDETECT.COM. The support area of the NT installation CD (/support) contains a file NTDETECT.CHK. Follow these instructions to use it:

1. Using the Diskcopy command, create a copy of the first installation disk:

   ```
   diskcopy a: a: (/v)
   ```

2. Copy NTDETECT.COM from the support CD to the installation disk.

   ```
   copy d:\support\ntdetect.chk a:ntdetect.com
   ```

3. Then reboot the machine with the new version of the installation disk, and each item will be shown as it is detected.

NT ONLY

FAQ

4.2 Does NT have to be installed on the C drive?

No, NT can be installed on any drive; however, it does place a few files on the active partition in order for NT to boot.

NT4 ONLY

4.3 I have NT installed. How do I install DOS?

Follow these steps:

1. Make an Emergency Repair Disk (Start > Run > Rdisk > Update Repair Info).
2. Make sure you have NT installation disks (made by executing **`winnt32 /ox`**).
3. Reboot the machine and boot off of the MS-DOS disks.
4. Install DOS (same as performing a SYS a: c: from a DOS bootable disk).
5. Your computer will reboot into DOS.
6. Reboot your machine and boot off of NT installation disks.
7. After disk 2, the setup procedure will give options, press R for repair.
8. Deselect all options except Inspect Boot Sector and continue with the process.
9. Press Enter to detect hardware and insert disk 3.
10. The procedure will ask if you have an Emergency Repair Disk (ERD); say Yes and insert the ERD.
11. The machine will then reboot into NT again.
12. Once in NT, go to a DOS session.
13. Type the following

    ```
    attrib c:\boot.ini -r -s
    ```

14. Edit the BOOT.INI file and insert the following text at the bottom of the file

    ```
    c:\="MS-DOS"
    ```

15. After saving the file, in the DOS session type command

    ```
    attrib c:\boot.ini +r +s
    ```

16. Reboot the machine and you will have MS-DOS and NT options! Easy :-)

This procedure works only if the C drive is FAT.

NT ONLY

4.4 How do I remove NT from a FAT partition?

If you have NT installed on a FAT partition, then you will need to remove the NT operating system files and the NT boot loader. To remove the files and the boot loader, boot a MS-DOS disk with the DELTREE utility copied and perform the following in a CMD.EXE session:

1. C:
2. DELTREE WINNT
3. CD PROGRA~1
4. DELTREE WINDOW~1
5. CD \
6. DEL NTLDR.
7. DEL NTDETECT.COM
8. DEL BOOT.INI
9. DEL PAGEFILE.SYS (this file may not be on the active partition depending on your configuration)
10. DEL BOOTSECT.DOS
11. Boot up using a Win95 or DOS startup disk and type SYS a: c:
12. Reboot.

NT ONLY

FAQ 4.5 How do I remove NT from a NTFS partition?

The best way is to delete the partition. Start the computer from the NT installation disks. When the option to create/choose partitions is displayed, select the NTFS partition NT is installed on and press D to delete the partition. Then press L to confirm.

FAQ 4.6 What are symbol files? Do I need them?

Symbol files are created when images are compiled and are used for debugging an image. They allow someone with the correct tools to view code as the software is running. You do not need symbol filcs unlcss you are a developer.

FAQ 4.7 How do I install NT and Linux?

Linux has a boot manager called LILO (which is a separate utility), and it boots Linux on its native EXT2 partition and any other DOS/Windows boot images residing on a FAT16 partition. LILO doesn't care whether it is DOS/Windows 95/NT, it will boot it. So as long as NT is installed on a FAT16 partition, there is no problem with LILO.

Apparently the latest Linux kernel has FAT32 support, so that may also be an option as well. Actually Linux supports FAT16 and can mount the FAT16 partition under its filesystem and have all the DOS/Windows files visible if you want it to. An alternative to LILO is Grub, which can be downloaded from http://www.uruk.org/~erich/grub.

LOADIN allows Linux to be installed as a MS-DOS subdirectory in a DOS/ Windows system. LOADIN allows Linux to be run as an application after you started DOS. It does not work with NT as Linux needs to run in supervisor mode and not user mode, which is the mode NT will run applications. NT will not yield at all on this. Windows 95 is the same, but you can set LOADIN to run in DOS mode where it just sees DOS 7 and works fine.

Linux and NT will work even if Windows NT is on NTFS. You need to set in Linux fdisk for the Linux drive to be flagged bootable, not NT. Then install LILO and select to boot the Linux partition and NT (which will say OS/2 in LILO). This way you can use both NT and Linux and still have a NTFS partition. LILO must reside on the Linux root sector and not the MBR.

Another method is as follows:

1. Install NT as per normal.
2. Download the freeware utility, BOOTPART.EXE, from http://www.winimage.com/bootpart.htm.
3. Install Linux, and make sure LILO is not installed on MBR, but on the boot sector of the Linux root partition.
4. Boot NT.
5. Start a command prompt (CMD.EXE).
6. Run BOOTPART.EXE and add the Linux bootsector into the NT-OS loader.(This also works when NT boot partition is NTFS.)

You can learn more about it from the Linux documentation project and the FAQ inside. It is mirrored in a large number of locations. One of the mirrors is ftp://ftp.ox.ac.uk/pub/linux/LDP_WWW/linux.html.

NT4 ONLY

FAQ

4.8 How do I install NT over the network?

If you do not currently have any operating system installed on your machine, then you need to create a bootable floppy disk that contains a driver for your network card and network protocol. A tool is provided called Network Client Administrator that automatically creates a bootable disk used to install Windows 95 or Network Client. It is possible to use this tool to also create a disk that can be used to install NT with a bit of tweaking :-).

1. Format a system floppy drive using DOS:

```
format a: /s
```

2. Create a share on the NT box containing the entire i386 structure from the NT installation CD-ROM and set the permissions on the share to everyone read access.
3. Log on as the Administrator (or a member of the Administrator's group).
4. Start the Network Client Administrator (Start > Programs > Administrative Tools > Network Client Administrators).
5. Click the Make Network Installation Startup Disk option and click Continue.
6. Select Share files and accept the default of <CD-ROM>\clients.
7. Click the OK button, and the program will perform some background actions.
8. Next select the floppy drive, click Network Client V3.0 as the client, and choose your network card from the drop-down list. Click OK.
9. Enter the name of the computer that the installation will be known as. The username and domain will automatically be completed using the current user.
10. You need to choose the protocol. In this example, choose TCP/IP and uncheck DHCP. Enter an IP address, subnet mask, and gateway.
11. Insert the disk created in step 1 and click OK.
12. Files will be copied to the floppy disk. Once completed, exit Network Client Administrator.
13. The disk needs to be edited to stop the automatic installation of the Network Client. Start Explorer and open the A drive. Right-click on AUTOEXEC.BAT and select Edit, which will open Notepad with the file loaded.
14. Remove the last two lines of the file (echo running setup and the setup).
15. You can also change the net use command to point to the correct share where the NT installation files are located.
16. Click Save from the File menu and close Notepad.
17. Insert the disk into the machine where you want to install NT and power on.
18. Once the startup has completed, change the directory to Z (or whatever your net use pointed to).
19. Start a floppyless install:

```
winnt /b
```

If you plan to produce a large number of install disks, you can configure the Network Client Administrator to also create Workstation and Server network installation disks.

To do so, you need to have the client directory on a hard disk and create two subdirectories under it (\\server\client):

- winnt\netsetup (hierarchy of \i386 from NT Workstation CD-ROM)
- winnt.srv\netsetup (hierarchy of \i386 from NT Server CD-ROM)

When creating the network disk, you will now also have options for Windows NT Workstation and Windows NT Server.

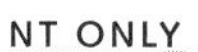
NT ONLY

4.9 Is it possible to use disk duplication to distribute Windows NT?

It is OK to use disk duplication to install NT but **not** a complete NT installation. You should follow these steps:

1. Use the winnt /b installation option on a machine.
2. Stop the setup at the second reboot, when it has finished the text portion of the installation and will be starting the GUI section.
3. Remove and duplicate the hard disk of the machine.
4. Install the duplicate hard drive in the new machine.
5. Start the new machine, and the GUI sections will start.

The traditional problems with cloning were that the security Identifier (SID) would be duplicated; however, now several third-party products enable you to change the SID of a duplicated machine. You can then create a new Computer Account on the PDC for the machine and then change the machine's name.

Following is a list of links for applications that can be used for disk duplication:

- NT Internals: http://www.sysinternals.com
- ImageCast: http://www.netversant.com
- DiskClone: http://www.qdeck.com
- DriveCopy: http://www.powerquest.com
- Ghost: http://www.ghostsoft.com

4.10 How do I perform an unattended installation?

It is possible to specify a text file that can be passed to the Windows NT installation program that contains answers to the questions the installation procedure asks. This file is usually called UNATTEND.TXT and is passed to the Windows NT installation program using the /u:unattend.txt qualifier. The answer file has to adhere to a strict format that can be very complex; however, a utility on the NT Server CD called SETUPMGR.EXE (in Support\Deptools\i386 or support\tools under 2000) allows the information to be filled into dialog boxes. The utility will then create UNATTEND.TXT (or any other name) for you. The following is an example of how to use the SETUPMGR.EXE file:

1. Load the NT Server Installation CD-ROM.
2. Run <CD-ROM>:/Support/Deptools/i386/setupmgr.exe.
3. Click the New button and click OK to the Advice dialog box.
4. Click the General Setup button.
5. Click the User Information tab and type your name (e.g., John Savill, not your domain logon name!), your company, a computer name, and the product ID (from the back of the NT installation CD-ROM).
6. Click the Computer Role tab, and from the drop-down list, select the type (in this case, Workstation in Domain), and then type the Domain name.
7. Click Install Directory and choose the NT install directory.
8. Click Time Zone tab, and from the drop-down list, select your time zone.
9. If you choose a PDC, then you can click the Licence Mode tab and choose the licensing to be used.
10. Click OK.
11. Click the Networking Setup button.
12. Enter in the information for adapters and protocols; then click OK.
13. If you want to use NTFS, click the Advanced button and click the File System tab. Select convert to NTFS.
14. Click OK.
15. Click Save and enter a filename.
16. Click Exit.

Microsoft provides a document on automated installations at http://www.microsoft.com/NTWorkstation called Deployment Guide to Windows NT Setup. A list of parameters for unattended installations: http://support.microsoft.com/support/kb/articles/q155/1/97.asp.

FAQ 4.11 Is it possible to specify unique items during an unattended install?

The unattended installation file contains details for settings that will apply to all machines; however, you may want some settings, such as username, computer name, and TCP/IP address, to be different from machine to machine. This can be accomplished by producing a text file in a certain format, with different sections for each computer. The Uniqueness Database File (UDF) file is used by specifying the /UDF:ID[,<database filename>]. An example UDF file follows:

```
[UniqueIds]
u1 = UserData,TCPIPParams
u2 = UserData,TCPIPParams
[u1:UserData]
FullName = "John Savill"
ComputerName = SavillComp
ProductID = xxx-xxxxxx
[u1:TCParamSection]
IPAddress = 200.200.153.45
[u2:UserData]
FullName = "Kevin Savill"
ComputerName = KevinComp
ProductID = xxx-xxxxxx
[u2:TCParamSection]
IPAddress = 200.200.153.46
```

The ID specified is (in this example) u1 or u2. If the preceding file was saved as UDF.TXT, to perform an unattended installation for machine one, you use

```
winnt /b /s:z: /u:unattend.txt /UDF:u1,udf.txt
```

which sets the installation as user John Savill, computer name SavillComp, and IP address 200.200.153.45. If a parameter is specified in both the unattended answer file and the UDF, the value in the UDF will be used. The /b in the preceding command line means it's a floppyless installation, and the /s specifies the source for the installation files and UDF, etc. You have to have created the connection to Z already (net use z: //savillcomp/dist).

The structure of the UDF uses a subset of the sections available in the unattended answer file.

FAQ 4.12 When I perform an unattended installation, how do I avoid clicking Yes at the license agreement?

In the [unattended] section of your unattended answer file, insert the line

```
OemSkipEula = yes
```

FAQ 4.13 How do I remove Windows 95/DOS from my NT system?

The following procedure should be used on systems with Windows 95 and/or DOS installed; however, be aware it is sometimes a good idea to have a small DOS installation for use with hardware setup, and so forth. Before you start this procedure, make sure you have an up-to-date ERD (rdisk -s) and the three NT installation disks (four in Windows 2000) (winnt32 /ox) just in case :-).

1. Modify the attributes on BOOT.INI to allow the file to be edited:

   ```
   attrib c:\boot.ini -r -s
   ```

2. Using Notepad (or another test editor), open c:\BOOT.INI and remove the lines for DOS and/or Windows95 from the [operating systems] section. For example, the lines to remove may be one of the following:

   ```
   c:\="MS DOS 6.22"
   c:\bootsect.622="MS DOS 6.22"
   c:\="Windows 95"
   ```

   Lines to avoid removing are structured like

   ```
   multi(0)disk(0)rdisk(0)partition(2)\WINNT="Windows NT Workstation
   Version 4.00"
   ```

3. Save the file, and put back the file attributes:

   ```
   attrib c:\boot.ini +r +s
   ```

4. If you are removing DOS, then delete the DOS tree structure:

   ```
   deltree c:\dos
   ```

5. If you are removing Windows 95, then delete the Windows 95 tree structure. Make sure it is not the same directory that NT is installed in; this is very unlikely, however.

   ```
   deltree d:\window95
   ```

6. You will also need to remove applications that were installed only for use with Windows 95/DOS—for example, programs under Program Files—however, NT will also install applications in this directory, so be careful.

7. DOS and Windows 95 place a number of files on the boot partition that can be deleted, e.g., the following:

   AUTOEXEC.BAT
   CONFIG.SYS
   IO.SYS
   MSDOS.SYS
   BOOTLOG.TXT
   COMMAND.COM

8. It will probably be safer to copy them somewhere before deleting them and just check that NT boots OK. You may need to set them to be deletable using

```
attrib <file> -r -h -s
```

   You can basically delete all files at the base of the boot partition except

   BOOT.INI
   NTLDR
   NTDETECT.COM
   NTBOOTDD.SYS (for SCSI systems)

   which are needed for NT startup.
9. Reboot the machine, and Windows95 and DOS are now removed.

FAQ 4.14 I can't create a NTFS partition over 4GB during installation. What should I do?

During the text-based portion of the NT installation, it is possible to create and format partitions. The maximum size for an NTFS partition is very large (16 exabytes); however, the maximum size for a FAT partition under NT is 4GB (2GB under DOS). If you format a partition as NTFS during NT installation, it originally formats it as FAT and then converts it in the final stages of the NT installation, and thus, you are limited to a maximum partition size of 4GB during the NT installation.

Windows 2000 does not have this problem as it formats directly as NTFS, and so does not hit the 4GB FAT limit.

To get around this problem, several paths of action are open to you:

1. Before starting the installation, insert the disk into an existing NT installation and partition/format the disk using Disk Administrator. Then insert the disk into the machine to be installed.

2. Partition the disk into smaller partitions. If you have a 5GB disk, you could have a 1GB system partition, and a 4GB boot partition. The system partition is the partition where NT's core startup files are located, BOOT.INI, NTLDR, and NTDETECT.COM (NTBOOTDD.SYS if SCSI), and will normally be the active partition. The boot partition is the partition where NT stores the rest of its files—for example, the %systemroot% directory.
3. Create a 4GB partition at installation time and then extend the NTFS partition after installation has completed.
4. Start Disk Administrator (Start > Programs > Administrative Tools > Disk Administrator). Select the NTFS partition and, holding down the Ctrl key, select the unpartitioned space of the rest of the disk.
5. From the Partition menu, select Extend Volume Set.

Note: *You cannot extend a NTFS partition if it is the boot or system partition (because the boot/system partition cannot be part of a volume set).*

If you are performing an unattended installation, it is possible to create a greater than 4GB partition using the ExtendOEMPartition flag in the unattended file. This key causes text-mode setup to extend the partition on which the temporary Windows NT sources are located into any available unpartitioned space that physically follows it on the disk. Under the [unattended] section, include the lines:

```
FileSystem = convertNTFS
ExtendOemPartition = 1, NoWait
```

The NoWait is only available from Service Pack 1 and above.

Also, if you are installing from a distribution kit, you can copy the Service Pack 3 version of SETUPDD.SYS and replace the version in i386 folder of the NT distribution set.

NT4 ONLY

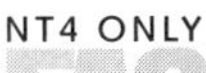

4.15 How can I use a network card that is not one of those shown with Network Client Administrator?

The Network Client Administrator tool located in the Administrative Tools section is a very useful tool but lacks the seemingly obvious function of Have disk to use a NDIS 2.0-compatible driver supplied with the network card. You can get around this though with a minimum of hassle.

1. Run Network Client Administrator as normal, selecting a network card similar to your card.
2. Once finished, locate the driver disk that was supplied with the network card (you did keep it ☺).
3. On the disk, there will be a NDIS folder and a DOS section.
4. Copy the .DOS file from this disk to the \net subdirectory on the disk created by Network Client Administrator.
5. Also in the directory should be a sample PROTOCOL.INI file; open this file and look for the line with a driver that has a $ on the end, for example:

   ```
   DriverName = "EL59X$"
   ```

   Write down this name.
6. Insert the disk created by the Network Client Administrator and move to the \net subdirectory.
7. Open the file SYSTEM.INI, edit the network drivers section, and change the netcard parameter to the name of the .DOS file you copied to the disk:

   ```
   [network drivers]
   netcard=EL59X.dos
   ```

8. After saving SYSTEM.INI, open PROTOCOL.INI (in the same directory), locate the DriverName parameter, and change to the name you found in the PROTOCOL.INI file supplied on the Network Card driver disk (the one you wrote down in step 5), for example:

   ```
   [ms$elnk3]
   DRIVERNAME=EL59X$
   ```

   If the card is a PCI card, make sure the I/O, slot, and so on are commented out, or set them to the correct values. Again, save the file.

The Network Client Administrator disk is now configured to use your network card. A known problem is with Irmatrac/Microdyne token ring adapters, and the procedure will not work unless the \net subdirectory on the disk is renamed to \dev.

This solution is fine for one-off disk creations; however, you may want to have the network card displayed as an option by the Network Card Administrator program. To do so, perform the following steps:

1. You have to have the clients directory shared on your hard disk—for example, d:\clients.

2. Copy the .DOS file from the network driver disk (windows for workgroups area) to the <client share name>\msclient\netsetup directory.
3. Edit the file <client share name>\msclient\netsetup\wcnet.inf and enter the following details. This information will be on the Network card installation disk as an OEMSETUP.INF or a similar file.

```
[netcard]
tcm$el59x="3Com Fast EtherLink/EtherLink III BusMaster Adapter
(3C59x)",0,ndis,ethernet,0x07,tcm$el59x,tcm$el59x_nif
```

   Also in the OEMSETUP.INF will be two sections that correspond to the last two parameters—for example, tcm$el59x and tcm$el59x_inf. Append these sections to the end of WCNET.INF, then save the file.

Network Client Administrator will now list the new card as an option as a network card.

FAQ 4.16 How can I make domain users members of local Administrators groups during an unattended installation?

The easiest way to do this is to use the **net localgroup** command; however, before you can use the command, you have to connect to the PDC and start the netlogon service. The following commands can be used in the unattended installation using the CMDLINES.TXT file:

```
net use \\<machine name of the PDC> /user:<domain name>\<username>
<password>
net start netlogon
net localgroup Administrators "<domain name>\<user>" /add
```

FAQ 4.17 Why do I have problems running a program as part of the unattended installation?

You can use the /e switch during the unattended installation to specify a program to run, for example,

```
winnt.exe /u:unattend.txt /s:w: /e:"w:\servpack\update -u -z"
```

The preceding can be used to install a service pack after the NT installation (-u for unattended, -z for no reboot); however, you may get an error, such as the following error in SETUPLOG.TXT:

```
Warning:
Setup was unable to invoke external program
<drive>:\<directory>\<program> because of the following error:
CreateProcess returned error 3.
```

This error occurs after the installation network drives are no longer mapped and w: no longer exists. Any source files need to be locally stored in order to be run, and then with the /e parameter, you need to use a local drive letter.

FAQ 4.18 I have Windows NT installed. How do I install Windows 98?

As with the installation of Windows 95, the system partition (the active partition, C) must be FAT and not NTFS because Windows 98 cannot read or write to an NTFS partition. Windows 98 places COMMAND.COM on the active partition (along with a blank AUTOEXEC.BAT).

If you system partition is not FAT, then you should back up your data, reformat the partition as FAT, and restore the backup.

Windows 98 is normally NT boot menu friendly, which means it will not replace the boot loader code of the disk but instead automatically adds an option to the boot menu (BOOT.INI) of the format:

```
C:\="Microsoft Windows 98"
```

This means upon booting, the machine Windows 98 or NT can be chosen.

To be on the safe side, before installing Windows 98, create a new Emergency Repair Disk (ERD) for NT using RDISK.EXE.

Windows 98 cannot be installed from within Windows NT, so if you have DOS also installed, boot from DOS (its boot menu item will be replaced after the Windows 98 installation with the Windows 98 name) and run SETUP.EXE on the Windows 98 installation disk.

If you do not have DOS installed, you should boot from a DOS boot disk with a driver for your CD-ROM and again run SETUP.EXE.

Once installation has started, you will be able to choose the installation drive and directory (only FAT partitions will be allowed). If NTFS partitions are on the system, a warning will be given that the contents will not be viewable under Windows 98.

Once installation has completed, no user action is needed, and you may boot from either installation.

If you find you **don't** have the NT boot menu and the machine boots straight into 98, perform the following:

1. Reboot the machine and boot from the NT installation disks.
2. After disk 2 you will be given a number of options, press R for repair.
3. Deselect all options except Inspect Boot Sector and continue.
4. Press Enter to detect hardware and insert disk 3.
5. The procedure will ask if you have an ERD; say Yes and insert the ERD.
6. The machine will then reboot into NT again.
7. Once in NT, go to a DOS session and type

   ```
   attrib c:\boot.ini -r -s
   ```

8. Edit BOOT.INI and insert the following at the bottom of the file:

   ```
   c:\=Microsoft Windows 98
   ```

9. Type the following:

   ```
   attrib c:\boot.ini +r +s
   ```

10. Reboot the machine, and you will have Windows 98 and NT options.

Make sure once you have completed the Windows 98 installation that you do **not** upgrade the active partition to FAT32. Windows NT 4.0 cannot read FAT32, and converting the active partition to FAT32 will render the NT boot menu unusable and unbootable.

FAQ 4.19 I have Windows 2000 installed, but when I try to install Windows NT 4.0 the installation fails. What should I do?

Windows 2000 has changed the boot loader and if you try to install Windows NT 4.0 afterward, Setup may continuously restart each time the computer is started without ever finishing.

Service Pack 4 provides an updated WINNT32.EXE file that allows Windows NT 4.0 to be installed after Windows 2000 so you will need to perform the following:

1. Copy the i386 directory structure from the Windows NT installation CD-ROM.
2. Rename the WINNT32.EXE filename to WINNT32.OLD.
3. Copy the WINNT32.EXE from the Service Pack 4 CD from the Support\Winnt32\i386 to your i386 directory structure.
4. Run WINNT32.EXE from your local stored copy.

FAQ 4.20 I want to install Windows 98 and NT. What filesystem should I use?

Windows 98 supports two filesystems, FAT and FAT32. Windows NT 4.0 supports two main filesystems FAT, and NTFS. The only common filesystem is FAT, which means the active partition, C, must be FAT. If you then partition the hard disk into one partition for the active partition, one for 98 (D) and one for NT (E), you could have FAT32 on D and NTFS on E, but you should be aware that the two operating systems will not be able to see the partition of the other. If you ever want a partition that can be seen by both, you will need FAT.

Windows 2000 introduces support for FAT32 so, in this case, the active partition could be FAT32, and you would need only one separate partition for NT if you wanted NTFS.

Some tools enable Windows 9x to read NTFS—for example, NTFSDOS from http://www.sysinternals.com; however, these tools are mainly read-only and may lead to corruption if not used correctly. Also bear in mind that Windows 2000 introduces NTFS 5.0, which these utilities will not be able to read.

FAQ 4.21 How do I manually install SCSI drivers before the autodetect of installation?

When you put in the first boot disk to install NT, for a brief moment, at the top of the screen in white lettering "Setup is inspecting your Hardware. . . ." is displayed. Press the F6 key at this point. Once the NT kernel is loaded, it will ask you to select which drivers to install at the end of reading disk 2 but before selecting the installation type.

FAQ 4.22 During the installation of Windows 2000 Server, why can the type of server not be set?

Unlike earlier versions of Windows NT, the role of a server can be changed at any time in its life—for example, from a member server to a domain controller, and from a domain controller back to a member server. This means that when initially installed, **all** servers are installed as standalone/member servers (even upgraded PDCs/BDCs), which then have to be promoted to domain servers.

For information on promoting a server to a domain controller, see FAQ 14.2.

FAQ 4.23 How do I delete the Recycle Bin as part of an unattended installation?

The Recycle Bin is just a Registry entry, so deleting the Registry entry removes the Recycle Bin.

Create the following in a file REMREYCL.INF:

```
[Version]
Signature = "$Windows NT$"
Provider=%Provider%
[Strings]
Provider="SavillTech Ltd"
[DefaultInstall]
AddReg = AddReg
DelReg = DelReg
UpdateInis = UpdateInis
[AddReg]
[DelReg]
HKEY_LOCAL_MACHINE\SOFTWARE\Microsoft\Windows\CurrentVersion\
Explorer\Desktop\NameSpace\{645FF040-5081-101B-9F08-00AA002F954E}
[UpdateInis]
```

You should then create a OEM folder in your i386 installation directory and copy the file REMREYCL.REG into the directory.

If the file CMDLINES.TXT exists, edit it; otherwise, create it (in the OEM directory) and add the following:

```
[Commands]
"rundll32 setupapi,InstallHinfSection DefaultInstall 128
.\remreycl.inf"
```

FAQ 4.24 How do I map a network drive during an unattended installation?

This may be useful if you want to install software, such as a service pack, during installation.

Using the CMDLINES.TXT file, it is easy to map to a network share. CMDLINES.TXT must be stored in the OEM directory under your NT installation area—for example, i386\OEM. A very basic UNATTEND.TXT consists of the following lines:

```
[Unattended]
OemPreinstall = yes
```

The map command should be under the [Commands] section of your CMDLINES.TXT file, for example,

```
[Commands]
".\net use <drive letter>: \\<server>\<share> /user:<domain>\<user>
[<password>] /persistent:no"
```

It is important to add the /user; otherwise, the system will attempt to use the System account, which does not have an actual user account, and thus the command would fail. The /persistent:no is used because the connection should not be remade at each logon.

One option is to enable the Guest account and give it access to the share, which means you could connect at /user:<domain>\Guest. This allows a connection to be made to the share even if the domain controller cannot be contacted.

FAQ 4.25 How can I install Windows 2000 on a machine with less than 64MB of memory?

By default you need 64MB of memory installed on a machine to install Windows 2000 Server; however, this limitation can be worked around.

1. Copy the Windows 2000 i386 installation structure to a hard disk/network drive.
2. Edit the file TXTSETUP.SIF located in the root of the i386 structure.
3. Search for "RequiredMemory".
4. Edit the line that allows you to change the amount of memory; however, change it only if you know what you are doing!

```
RequiredMemory=66584576
```

5. Save the file.
6. Install as normal.

Be aware that this will not work with upgrades/installs using WINNT32.EXE; it works only with WINNT.EXE.

FAQ 4.26 How do I use SmartDrv?

Why am I talking about the MS-DOS SmartDrv utility? Well, if you use the WINNT.EXE installation method for NT and do not use SmartDrv, the installation will take much more time.

At the most basic, you may create a DOS bootable disk (**format a: /s** from DOS) that just maps to a network drive and starts the installation. To take advantage of SmartDrv, copy the following files onto the disk:

- SMARTDRV.EXE
- HIMEM.SYS

You should then edit (or create) the file AUTOEXEC.BAT and add the line

```
<path>smartdrv.exe /q
```

For example, **a:smartdrv.exe /q**

Now edit (or again create) the file CONFIG.SYS and add the line:

```
device=himem.sys
```

HIMEM.SYS is needed by SmartDrv and allows access to higher areas of memory.

This applies equally to locally installed copies of DOS; however, SMARTDRV.EXE is automatically installed, but make sure you are using it by looking at AUTOEXEC.BAT.

Also, adding the following line to CONFIG.SYS on the bootable disk can speed up operations:

```
BUFFERS=99
```

FAQ 4.27 How can I recreate the Windows NT installation disks?

To recreate the installation disks, perform the following:

1 Start up an operating system (DOS, WFW, Windows 9x, or NT).
2. Insert the NT installation CD.
3. Start a command session (COMMAND.COM or CMD.EXE if NT).
4. Move to the i386 folder.
5. If you are running NT or Windows 9x, enter the command

   ```
   winnt32 /ox
   ```

   For any other 16-bit operating systems, type

   ```
   winnt /ox
   ```

6. You will be asked to insert three disks.

Done!

If you want to create Windows 2000 startup disks, perform the following:

1. Again start up an operating system.
2. Insert the 2000 installation CD.
3. Start a command session (COMMAND.COM or CMD.EXE if NT).
4. Move to the bootdisk folder.
5. Type the command

   ```
   makeboot a:
   ```

6. You will have to insert four disks.

Done.

FAQ 4.28 How can I stop the Welcome to Windows NT screen during setup?

Normally when a user logs on for the first time, a splash screen is displayed welcoming new users. This screen can be disabled in a number of ways.

1. Copy the i386 directory structure from the Windows NT installation CD to a distribution server.
2. Create the UNATTEND.TXT file as normal.
3. In the i386 directory on the distribution server, rename the file WELCOME.EX_ to WELCOME.BAK:

   ```
   rename welcome.ex_ welcome.bak
   ```

4. Create a backup of the file TXTSETUP.SIF (which is also in the i386 directory) to TXTSETUP.BAK.
5. Edit TXTSETUP.SIF and place a semicolon (;) in front of the WELCOME.EXE line, so the line

   ```
   welcome.exe=1,,,,,,,1,0,0
   ```

   becomes

   ```
   ;welcome.exe=1,,,,,,,1,0,0
   ```

   Save the modified file.
6. Create a backup of DOSNET.INF (again in the i386 directory) to DOSNET.BAK.
7. Edit DOSNET.INF and again place a semicolon (;) in front of the WELCOME.EXE line, so the link

   ```
   d1,welcome.exe
   ```

   becomes

   ```
   ;d1,welcome.exe
   ```

8. Save the modified file.
9. Perform the unattended installation from the distribution share.

The preceding just stops the installation of the WELCOME.EXE image and thus stops it from executing. An alternative is to create a Registry script that runs during installation. This script disables the Welcome dialog.

1. As before, copy the i386 directory from the NT CD to a distribution server.
2. Create an UNATTEND.TXT file as per normal.
3. Create a directory called oem under the i386 directory on the distribution server.
4. In the oem directory, create a file CMDLINES.TXT and enter the following lines:

```
[Commands]
".\regedit /s nowelcom.reg"
```

5. Again in the oem directory, create a file NOWELCOM.REG with the following lines (including the blank line):

```
REGEDIT4

[HKEY_CURRENT_USER\Software\Microsoft\Windows\CurrentVersion
\Explorer\Tips]
"DisplayInitialTipWindow"=dword:00000000
"Show"=hex:00,00,00,00
"Next"=hex:03,00
```

6. Copy the file REGEDIT.EXE from the directory into the oem directory.
7. Perform the unattended installation from the distribution share.

FAQ 4.29 I receive an error message "The System is not fully installed." What can I do?

This error is usually caused by using Sysprep with a third-party network client and is caused by a Registry entry being incorrectly updated.

To correct this situation, you need to install a second copy of NT onto the system and perform the following steps:

1. Boot into the second copy of NT.
2. Start the Registry editor (REGEDT32.EXE).
3. Select HKEY_LOCAL_MACHINE.
4. From the Registry menu, select Load Hive.

5. Move to the %systemroot%\system32\Config directory of the primary NT installation and select the System file. Click Open.
6. Type any name for the key—for example, System primary and click OK.
7. Double-click the new hive, expand Setup and double-click SystemSetupInProgress.
8. Change from 1 to 0. Click OK.
9. Select the key created in step 6 and select Unload Hive from the Registry menu.
10. Close the Registry editor and reboot into your primary installation.

NT4 ONLY

FAQ 4.30 How do I add a Network Install tab to Windows NT 4.0?

Windows 2000 provides the built-in ability to publish applications to users, groups of users, and domains; however, some of this functionality is still possible with Windows NT 4.0.

It's possible to add a Network Install tab to the 4.0-based clients with a list of installable applications as follows:

1. Copy the file APPS.INF from the %systemroot%\inf directory of a server to a network share on a server.
2. Open the copied version of APPS.INF and insert the underlined text (although your applications and their locations will be different):

```
[Version]
Signature = $Chicago$
ClassGUID={00000000-0000-0000-0000-000000000000}
LayoutFile = layout.inf

[appinstalllist]
Office 2000=\\titanic\Apps\off2000\setup.exe
Paint Shop Pro=\\titanic\Apps\psp\setup.exe

[PIF95]
123.COM=%123.COM%,moricons.dll,50,,123.COM
..
```

The clients must be configured to look at the updated APPS.INF file on the server by a Registry update:

3. Start the Registry editor (REGEDIT.EXE).
4. Move to HKEY_LOCAL_MACHINE\SOFTWARE\Microsoft\Windows\CurrentVersion.

5. From the Edit menu, select New > String Value.
6. Enter a name of **AppInstallPath**.
7. Double-click the new value and set to the location of the shares APPS.INF file—for example, \\titanic\inffiles\apps.inf.
8. Close the Registry editor.

Starting the Add/Remove Programs Control Panel applet will now show a new Network Install tab (see Figure 4-1).

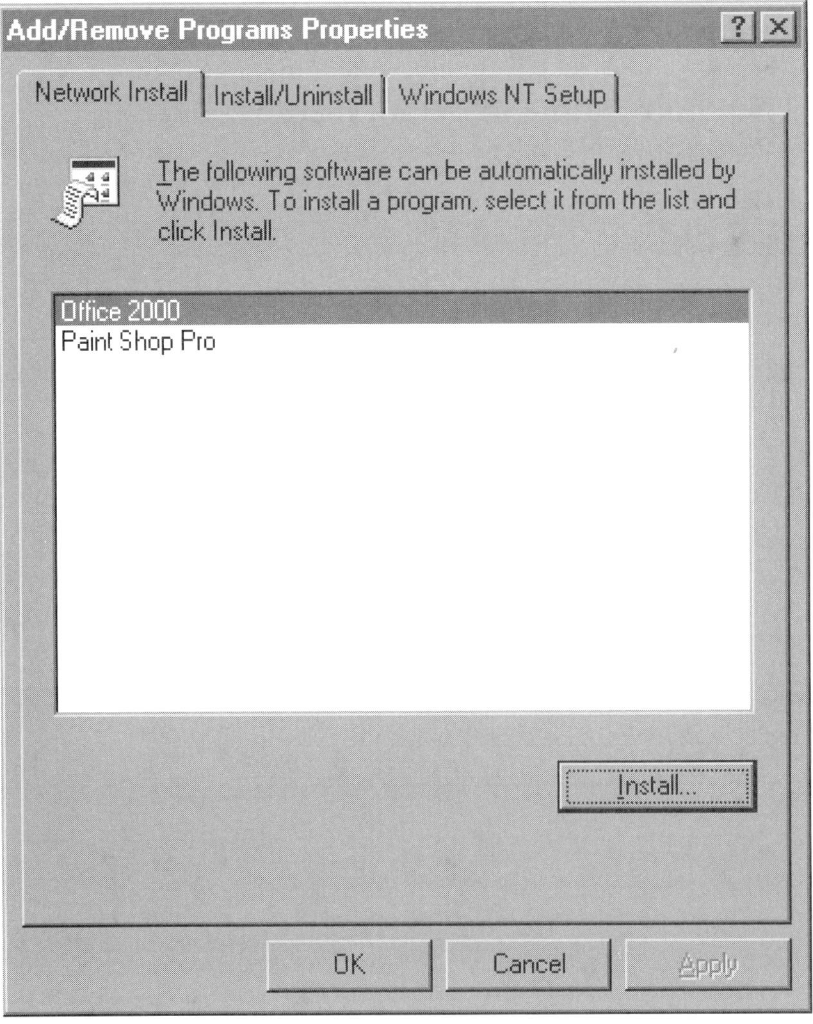

Figure 4-1 Installing software from the network

Obviously, editing the Registry on every client will be time-consuming, and so if you implement system policies, you can include this procedure as part of the policy, using the following .ADM file:

```
CLASS MACHINE

CATEGORY "Network Install"
 POLICY "Location of the Network install information"
 KEYNAME SOFTWARE\Microsoft\Windows\CurrentVersion
 PART "Locations" EDITTEXT
 VALUENAME "AppInstallPath"
 DEFAULT \\SERVER\INFSHARE\APPS.INF
 END PART
 PART "Create Network Install ability" TEXT END PART
 END POLICY
END CATEGORY ;
```

FAQ 4.31 How can I disable the Configure Server Wizard in Windows 2000?

When a user logs onto a 2000 machine for the first time, the Configure Server Wizard may start. It is possible to disable it by deselecting the Show this screen at startup checkbox; however, you may want this dialog to **never** be shown.

To disable an existing installation for any new users, perform the following steps:

1. Start the Registry editor (REGEDIT.EXE).
2. Move to HKEY_USERS\.DEFAULT\Software\Microsoft\Windows NT\CurrentVersion\Setup\Welcome.
3. Double-click srvwiz and set to 0. Click OK.
4. Close the Registry editor.

If you want to disable the wizard at installation time, perform the following:

1. Copy the contents of the installation folder (i386) to a share.
2. On the distribution share, locate the HIVEDEF.INF file.
3. Search for "srvwiz". Edit the line

```
HKCU,"Software\Microsoft\Windows
NT\CurrentVersion\Setup\Welcome","srvwiz",0x00010003,1
```

Change the end value 1 to 0:

```
HKCU,"Software\Microsoft\Windows
NT\CurrentVersion\Setup\Welcome","srvwiz",0x00010003,0
```

4. Save the file.

Any installations installed from this distribution point will not display the Configure Server Wizard.

FAQ 4.32 How do I install the Remote Installation Services?

Windows 2000 introduces the Remote Installation Services (RIS), which is a DHCP-based remote boot technology used to install an OS on a client's local hard disk from a remote source (CD or RIPrep image on a server share). A network boot can be initiated by either the system BIOS, a specific function key, or by a special remote boot floppy provided for existing unmanageable (ROM-less) client computers.

You must have a DNS, DHCP, and directory services server on the network before installing. Also RIS does not currently support either the Distributed or Encrypted File System.

To install on a server, perform the following steps:

1. Start the Add/Remove Programs Control Panel applet (Start > Settings > Control Panel > Add/Remove Programs).
2. Click the Add/Remove Windows Components button on the left side of the dialog.
3. Click Next on the Components Wizard dialog.
4. Check the Remote Installation Services option and click Next.
5. You will need to insert the Server CD-ROM.
6. Click Finish.
7. Click Close on the main dialog.
8. You will be asked to reboot the computer.

Once the reboot has finished, you need to complete the installation as follows:

1. Start the Add/Remove Programs Control Panel applet (Start > Settings > Control Panel > Add/Remove Programs).
2. Click the Add/Remove Windows Components button on the left side of the dialog.

3. Under Set up services, click Configure in the Configure Remote Installation Services area. (You can start the wizard directly by running RISETUP.EXE.)
4. Click Next on the welcome screen.
5. You will be asked for a location for the RemoteInstall path, which by default is d:\remoteInstall. This drive must be NTFS and **not** the system or boot partition. Click Next.
6. Enter the location of the Windows Professional files (a disk or network share), for example, f:\i386. Click Next.
7. Enter a folder name to store the installation (by default, WIN2000.PRO). Click Next.
8. Enter a friendly description for the installation and help text. Click Next. (See Figure 4-2.)

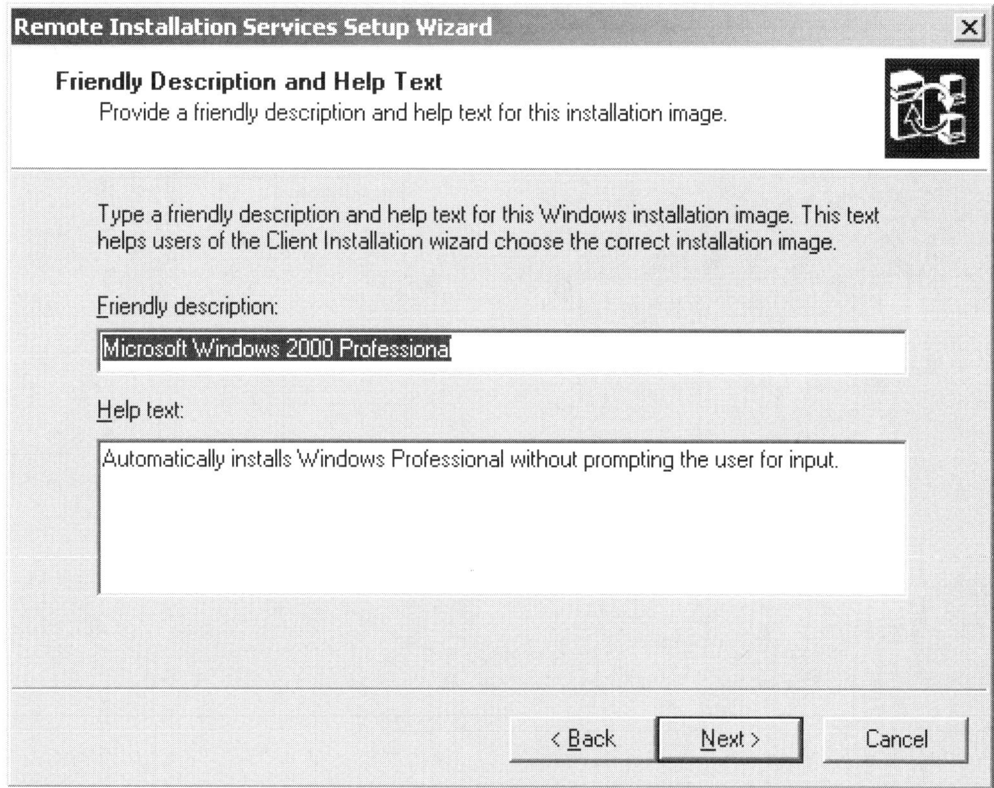

Figure 4-2 Entering a friendly description for the installation with Help

9. A summary will be shown detailing the source, destination, and OS version (see Figure 4-3). Click Finish.

   The files will be copied from the source to the destination, and the trivial FTP (tftpd) and NetPC Boot Service Manager services (binlsvc) will be installed and started.

10. Click Done.

If the server is not already DHCP authorized, you will need to authorize it (even if it's not a DHCP server), see FAQ 19.13.

The server is now ready to provide a network-based installation for Windows 2000 Professional using a standard Microsoft-provided template file, which can be changed. If you right-click on the server and select Properties within the Active Directory Users and Computers MMC snap-in, you will see a new tab Remote Install, which is used to manage the service.

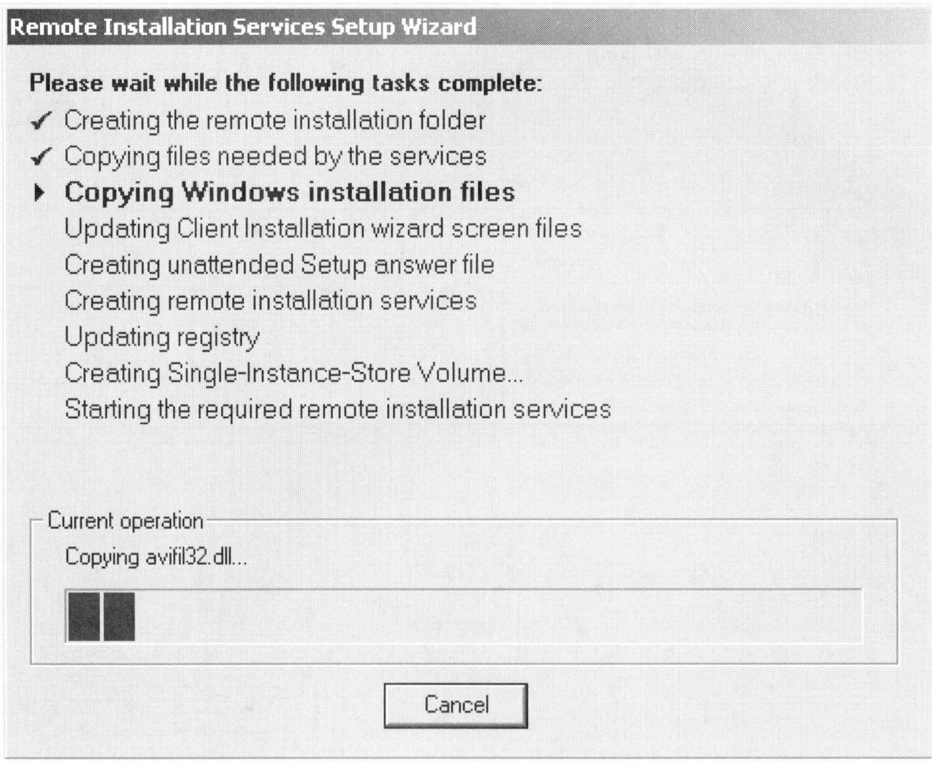

Figure 4-3 File copy in progress

Extra Information

The reason the RemoteInstall path cannot be the boot or system partition is that this volume will get accessed heavily by remote clients and the SIS (Single Instance Store) service runs on this volume. If the volume utilized is the system/boot volume, the SIS service cannot run.

SIS reduces the amount of disk space required on these volumes by removing duplicate files and placing the data in a common directory. The duplicate files are then truncated into reparse points that refer to the common directory for the file data.

FAQ 4.33 How do I move the distribution point for Remote Installation Services?

To move the distribution point for the Remote Installation Services, perform the following actions. The destination must still be NTFS and **not** the boot or system partition.

1. Stop both the trivial FTP and NetPC Boot Service Manager services:

   ```
   net stop binlsvc
   net stop tftpd
   ```

2. Copy the remoteinstall directory from the current drive to the destination:

   ```
   xcopy <current drive>:\remoteinstall <dest drive>:\remoteinstall
   ```

3. Delete the old reminst share:

   ```
   net share reminst /d
   ```

4. Recreate pointing to the new location:

   ```
   net share reminst=<new drive>:\remoteinstall
   ```

5. Invoke the RIS self-check mechanism. (The wizard will be started; click Next and then Finish.)

   ```
   risetup -check
   ```

6. Restart the services:

   ```
   net start binlsvc
   net start tftpd
   ```

If you get an error from the client such as "File not Found," change HKEY_LOCAL_MACHINE\System\CCS\Services\Tftpd\paramters\Directory to point to the new directory (<new drive>:\RemoteInstall).

Installation images stored in locations other than \\<server name>\<share name>\RemoteInstall\Setup\<language>\Images and referenced through junction points are not acted upon by the SIS Groveler agent and may use extra disk space.

4.34 How do I create a bootable Remote Installation Services client disk?

A special utility is used to create a boot disk to allow clients without PXE (Preboot eXecution Environment) to boot and install using the Remote Installation Services (providing they have a support NIC).

To create the boot disk, perform the following steps:

1. Click Start and select Run.
2. Type

   ```
   \\<RIS server name or IP
   address>\RemoteInstall\Admin\i386\rbfg.exe
   ```

3. Select the disk drive (A or B).
4. Insert a floppy disk.
5. Click Create Disk (see Figure 4-4).
6. Click No to create another disk.

You can now use this disk to boot a machine. To check which adapters it supports, click the "Adapter List" button in the RBFG utility.

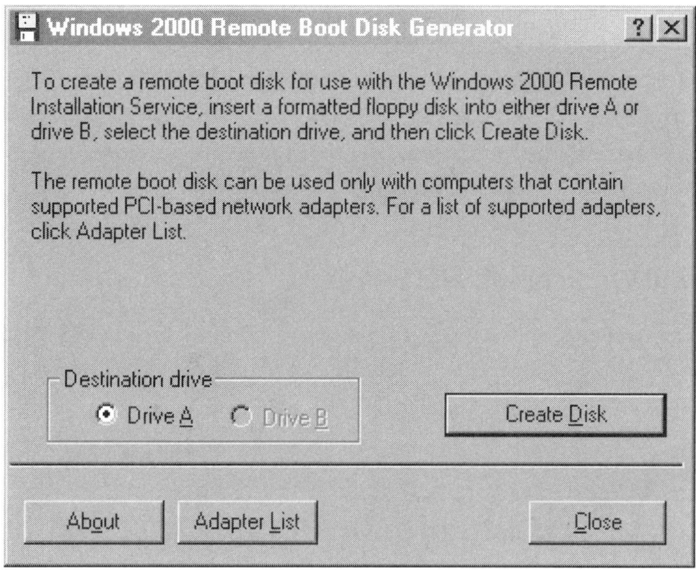

Figure 4-4 Creating a boot disk for use with RIS

FAQ 4.35 What operating systems can I clone?

The following is a brief summary of each operating system's ability to be cloned:

Windows 95

Windows 95 was not designed to support disk-image copying and is not supported, although copying on systems with similar hardware should work.

Windows 98

Windows 98 duplication is supported if the Microsoft Windows 98 Image Preparation Tool is used to prepare the master disk image.

Windows NT Workstation and Server 4.0

Microsoft supports cloning as a method of distribution in the following scenarios but **not** for domain controllers:

1. The master disk is copied at the end of the text portion of the setup procedure but **before** the GUI phase begins. This is because a local SID has not yet been created and no major specific hardware specific configuration has been completed.
2. The master system has the system preparation tool used, then cloned and the target system has identical hardware.

Windows 2000 Workstation and Server

The procedure is the same as with the 4.0 procedure but with the 2000 version of SYSPREP.EXE and you can completely install Windows 2000, configure it, add applications, and then run Sysprep and copy the master disk.

FAQ

4.36 How can I configure the Remote Installation Services options?

To configure an RIS server, perform the following steps:

1. Start the Active Directory Users and Computers MMC snap-in (Start > Programs > Administrative Tools > Active Directory Users and Computers).
2. Select the computer's container.
3. Right-click on the computer and select Properties.
4. Select the Remote Install tab.
5. You can now select the clients that the server responds to, and you can also select to let the service perform a self-check by clicking Verify Server. Clicking Advanced Settings allows rules for new computer names to be set and also extra images and tools can be added.

Client options are configured using the domain/site/OU policy object, and in the following example, we look at the domain Group Policy Object (GPO):

1. Start the Active Directory Users and Computers MMC snap-in (Start > Programs > Administrative Tools > Active Directory Users and Computers).
2. Right-click on the domain and select Properties.
3. Select the Group Policy tab.
4. Select the domain policy object and click Edit.

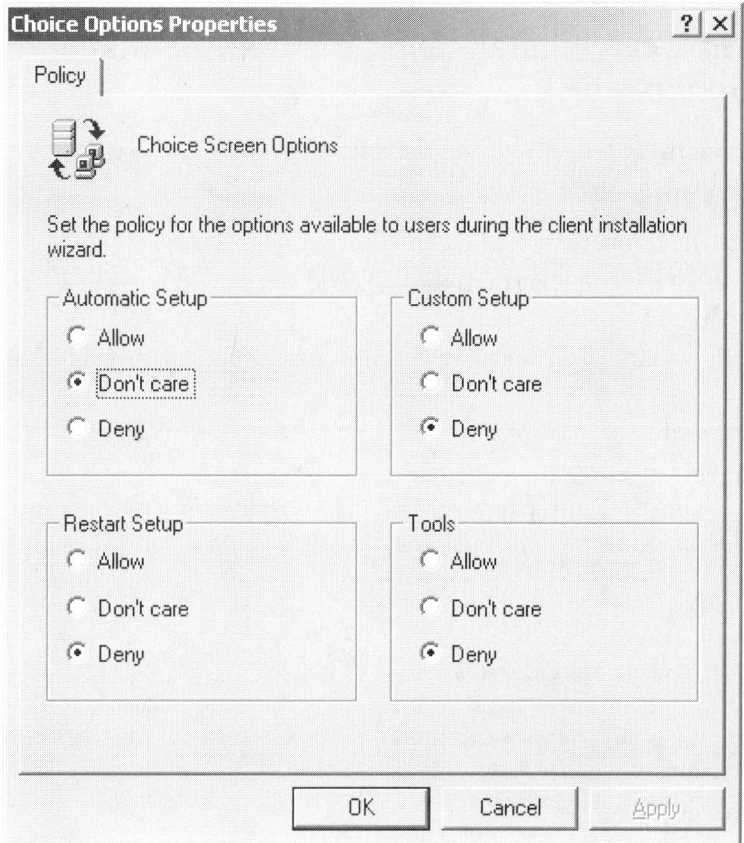

Figure 4-5 User options allowed for installation

5. Expand the User Configuration\Windows Settings\Remote Installation Service.
6. Double-click Choice Options (see Figure 4-5).

   Allow and Deny are obvious, but the Don't care option means that other policies might take effect (because you often will have multiple GPOs affecting a single client).
7. Make any changes.
8. Click Apply, then OK.

   Once you have made the changes, force a reload of the policy:

```
secedit /refreshpolicy user_policy
```

FAQ 4.37 How can I install using the Remote Installation Services disk?

To install using the RIS disk, perform the following:

1. Insert the RIS disk.
2. Reboot the computer.
3. Upon reboot, it will boot from the disk, and you should press F12 for a network boot.
4. A DHCP address will be negotiated, and a welcome screen will be shown. Press Enter.
5. Enter a username, password, and domain. The Client Installation Wizard is displayed.
6. Type a valid username, password, and domain name. You may use the Internet-style logon format (for example, Username@Company.com).

   ```
   Username: [savillj ]
   Password: [pass]
   Domain name: [savilltech.com]
   ```

7. Depending on the options configured in the Group Policy Object, you may have options to:
   - Automatic setup
   - Custom setup
   - Restart a previous setup attempt
8. Press Enter.
9. If you have more than one client image, you can select the image to install. Press Enter.
10. A warning that all data will be deleted will be shown. Press Enter.
11. The computer account name and a Global Unique ID will be shown. To start installation, press Enter.
12. The normal installation actions of NTDETECT will start, and NT installation will commence.

FAQ 4.38 How do I create a new Remote Installation Services image?

It's possible to create new images based on existing installations. Doing so has the advantage of having applications already installed and configured. To configure the new image, perform the following steps:

1. Create a 2000 Professional installation with applications installed. Both the system and boot partition must be the same partition—for example, C.
2. Log on to the machine as an Administrator.
3. Run the RIPrep image from the RIS server (Start > Run > \\<RIS server>\REMINST\Admin\i386\riprep.exe)—for example, \\titanic\REMINST\Admin\i386\riprep.exe.
4. Click Next at the Welcome dialog (see Figure 4-6).
5. Enter the server name of the RIS server. Click Next.

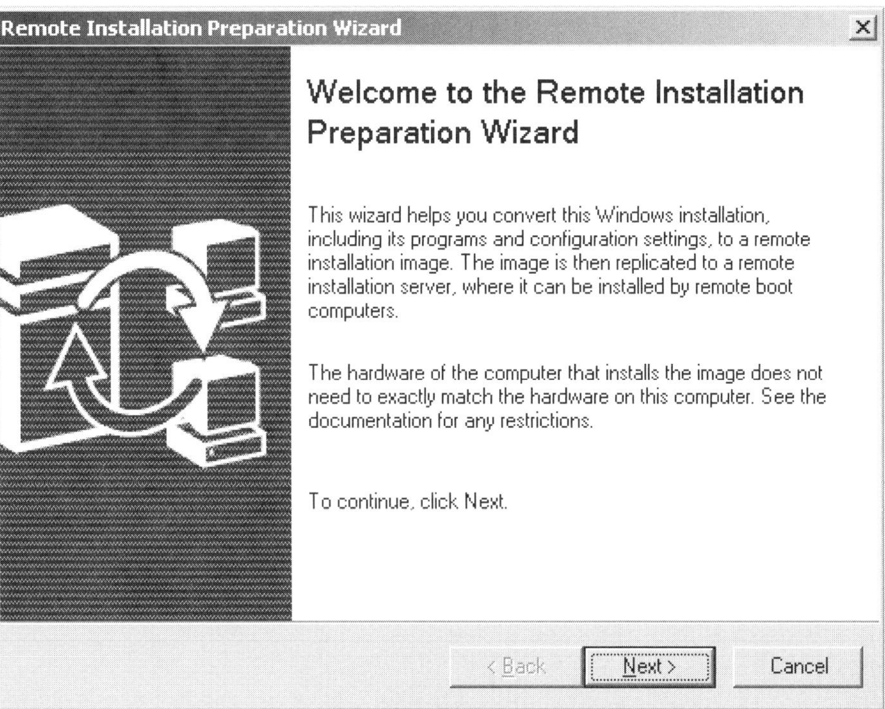

Figure 4-6 The first page of the Remote Installation Preparation Wizard

6. Enter a folder name for the new install—for example, 2000andapps. Click Next.
7. Enter a friendly description and help text (see Figure 4-7). Click Next.
8. Any running applications will be displayed, and you will be asked to stop them. Click Next after stopping them.
9. A summary of the remote installation server and folder name will be displayed. Click Next.
10. A screen explaining the next step will be shown. Click Next to begin the image preparation.
11. The program will verify the Windows version; check the partitions are OK and then copy files to the RIS server. This process may take some time.
12. The machine will then shut down, and you may reboot and use as normal.

If you examine the RIS server, you now have an extra client image.

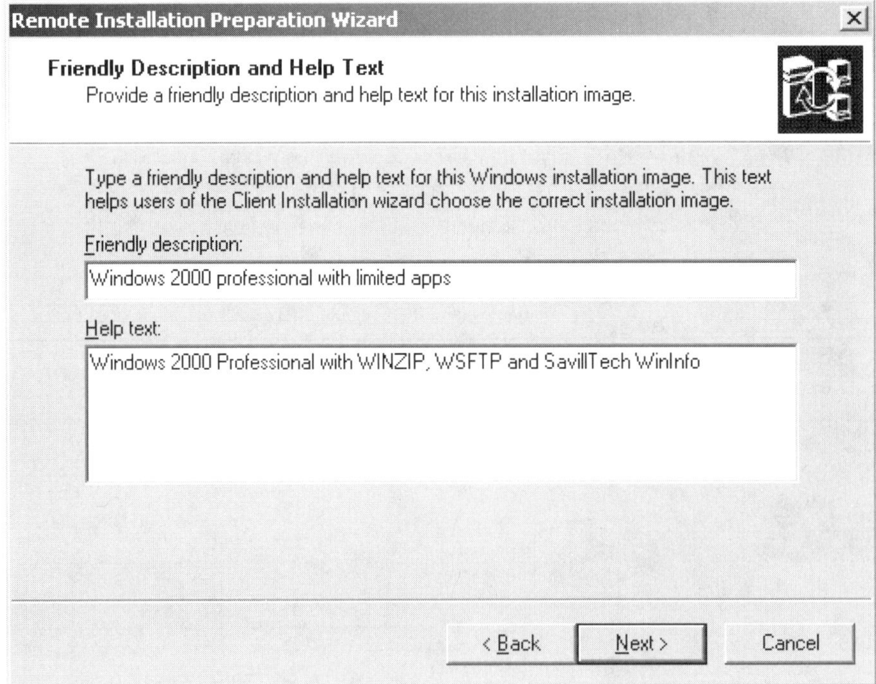

Figure 4-7 A description for the RIS instance

FAQ 4.39 How do I create a bootable Windows 2000/NT installation CD-ROM?

It's possible to create a bootable CD-ROM from the basic i386 structure. You will require version 3.7D of CDRWIN from http://www.goldenhawk.com and will need to load the necessary ASPI drivers. The free download version is fully functional but will only write at one speed.

Before starting the CD creation, create a directory and copy into it the i386 structure of 2000 and the CDROM_IS.5 file from the CD-ROM. As of Release Candidate 2, the name is CDROM_IS.5. You can check which CSROM_IS file it's expecting by looking at file i386\layout.inf, for example:

```
[Version]
signature="$Windows NT$"
ClassGUID={00000000-0000-0000-0000-000000000000}

[SourceDisksNames]

_x = %srvcd%,\cdrom_is.5,,""
_1 = %srvcd%,\cdrom_is.5,,""
_2 = %srvcd%,\cdrom_is.5,,""
_3 = %srvcd%,\cdrom_is.5,,""
_4 = %srvcd%,\cdrom_is.5,,""
etc...
```

Now you have a directory on disk with the i386 structure, and the CDROM_IS.5 file.

1. Start the CDRWIN program.
2. Insert your CD-ROM.
3. Select the Extract Disc/Tracks/Sectors option (the third button from the left on the top row—see Figure 4-8).

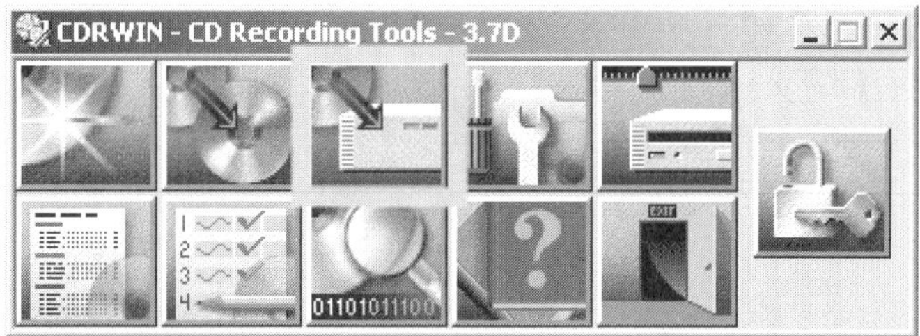

Figure 4-8 CDRWIN's main screen

4. Select extract mode Select Sectors. Enter a image filename—for example, CDSECTORBIN. Leave the file format as automatic and set the sector selection to start 20, end 20, and datatype Mode1 (2048). (See Figure 4-9) Click Start.
5. Click OK to the success message and close the Extract dialog.
6. Now select the File Backup and Tools CDRWIN option (see Figure 4-10).

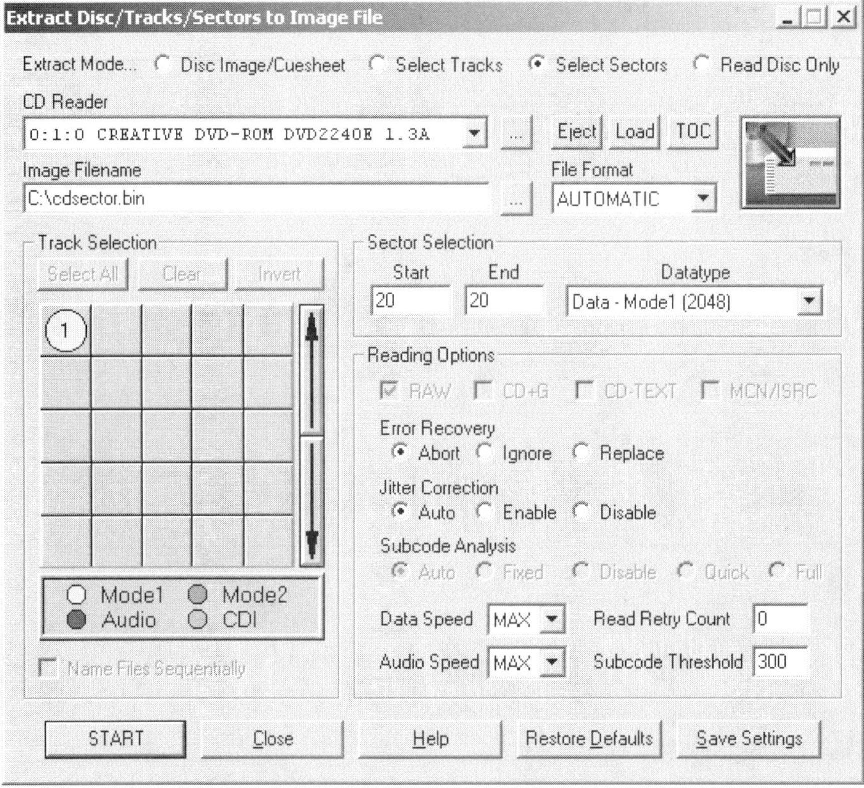

Figure 4-9 Options required to extract the required area

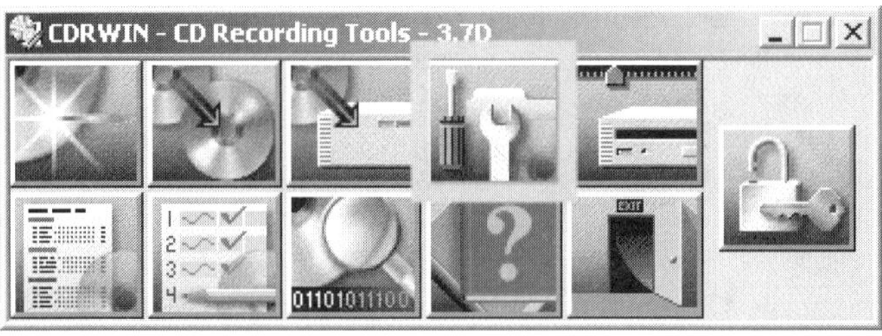

Figure 4-10 Select the CDRWIN write component

7. Select the option to Build and Record an ISO9660 Image File (see Figure 4-11). Click Add and select your server directory. Enter an ISO9660 image file—for example, ntsrv2072.
8. Select the options as shown in Figure 4-11.
9. Click Advanced Options.
10. Under Volume Label, type **NTSRV2195** (if it was build 2195).
11. Select the Bootable Disk tab.
12. Check the Make Bootable Disc and select Custom for the Media Emulation Type (see Figure 4-12). The image file should be the file created in step 4. Enter the Developer Name of Microsoft Corporation; for Load Segment, enter **07C0**, and for Load Sector Count, **4**. Click OK.
13. Click Start to begin making the CD.

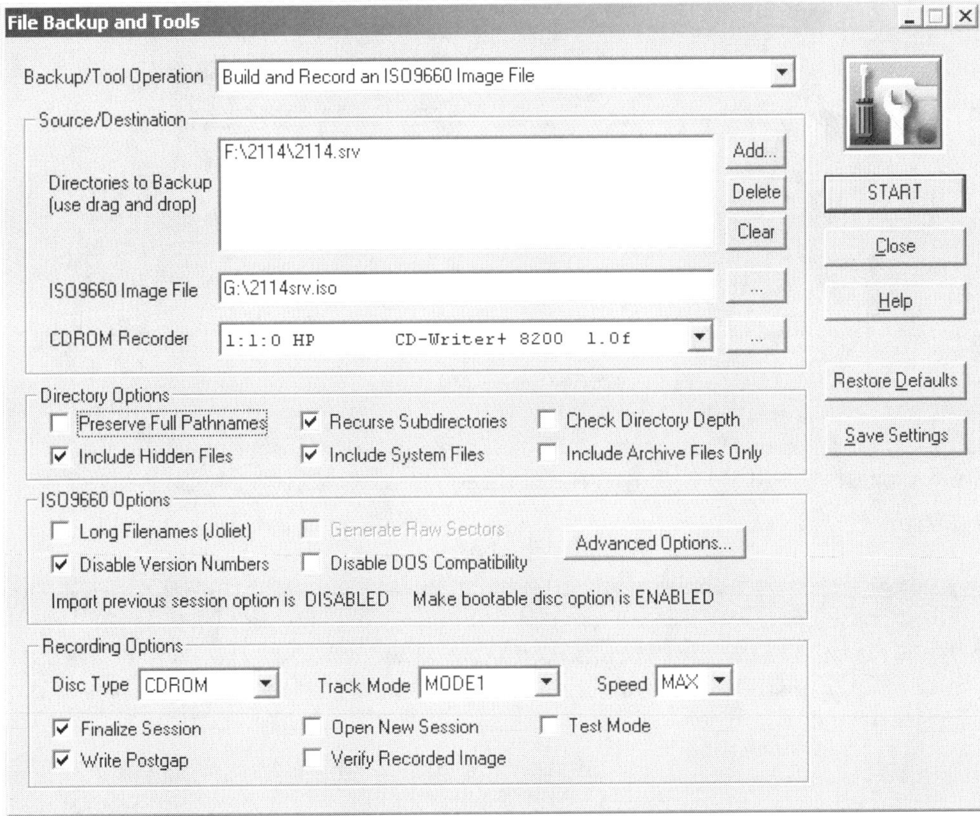

Figure 4-11 The options used to write a CD

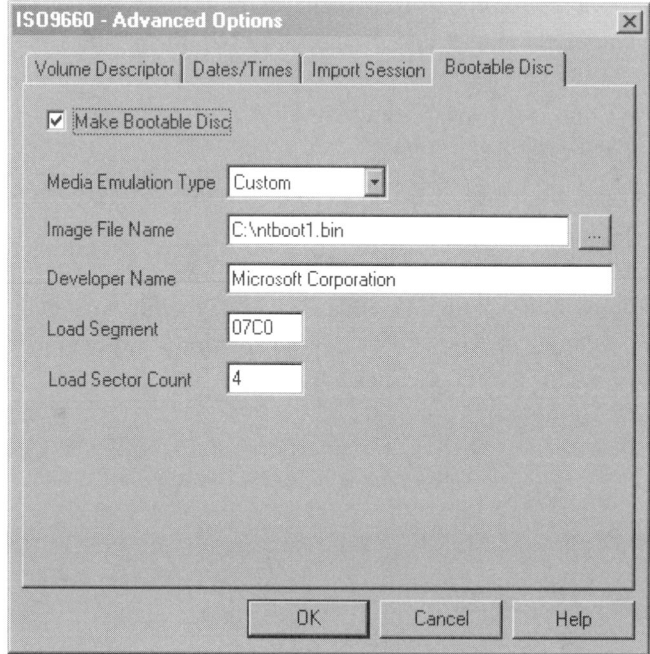

Figure 4-12 Selecting values for a bootable CD

Once CD completion is complete, you will have a file where you specified the ISO9660 image file of around 400MB, which may be deleted (it's just the ISO image that was copied to the CD).

You will now be able to boot with the CD (providing the motherboard and BIOS support CD-ROM booting). I tested the preceding procedure on build 2195 of Windows 2000.

This is thanks to Joseph R. Worrall, who provided most of the preceding procedure originally for Beta 2—I've updated it for build 2114 and the final version.

You can also use this procedure to make a Windows NT 4.0 bootable CD in the same way. You use the same instructions as Windows 2000, except that instead of CDROM_IS.5 (for the server), you need the CDROM_S.40 (or an equivalent _W.40 for the workstation). You also need the BOOTFIX.BIN file from a Windows 2000 i386 directory (this is the cool bit that says "Press any key to boot from CD-ROM"—another bonus!). Thanks goes to Steve Randall for pointing this out.

FAQ 4.40 Where is Setup Manager in Windows 2000?

Windows 2000 includes Setup Manager, which can be used to create distribution scripts for various types of installation including:

- Windows 2000 Professional unattended installation
- Windows 2000 Server unattended installation
- Remote Installation Services
- Sysprep installation

Setup Manager is shipped with the Resource Kit and is contained in DEPLOY.CAB as SETUPMGR.EXE and can be extracted using a utility such as Winzip. It is self-contained and does not require installation; you can just run the image, which will then start a wizard that allows you to specify the information you require (see Figure 4-13).

Figure 4-13 First page of the Windows 2000 Setup Manager Wizard

4.41 What is the Microsoft Installer Package format?

Windows 2000 introduces the concept of publishing applications using the Active Directory; however, to support this new ability, the application has to be supplied with a new type of installation file, a .MSI file, which is of the Microsoft Windows Installer Server package format.

These MSI files include information about Registry entries, core files, and so on, and they include a summary of the application details such as name and publisher. This knowledge of the Registry entry and file usage means that when the application starts and it detects that a Registry entry or a core file is missing, the Installer can automatically redownload information from the distribution server and fix itself.

Once you have your .MSI package, you can publish via the Group Policy editor to domains, organizational units, and sites. It's also easy to upgrade and retire packages, all via the .MSI file. Current applications that support Microsoft installer packages are Microsoft Office 2000 and the Windows 2000 Resource Kit (among others) as well as any other package that meets the Windows 2000 Logo requirement.

Service packs are shipped with MSI files, allowing you to deploy them via Group Policies with very little effort.

The Installer is best paired with the Remote Installation Services allowing RIS to install the operating system and allowing Group Policies to install the applications and settings. Of course, you may still want to use Systems Management Server (SMS) for some features; Windows 2000 has been designed to work with and not against SMS 2.0.

4.42 How do I create an MSI file from a legacy application?

The problem at the moment is that many applications (especially older programs) do not ship with MSI files, and so deploying legacy applications via Group Policies is not possible. Windows 2000 ships with WinINSTALL LE, which can be used in the same way as SYSDIFF. You take a snapshot of your system, install the application, and take an after snapshot. Then a discover program runs, extracting the different files and Registry entries that have been made.

It's important to run WinINSTALL LE on a clean system. By "clean system," I mean don't run it on an installation that has applications installed on it because when you install an application, WinINSTALL may check if certain runtimes and so on are installed. If runtimes are already present, the setup will not bother to recopy over, and this will mean your distribution package will be missing vital files.

To install WinINSTALL LE, perform the following steps. It's recommended that you **not** install the application on the PC that's going to act as the package-creation computer in case the program itself affects the installation of the applications:

1. Insert the Windows 2000 Server CD.
2. Move to the valuadd\3rdparty\mgmt\winstle folder.
3. Double-click the SWIADMLE.MSI file.
4. The Installer will begin, and a progress bar displays showing the progress of the installation.

A folder, Seagate Software, will be created under the Start menu's Program folder-Seagate Software.

The first stage is to take a snapshot of the blank Windows 2000 Professional installation so any changes made by the application installation will be detected.

1. Log on to the Professional reference installation as an Administrator.
2. Run the Discover Wizard from the distribution server. (Do not map a drive; use the Run dialog or Network Neighborhood.) For example, \\titanic.savilltech.com\d$\Program Files\Seagate Software\Winstall\DiscoZ.exe.
3. The wizard will start; click Next.
4. Enter a name for the package (the name of the software for which you are creating a package) and a path for the .MSI file (see Figure 4-14). (Make sure the path is on a drive other than one that forms part of the package and select a new empty directory.) Click Next.
5. Select a drive for the temporary files and click Next.
6. Select the drives that the discover program should scan and click Next.
7. Select the files to exclude from the scan (leave as the default unless you know what you're doing—see Figure 4-15). Click Next.
8. The WinINSTALL Discover program will then start.
9. Once complete, the program will ask you to click OK, which will prompt you for a setup program to run. This setup program is the legacy application that you want to create an .MSI file for.
10. Select the setup program you want to run and click Open.
11. Continue the application setup as per normal.

Once you have installed the application and made configuration changes, you need to create the after snapshot:

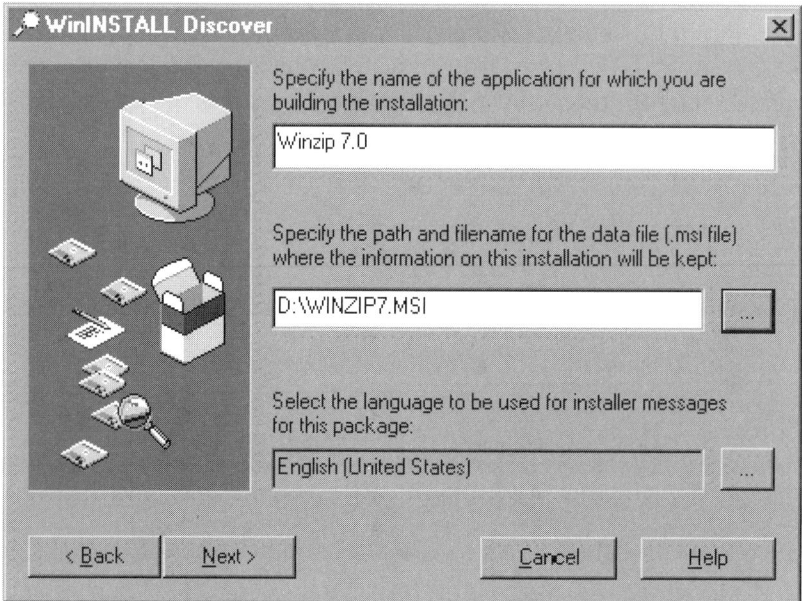

Figure 4-14 Creating a .MSI package

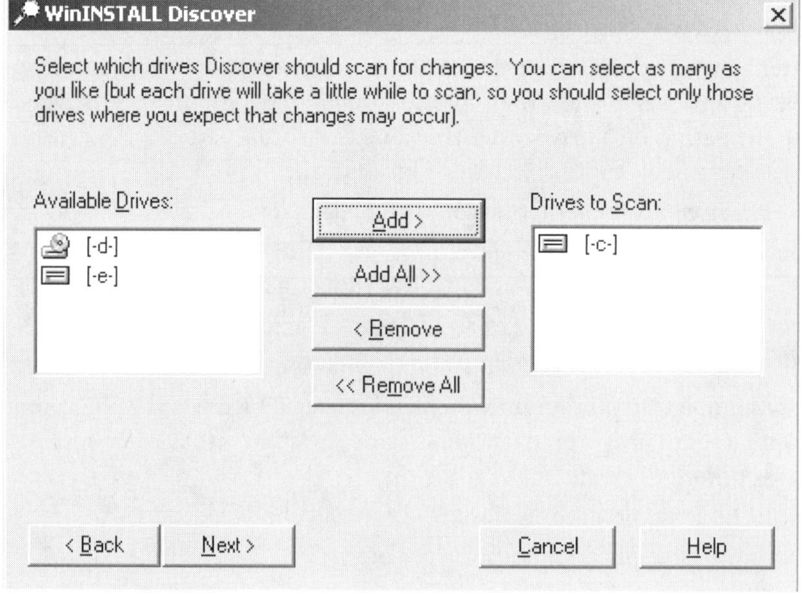

Figure 4-15 Selecting the partitions that will be checked

1. Log on again to the Professional reference installation as an Administrator.
2. Run the Discover Wizard from the distribution server. (Again, do not map a drive; use the Run dialog or Network Neighborhood.) For example, \\titanic.savilltech.com\d$\Program Files\Seagate Software\Winstall\DiscoZ.exe.
3. The wizard will detect that a before snapshot exists and will ask if you want to create the after snapshot. Click the Perform the Aftersnapshot now box and click Next (see Figure 4-16).
4. The check will begin on both the Registry and filesystem.
5. Any potential problems will be displayed. Click OK.
6. A notice is displayed saying the procedure is finished after the snapshot is completed and the package created.

Before running any other package creations, remove the application you installed, or better yet, reinstall the machine (RIS is useful for this).

It's possible to fine-tune your created package using the Seagate Software Console MMC snap-in (see Figure 4-17). Select Open from the File menu, and you can then change and view the files and Registry components that will be changed if installed. Select Save after any changes.

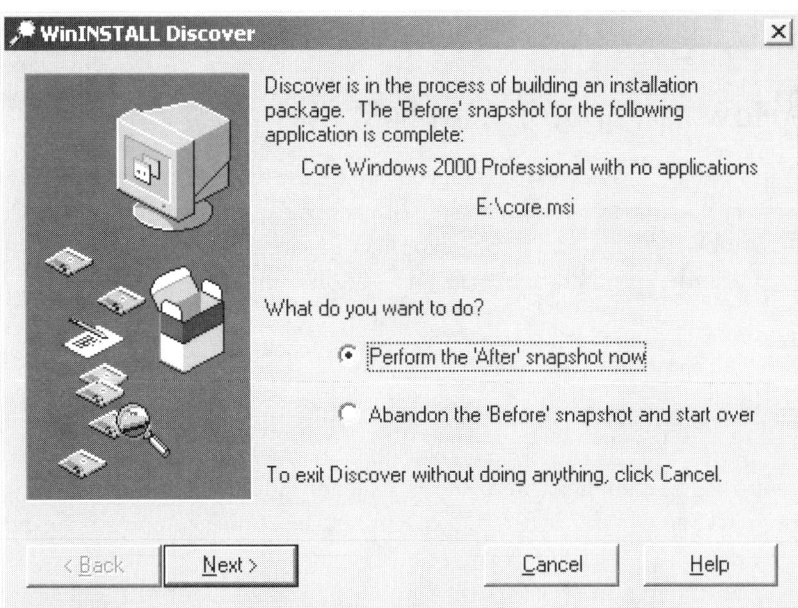

Figure 4-16 Creating the after snapshot of the WinINSTALL process

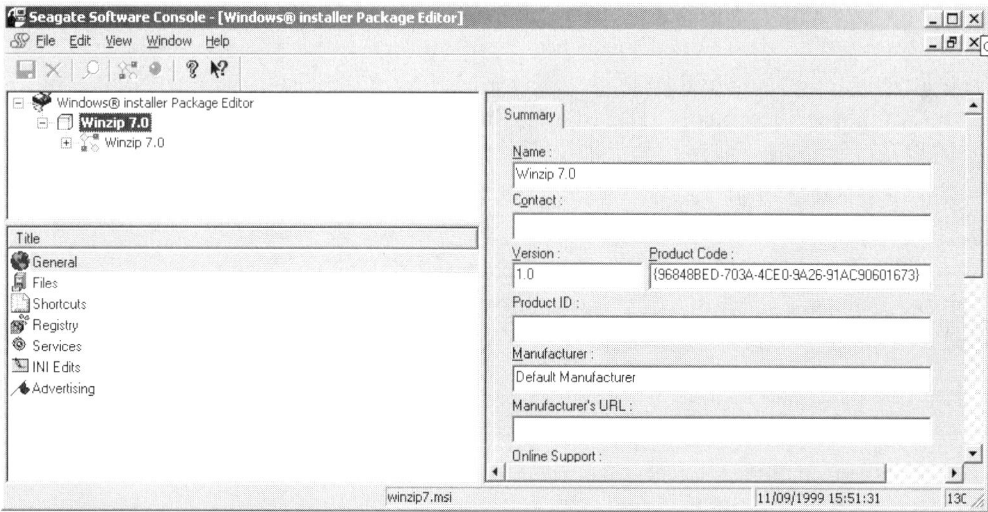

Figure 4-17 Setting optional information for your created MSI package

Once you have finished, you must not only place the .MSI file on the distribution server but put all files and subdirectories in the directory chosen for the MSI file.

4.43 How can I publish an MSI file?

With Group Policies in Windows 2000, you can do far more than just restrict and set certain Registry entries. You can set startup/shutdown/logon/logoff scripts, redirect folders like My Documents, and publish applications (and more). It's the last item that interests us presently, and there are four main options:

- Assign to a computer
- Publish to a computer
- Assign to a user
- Publish to a user

When you assign an application to a user, its icons are set up, and the software installed on first usage. If you assign to a computer, the application will be installed the next time the computer starts up. If you publish an application, the user has the option of installing the application via the Add/Remove Programs Control Panel applet or by clicking on an extension that is linked to the published program.

Any deployed application cannot be uninstalled by the user. Published applications can be uninstalled because they are optional.

You can publish/assign applications to any Group Policy object, which means you can assign applications on a per-domain, per-site, or per-organizational unit basis.

To assign an application to a GPO, perform the following steps:

1. Start the Active Directory Users and Computers MMC snap-in (Start > Programs > Administrative Tools > Active Directory Users and Computers).
2. Right-click on the domain, OU, or site and select Properties.
3. Select the Group Policy tab.
4. Select the GPO you wish to assign/publish the application with and click edit.
5. Select either Computer Configuration or User Configuration depending on whether the application is for a user or computer assignment.
6. Select the Software Settings\Software installation branch.
7. Right-click on Software installation, and select New > Package from the context menu.
8. Select the MSI file you wish to deploy; make sure you access via a network path or clients will be unable to install it—for example, \\titanic\data\winzip\winzip.msi. Click Open.
9. You will have the option to either publish/assign or advanced publish/assign. Click OK. If you select advance, you have options to select an existing package that this one will upgrade and various other settings including Security.
10. The program will now be shown under the Software installation branch and will be assigned/published to any user/computer who has the GPO applied to it.

FAQ 4.44 How can I run programs during the GUI phase of 2000 installation?

It's sometimes useful to enter commands and run processes during an installation of the operating system. With Windows 2000 GUI installation phase, you can press Shift+F10 to open a command window, and from there, you can start other programs such as TASKMGR.EXE and REGEDT32.EXE.

FAQ 4.45 How can I use an unattended answer script when installing a bootable CD-ROM?

With new machines being able to boot from CD-ROMs, it's obviously not possible to specify an unattended answer file via the CD-ROM.

Create your .SIF file (the Windows 2000 unattended answer format) and save to a floppy disk and name WINNT.SIF. Insert the disk when booting from the CD-ROM, and the WINNT.EXE program searches for a:\winnt.sif during installation.

FAQ 4.46 Underscores (_) in my computer names are changing to dashes (-) in Windows 2000. Why?

While the DNS server supplied with Windows 2000 supports the underscore (_) character as a valid DNS character (in accordance with RFC 2181), other DNS solutions may not. To avoid possible problems, Windows 2000 changes any underscore character to a dash in a computer name during Setup.

After Setup is complete, you can change the computer name back to include the underscore. If you do so, you receive a warning that the computer name may not work.

FAQ 4.47 How can I specify an alternate HAL during Windows 2000 installation?

During installation of Windows 2000, you can press F5 and select an alternate HAL to be used:

- Advanced Configuration and Power Interface (ACPI)Multiprocessor PC
- ACPI Uniprocessor PC
- ACPI PC
- Compaq SystemPro Multiprocessor or 100% Compatible
- MPS Uniprocessor PC
- MPS Multiprocessor PC
- Standard PC
- Standard PC with C-Step i486
- Other

Selecting Other allows a third-party HAL to be specified.

FAQ 4.48 How can I test whether my installation can be upgraded to Windows 2000?

WINNT32.EXE has a switch, /checkupgradeonly, that will check your system for upgrade compatibility. To use it, just enter the following in the Run box (Start > Run):

```
<CD drive>:\i386\winnt32 /checkupgradeonly
```

This will start the Windows 2000 Readiness Analyzer (see Figure 4-18) and will list any problem drivers and software. Selecting an item and clicking Details will provide more information and will describe the actions you should perform—for example, uninstalling or installing a newer version. Once you have made a note of all problems, click Finish to close the wizard.

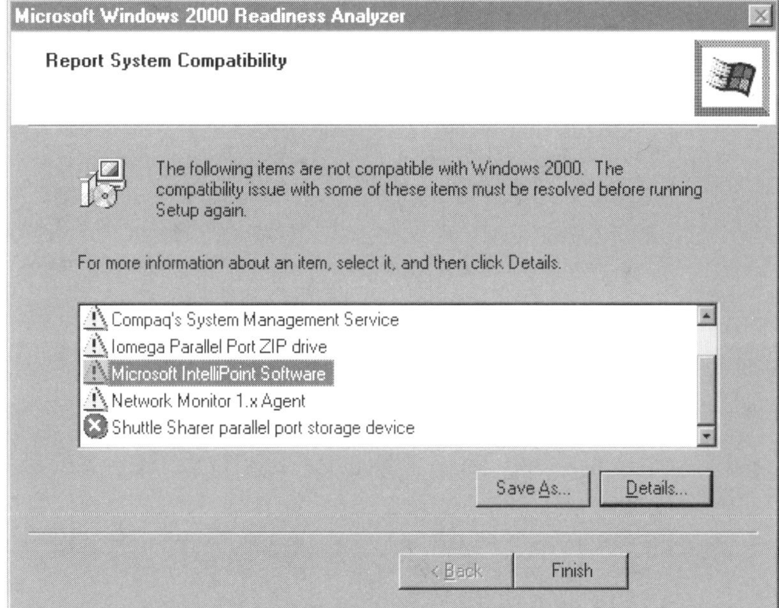

Figure 4-18 Readiness Analyzer Wizard in action

FAQ 4.49 What switches are available for Windows 2000 installation?

Some of the switches have changed for WINNT32.EXE in Windows 2000 to make them more understandable, and they are listed in the following table:

/s:<source path>	Source location for the Windows 2000 files.
/tempdrive:<drive letter>	The drive used for any temporary files.
/unattended	Upgrades in unattended mode if no answer file is specified. If an answer file is used, a new installation is installed. /unattended<seconds to wait before rebooting>:<name of answerfile>
/copydir:<folder name>	Creates an additional folder under %systemroot% with the name specified.
/copysource:<folder name>	Creates a temporary additional folder within the folder in which the Windows2000 files are installed. For example, if the source folder contains a folder called Private_drivers that has modifications just for your site, you can type **/copysource:Private_drivers** to have Setup copy that folder to your installed Windows2000 folder and use its files during setup. So then the temporary folder location would be C:\Winnt\Private_drivers. Unlike the folders /copydir creates, /copysource folders are deleted after setup completes.
/cmd:<command_line>	Runs the specified command after the second reboot but before setup is complete.
/debug<level>:<filename>	Creates a debug file in %windir%. By default, WINNT32.LOG is created at level 2, but the other options are 0—Severe errors 1—Errors 2—Warnings 3—Information 4—Detailed information for debugging
/udf:<id>[,<UDB>]	Specifies unique information. If no UDB file is named, the user will have to insert a disk with file $Unique$.udb on it.

/syspart	This copies the setup startup files to the hard disk, marks the disk as active, and then allows you to move the disk to another computer. When the computer is then turned on, it will start at the next phase of installation. Use the /tempdrive switch as well. /syspart cannot be used if upgrading from Windows 9x.
/checkupgradeonly	Checks your machine for any upgrade issues in advance.
/cmdcons	Installs the Recovery Console.
/m:<folder>	Copies replacement files from this alternate location first, and if not found, then uses the normal location.
/makelocalsource	Makes Setup copy all installation source to the local hard disk. Useful if you're installing from a CD and you don't wish to use the CD for any further component installations on the machine.
/noreboot	Stops the automatic reboot after the file copy stage of Setup.

WINNT.EXE is useful for installing from a DOS client or boot disk, and full help can be found with winnt /?:

```
winnt.exe /?
```

Sets up Windows 2000 Server or Windows 2000 Professional.

```
WINNT [/s[:sourcepath]] [/t[:tempdrive]]
[/u[:answer file]] [/udf:id[,UDF_file]]
[/r:folder] [/r[x]:folder] [/e:command] [/a]

/s[:sourcepath]
Specifies the source location of the Windows 2000 files.
The location must be a full path of the form x:[path] or
\servershare[path].

/t[:tempdrive]
Directs Setup to place temporary files on the specified
drive and to install Windows 2000 on that drive. If you do
do not specify a location, Setup attempts to locate a drive
for you.

/u[:answer file]
Performs an unattended Setup using an answer file (requires
```

```
/s). The answer file provides answers to some or all of the
prompts that the end user normally responds to during Setup.

/udf:id[,UDF_file]
Indicates an identifier (id) that Setup uses to specify how
a Uniqueness Database File (UDF) modifies an answer file
(see /u).The /udf parameter overrides values in the answer
file, and the identifier determines which values in the UDF
file are used. If no UDF_file is specified, Setup prompts
you to insert a disk that contains the $Unique$.udb file.

/r[:folder]
Specifies an optional folder to be installed. The folder
remains after Setup finishes.

/rx[:folder]
Specifies an optional folder to be copied. The folder is
deleted after Setup finishes.

/e Specifies a command to be executed at the end of GUI-mode Setup.

/a Enables accessibility options.
```

FAQ 4.50 How do I install Windows 2000?

We will look at a fresh Server installation, and the Professional installation is basically the same.

Overall, the installation is very similar to that of NT 4.0, except there is no PDC/BDC stage as we shall see. In this example, we will boot from the CD because many computers now support this.

1. Insert the Windows 2000 CD and reboot the computer.
2. The text-based portion of Setup will start.
3. Hardware will be detected by the Setup program, and you can press F6 to install any third-party drivers needed for disk detection and so forth. The standard drivers will then be loaded.
4. Press Enter to set up Windows 2000 (other options include R to repair a damaged existing installation or F3 to abort installation).
5. Read the license and press F8 (you no longer need to read all of it to press F8).

6. A list of your disks and partitions will be shown. Select/create a partition to install on and press Enter.
7. If it's an existing partition, a warning will be given. To continue, press C.
8. You have the option to install NTFS, FAT, or, if it was an existing partition, to leave as is. Make you selection and press Enter.
9. Files will be copied, and the machine will reboot to the GUI phase of the installation (see Figure 4-19).
10. When the GUI phase starts, Click Next.
11. The Setup program will detect hardware present in the machine; this may take a while.
12. The next stage allows the user to select the locales for the computer; click Customize.
13. Under the General tab, select the locale—for example, "English (United Kingdom)". Also click Set Default to select the system locale and click OK. Click Apply, then OK. Under the Input Locales tab, you can also set the default locale and remove U.S. if that is not a required installed locale.
14. Click Next.

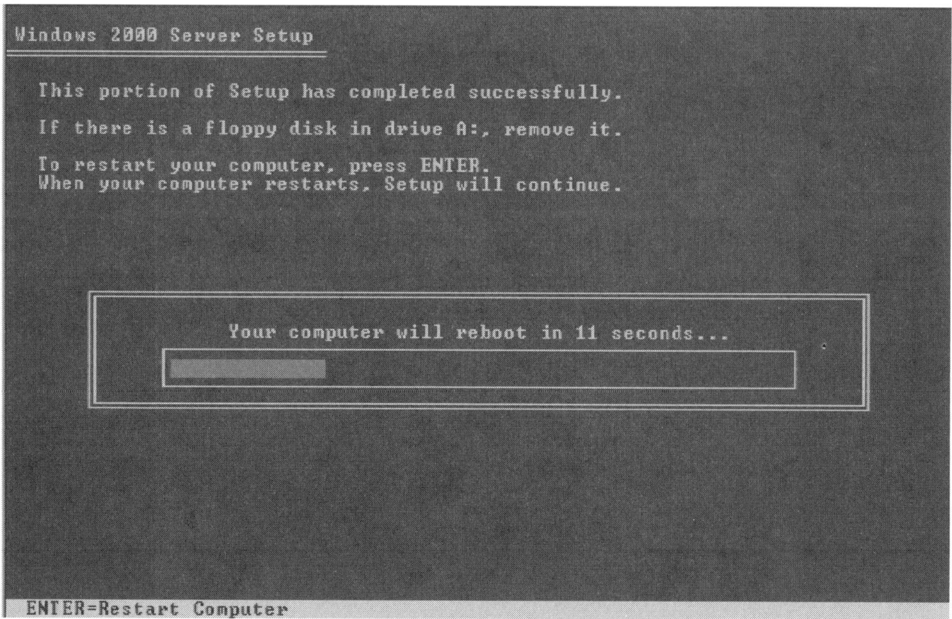

Figure 4-19 Text-mode portion of Windows 2000 setup completed

15. Enter a name and organization.
16. Enter the license key for the software (see Figure 4-20) and click Next.
17. Select the license mode, per-seat or per-server, and click Next. You don't have this stage for a Professional installation.
18. Enter a computer name and an Administrator password. Click Next.
19. Select the components you wish to install and click Next (e.g., DNS under Networking Services).
20. Select a Data and Time Zone and click Next. The networking components will be installed.
21. Once installed, select if you want Typical network settings, which is TCP/IP using DHCP, or use Custom to enter IP addresses, install extra protocols, and so forth. Click Next.

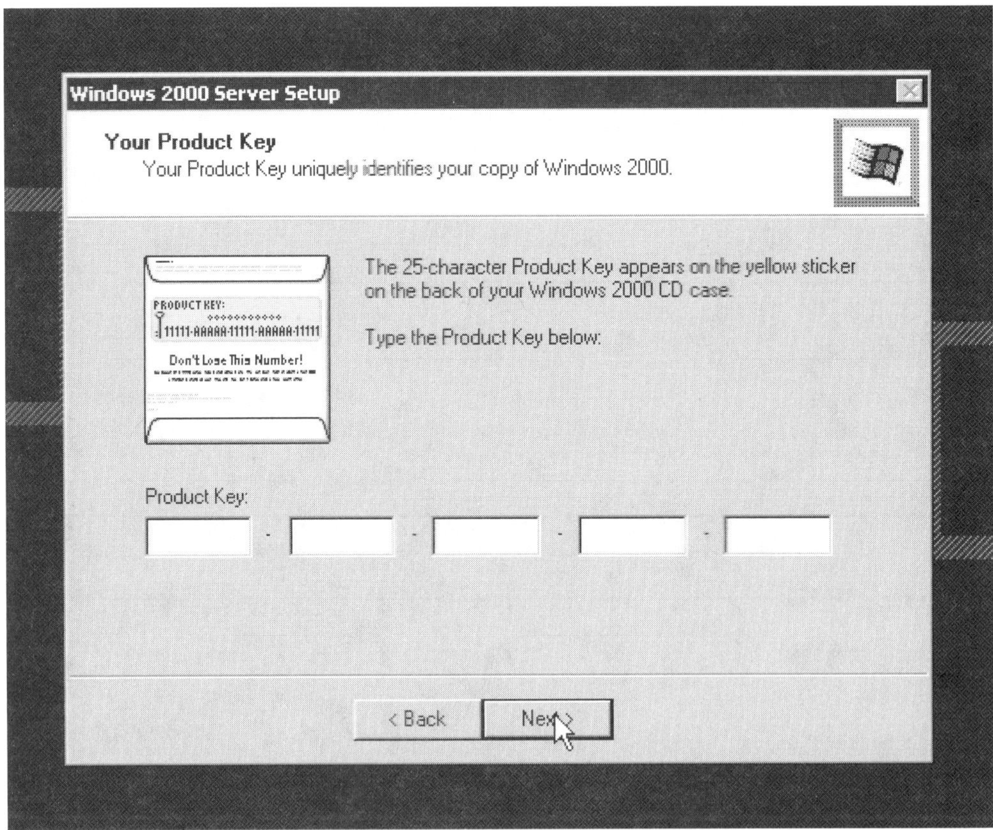

Figure 4-20 Entering your Windows 2000 install key

22. Select a workgroup or domain for the computer and click Next. If joining a domain, an account for the domain may be needed if an account has not already been added. The components will now be installed on the machine. The Start menu items will be added, components registered, and temporary files are removed.
23. Click Finish.

The machine will now reboot, and installation is complete. You should now configure any components. The first time you log on to a Professional installation, it gives the option to create an account to automatically log on as for future startups. You should now install the Command Console as it may save your life!

FAQ 4.51 How do I install the Recovery Console?

To create a domain controller, see FAQ 14.2.

FAQ 4.52 How do I deploy old applications in Windows 2000 via ZAP files?

New applications in Windows 2000 have .MSI files, which are used to deploy software via Group Policies; however, your older applications will not have MSI files.

In FAQ 4.42, we saw how to create an MSI file from a legacy application; however, a large amount of work is involved with this procedure, and an alternative method is available via ZAP files. I should stress MSI is the approach to take whenever possible.

ZAP files are just text files that provide instructions for deploying older applications, but there are some restrictions:

- Applications cannot be assigned to users or computers; they can only be published.
- Applications do not automatically repair themselves.
- Normally ZAP files require user intervention.
- ZAP files do not install with elevated privileges; users require the privilege to install software.

The ZAP file consists of two sections: the [Application] and [Ext] sections. The application section contains the name of the setup command, a version to display, a friendly name, and a URL, for example:

```
[Application]
FriendlyName = WinInfo Version 2.2
SetupCommand = setup.exe /unattend
DisplayVersion =2.2
Publisher = SavillTech
URL = http://www.savilltech.com/wininfo.html
```

The file extension section just lists extensions, which should be associated with the new application, for example,

```
[Ext]
SAV=
```

To publish a ZAP file, perform the following:

1. Start the Group Policy editor and open a Group Policy.
2. Select the User Configuration branch.
3. Expand Software Settings.
4. Right-click on Software installation, and select New > Package.

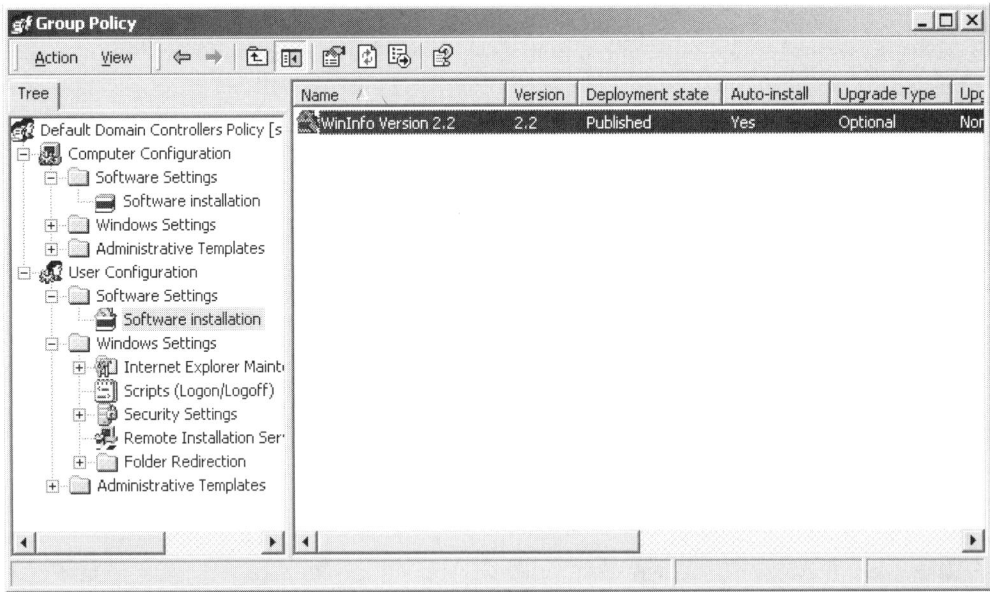

Figure 4-21 A published package via the Group Policy

5. Select the File type ZAW Down-level application packages (*.ZAP), and select the created ZAP file. Click Open.
6. Select Published from the deployment method and click OK.
7. The ZAP file will now be displayed as a published application (see Figure 4-21).

FAQ 4.53 What are the upgrade paths for Windows 2000?

In some ways, the upgrade paths are stricter than in NT 4.0 when you consider that you used to be able to upgrade from NT Workstation to NT Server (but not to a PDC or BDC), but this is not possible in Windows 2000. Windows 2000 gives better upgrade paths from the Windows 9x operating systems. The upgrade paths you can perform are

- Windows NT Workstation to Windows 2000 Professional
- Windows NT Server to Windows 2000 Server, Advanced Server, Datacenter
- Windows 2000 Advanced Server to Windows 2000 Datacenter

You **cannot** perform the following upgrades:

- Windows NT Workstation to Windows 2000 Server, Advanced Server, Datacenter
- Windows 2000 Professional to Windows 2000 Server, Advanced Server, Datacenter
- Windows 2000 Server to Windows 2000 Advanced Server, Windows 2000 Datacenter

FAQ 4.54 Why am I unable to upgrade Windows 9x to Windows 2000 in a dual-boot environment?

Microsoft does not support the upgrade of Windows 9x to Windows 2000 in a dual-boot environment. The problem seems to occur if Windows 2000 is already installed on another partition. You may get the errors:

```
Windows 2000 Setup does not support upgrading from Windows if you
have multiple operating systems installed. Setup will now exit.
```

or

```
Other Operating Systems Found
You cannot upgrade this Windows installation to Windows 2000,
because you have more than one operating system installed on your
```

```
computer. Upgrading one operating system can cause problems with
files shared by the other operating system, and is therefore not
permitted.
```

The official solution is to uninstall the other Windows 2000 installation and remove the files NTLDR, NTDETECT.COM, and BOOT.INI from the system partition (c:\). You can try to just delete those files and leave your other installation intact. Once the Win9x upgrade is complete, modify BOOT.INI to include a link to the existing Windows 2000 installation.

FAQ 4.55 How can I configure extra plug-and-play drivers for a Windows 2000 installation?

If you are installing Windows 2000 over the network (including RIS) and have the i386 structure on disk, it's possible to add extra plug-and-play drivers that will be loaded as needed during installations:

1. Move to your i386 structure and create a subdirectory \$OEM$\$1.
2. Under the $1 directory, create a directory of no more than eight characters of the name of the company who makes the driver—for example, **creative**.
3. Under that directory, create a subdirectory for the type of hardware—for example, video, sound, and so on (again no more than eight characters). At this point, you might have structure:

   ```
   - d:\i386\$OEM$\$1\creative\video
   - d:\i386\$OEM$\$1\creative\audio
   ```

4. Copy the drivers and the .INF files into the appropriate subfolder.
5. Open you answer file (or your SIF file) and add the directories to the OEMPnPDriversPath under the [Unattended] section, for example,

   ```
   [Unattended]
   OEMPnPDriversPath = "creative\video;creative\audio"
   ```

   Use a semicolon (;) to separate the entries.
6. If any of the drivers are unsigned, it will interrupt the unattended installation, so also add the following line under the OemPnPdriversPath line:

   ```
   DriverSigningPolicy = Ignore
   ```

You may, if you wish, just create a single directory under OEM\$1 such as pnpdriv and just copy everything into it as long as you have no filename clashes. If you do this, the OEMPnPDriversPath would be just pnpdriv. It is recommended that you keep the paths and files separated to improve organization, and also remember this structure will be copied locally to the system drive.

FAQ 4.56 Unsigned drivers are stopping my unattended installations. How should I handle this?

Windows 2000 uses a driver-signing system, and when a driver is signed, it has been tested and is known to work with Windows 2000. You should always use signed drivers where possible.

If a driver is not signed, and you try to use it as part of an unattended installation, your installation will stop. You will prompted to continue to use it, and this obviously defeats the purpose of an unattended installation, so it's possible to configure the installation to ignore driver signing.

Open your unattended\sif file. Go to the [Unattended] section and add the line

```
DriverSigningPolicy = ignore
```

There are actually three values for DriverSigningPolicy; you can ignore warn and block. They speak for themselves I think ☺.

Note that if you are using drivers that supercede those supplied with Windows 2000 and they are **not** signed, the installation process will ignore them and instead use the built-in signed versions.

FAQ 4.57 What are the directories I can have under OEM for an unattended installation in Windows 2000?

It's possible to configure extra files for an installation that might be specific to your organization or to the hardware in the machine. These files are placed under the OEM directory of the i386 structure. Under OEM, you can have the following:

\OEM\textmode	Hardware-dependent files for use during the initial Windows 2000 install and text-mode setup such as OEM HALs, SCSI drivers, etc.
\$OEM$\$$	Used to replace any core system files and required to match the structure of the Winnt structure. For example, to replace files in the winnt\system32 directory, you would create \$OEM$\$$\system32.
\$OEM$\$1	Files that you want to be copied to the drive where Windows 2000 is installed (%systemroot%).
\OEM\<drive letter>	Same as $1 but allows you to set a specific drive letter, e.g., \$OEM$\C copies everything under it (including subdirectories) to C.

4.58 Why is the DontDisplayLastUserName setting lost in upgrade from NT 4.0 to Windows 2000?

When you upgrade to Windows 2000 and select for the Terminal Services component to be installed, the DontDisplayLastUserName setting is reset to 0. To fix this, you will need to manually set it back to 1:

1. Start the Registry editor.
2. Move to HKEY_LOCAL_MACHINE\SOFTWARE\Microsoft\Windows\CurrentVersion\policies\system.
3. Double-click DontDisplayLastUserName.
4. Set to 1. Click OK.
5. Close the Registry editor.

It's actually been moved in 2000, as you may notice from the new Registry location in the preceding procedure.

4.59 How do I enable ACPI on my machine and/or change the HAL?

If during installation, you disabled ACPI to solve a problem (as seen in FAQ 4.47), you may want to enable again at a later time. You can do so as follows:

1. Right-click on My Computer and select Properties from the context menu.
2. Select the Hardware tab.

3. Click the Device Manager button.
4. Expand the Computer object.
5. Its type will be shown, probably Standard PC. If iAdvanced Configuration and Power Interface (ACPI) PC is displayed, then ACPI is enabled already. See Figure 4-22.
6. Right-click on the Computer type and select Properties.
7. Select the Driver tab.
8. Click Update Driver.
9. The Upgrade Device Driver Wizard will start. Click Next.
10. You can now either ask it to find a driver or manually select one.
11. If you select Manual, select the Show all hardware of this device class, and select the ACPI driver. Click Next.
12. Click Next to install the driver.
13. Click Finish, and click Close to close the Computer Property Driver dialog.
14. Click Yes to restart your computer.

Be careful with this process though. If you select a HAL that your computer is not compatible with, you may experience problems.

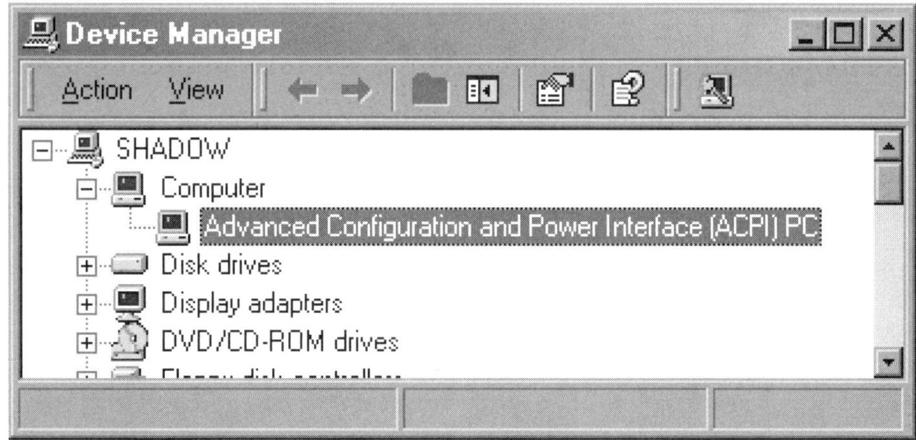

Figure 4-22 ACPI already enabled on this machine

FAQ 4.60 How do I disable/enable ACPI on my machine during installation?

We saw in FAQ 4.47 how to manually select an alternate HAL during installation, but it can also be done via modifying a file during installation.

1. After the text-mode phase of Setup completes but before the GUI stage, boot into an alternate installation (or via a boot disk CD).
2. Remove the read-only, hidden, and system flags from the TXTSETUP.SIF file:

```
attrib c:\txtsetup.sif -r -s -h
```

3. Edit the TXTSETUP.SIF file and search for ACPIEnable=.
4. To force ACPI to be enabled, change to ACPIEnable=1.
5. To force ACPI to be disabled, change to ACPIEnable=0.
6. Save the file.
7. Reapply the attributes:

```
attrib c:\txtsetup.sif +r +s +h
```

8. Continue with the Windows 2000 Setup Wizard.

You can also press F7 during installation to load a non-ACPI HAL.

FAQ 4.61 Why is the Administrator password I set during unattended installation ignored?

When using the AdminPassword unattended installation option and the password contains an asterisk (*), it means the install procedure should set the Administrator account to use a blank password. This means that if the asterisk appears anywhere in the password, then a blank Administrator password will be set.

```
[GuiUnattended]
AdminPassword=John*Savill
```

The fix is to not include an asterisk (*) in the Administrator password.

FAQ 4.62 My FAT32 partitions are not converted to NTFS during a Sysprep clone. Why?

When converting from a FAT32 to NTFS partition, if the volume has a volume name, you will be prompted to enter it. Obviously, if this is an automated operation, there is no way to enter that volume name, so the operation fails.

To request an NTFS upgrade during a Sysprep clone operating, the following is added to the SYSPREP.INF file:

```
[UNATTEND]
FileSystem=ConvertNTFS
```

To resolve the issue, one option is to issue the convert command for the filesystem before running Sysprep. This will enter the convert action in the Registry to be completed during Sysprep:

```
convert c: /fs:ntfs
```

The other option is to remove the volume label:

1. Double-click My Computer.
2. Right-click the drive and select Properties.
3. Remove the name of the volume and click OK.

FAQ 4.63 Why does Setup stop after reformatting my system/boot partition, which was a dynamic disk?

Windows 2000 introduces the dynamic disk, which allows some of the new disk functionality; however, it's not without problems.

If you reformat a dynamic disk during installation, then Setup may fail when trying to start the GUI portion:

```
Cannot find NTLDR
Press any key to restart
```

This error occurs because the boot sector's BIOS parameter block (BPB) contains invalid drive translation values that prevent the system from booting. This problem has been resolved in Windows 2000 Service Pack 1; however, if you don't have SP1, then perform the following:

To Fix a FAT32 System/Boot Partition

> **Warning:** *For FAT32 partitions, do not view the boot sector as a FAT boot sector from the View menu and then save it. Doing so corrupts the partition further. Instead, leave the tool in byte mode when you are editing.*

1. You will need either a parallel installation of Windows 2000 or to move the disk into an existing system.
2. Start DSKPROBE.EXE.
3. On the Drives menu, click Physical Drive and then double-click the physical drive that represents the system/boot drive.
4. Click to clear the Read Only checkbox, click Set Active and then click OK.
5. On the Sectors menu, click Read using the default settings.
6. On the Drives menu, click Volume Information and then note the following values:

```
-Sectors / Track
-Tracks / Cylinder
```

7. Using Calculator (CALC.EXE), convert the values you noted from decimal to hexadecimal. Note those hexadecimal values for later use. For example:

```
Sectors / Track of 63 decimal converts to 3F hexadecimal.
Tracks / Cylinder of 255 decimal converts to FF hexadecimal.
```

8. On the View menu, click Partition Table.
9. Locate the active partition (the Boot Indicator field lists "SYSTEM") by double-clicking each partition table index entry. Note the Relative Sector number for the active (SYSTEM) partition.
10. Click the Go button next to the Relative Sector number for the active partition.
11. On the View menu, click Bytes. This displays the BPB information in hexadecimal.
12. Change the value at offset 0x018 from 01 hexadecimal to equal the Sectors / Track value in hexadecimal that you noted in step 7.
13. Change the value at offset 0x01A from 01 hexadecimal to equal the Tracks / Cylinder value in hexadecimal that you noted in step 7.

14. After you verify that both BPB entries equal the correct hexadecimal values, click Write on the Sectors menu.
15. Verify that you are writing to the same sector that you recorded for the Relative Sectors setting and then click Write It.
16. Quit the DSKPROBE.EXE tool and boot into the original setup installation.

To Fix a FAT (Non-FAT32) or NTFS System/Boot Partition

1. Again you need a parallel installation.
2. Start DSKPROBE.EXE.
3. On the Drives menu, click Physical Drive and then double-click the physical drive that represents the system/boot drive.
4. Click to clear the Read Only checkbox, click Set Active and then click OK.
5. On the Sectors menu, click Read using the default settings.
6. On the Drives menu, click Volume Information and then note the following values

```
-Sectors / Track
-Tracks / Cylinder
```

7. On the View menu, click Partition Table.
8. Locate the active partition (the Boot Indicator field lists "SYSTEM") by double-clicking each partition table index entry. Note the Relative Sector number for the active (SYSTEM) partition.
9. Click the Go button next to the Relative Sector number for the active partition.
10. Based on the filesystem type (FAT or NTFS), click FAT Boot Sector or NTFS Boot Sector on the View menu. This displays the BPB information for editing.
11. Change the Sectors Per Track entry from 1 to equal the Sectors / Track value that you noted in step 6.
12. Change the Heads entry from 1 to equal the Tracks / Cylinder value that you noted in step 6.
13. After you verify that both BPB entries equal the correct values, click Write on the Sectors menu.
14. Verify that you are writing to the same sector that you recorded for the Relative Sectors setting and then click Write It.
15. Quit the DSKPROBE.EXE tool and restart the computer with original setup installation.

FAQ 4.64 How do I enable verbose logging in Windows 2000 GUI-mode setup?

If you are having problems with the installation of Windows 2000, it's possible to enable extensive logging to aid in diagnostics. To enable the extra logging, you have to create the value HKEY_LOCAL_MACHINE\Software\Microsoft\Windows\CurrentVersion\Setup\LogLevel and set to 0xFFFF. But obviously you can't create this using REGEDIT.EXE during setup, so we need to update a setup file to create the value for us.

1. On the distribution share or local hard disk containing the Windows 2000 files, locate the HIVESFT.INF file in the i386 folder.
2. Using any text editor (such as Notepad), locate the following line in the HIVESFT.INF file:

```
HKLM,"SOFTWARE\Microsoft\Windows\CurrentVersion\Setup",
"DriverCachePath",0x00020002,"%SystemRoot%\Driver Cache"
```

3. Below the line listed in the previous step, add the following line:

```
HKLM,"SOFTWARE\Microsoft\Windows\CurrentVersion\Setup","LogLevel",
0x00010003,0xFFFF
```

Note: The preceding two lines may be wrapped for readability, but are each a separate single line.

4. When you are done, the file should look like the following example. Verify this before saving the file to disk:

```
HKLM,"SOFTWARE\Microsoft\Windows\CurrentVersion\Setup",
"DriverCachePath",0x00020002,"%SystemRoot%\Driver Cache"
; added the following line

HKLM,"SOFTWARE\Microsoft\Windows\CurrentVersion\Setup","LogLevel",
0x00010003,0xFFFF
; ends here
HKLM,"SOFTWARE\Microsoft\Windows\CurrentVersion\Setup\
BaseWinOptions",,0x00000012
```

5. Save the file and quit the text editor.

The extra logging will now be enabled to the SETUPAPI.LOG file. This file will probably be around 4MB larger with logging enabled.

To check that logging is enabled via the GUI, press Shift+F10 to start a command prompt and use REGEDT32.EXE to verify that the value has been created.

FAQ 4.65 Why does Windows 2000 not detect my bus mouse?

If you perform a clean install of Windows 2000, your bus mouse will not be detected and installed. There is sadly no workaround for this.

If you, however, upgraded from Windows NT 4.0, you can edit c:\boot.ini and remove the /fastdetect switch and save the file. When you restart the computer, your bus mouse will function.

1. Start a command session (CMD.EXE).
2. Remove the read-only attribute from BOOT.INI.

```
attrib c:\boot.ini -r -s -h
```

3. Edit the file:

```
notepad c:\boot.ini
```

4. Remove the /fastdetect switch.
5. Save the file.
6. Reset the attributes

```
attrib c:\boot.ini +r +s +h
```

Note that removing the /fastdetect switch will increase the boot time.

FAQ 4.66 I'm trying to perform an unattended upgrade from Windows NT 4.0 to Windows 2000, but I receive an Inf corrupt message. What's wrong?

During an unattended upgrade of NT 4.0 to Win2K, you might receive the message "Line [line number] of the Inf is corrupt or invalid. Setup cannot continue."

One common cause of this problem is the inclusion of the following text in the unattended file:

```
[OEM_ADS]
Banner=""Windows 2000 Unattended Install Banner Message""
```

To resolve the problem, open the unattended file and comment out the above two lines using a semicolon (;) at the beginning of each line. Save the updated file and try the unattended upgrade again.

FAQ 4.67 How can I set up my computer account organizational unit (OU) during unattended installation?

Typically, when you create a computer account, it is added to the computer's OU of the domain. Using an unattended answer file, you can configure an OU to house the computer account.

1. Open the unattended answer file (UNATTEND.TXT).
2. Under the [Identification] section, add the following line:

```
MachineObjectOU = [full LDAP path]
```

For example, you might add the line

```
MachineObjectOU = "OU = London,OU = Sales,DC = SavillTech,DC =
com"
```

3. Save the change.

You can also use MachineObjectOU in the SYSPREP.INF file if you are using the Windows 2000 System Preparation Tool (Sysprep) 1.1. Sysprep is a utility that helps prepare a Win2K Server or Win2K Pro machine for disk duplication or imaging. You can download Sysprep 1.1 from the Microsoft Web site at http://www.microsoft.com/windows2000/downloads/tools/sysprep/default.asp.

FAQ 4.68 Why can't I install the Recovery Console (RC) on a mirrored system drive?

When you attempt to locally install the RC on a mirrored system partition (basic or dynamic disk) using WINNT32.EXE's /cmdcons switch, the installation fails with the message "No valid system partitions were found. Setup cannot continue."

During the RC installation, the system performs the same disk checks that it performs for a full installation, which also fails on a mirrored system partition. To work around this problem, you need to break the mirror, install the RC, then recreate the mirror.

But there is one caveat. In Windows 2000, you can create mirrors only on dynamic disks. If you have a mirrored volume on a basic disk that was created in Windows NT 4.0 and you break the mirror, you can recreate it only if you upgrade to dynamic disks. However, dynamic disks cause problems if you multiboot with non-Win2K installations. In this case, you can't install the RC.

FAQ 4.69 I am trying to create a partition for the full size of a disk. Why is some space left at the end of the disk?

During setup, if you try to create a partition that uses the remaining space on a disk, you can't use the maximum space available on the disk because space is reserved at the end of the disk to enable a later upgrade of the disk from basic to dynamic. Dynamic disk information is saved at the end of the disk. The amount that is reserved is a minimum of one cylinder, or 1MB, whichever is greater. (One cylinder can be up to 8MB, depending on drive geometry and translation.)

FAQ 4.70 How do I dual-boot Windows 2000 and Linux from NTLoader?

If you stubbornly insist on using Linux, here is a procedure you can use to enable a boot to Linux with Win2K NTLoader:

1. Install Win2K as usual onto NTFS and ensure you have also created the four Win2K boot/recovery disks.
2. Boot the system with the boot disk that comes with Red Hat Linux 6.2; then install Linux from the Red Hat CD-ROM.

3. Create your Linux "/" and swap partitions on a spare disk or partitions.
4. When prompted, select Yes, make a BOOT DISK. You use this disk in step 8 to get into Linux. If you choose put LILO to LINUX partition boot record instead of MBR, you may skip the next three steps.
5. Linux overwrites the Win2K master boot record (MBR). Boot Win2K using the four recovery disks, go into Recover, then select Command mode.
6. When prompted, log on as Administrator.
7. Execute the fixboot and fixmbr commands. You can now boot Win2K again as usual.
8. To boot Linux from NTLoader, insert the Linux boot disk and restart the system.
9. Log on to Linux as root.
10. Type **cd /etc** and examine the LILO.CONF file. At the beginning of this file, you will find an entry that shows where the default boot partition is (e.g., /dev/had).
11. Modify this entry (e.g., using emacs) so that it points to the disk and partition you installed Linux to. For example, if you installed Linux to /dev/hdc1, alter the original entry to reflect the appropriate disk and partition. In this case, you would change /dev/hda to /dev/hdc1. (If you don't remember where you installed Linux to, the last entry in LILO.CONF will have an "image" entry that specifies the root disk/partition.
12. Now execute LILO to write out the boot entry to /dev/hdc1 (type the command LILO without arguments). You should see a warning about this disk/partition not being on the first disk. Ignore it; we're happy that it's not stomping on the Win2K MBR!
13. You need to copy this boot sector to your Win2K partition so that BOOT.INI can reference it for your Linux entry. While you are still in Linux, use dd to raw-copy the boot sector to an appropriate file.

```
# cd
# dd if=/dev/hdc1 bs=512 count=1 of=bootsect.lnx
```

14. Now use mcopy to copy this file to a DOS disk.

```
# mcopy bootsect.lnx a:
```

15. You can now shut down Linux.

```
# shutdown -h now
```

16. Boot into Win2K.

17. Copy BOOTSECT.LNX onto C (and make it read-only).
18. Add to your BOOT.INI a Linux entry—for example,

```
bootsect.lnx="Linux"
```

When you reboot, if you select Linux, you will see a LILO: prompt for a few seconds, then the system will boot into Linux (press Enter if you don't want to wait, and the system will boot into Linux instantly).

FAQ 4.71 How can I install the Windows 2000 MultiLanguage version as part of an unattended installation?

Each Win2K MultiLanguage version install option uses about 50MB of disk space, so you must perform an installation that incorporates the Win2K MultiLanguage version from a network share.

1. In the install source directory, create folder MUITEMP and copy all the files from the Win2K MultiLanguage CD-ROM to it (the system will copy these files to destination drive %windir% during the final phase of a Win2K installation from the distribution share).
2. Open your answer file (or create one).
3. Using the tables of language IDs and language groups (see table to follow), add a RegionalSettings section for your default language. For example, for English (language ID 0409, language group 1), you would add the following statements to your answer file:

```
[RegionalSettings]
LanguageGroup=1
Language=0409
```

4. In the GuiRunOnce section, add a command to run MUISETUP.EXE to install the languages required, then include a command to run rmdir to delete the temp files:

```
[GuiRunOnce]
"%windir%\MUITEMP\MUISETUP.exe [-i LangID LangID...] [-d ] -r -s"
"%windir%\SYSTEM32\CMD.EXE /c RMDIR %WINDIR%\MUITEMP /s /q"
```

5. Use the following command to run the installation:

```
winnt32.exe /unattend:"unattend.txt" /copysource:"lang"
/copydir:"MUITEMP" /s:"path to install source"
```

For more information, see "How to Perform an Unattended Install of the Windows 2000 MultiLanguage version" on Microsoft's Global Software Development Web site.

Language Name	Language ID
English (default)	0409
French	040c
Spanish	0c0a
Italian	0410
Swedish	041D
Dutch	0413
Brazilian	0416
Finnish	040b
Norwegian	0414
Danish	0406
Hungarian	040e
Polish	0415
Russian	0419
Czech	0405
Greek	0408
Portuguese	0816
Turkish	041f
Japanese	0411
Korean	0412
German	0407
Chinese (Simplified)	0804

Language Name	Language ID
Chinese (Traditional)	0404
Arabic	0401
Hebrew	040d
Group Name	Group ID
Western Europe and United States	1
Central Europe	2
Baltic	3
Greek	4
Cyrillic	5
Turkic	6
Japanese	7
Korean	8
Traditional Chinese	9
Simplified Chinese	10
Thai	11
Hebrew	12
Arabic	13
Vietnamese	14
Indic	15
Georgian	16
Armenian	17

FAQ 4.72 I created a slipstreamed CD-ROM. Why do I get an error message when I boot from the installation disks?

Windows 2000 introduced the idea of slipstreaming an installation, which lets you apply a service pack to an installation area. If you then copy the installation area to a CD-ROM and boot from the regular installation disks, you might receive the following error message:

The following value in the .SIF file used by setup is corrupted or missing:

```
Value >\#39>0' on the line in section [SourceDiskFiles] with key
"SP1.CAB".
```

To resolve the problem, copy TXTSETUP.SIF from the i386 folder on the CD-ROM to the first of the four installation disks. Doing so should let you proceed with the installation.

FAQ 4.73 During Windows 2000 installation, how can I choose my network card instead of having the system select it automatically?

During Win2K installation, the system must select your network card automatically. All you can do is complete the installation, remove the device, and add it manually.

1. After your installation completes, start the Add/Remove Hardware Control Panel applet (Start > Settings > Control Panel > Add/Remove Hardware).
2. Click Next on the Welcome page, select Uninstall/Unplug a device and click Next.
3. Select Uninstall a device and click Next.
4. In the Devices box, select your network card (see Figure 4-23).
5. Click Next; click Yes, I want to uninstall this device; click Next; and then click Finish.
6. Start the Add/Remove Hardware Control Panel applet again (Start > Settings > Control Panel > Add/Remove Hardware).
7. Click Next on the Welcome page, select Add/Troubleshoot a device, and click Next.

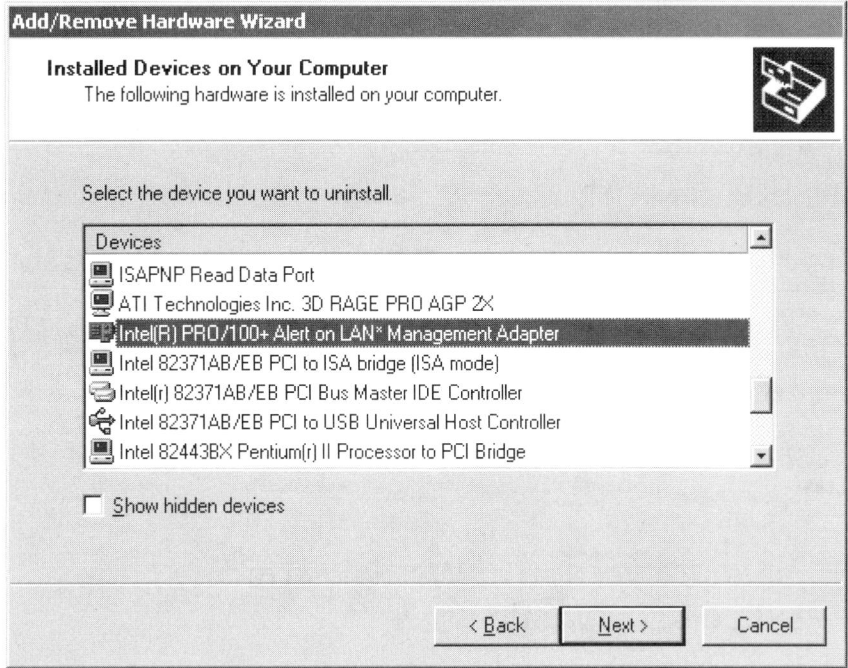

Figure 4-23 Preparing to remove a device

8. In the Devices box, select Add a new device; click Next; click No, I want to select the hardware from a list; and click Next.
9. In the Hardware types box, select Network Adapters, and click Next.
10. Select the appropriate network adapter manufacturer and model, click Next, click Next again, and click Finish.
11. Restart your computer.

FAQ 4.74 When I use the RIS, why doesn't the SIS service seem to save disk space?

RIS is very useful for deploying Windows 2000 when you have multiple RIS packages, each with different configurations. The bulk of each package contains the same files (the core Win2K Professional files). The idea of the Single Instance Store (SIS) service is that it examines these folders, removes duplicate files, and replaces them with a link to one instance. After the SIS service runs, the files consume less storage. However, SIS runs only during times of low CPU usage. If your server is always busy and SIS never gets the chance to run, you might need to manually run the SIS Groveler:

1. On the Win2K Server CD-ROM, go to the i386 folder in a command session (CMD.EXE).
2. Extract the GROVCTRL.EX_ file:

```
\i386\> expand grovctrl.ex_ %systemroot%\system32\grovctrl.exe
```

3. Use the following command to force the Groveler to run in the foreground:

```
grovctrl f
```

After the SIS Groveler runs, it will return to the usual low CPU execution.

FAQ 4.75 Is there a version of Windows Update more suited to corporate use?

Windows Update is great for single machines that can connect to the Microsoft site and download the required fixes, which are then automatically applied. However, Windows Update isn't much use in a corporate environment where you don't want every user connecting to get fixes (each user would have to have Admin privileges!).

The corporate Windows Update site at http://corporate.windowsupdate.microsoft.com/ provides a great way for administrators to download a fix or group of fixes in a packaged format that enables easy distribution to the network. The package contains fixes for the following OS and Internet Explorer (IE) versions:

- Windows 2000 (IE 5.01, 5.01 Service Pack 1—SP1)
- Win2K (IE 5.5)
- Windows NT 4.0 (IE 4.0, 4.01 SP2)
- NT 4.0 (IE 5.0, 5.01 SP1)
- NT 4.0 (IE 5.5)
- NT 4.0 Alpha (IE 4.0)
- NT 4.0 Alpha (IE 5.0, 4.01 SP2)
- Windows Millennium Edition—Windows Me (IE 5.5)
- Windows 98 (IE 4.0, 4.01 SP2)
- Win98 (IE 5.0, 5.01 SP1)

- Win98 (IE 5.5)
- Win98 Second Edition—Win98SE
- Windows 95 (IE 4.0, 4.01 SP2)
- Win95 (IE 5.0, 5.01 SP1)
- Win95 (IE 5.5)

When you download from this site, the system asks for a destination directory. In this directory, the system creates the following structure:

Software\[language]\[operating system]\[fix id]—For software updates
Drivers\[language]\[operating system]\[fix id]—For driver updates

For each fix, the system downloads the installation image and the README file.

FAQ 4.76 Why can't I install Windows 2000 on a disk formatted with Windows Me?

A known problem exists if you format your partitions with a Windows Millennium Edition (Windows Me) startup disk. Setup fails with the following error message:

```
Setup was unable to install Windows Boot Loader.
Ensure that your C: drive is formatted and that the drive is not
damaged. Setup cannot continue. Press ENTER to exit.
```

To resolve this problem, format the partition with a Windows 98 or Windows 95 startup disk and rerun Win2K setup.

FAQ 4.77 How can I send a product's CD key during a Windows Installer installation?

Usually, when you use Windows Installer to install a program, you must still enter the product ID; however, you can send this information with the MSIEXEC command:

```
msiexec /a [msi file] PIDKEY="[CD key]"
```

Optionally, you can supply USERNAME=[user name], COMPANYNAME=[company name], USERINITIALS=[user initials].

FAQ 4.78 Why can't I install Windows 2000 from certain USB CD-ROM drives?

Some new legacy-free machines don't ship with standard CD-ROM drives. As a result, you must use a USB CD-ROM drive on these systems. However, Win2K doesn't support some USB CD-ROM drives. If you have an unsupported drive, you can receive a "Stop 0x0000007B" error. The only course of action available at present is to contact the computer manufacturer and ask for a Windows 2000 Restoration CD that works with the USB CD-ROM drive.

FAQ 4.79 How can I activate Windows XP during an unattended installation?

To activate Windows XP during an unattended installation, you must add the following information into your unattended-install script:

```
[Unattended]
Unattendmode = FullUnattended
Filesystem = LeaveAlone
TargetPath = *
Win9XUpgrade = No
NtUpgrade = Yes
AutoActivate = Yes
ActivateProxy = Proxy
[userdata]
ProductKey = XXXXX-XXXXX-XXXXX-XXXXX-XXXXX

[Branding]
BrandIEUsingUnattended = Yes
[Proxy]
Proxy_Enable = 1
Use_Same_Proxy = 1
HTTP_Proxy_Server = myproxyserver:80
Proxy_Override = <local>
```

Notice that you can use the Proxy section of the script to specify a proxy server. Also, be sure that you replace the ProductKey with a real activation key.

Users in large organizations will be able to purchase versions of XP that don't require Windows Product Activation, which will save you from having to perform this operation.

FAQ 4.80 Why do I receive errors when I try to upgrade Windows Me or Windows 98 to Windows XP Professional?

When you upgrade Windows Me or Win98 to XP Pro, you might receive any of the following errors:

- `Error: Cannot get main entry point for C:WINDOWSSYSTEMVIPERSTI.CPL. Error:127 [ERROR=127 (7Fh)]`
- `Error: The signature for Windows XP Professional Edition Setup is invalid. The error code is fffffdf0. The system cannot find message text for message number 0xfffffdf0 in the message file for Syssetup.dll.`
- `Fatal Error: Setup failed to install the product catalogs. This is a fatal error. The setup log files should contain more information.`

These errors can occur if the setup process didn't delete all files in the %systemroot%\system32\catroot2 folder during the removal of the old OS phase of the upgrade. To resolve this problem, perform the following steps to manually delete the folder contents:

1. Start Windows Explorer.
2. Navigate to %systemroot%\system32\catroot2 (e.g., c:\windows\system32\catroot2).
3. Select all files (Ctrl+A).
4. Press Delete.

FAQ 4.81 Why does the installation process hang when I try to initiate a new Windows XP installation from within Windows 95?

The XP installation might hang during the Preparing Installation phase, at which point the Installation Wizard displays the message

```
Setup will complete in approximately 52 minutes
```

Because the XP Installation Wizard requires more pages during the installation than Win95 typically supports, the installation process might stop responding. To resolve this problem, either install Microsoft Internet Explorer (IE) to update the common controls and restart the XP installation or boot the computer from the XP CD-ROM to perform the installation. Machines running Win95 OEM Service Release 2 (SR2) or later won't experience this problem.

FAQ 4.82 How can I create Windows XP boot disks?

All XP installation CD-ROMs are bootable. As a result, Microsoft has removed the ability to create boot disks from the CD-ROM. However, Microsoft has added downloadable files to its Web site that you can use to create XP boot disks:

- Windows XP Home Edition boot disks—http://www.microsoft.com/downloads/release.asp?releaseid=33290
- Windows XP Professional boot disks—http://www.microsoft.com/downloads/release.asp?releaseid=33291

You can't use XP Home Edition boot disks with XP Pro or vice versa, and you can use boot disks to initiate an upgrade; you can only use them for new installations.

FAQ 4.83 How do I uninstall Windows XP?

If you upgraded to XP from Windows Me or Windows 98, go to the Add/Remove Programs Control Panel applet and click Uninstall Windows XP. If you've upgraded to NTFS or repartitioned disks, however, this uninstall will not function correctly. Under this same set of circumstances, you can also uninstall XP from the command prompt by performing the following steps:

1. Start the computer in Safe Mode with Command Prompt support (press F8 during startup).
2. Navigate to %systemroot%\system32.
3. Type

   ```
   osuninst.exe
   ```

   and press Enter.
4. Follow the onscreen instructions.

FAQ 4.84 How can I avoid having to reactivate my installation if I reinstall Windows on my machine?

If you simply are going to reinstall Windows on the same hardware, you can back up the activation status and then restore after upgrade. Back up the WPA.DBL file from the %systemroot%\system32 folder to a disk/other location.

Once you have reinstalled, perform the following:

1. Start your Windows installation in Minimal Safe mode.
2. Move to the \%systemroot%\system32 folder.
3. Rename WPA.DBL to WPA.NOACT.
4. Copy your backed up WPA.DBL to the system32 folder.
5. Reboot your system as normal.

This is **not** a hack to avoid activating installations and will only work on an installation on the same hardware that has already been activated.

FAQ 4.85 I'm receiving an INACCESSIBLE_BOOT_DEVICE error during setup of Windows 2000/NT 4 with a Promise ATA-100 card. How should I handle this problem?

As new hardware types are created, Microsoft attempts to add the drivers into the next version of Windows. The Ultra ATA-100 card is supported by default in Windows XP (just as the ATA-66 is in Windows 2000 but was not in NT 4.0).

To work around this problem, although the card is an IDE card, you need to treat it as a SCSI controller and load the driver accordingly:

1. Go to the Promise Web site (http://www.promise.com), and from the Tech Support section, download the driver for the Ultra 100.
2. Extract the downloaded ZIP file to a floppy disk (you should have a file TXTSETUP.OEM at the root for the disk).
3. Restart Windows installation, but when you are prompted to install a third-party RAID or SCSI, press F6.
4. Specify TXTSETUP.OEM on your floppy disk.
5. Installation should continue.

In general, whenever you get an INACCESSIBLE_BOOT_DEVICE, always check the controller your disks are connected to and ensure they are supported by Windows, or if you need to, manually specify the driver.

5 SERVICE PACKS

Service Packs contain product updates, which can be fixes or minor functionality changes. Service packs are cumulative so if you install Service Pack 4, there is no need to install Service Pack 1, 2, or 3 beforehand.

Windows 2000 removed the requirement of FTPing to Microsoft and downloading the latest service pack or hotfix after scouring for information about what you need. Windows Update now checks your machine for what fixes it needs, downloads them, and then installs them.

With Windows XP, this check is also performed during installation by connecting to Microsoft or to a local "fixes" server.

FAQ 5.1 What are the Q numbers and how do I look them up?

The Q numbers relate to Microsoft Knowledge Base articles and can be viewed at http://support.microsoft.com/support/.

FAQ 5.2 Why do I get an error message when I try to reinstall a hotfix after installing a service pack?

When you try to reinstall a hotfix (after reapplying a service pack), if you get the error

```
Hotfix: The fix is already installed.
Hotfix: Internal consistency error: Invalid Tree pointer = <garbage
characters displayed>.
```

you need to remove the hotfix before trying to reinstall.

To remove a hotfix, you would usually use **hotfix /r** or **hotfix -y** (depending on the version—to check the syntax for remove, use /? on the hotfix for the syntax); however, in some situations, the hotfix executable will refuse to remove the hotfix:

```
Hotfix: Fix <name of hotfix> was not removed.
```

All the hotfix actually does when you install one is to check a Registry entry to see if it is already there, so to get around this problem, we can go into the Registry and remove the hotfix's corresponding entry.

1. Start the Registry editor (REGEDIT.EXE).
2. Move to HKEY_LOCAL_MACHINE\SOFTWARE\Microsoft\Windows NT\CurrentVersion\Hotfix.
3. Under this key will be a number of subkeys with the name of the Knowledge Base article the hotfix is referenced by—for example, Q123456 (the True Color adapter fix).
4. To get more details about the hotfix, select the key (e.g., Q123456) and look at the Fix Description value.
5. To remove NT's knowledge of the fix being installed, select the specific hotfix you want to remove (e.g., Q123456) and select Delete from the Edit menu. Click Yes to the confirmation.
6. Close the Registry editor.

The fix is still installed on the system; all you have done is remove NT's knowledge of its installation so you will now be able to reinstall the hotfix in the normal way.

FAQ 5.3 When should I reapply a service pack?

For versions of Windows previous to Windows 2000, you should reapply any service pack (and subsequent hotfixes) whenever you add any system utilities, services, hardware, and/or software. A good rule of thumb is when the computer displays, "Changes have been made. You must shut down and restart your computer," reapply your service pack before the reboot.

The only problem is once you reinstall a service pack, unless you uninstall then reinstall, you will lose the ability to uninstall it again.

For Windows 2000 and above, you no longer need to reinstall a service pack unless you repair/reinstall the operating system.

FAQ 5.4 How can I tell which version of a service pack I have installed?

When a service pack is installed using the normal method (e.g., not just copying the files to a build location), the service pack version is entered into the Registry value

CSDVersion, which is under HKEY_LOCAL_MACHINE\SOFTWARE\Microsoft\Windows NT\CurrentVersion.

The value is of the formal "Service Pack n"—for example, "Service Pack 4"—but can have extra information if it is a beta or release candidate—for example, "Service Pack 4, RC 1.99."

To check this from the command line, you could use the REG.EXE Resource Kit supplement 2 utility:

```
reg query "HKLM\SOFTWARE\Microsoft\Windows
NT\CurrentVersion\CSDVersion"
REG_SZ CSDVersion Service Pack 4, RC 1.99
```

Make sure you put the value in double quotes (" ").

An alternative is to just run WINVER.EXE, which tells you your current build and service pack version. You can also use WINMSD.EXE or Help/About in Explorer. On Windows 2000 or Windows XP, you can simply look at the properties of My Computer, General tab.

FAQ 5.5 How can I tell who installed/uninstalled a service pack?

When Service Pack 4 is installed or uninstalled, an event is written to the System event log. The event ID is 4353 so you could just create a filter (View > Filter Events) to view only event ID 4353. It provides information such as the person and time it was actioned (see Figure 5-1).

The messages are

```
Windows NT Service Pack 4 was installed (Service Pack 3 was
previously installed).
```

or

```
Windows NT Service Pack 4 was uninstalled. Restoring Windows NT
to Service Pack 3.
```

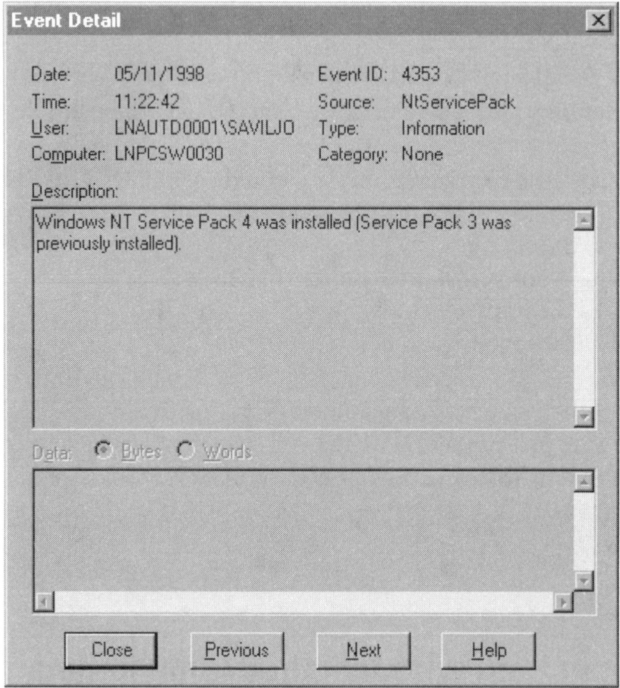

Figure 5-1 Event log showing service pack installation

5.6 How can I perform a function in a logon script depending on a machine's service pack version?

A new utility from SavillTech, CmdInfo (which can be downloaded from http://www.savilltech.com/download/cmdinfo.zip), sets error-level values depending on the service pack version of the client machine. A script calling the utility can then take different actions depending on the error-level value.

CmdInfo can also perform actions depending on the OS version and installation type. The following is an example of usage to detect the SP version in a logon script:

```
@ECHO OFF

CMDINFO.EXE /sp
IF ERRORLEVEL 5 GOTO SP5
IF ERRORLEVEL 4 GOTO SP4
```

```
IF ERRORLEVEL 3 GOTO SP3
IF ERRORLEVEL 2 GOTO SP2
IF ERRORLEVEL 1 GOTO SP1
IF ERRORLEVEL 0 GOTO SP0

:SP5
ECHO Service Pack 5 is installed on this NT computer.
ECHO No further upgrades are necessary.
GOTO END

:SP4
ECHO Service Pack 4 is installed on this NT computer.
ECHO Press any key to install Service Pack 5...
PAUSE > NUL
rem Let's assume drive X: is mapped to a sharepoint...
rem X:\SP5\UPDATE\UPDATE.EXE -u -f -o
GOTO END

rem (etc. ...)
:END
EXIT
```

FAQ 5.7 Is there a script that will reinstall a service pack and hotfixes, and then reboot?

Whenever you add/modify a core component on Windows NT, you have to reinstall the last service pack and any hotfixes, and this can be quite a job. This is not a problem in Windows 2000 because the system automatically uses the newest files from the base install or from the service pack when adding components.

I knocked together the following script, which just applies the service pack and any hotfixes and then lets the server/workstation reboot. Ideally, store the expanded service pack and hotfixes on a network location, and then you and/or your users can run the script to reinstall the service pack/hotfixes.

```
\\morpheus\installation\nt4ws\sp6a\update\update -u -n -o -z -q
\\morpheus\installation\nt4ws\sp6a\c2-fix\hotfix -n -z -q -m
\\morpheus\installation\nt4ws\sp6a\winlogon-fix\hotfix -n -f -q -m
```

Basically I've got a share called installation on a server Morpheus. Under that I've expanded Service Pack 6a and the two recent hotfixes.

The first command installs Service Pack 6. The -u means unattended mode; -n means not to back up files for uninstall purposes; -o means overwrite OEM files without asking; -z says not to reboot after installing (as we need to install the hotfixes); and -q means quiet mode.

Next we install the first hotfix; here -n means not to create an uninstall directory, -z means no reboot, -q means quiet, and -m means unattended.

The preceding script would be repeated for all hotfixes except the last one applied because after the last one, we want to reboot so the -z changes to a -f, which forces the applications to close at shutdown and allows the reboot.

You may want to modify bits of this script; maybe add some logic to check the users' current service pack version (you could use CmdInfo to check it—http://www.savilltech.com/cmdinfo.html) and then run different service pack/hotfixes depending on the service pack version.

I don't create uninstalls for any of the installations because this procedure is a reinstallation so the uninstall would already have been done on the initial installation. If you want to use this script to perform an initial installation, consider removing the -n switch from all commands.

FAQ 5.8 How do I expand a service pack/hotfix without installing?

It's often useful to have a directory with an expanded service pack/hotfix in to allow faster installation. To expand a service pack to a directory, perform the following steps:

1. Download the full service pack.
2. Run the downloaded service pack with a /x at the end—for example:

```
sp6i386.exe /x
```

3. You will be asked for a directory to expand to; enter your selection and click OK.
4. A completion dialog will be displayed; click OK.
5. In the selected folder, a subfolder called update will be created. In this folder is UPDATE.EXE, which can be used to install the service pack.

To expand a hotfix, perform the following:

1. Download the hotfix via FTP from ftp://ftp.microsoft.com/bussys/winnt/winnt-public/fixes/usa/nt40/.
2. Run the downloaded hotfix with a /x at the end—for example,

```
q244599i /x
```

3. You will be asked for a directory to expand to; enter your selection and click OK.
4. A completion dialog will be displayed; click OK.
5. You will now have a list of files in a directory including HOTFIX.EXE, which is used to install the hotfix.

FAQ 5.9 Where can I get service packs for Windows 2000 and what's new?

Service Pack 1 for Windows 2000 is available from http://www.microsoft.com/windows2000/downloads/recommended/sp1/default.asp or from Windows Update at http://www.windowsupdate.com. Other later service packs can be found by replacing the "sp1" in the former URL with the new service pack number—for example, "sp2".

The first Windows 2000 service pack includes the long-promised ability to "slipstream" the service pack into a distribution area, which means you can apply the service pack directly to a copy of the CD on a network share, and when you install from that network share, the installed machine will already have the service pack installed!

Windows 2000 is now service pack aware, and so when you install a service pack, it remembers the service pack has been installed and where from. When you install a new service and/or component, it will get the files from the Windows 2000 media and updated files from the service pack distribution point, no longer having to reapply service packs after installing new components.

A new log is created, SVCPACK.LOG, which contains the command that was used to start the service pack install and also the files that were replaced.

The actual process is similar to that on NT 4.0 but with some new steps:

1. Copies the service pack files locally (if you just want to expand and not install, you can use the /x switch as with other service packs).
2. Backs up the current file set and Registry information on the local computer.
3. Based on the system catalog, modifies Windows File Protection (WFP) service to reflect the new service pack files.
4. Updates the encryption files according to the encryption level of the currently installed operating system (56 or 128, there are not separate versions of the service pack).
5. Updates the necessary system files.
6. Updates the Registry with any new or modified Registry keys.
7. Installs a new DRIVER.CAB file that Setup and other components can use to install device drivers without requiring access to the network or the Service Pack CD.

8. Updates DRVINDEX.INF with the new drivers contained in the service pack DRIVER.CAB file.
9. Updates LAYOUT.INF, which identifies which files to install from the operating system media and which files to install from the service pack media.
10. Writes a ServicePackSourcePath Registry key, which Setup uses to identify the location of the service pack media when it needs future files.
11. Creates the $NTServicePackUninstall$ folder to store the uninstall information and compresses if NTFS.
12. Creates a log file that identifies the command line used to initiate the UPDATE.EXE program and the files copied to the computer by the UPDATE.EXE program.
13. Makes an entry in the event log about the installation.

A number of good documents are available with the Service Pack CD, which you should read.

To install:

1. Run UPDATE.EXE (in the update folder, or if you downloaded the single file, it will decompress first and execute UPDATE.EXE for you).
2. Check the Accept the License Agreement box.
3. Click Install.
4. It will then back up the files that will be replaced.
5. You must then reboot the machine by clicking Restart (see Figure 5-2).

After reboot, you will be running with the new service pack. If you run Winver, it will show you running the new service pack (as will my Win Info utility, http://www.savilltech.com/wininfo.html). See Figure 5-3.

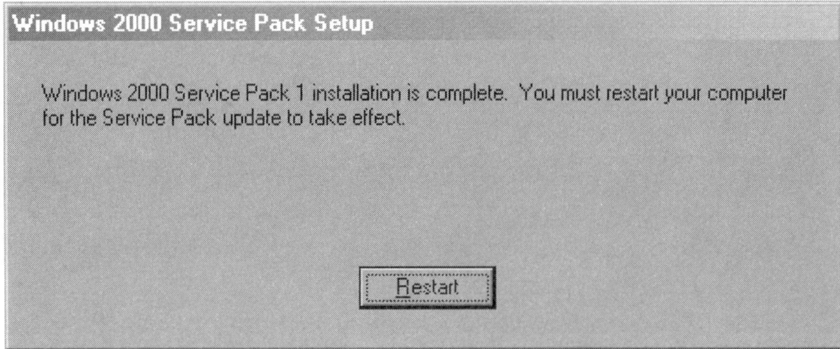

Figure 5-2 Service Pack installation complete confirmation. Reboot your machine.

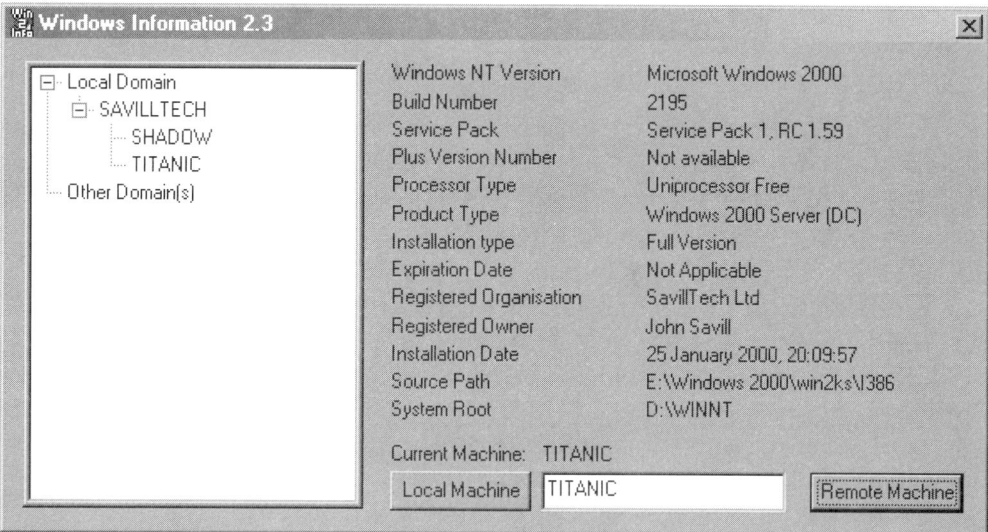

Figure 5-3 Showing the current service pack

FAQ 5.10 How do I use Windows 2000 service pack slipstreaming?

Windows 2000 service packs introduce the long sought after ability to be able to apply a service pack to a Windows 2000 distribution point (e.g., i386), and then when you install clients from that distribution point, they already have all of the updated files for the service pack.

This functionality is very easy to use as follows:

1. Copy your Windows 2000 CD (Professional, Server, or Advanced Server) to a distribution point—for example, F:\windows 2000\win2kp. You must copy the whole CD and not just i386. In this example, the procedure expects i386 to be at F:\windows 2000\win2kp\i386. At a minimum, you could just copy over the i386 folder and the CDROM_XX.5 (e.g., CDROM_IS.5 for server, CDROM_IP.5 for Professional) and CDROM_NT.5 to the root.
2. Run the update command from the service pack area with the -s switch, then the path of the Windows 2000 distribution point—for example,

```
update -s:"f:\windows 2000\win2kp"
```

You need to include the quotes if the path includes spaces. Notice I don't use the i386 folder; it needs the root as it checks for the CDROM_XX.5 file.

3. The service pack slipstream will then update all the files, and you are ready to install from that distribution share—easy! See Figure 5-4.

The key files replaced are a new LAYOUT.INF, DOSNET.INF, and TXTSETUP.SIF, which are the files that contain checksums for all files and are updated with new ones for the service pack files. Also, new entries may be added if new files are part of the service pack.

A new DRIVER.CAB **may** also be supplied if drivers which form the cabinet file have been updated.

You could then create a CD with this version to be able to install locally without a network connection using instructions in FAQ 11.9 for creating bootable CDs.

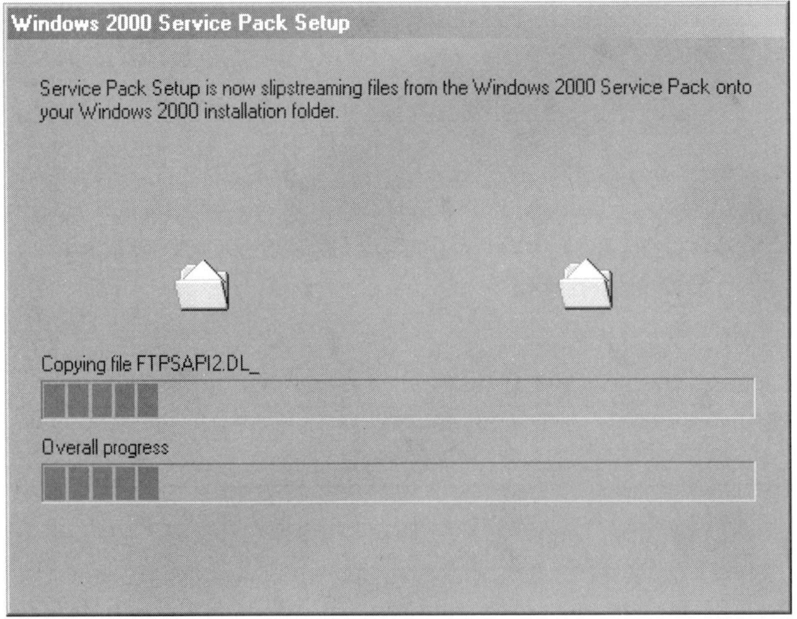

Figure 5-4 Slipstreaming a Windows 2000 installation area

FAQ 5.11 How can I change the location Windows 2000 expects to find the service pack files?

Windows 2000 remembers where the service pack was installed from, and so when new components are added, it can automatically get updated files from the service pack location without requiring the user to manually reinstall the service pack.

If this location is changed or you wish to modify it, perform the following steps:

1. Start the Registry editor (REGEDEIT.EXE).
2. Move to HKEY_LOCAL_MACHINE\SOFTWARE\Microsoft\Windows\CurrentVersion\Setup.
3. Double-click ServicePackSourcePath.
4. Modify the Registry value to the required path that contains the service pack files.
5. Click OK.
6. Close the Registry editor.

FAQ 5.12 How can I install Windows 2000 hotfixes during an unattended installation?

With the new slipstreaming ability of Windows 2000 service packs, it's easy to install them as part of an unattended installation by just applying them to the distribution point. However, this cannot be done with hotfixes, and so to install hotfixes during installation requires some manual configuration. This is described in the latest service pack release notes.

As a side note, if you wanted to install Windows 2000, a service pack, and hotfixes, just slipstream the service pack first into the distribution area, and then follow these instructions:

1. Edit your UNATTENDED.TXT file and ensure it contains the following:

   ```
   [Unattended]
   OemPreinstall = Yes
   ```

2. Copy the QXXXXXX.EXE images to the %OEM% folder (the same folder as the UNATTEND.TXT and the CMDLINES.TXT files).

3. Edit your %oem%\cmdlines.txt file and add the following:

```
[Commands]

"Q123456 /n /q /z"
"Q654321 /n /q /z"
```

4. Save the changes.

During installation, the hotfixes will automatically be installed.

5.13 How can I uninstall a Windows 2000 service pack?

One of the great points of Windows 2000 service packs are the improvements in the uninstall area. To uninstall from the GUI, perform the following steps:

1. Start the Add/Remove Programs Control Panel applet (Start > Settings > Control Panel > Add/Remove Programs).
2. Select Windows 2000 SP1 (e.g., works with all versions).
3. Click Change or Remove Programs (see Figure 5-5).
4. Follow the instructions and reboot as needed.

To uninstall from the command line, perform the following:

1. Open a command prompt (CMD.EXE).
2. Move to %systemroot%\$NtServicePackUninstall$\spuninst.
3. Run SPUNINSTL.EXE.
4. Close the command prompt by typing **exit**.
5. Follow the instructions.

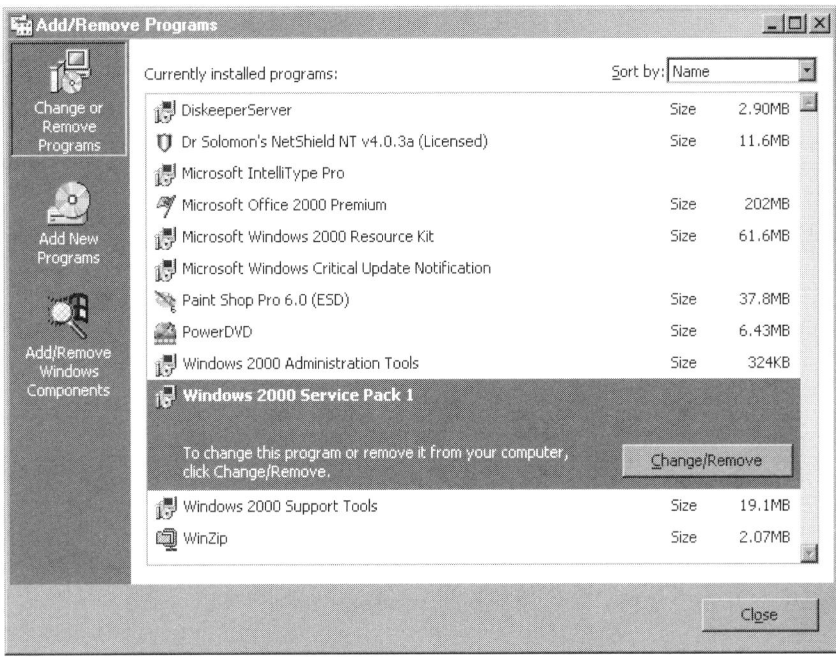

Figure 5-5 Uninstalling a service pack

5.14 I get an RPC error when trying to install Service Pack 1 for Windows 2000. What can I do?

A number of built-in shares exist on each NT/2000 installation, such as C$, which is the root of your C drive, and ADMIN$, which is your NT root—for example, C:\winnt.

It's possible to prevent these shares from being created as seen in FAQ 13.4.

If you receive the error "The RPC Service is not available," it is normally caused by a missing ADMIN$ share. Make sure ADMIN$ exists. You can check this with the NET SHARE command.

```
net share

Share name Resource Remark

-------------------------------------------------------------------
--------
```

```
D$ D:\ Default share
G$ G:\
ADMIN$ C:\WINNT Remote Admin
C$ C:\ Default share
IPC$ Remote IPC
The command completed successfully.
```

If the ADMIN$ share does not exist, then remove the Registry key as outlined in the previously mentioned FAQ or manually recreate it:

```
net share admin$=c:\winnt
```

FAQ 5.15 Why doesn't the slipstream switch for Win2K SP1 UPDATE.EXE work with RIS server images?

To review, slipstreaming lets you apply a service pack to a Windows 2000 installation folder (e.g., the i386 folder), which means that when you then install from the slipstreamed location, the system applies the service pack automatically (for more information, see FAQ 5.10.

When you try to slipstream Service Pack 1 (SP1) into a CD-ROM image on a Remote Installation Services (RIS) server, you receive the following error: "An error has occurred copying files from the Service Pack share to the distribution folder." Microsoft hasn't implemented slipstreaming for RIS images but may do so for a future version of the service packs.

You can work around this missing functionality by recreating the RIS image:

1. Copy the Win2K Professional CD-ROM to a folder accessible from the RIS server.
2. Slipstream the service pack files to this folder using the syntax

   ```
   update -s:"[Win2K Pro root location]"
   ```

3. Run RISETUP.EXE again on the RIS server and create a new image using the slipstreamed path.

FAQ 5.16 When I try to slipstream Win2K SP1 or SP2 from the downloaded file, why do I get an error?

Although this FAQ applies to both Windows 2000 SP1 and SP2, the following example addresses SP1 only. If you try to slipstream a Win2K distribution point from the downloaded SP1 file (SP1NETWORK.EXE from http://msvaus.www.conxion.com/download/win2000platform/SP/SP1/NT5/EN-US/sp1network.exe) with the -s switch (e.g., sp1network.exe -s:[2000 distribution location]), you receive an error message:

```
Not all files necessary to perform an integrated installation are
present.
```

You receive this error message because you didn't extract file CDTAG.1 before the installation. You don't encounter this problem when you use the SP1 CD-ROM (see Figure 5-6). To resolve the problem, first expand the service pack file to a temporary area:

```
sp1network.exe -x:[service pack 1 location]
```

For example,

```
sp1network.exe -x:d:\temp\sp1
```

After you extract the file, go to the folder [service pack 1 location]\i386\update subfolder. Run the following update command, and you should no longer receive a warning:

```
update -s:[2000 distribution location]
```

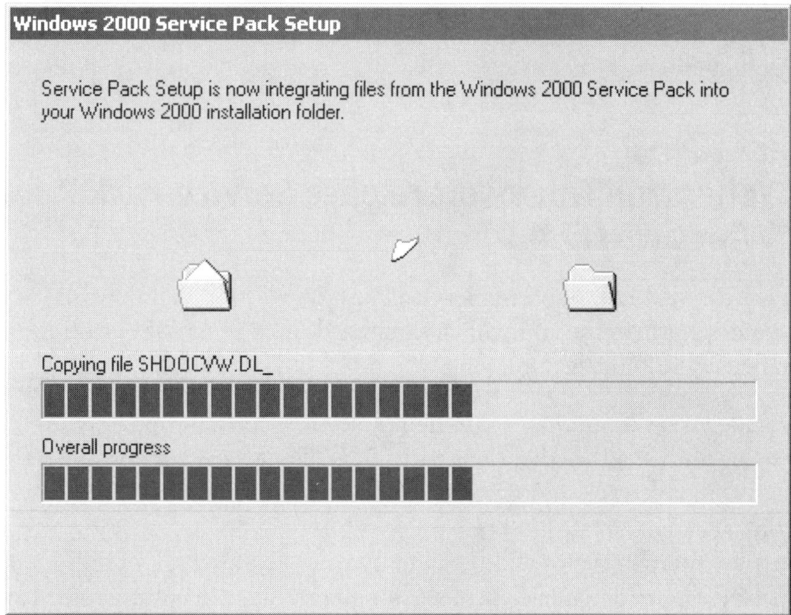

Figure 5-6 Avoiding the slipstream error and a successful file copy

Note that the [2000 distribution location] should be the folder in which the i386 folder exists, not the i386 folder itself. That is, if your Win2K folder is d:\deploy\win2kp\i386, the distribution location is d:\deploy\win2kp.

FAQ 5.17 I've upgraded to Windows 2000 Server with Service Pack 1 (SP1) slipstreamed. Why doesn't the Registry show that SP1 is installed?

Slipstreaming, which lets you integrate a service pack's content into a setup area for the OS, is a great addition to Win2K. However, a known problem exists: The system doesn't update the Registry key that indicates that SP1 is installed. This issue is minor, and you can resolve it by performing the following steps:

7. Start REGEDIT.EXE.
8. Go to HKEY_LOCAL_MACHINE\SOFTWARE\Microsoft\Windows NT\CurrentVersion.
9. From the Edit menu, select New > String value.
10. Enter a name of **CSDVersion** and press Enter.
11. Double-click the value and set it to Service Pack 1. Click OK.
12. Close Regedit.

FAQ 5.18 When will Microsoft release Service Pack 7 for Windows NT 4.0?

Microsoft has decided not to release Service Pack 7 (SP7) for Windows NT 4.0, despite the many hotfixes the company has released since SP6a. Microsoft originally planned to release SP7 for three reasons:

- To provide an easier mechanism to deploy security fixes/hotfixes
- To provide an NT 4.0 Active Directory (AD) client (you can download this separate component from http://www.microsoft.com/windows2000/news/bulletins/adextension.asp)
- To provide international versions of the Internet Explorer (IE) High Encryption pack (you can download these versions from http://www.microsoft.com/windows/ie)

Because Microsoft has addressed two of the three goals, the company feels that another service pack isn't justified.

FAQ 5.19 Where can I get the Windows 2000 Service Pack 1 Windows Installer file?

Win2K introduces the Windows Installer format, the .MSI file, which lets you deploy software via a Group Policy. In keeping with this new software deployment approach, Microsoft released an .MSI file that you can use to deploy Win2K SP1. You can download the .MSI file from http://www.microsoft.com/windows2000/downloads/servicepacks/sp1/msi/default.asp. Once you've downloaded it, run the executable and copy the created UPDATE.MSI file to the /update folder of your service pack distribution point.

If you downloaded SP1 via the Internet, you won't have the required folder structure. Use the /x switch with the downloaded file to extract the package (e.g., sp1network /x). Extracting the package will create the folder structure that includes the /update folder.

FAQ 5.20 How do I create a bootable Windows 2000 CD-ROM with a service pack slipstreamed?

Win2K introduced to service packs the slipstream ability, which lets you apply a service pack to a Win2K installation distribution point so that any clients you install from that location automatically have the service pack applied. Without much more effort, you can burn this slipstreamed installation to a CD-ROM to enable Win2K installs from a bootable CD-ROM.

1. Copy the entire structure of the Win2K CD-ROM to a folder on your local disk (e.g., c:\temp\win2000pro).
2. Slipstream the service pack to this installation point (you must point to the root of the CD-ROM's COPIED location and not to the i386 folder—e.g., c:\win2ksp2\i386\update\update -s:c:\temp\win2000pro).

   The installation point will now have the service pack applied, and the root will include a couple of extra files; the important file is the one that indicates that the service pack is installed. This is an empty file with a name of CDROM_SP.TST if SP1 is slipstreamed or CDROMSP2.TST if SP2 is slipstreamed.

Other important files that should be in the root of the distribution area are the following:

- CDROM_NT.5—Identifier indicating that the CD-ROM contains Windows 2000
- CDROM_IP.5—Identifier indicating that the CD-ROM contains the professional version
- CDROM_IS.5—Identifier indicating that the CD-ROM contains the server version
- CDROM_IA.5—Identifier indicating that the CD-ROM contains the advanced server version

3. Create the CD-ROM.
4. You need the boot sector for the CD-ROM, which I explain how to get in FAQ 11.9.
5. You should then burn the CD-ROM (see FAQ 11.9 mentioned in the previous step). You perform steps 8 through 18 if you use Adaptec's Easy CD Creator.
6. Start Easy CD Creator.
7. From the File menu, select New CD Project > Bootable CD.
8. For the boot settings, set the emulation to No Emulation, Load Segment to 0x7c0, and Sector Count to 4 (see Figure 5-7). Click Browse and select the boot image (e.g., W2KCDBT.BIN). Click OK.
9. Add all the files in the Win2K folder to the CD-ROM folder (so CDROM_NT.5, etc. will be at the root of the CD-ROM).
10. Right-click the root of the CD-ROM and select Properties.
11. Change the volume label to W2PFPP_EN for Win2K Professional, W2SFPP_EN for Win2K Server, and W2AFPP_EN for Win2K Advanced Server.
12. Change the filesystem to ISO9660.
13. Click OK.
14. Click Record.
15. Under Record Method, select Finalize CD, and under Record Options, select Record CD. Click Start Recording.
16. When the recording is complete, remove the CD-ROM. You can delete the temporary Win2K local folder.

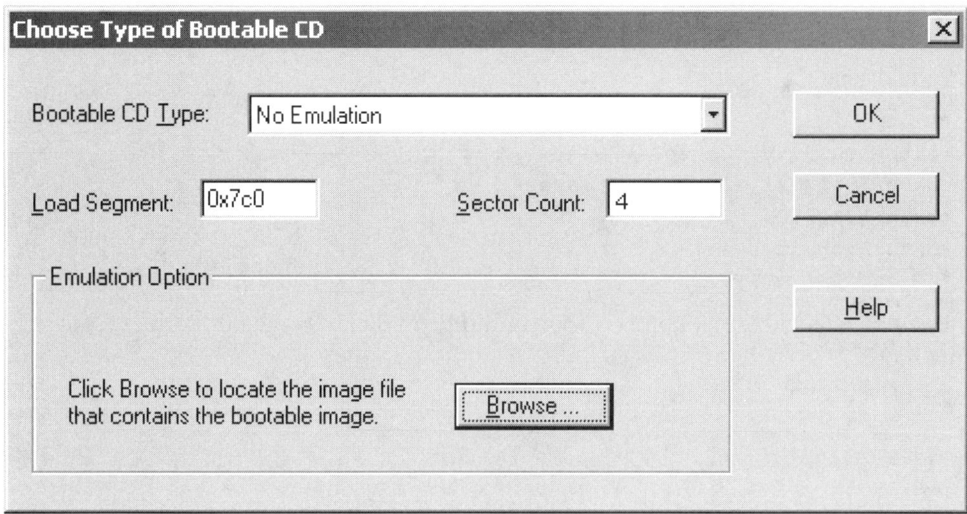

Figure 5-7 Bootable CD options

FAQ 5.21 How do I install the Windows 2000 Service Pack 2 Support Tools update?

Win2K SP2 includes a number of support tools updates that aren't installed when you install SP2. The updated tools reside in the \support\tools folder on the SP2 CD-ROM, or you can download them from http://www.microsoft.com/windows2000/downloads/servicepacks/sp2/supporttools.asp.

If you download the updated tools, you'll have a file SP2SUPPORTTOOLS.EXE that you should run and install (you should remove the old tools first by following the onscreen prompts). If you already have the current tools installed, a patch (which is only 700KB instead of 10MB for the full set) is available at http://www.microsoft.com/windows2000/downloads/servicepacks/sp2/supportpatch.asp.

FAQ 5.22 What is QCHAIN.EXE?

Qchain is a tool that Microsoft has released for Windows 2000 and Windows NT 4.0 to help users install multiple hotfixes at once without having to reboot after each installation. You can download the tool from Microsoft's Web site and run the download to obtain the QCHAIN.EXE image.

To use Qchain, you simply install each hotfix (without rebooting). Run Qchain to clean up the internal files (e.g., .INF files) and then reboot the system. So, for example, you could type

```
<path>\Q123456_w2k_sp2_x86.exe -z -m
<path>\Q123321_w2k_sp2_x86.exe -z -m
<path>\Q123789_w2k_sp2_x86.exe -z -m
<path>\qchain.exe
```

The -z flag tells the hotfix not to reboot, and the –m flag tells the hotfix to execute in quiet mode.

FAQ 5.23 When I try to install a service pack in Windows 2000, why does my machine complain about the Print Spooler service?

When you install a service pack, the installer activates the Print Spooler service if it's not already running. However, if you've disabled the startup type for this service, the service will fail to start, and the computer will display the following error message:

```
Cannot install the Service Pack.
The Print Spooler service is not started.
```

To resolve this problem, perform the following steps to set the service startup type to manual:

1. Start the Microsoft Management Console (MMC) Computer Management snap-in (go to Start > Programs > Administrative Tools and click Computer Management).
2. Select the Services and Applications branch.
3. Select Services.
4. Right-click Print Spooler and select Properties.
5. Under the Startup type setting, select Manual.
6. Click OK.

FAQ 5.24 Can any tools identify whether a system is missing important service packs?

In FAQ 9.14, I discuss CmdInfo, a freeware utility (available at http://www.savill tech.com/cmdinfo.html) that you can use to test whether a hotfix is installed on local and remote machines. Recently, Microsoft released a new tool, hfnetchk, that communicates with a constantly updated list of hotfixes stored on the Microsoft Web site and can determine whether your system is missing any critical fixes. You can use hfnetchk to scan one computer, a group of computers, or a whole domain. See Microsoft article Q303215 for further information.

You can download hfnetchk from http://www.microsoft.com/downloads/release.asp? releaseid=31154.

Here is a sample execution:

```
D:\temp>hfnetchk -i 200.200.200.1
Microsoft Network Security Hotfix Checker, 3.1
Developed for Microsoft by Shavlik Technologies, LLC
info@shavlik.com (www.shavlik.com)

** Attempting to download the XML from
http://download.microsoft.com/download/xml/security/1.0/NT5/
EN-US/mssecure.cab. **

** File was successfully downloaded. **

** Attempting to load D:\temp\mssecure.xml. **

Using XML data version = 1.0.1.137 Last modified on 8/21/2001.

Scanning 200.200.200.1

Done scanning 200.200.200.1
--------------
200.200.200.1
--------------

WINDOWS 2000 ADVANCED SERVER SP2
```

```
Patch NOT Found MS00-077 Q299796
Patch NOT Found MS00-079 Q276471
Patch NOT Found MS01-007 Q285851
Patch NOT Found MS01-013 Q285156
WARNING MS01-022 Q296441
Patch NOT Found MS01-025 Q296185
Patch NOT Found MS01-031 Q299553
Patch NOT Found MS01-036 Q299687
Patch NOT Found MS01-037 Q302755
Patch NOT Found MS01-040 Q292435
Patch NOT Found MS01-041 Q298012
Patch NOT Found MS01-043 Q303984
Patch NOT Found MS01-046 Q252795

Internet Information Services 5.0

Patch NOT Found MS01-025 Q296185
Patch NOT Found MS01-044 Q301625

Internet Explorer 5.5 SP1

Patch NOT Found MS00-093 Q279328
Patch NOT Found MS01-015 Q286043

SQL Server 2000 Gold

WARNING MS00-092 Q280380
WARNING MS01-032 Q299717
WARNING MS01-041 Q298012
```

It's important to note that Microsoft now offers several utilities to analyze your machine, including

- Windows Update—http://www.windowsupdate.microsoft.com
- Microsoft Personal Security Advisor—http://www.microsoft.com/technet/mpsa/start.asp
- The hfnetchk utility

It's best to use all of these resources to ensure your system is up-to-date.

The company that made this tool for Microsoft offers a professional version at http://www.shavlik.com/security/; however, a free download is available at http://www.multiply.org/software/hfnetchk/index.html, which takes the output from the utility and converts it into HTML-friendly output.

FAQ 5.25 How do I access the Windows Update Catalog for XP/.NET?

Windows Update (at http://windowsupdate.microsoft.com/) contains fixes to install onto a machine; however, they cannot be saved locally. To store them locally, you need to use the corporate catalog, which allows local storage and subsequent installation. To access this catalog, perform the following steps:

1. Go to the usual Windows Update, http://windowsupdate.microsoft.com.
2. Under Other Options, select Personalize Windows Update.
3. Check the Display the link to the Windows Update Catalog under See Also option.
4. Click Save Settings.
5. Under See Also, you will now have Windows Update Catalog.

The Windows Update Catalog can also be accessed directly from the URL http://v4.windowsupdate.microsoft.com/en/default.asp?corporate=true.

Once you access the Windows Update Catalog, you can add to your basket a number of fixes, which are then downloaded to your machine.

FAQ 5.26 How can I ensure hotfixes installed on my system are not corrupt or incomplete?

Microsoft has released a utility QFECHECK.EXE that scans your system for installed hotfixes and then ensures they are not compromised—that is, no files that make up the fix have been replaced with older or incorrect versions. QFECHECK.EXE is different from hfnetchk, which connects to the Internet and checks if your system is missing any operating system, Internet Explorer, SQL, fixes, and so on. QFECHECK just ensures those already installed are still fully installed.

The QFECHECK utility can be downloaded from http://support.microsoft.com/default.aspx?scid=kb;en-us;Q282784&ID=282784 and has versions for

- Windows 2000 i386
- Windows XP Professional and Home i386
- Windows XP IA64

After you downloaded the utility, you execute it, and this installs the application to the %systemroot%\system32 folder. To execute it, open a command window (CMD.EXE) and type **qfecheck**.

```
qfecheck
```

```
Windows XP Hotfix Validation Report for \\DBLON20344

Report Date: 1/23/2002 8:07pm

Current Service Pack Level: No Service Pack is installed.

Hotfixes Identified:
Application Compatibility Update: Current on system.
Q282784: Current on system.
Q307869: Current on system.
Q308210: Current on system.
Q309521: Current on system.
Q309691: Current on system.
Q310437: Current on system.
Q310507: Current on system.
Q311889: Current on system.
Q313484: This hotfix should be reinstalled.
Q315000: Current on system.
```

You can optionally use the /q (quiet) and /v (verbose) switches depending on the level of output required. Verbose mode is the same as normal unless a hotfix needs to be reinstalled where QFECHECK will identify the incorrect files to screen.

If you experience problems under Windows 2000 with SP1 installed identifying hotfixes, you may need an updated SP2.CAT file, which is included with the hotfixes from http://support.microsoft.com/default.aspx?scid=kb;en-us;Q281767.

6 SYSTEM CONFIGURATION

Windows is now so feature rich with so many components that form part of the operating system the configurations that can be performed are almost limitless. We cover the most common configurations in this chapter, but you should also check Chapter 7, "User Configuration," and Chapter 8, "Desktop Environment," for tips that relate to user and desktop settings.

FAQ 6.1 How do I decrease the boot delay?

There are three ways of performing this change; the first method just automates the second method.

Method 1

1. Log on as Administrator.
2. Start the System Control Panel applet (Start > Settings > Control Panel > System).
3. Select the Start-up/Shutdown tab.
4. In the Show list for box, set the number of seconds to the delay required.

Method 2

Method 1 just updates the timeout value in the [boot loader] section of BOOT.INI so we can do this manually:

1. Set the file to nonsystem and nonread-only

   ```
   attrib c:\boot.ini -r -s
   ```

2. Edit the file and change the timeout value to whatever you want—for example, to make it wait for 5 seconds change to

   ```
   timeout= 5
   ```

3. Save your changes.
4. Set the file back to system and read-only

```
attrib c:\boot.ini +r +s
```

Method 3

Windows XP supplies a new command-line utility BOOTCFG that allows boot configuration settings to be modified and used with the /timeout parameter, which allows the timeout to be modified. The following command changes the timeout to 10 seconds:

```
bootcfg /timeout 10
```

FAQ 6.2 Where do I load ANSI.SYS?

A file in your system32 directory, CONFIG.NT, tells NT how to run DOS 5 sessions. Add the line

```
device=c:\winnt\system32\ansi.sys
```

or

```
device=%systemroot%\system32\ansi.sys.
```

You will then have to start a command line using the COMMAND.COM that came with DOS 5 (dig out those old disks!).

FAQ 6.3 How do I schedule commands?

Windows NT has a built-in Scheduler service that enables applications to be started at specified times. To schedule events, the Scheduler service must be started:

1. From the Control Panel (Start > Settings > Control Panel), start Services.
2. Click Scheduler (or Task Scheduler on Workstation) and click Startup.
3. Select Automatic and click OK.
4. You can now reboot, or just click Start, which will start the Scheduler service.
5. Close the Services Control applet.

The Scheduler service only needs to be started on the **target** machine, not the issuing machine. If the Scheduler service is not started on the target machine, the error "The service has not been started." will be displayed.

To schedule a command, you use the AT utility. AT is used with the following syntax:

```
at [<computername>] <time> [/interactive] [/every:date/day..]
[/next:date/day..] <command>
```

For example: **at \\savmain 22:00 /interactive /every:M,T,W,Th,F sol.exe**. The example starts the solitaire game on the SAVMAIN machine at 10:00 p.m. every weekday. The /interactive means the application can interact with the desktop, that is, the currently logged on user. If /interactive is omitted and the application requires user interaction, it will just start and finish instantly.

When a command is submitted, it will be given an ID. To delete a scheduled command use

```
at [<computername>] <id> /delete /yes
```

For example, **at \\savmain 3 /delete /yes**—the /yes skips confirmation of the delete.

The preceding may seem quite a lot to take in if all you want to do is a backup (see FAQ 12.9, for an example of using AT with a backup), so a utility called WINAT is shipped with the NT Resource Kit that puts a graphical interface on the AT command, which you may find easier to use; however, the functionality is the same. The advantage with WINAT is that it automatically starts the Scheduler service on the target machine.

FAQ 6.4 How can I execute a batch file using WINAT with Administrator permissions?

From the Services Control Panel applet (Start > Settings > Control Panel), double-click Scheduler. Change the account/password to that of a user in the Administrative group. It may be wise to create a new account just for this use, which requires the following attributes:

- Nonblank password
- Nonexpiring password
- User rights—Log on as service and log on as batch job

After changing the Scheduler information, you will need to stop and start the service.

FAQ 6.5 How do I change the organization name on NT?

Your company changed names again? To change the company name in NT is easy:

1. Start the Registry editor (Start > Run > REGEDIT).
2. Go to the HKEY_LOCAL_MACHINE\Software\Microsoft\WindowsNT\CurrentVersion and select the CurrentVersion. On the right part of the screen is a number of values.
3. Double-click RegisteredOrganization and change the value data.
4. Click OK.
5. Exit the Registry editor.

NT ONLY.

FAQ 6.6 How do I change the default location where NT expects to find NT software for installation (that is, CD)?

To modify from the location from the media that installed NT, perform the following:

1. Start the Registry editor (REGEDIT.EXE).
2. Move to HKEY_LOCAL_MACHINE\SOFTWARE\Microsoft\Windows NT\CurrentVersion.
3. Double-click SourcePath and set to the new location.
4. Move to HKEY_LOCAL_MACHINE\SOFTWARE\Microsoft\Windows\CurrentVersion\Setup.
5. Double-click SourcePath again and set to the new location.

FAQ 6.7 How can I remove the Shutdown button from the logon screen?

To remove the Shutdown button, start the Registry editor (REGEDIT.EXE), change KHEY_LOCAL_MACHINE\SOFTWARE\Microsoft\Windows NT\CurrentVersion\Winlogon, and change ShutdownWithoutLogon from 1 to 0.

This can also be accomplished using the Policy Editor (POLEDIT.EXE). Expand the Windows NT System—Logon tree and blank out Enable shutdown from Authentication dialog box.

FAQ 6.8 How can I parse and/or not parse AUTOEXEC.BAT?

The value HKEY_CURRENT_USER\Software\Microsoft\Windows NT\CurrentVersion\Winlogon\ParseAutoexec should be set to 1 for AUTOEXEC.BAT to be parsed or 0 for AUTOEXEC.BAT not to be parsed.

FAQ 6.9 How do I add a path statement in NT?

Start the Control Panel (Start > Settings > Control Panel), double-click the System icon, and go to the Environment tab. Choose if a user or system path should be defined, click on the path variable, and then add the statement to the end of the current string (including a semicolon—;), then click Set.

Under Windows 2000 and XP, you must select the Advanced tab under System and click the Environment Variables button, but apart from that, the procedure is the same.

FAQ 6.10 Can I change the default Windows background?

Using the Registry editor (REGEDIT.EXE), edit the key HKEY_USERS\.DEFAULT\Control Panel\Desktop and double-click the Wallpaper Key and enter the value including directory (e.g., c:\winnt\savlogo.bmp).You can also change the background color HKEY_USERS\DEFAULT\Control Panel\Colors; double-click Background and change the value (e.g., 0 0 0 for black).

FAQ 6.11 How do I change the Start menu items under the line?

Items above the line are part of the logged on user's profile (winnt/profiles/<user name> /Start Menu/Programs). Items under the line are part of the all user group (winnt/profiles/All Users/Start Menu/Programs). To change these items, click on Start > Settings > Taskbar & Start Menu > Start Menu > Advanced and then move the directory to All Users and make changes. You can set the All Users folder only if you are logged on as a member with Administrative Privileges.

FAQ

6.12 How can I restore the old Program Manager?

NT 4.0 and above by default use the Explorer shell (EXPLORER.EXE); however, the old Program Manager (PROGMAN.EXE) is still delivered with the new Windows versions and can be configured to be the default shell using the Registry:

1. Start the Registry editor (Start > Run > REGEDIT.EXE).
2. Go to the HKEY_LOCAL_MACHINE\SOFTWARE\Microsoft\Windows NT\CurrentVersion\Winlogon.
3. Double-click on the value Shell.
4. Change from EXPLORER.EXE to PROGMAN.EXE and click OK.
5. Exit the Registry editor.
6. Log off and then log on.

Back to the old! :-)

NT ONLY

FAQ

6.13 Is there a way to start NT in DOS mode?

The command shell is COMMAND.COM, and NT can be started in this mode with COMMAND.COM as the default shell. Just perform the steps outlined in the previous FAQ, but instead of changing the shell value to PROGMAN.EXE, change it to COMMAND.COM or CMD.EXE.

Under Windows 2000 and XP, we also have the Safe mode option during system startup.

FAQ

6.14 How can I disable Lock Workstation when I press Ctrl+Alt+Del?

Windows NT 4.0 Service Pack 4 introduces a new Registry entry:

1. Start the Registry editor (REGEDIT.EXE).
2. Move to HKEY_CURRENT_USER\Software\Microsoft\Windows\CurrentVersion\Policies\System.
3. From the Edit menu, select New > DWORD Value.
4. Enter a name of **DisableLockWorkstation** and press Enter.

5. Double-click on the new value and set to 1. Click OK.
6. Close the Registry editor.

Lock Workstation will now be greyed out.

This is also possible if you don't mind hacking one of the system DLL files. The file that the Ctrl+Alt+Del dialog is stored in is MSGINA.DLL. Using any 32-bit resource editor (such as one with a Win32 C++ compiler, Visual C++, Borland C++), you can edit this DLL and remove the Lock Workstation button. The following are instructions for performing this with Visual C++; however, for another resource editor, find dialog #1650 and edit the attributes of the Lock Workstation to "inactive" or "invisible".

1. Rename %systemroot%\system32\msgina.dll to MSGINA_ORIG.DLL (this is so you have a backup).
2. Copy the file back to be called MSGINA.DLL—for example:

```
copy d:\winnt\system32\msgina_orig.dll
d:\winnt\system32\msgina.dll
```

3. Start Visual C++ and select Open.
4. Change the type to Executable Files (.DLL, .EXE, .OCX).
5. Move to the %systemroot%\system32 directory, select MSGINA.DLL, and click OK.
6. Once open, click on the dialog tree and double-click 1650.
7. Double-click on the Lock Workstation button and deselect Visible.
8. Close the dialog box and the from the File menu, select Save.
9. Exit Visual C++ and reboot the machine.

Once the machine has booted up again, the Lock Workstation button will no longer be displayed.

FAQ 6.15 How can I make NT power down on shut down?

Follow these procedures:

1. Start the Registry editor (REGEDIT.EXE).
2. Go to the Key HKEY_LOCAL_MACHINE\Software\Microsoft\Windows NT\CurrentVersion\Winlogon.
3. If the value PowerdownAfterShutdown exists, change it to1. Go to step 5.

4. If the value does not exist, add it as type REG_SZ and set to 1.
5. Exit the Registry editor.

You will need an ATX power supply and an updated HAL.DLL from the computer manufacturer in order for this to work; otherwise, the machine will just reboot.

Windows NT 4.0 Service Pack 4 and above ships with a file, HAL.DLL.SOFTEX, which works on many systems. To obtain HALL.DLL.SOFTEX (and HALMPS. DLLSOFTEX for multiprocessor systems), run the service pack executable of the service pack you actually have installed with the command-line parameter /X . This will extract all the files in the service pack to a temporary directory without installing them. You'll find HALL.DLL.SOFTEX and HALMPS.DLL.SOFTEX among the extracted files.

To install, enter the following:

```
cd %systemroot%\system32
WINNT\system32> rename hal.dll hal.old
WINNT\system32> copy g:\i386\hal.dll.softex hal.dll
```

Reboot.

An alternative to renaming HALL.DLL is to add option /hal=filename.ext in BOOT.INI.

Another file, HALMPS.DLL.SOFTEX, is shipped for multiprocessor systems. Some people have reported that after using the softex DLLs, the CPU misses the idle loops and stays at higher temperatures, so you may want to watch out for this. If you purchase Softex NT Power Management v2.19 and install it, the same happens on a Dell Inspiron 3500 Laptop with Mobile Celeron 366.

Windows 2000 and Windows XP include better support for Advanced Configuration and Power Interface (ACPI) and the previously described actions are not needed on most new systems.

FAQ 6.16 How do I enable Ctrl+Esc to start Task Manager?

This was removed in release 4.0 of NT and changed to Ctrl+Esc+Shift; however, it can be restored by editing the Registry:

1. Start the Registry editor (REGEDIT.EXE).
2. Go to the HKEY_LOCAL_MACHINE\Software\Microsoft\Windows NT\CurrentVersion\Winlogon.
3. Click Edit > New > String Value and enter the name as **TaskMan**.
4. Double-click the entry, set the value to **TASKMAN.EXE**, and press Enter.

5. Close the Registry.
6. Reboot the machine.

FAQ 6.17 How can I allow non-Administrators to issue AT commands?

By default only Administrators can issue AT commands (which use the Scheduler service). It is possible to allow Server operators to also submit AT commands:

1. Start the Registry editor (REGEDIT.EXE).
2. Move to the HKEY_LOCAL_MACHINE\SYSTEM\CurrentControlSet\Control\Lsa.
3. From the Edit menu, select New > DWORD.
4. The name is "SubmitControl" and press Enter.
5. Double-click on the name and set the value to 1.
6. Exit the Registry editor.
7. Reboot the machine.

You may want to recreate your Emergency Repair Disk after making this change.

FAQ 6.18 How do I control access to floppy drives and CD-ROM drives?

By default Windows NT allows any program to access the floppy and CD-ROM drives. In a secure environment, you may only want the interactive user to be able to access the drives, and this is accomplished using the Registry:

1. Start the Registry editor (REGEDIT.EXE).
2. Move to the HKEY_LOCAL_MACHINE\SOFTWARE\Microsoft\WindowsNT\CurrentVersion\Winlogon.
3. From the Edit menu, select New Reg_SZ type.
4. To allocate floppy drives, create a name "AllocateFloppies"; to allocate CD-ROM drives, "AllocateCDRoms".
5. Press Enter and then set the value to 1.
6. Log out and log on again.

6.19 How can I show DOS, Windows 95, and NT all on the boot menu?

To display all of your operating systems on the boot menu, you need the handy Bootpart utility from http://www.ntfaq.com/ntfaq/download/bootpart.zip, which creates multiple operating .SYS files enabling DOS and Windows 95 to be shown on the boot menu.

1. Create an Emergency Repair Disk (RDISK /s).
2. Reboot the machine and boot into Windows 95.
3. When Starting Windows 95 is displayed, press F8.
4. Select option 8 to boot to a previous version of DOS.
5. Once in DOS, go to where you unzipped BOOTPART.ZIP and type

```
BOOTPART DOS622 c:\BOOTSECT.622 "MS-DOS 6.22"
BOOTPART WIN95 c:\BOOTSECT.W95 "Windows 95"
BOOTPART REWRITEROOT:C:
```

6. Edit the BOOT.INI file to remove the old MS-DOS/Windows 95 option

```
attrib c:\boot.ini -r -s
edit c:\boot.ini and remove c:\="MS-DOS"
attrib c:\boot.ini +r +s
```

7. Reboot.

Be aware that using Bootpart may cause problems if you select Previous Windows version from Windows 95.

6.20 How do I remove an app from Control Panel?

Each item in the Control Panel corresponds to a .CPL file. When Control Panel starts, it searches %systemroot%/system32 for all .CPL files. To remove an item from Control Panel, rename the .CPL file (e.g., to .NOCPL).

If you only want certain users not to be able run a particular applet, an alternative is to have the boot partition on NTFS and remove the READ permission for these users/groups.

Have a look at the next FAQ for more information on the .CPL files.

FAQ 6.21 What are the .CPL files in the system32 directory?

Each .CPL file represents one or more Control Panel applets (Start > Settings > Control Panel). The following is a list of common .CPL files and what Control Panel applets they represent:

.CPL Filename	Control Panel Applets
ACCESS.CPL	Accessibility options
APPWIZ.CPL	Add/remove programs
CONSOLE.CPL	Console
DESK.CPL	Display
DEVAPPS.CPL	PCMCIA, SCSI adapters, and tape drives
INETCPL.CPL	Internet
INTL.CPL	Regional settings
JOY.CPL	Joystick
MAIN.CPL	Fonts, keyboard, mouse, and printers
MLCFG32.CPL	Mail
MMSYS.CPL	Sounds and multimedia
MODEM.CPL	Modems
NCPA.CPL	Network
NTGUARD.CPL	Dr Solomons
ODBCCP32.CPL	ODBC
PORTS.CPL	Ports
RASCPL.CPL	Dial-up monitor
SRVMGR.CPL	Server, services, and devices
SYSDM.CPL	System

(continued)

.CPL Filename	Control Panel Applets
TELEPHON.CPL	Telephony
TIMEDATE.CPL	Date/time
TWEAKUI.CPL	TweakUI
UPS.CPL	UPS

If you rename any of these files, then the items they represent in the Control Panel will not be shown—for example, the following removes the Date/Time Control Panel applet:

```
rename timedate.cpl timedate.non
```

Also, setting HKEY_CURRENT_USER\Software\Microsoft\Windows\CurrentVersion\Policies\Explorer\NoSetFolders (REG_DWORD) to 1 hides the Control Panel, Printers, and My Computer in Explorer and in the Start menu. You would normally need to create this value as it does not exist by default.

FAQ 6.22 How do I configure a default screensaver if no one logs on?

Configuring a default screensaver is accomplished using the Registry editor:

1. Start the Registry editor (REGEDIT.EXE).
2. Move to the HKEY_USERS\DEFAULT\Control Panel\Desktop.
3. Double-click ScreenSaveActive and set to 1.
4. Double-click SCRNSAVE.EXE and set to black16.scr.
5. Double-click ScreenSaveTimeOut and set to the number of seconds (e.g., 600 for 10 minutes).
6. Exit the Registry editor.

FAQ 6.23 How do I configure the default screensaver to be the Open GL Text Saver?

Follow this procedure:

1. Start the Registry editor (REGEDIT.EXE).
2. Change the value HKEY_USERS\.DEFAULT\Control Panel\Desktop\SCRNSAVE.EXE to "E:\WINNT\System32\sstext3d.scr".
3. Create a key called HKEY_USERS\.DEFAULT\Control Panel\Screen Saver.3DText (Edit > New > Key).
4. Under this new key, create two new values of string type (Edit > New > String Value) called "Font" and "Text".
5. Set Font (double-click on it) to Arial.
6. Set Text to the string you want to be displayed (you are limited to 16 characters).
7. Close the Registry editor.

A word of caution: The Open GL screensavers use a lot of system resources, so I recommend you not use them.

FAQ 6.24 How can I create a new hardware profile?

If you are about to change hardware, you may want to create a copy of your current hardware config before starting, which will enable you to revert to your old configuration:

1. From Control Panel, start the System Control Panel applet (Start > Settings > Control Panel), or right-click on My Computer and select Properties.
2. Click on the Hardware Profiles tab (or Hardware tab in Windows XP, then click the Hardware Profiles button).
3. Select the current Hardware Profile Original Configuration (Current).
4. Click Copy and then type in the new name in the dialog box that is shown.
5. Click OK, and the startup options will be set.

6.25 I have entries on the Remove software list that don't work. How can I remove them?

Each entry on this list (Start > Settings > Control Panel > Add/Remove Programs) is an entry in the Registry under HKEY_LOCAL_MACHINE\SOFTWARE\Microsoft\Windows\CurrentVersion\Uninstall. Just remove the key for any entries you don't want.

6.26 How can I disable Dr. Watson?

Dr. Watson can be disabled using the Registry editor:

1. Start the Registry editor (REGEDIT.EXE).
2. Go to HKEY_LOCAL_MACHINE\SOFTWARE\Microsoft\Windows NT\CurrentVersion\AeDebug.
3. Click on AeDebug and click Del.

Alternatively just set HKEY_LOCAL_MACHINE\SOFTWARE\Microsoft\Windows NT\CurrentVersion\AeDebug\AUTO to 0.

To reenable Dr. Watson, type **drwtsn32 -i**.

6.27 How do I create a network share?

It is possible to create a share from the command prompt by typing

```
net share <share name>=<drive>:<dir> /remark="<description>"
```

For example, **net share john=c:\data\johndrv /remark="Johns drive"**

A share can also be created using Explorer:

1. Start Explorer (Start > Programs > Windows NT Explorer).
2. Right-click on a directory and select Sharing.
3. Click the Sharing tab and select Shared as.
4. Enter a description and click OK. The directory will now have a hand on the directory.

It is possible to add a dollar sign ($) to the end of the share so it will appear hidden and not visible from a network browse.

FAQ 6.28 How do I connect to a network share?

You can connect to a network share using the command prompt:

```
net use <drive letter>: <UNC>
```

For example, **net use f: \\johnpc\john**.

A share can also be connected to using Explorer:

1. Start Explorer (Start > Programs > Windows NT Explorer).
2. From the Tools menu, select Map Network Drive.
3. Select a drive letter, and either enter the share path or browse the network and select.
4. Click OK.

The advantage of using the net use command is you can connect to hidden shares—that is, john$—(although you can also connect by manually typing the address in Explorer), and net use also can be used from within command files.

FAQ 6.29 How do I configure the boot menu to show forever?

The timeout is changed by editing the BOOT.INI file, which is on the boot partition, and by changing the timeout parameter:

1. Start a command session (Start > Run > Command).
2. Set the attributes on c:\boot.ini to nonread and nonsystem:

   ```
   attrib c:\boot.ini -r -s
   ```

3. Edit the file and change the timeout to -1:

   ```
   [boot loaded]
   timeout = -1
   ```

4. Save your changes and set the file back to read only and system:

   ```
   attrib c:\boot.ini +r +s
   ```

In Windows 2000/XP, this process can also be done through the GUI, select the Properties of My Computer, select the Advanced tab, click Setup and Recovery.

FAQ 6.30 How can I configure the machine to reboot at a certain time?

A command-line utility, SHUTDOWN.EXE, that is shipped with the Resource Kit can be used to reboot the local machine:

```
shutdown /l /r /y /c
```

Where /l tells the computer to shut down the local machine, /r to reboot, /c to close all programs, and /y to avoid having to say yes to questions. You can then combine this command with the AT command (don't forget you need the Scheduler service to be running—Start > Settings > Control Panel > Services—to use the AT command) to make this happen at a certain time:

```
AT <time> shutdown /l /r /y /c
```

For example, **AT 20:00 shutdown /l /r /y /c**.

Additions to the at command could be /every:M,T,W,Th,F so it happens every day—for example, **AT 20:00 /every:M,T,W,Th,F shutdown /l /r /y /c**. You will then be given 20 seconds before the machine is shut down, to abort the shutdown, type

```
shutdown /l /a /y
```

FAQ 6.31 How can I configure Explorer to start with drive x?

The following procedure is used to change the shortcut for Explorer in the Start menu; however, you could just as easily create a new shortcut on the desktop, then edit its properties, and change the target.

1. Start Explorer (Start > Programs > Windows NT Explorer or Win key+E).
2. Move to %SystemRoot%/profiles/<your username>/Start Menu/Programs—for example, d:/winnt/profiles/savillj/Start Menu/Programs.
3. Right-click on Windows NT Explorer and select Properties, or select Properties from the File menu.
4. The target will be %SystemRoot%\explorer.exe; change this to %SystemRoot%\explorer.exe /e, <drive letter>:\. For example, %SystemRoot%\explorer.exe /e, e:\

would make Explorer start at the E drive (make sure you type two commas); you can also use /root, which forces the right pane to show only E (not nice!). For example, %SystemRoot%\explorer.exe /e, /root, e:\ .

Also note that instead of just a drive letter, you can also specify a directory—for example, %SystemRoot%\explorer.exe /e, e:\winnt\system32.

5. Click OK and exit Explorer.

FAQ 6.32 How can I decrease the time my machine takes to shut down or reboot?

It is possible to manually shut down each service (well, some of them) and then shut down the machine. To identify which services are running, enter the command

```
net start
```

(You can add > [filename] to the end to make it output to a file—i.e., net start > services.lst.) You can then try to shut down each of the services by entering the command

```
net stop "<service name>"
```

For example, **net stop "spooler"**. Some services ask you to enter a y to confirm, and for these services, just add /y to the end. You will be able to build up a list of all the services that can be manually stopped, and you should put these in a .BAT file—for example,

```
net stop "Computer Browser""
net stop "Messenger"
.
.
net stop "Workstation"
```

To the end of the file, add the following command:

```
shutdown /r /y /l /t:0
```

To reboot the machine (leave off the /r to just shut down the machine). SHUTDOWN.EXE is part of the Windows NT Resource Kit or is supplied as standard in Windows

XP. You may also want to add @echo off to the start of the file. You could add a check to accept an input parameter to reboot or shut down—for example, save this file as SHUTFAST.BAT, and call using shutfast reboot, or shutfast shutdown:

```
@echo off
net stop "Computer Browser""
net stop "Messenger"
net stop "Net Logon"
net stop "NT LM Security Support Provider"
net stop "Plug and Play"
net stop "Protected Storage"
net stop "Remote Access Autodial Manager"
net stop "Server"
net stop "Spooler"
net stop "TCP/IP NetBIOS Helper" /y
net stop "Workstation"

if %1==reboot goto reboot
shutdown /l /y /t:0
exit
:reboot
shutdown /l /y /r /t:0
exit
```

You could add a shortcut on the desktop for this batch file with the relevant parameter. You can also decrease the time NT waits for a service to stop before terminating it by performing the following:

1. Start the Registry editor (REGEDIT.EXE).
2. Move to HKEY_LOCAL_MACHINE\SYSTEM\CurrentControlSet\Control.
3. Double-click on WaitToKillServiceTimeout (REG_DWORD) and change to the number of milliseconds after the logoff/shutdown before displaying the Wait, End Task, and Close dialog boxes—for example, 10,000 for 10 seconds; the default is 20,000.
4. Add HangAppTimeout (REG_DWORD) and change to the number of milliseconds to wait before displaying the Wait, End Task, and Close dialog boxes after trying to close an application.
5. Add AutoEndTasks (REG_DWORD) and change to 1 to avoid the dialog asking to Wait, End Task, and Close.

FAQ 6.33 How can I change the startup order of the services?

Each service belongs to a Service Group, and it is possible to modify the order that the groups start:

1. Start the Registry editor (REGEDT32.EXE, **not** REGEDIT.EXE unless you're using XP, in which case, REGEDIT.EXE is fine).
2. Move to HKEY_LOCAL_MACHINE\SYSTEM\CurrentControlSet\Control\ServiceGroupOrder.
3. Double-click on List in the right pane.
4. You can then move the groups around in the list order.
5. Click OK.
6. Close the Registry editor.

See Knowledge Base article Q102987 at http://support.microsoft.com/support/kb/articles/q102/9/87.asp for more information.

FAQ 6.34 How can I configure the system so that certain commands run at boot-up time?

The AUTOEXNT utility is supplied in a ZIP file as part of the Windows Resource Kit. To use it, perform the following steps:

1. From the AUTOEXNT.ZIP file, extract the files AUTOEXNT.EXE, AUTOEXNT.BAT, and SERVMESS.DLL to %systemroot%/system32.
2. Also extract the file INSTSRV.EXE to any directory (a temp directory will do).
3. At the command prompt, enter

   ```
   instsrv install
   ```

   This will create a new service called AutoExNT.
4. Edit the file %systemroot%/system32/autoexnt.bat and put in any commands you want to run when the machine boots (such as a CHKDSK, etc.).

When the system boots in the future, the AutoExNT service will check for the existence of the file AUTOEXNT.BAT and execute any commands in it.

A version of this utility is also shipped with the Resource Kit; however, it is better to use the downloadable version. To install the Resource Kit version, you have to type

```
instexnt install
```

FAQ 6.35 How can I create a non-network hardware configuration?

You may have some machines that are not always connected to the network, and a solution is to create an alternate hardware profile that has all network devices and services disabled.

1. Start Control Panel (Start > Settings > Control Panel).
2. Start the System Control Panel applet.
3. Select the Hardware Profiles tab (or Hardware tab—click the Hardware Profiles button in Windows 2000 or above).
4. Select the current configuration and click Copy.
5. In the To box, enter the name "No Network" and click OK.
6. From the Available Hardware Profiles box, select No Network and click Properties.
7. Click the Network tab, check the Network disabled hardware profiles box, and click OK.
8. Check that the wait for time is set—for example, 30 seconds—and then click OK.
9. You can also change the name of "Original Configuration" to "On Network" if you want by selecting it, clicking rename, and typing the new name.

To actually use this configuration when you boot up the machine, after you select the operating system to load—for example, "Windows NT Workstation 4.0"—you will receive another menu with your hardware profile choices. Select the required option and click Enter.

FAQ 6.36 How can I remove the option Press Spacebar for last known good config?

The choice is hard-coded into NT and therefore cannot be removed; however, you can remove its functionality.

Several sets of configuration information are stored in NT: the current configuration and one or more sets of old configuration that are known to work. In the Registry, NT points to the current configuration and a link to one of the other sets. It is possible to change the link to the last known good config; thus pressing the spacebar at bootup will have no effect.

1. Start the Registry editor (REGEDIT.EXE).
2. Move to HKEY_LOCAL_MACHINE\SYSTEM\Select (if you look at HKEY_LOCAL_MACHINE\SYSTEM, you can see the control sets).
3. Double-click on LastKnownGood and change to whatever value Current is.
4. Click OK and exit the Registry editor.

The option Press Spacebar for last known good config has caused lots of trouble, because of use with the Novell IntranetWare for Windows NT, which is unavailable after restoring the last known good configuration; the same is true for any self-created hardware profile.

An interesting solution for this and other related system crashes has been found. Save the whole registration key from Regedit (interestingly, this method doesn't work with the more detailed Regedt32) as a script file named, for example SAVE.REG. If a system is damaged, a simple double-click on this executable file regenerates the whole configuration without loss of information. Moreover, you can zip this file—usually as large as 5MB—to a volume of nearly 500KB. With these tools in hand, it is possible to restore a crashed system from the hard disk with rdisk and afterwards regenerate it with the Registry file to the last known standard.

FAQ 6.37 How can I disable the OS2/POSIX subsystems?

It is possible to disable one or both of these subsystems:

1. Start the Registry editor (REGEDT32.EXE, **not** REGEDIT.EXE if using NT 4.0).
2. Move to HKEY_LOCAL_MACHINE\SYSTEM\CurrentControlSet\Control\Session Manager\SubSystems.
3. Double-click on Optional.
4. On each line is one subsystem; simply remove the one you wish to disable. If you want to disable both, set the value to NULL.
5. Click OK.
6. Close the Registry editor and reboot.

FAQ 6.38 How can I run a Control Panel applet from the command line?

It is possible to run Control Panel applets from the command line by just typing

```
control <applet name>
```

In some instances, the .CPL file represents more than one Control Panel applet when you need to pass a parameter of which applet to run. The following is a list of such .CPL files:

- SRVMGR.CPL—Use services, devices, or server
- MAIN.CPL—Fonts, mouse, printers, or keyboard
- MMSYS.CPL—Sounds or multimedia

For example, **control main.cpl printers** runs the Printer Control Panel applet.

However, it is better to associate the .CPL extension with CONTROL.EXE, which means you need to type only the applet name, which is accomplished using the assoc and ftype commands:

```
assoc .cpl=ControlFile
ftype ControlFile=control.exe %1 %*
```

You can now just enter the command, and it will run (be sure to include the .CPL extension).

FAQ 6.39 How can I configure a program/batch file to run every x minutes?

NT comes with a powerful built-in scheduling tool, the at command. However, it is not really suitable for running a command every five minutes. To run a command every five minutes, you have to submit hundreds of at jobs to run at certain times of the day. A number of tools are supplied with the Windows NT Resource Kit that will help.

SLEEP.EXE is used to set a command file (like the timeout command) to wait for n seconds, and its usage is simply

```
sleep 300
```

which makes the batch file pause for five minutes. So if you wanted a command file/program to run every five minutes, you could write a batch file with the following (name RUN5.BAT)

```
<program name>
sleep 300
run5
```

There are a number of problems with this approach. The command session has to stay open, and the five minutes does not start until the program has closed. (However, this problem can be solved by running the program in a separate thread by putting the word **start** in front of the program—for example, **start <program>**.)

Another program is called SOON.EXE, and this schedules a task to run in n seconds from now. To use soon, the Scheduler service has to be running (Start > Settings > Control Panel > Services). Again you could create a batch file to use it (RUNSOON.CMD)

```
soon 300 runsoon.cmd
notepad.exe
```

Run the command file using the at command or soon—for example, from the command line—to get it started:

```
soon 300 runsoon.cmd
```

If you wanted to stop soon, you can use the AT command to get a list of current scheduled jobs.

```
at
Status ID Day Time Command Line -----------------------------------
---------------------------------------
0 Today 9:04 AM runsoon.cmd
```

Once its ID is known, it can be stopped using

```
at [\\computer name] <ID> /delete
```

For example, **at 0 /delete**.

With Windows 2000 / XP, this is quite easy with its built-in Scheduled Task Wizard, where in Advanced options, you can set an interval in which certain program should be run.

FAQ 6.40 What Registry keys do the Control Panel applets update?

The following table shows the Control Panel applets and the corresponding Registry areas; those not shown are stored in multiple areas.

Accessibility Options	HKEY_CURRENT_USER\Control Panel\Accessibility
Date/Time	HKEY_LOCAL_MACHINE\SYSTEM\CurrentControlSet\Control\TimeZoneInformation
Devices	HKEY_LOCAL_MACHINE\SYSTEM\CurrentControlSet\Services
Display	HKEY_CURRENT_USER\Control Panel\Desktop and HKEY_LOCAL_MACHINE\HARDWARE\RESOURCEMAP\VIDEO
Fonts	HKEY_LOCAL_MACHINE\SOFTWARE\Microsoft\Windows NT\CurrentVersion\Fonts
Internet	HKEY_LOCAL_MACHINE\SOFTWARE\Microsoft\Windows\CurrentVersion\Internet Settings
Keyboard	HKEY_CURRENT_USER\Control Panel\Desktop
Modems	HKEY_LOCAL_MACHINE\SOFTWARE\Microsoft\Windows\CurrentVersion\Unimodem
Mouse	HKEY_CURRENT_USER\Control Panel\Mouse
Multimedia	HKEY_LOCAL_MACHINE\SOFTWARE\Microsoft\Multimedia
Ports	HKEY_LOCAL_MACHINE\HARDWARE\RESOURCEMAP
Printers	HKEY_CURRENT_USER\Printers
Regional Settings	HKEY_CURRENT_USER\Control Panel\International
SCSI Adapters	HKEY_LOCAL_MACHINE\HARDWARE\RESOURCEMAP\ScsiAdapter
Services	HKEY_LOCAL_MACHINE\SYSTEM\CurrentControlSet\Services
Sounds	HKEY_CURRENT_USER\AppEvents\Schemes\Apps\.Default
Tape Devices	HKEY_LOCAL_MACHINE\HARDWARE\RESOURCEMAP\OtherDrivers\TapeDevices

Telephony	HKEY_LOCAL_MACHINE\SOFTWARE\Microsoft\Windows\CurrentVersion\Telephony
UPS	HKEY_LOCAL_MACHINE\SYSTEM\CurrentControlSet\Services\UPS

FAQ 6.41 How can I run a script at shutdown time?

There is no direct way to accomplish this; however, it is possible to write a script and then call the SHUTDOWN.EXE utility that is shipped with the NT Resource Kit.

```
shutdown /l /y
```

You could then add a shortcut to this script on the desktop.

You may also consider ShutdownPlus (http://www.wmsoftware.com/shutdownplus), which replaces the standard Windows shutdown and logoff dialog boxes. Shutdown-Plus allows you to run applications and stop services (stopping services only under NT/2000) at shutdown, restart, or logoff.

In Windows 2000 and XP, this can be accomplished using Group Policy Objects. Go to the User Configuration > Windows Settings > Scripts (Logon/Logoff) and set the Logoff option (see Figure 6-1).

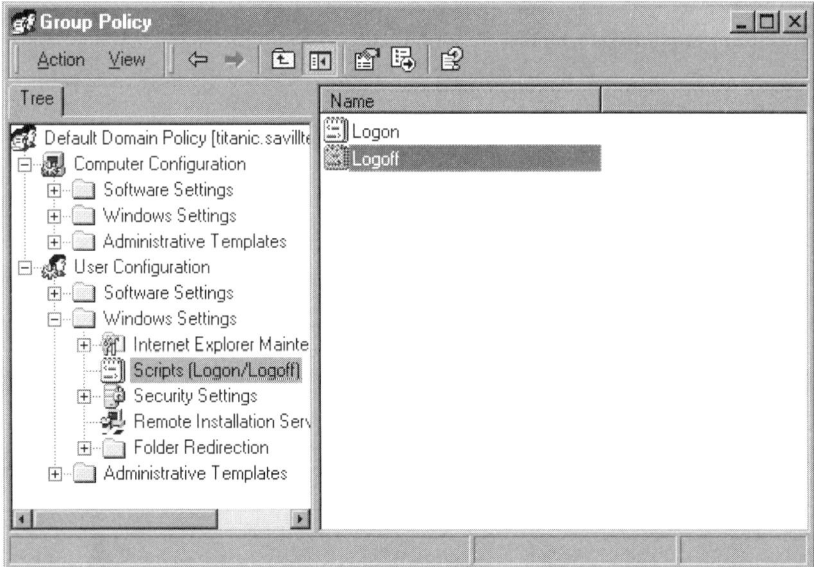

Figure 6-1 Setting the Logoff script

FAQ 6.42 How can I create my own tips to be shown when NT starts?

The tips that NT displays are stored in key HKEY_LOCAL_MACHINE\SOFTWARE\Microsoft\Windows\CurrentVersion\Explorer\Tips and can easily be edited using the Registry editor. You will notice that the names of the values are incremented by one. So to add a new tip, either edit an existing one or create a new value (of type string) and set its name to the next available number.

The tips are displayed sequentially, and the counter is stored in HKEY_CURRENT_USER\Software\Microsoft\Windows\CurrentVersion\Explorer\Tips\Next and can be changed if you want. The values are stored in hexadecimal.

To control whether tips are shown, set the value HKEY_CURRENT_USER\Software\Microsoft\Windows\CurrentVersion\Explorer\Tips\show to 01000000 to display and 00000000 to not display.

FAQ 6.43 How can I change the location of the event logs?

In Event Viewer, you will notice that there are three different logs: Application, System, and Security. Each of these logs is mapped to a .EVT file in the %systemroot%/system32/config directory; however, for performance/disk space reasons, you may wish to move them, which can be done by performing the following steps:

1. Start the Registry editor (REGEDIT.EXE).
2. Move to the HKEY_LOCAL_MACHINE\SYSTEM\CurrentControlSet\Services\EventLog key. Under this key are three other subkeys: Application, Security, and System. Select one of them.
3. Under each of the subkeys is a File value; double-click this value.
4. Edit the value to the location you require and click OK.
5. Repeat these steps for the other two log settings.
6. Close the Registry editor and reboot the machine for the change to take effect.

FAQ 6.44 How can I configure the default Internet browser?

When you start an Internet browser, it usually performs a check to see if it is the default browser. However, you may have turned off this check, and you may want to change the default browser.

1. Start the Registry editor (REGEDIT.EXE).
2. Move to HKEY_CLASSES_ROOT\http.
3. Expand the tree and move to HKEY_CLASSES_ROOT\http\shell\open\command. Double-click Default and set the string to the command you wish to run for Internet addresses. For example, for Internet Explorer:

   ```
   "E:\Program Files\Internet Explorer\iexplore.exe" -nohome
   ```

   For Netscape:

   ```
   E:\Program Files\Netscape\Communicator\Program\netscape.exe -h
   "%1"
   ```

   Click OK.
4. Move to HKEY_CLASSES_ROOT\http\shell\open\ddeexec\Application, and again. Double-click Default, change to the browser: **NSShell** for Netscape, **IExplore** for Internet Explorer.
5. You may also want to change the icon associated with the browser. Move to HKEY_CLASSES_ROOT\http\DefaultIcon; (do I need to say) double-click Default and set it to the icon. For Internet Explorer:

   ```
   %SystemRoot%\system32\url.dll,0
   ```

   For Netscape Navigator:

   ```
   E:\Program Files\Netscape\Communicator\Program\netscape.exe,0
   ```

6. You should repeat the preceding steps for https as well—that is, HKEY_CLASSES_ROOT\https\shell\open\command, etc.

FAQ 6.45 How can I change the alert for low disk space on a partition?

By default when a partition has less than 10% free disk space, an event ID 2013 is created with the following text:

```
The disk is at or near capacity. You may need to delete some files.
```

To view these events, use Event Viewer; however, it is possible to change the percentage at which the alert is created.

1. Start the Registry editor (REGEDIT.EXE).
2. Move to HKEY_LOCAL_MACHINE\SYSTEM\CurrentControlSet\Services\LanmanServer\Parameters.
3. If the value DiskSpaceThreshold exists, then double-click it and skip to step 5.
4. If the value does not exist, from the Edit menu, select New > DWORD Value. Enter a name of **DiskSpaceThreshold**. Click OK, then double-click on the new value.
5. Set the base to decimal and enter a value that you want the event to be generated at from 0–99.
6. Click OK.
7. Restart the machine.

FAQ 6.46 Is it possible to delete/rename the Administrator account?

It is not possible to delete the Administrator account. If you try to delete it, an error "Cannot delete built-in accounts" will be displayed. You can, however, rename it; in fact, it is recommended that the account be renamed to avoid the possibility of hacking. Most hackers try to enter a system using an Administrator account. To rename the Administrator account, perform the following

1. Log onto the machine as an Administrator.
2. Start User Manager (or User Manager for Domains).
3. Select the Administrator account and select Rename from the User menu.
4. Enter a new name and click OK.

For Windows 2000 and above:

1. Log onto the machine as an Administrator.
2. Start the Computer Management MMC snap-in, expand System Tools > Local Users and Groups > Users.
3. Right-click the Administrator account and select Rename from the context menu.
4. Enter a new name and press Enter.
5. Windows XP also has a Group Policy setting, Computer Configuration/Windows Settings/Security Settings/Local Policies/Security Options/Accounts: Rename administrator account.

NT ONLY

6.47 How can I tell NT how much secondary cache (L2) is installed?

NT will try to detect how much L2 cache is installed at startup time; however, it cannot always tell and will use a default of 256. If you have more, you can manually configure NT with your exact amount:

1. Start the Registry editor (REGEDIT.EXE).
2. Move to HKEY_LOCAL_MACHINE\SYSTEM\CurrentControlSet\Control\Session Manager\Memory Management.
3. Double-click on SecondLevelDataCache.
4. Click the decimal base and then enter the amount—for example, 512 if you have 512K of cache.
5. Click OK.
6. Close the Registry editor and reboot the machine.

The preceding steps apply only to processors below the Pentium II; processors at PII level or above will correctly identify the L2 cache size. For more information, see Q183063 at http://support.microsoft.com/support/kb/articles/Q183/0/63.ASP.

FAQ 6.48 What switches can be used in BOOT.INI?

The BOOT.INI file has a number of lines, and some of them relate to the Windows NT operating system—for example:

```
multi(0)disk(0)rdisk(0)partition(2)\WINNT="Windows NT Workstation
Version 4.00"
```

A number of switches can be appended to the Windows NT startup line to perform certain functions. To edit the file, perform the following steps:

1. Start a command session (CMD.EXE).
2. Modify the attributes on the file c:\boot.ini to make the file editable:

   ```
   attrib c:\boot.ini -r -s
   ```

3. Edit the file

   ```
   edit c:\boot.ini
   ```

4. Once finished, save the file and reset the files attributes

```
attrib c:\boot.ini +r +s
```

The switches that can be added are as follows:

/3GB	New to Service Pack 3, this switch causes the split between user and system portions of the Windows NT map to become 3GB for user applications, 1GB for system. To take advantage of this, the system must be part of the NT Enterprise suite, and the application must be flagged as a 3GB-aware application.
/BASEVIDEO	The computer starts up using the standard VGA video driver. Use this switch if you have installed a graphics driver that is not working.
/BAUDRATE	Specifies the baud rate to be used for debugging. If you do not set the baud rate, the default baud rate is 9600 if a modem is attached, and 19200 for a null-modem cable.
/BOOTLOG	Makes Windows 2000 write a log of the boot to the file %SystemRoot%\NTBTLOG.TXT Windows 2000 and XP Only
/BURNMEMORY=	Makes NT forget about the given amount of memory in MB. If /burnmemory=64 was given, then 64MB of memory would be unavailable.
/CRASHDEBUG	The debugger is loaded when you start Windows NT but remains inactive unless a kernel error occurs. This mode is useful if you are experiencing random, unpredictable kernel errors.
/DEBUG	The debugger is loaded when you start Windows NT and can be activated at any time by a host debugger connected to the computer. Use this mode when you are debugging problems that are regularly reproducible.
/DEBUGPORT=comx	Specifies the COM port to use for debugging, where x is the communications port that you want to use.

/FASTDETECT	Specifying FASTDETECT causes NTDETECT to skip parallel and serial device enumeration for a boot into Win2K, whereas omitting the switch has NTDETECT perform enumeration for a boot into NT 4.0. Win2K setup automatically recognizes dual-boot configurations and sets this switch for BOOT.INI lines that specify a Win2K boot. Windows 2000 and XP Only
/HAL=<hal>	Allows you to override the HAL used—for example, using a checked version.
/INTAFFINITY	Sets the multiprocessor HAL (HALMPS.DLL) to set interrupt affinities such that only the highest numbered processor in an SMP will receive interrupts. Without the switch, the HAL defaults to its normal behavior of letting all processors receive interrupts. Windows 2000 and XP Only
/KERNEL=<kernel>	Same as the /INTAFFINITY switch but for the kernel.
/MAXMEM:n	Specifies the maximum amount of RAM that Windows NT can use. This switch is useful if you suspect a memory chip is bad.
/NODEBUG	When this option is specified, no debugging information is being used.
/NOGUIBOOT	When this option is specified, the VGA video driver responsible for presenting bitmapped graphics during Win2K's boot process is not initialized. The driver is used to display boot progress information, as well as to print the blue crash screen, so disabling it will disable Win2K's ability to do those things as well. Windows 2000 and XP Only
/NOSERIALMICE=[COMx | COMx,y,z...]	Disables serial mouse detection of the specified COM port(s). Use this switch if you have a component other than a mouse attached to a serial port during the startup sequence. If you use /NOSERIALMICE without specifying a COM port, serial mouse detection is disabled on all COM ports.

(continued)

/NUMPROC=n	Enables only the first n processors on a multiple-processor system.
/ONECPU	Uses only the first CPU in a multiple-processor system.
/PCILOCK	Stops Windows NT from dynamically assigning IO/IRQ resources to PCI devices and leaves the devices configured by the BIOS.
/SAFEBOOT:	This is an automatic switch that NTLDR should complete for you when you use the F8 menu to perform a safe boot. Following the colon in the option, you must specify one of three additional switches: MINIMAL, NETWORK, or DSREPAIR. The MINIMAL and NETWORK flags correspond to safe boot with no network and safe boot with network support. The safe boot is a boot where Windows 2000 loads only drivers and services that are specified by name or group in the Minimal or Network Registry keys under HKLM\System\CurrentControlSet\Control\SafeBoot. The DSREPAIR (Directory Services Repair) switch causes NT to boot into a mode where it restores the Active Directory from a backup medium you present.
	An additional option that you can append is (ALTERNATE-SHELL), which tells NT to use the program specified by HKLM\System\CurrentControlSet\SafeBoot\AlternateShell as the graphical shell, rather than to use the default, which is Explorer. Windows 2000 and XP Only
/SOS	Displays the driver names while they are being loaded. Use this switch if Windows NT won't start up, and you think a driver is missing. This option is configured by default on the [VGA] option on the boot menu.
/WIN95	This switch is only pertinent on a triple-boot system that has DOS, Win9x, and Windows NT installed. Specifying the /WIN95 switch directs NTLDR to boot the Win9x boot sector stored in BOOTSECT.W40. See Microsoft KB article Q157992 for more information.
/WIN95DOS	This switch is only pertinent on a triple-boot system that has DOS, Win9x, and Windows NT installed. Specifying the

	/WIN95DOS switch directs NTLDR to boot the DOS boot sector stored in BOOTSECT.DOS. See Microsoft KB article Q157992 for more information.
/YEAR=	Specifying this value causes NT/Windows 2000 core time function to ignore the year that the computer's real-time clock reports and instead use the one indicated. Thus, the year used in the switch affects every piece of software on the system, including the NT kernel. Example: /YEAR=2005. Note: this option is available only on NT 4.0 Service Pack 4 and Windows 2000.

You can then edit the BOOT.INI file and either add Windows NT startup entries or modify existing entries—for example, you could add a debug entry in the file as follows:

```
multi(0)disk(0)rdisk(0)partition(2)\WINNT="Windows NT Workstation
Version 4.00 [debug]" /debug /debugport=com2
```

FAQ 6.49 How can I change the default editor used for editing batch files?

By default if you right-click on a batch file and select Edit, then the batch file will be opened in Notepad; however, the application used can be changed as follows:

1. Start the Registry editor (REGEDIT.EXE).
2. Move to HKEY_CLASSES_ROOT\batfile\shell\edit\command.
3. Double-click on default.
4. Change the value to the editor you want to use—for example, for Word, change it to

   ```
   D:\Program Files\Microsoft Office\Office\winword.exe %1
   ```

5. Once completed, click OK and close the Registry editor.

There is no need to reboot; the change takes immediate effect. To reset back to Notepad, change the entry to

```
%SystemRoot%\System32\NOTEPAD.EXE %1
```

FAQ 6.50 How do I configure the default keyboard layout during logon?

You can change the keyboard layout using the Keyboard Control Panel applet (Start > Settings > Control Panel > Keyboard > Input Locales); however, this does not affect the layout used during logon—which is by default English (United States). To change this layout, perform the following steps:

1. Start the Registry editor (REGEDIT.EXE).
2. Move to HKEY_USERS\.DEFAULT\Keyboard Layout\Preload.
3. Double-click on 1 and change the number to your local layout (you could get this by looking at HKEY_CURRENT_USER\Keyboard Layout\Preload1). Click OK.
4. You may also change HKEY_USERS\.DEFAULT\Control Panel\International\Locale to this value; however, it is not mandatory to do so.
5. Close the Registry editor.
6. Log off and then on again.

Make sure you select a country code that has been installed via the Control Panel, or your system will not boot.

A table of the codes to the countries follows:

00000402	Bulgarian
000004a	Croatian
00000405	Czech
00000406	Danish
00000413	Dutch (Standard)
00000813	Dutch (Belgian)
00000409	English (United States)
00000809	English (United Kingdom)
00001009	English (Canadian)
00001409	English (New Zealand)
00000c09	English (Australian)
0000040b	Finnish

0000040c	French (Standard)
0000080c	French (Belgian)
0000100c	French (Swiss)
00000c0c	French (Canadian)
00000407	German (Standard)
00000807	German (Swiss)
00000c07	German (Austrian)
00000408	Greek
0000040e	Hungarian
0000040f	Icelandic
00001809	English (Irish)
00000410	Italian (Standard)
00000810	Italian (Swiss)
00000414	Norwegian (Bokmal)
00000814	Norwegian (Nynorsk)
00000415	Polish
00000816	Portuguese (Standard)
00000416	Portuguese (Brazilian)
00000418	Romanian
00000419	Russian
0000041b	Slovak
00000424	Slovenian
0000080a	Spanish (Mexican)
0000040a	Spanish (Traditional Sort)
00000c0a	Spanish (Modern Sort)
0000041d	Swedish
0000041f	Turkish

These codes can also be seen in the Registry at HKEY_LOCAL_MACHINE\SYSTEM\CurrentControlSet\Control\Keyboard Layout\DosKeybCodes.

FAQ 6.51 How can I add my own information to General tab of the System Control Panel applet?

When you receive a PC from a manufacturer, you may see extra lines of description text and a company logo in the General tab of a System Control Panel applet. These lines of text and the logo can be changed or added to as follows:

1. Create a bitmap with the dimensions 180 by 114. Save the bitmap in the %systemroot%/system32 folder (e.g., d:\winnt\system32) with a name of OEMLOGO.BMP. If the picture is greater than this size, then it will be clipped from the top-left corner. If it is smaller, then a black border will be added.
2. Create the file %systemroot%/system32/OEMINFO.INI (e.g., d:\winnt\system32\oeminfo.ini) with the following format:

```
[general]
Manufacturer=SavillTech Ltd
Model=SuperDuper 1
[Support Information]
Line1=" "
Line2="For support ...."
Line3=" "
```

You do not need to reboot the machine; the System Control Panel applet will pick up the files when started. The preceding information gives the output shown in Figure 6-2.

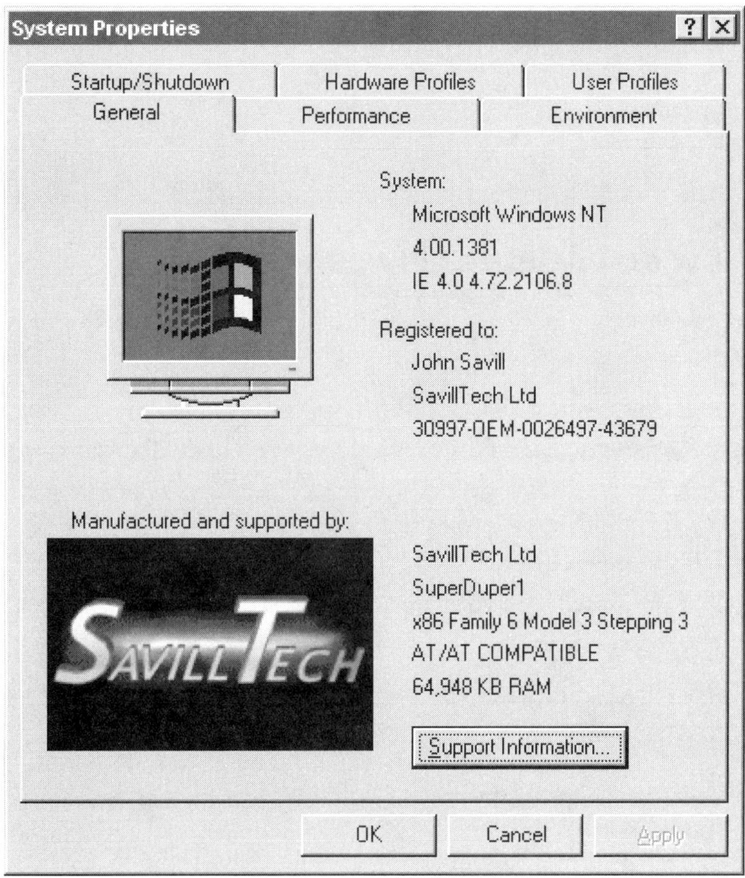

Figure 6-2 Added information to the System Control Panel applet in Windows NT 4.0

FAQ 6.52 How can I stop and start services from the command line?

This can be accomplished using the following:

```
net stop <service name>
net start <service name>
```

A full list of the exact services is found in the Registry (run REGEDIT.EXE) under the HKEY_LOCAL_MACHINE\SYSTEM\CurrentControlSet\Services key.

Alternatively, you can perform the stop and start using the name that is displayed in the Services Control Panel applet by putting the name in quotes—for example:

```
net stop "<service>"
net start "<service>"
```

6.53 How do I delete a service?

To delete a service that has not been automatically removed by a software uninstall, you need to edit the Registry:

1. Start the Registry editor (REGEDIT.EXE).
2. Move to the HKEY_LOCAL_MACHINE\SYSTEM\CurrentControlSet\Services key.
3. Select the key of the service you want to delete.
4. From the Edit menu, select Delete.
5. You will be prompted "Are you sure you want to delete this Key," click Yes.
6. Exit the Registry editor.

The INSTSRV.EXE utility supplied with the NT Resource Kit can be used to install and remove services:

```
instsrv <service name> remove
```

Alternatively, also with the Resource Kit is a utility SRVINSTW.EXE that again installs and removes services, but with a GUI wizard format allowing you to select the service either locally or remotely.

6.54 What are the long path names in the BOOT.INI file?

The path names in the BOOT.INI file are the ARC (Advanced RISC Computing) path names. They are used to locate the NT boot partition. The two main types of ARC names depend on whether the disks are IDE or SCSI. For IDE the path names follow this convention:

```
multi(x)disk(x)rdisk(x)partition(x)\%systemroot%
```

Both multi and disk are not really used for IDE and should always be 0. rdisk is the physical drive and will be 0 or 1 on the first IDE controller, or 2 and 3 on the second IDE controller. partition() is the partition number on the disk and starts from 1.

The scheme is slightly different for SCSI:

```
scsi(x)disk(x)rdisk(x)partition(x)\%systemroot%
```

scsi() is the controller number of the SCSI identified in NTBOOTDD.SYS. disk() is the SCSI ID of the physical disk. rdisk() is the SCSI logical unit number (LUN), which will nearly always be 0. partition() is the same as with IDE and is the partition number starting with 1.

The multi() designation means that the drive can respond to INT 13 calls, and most SCSI drives can, so you may use multi() with a SCSI drive also.

In a pure IDE system, the multi() syntax will work for up to the four drives maximum on the primary and secondary channels of a dual-channel controller. In a pure SCSI system, the multi() syntax will work for the first two drives on the first SCSI controller (i.e., the controller whose BIOS loads first). In a mixed SCSI and IDE system, the multi() syntax will work only for the IDE drives on the first controller.

In Windows 2000, you may also see a signature(xxxxxxxx) format, for example:

```
signature(8b467c12)disk(1)rdisk(0)partition(2)\winnt="description"
```

Signature() syntax is used only if one of the following conditions exists:

- The partition on which you installed Windows 2000 is larger than approximately 7.8GB in size, or the ending cylinder number is higher than 1024 for that partition, and the system BIOS or boot controller BIOS does not support INT13 extensions.
- The drive on which you installed Windows 2000 is connected to a SCSI controller whose BIOS is disabled, so INT13 BIOS calls cannot be used during the boot process.

The signature() syntax is equivalent to the scsi() syntax but is used instead to support the plug-and-play architecture in Windows 2000. Because Windows 2000 is a plug-and-play operating system, the SCSI controller number instance may vary each time you start Windows 2000, especially if you add new SCSI controller hardware after Setup is finished.

As with scsi() format, a NTBOOTDD.SYS file must be located at the root of the system partition for signature().

6.55 How can I open a file with an application other than the one it is associated with?

You usually can right-click on the file and select open. If you hold down the Shift key and right-click on the file, you will perform an "open with" operation.

6.56 How do I change the icon associated with a shortcut?

Follow these steps:

1. Right-click on the shortcut and choose Properties.
2. Click the Shortcut tab and click Change Icon.
3. Select your new icon. You can use several sets of icons that come with NT: SHELL32.DLL, PIFMGR.DLL, MORICONS.DLL, and PROGMAN.EXE.
4. Click OK.
5. Exit.

6.57 Is it possible to map a drive letter to a directory?

You can use the SUBST command to map a pseudo-drive letter to a drive and/or directory. The following maps the letter "r" to the directory winnt\system32 on the D drive:

```
subst r: d:\winnt\system32
```

6.58 How can I change the program associated with a file extension?

The easiest way is to

1. Start Explorer.
2. Hold down the Shift key and right-click on a file with the extension you wish to change.
3. From the context menu displayed, select the Open with option.

4. Select the Application from the list (or click Other) and check Always use this program to open this type of file.
5. Click OK.

An alternative method is to

1. Start Explorer.
2. Select Options (or Folder Options for IE 4.0 installations) from the View menu.
3. Click File Types tab.
4. Select the File type and click Edit.
5. You can edit the open and print actions for the file type. To change the open, select Open in the actions and click Edit. You can then change the command.
6. Click OK when finished.

FAQ 6.59 How can I move shares and their contents from one machine to another?

Moving the actual files and directories is simple; however, share information is not contained in the directories but rather is contained in the Registry (under LanmanServer). It is therefore necessary to copy this Registry information from the machine currently containing the shares, to the machine that **will** host the shares:

1. To copy the files, you will need to use the SCOPY utility that is supplied with the Resource Kit to keep the current permission/audit settings:

   ```
   SCOPY <current>:\<dir> <new>:\<dir> /o /a /s
   ```

2. On the machine that currently hosts the shares, start the Registry editor (REGEDT32.EXE, **not** REGEDIT.EXE).
3. Move to the key HKEY_LOCAL_MACHINE\SYSTEM\CurrentControlSet\Services\LanmanServer\Shares.
4. Click on Shares and select Save Key from the Registry menu.
5. Enter the name of a file—for example, SHARES.REG and click OK.
6. Copy this file to the target machine.
7. Again start the Registry editor (REGEDT32.EXE) and move to HKEY_LOCAL_MACHINE\SYSTEM\CurrentControlSet\Services\LanmanServer\Shares and select Shares.

8. From the Registry menu, select Restore and select the file you saved—for example, SHARES.REG and click Open.

   Warning: *You will lose all currently configured shares on the machine.*

9. You will prompted to continue, click Yes.
10. Close the Registry editor.
11. Reboot the machine, and once restarted, you will see the new shares.

FAQ 6.60 How do I create a shortcut on the desktop to a directory and/or disk?

The following procedure works for a file, directory, and disk (even the A drive).

1. Start Explorer (Start > Programs > Explorer or Win key+E).
2. Right-click on the file/directory/disk and drag to the desktop.
3. Release the right mouse button and, from the menu that will be displayed, select Create Shortcut(s) here.

FAQ 6.61 How can I show the context menu without the right mouse button?

Pressing Shift+F10 will bring up the context menu for any selected item. Just pressing F10 shifts the cursor focus to the first menu item (normally File).

FAQ 6.62 How do I set a process to use a certain processor?

This is called "processor affinity" where you set a process to use a specific processor on a multiprocessor system.

1. Start Task Manager (right-click on the taskbar and select Task Manager).
2. Click the Processes tab.
3. Right-click on the program and select Set Affinity.
4. You can check the processors you want the program to run on (uncheck the ones you don't want it to use).

You cannot set affinity for a service or set affinity for a program that has not yet been started.

FAQ 6.63 Why do I have duplicate entries on my boot menu?

This is easy to remedy and is usually caused by reinstalling Windows NT.

1. Start a command prompt (CMD.EXE).
2. Enter the command

   ```
   attrib c:\boot.ini -r -s
   ```

3. Now edit BOOT.INI.

   ```
   edit boot.ini
   ```

4. You will see lines like the following under the [operating systems] section of the file:

   ```
   multi(0)disk(0)rdisk(0)partition(2)\WINNT="Windows NT Workstation
   Version 4.00"
   multi(0)disk(0)rdisk(0)partition(2)\WINNT="Windows NT Workstation
   Version 4.00 [VGA mode]" /basevideo /sos
   C:\ = "MS-DOS"
   ```

If you see any duplicates, delete them. Make sure you delete the right ones if they differ with the “multi(0)disk(0)rdisk(0)partition(2)” part because it means you had NT installed on a different disk/partition before.

FAQ 6.64 How can I stop a service from the command line?

To get a list of the running services, enter the command

```
net start
```

You can add < **[filename]** to the end to make it output to a file—for example, **net start > services.lst**. You can then try to shut down each of them by entering the command

```
net stop "<service name>"
```

For example, **net stop "spooler"**. Some services will ask you to enter a y to confirm, and for these, just add **/y** to the end.

You can also use the Resource Kit SC.EXE command, use the following to get a list of the services:

```
sc query
```

then enter the following to stop the service:

```
sc stop <service name>
```

6.65 How can I add the Printer panel to the Start menu?

To add a Printer panel to the Start menu, perform the following:

1. Create a new folder (right-click the desktop and choose New > Folder). Name the folder:

   ```
   Printers.{2227A280-3AEA-1069-A2DE-08002B30309D}
   ```

2. Right-click Start and choose Open.
3. Drag the new folder to the Start menu window.

The Printer panel will now be on the Start menu and will be cascading, which means all printers can be viewed as subobjects of the menu item.

6.66 How can I hide the Administrative Tools on the Start menu?

Several options are open to you.

One alternative is to set the protections on the folder and its contents so only members of the Administrative group can read/execute it. This will work only if the boot partition is NTFS:

1. Start Explorer.
2. Move to %systemroot%\Profiles\All Users\Start Menu\Programs.
3. Select Administrative Tools (Common) and select Properties from the File menu (or right-click the file and select Properties).
4. Click the Security tab.
5. Click the Permissions button.

6. Select Everyone and click Remove.
7. Click Add and select Domain Admins, click Add, and select Access to Full Control. Click OK.
8. Back in the Directory Permissions dialog box, click OK.

Non-Administrative users will now see an empty Administrative Tools menu. You could select different users if you wish.

Another alternative is you could also just move the Administrative Tools folder from the All Users section to a specific account area on the machine. There may be complications with roaming profiles, and so on.

The previously described methods just hide the items from the menu; however, users could still run the applications from Run. The operating system prevents unauthorized users altering the system using these tools so that is not a problem. (You could always set the protections on the images as well if you don't want users to run them.)

FAQ 6.67 How do I restrict access to the floppy drive?

The NT Resource Kit and the Zero Administration Kit come with a FlopLock service:

1. Install the FlopLock service:

```
instsrv FloppyLocker c:\reskit\floplock.exe
```

2. Start the Service Control Panel applet (Start > settings > Control Panel > Services).
3. Double-click on FloppyLocker and make sure the System Account is selected.
4. Set the startup to Automatic and click OK.
5. You can manually start the service to avoid the reboot by selecting FloopyLocker and click Start.

With the service is started on Windows NT Workstation, only members of the Administrators and Power Users groups can access the floppy drives. When the service is started on Windows NT Server, only members of the Administrators group can access the floppy drives.

To remove the service, perform the following:

1. Stop the FloppyLocker service (Start > Settings > Control Panel > Services > FloppyLocker > Stop).
2. Enter the command

```
instsrv FloppyLocker remove
```

FAQ 6.68 How do I enable AutoLogon?

The easiest way is to install TweakUI, go to the Network tab, and just fill in the boxes. It can be done manually through the Registry by following these instructions:

1. Start REGEDIT.EXE (Start > Run > Regedit).
2. Open the HKEY_LOCAL_MACHINE\SOFTWARE\Microsoft\Windows NT\Current Version\Winlogon.
3. Double-click the DefaultDomainName and fill in your domain name.
4. Double-click the DefaultUserName and fill in logon name.
5. From the Edit menu, select New String Value and enter **DefaultPassword** as the name of the value.
6. Double-click the DefaultPassword and enter the password.
7. From the Edit menu, select New String Value and enter **AutoAdminLogon** as the name of the value.
8. Double-click the AutoAdminLogon and set the value to the number 1.
9. Close Regedit.
10. Log off, and you will be automatically logged on again.

You should also make sure DontDisplayLastUserName (also under the WinLogon key) is set to 0.

The preceding instructions should be done only by someone who is happy with using the Registry editor. The following is an example REG file that could be used:

```
REGEDIT4

[HKEY_LOCAL_MACHINE\SOFTWARE\Microsoft\Windows
NT\CurrentVersion\Winlogon]

"DefaultUserName"="User"
"DefaultDomainName"="Domain"
"AutoAdminLogon"="1"
"DefaultPassword"="Password"
```

It is also possible using a program called AUTOLOG.EXE that comes with the Resource Kit. Just run the executable, and you will be able to fill in the information.

To log on as a different user, you need to hold down the Shift key as you log off.

You will have to use REGEDIT32.EXE to disable write permissions to HKEY_LOCAL_MACHINE\SOFTWARE\Microsoft\Windows NT\Current Version\Winlogon if you want to be able to log off and log on as another user but still have the "original" user as the autologon.

1. Start REGEDT32.EXE.
2. Move to HKEY_LOCAL_MACHINE\SOFTWARE\Microsoft\Windows NT\Current Version\Winlogon.
3. Select Winlogon.
4. From the Security menu, select Permissions and adjust them so the Write permission is removed for normal users.

FAQ 6.69 How do I disable AutoLogon?

Again use TweakUI, or in Regedit, set AutoAdminLogon to 0 and clear the DefaultPassword.

FAQ 6.70 How do I add a warning logon message?

You need to use the Registry editor:

1. Start the Registry editor (REGEDIT.EXE).
2. Move to HKEY_LOCAL_MACHINE/SOFTWARE/Microsoft/Windows NT/CurrentVersion/ Winlogon (see the Note that follows this procedure).
3. Double-click LegalNoticeCaption and enter the text to go in the title bar; click OK.
4. Double-click LegalNoticeText, enter the warning text, and click OK.
5. Close the Registry and log off. When you log on, you will see a warning.

> **Note:** *In Windows 2000, in step 2 you move to HKEY_LOCAL_MACHINE\SOFTWARE\Microsoft\Windows\CurrentVersion\policies\system instead.*

This can also be done via the Policy Editor (POLEDIT.EXE) for NT 4.0:

1. Start the Policy Editor (POLEDIT.EXE).
2. Open the default Computer Policy.
3. Open the Windows NT System tree and then Logon.
4. Put a tick in the Logon banner and enter the caption and text.
5. Click OK and save the policy.

For Windows 2000 Group Policy Objects, move to Computer Configuration > Windows Settings > Security Settings > Local Policies > Security Options and set the Message text for users attempting to log on and Message title for users attempting to log on.

Alternatively, a text message can be displayed by creating the key LogonPrompt in HKEY_LOCAL_MACHINE/SOFTWARE/Microsoft/Windows NT/CurrentVersion/Winlogon.

Windows Scripting Host can also be used to create these messages as follows:

```
Set WSHShell = CreateObject("WScript.Shell")
s1 = "HKLM\Software\Microsoft\Windows\CurrentVersion\WinLogon\"
s2 = "LegalNoticeCaption"
s3 = "LegalNoticeText"
objShell.RegWrite s1+s2, "SavillTech Ltd"
objShell.RegWrite s1+s3, "Only Authorized Access Allowed!"
```

FAQ 6.71 How do I stop the last logon name being displayed?

For security reasons, it may be desirable to stop the last logon name from being displayed. To do so, perform the following steps:

1. Start the Registry editor (REGEDIT.EXE).
2. Move to HKEY_LOCAL_MACHINE\SOFTWARE\Microsoft\Windows NT\CurrentVersion\Winlogon.
3. Double-click DontDisplayLastUserName.
4. Set to 1 and click OK.
5. Close the Registry editor.

This can also be done using the Policy Editor and is under the Windows NT System > Logon tree and tick do not display last logged on username.

Under Windows 2000, dontdisplaylastusername has been moved to HKEY_LOCAL_MACHINE\SOFTWARE\Microsoft\Windows\CurrentVersion\policies\system.

To assign using a Group Policy Object, set under the Computer Configuration > Windows Settings > Security Settings > Local Policies > Security Options > Do not display last user name in logon screen.

FAQ 6.72 How can I stop people logging on to the server?

If you want to disable an NT server's ability to handle authentication, then it is possible to stop the Net logon service:

1. Start Control Panel.
2. Double-click on Services.

3. Click Net Logon and then click Pause.
4. Exit Control Panel.

To disable all of NT's server services, click on Server and click Stop, which will stop Net Logon, Computer Browser, and any other server services.

FAQ 6.73 Why do users fail to log on at a server?

By default members of domain users will not be able to log on to a server—that is, a PDC or a BDC—and if they try, the error "The local policy of this system does not allow you to logon interactively" is displayed. If you want users to be able to log on to a server (why, I don't know), follow this procedure:

1. Log on to the server as an Administrator.
2. Start User Manager for Domains (Start > Programs > Administrative Tools > User Manager for Domains).
3. Select User Rights from the Policies menu.
4. From the drop-down Rights list, select Log on locally.
5. Click Add and select Domain Users. Click Add and then click OK.
6. Close User Manager.
7. Log out, and a user will now be able to log on.

FAQ 6.74 How do I enable NumLock automatically?

The Registry entry HKEY_CURRENT_USER\Control Panel\Keyboard\ InitialKeyboardIndicators can be used to set the initial state of the NumLock key for the current user. To modify the state of NumLock for the logon screen:

1. Start the Registry editor (REGEDIT.EXE).
2. Move to HKEY_USERS\.DEFAULT\Control Panel\Keyboard (we are editing .default, which is the profile used prior to logon).
3. Double-click on InitialKeyboardIndicators.
4. Set to 2 and click OK.
5. Close the Registry editor.

An easier way is to turn NumLock on and then log off using Ctrl+Alt+Del Logoff, which will preserve the state of Numlock.

FAQ 6.75 How do I limit the number of simultaneous logons?

Perform the following:

1. Start the Registry editor (REGEDIT.EXE).
2. Move to HKEY_LOCAL_MACHINE\SYSTEM\CurrentControlSet\Services\LanmanServer\Parameters.
3. Double-click on the user's value in the right pane. Set the type to decimal and then enter the maximum number of simultaneous connections. This will be 10 on a workstation.
4. Click OK and close the Registry editor.

FAQ 6.76 Why is %SystemRoot% not expanded when I use it in a command?

If when you type SET or PATH at a command prompt, you notice that the %SystemRoot% environment variable has not been expanded. This problem needs to be corrected:

1. Start the Registry editor (REGEDT32.EXE).
2. Move to HKEY_LOCAL_MACHINE\SYSTEM\CurrentControlSet\Control\Session Manager\Environment.
3. Look at the Path in the right pane and check the type (it's the second part), for example:

   ```
   Path: REG_EXPAND_SZ: %SystemRoot% etc.
   ```

   If the type is **not** REG_EXPAND_SZ, then perform the next steps; if it is, exit the Registry editor.
4. Double-click on Path and select the contents. Press Ctrl+C to copy to the Clipboard.
5. While Path is still selected, select Delete from the Edit menu (or click the Del key). Confirm the deletion.
6. Make sure Environment is selected in the left pane and select Add Value from the Edit menu.
7. Enter a name for Path (note the capital "P" in "Path") and type **REG_EXPAND_SZ**. Click OK.

8. Double-click Path and press Ctrl+V to copy back in the information you copied into the Clipboard. Click OK.
9. Close the Registry editor.

You can also check HKEY_LOCAL_MACHINE\SOFTWARE\Microsoft\Windows NT\CurrentVersion\SystemRoot and make sure that this REG_SZ value contains the proper path (e:\winnt).

FAQ 6.77 How can I disable the Win key?

To disable both Windows keys, perform the following:

1. Start the Registry editor (REGEDT32.EXE).
2. Move to HKEY_LOCAL_MACHINE\SYSTEM\CurrentControlSet\Control\Keyboard Layout.
3. From the Edit menu, select New > Binary Value.
4. Enter a name of "Scancode Map" and press Enter.
5. Double-click on the new value and set to

   ```
   0000 0000 0000 0000 0300 0000 0000 5BE0 0000 5CE0 0000 0000
   ```

   Note: *Do not type the spaces; I include them only to help you view the data.*

6. Click OK.
7. Close the Registry editor and reboot the machine.

Once the machine has restarted, the Win key will no longer work.

You can automate this process by placing the command in a REGINI file and creating the file REMOVE_WIN.INI with the following contents:

```
\Registry\Machine\SYSTEM\CurrentControlSet\Control\Keyboard Layout
      Scancode Map = REG_BINARY 24        0x00000000 0x00000000 3
0xE05B0000 0xE05C0000          \
      0x0
```

To then run the script, enter the command

```
regini remove_win.ini
```

REGINI.EXE is supplied with the Windows NT Resource Kit.

To reenable the Win key, delete the Scancode Map value you created.

FAQ 6.78 How do I set the number of cached logons a machine stores?

By default an NT machine (since version 3.5; 3.1 only stored the last cached logon) caches the last 10 successful logons; however; this number can be changed from anywhere between 0 and 50.

1. Start the Registry editor (REGEDIT.EXE).
2. Move to HKEY_LOCAL_MACHINE\SOFTWARE\Microsoft\Windows NT\CurrentVersion\Winlogon.
3. From the Edit menu, select New > String Value.
4. Enter a name of CachedLogonsCount and press Enter.
5. Double-click on the new value and set between 0 and 50. 0 means no logons will be cached; 50 will cache the last 50. Click OK.
6. Close the Registry editor.
7. Reboot the machine.

If someone attempts to log on and the domain controller is not available but his or her information is cached, he or she will receive the following message:

```
A domain controller for your domain could not be contacted. You have
been logged on using cached account information. Changes to your
profile since you last logged on may not be available.
```

But he or she still will be logged on successfully. If his or her information is not cached, he or she will get the message

```
The system cannot log you on now because the domain <domain name> is
not available.
```

and not be logged on.

FAQ 6.79 How can I configure the system to run a program at logon time?

The easiest way is to add the program to the startup folder, and you can do this in one of two ways. The first is to add the program just to your startup menu (%systemroot%\Profiles\<username>\Start Menu) or to the all users startup menu (%systemroot%\Profiles\All Users\Start Menu).

If you don't want to do it that way (if you don't want users to be able to remove it, for example), a Registry key can be used to run programs.

1. Start the Registry editor (REGEDIT.EXE).
2. Move to HKEY_LOCAL_MACHINE\SOFTWARE\Microsoft\Windows\CurrentVersion\Run.
3. From the Edit menu, select New > String Value.
4. Give it any name you want—for example, notepad.
5. Double-click the new value and set it to the fully qualified pathname of the program (unless it is part of your system path, in which case you can just enter the image name)—for example, NOTEPAD.EXE. Click OK.
6. Close the Registry editor.
7. Log off and on.

If you want a program to run only once and then never run again, perform the preceding steps but add the values under HKEY_LOCAL_MACHINE\SOFTWARE\Microsoft\Windows\CurrentVersion\RunOnce. Once the program has run, it gets deleted from the RunOnce key.

You can also configure programs for your account only by adding values to HKEY_CURRENT_USER\SOFTWARE\Microsoft\Windows\CurrentVersion\Run.

NT 4.0 ONLY

FAQ 6.80 How can I install the Policy editor on a workstation?

The Policy editor consists of POLEDIT.EXE and a number of .ADM files. To install the Policy editor on a workstation, perform the following:

1. Copy POLEDIT.EXE from the %systemroot% on a Windows NT Server machine to the %systemroot% folder on the workstation.
2. Copy COMMON.ADM, WINDOWS.ADM, and WINNT.ADM from %systemroot%/inf on the NT Server to the %systemroot%/inf folder on the workstation.

You will now be able to run the Policy editor on a Windows NT workstation. You may want to create a shortcut to POLEDIT.EXE in your Administrative Tools folder.

FAQ 6.81 How can I delete the My Computer icon?

It is not possible to delete the icon; however, you can make it invisible.

1. Right-click on the desktop and select Properties.
2. Select the Plus tab.
3. Select My Computer and click Change Icon.
4. Change the filename to **%systemroot%\system32\tweakui.cpl**.
5. Select the fourth icon (a big blank) and click OK.
6. Click Apply, then click OK.

You could then move the icon to the bottom of the screen to hide the My Computer text.

Now, don't use autoarrange and don't select a greater screen resolution, and you will never see it again.

FAQ 6.82 How do I disable the file delete confirmation?

If you use the Recycle Bin, then you can disable the delete confirmation.

1. Right-click on the Recycle Bin and select Properties.
2. Uncheck the Display delete confirmation dialog box.
3. Click Apply, then OK.

FAQ 6.83 How can I switch the time between 24 hour and 12 hour?

This can be configured in two ways. The first is using the Regional Control Panel applet:

1. Start the Regional Control Panel applet (Start > settings > Control Panel > Regional Settings).
2. Select the Time tab. "HH" in capitals means 24 hour, "hh" (lowercase) means 12 hours.
3. Click Apply, then OK.

The second way to configure this is to directly edit the Registry:

1. Start the Registry editor (REGEDIT.EXE).
2. Move to HKEY_CURRENT_USER\Control Panel\International.
3. From the Edit menu, select New > String.
4. Enter a name of **iTime**.
5. Double-click the new iTime value and set to 0 for 12 hours and 1 for 24 hours. Click OK.
6. Close the Registry editor.
7. Log off and log back on again.

FAQ 6.84 How can I suppress boot error messages?

If you are developing or know of a problem, you may decide you wish to suppress the error pop-ups that are displayed when a problem arises. For example, when a driver can't be loaded or some other system component is not acting correctly, an error pop-up is displayed.

The pop-ups can be generated from either of the two main startup phases, and a separate Registry key needs to be set for each stage.

Errors that are displayed as a result of the boot phase can be disabled as follows:

1. Start the Registry editor (REGEDIT.EXE).
2. Move to HKEY_LOCAL_MACHINE\SOFTWARE\Microsoft\Windows NT\CurrentVersion\Windows.
3. From the Edit menu, select New > DWORD Value, enter a name of NoPopUpsOnBoot, and press Enter.
4. Double-click the new value and set to 1 to suppress boot errors. Click OK.
5. Close the Registry editor, and the change will take effect at the next reboot.

To suppress error messages that are displayed as part of the post-boot startup phase, which includes most device driver messages, perform the following:

1. Start the Registry editor (REGEDIT.EXE).
2. Move to HKEY_LOCAL_MACHINE\SOFTWARE\Microsoft\Windows NT\CurrentVersion\Windows.
3. From the Edit menu, select New > DWORD Value, enter a name of **ErrorMode**, and press Enter.
4. Double-click the new value and set to 1 to display only application errors or 2 to suppress all error dialogs. Click OK.
5. Close the Registry editor, and the change will take effect at the next reboot.

Instead of a blanket ban on all error messages, you may prefer to mark some services as "optional" and not to generate an error if they don't start correctly. This can be accomplished by setting HKEY_LOCAL_MACHINEM\SYSTEM\CurrentControlSet\Services\<service>\ErrorControl to 0.

FAQ 6.85 How can I enable/disable Ctrl+Alt+Del to enter logon information?

Windows 2000 introduces the ability to remove the necessity of pressing Ctrl+Alt+Del, the Security Attention Sequence (SAS), to log on. By default this is no longer needed on a workstation; however, on a server, it is still necessary. It can be configured with a single Registry entry:

1. Start the Registry editor (REGEDIT.EXE).
2. Move to HKEY_LOCAL_MACHINE\SOFTWARE\Microsoft\Windows NT\CurrentVersion\Winlogon.
3. Double-click on DisableCAD (create type REG_DWORD if it does not exist).
4. Set to 1 if you don't want to have to press Ctrl+Alt+Del and set to 0 if you do. Click OK.
5. Close the Registry editor.
6. Reboot the machine.

Disabling this feature does not decrease the security of Windows NT. To gain access to the computer, users are required to log on to Windows NT with a valid username and password. The Windows NT logon process suspends all other user-mode processes to protect the logon process and is the only process that can create the access tokens used by the Windows NT security system.

You can also enable/disable Ctrl+Alt+Del to enter logon information via a GUI on Windows 2000 Professional as follows:

1. Start the Users and Passwords Control Panel applet (Start > Settings > Control Panel > Users and Passwords).
2. Select the Advanced tab.
3. Unselect Require users to press Ctrl+Alt+Delete before logging on (see Figure 6-3).
4. Click Apply, then OK.

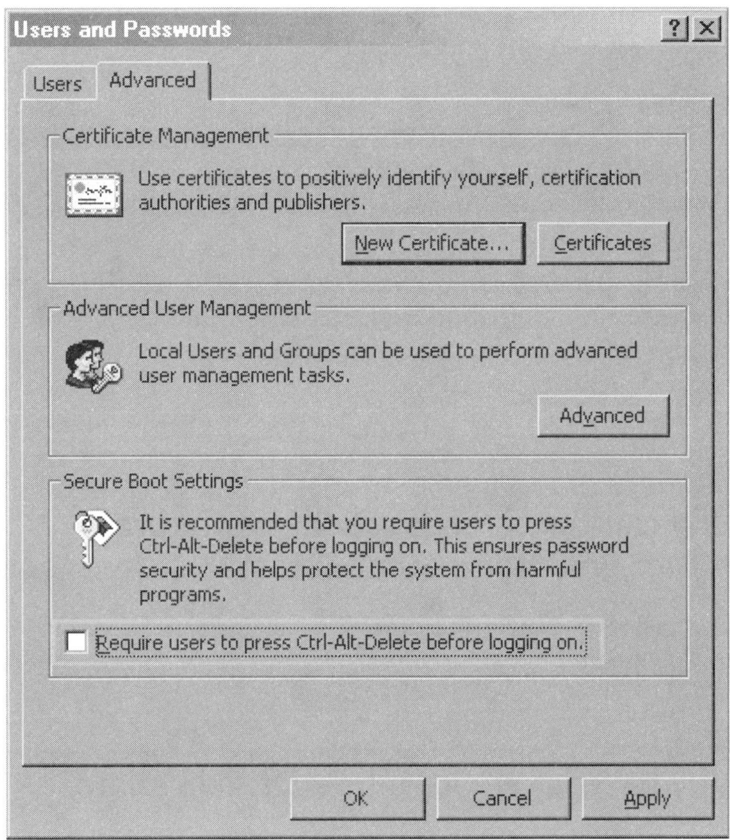

Figure 6-3 Requiring Ctrl-Alt-Delete for logon

FAQ 6.86 How can I stop the last username to log on from being displayed?

There are two ways of doing this, the easiest of which is with the TweakUI utility. Perform the following:

1. Start the TweakUI Control Panel applet (Start > Settings > Control Panel > TweakUI).
2. Select the Paranoia tab.
3. Check the Clear Last User at logon box.
4. Click Apply, then OK.

If you don't have TweakUI or you simply want to achieve the result through the Registry (maybe so you can set it from a logon script), follow these steps:

1. Start the Registry editor.
2. Move to HKEY_LOCAL_MACHINE\SOFTWARE\Microsoft\Windows NT\CurrentVersion\Winlogon for NT 4.0 or HKEY_LOCAL_MACHINE\SOFTWARE\Microsoft\Windows\CurrentVersion\policies\system for Windows 2000.
3. If the value DontDisplayLastUserName does not exist, select New > String Value and enter a name of **DontDisplayLastUserName**.
4. Double-click DontDisplayLastUserName and set to 1.
5. Close the Registry editor.

FAQ 6.87 Why can the screensaver be configured to start up only to 60 minutes?

This is a hard-coded restriction of Windows NT 4.0; however, Service Pack 4 increases this interval to 999 minutes.

FAQ 6.88 Why have I have lost the ADMIN$ share?

If you have configured the system to not automatically create system shares at startup time by setting the relevant Registry entry AutoSharexxx, then this share will not be created because that is what you are asking.

If however you do not have this Registry entry set and you have just lost the ADMIN$ share that points to the %SytemRoot% folder—for example, d:\winnt—then you can recreate it by entering the following command:

```
net share admin$
```

For more information on suppressing the system shares, see FAQ 13.4.

FAQ 6.89 How can I configure Notepad to wrap?

By default Notepad allows you to enter text and does not wrap when the screen is full; rather it just scrolls right. This behavior can be altered.

Under Notepad's Edit menu, you can check Word Wrap. However, if you want to configure this setting as the default for policies, as part of a logon script, or an as part of an unattended installation, this can also be configured using the Registry:

1. Start the Registry editor (REGEDIT.EXE).
2. Move to HKEY_CURRENT_USER\Software\Microsoft\Notepad.
3. Double-click on fWrap.
4. Set to 1 and click OK.
5. Close the Registry editor.

FAQ 6.90 How do I modify the logon timer for profiles?

When you log on and, for instance, your local profile is newer than the one stored on the profile server, you have an option of which to use, and a timer of 30 seconds is given. This 30 seconds can be modified as follows:

1. Start the Registry editor (REGEDIT.EXE).
2. Move to HKEY_LOCAL_MACHINE\SOFTWARE\Microsoft\Windows NT\CurrentVersion\Winlogon.
3. From the Edit menu, select New > DWORD Value, enter a name of **Show**, and press Enter.
4. Double-click the new value and set it to between 0 and 600. Make sure you set the type to decimal. Click OK.
5. Close the Registry editor. This will take effect at the next log on.

FAQ 6.91 How do I change the location for temporary files?

The values of the numerous "temp" variables—mainly temp and tmp—can be changed as follows:

1. Start the System Control Panel applet.
2. Select the Environment tab.

3. Under User Variables, select temp (or tmp), and its value will be displayed. Modify it in the Value box and click Set.
4. Once you have made all changes, click Apply and then OK.

Alternatively you can directly edit the Registry to make these changes:

1. Start the Registry editor.
2. Move to HKEY_CURRENT_USER\Environment.
3. Double-click on the variable—for example, temp—and edit the value. Once complete, click OK.
4. Close the Registry editor.

A final method from the command line is to use the SET command:

```
set temp=d:\temp
```

Most Windows applications such as Word check the variable "tmp" for the location of temporary files and not "temp" so make sure you modify "tmp" and not just "temp".

FAQ 6.92 How do I modify system variables?

As with user variables, system variables can be changed using the System Control Panel applet:

1. Start the System Control Panel applet.
2. Select the Environment tab.
3. Under System Variables, select a variable, and its value will be displayed. Modify it in the Value box and click Set.
4. Once you have made all changes, click Apply and then OK.

Alternatively you can directly edit the Registry to make these changes:

1. Start the Registry editor.
2. Move to HKEY_LOCAL_MACHINE\SYSTEM\CurrentControlSet\Control\Session Manager\Environment.
3. Double-click on the variable—for example, Path—and edit the value. Once complete, click OK.
4. Close the Registry editor.

A final method from the command line is to use the SET command:

```
set OS=OS2
```

Obviously setting our OS to OS2 is not a good idea ☺

FAQ 6.93 How do I disable the ability to change passwords?

Service Pack 4 introduces a new Registry entry:

1. Start the Registry editor (REGEDIT.EXE).
2. Move to HKEY_CURRENT_USER\Software\Microsoft\Windows\CurrentVersion\Policies\System.
3. From the Edit menu, select New - DWORD Value.
4. Enter a name of **DisableChangePassword** and press Enter.
5. Double-click on the new value and set to 1. Click OK.
6. Close the Registry editor.

When you press Ctrl+Alt+Del, Change Password will now be grayed out.

FAQ 6.94 How do I stop a process on a remote machine?

If you are playing a multiplayer game of Quake and are about to get killed for the sixth time, just stop the opponent's Quake process :-) (always works for me). To stop a remote process, perform the following:

> **Note:** *The utilities discussed are part of the NT Resource Kit.*

The target machine must have the RKILLSRV.EXE service running (either from the command line or installed as a service). To install as a service, enter the command

```
instsrv rkillsrv c:\ntreskit\RKILLSRV.EXE
```

This command will install the executable as a service and set its startup to automatic so it will restart at every boot-up. After being installed, the service will not be started, and so if it is to be used before a reboot, you should start via the Services Control Panel applet or start from the command line using

```
net start rkillsrv
```

Once the service has been configured and started on the remote machine, processes can be manipulated from client machines by users who have Administrative privileges via the command line RKILL.EXE and the GUI WRKILL.EXE utilities.

To view the running processes with the command-line tool, type

```
rkill /view \\<machine name>
```

For example, **rkill /view \\nt4pdc**.

Once you have identified the process to stop, enter the command

```
rkill /kill \\<machine name> <process id>
```

For example, **rkill /kill \\nt4pdc 84**.

Using the GUI utility, WRKILL.EXE, the process is simpler and allows you to stop a process by selecting it and clicking Kill Selected Process. Click Yes to the confirmation and then OK to the success dialog (see Figure 6-4).

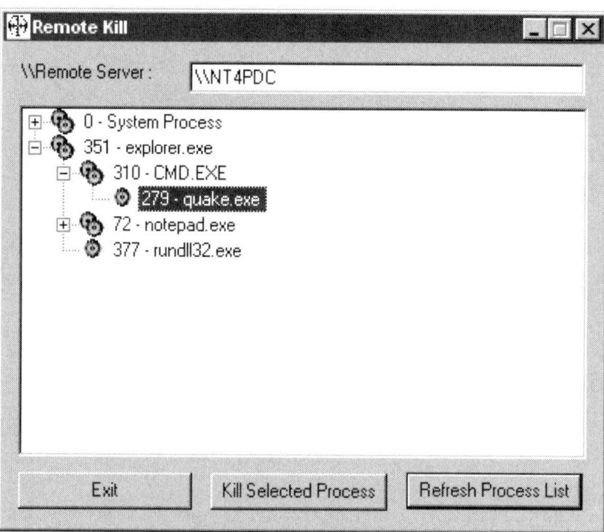

Figure 6-4 Remote kill of a process

Bye, bye quake, 1–0 to me! ☺

Under Windows XP, its built-in taskkill command can also kill processes on remote machines using the /s switch.

FAQ 6.95 How do I install the Security Configuration editor?

The Security Configuration editor, SECEDIT.EXE, is a new utility that forms part of Service Pack 4 for Windows NT 4.0 and is a core part of 2000 and XP. However, due to Microsoft's pledge not to provide new functionality with service packs, the utility was previously available only on the Service Pack 4.0 CD. After public demand, a Web download version is available from ftp://ftp.microsoft.com/bussys/winnt/winnt-public/tools/SCM/SCESP4I.EXE.

Once the file is downloaded, you should execute it and select an extraction directory.

Once the extraction is complete, move to the extracted file directory and double-click on MSSCE.EXE to install. The installation installs two versions of SCE (Security Configuration Editor)—a GUI and command-line version. If you want to install only the command-line tool, enter the command

```
mssce /c /s
```

The /c means command line only, and the /s means silent install (no prompts).

The SCE is a Microsoft Management Console snap-in, and to use it, you must follow these steps:

1. Start MMC (MMC.EXE).
2. From the Console menu, select Add/Remove Snap-in.
3. Click the Add button.
4. Select Security Configuration Manager and click OK.
5. Click OK to the main dialog.

You may want to save this configuration.

1. Select Save As from the Console menu.
2. Enter a name of **secedit** and click Save. The new console will be added to the My Administrative Tools program folder.
3. To edit a configuration, expand the Configurations branch and the directory and select a configuration (see Figure 6-5).

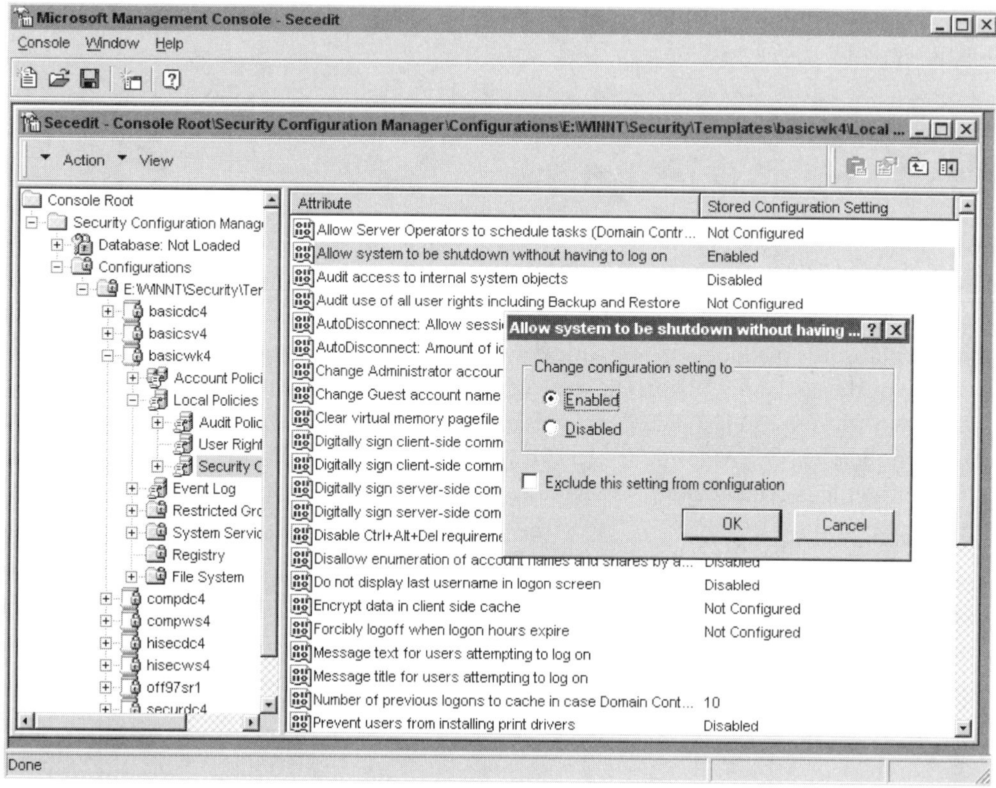

Figure 6-5 Setting the shutdown without logon via policy

Once you have modified a configuration and saved it, you need to activate it:

1. Right-click on database and select Import Configuration.
2. Select a security configuration file (a .INF file) and click Open.
3. Right-click again and select Configure system now.
4. Select a log filename and location. The policy will be applied to the system.

6.96 How do I increase the number of page table entries on my system?

To change the number of page table entries (or system pages) that are used for mapping I/O buffers and other information into the system address space, perform the following:

1. Start the Registry editor (REGEDIT.EXE).
2. Move to HKEY_LOCAL_MACHINE\SYSTEM\CurrentControlSet\Control\Session Manager\Memory Management.
3. Double-click SystemPages value and chose Decimal. Enter the amount of PTEs you need in the Data text box. Click OK. The maximum value is 50,000.
4. Reboot the computer for the change to take effect.

By default the value is 0, which means use the system default.

FAQ 6.97 How can I change the short date format from yy to yyyy?

Due to year 2000 concerns, you may want the NT short date format to show four-digit years as opposed to the short two-digit version. The normal method is as follows:

1. Start the Regional Control Panel applet (Start > Settings > Control Panel > Regional).
2. Select the Date tab.
3. Select M/d/yyyy and click Apply.
4. Click OK.
5. Close the dialog.

All this procedure actually does is set the Registry entry HKEY_CURRENT_USER\Control Panel\International\sShortDate, and so you can use this to automate the update. For example, using the REG.EXE utility,

```
reg update "HKCU\Control Panel\International\sShortDate=M/d/yyyy"
```

This could be incorporated in a logon script or even a custom system policy.

You will also notice under the Registry key the long date format can be set by changing sLongDate.

An alternate solution to set for new systems is by using an unattended installation, make the sShortDate change as part of the CMDLINES.TXT setup. This is then adopted by admin and any new accounts created on the workstation. Sample code:

```
***** CMDLINES.TXT *****
"rundll32 setupapi InstallHinfSection DefaultInstall 128 .\y2k.inf"
***** EOF ********

*** y2k.inf ***
[Version]
Signature="$Windows NT$"
```

```
[DefaultInstall]
AddReg=AddReg

[AddReg]
HKU,".DEFAULT\Control Panel\International","sShortDate",,"M/d/yyyy"
*** EOF ***
```

FAQ 6.98 How do I enable fast reboot on 4.0 SP3 and above?

Service Pack 3 introduces a new ability to reboot the machine by pressing Shift+Ctrl+Alt+Delete at the same time (basically the normal three finger plus Shift). This will then shut down all applications and reboot the machine. To enable this feature, perform the following:

1. Start the Registry editor (REGEDIT.EXE).
2. Move to HKEY_LOCAL_MACHINE\SOFTWARE\Microsoft\Windows NT\CurrentVersion\Winlogon.
3. From the Edit menu, select New > String Value.
4. Enter a name of EnableQuickReboot.
5. Double-click the new value and set to 1. Click OK.
6. Close the Registry editor.
7. Reboot the machine for the change to take effect.

An event will also be written to the System event Log (viewable using the Event Viewer):

```
Event ID - 6008
The previous system shutdown at <time> on <date> was unexpected.
```

FAQ 6.99 How can I create a program alias?

It is possible to create an alias for a program—for example, to define JOHNWORD.EXE to actually run WINWORD.EXE. To do this, perform the following:

1. Start the Registry editor (REGEDIT.EXE).
2. Move to HKEY_LOCAL_MACHINE\SOFTWARE\Microsoft\Windows\CurrentVersion\App Paths.
3. From the Edit menu, select New > Key.

4. Enter the name of the alias—for example, JOHNWORD.EXE and press Enter.
5. Move to the new key and double-click on the (Default) value (it is blank by default).
6. Set to the fully qualified filename, it should run—for example, C:\Program Files\Microsoft Office\Office\winword.exe. Click OK.
7. Optionally you can create a new String called Path, which is where the program will first start running (Edit > New > String Value > Path, double-click and set to the starting path).
8. Close the Registry editor.

If you now select Run from the Start menu and type JOHNWORD.EXE, Microsoft Word will start, cool!

If you type your alias from the command prompt, Windows will not find it; however, if you type

```
start <alias name>
```

it will work fine.

The actual program name does not have to be an .EXE program; it can be any file that has an association (such as C:\temp\ntfaq.url). The alias itself can remain as an .EXE.

If the alias is an .EXE, then the run or start command does not need to include the extension. If the alias is **not** an .EXE, then you need to use the full name, but then you are not limited to any extensions (but the alias must have some extension). Your alias can be John.Savill that you have aliased to C:\ProgramYadaYadaYada\Winword.exe, and Word will start up just fine.

FAQ 6.100 How can I share my ClipBook with other machines?

Windows NT machines have a built-in ClipBook server service, which allows other machines to use its ClipBook. This service is enabled as follows:

1. Start the Services Control Panel applet (Start > Settings > Control Panel > Services).
2. Select ClipBook Server and click Start.
3. You can also click Startup and set to Automatic so the service will start at each reboot.
4. Click Close.

You can also start the service from the command line by entering the command

```
net start clipsrv
```

or

```
net start "clipbook server"
```

You can then copy your data to the Clipboard as normal by pressing Ctrl+C, PrtScn, or Alt+PrtScn (to only copy the current window).

1. Start the Clipboard Viewer (Start > Programs > Accessories > Clipboard viewer).
2. From the Edit menu, select Paste and enter a name that this data will be known as (e.g., "Cat", though not if it's a picture of a dog :-)) and check the Share Item Now box.
3. Just click OK in response to the next dialog, which is about starting an application.

From the client, perform the following:

1. Start the Clipboard Viewer (Start > Programs > Accessories > Clipboard Viewer).
2. From the File menu, select Connect.
3. Enter the machine running the ClipBook Server service.
4. A window showing the machine's list of clips will be shown.
5. Double-click on one to display the data. You can then select Copy from the Edit menu to copy into the client's local Clipboard.

FAQ 6.101 How can I stop tips showing on startup?

To stop tips for the current user, you can uncheck the display checkbox on the dialog when it is displayed or edit the Registry:

1. Start the Registry editor (REGEDIT.EXE).
2. Move to HKEY_CURRENT_USER\Software\Microsoft\Windows\CurrentVersion\Explorer\Tips.
3. Double-click show.
4. Change the 01 to 00.
5. Click OK.
6. Close the Registry editor.

To stop it being shown for new users, edit the value under HKEY_USERS\.DEFAULT and set to 0, which new users will inherit. This works under Windows 2000.

FAQ 6.102 How can I configure Outlook Express to be the default news reader?

To configure Outlook Express as the default news reader, perform the following:

1. Start Outlook Express.
2. From the Tools menu, select Options.
3. Select the General tab.
4. At the bottom of the dialog box, click the Make Default button next to the This application is **not** the default News handler.

You can also manually perform the change by making the following Registry changes:

1. Start the Registry editor (REGEDIT.EXE).
2. Move to HKEY_CLASSES_ROOT\news\DefaultIcon.
3. Double-click (Default) and change to **%SystemDrive%\Program Files\Outlook Express\msimn.exe,-3**.
4. Move to HKEY_CLASSES_ROOT\news\shell\open\command.
5. Double-click (Default) and change to **"%SystemDrive%\Program Files\Outlook Express\msimn.exe" /newsurl:%1** (**do** type the quotes).
6. Move to HKEY_CLASSES_ROOT\snews\DefaultIcon.
7. Double-click (Default) and change to **%SystemDrive%\Program Files\Outlook Express\msimn.exe,-3**.
8. Move to HKEY_CLASSES_ROOT\snews\shell\open\command.
9. Double-click (Default) and change to **"%SystemDrive%\Program Files\Outlook Express\msimn.exe" /newsurl:%1** (**do** type the quotes).
10. Move to HKEY_CLASSES_ROOT\nntp\DefaultIcon.
11. Double-click (Default) and change to **%SystemDrive%\Program Files\Outlook Express\msimn.exe,-3**.
12. Move to HKEY_CLASSES_ROOT\nntp\shell\open\command.
13. Double-click (Default) and change to **"%SystemDrive%\Program Files\Outlook Express\msimn.exe" /newsurl:%1** (**do** type the quotes).
14. Close the Registry editor.
15. Reboot the machine.

FAQ 6.103 How can I modify the My Computer text to show logged on username and machine name?

It may be useful to have the My Computer icon show the current logged on user and computer name. This can be configured as follows:

1. Start the Registry editor (REGEDT32.EXE).
2. Move to HKEY_CLASSES_ROOT\CLSID\{20D04FE0-3AEA-1069-A2D8-08002B30309D}.
3. Select the <No Name> value and Delete.
4. From the Edit menu, select Add Value.
5. Leave the value name blank and set the type to REG_EXPAND_SZ.
6. Click OK and enter the text **User: %USERNAME% on: %COMPUTERNAME%**.
7. Click OK.
8. Click on the desktop and press F5 (for refresh), and the change takes effect.

Without changing the value type to REG_EXPAND_SZ, the %username% and %computername% does not get expanded to the actual username and computer name. This works for Windows NT 4.0; for Windows 2000, perform the following:

1. Start the Registry editor (REGEDT32.EXE).
2. Move to HKEY_CLASSES_ROOT\CLSID\{20D04FE0-3AEA-1069-A2D8-08002B30309D}.
3. Double-click the value LocalizedString to edit and cut and paste the contents to somewhere safe. It will be something like:

   ```
   @D:\WINNT\system32\shell32.dll,-9216@1033,My Computer
   ```

4. Use Registry/Save Subkey to save the current entry.
5. Delete the value LocalizedString.
6. Create a new value named LocalizedString of type REG_EXPAND_SZ and paste in the content saved at step 3. Edit the text My Computer at the end of the string and change it to **%USERNAME% on %COMPUTERNAME%**—for example, to:

   ```
   @D:\WINNT\system32\shell32.dll,-9216@1033,%username% on
   %computername%
   ```

7. Right-click on the desktop and choose Refresh; if you have desktop icons shifted to the taskbar, right-click on the desktop section and choose Refresh.

FAQ 6.104 How can I automatically kill hung processes when I log off?

When you tell NT to shut down, it first sends shutdown requests to any running processes. Most 32-bit applications honor these requests and shut down, but older 16-bit apps running in the virtual DOS machine often won't. When this occurs, the operating system prompts you with a dialog box asking if you want to kill the task, wait for the task to die on its own, or cancel the shutdown. By modifying the Registry, you can automate this process.

You can force NT to kill all running processes on shutdown by performing the following:

1. Start the Registry editor (REGEDIT.EXE).
2. Move to HKEY_CURRENT_USER\Control Panel\Desktop.
3. If a value "AutoEndTasks" does not exist from the Edit menu, select New > String Value. Enter a name of AutoEndTasks and press Enter.
4. Double-click on AutoEndTasks and set to 1. Click OK.
5. Close the Registry editor.

You can also add this key to HKEY_USERS\.DEFAULT\Control Panel\Desktop for new users to inherit.

FAQ 6.105 How can I change the InfoTip for icons?

In Windows 2000, when you move the cursor over an icon (such as My Network Places or My Computer), text is displayed, explaining the icon's use. This text is stored in a Registry entry InfoTip of type String for each CLSID entry and can be changed to any text you want.

For example, to change the My Network Places text:

1. Start the Registry editor (REGEDIT.EXE).
2. Move to HKEY_CLASSES_ROOT\CLSID\{208D2C60-3AEA-1069-A2D7-08002B30309D}.
3. Double-click InfoTip and change. Click OK.
4. Close the Registry editor.

The change takes immediate effect.

Other useful entries are (all under HKEY_CLASSES_ROOT\CLSID\):

{20D04FE0-3AEA-1069-A2D8-08002B30309D}	My Computer
{450D8FBA-AD25-11D0-98A8-0800361B1103}	My Documents
{645FF040-5081-101B-9F08-00AA002F954E}	Recycle Bin
{00020D75-0000-0000-C000-000000000046}	Microsoft Outlook
{21EC2020-3AEA-1069-A2DD-08002B30309D}	Control Panel
{2227A280-3AEA-1069-A2DE-08002B30309D}	Printers
{7007ACC7-3202-11D1-AAD2-00805FC1270E}	Network and dial-up connections
{85BBD920-42A0-1069-A2E4-08002B30309D}	Briefcase
{871C5380-42A0-1069-A2EA-08002B30309D}	Internet Explorer
{BDEADF00-C265-11d0-BCED-00A0C90AB50F}	Web folders

FAQ 6.106 How can I control who can eject Zip disks?

Windows 2000 introduces a new Registry key that allows you to configure who can eject Zip disks:

1. Start the Registry editor (REGEDIT.EXE).
2. Move to HKEY_LOCAL_MACHINE\SOFTWARE\Microsoft\Windows NT\CurrentVersion\Winlogon.
3. From the Edit menu, select New > String Value.
4. Enter a name of **AllocateDASD** and press Enter.
5. Double-click the new value and set to:

   0 = Admins only can eject

   1 = Admins and power users

   2 = Admins and the interactive user (this allows normal users)
6. Click OK.
7. Close the Registry editor.
8. Reboot the computer.

The preceding also works on NT 4.0 as long as you run the undocumented IomegaAccess utility included in the latest Iomegaware download. This utility installs a service that grants all users rights to format, eject, and so on. Note that the program must be run from the hard drive, as the service defaults to referencing the installation directory on startup.

FAQ 6.107 How can I configure monitor power off for the logon screen?

If you select the Screen Saver tab of the Desktop Control Panel applet, you can configure power-saving settings that include powering off the monitor after x minutes. To enable the monitor to power off for the logon screen, perform the following on each machine:

1. Start the Registry editor (REGEDIT.EXE).
2. Move to HKEY_USERS\.DEFAULT\Control Panel\Desktop.
3. Double-click PowerOffActive and set to 1. Click OK.
4. Double-click ScreenSaveActive and set to 1. Click OK.
5. Double-click SCRNSAVE.EXE (if present) and set to **(NONE)**. Click OK.
6. Move to HKEY_USERS\.DEFAULT\Control Panel\PowerCfg.
7. Double-click CurrentPowerPolicy and set to 0 (the Home/Office Desk power setting configuration). Click OK.
8. Close the Registry editor.
9. Reboot the machine.

To change the settings such as monitor timeout, change the settings on your local profile, export HKEY_CURRENT_USER\Control Panel\PowerCfg\PowerPolicies\0 to a file, and import to HKEY_USERS\.DEFAULT\Control Panel\PowerCfg\PowerPolicies\0.

If you need to do this on lots of machines, create an .ADM file and set it as part of the system policy.

FAQ 6.108 What are the problems with workstations having the same SID?

At the start of the GUI phase of installation, each NT/2000 installation generates a unique security identifier (SID). If you then clone a workstation, each installation would have the same machine SID. This is not a problem in a Windows NT 4.0 domain because users have a SID generated by the domain controller and do not use the local workstation SID for security. It **is** a problem in a Windows 2000 domain because the local machine SID is used in nearly all aspects of security, and before migrating to 2000, you should resolve any duplicate SID issues that may have been caused by cloning installations.

Duplicate local SIDs are also a major security risk in workgroups; lets look further. In a workgroup, the user accounts are based on the local workstation SID plus a relative identifier (RID). If all the workstations had the same SID, then the first account generated (and so forth) on each workstation is the same because of the duplicate local SID. This makes it impossible to secure files and folders on a user basis because different users will have the same SID, and all security is based on the user SID. An example best illustrates this situation.

Two workstations, wstation1 and wstation2, deployed using cloning software, each has duplicated SIDs.

User John on wstation1 has a local machine account on wstation1 of S-1-5-34-148593445-285934854-2859284934-1010. User Kevin on wstation2 has a local machine account on wstation1 of S-1-5-34-148593445-285934854-2859284934-1010.

User John saves private work on an NTFS drive and creates a share called private that only he can access. If Kevin browses the network and attempts connection, he will have full access because his SID is identical to John's. There is no way to differentiate between them. Expand this to 100 machines installed via duplication all with the same local SID, and you can see the lack of security. Any files stored on removable media with security would also be vulnerable.

Microsoft has a tool, SysPrep, that can be used on a workstation system **before** cloning, which resolves the SID problem by generating a new SID when the new cloned installations are started. SysPrep is provided as standard in Windows 2000 and a version for 4.0 can be requested from Microsoft.

SysPrep does have a few "problems" on Windows member servers. If a server with several local accounts is cloned, the SID of any extra accounts are not updated; only the two primary accounts, Administrator and Guest are fixed. This means other accounts would be left with the old SID and thus considered orphaned.

The following are other SID-fixing utilities:

- SIDchanger—http://www.powerquest.com
- GHOST Walker—http://www.ghostsoft.com
- NTSID—http://www.sysinternals.com

FAQ 6.109 Where is time zone information stored in NT/2000?

Start the Date/Time Control Panel applet, select the Time Zone tab, and unselect Automatically adjust clock for daylight saving. It can also be done directly in the Registry:

1. Start the Registry editor (REGEDIT.EXE).
2. Move to HKEY_LOCAL_MACHINE\SYSTEM\CurrentControlSet\Control\TimeZoneInformation.
3. From the Edit menu, select New > DWORD Value.
4. Enter a name **DisableAutoDaylightTimeSet** and press Enter.
5. Double-click the new value and set to 1. Click OK.
6. Close the Registry editor.

FAQ 6.110 How can I improve I/O performance?

If your system is fairly I/O intensive, you may benefit from raising the I/O Page Lock Limit, which can increase the effective rate the OS reads or writes data to the hard disks.

First, benchmark your common tasks. See how long it takes to load and save large files, how long it takes to search a database or run a common program; just do your normal tasks, timing them to record how fast they are. Then follow these steps:

1. Start the Registry editor (REGEDIT.EXE).
2. Move to HKEY_LOCAL_MACHINE\SYSTEM\CurrentControlSet\Control\Session Manager\Memory Management.
3. Double-click IoPageLockLimit.
4. Enter a new value.
5. This value is the maximum bytes you can lock for I/O operations. A value of 0 defaults to 512KB. Raise this value by 512KB increments (enter **512**, **1024**, etc.), then exit REGEDIT.EXE and benchmark your system after each adjustment. When an increase does not give you a significant performance boost, go back and undo the last increment.

Caution: *Do not set this value (in bytes) beyond the number of megabytes of RAM times 128. That is, if you have 16MB RAM, do not set IoPageLockLimit over 2048 bytes; for 32MB RAM, do not exceed 4096 bytes, and so on.*

6. Click OK.
7. Close the Registry editor.

Unless you do little I/O, this should give you a significant boost in performance.

I have recently learned that this value specifies the maximum amount of application memory that can be locked into physical memory at any given point in time. Device drivers typically lock user buffers in order to transmit them to a hardware device. If the limit is exceeded, an I/O operation will simply return a STATUS_QUOTA_EXCEEDED error to the application. Thus, the value should be raised only if I/O operations begin returning this error, and it has absolutely no effect on performance.

FAQ 6.111 How can I configure the Windows 2000 System File Checker?

Windows 2000 includes a new component that protects system files by scanning all protected system files and replacing incorrect versions with correct Microsoft versions. It is possible to modify the behavior of this protection using the SFC.EXE utility (you must be a member of the Administrators group).

```
SFC [/SCANNOW] [/SCANONCE] [/SCANBOOT] [/CANCEL] [/PURGECACHE]
[/CACHESIZE=x] [/QUIET]

/SCANNOW Scans all protected system files immediately.
/SCANONCE Scans all protected system files once at the next boot.
/SCANBOOT Scans all protected system files at every boot.
/CANCEL Cancels all pending scans of protected system files.
/QUIET Replaces all incorrect file versions without prompting
the user.
/PURGECACHE Purges the file cache and scans all protected system
files immediately.
/CACHESIZE=x Sets the file cache size
```

Setting the Quiet option updates HKEY_LOCAL_MACHINE\SOFTWARE\Microsoft\Windows NT\CurrentVersion\Winlogon\SFCDisable, and the other options modify HKEY_LOCAL_MACHINE\SOFTWARE\Microsoft\Windows NT\CurrentVersion\Winlogon\SFCScan.

You can disable SFC by performing the following:

1. Start the Registry editor (REGEDIT.EXE).
2. Move to HKEY_LOCAL_MACHINE\SOFTWARE\Microsoft\Windows NT\CurrentVersion\Winlogon.
3. From the Edit menu, select New > DWORD Value.
4. Enter a name of **EnableFileProtection**, press Enter.
5. Double-click the value and set to 0.
6. Close the Registry editor.

FAQ 6.112 How can I lock a workstation from the command line?

Windows 2000 enables you to lock the workstation by typing the following command:

```
rundll32.exe user32.dll,LockWorkStation
```

You could also use this command as a shortcut on you desktop.

This command will not work in Windows NT 4.0. To achieve a similar effect requires a bit more work. You can use the SendMessage call to send a SC_SCREENSAVE message to the top-most window, which locks the workstation if the current user has a screensaver configured to require a password.

To ensure that a screensaver is configured, you can create Registry entries. Run a Registry (.REG) file that adds the following entries from the command line:

```
HKCU\Control Panel\Desktop\ScreenSaveActive = 1
HKCU\Control Panel\Desktop\ScreenSaverIsSecure = 1
HKCU\Control Panel\Desktop\ScreenSaveTimeout = timeout in seconds
HKCU\Control Panel\Desktop\SCRNSAVE.EXE =
%SystemRoot%\System32\Appropriate screensaver.scr
```

Some screensavers require additional parameters in HKCU\Control Panel\Screen Saver.screensaver name as well.

After you create these Registry entries, the following call invokes the screensaver: SendMessage(HWND_TOPMOST, WM_SYSCOMMAND, SC_SCREENSAVE, 0)

You must write and compile a short program (an .EXE file) that contains this call. You can then call your program from the command line to activate the screensaver. Because the ScreenSaverIsSecure value in the Registry has been set to 1, this has the effect of locking the workstation.

FAQ 6.113 How do I create a default association for files with no extension?

Normal files with an extension can have a program association; however, this is not the case with files that don't have an extension. If you double-click on one, select an application, and check the box to always use that application, it is ignored. Every time you select a file, you have to choose the application.

You can force an association, using the Registry:

1. Start the Registry editor (REGEDIT.EXE).
2. Move to HKEY_CLASSES_ROOT.
3. From the Edit menu, select New > Key.
4. Enter a name of "." and press Enter (don't type the quotes).
5. Select the new "." key.
6. Double-click the (Default) value.
7. Change to the HKEY_CLASSES_ROOT used to open—for example, NOTEPAD for the NOTEPAD.EXE application (see Figure 6-6):

   ```
   NOTEPAD
   ```

8. Click OK.

If you now double-click on a file with no extension, it will open with the application selected.

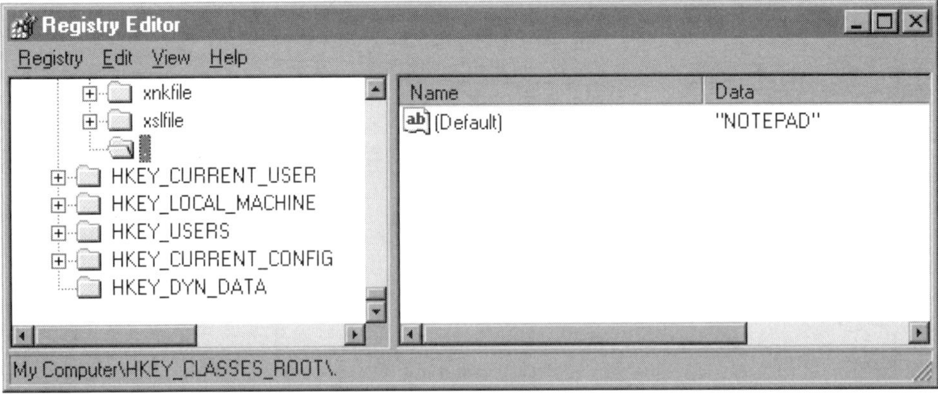

Figure 6-6 Creating a default association for files with no extension

To check what an existing application used, look at its entry under HKEY_CLASSES_ROOT—for example, HKEY_CLASSES_ROOT\.doc uses Word.Document.8. So if you want this as your default editor, you can change HKEY_CLASSES_ROOT\.\(Default) to Word.Document.8.

Here's a method that avoids the need to edit the Registry:

1. Open Explorer—View > Folder Options > File Types > New Type.
2. Description of type: Text (any description, you can type in)

```
Associated extension: . (just a period)
Actions: - new...
Action: open
Application used to perform action: c:\winnt\notepad.exe
```

3. Click OK, then OK again.

FAQ 6.114 How do I create a default association for files with an unknown extension?

Files with an unknown extension will bring up an "open with" dialog when you double-click on them; however, it is possible to associate an application with files of an unknown type.

You can force this using the Registry:

1. Start the Registry editor (REGEDIT.EXE).
2. Move to HKEY_CLASSES_ROOT\Unknown\shell.
3. From the Edit menu, select New > Key.
4. Enter a name of **open** and press Enter.
5. Select the new "open" key.
6. From the Edit menu, select New > Key.
7. Enter a name of **command** and press Enter.
8. Double-click the (Default) value.
9. Change to the application used to open—for example, NOTEPAD.EXE %1 for the NOTEPAD.EXE application (you need %1 to pass the document name to Notepad and, depending on the application, you may need %1 %*).
10. Click OK.

If you now double-click on a file with no extension, it will open with the application selected.

You can optionally delete the HKEY_CLASSES_ROOT\Unknown\shell\openas key and its content (but it is not necessary), and it will just remove the open with context menu option.

It is possible to just add a Notepad option to the context menu of Unknown by using the existing entry in HKEY_CLASSES_ROOT/Unknown/shell, adding a new key value of Notepad and a new key value of "open" underneath Notepad, then a new key called "command" under open. Set the (Default) value of command to Notepad.exe %1. Following is a Registry file to perform this configuration:

```
REGEDIT4

[HKEY_CLASSES_ROOT\Unknown\shell\notepad]

[HKEY_CLASSES_ROOT\Unknown\shell\notepad\open]

[HKEY_CLASSES_ROOT\Unknown\shell\notepad\open\command]
@="notepad %1"
```

FAQ 6.115 How do I set DLL files to use their own icon rather than the standard?

Windows displays DLL files in Explorer with a generic DLL icon. This generic icon conveys no information about the DLL file, other than the fact that the file is a DLL.

Many DLL files have one or more icons, and it's possible to have one displayed in Explorer.

1. Start the Registry editor (REGEDIT.EXE.
2. Move to HKEY_CLASSES_ROOT\dllfile\DefaultIcon.
3. Double-click (Default) and change from

```
%SystemRoot%\System32\shell32.dll,-154
```

to

```
%1
```

4. Click OK.
5. Close the Registry editor.

FAQ 6.116 How can I make Explorer show the extension of known file types?

Normally Windows Explorer will not show the extension of known file types; however, you can force Explorer to show them:

1. Start Explorer.
2. From the View menu, select Options.
3. Select the View tab.
4. Unselect Hide file extensions for known file types.
5. Click OK.

FAQ 6.117 What are super hidden files?

Windows 2000 introduces super hidden files, which, as the name implies, are files that are hidden from the user even more than normal hidden files. If you enable the ability to view hidden files and folders in Explorer, these super hidden files/folders will still not be displayed.

This super hidden file status is for folders like the cmdcons folder, which is used for the Emergency Recover console.

FAQ 6.118 How can I view super hidden files?

Super hidden files/folders can be viewed from the command line as normal files; you don't even need the /ah dir switch (/ah sets the mode to **a**ttribute **h**idden).

If you wish to view these files via the GUI, such as Explorer, perform the following:

1. Start Explorer.
2. From the Tools menu, select Folder Options.
3. Select the View tab.
4. Unselect the Hide protected operating system files (Recommended) box (see Figure 6-7).
5. Click Apply, then OK.

The super hidden files will now be visible in Explorer. This can also be done by directly editing the Registry.

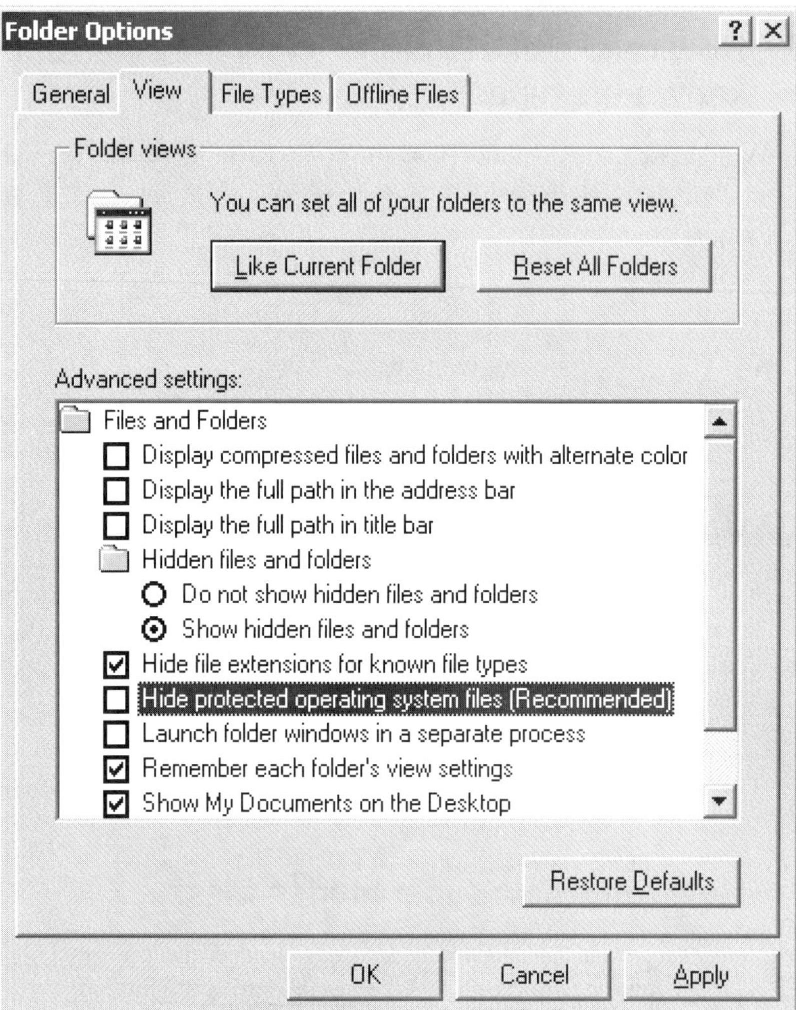

Figure 6-7 Enabling the viewing of operating system files

1. Start the Registry editor (REGEDIT.EXE).
2. Move to HKEY_LOCAL_MACHINE\SOFTWARE\Microsoft\Windows\CurrentVersion\policies\Explorer if using Server (or Advanced Server) or HKEY_CURRENT_USER\Software\Microsoft\Windows\CurrentVersion\Explorer\Advanced if using Professional (Workstation).

3. If the value does not exist, create a value named ShowSuperHidden of type DWORD.
4. Set to 1. Click OK.
5. Close the Registry editor.

FAQ 6.119 After upgrading from NT 4.0 to Windows 2000, the timeout in BOOT.INI has been reset to 30. Why?

The timeout value, which is the amount of time you have to pick your operating system during system startup, is defined in the BOOT.INI file. During an upgrade to 2000, this value is reset to 30, no matter what you may have set it to in the past. To change it back to your preferred value, perform the following:

1. Right-click My Computer on the desktop and then click Properties.
2. On the Advanced tab, click Startup and Recovery.
3. Change the value in the Display list of operating systems for N seconds to the value you want, in seconds.
4. Click OK and then click OK.

You can also do this by directly editing the BOOT.INI file and change the timeout value to the number of seconds you require:

```
[boot loader]
timeout=10
```

Remember the file BOOT.INI is a read-only file so you will first need to set it as write enabled:

1. Remove the system, hidden and read-only attributes from boot.ini

   ```
   attrib boot.ini -r -s -h
   ```

2. Edit BOOT.INI.
3. Add the system, hidden and read-only attributes to boot.ini

   ```
   attrib boot.ini +r +s +h
   ```

6.120 How can I force a check of protected system files in Windows 2000?

Windows 2000 includes a new component that protects critical system files. If they are replaced by an application, the correct original file will be replaced by the process, which should fix the common "DLL Hell" scenario.

A SFC.EXE (System File Checker) utility is supplied that can be used to perform various checks and configuration for this service. To force a check of files at any time just type:

```
sfc /scannow
```

A check of your system files will then be carried out. You may need to insert your Windows 2000 CD-ROM.

You can also use switches:

- /SCANONCE—Scans all protected system files once at the next boot.
- /SCANBOOT—Scans all protected system files at every boot.

6.121 How can I disable the DLL cache in Windows 2000?

To remove the DLL cache in Windows 2000 that the System File Checker service uses and that can take up about 200MB of space, enter the following commands:

```
sfc /cachesize=0
sfc /scannow
```

sfc /scannow forces Windows to remove the cached files.

6.122 Why can't I add or remove accessories on my Windows 2000 Professional machine?

Start the Control Panel Add/Remove Programs applet and select Add/Remove Windows components. In the section Accessories and Utilities, click Details to add accessories (e.g., Calculator, Games). If one of the options you want to add or remove is missing, you can add it.

1. Start Notepad.
2. Open the file \%systemroot%\inf\sysoc.inf.
3. Find the old base components section, which the following example shows, and remove the word HIDE. For example, change

```
Games=ocgen.dll,OcEntry,games.inf,HIDE,7
AccessUtil=ocgen.dll,OcEntry,accessor.inf,HIDE,7
CommApps=ocgen.dll,OcEntry,communic.inf,HIDE,7
media_clips=ocgen.dll,OcEntry,mmopt.inf,HIDE,7
MultiM=ocgen.dll,OcEntry,multimed.inf,HIDE,7
AccessOpt=ocgen.dll,OcEntry,optional.inf,HIDE,7
Pinball=ocgen.dll,OcEntry,pinball.inf,HIDE,7
MSWordPad=ocgen.dll,OcEntry,wordpad.inf,HIDE,7
```

to

```
Games=ocgen.dll,OcEntry,games.inf,,7
AccessUtil=ocgen.dll,OcEntry,accessor.inf,,7
CommApps=ocgen.dll,OcEntry,communic.inf,,7
media_clips=ocgen.dll,OcEntry,mmopt.inf,,7
MultiM=ocgen.dll,OcEntry,multimed.inf,,7
AccessOpt=ocgen.dll,OcEntry,optional.inf,,7
Pinball=ocgen.dll,OcEntry,pinball.inf,,7
MSWordPad=ocgen.dll,OcEntry,wordpad.inf,,7
```

4. Save the file.

You don't need to reboot the machine.

FAQ 6.123 How can I remove a device driver?

To remove a device driver, perform the following steps:

1. Stop the service or device driver. For services, run Control Panel and choose Services. For device drivers, run Control Panel and choose Devices. If the service or device driver doesn't stop, set the startup type to disabled and reboot the computer.
2. Start the Registry editor (REGEDT32.EXE).
3. Move to HKEY_LOCAL_MACHINE\SYSTEM\CurrentControlSet\Services.

4. Find the Registry key that corresponds to the service or device driver that you want to delete.
5. Select the key.
6. From the Edit menu, choose Delete.
7. Choose Yes to confirm the deletion of the key.
8. Close the Registry editor.
9. Shut down and restart the computer.

The Windows NT Resource Kit has the SRVINSTW tool that, on the third screen of the operation of the utility, lets you add device drivers for removal operations.

FAQ 6.124 How do I remove the Windows 2000 Resource Kit Time service?

To remove the TimeServ Windows 2000 Resource Kit utility, perform the following steps:

1. Start the Control Panel Services applet and stop the Time service.
2. Start the Registry editor (REGEDT32.EXE).
3. Move to HKEY_LOCAL_MACHINE\SYSTEM\ControlSet001\Services\Eventlog\Application.
4. Select TimeServ and click Del. Click Yes to the confirmation.
5. Move to HKEY_LOCAL_MACHINE\SYSTEM\ControlSet001\Services.
6. Select TimeServ and click Del. Click Yes to the confirmation.
7. Move to HKEY_LOCAL_MACHINE\SYSTEM\CurrentControlSet\Services\Eventlog\Application.
8. Select TimeServ and click Del. Click Yes to the confirmation.

If you start the Control Panel Services applet, the TimeServ service is disabled and unavailable. Reboot the computer, and the OS doesn't show the TimeServ service.

FAQ 6.125 How can I configure Event-log wrapping in Windows 2000?

When you start Windows 2000, you might receive warnings about log *x* being full. To action these requests and set log options, perform the following steps:

1. From the Start menu, select Programs > Administrative Tools, then the Microsoft Management Console (MMC) Computer Management snap-in.
2. Expand System Tools and select Event Viewer.
3. Right-click the relevant log (i.e., Application) and select Properties (see Figure 6-8).
4. Set the log size and the overwrite option that you want. Selecting Overwrite events as needed might be the easiest option to manage, but it leaves you exposed from an auditing perspective (see Figure 6-9).
5. Click Apply, then OK.

You'll notice that when you right-click the event log, you can also use the relevant context menu option to clear its contents.

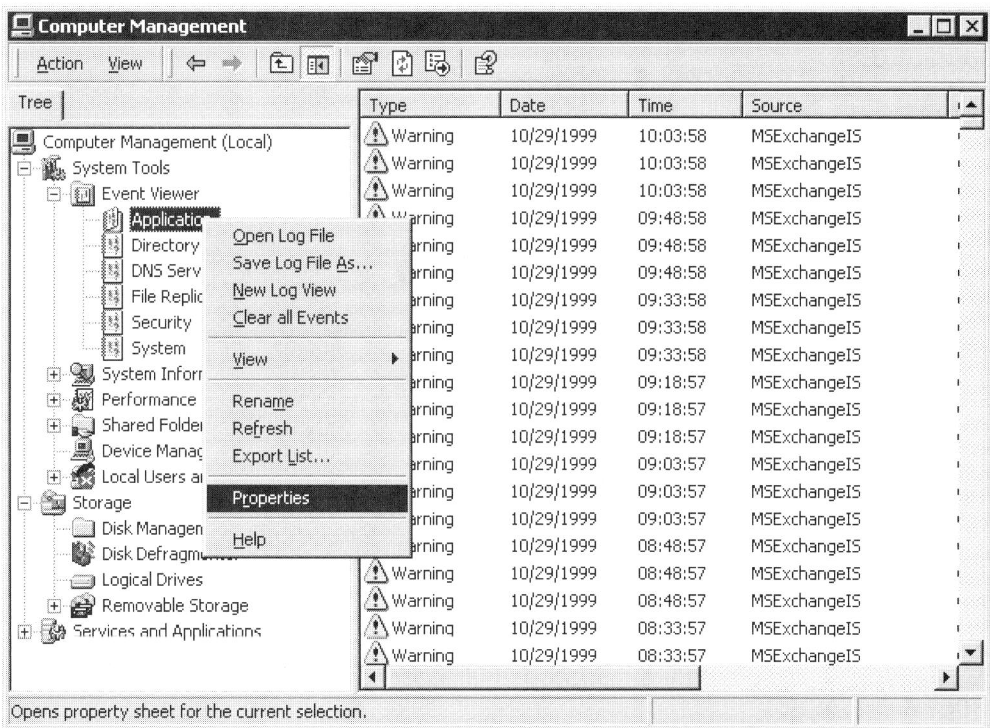

Figure 6-8 Properties of the Application event log

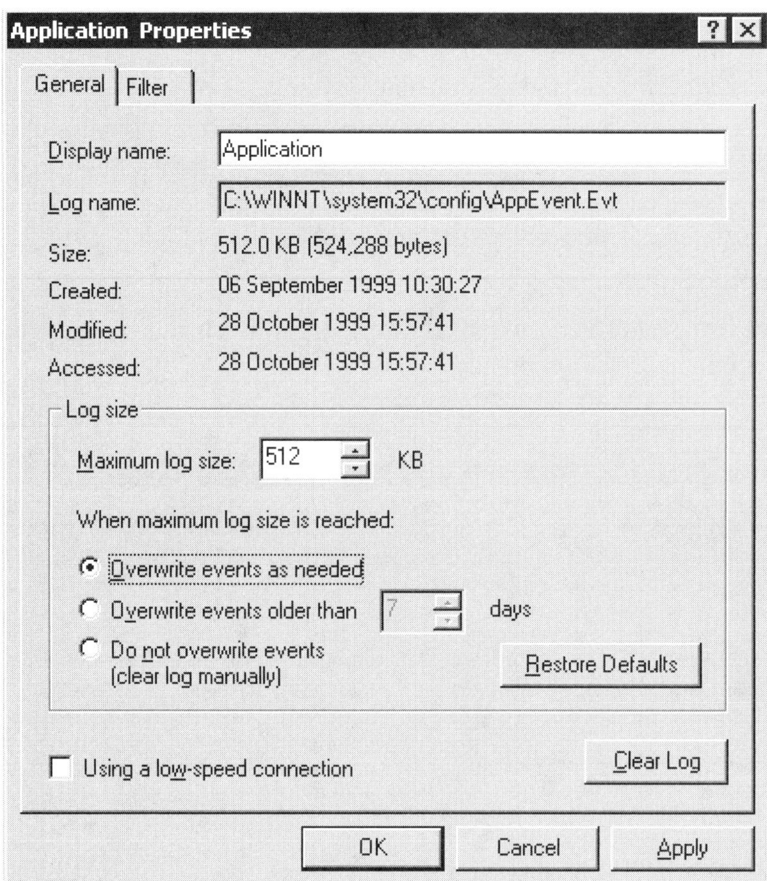

Figure 6-9 Enabling automatic overwrite of the event log

6.126 What are offline folders?

Windows 2000 introduces the concept of offline folders, which are locally cached versions of network files or folders. The contents of the locally cached versions are synchronized with network versions to assure that no changes to files are lost and that the access permissions are the same as if you were connected. This process of offline files doesn't bypass any ACLs.

When your connection status changes, an Offline Files icon appears in the status area, and the OS displays an informational balloon over the status area to notify you of the change (see Figure 6-10).

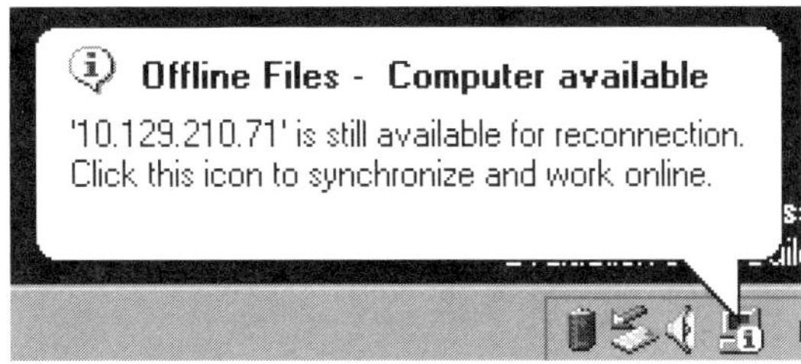

Figure 6-10 Source computer of offline file available again

You can make any shared files or folders on a Microsoft network available offline from any computer that supports Server Message Block (SMB)-based File and Printer Sharing, including Windows NT 4.0, Win98, and Win95. The offline folder and file feature isn't available on Novell NetWare networks.

FAQ 6.127 How do I set a folder as available and not available offline?

To make a file or folder available offline, right-click the file or folder. Select Make Available Offline to start a wizard and perform the following steps:

1. Click Next to the welcome screen.
2. Check the Automatically synchronize the option Offline Files when I log on and log off my computer. (This option slows logon and logoff slightly.) Click Next.
3. The program selects Enable reminders by default, which produces little reminder bubbles when you aren't connected (see Figure 6-11).
4. Click Finish.
5. If you select a folder that has subfolders, after you click Finish, the program asks you if you want the subfolders and content also available. A file copy operation will commence and will copy files from the network source to a local area to create the cached version.

To make a file or folder unavailable, right-click it and clear the Make Available Offline checkbox.

If you use a folder or file that isn't currently available, when the share becomes available, right-click the folder or file and select Synchronize. Choosing this option synchronizes the content and makes the folder or file available online again.

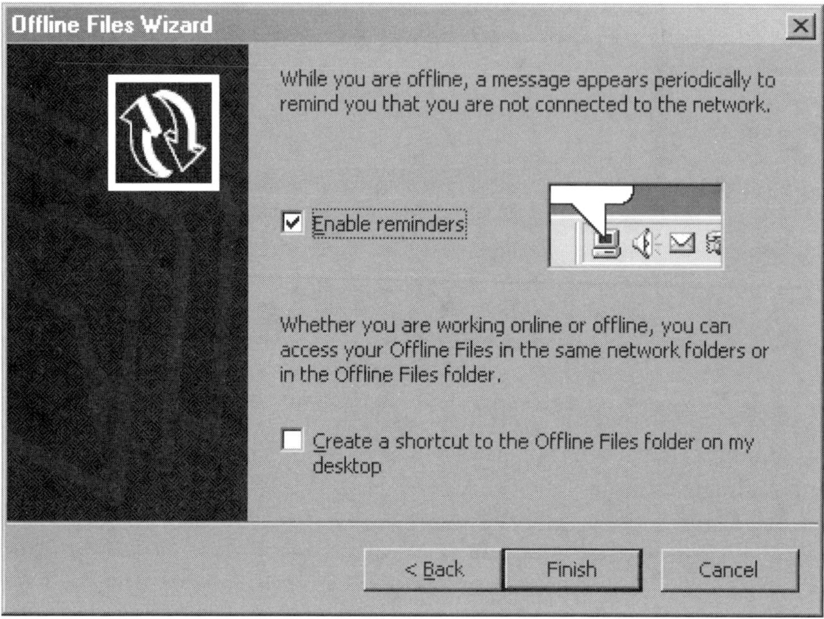

Figure 6-11 Offline files option for reminders

FAQ 6.128 How do I configure a shared folder as automatically available offline?

You can configure a shared folder to be automatically available offline to clients. To do so, perform the following steps:

1. Start Windows Explorer.
2. Right-click the shared folder.
3. Select Sharing from the context menu.
4. Click the Caching button.
5. Select the caching type (see Figure 6-12):

```
- Automatic Caching for Documents
- Automatic Caching for Programs
- Manual Caching for Documents
```

6. Click OK.
7. Click OK to the main share.

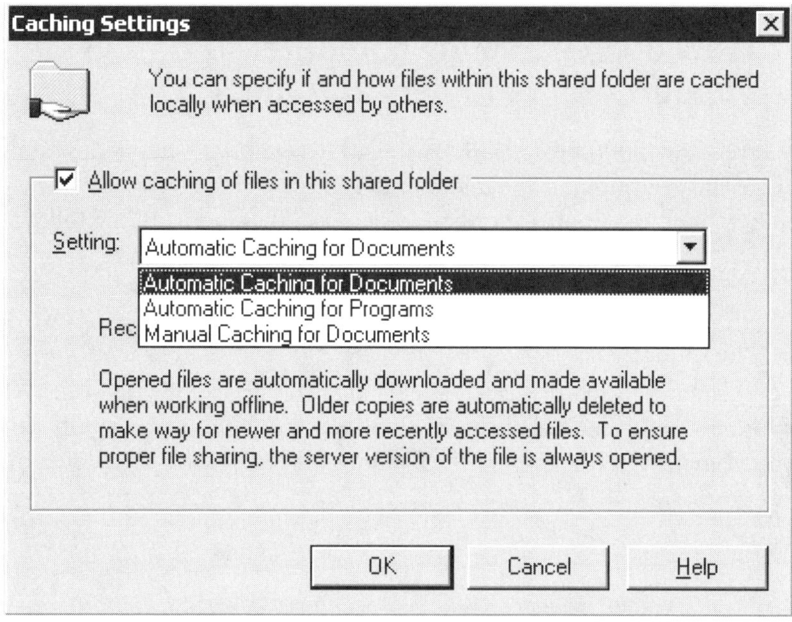

Figure 6-12 Setting the cache options for documents and programs

Clients connecting to the share (Windows 2000 clients) will automatically cache any opened files. Clients won't cache the entire content, only files and programs that are opened from the share. If the share is unavailable, only the previously opened files will be listed and are the only ones that the clients can open. When the share goes offline, you receive the standard notification that the share is no longer available online (see Figure 6-13), and you use the offline version.

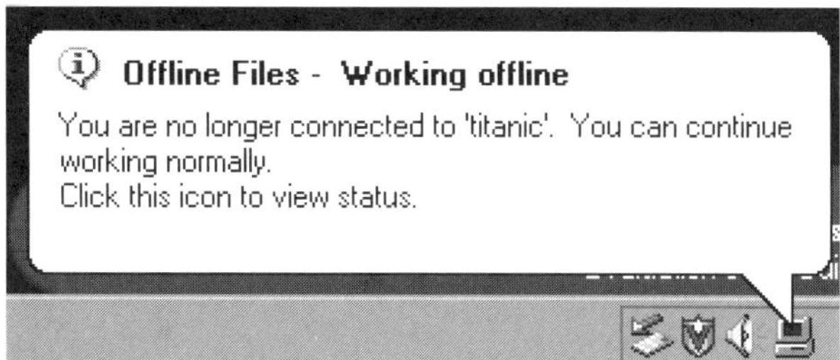

Figure 6-13 Notification of offline working

FAQ 6.129 How do I enable my computer to support offline folders and files?

By default, Windows 2000 Professional installations enable offline folders and files, and Win2K Server installations disable folders and files.

To enable or disable support for offline folders and files, perform the following steps:

1. Start Windows Explorer.
2. From the Tools menu, select Folder Options.
3. Select the Offline Files tab.
4. Make the required changes, such as checking the Enable Offline Files box (see Figure 6-14). The Synchronize all offline files before logging off option forces resynchronization before the OS logs off but doesn't slow down the logoff process.
5. Click Apply, then OK.

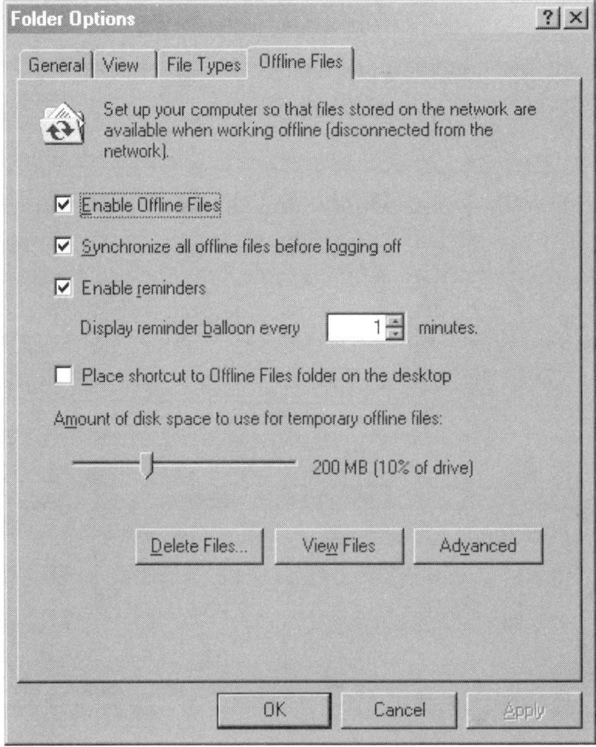

Figure 6-14 Enabled offline files

FAQ 6.130 How can I configure the Time service in Windows 2000?

Windows 2000 Kerberos authentication protocol relies heavily on domain controllers (DCs) having a common time. Therefore, Win2K ships with Windows Time Service (W32Time), which takes a hierarchical approach to assigning time, as the following bulleted items show:

- All client desktops and member servers use their authenticating DCs as the inbound time partner.
- All DCs in a domain use the PDC Flexible Single-Master Operation (FSMO) as the in-bound time partner.
- PDC FSMOs use the domain hierarchy to pick their in-bound time partner.

The PDC FSMO in the root domain becomes the authoritative time source for the enterprise, and you should, therefore, configure the PDC FSMO to gather the time from an external source. Until you complete this task, event log events will state that W32Time isn't configured (see Figure 6-15).

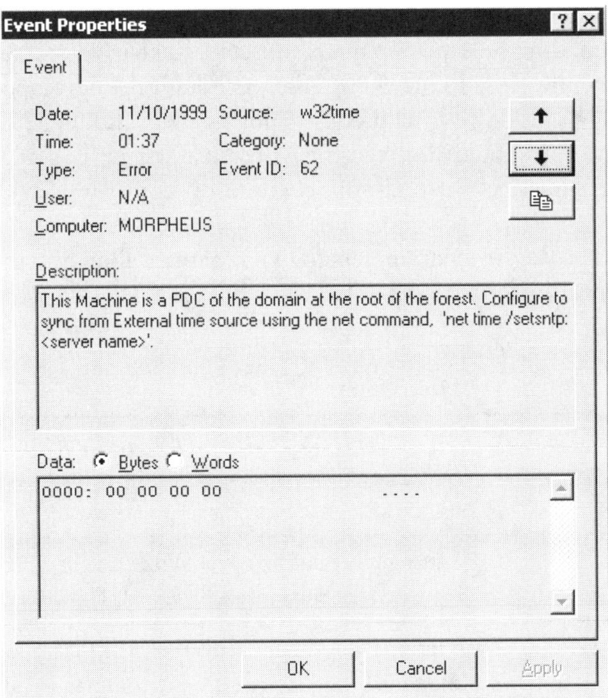

Figure 6-15 Event log when W32Time is not configured

To configure Win2K to use an external time server, use the command

```
net time /setsntp:192.4.41.40
```

You can use several external time servers that are based at the U.S. Naval Observatory, including the following examples:

- ntp2.usno.navy.mil—192.5.41.209
- tick.usno.navy.mil—192.4.41.40
- tock.usno.navy.mil—192.5.41.41

However, don't talk directly to the Navy Network Time Protocol (NTP) servers unless the domain administrator needs to operate a stratum-2 server (and will open it to a large community of users). Domain administrators shouldn't hit directly on tick.usno.navy.mil, tock.usno.navy.mil, or ntp2.usno.navy.mil. Instead, they should use their ISP's NTP server (they should have one), unless they have unusual requirements for precision.

When you perform the /setsntp command, it updates Registry entry HKEY_LOCAL_MACHINE\SYSTEM\CurrentControlSet\Services\W32Time\Parameters\ntpserver. Simple Network Time Protocol (SNTP) uses UDP port 123, so you need to ensure that proxy servers or firewalls don't block this port.

For more information, see ftp://ftp.microsoft.com/ResKit/y2kfix/x86/w32time/w32time.doc to see the W32TIME.DOC file. Although the developers wrote this file for Windows NT 4.0's w32time program, not for Win2K's W32Time, the file is still worth reading. You should also read the Microsoft article "Basic Operation of the Windows Time Service" (http://support.microsoft.com/support/kb/articles/Q224/7/99.ASP).

Some of the other Registry parameters for W32Time follow (my thanks to Matthew Ellis for this information):

Name	Description
LocalNTP (REG_DWORD)	According to W32TIME.DOC, setting this value to 1 (W32Time uses an .INI file and sets the value to Yes) sets up the local machine as an SNTP server.
Log (REG_DWORD)	Setting this value to 1 gets W32Time to write to the System log when the time is synchronized. The default value is 0.
NTPServer (REG_SZ)	This Registry parameter is the (S)NTP server to get the time from. You can use the command **net time /setsntp[:serverlist]** to set the parameter from the

	command line. The file W32TIME.DOC states that BroadcastClient and MulticastClient are reserved names and that you can't use them for NTP servers. However, I don't know what BroadcaseClient and MulticastClient stand for.
Period (REG_SZ)	See W32TIME.DOC and the Microsoft article that I noted previously.
PrimarySource (REG_SZ)	This Registry entry lists the NetBIOS names of all the network Master Time Servers. You must prefix each name with two backslashes (\\) and separate names by semicolons (;).
RandomPrimary (Unknown type, probably a REG_DWORD)	This Registry entry selects a random primary server from the PrimarySource list.
ReliableTimeSource	This value is presumably REG_SZ, with the name of the RTS server.
SecondaryDomain (REG_SZ)	Setting this value tells a secondary machine which domain to broadcast its Time Request to. The W32TIME.DOC file says that if you leave the entry blank, the secondary machine will query its domain for time information. This feature is very helpful in a master or multiple-master domain model in which network administrators don't want to set up each domain with its own Primary Time Server.
TAsync	See W32TIME.DOC for a detailed explanation.
Type (REG_SZ)	NTP/PRIMARY/SECONDARY. See W32TIME.DOC.

FAQ 6.131 How can I configure Administrative alerts in Windows 2000?

Windows 2000 Professional doesn't have a GUI interface that you can use to set Administrative alerts. Instead, you need to manually update the Registry. To do so, complete the following steps:

1. Start REGEDT32.EXE (not REGEDIT.EXE).
2. Move to HKEY_LOCAL_MACHINE\SYSTEM\CurrentControlSet\Services\Alerter\Parameters.

3. Double-click AlertNames.
4. On each line, enter the username or computer that you want to receive the alert.
5. Click OK.
6. Close the Registry editor.

For machines to receive the alerts, their Alerter service must be running. You can use the Control Panel Services applet to start this service, or in Win2K, use the Microsoft Management Console (MMC) Computer Management snap-in and select the Services branch.

Win2K Server still includes a Server Manager (SRVMGR.EXE) version that you can also use to configure alerts. To do so, select a computer, select Properties from the Computer menu, and choose the Alerts button.

FAQ 6.132 How can I tell if my Windows 2000 installation is registered?

When Windows 2000 is registered, it updates Registry key HKEY_LOCAL_MACHINE\SOFTWARE\Microsoft\Windows NT\CurrentVersion\RegDone with registration information. If the Registry value is blank, then your Win2K version isn't registered.

FAQ 6.133 How do I enable Telephony API (TAPI) 2.1 support?

Windows NT 4.0 Service Pack 4 (SP 4) includes an updated Telephony API (TAPI) version. NT 4.0 automatically installs the TAPI files when the OS installs SP4.

To enable the telephony server, perform the following steps:

1. Log on to the server as an administrator.
2. Use User Manager to create or configure a user account with Administrator privileges. This account is the user account in which the Telephony service process (TAPISRV) runs.
3. Open a command prompt window and enter the following command at a command prompt:

```
tcmsetup.exe /s domain\loginID password
```

The domain, loginID, and password refer to the user account that you configured. After you execute this command, you receive a message stating that the server was set up correctly.

4. Shut down your machine and restart the server.

After you install and enable the telephony server, enable the clients as follows:

1. Log on to the client computer as an administrator.
2. Enter the following command at a command prompt:

```
tcmsetup /c RemoteServerName
```

RemoteServerName is the telephony server's computer name.

FAQ 6.134 In what order does the OS process environment variables during logon?

When a user logs on, the system processes variables in the following order:

1. Dynamic variables, such as OS variables
2. System variables defined in System tools in the Control Panel
3. Variables defined in the AUTOEXEC.BAT file
4. Environment variables defined for the current user in System tools in the Control Panel

If a variable is defined several times, the last setting takes precedence.

FAQ 6.135 How can I change the display order for the hardware profile list at startup?

You can edit the Registry to modify the order of hardware profiles on your system. To do so, complete the following steps:

1. Start the Registry editor (REGEDIT.EXE).
2. Move to HKEY_LOCAL_MACHINE\SYSTEM\CurrentControlSet\Control\IDConfigDB\Hardware Profiles.
3. You'll see several subkeys (e.g., 0001, 0002), and each key has a FriendlyName and a PreferenceOrder under the name.

4. Select each subkey and modify the PreferenceOrder, starting from 0 and incrementing by one for each entry.
5. Close the Registry editor.
6. Reboot the computer to see your new order.

Make sure that you don't have any gaps, or you might experience problems.

You can also use the System Control Panel applet's Hardware Profiles tab to change the display order (use the arrows).

FAQ 6.136 How can I change the screen tip for a shortcut?

Windows 2000 introduces tips for shortcuts that the OS displays when you pause the mouse over a shortcut on the desktop or in a Start menu (or anywhere else). See Figure 6-16.

To change the shortcut tip, perform the following steps:

1. Right-click the shortcut.
2. Select Properties.
3. Modify the Comment (see Figure 6-17).
4. Click Apply.

Win2K will now display the new tip.

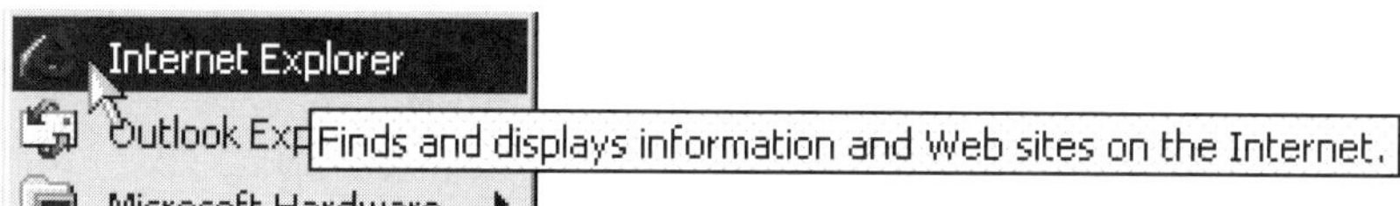

Figure 6-16 Default screen tip for Internet Explorer

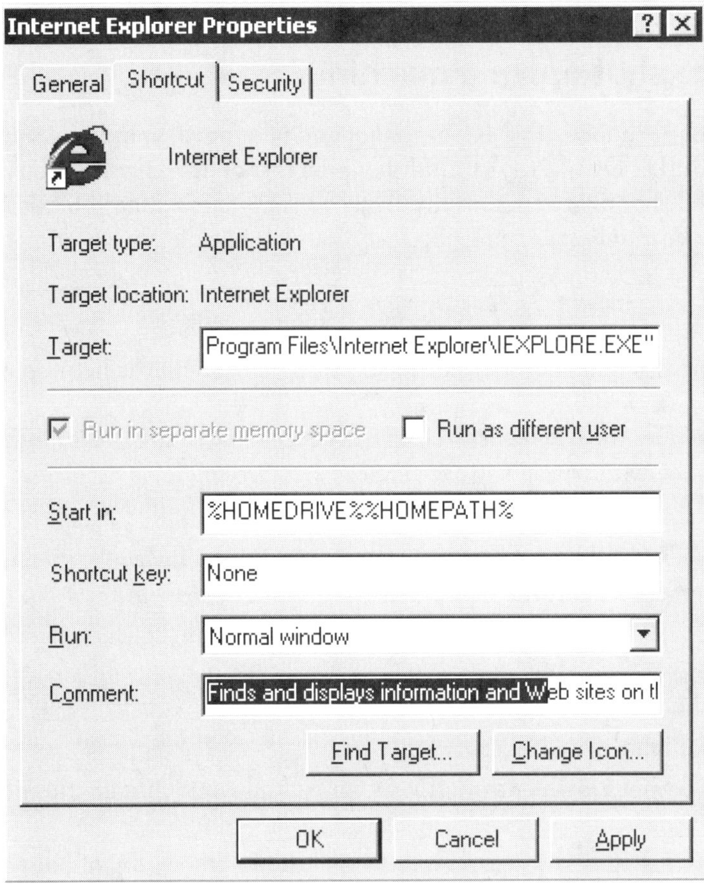

Figure 6-17 Modifying the screen tip for a shortcut

FAQ 6.137 How can I enable network lockout for the Administrator account?

Typically you can't lock out the Administrator account. However, you can use the Microsoft Windows 2000 Resource Kit utility PASSPROP.EXE to lock out the Administrator account via network access and prohibit the possibility of a password brute force attack. However, an administrator can still log on locally at the server. To enable Administrator lockout, enter the following command at a command prompt:

```
passprop /adminlockout
```

FAQ 6.138 How can I remotely log off from, reboot, or shut down a machine?

The Microsoft Windows 2000 Resource Kit and Microsoft Windows NT Resource Kit supply a SHUTDOWN.EXE utility (which is supplied as standard in XP) that you can use to shut down or reboot the local or a remote machine. This utility also lets you configure how to handle hung applications. For example, the command

```
shutdown \\morpheus /r /t:15 "bye bye"
```

reboots (/r) the machine morpheus in 15 seconds (/t:15) with the helpful message "bye bye."

Win2K includes the Microsoft Management Console (MMC) Computer Management snap-in that you typically use to manage services and local users, but you can also use the snap-in to shut down or reboot by completing the following steps:

1. From the Start menu, select Programs > Administrative Tools, then Computer Management to start the Computer Management snap-in.
2. Right-click the root of the tree (Computer Management) and select Properties from the context menu.
3. Select the Advanced tab.
4. Click the Startup and Recovery button.
5. Click the Shut Down button. (Don't worry. You won't shut anything down at this point.)
6. From the dialog box, you can select to shut down, reboot, log off, or power down (if supported). You can also choose how to handle hung applications (see Figure 6-18).
7. Make your selections and click OK.

If you select Log off Current User from a terminal services session, the application logs off the user, not your session, at the console so choose this option with care.

You can use the Computer Management snap-in to attach to other computers. After you connect to the computers, you can perform the same steps as previously described to reboot or shut down.

To connect to a remote machine, perform the following steps:

1. Start the Computer Management snap-in.
2. Right-click the root and select Connect to another computer (see Figure 6-19).
3. Select the computer you wish to connect to and click OK (see Figure 6-20).
4. Select Properties, then the Advanced tab. Click the Startup and Recovery button, then the Shut Down button as before.

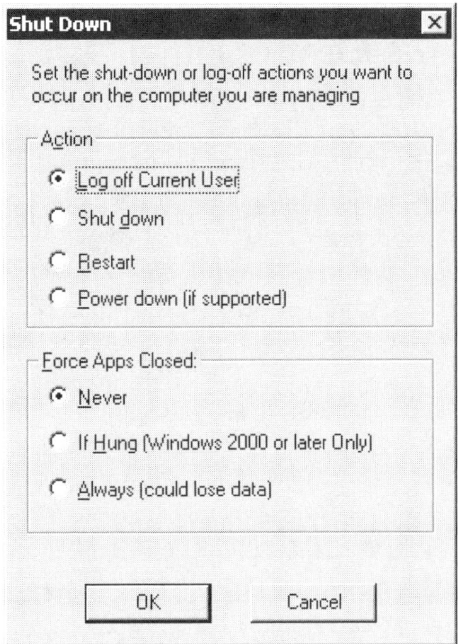

Figure 6-18 Shutdown options for a managed machine

Figure 6-19 Connecting to a remote computer from the Computer Management MMC

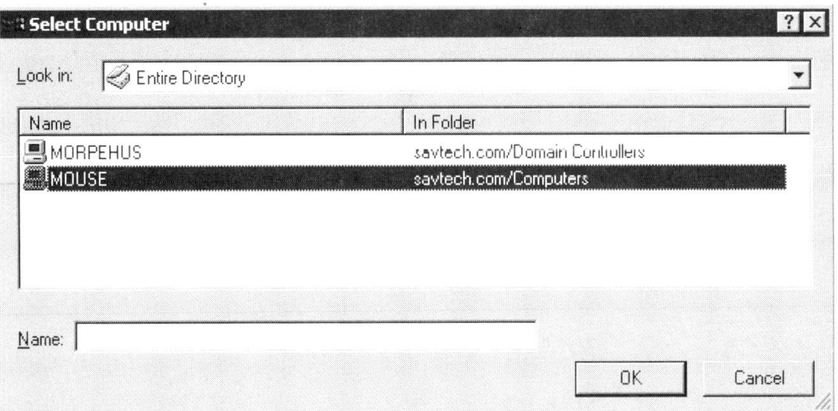

Figure 6-20 Selecting the remote computer

FAQ 6.139 Where is the Control Panel ODBC Data Sources applet in Windows 2000?

Windows 2000 moved many items from their Windows NT 4.0 locations. Although most Control Panel applets were left alone, the ODBC Data Sources applet is an exception. Microsoft removed it as a Control Panel applet in Win2K and now lists it in the Administrative Tools program groups folder. To view the program, from the Start menu, select Programs > Administrative Tools, then Data Sources (ODBC).

You can also call the program directly by running ODBCAD32.EXE. (This method also works in NT 4.0.)

The actual functionality of the utility is unchanged.

FAQ 6.140 How do I view and create saved Directory Service (DS), DNS, and File Replication Service event logs?

You can use the Microsoft Management Console (MMC) Computer Management snap-in to view and archive event logs. To stop your system from grinding to a halt, you need to archive old event logs regularly (or configure the system to loop around, which might result in a loss of important event logs as the system overwrites the oldest information as needed).

Windows 2000 shows the DS and File Replication Service event logs only in Event Viewer on Win2K domain controllers (DCs). The DNS Server event log is available only on DNS servers.

To save an event area and clear the current display, perform the following steps:

1. From the Start menu, select Programs, Administrative Tools, then Computer Management to start the Computer Management snap-in.
2. From the System Tools branch, select Event Viewer.
3. Right-click the selected log (e.g., DNS), and select Clear All Events from the context menu (see Figure 6-21).
4. The program asks you if you want to save the logs first. Answer Yes and select a location. Click Save. The program clears the events from the display.

After you save the log files, you can complete the following steps to open one of these files:

1. From the Computer Management snap-in, right-click the root Event Viewer.
2. Select Open Log File from the context menu.

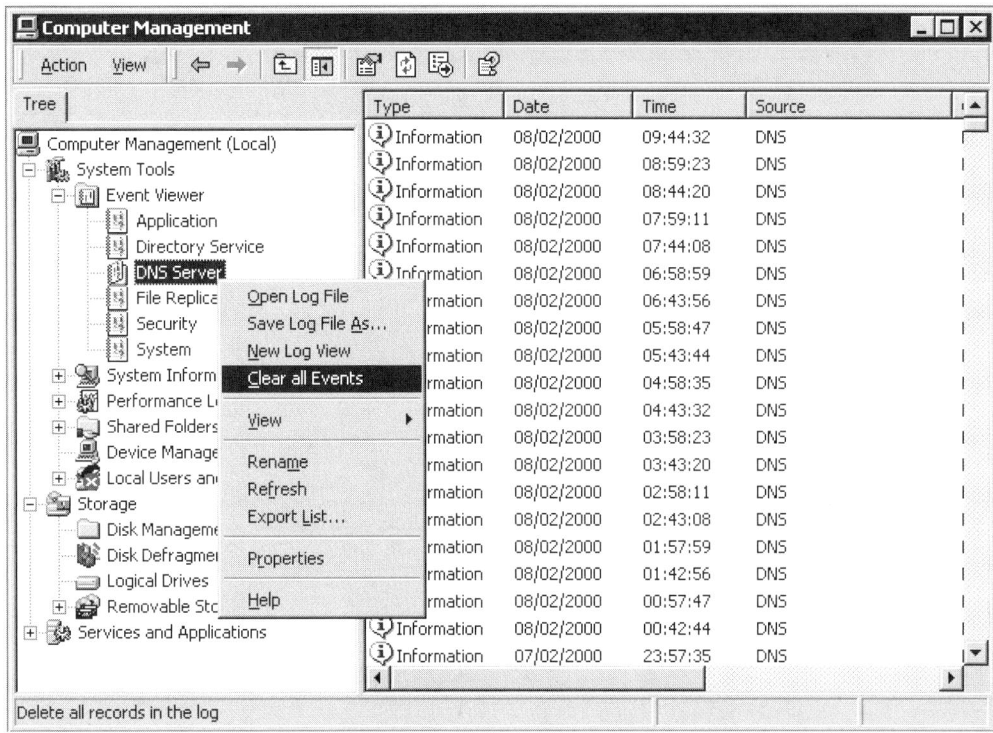

Figure 6-21 Clearing the DNS event log

3. Move to the location of the saved log files and select a file.
4. Select the type of log file (e.g., DNS Server) and enter the name that you want the OS to display the file as (see Figure 6-22).
5. Click Open. You'll see the opened log displayed under the Event Viewer branch beneath any other logs.

When you finish looking at the old data, right-click the Saved DNS Server Log and select Delete from the context menu. The system doesn't delete the actual file, just the view into the file.

Win2K Professional can't read any of the DNS/FRS/DS logs, but Win2K Pro does read the standard application, system, and security logs.

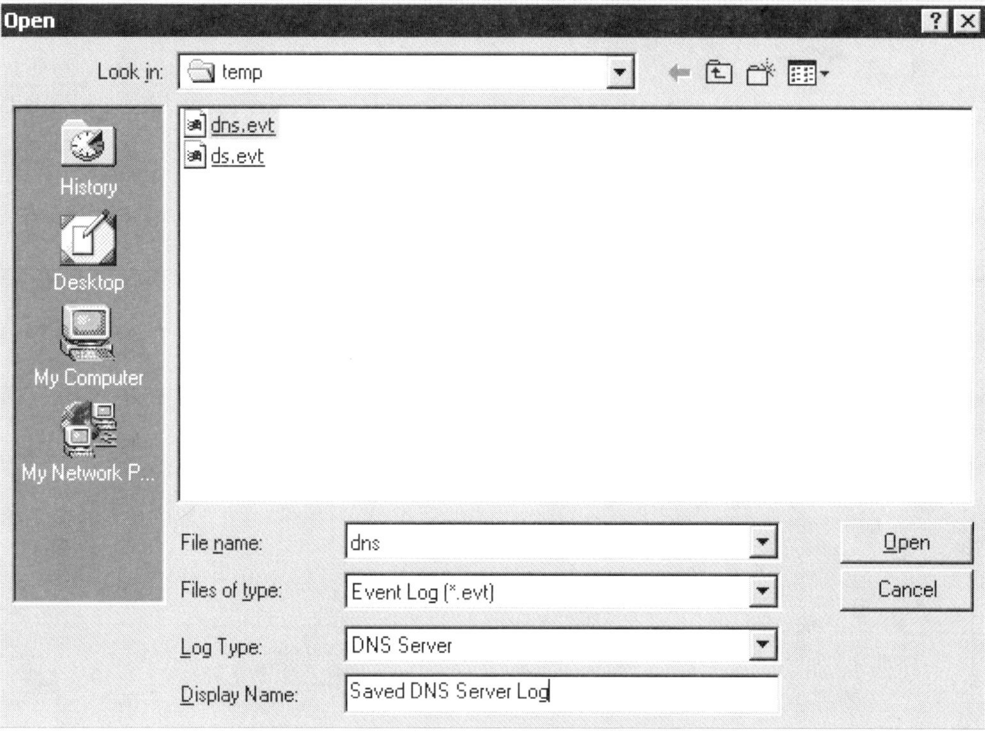

Figure 6-22 Opening a saved event log

6.141 How can I change the icon for drive letters?

Windows 2000 lets you assign a different icon to drive letters. To do so, complete the following steps:

1. Start the Registry editor (REGEDIT.EXE).
2. Move to HKEY_LOCAL_MACHINE\SOFTWARE\Microsoft\Windows\CurrentVersion\Explorer.
3. From the Edit menu, select New > Key. Enter the name **DriveIcons**.
4. Select the new key, select New > Key, then enter the name of the drive (e.g., C).
5. Select the created key, select New > Key, then enter the name **DefaultIcon**.
6. Move to DefaultIcon and double-click the (default) value.

7. Set the default value to the DLL containing the icon and the icon number (e.g., icons.dll,-24 is icon 24 in ICONS.DLL). Click OK.
8. Close the Registry editor.

You can click F5 (refresh) in Windows Explorer to show the new icons (see Figure 6-23).

For example, suppose I created a DLL that contains a C and D icon (ID 24 and 25, respectively) and a Registry file that configures them. To use the Registry file, the ICONS.DLL file would be at the root of C, but you can easily change the Registry file.

```
Windows Registry editor Version 5.00
[HKEY_LOCAL_MACHINE\SOFTWARE\Microsoft\Windows\CurrentVersion\
Explorer\DriveIcons]

[HKEY_LOCAL_MACHINE\SOFTWARE\Microsoft\Windows\CurrentVersion\
Explorer\DriveIcons\C]

[HKEY_LOCAL_MACHINE\SOFTWARE\Microsoft\Windows\CurrentVersion\
Explorer\DriveIcons\C\DefaultIcon]
@="c:\\icons.dll,-24"
```

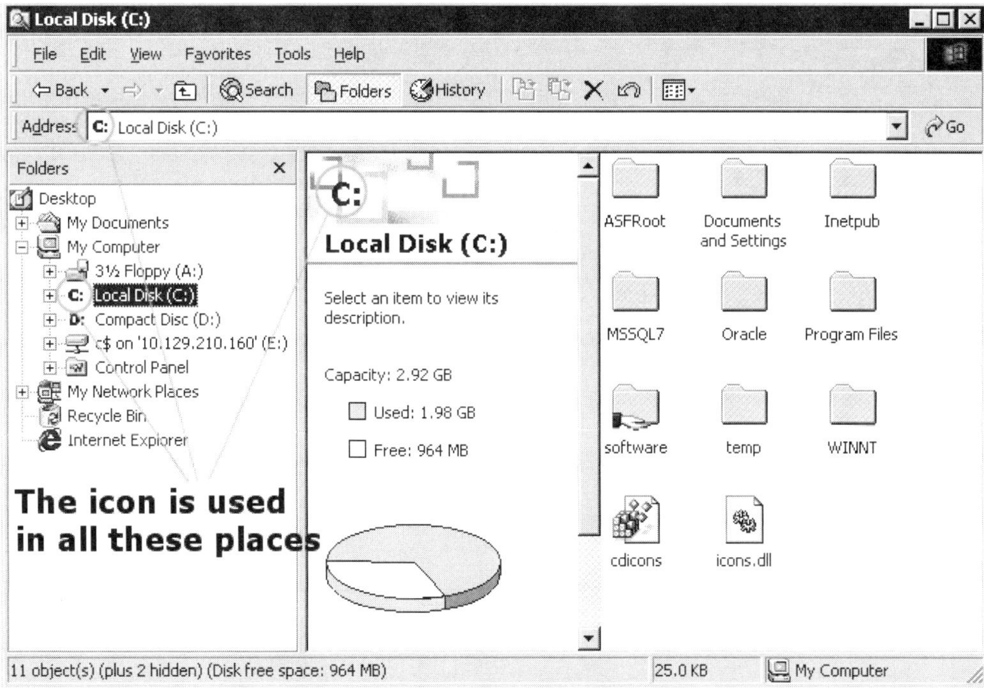

Figure 6-23 Modified drive letter icon

```
[HKEY_LOCAL_MACHINE\SOFTWARE\Microsoft\Windows\CurrentVersion\
Explorer\DriveIcons\D]

[HKEY_LOCAL_MACHINE\SOFTWARE\Microsoft\Windows\CurrentVersion\
Explorer\DriveIcons\D\DefaultIcon]
@="c:\\icons.dll,-25"
```

FAQ 6.142 How can I stop Windows 2000 from displaying the InfoTips for icons and drives?

Windows 2000 has InfoTips for some programs and folders. You can disable this feature in two ways.

The first method is via the GUI. To disable the feature, perform the following steps:

1. Start Windows Explorer.
2. From the Tools menu, select Folder Options.
3. Select the View tab.
4. Clear the checkbox for Show pop-up description for folder and desktop items (see Figure 6-24).
5. Click Apply, then OK.

You can also edit the Registry to disable the InfoTips feature. To do so, complete the following steps:

1. Start the Registry editor.
2. Move to HKEY_CURRENT_USER\Software\Microsoft\Windows\CurrentVersion\Explorer\Advanced.
3. Double-click ShowInfoTip and set the value to 0. Click OK. (You need to create the entry with value type REG_DWORD if it doesn't exist.)
4. Close the Registry editor.

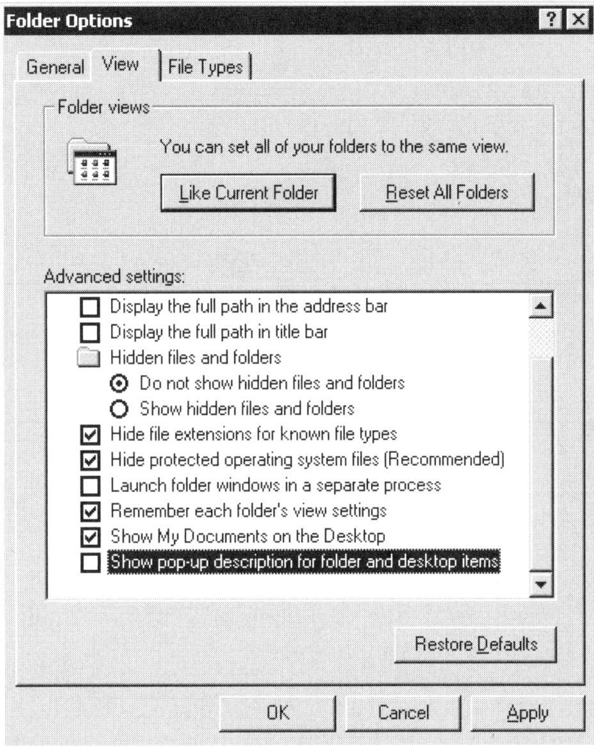

Figure 6-24 Disabling the pop-up description for folder and desktop items

FAQ 6.143 How can I enable the Windows 2000 System File Checker (SFC) to cache all DLLs?

The SFC maintains copies of the DLLs in a cache to protect them from application installation corruption or user removal.

The Windows 2000 Server family caches all protected files (e.g., .SYS, .DLL, .EXE, .TTF, .FON., .OCX) on the Win2K CD-ROM (until you have fewer than 300MB of free disk space). Win2K Professional will cache only 50MBs of DLLs. However, you can complete the following steps to change this amount:

1. Start the Registry editor (REGEDIT.EXE).
2. Move to HKEY_LOCAL_MACHINE\Software\Microsoft\Windows NT\CurrentVersion\Winlogon.

3. Double-click SFCQuota.
4. Set to 0xFFFFFFFF and click OK.
5. Close the Registry editor.
6. Start a command session (CMD.EXE) and run

```
sfc /scannow
```

All system files should now be cached (until you reach 150MB of free disk space, and then the SFC frees up DLL cache). The dllcache folder will reach about 250MB (the size on a server installation).

The SFC.EXE program also has a /cachesize=x option that lets you set cache size from the command line.

The DLL cache is located at \%systemroot%\system32\dllcache.

FAQ 6.144 How can I move the DLL cache?

By default, the DLL cache is stored in \%systemroot%\system32\dllcache. To move the DLL cache, complete the following steps:

1. Start the Registry editor (REGEDT32.EXE **not** REGEDIT.EXE).
2. Move to HKEY_LOCAL_MACHINE\Software\Microsoft\Windows NT\CurrentVersion\Winlogon.
3. From the Edit menu, select Add Value.
4. Set the name to SFCDllCacheDir and the type to REG_EXPAND_SZ. Click OK.
5. Enter the string for the cache's new location (e.g., C:\files\dllcache) and click OK. (The location must be a local path.)
6. Close the Registry editor.
7. Reboot your machine.

FAQ 6.145 How can I disable the Start menu program scroll?

In Windows 2000, the Start menu will scroll the content if more entries exist than can fit in a single column. In Windows NT 4.0, the Start menu uses multiple columns as needed. You can configure Win2K to use NT 4.0's multiple column method. To do so, complete the following steps:

1. Start the Registry editor (REGEDIT.EXE).
2. Move to HKEY_CURRENT_USER\Software\Microsoft\Windows\CurrentVersion\Explorer\Advanced.
3. Double-click StartMenuScrollPrograms, and enter No in the text box.
4. Click OK.
5. Close the Registry editor.
6. Reboot the computer.

You can also perform the following steps to make the change:

1. Select Start > Settings > Taskbar, then Start Menu Programs.
2. Select the Advanced tab.
3. Unselect Scroll the programs menu and click OK.

FAQ 6.146 How can I restrict network browsing to users' local workgroups or domains?

By default, when users browse the network with Windows Explorer or My Network Places (Network Neighborhood), they find many domains or workgroups listed. You can restrict the display to list only computers in the users' local workgroups or domains. To do so, complete the following steps:

1. Start the Registry editor (REGEDIT.EXE).
2. Move to HKEY_CURRENT_USER\Software\Microsoft\Windows\CurrentVersion\Policies\Network (create the key if it doesn't exist).
3. From the Edit menu, select New, then DWORD Value.
4. Enter the name **NoEntireNetwork**, then press Enter.
5. Double-click New Value and set the value to 1. Click OK.
6. Close the Registry editor.
7. Log off and log on again for the change to take effect.

You can also perform this procedure with a Group Policy Object (GPO) by selecting User Configuration > Administrative Templates > Windows Components > Windows Explorer, then No Entire Network in My Network Places.

6.147 How can I stop users from browsing computers in their local workgroups or domains?

To stop users from listing machines in their local workgroups or domains via Windows Explorer or My Network Places (Network Neighborhood), perform the following steps:

1. Start the Registry editor (REGEDIT.EXE).
2. Move to HKEY_CURRENT_USER\Software\Microsoft\Windows\CurrentVersion\Policies\Network (create the key if it doesn't exist).
3. From the Edit menu, select New, then DWORD Value.
4. Enter the name **NoComputersNearMe** and press Enter.
5. Double-click New Value and set the value to 1. Click OK.
6. Close the Registry editor.
7. Log off and log on for the change to take effect.

You can also perform this procedure with a Group Policy Object (GPO) by selecting User Configuration > Administrative Templates > Windows Components > Windows Explorer, then No Computers Near Me in My Network Places.

6.148 How can I hide all desktop icons?

You can perform the following steps to hide all icons, including any shortcuts. This procedure doesn't stop their functionality but only hides them from the desktop.

1. Start the Registry editor (REGEDIT.EXE).
2. Move to HKEY_CURRENT_USER\Software\Microsoft\Windows\CurrentVersion\Policies\Explorer.
3. From the Edit menu, select New, then DWORD Value.
4. Enter the name **NoDesktop** and press Enter.
5. Double-click New Value and set the value to 1. Click OK.
6. Close the Registry editor.
7. Log off and log on again for the change to take effect.

You can also perform this procedure with a Group Policy Object (GPO) by selecting User Configuration > Administrative Templates > Desktop, then Hide all icons on Desktop.

Note that after you enable Hide all icons Desktop, you can't right-click on the desktop to get a context menu.

FAQ 6.149 How do I upgrade my Windows 2000 installation to 128-bit encryption?

The United States relaxed the rules on exporting 128-bit encryption, so now it's generally available (except to certain countries).

If you purchased Windows 2000 in the United States or Canada, you have a floppy disk that came with the package and contains the 128-bit update. If you don't have the disk, you can download the update from http://www.microsoft.com/windows2000/downloads/recommended/encryption/default.asp.

To install 128-bit encryption, complete the following steps:

1. Expand the downloaded ENCPACK_WIN2000ADMIN_EN.EXE.
2. Run the ENCPACK.EXE file (this is the same step that you follow when you use the disk).
3. Click Yes to the confirmation to install.
4. Click Yes to the license.
5. Click Yes to reboot the computer.

After you reboot, you'll be using 128-bit encryption.

FAQ 6.150 How can I use System Monitor to create sequentially numbered performance logs?

Similarly to Windows NT, System Monitor (the Performance Monitor replacement in Windows 2000) can write to a file. System Monitor also lets you create sequentially numbered performance logs when each file reaches a certain size to make the file more manageable. To create sequentially numbered performance logs, complete the following steps:

1. Start System Monitor (PERFMON.EXE).
2. Expand Performance Logs and Alerts.
3. Right-click Counter Logs, then click New Log Settings.
4. Type the name of the appropriate log.
5. On the General tab, click Add to select the counter.

6. Click the object, click the counter you want to monitor, then click Add.
7. On the Log Files tab, type the location of the performance log and the filename.
8. Click to select the End filenames with checkbox, then click nnnnnn. If you click Date, the OS overwrites your log file if it reaches its maximum size in less than 24 hours.
9. Type a starting number for your log in the Start Numbering At section.
10. In the Log File Type section, click Binary File. You can type a comment if appropriate.
11. In the Log File Limit section, click Limit of, then type a reasonable size for your log file (see Figure 6-25).

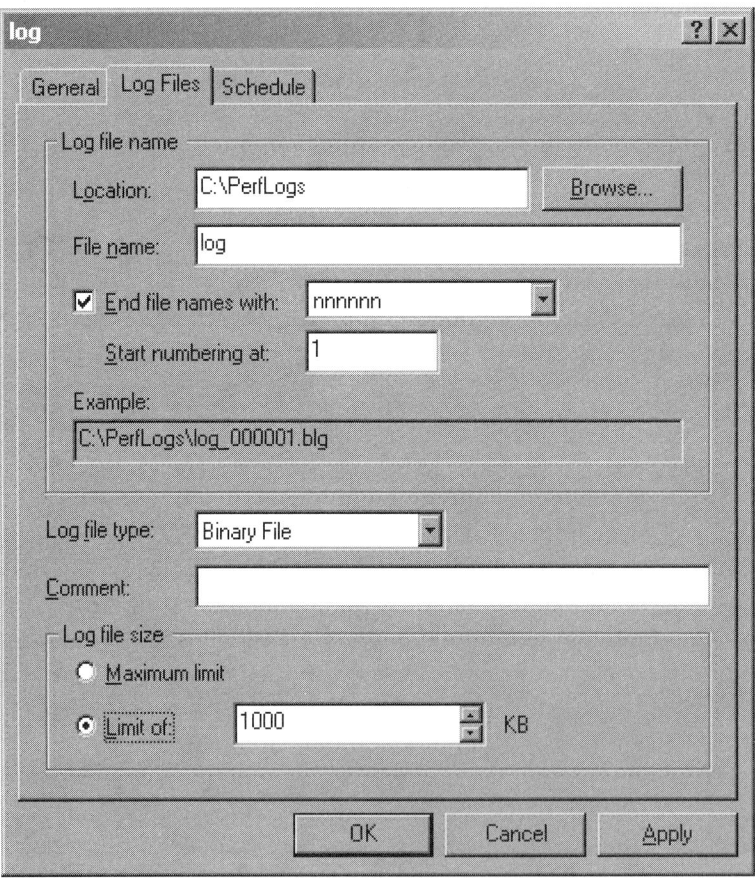

Figure 6-25 Performance log options

12. On the Schedule tab, click When the log file is full in the Stop Log section (the maximum size of the log file should be displayed).
13. Select the Start a new log file checkbox (see Figure 6-26).
14. To start logging, right-click the log name in System Monitor's right pane and click Start (or click the Start button).

System Monitor puts a British GMT date and time onto all counters. Microsoft acknowledges the fault and says that the company will fix the problem in the Win2K release. You can increment the date when it's imported into the database to resolve the problem.

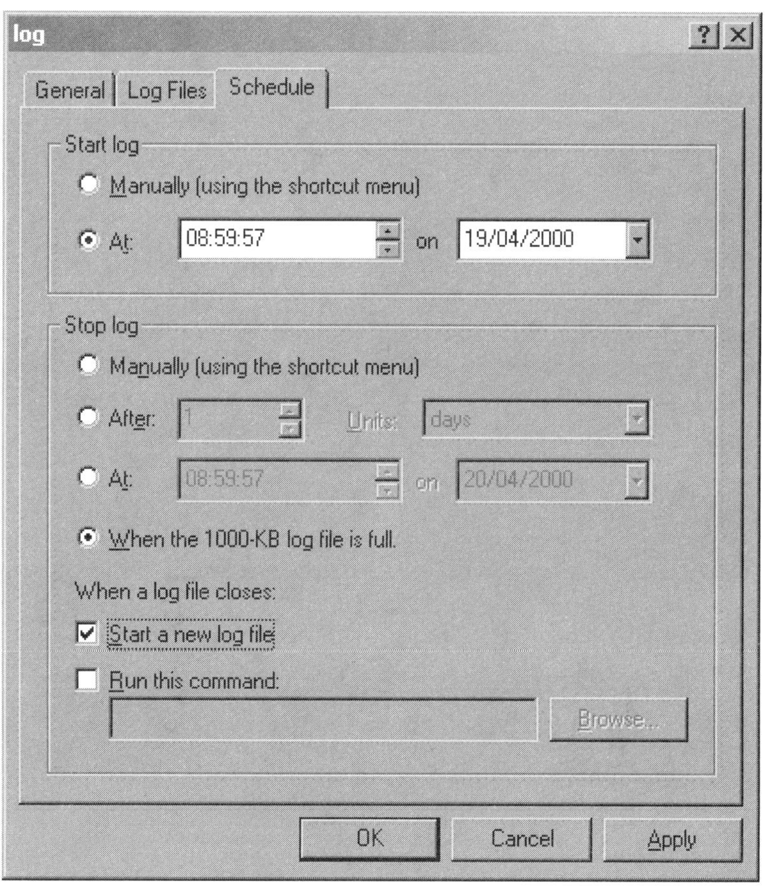

Figure 6-26 Options for starting and stopping the log

FAQ 6.151 How can I find unsigned third-party drivers?

Windows 2000 and above uses a driver-signing process to make sure that drivers are certified to work correctly with Win2K. If you're having problems, you might be using a driver that's not correctly written for Win2K. To identify these drivers, use the signature verification tool.

Microsoft makes the following statement:

> Microsoft is promoting driver signing for designated device classes as a mechanism to advance the quality of drivers, to provide a better user experience, and to reduce support costs for vendors and total cost of ownership for customers. Microsoft began digitally signing drivers for the Microsoft Windows 98 operating system that passed the Windows Hardware Quality Labs (WHQL) tests in 1998, and has been signing drivers for Windows 2000 since the RC3 release.

To use the signature verification tool, perform the following steps:

1. From the Start menu, select Run, then SIGVERIF.EXE.
2. Click Advanced.
3. Select Look for other files that are not digitally signed.
4. For the folder, select \%systemroot%\system32\drivers (see Figure 6-27).

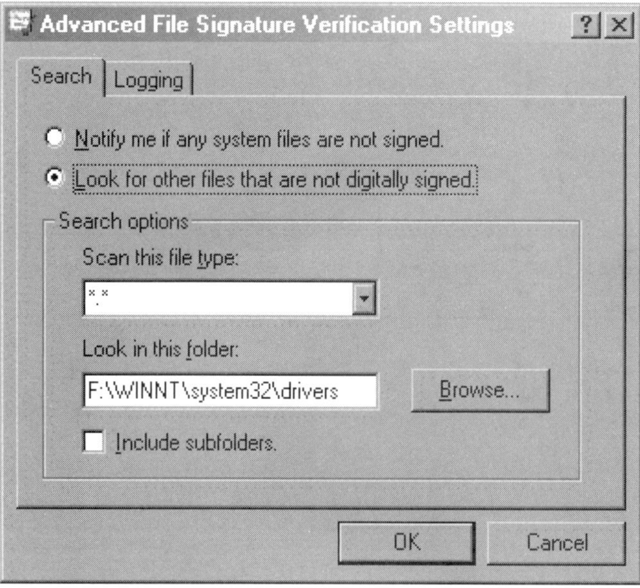

Figure 6-27 Advanced file signature verification settings

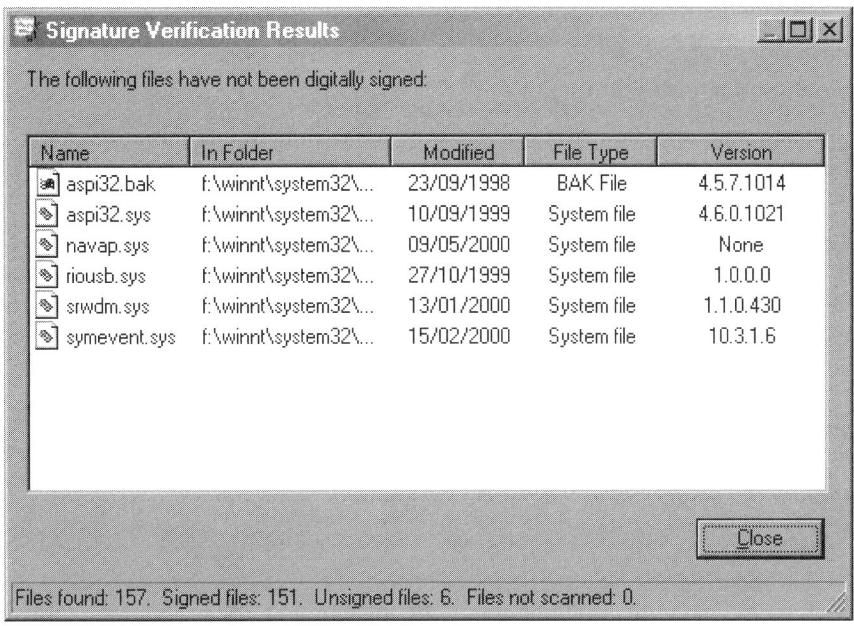

Figure 6-28 List of files that are not digitally signed

5. Under the Logging tab, make sure that logging is enabled.
6. Click OK.
7. Click Start to begin the search. The program will display a list of unsigned drivers, which you can then investigate (see Figure 6-28).

FAQ 6.152 How do I enable folder name completion?

You can set the Registry entry HKEY_CURRENT_USER\Software\Microsoft\Command Processor\CompletionChar to 9 and use the Tab key to enable filename completion. However, you can use another setting to enable path completion (but not filename completion). To do so, complete the following steps:

1. Start the Registry editor (REGEDIT.EXE).
2. Move to HKEY_CURRENT_USER\Software\Microsoft\Command Processor.
3. From the Edit menu, select New, then DWORD Value.
4. Enter the name **PathCompletionChar**.

5. Double-click New Value and set the value to the desired key (4 sets to Ctrl+D).
6. Click OK.
7. Close the Registry editor.

You don't need to restart Windows; just start a new command prompt window (CMD.EXE).

6.153 How do I create a new toolbar?

The QuickLaunch toolbar on the bottom of a screen gives you quick and easy access to your most common programs. However, you can create additional toolbars from any folder, including the Control Panel, Printers, and My Documents folders.

To create a toolbar, drag the folder to a corner of your screen where you want to create the new toolbar (see Figure 6-29).

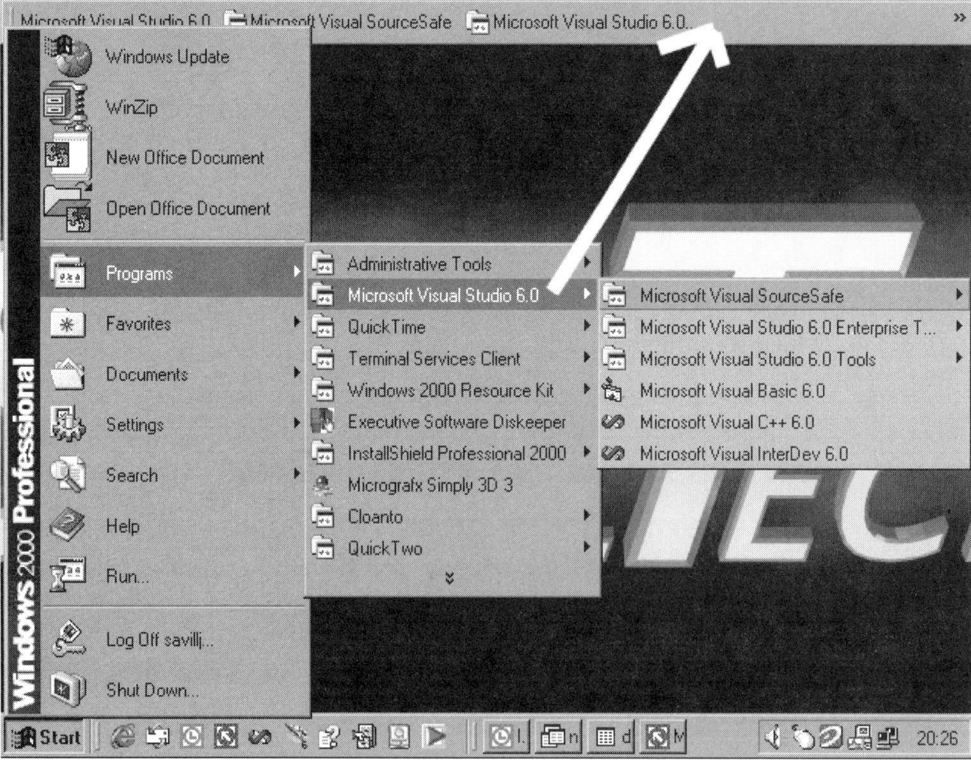

Figure 6-29 Creating a new toolbar

You can then drag the folder to other corners or down to the bottom of the screen and add the folder to the existing taskbar.

To remove the toolbar, right-click it. From the context menu, select Toolbars and clear the checkbox for the selected toolbar to remove it.

To create a new toolbar that's not based on an existing folder onscreen, you can perform the following steps:

1. Right-click the taskbar.
2. Select Toolbars, then New Toolbar.
3. Select a root folder and click New Folder.
4. Give the folder a name and press Enter.
5. Select the new folder and click OK to add it to the taskbar.

FAQ 6.154 Why can't I select the Customize this folder option for folders such as the winnt and winnt\system32 folders?

For most folders, you can select the Customize this folder option from the View menu. However, you don't have this option for the system folders.

The system folders already have hidden DESKTOP.INI files, but you can replace them with another DESKTOP.INI file as follows:

1. Create a new blank folder.
2. From the View menu, select Customize this folder.
3. Set your required preferences.
4. Copy the DESKTOP.INI file from the new folder to the winnt and /winnt/system32 folders (click Yes to overwrite the existing file).

After you complete the preceding steps, you don't need to click Show files every time you access the folder.

FAQ 6.155 How do I disable Secure Desktop?

The March 23, 2000, Microsoft Security Update introduced a security fix that prevents someone who is interactively logged on from performing unauthorized actions (e.g., gaining access to display and input devices that a computer process with higher privileges owns).

For example, if a malicious user can start a process in the computer desktop, which the Winlogon process owns, the new process can record the passwords that users enter when they log on to the computer.

If this security tool causes problems with some of your programs, you can perform the following steps to disable the utility:

1. Start the Registry editor (REGEDIT.EXE).
2. Move to HKEY_LOCAL_MACHINE\SOFTWARE\Microsoft\Windows NT\CurrentVersion\Windows.
3. From the Edit menu, select New, then DWORD Value.
4. Enter **SecureDesktop** and press Enter.
5. Double-click New Value and set the value to 0. Click OK.
6. Close the Registry editor.

FAQ 6.156 How can I add information to Windows 2000's System Properties General tab?

When you receive a PC from a manufacturer, you might see extra lines of description text and a company logo on the Control Panel System applet's General tab. You can change the logo and text.

1. Create a bitmap with the dimensions 172 by 172. Save the picture as OEMLOGO.BMP in the \%systemroot%\system32 folder (e.g., D:\winnt\system32). If the picture is larger than 172 x172, the OS clips the top left corner. If the picture is smaller, the OS adds a black border.
2. Create the file \%systemroot%\system32\oeminfo.ini (e.g., D:\winnt\system32\oeminfo.ini) with the format that Listing 1 shows.

LISTING 1: Format for OEMINFO.INI file

```
[general]
Manufacturer=SavillTech Ltd
Model=SuperDuper 1
SupportURL=http://www.savilltech.com
LocalFile=%windir%\web\savtech\support.htm
[OEMSpecific]
SubModel=Optional line
SerialNo=Optional line
OEM1=Optional private info
```

```
OEM2=More private info
[ICW]
Product=Your Product Name
[Support Information]
Line1=" "
Line2="For support ...."
Line3="
```

Figure 6-30 shows an example of how you can use OEMINFO.INI to customize the System Properties General tab. You don't need to reboot the machine, because the System applet will pick up the files when the applet starts.

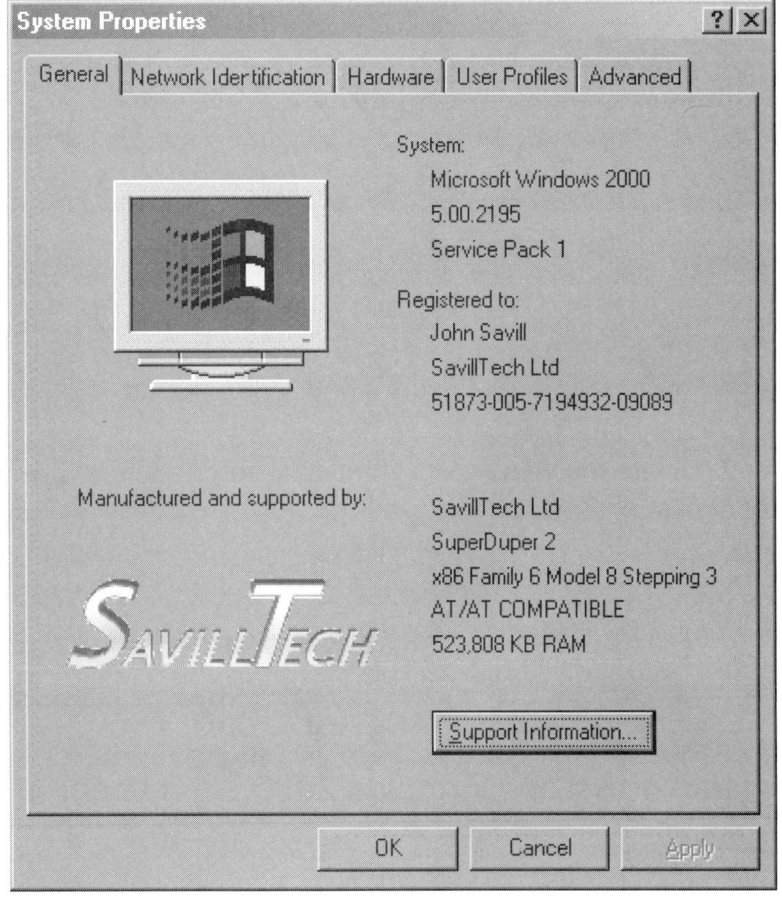

Figure 6-30 Adding information to System Control Panel applet in Windows 2000

6.157 How do I remove the Windows 2000 Service Pack Uninstall folder and Control Panel entry?

If you initially chose the option that would let you uninstall a Win2K service pack but now want to remove the uninstall folder and the Add/Remove Programs entry, perform the following steps:

- Delete the %SystemRoot%\$NtServicePackUninstall$ folder (because this entire folder is compressed, it will be blue if you opted to show encrypted files in a different color).
- Next, you need to delete the Add/Remove Programs entry. You can do this in one of two ways.

Alternative 1: Uninstall service pack:

1. Start Add/Remove Programs (Start > Settings > Control Panel > Add/Remove > Programs).
2. Select Windows 2000 Service Pack 1.
3. Click Change/Remove. You will see the message "An error occurred while trying to remove Windows 2000 Service Pack 1. It may have already been uninstalled. Would you like to remove Windows 2000 Service Pack 1 from the Add/Remove programs list?"
4. Click Yes to remove it.

Alternative 2: Delete the Win2K SP1 Uninstall program entry from the Registry:

1. Start a Registry editor (e.g., REGEDIT.EXE).
2. Go to HKEY_LOCAL_MACHINE\SOFTWARE\Microsoft\Windows\CurrentVersion\Uninstall.
3. Delete the Windows 2000 Service Pack 1 entry.

6.158 How do I stop Windows 2000 from beeping?

Perform the following steps to disable your machine's system beep:

1. Right-click My Computer and select Manage.
2. Expand System Tools and select Device Manager.

3. From the View menu, select Show hidden devices.
4. Expand Non-Plug and Play Drivers.
5. Right-click Beep and select Properties.
6. Select the Drivers tab.
7. Click Stop. You can also change the start-up type to Disabled so the beep service never starts.

FAQ 6.159 How do I switch between single- and double-click?

When you are in Explorer or on your desktop, the traditional way to launch a program is to double-click it. Enhancements in Internet Explorer (IE) allow a Web-like hyperlink approach that lets you move the mouse pointer over an object to select it and click the object once to execute it.

To switch between the traditional double-click model and the single-click Web model, perform the following steps:

1. Start Explorer (Start > Run > EXPLORER.EXE—or press the Win key+E).
2. From the Tools menu, select Folder Options.
3. Select the General tab.
4. In the Click items as follows section, select one of the following:
   - Single-click to open an item (point to select)
   - Double-click to open an item (single-click to select)
5. If you choose the single-click option, you can also choose when the system will underline titles of objects.
6. Click OK.

FAQ 6.160 Where can I get TweakUI for Windows 2000?

The Windows 2000 TweakUI can be downloaded from http://www.microsoft.com/ntworkstation/downloads/default.asp. This version is very similar to older versions, but it has some new Win2K tweaks. This is a new Windows XP version; however, it will not install under Windows 2000.

FAQ 6.161 How do I install ERD Commander 2000?

Winternals Software has released a new version of its Emergency Repair Disk (ERD) software. This new version, ERD Commander 2000, has many great features and great new ways to deploy the utility.

The previous version, ERD Commander Pro, created a set of Windows NT startup disks; however, ERD Commander 2000 lets you create boot disks **or** a bootable CD-ROM **or** install ERD Commander 2000 to the local hard disk (like the Windows 2000 Recovery Console—RC).

To install the new version of the software, simply perform the following steps:

1. Go to the directory to which you downloaded ERD Commander 2000.
2. Double-click e2KSETUP.EXE.
3. Click Next.
4. After reading the license agreement, click Yes.
5. Specify a destination folder and click Next (by default, the destination folder is C:\program files\Winternals\ERD Commander 2000).
6. Click Next to the program folder name, then click Next again.
7. The system will copy files and Registry entries, and the Setup Wizard will start.
8. Click Next when the license agreement appears again.
9. Select the type of installation and click Next.
10. The system will ask for the location of the i386 folder of a Win2K installation (Professional or Server). Specify the appropriate location and click Next.
11. If you have any special SCSI drivers, the system gives you the chance to add them; after you do so, click Next.
12. You can now set a password to access the installation. Set a password (this step is **very** important if you've chosen to install ERD Commander 2000 on the local hard disk, but it is also an option if you are creating a bootable CD-ROM) and click Next.
13. Click Next to create the disks/files.
14. Click Finish.

If you selected to create a bootable CD-ROM, you need to perform a few more steps. You will have a folder with the following items in it:

1. i386 folder (contains the files used for the console)
2. BOOTSECT.BIN (the file you will use as the boot sector for the CD-ROM)
3. CDROM_IS.5 (for Win2K Server) or CDROM_IP.5 (for Win2K Pro)

To create the CD-ROM, start your CD-ROM burner software and specify the following settings:

1. Use ISO 9660 filesystem (not Joliet)
2. Include hidden files
3. Include system files
4. Disable version numbers
5. Set as bootable CD_ROM
6. Set boot sector image to BOOTSECT.BIN
7. Set Media Emulation to Custom
8. Set Load Sector Count to 4
9. Set Load Segment to 07C0 (hex)

If you were using Golden Hawk CDRWIN software, your main screen would look like the one shown in Figure 6-31, and you can click Advanced Options to set the bootable parts.

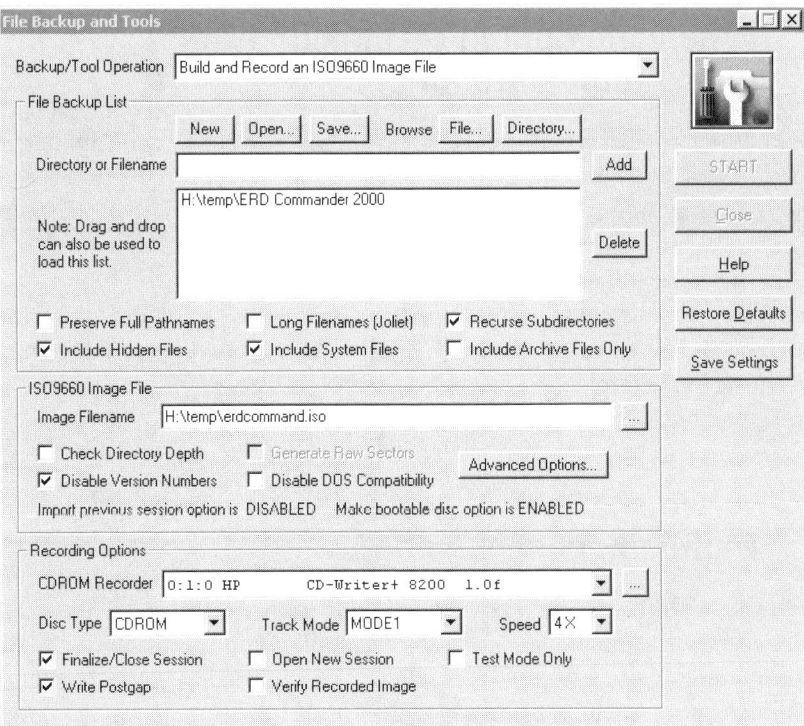

Figure 6-31 Creating the ERD Commander 2000 CD

One really neat feature of the new version is that it takes only **two** steps to change a password.

1. Use the following command to connect to the Registry:

```
Registry
```

2. Use the password command to change the password:

```
password [username] [new password]
```

I highly recommend this new version. The old version saved my neck a number of times, and this new version is even better. You can purchase ERD Commander 2000 for $349. An upgrade to ERD Commander Pro is available for $49. ERD Commander 2000 operates on both NT 4.0 and Win2K. For more information, visit the Winternals Software Web site at http://www.winternals.com/.

FAQ 6.162 Where are the QuickLaunch buttons on my toolbar defined?

The QuickLaunch toolbar, which provides easy access to your favorite applications, appears beside your Start button. Traditionally, you can add shortcuts to the QuickLaunch bar by simply dragging a file onto it and selecting Create shortcut here from the context menu. To remove items, simply right-click the shortcut and select Delete from the context menu.

You can also manually control these shortcuts by adding/removing entries in the C:\Documents and Settings\[user name]\Application Data\Microsoft\Internet Explorer\Quick Launch folder.

FAQ 6.163 What is the Windows 2000 MultiLanguage version?

The Windows 2000 MultiLanguage version is a Win2K Professional, Server, and Advanced Server add-on that lets one Win2K installation display menus and dialog boxes in different languages. This add-on eliminates the need to install language-specific Win2K versions, simplifying a global Win2K roll-out, especially in multi-lingual organizations. The add-on is especially useful on Win2K Server Terminal

Services servers because each remote connection can then use a different set of menus and dialog boxes!

A system running the Win2K MultiLanguage version will look and behave much like the local version except that the following items remain in the "master" language of the system: all 16-bit code, bitmaps, Registry keys and values, folders and filenames, and INF files.

To use the Win2K MultiLanguage version, install Win2K as usual, then perform the following steps:

1. Insert the MultiLanguage File Installation CD-ROM.
2. The file installation should run automatically; if it doesn't, run MUISETUP.EXE on the root of the CD-ROM.
3. Check the languages you want to install (Microsoft will add more languages in the future):
   Chinese (Simplified)
   Chinese (Traditional)
   Dutch
   English
   French
   German
   Italian
   Japanese
   Korean
   Spanish
   Swedish
4. Select the default language for current and new users (see Figure 6-32).
5. Click OK.
6. MUISETUP.EXE will install additional fonts, dictionaries, help files, and DLLs.
7. Click OK in response to the "Installation complete" message.
8. Click Yes to reboot the system. Any problems will be logged to the %systemroot%\muisetup.log file (in the current language).

See FAQ 4.71.

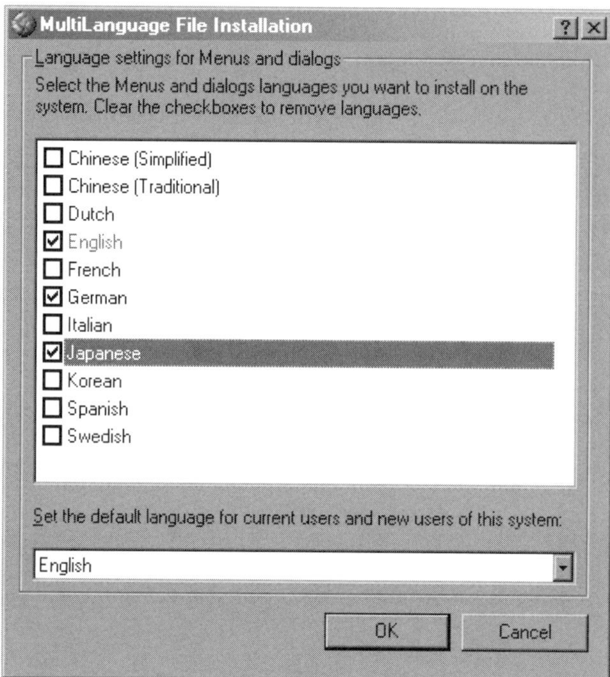

Figure 6-32 Extra languages with the MultiLanguage version of Windows 2000

FAQ 6.164 How do I change the language for the menus and dialog boxes after installing the Windows 2000 MultiLanguage version?

When you install the Windows 2000 MultiLanguage version, a new option appears on the General tab of the Regional Options Control Panel applet. You use this option to modify the language selection.

1. Start the Regional Options Control Panel applet (Start > Settings > Control Panel > Regional Options).
2. Select the General tab.
3. For the Menus and dialogs option, select the appropriate language from the drop-down list (see Figure 6-33).

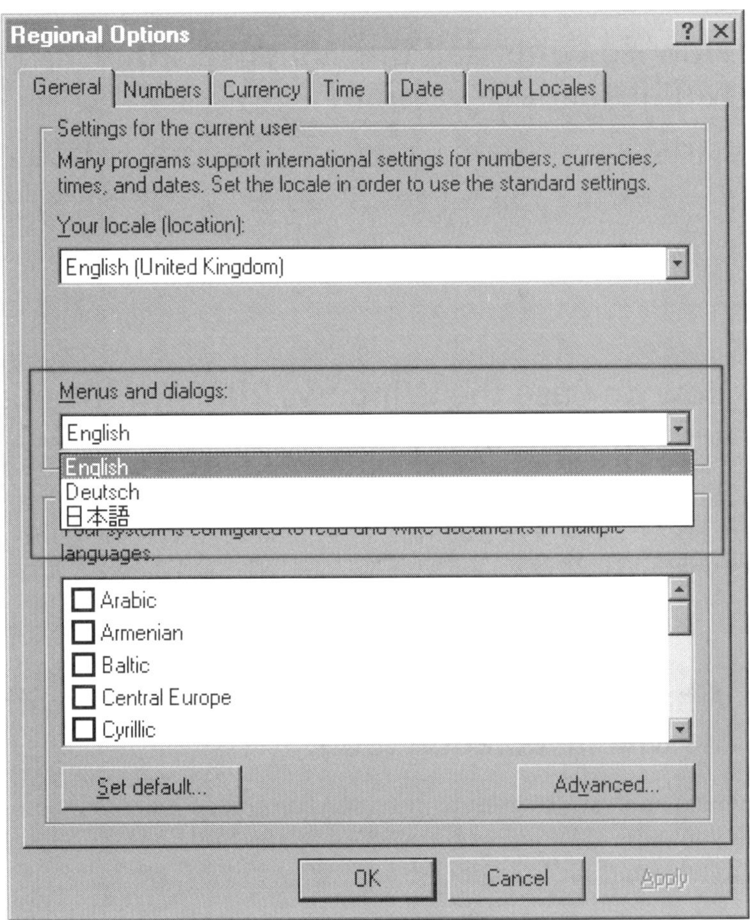

Figure 6-33 Selecting the language for menus and dialogs

4. Click OK.
5. Click No when asked whether the system should make the change for all users on the machine.
6. Log off, then log on for the new language option to take effect.

FAQ 6.165 How do I uninstall the Windows 2000 MultiLanguage version?

The Win2K MultiLanguage version doesn't have an uninstall option. Simply run MUISETUP.EXE and clear the checkboxes for all languages except your default language. When you've finished, you don't need to reboot. The Menus and dialogs option will be removed from the Regional Options Control Panel applet.

FAQ 6.166 How do I use the Windows 2000 MultiLanguage version without the English Win2K CD-ROM?

Currently, you can't use the Windows 2000 MultiLanguage version without the English Win2K CD-ROM. The MultiLanguage module works only with a primary language of English Win2K.

FAQ 6.167 What command-line switches can I use with the MSI installation tool?

From a command line, you can execute the new Microsoft Installer (Microsoft has renamed this application "Windows Installer") with the MSIEXEC.EXE statement, which has several command-line options:

/i	[package]	Installs the specified product
/f	p|o|e|d|c|a|u|m|s|v	p—Reinstalls a product only when a file is missing.
		o—Reinstalls a product when a file is missing or an older version of a file is installed.
		e—Reinstalls a product when a file is missing or an equal or older version of a file is installed.
		d—Reinstalls a product when a file is missing or a different version of a file is installed.
		c—Reinstalls a product when a file is missing or the stored checksum value doesn't match the calculated value.

		a—Forces all files to be reinstalled.
		u—Rewrites all required user-specific Registry entries.
		m—Rewrites all required computer-specific Registry entries.
		s—Overwrites all existing shortcuts.
		v—Runs from the source file and recaches the local product.
/a	[package]	Installs a product on the network.
/x	[package]	Uninstalls a product.
/j u|m	[package]	Advertises a product (u is current user; m is all users).
/l	i|w|e|a|r|u|c|m|p|v|+|!|* [log file]	Specifies the log file and the options you can use.
		i—Displays status messages.
		w—Displays nonfatal warnings.
		e—Displays all error messages.
		a—Action startups.
		r—Action-specific records.
		u—User requests.
		c—Initial user interface (UI) parameters.
		m—Out-of-memory.
		p—Terminal properties.
		v—Verbose output.
		+—Appends to the existing file.
		!—Clears each line in the log file.
		*—Wildcard. Logs all information, but the use of the v option isn't included. To include the v option, type **/l*v**.
/p	[patch]	Applies a patch. To patch an installed Administrator image, you should also use the /a switch (i.e., msiexec /p [patch] /a [package]).

(*continued*)

/	n/b/r/f	Sets the user interface (UI) level.
		n—No UI.
		b—Basic UI.
		r—Reduced UI.
		f—Full UI.
/y		Calls system API DLLRegisterServer to register the module—e.g., msiexec /y savill.dll.
/z		Calls system API DLLRegisterServer to unregister a module—e.g., msiexec /z savill.dll.

FAQ 6.168 How do I enable verbose boot, shutdown, logon, and logoff messages?

Windows 2000 provides the option of verbose event messages. You usually enable them through a Group Policy:

1. Open a policy in Group Policy editor (GPE).
2. Expand Computer Configuration > Administrative Tools > System.
3. Double-click verbose vs normal status messages (see Figure 6-34).
4. Set this option to Enabled or Disabled.
5. Click OK.
6. Close GPE.

You can also set this option via the Registry editor as long as no policy will override it (i.e., all policies applied to the machine must be set to "not configured").

1. Start REGEDIT.EXE.
2. Go to HKEY_LOCAL_MACHINE\SOFTWARE\Microsoft\Windows\CurrentVersion\policies\system.
3. From the Edit menu, select New > DWORD Value.
4. Enter a name of **VerboseStatus** and press Enter.
5. Double-click the new value and set it to 1 to enable verbose mode (set it to 0 for normal mode). Click OK.
6. Close REGEDIT.EXE.

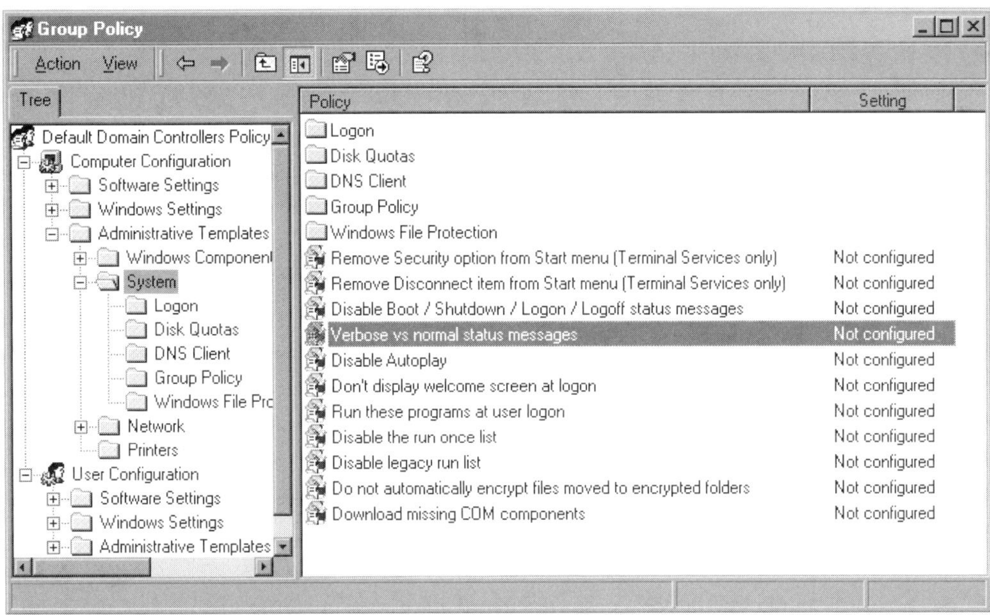

Figure 6-34 Status message options via policy

FAQ 6.169 How can I stop Windows Explorer from changing the case of my filenames?

By default, Explorer changes the case of your filenames so that a file you name c:\iLikeTOTypeTHiS appears as c:\Iliketotypethis. Microsoft calls this "PrettyPath," and you can disable it by performing the following steps:

1. Start REGEDIT.EXE.
2. Go to HKEY_CURRENT_USER\SOFTWARE\Microsoft\Windows\CurrentVersion\Explorer\Advanced.
3. Double-click DontPrettyPath (or create this key with a type of REG_DWORD if it doesn't exist).
4. Set the value to 1 to keep the case as you type it or 0 to adjust the case as Explorer requires.
5. Click OK.
6. Close Regedit.
7. Restart the machine.

FAQ 6.170 How can I stop Single Instance Storage (SIS) from parsing a certain folder?

When you install Microsoft Remote Installation Services (RIS), the SIS engine is installed. SIS is designed to cut down on wasted disk space by removing duplicate files. The problem is the SIS Groveler works on the entire volume, not just the RIS folders. To exclude folders on the SIS Common Store volume, perform the following steps:

1. Using Notepad, open GROVELER.INI from the SIS Common Store folder.
2. For each folder you want to exclude, add a line under [Excluded Paths] that has the following format:

   ```
   "A name to identify the folder" = \FolderName
   ```

   (Don't type the quotation marks.)

To exclude a folder on all volumes, perform the following steps:

1. Start REGEDIT.EXE.
2. Go to HKEY_LOCAL_MACHINE\SOFTWARE\Microsoft\Windows NT\CurrentVersion\Groveler\ExcludedPaths.
3. For each folder that you want to exclude, select New > String value from the Edit menu.
4. Enter a name to identify the folder and press Enter.
5. Double-click the new value and set it to the folder name.
6. When you finish adding values, use the following statements to stop and restart the Groveler service:

   ```
   net stop groveler
   net start groveler
   ```

FAQ 6.171 Why doesn't my new mail notification sound play?

If you've configured a sound to play when a new email message arrives and that sound doesn't play even after you've used the Control Panel Sound applet to confirm that it is correctly configured, you can configure the sound via the Registry:

1. Start REGEDIT.EXE.
2. Go to HKEY_CURRENT_USER\AppEvents\Schemes\Apps\.Default\MailBeep\.current.
3. Double-click (Default) and set its value to the WAV file to play.
4. Click OK.
5. Close Regedit.
6. Restart the machine.

FAQ 6.172 Can I disable the Microsoft Office copy clipboard dialog box?

In Microsoft Office 2000, when you copy multiple text blocks, the application brings up a dialog box with all the Clipboard data it knows about. This behavior can be very annoying. To disable this dialog box, perform the following steps:

1. Start REGEDIT.EXE.
2. Go to HKEY_CURRENT_USER\SOFTWARE\Microsoft\Office\9.0\Common\General.
3. From the Edit menu, select New > DWORD Value.
4. Enter a name of **AcbControl** and press Enter.
5. Double-click the new value and set it to 1 (0 will turn the dialog box back on).
6. Close Regedit.
7. Restart your Office applications.

You can still access the copy clipboard manually via the Clipboard toolbar (View > Toolbars > Clipboard).

FAQ 6.173 How can I prevent Microsoft Office 2000 Help from resizing my application window?

When you press F1 for Help, the system reduces the width of the current application window to make room for the Help text that appears. If you don't want this to happen, perform the following steps:

1. Start REGEDIT.EXE.
2. Go to HKEY_CURRENT_USER\SOFTWARE\Microsoft\Office\9.0\Common\HelpViewer.

3. Double-click the IsFloating value and set it to 1 (if this value doesn't exist, create a new value of type DWORD).
4. Close Regedit.
5. Restart your Office applications.

6.174 How can I configure my system so that the OS version displays on the desktop?

In beta versions of Windows, the system displays the version in the bottom-right corner. To enable this display on final versions of Windows, perform the following steps:

1. Start REGEDIT.EXE.
2. Go to HKEY_CURRENT_USER\Control Panel\Desktop.
3. Double-click PaintDesktopVersion (or create a new value of type DWORD if it doesn't exist).
4. Set PaintDesktopVersion to 1. Click OK.
5. Close Regedit.
6. Log off and then log on for the change to take effect.

If you are using Active Desktop, the system won't display the OS and build number. However if you aren't using Active Desktop, you will see text similar to the following:

```
Windows 2000 Professional
Build 2195
```

6.175 How can I disable the Show Files dialog box for system folders?

In FAQ 8.37, I describe how to modify the appearance of certain folders. You can use the same approach to remove the dialog box that warns you every time you try to view the contents of a folder that contains system files (e.g., winnt, system32). Perform the following steps:

1. Start Windows Explorer.
2. Go to the folder in question (e.g., c:\winnt).
3. Open FOLDER.HTT (this is a hidden file, so you might need to modify your options to see hidden files—Tools > Folder Options > View > Show hidden files

and folders). (Ensure that you have a backup copy of FOLDER.HTT in case you modify something incorrectly.)

4. Locate the occurrences of

```
if (gShowFiles)
```

and replace them with

```
if(true)
```

5. Save the updated FOLDER.HTT.

FAQ 6.176 How can I disable Win key+U?

Pressing the Windows key with U starts the Utility Manager, which provides a number of useful aids (e.g., the Narrator, magnifier, on-screen keyboard) for people who have poor vision. To disable this shortcut, perform the following steps:

1. Start the Microsoft Management Console (MMC) Services snap-in (Start > Programs > Administrative Tools > Services).
2. Right-click Utility Manager and select Properties.
3. Set the Start-up type to Disabled and click Apply. Then click OK.

To reenable the shortcut, simply perform the preceding steps, setting the Start-up type to Manual.

Note that disabling the Utility Manager service affects all users of the machine and may prevent users with physical and/or sensory disabilities from logging on. It's recommended that this tip be used only on the reader's personal machine and not deployed on a wide scale.

FAQ 6.177 How can I stop users from connecting to Windows Update?

Windows Update is a great resource for getting the latest fixes; however, you probably want to control change roll-outs, so it's a good idea to stop users from connecting directly to Windows Update. You can do so via a Group Policy:

1. Start the Microsoft Management Console (MMC) Active Directory Users and Computers snap-in (Start > Programs > Administrative Tools > Active Directory Users and Computers).

2. Right-click the container of the users (a site/domain or organizational unit—OU) and select Properties.
3. Go to the Group Policy tab.
4. Select the policy and click Edit.
5. Expand User Configuration > Administrative Templates > Start Menu & Taskbar.
6. Double-click Disable and remove links to Windows Update.
7. Set this policy to Enabled and click OK (see Figure 6-35).
8. Close all windows.

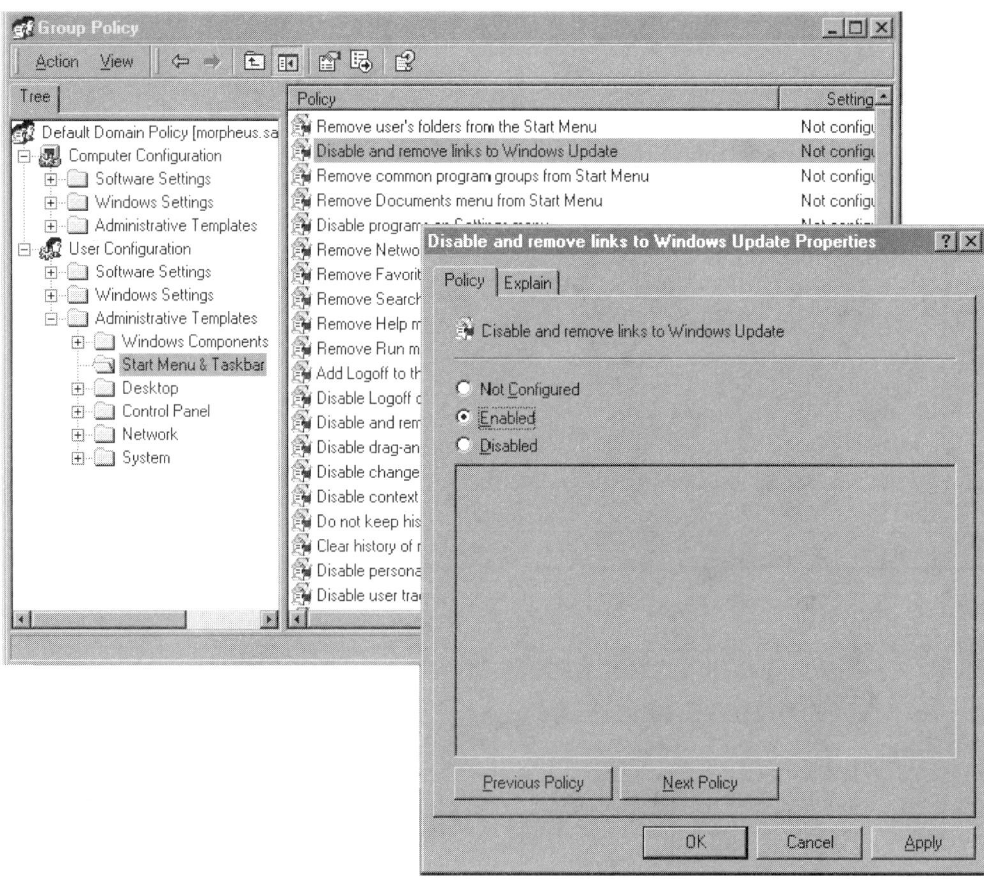

Figure 6-35 Remove Windows Update links via policy

FAQ 6.178 How can I increase the time that services have to shut down?

By default, the OS allows services 20 seconds to stop before it forcefully halts them. For services that have a large amount of information in memory (e.g., Internet Security and Acceleration—ISA—Server 2000), 20 seconds might not be enough time. To increase the time the system allows, perform the following steps:

1. Start REGEDIT.EXE.
2. Go to HKEY_LOCAL_MACHINE\SYSTEM\CurrentControlSet\Control.
3. Double-click WaitToKillServiceTimeout.
4. Set this value to the desired wait time in milliseconds—60000 is one minute.
5. Click OK.
6. Close Regedit.
7. Reboot the machine.

Note that this value applies to **all** services, so setting it to a longer interval might slow your computer's shut down: If a service doesn't shut down correctly, it will have a longer time before the OS halts it.

FAQ 6.179 How do I disable opportunist locking?

Windows XP and Windows 2000 support opportunist locking, which lets Server Message Block (SMB) clients lock a file on the server and cache the information, without having to worry whether another user might change the file (earlier Windows versions also support this feature, but the method is different). Opportunist locking leads to better performance for the user. However, it adds a workload to the server, which must maintain and manage the locks. You can use one of two methods to disable opportunist locking.

Method 1

1. Start REGEDIT.EXE.
2. Go to HKEY_LOCAL_MACHINE\SYSTEM\CurrentControlSet\Services\MRxSmb\Parameters.
3. From the Edit menu, select New > DWORD Value.
4. Enter a name of **OplocksDisabled** and press Enter.

5. Double-click the new value and set it to 1.
6. Click OK.

Method 2

1. Start REGEDIT.EXE.
2. Go to HKEY_LOCAL_MACHINE\SYSTEM\CurrentControlSet\Services\lanmanserver\parameters.
3. From the Edit menu, select New > DWORD Value.
4. Enter a name of **EnableOplocks** and press Enter.
5. Double-click the new value and set it to 0.
6. Click OK.

In addition, under the HKEY_LOCAL_MACHINE\SYSTEM\CurrentControlSet\Services\lanmanserver\parameters, you can set the following optional parameters to tune opportunist locking:

- MinLinkThroughput (DWORD)—The minimum number of bytes per second that must be maintained through the server before the lock is disabled (0 to infinite)
- MaxLinkDelay (DWORD)—The maximum time allowed for a delay in the link before the lock is disabled (0 to 100,000 seconds)
- OplockBreakWait (DWORD)—The time the server waits for a client holding a lock to respond to a lock break request before forcefully breaking the lock (10 to 180 seconds)

FAQ 6.180 How do I use Msconfig to modify BOOT.INI?

The Windows XP utility Msconfig is useful for configuring various OS elements:

- Startup type (e.g., which drivers are loaded, whether system.ini/win.ini are parsed)
- Which parts of system.ini are used
- Which parts of WIN.INI are used
- Which commands run at startup
- Which services start
- BOOT.INI

With the BOOT.INI option, you can check the current entries, specify additional options, and configure the timeout.

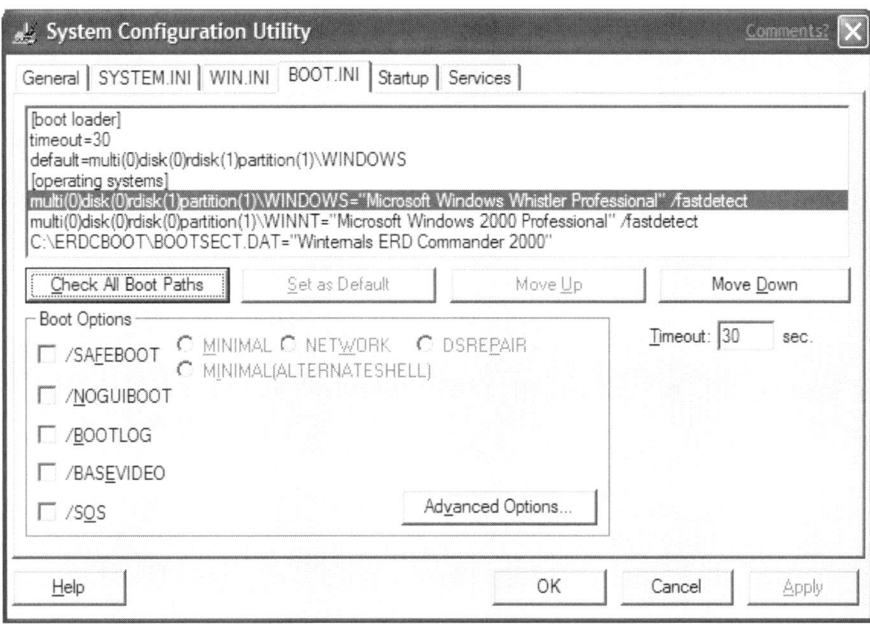

Figure 6-36 Configuring boot options via the system configuration utility

1. Start Msconfig (Start > Run > MSCONFIG.EXE).
2. Select the BOOT.INI tab.
3. The dialog box displays the current OSs (see Figure 6-36).
4. Click Check All Boot Paths to go through all the entries and ensure that they relate to a true installation.
5. If you select an actual installation, you can then set the various boot options, such as basevideo and SOS.
6. Once finished, click OK.

FAQ 6.181 What is the Shutdown Event Tracker?

Windows XP introduces the Shutdown Event Tracker, which is an optional task that, when enabled, lets the user who stops and reboots a box enter an option for the stop (e.g., a hardware modification) and a comment (you have to enter a comment). See Figure 6-37.

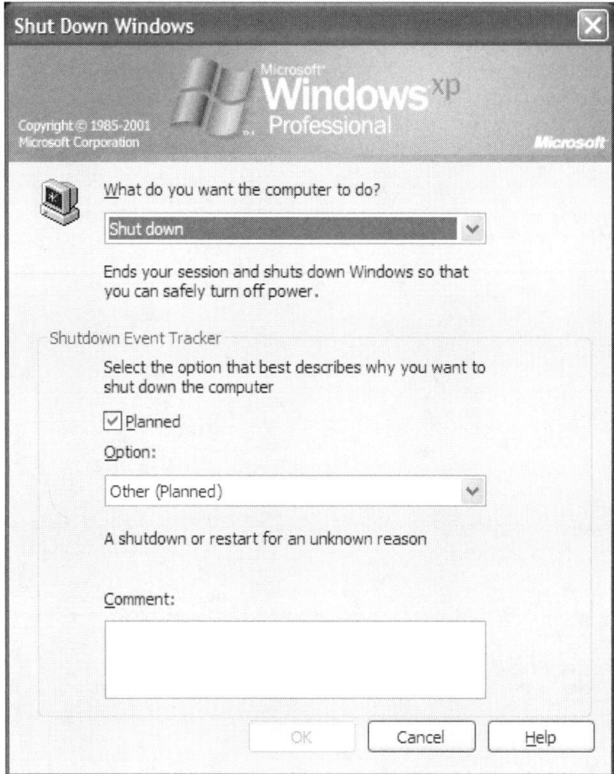

Figure 6-37 Enhanced logging for shutdowns

Also, if the system stops for an unknown reason, the next time the computer starts, it prompts the Administrator to enter a comment for the cause of the unexpected shutdown. These events are then written to the System event log (event ID 1075), which you can use to better log the reasons behind system actions.

This component is included with XP Professional, .NET Server, and .NET Enterprise Server, but—by default—it is disabled on XP Pro.

FAQ 6.182 How do I enable/disable the Shutdown Event Tracker?

To control the use of the Shutdown Event Tracker, perform the following steps:

1. Start REGEDIT.EXE.
2. Go to HKEY_LOCAL_MACHINE\SOFTWARE\Microsoft\Windows\CurrentVersion\Reliability.
3. Double-click ShutdownReasonUI and set it to 1 to enable or 0 to disable.
4. Click OK.
5. Close Regedit.

You don't need to reboot for this change to take effect.

FAQ 6.183 How do I enter a shutdown description from the command line?

In Windows XP, the new version of SHUTDOWN.EXE (the tool used to shutdown/reboot from the command line) contains support for tracker descriptions via the -d (description/reason code) and-c (comment) attributes. For example, the following shuts down the system in 10 seconds, with a description of "user-defined," "planned," "major reason 125," "minor reason 1," and a comment of "Testing":

```
shutdown -t 10 -d up:125:1 -c "Testing"
```

FAQ 6.184 How do I add my own Shutdown Event Tracker shutdown reasons?

Previously we looked at using the Shutdown Event Tracker for shutdowns. Although the tracker includes several built-in events, you might want to add your own events. To do so, perform the following steps:

1. Start REGEDIT.EXE.
2. Go to HKEY_LOCAL_MACHINE\SOFTWARE\Microsoft\Windows\CurrentVersion\Reliability\UserDefined.
3. From the Edit menu, select New > Multi-String value.

4. Set the name in the following format:
   - P—The shutdown is planned.
   - C or B—A comment is required.
   - S—The reason should be displayed in the user-initiated shutdown box.
   - D—The reason should be displayed in the sudden shutdown box (you must specify either S or D).
5. Define a major reason number and a minor reason number. For example, PCS;5;5 means a planned, comment required, user-initiated shutdown with a major reason of 5 and a minor reason of 5.
6. Double-click the new value and enter two lines. The first line is the title (up to 64 characters), and the second line is the description (up to 96 characters). See Figure 6-38.

```
Baby needs changing
Baby has soiled self and must begin de-stinking procedure.
```

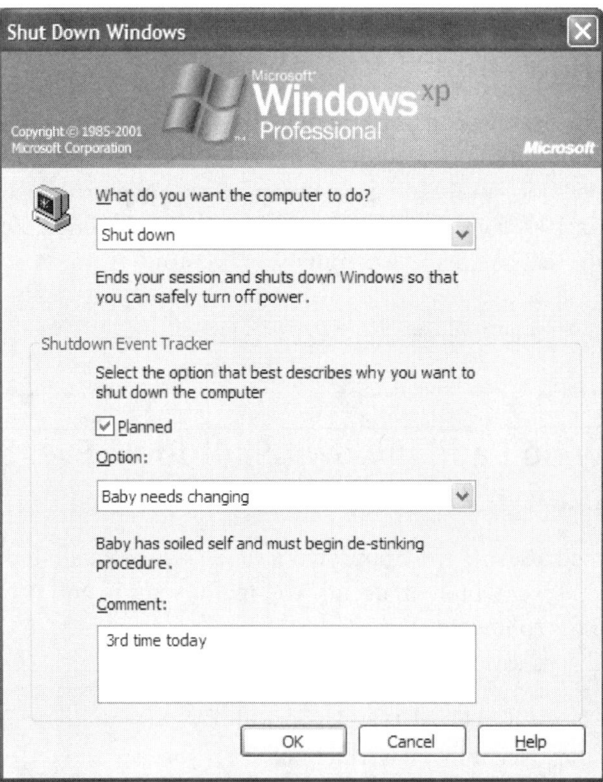

Figure 6-38 Our own reasons for having to stop the machine!

7. Click OK.
8. Close Regedit.

Note that because we specified C, a comment is required before the user can click OK.

FAQ 6.185 Can I make the Shutdown Event Tracker display only my options?

If you have at least one working user-defined reason, you can prevent the system from displaying the default ones by performing the following steps:

1. Start REGEDIT.EXE.
2. Go to HKEY_LOCAL_MACHINE\SOFTWARE\Microsoft\Windows\CurrentVersion\Reliability.
3. From the Edit menu, select New > DWORD Value.
4. Enter a name of **ShutdownIgnorePredefinedReasons** and press Enter.
5. Double-click the new value and set it to 1.
6. Click OK.

The system will no longer display the default reasons. To get the default reasons back, either set ShutdownIgnorePredefinedReasons to 0 or delete this value.

FAQ 6.186 How can I change the port that a service uses?

Changing the port that a service uses depends heavily on the service. For example, you can set HTTP's port with the Internet Service Manager (ISM).

As a general rule, you can change the port by changing the %systemroot%\system32\drivers\etc\services file with a text editor (e.g., Notepad). For example, to change the port SNMP uses, open the file and modify the following lines:

```
snmp 161/udp #SNMP

snmptrap 162/udp snmp-trap #SNMP trap
```

Change 161 and 162 to the ports you want to use and save the file. You must restart the computer for the change to take effect.

6.187 How do I disable NTFS tracking of broken shortcuts?

If a shortcut to a file breaks, Windows XP and Windows 2000 automatically attempt to locate the shortcut destination by searching all paths associated with the shortcut. If you want to prevent this behavior, perform the following steps:

1. Start REGEDIT.EXE.
2. Go to HKEY_CURRENT_USER\Software\Microsoft\Windows\CurrentVersion\Policies\Explorer.
3. From the Edit menu, select New > DWORD Value.
4. Enter a name of **NoResolveTrack** and press Enter.
5. Double-click the new value and set it to 1.
6. Click OK.

You can also prevent this behavior at a Group Policy level by selecting Do not use the tracking-based method when resolving shell shortcuts in the User Configuration\AdministrativeTemplates\Start Menu & Taskbar Group Policy branch.

6.188 How can I change a program's run mode from its Start menu shortcut?

When you run a program, it opens in one of three modes:

- Normal—The program appears on the desktop, and you can resize it.
- Minimized—The program appears on the taskbar but not on the desktop.
- Maximized—The program occupies the entire desktop.

While the program is running, you change how it runs by clicking one of the buttons in the top-right corner next to the X. You can also configure the program on the shortcut menu to control how the program starts. Perform the following steps:

1. Click Start > Programs, and right-click the shortcut of the program whose run behavior you want to modify.
2. Select Properties from the context menu.
3. Select the Shortcut tab.
4. From the Run drop-down box, select Normal, Minimized, or Maximized (see Figure 6-39).
5. Click OK.

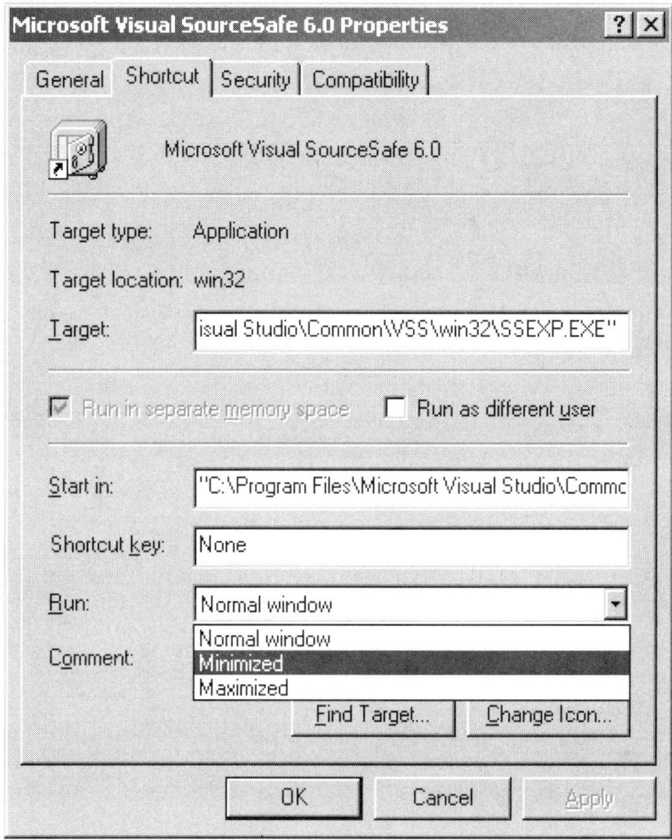

Figure 6-39 Options for running applications in minimized form

FAQ 6.189 How do I modify the Windows 2000 boot/system drive letter?

Microsoft doesn't recommend ever changing the Win2K boot/system drive; however, if an automatic cause, such as a mirror break, changes the drive, you can modify the drive letter as follows (perform a **full** system backup before you try this approach)—in this example, we swap drives C and D.

1. Log on as an Administrator.
2. Start REGEDT32.EXE.
3. Go to HKEY_LOCAL_MACHINE\SYSTEM\MountedDevices.
4. Click MountedDevices.

5. On the Security menu, click Permissions. Ensure that Administrators have full control (change this setting back to its original value when you finish these steps).
6. Quit Regedt32 and start REGEDIT.EXE (you **must** use Regedit to perform the next steps).
7. Go to HKEY_LOCAL_MACHINE\SYSTEM\MountedDevices.
8. Find the first drive letter you want to change to a new drive letter. In this example, we look for \DosDevices\C.
9. Right-click \DosDevices\C: and click Rename.
10. Rename this value to an unused drive letter (e.g., \DosDevices\Z:) to free up drive letter C to use later.
11. Find the second drive letter you want to change. In this example, we look for \DosDevices\D:.
12. Right-click \DosDevices\D: and click Rename.
13. Rename this value to the appropriate new drive letter—in this example, \DosDevices\C:.
14. Right-click the value for \DosDevices\Z:, click Rename, and name it \DosDevices\D:.
15. Quit Regedit and, if you changed the Administrators permissions setting, restart Regedt32.
16. Change the Administrators permissions setting back to the original setting.
17. Restart the computer.

FAQ 6.190 Each time I try to modify my Startup and Recovery settings on the System Properties Advanced tab, why do I receive a message asking me to enter a value between 0 and 999 seconds?

When you access the Startup and Recovery settings on the System Properties Advanced tab, you might receive the message shown in Figure 6-40.

You receive this message because your BOOT.INI file contains a -1 for the timeout value. BOOT.INI contains the startup information for your machine, including the amount of time it waits for user input before selecting the default. If you set this value to -1, the system waits forever.

```
[boot loader]
timeout=-1
```

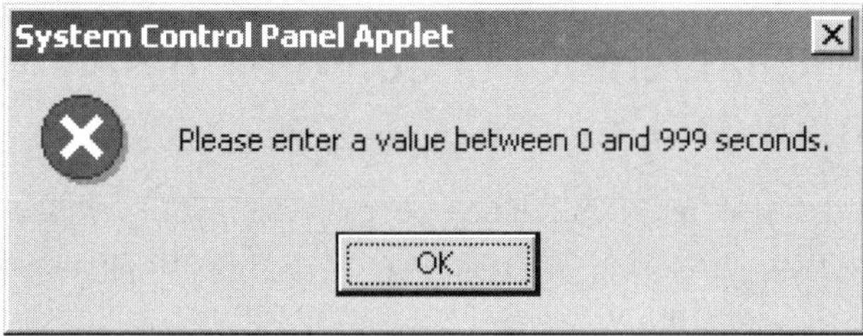

Figure 6-40 Invalid startup and recovery time

Unfortunately, the Control Panel System applet doesn't support a -1 timeout value. When you try to access the properties via the GUI, you receive the error message, and the system sets the default to 30. If you want to keep -1 as the timeout value, you need to edit the BOOT.INI file after you make any other changes. Remember that BOOT.INI is a system, hidden, read-only file, so you need to use the following command to remove these settings before you can edit it:

```
attrib c:\boot.ini -s -h -r
```

FAQ 6.191 How can I uninstall hidden Windows components?

When you start the Add/Remove Programs Control Panel applet and select Add/Remove Windows components, the system doesn't display all of the components because Windows doesn't want them uninstalled. However, you can change which components the system displays. Perform the following steps:

1. Open the SYSOC.INF file located in the %systemroot%\inf folder.
2. Go to the [Components] section.
3. Locate the entry you want to make uninstallable and remove the word "hide." For example, for MSN Messenger Service, change the line

   ```
   msmsgs=ocgen.dll,OcEntry,msmsgs.inf,hide,7
   ```

   to

   ```
   msmsgs=ocgen.dll,OcEntry,msmsgs.inf,,7
   ```

4. Save the SYSOC.INF file.

FAQ 6.192 How can I remove or edit the Comments text in Windows XP?

XP adds the "Comments?" text to all dialog boxes. When you click Comments?, the system opens a dialog box that lets you communicate with Microsoft. However, this text can be distracting and, in some cases, causes problems with the minimize, maximize, and shutdown buttons.

You can remove the Comments? link or change its text. Perform the following steps:

1. Start REGEDIT.EXE.
2. Go to HKEY_CURRENT_USER\Control Panel\Desktop.
3. Set LameButtonEnabled to 0 to disable the text (8—enabled—is the default). Or, if you don't want to disable the text, leave LameButtonEnabled set to 8 and set LameButtonText to the string you want the system to display.
4. Close Regedit.
5. Log off and then log back on for the change to take effect.

FAQ 6.193 How can I remove the view of other people's documents in Windows Explorer?

New to Windows XP is the view of other people's documents folders in Windows Explorer when you view the root of My Computer under the Other Files Stored on This Computer section. To remove this section, perform the following steps:

1. Start REGEDIT.EXE.
2. Go to HKEY_LOCAL_MACHINE\SOFTWARE\Microsoft\Windows\CurrentVersion\Explorer\MyComputer\NameSpace\DelegateFolders.
3. Delete the subkey {59031a47-3f72-44a7-89c5-5595fe6b30ee}.
4. Close Regedit.
5. Restart Explorer.

Note that this change affects all of the machine's users because you modify this setting at a machine, not user, level.

FAQ 6.194 How do I run Windows Explorer as an Administrator when I'm logged on as a different user?

The impersonation service, Runas, is a nice Windows 2000 and XP feature. But Runas can't run Windows Explorer impersonated because in Win2K, new Windows Explorer windows are spawned as threads of the main EXPLORER.EXE invocation. You can circumvent this behavior in the following way:

1. Select Start > Run and type

   ```
   runas /user:administrator "\"c:\program files\internet
   explorer\iexplore\" c:\\"
   ```

2. Click OK.
3. When the system prompts you, enter your Administrator password.

This command executes Windows Explorer in the desired context; adding a local path makes Windows Explorer emulate the default (i.e., no Windows Explorer bars or buttons).

FAQ 6.195 How can I disable Windows Update?

Windows Update is a great tool for updating your computers; however, if you want to control the deployment of fixes, you might want to disable Windows Update. To disable it at a Group Policy level, perform the following steps:

1. Start Group Policy editor (GPE) and load the desired Group Policy Object (GPO).
2. Expand User Configuration > Administrative Templates > Start Menu and Taskbar.
3. Double-click Disable and Remove Links to Windows Update (Windows 2000) or Remove links and access to Windows Update (Windows XP).
4. Select Enabled and click OK.
5. Close GPE.

You can also edit the Registry to disable Windows Update on a per user basis:

1. Start REGEDIT.EXE on the machine where you want to disable Windows Update.

2. Go to HKEY_CURRENT_USER\Software\Microsoft\Windows\CurrentVersion\Policies\Explorer.
3. From the Edit menu, select New > DWORD Value.
4. Enter a name of **NoWindowsUpdate** and press Enter.
5. Double-click NoWindowsUpdate and set it to 1.
6. Close Regedit.

You don't need to reboot. If the user tries to start Windows Update, the system will display the following error message:

```
Windows Update was disabled by your system Administrator.
```

FAQ 6.196 How can I add a boot option that starts with the alternate shell?

Under the Registry key HKEY_LOCAL_MACHINE\SYSTEM\CurrentControlSet\Control\SafeBoot is the value AlternateShell, which is set to CMD.EXE (the command prompt). When you press F8 during startup and select Safe Mode with Command Prompt, the system uses this alternate shell. You shouldn't change the AlternateShell value. You can, however, create a boot option so that you don't have to press F8, then select Safe Mode with Command Prompt.

1. Edit the BOOT.INI (c:\boot.ini) file attributes to make the file nonread-only, nonsystem, and nonhidden (**attrib c:\boot.ini -r -s -h**).
2. Open BOOT.INI.
3. Add a line similar to the following:

```
multi(0)disk(0)rdisk(0)partition(1)\WINDOWS="Microsoft Windows XP
Professional" /fastdetect /SAFEBOOT:MINIMAL(ALTERNATESHELL)
```

4. Save the file.
5. Reapply the correct permissions (attrib c:\boot.ini +r +s +h).

FAQ 6.197 How can I create a pagefile larger than 4GB on one volume?

The largest pagefile that you can create on one volume is 4GB, but you can edit the Registry to create multiple pagefiles in separate folders on one volume.

1. Open a Registry editor (Regedit for Windows XP; Regedt32 for Windows 2000 or earlier).
2. Go to the HKEY_LOCAL_MACHINE\SYSTEM\CurrentControlSet\Control\Session Manager\Memory Management Registry subkey.
3. Double-click PagingFiles. The entry will appear as in the following example:

   ```
   g:\pagefile.sys 380 480
   ```

   The entry shows the pagefile's location, name, initial size, and maximum size.
4. To create multiple pagefiles on one volume, specify the names of the desired number of folders on the volume. For example, to create three pagefiles on volume G, enter

   ```
   g:\pagefile1\pagefile.sys 3000 4000
   g:\pagefile2\pagefile.sys 3000 4000
   g:\pagefile3\pagefile.sys 3000 4000
   ```

5. Click OK.
6. Close the Registry editor.
7. Reboot the machine.

FAQ 6.198 How do I execute .EXE files without typing the extension?

Your computer knows the common extensions via the pathext environment variable. To view the extensions, go to a command prompt and type:

```
set pathext
```

When you type in this environment variable, you'll see a list of extensions that your computer recognizes, similar to the following:

```
PATHEXT=.COM;.EXE;.BAT;.CMD;.VBS;.VBE;.JS;.JSE;.WSF;.WSH
```

If your list doesn't look like this example, go to the command prompt and type:

```
set pathext=.COM;.EXE;.BAT;.CMD;.VBS;.VBE;.JS;.JSE;.WSF;.WSH
```

You can also set this variable for all users on your machine by editing the Registry:

1. Start the Registry editor (REGEDIT.EXE).
2. Go to HKEY_LOCAL_MACHINE\SYSTEM\CurrentControlSet\Control\Session Manager\Environment.
3. Double-click PATHEXT.
4. Modify the entry as required (ensure .EXE is present) and click OK.
5. Close the Registry editor.

You can also add new file extensions here so that you can execute those file types without having to type in the file extension.

FAQ 6.199 Where is the JVM in Windows XP?

Because of Microsoft's ongoing problems with Sun Microsystems over Java and Microsoft's new C# language, Microsoft is moving away from Java. As a result, the Microsoft Java Virtual Machine (JVM) is available only as a Web download. To obtain the latest 32-bit edition of the Microsoft JVM, go to Microsoft's Java site at http://www.microsoft.com/java or the Windows Update site. If you don't already have a JVM on your system and you visit a Web site running a Java applet, Internet Explorer (IE) will automatically ask whether you want to install the Microsoft JVM. To see an example of this functionality, go to my http://www.savilltech.com/spaceboulders/spaceBoulders.html.

FAQ 6.200 How do I enable and disable Windows XP's System Restore feature?

System Restore (i.e., RESTOREPT.API) is a new Windows XP feature that's similar to last known configuration. However, System Restore maintains multiple restore points instead of one last restore point. The user can manually create restore points, or System Restore can keep restore points during the following operations:

- Installing new software, if the application uses a current installer that is System Restore-compliant
- Using AutoUpdate
- During a restore operation
- During a Microsoft backup or recovery operation
- Installing an unsigned driver
- Automatically following 24 hours of inactivity

By default, System Restore monitors all partitions. So, for example, if you delete an executable file, you can have the system state revert to a specific restore point to recreate or repair the executable file. When you revert to a restore point, however, you lose all changes since that point, except for changes to files in the My Documents folder and documents you've created with applications such as Microsoft Word and Microsoft Excel.

If you use System Restore and don't like the new system state, you can undo the process and restore the machine to the system state it had before you ran System Restore. Alternatively, you can run System Restore to change the system state to a different restore point.

To enable or disable System Restore, perform the following steps:

1. Start the System Control Panel applet (go to Start > Settings > Control Panel > System).
2. Select the System Restore tab.
3. Clear the Turn off System Restore on all drives checkbox to enable System Restore or select this checkbox to disable System Restore (see Figure 6-41).
4. Click OK.

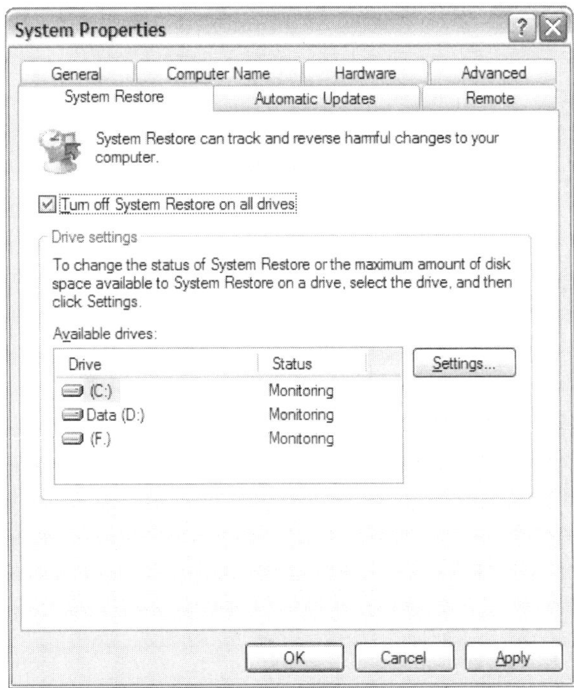

Figure 6-41 System Restore enabled

You can also click the Settings button to set a maximum amount of space that you want each drive to use for restore information. If the drive you select isn't the system drive, you can also disable System Restore on a per-drive basis. The maximum amount of space that you can use for restore information is 12% per drive.

An alternative to the usual method of enabling and disabling Windows XP's System Restore feature is to use the Registry. To use this alternative, perform the following steps:

1. Start the Registry editor (REGEDIT.EXE).
2. Go to HKEY_LOCAL_MACHINE\SOFTWARE\Microsoft\Windows NT\CurrentVersion\SystemRestore.
3. If a DisableSR value doesn't exist, go to the Edit menu, select New > DWORD Value, and create the value.
4. Set the value to 1 to disable System Restore or 0 to enable System Restore.
5. Go to HKEY_LOCAL_MACHINE\SYSTEM\CurrentControlSet\Services\sr to prevent the System Restore service from starting.
6. Double-click Start and set the value to 4 to stop the service from starting or to 0 for normal startup.
7. Close the Registry editor.

FAQ 6.201 How can I determine whether I've activated my Windows XP machine?

Go to Accessories and select System Tools. If you see an Activate icon, you haven't activated the OS. Alternatively, you can review the System Summary branch of System Information by running MSINFO32.EXE from the command prompt; if you don't see any information about activation status, then you've activated your system.

You can also use Win Info (version 2.4 or higher) from http://www.savilltech.com/wininfo.html to obtain the status of local and remote machines. Win Info tells you whether you've activated XP, and if you haven't, how much time is left before you must activate the system.

FAQ 6.202 Why do I receive error messages from various Microsoft Management Console (MMC) snap-ins?

If you're having problems with the Active Directory (AD) snap-ins (e.g., Users and Computers, Sites and Services) and have the Dr. Watson log, a missing Registry value might be causing the problem.

1. Start the Registry editor (REGEDIT.EXE).
2. Go to HKEY_CLASSES_ROOT\LDAP\Clsid.
3. If the key doesn't exist, you need to create it. Paste the following statements into a file (FIX.REG):

```
[HKEY_CLASSES_ROOT\LDAP\Clsid]
@="{228D9A81-C302-11cf-9AA4-00AA004A5691}"
```

4. Save the file, then double-click it to create the value and resolve many AD-related MMC problems.
5. Close REGEDIT.EXE.

If this approach doesn't resolve your problems, confirm that your version of ACTIVEDS.TLB (in the %systemroot%\system32 folder) is at least version 5.0.2143.1 (right-click ACTIVEDS.TLB and select Properties, then select the Version tab). If your version of ACTIVEDS.TLB is earlier than 5.0.2143.1, replace it with the latest version from a service pack.

FAQ 6.203 Why do I receive an error when joining a node to a Windows 2000 cluster?

If you've used the user principal name (UPN) format (e.g., username@domain.com) to enter the account that the Microsoft Cluster service is using on the first node, the second node can't validate the account properly and will return an error. To fix this problem, change the Cluster service account on the first node to use the pre-Win2K username (e.g., Domain\Username), then restart the service.

FAQ 6.204 How do I disable Windows XP's low-disk-check taskbar warning?

XP monitors the amount of available disk space and displays a warning in the taskbar when the hard disk is almost full. To disable this feature, perform the following steps:

1. Start the Registry editor (REGEDIT.EXE).
2. Navigate to HKEY_CURRENT_USER\Software\Microsoft\Windows\CurrentVersion\Policies\Explorer.
3. Go to the Edit menu and select New > DWORD Value.
4. Enter a name of **NoLowDiskSpaceChecks** and press Enter.
5. Double-click the new value, set it to 1, and click OK.
6. Close the Registry editor.
7. Log off and log on for the change to take effect.

You can also use Microsoft's TweakUI utility (version 1.9) to disable the low-disk-check feature. Access the utility from the taskbar and clear the Warn when low on disk space setting.

FAQ 6.205 How can I modify the title of the Windows Security dialog box in Windows XP and Windows 2000?

The dialog box, which appears when you press the Secure Attention Sequence (SAS—i.e., Ctrl+Alt+Del) has a title of Windows Security. To customize this title for your organization to include text after the Windows Security title, perform the following steps:

1. Start the Registry editor (REGEDIT.EXE).
2. Navigate to HKEY_LOCAL_MACHINE\SOFTWARE\Microsoft\Windows NT\CurrentVersion\Winlogon.
3. From the Edit menu, select New > String value.
4. Enter a name of **Welcome** and press Enter.
5. Double-click the new value, add the text you want to display after Windows Security (e.g., for SavillTech Domain), and click OK.
6. Close the Registry editor.
7. Press the SAS sequence to see the new dialog box title.

FAQ 6.206 How can I disable the Shift key override for autologon?

If you've configured your system to automatically log on to Windows, you can override the autologon feature and log on as another user by holding down the Shift key while you log off. To disable the override functionality, perform the following steps:

1. Start the Registry editor (REGEDIT.EXE).
2. Navigate to HKEY_LOCAL_MACHINE\Software\Microsoft\Windows NT\CurrentVersion\Winlogon.
3. From the Edit menu, select New > String value.
4. Enter a name of **IgnoreShiftOverride** and press Enter.
5. Double-click the new value and set it to 1.
6. Close the Registry editor.

FAQ 6.207 How can I set the number of times autologon executes?

By default, autologon will log on a defined user account each time the machine starts. However, in some circumstances, you might want automatic logon to occur only a defined number of times (e.g., unattended installations require autologon only once). To set the autologon count, perform the following steps:

1. Start the Registry editor (REGEDIT.EXE).
2. Navigate to HKEY_LOCAL_MACHINE\Software\Microsoft\Windows NT\CurrentVersion\Winlogon.
3. From the Edit menu, select New > String value.
4. Enter a name of **AutoLogonCount** and press Enter.
5. Double-click the new value and enter the number of times you want autologon to occur.
6. Close the Registry editor.

Each time autologon occurs, the AutoLogonCount will decrement by one. After this value reaches 0, Windows will disable autologon and remove all Registry values related to this setting.

FAQ 6.208 Why do programs scheduled to run using the Windows 2000 Scheduler stop running after 72 hours?

Win2K introduced a maximum running time of 72 hours for programs executed using the Scheduler. To remove or modify this timeframe, contact Microsoft and request the Q304288 fix, which consists of updated MSTASK.EXE and MSTASK.DLL files. After you apply these files, you can use a new Registry entry to set the timeout period. To edit the Registry, perform the following steps:

1. Start a Registry editor (e.g., REGEDIT.EXE).
2. Navigate to HKEY_LOCAL_MACHINE\SYSTEM\CurrentControlSet\Services\Schedule.
3. From the Edit menu, select New > DWORD Value.
4. Enter a name of **AtTaskMaxHours** and press Enter.
5. Double-click the new value, set the value to the number of hours (between 1 and 999, or set the value to 0 to disable a maximum time), and click OK.
6. Close the Registry editor.
7. Restart the machine for the changes to take effect.

Microsoft plans to release this fix in Win2K Service Pack 3 (SP3).

FAQ 6.209 Where can I find the updated Windows XP task switcher?

The XP PowerToys include an updated task switcher that replaces the simple dialog box that appears when you press Alt+Tab. The updated task switcher provides a screenshot as you cycle through each application. To download the updated task switcher and documentation as part of the XP PowerToys, visit Microsoft's XP Web site at http://www.microsoft.com/windowsxp/pro/downloads/powertoys.asp.

FAQ 6.210 Which ADMINPAK.MSI Windows Installer can I use with Windows XP and Windows 2000?

The XP and Win2K server family include an ADMINPAK.MSI Windows Installer that consists of tools to manage server services from either an XP Professional or

Win2K Professional client. You must use the correct version of ADMINPAK.MSI; otherwise, you risk corrupting your directory service. Use the Win2K ADMINPAK.MSI on only Win2K machines to manage a Win2K domain. Use the Windows .NET ADMINPAK.MSI on only XP machines to manage .NET and Win2K domains. You can't install either set on earlier OSs.

The .NET version can also be downloaded from http://www.microsoft.com/downloads/release.asp?ReleaseID=34032.

FAQ 6.211 How can I disable Windows XP's System Restore interface?

You can disable user access to XP's System Restore application (located at Start > Programs > Accessories > System Tools > System Restore) by performing the following steps:

1. Start the Registry editor (e.g., REGEDIT.EXE).
2. Navigate to HKEY_LOCAL_MACHINE\SOFTWARE\Policies\Microsoft\Windows NT.
3. From the Edit menu, select New > Key.
4. Enter a name of **SystemRestore** and press Enter.
5. Move to the new key, and select New > DWORD Value from the Edit menu.
6. Enter a name of **DisableConfig** and press Enter.
7. Double-click the new value, set the value to 1, and click OK.
8. Close the Registry editor.
9. Log off and log on for the change to take effect.

FAQ 6.212 Why do I receive System Event IDs 54 and 64 in the System log?

System Event IDs 54 and 64 will appear in your System log if the server's Time service can't find a domain controller (DC) to synchronize time with. To limit the amount of traffic on the network, the DC attempts this synchronization only every 960 minutes (16 hours), even if the connection between the server and DC is restored during that time.

To force the server and DC to resynchronize the time, go to the command prompt and execute one of the following sets of commands:

- **net stop w32time**
- **net start w32time**
- **w32tm -s (/resync in Microsoft .NET)**

If the server is the forest root DC, you'll need to configure it to synchronize the time with an external source.

FAQ 6.213 Where can I find a list of external time synchronization sources?

Within Microsoft .NET and Windows 2000 domains, time synchronization is vital to security. As a result, all domain controllers (DCs) automatically perform time synchronization. However, the forest root DC must synchronize with an external time source. A list of external U.S. time sources is available at http://www.boulder.nist.gov/timefreq/service/its.htm.

Microsoft maintains a list of external time sources at its site, http://support.microsoft.com/support/kb/articles/Q262/6/80.asp.

Microsoft's Web site also provides information about local time servers for other global locations. To set an authoritative time server, type the following command at the command prompt:

```
net time /setsntp:ntp0.uk.uu.net
```

where ntp0.uk.uu.net is an example of an SNTP time server. Time synchronization uses UDP port 123, so if you use a firewall, this port must be open.

FAQ 6.214 How can I suppress Windows XP's Windows Tour prompt?

The first three times that a user logs on to XP, the OS displays the Windows Tour balloon prompt. To suppress this action for all users, perform the following steps:

1. Start the Registry editor (e.g., REGEDIT.EXE).
2. Navigate to HKEY_LOCAL_MACHINE\SOFTWARE\Microsoft\Windows\CurrentVersion\Applets.
3. Select the Tour Registry key (if this key doesn't exist, go to Edit > New > Key and create the key).
4. From the Edit menu, select New > DWORD Value.

5. Enter a name of **RunCount** and press Enter.
6. Double-click the new value and set it to 0.
7. Click OK.
8. Close the Registry editor.

To perform the same function for a particular user, perform the same steps, but in step 2 navigate to HKEY_CURRENT_USER\SOFTWARE\Microsoft\Windows\CurrentVersion\Applets.

FAQ 6.215 How do I configure the lower graphics resolutions in Windows XP?

By default, XP hides the lower graphics resolutions (e.g., 256 colors, 640x480) from the user. To access these graphics resolutions, perform the following steps:

1. Start the Display Control Panel applet (go to Start > Settings > Control Panel > Display).
2. Select the Settings tab.
3. Click the Advanced button and select the Adapter tab.
4. Click List All Modes to select the graphics mode you want and click OK (see Figure 6-42).
5. Close all the dialog boxes.

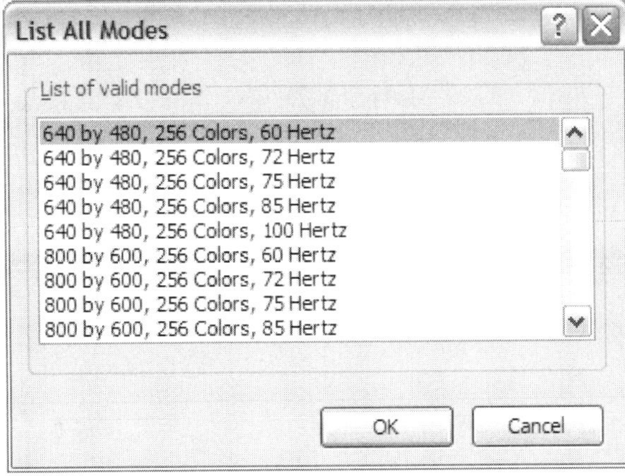

Figure 6-42 All possible graphical modes

6.216 How can I disable the new features of the Windows XP and Windows 2000 shell?

You can use Group Policy to disable the new features (e.g., Active Desktop, QuickLaunch, Web view) of the XP and Win2K shell and configure the classic shell. To configure the classic shell, perform the following steps:

1. Open Group Policy in Group Policy editor (GPE).
2. Expand User Configuration > Administrative Templates > Windows Components > Windows Explorer.
3. Double-click Enable Classic Shell.
4. Set to Enabled and click OK.
5. Close GPE.

You can also use the Registry to configure this setting by performing the following steps:

1. Start a Registry editor (e.g., REGEDIT.EXE).
2. Navigate to HKEY_CURRENT_USER\Software\Microsoft\Windows\CurrentVersion\PoliciesExplorer.
3. From the Edit menu, select New > DWORD Value.
4. Enter a name of **ClassicShell** and press Enter.
5. Double-click the new value, set it to 1, and click OK.
6. Close the Registry editor.

6.217 Where can I get the Task Scheduler?

The Task Scheduler works in conjunction with the standard Scheduler service that is normally accessible via the AT command (or Soon if using the Resource Kit); however, its syntax can sometimes be complex. To help resolve this situation, a new graphical interface was added. If this interface is installed on your machine, you will see a Scheduled Tasks icon in the following places:

- Control Panel (see Figure 6-43)
- Computer entry in My Network Places

If you are using Windows 2000 or above, Scheduled Tasks is built-in so no action is required.

Figure 6-43 Scheduled Tasks icon displayed in the Control Panel

For Windows NT 4.0, you will need to install either Internet Explorer 4 or above and install additional components.

1. Start the Add/Remove Programs Control Panel applet (Start > Settings > Control Panel > Add/Remove Programs).
2. Select Microsoft Internet Explorer 4/5.
3. Click Change/Remove.
4. Add a component.
5. If you're using IE4, you should select Task Scheduler under Additional Explorer Enhancements. With IE5, select the Offline Browsing Pack.

You now have the Task Scheduler.

FAQ 6.218 How do I schedule a task using the Task Scheduler?

To add a new task using the graphical front end, perform the following:

1. Start the Schedule Task Wizard (Start > Settings > Control Panel > Scheduled Tasks > Add Scheduled Tasks).
2. Click Next on the wizard.
3. A list of programs installed on your machine will be displayed. If not, click Browse and locate the executable. Click Next.

4. Select a task name that the task will be displayed as, and select when it should be run:
   - Daily
   - Weekly
   - Monthly
   - One time only
   - When my computer starts
   - When I log on
5. Click Next.
6. If you select any of the first four items, you will be shown a dialog allowing the day/month/time to be selected (see Figure 6-44). Click Next.
7. You will now be asked for a username and password that the scheduled task should be run as. Click Next.
8. Click Finish.

The task will now be displayed under Scheduled Tasks. If you wish to modify the task, right-click on the process and select Properties. An advanced dialog will be displayed allowing parameters to be changed.

Tasks scheduled with the normal AT command will be display with a name of at <status id>.

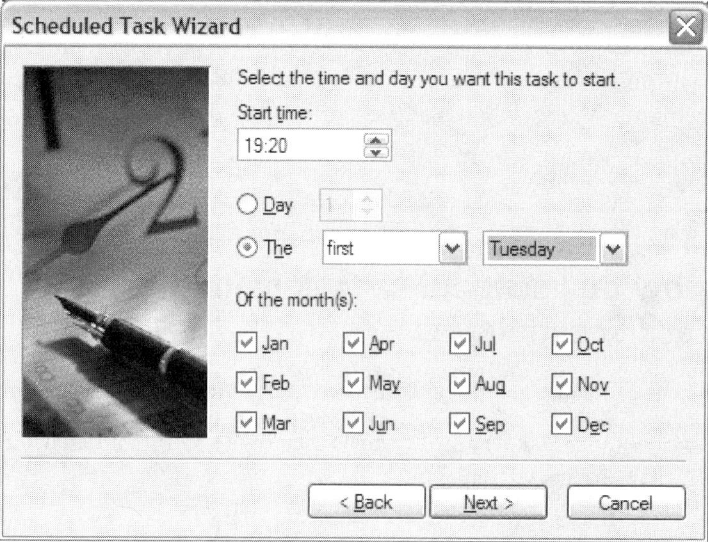

Figure 6-44 Using the Scheduled Task Wizard

FAQ 6.219 How can I move or copy scheduled tasks between machines?

It's possible to move and copy tasks between machines, thanks to the feature of scheduled tasks appearing as a property of computers under My Network Places. Schedule Task supports cut/copy and paste as follows:

1. Open Schedule Task on your local machine.
2. Right-click on the task your wish to move or copy (see Figure 6-45).
3. If you want to copy the task, select Copy; if you want to move it, select Cut.
4. Open My Network Places (Explorer), expand the domain/workgroup, and select the target machine.
5. Right-click on its Scheduled Tasks and click Paste.

The task will now show on the target machine under Scheduled Tasks. You should be careful the task will work on the remote machine; for example, the target application exists on the machine, parameters are valid, and so on.

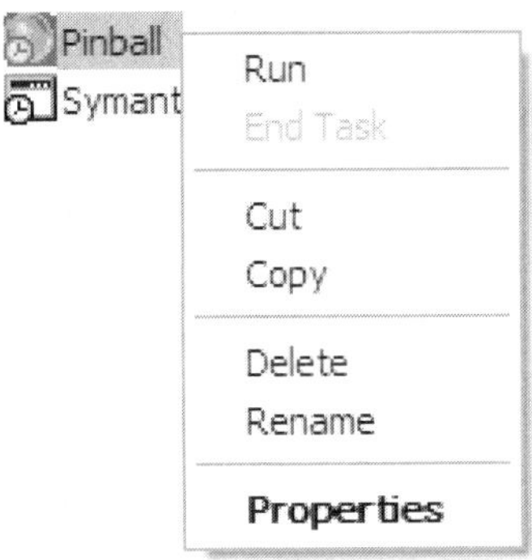

Figure 6-45 Selecting the actions for a scheduled task

FAQ 6.220 How can I execute a scheduled task immediately?

If you right-click on the task under Scheduled Tasks, you can select Run from the displayed context menu.

FAQ 6.221 How can I delete a scheduled task?

Right-click on the task under Scheduled Tasks and select Delete. Click Yes to the confirmation. You cannot delete tasks created with the Schedule Task Wizard using the AT command.

FAQ 6.222 How can I be notified of a missed scheduled task?

By default if a scheduled task is missed, there will be no notification. To enable a notification, perform the following:

1. Open Scheduled Tasks (Start > Settings > Control Panel > Scheduled Tasks).
2. Select Notify Me of Missed Tasks.

You can also configure this by directly editing the Registry:

1. Start the Registry editor (REGEDIT.EXE).
2. Move to HKEY_LOCAL_MACHINE\SOFTWARE\Microsoft\SchedulingAgent.
3. Double-click NotifyOnTaskMiss (if it does not exist, create of type DWORD).
4. Set to 1 to enable, 0 to disable.
5. Close the Registry editor.

The next time a task is missed, a pop-up will be displayed with an option to run the missed task.

FAQ 6.223 How do I add themes to the .NET Server product?

Both Windows XP and the .NET Server product lines support desktop themes that enable a modified window look, which are accessed via the Display Control Panel applet > Appearance tab. By default two options are available:

- Windows XP style
- Windows Classic style

With .NET, only the Windows Classic style is available because themes use extra resources; however, themes are included but disabled by default. To enable themes, start the Themes service:

```
net start themes
```

To ensure the Themes service starts at reboot, perform the following:

1. Start the Computer Management MMC snap-in (Start > Programs > Administrative Tools > Computer Management).
2. Expand the Services and Applications branch.
3. Select Services.
4. Double-click Themes.
5. Set Startup type to Automatic and click OK.
6. Close the snap-in.

FAQ 6.224 How can I create a shortcut to the Device Manager?

To create a shortcut to the Device Manager, which can normally be accessed via the System Control Panel Applet (Start > Settings > Control Panel > System > Hardware > Device Manager).

If you use Device Manager frequently, you can create a shortcut as follows:

1. Right-click on the desktop.
2. Select New > Shortcut from the displayed context menu.
3. Under location, type **DEVMGMT.MSC**. Click Next.
4. Select a name for the shortcut Device Manager and click Finish.

FAQ 6.225 How can I execute .MSC files without typing the .MSC extension?

Some file types do not need their extension typed when running, for example, .EXE, .BAT. To add the Microsoft Snap-in Console to this list, add .MSC to your PATHEXT variable. To perform this for a single command session, type

```
set pathext=%pathext%;.MSC
```

To set for all of Windows, modify the system environment variable:

1. Start the System Control Panel applet (Start > Settings > Control Panel > System).
2. Select the Advanced tab.
3. Click Environment Variables button.
4. Under System variables, double-click PATHEXT.
5. Add **;.MSC** to the end of the string and click OK.
6. Click OK to all dialogs.

You will now be able to start .MSC without typing the extension, for example, DEVMGMT.

FAQ 6.226 How can I run scheduled tasks in the background when they run as the current logged on user?

Normally scheduled tasks run under the SYSTEM context and run in the background, but if you change a service to run as a user account and that account is currently logged onto the machine, the scheduled task will run in the foreground, which can be annoying.

To resolve this, perform the following:

1. Start the Registry editor (REGEDIT.EXE).
2. Move to HKEY_LOCAL_MACHINE\SOFTWARE\Microsoft\Windows NT\CurrentVersion\Winlogon.
3. Double-click Shell (this will be EXPLORER.EXE).
4. Modify to **c:\windows\Explorer.exe**, (do type the comma). You need to change c:\windows to that of your local machine system root.
5. Click OK.

FAQ 6.227 How can I print the Euro (€) symbol?

You must first ensure the font you are using supports the Euro (information can be found at the Microsoft Web site http://www.microsoft.com/euro).

To enter the Euro character, perform the following

1. Ensure NumLock is enabled (you should have a NumLock light on your keyboard).
2. Hold down the Alt key and type 0128 on the numeric keypad.
3. The Euro symbol will be output.

Simpler ways are available for most Windows locales (a full list can be found at http://www.microsoft.com/typography/faq/faq12.htm), but for most locales, it is AltGr+e; for the U.K., it's AltGr+4 (a few others use AltGr+5 or AltGr+u).

FAQ 6.228 How can I modify how many most recent documents are shown on the Start menu?

By default only the 15 most recently accessed documents are displayed on the Start > Documents menu; however, this number can be changed as follows:

1. Start the Registry editor (REGEDIT.EXE)
2. Move to HKEY_CURRENT_USER\Software\Microsoft\Windows\CurrentVersion\Policies\Explorer.
3. From the Edit menu, select New > DWORD Value.
4. Enter a name of **MaxRecentDocs** and press Enter.
5. Double-click the new value and set the base to Decimal.
6. Set to the number of documents you wish to be shown in multiples of 15 (e.g., 15,30,45) and click OK.
7. Close the Registry editor.

FAQ 6.229 What is SCHTASKS.EXE?

Previous versions of Windows introduced the Scheduled Tasks interface that gave a graphical view of scheduled tasks; however, it was not always compatible with the command-line scheduler utility, AT.

To rectify this situation, Windows XP/.NET and above include a new utility, SCHTASKS.EXE, which is the replacement for AT (although AT is still shipped) and provides all the functionality of AT but with a superset of features.

Schtasks when run with no switches will perform a query on pending scheduled tasks, for example:

```
C:\>at

There are no entries in the list.

C:\>schtasks

TaskName                               Next Run Time           Status
========================               ================        ========
Symantec NetDetect                     20:51:00, 23/01/2002
Symantec NetDetect                     At logon time
```

The AT output is included to demonstrate how Schtasks supports the full scheduled task types.

Additionally Schtasks can create new scheduled tasks, change existing jobs, run a scheduled job immediately, end a program started by a task, delete a scheduled task, and query all scheduled tasks including those scheduled by other users.

Detailed information can be found about tasks using combinations of switches—for example, to get detailed information about all tasks in a list output:

```
schtasks /query /v /fo LIST

HostName:                 CONAN
TaskName:                 Symantec NetDetect
Next Run Time:            20:51:00, 23/01/2002
Status:
Last Run Time:            16:51:00, 23/01/2002
Last Result:              101
Creator:                  savijo
Schedule:                 Every 5 minute(s) from 20:51 for 24 hour
                          ) every day, starting 23/01/2002
Task To Run:              C:\Program Files\Symantec\LiveUpdate\
                          NDECT.EXE
Start In:                 C:\Program Files\Symantec\LiveUpdate
Comment:                  Symantec NetDetect
Scheduled Task State:     Enabled
Scheduled Type:           Minute
```

```
Start Time:                20:51:00
Start Date:                23/01/2002
End Date:                  N/A
Days:                      Everyday
Months:                    N/A
Run As User:               savilltech\john
Delete Task If Not Rescheduled: Disabled
Stop Task If Runs X Hours and X Mins: 72:0
Repeat: Every:             5 Minute(s)
Repeat: Until:             Time: None
Repeat: Until:             Duration: 24 Hour(s): 0 Minute(s)
Repeat:                    Stop If Still Running: Disabled
Idle Time:                 Disabled
Power Management:          Disabled
```

For detailed help, search for SCHTASKS in the Help and Support utility (on the Start menu).

7 USER CONFIGURATION

This chapter discusses configuring users in domains and local machines. We look at the basic features and some more advanced issues such as delegating authority in Windows 2000 and above.

FAQ 7.1 What should be in the logon script?

The contents of this script will vary from site to site; however, generally a logon script will synchronize the time of the workstations with the server (providing the server's time is accurate!), and perhaps connect a home area. The command Net use x: /home will ask the domain server for your home area location and connect to it. A logon script may be

```
@echo off
net time \\johnserver /set /yes
net use p: /home
```

NT4.0 ONLY

FAQ 7.2 Is there a way of performing operations depending on a user's group membership?

On the Resource Kit for NT, you'll find the Ifmember program, which you base your logon script on.

> **Warning:** *Ifmember works by checking for membership in a group and returning an ERRORLEVEL; hence, you'll have a bunch of IF THENS.*

Ifmember sets errorlevel to the number of groups in the list that the user is actually a member of, for example:

	Group1	Group2	Group3
savillj	Y	Y	N

If you typed the following command, an errorlevel of 2 would be returned:

```
ifmember group1 group2
ifmember group1
if %errorlevel%==1 <command>
```

FAQ 7.3 How do I limit the disk space for a user?

NT server has no way to do this; Windows 2000 and XP have per-volume quotas on NTFS 5.0 volumes.

There is third-party software for NT 4.0 such as

- Quota Server from http://www.northern.se
- Quota Manager from http://www.softshelf.com/winnt/qm/so02003.htm
- Disk Guard from http://www.spaceguard.com
- QuotaAdvisor from http://www.wquinn.com
- Space Guard from http://www.tools4nt.com/Products/SpaceGuard/SpaceGuard.htm

FAQ 7.4 Is there a utility that shows who is currently logged on?

The Resource Kit includes the WHOAMI.EXE utility (which is supplied as standard in Windows XP). It displays the domain/workgroup and username. You can also press Ctrl+Alt+Del, and the current logged on user will be shown.

Alternatively you could just display the %userdomain% and %username% variables—for example,

```
Zecho %userdomain%\%username%
```

FAQ 7.5 How can I change environment variables from the command line?

The Resource Kit has the SETX.EXE utility (again part of the core package with Windows XP). It enables the user to change environment settings—for example,

```
setx johnvariable 1
setx johnvariable -k HKEY_LOCAL_MACHINE\...\DefaultDomainName
```

FAQ 7.6 How can I hide drive x from users?

This can be done using the TweakUI utility from the My Computer tab. Just deselect the tick next to the drives you want to hide. Doing so changes the Registry value HKEY_CURRENT_USER\Software\Microsoft\Windows\CurrentVersion\Policies\Explorer\NODRIVES, which is a 32-bit word (DWORD). The lower 26 bits of the 32-bit word correspond to drive letters A through Z. Drives are visible when set to 0 and hidden when set to 1.

Drive A is represented by the right-most position of the bitmask when viewed in binary mode—for example, a bitmask of 00000000000000000000010101(0x7h) hides local drives A, C, and E.

Drives hidden using the NODRIVES setting are not available through Windows Explorer, under the My Computer icon, or in the File Open\Save dialog boxes of 32-bit Windows applications. File Manager and the Windows NT command prompt are not affected by this Registry setting.

FAQ 7.7 How do I make the shell start before the logon script finishes?

Change the Registry value HKEY_CURRENT_USER\software\microsoft\windows nt\currentversion\winlogon\RunLogonScriptSync to 0, which means the shell starts before the logon script has finished. A value of 1 means the shell will not start until the logon script is finished.

FAQ 7.8 How can I find out which groups a user is in?

NT provides a means of getting information about your domain account using the following, which provides information about group membership:

```
net user <username> /domain
```

FAQ 7.9 I can no longer see items in the common groups from the Start menu. How can I change this?

A Registry flag sets whether or not the common groups are displayed on the Start menu. To disable this setting, set HKEY_CURRENT_USER\Software\Microsoft\Windows\CurrentVersion\Policies\Explorer\NoCommonGroups to 0 using the Registry editor (REGEDIT.EXE). By default this value will not exist.

FAQ 7.10 How can I configure each user to have a different screen resolution?

You cannot; the screen resolution is stored in the Registry, in a nonuser-specific area and is therefore not configurable for individual users. The resolution has to be changed manually when the user logs on.

FAQ 7.11 How can I add a user from the command line?

The simple answer is to use net user <username> <password> /add (/domain); however, it is possible to automate not only the addition of the user, but also his/her addition to groups and the creation of a template user account directory structure. Many organizations have a basic structure with Word and Excel directories and some template files. This can be automated with a basic script. For example:

```
addnew.bat

net user %1 password /add /homedir:\\<server>\users\%1
/scriptpath:login.bat /domain

net localgroup "<local group>" %1 /add
```

Repeat for local groups:

```
net group "<groups>" %1 /add /domain
```

Repeat for global groups:

```
xcopy \\<server>\users\template \\<server>\users\%1 /e

sleep 20

cacls \\<server>\users\%1 /e /r Everyone
```

Remove the Everyone permission to the directory:

```
cacls \\<server>\users\%1 /g %1:F /e

cacls \\<server>\users\%1 /g Administrators:F /e
```

FAQ 7.12 How can I remotely change the local Administrator passwords?

As you may be aware, it is possible to change your password from the command line using the net user command, and if you combine it with the at command, you can run the command on different machines—for example,

```
at \\<machine name> <time> cmd /c net user Administrator
anythingyouwant
```

For example, at \\savilljohn 18:00 cmd /c net user Administrator password.

The /c after cmd causes the command window to close after the command has been executed. An alternative to the at command is the soon command:

```
soon \\<machine name> cmd /c net user Administrator password
```

For this to work, you need to ensure the Scheduler (Task Scheduler) service is running on the destination machines.

7.13 How do I change my password?

Perform the following:

1. Press Ctrl+Alt+Delete.
2. Click the Change Password button.
3. Enter you old password and new password twice and click OK.

To change your password from the command line, use the net user command—for example:

```
net user <username> <password> (/domain)
```

To change your password from a program, use the NetUserChangePassword()call.

7.14 How can I tell which user has which SID?

To determine which user has which security identifier, perform the following:

1. Start the Registry editor.
2. Move to HKEY_LOCAL_MACHINE\SOFTWARE\Microsoft\Windows NT\CurrentVersion\ProfileList.
3. Select each SID under the Registry value in turn and look at the ProfileImagePath; at the end of this string is the name of the user.
4. Close the Registry editor.

If you knew the SID and just wanted to know the username, you could use the REG.EXE command (with Resource Kit Supplement 2)—for example:

```
reg query "HKEY_LOCAL_MACHINE\SOFTWARE\Microsoft\Windows
NT\CurrentVersion\ProfileList\<SID>\ProfileImagePath"
```

For example:

```
reg query "HKEY_LOCAL_MACHINE\SOFTWARE\Microsoft\Windows
NT\CurrentVersion\ProfileList\S-1-5-21-1843332746-572796286-
2118856591-1000\ProfileImagePath"
```

And again this will show the ProfileImagePath giving you the user.

In the Windows 2000 Resource Kit, a GETSID.EXE utility is supplied, which is part of the core operating system in Windows XP. When passed a username and server, this utility will return the SID value for the user.

FAQ 7.15 How can I modify the size of icons on the desktop?

As you may be aware, you can change the size of icons in Explorer by selecting Large icon/Small icon from the View menu. You can actually make the icons even bigger!

1. Start the Registry editor (REGEDIT.EXE).
2. Move to HKEY_CURRENT_USER\Control Panel\Desktop\WindowMetrics.
3. Double-click on Shell Icon Size.
4. Modify the icon to the size you want (increase the value by 16)—for example, change the value to 48 or 64. Click OK.
5. Close the Registry editor.

If large icons are selected in Explorer, you will now see the new size. You don't need to log off; just change folders.

It's also possible to change the icons for the small icon/Start menu:

1. Start the Registry editor (REGEDIT.EXE).
2. Move to HKEY_CURRENT_USER\Control Panel\Desktop\WindowMetrics.
3. From the Edit menu select New > String.
4. Enter a name of **Shell Small Icon Size**.
5. Double-click the new value and set to the size you want. The value is 16 by default, but again it could be 32, 48, 64, and so on.

Log off and on again for the change to take effect.

To change the number of colors the icons use, perform the following:

1. Start the Registry editor (REGEDIT.EXE).
2. Move to HKEY_CURRENT_USER\Control Panel\Desktop\WindowMetrics.
3. Double-click on Shell Icon BPP.
4. Modify to 4 for 16 colors, 8 for 256, 16 for 65,536, 24 for 16 million, and 32 for true color.
5. Close the Registry editor.

Again you need to log off for the change to take effect.

7.16 How can I disable Alt+Tab?

This can be disabled via the Registry:

1. Start the Registry editor (REGEDIT.EXE).
2. Move to HKEY_CURRENT_USER\Control Panel\Desktop.
3. Double-click on CoolSwitch.
4. Set to 0 and click OK.
5. Close the Registry editor.

You need to restart the computer for this to take effect.

7.17 How can I configure the Alt+Tab display?

Again you can configure this through the Registry:

1. Start the Registry editor (REGEDIT.EXE).
2. Move to HKEY_CURRENT_USER\Control Panel\Desktop.
3. Double-click on CoolSwitchColumns to change the number of columns displayed; double-click on CoolSwitchRows to change the number of rows.
4. Close the Registry editor.

Restart the computer for the change to take effect.

7.18 How can I edit the list of connections listed in Explorer when I map a connection?

When you select Map Network Drive from Tools menu in Explorer and click the drop-down box for the path, Explorer checks the HKEY_CURRENT_USER\Software\Microsoft\Windows NT\CurrentVersion\Network\Persistent Connections area of the Registry for a list of old/current drive mappings. To remove items from the list (or to add itcms to thc list), pcrform the following:

1. Start the Registry editor (REGEDIT.EXE).
2. Move to HKEY_CURRENT_USER\Software\Microsoft\Windows NT\CurrentVersion\Network\Persistent Connections.
3. In the right pane, you will see a list of values, a–z, and each Registry value will have a value such as "\\<machine name>\<share>".

4. To remove a map, select the letter associated with it and press the Delete key.
5. You should now edit the Order value and remove the letter you have just deleted.
6. If you wish to add a mapping, select New > String Value, enter a name of a–z (use one that is not in use), and press Enter. Double-click on your new value and set it to the share name—for example, \\johnmachine\d$.
7. Edit the Order value and add your new letter to the end of the string.
8. Close the Registry editor.
9. Start Explorer, and your new share or removed share will have taken effect.

FAQ 7.19 How can I exclude the Temporary Internet Files folder from the user profile?

By default the storage area for temporary Internet files is %systemroot%\Profiles\<user>\Temporary Internet Files. If you implemented roaming profiles, these files would count as part of your profile, taking up valuable server space. To change the location from the browser, perform the following:

1. Start Internet Explorer.
2. Select Internet Options from the View menu.
3. Select the General tab.
4. Click the Settings button.
5. Click the Move Folder button.
6. Click Yes to the confirmation dialog.
7. Select the new location and click OK.

You will need to restart the machine for the new location to take effect.

Alternatively you could create a .REG file to manually update the following Registry values and include it as part of a logon script:

- HKEY_LOCAL_MACHINE\SOFTWARE\Microsoft\Windows\CurrentVersion\Internet Settings\Cache\Paths\path1\CachePath
- HKEY_LOCAL_MACHINE\SOFTWARE\Microsoft\Windows\CurrentVersion\Internet Settings\Cache\Paths\path2\CachePath
- HKEY_LOCAL_MACHINE\SOFTWARE\Microsoft\Windows\CurrentVersion\Internet Settings\Cache\Paths\path3\CachePath
- HKEY_LOCAL_MACHINE\SOFTWARE\Microsoft\Windows\CurrentVersion\Internet Settings\Cache\Paths\path4\CachePath
- HKEY_CURRENT_USER\Software\Microsoft\Windows\CurrentVersion\Explorer\Shell Folders\Cache

- HKEY_CURRENT_USER\Software\Microsoft\Windows\CurrentVersion\Explorer\User Shell Folders\Cache

Here's an example .REG file:

```
REGEDIT4

[HKEY_LOCAL_MACHINE\SOFTWARE\Microsoft\Windows\CurrentVersion\
Internet Settings\Cache\Paths\path1]
"CachePath"="E:\\TEMP\\Cache1"
[HKEY_LOCAL_MACHINE\SOFTWARE\Microsoft\Windows\CurrentVersion\
Internet Settings\Cache\Paths\path2]
"CachePath"="E:\\TEMP\\Cache2"
[HKEY_LOCAL_MACHINE\SOFTWARE\Microsoft\Windows\CurrentVersion\
Internet Settings\Cache\Paths\path3]
"CachePath"="E:\\TEMP\\Cache3"
[HKEY_LOCAL_MACHINE\SOFTWARE\Microsoft\Windows\CurrentVersion\
Internet Settings\Cache\Paths\path4]
"CachePath"="E:\\TEMP\\Cache4"
[HKEY_CURRENT_USER\Software\Microsoft\Windows\CurrentVersion\
Explorer\Shell Folders]
"Cache"="E:\\TEMP"
[HKEY_CURRENT_USER\Software\Microsoft\Windows\CurrentVersion\
Explorer\User Shell Folders]
"Cache"="E:\\TEMP"
```

Make sure you use two backslashes (\). This sets the cache area to e:\temp; however, you could change this setting to anything you want. Save the file as CACHE.REG and run it as

```
regedit /s cache.reg
```

Netscape does not store temporary files under the user profile (it is stored in the Registry location HKEY_LOCAL_MACHINE\SOFTWARE\Netscape\Netscape Navigator\Users\<user>\DirRoot ;-)).

7.20 How can I stop the programs in my startup folders from running when I log on?

Hold down Shift during your logon, and any programs in the startup folders will not run.

If Administrators wish to disable this behavior, add IgnoreShiftOveride of type String to HKEY_LOCAL_MACHINE\SOFTWARE\Microsoft\Windows NT\CurrentVersion\Winlogon and set the value to 1.

NT 4 ONLY

FAQ 7.21 Why can't I can't delete user x?

This behavior can be caused by a number of things. You can try deleting the user from the command line:

```
net user <username> /delete [/domain]
```

If this does not work, try renaming the account and then deleting it:

1. Start User Manager (for domains).
2. Select the user you can't delete.
3. From the User menu, select Rename.
4. Enter the new name and click OK.
5. Now select the new username, press Delete, and click OK to the confirmation.

The preceding solution works if you have an invalid username (like AAAAAAAAAAA).

FAQ 7.22 How can I stop users from being able to map and disconnect network drives?

This is accomplished using the Policy editor under normal conditions. It can also be performed by directly editing the Registry.

1. Start the Registry editor (REGEDIT.EXE).
2. Move to HKEY_CURRENT_USER\Software\Microsoft\Windows\CurrentVersion\Policies\Explorer.
3. From the Edit menu, select New > DWORD Value.
4. Enter a name of **NoNetConnectDisconnect** and press Enter.
5. Double-click the new value and set to 1.
6. The user will need to log off and on for the change to take effect.

FAQ 7.23 How can I remove a user from a group from the command prompt?

If the group is a local group, perform the following:

```
net localgroup <group name> <user> /delete
```

For example, net localgroup Administrators savillj /delete. If the group is part of a domain user:

```
net group <group name> <user> /delete /domain
```

FAQ 7.24 How can I remove the colon (:) from the time?

This can be accomplished by editing the Registry:

1. Start the Registry editor (REGEDIT.EXE).
2. Move to HKEY_CURRENT_USER\Control Panel\International.
3. Double-click on the sTimeFormat.
4. Remove the colon (:) between the HH:mm.
5. Click OK.
6. Close the Registry editor.

To see the change, log off and on again.

FAQ 7.25 How can I rename a user from the command prompt?

A utility, RENUSER.EXE, (which can be downloaded from http://www.ntfaq.com/download/renuser.zip) has the following usage:

```
renuser <old username> <new username> [<domain name>]
```

For example, renuser savillj johns savilltech.

FAQ 7.26 Why are roaming profiles not saved to the server?

If a user is a member of the Domain Guests group, then no changes to profiles are stored; therefore, you should check the members of the Domain Guests group. Ensure users who are experiencing their profiles not being saved are not in this Domain Guests group.

FAQ 7.27 Why does my connection fail now that I've made user shares hidden?

To hide a share, all you need to do is add the dollar sign ($) to the end, for example, \\server\share$.

If previously your logon scripts included the command

```
net use f: \\<server>\%username%
```

the scripts will no longer work because the share is hidden with the dollar sign. To connect, you will need to specify the dollar sign, so change the command to

```
net use f: \\<server>\%username%$
```

FAQ 7.28 How can I disable the Display Control Panel applet?

Using policies, it is possible to disable the Display Control Panel applet. It can also be accomplished using the Registry editor:

1. Start the Registry editor (REGEDIT.EXE).
2. Move to HKEY_CURRENT_USER\Software\Microsoft\Windows\CurrentVersion\Policies\System.
3. From the Edit menu, select New > DWORD Value.
4. Enter a name of **NoDispCPL** and press Enter.
5. Double-click the new value and set to 1.
6. Close the Registry editor.

The change takes immediate effect. If you try to run the Display Control Panel applet either by right-clicking on the desktop and selecting Properties or starting from the Control Panel applet, you will receive the message "Your system administrator disabled the Display control panel."

FAQ 7.29 How can I disable elements of the Display Control Panel applet?

Again, using policies, it is possible to disable elements of the Display Control Panel applet. It can also be accomplished using the Registry editor.

1. Start the Registry editor (REGEDIT.EXE).
2. Move to HKEY_CURRENT_USER\Software\Microsoft\Windows\CurrentVersion\Policies\System.
3. From the Edit menu, select New > DWORD Value.
4. Enter any of the following values as outlined in the following table:

NoDispAppearancePage	Removes the Appearance tab, which means users cannot change the colors or color scheme
NoDispBackgroundPage	Removes the Background tab, meaning no more matrix background (darn!)
NoDispScrSavPage	Removes the Screen Save tab
NoDispSettingsPage	Removes the Settings and the Plus tab

5. Double-click the new value and set to 1.
6. Close the Registry editor.

These changes take immediate effect, and any disabled Tab will not be displayed.

Of course the user can go into the Registry and change these settings back, which is why it is better to implement these changes as policies (which is what I do). Because they take immediate effect, there is nothing to stop someone creating a REG script to run as part of the startup group, which sets the values to how users may want to get around the policy.

FAQ 7.30 When I log off, all my home directory files are deleted. Why?

The most common cause for this behavior is when your roaming profile path and your home directory path are the same. It seems that part of the update makes sure the contents of the directories (and subdirectories) are the same, and because the local profile directory does not contain your home directory files, they are deleted!

You should therefore change the location of the roaming profile so it is different from the user's home directory. The directory may be a subdirectory if you wish. This can be changed by using the User Manager application; click the Profiles button and change the locations.

FAQ 7.31 How can I log off from the command prompt?

The Windows NT 4.0 Resource Kit Supplement 2 ships with the utility LOGOFF.EXE (which is part of core Windows XP), and it can be used to log off from the command line. The syntax is

```
logoff [/f] [/n]
```

Where the option /f means running processes will be closed without asking to save unsaved data but will ask for confirmation. /n will logoff without confirmation but will ask to save unsaved data.

Using both together will result in no confirmation and all unsaved data being lost.

FAQ 7.32 Where is User Manager in Windows 2000?

Windows 2000 no longer uses User Manager for domain account administration. The new tool is the Active Directory Users and Computers Microsoft Management Console (MMC). See FAQ 7.33 for more information.

FAQ 7.33 How do I administer domain users in Windows 2000?

Windows 2000 has a whole new look for its administration tools with Microsoft Management Console (MMC) snap-ins, and for the administration of domain users, the Active Directory Users and Computers MMC snap-in is used. The snap-in is selected from the Administrative Tools folder (Start > Programs > Administrative Tools—Active Directory Users and Computers).

Once started, expand the domain and users branch to see the users (see Figure 7-1).

Context menus are heavily used in Windows 2000. For example, to change a user's password, simply right-click on the user and select Reset Password (see Figure 7-2).

Selecting Properties allows other properties of the user to be set, such as group membership and profile location.

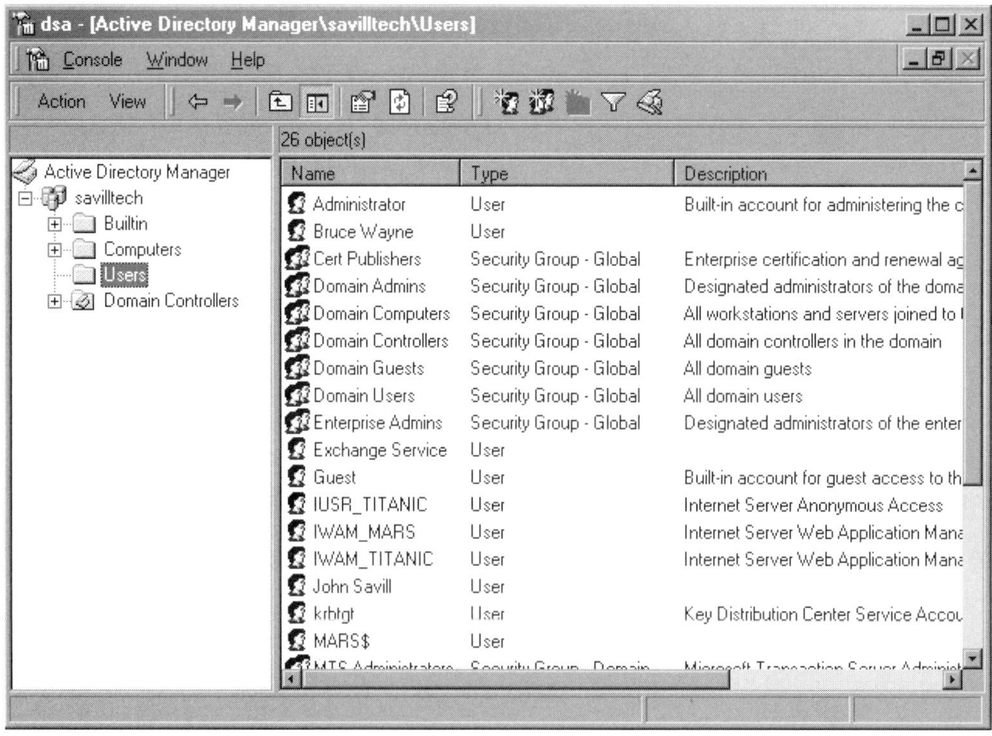

Figure 7-1 The users branch of my Active Directory domain

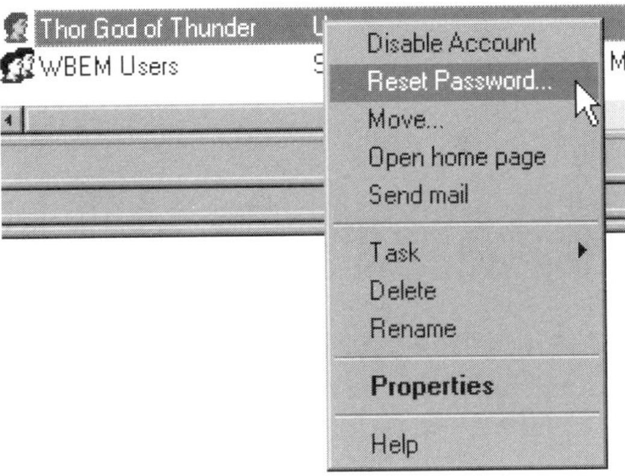

Figure 7-2 Resetting a user's password via the user's context menu

FAQ 7.34 How do I remove the Goto menu from Explorer?

Service Pack 4 for Windows NT 4.0 and Windows 2000 support a system policy Remove Tools > GoTo menu from Explorer. To configure this feature via the Policy editor, POLEDIT.EXE, perform the following:

1. Start the Policy editor.
2. Load a policy or create a new one.
3. Select Default User.
4. Expand Windows NT Shell > Restrictions.
5. Check Remove Tools > GoTo menu from Explorer.
6. Click OK.
7. Save your changes.

Alternatively you can perform this directly in the Registry:

1. Start the Registry editor (REGEDT32.EXE).
2. Move to HKEY_CURRENT_USER\Software\Microsoft\Windows\CurrentVersion\Policies\Explorer .
3. From the Edit menu select New > Binary value.
4. Enter a name of **NoGoTo** and press Enter.
5. Double-click the new value and set to 1.

6. Click OK.
7. Close the Registry editor.

7.35 How can I disable the Logon Using Dial-Up Networking at logon time?

It is possible to disable the Logon Using Dial-Up Networking checkbox when logging on by performing the following:

1. Start the Registry editor (REGEDIT.EXE).
2. Move to HKEY_LOCAL_MACHINE\SOFTWARE\Microsoft\Windows NT\CurrentVersion\Winlogon.
3. From the Edit menu select New > String Value.
4. Enter a name of **RASDisable**.
5. Double-click the new value and set to 1. Click OK.
6. Close the Registry editor.

The change will take effect at next reboot, and the Logon Using Dial-Up Networking checkbox will be grayed out.

7.36 How can I stop a user closing the logon script before it completes?

It is possible to modify GINA.DLL, and it has been done in the past. But no modified GINA.DLLs are available for download at this time.

An alternative is to hide the script, which can be done by creating DWORD Value HKEY_USERS\\Console\WindowSize and setting it to 050005 in hexadecimal and HKEY_USERS\\Console\WindowPosition and setting it to 04FF06FF in hexadecimal. Doing so makes the window very small and positions it off the screen.

7.37 How can I tell at what time I logged on?

If you type

```
net statistics workstation
```

from the command prompt, it will show you the time the workstation service started, which does **not** necessarily reflect the last logon time, as some sources would have you believe.

If you press Ctrl+Alt+Del, then you will also be shown the logon date and time. The best way is to use the Event Viewer:

1. Start the Event Viewer (Start > Programs > Administrative Tools > Event Viewer).
2. From the File menu, select Security.
3. Look for the latest event 528, which is a Success Audit.
4. Double-click it for complete information.

You will need to ensure auditing is enabled for logon success and failure:

1. Start the User Manager (Start > Programs > Administrative Tools > User Manager).
2. Select Audit from the Policies menu.
3. Enable Audit These Events and select Logon and Logoff success and failure. Click OK.
4. Close User Manager.

FAQ 7.38 How can I stop certain folders being replicated as part of the user profile?

Service Pack 4 introduced a new Registry setting, ExcludeProfileDirs, which can be used to exclude certain directories from the replication of user profiles. To implement this setting, perform the following:

1. Start the Registry editor (REGEDIT.EXE).
2. Move to HKEY_CURRENT_USER\Software\Microsoft\Windows NT\CurrentVersion\Winlogon.
3. From the Edit menu, select New > String value.
4. Enter a name of **ExcludeProfileDirs** and press Enter.
5. Double-click the new value and set to the relevant areas, separating them by semicolons, for example

   ```
   Local Settings\Application Data\Microsoft\Outlook;Temporary
   Internet Files;Personal
   ```

6. Click OK.
7. Close the Registry editor.

This can also be done via a system policy:

1. Start the Policy Editor (POLEDIT.EXE).
2. Create a new policy (or open an existing one, providing it was created after SP4 installation).
3. Double-click Default User.
4. Expand the Windows NT User Profiles branch.
5. Check Exclude directories in roaming profile.
6. In the data box, type the name of the directories to be excluded (see Figure 7-3).
7. Click OK.
8. Save the policy to the netlogon share of the PDC.

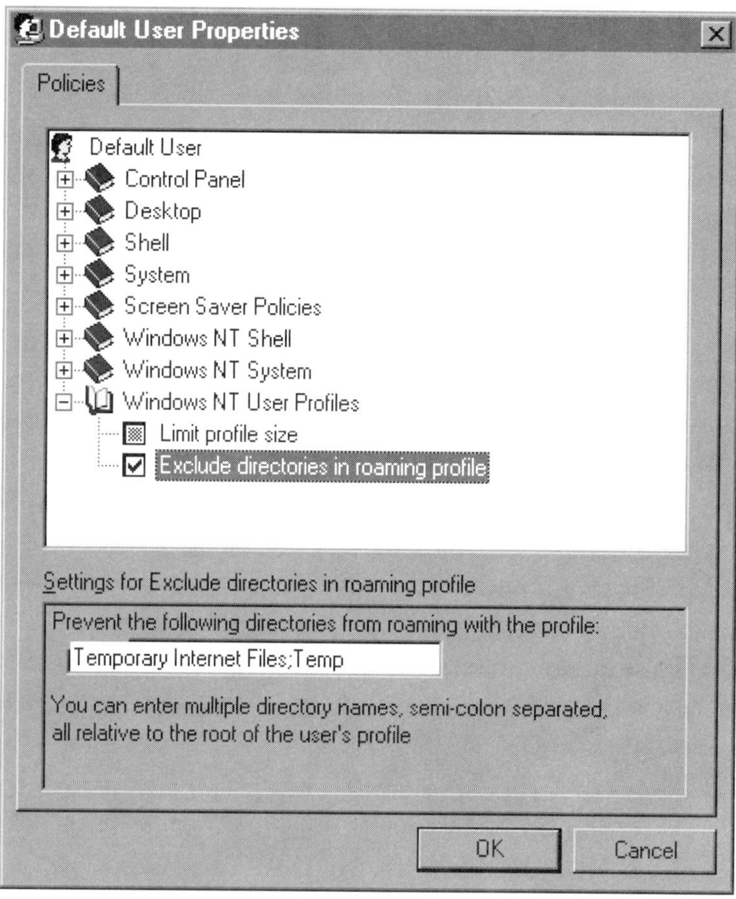

Figure 7-3 Excluding folders from the roaming profile

FAQ 7.39 How can I prevent users from creating persistent connections?

Persistent connections are those that are recreated after you log off and log on again. It may be desirable to prevent persistent connections. A Registry entry exists to disable users from creating them:

1. Start the Registry editor (REGED32.EXE).
2. Move to HKEY_USERS\.DEFAULT\Software\Microsoft\Windows NT\CurrentVersion\Network\Persistent Connections.
3. Double-click on SaveConnections.
4. Change to **no**. Click OK.
5. Close the Registry editor.

The preceding disables persistent connections for new users. To disable them for current users, perform the same procedure but on the HKEY_CURRENT_USER\Software\Microsoft\Windows NT\CurrentVersion\Network\Persistent Connections\SaveConnections value.

FAQ 7.40 I'm not given a warning if I'm logged on using cached credentials in Windows 2000. Why?

In Windows NT 4.0, if you log on and no domain controller can be found, you are logged on using cached information (assuming you have previously logged onto the machine). You are given a warning "A domain controller could not be contacted and you have been logged on using cached information."

This warning is disabled by default in Windows 2000 but can be enabled by performing the following on each computer:

1. Start the Registry editor (REGEDIT.EXE).
2. Move to HKEY_LOCAL_MACHINE\SOFTWARE\Microsoft\Windows NT\CurrentVersion\Winlogon.
3. From the Edit menu, select New > String Value.
4. Enter a name of **ReportControllerMissing** and press Enter.
5. Double-click the new value and set to **TRUE** (must be uppercase). Click OK.

Now for each user who you wish to controller-missing message to be displayed, perform the following:

1. Start the Registry editor (REGEDIT.EXE).
2. Move to HKEY_CURRENT_USER\Software\Microsoft\Windows NT\CurrentVersion\Winlogon.
3. From the Edit menu, select New > DWORD Value.
4. Enter a name of **ReportDC** and press Enter.
5. Double-click the new value and set to 1. Click OK.

You may want to automate this via a logon script or via a policy template.

This warning was probably removed by default because most users would not understand the warning and would just ignore it. Be selective about reenabling it.

FAQ 7.41 How do I manually delegate authority in Windows 2000?

Windows NT basically had two types of users, Administrators and Users. While other groups exist such as Print Operators and Server Operators, when it comes to authority of users, you had all or none.

Now with the Directory service holding much more than just passwords and profile settings, it's desirable for people other than Administrators to update information like address and telephone number (you don't want your highly paid Administrators managing the phone numbers!).

It's possible to allow certain users and/or groups to manually manage the properties of other users as follows:

1. Start the Active Directory Users and Computers MMC snap-in (Start > Programs > Administrative Tools > Active Directory Users and Computers).
2. Enable the Advanced View (View Menu > Advanced Features).
3. Right-click on the User/Group/OU/Domain and select Properties from the context menu.
4. Select the Security tab.
5. Click the Advanced button.
6. Under the Permissions tab, either add a new user/group or select an existing permission entry and click the View/Edit button.
7. Select the Object or Properties tab and set the relevant Allow/Deny option for the specific option (see Figure 7-4).
8. Click OK to all dialogs.

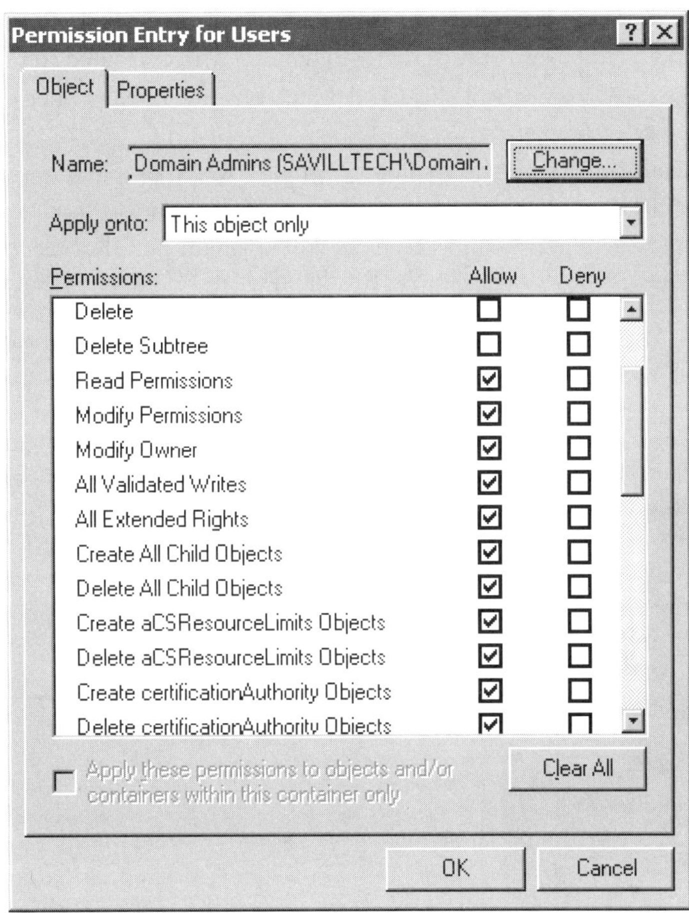

Figure 7-4 Modifying permissions on the Users container

FAQ 7.42 How do I delegate authority in Windows 2000 using the wizard?

It's possible to delegate authority in the Active Directory using a wizard, which is simpler than manually delegating authority:

1. Start the Active Directory Users and Computers MMC snap-in (Start > Programs > Administrative Tools > Active Directory Users and Computers).
2. Right-click on the container (domain/OU/built-in) and select Delegate Control from the context menu.

3. Click Next to the Delegation of Control Wizard.
4. Click Add to add users/groups that will have control delegated to them.
5. Select the users/groups and click Add. Click OK. Click Next once users/groups have been selected.
6. Select whether all objects in the folder will be covered or whether only certain objects—for example, select User objects only. Click Next.
7. Select the type of permissions; General will normally be OK. Select the type of Permissions—for example, Read and write Phone and Mail Options. Click Next.
8. Click Finish to the wizard (see Figure 7-5).

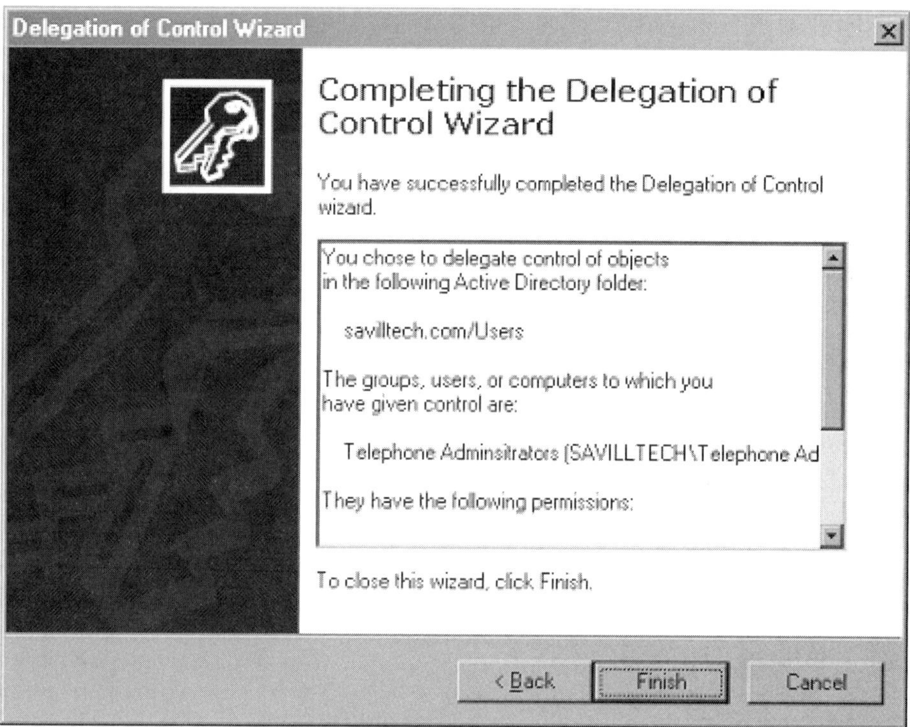

Figure 7-5 Using the Delegation of Control Wizard

FAQ 7.43 Why do the files and folders I delete from my profile reappear when using roaming profiles?

With roaming profiles, the user's profile is stored centrally on a server, and a copy is cached locally on machines the user logs onto.

If a user logs onto computer a and logs off, computer a has a cached version of the profile. If the user then logs onto computer b and deletes a number of files/folders and logs off, the central profile is updated without the files.

The problem is if the user logs back onto computer a, the locally cached version has the deleted files and folders so they will be copied back to the server!

The solution is to disable profile caching on each machine, which is explained in FAQ 7.44.

FAQ 7.44 How do I disable locally cached profiles?

To disable a locally cached version of the user's profile, perform the following on each machine:

1. Start the Registry editor (REGEDIT.EXE).
2. Move to HKEY_LOCAL_MACHINE\SOFTWARE\Microsoft\Windows NT\CurrentVersion\Winlogon.
3. From the Edit menu, select New > DWORD Value.
4. Enter a name of **DeleteRoamingCache** and press Enter.
5. Double-click the new value and set to 1.
6. Click OK.

FAQ 7.45 How do I create a new local user in Windows 2000?

As long as your machine is not a domain controller, you can add local users to it. While it's possible to use the Local users and groups branch of the System tools root of Computer Management, a nice quick method is available.

1. Start Control Panel (Start > Settings > Control Panel).
2. Double-click User Accounts.
3. Select the Users tab (see Figure 7-6).

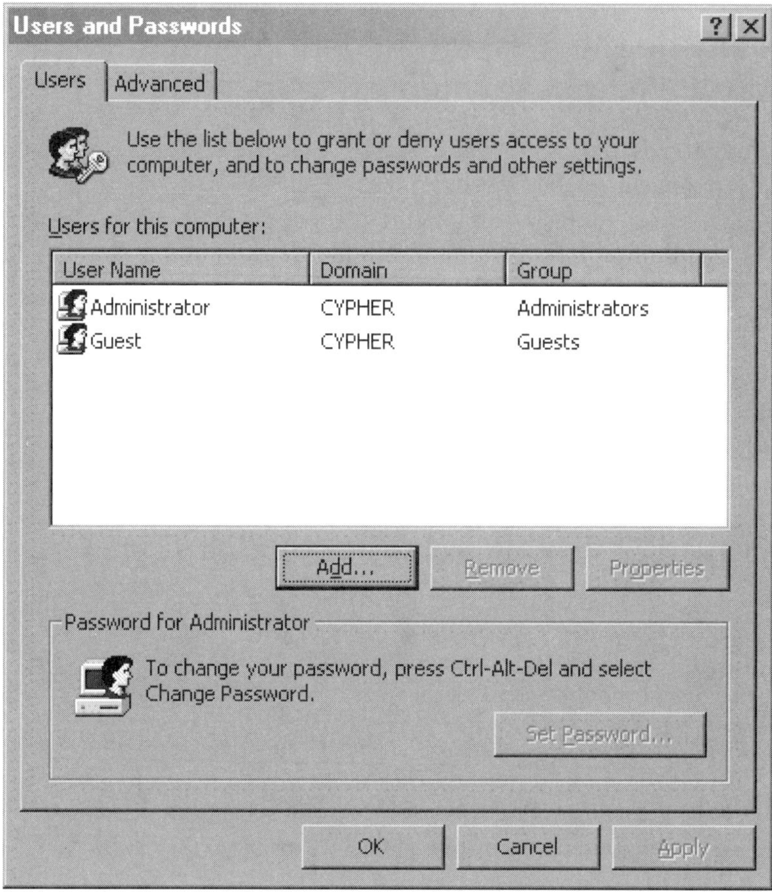

Figure 7-6 The Users tab of the Users and Passwords Control Panel applet

Selecting the Advanced tab shows the same information as the Local Users and Groups branch from Computer Management.

4. Click Add.
5. Enter a username, password, and description and click Next.
6. Enter the specified password again for verification.
7. Select the type of user: standard, restricted, or other (e.g., Administrator, Backup operator, etc.—see Figure 7-7).
8. Click Finish.

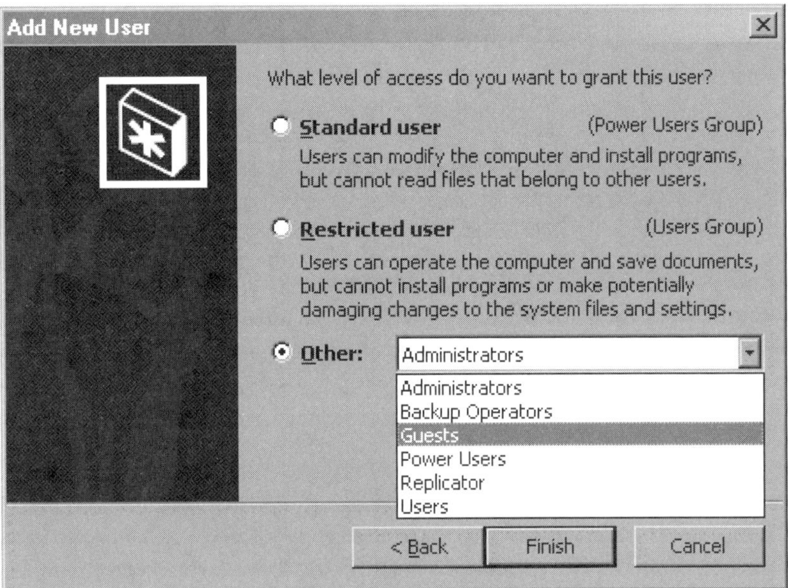

Figure 7-7 Selecting the access for a new user

FAQ 7.46 How can I configure the system to let users change their passwords without logging onto the domain?

If you use a password policy in a Windows 2000 domain and you migrated some or all of the users to Active Directory (AD) with the AD Migration tool, users who attempt to change their passwords as soon as they receive the Password Change Notification message might receive the following error message:

```
You do not have permission to change your password.
```

However, users who choose not to change their passwords when the Password Change Notification message appears (by clicking No) are logged on with their old passwords and then can change their passwords.

This system behavior occurs when the Everyone group hasn't been granted the Change Password right on the user object. Users can't change their passwords over the null session connection (anonymous logon relies on the Everyone group to carry out this action) established between the workstation and a domain controller. Instead, an authenticated session is required to change a password (i.e., users must be logged on to change their passwords).

To change the permissions setting for the Everyone group, take the following steps:

1. Start the AD Users and Computers snap-in (Start > Programs > Administrative Tools > Active Directory Users and Computers).
2. Select the View menu and enable Advanced Features.
3. Right-click the container hosting the user object to which you want to grant the Change Password right (e.g., Users); then click Properties.
4. Select the Security tab. Ensure that the Everyone group is listed in the Name box. If it isn't, click Advanced; then add the Everyone group to the list from the Advanced Access Control Settings dialog box. If the Everyone group is listed, click Advanced.
5. Click the Everyone group in the list; then click View/Edit to edit the group's permissions. In the Apply Onto box, click User Objects. In the Permissions section, select the Allow checkbox for "Change Password" (see Figure 7-8).
6. Click OK to accept the changes.

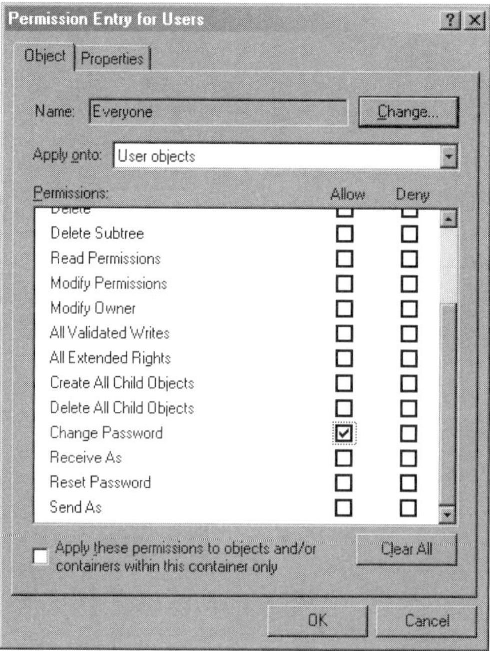

Figure 7-8 Allowing Everyone to change password for the Users container

FAQ 7.47 How can I move the My Documents and My Pictures folders?

You can change where the My Documents and My Pictures shortcuts point to by performing the following steps:

1. Start REGEDIT.EXE.
2. Go to HKEY_CURRENT_USER\SOFTWARE\Microsoft\Windows\CurrentVersion\Explorer\User Shell Folders.
3. Double-click Personal (for My Documents) and change the value.
4. Double-click My Pictures and change the value.
5. Close Regedit.
6. Log off and restart the machine for the change to take effect.

You can also redirect these folders using a Group Policy Object (GPO)—look under User Configuration > Windows Settings > Folder Redirection. Right-click a folder and select its redirection.

Another method to move the My Documents is as follows:

1. On the desktop, right-click the My Documents folder icon.
2. Select Properties.
3. Click Move and select your new location.

Everything is moved automatically, including the My Picture reference.

FAQ 7.48 How do I change the directory in which the system stores profiles?

Windows NT 4.0 and earlier versions of NT store profiles in the %systemroot%\Profiles folder. Windows 2000 stores profiles in %systemdrive%\Documents and Settings, but the OS lets you specify a different location. To change the location, take the following steps:

1. Create a new folder to host the profiles.
2. Copy all existing profiles from the %systemdrive%\Documents and Settings folder to the folder you just created. (Note: If you're copying from NTFS to NTFS, use the XCOPY command with the /o switch to maintain any access control lists—ACLs—on the files.)

3. Launch REGEDIT.EXE, and go to HKEY_LOCAL_MACHINE\SOFTWARE\Microsoft\Windows NT\CurrentVersion\ProfileList.
4. Double-click ProfilesDirectory.
5. Enter the path to the new folder and click OK.

You can change the profile Win2K uses for default users by modifying the DefaultUserProfile string value, and you can change the profile Win2K uses for all users by modifying AllUsersProfile.

FAQ 7.49 Why are some dial-in options missing for users who use the Active Directory Users and Computers snap-in?

With the Microsoft Management Console (MMC) Active Directory Users and Computers snap-in, the following dial-in options might not be available (see Figure 7-9):

- Control access through Remote Access Policy
- Verify Caller ID
- Assign a Static IP Address
- Apply Static Routes
- Static Routes

These Windows 2000 options aren't available because the domain is in mixed mode. Windows NT 4.0 domain controllers (DCs) don't support the Win2K options, so the options aren't available. To enable the options, you must switch to native mode (although this switch is a one-way operation, so be certain before you perform this action).

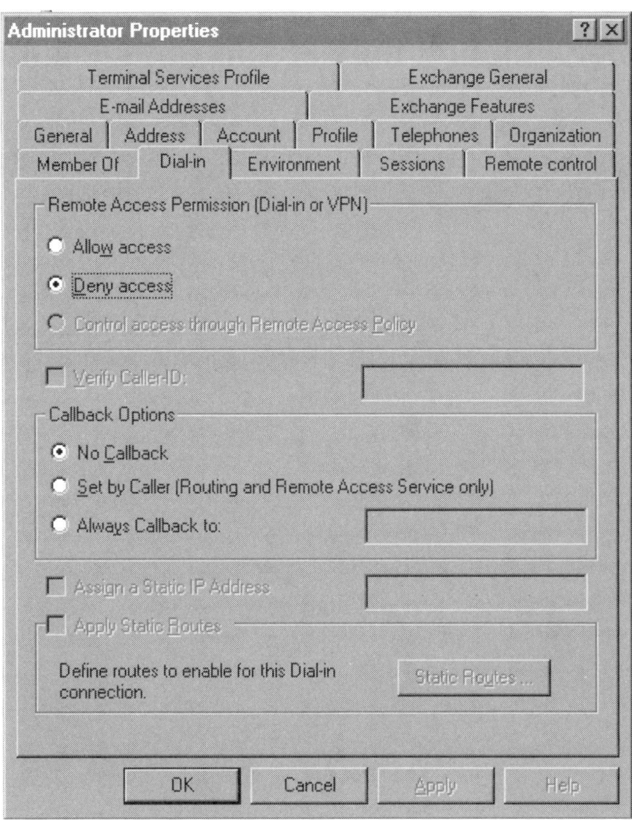

Figure 7-9 Setting the RAS permissions for a user

FAQ 7.50 Why does the system ignore my ExcludeProfileDirs when the entry is more than 260 characters?

In FAQ 7.38, we explored how to stop certain areas of a profile from replicating when you use roaming profiles. A problem in Windows 2000 causes the ExcludeProfileDirs entry to be set to NULL if the entry is longer than 260 characters. To address this problem, check the value at HKEY_CURRENT_USER\Software\Microsoft\WindowsNT\CurrentVersion\Winlogon\ExcludeProfileDirs to ensure that it is less than 260 characters. Or you can modify your system policy, as described in FAQ 7.38.

FAQ 7.51 How do I modify the default Telnet client terminal type?

When you connect via Telnet, your session can emulate one of a number of types. You usually can set the type by starting Telnet and running the following command:

```
set term x
```

where x is ANSI, VT100, VT52, or VTNT.

You can also set the type in the Registry. To avoid having to set each type, perform the following steps:

1. Start REGEDIT.EXE.
2. Go to HKEY_CURRENT_USER\SOFTWARE\Microsoft\Telnet.
3. From the Edit menu, select New > DWORD Value.
4. Enter a name of **TERMTYPE**.
5. Set TERMTYPE to one of the following:
   0—Default VTNT
   1—VT100
   2—VT52
   3—ANSI
6. Click OK.
7. Close Regedit.

FAQ 7.52 How can I prevent a user from running or stopping a scheduled process?

You can block user access to scheduled tasks in a number of ways. To block access at a Group Policy level, perform the following steps:

1. Start Group Policy editor (GPE) for the container you want to modify.
2. Expand either User Configuration or Computer Configuration.
3. Expand Administrative Templates > Windows Components > Task Scheduler.
4. Double-click Prevent Task Run or End.
5. Select Enabled and click OK.

You can also edit the Registry to block access on a per-computer or per-user basis:

1. Start REGEDIT.EXE on the machine where you want to block access.
2. Go to HKEY_LOCAL_MACHINE\SOFTWARE\Policies\Microsoft\Windows\Task Scheduler5.0 or HKEY_CURRENT_USER\Software\Policies\Microsoft\Windows\Task Scheduler5.0 (you might need to create the key).
3. From the Edit menu, select New > DWORD Value, enter a name of **Execution**, and press Enter.
4. Double-click the new value and set it to 1. Click OK.
5. Close Regedit.

FAQ 7.53 How do I toggle Windows XP's new menu mode and Classic Start menu mode?

Windows XP has a new Start menu mode. However, the old Classic Start menu mode is still available. To toggle between these two modes, perform the following steps:

1. Right-click the Start button and select Properties.
2. Select either Start menu for the new format or Classic Start menu (see Figure 7-10).
3. Click OK.

You can also use the Registry to toggle the menu modes, but this procedure can get tricky. To use the Registry to set the menu mode, perform the following steps:

1. Start the Registry editor (REGEDIT.EXE).
2. Go to HKEY_CURRENT_USER\Software\Microsoft\Windows\CurrentVersion\Explorer.
3. Double-click ShellState.
4. Modify byte 32 from 00 to 02 for the new XP Start menu mode or vice versa for the Classic Start menu mode (see Figures 7-11 and 7-12).
5. Click OK.
6. Close the Registry editor.
7. Log off and log on to your system for the change to take effect; alternatively, terminate and recreate the Windows Explorer task.

Figure 7-10 Switching between the Classic and new Start menus

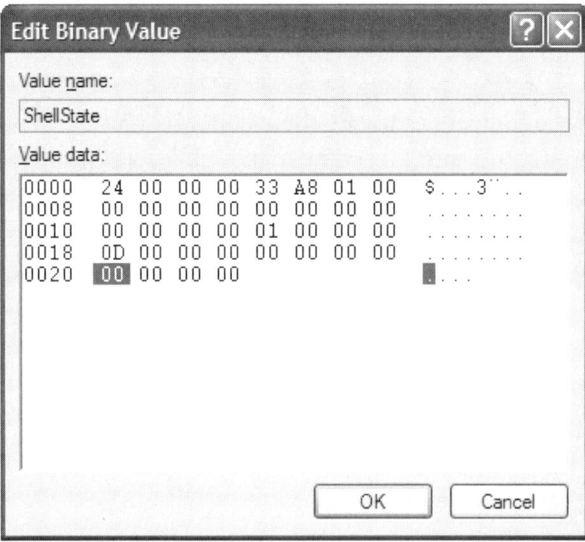

Figure 7-11 The Registry view for Classic mode

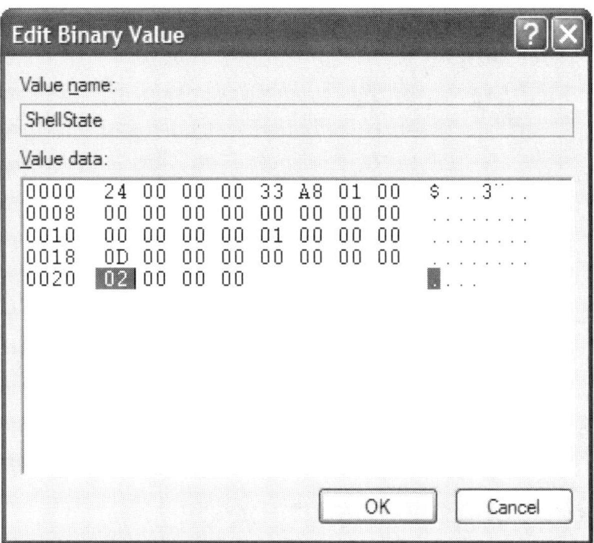
Edit Binary Value

Value name:

ShellState

Value data:

```
0000  24 00 00 00 33 A8 01 00  $...3"..
0008  00 00 00 00 00 00 00 00  ........
0010  00 00 00 00 01 00 00 00  ........
0018  0D 00 00 00 00 00 00 00  ........
0020  02 00 00 00              ....
```

OK Cancel

Figure 7-12 The Registry view after change

FAQ 7.54 How do I disable the ToolTips in Windows XP and Windows 2000 for the Minimize, Maximize, and Close buttons?

XP and Win2K display a tip when you position the mouse on the Minimize, Maximize, or Close buttons. To disable this functionality, perform the following steps:

1. Start the Registry editor (REGEDIT.EXE).
2. Go to HKEY_CURRENT_USER\Control Panel\Desktop.
3. Double-click UserPreferencesMask.
4. Modify the first number in the string using the following equivalent values (e.g., change 9e 3e 07 80 to 1e 3e 07 80):

   Change 8 to 0

   Change 9 to 1

   Change a to 2

   Change b to 3

   Change c to 4

   Change d to 5

   Change e to 6

5. Click OK.
6. Close the Registry editor.
7. Log off, then log on again for the change to take effect.

FAQ 7.55 Why can't I rename or enable the KRBTGT account?

The Windows 2000 (and later) Server family uses the KRBTGT account as part of Kerberos authentication. You can't use this account to log on to a server, and you can't rename or enable it.

FAQ 7.56 How do I enable clear type on the welcome screen?

Windows XP introduces clear type, which greatly improves the readability on LCD screens. You usually enable clear type on a per-user basis, so it isn't enabled for the logon screen. To enable clear type for the logon screen, perform the following steps:

1. Start the Registry editor (REGEDIT.EXE).
2. Go to HKEY_USERS\.DEFAULT\Control Panel\Desktop.
3. Double-click FontSmoothing and set it to 2. Click OK.
4. Double-click FontSmoothingType and set it to 2. Click OK.
5. Close the Registry editor.

The logon screen will now use clear type.

FAQ 7.57 How do I change the location of the shortcuts in the Windows Start menu?

Windows typically loads the Start menu shortcuts for the user profile from the %USERPROFILE%\Start Menu folder. To modify these shortcuts, perform the following steps:

1. Start a Registry editor (e.g., REGEDIT.EXE).
2. Navigate to HKEY_CURRENT_USER\Software\Microsoft\Windows\CurrentVersion\ExplorerUser Shell Folders.

3. Double-click the Start Menu Registry value.
4. Change the path to point to the new location of the Start menu shortcuts and click OK.
5. Close the Registry editor.
6. Log off and log on for the change to take effect.

You can also use Group Policy in Windows 2000 to accomplish this same change. Go to User Configuration > Windows Settings > Folder Redirection; right-click the Start Menu option and enter the new shortcut path.

FAQ 7.58 How do I create a password-reset disk for a computer that's a member of a domain under Windows XP?

You can't create a password-reset disk for a domain account, but you can create this disk for a local account on a machine that's a member of a domain. To create the disk, perform the following steps:

1. Press Ctrl+Alt+Delete to open the Security dialog box.
2. Click Change Password.
3. Select Log on to specify the local computer.
4. Click Backup to start the Forgotten Password Wizard.
5. In the Current user account password box, type your password and click Next. The Forgotten Password Wizard creates the password-reset disk.
6. When the progress bar reaches 100% complete, click Next, then click Finish. The Forgotten Password Wizard returns you to the Change Password dialog box.
7. Remove the password-reset disk. Label the disk and store it in a safe place.
8. Click Cancel to exit the Change Password dialog box.
9. Click Cancel to exit the Windows Security dialog box.

FAQ 7.59 How do I disable the Windows XP balloon tips?

To disable the XP balloon tips, perform the following:

1. Start the Registry editor (REGEDIT.EXE).
2. Move to HKEY_CURRENT_USER\Software\Microsoft\Windows\CurrentVersion\Explorer\Advanced.

3. From the Edit menu, select New > String value.
4. Enter a name of **EnableBalloonTips** and press Enter.
5. Double-click the new value and set to 0. Click OK.
6. Close the Registry editor.

You can also set this via TweakUI (Taskbar > Uncheck Enable balloon tips).

8 DESKTOP ENVIRONMENT

In this chapter, we discuss configurations that we can perform at a desktop level to change appearance and performance on our desktops. Many of these tips are for the current user—for example, the HKEY_CURRENT_USER Registry hive. However, if you want to perform the changes for another user or the default user, simply substitute HKEY_CURRENT_USER for HKEY_USERS\<SID of user> or HKEY_USERS\.DEFAULT, respectively.

8.1 How do I reduce or increase the delay for cascading menus?

You can use TweakUI's Mouse tab and decrease/increase the menu time; however, this can also be accomplished using the Registry editor, by changing the value HKEY_CURRENT_USER\Control Panel\Desktop\MenuShowDelay to the required value.

8.2 How do I delete or rename the Recycle Bin?

When you right-click on the Recycle Bin, its context menu does not display a rename or delete option as on other desktop shortcuts and components. To add the rename option, perform the following:

1. Start the Registry editor (REGED32.EXE, don't use REGEDIT.EXE).
2. Move to HKEY_CLASSES_ROOT\CLSID\{645FF040-5081-101B-9F08-00AA002F954E}\ShellFolder.
3. Double-click on the Attributes value in the right pane.
4. Change from 40010020 to **50010020**.
5. Click OK.

If you right-click on Recycle Bin, you now have a rename option.

If you want to delete the icon, change the Attribute's value to **60010020** by following the preceding procedure. To have the rename **and** delete options, change the Attribute's value to **70010020**. You can now delete by right-clicking on the icon and selecting Delete. Click Yes to the confirmation.

You may want to avoid manually updating the Registry. You can delete the icon by using the TweakUI utility. If you have TweakUI installed, perform the following:

1. Start the TweakUI Control Panel applet (Start > Settings > Control Panel > TweakUI).
2. Click the Desktop tab.
3. Unselect the Recycle Bin box and click OK.

8.3 How do I disable Window Animation?

Using TWEAKUI on the General tab, you can unselect Window Animation, which will stop the animation when a window is minimized or restored. This can also be accomplished using the Registry:

1. Start the Registry editor (REGEDIT.EXE).
2. Goto the key HKEY_CURRENT_USER\Control Panel\Desktop\WindowMetrics.
3. Double-click MinAnimate.
4. Set to 1 for normal animation and set to 0 for none.
5. Close the Registry editor.
6. Log out and log on again (if you use TweakUI, you don't have to log out).

Under Windows XP, in the System Control Panel applet, select the Advanced tab, and under the Performance section, click Advanced. Under the Visual Effects area, you can uncheck the option Animate windows when minimizing and maximizing.

8.4 How do I disable the Task Manager?

You can disable the Task Manager by using the Registry as follows

1. Start the Registry editor.
2. Move to HKEY_CURRENT_USER\Software\Microsoft\windows\currentversion\Policies.
3. If the \System key does not exist create it.

4. Add a new value of type DWORD called DisableTaskMgr and set to 1.
5. Exit the Registry editor.

This can also be done using the Policy editor.

1. Start the Policy editor.
2. Select the user or edit the default user.
3. Go to Shell/Restrictions and select Remove Taskbar from user.

To remove Task Manager for all users, just rename TASKMGR.EXE to something else, or if it is on a NTFS partition, you can set the permissions so normal users cannot access it.

FAQ 8.5 How can I remove the Documents menu?

There is no way to remove the Documents menu from the Start button without Active Desktop installed, and you have to empty it at the start of each session. With Windows 98, you can remove the Documents menu.

1. Start the Registry editor (REGEDIT.EXE).
2. Move to HKEY_CURRENT_USER\Software\Microsoft\Windows\CurrentVersion\Policies\Explorer.
3. From the Edit menu, select New > DWORD Value.
4. Enter a name of **NoFavoritesMenu** and press Enter.
5. Double-click the new value and set to 1. Click OK.
6. Close the Registry editor.

Log off and on again, and the Documents menu is removed.

For NT, the documents menu is actually the contents of %systemroot%\Profiles\<username>\Recent—for example, d:\winnt\Profiles\savillj\Recent. If you delete the contents of this folder, then nothing will be shown in the Documents menu. The easiest way to do this is to create a batch file and place it in your startup group:

1. Start Notepad.
2. Enter into the file

   ```
   del /q %systemroot%\Profiles\%username%\Recent\*.*
   ```

   Type **%systemroot%** and **%username%** unless you are performing this procedure on a Windows 95 machine, in which case, you should type in real values.

3. Save the file as **"DELDOC.BAT"** (put the filename in quotes; otherwise, Notepad will add ".txt" to the end of the filename) in a directory of your choice.
4. Start Explorer.
5. Move to the folder you saved DELDOC.BAT to and right-click on it.
6. Drag the file to %systemroot%\Profiles\%username%\Start Menu\Programs\Startup (e.g., d:\winnt\Profiles\savillj\etc.) and release. Select create shortcut here from the displayed context menu.

When you log on from now on, the batch file will be run, and it will delete your Documents menu.

The same effect can be achieved if you have TweakUI installed by clicking the Paranoia tab and checking Clear Document history at logon.

If you have Active Desktop in NT 4.0 or Windows 2000 using TweakUI 98, select the IE tab and unselect Show Documents on Start Menu, which can also be done by directly editing the Registry and setting HKEY_CURRENT_USER\Software\Microsoft\Windows\CurrentVersion\Policies\Explorer\NoRecentDocsMenu to 1 (of type REG_BINARY).

FAQ 8.6 How can I configure the wallpaper to be displayed somewhere other than the center of the screen?

It is possible to configure NT to display wallpaper anywhere on the screen; however, you have to manually update the Registry:

1. Start the Registry editor (REGED32.EXE).
2. Move to HKEY_CURRENT_USER\Control Panel\Desktop.
3. From the Edit menu, select Add Value.
4. Enter a name of **WallpaperOriginX** with a type of REG_SZ and click OK. You will then be prompted for a value, which is the number of pixels the left side of the image will be from the left side of the screen.
5. Next select Add Value again from the Edit menu, and this time, the name WallpaperOriginY. Click OK and enter the number of pixels the top of the image should be from the top of the screen.
6. Log off and log back on to see the change take effect.

FAQ 8.7 How can I configure NT to display a thumbnail of bitmaps instead of the Paint icon?

Perform the following; for best effect, make Explorer use large icons:

1. Start the Registry editor (REGEDIT.EXE).
2. Move to HKEY_CLASSES_ROOT\Paint.Picture\DefaultIcon.
3. Double-click on Default in the left pane and change to %1. Click OK.
4. Close the Registry editor. The change will take immediate effect.

FAQ 8.8 How can I configure the Windows XP and Windows 2000 Start menus to display items in alphabetical order?

The XP and Win2K Start menus can maintain a user-configured order; however, you might want to sort the Start menu items alphabetically. To sort the folders, right-click one of the folders in the Start menu and select Sort by Name from the displayed context menu.

You can also sort the folders using the Registry by performing the following steps:

1. Start a Registry editor (e.g., REGEDIT.EXE).
2. Navigate to HKEY_CURRENT_USER\Software\Microsoft\Windows\CurrentVersion\Explorer\MenuOrder.
3. Delete the MenuOrder key.
4. Close the Registry editor.

FAQ 8.9 How can I set a background picture for Windows Explorer toolbars in Windows XP and Windows 2000?

To configure a background for Windows Explorer toolbars, perform the following steps:

1. Start a Registry editor (e.g., REGEDIT.EXE).
2. Navigate to HKEY_CURRENT_USER\Software\Microsoft\Internet Explorer\Toolbar.

3. From the Edit menu, select New > String Value.
4. Enter a name of **BackBitmapShell** and press Enter.
5. Double-click the new value, set it to the name and location of the bitmap file you want to use for your background (e.g., c:\windows\zapotec.bmp), and click OK.
6. Close the Registry editor.

FAQ 8.10 How can I add a Copy to Folder option to the context menu?

It's possible to add a context menu option to copy a file to a folder by adding the following Registry key:

1. Start the Registry editor (REGEDIT.EXE).
2. Move to HKEY_CLASSES_ROOT\AllFilesystemObjects\shellex\ContextMenuHandlers.
3. From the Edit menu, select New > Key.
4. Enter a name of **Copy To** and press Enter.
5. Move to the Copy To key and double-click on the (Default) value.
6. Set to **{C2FBB630-2971-11D1-A18C-00C04FD75D13}**. Click OK.
7. Close the Registry editor.
8. Restart Explorer for the change to take effect (you don't need to reboot).

If you now right-click on a file or folder, an option to copy to a folder will be listed (see Figure 8-1).

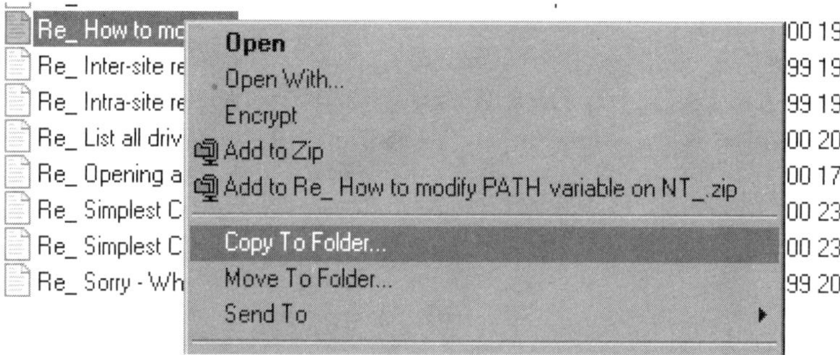

Figure 8-1 The Copy To Folder context menu

FAQ 8.11 How do I add an item to the Right-Click menu?

Follow this procedure:

1. Start the Registry Editor (REGEDIT.EXE).
2. Expand the HKEY_CLASSES_ROOT by clicking the plus sign.
3. Scroll down and expand the Unknown subkey.
4. Right-click on the Shell key.
5. Select New from the displayed context menu and choose Key.
6. Enter the name you want to be displayed—for example, the name of the application. Click Enter.
7. Right-click on the new subkey and click New. Again select Key, enter the name **Command**, and click Enter
8. Click on the newly created Command and double-click on (Default).
9. Enter the path and name of the executable with %1—for example, d:\program files\savedit\savedit.exe %1.
10. Close the Registry editor.

When you right-click on a file, the new entry will be displayed.

FAQ 8.12 How can I clear the Run history?

The Run history is stored in the Registry in location HKEY_CURRENT_USER\Software\Microsoft\Windows\CurrentVersion\Explorer\RunMRU as a series of values a–z. To delete an entry from the run menu, perform the following:

1. Start the Registry editor (REGEDIT.EXE).
2. Move to HKEY_CURRENT_USER\Software\Microsoft\Windows\CurrentVersion\Explorer\RunMRU.
3. Select the entry you wish to remove—for example, h.
4. Press the Del key (or select Edit > Delete) and click Yes to the confirmation.
5. Double-click the MRUList value and remove the letter you just deleted. Click OK to save the change.
6. Close the Registry editor.

If you want to clear the whole Run list, you can use the TweakUI utility:

1. Start the TweakUI Control Panel applet (Start > Settings > Control Panel > TweakUI).
2. Click the Paranoia tab :-).
3. Check Clear Run history at logon.
4. Click the Clear Selected Items Now.
5. You can then either clear the check on Clear Run history at logon and click OK, or leave it checked to automatically clear the Run at logon.

FAQ 8.13 How do I change the Internet Explorer icon?

For Internet Explorer version prior to 4.0, follow this procedure:

1. Start the Registry editor (REGEDIT.EXE).
2. Move to HKEY_CLASSES_ROOT\CLSID\{FBF23B42-E3F0-101B-8488-00AA003E56F8}\DefaultIcon.
3. Double-click Default on the right side and change to the icon you require (use Browse).
4. Select OK.
5. Close the Registry editor.

The MicroAngelo program, which automates this procedure, is available from http://www.iconstructions.com.

The preceding solution does not work for Internet Explorer 4.0 and above. For Internet Explorer 4.0 and above, the method is as follows:

1. Start the Registry editor (REGEDIT.EXE).
2. Move to HKEY_CLASSES_ROOT\CLSID\{871C5380-42A0-1069-A2EA-08002B30309D}.
3. From the Edit menu, select New > Key and enter the name of **DefaultIcon** and press Enter.
4. Double-click Default on the right side and change to the icon you require (use Browse).
5. Select OK.
6. Close the Registry editor.

Some really nice IE icons are available at http://www.blably.com/iconstructions/.

FAQ 8.14 How do I change the Network Neighborhood icon?

This icon can be changed using Themes for NT or the Plus Tab of Display settings. It can also be changed using the Registry editor:

1. Start the Registry editor (REGEDIT.EXE).
2. Move to the HKEY_LOCAL_MACHINE\SOFTWARE\Classes\CLSID\{208D2C60-3AEA-1069-A2D7-08002B30309D}\DefaultIcon.
3. Double-click on (Default).
4. Set to the icon required—for example, d:\Prog Files\Plus\Themes\John.ico,0. The 0 shows it is icon 1 in the file.
5. Exit the Registry editor.

FAQ 8.15 How do I change the Recycle Bin icons?

There are two icons for the Recycle bin, an empty and a full. To change them, use the following:

1. Start the Registry editor (REGEDIT.EXE).
2. Move to the HKEY_LOCAL_MACHINE\SOFTWARE\Classes\CLSID\{645FF040-5081-101B-9F08-00AA002F954E}\DefaultIcon.
3. To change the empty icon, double-click on Empty. To change the full icon, double-click on Full.
4. Set to the icon required—for example, d:\Prog Files\Plus\Themes\John.ico,0. The 0 shows it is icon 1 in the file.
5. Exit the Registry editor.

You can also change the icons using the Plus tab of Display properties.

FAQ 8.16 I have deleted the Recycle Bin. How can I recreate it?

If you have TweakUI, click the Desktop tab, check the Recycle Bin, and click Apply. Then click OK. If you do not have TweakUI, you can readd the Recycle Bin by directly updating the Registry:

1. Start the Registry editor (REGEDIT.EXE).
2. Move to HKEY_LOCAL_MACHINE\SOFTWARE\Microsoft\Windows\CurrentVersion\Explorer\Desktop\NameSpace.
3. From the Edit menu, select New > Key.
4. Enter a name of **{645FF040-5081-101B-9F08-00AA002F954E}**.
5. Select the new key and double-click on (Default). Set to Recycle Bin and click OK.
6. Close the Registry editor.
7. Press F5 on the desktop for the Recycle bin to appear.

FAQ 8.17 I have deleted Internet Explorer from the desktop. How can I recreate it?

Again you can use TweakUI. Select Desktop, check the Internet box, click Apply, and then OK. Alternatively you can directly edit the Registry:

1. Start the Registry editor (REGEDIT.EXE).
2. Move to HKEY_LOCAL_MACHINE\SOFTWARE\Microsoft\Windows\CurrentVersion\Explorer\Desktop\NameSpace.
3. From the Edit menu, select New > Key.
4. Enter a name of **{FBF23B42-E3F0-101B-8488-00AA003E56F8}**.
5. Select the new key and double-click on (Default). Set to The Internet and click OK.
6. Close the Registry editor.
7. Press F5 on the desktop for the Internet Explorer icon to appear.

FAQ 8.18 How can I add a shortcut to launch a screensaver on the desktop?

Screensavers are just programs with a .SCR extension. To create a shortcut of a screensaver, perform the following:

1. Start Explorer (Win+E or Start > Programs > NT Explorer).
2. Move to the %systemroot%\system32 directory (e.g., d:\winnt\system32).
3. Find the .SCR file of the screensaver. (You could perform a search; Tools > Find > Folders of Files. Enter a name of ***.SCR** and unselect Include subfolders, then click Find Now.)

4. Right-click on one of them, drag it to the desktop, release the right mouse button, and select Create shortcut here.
5. Next right-click on the new shortcut and select Properties.
6. In the target box, add to the end **-s**—for example, C:\WINNT\system32\sspipes.scr -s.
7. Click OK.

This screensaver is not password protected.

FAQ 8.19 How do I delete/rename the Inbox icon?

When you right-click on the Inbox icon, its context menu does not display a rename or delete option as on other desktop shortcuts and components. To add the rename option, perform the following:

1. Start the Registry editor (REGED32.EXE, don't use REGEDIT.EXE).
2. Move to HKEY_CLASSES_ROOT\CLSID\{00020D75-0000-0000-C000-000000000046}\ShellFolder.
3. Double-click on the Attributes value in the right pane.
4. Change from 72000000 to **50000000**.
5. Click OK.

If you right-click on the Inbox icon, you now have a rename option.

If you want to be able to delete the icon, change the Attributes value to **60000000** by following the preceding procedure. You can now delete by right-clicking the icon and selecting Delete. Click Yes to the confirmation.

You may want to avoid manually updating the Registry. You can delete the icon by using the TweakUI utility. If you have TweakUI installed, perform the following:

1. Start the TweakUI Control Panel applet (Start > Settings > Control Panel > TweakUI).
2. Click the Desktop tab.
3. Unselect the Inbox box, click Apply and then OK.

FAQ 8.20 Can I remove one of the startup folders on the Start menu?

Unfortunately no. One of the startup folders is your own user startup folder (%system-root%\Profiles\<Username>\Start Menu\Programs\Startup), and the other is the All Users (%system root%\Profiles\All Users\Start Menu\Programs\Startup). Both are system files and therefore undeletable.

It is possible to **hide** one or both of the startup folders by setting the hidden attribute on the folder:

```
attrib +h %system root%\Profiles\<Username>\Start Menu\Programs\
Startup
```

A trick has been found to remove one of the startup menus by copying the All Users Startup group over the Administrator Startup group, which then deletes the All Users startup group.

To be precise, you cannot delete either of the two Startup groups; the settings for both must exist, and the paths for both must exist.

However, the Startup group setting is independent of the Start menu setting. The problem is Microsoft defaults to putting the Startup group nested inside the Start menu.

Change the Startup group path in the Registry (key HKEY_CURRENT_USER\Software\Microsoft\Windows\CurrentVersion\Explorer\Shell Folders) to something like:

```
%systemroot%\Profiles\<Username>\Startup
```

You can leave the Start menu path as:

```
%systemroot%\Profiles\<Username>\Start Menu
```

Any shortcuts existing in the Startup group will still get launched, even though you do not see them in the Start menu.

FAQ 8.21 How do I change the color used to display compressed files/directories?

The color used is stored in the Registry in hexadecimal format; therefore, before you try to change the color, you need to work out what the value is in hex. You usually know a color as an RGB value like 255,0,0 for red. To convert this value to hex, use the calculator supplied with Windows NT (CALC.EXE):

1. Start the Calculator (Start > Run > CALC.EXE).
2. From the View menu, select Scientific.
3. Select Dec and enter in the first part of the RGB value.
4. Click Hex, and it will be displayed in hex—for example, 255 would show ff.
5. Repeat for the G and B parts of the color.

You will now have a hex value for the color—for example, 255,128,0 would be ff, 80, 0.

1. Start the Registry editor (REGEDIT.EXE).
2. Move to HKEY_CURRENT_USER\Software\Microsoft\Windows\CurrentVersion\Explorer.
3. Double-click on the AltColor value in the right pane.
4. You will see the actual value as something like "0000 00 00 FF 00 ..y". Ignore the set of four zeros and modify only the three sets of numbers after that—that is, the 00, 00 and FF; ignore the last two. To edit, click once to the right of the value you wish to change, then press the backspace key. You will have deleted **both** parts of the number; then type in your new value.
5. Click OK and then close the Registry editor.
6. You will need to log off and on again for the change to take effect.

If you would prefer to avoid the Registry, you can make the same change using the TweakUI utility.

1. Start the TweakUI Control Panel applet (Start > Settings > Control Panel > TweakUI).
2. Click on the Explorer tab.
3. At the bottom of the dialog is the color of compressed files (why can't Americans spell "colour"? ☺); click Change Color.
4. You can now just select the color you want and click OK.
5. Click OK.
6. You will need to log off and on again for the change to take effect.

8.22 How can I get rid of the arrow over the shortcuts?

You can remove the overlay by using TweakUI.

1. Start TweakUI Control Panel applet (Start > Settings > Control Panel > TweakUI).
2. Click the Explorer tab.
3. Select the arrow type (Arrow, Light arrow, None, or Custom).
4. Click Apply, then OK.
5. Close the TweakUI applet.

You can also remove the arrow by editing the Registry:

1. Start the Registry editor (REGEDIT.EXE).
2. Move to HKEY_CLASSES_ROOT\lnkfile.
3. Select IsShortcut and then Delete from the Edit menu.
4. Restart the machine.

8.23 How can I check for dead shortcuts on my system?

The Windows 2000 Resource Kit supplies CHKLNKS.EXE, which checks all your system's shortcuts. If the target of the shortcut is not found, it provides the option to delete one or all of the dead shortcuts.

To use it, just start the Chklnks utility, click Next, and select the dead shortcuts to remove (see Figure 8-2).

The utility also runs on NT 4 boxes with no obvious problems.

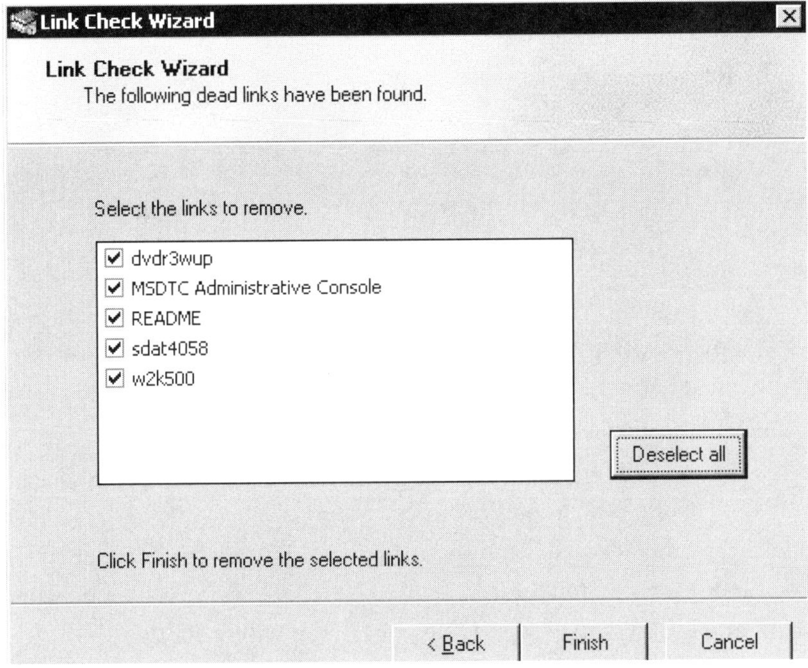

Figure 8-2 Dead links identified

FAQ 8.24 How can I minimize all open windows?

To minimize all open Windows, press Win key+M. To restore, press Win key+Shift+M. If you have the QuickLaunch toolbar, you can also select the Show desktop button.

FAQ 8.25 How do I change the My Computer icon?

This icon can be changed using Themes for NT or the Plus Tab of the Display settings. It can also be changed using the Registry editor:

1. Start the Registry editor (REGEDIT.EXE).
2. Move to HKEY_LOCAL_MACHINE\Software\Classes\CLSID\{20D04FE0-3AEA-1069-A2D8-08002B30309D}\DefaultIcon.
3. Double-click on (Default).

4. Set to the icon required—for example, d:\Prog Files\Plus\Themes\John.ico,0. The 0 shows it is icon 1 in the file.
5. Exit the Registry editor.

8.26 How do I hide the Network Neighborhood icon?

You can use TweakUI, and on the Desktop tab, unselect Network Neighborhood. This can also be done using the Registry:

1. Start the Registry editor (Regedit).
2. Move to the HKEY_CURRENT_USER\Software\Microsoft\Windows\CurrentVersion\Policies\Explorer.
3. From the Edit menu, select New > DWORD Value.
4. Enter a name of **NoNetHood** and press Enter.
5. Double-click the new value and set to 1. Click OK.
6. Close the Registry editor.
7. Log off and log on, and Network Neighborhood will be hidden.

8.27 Is it possible to move the taskbar?

The taskbar can be moved to any of the four sides—left, right, top, and bottom. To move it, just single-click on the taskbar and drag to the side of your screen you wish the taskbar to reside on.

If you have lost the taskbar, just press Ctrl+Esc to redisplay it.

8.28 How can I disable the right mouse button?

For those systems running with Windows NT 4.0 Service Pack 2 or above, it is possible to disable the context menu as follows:

1. Start the Registry editor (REGEDIT.EXE).
2. Move to HKEY_CURRENT_USER\Software\Microsoft\Windows\CurrentVersion\Policies\Explorer.
3. From the Edit menu, select New > DWord value.
4. Enter the name **NoViewContextMenu** and press Enter.

5. Double-click the new value, set the value to 1, and click OK.
6. Close the Registry editor.
7. Log out and log on again.

To remove the right mouse button context menu action, just delete the value NoViewContextMenu (or set it to 0) and log out and log on again.

FAQ 8.29 How do I change the Briefcase icon?

To change this icon, perform the same procedure as in FAQ 8.14, explained earlier in this chapter, but in step 2 move instead to HKEY_LOCAL_MACHINE\SOFTWARE\Classes\CLSID\{85BBD920-42A0-1069-A2E4-08002B30309D}\DefaultIcon.

FAQ 8.30 How can I prevent the "Click here to begin" message?

There are two ways to prevent this message. If you have the TweakUI utility, perform the following:

1. Start the TweakUI Control Panel Applet (Start > Settings > Control Panel > TweakUI).
2. Click the Explorer Tab.
3. Deselect Animated click here to begin.
4. Click OK.

If you don't have TweakUI, you will need to edit the Registry directly.

5. Start the Registry editor (REGEDIT.EXE).
6. Move to HKEY_CURRENT_USER\Software\Microsoft\Windows\CurrentVersion\Policies\Explorer.
7. Double-click on NoStartBanner and change to **01 00 00 00**.
8. Click OK.
9. Close the Registry editor.

FAQ 8.31 How do I remove a template from the New menu?

If you select New withinExplorer, for example, you will be given a large list of document templates that have registered themselves on your machine.

If you would like to trim away some of these, perform the following:

1. Start the Registry editor (REGEDIT.EXE).
2. Move to HKEY_CLASSES_ROOT.
3. Move to the file extension of the template you no longer want to be displayed—for example, .S3D for Simply 3D, .PSP for Paint Shop Pro, .DOC for Word.
4. If the template appears on the New menu, there will be a subkey, ShellNew. Select this key and press Del. Click YES to the confirmation.
5. Close the Registry editor.

It will now be removed from the new menu. (You have to restart Explorer if it is running so it reloads in the Registry information.)

FAQ 8.32 How can I get more room on the taskbar?

If you move the cursor over the top of the taskbar, it turns into a double-headed arrow. When the cursor is the double arrow, hold down the left button and drag upwards, and the task bar's area will be increased one row at a time. Likewise you can shrink it by dragging downwards.

FAQ 8.33 How do I add the Control Panel to the Start menu?

Create a new folder under the start menu profile you wish to have it on (Administrator or All users) using Explorer. Name the new folder as follows:

```
Control Panel.{21EC2020-3AEA-1069-A2DD-08002B30309D}
```

The name should contain the period, brackets, and dashes. Once the name is entered, the folder will automatically be renamed to Control Panel, and unlike the Settings Control Panel, it will be cascading, meaning all Control Panel applets will be shown as subobjects.

If you have a problem, try pressing F5 to refresh the screen, or log off and on again.

FAQ 8.34 How do I stop Windows 2000 Explorer from opening a new window when I map a network drive?

When you map a new network drive in Explorer, the system opens the newly mapped drive in a new window by default. To stop Win2K Explorer from opening a new window when you map a network drive, press the Shift key before you click Finish and continue to hold down the Shift key for a short time after you click Finish.

FAQ 8.35 How can I remove a program from Open With when right-clicking?

Each entry in Open With has an entry in the Registry HKEY_CLASSES_ROOT called "<extension>_auto_file"—for example, doc_auto_file for work. To remove the entry, just delete the base <extension>_auto_file tree in the Registry. If you are unsure, you could use the following:

1. Start the Registry editor (REGEDIT.EXE).
2. Search for the name of the EXE you want to remove from the Open With menu.
3. If a match is found, and its root is HKEY_CLASSES_ROOT/xxx_auto_file, then delete the tree HKEY_CLASSES_ROOT/xxx_auto_file.
4. Close the Registry editor.

FAQ 8.36 Why can't I move any icons?

It is possible to configure NT to autoarrange the icons, which means you cannot manually move them. To turn off this feature, right-click on the desktop (anywhere a window is not located), select Arrange Icons, and unselect Auto-Arrange.

FAQ 8.37 How do I customize the appearance of a folder?

With Windows 2000's integration with the Web, any folder on your machine can be customized to have its own look, links, background. Windows 2000 even has a neat wizard to help you do this. Let's explore this wizard.

You need to ensure that Web Content for Folders is enabled on your machine to be able to customize folders. This topic is covered in the next FAQ.

To customize a folder using the wizard, perform the following:

1. Start Explorer.
2. Select the folder you wish to customize.
3. From the View menu, select Customize This Folder.
4. Click Next to the wizard.
5. Select the options you wish to change for the folder (see Figure 8-3)
   - Custom HTML template
   - Select a background picture
   - Add a folder comment
6. Click Next.

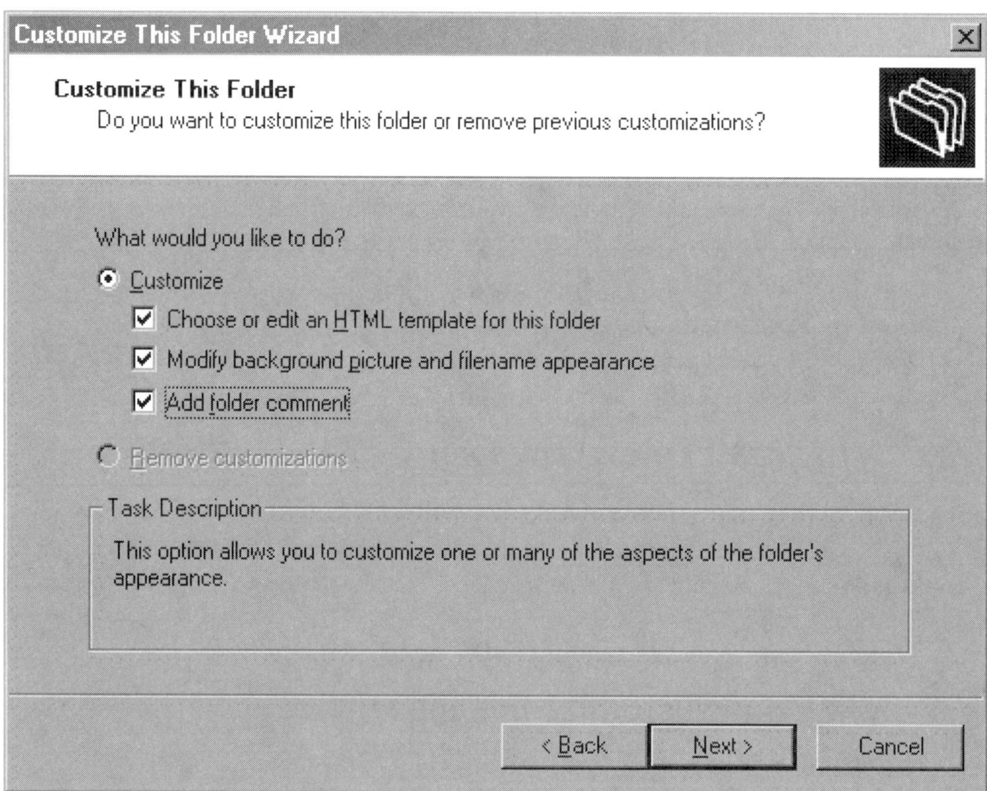

Figure 8-3 Customize options for a folder

7. If you selected a custom HTML template, a list of templates will be displayed:
   Standard
   Classic
   Simple
   Image Preview
   You can also select to edit the HTML for the template and click Next.
8. The next option is to select a background text color. Click Next.
9. Enter a comment for the folder and click Next.
10. Click Finish.

A new file DESKTOP.INI is created with your settings in it. A folder, Folder Settings, is also created, which contains the background picture. FOLDER.HTT is created, which is the information used to display the folder content.

FAQ 8.38 How do I remove the Favorites branch of the Start menu?

If you wish to remove your Favorites from the Start menu, perform the following:

1. Start the Registry editor (REGEDIT.EXE).
2. Move to HKEY_CURRENT_USER\Software\Microsoft\Windows\CurrentVersion\Policies\Explorer.
3. From the Edit menu, select New > DWORD Value.
4. Enter a name of **NoFavoritesMenu** and press Enter.
5. Double-click the new value and set to 1. Click OK.
6. Close the Registry editor.

Log off and on again and voilà, the Favorites menu is gone.

FAQ 8.39 I've lost the My Documents shortcut. How do I get it back?

If you deleted the My Documents shortcut from the desktop and want it back, just, perform the following:

1. Double-click My Computer.
2. Select Folder Options from the Tools menu.

3. Select View tab.
4. Check Show My Documents on the Desktop.
5. Click Apply, then OK.

FAQ 8.40 How do I disable the logoff buttons?

If you wish to disable the logoff buttons on the Start menu/NT Security dialog, perform the following:

1. Start the Registry editor (REGEDIT.EXE).
2. Move to HKEY_CURRENT_USER\Software\Microsoft\Windows\CurrentVersion\Policies\Explorer.
3. From the Edit menu, select New > DWORD Value.
4. Enter a name of **NoLogoff** and press Enter.
5. Double-click the new value and set to 1. Click OK.
6. Close the Registry editor.

The change takes immediate effect. To undo it, simply set to the value to 0.

FAQ 8.41 How can I disable personalized menus?

Personalized menus (or IntelliMenus as they are also known) are a new addition to Windows 2000. IntelliMenus display only the most commonly used shortcuts on your Programs and Favorites Start menu. If you find this feature annoying and not required, it can be disabled by performing the following:

1. Click the Start button.
2. Select Settings and select TaskBar & Start Menu.
3. Select the General tab.
4. Unselect Use Personalized Menus (see Figure 8-4).
5. Click Apply and then OK.

This can also be done by directly editing the Registry:

1. Start the Registry editor (REGEDIT.EXE).
2. Move to HKEY_CURRENT_USER\Software\Microsoft\Windows\CurrentVersion\Explorer\Advanced.
3. Double-click IntelliMenus (or create it of type String if it does not exist).

Figure 8-4 Personalized menus disabled here

4. No to disable.
5. Click OK.
6. Close the Registry editor.

FAQ 8.42 How do I add the Printers Settings applet to the Start menu?

Create a new folder under the Start menu you wish to have the Printer Settings applet shortcut on (Administrator, All users, or your specific profile)—for example, c:\winnt\Profiles\savillj\Start Menu. Name the new folder:

```
Printers.{2227A280-3AEA-1069-A2DE-08002B30309D}
```

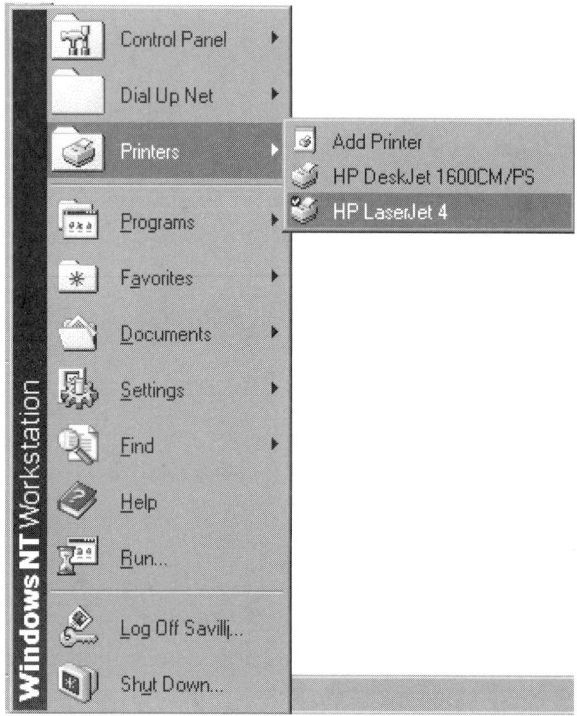

Figure 8-5 The expanded printers branch of the context menu

The name must include the period, brackets, and dashes. Once the name is entered, the folder will automatically be renamed to Printers, and unlike Settings Printers, it will be cascading, meaning all printers will be shown as subobjects (see Figure 8-5).

If you have a problem, try pressing F5 to refresh the screen or log off and on again.

FAQ 8.43 How can I configure Control Panel to cascade on the Start menu in Windows 2000?

This is normally done by selecting Taskbar & Start Menu from the Settings menu of the Start button. Select Start Menu Options and check the Expand Control Panel option. You can also accomplish this by directly editing the Registry:

1. Start the Registry editor (REGEDIT.EXE).
2. Move to HKEY_CURRENT_USER\Software\Microsoft\Windows\CurrentVersion\Explorer\Advanced.

3. From the Edit menu, select New > String value and enter a name of **CascadeControlPanel** (if it does not exist).
4. Double-click the new value and set to YES.
5. Close the Registry editor.
6. Log off and then log on.

FAQ 8.44 How can I remove the Scheduled Tasks icon from My Computer?

The Scheduled Tasks icon can be removed by editing the Registry as follows:

1. Start the Registry editor (REGEDIT.EXE).
2. Move to HKEY_LOCAL_MACHINE\SOFTWARE\Microsoft\Windows\CurrentVersion\Explorer\MyComputer\NameSpace.
3. Select {D6277990-4C6A-11CF-8D87-00AA0060F5BF}.
4. This step is optional: From the Registry menu, select Export Registry File. Enter a name for the REG file that will be created. This file will enable you to automatically undo this if you wish.
5. Press the Del key to delete the key.
6. Click Yes to the deletion confirmation dialog.

Scheduled Tasks will no longer be visible from My Computer.

To restore it using your REG file, just double-click on the REG file from Explorer, and scheduled tasks will be restored.

FAQ 8.45 How can I configure Administrative Tools to show on the Start menu?

By default under Windows 2000 Professional, the Administrative Tools branch is not shown as it is on the Windows 2000 Server, Advanced Server, and Datacenter products.

It can be configured as follows:

1. Start the Taskbar and Start menu configuration (Start > Settings > Taskbar and Start menu).
2. Select the Start Menu Options tab.
3. Check or uncheck the Display Administrative Tools.
4. Click Apply, then OK.

This updates the Registry entry HKEY_CURRENT_USER\Software\Microsoft\Windows\CurrentVersion\Explorer\Advanced\StartMenuAdminTools to either NO or YES.

8.46 How can I recreate My Briefcase if I deleted it?

To recreate the My Briefcase icon on your desktop, just type the following command either from a CMD.EXE session or the RUN box:

```
syncapp
```

You can also recreate My Briefcase by right-clicking on the desktop and selecting New > Briefcase.

8.47 How do I use My Briefcase?

My Briefcase allows you to synchronize multiple copies of files and keeps track of changes such as modifications, additions, and deletions. The normal usage method is as follows:

1. Insert a floppy disk into your floppy drive.
2. Create a new briefcase on the disk (from Explorer, select the drive, File > New > Briefcase). By default it will be called "New Briefcase," but you can rename by selecting and pressing F2.
3. Copy the files from your hard disk to the new briefcase.
4. You can now edit the files on the floppy to the hard disk. The files on the floppy can also be edited on other computers.

To sync the folders after making any changes, open the briefcase in Explorer (see Figure 8-6) and click the Update All button or select from the briefcase menu. Any modifications will be displayed, and you have the option to perform the actual update.

If you would actually like to be able to edit the files locally on different machines, then you should perform the following:

1. Insert a floppy disk.
2. Move the files you wish to keep synchronized to the floppy disk.
3. Create a briefcase on the local hard disk.

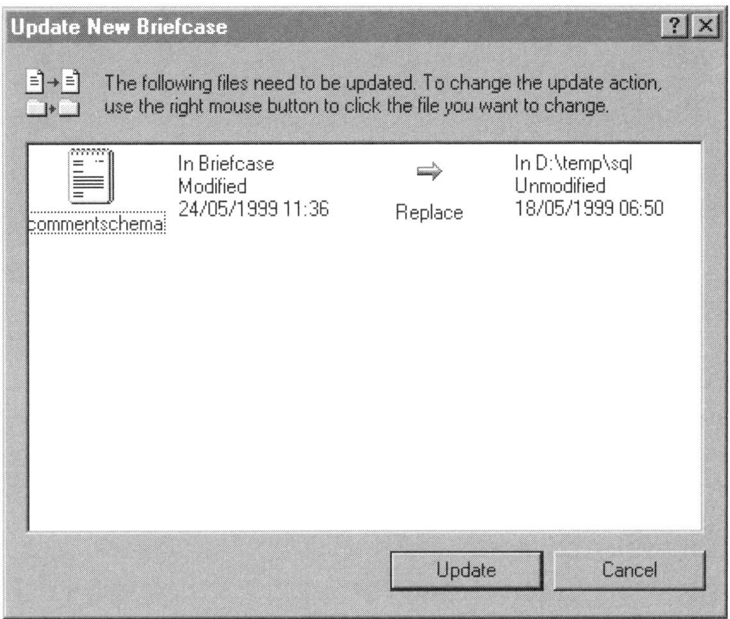

Figure 8-6 Out-of-date files identified for briefcase

4. Copy the files from the floppy to the local briefcase.
5. Repeat steps 3 and 4 on the other machine.

You now edit the files locally from the briefcase folder, which will be synchronized with the floppy disk. You have two briefcases, one on each machine. To synchronize the two briefcases, you select Update All after selecting the briefcase on the hard disk and inserting the floppy disk with the original files on it.

If two computers are connected via a network, just create a briefcase on one machine, which is accessible via a network share to the other, and copy the files accordingly.

If you create a briefcase on a hard disk and wish to move it to a floppy, do **not** copy it; you must **move** it or the associations between the files will be lost.

FAQ 8.48 Where are the Active Desktop background image settings located in the Registry?

The system stores the usual background wallpaper bitmap in the HKEY_CURRENT_USER\Control Panel\Desktop\Wallpaper Registry key. If you've enabled Active

Desktop and selected a different background picture, such as a JPEG, the system stores this wallpaper in the HKEY_CURRENT_USER\Software\Microsoft\Internet Explorer\Desktop\General\Wallpaper Registry key.

As with a standard wallpaper, with the Active Desktop wallpaper, you can tile the wallpaper by setting the value TileWallpaper to 1, and you can center or stretch the wallpaper by setting the WallpaperStyle. A value of 0 centers the wallpaper; a value of 2 stretches it. When you first log on, the system displays the standard wallpaper until all processes start and the Active Desktop is enabled.

FAQ 8.49 How do I use desktop themes in Windows 2000?

Windows 2000 has built-in support for themes but has no Control Panel icon for it. To use themes, you need to manually run the THEMES.EXE image, which is located in the %windir%\system32 directory.

There are some compatibility issues between Windows 2000 and older themes because themes for use with Windows 2000 must have the extension .THEME (in Windows 9x, the extension is .THE or .THM) so you must rename them.

Also Windows 9x sometimes uses an environment variable, %THEMESDIR%, that is not used in Windows 2000 so you may need to manually edit the themes file to correct these kinds of problems.

FAQ 8.50 How can I remove an item from the New context menu?

Many applications such as Office and other document-based programs may add options to the New context menu. This can slow down the system because systems with IE 4 or above have to generate this list, which involves fetching the icons for each of the documents (see Figure 8-7).

It's possible to remove items from the new context menu by performing the following:

1. Identify the file extension for the context menu item—for example, .OBD for Microsoft Office Binder (if you are unsure of the extension, just create a document of the file type and then check the extension).
2. Start the Registry editor (REGEDIT.EXE).
3. Move to HKEY_CLASSES_ROOT\.<extension>—for example, HKEY_CLASSES_ROOT\.obd.

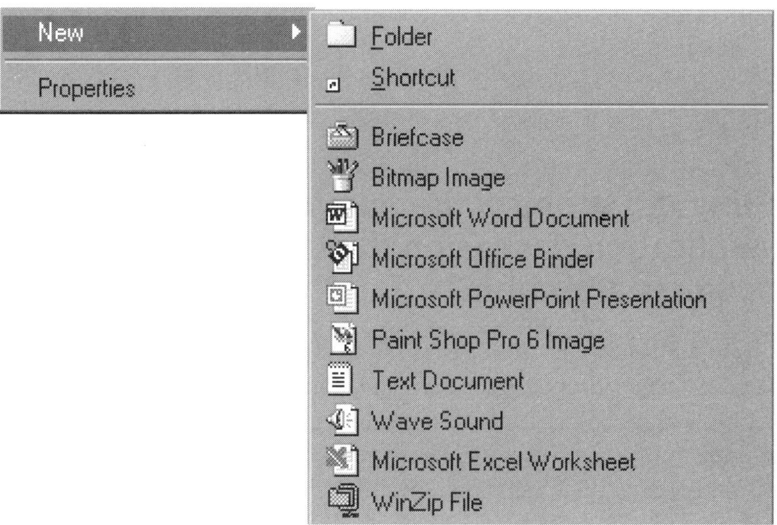

Figure 8-7 New file options

4. Delete or rename the ShellNew key. It may not always be at the root of the key—for example, to disable .OBD, I had to go to HKEY_CLASSES_ROOT\.obd\Office.Binder.9\ShellNew.
5. Close the Registry editor.
6. The context item should no longer be displayed.

This can also be accomplished using the TweakUI utility.

FAQ 8.51 How do I add the Dial Up Networking shortcut to the Start menu?

Create a New folder under the Start menu you wish to have it on (Administrator > All users or your specific profile)—for example, c:\winnt\Profiles\savillj\Start Menu. Name the new folder:

```
Dial Up Net.{992CffA0-F557-101A-88EC-00DD010CCC48}
```

The name of the folder should include the period, brackets, and dashes. Once the folder name is entered, the folder will automatically be renamed to "Dial Up Net" and unlike

Settings Dial Up Networking, it will be cascading, meaning all dial-up connections will be shown as subobjects.

If you have a problem, try pressing F5 to refresh the screen or log off and on again.

FAQ 8.52 How can I control the number of times an application flashes on the taskbar when it requires attention?

When you have multiple applications running and an application that isn't currently in the foreground wants user input, its taskbar entry flashes three times and, after 200 seconds, the application comes to the foreground.

To change the number of times the taskbar entry flashes and/or the delay time before the application comes to the foreground, perform the following steps:

1. Start REGEDIT.EXE.
2. Go to HKEY_CURRENT_USER\Control Panel\Desktop.
3. Double-click ForegroundFlashCount.
4. Set the Base value to Decimal, change the number of times the taskbar entry should flash, then click OK.
5. Double-click ForegroundLockTimeout.
6. Set the Base value to Decimal, change the number of milliseconds to wait before coming to the foreground (or set this value to 0 if you want the application to come to the foreground immediately), then click OK.
7. Close Regedit.

FAQ 8.53 How do I enable and disable the new Windows XP UI?

XP includes a new task-based UI that might take some getting used to but will no doubt prove popular with new users (see Figure 8-8). XP Home and XP Professional enable the new UI by default, but the Windows .NET Server family will retain the classic Windows UI. To switch between the UIs, perform the following steps:

1. Right-click the Start button and select Properties.
2. Select either Start Menu for the new interface or Classic Start Menu for the standard Windows interface.
3. Click OK.

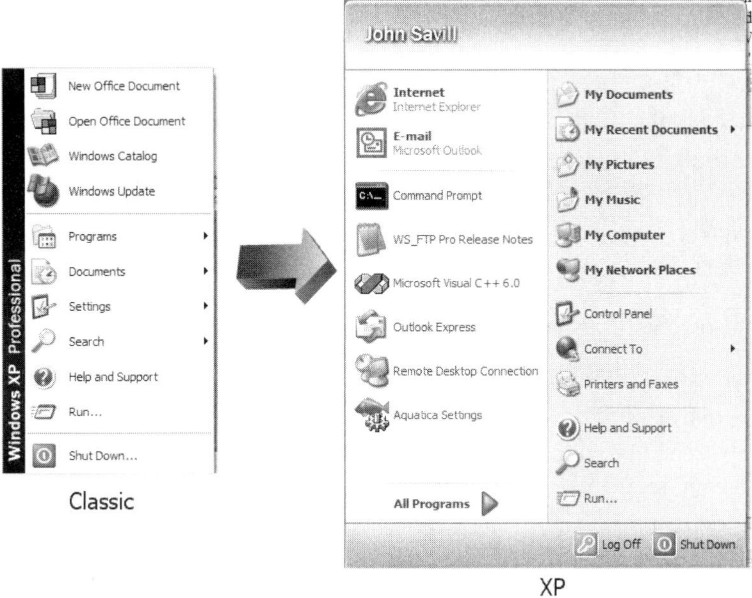

Figure 8-8 The Classic and new XP versions of the Start menu

FAQ 8.54 How can I configure the grouping of similar taskbar buttons in Windows XP?

XP lets you group multiple instances of the same executable on the taskbar in one of two ways:

- Clustering—XP places multiple instances of the same executable next to each other on the taskbar.
- Grouping—XP displays multiple instances of the same executable as one taskbar program instance (see Figure 8-9).

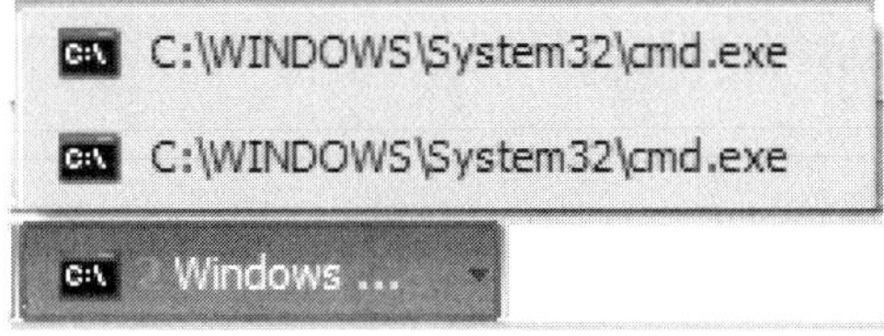

Figure 8-9 Multiple instances of one program grouped on the Start menu

By default, XP groups multiple instances of the same executable when insufficient space exists on the taskbar to display the appropriate text for each button. To disable grouping, perform the following steps:

1. Right-click the taskbar and select Properties.
2. Select the Taskbar tab.
3. Clear the Group similar taskbar buttons checkbox in the Taskbar appearance section (see Figure 8-10).
4. Click OK.

You can also adjust this setting in the Registry by performing the following steps:

1. Start the Registry editor (REGEDIT.EXE).
2. Navigate to HKEY_CURRENT_USER\Software\Microsoft\Windows\CurrentVersion\Explorer\Advanced.
3. Double-click TaskbarGlomming (or create this DWORD Value if it doesn't already exist).
4. Set this value to 1 to enable or 0 to disable, and click OK.

Figure 8-10 Option to enable grouping of similar tasks

5. Close the Registry editor.
6. Log off and log back on for the change to take effect, or if you feel brave, kill the Windows Explorer process and use Task Manager to recreate this process.

FAQ 8.55 How can I lock and unlock the Windows XP taskbar?

You can lock the taskbar in XP by right-clicking the taskbar and selecting Lock the Taskbar. You can also edit the Registry to lock the taskbar by performing the following steps:

1. Start the Registry editor (REGEDIT.EXE).
2. Navigate to HKEY_CURRENT_USER\Software\Microsoft\Windows\CurrentVersion\Explorer\Advanced.
3. Double-click TaskbarSizeMove.
4. Set the TaskbarSizeMove value to 0 to lock the taskbar or to 1 to unlock the taskbar, then click OK.
5. Close the Registry editor.

FAQ 8.56 How can I prevent users from using a nonbitmapped wallpaper?

Active Desktop lets you easily use most formats for the background picture. When you choose a picture that isn't a bitmap, the system asks whether you want to enable Active Desktop and use the image you selected. You can use Group Policy to restrict users to bitmapped images.

1. Start the Microsoft Management Console (MMC) Group Policy Editor (GPE) snap-in and load the Group Policy Object (GPO) you want.
2. Expand User Configuration > Administrative Templates > Desktop > Active Directory.
3. Double-click Allow only bitmapped wallpaper.
4. Select Enabled and click OK.
5. Close GPE.

You can also edit the Registry to restrict users to bitmapped images.

1. Start Regedit on the machine where you want to restrict users to bitmapped images.
2. Go to the HKEY_CURRENT_USER\Software\Microsoft\Windows\CurrentVersion\Policies\ActiveDesktop Registry subkey.
3. From the Edit menu, select New > DWORD Value.
4. Enter the name **NoHTMLWallPaper** and press Enter.
5. Double-click NoHTMLWallPaper, enter 1 for the Value data, and click OK.
6. Close the Registry editor.

FAQ 8.57 How do I enable ClearType in Windows XP?

XP, like Windows Me, supports ClearType. On LCD screens, ClearType offers a 300% higher than usual horizontal resolution, providing much clearer text than usual. To enable ClearType, perform the following steps.

1. Right-click the desktop and select Properties.
2. Click the Appearance tab.
3. Click Effects.
4. Under Use the following method to smooth edges of screen fonts, select ClearType.
5. Click OK.
6. Click OK on the main dialog box.

You can also edit the Registry to enable ClearType:

1. Go to the HKEY_CURRENT_USER\Control Panel\Desktop\FontSmoothing Registry subkey, and set the value to 0 to disable font smoothing or 2 to enable font smoothing.
2. Go to the HKEY_CURRENT_USER\Control Panel\Desktop\FontSmoothingType Registry subkey, and set the value to 0 for no smoothing, 1 for standard smoothing, or 2 for ClearType.

To enable font smoothing for the logon screen, go to the HKEY_USERS\.DEFAULT\Control Panel\Desktop Registry subkey and use the same values as previously described.

FAQ 8.58 How can I create a process for the desktop separate from Windows Explorer instances?

The Windows shell in Windows XP, Windows 2000, and Windows NT 4.0 typically executes in the same process as Windows Explorer instances but in separate threads. When a Windows Explorer instance hangs and restarts, the process causes the desktop to also restart. To put the desktop and taskbar into a separate process, perform the following steps:

1. Start the Registry editor (REGEDIT.EXE).
2. Navigate to HKEY_CURRENT_USER\Software\Microsoft\Windows\CurrentVersion\Explorer.
3. From the Edit menu, select New > DWORD Value.
4. Enter a name of **DesktopProcess** and press Enter.
5. Double-click the new value, set it to 1, and click OK.
6. Log off your Windows session, then log on.

The success of this change is subject to a known issue related to drive mappings. If you make this Registry change, then disconnect from a mapped drive and reuse the same drive letter for another share, Windows might display the old mapping name (but the correct drive contents). If you experience this problem, you should remove the DesktopProcess value or set it to 0, which will result in the desktop and taskbar no longer being in a separate process.

FAQ 8.59 How can I remove the icon that appears in Windows Explorer for shared folders or drives in Windows 2000 and Windows NT 4.0?

When you share a folder or drive, the icon that appears in Windows Explorer changes from a typical-looking folder or drive to a folder or drive being cradled by a hand. To change this shared icon back to the default disk or drive icon, perform the following steps:

1. Start the Registry editor (e.g., REGEDIT.EXE).
2. Navigate to HKEY_CLASSES_ROOT\Network\SharingHandler.
3. Double-click the Default value.
4. Highlight NTSHRUI.DLL, press Delete, and click OK.

5. Close the Registry editor.
6. Reboot the machine.

FAQ 8.60 How can I avoid having to click Show Files in 2000's Explorer all the time?

In Windows 2000, certain directories' content is automatically hidden (such as the %systemroot%, system32 etc folder) to avoid the user accidentally corrupting the system. In order to see the files, you have to click the Show Files text (see Figure 8-11).

If you know what you are doing, this can get annoying, quickly and you can disable the hiding of folder contents as follows:

1. Start Explorer (Win+E or right-click My Computer and select Explore).
2. From the Tools menu, select Folder Options.
3. On the View tab, select Show hidden files and folders. Click OK.
4. Move to the %systemroot% directory (e.g., c:\winnt).

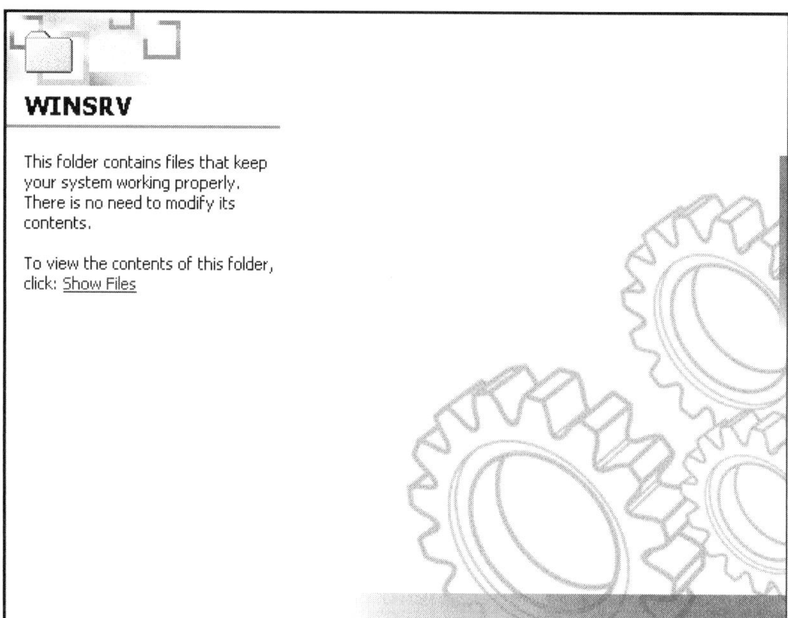

Figure 8-11 System files hidden from the user

5. Click Show Files.
6. Rename the DESKTOP.INI file to something else—for example, DESKTOPBAK.INI.

Repeat this process for any other folders such as %systemroot%\system32 and for program files.

FAQ 8.61 How do I disable the context menu for the Start button?

The context menu is displayed when you right-click on an object. If you right-click on the Start button, options to start Explorer, access Find, and other options are displayed. To disable this menu, perform the following:

1. Start the Registry editor (REGEDIT.EXE).
2. Move to HKEY_CLASSES_ROOT\Directory\shell.
3. Delete the subkeys under this key—for example, DosHere, find.
4. Move to HKEY_CLASSES_ROOT\Folder\shell.
5. Delete the keys under this—for example, explore, open.

Right-clicking on Start will now demonstrate that you have removed these options.

To disable the context menu entirely, perform the following:

1. Start the Registry editor (REGEDIT.EXE).
2. Move to HKEY_CURRENT_USER\Software\Microsoft\Windows\CurrentVersion\Policies\Explorer.
3. From the Edit menu, select New > DWORD Value.
4. Enter a name of **NoTrayContextMenu** and press Enter.
5. Double-click the new value and set to 1.

To reenable the context menu, you would set the value to 0. Log out and log on again for it to take effect.

FAQ 8.62 How can I stop and start Explorer (the shell)?

Explorer is just a process, so you can stop the Explorer process and then start a new one. You should use caution with this procedure though. You will also lose the service type icons on the taskbar when Explorer restarts.

1. Right-click on the taskbar and select Task Manager.
2. Click the Processes tab, select Explorer, and click End Process.
3. Click the Applications tab and click New Task.
4. Enter a name of **explorer** and click OK.
5. Close Task Manager.

FAQ 8.63 How can I set the default view for all drives/folders?

Set the view to what you want (perhaps Details) and close the window while holding the Ctrl key.

FAQ 8.64 How can I prevent my environment changes from being saved when I log off?

By default when you log off, Windows stores your settings in your profile, which includes any open Explorer windows, position changes, and so forth. It is possible to prevent NT from saving these settings:

1. Start the Registry editor (REGEDIT.EXE).
2. Move to HKEY_CURRENT_USER\Software\Microsoft\Windows\CurrentVersion\Policies\Explorer.
3. From the Edit menu, select New > DWORD Value. Enter a name of **NoSaveSettings**.
4. Double-click the new value and set it to 1.

When you log off, any open windows will not be reopened, and savings will not be saved. This setting can also be set domainwide using the Policy editor.

1. Start the Policy editor (POLEDIT.EXE).
2. Open your domain's policy (or create a new one).
3. Double-click Default User.
4. Expand Shell > Restrictions.
5. Check the Don't save settings at exit.
6. Click OK.
7. Save the policy to the netlogon share of the domain controllers.

FAQ 8.65 How can I enable Hi-Color icons?

If you run the Desktop Control Panel applet (Start > Settings > Control Panel > Desktop) and select the Plus! tab, you can check the box Show icons using all possible colors to get better resolution icons. This can also be done by directly editing the Registry (for example, if you don't have the Plus! tab or if you wish to perform via a logon script, etc.):

1. Start the Registry editor (REGEDIT.EXE).
2. Move to HKEY_CURRENT_USER\Control Panel\Desktop\WindowMetrics.
3. From the Edit menu, select New > String Value.
4. Enter a name of **Shell Icon BPP** and press Enter.
5. Double-click the new value and set to 16 if you have a 16-bit graphic card or 24 for a 24-bit graphics card. Click OK.
6. Close the Registry editor.

Pressing F5 to refresh your screen should make the change take effect; if not reboot.

FAQ 8.66 The underlines under the hot keys are not displayed. How do I display them?

Some menus have underlines under certain letters, which are their hot keys—for example, Alt+F for File. Some applications don't display these underlines until Alt is pressed. If you don't wish to press Alt to see the underlines, you can disable the hiding of the keyboard navigation indicators as follows:

1. Right-click on the desktop and select Properties.
2. Select the Effects tab.
3. Unselect Hide keyboard navigation indicators until I use the Alt key (see Figure 8-12).
4. Click Apply.
5. Click OK.

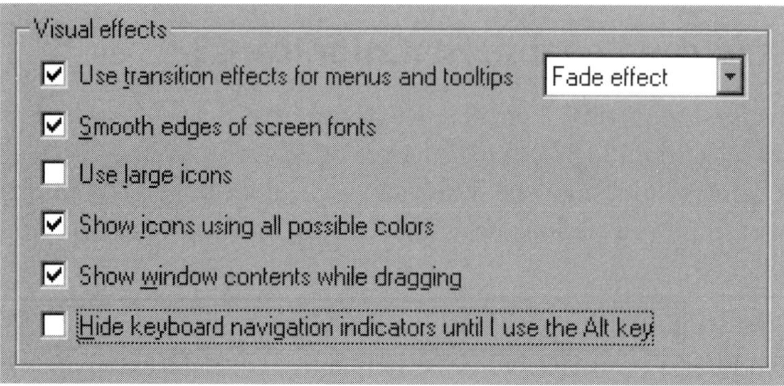

Figure 8-12 Enabling keyboard navigation indicators to be hidden

FAQ 8.67 How can I set the taskbar autohide from a program or another method?

It's possible to configure the taskbar to automatically hide (Start > Settings > Taskbar & Start Menu > Auto hide > OK), but a number of people have asked if this feature can be set another way. Basically the answer is no ☹.

MSDN says this:

> The taskbar supports two display options: Auto Hide and Always On Top. To set these options, the user must open the taskbar shortcut menu, click Properties, and select or clear the Auto Hide check box or the Always On Top check box. There is no way to set these options programmatically. To retrieve the state of these display options, use the ABM_GETSTATE message. If you would like to be notified when the state of these display options changes, process the ABN_STATECHANGE notification message in your window procedure.
>
> The work area is the portion of the screen not obscured by the taskbar. To retrieve the size of the work area, call the SystemParametersInfo function with the SPI_GETWORKAREA value set. To retrieve the rectangle coordinates that describe the location of the taskbar, use the ABM_GETTASKBARPOS message.

So there is no Registry entry way to change this.

FAQ 8.68 How can I configure the wallpaper to stretch across the screen?

If you run the Desktop Control Panel applet (Start > Settings > Control Panel > Desktop) and select the Plus! tab, you can check the box Stretch desktop wallpaper to fill the screen to force the wallpaper to fill the entire screen. This can also be done by directly editing the Registry (if you don't have the Plus! tab or if you wish to perform via a logon script, etc.):

1. Start the Registry editor (REGEDIT.EXE).
2. Move to HKEY_CURRENT_USER\Control Panel\Desktop.
3. From the Edit menu, select New > String Value.
4. Enter a name of **WallpaperStyle** and press Enter.
5. Double-click the new value and set to 2 if you want the wallpaper to be stretched or 0 for normal display. Click OK.
6. Close the Registry editor.

To make the change take effect, either log off and then log on, or run the Desktop Control Panel applet and change anything to refresh the screen.

FAQ 8.69 How can I configure dialog box content to be shown while dragging windows?

If you run the Desktop Control Panel applet (Start > Settings > Control Panel > Desktop) and select the Plus! tab, you can check the box Show window contents while dragging. This can also be done by directly editing the Registry (if you don't have the Plus! tab or if you wish to perform via a logon script, etc.):

1. Start the Registry editor (REGEDIT.EXE).
2. Move to HKEY_CURRENT_USER\Control Panel\Desktop.
3. If a value DragFullWindows does not exist from the Edit menu, select New > String Value and enter a name of **DragFullWindows**. Press Enter.
4. Double-click the new value and set to 1. Set to 0 to disable. Click OK.
5. Close the Registry editor.

To make the change take effect, either log off and then log on, or reboot the machine.

FAQ 8.70 How can I configure Font Smoothing?

If you run the Desktop Control Panel applet (Start > Settings > Control Panel > Desktop) and select the Plus! tab, you can check the box Smooth edges of screen fonts. This can also be done by directly editing the Registry (if you don't have the Plus! tab or if you wish to perform via a logon script, etc.):

1. Start the Registry editor (REGEDIT.EXE).
2. Move to HKEY_CURRENT_USER\Control Panel\Desktop.
3. If a value FontSmoothing does not exist from the Edit menu, select New > String Value, enter a name of **FontSmoothing**, and press Enter.
4. Double-click the new value and set to 2. Set to 0 to disable. Click OK.
5. Close the Registry editor.

To make the change take effect, either log off and then log on, or reboot the machine.

FAQ 8.71 How can I modify the grace timeout for password-protected screensavers?

When a password protected screensaver starts, there is a grace period before a password must be entered to deactivate the screensaver. This can be changed as follows:

1. Start the Registry editor (REGEDIT.EXE).
2. Move to HKEY_LOCAL_MACHINE\SOFTWARE\Microsoft\Windows NT\CurrentVersion\Winlogon.
3. From the Edit menu, select New > String Value.
4. Enter a name of **ScreenSaverGracePeriod** and press Enter.
5. Double-click and set to the number of seconds grace period. Click OK.
6. Close the Registry editor.
7. Reboot the machine.

FAQ 8.72 How can I configure logoff to show on the Start menu in Windows 2000?

You can do this by selecting Taskbar & Start Menu from the Settings menu of the Start button; then select Start Menu Options and check the Display Logoff option.

You can also accomplish this configuration by directly editing the Registry:

1. Start the Registry editor (REGEDIT.EXE).
2. Move to HKEY_CURRENT_USER\Software\Microsoft\Windows\CurrentVersion\Explorer\Advanced.
3. From the Edit menu, select New > DWORD Value and enter a name of **StartMenuLogoff** (if it does not exist).
4. Double-click the new value and set to 1.
5. Close the Registry editor.
6. Log off and then log on.

FAQ 8.73 How can I change the color used to display selected files and folders in Windows XP's and Windows 2000's single-click view mode?

By default, when you hover over a file or folder in single-click view mode, the object will change color to a light blue (RGB value 100 139 203). To change the color, perform the following steps:

1. Start a Registry editor (e.g., REGEDIT.EXE).
2. Navigate to HKEY_CURRENT_USER\Control Panel\Colors.
3. Double-click HotTrackingColor.
4. Change to the desired RGB value (e.g., 255 0 0 for red) and click OK.
5. Close the Registry editor.
6. Log off and log on again for the change to take effect.

FAQ 8.74 How do I enable Web content for a folder?

To enable Web content for a folder, which enables it to be customized and display previews of images/Web pages, perform the following:

1. Start Explorer.
2. From the Tools menu, select Folder Options.
3. Under Web View, select Enable Web content in folders (see Figure 8-13).
4. Click Apply, then OK.

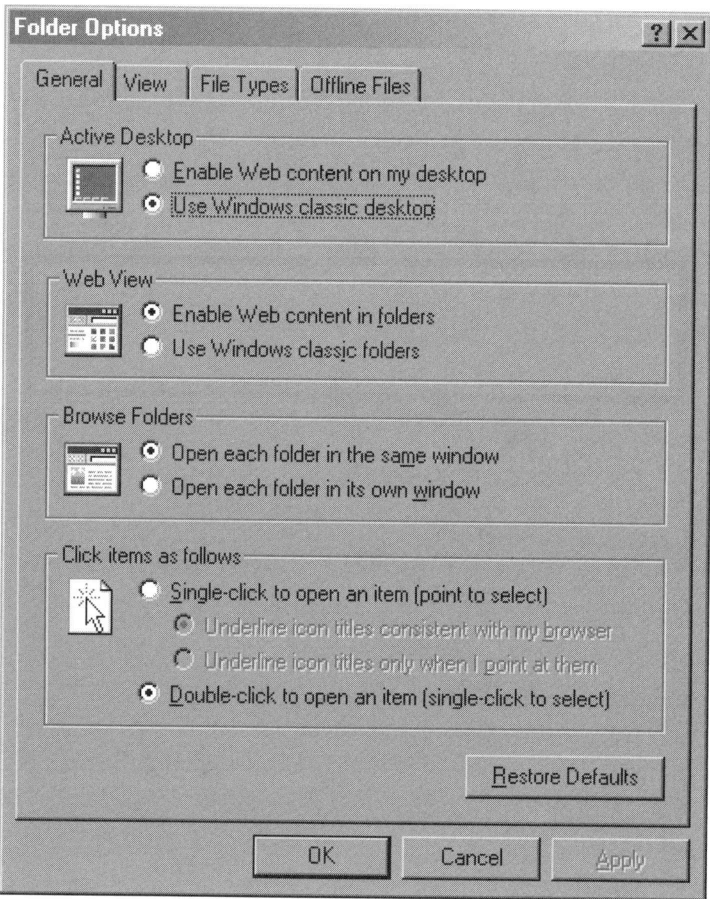

Figure 8-13 Options for Web view

8.75 How do I remove the icons that appear in my system tray?

The system tray icons are midway between a service and an application and have the advantage of a UI. They are listed under the Registry key HKEY_LOCAL_MACHINE\SOFTWARE\Microsoft\Windows\CurrentVersion\Run. You can remove them; however, be aware that doing so not only removes the icon but also stops the application from performing its actions.

To remove one of these icons from your system tray, perform the following steps:

1. Start REGEDIT.EXE.
2. Go to HKEY_LOCAL_MACHINE\SOFTWARE\Microsoft\Windows\CurrentVersion\Run.
3. Select the run value you want to remove (e.g., Microsoft IntelliType).
4. Click Del.
5. Close Regedit.

FAQ 8.76 How do I remove customization for a folder?

To remove customization for a folder and return to the system default, perform the following:

1. Start Explorer.
2. Select the folder with the customization.
3. From the View menu, select Customize This Folder.
4. Click Next.
5. Select Remove customizations and click Next.
6. Leave all the checks to restore the various components and click Next.
7. Click Finish.

You can then manually delete the DESKTOP.INI file and the Folder Settings folder, which don't get automatically deleted.

FAQ 8.77 How do I enable the mouse snap-to?

It's possible to configure windows to move the mouse to the default button to speed up general operations. To enable this, perform the following:

1. Start the Registry editor (REGEDIT.EXE).
2. Move to HKEY_CURRENT_USER\Control Panel\Mouse.
3. If the value SnapToDefaultButton exists, go to step 4; otherwise, select New > String Value from the Edit menu and enter a name of **SnapToDefaultButton** (watch the case of the letters).
4. Double-click on the value and set to 1. Click OK.

5. Close the Registry editor.
6. Log off and on for the change to take effect.

This can also be accomplished using the Mouse Control Panel applet; select the StepSavers tab and check the SnapTo box if you have the IntelliMouse software\ installed. Or select the Motion tab and check the Snap Mouse to the default button in dialog box if you don't. Click Apply, then OK, and you won't have to reboot.

FAQ 8.78 I have deleted the Inbox icon. How can I recreate it?

If you have TweakUI, click the Desktop tab, check the Inbox, and click Apply, then OK. If you do not have TweakUI, you can readd the Inbox icon, by directly updating the Registry:

1. Start the Registry editor (REGEDIT.EXE).
2. Move to HKEY_LOCAL_MACHINE\SOFTWARE\Microsoft\Windows\CurrentVersion\Explorer\Desktop\NameSpace.
3. From the Edit menu, select New > Key.
4. Enter a name of **{00020D75-0000-0000-C000-000000000046}**.
5. Select the new key and double-click on (Default). Set to Inbox and click OK.
6. Close the Registry editor.
7. Press F5 on the desktop for the Inbox icon to appear.

FAQ 8.79 How do I enable X Windows-Style auto-raise?

Is it possible to configure Windows so when you move the mouse over a window it will come into focus:

1. Start the Registry editor (REGEDIT.EXE).
2. Move to HKEY_CURRENT_USER\Control Panel\Mouse.
3. If the value ActiveWindowTracking exists, go to step 4; otherwise, select New > DWORD Value from edit value and enter a name of **ActiveWindowTracking** (watch the case).

4. Double-click on the value and set to 1. Click OK.
5. Close the Registry editor.
6. Log off and on for the change to take effect.

An undesirable side effect of this is when turning on X-Windows-style auto-raise, Netscape Navigator button-based menus (i.e., for bookmarks, etc.) do not work at all because auto-raise causes somewhat of an infinite loop between the browser and its menus (which are implemented as windows).

For Windows 2000 and XP, you need to perform the following:

1. Start the Registry editor (REGEDIT.EXE).
2. Move to HKEY_CURRENT_USER\Control Panel\Desktop.
3. Double-click UserPreferencesMask.
4. This value will have 4 bytes of data—for example:

   ```
   9e 08 07 80
   ```

5. Change the first byte (in this case 9e) to

   `9f`

   To just have windows gain focus when the mouse moves over them but not to come to the front

   `df`

   For the window to gain focus and autoraise to the front of the screen

   `9e`

6. Turn off all focus/autoraise. Your value should now be

   ```
   df 08 07 80
   ```

   Your last 3 bytes may vary.
7. Click OK.
8. Close the Registry editor.
9. Log off and log on for the change to take effect.

You can also perform this using the version 2 of TweakUI and above via the Mouse > X-Mouse section.

FAQ 8.80 I don't have the new item on my desktop context menu. What should I do?

If when you right-click on the desktop and there is no New item, perform the following:

1. Start the Registry editor (REGEDIT.EXE).
2. Move to HKEY_CLASSES_ROOT\Directory\Background\shellex\ContextMenuHandlers.
3. From the Edit menu, select New > Key and enter a name of **New**. Press Enter.
4. Move to New.
5. Double-click on the default value and enter data **{D969A300-E7FF-11d0-A93B-00A0C90F2719}**.
6. Click OK.
7. Close the Registry editor.

You should now have a New item on the desktop context menu. A reboot is not needed.

FAQ 8.81 What is Windows skinning/styles?

If you use Windows Media Player 7 (WMP7) or later, you know that each application can use a different GUI style, known as a *skin*. Microsoft has added this skinning capability to Windows XP, so you can specify a different style for your Start menu and other windows—in fact, you can specify a different style for everything (for more information, see the FAQ 8.82). Some third-party packages add this feature to Windows 2000 (e.g., Windows Blinds from Stardock—http://www.stardock.com). This software provides the same skinning that you get in XP, but you can download extra skins (even a cool Matrix one!) and totally change the OS's look.

FAQ 8.82 How do I use Windows XP styles?

XP has many improvements, one of which is a change to the core that lets you skin the OS and offers a new API for third-party applications to use this feature. XP includes a limited implementation of skinning to give you an idea of what's possible. To access this feature, perform the following steps:

1. Right-click the Desktop and select Properties (or start the Control Panel Display applet).

2. Select the Appearance tab.
3. Under Windows and buttons, select either Windows XP style or Windows Classic.
4. Click OK.

FAQ 8.83 Where can I get more skins for Windows XP?

Unless someone outside of Microsoft makes a tool to create visual styles in the same format as Microsoft, you won't be able to add new skins to the OS without a third-party add-on. Microsoft has said that it won't support third-party skins for XP because the skins could cause inconsistency and confusion. If someone else makes a skin for the OS that has a 5MB title, the OS might experience problems, and people would blame Microsoft (a scenario the company, understandably, wants to avoid). However, Microsoft has provided an API that lets third parties extend this skinning capability.

Note that Stardock (http://www.stardock.com) has released Windows Blinds XP, which provides skinning; however, Stardock uses its own format for the skin and not the Microsoft format.

FAQ 8.84 How can I modify the icon spacing on the desktop?

Icons displayed on the desktop are spaced according to values defined in the display properties. To change these values in Windows 2000 and Windows NT, perform the following steps:

1. Start the Display Control Panel applet (go to Start > Settings > Control Panel and click Display).
2. Select the Appearance tab.
3. Under Item, select Icon Spacing (Horizontal) and modify the size.
4. Select Icon Spacing (Vertical) and modify the size.
5. Click OK to close all dialog boxes.

For the change to take effect, you need to unselect Auto Arrange from the Arrange Icons context menu that displays when you right-click the desktop.

You can also set the icon spacing in Win2K and NT by changing the IconSpacing and IconVerticalSpacing values under the HKEY_CURRENT_USER\Control Panel\Desktop key in the Registry.

8.85 How can I add an Encrypt/Decrypt option to the context menu?

It's possible to add a context menu option to encrypt/decrypt files by adding the following Registry key:

1. Start the Registry editor (REGEDIT.EXE).
2. Move to HKEY_LOCAL_MACHINE\SOFTWARE\Microsoft\Windows\CurrentVersion\Explorer\Advanced.
3. From the Edit menu, select New > DWORD Value.
4. Enter a name of **EncryptionContextMenu** and press Enter.
5. Double-click the new value and set to 1. Click OK.
6. Close the Registry editor.
7. Reboot the computer for the change to take effect (or you can start Task Manager, stop EXPLORER.EXE, and start a new occurrence).

If you now right-click on a file/folder, Encrypt will be listed for unencrypted files, Decrypt for encrypted files.

8.86 How can I add a Move to Folder option to the context menu?

It's possible to add a context menu option to move a file to a folder by adding the following Registry key:

1. Start the Registry editor (REGEDIT.EXE).
2. Move to HKEY_CLASSES_ROOT\AllFilesystemObjects\shellex\ContextMenuHandlers.
3. From the Edit menu, select New > Key.
4. Enter a name of **Move To** and press Enter.
5. Move to the Move To ☺ key and double-click on the (Default) value.
6. Set to **{C2FBB631-2971-11D1-A18C-00C04FD75D13}**. Click OK.
7. Close the Registry editor.
8. Restart Explorer for the change to take effect (you don't need to reboot).

If you now right-click on a file/folder, an option to move to folder will be listed.

FAQ 8.87 How do I stop the default shortcut to text added to new shortcuts?

Perform the following Registry change to prevent the shortcut being prefixed to the name of your shortcuts:

1. Start the Registry editor (REGEDT32, **not** REGEDIT.EXE).
2. Move to HKEY_CURRENT_USER\Software\Microsoft\Windows\CurrentVersion\Explorer.
3. Double-click on link.
4. Change to **00000000** and click OK.
5. Close the Registry editor.
6. Log off and on again for the change to take effect.

FAQ 8.88 How do I modify the shortcut arrow?

Perform the following Registry change to modify the arrow used on shortcuts:

1. Start the Registry editor (Regedt32 or REGEDIT.EXE).
2. Move to HKEY_LOCAL_MACHINE\SOFTWARE\Microsoft\Windows\CurrentVersion\Explorer\Shell Icons.
3. Double-click on 29.
4. Change to the name of the icon and icon number separated by a comma—for example, shell32.dll,30 is a big arrow icon.
5. Click OK.
6. Close the Registry editor.

The changes take effect at the next logon.

To avoid having to log off, you can modify an icon-related entry, make the screen repaint by changing the background and setting it back to the original background—for example, HKEY_CURRENT_USER\Control Panel\Desktop\WindowMetrics\Shell Icon Size.

If the Shell Icons\29 value does not exist, then you must create the Shell Icons branch and then create the 29 value of type String.

9 SYSTEM INFORMATION

Gathering information about your systems is vital to diagnosing performance and to making upgrades. This information can be obtained by using built-in and third-party tools and with new features such as product activation. In this chapter, we look at tools that help detect the activation status of an installation.

FAQ 9.1 How can I tell what my Windows NT machine's role is?

There are several ways to determine what your Windows NT machine's role is. However, the easiest method is to type the command

```
net accounts
```

The bottom of the output shows the computer's role as one of the following items:

```
Workstation: A normal NT Workstation machine
Server: A standalone NT Server machine
Primary: A PDC
Backup: A BDC
```

FAQ 9.2 How do I view all the applications and processes on the system?

You can use the Windows NT Task Manager to view your applications. To access Task Manager, right-click the taskbar and select Task Manager. You can also use the PVIEW program that comes with Visual C++. For command-line viewing, you can use TLIST, which comes with the Windows Resource Kit or TASKLIST, which is a core Windows XP command.

FAQ 9.3 Where can I get information about my machine?

Windows ships with msinfo32, which gives easy access to a graphical view of information about your machine, or you can use WinInfo, from http://www.savilltech.com/download/wininfo.zip, which gives enhanced information such as activation status, Windows trial status, and so forth.

SavillTech has a command-line utility, CMDINFO (http://www.savilltech.com/cmdinfo.html), which can give information about a local or remote machine from the command line. It can also be passed a switch to test a certain value (e.g., service pack version) and set %errorlevel% accordingly allowing values to be tested via scripts and actions performed.

```
cmdinfo

Version Type        Full Version
Installation Date   30 November 2001, 09:49:41
Expiry Date         Not Applicable
OS Type             Microsoft Windows XP
Product Type        Windows XP Professional
Plus Version        Not Available
IE Version          Internet Explorer 6 (XP) (6.0.2600.0000)
Service Pack        Not available
Processor Type      Multiprocessor Free
Activation Status   Activated
Build Number        2600
Source Path         F:\I386
System Root         G:\WINDOWS
Owning Org          SavillTech Ltd
Owner Name          John Savill
Uptime              0 days, 3 hours, 49 minutes and 15 seconds
Hotfixes:
Application Compatibility Update Windows XP Hotfix (SP1) [See
Q308381 for more information]
Q147222 No Description
Q282784 Windows XP Hotfix (SP1) [See Q282784 for more information]
Q307869 Windows XP Hotfix (SP1) [See Q307869 for more information]
Q308210 Windows XP Hotfix (SP1) [See Q308210 for more information]
Q309521 Windows XP Hotfix (SP1) [See Q309521 for more information]
Q309691 Windows XP Hotfix (SP1) [See Q309691 for more information]
Q310437 Windows XP Hotfix (SP1) [See Q310437 for more information]
```

```
Q310507 Windows XP Hotfix (SP1) [See Q310507 for more information]
Q311889 Windows XP Hotfix (SP1) [See Q311889 for more information]
Q313484 Windows XP Hotfix (SP1) [See Q313484 for more information]
Q315000 Windows XP Hotfix (SP1) [See Q315000 for more information]
```

Windows XP includes a new utility SYSTEMINFO, which outputs similar information but has additional information about memory, network, and process but does not give activation, installation type (e.g., trial limited, full, NFR) or Internet Explorer information. It also duplicates some hotfix entries.

```
systeminfo

Host Name: CONAN
OS Name: Microsoft Windows XP Professional
OS Version: 5.1.2600 Build 2600
OS Manufacturer: Microsoft Corporation
OS Configuration: Standalone Workstation
OS Build Type: Multiprocessor Free
Registered Owner: John Savill
Registered Organization: SavillTech Ltd
Product ID: 55274-005-0147286-22895
Original Install Date: 30/11/2001, 09:49:41
System Up Time: N/A
System Manufacturer: Compaq
System Model: Professional Workstation AP550
System type: X86-based PC
Processor(s): 2 Processor(s) Installed.
[01]: x86 Family 6 Model 8 Stepping 6 GenuineIntel ~863 Mhz
[02]: x86 Family 6 Model 8 Stepping 6 GenuineIntel ~863 Mhz
BIOS Version: COMPAQ - 20010410
Windows Directory: G:\WINDOWS
System Directory: G:\WINDOWS\System32
Boot Device: \Device\HarddiskVolume1
System Locale: en-gb;English (United Kingdom)
Input Locale: en-gb;English (United Kingdom)
Time Zone: (GMT) Greenwich Mean Time : Dublin, Edinburgh, Lisbon,
London
Total Physical Memory: 512 MB
Available Physical Memory: 197 MB
Virtual Memory: Max Size: 994 MB
Virtual Memory: Available: 460 MB
Virtual Memory: In Use: 534 MB
Page File Location(s): N/A
```

```
Domain: FMMS
Logon Server: \\CONAN
Hotfix(s): 16 Hotfix(s) Installed.
[01]: File 1
[02]: Q147222
[03]: Q282784 - Windows XP Hotfix (SP1) [See Q282784 for more
information]
[04]: Q307869 - Windows XP Hotfix (SP1) [See Q307869 for more
information]
[05]: Q308210 - Windows XP Hotfix (SP1) [See Q308210 for more
information]
[06]: Q309521 - Windows XP Hotfix (SP1) [See Q309521 for more
information]
[07]: Q309691 - Windows XP Hotfix (SP1) [See Q309691 for more
information]
[08]: Q310437 - Windows XP Hotfix (SP1) [See Q310437 for more
information]
[09]: Q310507 - Windows XP Hotfix (SP1) [See Q310507 for more
information]
[10]: Q311889 - Windows XP Hotfix (SP1) [See Q311889 for more
information]
[11]: Q313484 - Windows XP Hotfix (SP1) [See Q313484 for more
information]
[12]: Q315000 - Windows XP Hotfix (SP1) [See Q315000 for more
information]
[13]: Q282784 - Update
[14]: Q311889 - Update
[15]: Q313484 - Update
[16]: Q315000 - Update
NetWork Card(s): 1 NIC(s) Installed.
[01]: Intel(R) 82559 Fast Ethernet LOM with Alert on LAN*
Connection Name: Local Area Connection
DHCP Enabled: No
IP address(es)
[01]: 200.200.200.2
```

FAQ 9.4 How can I tell when Windows NT was last started?

From the command prompt, enter the command

```
net statistics workstation | more
```

At the top of the display, you'll see "statistics since. . . ." This statement gives the time since the workstation service was started. The uptime will be incorrect if someone has performed the commands:

```
net stop workstation
net start workstation
```

The PVIEW utility also displays the time that Windows NT has been running. A set of applications called 3UPTIMES.ZIP displays this information. The set includes a command-line and a Windows version. You can find information about these applications from http://barnyard.syr.edu/~vefatica/. Be aware that this utility gives incorrect information if the system has been running more than 50 days.

The last line of output from the Windows NT Server Resource Kit utility SRVINFO.EXE displays the total uptime in the format:

```
System Up Time: 24 Hr 3 Min 29 Sec
```

A performance monitor object is available from the Performance Monitor tool (PERFMON.EXE):

```
Object: System
Counter : System Up time
```

FAQ 9.5 How can I tell when Windows NT was installed?

Windows NT stores its install time in the Registry key HKEY_LOCAL_MACHINE\SOFTWARE\Microsoft\Windows NT\CurrentVersion\InstallDate in seconds from January 1, 1970. I've written a utility you can use that will display this and other information (in converted form—see Figure 9-1). You can download the utility from http://www.savilltech.com/download/wininfo.zip.

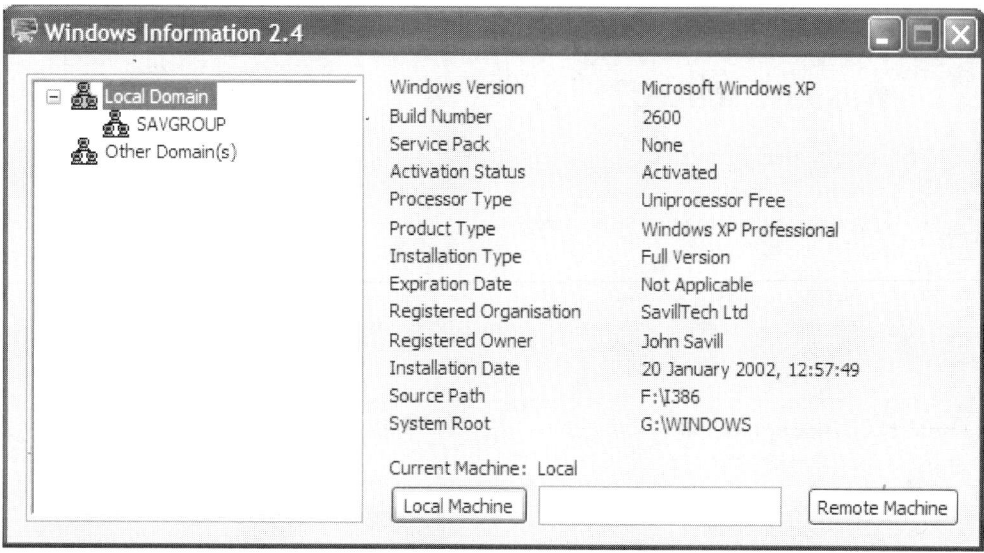

Figure 9-1 The installation date (among other things)

9.6 How can I tell whether my Windows NT installation is a 120-day evaluation or a full version?

If you use setup disks that you created with an evaluation CD-ROM, your installation will expire, even if you entered a full-version registered product ID code. However, Microsoft doesn't provide a method to determine whether or not your installation will expire, which is very annoying because after the evaluation expires the OS gives you only a one-hour notice before shutting down.

Download WinInfo from http://www.savilltech.com/download/wininfo.zip, and the Installation Type value will show either

- Full version
- Time Limited Version (nnn days)

FAQ 9.7 How can I check what type of Windows NT installation I have?

Several Windows NT installation types exist, such as NT Workstation; NT Server; NT domain controllers; NT Server 4.0, Terminal Server Edition (WTS); and NT Enterprise Edition. To check the installation version, type

```
net accounts
```

However, this command sometimes doesn't provide all the necessary information. Another way to check your version is to look in the Registry. To do so, complete the following steps:

1. Start the Registry editor (REGEDT32.EXE).
2. Move to HKEY_LOCAL_MACHINE\SYSTEM\CurrentControlSet\Control\ProductOptions.
3. Look at ProductType; it will be one of the following types:
   WinNT—Windows NT Workstation
   ServerNT—Windows NT Server standalone
   LanmanNT—Windows NT Server Domain Controller
4. You can also look at ProductSuite (if it exists), and depending on your version, you might see one of the following types:
   Terminal Server—WTS
   Enterprise—Enterprise Edition
5. Close the Registry editor.

If you attempt to open or edit these values (depending on your service pack), the OS gives you a warning and changes the value back to its original setting. Don't try to change these values.

If you don't want to search the Registry, WinInfo (from http://www.savilltech.com/download/wininfo.zip) displays the product type (and much more), which will be one of the following versions:

- NT Workstation
- NT Server
- NT Domain Controller
- WTS
- NT Enterprise Edition

FAQ 9.8 How can I tell whether my Windows NT installation is a Not For Resale installation?

Microsoft provides Not For Resale versions of Windows NT Server as part of kits such as Microsoft Developer Network (MSDN). This software is fully functional, except that it has a set number of licenses (i.e., 5 or 10), and you can't increase the set number.

To test if your installation is a Full or Not For Resale version, download WinInfo from the previously provided URL and check the Installation type value. If it says Not For Resale Version, then your limit is 10 clients.

FAQ 9.9 Where do Windows 2000 and Windows NT store time zone information?

From the Control Panel Date/Time applet, select the Time Zone tab to set the local country and its associated time difference. You can select the same tab to enable daylight saving.

Changing these settings updates the Registry values under the HKEY_LOCAL_MACHINE\SYSTEM\CurrentControlSet\Control\TimeZoneInformation key. The most useful time-zone values follow:

ActiveTimeBias	This value is the current time difference from Greenwich Mean Time (GMT) in minutes and is the difference for GMT. For example, if you're one hour ahead, GMT is one hour behind. The value would be ffffffc4, which is hexadecimal for -60.
Bias	This value is the normal time difference from GMT, excluding daylight saving in minutes. The value is the difference for GMT, so if you're three hours ahead (e.g., if you live in Moscow), the Bias would be ffffff4c, which is hex for 180. If you're two hours behind GMT (e.g., if you're on a boat in the middle of the Atlantic ocean), GMT is two hours ahead, so the value is 120.
DaylightBias	This value is the time difference used for daylight saving for GMT. If you're one hour ahead, the value is ffffffc4, which is hex for -60. Notice that the ActiveTimeBias is the sum of Bias and DaylightBias in daylight saving months, which is the same as Bias for standard months.

DaylightName	The OS uses this name during daylight saving months.
StandardName	The OS uses this name during nondaylight saving months.
DaylightStart	This value tells the computer when to start daylight mode.
StandardStart	This value tells the computer when to start standard mode.
DisableAutoDaylightTimeSet	This value exists only if you clear the checkbox for the option Automatically adjust clock for daylight saving and if you set the value to 1.

Using the Microsoft Windows 2000 Resource Kit or the Microsoft Windows NT Resource Kit REG.EXE utility, you can use the following command to query these values from the command line:

```
reg query
hklm\system\currentcontrolset\control\timezoneinformation\bias
REG_DWORD bias 0

C:\>reg query
hklm\system\currentcontrolset\control\timezoneinformation\
daylightname
REG_SZ daylightname GMT Daylight Time
```

FAQ 9.10 How can I tell which process has file x open?

You can view files that a user accesses over the network with the net-file command:

```
net file
ID Path User name # Locks

---------------------------------------------------------------------
51 G:\www.ntfaq.com ADMINISTRATOR 0
The command completed successfully.
```

You can't use this command to access information about files that local processes open. Two programs, NTHandle (a command-line tool) and HandleEx (a GUI version—see Figure 9-2) let you view which process has file x open. Both programs are available from http://www.sysinternals.com.

HandleEx - Systems Internals: http://www.sysinternals.com

File View Search Help

Process	PID	Descript...	Owner	Priority	Handles	Window...
winlogon.exe	180		NT AUTHORITY:SYSTEM	13	457	
services.exe	208		NT AUTHORITY:SYSTEM	9	528	
lsass.exe	220		NT AUTHORITY:SYSTEM	9	305	
svchost.exe	376		NT AUTHORITY:SYSTEM	8	259	
SPOOLSV.EXE	408		NT AUTHORITY:SYSTEM	8	112	
amgrsrvc.exe	460		NT AUTHORITY:SYSTEM	8	87	
svchost.exe	500		NT AUTHORITY:SYSTEM	8	444	
Mcshield.exe	524	McShield	NT AUTHORITY:SYSTEM	13	80	
VsTskMgr.exe	580		NT AUTHORITY:SYSTEM	8	95	

Handle	Type	Name
14	ObjDirectory	\KnownDlls
18	File	D:\WINNT\system32
20	ObjDirectory	\Windows
28	Mutant	\NlsCacheMutant
34	WinStation	\Windows\WindowStations\WinSta0
3C	WinStation	\Windows\WindowStations\WinSta0
40	Key	HKLM
58	Thread	Mcshield.exe(524): 520
64	ObjDirectory	\BaseNamedObjects

Mcshield.exe pid: 524

Figure 9-2 File handles open

Under Windows 2000/XP is the Computer Management tool > System Tools > Shared Folders > Open Files, which shows you open files graphically as well as allowing you to close them.

9.11 How can I tell which DLL and API calls a program makes?

The Microsoft Windows 2000 Resource Kit and Microsoft Windows NT Resource Kit supply the API Monitor utility that you can use to monitor all DLL and API calls. To use the utility, perform the following steps:

1. From the Start menu, select Run, then APIMON.EXE.
2. From the File menu, select Open.
3. Select the image you want to monitor and click OK. (I'm using %systemroot%\system32\notepad.exe.) Two blank windows, DLLs in use and Api Counters, will open.

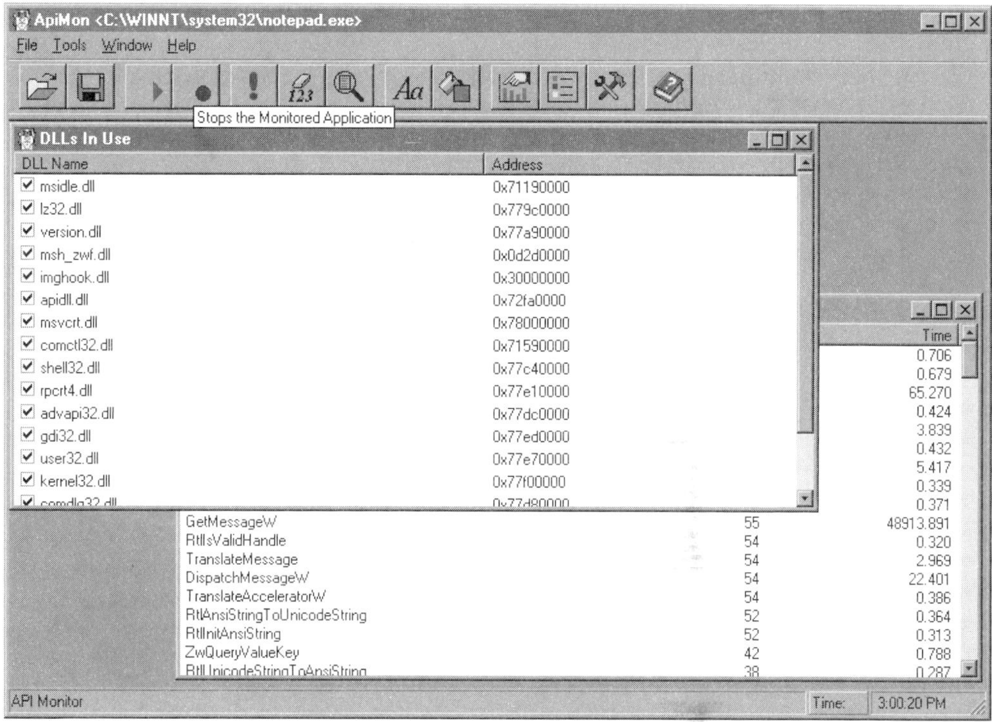

Figure 9-3 Viewing DLLs in use by an application

4. The next task is to start the selected image. Click the green Play arrow (or select Start Monitor from the Tools menu).

   The application will start, and the two blank windows will now include DLL and API information.

5. When the program monitoring is complete and the program is closed, click Stop or select Stop Monitor from the Tools menu (see Figure 9-3).
6. Stopping the API Monitor program also stops the image that the program had loaded, so make sure you don't lose any work.

FAQ 9.12 Why are there so many copies of SVCHOST.EXE on my machine?

Svchost is a generic host process that hosts services run from DLLs. During development, it's customary to separate new or changing services to increase the reliability and ease of troubleshooting; thus, on a beta OS version, you see more Svchost processes running than on a release version.

To find out what's inside each copy of SVCHOST.EXE, use the Resource Kit Support Tools' TLIST.EXE (with the -s switch). (You need to install the Support Tools from \support\tools on your product CD-ROM; they don't install by default.) The following is sample output from the tlist command:

```
tlist -s

0 System Process
4 System
176 smss.exe
208 csrss.exe Title:
172 winlogon.exe Title: NetDDE Agent
256 services.exe Svcs: Eventlog,PlugPlay
268 lsass.exe Svcs: Netlogon,PolicyAgent,ProtectedStorage,SamSs
320 svchost.exe Svcs: RpcSs
420 svchost.exe Svcs: AudioSrv,Browser,CryptSvc,Dhcp,dmserver,
EventSystem,FastUserSwitchingCompatibilityServices,helpsvc,HidServ,
lanmanserver,lanmanworkstation,Netman,Nla,Schedule,seclogon,SENS,
ShellHWDetection,TermService,ThemeService,TrkWks,uploadmgr,W32Time,
WmdmPmSp,wuauser
480 svchost.exe Svcs: Dnscache
500 svchost.exe Svcs: LmHosts,Messenger,RemoteRegistry,SSDPSRV,
WebClient
544 spoolsv.exe Svcs: Spooler
660 DKService.exe Svcs: Diskeeper
800 svchost.exe Svcs: winmgmt
1092 explorer.exe Title: Program Manager
1244 ctfmon.exe Title:
900 ISATRAY.EXE Title: IsaTray
1344 NAVAPW32.EXE Title: Norton AntiVirus Auto-Protect
1212 FRONTPG.EXE Title: Microsoft FrontPage - D:\asp
www.ntfaq.com\NTFAQ\5apr2001.htm
428 NAVAPSVC.EXE Svcs: NAV Auto-Protect
1376 ALERTSVC.EXE Svcs: NAV Alert
1372 PowerDVD.exe Title: PowerDVD
444 OUTLOOK.EXE Title: Tasks - Microsoft Outlook
1268 msmsgs.exe Title:
1436 MDM.EXE Title: OleMainThreadWndName
632 WINWORD.EXE Title: DDE Server Window
1404 IEXPLORE.EXE Title: Q250320 - Description of Svchost.exe -
Microsoft Internet Explorer
```

```
1348 cmd.exe Title: E:\WINDOWS\System32\cmd.exe - tlist -s
1428 tlist.exe
```

Many services, drivers, and modules load at system startup and are essential to system operation. Even though they show up in Task Manager, they're still critical.

The svchosts are defined in the Registry key HKEY_LOCAL_MACHINE\SOFTWARE\Microsoft\Windows NT\CurrentVersion\Svchost.

FAQ 9.13 What is the Task Manager tiny footprint mode?

Task Manager can run in a small footprint mode, which removes the menu bar and the page tabs. To enable tiny footprint mode, double-click in the border around the tabs (see Figure 9-4). To switch back, double-click the border area again.

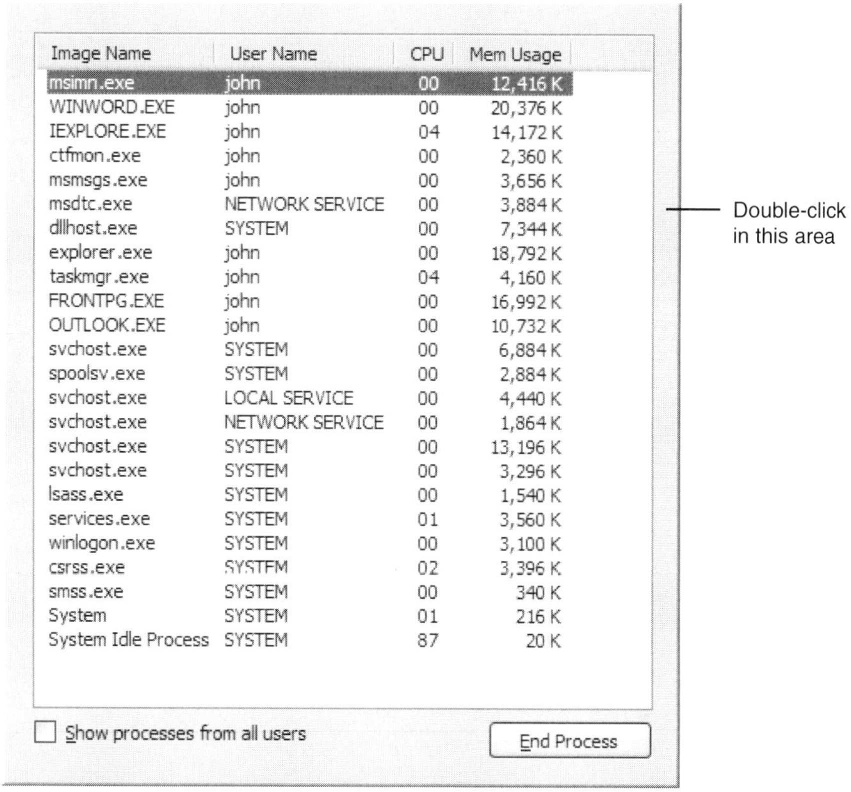
Image Name User Name CPU Mem Usage
msimn.exe john 00 12,416 K
WINWORD.EXE john 00 20,376 K
IEXPLORE.EXE john 04 14,172 K
ctfmon.exe john 00 2,360 K
msmsgs.exe john 00 3,656 K
msdtc.exe NETWORK SERVICE 00 3,884 K
dllhost.exe SYSTEM 00 7,344 K
explorer.exe john 00 18,792 K
taskmgr.exe john 04 4,160 K
FRONTPG.EXE john 00 16,992 K
OUTLOOK.EXE john 00 10,732 K
svchost.exe SYSTEM 00 6,884 K
spoolsv.exe SYSTEM 00 2,884 K
svchost.exe LOCAL SERVICE 00 4,440 K
svchost.exe NETWORK SERVICE 00 1,864 K
svchost.exe SYSTEM 00 13,196 K
svchost.exe SYSTEM 00 3,296 K
lsass.exe SYSTEM 00 1,540 K
services.exe SYSTEM 01 3,560 K
winlogon.exe SYSTEM 00 3,100 K
csrss.exe SYSTEM 02 3,396 K
smss.exe SYSTEM 00 340 K
System SYSTEM 01 216 K
System Idle Process SYSTEM 87 20 K
Show processes from all users
End Process
Double-click in this area

Figure 9-4 Modify the Task Manager process tab

FAQ 9.14 How can I check which hotfixes a remote system has installed?

The CmdInfo command-line utility lists installed hotfixes and provides full Windows XP support. CmdInfo 2.4 is available at http://www.savilltech.com/cmdinfo.html. To use the utility to view a list of hotfixes on a remote system, go to a command prompt and enter

```
cmdinfo \\<remote system name>
```

CmdInfo can also check for a particular hotfix and return a value based on whether the hotfix is installed. For example, if you enter

```
cmdinfo /ht:Q293826
```

and hotfix Q293826 is installed, CmdInfo returns a 1 for %errorlevel%. If the hotfix isn't installed, CmdInfo returns a 0. You can include the cmdinfo /ht:KBarticle statement in a logon script that determines whether a hotfix is installed and, if not, triggers an action to install the hotfix. In addition to hotfix information, CmdInfo's return values can identify current activation status, trial version, and other displayed information.

FAQ 9.15 What environment variables are available in Windows?

Environment variables are very useful for gaining information about a system. The following is a complete list of environment variables:

ALLUSERSPROFILE	Local—Returns the location of the All Users profile.
APPDATA	Local—Returns the location where applications store data by default.
CD	Local—Returns the current directory string.
CMDCMDLINE	Local—Returns the exact command line used to start the current CMD.EXE.
CMDEXTVERSION	System—Returns the version number of the current Command Processor extensions.

COMPUTERNAME	System—Returns the name of the computer.
COMSPEC	System—Returns the exact path to the command shell executable.
DATE	System—Returns the current date. Uses the same format as the date /t command. Generated by CMD.EXE.
ERRORLEVEL	System—Returns the error code of the most recently used command. A nonzero value usually indicates an error.
HOMEDRIVE	System—Returns which local workstation drive letter is connected to the user's home directory. Set based on the value of the home directory. The user's home directory is specified in Local Users and Groups.
HOMEPATH	System—Returns the full path of the user's home directory. Set based on the value of the home directory. The user's home directory is specified in Local Users and Groups.
HOMESHARE	System—Returns the network path to the user's shared home directory. Set based on the value of the home directory. The user's home directory is specified in Local Users and Groups.
LOGONSEVER	Local—Returns the name of the domain controller that validated the current logon session.
NUMBER_OF_PROCESSORS	System—Specifies the number of processors installed on the computer.
OS	System—Returns the operating system name. Windows 2000/XP displays the operating system as Windows_NT.
PATH	System—Specifies the search path for executable files.
PATHEXT	System—Returns a list of the file extensions that the operating system considers to be executable.

(continued)

PROCESSOR_ARCHITECTURE	System—Returns the chip architecture of the processor. Values: x86, IA64.
PROCESSOR_IDENTFIER	System—Returns a description of the processor.
PROCESSOR_LEVEL	System—Returns the model number of the processor installed on the computer.
PROCESSOR_REVISION	System—Returns the revision number of the processor.
PROMPT	Local—Returns the command prompt settings for the current interpreter. Generated by CMD.EXE.
RANDOM	System—Returns a random decimal number between 0 and 32767. Generated by CMD.EXE.
SYSTEMDRIVE	System—Returns the drive containing the Windows root directory (that is, the system root).
SYSTEMROOT	System—Returns the location of the Windows root directory.
TEMP or TMP	System and User—Returns the default temporary directories that are used by applications available to users who are currently logged on. Some applications require TEMP and others require TMP.
TIME	System—Returns the current time. Uses the same format as the time /t command. Generated by CMD.EXE.
USERDOMAIN	Local—Returns the name of the domain that contains the user's account.
USERNAME	Local—Returns the name of the user who is currently logged on.
USERPROFILE	Local—Returns the location of the profile for the current user.
WINDIR	System—Returns the location of the operating system directory.

To access these environment variables, you must place a percent sign (%) before and after the name of the environment variable. For example, the following displays the processor type (still not IA64!):

```
echo %PROCESSOR_ARCHITECTURE%
x86
```

Some environment variables are available only in later versions of operating systems—for example, %RANDOM% is not available in Windows NT 4.0.

10 REGISTRY

Windows originally contained.INI files; however, there are many problems with .INI files: size limitations, no standard layout, slow access, no network support, and so on. Windows 3.1 (yes, Windows, not Windows NT) had a Registry, which was stored in REG. DAT, could be viewed using REGEDIT.EXE, and was used for DDE, OLE, and File Manager integration. The Registry is at the heart of Windows NT and is where nearly all information is stored. The Registry is split into a number of subtrees (see the list that follows), each starting with HKEY_ to indicate that it is a handle that can be used by a program.

HKEY_LOCAL_MACHINE	This tree contains information about the hardware configuration and installed software.
HKEY_CLASSES_ROOT	This is just a link to HKEY_LOCAL_MACHINE\SOFTWARE\Classes. It contains links between applications and file types as well as information about OLE.
HKEY_CURRENT_CONFIG	Again this link is to HKEY_LOCAL_MACHINE\SYSTEM\CurrentControlSet\Hardware Profiles\Current and contains information about the current configuration.
HKEY_CURRENT_USER	This is a link to HKEY_USERS\<SID of User> and contains information about the currently logged on users such as environment, network connections, printers, etc.
HKEY_USERS	This subtree contains information about actively loaded user profiles, including .DEFAULT, which is the default user profile.

Each of the subtrees has a number of keys, which in turn have a number of subkeys. Each key/subkey can have a number of values, which have three parts:

- The name of the value—for example, Wallpaper
- The type of the value—for example, REG_SZ (which is a text string)
- The actual value of the value—for example, c:\winnt\savilltech.bmp

To edit the Registry, two tools are available, REGEDT32.EXE and REGEDIT.EXE. REGEDIT.EXE has better search facilities but does not support all of the Windows NT Registry value types. If you want to just have a look around the Registry:

1. Start a Registry editor (REGEDIT.EXE or REGEDT32.EXE).

   In REGEDT32.EXE, you can set the Registry to read-only mode, which means you won't corrupt anything :-) (Options > Read Only Mode).
2. Select the HKEY_USERS subkey.
3. Move to the .default > Control Panel > Desktop, and you will see a number of values in the right pane.

One of them is wallpaper, which is the background that is displayed before you log on.

FAQ 10.1 What files make up the Registry, and where are they?

The files that make up the Registry are stored in %systemroot%/system32/config directory and consist of

- SAM—HKEY_LOCAL_MACHINE\SAM
- SECURITY—HKEY_LOCAL_MACHINE\Security
- Software—HKEY_LOCAL_MACHINE\Software
- System—HKEY_LOCAL_MACHINE\System & HKEY_CURRENT_CONFIG
- Default—HKEY_USERS\.DEFAULT
- NTUSER.DAT—HKEY_CURRENT_USER (This file is stored in %System-Root%\Profiles\%username%.)

There are also other files with different extensions for some of them:

- .ALT—Contains a backup copy of the HKEY_LOCAL_MACHINE\System hive. Only System has a .ALT file.
- .LOG—A log of changes to the keys and values for the hive.
- .SAV—A copy of the hive as it looks at the end of the text-mode stage in setup.

FAQ 10.2 How do I restrict access to the Registry editor?

You can restrict access using the Registry editor (REGEDT32.EXE):

1. Highlight HKEY_USERS and select Load Hive from the Registry menu.
2. Browse to the user's profile directory belonging to the user for whom you want to restrict the Registry tools and select NTUSER.DAT.
3. When prompted for Key Name, input the user's UserID.
4. Navigate to \Software\Microsoft\Windows\CurrentVersion\Policies.
5. If no System subkey exists, add the System key using New > Key from the Edit menu. Then add a value of DisableRegistryTools (under the System key), using type REG_DWORD and set it to 1.
6. Unload hive from the Registry menu.

FAQ 10.3 What is the maximum Registry size?

The maximum size is 102MB; however, it is slightly more complicated than this.

The Registry entry that controls the maximum size of the Registry is HKEY_LOCAL_MACHINE\SYSTEM\CurrentControlSet\Control\RegistrySizeLimit. By default this entry will not exist so it will need to be created:

1. Start the Registry editor (REGEDIT.EXE).
2. Move to the HKEY_LOCAL_MACHINE\SYSTEM\CurrentControlSet\Control key.
3. From the Edit menu, select New > DWORD Value and enter the name as **RegistrySizeLimit**.
4. Double-click the new entry and enter a value in bytes (choose decimal as the type).

The minimum size is 4MB, and if anything less than this amount is entered in the Registry, then it will be forced up to 4MB. The maximum is 80% of the paged pool (which has a maximum size of 128MB, hence 102MB which is 80% of 128MB). If no entry is entered, then the maximum size is 25% of the paged pool. The paged pool is an area of physical memory used for system data that can be written to disk when not in use.

An important point to note is that the RegistrySizeLimit is a maximum, not an allocation, and so setting a high value will not reserve the space. It does not guarantee the space will be available.

This can also be configured using the System Control Panel applet; click on the Performance tab, and the maximum Registry size can be set there. You must then reboot.

For more information, see Knowledge Base article Q124594.

Another complication occurs during early boot when NTLDR loads some code, allocates working memory, and reads in parts of the Registry. All of this has to fit in the first 16MB of memory, regardless of how much memory is physically installed. The entire system file is read; enough memory is required to contain the whole file as stored on disk without regard to how much of it is useful.

Here are some problems:

- The Registry contains wasted space (sometimes a **lot**). Try saving the SYSTEM key from REGEDT32 and then comparing the saved file size with that of the SYSTEM hive in \%systemroot%\system32\config\. On one machine, I reduced the SYSTEM hive from 9,720KB to 864KB in this manner.
- Creation of the LastKnownGood ControlSet (usually #2) soon after boot almost doubles the size of the file. Depending on circumstances, such as reclaimable space in the "gas," additions to the Registry may require new space to be allocated beyond the end of the combined Current and LastKnownGood SYSTEM hive. Now after the next boot, another LastKnownGood is tacked onto the end of the file, adding about a third to its size. In my case, a Registry with a "true" size of 4MB was thus inflated to 12MB and caused boot failure.

Here are a number of ways to get rid of the excess space:

- If your system is FAT: merely boot from DOS floppy, then replace the SYSTEM file.
- If NTFS: boot from another NT partition and replace file in previous partition.
- Use REGBACK/REGREST from the NT Resource Kit (maybe easiest of all).
- Run rdisk, shut down, and repair the system. Make sure you use rdisk /s when using this to also back up the user database.
- Use ERD Commander from Winternals Software.

To turn off the boot reporting, use REGEDT32 to add the value ReportBootOk: REG_SZ:0 [zero] to HKEY_Local_Machine\SOFTWARE\Microsoft\WindowsNT\CurrentVersion\Winlogon. This will prevent creation of the LastKnownGood ControlSet. If a boot fails because the 16MB limit with NTLDR is exceeded, no dump can be produced, and MS will not solve the problem. This 16MB problem will not be changed in Windows 2000.

FAQ 10.4 Should I use REGEDIT.EXE or REGEDT32.EXE?

Prior to Windows XP, two Registry editing tools were supplied, and the following was true:

- Regedit did not support the full Regedit data types such as REG_MULTI_SZ, so if you edit this type of data with Regedit, it will change its type.
- REGEDT32.EXE allows full access control list (ACL) modification on all Registry values, which REGEDIT.EXE did not.

This functionality is now part of the Windows 2000 version of REGEDIT.EXE, and in Windows XP, REGEDT32.EXE is no longer supplied.

FAQ 10.5 How do I restrict access to a remote Registry?

Access to a remote Registry is controlled by the ACL on the key winreg.

1. Start the Registry editor (REGEDT32.EXE).
2. Move to HKEY_LOCAL_MACHINE\SYSTEM\CurrentControlSet\Control\SecurePipeServers.
3. Check for a key called "winreg". If it does not exist, create it (Edit > Add Key).
4. Select the winreg key (by clicking on it).
5. From the Security menu, select Permissions.
6. Click the Add button and give the user you want read access.
7. Once added, click on the user and select Special Access.
8. Double-click on the user, and you can select which actions the user can perform.
9. Click OK when finished.

It is possible to set up certain keys to be accessible even if the user does not have access by editing the value HKEY_LOCAL_MACHINE\SYSTEM\CurrentControlSet\Control\SecurePipeServers\winreg\AllowedPaths\Machine (use Regedt32). You can add paths to this list.

FAQ 10.6 How can I tell what changes are made to the Registry?

Using the REGEDIT.EXE program, it is possible to export portions of the Registry. This feature can be used as follows:

1. Start the Registry editor (REGEDIT.EXE).
2. Select the key you want to monitor.
3. From the Registry menu, select Export Registry file.
4. Enter a filename (if you want to export the whole Registry, just select the Export Range All) and click OK.
5. Perform the change (install some software or change a system parameter).
6. Rerun steps 1 to 4 using a different filename.
7. Run the two files through a comparison utility (for example, WINDIFF.EXE).
8. If you are using windiff, select Compare Files from the File menu. You will then be prompted to select the two files to compare.
9. Once the files are compared, a summary will be displayed stating the differences. To view the changes, double-click on the message.
10. Press F8 to view the next change (or select Next Change from the View menu.)

You have now found what changed!

FAQ 10.7 How can I delete a Registry value/key from the command line?

Using the Windows utility REG.EXE, you can delete a Registry value from the command line or batch file—for example:

```
reg delete HKLM\Software\test
```

The preceding command deletes the HKEY_LOCAL_MACHINE\Software\test value. When you enter the command, you are prompted whether you really want to delete; enter Y. To avoid the confirmation, add /force to the command—for example:

```
reg delete HKLM\Software\test /force
```

A full list of the codes to be used with REG DELETE follows:

HKCR	HKEY_CLASSES_ROOT
HKCU	HKEY_CURRENT_USER
HKLM	HKEY_LOCAL_MACHINE
HKU	HKEY_USERS
HKCC	HKEY_CURRENT_CONFIG

To delete a entry on a remote machine, add the name of the machine, \\<machine name>—for example:

```
reg delete HKLM\Software\test \\johnpc
```

FAQ 10.8 How can I audit changes to the Registry?

Using the REGEDIT.EXE utility, it is possible to set auditing on certain parts of the Registry. You should note that any type of auditing is very sensitive lately, and you may want to provide some sort of warning, letting people know that their changes are being audited.

1. Start the Registry editor (REGEDIT.EXE).
2. Select the key you wish to audit (e.g., HKEY_LOCAL_MACHINE\Software).
3. From the Edit menu, select Permissions.
4. Click the Advanced button.
5. Select the Auditing tab and click Add.
6. Add the users and which properties to audit.
7. Click OK.

You also need to ensure that audit logging is enabled via the policy:

1. Start the Policy editor (Start > Programs > Administrative Tools > Local Security Policy).
2. Expand Local Policies and select Audit Policy.
3. Double-click on Audit object access.
4. Select Success and Failure and click OK.
5. Close the Policy editor.

To view the information, use Event Viewer and look at the Security information.

10.9 How can I clean up/remove invalid entries from the Registry?

Microsoft has released a utility called RegClean, which will go through your machine's Registry and delete any unused/unnecessary keys. The current version is 4.1a. Unfortunately, Microsoft has removed it as a download, but you may find it on the Web via a search.

Once you've downloaded it, just click on the executable, and it will check your Registry. After the check is completed, you will be given the option to fix errors via the Fix Errors button. You can click the Exit button to exit.

RegClean creates an uninstall file (UNDO.REG) in the directory the image is located in—for example, Undo workstation 19980320 104323.reg.

To undo the changes, just double-click this file (or single-click it, depending on your config ☺).

10.10 I make changes to HKEY_LOCAL_MACHINE, but they are lost on reboot. Why?

This is because HKEY_LOCAL_MACHINE\HARDWARE is recreated by the system at boot time, which means any settings such as ACLs are lost. The rest of HKLM (HKEY_LOCAL_MACHINE) SOFTWARE, SYSTEM, SAM, SECURITY) is stored on disk and is not recreated during system boot.

10.11 What data types are available in the Registry?

The following table lists data types supported by REGED32.EXE. REGEDIT.EXE does not support REG_EXPAND_SZ or REG_MULTI_SZ.

REG_BINARY	This data type is raw binary data.
REG_DWORD	This is a double word (4 bytes). It can be displayed in binary, hexadecimal, or decimal format.
REG_EXPAND_SZ	This data type is an expandable text string that contains a variable (e.g., %systemroot%).
REG_MULTI_SZ	This is a multiple line string. Each line is separated by a NULL.
REG_SZ	This is a text string.

10.12 How can I automate updates to the Registry?

You can use two main methods to create scripts that can be run to automate the updates. The first is to create a .REG file that can then be run using

```
regedit /s <reg file>
```

The format of the file is

```
Windows Registry Editor Version 5.00
[<key name>]
"<value name>"="<value>" a string value
"<value name>"=hex:<value> a binary value
"<value name>"=dword:<value> a dword value
```

For example

```
Windows Registry Editor Version 5.00

[HKEY_USERS\.DEFAULT\Control Panel\Desktop]
"Wallpaper"="E:\\WINNT\\savtech.bmp"
"TileWallpaper"="0"

[HKEY_USERS\.DEFAULT\Control Panel\Colors]
"Background"="0 0 0"
```

The preceding sets the default background and color before anyone logs on.

The second method is to user a Windows 95-style .INF file. These files are run using the command

```
rundll32 syssetup,SetupInfObjectInstallAction DefaultInstall 128
<inf file>
```

The format of the file is as follows

```
[Version]
Signature = "$Windows NT$"
Provider=%Provider%

[Strings]
Provider="SavillTech Ltd"
```

```
[DefaultInstall]
AddReg = AddReg

DelReg = DelReg
UpdateInis = UpdateInis

[AddReg]
[DelReg]
[UpdateInis]
```

The following are the keys to be used:

HKCR	HKEY_CLASSES_ROOT
HKCU	HKEY_CURRENT_USER
HKLM	HKEY_LOCAL_MACHINE
HKU	HKEY_USERS

The following file is an .INF file that performs the same as the previously described .REGfile:

```
[Version]
Signature = "$Windows NT$"

[DefaultInstall]
AddReg = AddReg

[AddReg]
HKU,".DEFAULT\Control Panel\Colors","Background",0000000000,"0 0 0"
HKU,".DEFAULT\Control
Panel\Desktop","Wallpaper",0000000000,"E:\WINNT\savtech.bmp"
HKU,".DEFAULT\Control Panel\Desktop","TileWallpaper",0000000000,"1"
```

INF files can be generated automatically using the SysDiff utility if you have a difference file (sysdiff /inf <name of difference file> <dir to create to>).

A Registry entry can also be deleted using .REG files. That is, if one has a .REG file with—for example:

```
[HKEY_CURRENT_USER\Test]
```

to enter a key, then one can use the following to remove it:

```
[-HKEY_CURRENT_USER\Test]
```

FAQ 10.13 How do I apply a .REG file without the success message?

To apply a .REG file (a Registry information file), using the normal method from the command prompt, enter

```
regedit <registry file>.reg
```

The preceding command applies the change and gives the following confirmation message:

```
Information is <filename>.reg has been successfully entered into the
registry
```

If you would like to avoid this confirmation message and apply the change silently use the /s switch—for example:

```
regedit /s <registry file>.reg
```

FAQ 10.14 How can I remotely modify the maximum Registry size?

The maximum Registry size is usually defined using the System properties Control Panel applet, Performance tab. When you change this value, all it actually does is to update the Registry entry

```
HKEY_LOCAL_MACHINE\SYSTEM\CurrentControlSet\Control\RegistrySizeLimit
```

You could therefore modify this value from the command line using a Registry script. For example:

```
REGEDIT4

[HKEY_LOCAL_MACHINE\System\CurrentControlSet\Control]
"RegistrySizeLimit"="24000000"
```

You can run it using

```
regedit /s
```

You could add this command to a login script.

Alternatively, run this command remotely by submitting it with the AT command. The change will not take effect until the machine reboots. If you wanted the reboot to occur, you could add a reboot using the Resource Kit SHUTDOWN.EXE utility (as explained in FAQ 6.30).

Ensure on the machines that HKEY_LOCAL_MACHINE\SYSTEM\CurrentControlSet\Control\Session Manager\Memory Management\PagedPoolSize is set to 0, which allows it to automatically set itself. If it's set to a value that does not correlate to registrysizelimit, you may experience problems.

FAQ 10.15 How can I install an .INF file from the command line?

The normal method to install an .INF file is to right-click on it and select Install from the context menu. It is also possible to install it from the command line. The syntax is

```
rundll32 syssetup,SetupInfObjectInstallAction DefaultInstall 128
.\<file>.inf
```

FAQ 10.16 How can I compress the Registry?

The following procedure can be used to compact the Registry files and also to restore the repair disk data when you mess up the Registry:

1. As always, make sure you have a backup of your system, including the Registry.
2. Update the repair information located under %systemroot%\repair. The Registry data are reorganized and compressed. (For XP/2000, this is via the NTBACKUP utility and create backup disk/ASR.)
3. Check your %temp% folder and %systemroot%\system32\config to find the difference in size between the different files that make up the Registry. Probably the SOFTWARE hive will have a remarkable difference. In my case, it shrank from over 10MB to 3.5MB.
4. The Registry files in %systemroot%\system32\config should be replaced by the reorganized ones in your %temp% folder. You can do this by:
   - Booting to DOS or Win3.x/95/98 and simply replacing the files (in case your system files are on a FAT partition).

- Replacing these files while booting from a second Windows NT installation.
- Or by using the MV command (move) from the Resource Kit to move these files at boot time:

```
MV /X /D %systemroot%\repair\DEFAULT
%systemroot%\SYSTEM32\CONFIG\DEFAULT

MV /X /D %systemroot%\repair\SAM %systemroot%\SYSTEM32\CONFIG\SAM
MV /X /D %systemroot%\repair\SECURITY
%systemroot%\SYSTEM32\CONFIG\SECURITY
MV /X /D %systemroot%\repair\SOFTWARE
%systemroot%\SYSTEM32\CONFIG\SOFTWARE
MV /X /D %systemroot%\repair\SYSTEM
%systemroot%\SYSTEM32\CONFIG\SYSTEM
```

When I performed these steps, I noticed a serious performance gain during system startup.

FAQ 10.17 Access to the Registry tools has been prevented. Is there any way to get access?

I include this FAQ because I had the exact problem, and I want Administrators to be aware that access can be enabled.

If the Scheduler service is running on your PC (or if you can start it), you can submit the Registry editor to start via the Scheduler, and it will then be started under the system context. For example:

```
at <1 minute in the future> /interactive regedt32.exe
```

One minute from submission, REGEDT32.EXE will be started, giving you full access to the Registry. Cool!

You can also reenable the tools by writing a small .REG file. Double-click on it, which gives full access:

```
REGEDIT4

[HKEY_CURRENT_USER\Software\Microsoft\Windows\CurrentVersion\
Policies\System]
"DisableRegistryTools"=dword:00000000
```

Save it as DISABLEREGISTRYTOOLS.REG, double-click it from Explorer, and you will have full Registry access.

10.18 Where does Windows 2000 store the last key accessed?

In Windows 2000, when you start the Registry editor, it remembers where you last were and automatically reopens that key. This information is actually stored in the Registry in location:

```
HKEY_CURRENT_USER\Software\Microsoft\Windows\CurrentVersion\Applets\
Regedit\LastKey
```

If this annoys you, it could be reset at each logon to NULL via a script with a .REG file—for example:

```
Windows Registry Editor Version 5.00

[HKEY_CURRENT_USER\Software\Microsoft\Windows\CurrentVersion\Applets
\Regedit]
"LastKey"=""
```

10.19 What's new in the Windows 2000 version of Regedit?

As we saw in the last FAQ, the Windows 2000 version of REGEDIT.EXE now remembers the last key that was opened before you started the application. The second major change is the introduction of a Favorites menu to which you can add your most used and favorite Registry keys (you would have to be sad to have favorite Registry keys:-)).

Another change is the addition of the ability of new Regedit to save files in the old (REGEDIT4) format from the command line, using a command-line switch -ea.

REGEDT32.EXE has not had any major functionality changes.

FAQ 10.20 How do I add a DWORD value from a .INF file?

An INF file has many uses, including the creation of Registry keys. Normally a string value is created, but to create a DWORD, use the following format:

```
[Version]
Signature = "$Windows NT$"
Provider=%Provider%

[Strings]
Provider="SavillTech Ltd"

[DefaultInstall]
AddReg = AddReg

DelReg = DelReg
UpdateInis = UpdateInis

[AddReg]
HKLM,"Software\SavillTech","A DWORD",65537,ee,ff,c0,00
[DelReg]
[UpdateInis]
```

The important part is after the value name "A DWORD" is the type, a 0 in lowest bit means a string value, and a 1 means another type. 0x10000 is a DWORD value, hence 65537. The rest of the value is in four hexadecimal numbers.

FAQ 10.21 Where in the Registry is the language setting for each user stored?

The ID for the current language is stored in the Registry value HKEY_CURRENT_USER\Control Panel\Desktop\MultiUILanguageId. When you request a change to the language, the ID for the new language is stored in HKEY_CURRENT_USER\Control Panel\Desktop\MUILanguagePending and takes effect at the next logon. Both Registry values store a number that corresponds to the language ID you've chosen. The following table lists the available values:

Language Name	Language ID
English (default)	0409
French	040c
Spanish	0c0a
Italian	0410
Swedish	041D
Dutch	0413
Brazilian	0416
Finnish	040b
Norwegian	0414
Danish	0406
Hungarian	040e
Polish	0415
Russian	0419
Czech	0405
Greek	0408
Portuguese	0816
Turkish	041f
Japanese	0411
Korean	0412
German	0407
Chinese (Simplified)	0804
Chinese (Traditional)	0404
Arabic	0401
Hebrew	040d

If you request a language change and then want to cancel the change, you can open a Registry editor and change the MUILanguagePending value to that of the MultiLanguageId value.

FAQ 10.22 Where can I find the RegClean utility on Microsoft's Web site?

Microsoft no longer provides this utility on its Web site, but you can download the utility from either Tweakfiles.com or CNET's Download.com. RegClean is still a neat utility that parses the entire Registry and finds inconsistencies and dead links and removes them.

FAQ 10.23 How do I delete a value from a .REG file?

You can use Registry files to import information into the Registry, but you can also use them to delete a value by including a hyphen (-) as the value's data. In the following example, I delete the valueName value from the key HKEY_LOCAL_MACHINE\SOFTWARE\SavillTech\key:

```
[HKEY_LOCAL_MACHINE\SOFTWARE\SavillTech\key]

"valueName"=-
```

FAQ 10.24 How do I delete a key and all its values from a .REG file?

To completely remove a key from a .REG file, place a hyphen (-) in front of the key. In the following example, I delete the key HKEY_LOCAL_MACHINE\SOFTWARE\SavillTech\key and all its values:

```
[-HKEY_LOCAL_MACHINE\SOFTWARE\SavillTech\key]
```

10.25 How do I place comments in a .REG file?

To include comments in a Registry file, place a semicolon (;) at the beginning of the line, as follows:

```
; This will delete the key below because of the - sign
[-HKEY_LOCAL_MACHINE\SOFTWARE\SavillTech\key]
```

10.26 How do I export a key in ANSI format from the Registry?

To export a key from the Registry in ANSI format, use the /a switch:

```
regedit /a <registry file> "<registry key>"
```

For example, the following command exports the HKEY_LOCAL_MACHINE\Software key in ANSI format from the HKLM.REG file:

```
regedit /a c:\hklm.reg "HKEY_LOCAL_MACHINE\Software"
```

10.27 Why do I receive the error "Installation ended prematurely because of an error" when I try to install Office XP?

An error message indicating that the installation didn't complete might be the result of incorrect Registry permissions on the Registry key HKEY_LOCAL_MACHINE\SOFTWARE\Microsoft\Office. To confirm that these permissions are correct, perform the following steps:

1. Start the Registry editor (REGEDT32.EXE on Windows 2000 or REGEDIT.EXE on Windows XP and Microsoft .NET Server).
2. Navigate to HKEY_LOCAL_MACHINE\SOFTWARE\Microsoft\Office.
3. From the Security menu (or the Edit menu in Windows XP), select Permissions. The permissions should be

   Administrators—Full Control

   Creator Owner—Full Control

Power Users—Special
System—Full Control
Users—Read

4. If the permissions onscreen don't match the permissions in step 3, go to step 5; otherwise, skip to step 6.
5. Ensure that the Reset permissions on all child objects checkbox is selected and that the Allow Inheritable permissions from parent to propagate to this object checkbox is cleared, click OK, and click Yes to overwrite existing permissions.
6. Close the Registry editor.

11 RECOVERY

Windows XP is the most reliable version of Windows ever, and tests have found it far less likely to error. However, it still can and still will!

We look at a number of problems in this chapter—and not just faults. We look at what to do if you forget the Administrator password, and we describe some third-party tools.

FAQ 11.1 Why do I get the error "Can't find NTLDR."?

This is a core file that must be in the root directory, and the fact that the file cannot find this file may mean other files are also missing. To fix this problem, perform the following:

1. Boot the system with a DOS bootable floppy disk if it is a FAT partition. If it is a NTFS partition, use the NT boot disk. If you're using Windows 2000 or above, use the Recovery Console.
2. In the i386 directory of the CD-ROM is a file NTLDR._, which is the compressed version of NTLDR. You can expand this file using EXPAND.EXE, which comes with DOS and Windows for Workgroups:

```
expand d:\i386\ntldr._ c:\ntldr
```

FAQ 11.2 How do I recover a lost Administrator password?

If no other accounts are in the Administrator group, and the machine is not part of a domain where the Domains Administrator account could be used to log on and change the local Administrator password (the domain's Administrator group is automatically made a member of the machine's Administrator group when the machine joins the domain), then the only way to recover the password is to reinstall NT into a new directory (not the same folder, because it will upgrade and see the old password), and Setup will let you enter a new Admin password. Also if you have an old ERD that you knew the password of at the time of making the ERD disk, you could use this and restore the SAM and security portions of the Registry.

The software LockSmith, available from http://www.winternals.com, can break into an NT system and will change any password. The software is not free and will cost around US$100. A new product, ERD Professional (from the same company that develops LockSmith) can also change passwords and is available from the same site.

A similar piece of software is also available from http://www.mirider.com. It allows you to boot from a set of disks and change the Administrator password.

The following instructions require a second installation of NT on the machine you have forgotten the password to. I use the SRVANY.EXE Resource Kit utility.

1. Install a second copy of NT onto the machine into a different directory/drive (it has to be only a minimal installation) and boot into this installation.
2. Copy SRVANY.EXE from the Resource Kit into a directory—for example, c:\temp.
3. Start Regedt32.
4. Move to HKEY_LOCAL_MACHINE and select the root.
5. From the Open menu, select Load Hive.
6. Move to %systemroot%\system32\config of the **main** NT installation—that is, if your main installation (the one whose password you are trying to change) is installed at d:\winnt, you would move to d:\winnt\system32\config.
7. Select System and click Open.
8. You will be asked for a key name, enter **Mainreg** and click OK.
9. Select the Select branch and write down the Default value—for example, 0xn, 0x1. This will be used to load ControlSet00n.
10. Move to HKEY_LOCAL_MACHINE\Mainreg\ControlSet00n\Services\Spooler and take a note of the ImagePath value (it will usually be %SystemRoot%\system32\spoolss.exe).
11. Change ImagePath to c:\temp\srvany.exe (or wherever you copied the file to), click OK.
12. Move to Parameters and add a value of type REG_SZ called **Application**. Once added, double-click the new value and set to **%systemroot%\system32\net.exe**.
13. Add another value of type REG_SZ called **AppParameters**. Once added double-click the new value and set to user Administrator password.
14. Move back to HKEY_LOCAL_MACHINE\Mainreg and select Unload Hive from the open menu. Click Yes to the confirmation.
15. You should now reboot and boot off of your original NT installation. Wait a few minutes and then log on as the Administrator with password "password".

You now need to correct the changes made:

1. Start REGED32.EXE.
2. .Move to HKEY_LOCAL_MACHINE\SYSTEM\CurrentControlSet\Services\Spooler\Parameters and delete Application and AppParameters values.
3. Move down to HKEY_LOCAL_MACHINE\SYSTEM\CurrentControlSet\Services\Spoole and change ImagePath back to its original value (%SystemRoot%\system32\spoolss.exe).

You may now delete the second installation of NT if you wish and remove it from the boot menu (edit BOOT.INI after removing the hidden, read-only, and system attributes—**attrib c:\boot.ini -r -s -h**).

All this actually does is change the Spooler service to use the SRVANY.EXE program, which runs the NET command as the service with the parameters user Administrator password. These parameters are the same as the net user Administrator password, which is a way to change the password. Check the Resource Kit for more information on SRVANY.

FAQ 11.3 I have set a drive to no access, and now no one can access it. What can I do?

Log on as an Administrator and then perform the following

1. Start Explorer.
2. Right-click on the drive and select Properties.
3. Select the Security tab and click Advanced.
4. Select the Owner tab.
5. Under Change owner to, select the new owner and click OK.
6. Click OK to the main properties dialog.

FAQ 11.4 If I copy a file with Explorer or from the command line, the permissions get lost. Why?

The only time a file keeps its permissions is when it is moved on the same partition. When it is copied, it inherits the protection of the owning directory (a move across drives is a copy and delete). Also FAT does not support permissions, so anything copied to FAT will lose protections.

The SCOPY command can be used to maintain permissions (this command has been merged into XCOPY under Windows XP).

FAQ 11.5 How can I get my taskbar back?

Press Ctrl+Alt+Del and then select Task Manager. Click the Applications tab, select New Task, and type **Explorer**.

FAQ 11.6 I get the error "NTOSKRNL.EXE missing or corrupt" on boot-up. Why?

This error is usually due to an error in the BOOT.INI file. The entry for NT is either missing or incorrect. Edit the BOOT.INI file and check that the entry for NT is correct—for example, for an IDE disk, the entry should look something like

```
multi(0)disk(0)rdisk(0)partition(2)\winnt="Windows NT workstation"
```

Check that the disk and partition are correct. If you have recently added a new disk or altered the partitions, try changing the disk() and partition() values. If you are sure everything is OK, then the actual file may be corrupt. Copy NTOSKRNL.EXE off of the installation CD onto the %systemroot%/system32 directory.

You may need to edit the BOOT.INI if Linux is installed onto a system. During installation, DiskDruid (Red Hat's disk configuration utility) may create a primary partition (depending on disk configuration), and although the extended NT partition was there first (and at the beginning of the disk), the primary partition affects the numbering of the partition() parameter of BOOT.INI. Changing it from (1) to (2) (for example) allows the successful boot of NT.

FAQ 11.7 Where is rdisk in Windows 2000?

The RDISK.EXE utility has been replaced with an option in the NTBACKUP.EXE utility.

1. Start NTBACKUP.EXE (Start > Run > NTBACKUP.EXE).
2. Select Create an Emergency Repair Disk from the Tools menu.
3. Insert a blank formatted disk in drive A and click OK.
4. Click OK to the completion message and click OK

The recovery disk can no longer be used to restore user accounts and other functions. You must back up or restore the Active Directory, which is covered in Chapter 12.

FAQ 11.8 How do I install the Recovery Console?

The Windows 2000 Recovery Console (RC) enables an Administrator to gain access to a 2000 system from a command session to replace damaged files and to disable or enable services. When installed, it adds an option to the Windows 2000 Start menu.

To install, perform the following:

1. Boot into Windows 2000.
2. Insert the installation CD.
3. From a command prompt, move to the i386 directory and type

   ```
   winnt32 /cmdcons
   ```

4. A dialog will be displayed asking for confirmation. Click Yes.

   Several files will be copied to the computer, and an extra item added to the boot menu:

   ```
   C:\CMDCONS\BOOTSECT.DAT="Microsoft Windows 2000 Command Console"
   /cmdcons
   ```

5. A completion message will be displayed. Click OK.

   Rebooting the computer will enable the option “Microsoft Windows 2000 Command Console” to be selected and enable you to start Windows 2000 in command mode.

6. You will be asked which 2000 installation to repair and to enter the Administrator password:

   ```
   Microsoft Windows 2000(TM) Recovery Console.
   The Recovery Console provides system repair and recovery
   functionality.
   Type EXIT to quit the Recovery Console and restart the computer.
   1: C:\Winnt
   2: F:\WINNT
   Which Windows 2000 installation would you like to log onto
   (To cancel, press ENTER)? 2
   Type the Administrator password: ***
   ```

Once you have entered the password, you will be able to enter a number of commands such as DISABLE to disable a service, DISKPART to create and remove partitions, and many others. Just type **HELP** for a list of all commands.

It's also possible to activate the console directory from the installation CD by booting off the CD (if your motherboard supports CD booting), select Repair and press C to repair using the console.

If you have renamed the Administrator account, the console will still work; however, deleting the Administrator account will render the console inoperative.

The Recovery Console does have built-in security, and you can access only the root of the system driver, the %systemroot% directory, and its subdirectories.

Some of the most useful commands are

LISTSVC	List services
ENABLE/DISALBE	Enable/disable service
DISKPART	Equivalent of FDISK
FIXBOOT	Create a new boot sector on the system partition
FIXMBR	FDISK /MBR equivalent (repair problems with RAID, etc)
LOGON	List installation of Windows 2000 and can choose which installation to work on
SYSTEMROOT	Move to the system root
MAP	Display a list of drives and their ARC paths. Useful to fix BOOT.INI problems

11.9 How do I create a bootable CD-ROM containing ERD Commander/Professional?

ERD Commander is a fantastic tool by Winternals (http://www.winternals.com) that provides access to NT systems by booting off modified Windows NT setup disks. ERD Commander allows access to not only the filesystem but also to the Registry and many other items to enable you to recover an unbootable NT system. It also provides access to removable media, allowing you to replace corrupted system files, something you otherwise can't do without a second NT installation on the machine. The professional version also allows you to change passwords from outside of NT!

It's now possible to create a bootable CD-ROM containing ERD Commander, which allows you to just insert the CD-ROM, reboot, and you have an ERD Commander session.

Following are the steps I used. I have included some additional files to make it easier for you.

1. Install ERD Commander/Professional as usual. Doing so creates a number of startup disks based on the NT installation diskettes (three for Commander, four for Professional).
2. Create a directory on a partition called ERD.
3. Create a subdirectory i386 (e.g., c:\ERD\i386).
4. Copy the content of all disks to this i386 directory.
5. Download and extract Service Pack 5:

   ```
   SP5I386 /X
   ```

6. Replace any files that are in the ERD\i386 directory that are also included with SP5 with the SP5 version (including files in the system32 directory **except SMSS.EXE**, which is core to ERD Commander). There are a lot of these files, but replacing them will allow you to access NTFS 5.0 partitions, which contain a number of fixes. This step is not compulsory but recommended.
7. Download the files BOOTSEC.BIN and CDROM_W.40 from http://www.ntfaq.com/ misc/. Place them both in the ERD directory.
8. Copy the following files from the ERD\i386 directory to the ERD directory (but do **not** remove them from the ERD\i386 directory):

   NTDETECT.COM
   SETUPLDR.BIN
   TXTSETUP.SIF

9. Start your CD-ROM-burning software (CDRWIN from http://www.goldenhawk.com is recommended). Whatever software you use, it must support creating a bootable CD-ROM.
10. Add the ERD directory to the CD image, **but** ERD should be the root. i386 should only be a subdirectory of the root of the CD, so you should not have a directory ERD/i386 on the CD. Just have the directory i386 and the three files in the ERD directory on the root of the CD.
11. Remember the following options:

    ISO9660 File system (no Joliet)
    No version numbers

BOOTABLE CD : emulation : none (custom) load sector count : 4 load segment (default) 07C0H

The boot sector image is the BOOTSEC.BIN you downloaded.

An example of creating a 2000 disk is shown at FAQ 11.9, which is basically the same as this step (see step 7 of FAQ 11.9).

12. Create your CD! You should now be able to boot off it. I tried this procedure last night, and it worked great. If you have problems, download the Word document listed at the start of this FAQ. I never had to edit SETUPLDR.BIN, and if you use my boot sector image, you won't need to do that part either.

Note: *If you create a bootable ERD Commander Professional CD (versions 1.06a or below), the program continues to ask for disk 4 for the FTDISK, PASSWORD, and CHKDSK commands, which will be fixed in the next version.*

If you're using ERD Professional, it's a good idea to get the new password update from Winternals.com's support page.

The full list of files from SP 5 to be copied to ERD\i386 are:

- i8042PRT.SYS
- HALNCR.DLL
- HALMCA.DLL
- HAL486C.DLL
- L_INTL.NLS
- FASTFAT.SYS
- DISK.SYS
- KBDUS.DLL
- C_1252.NLS
- CPQFWS2E.SYS
- CPQARRAY.SYS
- CLASS2.SYS
- HALAPIC.DLL
- NTFS.SYS
- NTKRNLMP.EXE
- CDROM.SYS
- PCMCIA.SYS
- CDFS.SYS
- NTDETECT.COM
- AUTOCHK.EXE

- QL10WNT.SYS
- SCSIPORT.SYS
- ATDISK.SYS
- ATAPI.SYS
- AIC78XX.001
- SFLOPPY.SYS
- FTDISK.SYS
- SYMC810.SYS
- VGA.SYS
- VIDOPRT.SYS
- SYSTEM32\NTDLL.DLL

FAQ 11.10 How do I enable kernel-only crash dumps?

When a crash occurs in Windows NT 4.0, the entire memory is dumped out to file MEMORY.DMP to aid in the debugging of a crash. In reality, only information stored within the kernel portion of memory is needed, and Windows 2000 introduces the ability to dump out only the kernel area of memory.

Why? Well, if we have 128MB of memory and the machine crashes, we get a 128MB file, which is big, but not too big to FTP to Microsoft. Now imagine you have a huge data store server with terabytes of memory. While Microsoft has the ability to accept files this big, a smaller file would be better for everyone.

Using the 128MB machine, dumping out the kernel-only portion of memory results in a dump of around 35MB—about 27% of the original file size.

To enable kernel-only crash dumps, perform the following:

1. Start the System Control Panel applet.
2. Select the Advanced tab and click the Startup and Recovery button.
3. Under the Write Debugging Information section, select Kernel Memory Dump(see Figure 11-1).
4. Click OK.
5. Restart the computer for the change to take effect.

You can also enable kernel-only crash dumps by changing values under HKEY_LOCAL_MACHINE\SYSTEM\CurrentControlSet\Control\CrashControl key. CrashDumpEnabled should be set to 2 for a kernel dump, 3 for a mini-memory dump, and DumpFile should be set to %SystemRoot%\Memory.dmp.

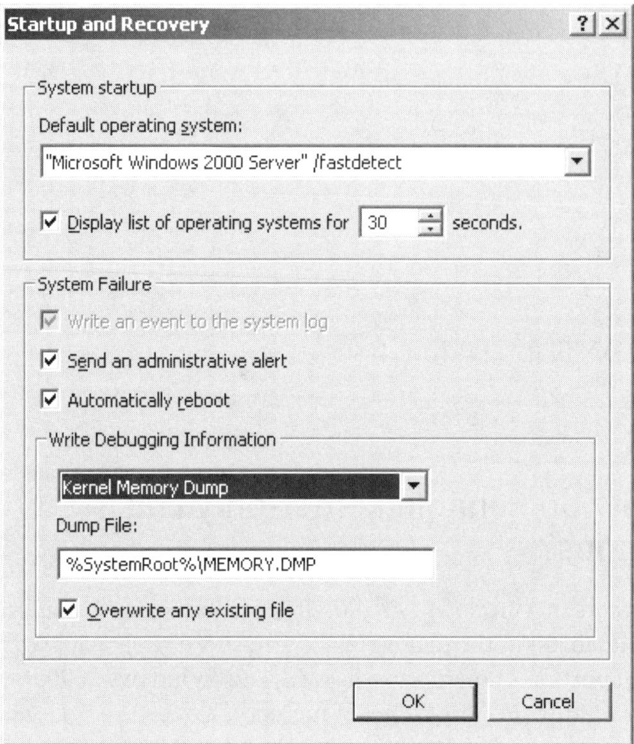

Figure 11-1 Debug write options

FAQ 11.11 What's the difference between manual and fast recovery in Windows 2000?

Windows 2000 has two options when performing recovery—Fast or Manual. When you select manual, you have a number of options:

- Inspect startup environment—Checks the existence of BOOT.INI and the ARC paths therein
- Verify Windows 2000 system files—Performs a cyclic redundancy check (CRC) on the core boot/system files except NTBOOTDD.SYS
- Inspect Boot Sector—Repairs the active system partition boot sector and reinstalls boot-loaded functionality

If you select Fast repair, it performs all of the previously listed options and additionally tries to load each Windows 2000 Registry file (SAM, SECURITY, SYSTEM, and

SOFTWARE). If a Registry file is damaged or cannot be loaded, the Repair process copies the missing or corrupted Registry file from the %SystemRoot%\Repair folder to the %SystemRoot%\System32\Config folder.

Because it may restore old Registry backup files, Repair may revert your installation back to an older configuration. If this happens, you will need to manually restore a more up-to-date system state backup.

FAQ 11.12 I've deleted NTBOOTDD.SYS and can't find it anywhere. What should I do?

If in your BOOT.INI file, your ARC paths consist of either SCSI() or SIGNATURE(), you are using a SCSI connection for the installation. The file NTBOOTDD.SYS contains the miniport device driver for the initial boot to communicate with the SCSI controller.

No such file as NTBOOTDD.SYS is supplied with Windows NT/2000 because it's created during installation, depending on your exact SCSI card. This file is the specific SCSI miniport device driver for the SCSI adapter from which you are booting, renamed to NTBOOTDD.SYS and placed in the root folder of the system drive.

To fix the missing file problem, copy the correct device driver for the SCSI controller in use on the computer and then rename it to NTBOOTDD.SYS at the root of the system partition (C normally).

For example, you would rename AIC78XX.SYS for a 2940UW Adaptec card (either from the NT installation media or better from the latest service pack if supplied).

FAQ 11.13 How can I change the Recovery Console Administrator password on a domain controller?

When you use the Recovery Console (RC), the system uses the account passwords in the local SAM file. But if a system is a domain controller (DC), it doesn't use the local SAM file, so changing the Administrator password changes the Active Directory (AD) account and not the local SAM password. To modify the SAM password, perform the following steps:

1. Shut down the DC on which you want to change the password.
2. Restart the computer. When the system displays the selection menu during the restart process, press F8 to view advanced startup options.
3. Select Directory Service Restore Mode.

4. After you successfully log on, to change the local Administrator password at a command prompt, type the following command:

```
net user administrator *
```

5. Restart the computer.

If you don't know the password, you can demote the DC to a regular server, change the password, then promote the system to a DC. You can also copy the SAM in the %SystemRoot%\Repair folder to the %SystemRoot%\System32\Config folder.

FAQ 11.14 How can I determine whether my machine started in safe mode, safe mode with command prompt, or safe mode with networking?

When you start your machine in safe mode in Windows 2000 or later Windows OSs, you can select from several options: safe mode with command prompt, safe mode, and safe mode with networking. The OS sets the Safeboot_Option environment variable when you start a machine in safe mode. To examine the status of this variable, enter the following at the command prompt:

```
echo %safeboot_option%
```

Possible values include

- Minimal—If the machine is in safe mode
- Minimal—If the machine is in safe mode with command prompt
- Network—If the machine is in safe mode with networking

12 BACKUP

In an ideal world, backups would not be necessary; however, mere mortals make mistakes—users accidentally delete files, which makes it sometimes necessary to restore files.

With Windows 2000 it became possible to back up to nontape devices such as file systems, ZIP drives, and so on, opening up NTBACKUP to regular desktop users.

Windows XP added native CD-ROM-burning abilities with a scaled-down version of Roxio's Easy-CD incorporated into the product giving an additional backup target.

FAQ 12.1 What types of backup does NT Backup support?

NT Backup supports the following five types of backup:

- Normal—Backs up the files you select, and marks the files as backed up.
- Incremental—Backs up the files that changed since the last backup, and marks the files as backed up.
- Differential—Backs up the files that changed since the last backup, but doesn't mark the files as backed up.
- Copy—Backs up the files you select, but doesn't mark the files as backed up.
- Daily—Backs up the files that changed that day, but doesn't mark the files as backed up.

FAQ 12.2 What backup strategy should I use?

The most common backup strategy is to perform incremental backups Monday through Thursday and a normal backup Friday. Incremental backups are fast because they back up only those files that changed since the last backup, marking the files as backed up. In the event of a failure, you need to first restore the normal backup, then restore any subsequent incremental backups.

An alternative backup strategy is to perform differential backups Monday through Thursday and a normal backup Friday. Differential backups and incremental backups are similar, except that a differential backup doesn't mark the files as backed up. Therefore, files backed up Monday are still backed up Tuesday, and so forth. In the event of a failure, you need to restore only the normal backup and the latest differential backup.

Be sure to maintain more than one week's worth of tapes. The best strategy is to have a rotation of at least ten tapes and to rotate the tapes every two weeks.

If you want an extra backup for one-time use, consider a copy backup. A copy backup is a full backup, but the files aren't marked as backed up. This type of backup doesn't interfere with the backup scheme you're using.

FAQ 12.3 What NT Backup options are available?

After you start NT Backup, you'll see a list of all the drives on the machine. You can select an entire drive, or you can double-click the drive and select directories. After you select the drives or directories, click Backup.

When you perform a backup, you need to complete the following fields:

- Current Tape—The inserted tape's name. You can't edit this field.
- Creation Date—Date of original backup set creation. You can't edit this field.
- Owner—Tape owner. You can't edit this field.
- Tape Name—A 32-character (maximum) string describing the tape.
- Operation Append/Replace—If you select append, the new saveset adds to the end of the tape. If you select replace, NT Backup overwrites any information on the tape.
- Verify After Backup—After the files copy to tape, this field verifies the files against the files on disk.
- Back Up Local Registry—Backs up the local computer's Registry. (You can't back up a remote computer's Registry.)
- Restrict Access to Owner or Administrator—Makes the tape secure. Only the tape's owner or a member of the Administrators group or Backup Operators group can access the tape.

FAQ 12.4 How do I run NT Backup from the command line?

To run NT Backup from the command line, simply use the following syntax:

```
ntbackup <operation> <path> /a /b /d "text" /e /hc:<on/off> /l
"<filename>" /r /missingtape /t <backup type> /tape:n /v
```

The following table explains each parameter:

<operation>	The operation to perform. If you want to eject a tape, add the eject command and include the /tape parameter.
>path>	The list of drives and directories to back up. You can't use filenames or the wildcard character. To back up multiple drives, insert a space between the drives (e.g., ntbackup backup c: d:).
/a	Appends backup sets to the end of the tape. If you omit this parameter, the tape will erase.
/b	Backs up the local Registry.
/d "text"	A description of the tape.
/e	Logs only exceptions.
/hc:<on/off>	If you use /hc:on, hardware compression is enabled. If you use /hc:off, no hardware compression is used.
/l "<filename>"	Location and name for the log file.
/r	Restricts access (ignored if you use the /a parameter).
/missingtape	Specifies that a tape is missing from the backup set when the set spans several tapes. Each tape becomes one unit rather than part of the set.
/t <backup type>	The type of backup (i.e., normal, incremental, differential, copy, or daily).
/tape:n	Specifies which tape drive to use (from 0 to 9). If you omit this parameter, NT Backup uses tape drive 0.
/v	Performs verification.

FAQ 12.5 How do I use NT Backup to erase a tape?

When NT Backup starts and you insert a tape, NT Backup scans the device. If the program finds an error, you'll see one of the following messages:

- `Tape Drive Error Detected`
- `Tape Drive Not Responding`
- `Bad Tape`

You won't be able to perform any actions on the tape, including erasing it. You can use the /nopoll parameter to force NT Backup to not check a tape when you insert it:

```
ntbackup /nopoll
```

You can then use NT Backup to erase a tape.

If you have multiple tape drives, you might want to use the /tape:n parameter to instruct NT Backup to ignore a tape drive.

After you erase the tape, you need to exit NT Backup. Then, restart NT Backup, without using the /nopoll parameter, to use the tape.

FAQ 12.6 How do I back up the Registry?

Most Registry hives are open, making them impossible to copy in the normal way. However, you can use one of the following methods:

- If you have a tape drive attached to a Windows NT machine, NT Backup can perform a full Registry backup. Simply select the "back up local Registry" option when you start the backup. NT Backup can't back up Registries on remote machines.
- The command rdisk /s backs up the Registry to the %SystemRoot%/repair directory. Windows 2000 and XP don't include this command; for more information, see FAQ 11.7.
- The Microsoft Windows 2000 Resource Kit's Regback utility backs up the Registry's **open** files. To back up unopened files, you must use the xcopy or scopy command to manually copy the files. You can also use the Resource Kit's Regrest utility to restore the Registry.
- You can use the Resource Kit's REG.EXE utility with the backup option (e.g., reg backup) to back up sections of the Registry.

FAQ 12.7 What permissions does a user need to perform a backup?

To perform a backup, a user needs the back up files and directories user right. You can use User Manager to grant this right, or you can make the user a member of the Administrators group or Backup Operators group. One of the latter methods is preferable.

FAQ 12.8 How do I back up open files?

Running a backup program while you have files open might corrupt some of those files. To prevent NT Backup from backing up open files, perform the following steps:

1. Start a Registry Editor.
2. Go to the HKEY_CURRENT_USER\Software\Microsoft\Ntbackup\Backup Engine Registry entry.
3. Select Backup files in use. If the value is set to 1, double-click the value and set it to 0. Click OK.
4. Close the Registry Editor.

If the Backup files in use value was set to 1, you also need to set the parameter for the HKEY_CURRENT_USER\Software\Microsoft\Ntbackup\User Interface\Skip open files Registry entry. The values for this parameter are as follows:

- 0—Don't skip the file; wait until it can be backed up.
- 1—Skip files that are open or unreadable.
- 2—Wait for open files to close for (which is another Registry value stored in) seconds.

To back up open files without corrupting them, you can try St. Bernard Software's Open File Manager. You can download a 15-day trial version from the company's Web site at http://www.stbernard.com.

FAQ 12.9 How do I schedule a backup?

Before you can schedule a backup, you need to ensure that the Scheduler service is running on the target machine. The service doesn't need to be running on the issuing machine (for information about the Scheduler service, see FAQ 6.3.

As long as the Scheduler service is running, you can use NT Backup to submit a backup command. Enter a command similar to the following:

```
at 22:00 /every:M,T,W,Th,F ntbackup backup d: /v /b
```

The example command schedules a backup of drive D, as well as the local Registry (with verification), every weekday at 10:00 p.m.

If you're having scheduling problems, you might want to use the /interactive switch. This option lets you interact with NT Backup.

FAQ 12.10 How do I kill a stalled backup process?

If you use the AT command (i.e., the schedule command) to start a backup and NT Backup has a problem, you'll receive an error message saying you don't have the proper authority when you try to run Task Manager to kill the process. The only solution is to reboot the server.

If you use the /interactive switch with the ntbackup command, you can create a special version of Task Manager to kill the rogue NT Backup process, rather than rebooting the server. Simply use the AT command to start Task Manager one minute in the future:

```
at [\\<computer name>] <time in future> /interactive taskmgr
```

The computer name field is optional and starts Task Manager on another machine.

Alternatively, use the Microsoft Windows NT Resource Kit's Soon utility:

```
soon 30 /interactive taskmgr
```

Task Manager will display in 30 seconds, and you can kill the NT Backup process.

Yet another method is to use the Resource Kit's Tlist and Kill commands. Although you need administrative privileges to run the Kill program, you might find this method preferable to fumbling with the AT command and waiting for the command to start Task Manager as a system account. First, use Tlist to see the active tasks and their process identifiers (PIDs):

```
tlist -t | more
```

You'll see the following output:

```
ATSVC.EXE (315)
CMD.EXE (345)
NTVDM.EXE (348)
NTBACKUP.EXE (314)
```

The PID varies depending on the system. The -t option is important and provides a treelike output to show which process is the parent or child.

Use Kill to end the parent process (i.e., CMD.EXE) and the NT Backup command:

```
kill -f 345
```

Killing the parent process doesn't kill the child processes the parent created. After you kill CMD.EXE, you need to kill the child processes that CMD.EXE called.

Be sure not to kill the ATSVC.EXE process, or you'll kill the Scheduler service. Then, you'll need to restart the service.

If you need to kill a backup process on a remote server and can't get to the console, load the Resource Kit's Rkillsrv utility as a service on the remote machine. Then, use the Resource Kit's Rkill utility on your local machine. You need administrative privileges on the target system to kill the stalled process.

To obtain the process list on the server, enter

```
rkill /view \\<servername>
```

To kill the PID process on the server, enter

```
rkill /kill \\<servername> pid
```

To put your remote security token on the server, enter

```
rkill /token \\<servername>
```

A final hint is to always run the following command at the beginning of a scheduled NT Backup job. This command kills any old backup jobs that are running:

```
kill.exe -f ntbackup.exe
```

FAQ 12.11 What backup software is available for Windows NT?

Windows NT includes NT Backup. Although this program's features are basic, it is suitable for backing up most installations. For large or complex installations, you might want to try one of the following products:

- Tivoli's ADSM, http://www.storage.ibm.com/software/adsm/index.htm
- Computer Associates' ARCserveIT, http://www.cai.com/arcserveit
- Computer Data Strategies' Back Again II, http://www.cds-inc.com
- VERITAS Software's VERITAS Backup Exec, http://www.veritas.com/us/products/backupexec
- Syncsort's Backup Express, http://www.syncsort.com/infobex.htm
- KieSoft's EaseBackup, http://www.kiesoft.com

- Legato Systems' Legato NetWorker, http://www.legato.com/products/protection/networker
- Storactive's LiveBackup, http://www.storactive.com/products/products.html
- VERITAS Software's VERITAS NetBackup, http://www.veritas.com/us/products/netbackup
- NovaStor's NovaBACKUP, http://www.novastor.com
- HP's OpenView OmniBack II, http://www.managementsoftware.hp.com/products/omniback/index.asp
- Stac Software's Replica, http://www.stac.com
- Dantz's Retrospect 5.0, http://www.dantz.com
- BEI's UltraBac, http://www.ultrabac.com

FAQ 12.12 Why can't I back up the NT Event Viewer files when I'm logged on as a member of the Backup Operators group?

If you're a member of the Backup Operators group and you use NT Backup to back up the boot partition, NT Backup might not back up the Event Viewer (.EVT) files because members of the group might not have the necessary security credentials. To resolve this problem, log on as a domain or local administrator to back up the system.

13 NETWORK

Even homes sometimes have more than one computer, now making home networks more common. Certainly in the office, a network is now mandatory.

This ability to share information and resources is great. With more networks on the Internet, security is an important issue, and care must be taken. We also look at hosting some Net-based services such as FTP servers.

FAQ 13.1 I can't FTP to my server, although the FTP service is running. Why?

Have you unchecked the Allow only anonymous connections option but still receive a "530 User xyz cannot log in. Login failed." message? To log onto the FTP server with your domain account, it is not sufficient to specify your name at the user prompt. The FTP service checks local accounts only, even if the computer is participating in a domain. Use domainname\username instead. For example, if the domain name was savilltech and the user was john, enter **savilltech\john** as the username.

I have heard of problems where the users must have the logon locally right or the FTP logon may fail.

FAQ 13.2 Can I synchronize the time of a workstation with a server?

Yes, enter the command

```
NET TIME \\<name of the server to set time to> /SET /YES
```

Note that users will require the Change System Time user right, via User Manager\User rights. The TimeServ utility on the Resource Kit runs the time synchronization as a service and works even when there are no logged-on users.

On Windows 2000/XP, it is not necessary that users be part of a domain because they automatically synchronize to the domain controller that authenticates them.

FAQ 13.3 How can I send a message to all users?

Ensure the Messenger service is started (Control Panel > Services > Messenger > Auto). To send a message type

```
net send <machine name> "<message>"
```

Or instead of a machine name, type an asterisk (*) to broadcast to all stations.

FAQ 13.4 How do I stop the default admin shares from being created?

This can be done through the Registry:

1. Start the Registry editor.
2. Move to HKEY_LOCAL_MACHINE\System\CurrentControlSet\Services\LanmanServer\Parameters.
3. If you are using Workstation, create a value (Edit > Add Value) called **AutoShareWks** (**AutoShareServer** for Server) of type DWORD and press OK. It will ask for a value; type the number **0**.
4. Close the Registry editor.
5. Reboot.

A few other options are available though. The first is to use NTFS and set protections on the files so users can connect to the share, but they will not be able to see anything. The second is to delete the shares each time you log on; this can be done through Explorer. It would be better to have a command file run each time with the lines

```
net share c$ /delete
```

and for all the other administration shares. However, these shares are there for a reason, so your machine can be administered by the servers. If you delete them, system managers may have something to say about it!

FAQ 13.5 How do I disconnect all network drives?

Use **net use * /del /yes**.

FAQ 13.6 How do I hide a machine from network browsers?

Using the Registry editor, set the key HKEY_LOCAL_MACHINE\System\CurrentControlSet\Services\LanManServer\Parameters and set value Hidden from 0 to 1, which should be of type DWORD. You should then reboot. You can also type

```
net config server /hidden:yes
```

The preceding command also automatically creates quite a lot of other values under \Parameters key.

You can still connect to the computer, but it is not displayed on the browser.

NT ONLY

FAQ 13.7 How do I remote-boot NT?

NT does not support remote boot. It is possible to reboot a machine from another computer using the Shutdown Manager that comes with the NT Resource Kit.

You could also reboot by using the SHUTDOWN.EXE Resource Kit utility and specify another machine name:

```
shutdown \\<machine name> /r /y /c
```

Software such as PC Anywhere can also remotely reboot machines.

NT4.0 ONLY

FAQ 13.8 How can I get a list of users currently logged on?

Use the net sessions command, which works only if you are an Administrator. You can also use the Control Panel and choose Server.

The Resource Kit utility, Net Watch, can also show currently logged-on users who are connected to the netlogon share if you connect to the domain controller. However, these connections terminate after a finite amount of time, so netlogon will not necessarily show all users.

FAQ 13.9 How can I prevent a user from logging on more than once?

There is no way in NT to prevent a user from logging on more than once. It is possible to restrict a workstation so that only a certain user can log on, and with this method, each user is tied to one workstation. Thus each user can log on only once:

1. Log on to the workstation as the Domain Administrator.
2. Start User Manager (Start > Administrative Tools > User Manager).
3. Double-click the Users group, select Domain\Everyone, and click Remove.
4. Next click Add, select the specific domain user, and click Add.
5. Close User Manager.
6. Log off and only that specific user will be able to log on (be careful that Administrators still include Domain\Administrators, or you will not be able to log on).

This solution is far from ideal. It may be plausible to write a logon script that checks whether a user is currently logged on, and if so, log off straight away (using the logout command-line tool).

Another method is to set the user's netlogon share to one connection only. Then the script could open a file from the logon share, which means if the user was already logged on, a second logon would be unable to connect to the share, and the logon would fail.

The Windows 2000 Resource Kit introduces the CCONNECT.EXE (Con-Current Connection Limiter) utility that:

- Is completely hidden from the end user's view
- Keeps track of all computers that users are logged on
- Tracks the last known user of the computer
- Monitors what logon server users are logging into
- Allows concurrent connection limitations to be set on a per-user or per-group basis
- Stores all information in a Microsoft SQL Server database assigned by the Administrator

Con-Current Connection Limiter is not installed by the Windows 2000 Resource Kit setup program. The files required for this tool are located on the Apps\Cconnect\ folder of the Resource Kit companion CD.

Before using CConnect Client or CConnect Administrator, you must first install it using the installation programs (SETUP.EXE) located in the Apps\Cconnect\Client and Apps\Cconnect\Admin folders.

FAQ 13.10 How can I get information about my domain account?

From the command prompt, type

```
net user <username> /domain
```

And all your user information will be displayed; this information includes last logon time and password change.

FAQ 13.11 How do I automatically FTP using NT?

I use a basic script to update my main site and the mirrors using two batch files. The first consists of a few lines:

```
d:
cd \savilltechhomepage
ftp -i -s:d:\savmanagement\goftp.bat
```

The -i suppresses the prompt when performing a multiple put, and the -s defines an input file for the FTP like:

- open ftp.savilltech.com—The name of the FTP server
- johnny—Username
- secret—Password
- cd /www—Remotely move to a base directory
- lcd download—Locally change directory
- cd download—Remotely move to a sub directory of the current directory
- binary—Set mode to binary
- put faqcomp.zip—Send a file
- cd . . . —Move down a directory remotely
- lcd . . . —Move down a directory locally
- cd ntfaq
- lcd ntfaq
- mput *.HTML—Send multiple files (this is why we needed -i)
- close—close the connection

FAQ 13.12 How can I change the time period used for displaying the password expiration message?

Follow these instructions:

1. Start the Registry editor (REGEDIT.EXE).
2. Go to the key HKEY_LOCAL_MACHINE\SOFTWARE\Microsoft\Windows NT\CurrentVersion\Winlogon.
3. From the Edit menu, click New > DWORD.
4. Type the name **PasswordExpiryWarning** and press Enter.
5. Double-click on the new value you have created and set to the number of days prior to the expiration you want the message to appear.

FAQ 13.13 How can I change the protocol binding order?

Network bindings are links that enable communication between the network adapter(s), protocols, and services. If you have multiple protocols installed on a machine, you can configure NT to try a certain protocol first for communication:

1. Log on to the machine as a member of the Administrators group.
2. Start the Network Control Panel applet (Start > Settings > Control Panel > Network, or right-click Network Neighborhood and select Properties).
3. Click the Bindings tab.
4. Select All services from the drop-down list of bindings.
5. Select the service you wish to change the binding order for by clicking its plus sign (usually you change the Workstation service because it is used for connecting to resources, etc.).
6. A list of all the protocols installed is displayed and can be ordered by selecting the protocol and clicking Move up or Move down.
7. Click OK when finished, and you will have to reboot for the changes to take effect.

At first glance, this option seems to have disappeared from Win2K, but don't worry. Microsoft has simply moved it.

1. Open the Network and Dial-up Connections window (Start > Settings > Network and Dial-up Connections).
2. Select the connection you want to modify (e.g., Local Area Connection).

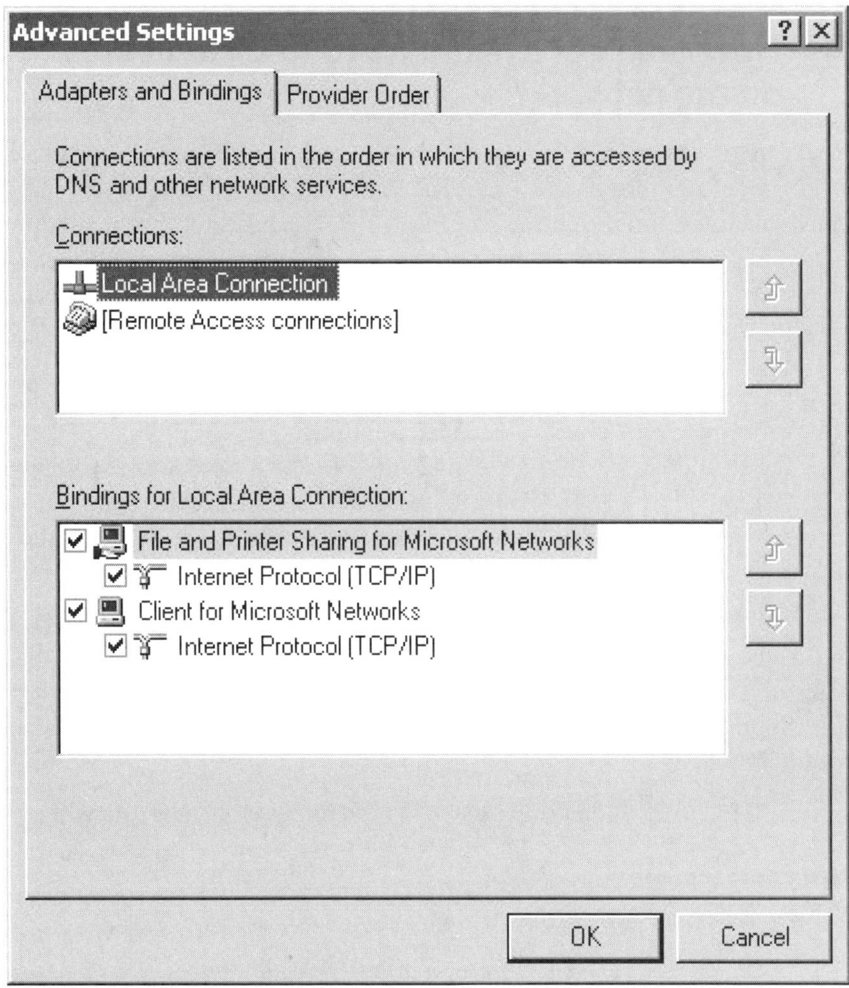

Figure 13-1 Binding options for a Local Area Connection

3. From the Advanced menu, select Advanced Settings.
4. Select the Adapters and Bindings tab (see Figure 13-1).
5. Modify the bindings as required.
6. Click OK.

FAQ 13.14 How can I get a list of MAC to IP addresses on the network?

An easy way to get a list of MAC to IP addresses on the local subnet is to ping every host on the subnet and then check your ARP cache. However, pinging every individual node would take ages, and the entries stay in the ARP cache for only two minutes. An alternative is to ping the broadcast mask of your subnet, which pings every host on the local subnet. (You can't ping the entire network because you communicate directly only with nodes on the same subnet. All other requests are via the gateway—so you would just get an ARP entry for the gateway.)

What is the broadcast mask? The broadcast mask is easy to calculate if the subnet mask is in the format 255.255.255.0 or 255.255.0.0, etc. (i.e., multiples of 8 bits). For example, if the IP address was 134.189.23.42 and the subnet mask was 255.255.0.0, the broadcast mask would be 134.189.255.255, where 255 is in the subnet mask the number from the IP address is copied over; where 0 is replaced with 255, basically the network ID part is kept. If the subnet mask is not the basic 255.255 format, you should use the following; all you need is the IP address and the subnet mask:

- For each bit set to 1 in the subnet mask, copy the corresponding bit from the IP address to the broadcast mask.
- For each bit set to 0 in the subnet mask, copy a 1 into the corresponding bit of the broadcast mask.

To get the MAC to IP addresses, you would therefore perform the following:

```
ping <broadcast mask>
arp -a
```

Voilà, a list of IP addresses and their corresponding MAC addresses (you can add > **filename** to get the list to a file—e.g. **arp -a > iptomac.lst**). You could repeat this exercise on the various subnets of your organization.

Unfortunately due to limitations in NT's implementation of Ping, the preceding will not work correctly, so put the following into a file:

```
REM arpping.bat
ping -n 1 -l 1 %1.%2
arp -a %1.%2
```

You can then call the batch file as follows:

```
for /l %i in (1,1,254) do arpping 160.82.220 %i
```

In this case, the command would generate a list of all MAC to IP addresses for 160.82.220.1 to 160.82.220.254. Again you could put this all in a file, redirect to a file, and then search—for example:

```
REM test.bat
for /l %%i in (1,1,254) do arpping.bat 160.82.220 %%i
```

Notice you have to use two percent signs (%%). You could it run as

```
test.bat > file.txt
```

Then search LISTING.TXT for (example) the dynamic word

```
findstr dynamic file.txt
160.82.220.1 00-00-0c-60-8b-41 dynamic
160.82.220.9 00-60-97-4b-bf-4c dynamic
160.82.220.13 00-10-4b-49-94-e1 dynamic
160.82.220.17 00-80-5f-d8-a4-8b dynamic
160.82.220.22 00-a0-d1-02-a4-cf dynamic
160.82.220.25 00-60-08-75-0d-7a dynamic
160.82.220.26 00-10-4b-44-e4-73 dynamic
160.82.220.33 00-10-4b-44-d6-33 dynamic
160.82.220.34 00-10-4b-4e-67-6a dynamic
160.82.220.35 00-60-97-4b-c4-53 dynamic
160.82.220.39 00-10-4b-44-eb-ae dynamic
160.82.220.41 00-10-4b-49-7b-f7 dynamic
160.82.220.42 00-00-f8-21-7a-7f dynamic
160.82.220.43 08-00-20-88-82-57 dynamic
160.82.220.221 00-80-5f-88-d0-55 dynamic
```

You can consolidate the last couple of steps, so you just create ARPPING.BAT as before; then just issue the command

```
for /l %i in (1,1,254) do arpping.bat 10.129.210 %i |findstr dynamic

C:\>arpping.bat 10.129.210 1 | findstr dynamic
10.129.210.1 00-08-c7-d3-24-f5 dynamic

C:\>arpping.bat 10.129.210 2 | findstr dynamic
10.129.210.2 00-08-c7-df-81-60 dynamic

C:\>arpping.bat 10.129.210 3 | findstr dynamic
10.129.210.3 00-80-5f-9b-ea-93 dynamic
```

```
C:\>arpping.bat 10.129.210 4 | findstr dynamic
10.129.210.4 00-80-5f-9b-36-ea dynamic

C:\>arpping.bat 10.129.210 5 | findstr dynamic
10.129.210.5 00-04-ac-37-78-92 dynamic
C:\>arpping.bat 10.129.210 6 | findstr dynamic
```

Notice we only use one percent sign (%) because we are not in a batch file. The command automatically lists only found entries, or you can use a combination of the different methods to match your exact needs.

FAQ 13.15 How can I control the list of connections shown when mapping a network drive?

When you map a network drive (Explorer > Tools > Map network drive) and you click the down arrow on the directory path, a list of previous connections will be shown. These connections are stored on the Registry and can be edited:

1. Start the Registry editor (REGEDIT.EXE).
2. Move to HKEY_CURRENT_USER\Software\Microsoft\Windows NT\CurrentVersion\Network\Persistent Connections.
3. In the left pane, you'll notice a number of string values—a, b ,c, etc. For the connections you do not want shown, click on the entry and then either press the Delete key and respond Yes to the confirmation, or select Delete from the Edit menu.
4. Once you have deleted entries, you need to update which ones Explorer will show by double-clicking Order and removing the letters of the entries you deleted.
5. Click OK.
6. Close the Registry editor.

FAQ 13.16 How do I grant users access to a network printer?

The same way that files have security information, so do printers, and you need to set which users can perform actions on each network printer.

1. Log on as an Administrator.
2. Double-click My Computer and then select Printers.

3. Right-click on the printer whose permissions you wish to change and select Properties.
4. Click the Security tag and select Permissions.
5. You can now add users/groups and grant them the appropriate privilege.
6. Click OK when finished.

FAQ 13.17 Why do I get errors accessing a Windows NT FTP server from a non-Internet Explorer browser?

If you run the Microsoft FTP Server service, then you may find problems accessing an area other than the root from a non-Internet Explorer browser. This is because most other FTP servers use the UNIX-type naming conventions, which is what browsers such as Netscape expect. However the Microsoft FTP service outputs using **DOS** naming conventions. This can be resolved by forcing the FTP server service to use UNIX conventions rather than DOS.

1. Start the Registry editor (REGEDIT.EXE).
2. Move to HKEY_LOCAL_MACHINE\SYSTEM\CurrentControlSet\Services\ftpsvc\Parameters.
3. If the value MsdosDirOutput exists, double-click it and set it to 0. Click OK.
4. If it does not exist, from the Edit menu, select New > DWORD Value and enter the name **MsdosDirOutput**. Click OK, then perform step 3.

You will need to stop and start the FTP Server service for this change to take effect (Start > Settings > Control Panel > Services > FTP Service > Stop > Start).

FAQ 13.18 Is there any way to improve the performance of my modem Internet connection?

By default, NT will use a Maximum Transmission Unit (MTU—packet size) over the path to a remote host of 576. Problems can arise if the data is sent over routes, and other transport components that cannot handle data of this size, and the packets get fragmented.

The parameter EnablePMTUDiscovery set to 1 forces NT to discover the maximum MTU of all connections that are not on the local subnet. To change value, this perform the following:

1. Start the Registry editor (REGEDIT.EXE).
2. Move to HKEY_LOCAL_MACHINE\SYSTEM\CurrentControlSet\Services\Tcpip\Parameters.
3. From the Edit menu, select New > DWORD Value.
4. Enter a name of **EnablePMTUDiscovery** and press Enter.
5. Double-click on this new value and set to 1; then click OK.
6. Close the Registry editor and reboot the machine.

By discovering the path MTU and limiting TCP segments to this size, TCP can eliminate fragmentation at routers along the path that connect networks with different MTUs. Fragmentation adversely affects TCP throughput and network congestion.

FAQ 13.19 How can I remotely tell who is logged on at a machine?

The easiest way is to use the NBTSTAT command. There are two ways to use this command, depending on whether you know the machine's name or just its IP address. If you know the machine's name, enter the command

```
nbtstat -a <machine name>
```

For example, **nbtstat -a pdc**.

The output will be of the format:

```
NetBIOS Remote Machine Name Table
Name Type Status
---------------------------------------------
PDC <00> UNIQUE Registered
PDC <20> UNIQUE Registered
SAVILLTECH <00> GROUP Registered
SAVILLTECH <1C> GROUP Registered
SAVILLTECH <1B> UNIQUE Registered
SAVILLTECH <1E> GROUP Registered
PDC <03> UNIQUE Registered
SAVILLJ <03> UNIQUE Registered
SAVILLTECH <1D> UNIQUE Registered
INet~Services <1C> GROUP Registered
..__MSBROWSE__.<01> GROUP Registered
IS~PDC.........<00> UNIQUE Registered
```

```
MAC Address=00-A0-24-B8-11-F3
The user name is the <03>.
```

If you know only the IP address, use the command

```
nbtstat -A <IP address>
```

For example, **nbtstat -A 10.23.23.12**.

The output is the same. Notice I just use a capital "A" instead of a lowercase "a". This command will work only if the remote machine in question is running its messenger service; otherwise, the username is not returned.

FAQ 13.20 How can I shut down a number of machines without going to each machine?

I have a number of machines set up in my lab, and at the end of an entertaining evening of computing, I don't want to have to go to each machine and shut them down. I wrote a small batch file that uses the **SHUTDOWN.EXE** Resource Kit utility. Just enter the following into a file with a .BAT extension:

```
rem Batch file to shutdown local machine and the PDC, BDC
```

The following shuts down a machine called PDC in two seconds; repeat with other machine names:

```
shutdown \\pdc /t:2 /y /c
```

The following shuts down a machine called BDC in two seconds:

```
shutdown \\bdc /t:2 /y /c
```

The following line shuts down the local machine in five seconds:

```
shutdown /l /y /c /t:5
```

You can then just right-click the file in Explorer and drag it onto the desktop. Release the file and select the Create shortcut icon. Clicking this icon will then shut down all the machines in the file. On a NT Server, these shutdowns are not graceful, and the users will not be asked to save their work if they are not logged on or if the machine is locked. If they are logged on, then they have the option of saving their files (unless a force switch is used).

If you have installed an SP4 or SP5 on WinNT, the remote shutdown command will shut down a machine immediately without stopping the services (dirty shutdown event ID 6008).

13.21 How can I close all network sessions/connections?

The following command will close all network sessions:

```
net session /delete
```

13.22 How can I connect to a server using different user accounts?

It is possible to specify a user account to use when connecting to a share using the /user switch—for example:

```
net use k: \\server\share /user:domain\user
```

If you then attempt to connect to the server again with a different username, an error will be displayed. A work around is to connect to the server using its IP address rather than its NetBIOS name—for example:

```
net use l: \\<ip address>\share /user:domain\user
```

This can also be accomplished using the Explorer interface by clicking Connect, using a different username when mapping to the drive.

13.23 How do I set the comment for my machine that is displayed in Network Neighborhood?

There are three ways to set this comment: from the command line, by editing the Registry, or via the GUI. The easiest way is via the GUI using the System Control Panel applet:

1. Start the server Control Panel applet (Start > Settings > Control Panel > System).
2. Select the Computer Name tab.

3. Enter the new description of the machine in the Computer Description field.
4. Click OK.

An alternative method is from the command prompt using the net config command:

```
net config server /srvcomment:"machine comment"
```

Note that even if you are performing this on a workstation machine, you still use net config server because this is a configuration on the Server service of the machine.

Both of the methods shown update a single Registry value so it can also be edited directly:

1. Start the Registry editor (REGEDIT.EXE).
2. Move to HKEY_LOCAL_MACHINE\SYSTEM\CurrentControlSet\Services\LanmanServer\Parameters.
3. Double-click on srvcomment.
4. In the Value data box, enter the new description and click OK.
5. Close the Registry editor.

This method only works once the Server service has been restarted; however, both other methods work instantly. This is because the Registry area is only read during startup of the service.

Under Windows 2000 and above, right-click on My Computer and choose Manage. Then right-click on Computer Management (Local) and choose Properties. The option for the Description is under the Network Identification tab.

FAQ 13.24 How can I define multiple NetBIOS names for a machine?

This would be useful if, for instance, you wanted to migrate a number of shares to a different machine. Rather than having to switch all clients to the new machine instantly, you could define the new machine to also answer to the old machine's NetBIOS name and then slowly migrate the machines. To define extra names for a machine, perform the following:

1. Start the Registry editor (REGEDT32.EXE).
2. Move to HKEY_Local_Machine\System\CurrentControlSet\Services\LanmanServer\Parameters.
3. From the Edit menu, select Add Value.

4. Set the type to REG_SZ if you want one extra name, or REG_MULTI_SZ if you want more than one. Enter a name of **OptionalNames**. Click OK.
5. You will then be prompted for a value. Enter the other name (or names if type REG_MULTI_SZ, one on each line) you want it to be known as and click OK.
6. Close the Registry editor.
7. Reboot the machine.

There may be a WINS resolution problem. The entries for the additional NetBIOS names will have been dynamically added to the WINS database, complete with IP number. However, a "real" server machine in the WINS dbase normally has three WINS entries, 00h, 03h, and 20h. Your aliases may only have one, 03h. Therefore you may need to add static entries for the additional NetBIOS names, which created all three entries. You should now be able to ping by NetBIOS name.

FAQ 13.25 How can I remotely manage services?

SC.EXE allows remote services to be managed. To view the services on a remote machine, use

```
sc \\<server name> goofy
```

To see the current state of a service, use

```
sc \\<server name> queryex <service>
```

You can then modify the state of the service, using the start, stop, pause, and continue switches—for example:

```
sc \\<server name> stop <service>
```

Under Windows 2000 and above, you can use the Connect to another computer option of the Computer Management MMC snap-in and then select the Services branch.

FAQ 13.26 Is there a reference for NET.EXE?

The following is a summary of all the NET.EXE usage methods:

```
net accounts
```

Used to modify user accounts. Specified on its own, this command will provide information about the current logon.

Options:

/forcelogoff:<minutes or no>	Minutes until the user gets logged off after logon hours expire. No means a forced logoff will not occur.
/lockoutthreshold: <number of failed attempts>	This parameter allows you to configure the number of failed logon attempts before the account is locked. The range is 1 to 999.
/lockoutduration:<minutes>	This parameter specifies the number of minutes accounts remain locked before automatically becoming unlocked. The range is 1 to 99999.
/lockoutwindow:<minutes>	This parameter lets you configure the maximum number of minutes between two consecutive failed logon attempts before an account is locked. The range is 1 to 99999.
/minpwlen:<length>	Minimum number of characters for the password. Default is 6; valid range is between 0 and 14.
/maxpwage:<days>	Maximum number of days a password is valid. Default is 90; valid range is between 0 and 49710.
/minpwage:<days>	Number of days that must occur before the password can be changed. Default is 0; valid range is between 0 and maxpwage.
/uniquepw:<number>	Password may not be reused for number attempts.
/sync	Forces a domain sync.
/domain	Performs any of the preceding actions on the domain controller.

```
net computer
```

Used to add and remove computer accounts from the domain.

Options:

\\<computer name>	Name of the computer to be added or removed.
/add	Adds the specified computer.
/del	Removes the specified computer.

```
net config server
```

Allows modifications to the Server service. Entered with no parameters gives details of the current configuration.

Options:

/autodisconnect:<minutes>	Number of minutes an account may be inactive before disconnection. Default is 15; valid range between 1 and 65535. -1 means never disconnected.
/srvcomment:"text"	Sets the comment for the machine.
/hidden:<yes or no>	Specifies whether the computer is hidden in the listing of computers.

```
net config workstation
```

Allows modifications to the Workstation service. Entered with no parameters, this command provides details of the current configuration.

Options:

/charcount:<bytes>	Number of bytes to be collected before data is sent. The default is 16; valid range is between 0 and 65535.
/chartime:<msec>	Number of milliseconds NT waits before sending data. If charcount is also set, whichever is satisfied first is used. Default is 250; valid range is between 0 and 65535000.
/charwait:<seconds>	Number of seconds NT waits for a communications device to become available. Default is 3600; valid is between 0 and 65535.

```
net continue <service name>
```

Restarts the specified paused service.

```
net file
```

Lists any files that are open/locked via a network share.

Options:

id	Identification of the file (given by entering net file on its own).
/close	Close the specified lock.

net group

Adds/modifies global groups on servers. Without parameters, this command lists global groups.

Syntax:

```
net group <group name> [/command:"<text>"] [/domain]
net group <group name> [/add [/comment:"<text>"] or /delete] [/domain]
net group <group name> <user name> /add or /delete [/domain]
```

Options:

groupname	Name of the global group.
/comment:"<text>"	Comment if a new global group is created. Up to 48 characters.
/domain	Performs the function on the primary domain controller.
username	Username to which to apply the operation.
/add	Adds the specified user to the group or the group to the domain.
/delete	Removes a group from a domain or a user from a group.

net localgroup

Performs actions on local groups. Same parameters as net group.

net name

Adds/removes a name to which messaging may be directed to. Running the command on its own will list all messaging names eligible on the machine.

Options:

name	The messaging name to be added/removed.
/add	Add the name.
/delete	Remove the name.

```
net pause <service name>
```

Used to pause a service from the command line.

```
net print
```

Used to list/modify print jobs.

Options:

\\computername	Computer that hosts the printer queue.
sharename	Name of the printer queue.
job	Job number to modify.
/hold	Pauses a job on the print queue.
/release	Removes the hold status of a job on the print queue.
/delete	Deletes a job off of the print queue.

```
net send
```

Sends a message to a computer, user, or messaging name.

Options:

name	Name of the user, computer, or messaging name. Can also use an asterisk (*) to send to everyone in the group.
/domain:<domain name>	All users in the current domain or the specified domain.
/users	All users connected to the server.
message	Message to send.

```
net session
```

Lists or disconnects sessions. Used with no options, this command lists the current sessions.

Options:

\\<computer name>	Computer of whose session to close.
/delete	Closes the session to the computer specified. Omitting a computer name will close all sessions.

```
net share
```

Used to manage shares from the command line.

Syntax:

```
net share <sharename>=<drive>:\<directory> [/users=<number> or
/unlimited] [/remark:"text"]
net share <sharename> [/users=<number> or /unlimited]
[/remark:"text"]
net share <sharename or device name or drive and path> /delete
```

Options:

<sharename>	Name of the share.
<device name>	Specifies the printer name if specifying a printer share.
<drive>:<path>	Absolute path.
/users:<number>	Number of simultaneous connections to the share.
/unlimited	Unlimited usage.
/remark:"<text>"	Comment for the share.
/delete	Delete the specified share.

```
net start <service name>
```

Starts the specified service.

```
net statistics [workstation or service]
```

Gives information about either the server or workstation service.

```
net stop <service name>
```

Stops the specified service

```
net time
```

Synchronizes the time of a computer.

Options:

\\<computer name>	The name of the computer to which synchronize the time.
/domain:<domain>	Synchronizes the time with the specified domain.
/set	Sets the time.

```
net use
```

Connects or disconnects to a network share. Used with no qualifiers lists the current network mappings.

Syntax:

```
net use <device name> or * \\<computer name>\<share name> [password
or *] [/user:[domain\user] /delete or [persistent:[yes or no]]
net use <device name> /home /delete or /persistent:[yes or no]
```

Options:

<device name>	Name of the device to map to. Use the asterisk (*) to use the next available device name.
\\computer name	Name of the computer controlling the resource.
\sharename	Name of the share.
\volume	Name of the volume if on a NetWare server.
password	Password to which to map.
*	Gives a prompt to which to enter the password.
/user:<domain>\<user>	Specifies the user to connect as.
/home	Connects to a user's home directory.
/delete	Closes a connection.
/persistent:[yes or no>	Sets if the connection should be reconnected at next logon.

net user

Adds/creates/modifies user accounts.

Syntax:

```
net user <username> [password or *] [/add] [options] [/domain]
net user <username] /delete /domain
```

username	The name of the account.
password	Assigns or changes a password.
*	Gives a prompt for the password.
/domain	Perform on a domain.
/add	Creates the account.
/delete	Removes the account.
/active:[yes or no]	Activates or deactivates the account.
/comment:“<text>”	Adds a descriptive comment.
/counterycode.nnn	nnn is the number of the operating system code. Use 0 for the operating systems default.
/expires:<date or never>	The expiry date of the account. Date format is mm,dd,yy or dd,mm,yy, which is determined by the country code.
/fullname:“<name>”	The full name of the account.
/homedir:<path>	Path for the user’s home directory.
/passwordchg:[yes or no]	Used to specify whether the user can modify the password.
/passwordreq:[yes or no]	Used to determine whether the account needs a password.
/profilepath:<path>	Profile path.
/scriptpath:<path>	Path of the logon script.
/times:<times or all>	Hours user may logon.
/usercomment:“<text>”	Comment for the account.
/workstations:<machine names>	Names the user may log onto. An asterisk (*) means all.

```
net view
```

Lists shared resources on a domain. Used with no parameters, this command lists all machine accounts in a domain.

Options:

\\computer name	Computer whose resource should be viewed.
/domain:<domain name>	Domain to be used.
/network:<NetWare network>	NetWare network to be used.

FAQ 13.27 How can I make NET.EXE use the next available drive letter?

The normal syntax to map a network drive is

```
net use <drive letter>: \\<server>\<share>
```

This can be modified to

```
net use * \\<server>\<share>
```

which makes the net use command utilize the next available drive letter.

FAQ 13.28 How can I check if servers can communicate via RPCs?

Exchange ships with RPINGS.EXE and RPINGC32.EXE, which can be used to test RPC communication between two servers. These programs are located in the SERVER\SUPPORT\RPCPING directory of the Exchange CD. Test as follows:

1. On one server, start Command (CMD.EXE) and enter

   ```
   rpings
   ```

2. On the other server, run the RPINGC32.EXE utility.

3. You should then enter the name of the Exchange server to test communication with—for example, **NT4PDC**.
4. Click Start.

The connection will then be checked. Once complete, close the RPINGC32.EXE utility by clicking Exit. On the target machine, enter the sequence **@q**.

Figure 13-2 is an example of a successful test.

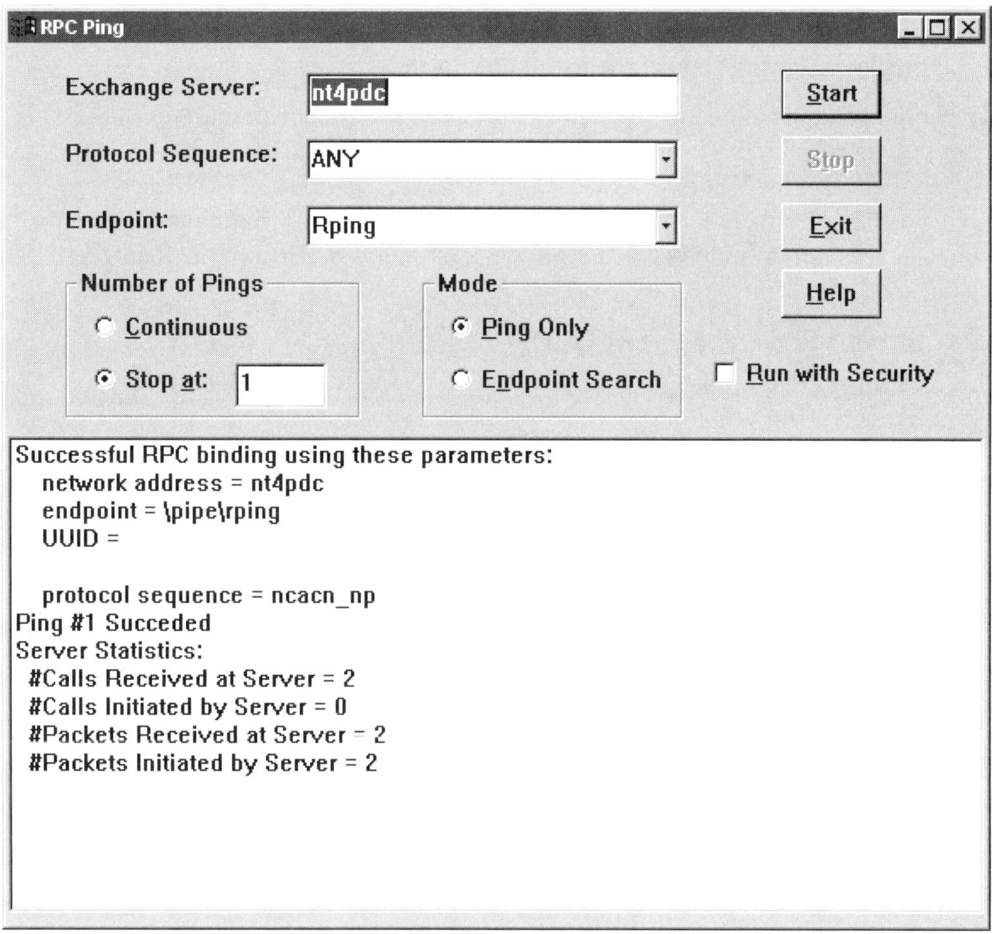

Figure 13-2 The RPC Ping utility

13.29 How can I reduce the delay when using multiple redirectors?

The MUP (Multiple UNC Provider) first establishes whether Distributed File System (DFS) is in use and passes the request to DFS. The delays come from two locations:

- The attempt to access the resource through DFS.
- The MUP must wait and accept all responses from all redirectors before completing the request. Therefore, even if a resource is readily available and accessible over one redirector, the request must still be made over the other installed redirectors before the request completes.

Depending on the number of redirectors, protocols, and timer configurations for connectivity, these delays can exceed 13 seconds for each initial connection.

Service Pack 4 for Windows NT 4.0 has introduced an updated MUP.SYS, giving better performance and a new Registry entry, which may speed up the initial connection to non-Windows UNC resources, DisableDFS. Perform the following change on each client:

1. Start the Registry editor (REGEDIT.EXE).
2. Move to HKEY_LOCAL_MACHINE\SYSTEM\CurrentControlSet\Services\Mup.
3. From the Edit menu, select New > DWORD Value.
4. Enter a name of **DisableDFS** and press Enter.
5. Double-click the new value and set to 1. Click OK.
6. Close the Registry editor.
7. Reboot the machine.

Setting the DisableDFS value to 0 or deleting it will set the machine back to its old behavior.

If you have the Novell IntranetWare client installed, you must also perform the following before rebooting:

1. Start the Registry editor (REGEDIT.EXE).
2. Move to HKEY_LOCAL_MACHINE\SYSTEM\CurrentControlSet\Services\NetwareWorkstation\NetworkProvider.
3. Double-click DeviceName and change from \Device\NetwareWorkstation to \Device\NetwareRedirector. Click OK.
4. Close the Registry editor.

Knowledge Base article Q171386 at http://support.microsoft.com/support/kb/articles/q171/3/86.asp has more information on this issue.

NT4 ONLY.

FAQ 13.30 How can a DOS machine connect to an NT domain?

Microsoft provides software to enable a DOS machine to participate on a network using a variety of protocols and to connect to a Windows NT domain.

NT Server ships with the Network Client Administrator, which allows the creation of an installation disk set or a disk to allow network-based installation of a variety of clients, including a network client for DOS.

FAQ 4.8 includes an example of creating a network installation disk. Here we will concentrate on creating an installation disk set:

1. Start Network Client Administrator (Start > Programs > Administrative Tools > Network Client Administrator).
2. Select Make Installation Disk Set and click Continue.
3. You will need to specify the location of the clients directory that is on the Windows NT Server CD-ROM. (It's easiest to copy clients from the CD-ROM. Enter the location in the path box and select Share Files. Click OK.)
4. Select the client to install Network Client v3.0 for MS-DOS and Windows. Select the destination and click OK.
5. Insert the first disk and click OK to the dialog.
6. Files will be copied to the disk.

To install on a DOS machine, you perform the following:

1. Insert disk 1.
2. Change to the disk drive A.
3. Run SETUP.EXE.
4. Press Enter to start the installation.
5. Select the installation target directory—by default C:\NET. Press Enter.
6. Select the network adapter from the displayed list or use a custom adapter by selecting Network adapter now shown on list below. Press Enter. If you are using a custom disk, the program looks for PROTOCOL.INI. On my test machine, I specified the NDIS\WFW directory on the install disk because the DOS directory did not have all the necessary files.

7. You now have the option of changing the setup. By default only IPX will be installed; select Change Network Configuration, and you can remove protocols and add the Microsoft TCP/IP protocol. You can then change the TCP/IP settings to configure IP address/subnet mask, etc. Make sure if you are not using TCP/IP to set Disable Automatic Configuration to 1.
8. Restart the machine.

When the machine reboots, it will load all the network and protocol drivers and then attempt to log on to the network by issuing the following command:

```
net start
```

You will then be asked for a username and password:

```
Type your user name, or press ENTER if it is ADMINISTRATOR:
Type your password:
```

You will be asked if you want to create a password file. If you select Yes, then you will no longer be asked for a password at startup time, like an auto-logon. Be aware: It means anyone accessing your computer can log on as you.

FAQ 13.31 Where are Windows 2000 network connections stored in the Registry?

The Windows 2000 connections consist of entries of not only remote connections such as to your ISP, but also your local area connection. The latter is contained under the HKEY_LOCAL_MACHINE\SYSTEM\CurrentControlSet\Control\Network\GUID\Connection Registry key, which GUID is the Globally Unique IDentifier of the connection.

It's interesting to know this because if you have a stray connection that gets corrupted, maybe if you remove the network card, you can manually remove it by editing the Registry.

FAQ 13.32 How do I install the loopback adapter in Windows 2000?

The loopback adapter is useful for those machines with no network card, and it's useful for you if you want to experiment with installing network protocols and other network-related items. Obviously because there is no physical network connection, you cannot talk to other machines.

1. Start the Add/Remove Hardware Control Panel applet (Start > Settings > Control Panel > Add/Remove Hardware).
2. Click Add/Troubleshoot a device and then click Next.
3. Click Add a new device and then click Next.
4. Click No, I want to select the hardware from a list and then click Next.
5. Click Network adapters and then click Next.
6. In the Manufacturers box, click Microsoft.
7. In the Network Adapter box, click Microsoft Loopback Adapter and then click Next.
8. Click Finish.

You should then configure the device with an IP address, etc. If you select DHCP, the IP component will use an address 169.254.x.x/16 (subnet mask 255.255.0.0) because no DHCP server can be contacted due to the lack of network connectivity.

FAQ 13.33 How can I turn off/on connection ghosting?

Windows uses ghosted connections for when a user doesn't need or want an actual connection until there is a need for the connection to be utilized. Once the user uses the connection, Windows NT/2000 will make the necessary connection. In some instances, this technique can cause problems; for example, there will be a delay the first time that an inactive, ghosted connection is used.

To turn off the ghosting and eliminate the initial delay when connecting, perform the following:

1. Start the Registry editor (REGEDIT.EXE).
2. Move to HKEY_LOCAL_MACHINE\SYSTEM\CurrentControlSet\Control\NetworkProvider.
3. From the edit menu, select New > DWORD Value.
4. Enter a name of **RestoreConnection** and press Enter.
5. Double-click the new value. Set to 0—Windows NT/2000 will ghost the connections or 1—Windows NT/2000 will not ghost the connections. Windows will restore connections when the user logs in.
6. Click OK.

7. Close the Registry editor.
8. Restart the computer.

13.34 How can I map to an FTP server as a drive?

It's possible to configure a machine to map to a FTP server (for instance, the Microsoft site) because a drive providing the machine runs both NetBEUI and TCP/IP. Perform the following:

1. Perform a NSLOOKUP for the FTP site—for example:

   ```
   nslookup ftp.microsoft.com
   ```

   Make a note of the IP address.
2. Edit the LMHOSTS file (in %systemroot%\system32\drivers\etc).
3. Add line

   ```
   <ip address> MicrosoftFTP #PRE
   ```

   For example, 207.46.133.140 MicrosoftFTP #PRE.
4. Save the file.
5. Open a CMD.EXE session. Enter the command:

   ```
   nbtstat -R
   ```

   This purges and reloads the name table cache.
6. Type the command:

   ```
   net view \\MicrosoftFTP
   ```

   You should see information on the site.
7. Now map a drive (to share data):

   ```
   net use * \\MicrosoftFTP\data /user:anonymous
   ```

All done. It will pass a drive letter for the connection.

FAQ 13.35 How can I create a browse election log file?

Using the checked version of RDR.SYS, it's possible to create a log file of the browser elections so you can monitor exactly what is happening. To turn on the log, perform the following:

1. Back up the original file to replace after troubleshooting by renaming %Systemroot%\System32\Drivers\rdr.sys to %Systemroot%\System32\Drivers\rdr.bak.
2. Place the checked version of RDR.SYS in the %systemroot%\system32\drivers directory (you may have to rename it from .CHK to .SYS).
3. After you replace the original file with the checked version, start the Registry editor (REGEDIT.EXE).
4. Move to HKEY_LOCAL_MACHINE\System\CurrentControlSet\Services\Rdr\Parameters.
5. From the Edit menu, select New > DWORD Value and enter a name of **BowserDebugLogLevel**.
6. Double-click the new value and set to **ffffffff** (in hex).
7. From the Edit menu, select New > DWORD Value and enter a name of **BowserDebugTraceLevel**.
8. Double-click the new value and set to **ffffffff** (in hex).
9. Close the Registry editor.

Note: *Yes, it's "Bowser" not "Browser"; it's not a typo.*

A log file BOWSER.LOG will be created in the %systemroot% folder. Here's example content:

```
Bowser::Find_Master: Master not found, forcing election. = Could not
find the master browser, so force an election.

Bowser: Last election long enough ago, forcing election on
\Device\NetBT_El90x1 = Wait a little while to decrease the chance of
a browser storm.

Send true election. = The need to force an election that we think we
can win is seen.
```

```
Send dummy election. = Force an election that we are not hoping to
win, for example, shutting down the browser or because we cannot
find a backup browser. The criteria of the election is 0x0.

New server: TITANIC. Periodicity: 240 = A new server (TITANIC) was
found in our domain that we need to remember.

#New domain: SAVILLTECH. Periodicity: 900 = A new domain
(SAVILLTECH) was found to add to our list of domains.

Domain pass for \Device\NetBT_El90x1 = We are going to search for
new domains on the transport \Device\NetBT_El90x1.

Received election packet on net \Device\NetBT_El90x1 from machine
TITANIC. Version: 1; Criteria: 20010fa8; TimeUp: 8750 = A computer
(named TITANIC) forced an election, on the network transport
\Device\NetBT_El90x1, it is running Browser version 1, its criteria
is 20010fa8, and it has been up for 8750 seconds.

We lost the election = There was an election and we lost it.

Dummy election request ignored during election. = There is an
election in process so we can discard the election packets with the
criteria of 0x0.
```

FAQ 13.36 How do I enable the Telnet server in Windows 2000?

Windows 2000 and above includes a Telnet service that is installed by default, but the service is not automatically started. To start via the GUI, perform the following:

1. Start the Computer Management MMC snap-in (Start > Programs > Administrative Tools > Computer Manager).
2. Expand the Services and Applications branch.
3. Select the Services leaf.
4. Right-click on Telnet and select Start.
5. You could also right-click, select Properties, and set the startup type to Automatic so it will always be started. Click OK.

To start from the command line, use

```
net start tlntsvr

The Telnet service is starting.
The Telnet service was started successfully.
```

The Telnet service uses %systemroot%\system32\tlntsvr.exe so if you want to prevent it being started on a machine, you can set an access control list (ACL) on the image or delete it.

Unlike normal Telnet services, passwords are not set clear text and are encrypted using NTLM. You need a special client, which is provided with Windows 2000 Professional (luckily :-)).

FAQ 13.37 How do I enable plain-text passwords with the Telnet server in Windows 2000?

Windows 2000 uses NTLM to encrypt passwords sent from Telnet for security reasons, but not all Telnet clients are compatible. It's possible to configure the Telnet service to not require NTLM as follows:

```
tlntadmn

Microsoft (R) Windows 2000 (TM) (Build 2194)
Telnet Server Admin (Build 5.00.99201.1)

Select one of the following options:

0) Quit this application
1) List the current users
2) Terminate a user session ...
3) Display / change registry settings ...
4) Start the service
5) Stop the service
Type an option number [0 - 5] to select that option: 3

Select one of the following options:
```

```
0) Exit this menu
1) AllowTrustedDomain
2) AltKeyMapping
3) DefaultDomain
4) DefaultShell
5) LoginScript
6) MaxFailedLogins
7) NTLM
8) TelnetPort
Type an option number [0 - 8] to select that option: 7
Current value of NTLM = 2
Do you want to change this value ? [y/n]y
NTLM [ current value = 2; acceptable values 0, 1 or 2 ] :1
Are you sure you want to set NTLM to : 1 ? [y/n]y

setting will take effect only when Telnet Service is re-started

Select one of the following options:

0) Exit this menu
1) AllowTrustedDomain
2) AltKeyMapping
3) DefaultDomain
4) DefaultShell
5) LoginScript
6) MaxFailedLogins
7) NTLM
8) TelnetPort
Type an option number [0 - 8] to select that option: 0

Select one of the following options:

0) Quit this application
1) List the current users
2) Terminate a user session ...
3) Display / change registry settings ...
4) Start the service
5) Stop the service
Type an option number [0 - 5] to select that option: 0

E:\>net stop tlntsvr
The Telnet service is stopping.
The Telnet service was stopped successfully.
```

```
E:\>net start tlntsvr
The Telnet service is starting..
The Telnet service was started successfully.
```

Now the Telnet service will not require NTLM authentication. You can also directly set Registry value HKEY_LOCAL_MACHINE\SOFTWARE\Microsoft\TelnetServer\1.0\NTLM to 1 for the same change.

FAQ 13.38 What is REXEC?

Windows NT/2000 ships with a command REXEC.EXE, which when used in conjunction with a REXEC daemon (REXECD), can run commands on remote systems—hence, the name Remote EXECution.

```
C:\>rexec 10.129.210.71 -l john@savtech.com dir
Password (10.129.210.71:):
> rexec:connect:Connection refused
rexec: can't establish connection
```

The -l is the name to use on the remote system; here I've used the Windows 2000 format, name@domain.com; however, you could also use the older domain\name format.

Notice in the example the command failed, which is because the remote machine did not have the REXEC daemon installed. This is actually a problem; Windows NT/2000 does not have a REXEC daemon, only the client. REXEC works not only for NT servers, but also for UNIX, VMS and anything else that supports REXEC.

There are third-party solutions; see FAQ 13.39.

FAQ 13.39 What REXEC daemons (REXECD) are available for NT/2000?

Microsoft does not provide an EXEC daemon for NT; however, there are third-party solutions:

- http://www.denicomp.com/rexecnt.htm—Winsock REXECD/NT
- http://www.ataman.com/products.html#ATRLS—Ataman TCP Remote Logon Services

13.40 How do I add a network place in Windows 2000?

Windows 2000 adds support for network places that work in a similar method to mapped drives except they are not mapped as drive letters and are instead accessed via the My Network Places branch of the desktop (see Figure 13-3).

To add a My Network Place, just perform the following:

1. Start Explorer.
2. Select My Network Places.
3. Double-click on the Add Network Place Wizard.
4. You will be asked for the location to point to—for example, \\titanic\c$ for the C drive of machine Titanic.
5. Click Next.
6. You will then be asked for a description for the new network place—for example, C drive on Titanic—click Finish.

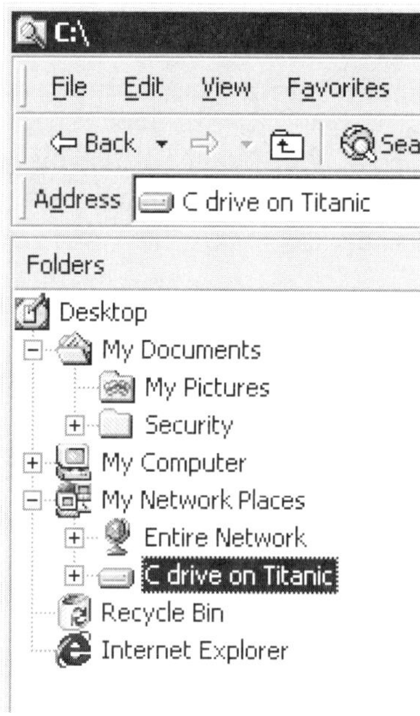

Figure 13-3 A network place on a remote machine

The new network place will now be listed.

The places are actually stored under your user profile in the folder c:\documents and settings\\NetHood as folder shortcuts.

FAQ 13.41 What are the NetBIOS suffixes (sixteenth character)?

NetBIOS names are 16 characters long with the sixteenth character always being a special character identifying the type of name—for example, a domain NetBIOS record with 1C as the sixteenth character as a domain controller (this is how they are located). The full list is as follows:

```
Name                    Number(h)  Type  Usage
-------------------------------------------------------------------
<computername>             00        U    Workstation Service
<computername>             01        U    Messenger Service
<\\-__MSBROWSE__>          01        G    Master Browser
<computername>             03        U    Messenger Service
<computername>             06        U    RAS Server Service
<computername>             1F        U    NetDDE Service
<computername>             20        U    File Server Service
<computername>             21        U    RAS Client Service
<computername>             22        U    Microsoft Exchange
                                          Interchange(MSMail Connector)
<computername>             23        U    Microsoft Exchange Store
<computername>             24        U    Microsoft Exchange Directory
<computername>             30        U    Modem Sharing Server Service
<computername>             31        U    Modem Sharing Client Service
<computername>             43        U    SMS Clients Remote Control
<computername>             44        U    SMS Administrators Remote
                                          Control Tool
<computername>             45        U    SMS Clients Remote Chat
<computername>             46        U    SMS Clients Remote Transfer
<computername>             4C        U    DEC Pathworks TCPIP service
                                          on Windows NT
<computername>             52        U    DEC Pathworks TCPIP service
                                          on Windows NT
<computername>             87        U    Microsoft Exchange MTA
<computername>             6A        U    Microsoft Exchange IMC
```

(*continued*)

```
<computername>       BE     U    Network Monitor Agent
<computername>       BF     U    Network Monitor Application
<username>           03     U    Messenger Service
<domain>             00     G    Domain Name
<domain>             1B     U    Domain Master Browser
<domain>             1C     G    Domain Controllers
<domain>             1D     U    Master Browser
<domain>             1E     G    Browser Service Elections
<INet~Services>      1C     G    IIS
<IS~computer name>   00     U    IIS
```

Where the record is U, only one IP address may be assigned; where G, it's a group and may have multiple IP addresses. M is a multihomed machine (a machine with more than one network card), and I is an Internet group.

13.42 How can I stop UNC shares automatically being added to My Network Places?

In Windows 2000, if you open a file or a Web site via a UNC name, it will automatically be added to the My Network Places area. To stop this from happening, perform the following:

1. Click Start > Run and type **mmc.exe**. Then click OK.
2. In Microsoft Management Console (MMC), click Add/Remove Snap-in on the Console menu.
3. Click Add.
4. Click Group Policy and then click Add.
5. Accept the default (which is Local Computer) and then click Finish.
6. Click Close and then click OK.
7. Under Local Computer Policy, expand the User Configuration entry.
8. Expand the Administrative Templates entry.
9. Expand the Desktop entry.
10. Right-click Do not add shares of recently opened documents to My Network Places and then click Properties.
11. Click Enabled and then click OK.

The preceding works on a local machine; for a domain/site/OU Group Policy, you open the corresponding Group Policy Object, go to the User Configuration\Administrative Templates\Desktop area and make the change.

You can also make the change in the Registry by setting HKEY_CURRENT_USER\Software\Microsoft\Windows\CurrentVersion\Policies\Explorer\NoRecentDocsNetHood to 1.

FAQ 13.43 Where do I get NETDIAG.EXE, and what is it?

NETDIAG.EXE is new to Windows 2000 but is not installed as part of a core installation; instead it is part of the Windows 2000 Support Tools. To install it, perform the following:

1. Insert your Windows 2000 CD.
2. Move to the Support\Tools directory.
3. Run SETUP.EXE.

A new program files\support tools folder will be created and populated with the utilities. It is adding to the path variable but any open cmd sessions will need to be closed and restarted to load the new path environment string.

What does it do? It's similar to Network Monitor but not quite as good. If you run NETDIAG.EXE with no options, it will run tests on the adapters including domain membership and connection tests.

If you run netdiag /? you will see you can run specific tests that may be more pertinent to your problem.

FAQ 13.44 How do I configure LAN autodisconnect?

As with RAS, it's possible to configure a timeout for LAN connections. After this idle time, the connection will be closed. If you then try to use the connection, the connection will be reconnected. This will be invisible to you, but you will experience a slight delay.

By default this timeout is 15 minutes; however, it can be changed by directly editing the Registry:

1. Start the Registry editor (REGEDIT.EXE).
2. Move to HKEY_LOCAL_MACHINE\SYSTEM\CurrentControlSet\Services\lanmanserver\parameters.
3. Double-click autodisconnect.
4. Set to decimal and set the number of minutes (from -1 to 4294967295).
5. Click OK.

6. Close the Registry editor.
7. Reboot the machine.

You can also configure this timeout from the command line but doing so from the Registry is preferred because it does not interfere with any of the built-in tuning. To configure the timeout from the command line, the following disconnects after 60 minutes (valid is from -1 to 65535):

```
Net Config Server /autodisconnect:60
```

To turn off the disconnect, set to -1 (Registry or net config command); **don't** set to 0 because it will autodisconnect all the time!

FAQ 13.45 Why can't I map a drive via its IP address?

When you try to map a drive via an IP address, you might receive the following error message:

```
System error 53 has occurred.
```

This error occurs when you try to map a drive to a server running one of the following applications:

- IBM OS/2 1.3
- LAN Manager 2.2
- Microsoft Net Server 1.11
- Hewlett-Packard UNIX LAN Manager X

To resolve this problem, use the server's NetBIOS name to map the drive:

1. Start Windows Explorer.
2. From the Tools menu, select Map Network Drive.
3. In the Drive box, click the drive letter you want to use.
4. In the Folder box, type

   ```
   \\[server]\[share]
   ```

   where [server] is the NetBIOS name of the server to which you want to connect and [share] is the name of a shared folder on that server.
5. Click Finish.

FAQ 13.46 How can I change a network adapter card's MAC address?

Each network card has a media access control (MAC) address that machines on local subnets use to talk to each other. These MAC addresses are usually burned into the units as part of the manufacturing process, but some network adapter cards have the ability to change the MAC address through software. If your network adapter card and driver support this feature, Windows 2000 can change it via its standard interface:

1. From the Start menu, select Settings > Network and Dial-Up Connections. Right-click the LAN instance that uses the network adapter card you want to modify and select Properties.
2. In the Connect using section, under the name of the network adapter card, click Configure.
3. Select the Advanced tab.
4. Select Locally Administered Address.
5. Type the new MAC address in the Value section.
6. Click OK.

If Locally Administered Address isn't available as an option, your network adapter card or driver doesn't support MAC address alteration.

FAQ 13.47 What is Pathping?

Pathping, a utility that's new to Windows 2000, is something of a cross between the Ping and Tracert utilities. The Pathping utility sends packets to each router on the way to a final destination over a period of time and computes results based on the packets that return from each hop. Because Pathping shows the degree of packet loss at any given router or link, you can determine which routers or links might be causing network problems. Following is the Pathping syntax:

```
pathping [-n] [-h maximum_hops] [-g host-list] [-p period] [-q
num_queries] [-w timeout] [-T] [-R] target_name
```

Parameters:

- **-n:** Doesn't resolve addresses to host names.
- **-h maximum_hops:** Specifies maximum number of hops to search for the target; the default is 30 hops.

- **-g host-list:** Lets you separate consecutive computers by intermediate gateways (loose source route) along a host list.
- **-p period:** Specifies number of milliseconds to wait between consecutive pings; the default is 250 milliseconds (1/4 second).
- **-q num_queries:** Specifies number of queries to each computer along the route; the default is 100.
- **-w timeout:** Specifies number of milliseconds to wait for each reply; the default is 3000 milliseconds (3 seconds).
- **-T:** Attaches a layer-2 priority tag (e.g., 802.1p) to the Ping packets that it sends to each of the network devices along the route. This helps identify network devices that don't have layer-2 priority configured. You must capitalize this parameter.
- **-R:** Checks whether each network device along the route supports the Resource Reservation Protocol (RSVP), which lets the host computer reserve a certain amount of bandwidth for a data stream. You must capitalize this parameter.
- **target_name:** Specifies the destination endpoint, identified either by IP address or host name.

FAQ 13.48 How do I make my computer's host (DNS) and computer (NetBIOS) names different?

The online help under NetBIOS names in mixed environments states, "If you are supporting both NetBIOS and DNS namespaces on your network, you can use a different computer name within each namespace." Although this was possible in Windows NT, Windows 2000 doesn't support separate names, and the NetBIOS name is simply the computer's host name (default to first 15 characters). Win2K host names, not the computer names, are the actual point of reference; the computer name is provided to allow for backward compatibility.

FAQ 13.49 How can I create an MS-DOS network boot disk in Windows 2000?

Windows NT has the network client creation utility (NCADMIN.EXE) that lets you create floppy disks that have network support. Microsoft dropped this utility in Win2K and replaced it with Microsoft Remote Installation Services (RIS). However,

NCADMIN.EXE still works under Win2K. You can copy the following files from an NT server to a Win2K machine to use the utility:

- NCADMIN.CNT
- NCADMIN.EXE
- NCADMIN.HLP

If you don't have an NT server to copy the files from, perform the following steps:

1. Create a folder on your Win2K machine for the three files you'll need.
2. Insert your NT Server CD-ROM.
3. Go to the i386 folder on the CD-ROM.
4. Copy the following files to the folder you created on the Win2K machine:
    - NCADMIN.CN_
    - NCADMIN.EX_
    - NCADMIN.HL_
5. Use the following command to expand the files:

```
ncadmin>expand -r ncadmin.*
```

FAQ 13.50 I've joined a domain with a Windows XP client. Why have I lost the cool logon screen?

XP has a new logon screen that lists the accounts on the machine. You can click your account and type your password. After you join a domain, however, the system replaces this screen with the standard Windows 2000 logon screen because the system can't list domain accounts.

If you want the XP logon screen, you need to join a workgroup again.

FAQ 13.51 Where's NetBEUI in Windows XP?

NetBEUI is a legacy protocol, and Microsoft has removed it from the final version of XP. It is still supplied in the \valueadd\msft\net\netbeui folder on Windows XP CD.

13.52 Why am I receiving 30020 event IDs on my Routing and Remote Access Server (RRAS) server?

The 30020 event ID might be added to the event log every 30 seconds. The full log entry appears as follows:

```
Event ID: 30020
Source: Iprip2
Type: Error
Description: Ipripv2 was unable to receive an incoming message on
the local interface with IP address [IP address]. The data is in
the error code. 0000: 00002746
```

An unreachable or incorrectly configured device that receives a Routing Information Protocol (RIP) request from the server causes this error. To resolve the problem, locate the device that the event log identifies and resolve the problem with that device.

13.53 How can I check to see which TCP ports are in use?

The Netstat command can list currently used ports, which might be helpful if you suspect an application is clashing with another one on an active port. Use the -an switch to show all connections and listening ports in numeric form.

```
netstat -an
```

Check the output for any port that you think your program might use.

13.54 How can I configure the LAN autodisconnect?

You can configure some Registry entries:

- **announce**—The network announce rate, in seconds. This rate determines how often the server is announced to other computers on the network.
- **anndelta**—The number of milliseconds the announce rate can vary, allowing a degree of randomness. The default is 3000 milliseconds.

For example, if the announce member has a value of 10 and the anndelta member has a value of 1, the announce rate can vary from 9.999 seconds to 10.001 seconds.

FAQ 13.55 The Ipconfig command returns "Fatal Error: Inconsistent Registry Contents." What can I do?

This problem can occur if you use Checkpoint Firewall or VPN software and you delete the Registry key for a NIC or make substantial changes to the network on a Windows NT 4.0 Server/Workstation. To resolve the problem, perform the following steps:

1. Remove CheckPoint Firewall or your VPN software.
2. Copy TCPIP.SYS from the latest service pack to %systemroot%\system32.
3. If the TCPIP.SYS file is compressed (TCPIP.SY_), use the following command to extract it:

   ```
   expand c:\winnt\system32\tcpip.sy_ c:\winnt\system32
   ```

4. Reboot the PC.
5. Reinstall CheckPoint Firewall or your VPN software.

FAQ 13.56 How can I easily configure my Windows 2000 notebook for different networks?

If you use your Win2K notebook in a variety of networks (e.g., at different customer sites), you probably always have to change the network settings. The Netsh utility lets you save your settings in a file that you can later use to restore your complete network settings.

To save the current settings, type the following command:

```
netsh -c interface dump >networksetting.txt
```

You can then create a dump file for every network that you use.

To load a set of settings again, type the following command:

```
netsh -f networksetting.txt
```

Using the Netsh utility, you can also easily switch between different configuration settings.

FAQ 13.57 Why are local copies that use UNC names so slow?

Using Uniform Naming Convention (UNC) names (e.g., \\<computer name>\<share name>) rather than native drive letters to copy files locally is about 10% slower. However, a longer slowdown in making local UNC copies (e.g., a copy that takes about 50 times as long as a copy that uses native drive letters) is the result of a bug in Norton AntiVirus (NAV) Autoprotect (including in NAV 2001, version 7). To work around this bug, you must stop the Autoprotect service from the Services applet in Control Panel and clear Autoprotect as an option from the NAV window. After you turn off Autoprotect, local UNC copies will behave normally.

FAQ 13.58 How do I determine which process has TCP ports or UDP ports open?

To display which process ID is using a certain TCP port or UDP port, you can start by using the Netstat command with the n (display in numeric form), o (display the owning process ID—this works on Windows XP only)—and a (display all connections and listening ports) switches as follows:

```
netstat -noa
```

For example, the command

```
netstat -noa
```

might produce output like the following:

```
Active Connections

Proto Local Address Foreign Address State PID
TCP 0.0.0.0:135 0.0.0.0:0 LISTENING 888
TCP 0.0.0.0:445 0.0.0.0:0 LISTENING 4
TCP 0.0.0.0:1025 0.0.0.0:0 LISTENING 988
TCP 0.0.0.0:1076 0.0.0.0:0 LISTENING 4
TCP 0.0.0.0:5000 0.0.0.0:0 LISTENING 1144
TCP 127.0.0.1:1063 0.0.0.0:0 LISTENING 1380
TCP 127.0.0.1:1064 0.0.0.0:0 LISTENING 500
```

```
TCP 127.0.0.1:1065 0.0.0.0:0 LISTENING 500
TCP 127.0.0.1:1199 0.0.0.0:0 LISTENING 356
TCP 200.200.200.206:139 0.0.0.0:0 LISTENING 4
TCP 200.200.200.206:1150 0.0.0.0:0 LISTENING 4
TCP 200.200.200.206:1150 200.200.200.1:139 ESTABLISHED 4
TCP 200.200.200.206:1152 0.0.0.0:0 LISTENING 4
TCP 200.200.200.206:1152 200.200.200.200:139 ESTABLISHED 4
UDP 0.0.0.0:135 *:* 888
UDP 0.0.0.0:445 *:* 4
UDP 0.0.0.0:500 *:* 712
UDP 0.0.0.0:1026 *:* 1124
UDP 0.0.0.0:1027 *:* 1124
UDP 0.0.0.0:1028 *:* 712
```

After you have this information, you can use the Tasklist command to match a particular process ID to a task name. To search for a specific process ID, use the following format:

```
tasklist | findstr
```

A sample command and output might look like

```
tasklist | findstr 712
```

```
lsass.exe 712 Console 0 1,792 K
```

The sample output indicates that the task LSASS.EXE is using process ID 712. If you're using Windows 2000, you can accomplish the same task by using Tlist instead of Tasklist.

FAQ 13.59 What is a 1394 network connection?

New Windows XP users might notice a new network device labeled "1394 Connection" on their system. This network device is actually your FireWire card. Although most users use FireWire to connect video and storage peripherals, Microsoft chose to list FireWire as a network device, which might confuse some users. Either you can ignore this connection, or you can disable it by right-clicking the connection from within Network Connections (from the Start menu, go to Settings > Network Connections) and selecting Disable.

FAQ 13.60 How do I use Network Monitor to determine a Preboot Execution Environment (PXE) client's globally unique identifier (GUID)?

To use Network Monitor to capture the GUID of a PXE client (e.g., a NetPC, PC98, or PC99 client), perform the following steps:

1. Start Network Monitor by selecting Network Monitor from the Network Analysis Tools Start menu Programs folder.
2. Start a packet capture.
3. Reboot the PXE client and press F12 to begin a network boot (you might have to enable network boot in the BIOS).
4. Stop the packet capture and look for a DHCP Discover packet.
5. Double-click the DHCP Discover packet, expand the DHCP Discover section, and expand the DHCP Option section.
6. Click unrecognized option 97 (0x61) to display a hexadecimal string of digits.
7. Skip the first 6 highlighted digits and record the remaining 32 highlighted digits. Those 32 digits are your client's GUID. You can use the GUID to prestage your Microsoft Remote Installation Services (RIS) clients.

FAQ 13.61 How can I enable load balancing with multiple network adapter cards?

If you have two or more network adapter cards in your system, you can use a randomizing algorithm to distribute the number of connections or sessions among the adapters. To use the algorithm, perform the following steps:

1. Start the Registry editor (e.g., REGEDIT.EXE).
2. Navigate to HKEY_LOCAL_MACHINE\SYSTEM\CurrentControlSet\Services\NetBT\Parameters.
3. From the Edit menu, select New > DWORD Value.
4. Enter a name of **RandomAdapter** and press Enter.
5. Double-click the new value, enter **1** to enable or **0** to disable, and click OK.
6. Close the Registry editor.
7. Reboot the machine.

FAQ 13.62 How can I control how many IP addresses the OS sends in response to a WINS request on a multihomed machine?

If a machine has multiple network adapter cards, the OS can send one IP address for each adapter when it receives a WINS request. You can configure this behavior by performing the following steps:

1. Start the Registry editor (e.g., REGEDIT.EXE).
2. Navigate to HKEY_LOCAL_MACHINE\SYSTEM\CurrentControlSet\Services\NetBT\Parameters.
3. From the Edit menu, select New > DWORD Value.
4. Enter a name of **SingleResponse** and press Enter.
5. Double-click the new value, enter **1** to enable or **0** to disable, and click OK.
6. Close the Registry editor.
7. Reboot the machine.

14 DOMAINS

Windows NT introduced the concept of domains to replace the limited scope of workgroups. Domains enable users to be authenticated against a single user authentication database.

With Windows NT 4.0 and previous versions, domains were created during Windows NT installation, and a domain was identified by a 15-character NetBIOS name.

With Windows 2000, domain names are no longer NetBIOS but are now DNS (Domain Name Service) names—for example, it.savilltech.com is a valid domain name. A NetBIOS domain name is also created for backwards compatibility, which is normally the left-most part of the DNS name—for example, IT—or if the domain is upgraded from an NT 4.0 domain, the NetBIOS domain renames that of the original.

This chapter also looks at trust relationships, which allow domains to communicate with other domains in a trusted manner. This leads to a number of domain models, or basic configurations of domains. This all changes in Windows 2000. More information can be found in Chapter 15.

FAQ 14.1 How can I force a client to validate its logon against a specific domain controller in Windows NT 4.0 domains?

Before answering this FAQ, it is best to understand what happens when a logon occurs.

When a logon request is made to a domain, the workstation sends out a request to find a domain controller for the domain. The domain name is actually a NetBIOS name that is a 16-character name with the sixteenth character used by Microsoft networking services to identify the NetBIOS type.

The type used for a domain controller is <1C> and so the NetBIOS name for domain controller of domain "SAVILLTECH" is "SAVILLTECH <1C>". The NetBIOS type has to be the sixteenth character; hence, the name of the domain has to be filled with blanks to make its length up to 15 characters.

If the client is WINS enabled, then a query for the resolution of "<domain name> <1C>" is sent to the WINS server as defined in the client's TCP/IP properties. The WINS server will return up to 25 IP addresses that correspond to domain controllers of the requested domain. A \mailslot\net\ntlogon is broadcast to the local subnet, and if the workstation receives a response, then it will attempt logon with the local domain controller.

If WINS is not configured, then it is possible to manually configure the LMHOSTS file on the workstations to specify the domain controller. This file is located in the %systemroot%\system32\drivers\etc directory.

An example entry in LMHOSTS is as follows:

```
200.200.200.50 titanic #PRE #DOM:savilltech #savilltech domain
controller
```

The preceding sets up IP address 200.200.200.50 to be host Titanic, which is the domain controller for savilltech and instructs the machine that this entry is to be pre-loaded into the cache.

To check the NetBIOS name cache, you can use the command nbtstat -c, which will show all the entries including their type. If WINS is not configured and no entry is in LMHOSTS, then the workstation will send out a series of three broadcasts. In the situation where no response is received and WINS is configured to use DNS for WINS resolution, a request to the DNS server will be sent, and finally the HOSTS file is checked. If all of this fails, then an error "A domain controller for your domain could not be contacted."

To force a client to use a specific domain controller, you need only do the following:

1. Start the Registry editor.
2. Move to HKEY_LOCAL_MACHINE\SYSTEM\CurrentControlSet\Services\NetBT\Parameters.
3. From the Edit menu, select New > DWORD Value.
4. Enter a name of **NodeType** and press Enter.
5. Double-click on the new value and set it to 4. (This sets the network to an M-mode/mixed, which means it will perform a broadcast before querying name servers for resolution). By default a system is 1 if no WINS servers are configured (B-node/broadcase) or 8 if at least one WINS server is configured (H-node/queries name resolution first then broadcasts).
6. Double-click on the EnableLMHOSTS value and set it to 1. If it does not exist, select New > DWORD Value from the Edit menu and enter a name of **EnableLMHOSTS**.

7. Close the Registry editor.
8. Reboot the machine.

The machine is now configured to broadcase for a domain controller on a local subnet and then query a name server. If no domain controllers are found on the WINS server, or WINS is not used, it will then search the LMHOSTS file. The next stage is to edit this file:

1. Check for the LMHOSTS file:

   ```
   dir %systemroot%\system32\drivers\etc\lmhosts
   ```

2. If the file does not exist, copy the sample host file:

   ```
   copy %systemroot%\system32\drivers\etc\lmhosts.sam
   %systemroot%\system32\drivers\etc\lmhosts

   1 file(s) copied.
   ```

3. Edit the file using EDIT.EXE; don't use NOTEPAD.EXE:

   ```
   edit %systemroot%\system32\drivers\etc\lmhosts
   ```

4. Go to the end of the comments and add a new line of the format:

   ```
   <ip address> <name of DC> #PRE #DOM:<domain name> #<comment>
   e.g. 200.200.200.50 titanic #PRE #DOM:savilltech #savilltech
   domain controller
   ```

5. Save the changes to the file and exit EDIT.EXE.
6. Force the machine to reload the LMHOSTS file (or just reboot):

   ```
   NBTSTAT -R
   ```

   The -R must be in capitals; the command is case sensitive.
7. Check the cache:

   ```
   NBTSTAT -c
   ```

8. At this point, the configuration is complete, and a reboot is advisable.

Service Pack 4 includes a new utility, SETPRFDC.EXE, which will direct a secure channel client to a preferred list of domain controllers. The syntax is

```
SETPRFDC <Domain Name> <DC1, DC2, ....., DCn>
```

SETPRFDC will try each DC in the list in order, until a secure channel is established. If DC1 does not respond, DC2 is tried, and so on. Once you run SETPRFDC on a Win NT 4.0, SP4 computer, the list is remembered until you change it. You can run SETPRFDC in batch, via the Scheduler, or even in a logon script (for future logons). Don't forget to undo any LMHOSTS entries you might have set.

FAQ 14.2 How do I promote a server to a domain controller?

Windows 2000 ships with a utility, DCPROMO.EXE, which is used to promote a standalone/member server to a domain controller and vice versa.

In Windows 2000, domains are DNS names, which means you can have a hierarchy of domains leading to parent-child domain relationships. The advantage of these parent-child relationships is that they have a bidirectional transitive trust, which means that if domain b is a child of domain a, and domain c is a child of domain b, domain c implicitly trusts domain a. This is very different from the way trusts work in earlier versions of Windows NT.

Because Windows 2000 domains rely on DNS, it is vital that DNS is correctly configured to enable the domain to be created (if you are creating a new top-level domain). Information on configuring DNS for a domain can be found in Chapter 18.

A final prerequisite is that an NTFS 5.0 volume is required to house the SYSVOL volume, and so make sure you have at least one NTFS 5.0 volume (use CHKNTFS to check the versions of your partitions).

To upgrade a standalone/member server to a domain controller, perform the following:

1. Start the DCPROMO utility (Start > Run > DCPROMO).
2. Click Next to the introduction screen.
3. You will have a choice of New domain or Replica domain controller in existing domain. There is no concept of a Backup Domain Controller (BDC) in Windows 2000, and all domain controllers are equal (more or less ☺). Select New Domain and click Next.
4. A new concept is *trees,* which enable the idea of child domains. If you are starting a new top-level domain, select Create new domain tree; to create a child domain, select Create new child domain. Click Next.
5. If you selected to create a new domain tree, you will be asked if you want to Create a new forest of domain trees or put this new domain tree in an existing forest. Forests enable you to join a number of separate domain trees and again a transitive trust relationship is created between them. If this is your first Windows 2000 domain tree, you should create a new forest. Click Next.

6. You will then be asked for the DNS name of your domain—for example, savilltech.com is a valid domain name. It is important this name matches information configured on the DNS server. Click Next.
7. You will then be asked for a NetBIOS domain name, which by default will be the left-most part of the DNS domain name (up to the first 15 characters)—for example, savilltech—however, this part can be changed. Click Next to continue.
8. You will then have to provide a storage area for the Active Directory and the Active Directory log. Except the defaults and click Next.
9. Finally you must select an area on an NTFS **5.0** partition for the SYSVOL volume for storage of the server's public files, %systemroot%\SYSVOL by default. Click Next.
10. Next an option to weaken security for pre-Windows 2000 services such as a 4.0 RAS server is displayed. Select your option and click Next.
11. You will be asked for an Administrator password to be used in Directory Server restore mode. Click Next.
12. A summary screen will be displayed; click Next to start the upgrade. It sets security and creates the Directory Server schema container. Information from the default directory service file and the old SAM is then read in if the machine is an upgraded Primary Domain Controller (PDC).
13. You should then click Finish and reboot the machine.

You now have a Windows 2000 domain controller. Additional domain controllers (old BDCs) can be added by performing the preceding procedure and selecting Replica domain controller in existing domain in step 3. The wizard then asks you the name of the domain to replica.

FAQ 14.3 How can I generate a list of all computer accounts in a domain?

The normal method under Windows NT 4.0 and earlier is to use Server Manager (Start > Programs > Administrative Tools > Server Manager), and computer accounts can be viewed, added, and deleted.

Under Windows 2000, this information can be viewed using the Active Directory MMC (Microsoft Management Console) snap-in and by browsing the domain/computers group. Of course, under Windows 2000 and the Active Directory, computers can also be created in organization units, so would not all be shown under this tree. (As shown in Figure 14-1, the computer account in the law OU would not be listed in the Computers group.)

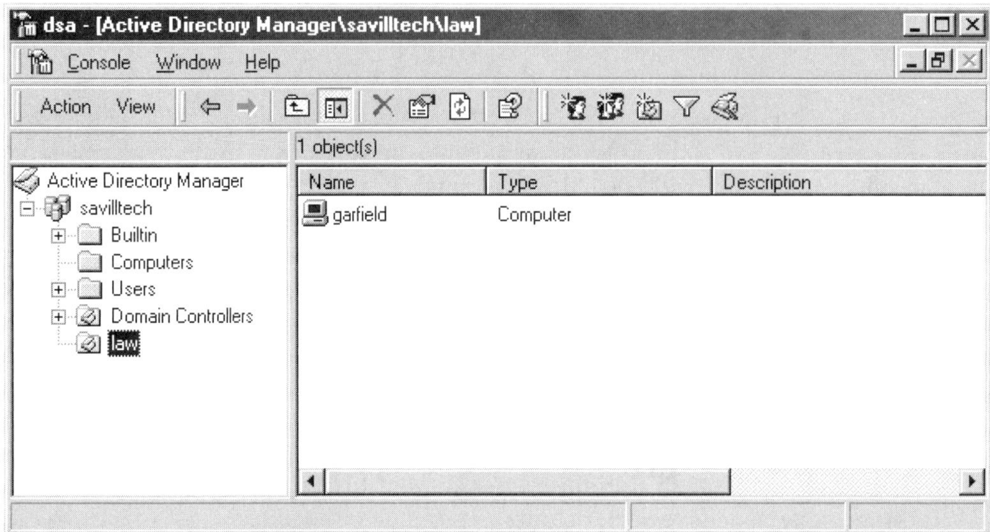

Figure 14-1 A new organizational unit with a machine in it

A more complete method is to use the Windows NT Resource Kit NETDOM.EXE utility (which runs under Windows 2000) to generate the list—for example:

```
netdom member
Searching PDC for domain SAVILLTECH ...
Found PDC \\TITANIC
Listing members of domain SAVILLTECH ...

Member 1 = \\ODIN
Member 2 = \\garfield
```

It is also possible to list other domains using a mixture of command-line switches—for example:

```
netdom /d:<domain name> [/u:<domain>\<user to which query>
/p:<password] member
```

The information in the square brackets ([]) is needed only if your account does not have privileges in the requested domain.

The advantage of the command-line tool is it lists **all** computer accounts, even those in OUs in the Active Directory.

An alternative method is to use the net view /domain:<domain> command, which has the advantage that you can pipe the output to a file or another command—for example:

```
net view /domain:savtech
```

14.4 How can I verify my Windows 2000 domain creation?

To verify the TCP/IP configuration is OK, check for the LDAP.TCP.<domain> service record—for example, ldap.tcp.savilltech.com:

```
nslookup
> set type=srv
> _ldap._tcp.savilltech.com
Server: [200.200.200.50]
Address: 200.200.200.50
_ldap._tcp.savilltech.com SRV service location:
priority=0
weight=0
port=389
svr hostname=titanic.savilltech.com
titanic.savilltech.com internet address=200.200.200.50
```

The ldap record used to be LDAP.TCP.<domain> in beta versions of 2000 but was modified in build 1946 onwards. The underscore is necessary to definitively differentiate our unique names in the DNS namespace from InterNIC registered domain names on the Internet. In this way, we can ensure that a DNS name clash will never occur. My understanding is that RFC 1034\1035 (these may be the wrong numbers because they may have been superceded) state that the underscore character is **not** a valid character to use in a domain name. All Internet registered names should never contain the underscore. Now, RFC 2181 states that the underscore (as well as plenty of other characters) is a valid label to use in DNS so the underscore is used to prevent a possible clash with Internet names. This change was introduced in earlier builds of Windows 2000. For a while DCs generated both styles of names in DNS to support both styles of clients (i.e., newer and older builds). Now that client code is changed to look for underscores, we have now retired the LDAP.TCP names in favor of the _LDAP.TCP names.

Also make sure the NetBIOS computer name is OK:

```
net view \\<computer name>
```

Finally, check that the NetBIOS domain name works:

```
usrmgr <domain name>
```

The NetBIOS domain name is used for backwards compatibility. Use a 4.0 version of usrmgr.

FAQ 14.5 How can I configure multiple logon servers with LMHOSTS?

Service Pack 4 adds support for multiple domain controllers for a single domain to be configured in the LMHOSTS file (located in %systemroot%\system32\drivers\etc). Normally when a computer starts, the WINS server is queried for any [1C] entries or domain controllers, and the WINS server will return a list. This list is not geographically aware, and you could be given a domain controller on the other side of the world.

An alternative is to specify a list of domain controllers in the LMHOSTS file (which is now checked before WINS is #PRE in the entry) and have different LMHOSTS files in different regions.

Example entries in the file are

```
200.200.200.50 titanic #PRE #DOM:SAVILLTECH
200.200.200.80 cuttysark #PRE #DOM:SAVILLTECH
```

You will need to ensure the computer is configured to use the LMHOSTS file:

1. Right-click on Network Neighborhood and select Properties.
2. Select the protocol's tab.
3. Select TCP/IP Protocol and click Properties.
4. Select WINS address.
5. Check the Enable LMHOSTS Lookup box.
6. Click Apply, then OK.
7. You will need to restart the computer.

FAQ 14.6 Are trust relationships kept when upgrading from a 4.0 domain to a Windows 2000 domain?

When a 4.0 PDC is upgraded to Windows 2000, all trust relationships are maintained.

FAQ 14.7 How are trust relationships administered in Windows 2000?

Instead of using User Manager as in NT 4.0, a new MMC snap-in, Active Directory Users and Computers, is used. Although the host application is different, the usage is exactly the same.

To view, add, or remove domains, perform the following:

1. Start the Domain Tree Manager (Start > Programs > Administrative Programs > Active Directory Domains and Trusts).
2. Expand the root and right-click on the domain.
3. Select Properties from the displayed context menu.
4. Select the Trusts tab and add/view as required (see Figure 14-2).
5. Click Apply, then OK.

Obviously you should try to use the tree and forest concept rather than manual trust relationships with pure Windows 2000 domains. This topic is discussed in FAQ 14.2.

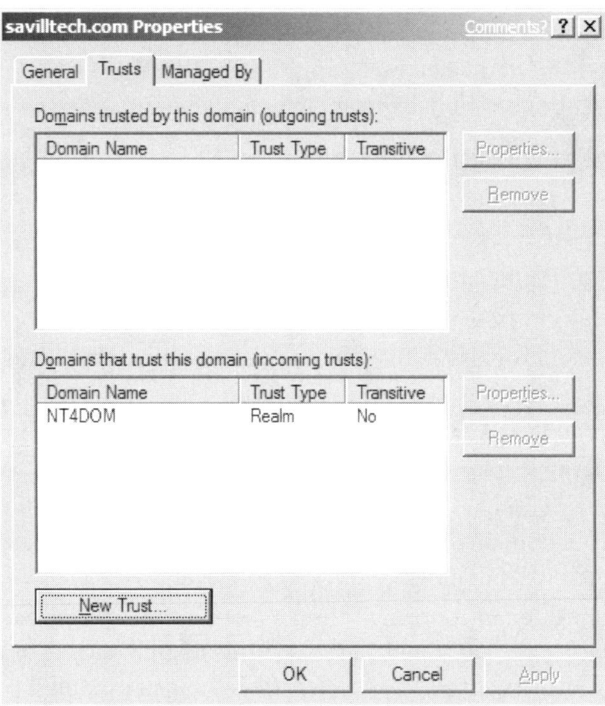

Figure 14-2 The Trusts tab of a .NET server showing a trusting domain

NT4 ONLY

FAQ 14.8 Why can't I promote a BDC to PDC?

If you receive an "Access Denied" message when attempting to promote a BDC to the PDC, it may be due to the fact the PDC has Service Pack 4 installed.

Service Pack 4 upgraded the security mechanism so you will either have to perform the promotion from a SP4 domain controller or upgrade the BDC to SP4.

Another reason for this error is trying to get a renamed and upgraded (3.51 to NT4) server to sync with the domain. The accounts database may have become out-of-date and thus couldn't be synchronized. netlogon may not even be startable.

The way around this problem is to do a "connect as" from the PDC to the rogue BDC using an admin ID known to be good by the BDC before it was upgraded. Once the "connect as" (say to Cc) is accepted, the BDC then accepts the synchronize request from the PDC's Server Manager, restarting netlogon in the process.

FAQ 14.9 How can I create a child domain?

Windows 2000 allows the creation of a domain as a child of another domain. When two or more domains are joined in a parent-child relationship, a domain tree is formed.

A child domain is created when executing the DCPROMO.EXE image, and the parent domain must be accessible to create the child domain.

1. Install Windows 2000 on the machine.
2. Ensure the machine has TCP/IP and DNS configured correctly.
3. Execute DCPROMO.
4. Click Next to continue the upgrade.
5. Select Domain controller for a new domain and click Next.
6. Select Create a new child domain in an existing domain tree and click Next.
7. Enter a username, password, and domain you will be using to join the domain tree. This account must reside in the parent domain, a domain in the forest you are joining. Click Next.
8. Select the parent domain name by selecting Browse—for example, savilltech.com. Enter the child domain (just the left-most part)—for example, legal. The new complete name will be shown—for example, legal.savilltech.com. Click Next.
9. If this is a new domain controller, enter a NetBIOS name for backwards compatibility. By default it will be the left-most 15 characters of the DNS domain name (up to the first dot—.). If you are upgrading an existing DC, then the NetBIOS name cannot be changed. Click Next.

10. Database and log locations will be shown. Click Next.
11. The System Volume area will be shown. Click Next.
12. An option to weaken security for 4.0 RAS servers is displayed. Select your option and click Next.
13. A summary will be shown. Click Next. The new domain creation will begin.
14. Click Finish and reboot the machine.

FAQ 14.10 How can I create a domain trust through a firewall?

When creating trust relationships, communications between the two domains is carried out over a number of protocols with each protocol using different TCP/IP ports. Following is a list of ports that need to be enabled on the firewall for a trust relationship:

- PORT 135 (TCP or UDP) for Remote Procedure Call (RPC) service
- PORT 137 (UDP) for NetBIOS Name service
- PORT 138 (UDP) for NetBIOS datagram (browsing)
- PORT 139 (TCP) for NetBIOS session (NET USE)
- ALL ports above 1024 for RPC communication

You may use LMHOSTS for name resolution (which has #pre #dom entries for the domain controllers), or WINS can be used which requires:

- PORT 53 (TCP and UDP) for DNS
- PORT 42 (TCP and UDP) for WINS Replication

Alternatively, a trust can be established through Point-to-Point Tunneling Protocol (PPTP). For PPTP, the following ports must be enabled:

- PORT (TCP) 1723 for PPTP
- IP PROTOCOL 47 (GRE)

If you wish to perform management through a firewall and/or RRAS, you can only allow TCP any-139, TCP 139-any, and UPD 138-138 through the firewall. Also allow UDP 137-137 to the WINS servers. This allows all the remote management tools to run from the management NT workstations.

Also see the following Knowledge Base articles:

- Q167128 (http://support.microsoft.com/support/kb/articles/Q167/1/28.asp) "SMS: Network Ports Used by Remote Helpdesk Functions"
- Q174395 (http://support.microsoft.com/support/kb/articles/Q174/3/95.asp) "Event ID 4202 Attempting WINS Replication across Router"

FAQ 14.11 How can I check the browse masters for a domain?

The Resource Kit has a utility BROWSTAT.EXE that allows the status of the browse service to be ascertained. To check browse masters for a domain, use the following command:

```
browstat status <domain>
```

To check statistics for a single server, use the command

```
browstat stats \\<server>
```

FAQ 14.12 How can I stop a remote master browser?

The Resource Kit utility BROWSTAT can be used to remotely stop a browse master with the following command:

```
BROWSTAT TICKLE <transport> <domain> | \\<server name>
```

Where <transport> is the Windows NT transport device name, <domain> is the domain in which the master browser is located, and <server name> is the computer name of the master browser.

To check which transport, use the command:

```
net config rdr
Workstation active on NetbiosSmb (000000000000) NetBT_Tcpip_{C2F....
```

The transport device is indicated by "<network service>_<NIC type>", where <network service> is the session-layer network service, and <NIC type> is the type of network interface card on your computer. The session-layer network services are NetBT for NetBIOS over TCP/IP, NwlnkNb for IPX, or Nbf for NetBEUI—for example, NetBT_Tcpip.

```
browstat tickle NetBT_Tcpip_{C2F8C130-F2AF-11D2-B748-DAEDF5F58140}
\\titanic
```

FAQ 14.13 How can I force a browser election?

The Resource Kit utility BROWSTAT can be used to force a browser election:

```
BROWSTAT ELECT <transport> <domain> | \\<server name>
```

Where <transport> is the Windows NT transport device name, <domain> is the domain in which the master browser is located, and <server name> is the computer name of the master browser.

To check which transport, use the command:

```
net config rdr
Workstation active on NetbiosSmb (000000000000) NetBT_Tcpip_{C2F....
```

The transport device is indicated by "<network service>_<NIC type>", where <network service> is the session-layer network service, and <NIC type> is the type of network interface card on your computer. The session-layer network services are NetBT for NetBIOS over TCP/IP, NwlnkNb for IPX, or Nbf for NetBEUI—for example, NetBT_Tcpip.

```
browstat elect NetBT_Tcpip_{C2F8C130-F2AF-11D2-B748-DAEDF5F58140}
savilltech
```

FAQ 14.14 How can I modify the domain refresh interval?

Windows refreshes the domain list whenever the machine is locked for more than two minutes (120 seconds). While Windows is refreshing the domain list, the user experiences a delay until the user gets control of the system again.

You can modify the amount of time the refresh process waits until refreshing by performing the following:

1. Start the Registry editor (REGEDIT.EXE).
2. Move to HKEY_LOCAL_MACHINE\SOFTWARE\Microsoft\Windows NT\CurrentVersion\Winlogon.
3. Double-click on DcacheMinInterval (or if it does not exist, create it of type REG_DWORD).
4. Modify between 120–86400 seconds.
5. Click OK.

6. Close the Registry editor.
7. Restart the computer.

14.15 How is the list of cached domains stored?

When you log on, a list of known (trusted) domains are displayed that you may log onto. You can view these entries by performing the following:

1. Start the Registry editor (REGEDIT.EXE).
2. Move to HKEY_LOCAL_MACHINE\SOFTWARE\Microsoft\Windows NT\CurrentVersion\Winlogon\DomainCache. You will be able to see all known domains.
3. Close the Registry editor.

There is no point editing this list because it will be recreated the next time the machine is started and/or locked.

14.16 How can I disable trust password changes?

After a trust is established using a defined password, it is changed automatically every seven days. If this password change is missed two cycles running, then the trust is broken. This also applies to machines in a domain that have a secure channel with the domain controller and change their passwords every 7 days on NT 4.0, and for Windows 2000 every 30 days.

To disable the trust password changes, perform the following change on the domain controllers/workstations:

1. Start the Registry editor (REGEDIT.EXE).
2. Move to HKEY_LOCAL_MACHINE\SYSTEM\CurrentControlSet\Services\Netlogon\Parameters.
3. Double-click on DisablePasswordChange.
4. Set to 1.
5. Click OK.
6. Close the Registry editor.

Another option to stop the computer account password changes is to refuse the change at the domain controller:

1. Start the Registry editor (REGEDIT.EXE).
2. Move to HKEY_LOCAL_MACHINE\SYSTEM\CurrentControlSet\Services\Netlogon\Parameters.
3. From the Edit menu, select New > DWORD Value.
4. Enter a name of **RefusePasswordChange**.
5. Double-click on the new value and set to 1.
6. Click OK.
7. Close the Registry editor.

FAQ 14.17 How can I change the password change interval for computer/trust accounts?

The default interval for password changes for a computer/trust account can be modified as follows:

1. Start the Registry editor (REGEDIT.EXE).
2. Move to HKEY_LOCAL_MACHINE\SYSTEM\CurrentControlSet\Services\Netlogon\Parameters.
3. From the Edit menu, select New > DWORD Value.
4. Enter a name of **MaximumPasswordAge**.
5. Double-click the new value and set to the number of days.
6. Click OK.
7. Close the Registry editor.

In NT 4.0, this value is available only for machines with Service Pack 4 and for all versions of Windows 2000. Values can be in the range of 1 to 1,000,000.

FAQ 14.18 The list of domains in the logon box is not updated. What can I do?

The list of trusted domains should be updated whenever a trust relationship is terminated or created, but this is not always the case.

To clear the machines cache of domains, perform the following:

1. Start the Registry editor (REGEDIT.EXE).
2. Move to HKEY_LOCAL_MACHINE\SOFTWARE\Microsoft\Windows NT\CurrentVersion\Winlogon.

3. Delete the DCache and DCacheUpdate values.
4. Close the Registry editor.
5. Restart the computer.

FAQ 14.19 Is it possible to administer a 4.0 domain from a Windows 2000 machine?

Many utilities used to administer an NT 4.0 domain do not come with Windows 2000 or work in a different way. However, you can copy over the NT 4.0 administration utilities to a Windows 2000 machine and administer the domain with no adverse effects.

FAQ 14.20 What are the differences between NT 4.0 and 2000 domains?

Domain implementation in Windows 2000 was basically written from the ground up with its directory service roots. The following table shows the major differences:

Feature	Windows NT 4	Windows 2000 Mixed Mode	Windows 2000 Native Mode
Number of objects	40,000 (20,000 recommended)	40,000 (20,000 recommended)	1,000,000 although 100,000,000 has been listed by Compaq
Multimaster replication	No	Yes	Yes
Group types	Global, Local	Global, Domain Local	Universal, Global, Domain Local
Nested groups	No	No	Yes
Cross-domain administration	Limited	Limited	Full
Password filters	Manually installed with SP2 and above	Manually installed	Automatically installed
Queries using desktop change/configuration management	No	2000 DCs only	Yes

Authentication protocols	NTLM	NTLM, Kerberos	Kerberos (but NTLM supported for NT 4 and Windows 9x clients)

FAQ 14.21 I've removed all Windows 2000 domain controllers from my domain. Why won't Windows NT 4.0 domain controllers authenticate Win2K Professional clients?

By default, when you install a Win2K client into a domain with Win2K DCs, the secure channel that the system uses for communication with the DCs is configured to use Kerberos. NT 4.0 doesn't support Kerberos; it supports only NT LAN Manager (NTLM). Thus, when a Win2K client tries to authenticate through an NT 4.0 DC, the client receives the following error message:

```
The system cannot log you on to this domain because the system's
machine account in its primary domain is missing or the password on
that account is incorrect.
```

To solve this problem, remove the client from the domain and then add the client back to the domain, which forces the client to use NTLM when its attempts to use Kerberos fail. You should remove the computer account using the Server Manager NT 4.0 tool and then recreate a new computer account. To use the client GUI, perform the following steps:

1. Right-click My Computer and select Properties.
2. Select the Network Identification tab.
3. Click Properties.
4. Under Member Of, click Workgroup and type the name of a work group to join (e.g., Workgroup).
5. Click OK twice.
6. Restart the computer.
7. Right-click My Computer and select Properties.
8. Select the Network Identification tab.
9. Click Properties.
10. Under Member Of, click Domain and type the name of the domain to join.
11. When the system prompts you for a domain administrator's credentials, enter the appropriate information.
12. Restart the computer.

You can also remove the client computer and add it back using the NETDOM tool:

```
NETDOM REMOVE /Domain:[domain name] [workstation name]
/UserD:[domain name]\[administrator account] /PassworD:[password]
NETDOM ADD/Domain:[domain name] [workstation name] /UserD:[domain
name]\[administrator account] /PassworD:[password]
```

FAQ 14.22 Why don't trusts created on my Windows 2000 PDC replicate to the BDCs?

You've encountered a known bug. The trust relationships created during a Win2K upgrade from a Windows NT 4.0 PDC domain don't replicate to existing NT 4.0 BDCs. When a machine joins a Win2K forest, the system automatically creates transitive trust relationships between this new domain and the other domains in the forest. The bug causes these new trust relationships to not replicate to the BDCs because the system doesn't update the change log (NETLOGON.CHG) with the change. You can work around this bug two ways.

Workaround 1

On each BDC, initiate a full synchronization with the following command:

```
net accounts /sync
```

To ensure that the full synchronization occurred, check the event log for the following events:

```
Event ID: 5717
Source: NETLOGON
Description: The full synchronization replication of the SAM
database from the primary domain controller  completed
successfully.

Event ID: 5717
Source: NETLOGON
Description: The full synchronization replication of the BUILTIN
database from the primary domain controller  completed
successfully.

Event ID: 5717
Source: NETLOGON
```

```
Description: The full synchronization replication of the LSA
database from the primary domain controller  completed
successfully.
```

When a full synchronization occurs, the system doesn't use the change log, so all trusts replicate.

Workaround 2

On the Win2K PDC Flexible Single-Master Operation (FSMO) roles, delete the change log (%systemroot%\netlogon.chg), which causes the system to create a new file and initiate a full synchronization to all down-level BDCs.

FAQ 14.23 How can I view the contents of the netlogon change file (NETLOGON.CHG)?

You can't read NETLOGON.CHG using a standard text editor, but Windows 2000 Support Tools supplies the NLTEST.EXT utility that you can use to view the contents of NETLOGON.CHG. Execute the following command:

```
nltest /list_deltas:netlogon.chg
```

The system will display a lot of information, listing all changes made to the domain. The trust entry that appears in the Local Security Authority (LSA) Database section consists of entries similar to the following:

```
Order: 1 DeltaType AddOrChangeLsaSecret (18) SerialNumber: 100 77bb
Immediately Name: 'G$$SAVTECHLON'
Order: 2 DeltaType AddOrChangeLsaSecret (18) SerialNumber: 100 77bc
Immediately Name: 'G$$SAVTECHLON'
Order: 3 DeltaType AddOrChangeLsaTDomain (14) SerialNumber: 100 77bd
Rid:
0x6d2637de Sid: S-1-5-21-239443569-258070511-1831221214
```

FAQ 14.24 How do I fix broken trust relationships in my mixed domain after I implement the RestrictAnonymous Registry setting?

The HKEY_LOCAL_MACHINE\SYSTEM\CurrentControlSet\Control\Lsa\RestrictAnonymous Registry subkey can have a value of 0, 1, or 2. The value 0 means rely on default permissions; the value 1 means don't allow enumeration of SAM accounts and names; the value 2 means no access without explicit anonymous permissions. You can use a value of 0 or 1 on any domain controller (DC), but you should use a value of 2 only on Windows 2000 machines.

If you work in a mixed networking environment with Win2K and Windows NT 4.0 DCs, don't set the RestrictAnonymous subkey to a value of 2 on any participating DC, because doing so will break two-way trust relationships that involve NT 4.0 DCs. To correct this problem, set the subkey to a value of 0 or 1.

1. Start Regedit.
2. Go to the HKEY_LOCAL_MACHINE\SYSTEM\CurrentControlSet\Control\Lsa Registry subkey.
3. Double-click RestrictAnonymous.
4. Set the value to 0 or 1 and click OK.
5. Close the Registry editor.
6. Break and reestablish all trust relationships.

FAQ 14.25 Why can't I join a Windows NT 4.0 domain from a Windows XP or Windows 2000 client?

XP and Win2K use DNS instead of NetBIOS to name domains. As a result, if you've installed only TCP/IP on the XP or Win2K client and you've disabled NetBIOS over TCP/IP, the client can't join an NT 4.0 domain. To enable NetBIOS over TCP/IP, perform the following steps:

1. From the Start menu, select Settings and click Network and Dial-up Connection.
2. Right-click Local Area Connection and select Properties from the context menu.
3. Click Internet Protocol (TCP/IP) and click Properties.
4. Click Advanced and select the WINS tab.

5. Click Enable NetBIOS over TCP/IP.
6. Click OK and ignore the WINS error.
7. Click OK to close all dialog boxes.

If you don't want to use NetBIOS over TCP/IP, you can instead use NetBEUI on all clients.

15 ACTIVE DIRECTORY

Active Directory (AD) is Microsoft's implementation of a Directory Service. DSs store data in an organized format and can publish and access the data. AD isn't a Microsoft innovation but is an implementation of an existing model (i.e., X.500), communication mechanism (i.e., Lightweight Directory Access Protocol—LDAP), and location technology (i.e., DNS).

To understand AD, you must understand what it is supposed to achieve. A directory is simply a container for other information.

A telephone directory is an example of a DS, because a telephone directory contains data and a means to access and use the data. For example, a telephone directory has various entries, and each entry has values. A telephone directory entry consists of name, address, and telephone number values. A large directory might group entries by location (e.g., city) or type (e.g., lawyers), or by both. Thus a hierarchy of types could exist for each location. You might also consider a telephone operator a DS, because the operator has access to the data. You can request data, and the operator presents the answer to your query.

AD is a type of DS that holds information about all the resources on a network. Clients can query AD for information about any aspect of the network. AD's features include the following.

- Secure information storage. Each object in AD has an ACL with a list of resources that can access the object and to what degree.
- A flexible query mechanism based on an AD-generated Global Catalog (GC). Any client that supports AD can query the catalog.
- Directory replication to all domain controllers (DCs) in the domain, for easy accessibility, high availability, and fault tolerance.
- An extensible design that lets you add new object types or build on existing objects. For example, you could add a salary attribute to the user object.
- Multiple-protocol communication. AD's X.500 foundation lets you communicate over various protocols, such as LDAPv2, LDAPv3, and HTTP.
- DNS rather than NetBIOS names for DC naming and location.
- Directory information partitioned by domain to avoid replicating an excessive amount of information.

Although AD partitions directory information into different stores, you can still query AD for information from other domains. GCs contain information about every object in the enterprise forest, so that you can perform a forestwide search.

When you run DCPROMO (the domain controller promotion program) on a Windows 2000 machine for the first time to create a new domain, DCPROMO creates a domain on the DNS server. A client then contacts the DNS server to look up the client's domain. The DNS server will discover not only the domain, but also the domain's DCs. The server then sends the client the closest DC's address. The client in turn connects and accesses the AD domain database on the closest DC to find objects (e.g., printers, file servers, users, groups, organizational units—OUs) in the domain. Because each DC stores links to other domains in the tree, the client can search an entire tree of domains.

A version of AD that lists all the objects in the forest is also available in case you need to perform a search beyond the client's tree of domains. This version is the GC. You can store the GC on any or all of the DCs in the forest.

The GC provides shorthand access to objects anywhere in the forest. However, the GC contains only some of an object's attributes. For the whole object, you must go to the domain AD (which is on a DC in the domain). You can configure the GC to provide the object attributes you want.

To help you create AD objects, the DC maintains a copy of the classes and hierarchy of classes for the whole forest. AD stores class structures in the schema. The schema is extensible, which means that you can add classes to it.

The schema is part of Win2K's configuration namespace, which all the DCs in a forest maintain. A namespace is a range of labels. Win2K's configuration namespace consists of several defined items such as physical locations, Win2K sites, and subnets. A site is stored within a forest; a site can contain machines from any domain, but all the machines in a site should have fast and reliable connections for DC replication. A subnet is an IP address grouping assigned to a site; subnets help speed up AD replication among DCs.

Because DCs store records in an LDAP distinguished name format, AD uses LDAP to access the records. In case an application uses a name format other than the LDAP distinguished name, you can also use the LDAP URL or AD canonical name formats to access AD.

FAQ 15.1 Which naming conventions does Active Directory use for objects?

Active Directory (AD) uses several naming conventions for objects. These naming conventions include the distinguished name (DN), relative distinguished name (RDN), Lightweight Directory Access Protocol (LDAP) URL name, LDAP canonical name, user principal name, and Security Access Manager (SAM) account name.

The most popular method for naming AD objects is to use the DN. Every AD object has a DN that uniquely identifies the object in the DS. For example, the following DN

```
/O=Internet/DC=COM/DC=SavillTech/CN=Users/CN=John Savill
```

identifies an object as follows:

- /O=Internet—Organization=Internet
- /DC=COM—Domain Component=COM
- /DC=SavillTech—Domain Component=SavillTech (the full Domain Component is SavillTech.com)
- /CN=Users—Common Names=Users
- /CN=John Savill—Common Names=John Savill

A DN might also include an organizational unit (OU). For more information about DNs, see RFC 1779, "A String Representation of Distinguished Names" at (http://www.cis.ohio-state.edu/htbin/rfc/rfc1779.html).

The RDN is also known as the *friendly* name. The RDN for the previous example is CN=John Savill. The RDN for the users container is CN=Users.

LDAP URL names begin with LDAP://, then include an LDAP server and a modified DN that identifies the object (e.g., LDAP://titanic.savilltech.com/ou=Sales, cn=JSavill,dc=SavillTech,dc=com).

An LDAP canonical name is the LDAP name without certain information (i.e., ou=, cn=, dc=). An example LDAP canonical name is savilltech.com/Sales/Jsavill. Many administrative tools use these names.

The user principal name contains the username and DNS domain name, linked with an asterisk (@—e.g., jsavill@savilltech.com).

The SAM account name (e.g., savillj) is in the Windows NT 4.0 format. Because of this name's single-layer convention, each name must be unique within an organization.

Objects are actually stored as globally unique IDs. A GUID is a 128-bit number that generates at object creation and is stored in the object attribute object GUID. GUIDs don't change.

FAQ 15.2 What are X.500 and LDAP?

X.500 is the most common directory-management protocol. Two X.500 standards exist: the 1988 version and the 1993 version. Windows 2000's Directory Service (DS) implementation is derived from the 1993 X.500 standard.

The X.500 model uses a hierarchical approach to objects in the namespace. The namespace has a root at the top, with children coming off the root. Win2K domains have DNS names (e.g., savilltech.com is a domain name, and legal.savilltech.com is a child domain of savilltech.com).

Figure 15-1 shows an example domain with a DS root and several children. The first layer of children is countries.

Imagine each country as a child domain of the root (e.g., usa.root.com, england.root.com). You can break each child domain into several organizations, and you can break the organizations into OUs. Various privileges and policies apply to each OU. Each OU has several objects, such as users, computers, and groups.

Although Win2K's DS is based on X.500, the access mechanism uses LDAP, which solves several X.500 problems.

X.500 is part of the Open System Interconnection (OSI) model, but OSI doesn't translate well into a TCP/IP environment. Thus, LDAP uses TCP/IP as its communication medium. LDAP reduces the number of functions available with a full X.500 implementation, providing a lean and fast DS while maintaining X.500's overall structure. LDAP is the mechanism that communicates with AD and performs basic read, write, and modify operations. You can find more information about X.500 in D.W. Chadwick's, "Understanding X.500—The Directory" (http://www.salford.ac.uk/its024/Version.Web/Contents.htm).

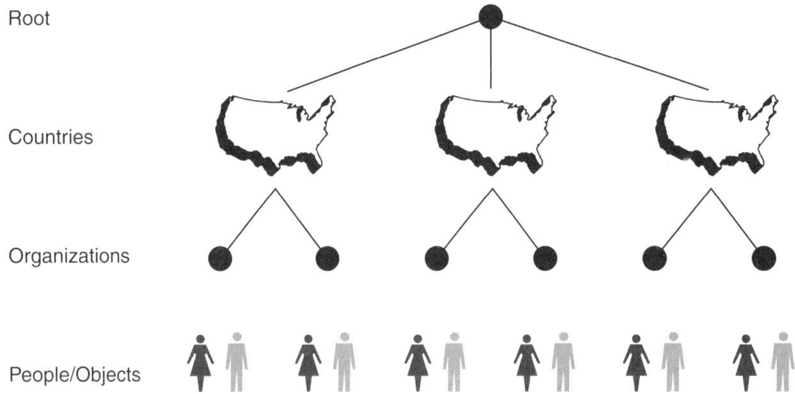

Figure 15-1 The X.500 hierarchical structure

FAQ 15.3 What DNS entries does Windows 2000 add when you create a domain?

Windows 2000 domains rely heavily on DNS entries. If you enable dynamic update on the relevant DNS zones, Win2K creates these entries automatically. Following is an explanation for each entry:

```
_ldap._tcp.<DNSDomainName>
```

Lets a client locate a Win2K domain controller in the domain named by <DNSDomainName>. A client searching for a domain controller in the domain savilltech.com would query the DNS server for _ldap._tcp.savilltech.com. (see Figure 15-2)

```
_ldap._tcp.<SiteName>._sites.<DNSDomainName>
```

Lets a client find a Win2K domain controller in the domain and site specified (e.g., _ldap._tcp.london._sites.savilltech.com for a domain controller in the London site of savilltech.com).

```
_ldap._tcp.pdc._ms-dcs.<DNSDomainName>
```

Lets a client find the PDC Flexible Single Master Operation (FSMO) role holder of a mixed-mode domain. Only the PDC of the domain registers this record.

```
_ldap._tcp.gc._msdcs.<DNSTreeName>
```

Lets a client find a Global Catalog (GC) server. Only domain controllers serving as GC servers for the tree will register this name. If a server ceases to be a GC server, the server will deregister the record.

```
_ldap._tcp.._sites.gc._msdcs.<DNSTreeName>
```

Lets a client find a GC server in the specified site (e.g., _ldap._tcp.london._sites.gc._msdcs.savilltech.com).

```
_ldap._tcp.<DomainGuid>.domains._msdcs.<DNSTreeName>
```

Lets a client find a domain controller in a domain based on the domain controller's globally unique ID. A GUID is a 128-bit (8 byte) number that generates automatically for referencing AD objects.

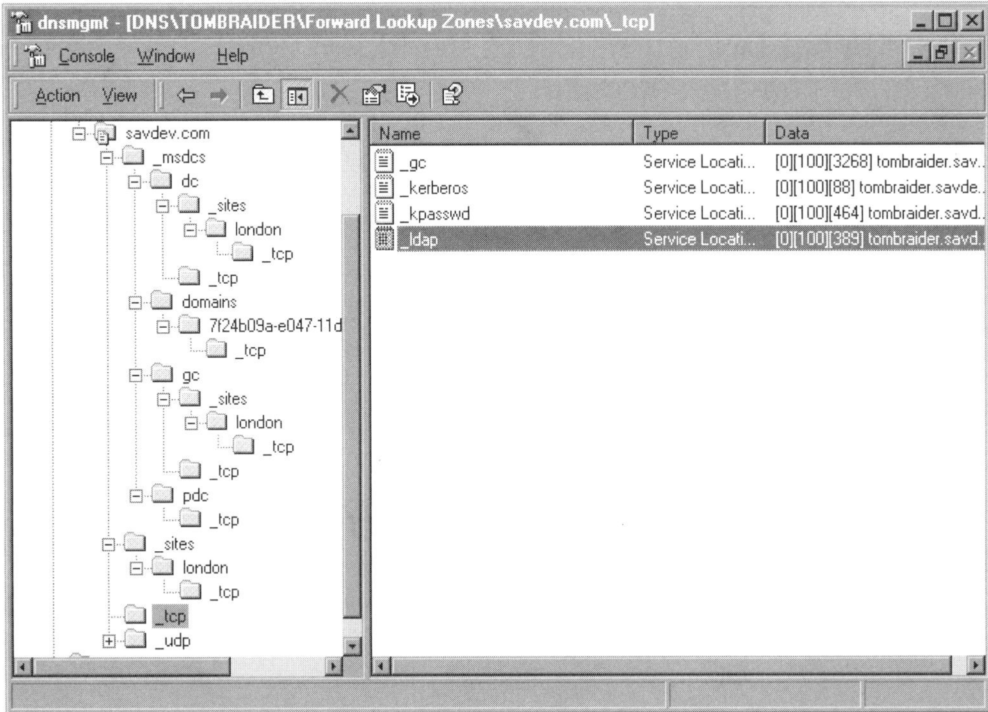

Figure 15-2 TCP entries added during the creation of an Active Directory domain controller

```
<DNSDomainName>
```

Lets a client find a domain controller through a normal host record.

Figure 15-2 is an example DNS screen for a domain.

15.4 What is the schema?

The schema is a blueprint of all the objects in a domain. When you create a new forest, a default schema contains definitions for users, computers, and domains. Because you can't have multiple definitions of an object, you can have only one schema per forest.

The file SCHEMA.INI contains the default schema's definition, as well as the initial structure for the file NTDS.DIT (which stores directory data). The %systemroot%\ntds directory contains the file SCHEMA.INI (although this can be changed during domain controller creation). The file is in plain ASCII format so that you can type it.

FAQ 15.5 What is a domain tree?

In Windows 2000, a domain can be a child of another domain (e.g., child.domain.com is a child of domain.com). A child domain name always includes the complete parent domain name. A child domain and its parent share a two-way transitive trust.

A domain tree exists when one domain is the child of another domain. A domain tree must have a contiguous namespace, as in the left-most diagram in Figure 15-3. In the right-most diagram in Figure 15-3, the lack of contiguous names means that the domains can't be part of the same tree.

The tree's name is the root domain name of the tree. In my example, the tree is root.com. Because domains are DNS names and because domains inherit the parent part of the name, if you rename part of a tree, all of the parent's children are also implicitly renamed. For example, if you renamed the parent domain ntfaq.com to backoffice.com, the child domain sales.ntfaq.com would change to sales.backoffice.com. Although you can't currently rename part of a tree, this problem will arise in future versions of the OS.

You can currently create domain trees only when DCPROMO promotes a server to a DC. This restriction might change in a future OS.

Placing domains in a tree yields several advantages. The most useful benefit is that all members of a tree have Kerberos transitive trusts with the domain's parent and all the domain's children. Transitive trusts also let any user or group in a domain tree obtain access to any object in the tree. In addition, you can use one network logon at any workstation in the domain tree.

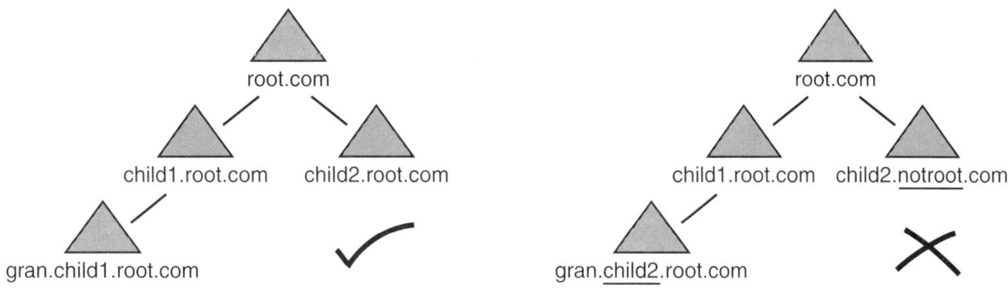

Figure 15-3 Legal and illegal parent-child relationships

15.6 What is a domain forest?

You might have several domain trees in your organization that need to share resources. To solve this problem, you can join the trees to form a forest.

A forest is a collection of trees that don't necessarily form a contiguous namespace (although each tree must be contiguous). This arrangement might be useful if your company has multiple root DNS addresses, as in Figure 15-4.

As Figure 15-4 shows, two root domains connect through a transitive, two-way Kerberos trust (much like the trust between a child and parent). Forests always contain a domain's entire domain tree. You can't create a forest that contains only part of a domain tree.

When you promote a server to a domain controller (DC), DCPROMO creates a forest if the user selects to create a new forest. Forest creation can't occur at any other time, although this restriction may change in a future OS.

You can add as many domain trees to a forest as you want. All the domains in a forest can grant object access to any user in the forest. Thus, the administrator doesn't need to manually manage the trust relationships.

Creating a forest provides the following benefits:

- All the trees have a common Global Catalog (GC) that contains specific information about every object in the forest.
- All the trees contain a common schema. Microsoft hasn't confirmed what happens if two trees have different schemas before you join the trees, because you currently can't join two trees (although in .NET you can link trees using transitive trusts). However, this problem will arise in future versions of the OS. I assume the changes will merge.

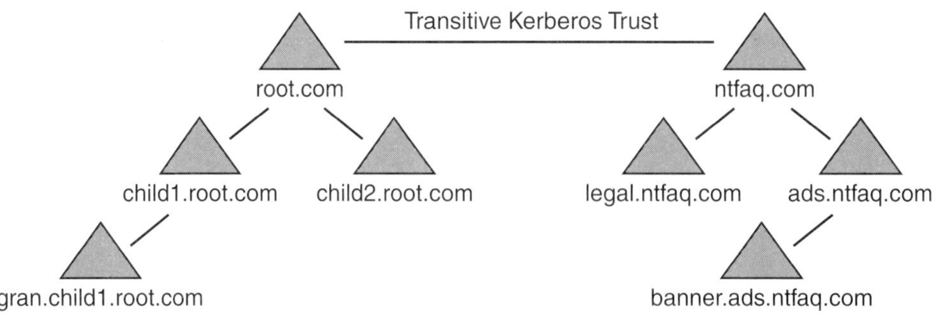

Figure 15-4 Two trees connected via a transitive Kerberos trust to create a forest

- Performing a search in a forest initiates a deep search of the entire tree in the domain you initiate the request from and uses the GC entries for the rest of the forest.

You might prefer not to join trees into a forest. Instead, you can create normal trusts between individual tree domains.

FAQ 15.7 What is a Kerberos trust?

Windows NT 4.0 trust relationships aren't transitive. Therefore, if domain2 (e.g., Marketing, in Figure 15-5) trusts domain1 (Sales), and domain3 (Development) trusts domain2 (Marketing), domain3 (Development) doesn't trust domain1 (Sales).

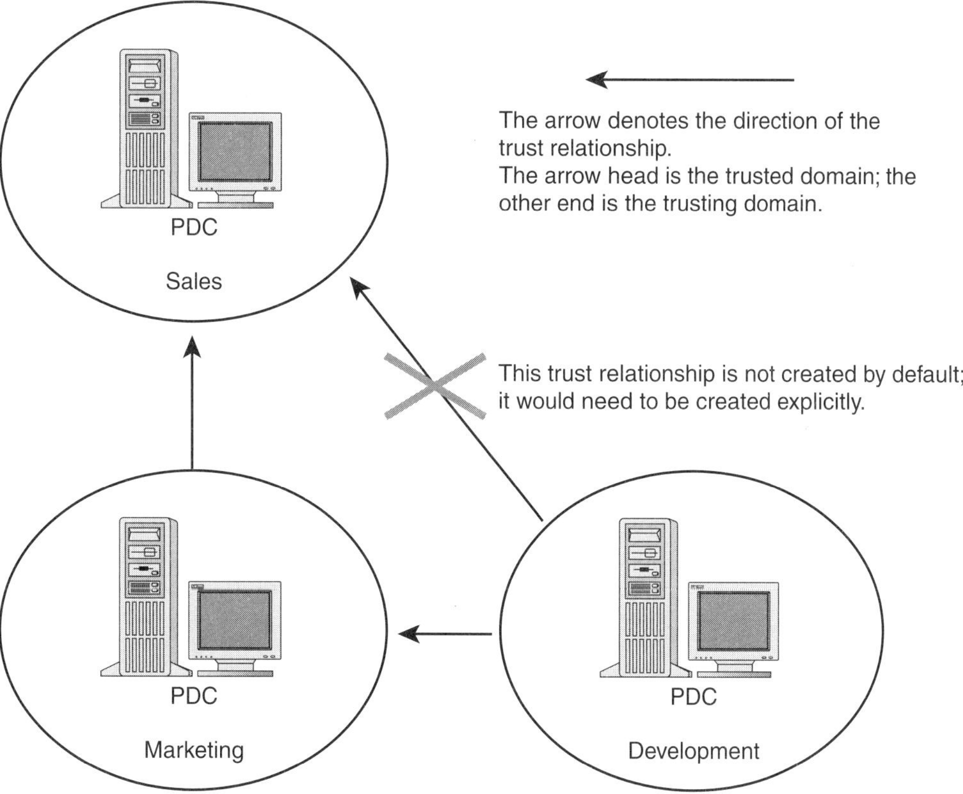

Figure 15-5 A nontransitive trust environment showing that the Development domain would not implicitly trust the Sales domain

In Windows 2000, the trust relationships that connect members of a tree or forest are two-way, transitive Kerberos trusts. Thus, all the domains in a tree implicitly trust all the other domains in the tree or forest. Because trusts occur automatically when a domain joins a tree, time-consuming trust administration is unnecessary.

Kerberos is Win2K's primary security protocol. Kerberos verifies a user's identity and a session's data integrity. Each DC has Kerberos services on it, and every Win2K workstation and server has a Kerberos client. A user's initial Kerberos authentication gives the user one logon session to enterprise resources. Kerberos isn't a Microsoft protocol but is based on MIT's Kerberos 5.0. For more information about Kerberos, see the Internet Engineering Task Force (IETF) Requests for Comments (RFC) 1510, "The Kerberos Version 5 GSS-API Mechanism" (http://www.ietf.org/rfc/rfc1510.txt?number=1510).

FAQ 15.8 How do I automatically upgrade a server to a domain controller during installation?

You can automatically run DCPROMO during an unattended installation. Enter the command

```
dcpromo /answer:%path_to_answer_file%
```

In my example, the DCInstall section and parameters are added directly to the unattended answer file. The Microsoft Windows 2000 Resource Kit details the DCInstall section's parameters in the file UNATTEND.DOC. I've listed the main entries in the following table:

AdministratorPassword	The new password for the domain Administrator account
AutoConfigDNS	Specifies whether the wizard should configure DNS
ChildName	Name of the child part of the domain
CreateOrJoin	Specifies whether the domain will join an existing forest or create a new one
DatabasePath	Location for the Active Directory database
DNSOnNetwork	Used when a new forest of domains is installed and no DNS client is configured on the computer
DomainNetBiosName	NetBIOS name for the domain

IsLastDCInDomain	Only valid when demoting an existing domain controller to a member server
LogPath	Path for the Directory Service (DS) logs
NewDomainDNSName	Name of the new tree or when a new forest is created
ParentDomainDNSName	Specifies the name of the parent domain
Password	Password for the username used to promote the server
RebootOnSuccess	Specifies whether an automatic reboot should be performed
ReplicaDomainDNSName	Name of the domain to be replicated from
ReplicaOrMember	Specifies whether a Windows NT 4.0 or 3.51 BDC being upgraded should become a replica domain controller or be demoted to a regular member server
ReplicaOrNewDomain	Specifies whether the machine is a new domain controller in a new domain or a replica of an existing domain
SiteName	Name of the site (Default-First-Site by default)
SysVolPath	Path of SYSVOL
TreeOrChild	Specifies whether entry is a new tree or child of existing domain
UserDomain	Domain for the user being used in promotion
UserName	Name of the user performing the upgrade

Because the DCPROMO process occurs after setup, the created answer file is called $WINNT$.INF and copies to the \system32 folder. The parameters are in this file, so you need to add the following text to the GUIRunOnce section of the unattended Setup answer file:

```
[GUIRunOnce] "DCpromo /answer:%systemroot%\system32\$winnt$.inf"
```

After the DCPROMO process completes, DCPROMO removes password information from the $WINNT$.INF file. To make this process easier because the RunOnce command doesn't execute until someone logs on to the computer, you can add the following text to the unattended answer file:

```
[GUIUnattended]
Autologon = yes ; automatically logs on the administrator account
AutoLogoncount = n ; number of times to perform auto-admin logon
```

Don't use items such as %systemroot% or %windir% because the unattended installation process doesn't understand them.

You can just create a DCInstall section directly in your UNATTEND.TXT file to avoid having multiple unattended setup files. Enter text such as the following.

```
[DCInstall]
AdministratorPassword = cartman
CreateOrJoin = Create
DomainNetBiosName = savtech
NewDomainDNSName = savtech.com
RebootOnSuccess = Yes
ReplicaOrNewDomain = Domain
SiteName = "London"
TreeOrChild = Tree
```

My example script would create a new forest with domain savtech.com at the top and the new domain controller in the site London. The SYSVOL, logs, and Active Directory (AD) files would be in the default locations. The new domain Administrator account password would be cartman.

If you want to use DCPROMO outside an unattended installation, enter

```
dcpromo /answer:<DCInstall answer filename>
```

You'll see a dialog box that says "DCPROMO is running in unattended mode". Then, the machine will reboot.

FAQ 15.9 How do I change my Windows 2000 domain's NetBIOS name?

Although Windows 2000 domain names are DNS based (e.g., savilltech.com), when Win2K launches the domain controller promotion program DCPROMO, this program also specifies a NetBIOS name for backwards compatibility with older clients and domain controllers. This NetBIOS name is typically the leftmost part of the DNS name (e.g. savilltech), although the user can specify a different NetBIOS name.

After DCPROMO sets a NetBIOS name, you must demote all the domain controllers and recreate the domain if you want to change the NetBIOS name. However, doing so would cause you to lose all domain objects. To prevent this problem, you can back up the objects before you recreate the domain and then reimport the objects.

If you're upgrading a Windows NT 4.0 domain to Win2K, you can't change the NetBIOS name while DCPROMO is running. You must use the NT 4.0 domain's NetBIOS name, although you can have a different DNS name.

FAQ 15.10 How do I create a new Active Directory site?

Active Directory (AD) has sites, which you can use to group servers into containers that mirror your network's physical topology. Sites also let you configure replication between domain controllers (DCs). In addition, you can map several TCP/IP subnets to sites so that new servers can automatically join the correct site depending on their IP address and so that clients can easily find the DC closest to them.

When you create the first DC, AD creates the default site Default-First-Site-Name and assigns the DC to this site. Subsequent DCs also add to this site, although you can later move the DCs to other sites. You can rename the default site if you want.

You use the Microsoft Management Console (MMC) Active Directory Sites and Services snap-in to create and administer sites. To create a new site, perform the following steps.

1. Start the MMC Active Directory Sites and Services snap-in. (From the Start menu, select Programs > Administrative Tools > Active Directory Sites and Services.)
2. Right-click the Site branch and select New > Site from the context menu.
3. Enter a name for the site (e.g., NewYork). The name must be 63 characters or fewer and can't contain spaces or periods. You must also select a site link (only one site link, DEFAULTIPSITELINK, exists by default). Alternatively, enter

   ```
   IP
   ```

4. Click OK.

After you create the site, you can assign various IP subnets to the site as follows.

1. Start the MMC Active Directory Sites and Services snap-in. (From the Start menu, select Programs > Administrative Tools > Active Directory Sites and Services.)
2. Expand the Sites branch.
3. Right-click Subnets and select New > Subnet, as the screen shows.
4. In the past, you needed to enter the subnet name in the form "network/bits masked" (e.g., for network 200.200.201.0 with subnet mask 255.255.255.0,

you'd enter 200.200.201.0/24). However, this method proved too complicated. Now, you simply enter the address and mask, as shown in Figure 15-6.

5. Then select the site to associate the subnet with.
6. Click OK.

After you have a subnet linked to a site, you can assign multiple subnets to the site.

Determining the *bits masked* portion of the subnet name can be confusing. This value is the number of bits set in the subnet mask. The subnet mask consists of four sets of 8 bits. You can use Figure 15-7 to convert the subnet mask to bits.

For example, the subnet mask 255.255.255.0 is 11111111.11111111.11111111.00000000 in binary, which uses 8 + 8 + 8 bits (i.e., 24) to define the subnet mask. The subnet mask 255.255.252.0 is 11111111.11111111.11111100.00000000 in binary, which is 8 + 8 + 6, or 22.

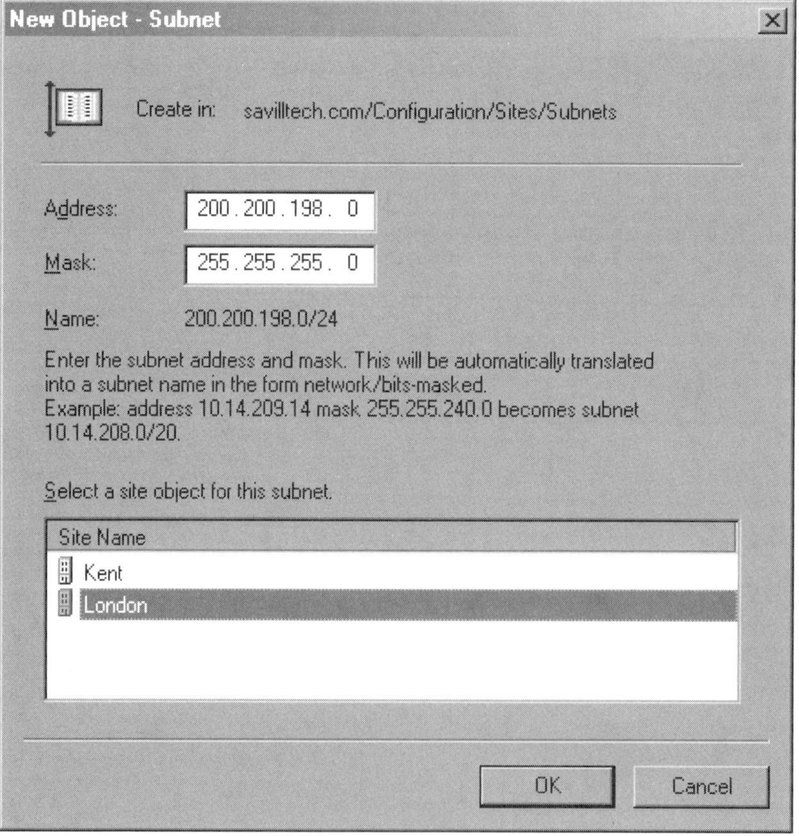

Figure 15-6 Creating a new subnet for a site

1	1	1	1	1	1	1	1		
128	64	32	16	8	4	2	1	=	255

Figure 15-7 How the 8-bit part of an IP address is calculated

After you define multiple sites, new DCs that you use DCPROMO to create will automatically join the site that matches their IP address. If no site exists for a DC's IP subnet, the DC will join the site that authorized the DC's promotion.

FAQ 15.11 How do I create a new site link?

After you create sites of IP subnets, you must link the sites together. You can add new sites to the default IP site link DEFAULTIPSITELINK as you create the sites, or you can select another existing site link. You can also create a new site link.

1. Start the Active Directory Sites and Services MMC snap-in. (Select Programs > Administrative Tools > Active Directory Sites and Services from the Start menu.)
2. Expand the Sites branch.
3. Expand the Inter-Site Transports branch.
4. Right-click the protocol for the type of site link you want to create (i.e., IP or SMTP) and select New Site Link.
5. Enter a name for the link and select the sites that you want to be part of the link, as shown in Figure 15-8. Then click OK.

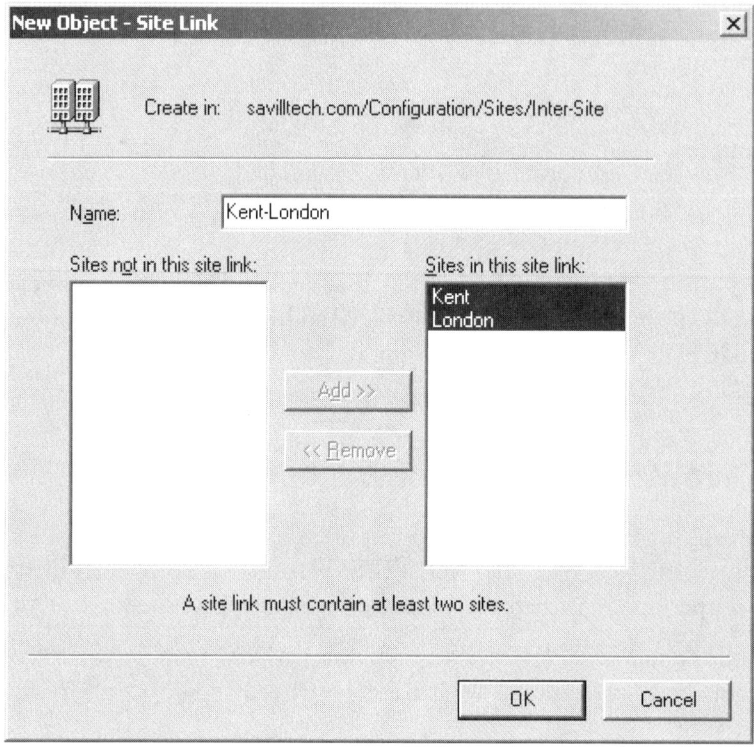

Figure 15-8 Selecting the sites for a site link

FAQ 15.12 How do I disable site link transitivity?

Site links are bridged together to make them transitive so that the Knowledge Consistency Checker (KCC) can create connection objects between domain controllers. You can disable site link transitivity, then manually bridge specific site links to achieve more control.

1. Start the Active Directory Sites and Services MMC snap-in. (Select Programs > Administrative Tools > Active Directory Sites and Services from the Start menu.)
2. Expand the Sites branch.
3. Expand the Inter-Site Transports branch.
4. Right-click the protocol you want to disable transitivity for (i.e., IP or SMTP) and select Properties.
5. Clear the Bridge all site links checkbox, as shown in Figure 15-9, and click Apply.
6. Click OK.

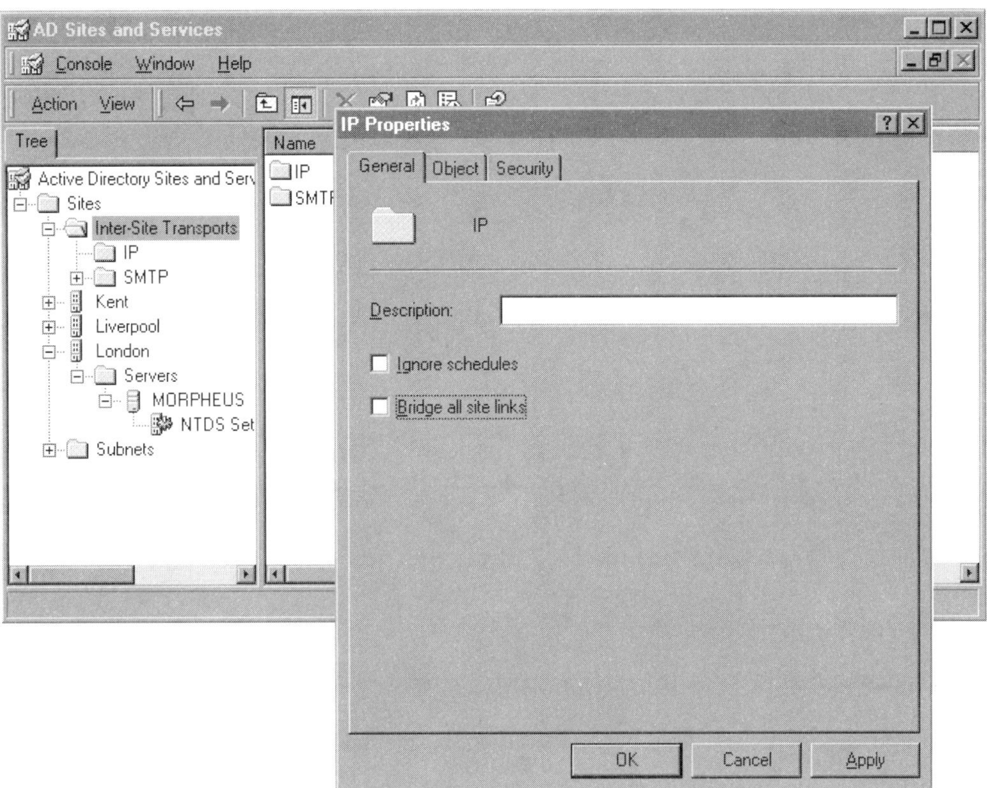

Figure 15-9 Disabling the bridging of all site links

15.13 How do I rename a site?

When you install your first domain controller, the domain controller creates the default site Default-First-Site-Name. This name isn't helpful, so you might want to rename it.

1. Start the Microsoft Management Console (MMC) Active Directory Sites and Services snap-in. (Select Programs > Administrative Tools > Active Directory Sites and Services from the Start menu.)
2. Expand the Sites branch.
3. Right-click the site you want to rename (i.e., Default-First-Site-Name) and select Rename, as shown in Figure 15-10. (Alternatively, select the site and press F2.)
4. Enter the new name and press Enter.

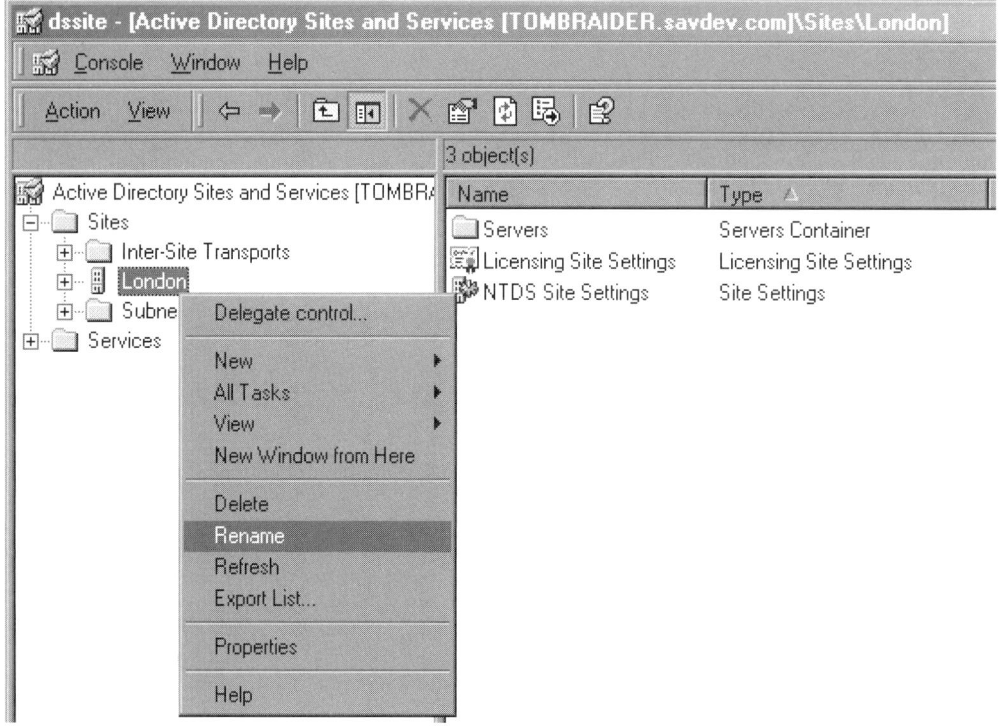

Figure 15-10 Rename option from a site context menu

15.14 How can a server belong to more than one site?

By default, a server belongs to only one site. However, you might want to configure a server to belong to multiple sites.

Because sites are necessary for replication, for clients to find resources and to decrease traffic on intersite connections, simply modifying a site's membership might cause performance problems.

To configure a server for multiple site membership, perform the following steps.

1. Log on to the server you want to join multiple sites.
2. Start Regedt32.
3. Go to the HKEY_LOCAL_MACHINE\SYSTEM\CurrentControlSet\ServicesNetlogon\Parameters Registry entry.

4. Select Add Value from the Edit menu.
5. Enter the name **SiteCoverage** and the type REG_MULTI_SZ.
6. Click OK.
7. Enter the names of the sites to join, each on a new line. (Press Shift+Enter to move to the next line.)
8. Click OK.
9. Close the Registry editor.

This process doesn't create the objects in Active Directory (AD) to evaluate the sites. You must add these objects manually.

FAQ 15.15 How do I move a server to a different site?

If your sites and subnets are configured, new servers automatically add to the site that owns the subnet. However, you can manually move a server to a different site.

1. Start the Microsoft Management Console (MMC) Active Directory Sites and Services snap-in. (From the Start menu, select Programs > Administrative Tools > Active Directory Sites and Services Manager.)
2. Expand the Sites container.
3. Expand the site that currently contains the server and expand the Servers container.
4. Right-click the server and select Move from the context menu, as shown in Figure 15-11.
5. You'll see a list of all the sites. Select the new target site and click OK.

The move takes effect immediately.

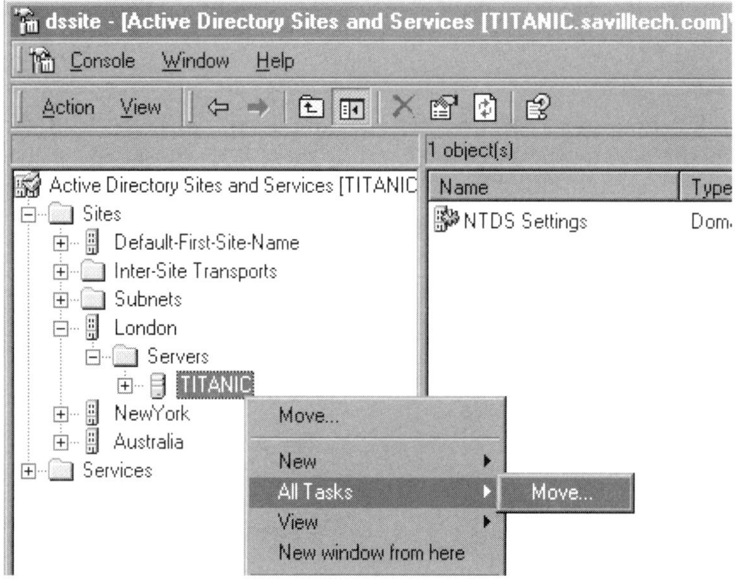

Figure 15-11 Selecting the Move option for a server within a site

FAQ 15.16 What is multimaster replication?

In a Windows 2000 domain, all domain controllers (DCs) are equal. Thus, you can make changes on any DC. Servers' complete domain directories are kept up-to-date with one another through a process of multimaster replication.

Each time you make a change to AD, the servers' update sequence number (USN), where the change implements, increases by one. AD then stores the new USN, as well as the change. These changes must replicate to all the DCs in the domain; the USN provides the key to multimaster replication.

USN increments are atomic in operation, which means that the increment to the USN and the actual change occur simultaneously. If one part fails, the whole change fails (except the USN would still have been incremented). A change can't occur without the USN being incremented; therefore, changes can't be lost. Each DC keeps track of the highest USNs of the DCs it replicates with. This procedure lets a DC calculate which changes must replicate on a replication cycle.

At the start of a replication cycle, each server checks its USN table and queries the DCs it replicates with for the DCs' latest USNs. The following is an example USN table for Server A.

Domain Controller B	Domain Controller C	Domain Controller D
54	23	53

Server A queries the DCs for their current USNs and gets the following information.

Domain Controller B	Domain Controller C	Domain Controller D
58	23	64

From this information, Server A can calculate the changes it needs from each server, as follows.

Domain Controller B	Domain Controller C	Domain Controller D
55-58	None	54-64

Server A then queries each DC for the necessary changes.

Multiple changes to an object's property can occur. Every property has a property version number, which helps detect collisions. Property version numbers work like USNs: Each time you modify a property, the property version number increases by one.

If you try to modify an object's property multiple times, the change with the highest property version number takes precedence. A collision occurs when the property version numbers are the same for two or more property updates. When two property version numbers match, the timestamp helps resolve the conflict. Because every change has a timestamp, DCs must be accurate with one another. In the unlikely event that the property version numbers match and the timestamps match, a binary buffer comparison occurs; the larger buffer size change takes precedence. Property version numbers increase only on original writes (not on replication writes, as USNs do) and aren't server specific. Instead, a property version number travels with a property.

A propagation-dampening scheme prevents changes repeatedly going to other servers. Each server keeps a table of up-to-date vectors, which are the highest originating writes received from each controller. The vectors take the following form.

```
<the change>,<the DC making the original change>,<the USN of the change>
```

For example,

```
<object savillj, property Password xxx>,Titanic,54
```

DCs send this information with the USNs so that they can calculate whether they already have the change the other DCs are trying to replicate.

FAQ 15.17 What are tombstone objects?

Because of Windows 2000's and Active Directory's (AD's) complex replication, if you simply delete an object, Win2K's replication algorithm might recreate the object at the next replication interval. Thus, AD marks deleted objects with tombstones.

When we create an object, it gets replicated to all other DCs in the domain. If deletion would mean to simply remove it from the DC, then there would be no sign on this DC that it ever existed, so during the next replication cycle, it would be simply replicated from another DC (and we won't be able to get rid of it). So, when we delete an object from an AD, it's not immediately removed from the AD—just most of its attributes are removed and the object is marked as deleted—tombstoned—and moved to a special hidden container. This tombstone is then replicated to all other DCs, and after a certain period of time (two months by default), a special process, the garbage collector, which runs on each DC, purges the tombstone from the AD database.

Win2K deletes tombstone objects 60 days after their original tombstone status setting. To change this default time (which I don't recommend), modify the tombstone-lifetime setting under the cd=DirectoryServices,cn=WindowsNT,cn=Services,cn=Configuration,dc=DomainName parameter.

FAQ 15.18 How do I modify the Active Directory's garbage-collection period?

The Active Directory (AD) garbage-collection process performs two vital functions. First, it cleans up deleted objects. When you delete an object in AD, the system doesn't immediately delete the object because when replication occurs, a replication partner would recreate the object. Instead, the system uses a tombstone with a finite lifetime to mark the object as deleted. The tombstone replicates to all DCs, and after it expires, the garbage-collection agent deletes the object.

The garbage-collection process also performs online AD defragmentation. By default this process runs every 12 hours on each DC. However, you can change this frequency by modifying the attribute garbageCollPeriod under the path CN=Directory Service,CN=Windows NT,CN=Services,CN=Configuration,DC=,DC=,DC=COM. The best way to modify the attribute is to use the Windows 2000 Support Tools' LDP.EXE utility.

FAQ 15.19 How does intrasite replication work in Windows 2000?

Windows 2000's Knowledge Consistency Checker (KCC) automatically manages replication within a site. The KCC uses a bidirectional ring topology that uses Remote Procedure Call (RPC) over TCP/IP without compression. DCs within a site are typically on a fast network (per the definition of a site), and the extra processing necessary for compression and decompression is undesirable.

The KCC runs every 15 minutes, adjusting the topology as necessary. As you create new DCs, the KCC automatically places them in the ring. To view the DC links, you can use the Microsoft Management Console (MMC) Active Directory Sites and Services snap-in. Expand the site, the Servers container, and the server. Under the NTDS Settings branch are the created connection objects.

Because the KCC runs on all DCs, the rings are in order of the DCs' globally unique IDs (GUIDs) to ensure convergence on one topology. An exception to the ring rule is that no more than three hops can exist between two DCs within the ring. To protect the three-hop rule, the KCC adds extra links for seven or more DCs, as shown in Figure 15-12.

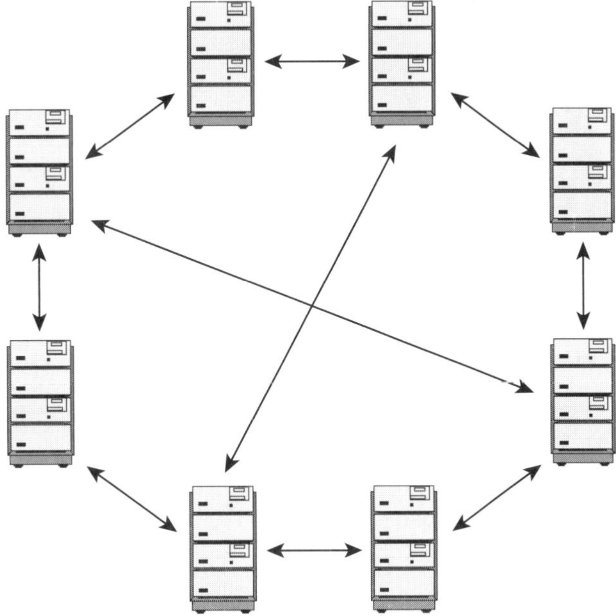

Figure 15-12 The three-hop rule in action

These rings are for same-naming context (i.e., domains) in one site. If you have multiple domains in a site, rings exist for each domain in the site.

Another type of ring that exists replicates schema and configuration information between DCs, as shown in Figure 15-13. Because all the domains share this information (i.e., the information is forestwide), each site has only one ring. Thus, if you have two domains in a site, you have three rings: one ring for each domain and one ring for the schema and configuration information. If you have only one domain in a site, one ring functions as two.

Manual configuration of intrasite replication is unnecessary, and Microsoft doesn't recommend such configuration. The only task you might need to perform is adding extra connection objects to reduce the hop count between DCs.

When you make a change to the naming context (i.e., domain) data, the DC's local copy of AD records the change, then the DC waits five minutes (by default) before notifying its replication partners of the change. You can continue to make changes during this time period. The delay exists so that all changes transmit at once. If no changes occur during a particular time period (which you can configure in the intrasite connection object schedule), a replication sequence initiates to ensure no changes were missed.

The SAM or the Local Security Authority (LSA) can trigger urgent replication during the following events: replication of a newly locked-out account (e.g., if you fire someone), change of an LSA secret (i.e., a trust account), and state changes to the

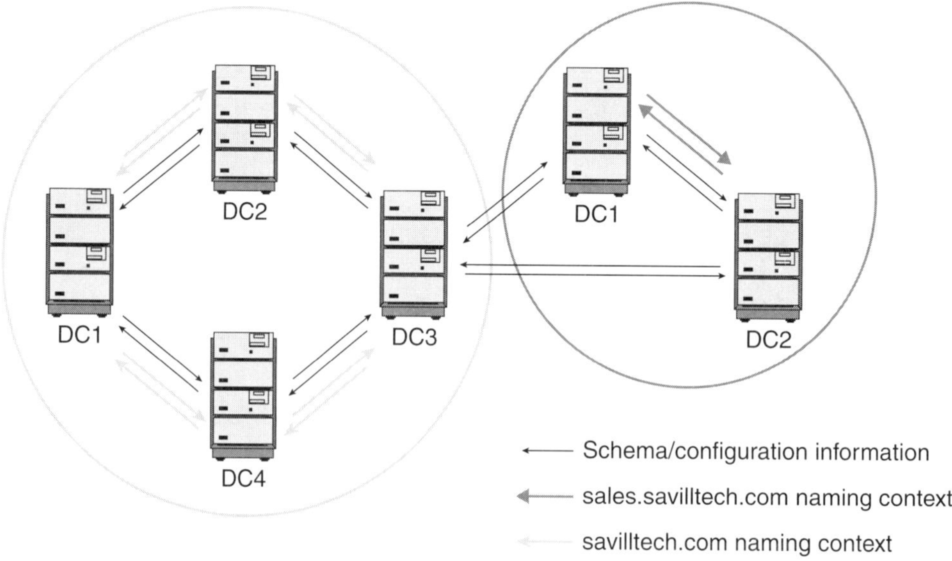

Figure 15-13 Different rings for the different domain/forest elements

relative identifier (RID) master These events trigger immediate replication. Because urgent replication requires notification, this type of replication occurs only within a site (i.e., intrasite). However, you can modify site links to enable notification.

An exception to multimaster normal replication is user passwords. As in other attribute changes, you can change a user password at any DC. However, the DC pushes the change to the PDC Flexible Single-Master Operation (FSMO) role holder on a best-attempt basis. Other DCs receive the password through normal replication. The reason for the extra password work is that if password validation fails, the validating DC will pass the request to the PDC FSMO in case the password has changed and the DC hasn't yet received the new password via standard replication.

The schema and configuration data replicates between DCs once an hour by default. For information about changing the replication interval, see FAQ 15.22.

FAQ 15.20 How do I change the intrasite replication interval in Windows 2000 for domain information?

As FAQ 15.99 explains, intrasite replication for naming context data doesn't occur until five minutes after a change. This delay lets all changes transmit at once. You can change this five-minute delay.

1. Start Regedit.
2. Go to the HKEY_LOCAL_MACHINE\SYSTEM\CurrentControlSet\Services\NTDS\Parameters Registry entry.
3. Double-click Replicator notify pause after modify (secs).
4. Enter the number of seconds you want for the delay and click OK.
5. Close the Registry editor.
6. Reboot the machine.

You might notice the parameter Replicator notify pause between DSAs (secs). This parameter determines the number of seconds between notification of directory service agents (DSAs). This parameter prevents simultaneous replies by replication partners.

FAQ 15.21 How do I force replication between two domain controllers in a site?

In Windows NT 4.0, you can use Server Manager to force replication between DCs. In Windows 2000, you can force replication between DCs as follows:

1. Start the Microsoft Management Console (MMC) Active Directory Sites and Services snap-in.
2. Expand the Sites branch to show the sites.
3. Expand the site that contains the DCs. (The default site Default-First-Site-Name might be the only site.)
4. Expand the servers.
5. Select the server you want to replicate to and expand the server.
6. Double-click NTDS Settings for the server.
7. Right-click the server you want to replicate from.
8. Select Replicate Now from the context menu, as shown in Figure 15-14.
9. Click OK in the confirmation dialog box.

This replication is one-way. If you want two-way replication, you need to replicate in each direction.

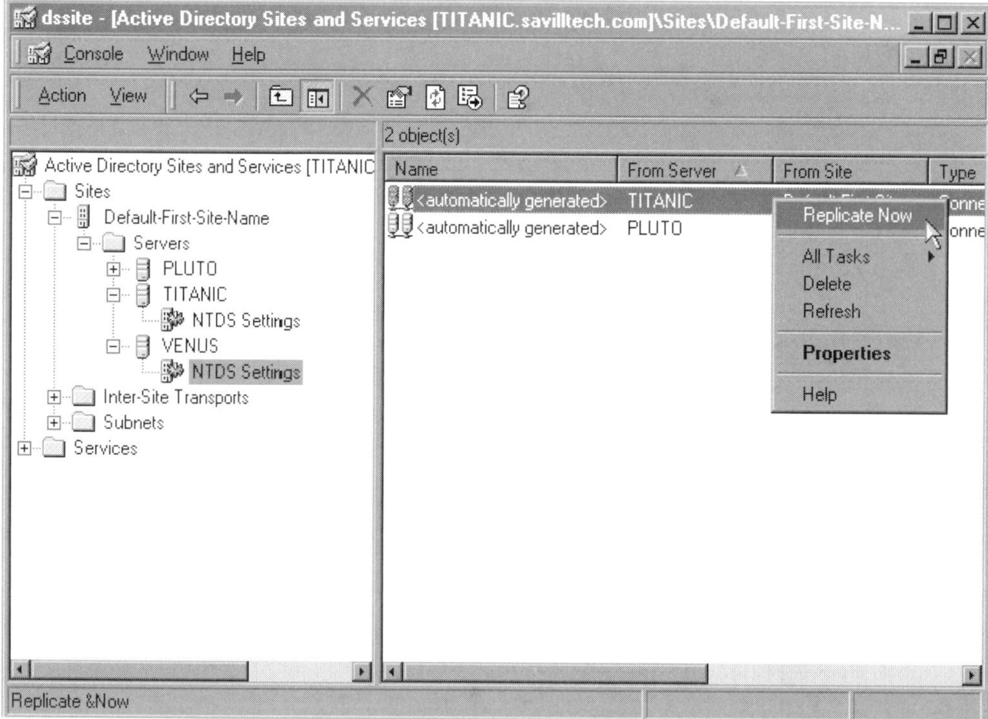

Figure 15-14 Forcing a replication

15.22 How do I change the schedule for replication between two domain controllers in a site?

By default, domain controllers replicate schema and configuration information once an hour. (For information about the type of data replicated, see FAQ 15.19.) To change this interval for domain controllers in one site, perform the following tasks:

1. Start the Microsoft Management Console (MMC) Active Directory Sites and Services snap-in. (Select Programs > Administrative Tools > Active Directory Sites and Services from the Start menu.)
2. Expand the Sites branch to show the various sites.
3. Expand the site that contains the domain controllers. (The default site Default-First-Site-Name might be your only site.)
4. Expand the servers.
5. Select the server you want to configure replication to and expand it.
6. Double-click NTDS Settings for the server.
7. Right-click the server you want to set replication from.
8. Select Properties from the context menu.
9. Select the Active Directory Service connection tab.
10. Click Change Schedule.
11. Modify the replication as necessary (see Figure 15-15) and click OK.

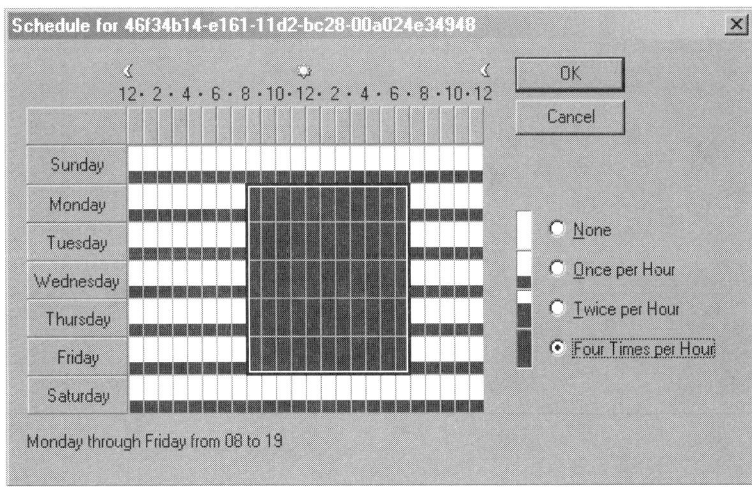

Figure 15-15 Setting the replication interval

12. Click Apply.
13. Click OK.

The schedule you set is for minimum replication. The replication schedule is one-way; you need to repeat the steps to configure the other direction. If you make a change, the notification and replication will occur after a five-minute delay.

FAQ 15.23 How do I tune Active Directory replication?

You can use one of several settings under the HKEY_LOCAL_MACHINE\SYSTEM\CurrentControlSet\Services\NTDS\Parameters Registry entry to modify elements of AD replication. When you make a change to AD, a timer starts. This timer specifies how long the domain controller will wait before notifying its first replication partner about replication between domain controllers. The default time is five minutes. To change this time period, edit the Replicator notify pause after modify (secs) value in the HKEY_LOCAL_MACHINE\SYSTEM\CurrentControlSet\Services\NTDS\Parameters Registry entry, as shown in Figure 15-16.

After the domain controller notifies its first replication partner, the DC waits before it notifies each subsequent replication partner. This delay prevents simultaneous replies from the replication partners. The default time is 30 seconds. To change this time period, edit the Replicator notify pause between DSAs (secs) value in the HKEY_LOCAL_MACHINE\SYSTEM\CurrentControlSet\Services\NTDS\Parameters Registry entry, as shown earlier in Figure 15-16.

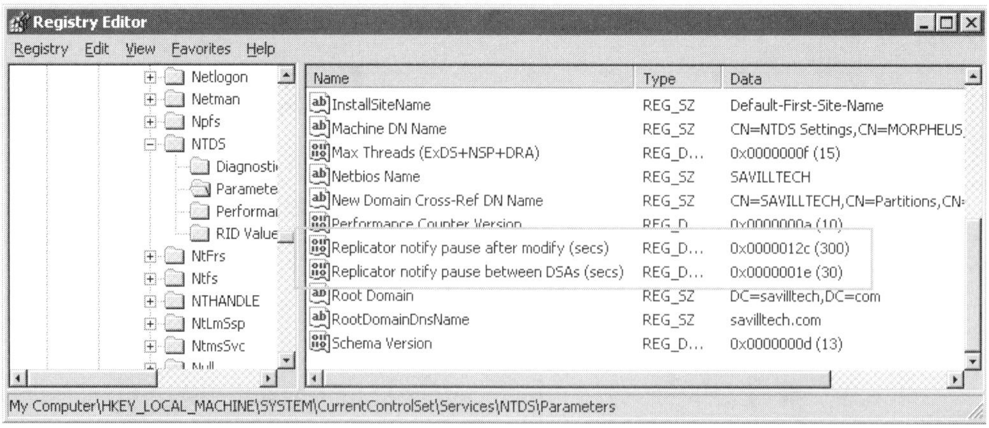

Figure 15-16 Detailed replication options via the Registry

You can modify other values to enhance a multiple-CPU system's performance. For example, set the replication thread priority high value to 1 to run replication at high priority. If you don't set this value, or you set it to 0, replication will run at low priority. Set the replication thread priority low value to 1 to run replication at low priority. If you set this value to -1, the value is ignored.

FAQ 15.24 How do I specify a bridgehead server?

To minimize bandwidth usage during intersite communication, the Knowledge Consistency Checker (KCC) dynamically chooses a server from each site to handle the communication. These servers are the bridgehead servers. Rather than letting the KCC choose the servers, you might prefer to nominate domain controllers (e.g., a domain controller with the best network connectivity, a DC that is the proxy server in a firewall environment).

A server that you nominate is a preferred bridgehead server. You can select multiple preferred bridgehead servers for a site, but only one of the servers is active at a time. If the active preferred bridgehead server fails, then another preferred bridgehead server becomes the active server. If no preferred bridgehead servers are available, a regular Windows 2000 DC becomes active for intersite communication. Letting a regular Win2K DC handle intersite communication might cause problems if the server lacks sufficient resources.

1. To nominate a server as a bridgehead server, start the Active Directory Sites and Services MMC snap-in. (Select Programs > Administrative Tools > Active Directory Sites and Services from the Start menu.)
2. Expand the Sites branch.
3. Expand the site containing the server and select the Servers container.
4. Right-click the server and select Properties.
5. Select the protocol you want the server to act as a preferred bridgehead server for (i.e., SMTP or IP), as shown in Figure 15-17, and click Add. Then click OK.

When the KCC runs the next time, the connection objects will change to use the bridgehead server you specified.

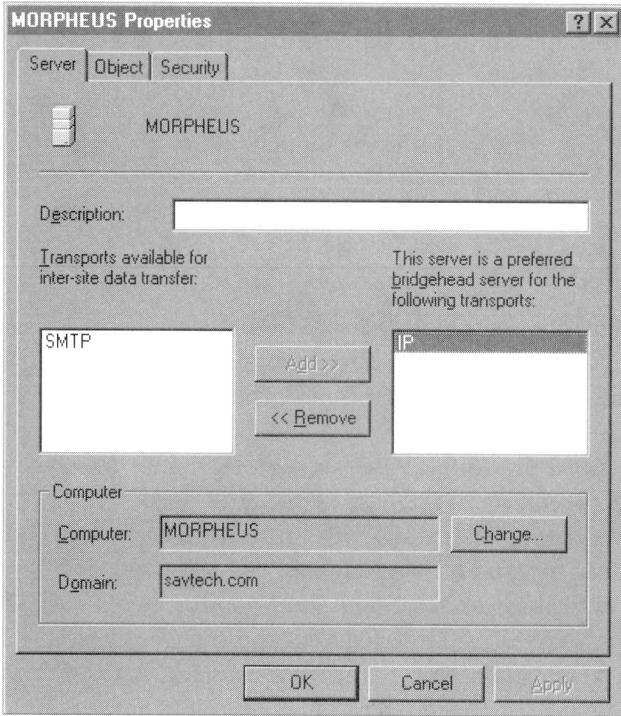

Figure 15-17 Specifying bridgehead transport options

FAQ 15.25 How do I create a site link bridge?

Site link bridges are important for intersite communication. Imagine you have the sites Liverpool, London, and Kent, and you have site links between Liverpool and London and between Kent and London (see Figure 15-18). If site link transitivity is disabled, Liverpool and Kent can't communicate. A site link bridge lets London act as a router for communication between Liverpool and Kent.

If site link transitivity is disabled, you must manually bridge sites so that replication can complete, and the Knowledge Consistency Checker (KCC) can create the necessary connection objects.

1. Start the Active Directory Sites and Services MMC snap-in. (Select Programs > Administrative Tools > Active Directory Sites and Services from the Start menu.)
2. Expand the Sites branch.
3. Expand the Inter-Site Transports branch.

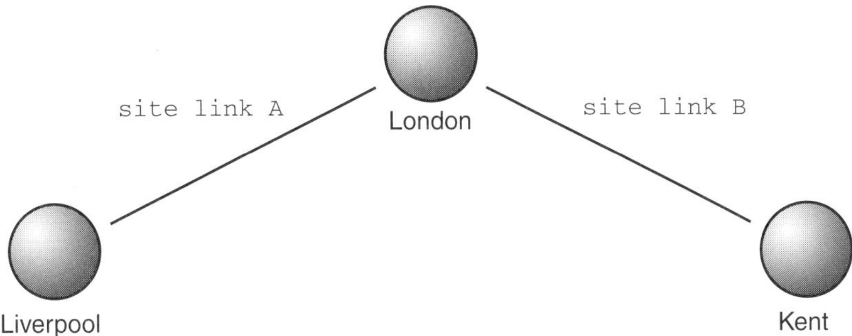

Figure 15-18 Site links between sites

4. Right-click the protocol you want to create the bridge for (i.e., IP or SMTP) and select New Site Link Bridge.
5. Enter a name for the bridge and select the site links that will form the bridge.
6. Click OK.

FAQ 15.26 I have several sites connected over a virtual private network. How should I configure my site links?

Obviously, with the Internet, the speed between sites is unknown. In addition, the route varies every time, so you can't place an accurate link cost, which controls the desirability of remote sites as sources of replication information, between sites—which negates the usefulness of site links and bridges. Your best option is to place all sites in a single site link.

FAQ 15.27 How does intersite replication work in Windows 2000?

You can use Remote Procedure Call (RPC) over IP or Simple Mail Transport Protocol (SMTP) to link sites. After you define the site links, replication schedules, cost factors, and site link bridges (if appropriate), the Knowledge Consistency Checker (KCC) can create the connection objects as long as the site links are transitive.

Using SMTP has some limitations. You can use SMTP to replicate the Global Catalog (GC) information, as well as schema and configuration data. However, SMTP can't replicate full domain name context data such as the data that DCs in a domain exchange, because some domain operations require the File Replication Service (FRS) (e.g., the Group Policy), which SMTP doesn't support.

Intersite replication uses a spanning tree topology. As long as the KCC can establish a replication route between all the sites in the enterprise forest, the replication tree is complete. The administrator manually creates the links between sites. Creating the links involves defining costs for each link (the cost relates the network's speed and reliability) and establishing a replication schedule.

You use the Microsoft Management Console (MMC) Active Directory Sites and Services snap-in to create and maintain site links. By default, your original site is part of the site link DEFAULTIPSITELINK. You can add sites to this site link when you create them. (When you create a site, you must specify a site link.)

Replication data that travels between sites is 10% to 15% of its original size due to data compression. This smaller size is important because intersite links are usually over WAN links, which tend to be slow.

You need to create only the necessary links between sites. The KCC creates the required connection objects.

FAQ 15.28 How do I monitor when the Knowledge Consistency Checker runs?

The KCC, which manages connection objects for inter- and intrasite replication, ascertains whether you need to create new objects or delete existing objects. The KCC runs every 15 minutes by default. FAQ 15.30 explains how to change this time period. To determine when the KCC starts and stops, start Regedit and go to the HKEY_LOCAL_MACHINE\SYSTEM\CurrentControlSet\Services\NTDS\Diagnostics Registry entry.

Double-click Knowledge Consistency Checker. Set the value to 3 or greater and click OK. Close the Registry editor. You don't need to restart the machine for the change to take effect.

A value of 3 or greater in Knowledge Consistency Checker causes the KCC to log extra events that you can use Event Viewer's Directory Service branch to view. Some common events that are useful to view include

- Event 1007 signifies the KCC starting
- Event 1009, as shown in Figure 15-19, signifies the beginning of the KCC check.
- Event 1013 signifies the end of the KCC check
- Event 1015 signifies the KCC stopping
- Event 1133 provides information about the KCC check

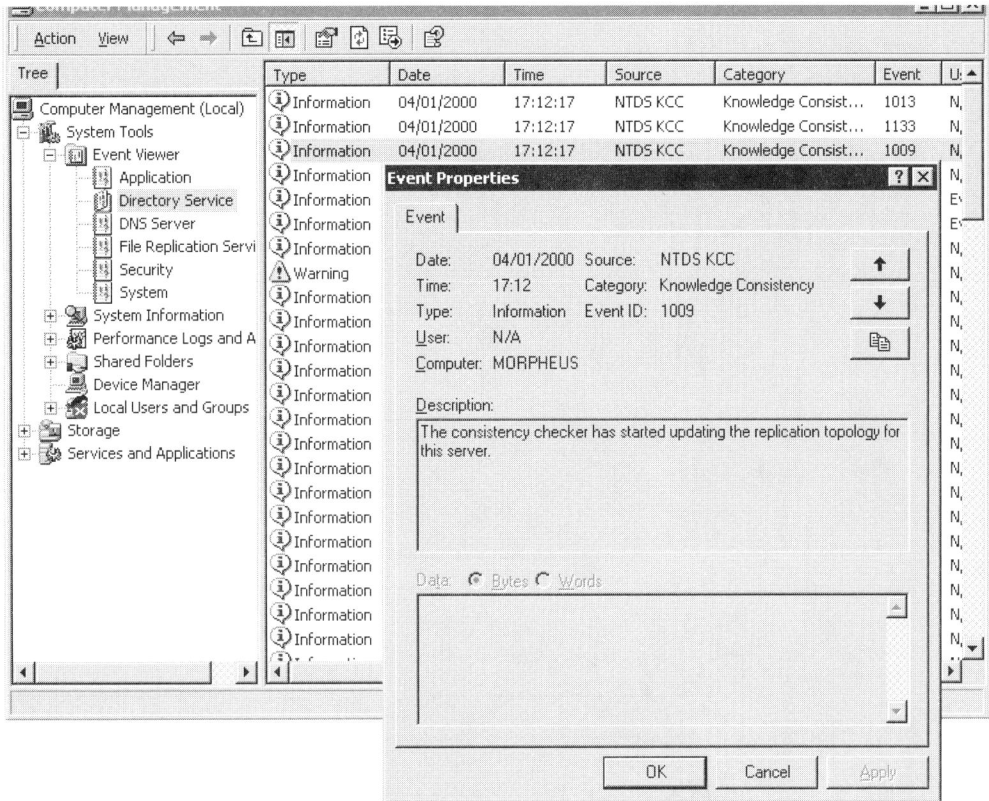

Figure 15-19 Event log showing the Knowledge Consistency Checker in action

FAQ 15.29 How do I disable the Knowledge Consistency Checker?

FAQ 15.19 explains how the KCC automatically creates and maintains connection objects for intra- and intersite replication. To manually maintain connection objects (which I don't recommend), you must disable the KCC.

To disable the KCC, use the Microsoft Windows 2000 Resource Kit's LDP tool. This program is in Win2K's %SystemDrive%:\Program Files\Support Tools folder.

1. Start LDP.EXE.
2. From the Connection menu, select Connect.

3. Enter the domain controller's DNS name, leave the port as 389 (LDAP), and make sure the Connectionless checkbox is clear. Click OK.
4. Some text will appear in the right-most pane. Next, select Bind from the Connection menu.
5. Enter an Administrator username, password, and domain, as shown in Figure 15-20. Click OK.
6. From the View menu, select Tree.
7. A dialog box will prompt you for the base distinguished name (DN), which includes a site and your domain. For example, in the London site savtech.com I enter

```
CN=London,CN=Sites,CN=Configuration,DC=SAVTECH,DC=COM
```

8. Expand the route and double-click CN=NTDS Site Settings. The results will display in the right-most window. Next, look for the options Attribute. If this attribute is missing or set to 0, you can proceed. Otherwise, you need to contact Microsoft Support for help checking your configuration before you can continue.

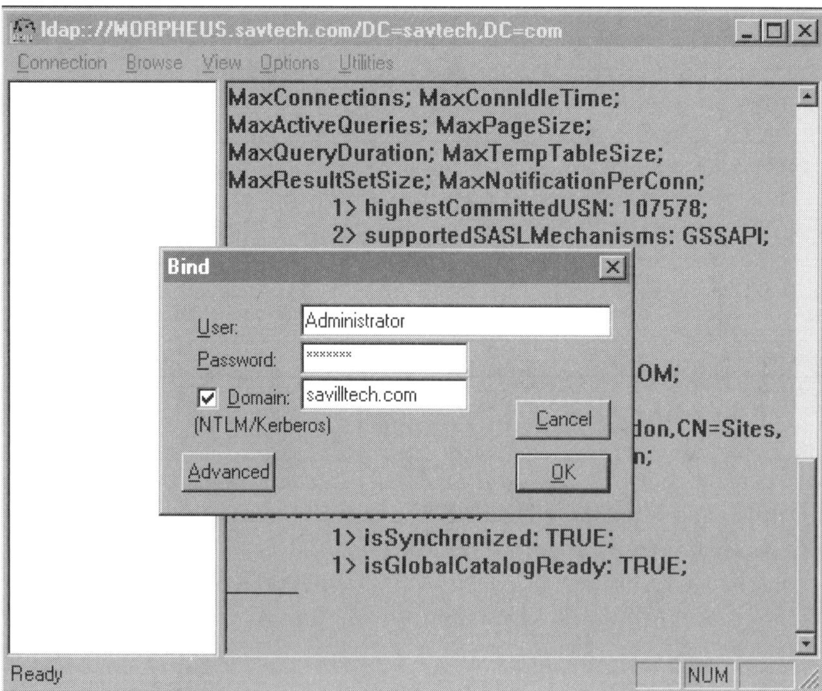

Figure 15-20 Binding to the LDAP interface

9. The text you see in the right-most window will look like

```
Expanding base 'CN=NTDS Site Settings,CN=London,CN=Sites,
CN=Configuration,DC=savtech,DC=com'...
Result : (null)
Matched DNs:
Getting 1 entries:
>> DN: CN=NTDS Site
Settings,CN=London,CN=Sites,CN=Configuration,DC=savtech,DC=com
```

10. Copy the last line, except the DN: portion, onto the Clipboard (e.g., CN=NTDS Site Settings,CN=London,CN=Sites,CN=Configuration,DC=savtech, DC=com).
11. From the Browse menu, select Modify.
12. In the Dn field, enter the string you copied in Step 9, as shown in Figure 15-21.
13. In the Attribute field, enter

```
options
```

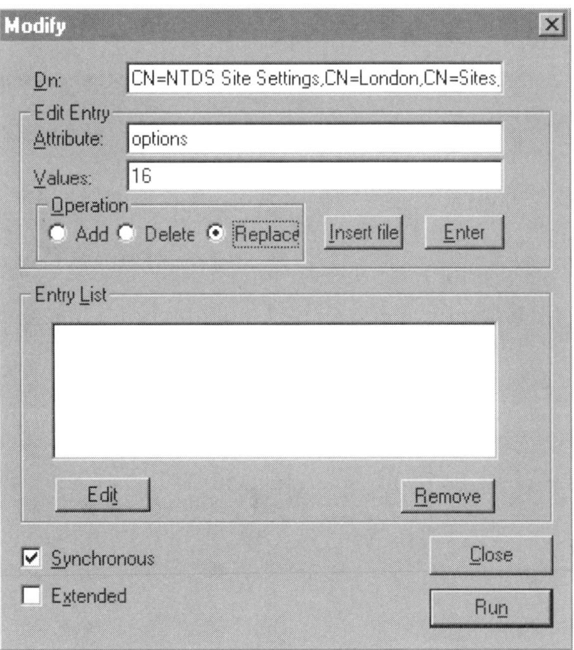

Figure 15-21 Replacing a value with the LDAP utility

14. In the Values field, enter the appropriate value. A value of 1 disables automatic intrasite topology generation, a value of 16 disables automatic intersite topology generation, and a value of 17 disables both types of topology generation.
15. In the Operation field, select Replace.
16. Click Enter.
17. Click Run.
18. Click Close.

    The right-most LDP.EXE window will display text such as

```
***Call Modify...
ldap_modify_s(ld, 'CN=NTDS Site
Settings,CN=London,CN=Sites,CN=Configuration,DC=savtech,DC=com',
[1] attrs);
Modified "CN=NTDS Site
Settings,CN=London,CN=Sites,CN=Configuration,DC=savtech,DC=com".
```

19. Close LDP.EXE.

To check whether the KCC is disabled, use Active Directory Replication Monitor (REPLMON.EXE) to generate a report on the site configuration.

1. Start REPLMON.EXE.
2. Right-click Monitored Services in the left-most window and select Add Monitored Server from the context menu.
3. Select Add the server explicitly by name and click Next.
4. Enter the server name and click Finish.
5. Right-click the server (under the site) and select Generate Status Report.
6. Enter a name and location for the log and click Save.
7. In the Options field, select Server/DC Configuration Data and Extended Site Configuration, as shown in Figure 15-22.
8. Click OK.
9. Click OK again to finish.

Open the file you specified, and you'll see site information such as the following.

```
*********************************************************************
Enterprise Data
*********************************************************************

Globally Unique Identifiers (GUIDs) for each domain controller in
the enterprise
```

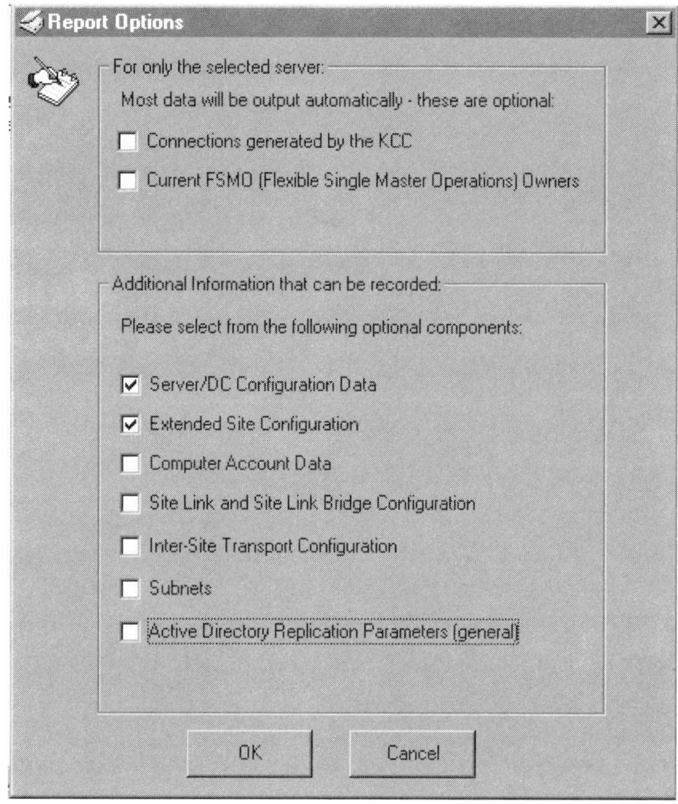

Figure 15-22 Report options

```
NOTE: the absence of a GUID means that the server has been demoted.
--------------------------------------------------------------------

Site Name: London
---------------------------------------
Site Options : NTDSSETTINGS_OPT_IS_INTER_SITE_AUTO_TOPOLOGY_DISABLED
Site Topology Generator: CN=NTDS
Settings,CN=MORPHEUS,CN=Servers,CN=London,CN=Sites,CN=Configuration,
DC=savtech,DC=com
Site Topology Renewal :
Site Topology Failover :

MORPHEUS
Server GUID (used for DNS) : DA644BE4-A8C9-47AF-AC4A-71F8DA4D50F0
```

```
Replication Database GUID (used to identify partner in replication) :
DA644BE4-A8C9-47AF-AC4A-71F8DA4D50F0
DSA Options : NTDSDSA_OPT_IS_GC
DSA Computer Path : CN=MORPHEUS,OU=Domain Controllers,DC=savtech,
DC=com
DSA Schema Location : CN=Schema,CN=Configuration,DC=savtech,DC=com
DSA Mail Address : _IsmService@da644be4-a8c9-47af-ac4a-71f8da4d50f0
._msdcs.savtech.com
DSA DNS Host Name : MORPHEUS.savtech.com
DSA BridgeHead Transports : IP
```

In the Site Options field, the text NTDSSETTINGS_OPT_IS_INTER_SITE_AUTO_TOPOLOGY_DISABLED means intersite topology management is disabled. The text NTDSSETTINGS_OPT_IS_AUTO_TOPOLOGY_DISABLED means intrasite topology management is disabled.

To reenable the KCC, follow steps 1 through 20, but set the value in step 14 to 0. If the KCC is fully enabled, Replmon's output won't include Site Options information.

FAQ 15.30 How do I change how often the Knowledge Consistency Checker runs?

The KCC, which manages connection objects for inter- and intrasite replication, runs every 15 minutes by default. To change this time period, start Regedit and go to the HKEY_LOCAL_MACHINE\SYSTEM\CurrentControlSet\Services\NTDS\Parameters Registry entry.

From the Edit menu, select New > DWORD Value. Enter the following and press Enter:

```
Repl topology update period (secs)
```

Double-click the new value and enter the number of seconds for how often you want the KCC to run. Click OK then close the Registry editor. Restart the machine for the change to take effect.

FAQ 15.31 What tools are available for monitoring or changing replication?

To monitor or change replication, you must use the Microsoft Management Console (MMC) Active Directory Sites and Services snap-in. This tool lets you view, create, or delete connection objects. Other tools you can use include the Microsoft Windows 2000 Supplemental Tools Repadmin and Replmon tools.

Repadmin is a command-line tool that lets you check replication consistency (e.g., for a KCC recalculation). The switch /showreps displays a list of replication partners, as well as reasons for problems. The invocation ID is the database globally unique ID (GUID).

When you use Repadmin with the switch /showreps, you'll see text such as the following:

```
D:\>repadmin /showreps
London\TITANIC
DSA Options : IS_GC
objectGuid : 221d9d34-540e-4a7b-bd26-054c11e2d1ad
invocationID: 221d9d34-540e-4a7b-bd26-054c11e2d1ad

==== INBOUND NEIGHBORS ======================================

CN=Schema,CN=Configuration,DC=savilltech,DC=com
London\TITUS via RPC
objectGuid: 2000eb93-cc24-4af7-9ad2-c52129c98c7a
Last attempt @ 1999-12-06 20:32.20 failed, result 8524:
Can't retrieve message string 8524 (0x214c), error 1815.
Last success @ 1999-09-17 20:53.45.
463 consecutive failure(s).
London\TRINITY via RPC
objectGuid: df3694d2-b4e9-4d9a-a560-3e8c26c48a89
Last attempt @ 1999-12-06 20:32.21 failed, result 8524:
```

The switch /showmeta shows object information, version numbers, and other information. When you use this switch, you'll see text such as the following:

```
C:\>repadmin /showmeta cn=garfield,DC=savtech,DC=com

45 entries.

Loc.USN Originating DSA Org.USN Org.Time/Date Ver Attribute
======= ============ ======= =========== === ======
99649 London\MORPHEUS 99649 1999-12-08 09:50.10 1 objectClass
99649 London\MORPHEUS 99649 1999-12-08 09:50.10 1 cn
99650 London\MORPHEUS 99650 1999-12-08 09:50.10 1 description
99649 London\MORPHEUS 99649 1999-12-08 09:50.10 1 givenName
99649 London\MORPHEUS 99649 1999-12-08 09:50.10 1 instanceType
```

Replmon is a GUI tool you can use to display and monitor replication status on domain controllers (DCs).

FAQ 15.32 In a Windows 2000 domain, how can I configure the site name information known to member servers and workstations?

Win2K introduced the concept of sites, which let you group machines that reside in similar TCP subnets. When a Win2K or later machine logs on, the system stores the site name in HKEY_LOCAL_MACHINE\SYSTEM\CurrentControlSet\Services\Netlogon\Parameters in the subkey named DynamicSiteName. The DC updates this name every 300 seconds (5 minutes); however, you can perform the following steps to modify the update time frame:

1. Start REGEDIT.EXE.
2. Go to HKEY_LOCAL_MACHINE\SYSTEM\CurrentControlSet\Services\Netlogon\Parameters.
3. From the Edit menu, select New > DWORD Value.
4. Enter a name of **SiteNameTimeout** and press Enter.
5. Double-click the new value and set it to the number of seconds.
6. Click OK.

To override the assigned site name, you can add a String value named SiteName in the Netlogon\Parameters subkey. If you use this approach, the system will never use the SiteNameTimeout value.

FAQ 15.33 How can I set the RPC port that intrasite replication uses?

By default, AD replication via Remote Procedure Calls (RPCs) takes place dynamically over an available port via the RPC Endpoint Mapper using port 135 (the same as Microsoft Exchange). An administrator may override this functionality and specify the port that all replication traffic passes through, thereby locking down the port.

1. Start Regedit.
2. Go to the HKEY_LOCAL_MACHINE\SYSTEM\CurrentControlSet\Services\NTDS\Parameters Registry entry.

3. From the Edit menu, select New > DWORD Value.
4. Enter the following and press Enter:

```
TCP/IP Port
```

5. Double-click the new entry and enter the port you want to use. (Make sure the port isn't already in use.) Click OK.
6. Close the Registry editor.
7. Reboot the machine.

After monitoring finishes, you need to remove the Registry entry you created. Removing this entry reinstates the security that dynamic RPC port allocation provides.

FAQ 15.34 How do I back up Active Directory and the system state?

You can use the Microsoft Windows Backup utility to back up Active Directory. AD is part of a machine's system state.

On Windows 2000 machines, the system state includes the Registry, class registration database, and system boot files. On a Win2K server that is a certificate server, the system state also contains the Certificate services database. On a Win2K machine that is a domain controller (DC), the system state also includes AD and the Sysvol directory.

To use Win2K's Backup Wizard to back up the system state, perform the following steps:

1. Start Windows Backup.
2. Click Backup Wizard.
3. Click Next in the introduction dialog box.
4. In the dialog box that asks what to back up, select Only back up the System State data and click Next.
5. Continue the backup process (i.e., select the backup media, etc.).

To manually back up the system state, perform the following steps:

1. Start Windows Backup.
2. Select the Backup tab.
3. Select the System State checkbox, as shown in Figure 15-23, as well as any other drives.

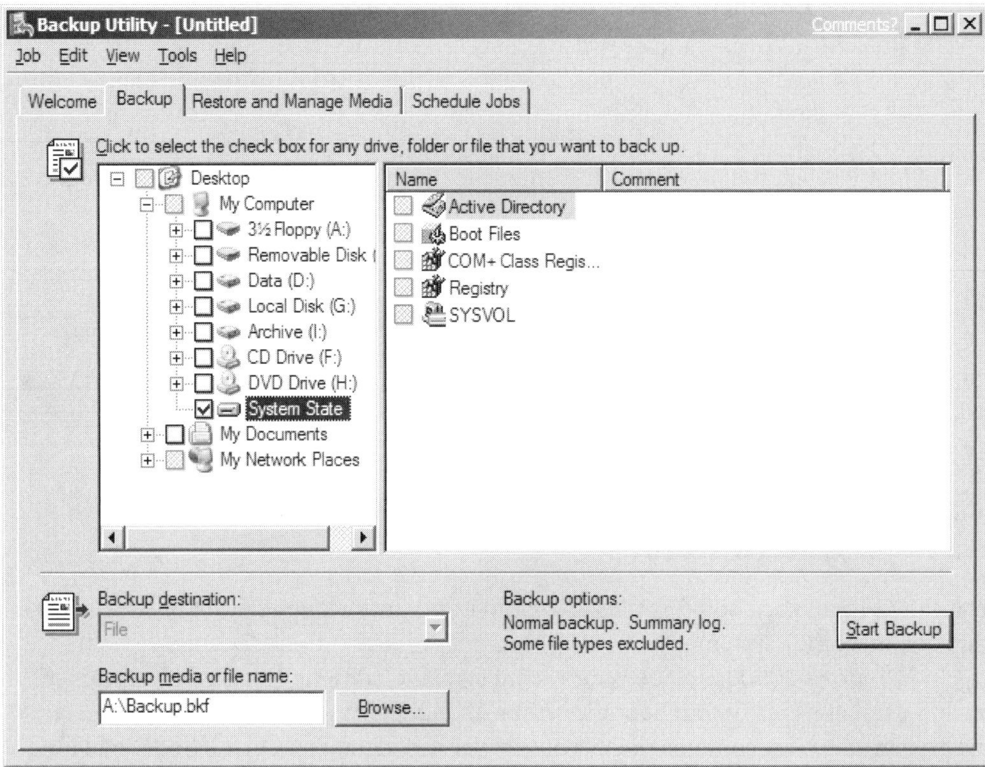

Figure 15-23 Backup of the system state on a domain controller

4. Select the backup destination.
5. Click Start Backup.
6. Confirm the backup description and click Start Backup.

To back up only the system state from the command line, enter

```
ntbackup backup systemstate /f d:\active.bkf
```

This command is a basic backup to file command. You can use more complex options if you prefer.

FAQ 15.35 How do I restore Active Directory?

You can't restore AD to a domain controller (DC) while the Directory Service (DS) is running. To restore AD, perform the following steps.

1. Reboot the computer.
2. At the boot menu, select Windows 2000 Server. Don't press Enter. Instead, press F8 for advanced options. You'll see the following text:

```
OS Loader V5.0

Windows NT Advanced Options Menu
Please select an option:

Safe Mode
Safe Mode with Networking
Safe Mode with Command Prompt

Enable Boot Logging
Enable VGA Mode
Last Known Good Configuration
Directory Services Restore Mode (Windows NT domain controllers
only)
Debugging Mode

Use | and | to move the highlight to your choice.
Press Enter to choose.
```

3. Scroll down and select Directory Services Restore Mode (Windows NT domain controllers only).
4. Press Enter.
5. When you return to the Windows 2000 Server boot menu, press Enter. At the bottom of the screen, you'll see in red text "Directory Services Restore Mode" (Windows NT domain controllers only).

The computer will boot into a special safe mode and won't start the DS. Be aware that during this time, the machine won't act as a DC and won't perform functions such as authentication.

1. Start Windows Backup.
2. Select the Restore tab.
3. Select the backup media and select System State.

4. Click Start Restore.
5. Click OK in the confirmation dialog box.

After you restore the backup, reboot the computer and start in normal mode to use the restored information. The computer might hang after the restore completes; I've experienced a 30-minute wait on some machines.

15.36 How do I manually defragment Active Directory?

Windows 2000 servers running Directory Services (DSs) perform a directory online defragmentation every 12 hours by default as part of the garbage-collection process. This defragmentation only moves data around the database file (NTDS.DIT) and doesn't reduce the file's size.

To create a new, smaller NTDS.DIT file and to enable offline defragmentation, perform the following steps:

1. Back up AD (see FAQ 15.34).
2. Reboot the server, select the OS option, and press F8 for advanced options.
3. Select the Directory Services Restore Mode option and press Enter. Press Enter again to start the OS.
4. Win2K will start in safe mode, with no DS running.
5. Use the local SAM's administrator account and password to log on.
6. You'll see a dialog box that says you're in safe mode. Click OK.
7. From the Start menu, select Run and type

   ```
   cmd.exe
   ```

8. In the command window, you'll see the following text. (Enter the commands in bold.)

   ```
   C:\> ntdsutil
   ntdsutil: files
   file maintenance:info
   ....
   file maintenance:compact to c:\temp
   ```

9. You'll see the defragmentation process. If the process was successful, enter the following to return to the command prompt:

   ```
   quit
   quit
   ```

10. Then, replace the old NTDS.DIT file with the new, compressed version.

```
copy c:\temp\ntds.dit %systemroot%\ntds\ntds.dit
```

11. Restart the computer and boot as normal.

The following is an example of the entire procedure.

```
D:\> ntdsutil
ntdsutil: files
file maintenance: info

Drive Information:

C:\ FAT (Fixed Drive) free(1.2 Gb) total(1.9 Gb)
D:\ NTFS (Fixed Drive) free(152.4 Mb) total(1.9 Gb)

DS Path Information:

Database : D:\WINNT\NTDS\ntds.dit - 8.1 Mb
Backup dir : D:\WINNT\NTDS\dsadata.bak
Working dir: D:\WINNT\NTDS
Log dir : D:\WINNT\NTDS - 30.0 Mb total
res2.log - 10.0 Mb
res1.log - 10.0 Mb
edb.log - 10.0 Mb
file maintenance: compact to c:\temp
Opening database [Current].
Using Temporary Path: C:\
Executing Command: D:\WINNT\system32\esentutl.exe /d
"D:\WINNT\NTDS\ntds.dit" /
/o /l"D:\WINNT\NTDS" /s"D:\WINNT\NTDS" /t"c:\temp\ntds.dit"
/!10240 /p

Initiating DEFRAGMENTATION mode...
Database: D:\WINNT\NTDS\ntds.dit
Log files: D:\WINNT\NTDS
System files: D:\WINNT\NTDS
Temp. Database: c:\temp\ntds.dit

Defragmentation Status (% complete )

0 10 20 30 40 50 60 70 80 90 100
|--|--|--|--|--|--|--|--|--|--|
...................................................
```

```
Note:
It is recommended that you immediately perform a full backup
of this database. If you restore a backup made before the
defragmentation, the database will be rolled back to the state
it was in at the time of that backup.

Operation completed successfully in 17.896 seconds.

Spawned Process Exit code 0x0(0)

If compaction was successful you either need to
copy "c:\temp\ntds.dit" to "D:\WINNT\NTDS\ntds.dit"
or run:
D:\WINNT\system32\ntdsutil.exe files "set path DB \"c:\temp\"" quit
quit
file maintenance: quit
ntdsutil: quit

D:\> copy c:\temp\ntds.dit %systemroot%\ntds\ntds.dit
Overwrite D:\WINNT\ntds\ntds.dit? (Yes/No/All): y
1 file(s) copied.
```

FAQ 15.37 I heard that more than one utility is available to defragment the Active Directory database. Is this true?

In Windows 2000, Microsoft included a version of an Exchange Server utility—ESENTUTL.EXE—that can defragment database files. At a command prompt, type the following command to defragment NTDS.DIT (the default name for the Active Directory—AD—database file):

```
ESENTUTL /D ntds.dit [options]
```

For a list of the command options, type

```
ESENTUTL /?
```

or

```
ESENTUTL /help
```

Usually, you use Ntdsutil to defragment your AD database; Ntdsutil is still the most supported version.

FAQ 15.38 Why can't I have spaces in my Windows 2000 NetBIOS domain name?

In Windows NT 4.0-based domains, the space is a legal character in NetBIOS domain names. Windows 2000 domains are DNS based and therefore use DNS names (although a NetBIOS name is available for backwards compatibility). DNS doesn't allow spaces in names. For consistency, Microsoft removed the space as a legal character in Win2K NetBIOS domain names.

Win2K NetBIOS domain names can contain the following special characters:

```
! @ # $ % ^ & ( ) - _ ' { } . ~
```

The following characters aren't allowed:

```
\ * + = | : ; " ? < > ,
```

FAQ 15.39 How do I create trusts from the command line in Windows 2000?

The Microsoft Windows 2000 Resource Kit's Trustdom tool lets you define trust relationships between Windows 2000 domains and one-way relationships with Windows NT 4.0 domains. You can create two types of one-way trusts: an outbound trust on the local or specified domain, and an inbound trust on the specified target domain. Trustdom's syntax is

```
trustdom [[domain[:dc],]target_domain[:dc]] [Options]
```

The default switch is -out. To see a list of other switches, use the /? switch.

FAQ 15.40 What is the Global Catalog?

The Global Catalog (GC) contains an entry for every object in an enterprise forest but only a few properties for each object. An entire forest shares a GC, with multiple servers holding copies. You can perform an enterprisewide forest search only on the properties in the GC, whereas you can search for any property in a user's domain tree. Only domain controllers (DCs) can hold a copy of the GC.

Configuring an excessive number of GCs in a domain wastes network bandwidth during replication. One GC server per domain in each physical location is sufficient. Windows sets servers as GCs as necessary, so you don't need to configure additional GCs unless you notice slow query response times.

Because full searches involve querying the whole domain tree rather than the GC, grouping the enterprise into one tree will improve your searches. Thus, you can search for items not in the GC.

FAQ 15.41 How do I configure a server as a Global Catalog?

To configure a Windows 2000 domain controller (DC) as a Global Catalog (GC) server, perform the following steps.

1. Start the Microsoft Management Console (MMC) Active Directory Sites and Services (From the Start menu, select Programs > Administrative Tools > Active Directory Sites and Services Manager.)
2. Select the Sites branch.
3. Select the site that owns the server and expand the Servers branch.
4. Select the server you want to configure.
5. Right-click NTDS Settings and select Properties.
6. Select or clear the Global Catalog Server checkbox, shown in Figure 15-24.
7. Click Apply, then OK.

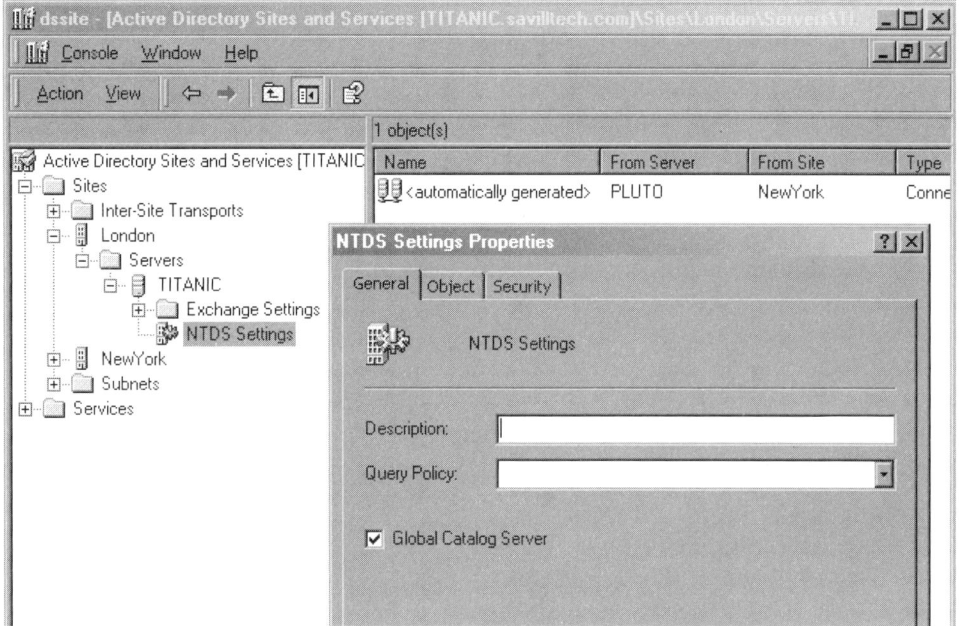

Figure 15-24 Global Catalog enabling of a server

FAQ 15.42 Why can't I use my user principal name to change my password if the Global Catalog is unavailable?

In Windows 2000, users have a user principal name (UPN)—e.g., john@savilltech.com—as well as the usual down-level SAM name—e.g., savillj. If you change your password using the down-level SAM username, the change works fine, even if the Global Catalog (GC) isn't available. If you change your password using your UPN and the GC isn't available, you receive the following error message if the account is in the parent domain:

```
The user name or old password is incorrect. Letters in passwords
must be typed using the correct case. Make sure the Caps is not
accidentally on.
```

Or you receive the following error message if the account is in the child domain:

```
Unable to change the password on this account due to the following
error:
```

```
1359: An internal error occurred
Please consult your system administrator.
```

To confirm that the GC's absence is the problem, use the following command to find your logon server:

```
echo %logonserver%
```

When you find the logon server, check the Directory Service event log for the following event:

```
Event 1126 Unable to establish connect with global catalog
```

To fix this problem, you need to ensure that the GC is available. You need the GC to change passwords using your UPN because domains store information only about their local domain whereas the GC includes information about objects in the entire forest. Thus, the GC must be available when you use the UPN, unless you have only one domain.

FAQ 15.43 What are the FSMO roles in Windows 2000?

In Windows 2000, all domain controllers (DCs) are equal. Changes replicate to all the DCs in a domain through a process known as *multimaster replication*. Multimaster replication resolves conflicts.

In some situations, **preventing** conflicts is preferable. Five Flexible Single-Master Operation (FSMO) roles, formerly known as *Floating* Single-Master Operation roles, manage an aspect of the domain or forest to prevent conflicts. You can manually move these roles between DCs.

Two types of roles exist: domain and forest. Only a DC in the domain can hold a domain-specific FSMO role, whereas any DC in the forest can hold a forest FSMO role. DCs can't hold FSMO roles in other domains or forests.

You can use the Ntdsutil utility or one of several GUI methods to assign FSMO roles. The following table summarizes each role:

Role Name	Description	Per Domain or Forest
Domain Naming Master	If you want to add a domain to a forest, the domain's name must be verifiably unique. The forest's Domain Naming Master FSMOs authorize the domain name operation.	One per forest
Infrastructure Master	When a user and group are in different domains, a lag can exist between changes to the user (e.g., a name change) and the user's display in the group. The Infrastructure Master of the group's domain fixes the group-to-user reference to reflect the change. The Infrastructure Master performs its fixes locally and relies on replication to bring all other replicas of the domain up-to-date.	One per domain
PDC Emulator	For backward compatibility, one DC in each Win2K domain must emulate a PDC for the benefit of Windows NT 4.0 and NT 3.5 DCs and clients.	One per domain
RID Master	Any DC can create new objects (e.g., users, groups, computer accounts). However, after creating 512 user objects, a DC must contact the domain's relative identifier (RID) Master for another 512 RIDs. (A DC actually contacts the RID Master when the DC has fewer than 100 RIDs left. Thus, the RID master can be unavailable for short periods of time without causing object creation problems.) This procedure ensures that each object has a unique RID. When a DC creates a security principal object, the DC attaches a unique SID to the object. The SID consists of the domain SID and a RID. The RID master must be available for you to use the Microsoft Windows 2000 Resource Kit's Movetree utility to move objects between domains.	One per domain

(continued)

Role Name	Description	Per Domain or Forest
Schema Master	At the heart of Active Directory (AD) is the schema, which is like a blueprint of all objects and containers. Because the schema must be the same throughout the forest, only one machine can authorize schema modifications.	One per forest

Even in native mode, the PDC Emulator has the following special roles:

- Failed authentication requests.
- For downlevel clients who issue a change (e.g., a password change) that would normally go to the PDC in an NT4.0 domain.
- Focus of best-effort push of password changes an account lockouts.
- In cases in which a time server client contacts the DC, the DC contacts the PDC Emulator, and the PDC Emulator contacts the PDC one level up, the PDC Emulator root domain could use Simple Network Time Protocol (SNTP) to contact an atomic Internet clock.
- Focus of group policies: If you edit or create a group policy, you contact the PDC; if the PDC isn't available, you can select another DC.

FAQ 15.44 How do I change the RID master FSMO?

FAQ 15.43 defines the relative identifier (RID) Master. To modify the role, perform the following steps:

1. Start the Microsoft Management Console (MMC) Active Directory Users and Computers snap-in on the domain controller (DC). (From the Start menu, select Programs > Administrative Tools > Active Directory Users and Computers.)
2. In the left-most pane, right-click the domain and select Connect to Domain Controller.
3. Select the DC you want to make the Flexible Single-Master Operation (FSMO) role owner, as shown in Figure 15-25, and click OK.
4. Right-click the domain again and select Operations Master from the context menu.
5. Select the RID Pool tab.
6. You'll see the name of the machine that holds the RID Master FSMO role, as the shown in Figure 15-26.

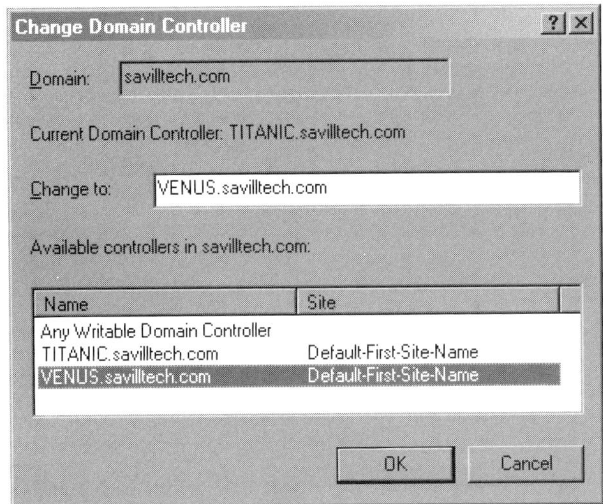

Figure 15-25 Selecting an alternate domain controller

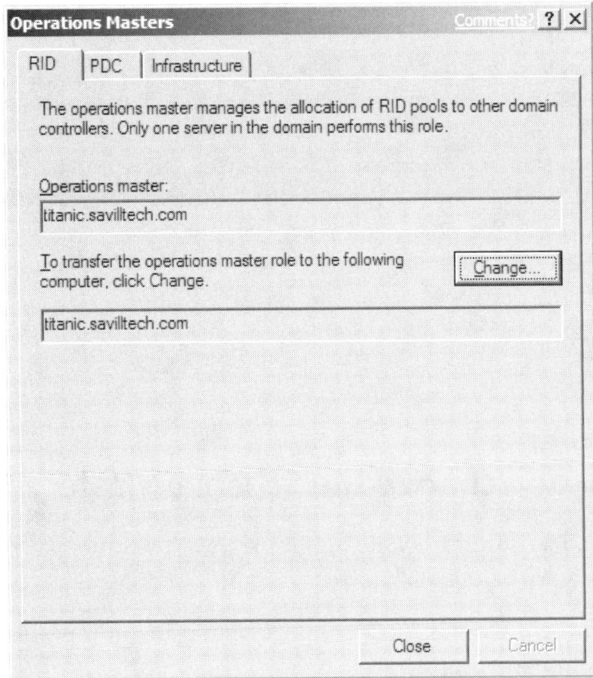

Figure 15-26 Modifying a RID operations master

7. To make a change, click Change.
8. Click OK in the confirmation dialog box.
   Finally, you'll see a dialog box confirming the role change.

You can also use the Ntdsutil utility to change the RID Master FSMO. In the following code, enter the commands in bold.

```
C:\> ntdsutil
ntdsutil: roles
fsmo maintenance: connections
server connections: connect to server <server name>
server connections: quit
fsmo maintenance: transfer rid master
```

Click Yes in the role-transfer dialog box. Then, enter the commands in bold in the following code:

```
Server "titanic" knows about 5 roles Schema - CN=NTDS
Settings,CN=TITANIC,CN=Servers,CN=Default-First-Site-
Name,CN=Sites,CN=Configuration,DC=savilltech,DC=com Domain - CN=NTDS
Settings,CN=TITANIC,CN=Servers,CN=Default-First-Site-
Name,CN=Sites,CN=Configuration,DC=savilltech,DC=com PDC - CN=NTDS
Settings,CN=TITANIC,CN=Servers,CN=Default-First-Site-
Name,CN=Sites,CN=Configuration,DC=savilltech,DC=com RID - CN=NTDS
Settings,CN=TITANIC,CN=Servers,CN=Default-First-Site-
Name,CN=Sites,CN=Configuration,DC=savilltech,DC=com Infrastructure -
CN=NTDS Settings,CN=TITANIC,CN=Servers,CN=Default-First-Site-
Name,CN=Sites,CN=Configuration,DC=savilltech,DC=com

fsmo maintenance: quit
ntdsutil: quit
```

FAQ 15.45 How do I change the Schema Master FSMO?

To change the Schema Master Flexible Single-Master Operation (FSMO), you must use the Active Directory Schema Manager.

1. First, register the .DLL for the Microsoft Management Console (MMC) snap-in. Go to a command prompt and enter

```
regsvr32 schmmgmt.dll
```

2. Then, use the Microsoft Windows 2000 Resource Kit's Tools console to start the Schema Manager. Alternatively, create a custom MMC and add the Active Directory Schema snap-in to it. (From the Start menu, select Run and enter

```
MMC
```

3. From the Console menu, select Add/Remove Snap-in. Click Add and select Active Directory Schema.
4. Click Add, Close, and then OK.
5. Start the MMC Active Directory Schema snap-in on the domain controller (DC).
6. In the left-most pane, right-click Active Directory Schema and select Change Domain Controller from the context menu.
7. Enter the DC to connect to.
8. Right-click Active Directory Domains Schema and select Operations Master from the context menu.

   You'll see the name of the machine that holds the domain name operations FSMO role, as shown in Figure 15-27.

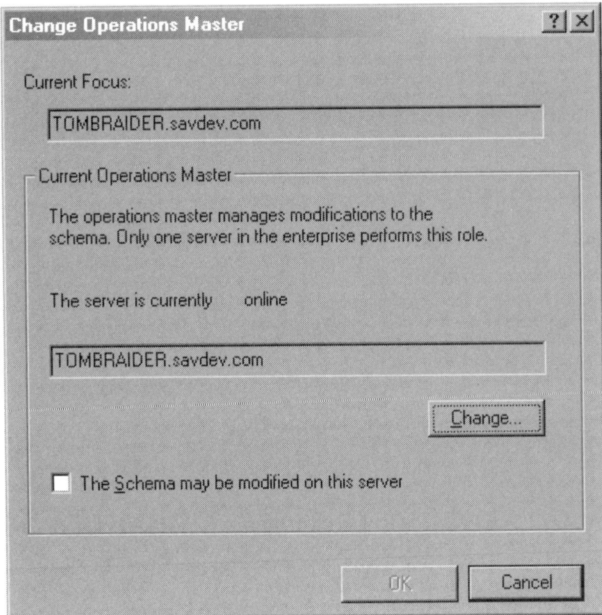

Figure 15-27 Changing the schema operations master

9. To make a change, click Change.
10. To set the Registry to allow changes to the schema, select the checkbox labeled "The Schema may be modified on this server". (Notice in Figure 15-27 that the machine is already the Schema Master.)
11. Click OK in the confirmation dialog box.

    Finally, you'll see a dialog box confirming the role change.

You can also modify the role from the command line. (In the following code, enter the commands in bold.)

```
C:\> ntdsutil
ntdsutil: roles
fsmo maintenance: connections
server connections: connect to server <server name>
server connections: quit
fsmo maintenance: transfer schema master
```

Click Yes in the role-transfer dialog box. Then, enter the commands in bold in the following code:

```
Server "titanic" knows about 5 roles Schema - CN=NTDS
Settings,CN=TITANIC,CN=Servers,CN=Default-First-Site-
Name,CN=Sites,CN=Configuration,DC=savilltech,DC=com Domain - CN=NTDS
Settings,CN=TITANIC,CN=Servers,CN=Default-First-Site-
Name,CN=Sites,CN=Configuration,DC=savilltech,DC=com PDC - CN=NTDS
Settings,CN=TITANIC,CN=Servers,CN=Default-First-Site-
Name,CN=Sites,CN=Configuration,DC=savilltech,DC=com RID - CN=NTDS
Settings,CN=TITANIC,CN=Servers,CN=Default-First-Site-Name,CN=Sites
,CN=Configuration,DC=savilltech,DC=com Infrastructure - CN=NTDS
Settings,CN=TITANIC,CN=Servers,CN=Default-First-Site-
Name,CN=Sites,CN=Configuration,DC=savilltech,DC=com

fsmo maintenance: quit
ntdsutil: quit
```

FAQ 15.46 How do I change the PDC Emulator FSMO?

To modify the role, perform the following steps.

1. Start the Microsoft Management Console (MMC) Active Directory Users and Computers snap-in on the domain controller (DC). (From the Start

menu, select Programs > Administrative Tools > Active Directory Users and Computers.)

2. In the left-most pane, right-click the domain and select Connect to Domain Controller.
3. Select the DC you want to make the Flexible Single-Master Operation (FSMO) role owner and click OK
4. Right-click the domain again and select Operations Master from the context menu.
5. Select the PDC tab.
6. You'll see the name of the machine that holds the PDC Emulator FSMO role.
7. To make a change, click Change.
8. Click OK in the confirmation dialog box.

   Finally, you'll see a dialog box confirming the role change.

You can also use the Ntdsutil utility to change the PDC Emulator FSMO. In the following code, enter the commands in bold:

```
C:\> ntdsutil
ntdsutil: roles
fsmo maintenance: connections
server connections: connect to server <server name>
server connections: quit
fsmo maintenance: transfer pdc
```

Click Yes in the role-transfer dialog box. Then, enter the commands in bold in the following code:

```
Server "titanic" knows about 5 roles Schema - CN=NTDS
Settings,CN=TITANIC,CN=Servers,CN=Default-First-Site-
Name,CN=Sites,CN=Configuration,DC=savilltech,DC=com Domain - CN=NTDS
Settings,CN=TITANIC,CN=Servers,CN=Default-First-Site-
Name,CN=Sites,CN=Configuration,DC=savilltech,DC=com PDC - CN=NTDS
Settings,CN=TITANIC,CN=Servers,CN=Default-First-Site-
Name,CN=Sites,CN=Configuration,DC=savilltech,DC=com RID - CN=NTDS
Settings,CN=TITANIC,CN=Servers,CN=Default-First-Site-
Name,CN=Sites,CN=Configuration,DC=savilltech,DC=com Infrastructure -
CN=NTDS Settings,CN=TITANIC,CN=Servers,CN=Default-First-Site-
Name,CN=Sites,CN=Configuration,DC=savilltech,DC=com

fsmo maintenance: quit
ntdsutil: quit
```

FAQ 15.47 How do I change the Infrastructure Master FSMO?

To modify the role, perform the following steps:

1. Start the Microsoft Management Console (MMC) Active Directory Users and Computers snap-in on the domain controller (DC). (From the Start menu, select Programs, Administrative Tools > Active Directory Users and Computers.)
2. In the left-most pane, right-click the domain and select Connect to Domain Controller.
3. Select the DC you want to make the FSMO role owner and click OK.
4. Right-click the domain again and select Operations Master from the context menu.
5. Select the Infrastructure tab. You'll see the name of the machine that holds the infrastructure FSMO role.
6. To make a change, click Change.
7. Click OK in the confirmation dialog box.

   Finally, you'll see a dialog box confirming the role change.

You can also use the Ntdsutil utility to change the Infrastructure Master FSMO. In the following code, enter the commands in bold:

```
C:\> ntdsutil
ntdsutil: roles
fsmo maintenance: connections
server connections: connect to server <server name>
server connections: quit
fsmo maintenance: transfer infrastructure master
```

Click Yes in the role-transfer dialog box. Then, enter the commands in bold in the following code:

```
Server "titanic" knows about 5 roles Schema - CN=NTDS
Settings,CN=TITANIC,CN=Servers,CN=Default-First-Site-
Name,CN=Sites,CN=Configuration,DC=savilltech,DC=com Domain - CN=NTDS
Settings,CN=TITANIC,CN=Servers,CN=Default-First-Site-
Name,CN=Sites,CN=Configuration,DC=savilltech,DC=com PDC - CN=NTDS
Settings,CN=TITANIC,CN=Servers,CN=Default-First-Site-
Name,CN=Sites,CN=Configuration,DC=savilltech,DC=com RID - CN=NTDS
Settings,CN=TITANIC,CN=Servers,CN=Default-First-Site-
Name,CN=Sites,CN=Configuration,DC=savilltech,DC=com Infrastructure -
```

```
CN=NTDS Settings,CN=TITANIC,CN=Servers,CN=Default-First-Site-
Name,CN=Sites,CN=Configuration,DC=savilltech,DC=com

fsmo maintenance: quit
ntdsutil: quit
```

FAQ 15.48 How do I change the Domain Naming Master FSMO?

To modify the role, make sure the machine is a Global Catalog (GC). Then, perform the following steps:

1. Start the Microsoft Management Console (MMC) Active Directory Domains and Trusts snap-in on the domain controller (DC). (From the Start menu, select Programs > Administrative Tools > Active Directory Domains and Trusts.)
2. In the left-most pane, right-click Active Directory Domains and Trusts and select Connect to Domain Controller from the context menu.
3. Enter the DC to connect to and click OK.
4. Right-click Active Directory Domains and Trusts and select Operations Master from the context menu. You'll see the name of the machine that holds the domain name operations FSMO role.
5. To make a change, click Change.
6. Click OK in the confirmation dialog box. Finally, you'll see a dialog box confirming the role change.

You can also use the Ntdsutil utility to change the Domain Naming Master FSMO. In the following code, enter the commands in bold:

```
C:\> ntdsutil
ntdsutil: roles
fsmo maintenance: connections
server connections: connect to server <server name>
server connections: quit
fsmo maintenance: transfer domain naming master
```

Click Yes in the role-transfer dialog box. Then, enter the commands in bold in the following code:

```
Server "titanic" knows about 5 roles Schema - CN=NTDS
Settings,CN=TITANIC,CN=Servers,CN=Default-First-Site-Name,
```

```
CN=Sites,CN=Configuration,DC=savilltech,DC=com Domain - CN=NTDS
Settings,CN=TITANIC,CN=Servers,CN=Default-First-Site-
Name,CN=Sites,CN=Configuration,DC=savilltech,DC=com PDC - CN=NTDS
Settings,CN=TITANIC,CN=Servers,CN=Default-First-Site-
Name,CN=Sites,CN=Configuration,DC=savilltech,DC=com RID - CN=NTDS
Settings,CN=TITANIC,CN=Servers,CN=Default-First-Site-
Name,CN=Sites,CN=Configuration,DC=savilltech,DC=com Infrastructure -
CN=NTDS Settings,CN=TITANIC,CN=Servers,CN=Default-First-Site-
Name,CN=Sites,CN=Configuration,DC=savilltech,DC=com

fsmo maintenance: quit
ntdsutil: quit
```

FAQ 15.49 How can I find the current FSMO role holders in a domain/forest?

The five Flexible Single Master of Object (FSMO) roles are Schema Master, Domain Naming Master, Relative Identifier (RID) Master, PDC Master, and Infrastructure Master.

You can use a GUI to find the FSMO role holders, but you need to perform several sets of steps (for this approach, see Q234790 at http://support.microsoft.com/support/kb/articles/Q234/7/90.ASP).

However, you can use other approaches to reduce the number of steps that the GUI requires to find the current FSMO role holders. First, you can use the command file DUMPFSMOS.CMD from the Win2K Server Resource Kit. This command uses the built-in NTDSUTIL.EXE, which shows you all the FSMO role owners.

To find the current FSMO role holders, you simply execute the dumpfsmos command on a domain. For example, you could type the following command:

```
dumpfsmos.cmd savilltech.com
```

When the following information appears on the screen, find the line that reads "Server 'savilltech.com' knows about 5 roles," and read the lines below it to find information about each FSMO role holder.

```
Ntdsutil: roles
fsmo maintenance: Connections
server connections: Connect to server savilltech.com
Binding to savilltech.com ...
Connected to savilltech.com using credentials of locally logged on
user
```

```
server connections: Quit
fsmo maintenance: select Operation Target
select operation target: List roles for connected server
Server "savilltech.com" knows about 5 roles
Schema - CN=NTDS Settings,CN=TITANIC-DC,CN=Servers,CN=Default-First-
Site-Name,CN=Sites,CN=Configuration,DC=savilltech,DC=com
Domain - CN=NTDS Settings,CN=TITANIC-DC,CN=Servers,CN=Default-First-
Site-Name,CN=Sites,CN=Configuration,DC=savilltech,DC=com
PDC - CN=NTDS Settings,CN=TITANIC-DC,CN=Servers,CN=Default-First-
Site-
Name,CN=Sites,CN=Configuration,DC=savilltech,DC=com
RID - CN=NTDS Settings,CN=TITANIC-DC,CN=Servers,CN=Default-First-
Site-
Name,CN=Sites,CN=Configuration,DC=savilltech,DC=com
Infrastructure - CN=NTDS Settings,CN=TITANIC-DC,CN=Servers,
CN=Default-
First-Site-Name,CN=Sites,CN=Configuration,DC=savilltech,DC=com
select operation target: Quit
fsmo maintenance: Quit
Ntdsutil: Quit
Disconnecting from savilltech.com ...
```

You can also manually execute the NTDSUTIL.EXE tool by performing the following steps:

1. Click Start > Run. Type **cmd** in the Open box and press Enter.
2. Type **ntdsutil** and press Enter.
3. Type **domain management** and press Enter.
4. Type **connections** and press Enter.
5. Type **connect to server [server name]** and press Enter.
6. Type **quit** and press Enter.
7. Type **select operation target** and press Enter.
8. Type **list roles for connected server** and then press Enter.

Sample output from the command follows with the text you type shown in bold. Following the line that reads "Server 'titanic-dc' knows about 5 roles," you'll find information about your FSMO role holders.

```
C:\>ntdsutil
ntdsutil: domain management
domain management: connections
server connections: connect to server titanic-dc
Binding to titanic-dc ...
```

```
Connected to titanic-dc using credentials of locally logged on user
server connections: quit
domain management: select operation target
select operation target: list roles for connected server
Server "titanic-dc" knows about 5 roles
Schema - CN=NTDS Settings,CN=TITANIC-DC,CN=Servers,CN=Default-First-
Site-Name,CN=Sites,CN=Configuration,DC=savilltech,DC=com
Domain - CN=NTDS Settings,CN=TITANIC-DC,CN=Servers,CN=Default-First-
Site-Name,CN=Sites,CN=Configuration,DC=savilltech,DC=com
PDC - CN=NTDS Settings,CN=TITANIC-DC,CN=Servers,CN=Default-First-
Site-
Name,CN=Sites,CN=Configuration,DC=savilltech,DC=com
RID - CN=NTDS Settings,CN=TITANIC-DC,CN=Servers,CN=Default-First-
Site-
Name,CN=Sites,CN=Configuration,DC=savilltech,DC=com
Infrastructure - CN=NTDS Settings,CN=TITANIC-DC,CN=Servers,
CN=Default-
First-Site-Name,CN=Sites,CN=Configuration,DC=savilltech,DC=com
select operation target: quit
domain management: quit
ntdsutil: quit
Disconnecting from titanic-dc ...
```

A third option for finding the current FSMO role holders is to use the dcdiag utility, which you can find in the Support/Tools folder of the Win2K Support Tools. To use the dcdiag utility, type the following command:

```
dcdiag /test:Knowsofroleholders /v
```

Sample output for the command appears follows. You'll find information about your FSMO role holders below the line that reads "Starting test: KnowsOfRoleHolders."

```
DC Diagnosis
Performing initial setup:
* Verifing that the local machine titanic-dc, is a DC.
* Connecting to directory service on server titanic-dc.
* Collecting site info.
* Identifying all servers.
* Found 1 DC(s). Testing 1 of them.
Done gathering initial info.

Doing initial non skippeable tests
```

```
Testing server: Default-First-Site-Name\TITANIC-DC
Starting test: Connectivity
* Active Directory LDAP Services Check
* Active Directory RPC Services Check
......................... TITANIC-DC passed test Connectivity

Doing primary tests

Testing server: Default-First-Site-Name\TITANIC-DC
Test omitted by user request: Replications
Test omitted by user request: Topology
Test omitted by user request: CutoffServers
Test omitted by user request: NCSecDesc
Test omitted by user request: NetLogons
Test omitted by user request: Advertising
Starting test: KnowsOfRoleHolders
Role Schema Owner = CN=NTDS Settings,CN=TITANIC-DC,CN=Servers,
CN=Defaul
t-First-Site-Name,CN=Sites,CN=Configuration,DC=savilltech,DC=com
Role Domain Owner = CN=NTDS Settings,CN=TITANIC-DC,CN=Servers,
CN=Defaul
t-First-Site-Name,CN=Sites,CN=Configuration,DC=savilltech,DC=com
Role PDC Owner = CN=NTDS Settings,CN=TITANIC-DC,CN=Servers,
CN=Default-F
irst-Site-Name,CN=Sites,CN=Configuration,DC=savilltech,DC=com
Role Rid Owner = CN=NTDS Settings,CN=TITANIC-DC,CN=Servers,
CN=Default-F
irst-Site-Name,CN=Sites,CN=Configuration,DC=savilltech,DC=com
Role Infrastructure Update Owner = CN=NTDS Settings,CN=TITANIC-DC,
CN=Se
rvers,CN=Default-First-Site-
Name,CN=Sites,CN=Configuration,DC=savilltech,DC=com
......................... TITANIC-DC passed test KnowsOfRoleHolders
Test omitted by user request: RidManager
Test omitted by user request: MachineAccount
Test omitted by user request: Services
Test omitted by user request: OutboundSecureChannels
Test omitted by user request: ObjectsReplicated
Test omitted by user request: frssysvol
Test omitted by user request: kccevent
Test omitted by user request: systemlog
```

```
Running enterprise tests on : savilltech.com
Test omitted by user request: Intersite
Test omitted by user request: FsmoCheck
```

FAQ 15.50 Why can't I add a Windows NT 4.0 BDC to my Windows 2000 domain?

Although Windows 2000 supports Windows NT 4.0 BDCs, you'll run into problems if you try to create an NT 4.0 BDC machine account. You'll receive the error message "The Machine Account for This Computer either does not exist or is inaccessible." If you try to use Srvmgr to add the computer account from an existing Windows NT 4.0-based BDC, you'll receive the error message "The Network Request is not supported."

Your Win2K-based PDC will log the following error message:

```
Source: SAM
EVENT ID: 12298
DESCRIPTION:The Account "COMPUTER$" Cannot be converted to be a
domain controller account as its object class attribute in the
directory is not a computer or is not derived from a computer. If
this is caused by an attempt to install a pre-Windows 2000 Domain,
then you should recreate the account for the domain controller with
the correct object class.
```

To work around this problem, use Win2K's Srvmgr tool to create the account.

FAQ 15.51 How do I remove a nonexistent domain from Active Directory?

Windows 2000 tracks each domain in the metadata. If you remove all the domain controllers (DCs) for a domain and you don't select the option "This is the last domain controller in the domain," when you run DCPROMO to demote the DC to a normal server, DCPROMO won't clean up the domain information, and the server's domain information will remain.

You can use the utility NTDSUTIL to remove a domain from the metadata. (In the following code, enter the commands in bold.)

```
ntdsutil
ntdsutil: metadata cleanup
metadata cleanup: connections
```

Connect to a server or domain (e.g., the parent domain) that recognizes the domain you want to delete. (In the following code, enter the commands in bold.)

```
server connections: connect to server titanic
Binding to titanic ...
Connected to titanic using credentials of locally logged on user
server connections: quit
metadata cleanup: select operation target
```

Next, select the domain you want to delete. (In the following code, enter the commands in bold.)

```
select operation target: list domains
Found 3 domain(s)
0 - DC=savilltech,DC=com
1 - DC=dev,DC=savilltech,DC=com
2 - DC=deleteme,DC=savilltech,DC=com
select operation target: select domain 2
Site - CN=London,CN=Sites,CN=Configuration,DC=savilltech,DC=com
Domain - DC=deleteme,DC=savilltech,DC=com
No current server
No current Naming Context
select operation target: quit
metadata cleanup: remove selected domain
```

In the confirmation dialog box, which is shown in Figure 15-28, click Yes.

Close the utility. (In the following code, enter the commands in bold.)

```
"DC=deleteme,DC=savilltech,DC=com" removed from server "titanic"
metadata cleanup: quit
ntdsutil: quit
Disconnecting from titanic ...
```

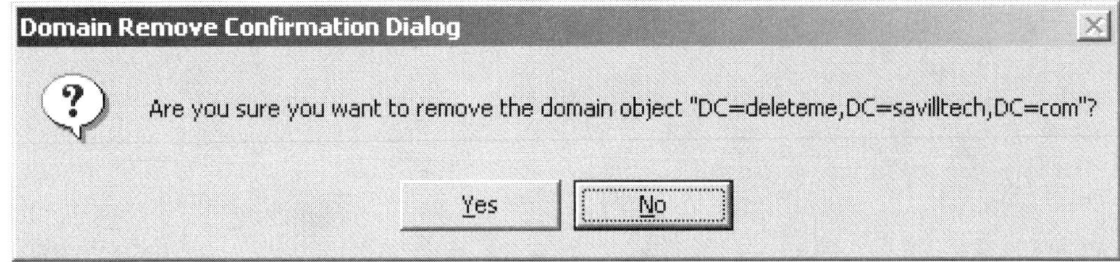

Figure 15-28 Confirming domain deletion (with a name like that are we surprised!)

FAQ 15.52 I canceled a domain controller demotion. Why can't I demote the domain controller now?

Once you start a domain controller (DC) demotion, you don't have an option to cancel it; however, you might have stopped the demotion via the Task Manager or by getting the process ID with tlist, then using the kill command. Neither approach is supported, and if you try to run DCPROMO again, you might get the following error message (depending on the stage the DCPROMO process was in when you stopped it):

```
Active Directory is already being installed or removed on this
computer. That operation must finish before another may be
attempted.
```

The only way to remove the DC information is to manually remove it using NTDSUTIL. See FAQ 15.53 for details.

FAQ 15.53 How do I remove a nonexistent domain controller?

Windows 2000 tracks each domain controller (DC) in the metadata. If you remove a DC (e.g., through reinstallation or hardware removal), and you don't run DCPROMO to clean up the DC's metadata, connection objects will remain.

You can use the utility NTDSUTIL to remove a server from the metadata. (In the following code, enter the commands in bold.)

```
ntdsutil
ntdsutil: metadata cleanup
metadata cleanup: select operation target
```

Next, you must connect to a server. In my example, I select a domain to accomplish this task. (In the following code, enter the commands in bold.)

```
select operation target: connections
server connections: connect to domain savilltech.com
Binding to \\TITANIC.savilltech.com ...
Connected to \\TITANIC.savilltech.com using credentials of locally
logged on user
server connections: quit
```

Next, you must select a site, a server (i.e., the server you want to delete), and the domain the server is in. The order isn't important. (In the following code, enter the commands in bold.)

```
select operation target: list sites
Found 2 site(s)
0 - CN=London,CN=Sites,CN=Configuration,DC=savilltech,DC=com
1 - CN=Kent,CN=Sites,CN=Configuration,DC=savilltech,DC=com
select operation target: select site 0
Site - CN=London,CN=Sites,CN=Configuration,DC=savilltech,DC=com
No current domain
No current server
No current Naming Context
select operation target: list servers in site
Found 4 server(s)
0 - CN=TITANIC,CN=Servers,CN=London,CN=Sites,CN=Configuration,
DC=savilltech,DC=com
1 - CN=TITUS,CN=Servers,CN=London,CN=Sites,CN=Configuration,
DC=savilltech,DC=com
2 - CN=MORPHEUS,CN=Servers,CN=London,CN=Sites,CN=Configuration,
DC=savilltech,DC=com
3 - CN=TRINITY,CN=Servers,CN=London,CN=Sites,CN=Configuration,
DC=savilltech,DC=com
select operation target: select server 2
Site - CN=London,CN=Sites,CN=Configuration,DC=savilltech,DC=com
No current domain
Server - CN=MORPHEUS,CN=Servers,CN=London,CN=Sites,CN=Configuration,
DC=savilltech,DC=com
DSA object - CN=NTDS
Settings,CN=MORPHEUS,CN=Servers,CN=London,CN=Sites,CN=Configuration,
DC=savilltech,DC=com
DNS host name - MORPHEUS.deleteme.savilltech.com
Computer object - CN=MORPHEUS,OU=Domain Controllers,DC=deleteme,
DC=savilltech,DC=com
No current Naming Context
select operation target: list domains
Found 3 domain(s)
0 - DC=savilltech,DC=com
1 - DC=dev,DC=savilltech,DC=com
2 - DC=deleteme,DC=savilltech,DC=com
select operation target: select domain 0
Site - CN=London,CN=Sites,CN=Configuration,DC=savilltech,DC=com
Domain - DC=savilltech,DC=com
```

```
Server - CN=MORPHEUS,CN=Servers,CN=London,CN=Sites,CN=Configuration,
DC=savilltech,DC=com
DSA object - CN=NTDS
Settings,CN=MORPHEUS,CN=Servers,CN=London,CN=Sites,CN=Configuration,
DC=savilltech,DC=com
DNS host name - MORPHEUS.deleteme.savilltech.com
Computer object - CN=MORPHEUS,OU=Domain Controllers,DC=deleteme,
DC=savilltech,DC=com
No current Naming Context
select operation target: quit
```

Next, remove the server you selected. (In the following code, enter the command in bold.)

```
metadata cleanup: remove selected server
```

In the confirmation dialog box, which is shown in Figure 15-29, click Yes. Close the utility. (In the following code, enter the commands in bold.)

```
"CN=MORPHEUS,CN=Servers,CN=London,CN=Sites,CN=Configuration,
DC=savilltech,DC=com
" removed from server "\\TITANIC.savilltech.com"
metadata cleanup: quit
ntdsutil: quit
Disconnecting from \\TITANIC.savilltech.com ...
```

Finally, you need to delete the server from the Microsoft Management Console (MMC) Active Directory Sites and Servers snap-in.

1. Select Programs > Administrative Tools > Active Directory Sites and Services from the Start menu.

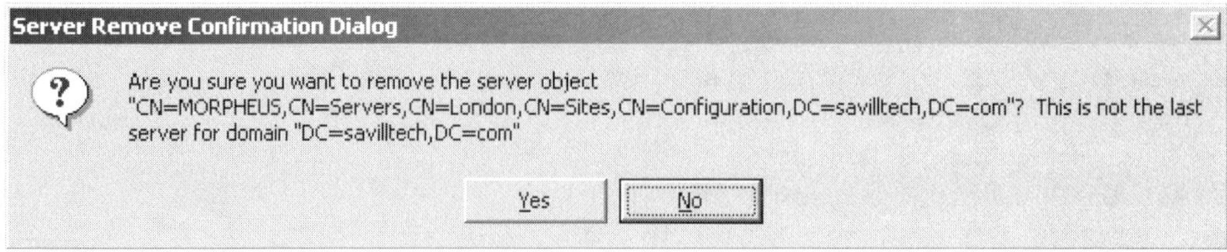

Figure 15-29 Confirming a server delete

2. Expand the Sites branch, select the site, expand the Services container, right-click the server, and select Delete.
3. Click Yes in the confirmation dialog box.

I have been informed of a possible problem with this if SP2 is installed, in which case, perform this procedure on a box without SP2 installed.

FAQ 15.54 Why can't I create a Kerberos-based trust between two domains in different forests?

When you manually create trusts, you can select one of two authentication protocols.

- Kerberos—The Kerberos V5 authentication protocol is the default authentication service for Windows 2000. You use it to verify that a user/host is who it says it is. This protocol is used for trusts between domains in a tree and between the root domains in a forest.
- NT LAN Manager (NTLM)—The NTLM authentication protocol is the default for network authentication in Windows NT 4.0 and earlier, but Win2K still supports it (although not as the default). NTLM is a challenge/response authentication protocol.

A transitive Kerberos-based trust links domains **within** a forest. Thus, when you create a trust between two domains in different forests, you can select only NTLM because Kerberos isn't available for cross-forest trust relationships. This limitation isn't a Kerberos one, but a limitation of the Microsoft implementation. If you use a third-party Kerberos implementation (e.g., MIT), you can use Kerberos for cross-forest trusts.

FAQ 15.55 How do I modify the number of Active Directory objects to search?

By default, AD searches 10,000 objects at a time. This policy affects all browse displays associated with AD (e.g., those in Local Users and Groups), the Microsoft Management Console (MMC) Active Directory Users and Computers snap-in, and the dialog boxes you use to set permissions for user or group objects in AD. As your organization grows, you might need to change the number of objects to search.

To set the number for a Group Policy Object:

1. Start the MMC Active Directory Users and Computers snap-in. (Select Programs > Administrative Tools > Active Directory Users and Computers from the Start menu.)
2. Right-click the container and select Properties.
3. Select the Group Policy tab.
4. Select the Group Policy Object and select Edit.
5. Select the User Configuration branch and expand Administrative Templates > Desktop > Active Directory.
6. Double-click Maximum size of Active Directory searches.
7. Select Enabled and set the number (e.g., 20000), as shown in Figure 15-30.
8. Click Apply.

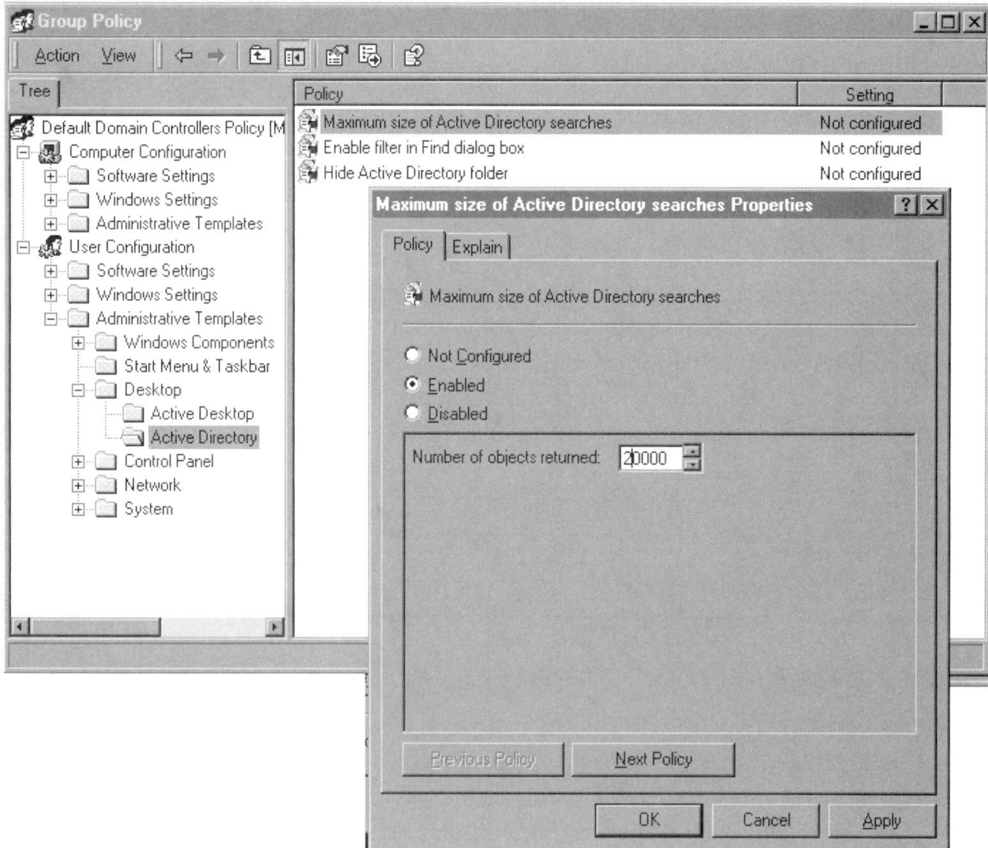

Figure 15-30 Modifying the number of Active Directory search results via Policy

9. Click OK.
10. Close the Group Policy editor.

To edit the Registry to set the number for a user:

1. Start Regedit.
2. Go to the HKEY_CURRENT_USER\Software\Policies\Microsoft Registry entry.
3. From the Edit menu, select New > Key.
4. Enter

   ```
   Windows
   ```

5. Select the Windows key, and from the Edit menu, select New > Key.
6. Enter

   ```
   Directory UI
   ```

7. Go to the Directory UI key, and from the Edit menu, select New > DWORD Value.
8. Enter

   ```
   QueryLimit
   ```

   and press Enter.
9. Double-click the new value and set the decimal value.
10. Click OK.
11. Close the Registry editor.

For both methods, the change will take effect when the user logs on the next time.

FAQ 15.56 How do I configure Group Policy to apply folder redirection settings to users who access the local network remotely?

By default, Windows 2000 doesn't apply Group Policy folder redirection settings to users on slow network connections. To modify this behavior, perform the following steps:

1. Start Group Policy editor (GPE) and load the policy in question (you can also right-click the Active Directory—AD—container that the policy applies to, select Properties, select the Group Policy tab, and click Edit).
2. Navigate to Computer Configuration > Administrative Templates > System > Group Policy.
3. Double-click Folder Redirection policy processing.
4. Select Enabled.
5. Select the Allow processing across a slow network connection checkbox (see Figure 15-31). (You can also double-click Group Policy slow link detection to set what constitutes a slow link.)
6. Click OK.

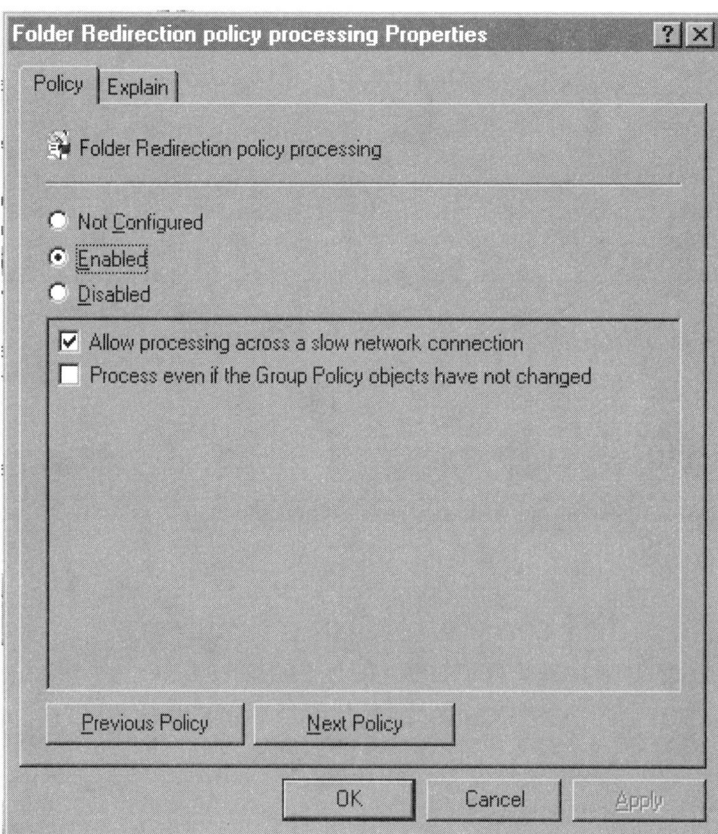

Figure 15-31 Folder Redirection options

7. Select Enabled to set the connection speed (500Kbps by default).
8. Click OK.
9. Close GPE.

FAQ 15.57 How can I replicate logon scripts between Windows 2000 and Windows NT 4.0 domain controllers?

NT 4.0 LAN Manager Replication (LMRepl) uses directory replication to replicate data from one export machine (%systemroot%\system32\Repl\export) to the import folders of the other domain controllers (DCs) (%systemroot%\system32\Repl\import), which then share the data as the Netlogon share. Win2K File Replication Service (FRS) uses the SYSVOL volume (%systemroot%\SYSVOL\sysvol), which replicates among DCs automatically. The Netlogon share points to %systemroot%\SYSVOL\sysvol\<domain name>\SCRIPTS.

The different system approaches are incompatible. Therefore, you must manually configure a script to periodically copy files from one of the Win2K Netlogon shares to the NT 4.0 export machine, which can then disseminate the files to the other NT 4.0 DCs. The Windows 2000 Resource Kit supplies LBRIDGE.CMD, a template for this script that can use either Xcopy or Robocopy to perform the file operations.

If you don't configure such a script, your NT 4.0 DCs will have out-of-date logon scripts.

FAQ 15.58 How can I stop password changes from being pushed to the PDC FSMO over WAN links?

By default, when someone changes a password, the change occurs on the local domain controller (DC), but Windows also pushes the change to the PDC Flexible Single-Master Operation (FSMO) role holder because such changes take time to replicate around the domain. If the change wasn't pushed to the FSMO role holder and someone tried to log on with the new password that wasn't replicated, the logon would fail. To avoid this kind of failure, Windows attempts to authenticate on the PDC FSMO role holder.

To prevent the system from pushing password changes over slow WAN links, make the following change on the relevant DCs:

1. Start REGEDIT.EXE.
2. Go to HKEY_LOCAL_MACHINE\SYSTEM\CurrentControlSet\Services\Netlogon\Parameters.
3. From the Edit menu, select New > DWORD Value.
4. Enter a name of **AvoidPdcOnWan** and press Enter.
5. Double-click AvoidPdcOnWan and set it to 1.
6. Click OK.
7. Close Regedit.

FAQ 15.59 How can I use the Registry to configure Group Policy update times?

You usually configure Group Policy update times under the Computer Configuration\Administrative Templates\System\Group Policy and the User Configuration\Administrative Templates\System\Group Policy branches; however, you can also directly set the Registry to configure Group Policy update times by performing the following steps:

1. Start REGEDIT.EXE.
2. Go to HKEY_LOCAL_MACHINE\SOFTWARE\Policies\Microsoft\Windows\System to set Computer refresh. Or, alternatively, go to HKEY_CURRENT_USER\Software\Policies\Microsoft\Windows\System to set User refresh.
3. Create a DWORD value with a name of GroupPolicyRefreshTime and set it to a number between 0 and 648000 minutes.
4. Create a DWORD value with a name of GroupPolicyRefreshTimeOffset and set it to a number between 0 and 1440 minutes. (You specify an offset value to prevent many clients from trying to refresh at the same time.)
5. Close Regedit.

FAQ 15.60 Why can't I create an organizational unit and child domain with the same name from one parent?

Although X.500 lets an organizational unit (OU) and child domain share a name, Active Directory (AD) doesn't. Shared names in AD cause problems with relative distinguished names (RDNs). If you try to create an OU and give it the same name as a child domain that already exists, you'll get the error message

```
Active Directory

Windows cannot create the object because: An attempt was made to add
an object to the directory with a name that was already in use.
Name-related properties on this object might now be out of sync.
Contact your network administrator.
```

If you try to create a child domain and give it the same name as an OU that already exists, you'll get the error message

```
Active Directory Installation Failed

The operation failed because: The Directory Service failed to create
the object CN=Sales, CN=Partitions, CN=Configuration, DC=Savilltech,
DC=Com. Please check for possible system errors. "The directory
service is busy"
```

Microsoft is aware of these restrictions, and no work arounds exist.

FAQ 15.61 I've upgraded one of my Windows NT 4.0 DCs to Windows 2000. Why do all of my Win2K Professional clients use the Win2K DC for authentication?

When you upgrade to Win2K, you should upgrade at least two domain controllers (DCs). Then, if you have to stop one Win2K DC, the other Win2K DC can act as the PDC to older NT 4.0 DCs. If you have only one Win2K DC and you have to stop it, you have to promote an NT 4.0 BDC to PDC. Doing so loses all AD information, and you can't bring the Win2K DC back into the domain because a Win2K DC can't act as a BDC to an NT 4.0 PDC.

The behavior you're encountering is actually a design "feature." The idea behind this feature was that the Win2K clients understand group policy concepts, so—where possible—they should log onto a Win2K DC. However, this feature causes the Win2K clients to use the Win2K DC for **all** authentication, which overloads the machine. This has been fixed in Service Pack 1 for Windows 2000.

FAQ 15.62 How can I move the Active Directory log files?

Along with the NTDS.DIT file, the AD keeps several log files that you might want to move to a faster disk. To do so, perform the following steps:

1. Restart the domain controller (DC).
2. Press F8 at the Startup menu when the system displays the list of OSs.
3. Select Directory Services Restore Mode.
4. Select the appropriate installation. If more than one exists, and then log on as an administrator at the logon prompt.
5. Start a command prompt (Start > Run > CMD.EXE).
6. Start the NTDS utility, NTDSUTIL.EXE.
7. At the ntdsutil prompt, type **files** as follows:

   ```
   ntdsutil: files
   ```

8. At the file maintenance prompt, type the following:

   ```
   file maintenance: move logs to [new location for file]
   ```

9. To view the log files, at the file maintenance prompt, type **info**:

   ```
   file maintenance: info
   ```

10. Type **quit** twice to return to a C prompt.
11. Restart the computer in Normal mode.

FAQ 15.63 How do I enable circular logging for Active Directory?

AD can record sequential or circular logs. The default logging method is sequential. Sequential log files aren't overwritten with new data. These files grow until they reach a specified size. After all the transactions in a log file are committed to the database, the log file is unnecessary. AD's garbage-collection process deletes unnecessary log files every 12 hours by default. If your server doesn't stay up longer than 12 hours between reboots, AD can't clean up old log files. Eventually, the files will use all your available disk space.

Circular logs overwrite transactions at specific intervals. Some administrators prefer circular logging because this method helps minimize the amount of logged data the physical disk must store. To enable circular logging, you need to edit the Registry.

1. Start Regedt32.
2. Go to the HKEY_LOCAL_MACHINE\SYSTEM\CurrentControlSet\Services\NTDS\Parameters Registry entry.
3. If the value CircularLogging doesn't exist, select New > String value from the Edit menu and enter

   ```
   CircularLogging
   ```

4. Double-click CircularLogging and set the value to 1 to enable circular logging. (Setting the value to 0 disables circular logging and enables sequential log files.)
5. Close the Registry editor.
6. Reboot the machine to restart the Directory Service (DS) and make the change effective.

FAQ 15.64 How do I audit Active Directory?

You can configure AD auditing to produce successful and failed entries in the Directory Service (DS) event log.

1. Start the Microsoft Management Console (MMC) Active Directory Users and Computers snap-in. (Select Programs > Administrative Tools > Active Directory Users and Computers from the Start menu.)
2. From the View menu, select Advanced Features.

3. Expand the domain, right-click the Domain Controllers container, and select Properties from the context menu.
4. Select the Group Policy tab.
5. Select Default Domain Controllers Policy and click Edit.
6. Expand the Computer Configuration branch, the Windows Settings branch, the Security Settings branch, and the Local Policies branch.
7. Select Audit Policy.
8. The right-most window will show auditing levels. Double-click Audit Directory Service Access.
9. Select the relevant checkboxes (e.g., Audit successful attempts, Audit failed attempts), as shown in Figure 15-32. Click OK.
10. Close the Group Policy window.
11. In the main Domain Controllers Properties dialog box, click OK.
12. Close the Active Directory Users and Computers MMC snap-in.

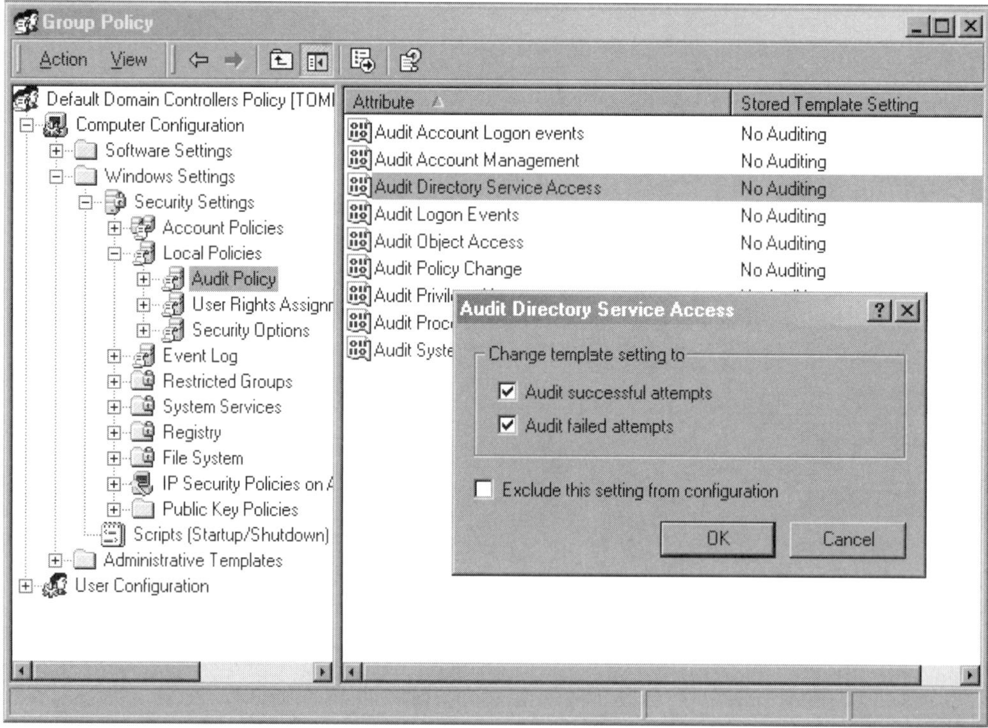

Figure 15-32 Directory Service audit options

You can use Event Viewer to view the logs in the Security log. Because domain controllers poll for policy changes every five minutes, the policy change might take as long as five minutes to take effect. Other domain controllers in the enterprise receive the changes after the five-minute interval, plus replication time.

FAQ 15.65 Why has my user group person icon's hair gone gray?

According to the Microsoft Knowledge Base, this behavior isn't a result of a stressed-out group but of a bug in Windows 2000 that results in the hair color changing from black to gray if a group has more than 500 users. Functionality doesn't change, and the hair-color change has no other effect (except that the group appears older and slightly more distinguished).

FAQ 15.66 How do I move objects within my forest?

You can use the Microsoft Windows 2000 Resource Kit's Movetree utility to move organizational units (OUs), users, or computers between domains in a forest. This capability is useful for consolidating domains or to reflect organizational restructuring.

You can't use Movetree to move certain objects, such as local and domain global groups. If you move the container that these objects are in, the utility places the objects in an orphan container in the source domain's LostAndFound container.

Movetree also doesn't move associated data, such as policies, profiles, logon scripts, and personal data. To move these items, use the Remote Administration Scripts tool to write custom scripts.

Movetree's syntax is

```
movetree [/start | /continue | /check] [/s SrcDSA] [/d DstDSA] [/sdn
SrcDN] [/ddn DstDN] [/u Domain\Username] [/p Password] [/quiet]
```

The following table describes each command:

/start	Starts a Movetree operation with the /check option by default. Use /startnocheck to start a Movetree operation without a check.
/continue	Continues a failed Movetree operation.
/check	Checks the whole tree before moving an object.
/s <SrcDSA>	Source server's fully qualified primary DNS name. Required.
/d <DstDSA>	Destination server's fully qualified primary DNS name. Required.
/sdn <SrcDN>	Source subtree's root distinguished name (DN). Required for /start and /check operations. Optional for /continue operations.
/ddn <DstDN>	Destination subtree's root DN. Relative distinguished name (RDN) plus destination parent DN. Required.
/u <Domain\UserName>	Domain name and user account name. Optional.
/p <Password>	Password. Optional.
/quiet	Quiet mode. Doesn't include screen output. Optional.

Run the Movetree utility in /check mode first, to perform a test without carrying out the action. You'll see any errors that will occur, and the utility will write these errors to the file MOVETREE.ERR in your current directory. If your test is OK, proceed with the /start option.

An example Movetree command is

```
movetree /check /s titanic.market.savilltech.com /d
pluto.legal.savilltech.com /sdn
OU=testing,DC=Market,DC=Savilltech,DC=COM /ddn
OU=test2,DC=Legal,DC=Savilltech,DC=COM
```

This command would move the OU testing from the domain market.savilltech.com to the OU test2 in the domain legal.savilltech.com.

15.67 How do I allow modifications to the schema?

The schema is extensible, which means that you can change it. However, modifying the schema is dangerous because doing so affects the entire domain forest. Microsoft warns against modifying the schema because changes to the schema cannot be undone.

If you insist on modifying the schema, you can use the GUI or edit the Registry. To use the GUI, you must first register the .DLL file for the Microsoft Management Console (MMC) snap-in. Go to a command prompt and enter

```
regsvr32 schmmgmt.dll
```

Then, use the Microsoft Windows 2000 Resource Kit's Tools console to start the Schema Manager. Alternatively, create a custom MMC to start the Schema Manager. Next, add the Active Directory Schema snap-in to the Schema Manager. From the Start menu, select Run and enter

```
MMC
```

From the Console menu, select Add/Remove Snap-in. Click Add and select Active Directory Schema. Finally, click Add, Close, and then OK.

1. Start the MMC Active Directory Schema snap-in on the domain controller (DC).
2. In the left-most pane, right-click Active Directory Schema, and select Operations Master from the context menu.
3. You'll see the name of the machine that holds the domain name operations Flexible Single-Master Operation (FSMO) role, as shown in Figure 15-33.

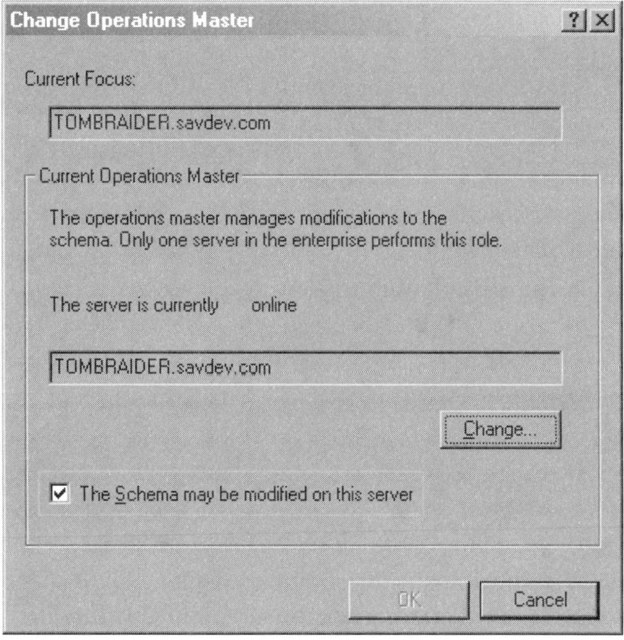

Figure 15-33 Enabling schema modification (Be careful!)

4. Select the Schema may be modified on this server checkbox.
5. Click OK in the confirmation dialog box.

Another way to modify the schema is to edit the Registry:

1. Start Regedit.
2. Go to the HKEY_LOCAL_MACHINE\SYSTEM\CurrentControlSet\Services\NTDS\Parameters Registry entry.
3. Double-click Schema Update Allowed (of type REG_DWORD).
4. Set the value to 1.
5. Click OK.
6. Close the Registry editor.

FAQ 15.68 How do I switch my Windows 2000 domain to native mode?

Windows 2000 domains have two modes: mixed and native. Mixed-mode domains let Windows NT 4.0 BDCs participate in a Win2K domain.

In a native mode domain, only Win2K-based domain controllers (DCs) can participate in the domain. In addition, NT 4.0-based BDCs can't act as DCs. Switching to native mode lets you use the new *universal security* groups, which you can nest inside one another (unlike cross domain global groups). NetBIOS-based clients can still use their NetBIOS domain names to log on, even in native mode.

To switch a Win2K domain to native mode, perform the following steps:

1. Start the Microsoft Management Console (MMC) Active Directory Domains and Trusts snap-in.
2. Right-click the domain you want to convert to native mode and select Properties.
3. Select the General tab.
4. Click Change Mode, as shown in Figure 15-34.
5. Click Yes in the confirmation dialog box.
6. Click Apply to return to the main dialog box.
7. Click OK.

Check all the DCs in the domain. If you can't contact a DC (e.g., if the DC is in a remote site and connects only periodically), the remote DC will switch to native mode the next time replication occurs.

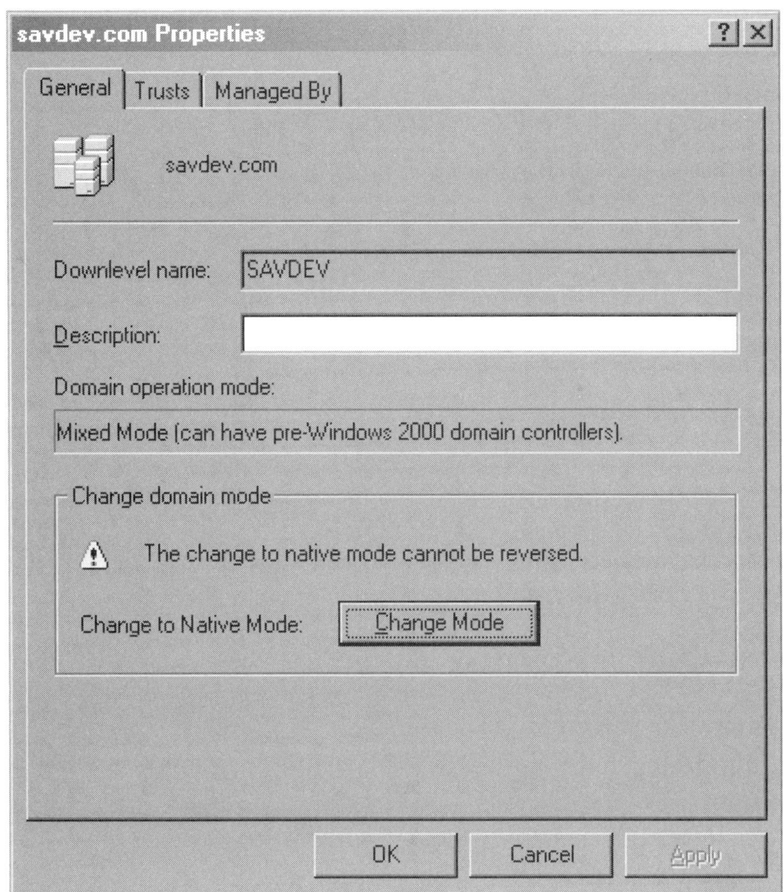

Figure 15-34 Switching the domain to native mode

15.69 How can I move the NTDS.DIT file?

The NTDS.DIT file contains the Active Directory (AD) data for your domain and is stored in the %systemroot%\ntds folder. This file can become very large. To improve performance, you might want to move this file to a faster drive. To do so, perform the following steps:

1. Restart the domain controller (DC).
2. Press F8 at the Startup menu when the system displays the list of OSs.
3. Select Directory Services Restore Mode.

4. Select the appropriate installation, if more than one exists, and then log on as an administrator at the logon prompt.
5. Start a command prompt (Start > Run > CMD.EXE).
6. Start the NTDS utility, NTDSUTIL.EXE.
7. At the ntdsutil prompt, type **files** as follows:

```
ntdsutil: files
```

8. At the file maintenance prompt, type the following:

```
file maintenance: move DB to
```

9. To view the database, at the file maintenance prompt, type **info** as follows:

```
file maintenance: info
```

10. To verify the integrity of the database at its new location, at the file maintenance prompt, type **integrity** as follows:

```
file maintenance: integrity
```

11. Type **quit** twice to return to a C prompt.
12. Restart the computer in Normal mode.

FAQ 15.70 Why is the size of the NTDS.DIT file different on different domain controllers?

The NTDS.DIT file contains Active Directory (AD) information, and because all domain controllers (DCs) replicate AD, you might expect the file to be the same size on all DCs. However, you might find differently sized files because the database file is created individually on each DC, and the data—not the database file—replicates. Thus, several factors can lead to files with different sizes:

- Over time, the database can become fragmented. Although objects are deleted while the database is online, you can't compact the database online (compacting requires a manual offline defragmentation).
- If a DC is a Global Catalog (GC), it contains information about objects of other domains in the forest, thus making it larger than non-GC servers.

- The displayed size of the NTDS.DIT file is the size of the file when you started the DC; if many objects are added and you restart one DC, that DC's NTDS.DIT file size will appear larger.

FAQ 15.71 How do I reset a machine account password?

Like user accounts, machine accounts in a domain have passwords that change automatically. The domain stores the previous and current passwords so that the previous password is accessible for authentication in case someone changes the current password but the domain controller hasn't yet fully replicated the password.

If a password changes twice, the computers that use the password might be unable to communicate. In this case, you would receive an error message (e.g., the error message "Access Denied" when Active Directory—AD—replication occurs). Passwords can also be out of sync during replication between domain controllers in the same domain.

You can manually change a machine account password. You must use the Microsoft Windows 2000 Resource Kit's Netdom tool rather than the Active Directory Users and Computers snap-in. Netdom is in Win2K's Support\Tools folder. To reset a machine account password, enter

```
netdom resetpwd /server:<servername> /userd:<username>\Administrator
/passwordd:*
```

After you enter the command, you'll see the following.

```
Type the password associated with the domain user:
The machine account password for the local machine has been
successfully reset.
The command completed successfully.
```

You need to run this Netdom command on the machine for which you want to change the password. The server must be a domain controller in the domain, and the user must have a domain account with administrative privileges over the machine account whose password you're changing.

You need to restart the machine for the password change to take effect. Simultaneously resetting the password on the local machine and a domain controller ensures that the two computers involved in the operation are synchronized, and starts AD replication so that other domain controllers receive the change.

FAQ 15.72 How can I let users search, but not browse, Active Directory?

You can use either a policy setting or the Registry to configure AD for browsing. To use the policy setting method, perform the following steps:

1. Open Group Policy with the Group Policy editor (GPE).
2. Navigate to User Configurations > Administrative Templates > Desktop > AD.
3. Double-click Hide Active Directory folder.
4. Select the Policy tab.
5. Click Enabled and click OK.
6. Close the policy.

To use the Registry to complete the same task, perform the following steps:

1. Start the Registry editor (e.g., REGEDIT.EXE).
2. Navigate to HKEY_CURRENT_USER\SOFTWARE\Policies\Microsoft.
3. If the Windows key doesn't exist, click Edit > New > Key to create the key.
4. Look for Directory UI under the Windows key, and if it doesn't exist, click Edit > New > Key to create the key.
5. From the Edit menu, select New > DWORD Value.
6. Enter a name of **HideDirectoryFolder** and press Enter.
7. Double-click the new value, set it to 1, and click OK.
8. Close the Registry editor.

FAQ 15.73 How does ntdsutil know it's in Directory Restore mode?

When you start the domain controller (DC) in Directory Restore mode, the DC sets the environment variable safeboot_option to dsrepair. If you want to check something in ntdsutil that is allowed only in Directory Restore mode, you can trick the program by typing the following statement at a command prompt:

```
set SAFEBOOT_OPTION=DSREPAIR
```

Don't use this approach on a live or important machine because it could result in system damage if you try to perform system modifications when the system isn't in Directory Restore mode.

FAQ 15.74 How can I prevent the OS from storing LAN Manager (LM) hashes in Active Directory and the SAM?

Both Windows XP and Windows 2000 support several authentication methods, including LAN Manager (LM), NT LAN Manager (NTLM), and NTLM version 2 (NTLMv2). LM stores passwords in a hashed format that's easy to crack. Starting with Win2K Service Pack 2 (SP2), Microsoft addressed this weakness by adding the ability to disable the storage of LM hashes.

To disable LM hashes in Win2K, perform the following steps:

1. Start the Registry editor (REGEDIT.EXE) on the domain controller (DC).
2. Navigate to HKEY_LOCAL_MACHINE\SYSTEM\CurrentControlSet\Control\Lsa.
3. From the Edit menu, select New > Key.
4. Enter a name of **NoLMHash**, set the value to 1, and press Enter.
5. Close the Registry editor.
6. Restart the computer for the change to take effect.

To disable LM hashes in XP, perform the previously described steps 1 and 2. At step 3, from the Edit menu, select New > DWORD Value. Complete the process by performing steps 4 through 6. This change won't take effect until each user changes his or her password.

In XP, you can also use Group Policy (GP) to disable LM hashes under Computer Configuration\Windows Settings\Security Settings\Local Policies\Security Options. To change the settings for this policy, locate the Network Security policy entitled "Do not store LAN Manager hash value on next password change." Be aware that if you set this option, some components that rely on LM hashes (e.g., the Windows 9x change password operation, Win9x client authentication if you don't have the Directory Services client pack installed) might not work as expected.

15.75 How do I publish a shared folder in Active Directory?

The usual method of connecting to a shared folder is to either browse a specific machine for visible machines (ones without a $ at the end) or know the complete share Uniform Naming Convention (UNC) in advance. However, you can publish shared folders to Active Directory (AD):

1. Start the Microsoft Management Console (MMC) Active Directory Users and Computers snap-in.
2. Select the container you want to house the shared folder and right-click it.
3. Select New > Shared Folder from the context menu.
4. In the display dialog box, enter a name for the share and the share's UNC.
5. Click OK.

The share you create will be visible in Windows Explorer under My Network Places > Entire Network – Directory > Domain. To remove the new share, simply right-click the shared folder in the Active Directory Users and Computers snap-in and select Delete.

15.76 What happens if two AD objects have the same RDN?

Every Active Directory (AD) object has a distinguished name (DN—e.g., CN=John Savill,CN=Users,DC=SavillTech,DC=Com) that uniquely identifies the object and its position in AD. The system also creates a relative distinguished name (RDN), which is a name relative to the container (e.g., CN=John Savill for the user).

Two objects with the same RDN can't exist in one container. For example, in the container CN=Users,DC=SavillTech, CN=John Savill and OU=John Savill are allowed because one is a user and the other is an organizational unit (OU). However, CN=John Savill and CN=John Savill aren't allowed.

The only way you can have a duplicate RDN is if two objects are created on different domain controllers (DCs). But at the next replication cycle, the system will rename the older object.

To find objects that the system has renamed because of RDN collisions, use the search.vbs script in \support\tools\support.cab as follows:

```
cscript search.vbs "LDAP://<server>/dc=<domain>,dc=com"

/C:"(CN=*\0ACNF:*)" /P:distinguishedName /S:SubTree
```

Any matches will display the RDN for the renamed objects.

FAQ 15.77 How can I move multiple users between organizational units?

You can move individual users between OUs by right-clicking the user in the Microsoft Management Console (MMC) Active Directory Users and Computers snap-in and selecting Move. To move multiple users, perform the following steps:

1. Start the Active Directory Users and Computers snap-in (go to Start > Programs > Administrative Tools, and click Active Directory Users and Computers).
2. Open the OU that contains the users you want to move.
3. Select multiple users by holding down Ctrl and selecting each user (if the users are in sequence, you can select them all by left-clicking the first name, holding down Shift, then left-clicking the last name).
4. Right-click the last user you selected and select Move from the context menu.
5. Select the destination OU and click OK.

FAQ 15.78 How do I create a certificate trust list for a domain?

To create a certificate trust list (CTL), you first need to configure each domain with a list of Certificate Authorities (CAs) the domain trusts, to let the domain's users request certificates. First, you need to install an Enterprise CA. (See FAQ 15.79.) You also need an Administrator certificate or an explicit Trust Signing certificate. The following steps outline how to request an Administrator certificate:

1. Start the Microsoft Management Console (MMC).
2. From the Console menu, select Add/Remove Snap-in.
3. Click Add.
4. Select Certificates and click Add.
5. Select My user account as the type and click Finish.
6. Click Close.

7. Click OK to return to the main dialog box.
8. Expand the Certificates root and right-click Personal.
9. From the All Tasks menu, select Request New Certificate, as shown in Figure 15-35.
10. Click Next in the Certificate Request Wizard dialog box.
11. Select the Administrator template and click Next.
12. Enter a user-friendly name and description, and click Next.
13. Click Finish when the confirmation screen displays.
14. When the dialog box displays to confirm the certificate creation, click Install Certificate.
15. Finally, click OK in the success dialog box.

As shown in Figure 15-36, you can use the MMC Certificates snap-in to view the certificate and see that the Enterprise CA rather than the local Administrator issued the certificate.

To create the CTL, perform the following steps:

1. Start the MMC Active Directory Users and Computers snap-in. (From the Start menu, select Programs > Administrative Tools > Active Directory Users and Computers.)
2. Right-click the domain and select Properties.
3. Select the Group Policy tab.
4. Select Default Domain Policy (or another policy) and click Edit.
5. Select User Configuration > Windows Settings > Security Settings > Public Key Policies > Enterprise Trust.
6. Right-click Enterprise Trust and select New > Certificate Trust List.
7. When the Certificate Trust List Wizard starts, click Next (see Figure 15-37).
8. You can enter a prefix for the CTL and the purpose (e.g., Encrypted File System—EFS).
9. Click Next.
10. Select a certificate, click Add from Store, select a domain certificate, and click OK. Click Next.
11. Select a signature (i.e., the Administrator you created), click Select from Store, select the certificate that displays, and click OK. Click Next.
12. You can add a timestamp if you want. Click Next.
13. Enter a user-friendly name and description. Click Next.
14. Click Finish when the summary page displays.
15. Click OK in the success dialog box.

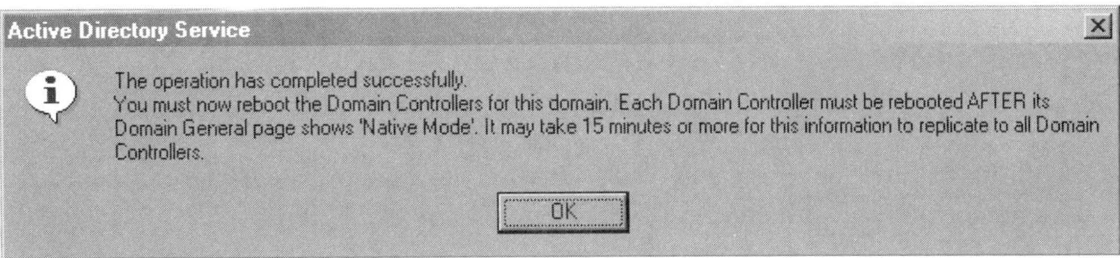

Figure 15-35 Confirmation of the native mode switch

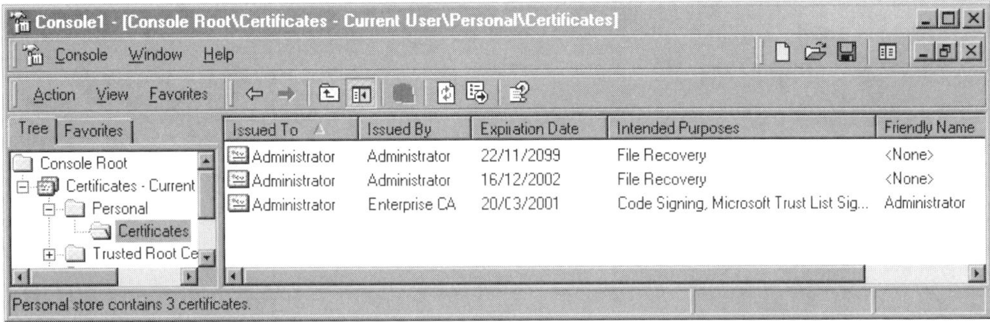

Figure 15-36 Viewing certificates for current user

Certificate Trust List Wizard

Certificate Trust List Purpose

This information identifies the certificate trust list (CTL) and the designated purposes.

Enter a prefix to use in identifying this CTL (optional):

EFS_

Valid Duration (optional):

months days

Select the purposes for this CTL:

- [ ] IP security user
- [x] Encrypting File System
- [ ] Windows Hardware Driver Verification
- [ ] Windows System Component Verification
- [ ] OEM Windows System Component Verification

Add Purpose...

< Back Next > Cancel

Figure 15-37 Purpose dialog of a certificate

FAQ 15.79 How do I install an Enterprise Certificate Authority?

A certificate server provides a trusted authority to confirm a private key user's identity. A domain normally has a hierarchy of certificate servers. An enterprise root Certificate Authority (CA) grants itself a certificate and creates subordinate CAs. The root CA gives the subordinate CAs their certificates, but the subordinate CAs can grant certificates to users.

For automatic certification, a domain needs an Enterprise CA to let clients request certificates, such as an Encrypted File System (EFS) recovery certificate. To install an Enterprise CA, perform the following steps.

1. Start the Control Panel Add/Remove Programs applet.
2. Click Add/Remove Windows Components to start the Windows Components Wizard.
3. Click Next when the welcome screen appears.
4. When the list of components displays, select the Certificate Services checkbox and click Next.
5. Then, you need to select the type. Types include the following:

   Enterprise root CA

   Enterprise subordinate CA

   Standalone root CA

   Standalone subordinate CA

   Select Enterprise root CA and click Next.
6. Enter a CA name and other information about the organization, as shown in Figure 15-38. Click Next.
7. Accept the default location for the certificate database (i.e., %systemroot%\System32\CertLog). Click Next.
8. If Microsoft IIS is running, the service will stop and a dialog box will display. Click OK.
9. A list of files to copy will generate, and the files will install. Service and system configurations will also install. You might need to insert the Windows 2000 Server CD-ROM.
10. When the wizard completes, click Finish.

The Microsoft Management Console (MMC) Certificate Authority snap-in will now contain a shortcut in the Administrative Tools folder.

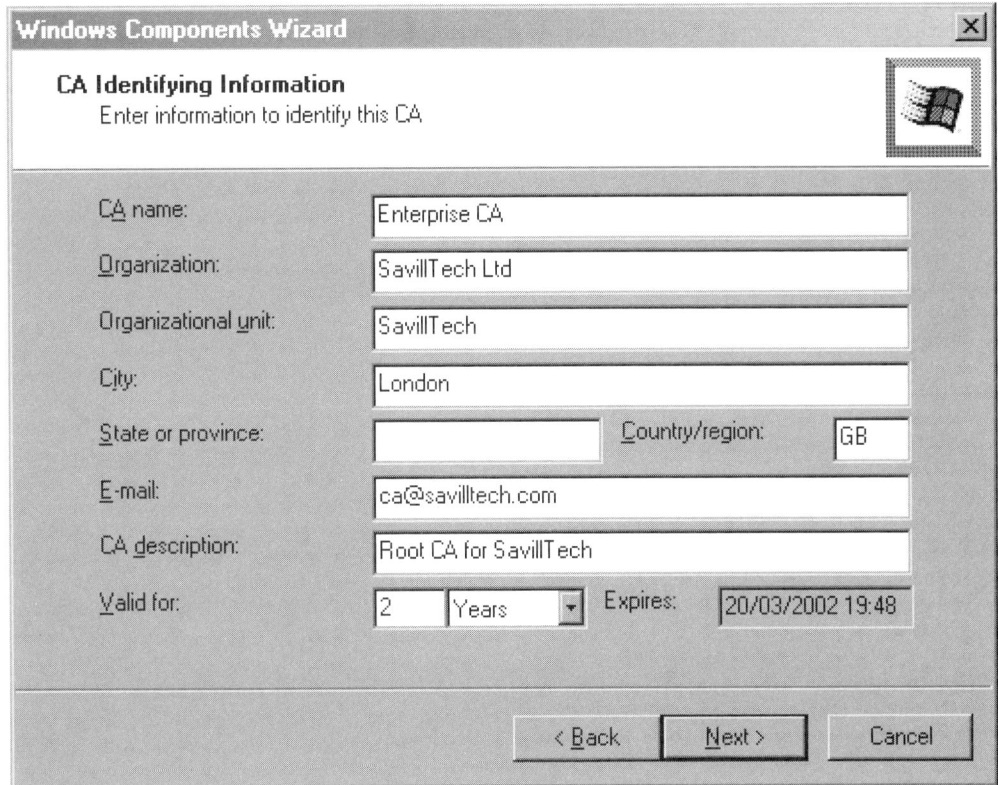

Figure 15-38 Certificate information

FAQ 15.80 How does a user request a certificate over the Web?

The Windows 2000 Certification Service installation adds a virtual directory called CertSrv pointing to %systemroot%\System32\CertSrv. You can use this directory to request certificates over an intranet.

1. Go to http://<Certificate Authority server>/certsrv.
2. Select Request a certificate and click Next.
3. Select User Certificate and click Next.
4. Click More Options to see various Cryptographic Service Providers (CSPs). Selecting Advanced lets you set the key size, hash algorithm, etc.

5. Click Submit.
6. After the certificate generates, click Install this certificate.
7. Close the Web page.

After the certificate installs, you can use the user's Microsoft Management Console (MMC) Certificates snap-in to view it.

16 GROUP POLICY

You will no doubt be familiar with the concept of system policies in NT 4.0. By utilizing the System Policy editor, you can configure various restrictions, save them as files in NTCONFIG.POL in the netlogon share, and the settings will be applied to all users of the domain. Effectively all the policies of Windows NT 4.0 allowed were Registry updates. These policy settings could be configured for users, computers, or groups of users.

Windows 2000 takes this to the next level and promises the following ideal: "The ability for the Administrator to state a wish about the state of their Users' environment once, and then rely on the system to enforce that wish."

In Windows 2000, the Group Policy model has been completely updated and now utilizes the Active Directory and offers much more than just Registry restrictions, for example:

- Application deployment
- Logon/logoff/startup/shutdown scripts
- Folder redirection

Group Policy Objects (GPOs) are a policy unit and can be applied to a site, domain, or organizational unit (OU); in fact it will often be the case that a user/computer will have multiple GPOs applicable to it and in the event of a clash of a setting, the order of precedence is **S**ite, **D**omain, then **OU**—SDOU. So any setting defined at a site level can be overwritten by a domain setting; anything defined on a domain can be overwritten by an OU setting. There is a fourth type, the **L**ocal computer policy, which has lowest priority, and any policies can be overwritten by any of the others, which gives us an order of LSDOU.

The three mechanisms to apply Group Policies for sites, domains, and OUs are as follows:

- Domain Group Policy Object
  Start the Active Directory Users and Computers MMC snap-in, right-click on the domain, and select Properties. Select the Group Policy tab.
- OU Group Policy Object
  Start the Active Directory Users and Computers MMC snap-in, right-click on the OU, and select Properties. Select the Group Policy tab.

- Sites Group Policy Object
  Start the Active Directory Sites and Services MMC snap-in, expand the sites, right-click on the required site, and select Properties. Select the Group Policy tab.

By default when you select Group Policy for a container, there will be no GPO, and you have the option of either adding an existing GPO to the container or creating a new one. To create a new GPO, just click the New button and enter a name for the GPO. Once created, clicking the Edit button can modify the specified policy. A new instance of the Microsoft Management Console will be started with the Group Policy editor loaded with the selected GPO at the root.

Windows NT 4.0 policies already in place are **not** upgraded to 2000, and you will need to redefine all your policies as GPOs. In a mixed environment of both 4.0 and 2000 clients, you will need to keep a NTCONFIG.POL in the netlogon share of the domain controllers (even the 2000 DCs as they may authenticate 4.0 client logons in a mixed environment) to ensure 4.0 clients still receive their policy settings. Windows 2000 clients will ignore NTCONFIG.POL unless you make a policy change to instruct them to implement the NTCONFIG.POL contents. If you do, then the order of reading is

1. GPO(s) computer at startup
2. Computer NTCONFIG.POL at logon
3. User NTCONFIG.POL at logon
4. GPO(s) user at logon

As has been said, GPO information is stored in the Active Directory, but the policy itself is stored on the SYSVOL container on each domain controller as %systemroot%\SYSVOL\sysvol\<domain>\Policies\<GUID of GPO> (GUID is globally unique identifier).

Under the folder, you will find a file GPT.INI, which for nonlocal GPO will contain

```
[General]
Version=<version number>
```

For example, the version may be 65539. The least four significant digits (four right-most digits) represent the Computer Settings version number (3), and the most four significant represent the User Settings version number (four left-most digits) (1). You have to convert to hexadecimal so:

```
65539 : 00010003
```

Also within the folder is an Adm folder, which contains the .ADM template files that are used in the GPO. Also in the folder are MACHINE and USER folders containing specific settings.

You can check the GUID for a GPO by right-clicking on its root, selecting Properties, and viewing the Unique name property (see Figure 16-1).

To avoid any conflicts with GPO modifications, only the PDC role holder can make changes to the GPO.

Another change is that old 4.0 policies are "tattooed" in the Registry, meaning that even after a policy has been removed, its settings stay in the Registry until changed by something else. An advantage of the Windows 2000 Group Policies is that this tattooing does not occur. The reason is that in Windows 2000, Registry settings written to the following two secure Registry locations are cleaned up when a Group Policy Object no longer applies:

- \Software\Policies
- \Software\Microsoft\Windows\CurrentVersion\Policies

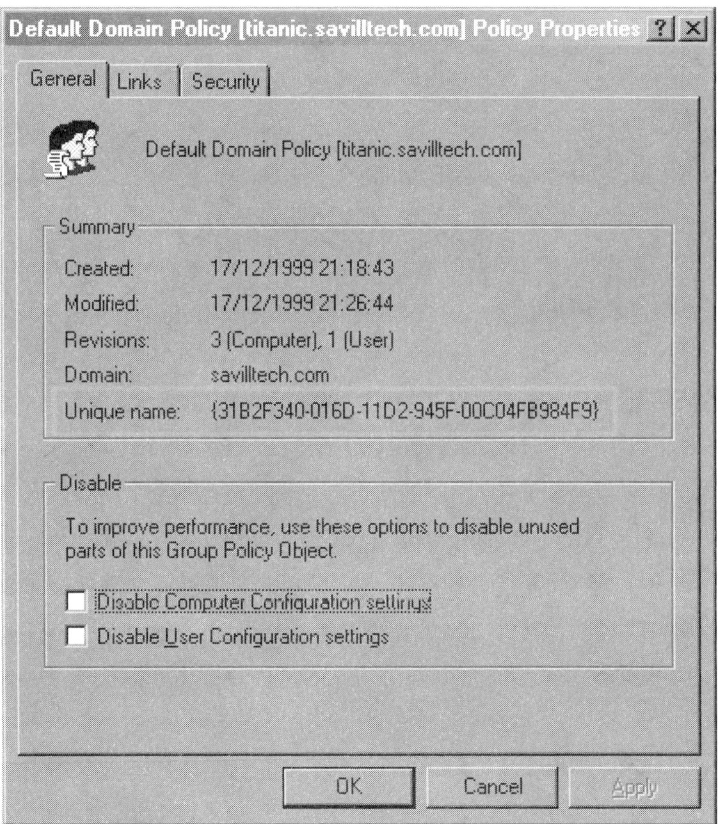

Figure 16-1 The GUID of a policy

Finally unlike the 4.0 System Policies, the policy actually gets refreshed at certain times. Well not **all** of the policy. Software deployment and folder redirection are not updated because, for example, you would be unhappy if the GPO was modified to remove Word, and you were using it at the time, and it suddenly uninstalled! All 2000 machines refresh the policy every 90 minutes except domain controllers who replicate every 5 minutes. These times and the parts to replicate can be modified within the GPO.

16.1 How can I force GPO updates to take effect?

Policies are refreshed every 90 minutes (5 on DCs). To force a machine to update the policy, use the SECEDIT command.

To update the computer policy, type

```
secedit /refreshpolicy machine_policy
```

To update the user policy, type

```
secedit /refreshpolicy user_policy
```

Adding /enforce to any of the preceding commands forces a reapply of the security policy even if there is no GPO change.

16.2 How can I enable the old NTCONFIG.POL to be used by Windows 2000 clients?

By default Windows 2000-based clients don't use NTCONFIG.POL but instead use Group Policy Objects (GPOs) as defined in the Active Directory. NT 4.0 clients still use NTCONFIG.POL even in a 2000 domain.

It **used** to be possible (pre RC2, build 2128) to enable the 2000 clients to use NTCONFIG.POL; however, you should have a good reason because GPOs are superior to the old system policies. This has been removed due to complications in implementation.

To enable system policies (NTCONFIG.POL), perform the following pre-build 2128 as follows:

1. Start the Active Directory Users and Computers MMC snap-in (Start > Programs > Administrative Tools > Active Directory Users and Computers).

2. Right-click on the root domain name—for example, savilltech.com—and select Properties.
3. Select the Group Policy tab.
4. Select the Default Domain Policy GPO and click Edit.
5. The Group Policy MMC snap-in will be started with the domain GPO at the root.
6. Move to Computer Configuration\Administrative Templates\System\Group Policy.
7. Double-click Disable system policy and set to Disabled (see Figure 16-2). Click OK.
8. Disabling disable system policy means enable the system policy; two minuses make a plus ☺.
9. Close the Group Policy MMC.

The updated GPO will take effect on the client the next time you log on. (It will actually take effect at the maximum 90 minutes after you make the change, but this only affects logon.)

This update actually changes Registry value HKEY_LOCAL_MACHINE\Software\Microsoft\Windows\CurrentVersion\Policies\System\DisableNT4Policy to 0.

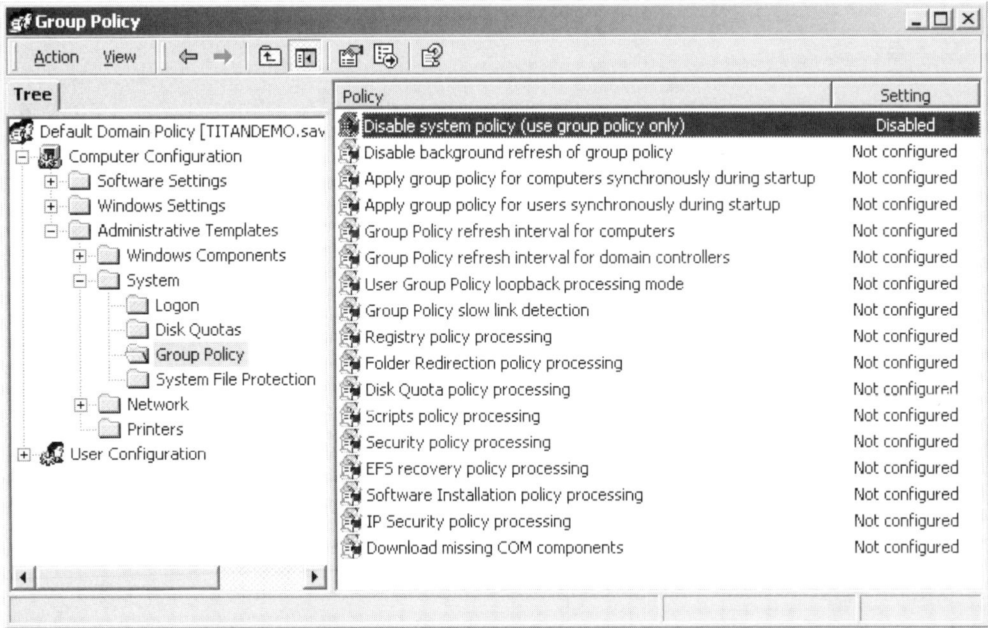

Figure 16-2 Disabling the use of system policy for Windows 2000 and above clients

FAQ 16.3 How can I add additional templates to a Group Policy Object?

The old style NT 4.0 templates (.ADM) are still supported in Windows 2000 Group Policy Objects (GPOs) and are listed in the Group Policy under the Administrative Templates branch. These settings are all Registry-based settings.

Windows 2000 ships with a number of .ADM files including

- SYSTEM.ADM (General system settings)
- INETRES.ADM (Internet Explorer specific settings)

When a ADM file is applied to a GPO, it is copied from the %systemroot%\inf folder to the %systemroot%\SYSVOL\domain\Policies\<GUID of GPO>\Adm folder.

To add/remove a new template to a GPO, perform the following:

1. Start the Active Directory Users and Computers MMC snap-in (Start > Programs > Administrative Tools > Active Directory Users and Computers).
2. Right-click on the container whose GPO you wish to change—for example, savilltech.com—and select Properties.
3. Select the Group Policy tab.
4. Select the GPO and click Edit.
5. The Group Policy MMC snap-in will be started with the GPO at the root.
6. Under User or Computer configuration, right-click on Administrative Templates and select Add/Remove Templates.
7. Click Add (or to remove select one and click Remove).
8. Select the ADM to add and click Open.
9. Click Close.
10. The new options will now be available.

The ADM file will be copied to the GPOs Adm folder.

FAQ 16.4 How can I apply a Group Policy to a security group?

It's not possible to apply a Group Policy to a security group; however, what you can do is to filter a Group Policy by changing the permissions on the Group Policy so that only certain users/groups have read and apply privileges.

1. Start the Active Directory Users and Computers MMC snap-in (Start > Programs > Administrative Tools > Active Directory Users and Computers).

2. Right-click on the container (OU or domain) that has the Group Policy Object whose permissions you wish to change and select Properties.
3. Select the Group Policy tab.
4. Select the GPO from the list and click Properties.
5. Select the Security tab.

   Modify the permissions so that only the required users have the read and apply privileges and the Administrators who need to modify the GPO have read and write privileges (see Figure 16-3).
6. Click OK to the dialog.
7. Click Close the containers properties.

Now only the selected users will run the GPO.

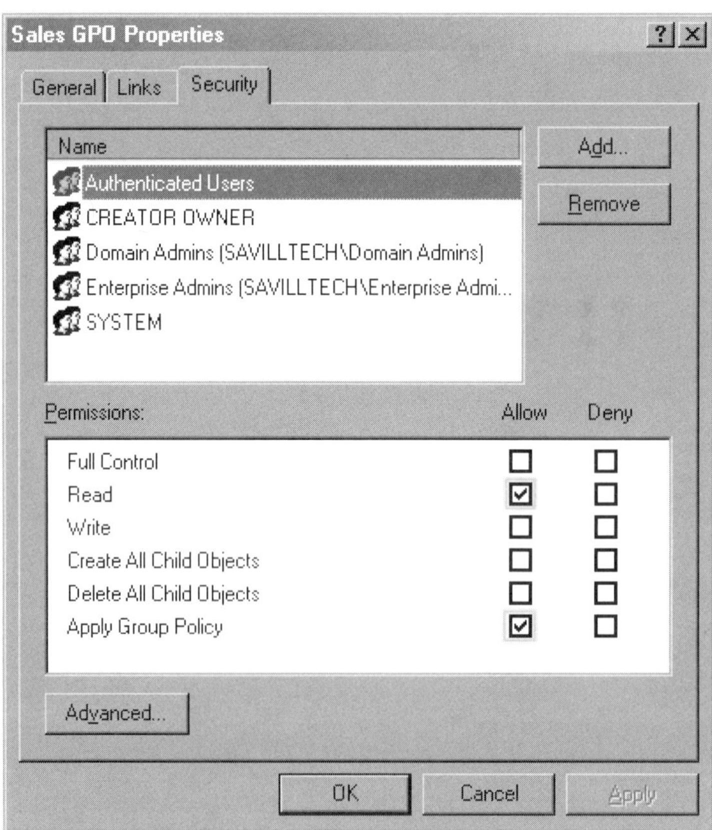

Figure 16-3 Specifying required options to read a Group Policy

16.5 Why don't password policies assigned to an OU/site GPO work?

Although the password policy branch is available for all Group Policy Objects, it is only implemented for GPOs at the domain level. Even if you make settings for a GPO for an OU or a site, it will have no effect. The only way to apply password settings is as follows:

1. Start the Active Directory Users and Computers MMC snap-in (Start > Programs > Administrative Tools > Active Directory Users and Computers).
2. Right-click on the domain and select Properties.
3. Select the Group Policy tab.
4. Select the domain Group Policy Object and select Edit.
5. Expand the Computer Configuration branch > Windows Settings > Security Settings > Account Policies > Password Policy.
6. You will now be able to set the relevant options (see Figure 16-4).
7. When complete close the Group Policy Editor.

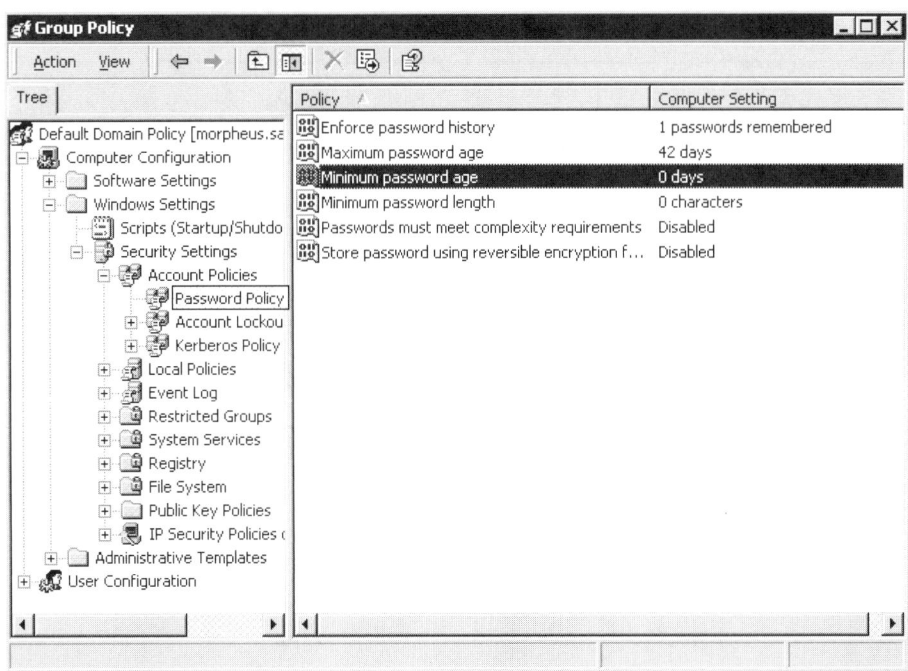

Figure 16-4 Setting password options via policy

FAQ 16.6 How can I convert a NT 4.0 .POL file to a Windows 2000 Group Policy Object?

The Windows 2000 Resource Kit has the GPOLMIG.EXE utility, which can convert a NT 4.0 system policy .POL file to a Windows 2000 Group Policy Object. The GPOLMIG.EXE utility is a **very** useful tool! For help, just enter

```
gpolmig /?
```

The example syntax to migrate a system policy for the user policy is

```
Zgpolmig c:\temp\ntconfig.pol /migrate user user1 {00000000-0000-
0000-0000-000000000000}User
```

FAQ 16.7 How can I restrict access to MMC snap-ins?

It's possible to restrict access to MMC snap-ins using the Group Policy settings:

1. Start Active Directory Users and Computers snap-in (Start > Programs > Administrative Tools > Active Directory Users and Computers).
2. Right-click on the domain or OU with the Group Policy set and select Properties.
3. Select the Group Policies tab.
4. Select the Group Policy you wish to change and click Edit.
5. Move to User Configuration\Administrative Templates\Windows Components\Microsoft Management Console.
6. Double-click Restrict Users to the explicitly permitted list of snap-ins.
7. Set to Enabled or Disabled.
8. You can then move to Restricted/Permitted snap-ins and enable or disable specific snap-ins.

If Restrict Users to the explicitly permitted list of snap-ins is set to Disabled or Not Configured, then the snap-ins are available unless they are explicitly set to Disabled under the Restricted/Permitted snap-ins folder.

If the Restrict Users to the explicitly permitted list of snap-ins is set to Enabled, then no snap-ins are available unless the snap-in is explicitly set to Enabled.

FAQ 16.8 How can I tell which containers link to a Group Policy?

Windows 2000 allows a Group Policy to be linked to a number of different domains, sites, and organizational units. Before ever deleting a Group Policy, you need to be sure no container still links to the Group Policy.

To check all links of a Group Policy, perform the following:

1. Start the Active Directory Users and Computers snap-in (Start > Programs > Administrative Tools > Active Directory Users and Computers).
2. Right-click on a container that links to the Group Policy you wish to check.
3. Select the Group Policy tab.
4. Select the Links tab.
5. Select the domain you wish to search for the Group Policy and click Find Now.

A list of all containers linking to the Group Policy will be shown in the result pane (see Figure 16-5).

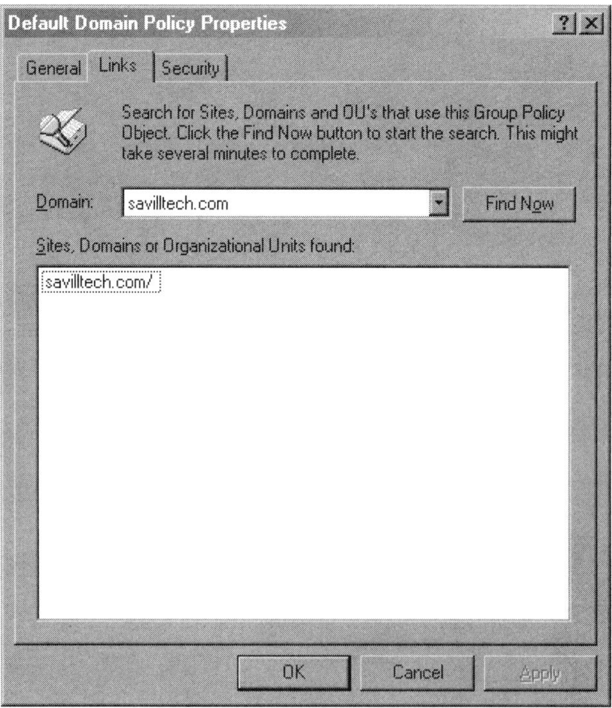

Figure 16-5 Find who is using a Group Policy Object

FAQ 16.9 How do the Group Policy No Override and Block Inheritance options work?

Group Policies can be applied at multiple levels (sites, domains, organizational units) and multiple GPs can be applied for each level. Obviously it may be that some policy settings conflict; hence the application order of site, domain, organizational unit. Within each layer, you set the order for all defined policies, but you may want to force some polices never to be overridden (No Override), and you may want some containers not to inherit settings from a parent container (Block Inheritance).

Helpful definitions follow:

- No Override—This prevents child containers from overriding policies set at higher levels
- Block Inheritance—Stops containers inheriting policies from parent containers
- No Override takes precedence over Block Inheritance. So if a child container has Block Inheritance set, but on the parent a Group Policy has No Override set, then the policy will get applied.

Also the highest No Override takes precedence over lower No Overrides set.

To block inheritance, perform the following:

1. Start the Active Directory Users and Computer snap-in (Start > Programs > Administrative Tools > Active Directory Users and Computers).
2. Right-click on the container you wish to stop inheriting settings from its parent and select Properties.
3. Select the Group Policy tab.
4. Check the Block Policy inheritance option (see Figure 16-6).
5. Click Apply and then OK.

To set a policy never to be overridden, perform the following:

1. Start the Active Directory Users and Computer snap-in (Start > Programs > Administrative Tools > Active Directory Users and Computers).

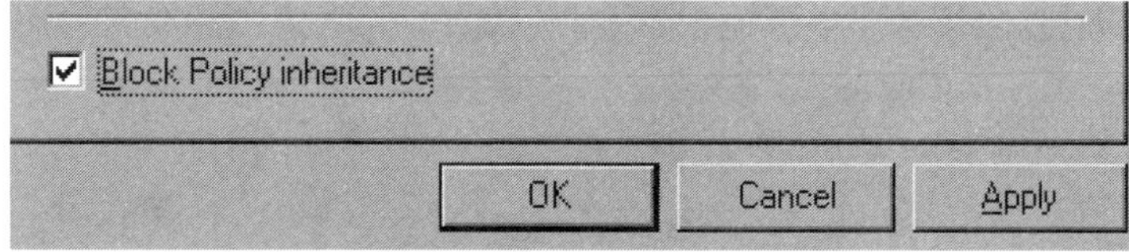

Figure 16-6 Stopping policy inheritance

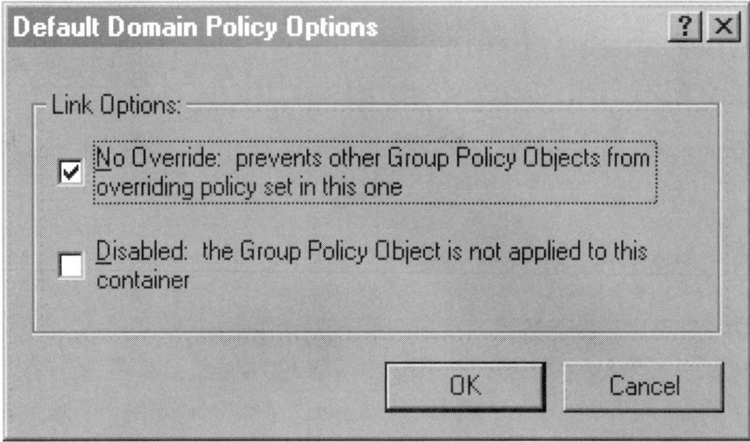

Figure 16-7 Selecting to stop override for Group Policy Object

2. Right-click on the container you wish to set a Group Policy not to be overridden and select Properties.
3. Select the Group Policy tab.
4. Click Options.
5. Check the No Override option (see Figure 16-7).
6. Click OK.
7. Click Apply, then OK.

16.10 How can I set only the user/computer part of a Group Policy to be applied?

Group Policies consist of two root parts, the user component and the computer component. It's possible to configure either part to be applied as follows:

1. Start the Active Directory Users and Computers snap-in (Start > Programs > Administrative Tools > Active Directory Users and Computers).
2. Right-click on the container whose Group Policy link you wish to set the active part (e.g., user or computer) and select Properties.
3. Select the Group Policy tab.
4. Select the Group Policy whose effect you wish to change and click Properties.

5. Select the General tab.
6. Under the Disable section, select to disable the Computer and/or User part (see Figure 16-8).
7. Click Apply, then OK.

You should also now refresh the policy for both parts:

```
secedit /refreshpolicy machine_policy
secedit /refreshpolicy user_policy
```

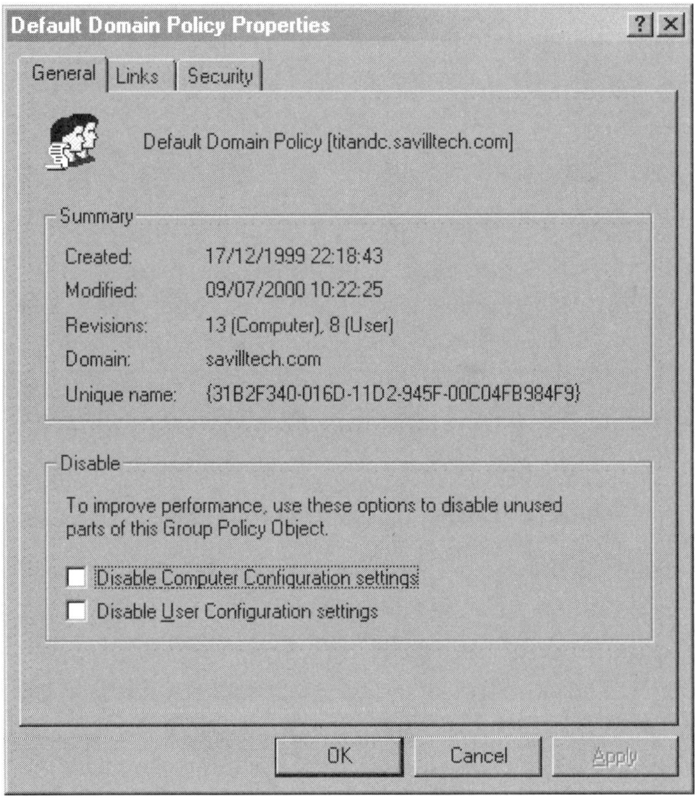

Figure 16-8 Selective enabling of Group Policy Object components

FAQ 16.11 How can I tell the resultant set of policy (RSoP) for a user/computer?

The resultant set of policy is the policy that gets applied to the end client from all the Group Policies applied to any domains, sites, and OUs it belongs to.

Windows 2000 does not provide a tool to show this, but FAZAM 2000 from http://www.FullArmor.com has the ability to show this information for any object. Windows .NET now provides this ability built in, and Windows XP's RsoP tool can be used if it's a member of a Windows 2000 domain.

FAQ 16.12 How can I copy a GPO from one domain to another?

Windows 2000 stores information about a Group Policy Object (GPO) in Active Directory (AD) and as part of the SYSVOL structure that replicates among all domain controllers (DCs) within a domain. The AD GPO information consists of the GPO's name and globally unique identifier (GUID). To determine a GPO's GUID, you must load the GPO in Group Policy Editor (GPE) and select Properties from the root context menu. Alternatively, you can open a container that has the GPO applied to it, select the GPO, and click Properties. Whichever method you use, the Unique name under the Summary section of the General tab displays the GUID.

Win2K stores the actual GPO data in %SystemRoot%\SYSVOL\sysvol\\Policies\{}. To copy a GPO, perform the following steps:

1. Determine the GUID of the GPO that you want to copy.
2. Create a new GPO in the target domain.
3. Determine the new GPO's GUID.
4. Navigate to the new GPO's storage area (%SystemRoot%\SYSVOL\sysvol\\Policies\{}) and delete the contents of that folder.
5. Copy the contents of the GPO folder from the original domain into the new GPO location.

For example, imagine I have an original GPO named Test in the savilltech.com domain and a GUID of 5AA140D1-397A-4B5C-B4DC-DF60FF731FC0. To copy this GPO to a new GPO named Sales in the ntfaq.com domain, I would perform the following steps:

1. Create a new GPO named Sales in the ntfaq.com domain.
2. Determine the new GPO's GUID (e.g., 600140D1-397A-4B5C-B4DC-DF60FF73XXXX).
3. Navigate to the new GPO's storage area (%SystemRoot%\SYSVOL\sysvol\ntfaq.com\Policies\{600140D1-397A-4B5C-B4DC-DF60FF73XXXX}) and delete the contents of that folder.
4. Copy the contents of %SystemRoot%\SYSVOL\sysvol\savilltech.com\Policies\{5AA140D1-397A-4B5C-B4DC-DF60FF731FC0} to %SystemRoot%\SYSVOL\sysvol\ntfaq.com\Policies\{600140D1-397A-4B5C-B4DC-DF60FF73XXXX}.

Be aware that you won't have both folders on one machine; instead, you'll be copying files between DCs.

FAQ 16.13 Why are Group Policy Objects set at organizational unit (OU) level not applied to members of that OU?

If a GPO is set at OU level, and regardless of ensuring that everything related to it is seemingly OK at levels above (in the AD structure), the settings are still not being applied, you should perform the following actions.

Log on as Administrator to a client PC and start the Computer Management MMC snap-in (Start > Programs > Administrative Tools > Computer Management or right-click on My computer and select Manage). Click the plus sign (+) next to Event Viewer and then access the Application Log. Check the log for entries:

```
Event ID: 1000
Event Source: Userenv
Description: Windows cannot determine the user or computer name.
Return value (1722).
```

If these exist, it means that the address for the configured preferred DNS server on the client is invalid or unreachable, which prevents access to the DNS and in turn AD information, and thus applicable GPOs.

To resolve this issue, correct the DNS address in the Internet Protocol (TCP/IP) properties for the LAN connection:

1. Right-click My Network Places and then click Properties.
2. Right-click Local Area Connection and then click Properties.

3. Click Internet Protocol (TCP/IP) and then click Properties.
4. Type the correct DNS address in the Preferred DNS server box.

Afterwards, log on as a user of the OU whose GPOs were not being applied, and you'll notice that the GPO is now applied.

For further information on the Application Log error, see http://support.microsoft.com/default.aspx?scid=kb;EN-US;q261007.

17 TCP/IP

TCP/IP is a suite of related protocols and utilities used for network communications. TCP/IP is actually two protocols, Internet Protocol (IP) and Transmission Control Protocol (TCP). There are many different implementations of TCP/IP; however, they all conform to a standard, which means different implementations can communicate with each other.

Each machine that uses TCP/IP must have a unique TCP/IP address that is a 32-bit number, which is usually displayed in the dotted quad (or dotted decimal) format xxx.xxx.xxx.xxx, where xxx is a number from 0 to 255—for example, here the IP address 147.98.26.11 is shown in its 32-bit form, and how it breaks down into the dotted quad format:

10010011	01100010	00011010	00001011
147	98	26	11

TCP/IP was originally used on ARPANET, a military network, grew to be used on universities, and is now used on virtually every computer system.

FAQ 17.1 How can I install TCP/IP if I don't have a network card?

Microsoft provides a loopback adapter that can be used for the testing of TCP/IP. The loopback adapter is useful for those users with no network card in their machine but who would like to experiment with installing network protocols and other network-related items. Obviously because there is no physical network connection, you cannot talk to other machines.

1. Start the Add/Remove Hardware Control Panel applet (Start > Settings > Control Panel > Add/Remove Hardware).
2. Click Add/Troubleshoot a device and then click Next.

3. Click Add a new device and then click Next.
4. Click No, I want to select the hardware from a list and then click Next.
5. Click Network adapters and then click Next.
6. In the Manufacturers box, click Microsoft.
7. In the Network Adapter box, click Microsoft Loopback Adapter and then click Next.
8. Click Finish.

You should then configure the device with an IP address, etc. If you select DHCP, TCP will use an address 169.254.x.x/16 (subnet mask 255.255.0.0) for Windows 2000 and above because no DHCP server can be contacted due to the lack of network connectivity.

17.2 I have installed TCP/IP. What steps should I use to verify the setup is correct?

Follow these steps:

1. From a command prompt, type

   ```
   ipconfig /all
   ```

   This will show information such as IP address, subnet mask, and the physical address. Check the IP address and subnet mask are what you expect.
2. Next a special IP address is used for loopback testing: 127.0.0.1. Try to ping this address:

   ```
   ping 127.0.0.1
   ```

   You should get four lines of

   ```
   Reply from 127.0.0.1: bytes=32 time<10ms TTL=128
   ```

   Pinging 127.0.0.1 does not send any traffic out on the network. If this does not work, it means the TCP/IP stack is not loaded correctly. Go back and check your configuration.
3. Next try to ping your own IP address. Once again this will not send any traffic out on the network, but it just confirms the software:

   ```
   ping 200.200.200.53
   ```

Once again you should get four reply messages. If this does not work, but the loopback did, you probably have typed the IP address wrong. Go back and check your configuration.

4. Try and ping the gateway:

   ```
   ping 200.200.200.1
   ```

   This is the first traffic going out over the network. The gateway should be on your subnet. If you fail to ping the gateway, check the gateway is up and that your network is correctly connected.

5. Ping something on the other side of the gateway, that is, something not on your subnet:

   ```
   ping 158.234.26.46
   ```

   If this does not work, then the gateway may not be functioning correctly.

6. If all of the preceding worked, then name resolution should be tested by pinging by name, which will test the HOSTS and/or DNS. If your machine name was john, and the domain savilltech.com, you would ping john.savilltech.com

   ```
   ping john.savilltech.com
   ```

   If this does not work, check in Network Settings > Protocols > TCP/IP that the domain name is correct. In addition, check the hosts file and the DNS.

7. Next try to ping a name outside the network:

   ```
   ping www.windows2000faq.com
   ```

   If this does not work, then check with your ISP (Internet Service Provider). Also make sure the site you are trying to ping supports ICMP; otherwise, Ping will not work.

If all of the preceding works, then get down to the serious stuff and start surfing!

FAQ 17.3 How can I trace the route the TCP/IP packets take?

In general TCP/IP packets will not always take the same route to a destination; however, the start of the journey is likely to be the same—that is, to your gateway, to the firewall, and so on. The command is **tracert**, and the syntax is as follows

```
tracert <host name or IP address>
```

For example:

```
tracert news.savilltech.com

Tracing route to news.savilltech.com [200.200.8.55]
over a maximum of 30 hops:

1 <10 ms <10 ms <10 ms 200.200.24.1 200.200.200.24.1 is the gateway
2 <10 ms 10ms <10 ms 200.200.255.81
3 30 ms 10 ms 10 ms news.savilltech.com [200.200.8.55]

Trace complete
```

The first column is the hop count, the next three columns (i.e., "<10 ms <10 ms <10 ms") show the time taken for the cumulative round-trip times (in milliseconds), the fourth column is the host name if the IP address was resolved, and the last column is the IP address of the host. It is really like a street map telling you each turn to take. An important thing to note is to look for looping routes, so host a goes to b, then c, then back to a, because this usually indicates a problem.

Tracert will not always work with some firewall products for those hosts that are outside the firewall.

FAQ 17.4 What is the subnet mask?

As has been shown, the IP address consists of 4 octets and is usually displayed in the format 200.200.200.5; however, this address on its own does not mean much. A subnet mask is required to show which part of the IP address is the network ID, and which part is the host ID. Imagine the network ID as the road name and the host ID as the house number. So with "54 Grove Street", 54 is the host ID and Grove Street is the network ID. The subnet mask shows which part of the IP address is the network ID, and which part is the host ID.

For example, with an address of 200.200.200.5, and a subnet mask of 255.255.255.0, the network ID is 200.200.200 and the host ID is 5. This is calculated using the following:

IP Address	11001000	11001000	11001000	00000101
Subnet Mask	11111111	11111111	11111111	00000000
Network ID	11001000	11001000	11001000	00000000
Host ID	00000000	00000000	00000000	00000101

A bitwise AND operation between the IP address and the subnet mask takes place—for example:

```
1 AND 1=1
1 AND 0=0
0 AND 1=0
0 AND 0=0
```

There are default subnet masks, depending on the class of the IP address as follows:

```
Class A : 001.xxx.xxx.xxx to 126.xxx.xxx.xxx uses subnet mask
255.0.0.0 as default
Class B : 128.xxx.xxx.xxx to 191.xxx.xxx.xxx uses subnet mask
255.255.0.0 as default
Class C : 192.xxx.xxx.xxx to 224.xxx.xxx.xxx uses subnet mask
255.255.255.0 as default
```

Where's 127.xxx.xxx.xxx ??? This is a reserved address that is used for testing purposes. If you ping 127.0.0.1, you will ping yourself ☺.

The subnet mask is used when two hosts communicate. If the two hosts are on the same network, then host A will talk directly to host B; however, if host B is on a different network, then host A will have to communicate via a gateway, and the way host A can tell if it is on the same network is using the subnet mask. For example

```
Host A 200.200.200.5
Host B 200.200.200.9
Host C 200.200.199.6
Subnet Mask 255.255.255.0
```

If Host A communicates with Host B, they both have network ID 200.200.200 so Host A communicates directly to Host B. If Host A communicates with Host C, they are on different networks, 200.200.200 and 200.200.199, respectively, so Host A would send via a gateway.

FAQ 17.5 What diagnostic utilities are there for TCP/IP?

We have already discussed Ping and Tracert. Following is a complete list:

- arp—This utility displays and modifies the IP to physical address translation tables used by the ARP (Address Resolution Protocol).

- finger—Displays information about a user on a specified system that is running the finger service.
- hostname—Displays the name of the current host.
- ipconfig—Displays information about the current TCP/IP configuration, including details about DNS servers, etc. Can also be used to renew and release DHCP address leases.
- nbtstat—Displays protocol statistics and current TCP/IP connections using NBT (NetBIOS over TCP/IP).
- netstat—Displays protocol statistics and current TCP/IP connections.
- Ping—Used to check if a destination host is receiving TCP/IP packets.
- route—Used to maintain and display routing tables.
- Tracert—Used to view the route packets take to a destination host.
- pathping—A Ping/Tracert merge tool new to XP.

For more information on these commands, just enter the command with a -?—for example, **netstat -?**.

FAQ 17.6 What is routing and how is it configured?

When host a wants to send to host b and they are on the same local network, then the IP protocol resolves the IP address to a physical address using ARP (Address Resolution Protocol). The physical address (e.g., 00-05-f3-43-d3-3e) of the source and destination hosts are added to the IP datagram to form a frame. Using the frame, the two hosts can communicate directly with each other.

If the two hosts are not on the same local network, then they cannot communicate directly with each other. Instead they have to go through a *router*. You have probably already come across a router when you install TCP/IP, as the default gateway is just a router that you have chosen to use as a means of communicating with hosts outside your local network if no specific route is known. A router can be a Windows NT computer with two or more network cards (one card for connection to each separate local network) or it can be a physical hardware device, such as Cisco routers.

Assuming our two hosts are not on the same local network, host A will check its routing table for a router that connects to the local network of host B. If it does not find a match, then the data packets will be send to the "default gateway". In most cases, no one router connects straight to the intended recipient; rather the router will know of another route to pass on your packet, which will then go to another router, and so on.

For example:

```
Host A—200.200.200.5
Host B—200.200.199.6
```

```
Subnet Mask—255.255.255.0
Router—200.200.200.2 and 200.200.199.2
Host A's routing table—Network 200.200.199.0 use router 200.200.
200.2
```

In this example, Host A would deduce that Host B is on a separate network, as its network ID is 200.200.199. Host A would then check its routing table and see that it knows for network 200.200.199 (the zero means all) it should send to 200.200.200.2. The router would receive the packets and then forward them to network 200.200.199.

What actually happens is each router will have its own routing table that will point to other routes.

To actually configure a route, you use the route command. For example, to configure a route for network 200.200.199 to use router 200.200.200.2, you type

```
route -p add 200.200.199.0 mask 255.255.255.0 200.200.200.2
```

The -p makes the addition permanent; otherwise, it will be lost with a reboot.

To view your existing information, type **route print.**

FAQ 17.7 What is ARP?

ARP stands for Address Resolution Protocol, and this topic was touched on in the previous FAQ as a means of resolving an IP address to an actual physical network card address.

All network cards have a unique 48-bit address, which is written as six hexadecimal pairs (e.g. 00-A0-24-7A-01-48), and this address is hard-coded into the network card. You can view your network card's hardware address by typing

```
ipconfig /all

Ethernet adapter Elnk31:
Description . . . . . . . . . : ELNK3 Ethernet Adapter.
Physical Address. . . . . . . : 00-A0-24-7A-01-48
DHCP Enabled. . . . . . . . . : No
IP Address. . . . . . . . . . : 200.200.200.5
Subnet Mask . . . . . . . . . : 255.255.255.0
Default Gateway . . . . . . . : 200.200.200.1
Primary WINS Server . . . . . : 200.200.50.23
Secondary WINS Server . . . . : 200.200.40.190
```

As discussed in FAQ 17.6, when a packet's destination is on the same local network as the sender's, then the sender needs to resolve the destination's IP address into a physical hardware address; otherwise, the sender needs to resolve the router's IP address into a physical hardware address. When a NT machine's TCP/IP component starts, it broadcasts an ARP message with its IP-to-hardware address pair. The basic order of events for sending to a host on the local network is as follows:

1. ARP checks the local ARP cache for an entry for destination's IP address. If a match is found, then the hardware address of the destination is added to the frame header and the frame is sent.
2. If a match is not found, then an ARP request broadcast is sent to the local network (remember it knows the destination is on the local network by working out the network ID from the IP address and the subnet mask). The ARP request contains the sender's IP address and hardware address—the IP address that is being queried and is sent to 255.255.255.255 (everyone, but it won't get routed).
3. When the destination host receives the broadcast, it sends a ARP reply with its hardware address and IP address.
4. When the source receives the ARP reply, it will update its ARP cache and then create a frame and send it.

If you are sending to a destination not on your local network, then the process is similar except the sender will resolve the route's IP address instead.

To inspect your machines ARP cache, type the following and a list of IP address-to-hardware address pairs will be shown:

```
arp -a
```

Try pinging a host on your local network and then displaying the ARP cache again, and you will see an entry for the host. Try pinging a host outside your local network, check the ARP cache, and an entry for the router will have been added.

You will notice that the word *dynamic* is listed with the records because they were added as needed and are volatile. Hence they will be lost on reboot. In fact the entries will be lost quicker than this! If an entry is not used again within two minutes, then it will be deleted from the cache. If it is used within two minutes, it will not be deleted for a further ten minutes, unless used again, and then it would be ten minutes from when used :-).

You may wish to add static entries for some hosts (to save time with the ARP requests) and the format is

```
arp -s <IP address> <hardware address>
```

For example:

```
arp -s 200.200.200.5 00-A0-24-7A-01-48
```

FAQ 17.8 My Network is not connected to the Internet. Can I use any IP address?

The basic answer would be Yes; however, it is advisable to use one of the following ranges that are reserved for use by private networks:

- 10.0.0.0–10.255.255.255: This is a single class A network.
- 172.16.0.0–172.31.255.255: This is a group of 16 contiguous class B networks.
- 192.168.0.0–192.168.255.255: This is a contiguous group of 256 class C networks.

The preceding addresses are detailed in RFC 1918. Obviously if one day you did want part of your network on the Internet, you would need to apply for a range of IP addresses (from InterNIC or from your ISP).

These addresses are routable, and routers will route them by default. You aren't supposed to route them publicly and need to configure your router accordingly. Internet backbone routers have been specifically configured not to route these addresses, but that is a specific configuration choice.

People using these addresses must specifically configure their routers not to route these addresses. Routers route these addresses by default because they don't know whether they are gateway routers or some intermediate router on a WAN (behind a gateway). Obviously if you're using them internally, you want your Intranet routers to route the addresses, or you won't be able to communicate intersubnet.

FAQ 17.9 How can I increase the time entries that are kept in the ARP cache?

The default two minutes can be changed by performing the following:

1. Start the Registry editor (REGEDIT.EXE).
2. Move to HKEY_LOCAL_MACHINE\SYSTEM\CurrentControlSet\Services\Tcpip\Parameters.
3. From the Edit menu, select New > DWord Value, enter a name of **ArpCacheLife**, and click OK.
4. Double-click the new value, set to the new value in seconds, and click OK.

5. Close the Registry editor.
6. Reboot.

NT4.0 ONLY

FAQ

17.10 How can I configure more than six IP addresses?

Using the TCP/IP configuration GUI, you are limited to six IP addresses; however, more can be added by directly editing the Registry:

1. Log on as an Administrator.
2. Start the Registry editor (REGEDIT.EXE).
3. Move to HKEY_LOCAL_MACHINE\SYSTEM\CurrentControlSet\Services and scroll down to the service for your adapter card (look at the Adapters tab on the Network Control Panel applet). For example, the Etherlink 3 card is Elnk3; however, you want the first occurrence, so go to Elnk31.
4. Move to the Parameters\TCPIP subkey.
5. Double-click the IPAddress value. Enter in additional IP addresses separated by a new line (see Figure 17-1).
6. When finished, click OK.
7. Next edit the SubnetMask and again, add an entry for each IP address added (in the same order). Click OK when finished.
8. Close the Registry editor.
9. Reboot the machine.

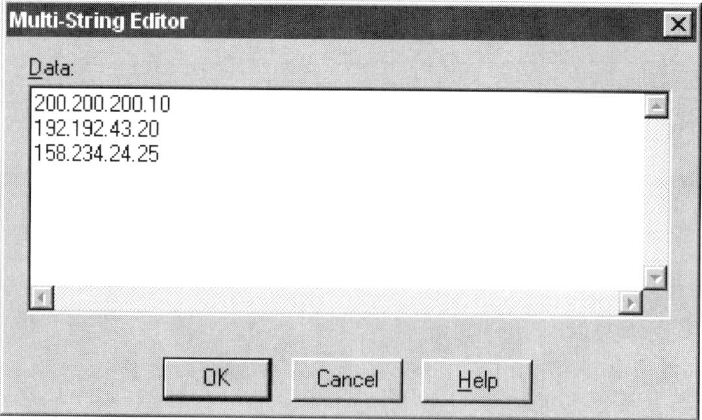

Figure 17-1 Multiple IP addresses via the Registry

FAQ 17.11 What are the common TCP ports?

Following is a list of the most common TCP ports:

Keyword	Port	Description
echo	7	Echo
systat	11	Active users
qotd	17	Quote of the day
msp	18	Message send protocol
ftp-data	20	File transfer (data channel)
ftp	21	File transfer (control)
telnet	23	Telnet
smtp	25	Simple mail transfer
name	42	TCP name server
bootps	67	Bootstrap protocol server
bootpc	68	Bootstrap protocol client
tftp	69	Trivial file transfer
gopher	70	Gopher
finger	79	Finger
www	80	World Wide Web
kerberos	88	Kerberos
pop3	110	TCP post office
nntp	119	Usenet
nfs	2049	Network file system

FAQ 17.12 How can I perform a migration to DHCP?

There are only a few basic Registry entries that define a client as a DHCP client, so an easy way to migrate clients to DHCP is to create a Registry script that sets the required values via logon script. You should obviously be careful that there is no overlap between the addresses in the DHCP address pool and those statically assigned.

The DHCP service needs to be configured to start at system startup. Go to HKEY_LOCAL_MACHINE\SYSTEM\CurrentControlSet\Services\DHCP\ and change the value entry Start from 1 to 2.

TCP/IP parameters are defined to each NIC (network interface card).

The following is an example Registry script you may consider using. If you are unsure of the card service, go to HKEY_LOCAL_MACHINE\SOFTWARE\Microsoft\Windows NT\CurrentVersion\NetworkCards\1 and write down the data for the value entry ServiceName:

```
REGEDIT4

[HKEY_LOCAL_MACHINE\SYSTEM\CurrentControlSet\Services\<card
service>\Parameters\Tcpip]
"EnableDHCP"=dword:00000001
"IPInterfaceContext"=dword:00000001
"IPInterfaceContextMax"=dword:00000001
```

You should then add something into the logon script to detect the NIC installed into the computer, run the REG script and request an IP address—for example:

```
if reg=elpc575 (for the 3com575tx) goto dhcp
..
..
..
:dhcp
regedit /s NIC_dhcp.reg
ipconfig /renew
net send %computername% Congrats Your computer has been configured
for DHCP!
endif
```

A quick way to find out which network card you are using is on your LAN; you will have various types of NIC. For instance, you may have the 3c89d, netflx3,3c575tx for the Neflx3 driver. When the install takes place, it adds a Registry key in the

HKEY_LOCAL_MACHINE\systems\Current control set\system\services\cpqNF31 with the parameters:

```
[HKEY_LOCAL_MACHINE\SYSTEM\CurrentControlSet\Services\CpqNF31\
Parameters\Tcpip]
"EnableDHCP"=dword:00000000.
```

You have to find out what the key name is because it is different for each NIC. Then you can run KIX32.EXE and use the argument:

```
EXISTKEY (
"Key"
)
```

This checks for the existence of a Registry key.

The Key parameter identifies the key you want to check the existence of. It returns:

- 0—The key specified exists (Note : this is different from the way the EXIST function works.)
- >0—The key does not exist, returncode represents an errorcode.

```
$ReturnCode=ExistKey (
"HKEY_LOCAL_MACHINE\SYSTEM\CurrentControlSet\Services\CpqNF31" )

If $ReturnCode=0
? "Key exists...."
Endif
```

To determine whether the key exists and then execute accordingly for that specific card.

You may also set the value IPAddress=0.0.0.0 and value SubnetMask=0.0.0.0 for the card service; however, they will be ignored anyway. Fill in the IPAddress and Subnet-Mask with 0.0.0.0. Blanking out or deleting the values won't work. Restart the work-station to complete the change.

This can also be done using Windows Scripting Host:

```
From MS SupportOnline Article ID: Q197424

'-------------------------------------------------------------------
   ' The following script reads the registry value name IPAddress to
   ' determine which registry entries need to be changed to enable
DHCP.
' This sample checks the first 11 network bindings for TCP/IP, which is
```

```
' typically sufficient in most environments.
' -----------------------------------
  Dim WSHShell, NList, N, IPAddress, IPMask, IPValue, RegLoc
  Set WSHShell = WScript.CreateObject("WScript.Shell")

  NList = array("0000","0001","0002","0003","0004","0005","0006", _
                "0007","0008","0009","0010")

  On Error Resume Next
  RegLoc = "HKLM\System\CurrentControlSet\Services\Class\NetTrans\"

  For Each N In NList
    IPValue = ""      'Resets variable
    IPAddress = RegLoc & N & "\IPAddress"
    IPMask = RegLoc & N & "\IPMask"
    IPValue = WSHShell.RegRead(IPAddress)
    If (IPValue <> "") and (IPValue <> "0.0.0.0") then
      WSHShell.RegWrite IPAddress,"0.0.0.0"
      WSHShell.RegWrite IPMASK,"0.0.0.0"
    end If
  Next

  WScript.Quit        ' Tells the script to stop and exit.
```

FAQ 17.13 How do I assign multiplied IP addresses to a single NIC?

It is possible to assign more than one IP address to a single NIC (network interface card). To configure extra IP addresses under NT 4.0, perform the following:

1. Right-click on Network Neighborhood and select Properties (if you are unable to do this, start the Network Control Panel applet via Control Panel).
2. Select the Protocols tab.
3. Select TCP/IP Protocol and click the Properties button.
4. Select the IP Address tab, and you will see your normal IP address. Click the Advanced button at the bottom of the dialog.
5. Select the Adapted and click Add under the IP addresses section.
6. Enter the new IP address and subnet mask (see Figure 17-2). Click Add.
7. Click OK to the Advanced dialog.
8. Click Apply, then OK to the TCP/IP dialog.

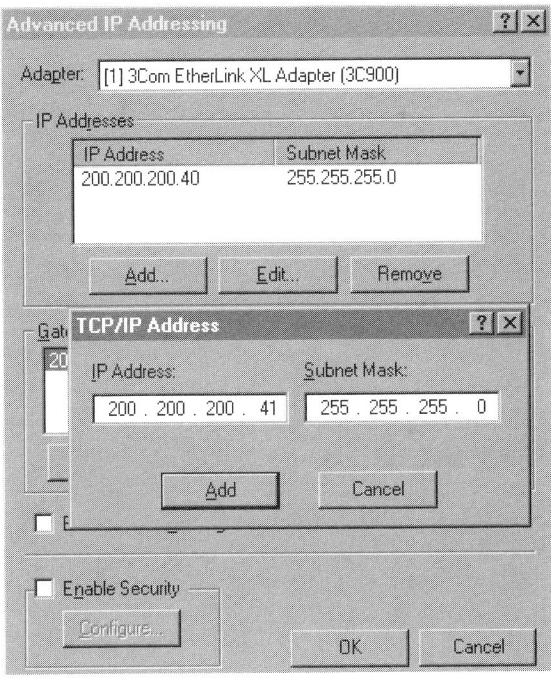

Figure 17-2 Additional IP address via the GUI

9. Close all other dialogs.
10. Reboot the computer.

Under Windows 2000/XP, the procedure is the same, except to get the TCP/IP Protocol Properties, you need to

1. Right-click on My Network Places and select Properties.
2. Right-click on Local Area Connection and select Properties.
3. Select Internet Protocol (TCP/IP) and select Properties.

The procedure is then the same as described earlier except the reboot is not necessary.

17.14 What is IPv6?

IPv6 is the next version of the Internet Protocol—version 6.0, hence IPv6.

Current computers use IP version 4.0, which despite being created in the mid-1970s has done very well; however, it has reached its limit and is about to run out of addresses. Version 4.0 is not the most bandwidth-friendly protocol so it's time for an upgrade.

Following are the four main reasons that IP version 4.0 needs an upgrade:

- Address space limitation—Basically not many IP addresses are left, and with everything from watches having IP addresses we need more.
- Performance—IP has a very strict header format that can waste a great deal of bandwidth.
- Security—The next version of IP has excellent security measures that up to now have had to be handled by higher layers.
- Autoconfiguration—IP configuration is quite complex, and DHCP tries to improve it. The next version of IP allows a computer to just plug into the network and go.

Current IP addresses consist of 32 bits, represented as 4 bytes, dotted-quad format—for example, 200.200.200.202. IP version 6 uses 128 bits for addresses!

IPv6 is defined in the following RFCs (Request for Comments) and can be downloaded from the Microsoft research site.

- RFC 1287—"Towards the Future Internet Architecture"
- RFC 1454—"Comparison of Proposals for Next Version of IP"
- RFC 2373—"IPv6 Addressing Architecture"
- RFC 2374—"IPv6 Global Unicast Address Format"
- RFC 2460—"IPv6 Specification"

FAQ 17.15 How will IPv6 addresses be written?

IPv6 addresses are 128 bit and four times longer than IPv4 addresses. IPv6 addresses are expressed as

```
X:X:X:X:X:X:X:X
```

where each X is a 4-digit hexadecimal integer (16 bits), and each digit is 4 bits. So each digit can be between 0 and F (F is 15 in hexadecimal), and so examples of valid addresses are

```
FEDC:BA98:7654:3210:FEDC:BA98:7654:3210
1080:0:0:0:8:800:200C:417A
```

Notice in the second address, you can leave off any leading zeros, but you must have at least one numeral in each part. For example :0800: can be written as :800:.

Obviously you may have a large sequence of zeros in the address, and so it is possible to have a single gap by writing :: which will fill the gap with zeros—for example 1080:0:0:0:8:800:200C:417A may be written as

```
1080::8:800:200C:417A
```

0:0:0:0:0:0:0:1, the loopback address (the same as 127.0.0.1 in IPv4), can be written as ::1.

A third format is available, when dealing with a mixed environment of IPv4 and IPv6 nodes:

```
x:x:x:x:x:x:d.d.d.d
```

where the x's are the hexadecimal values of the six high-order 16-bit pieces of the address, and the d's are the decimal values of the four low-order 8-bit pieces of the address (standard IPv4 representation). Examples:

```
0:0:0:0:0:0:13.1.68.3
0:0:0:0:0:FFFF:129.144.52.38
```

or in compressed form:

```
::13.1.68.3
::FFFF:129.144.52.38
```

The subnet mask is now replaced by a number appended to the network address specifying the number of bits making up the network part (CIDR notation)—for example, ipv6-address/prefix-length:

```
12AB:0000:0000:CD30:0000:0000:0000:0000/60
12AB:0000:0000:CD30::/60
```

means the first 60 bits make up the network part of the address.

When writing both a node address and a prefix of that node address (e.g., the node's subnet prefix), the two can be combined as follows:
The node address: `11AC:0:0:CA20:123:4567:89AB:CDEF`
and its subnet number: `11AC:0:0:CA20::/60`
can be abbreviated as `11AC:0:0:CA20:123:4567:89AB:CDEF/60`

FAQ 17.16 What is the IPv6 header format?

Following is the specification for the header format of IPv6:

Version	Traffic Class	Flow Label
Payload Length	Next Header	Hop Limit
Source address		
Destination address		

Following is a breakdown of the header:

- Version—4-bit Internet Protocol version number.
- Traffic Class—8-bit traffic class field
- Flow Label—20-bit flow label
- Payload Length—16-bit unsigned integer. Length of the IPv6 payload—that is, the rest of the packet following this IPv6 header, in octets. (Note that any data present is considered part of the payload—i.e., included in the length count.)
- Next Header—8-bit selector. Identifies the type of header immediately following the IPv6 header. Uses the same values as the IPv4 protocol field (RFC 1700).
- Hop Limit—8-bit unsigned integer. Decremented by 1 by each node that forwards the packet. The packet is discarded if the hop limit is decremented to zero.
- Source Address—128-bit address of the originator of the packet.
- Destination Address—128-bit address of the intended recipient of the packet (possibly not the ultimate recipient, if a routing header is present).

Notice that the IPv6 header has far less fields than the IPv4 header, and IPv6 introduces a number of extension headers as defined in RFC 2460.

FAQ 17.17 I am unable to install TCP/IP. Why?

If you are trying to reinstall TCP/IP after previously uninstalling it, the problem may be due to certain TCP/IP Registry values not being removed correctly.

To manually remove the TCP/IP Registry values, perform the following:

1. Start the Registry editor (REGEDIT.EXE).
2. Select the key you want to delete.
3. Select the Security menu and select Owner. The Owner dialog box appears.
4. Click Take Ownership.
5. Select the Security menu and select Permissions. The Registry Key Permissions dialog box appears.
6. In the Name list box, select Everyone.
7. Select Full Control from the Type of Access drop-down list box.
8. Select the Replace Permission on Existing Subkeys checkbox.
9. Click OK.
10. Repeat steps 2 to 8 for all Registry keys to be deleted.
11. Reboot the computer so that Registry changes are recognized by Windows NT.

An alternative that avoids having to change security is to start REGEDT32.EXE under the System account by submitting it via the Scheduler service. Use the following only if the Scheduler is not already running:

```
net start schedule
at <time> /inter regedt32.exe
```

Enter the following only if you had to start it:

```
net stop schedule
```

Once the computer has rebooted, restart REGEDT32.EXE and ensure all of the following are deleted (these are the keys whose security you must set):

Connectivity utilities:

- HKEY_LOCAL_MACHINE\Software\Microsoft\NetBT
- HKEY_LOCAL_MACHINE\Software\Microsoft\Tcpip
- HKEY_LOCAL_MACHINE\Software\Microsoft\TcpipCU
- HKEY_LOCAL_MACHINE\SYSTEM\CurrentControlSet\Services\DHCP
- HKEY_LOCAL_MACHINE\SYSTEM\CurrentControlSet\Services\Lmhosts
- HKEY_LOCAL_MACHINE\SYSTEM\CurrentControlSet\Services\'NetDriver'x\Parameters\Tcpip (where "x" is the number of the network adapter).
- HKEY_LOCAL_MACHINE\SYSTEM\CurrentControlSet\Services\NetBT
- HKEY_LOCAL_MACHINE\SYSTEM\CurrentControlSet\Services\Tcpip

SNMP service:

- HKEY_LOCAL_MACHINE\Software\Microsoft\RFC1156Agent
- HKEY_LOCAL_MACHINE\Software\Microsoft\SNMP
- HKEY_LOCAL_MACHINE\SYSTEM\CurrentControlSet\Services\SNMP

TCP/IP network printing support:

- HKEY_LOCAL_MACHINE\Software\Microsoft\LPDSVC
- HKEY_LOCAL_MACHINE\Software\Microsoft\TcpPrint
- HKEY_LOCAL_MACHINE\SYSTEM\CurrentControlSet\Services\LPDSVC

FTP Server service:

- HKEY_LOCAL_MACHINE\Software\Microsoft\FTPSVC
- HKEY_LOCAL_MACHINE\SYSTEM\CurrentControlSet\Services\FTPSVC

Simple TCP/IP services:

- HKEY_LOCAL_MACHINE\Software\Microsoft\SimpTcp
- HKEY_LOCAL_MACHINE\SYSTEM\CurrentControlSet\Services\SimpTcp

DHCP Server service:

- HKEY_LOCAL_MACHINE\Software\Microsoft\DhcpMibAgent
- HKEY_LOCAL_MACHINE\Software\Microsoft\DhcpServer
- HKEY_LOCAL_MACHINE\SYSTEM\CurrentControlSet\Services\DhcpServer

WINS Server service:

- HKEY_LOCAL_MACHINE\Software\Microsoft\Wins HKEY_LOCAL_MACHINE\Software\Microsoft\WinsMibAgent
- HKEY_LOCAL_MACHINE\SYSTEM\CurrentControlSet\Services\Wins

Windows sockets:

- HKEY_LOCAL_MACHINE\SYSTEM\CurrentControlSet\Services\Winsock
- HKEY_LOCAL_MACHINE\SYSTEM\CurrentControlSet\Services\Winsock2

It may also be necessary to remove the following keys:

- HKEY_LOCAL_MACHINE\System\CurrentControlSet\Enum\Root\Legacy_DHCP
- HKEY_LOCAL_MACHINE\System\CurrentControlSet\Enum\Root\Legacy_Lmhosts
- HKEY_LOCAL_MACHINE\System\CurrentControlSet\Enum\Root\Legacy_LPDSVC
- HKEY_LOCAL_MACHINE\System\CurrentControlSet\Enum\Root\Legacy_NetBT
- HKEY_LOCAL_MACHINE\System\CurrentControlSet\Enum\Root\Legacy_TCPIP
- HKEY_LOCAL_MACHINE\System\CurrentControlSet\Services\LanManServer\Linkage\Bind
- HKEY_LOCAL_MACHINE\System\CurrentControlSet\Services\LanManWorkstation\Linkage\Bind

FAQ 17.18 What switches can be used with Ping?

Ping is used to test TCP/IP connectivity with another host and gives information about the length of time test data takes to be sent to the host and a reply received. Its most basic use is as follows:

```
C:\>ping <IP address or hostname>
Pinging 160.82.52.11 with 32 bytes of data:

Reply from 160.82.52.11: bytes=32 time=10ms TTL=252
Reply from 160.82.52.11: bytes=32 time<10ms TTL=252
Reply from 160.82.52.11: bytes=32 time<10ms TTL=252
Reply from 160.82.52.11: bytes=32 time<10ms TTL=252
```

From the preceding, you can see Ping send 32 bytes to host 160.82.52.11, and each time, a reply was received in 10ms or less. This shows a good connection.

Ping does have a number of option parameters to accomplish different objectives:

```
ping [-t] [-a] [-n count] [-l size] [-f] [-i TTL] [-v TOS] [-r
count] [-s count] [[-j host-list] | [-k host-list]] [-w timeout]
destination-list
```

-t	Ping the specified host until interrupted
-a	Resolve addresses to host names
-n	count Number of echo requests to send
-l size	Send buffer size
-f	Set Don't Fragment flag in packet
-i TTL	Time to live
-v TOS	Type of service
-r count	Record route for count hops
-s count	Timestamp for count hops
-j host-list	Loose source route along host-list
-k host-list	Strict source route along host-list
-w timeout	Timeout in milliseconds to wait for each reply

In Windows 2000, you can press Ctrl+Break when running the -t option for a list of statistics. Press Ctrl+C to actually stop Ping.

It can be useful to have a small batch file ping various hosts and terminal servers at regular intervals to ensure all are still present (although commercial software packages can do this). A simple command like

```
C:\>ping -f -n 1 -l 1 148.32.43.23
Pinging 148.32.43.23 with 1 bytes of data:
Reply from 148.32.43.23: bytes=1 time<10ms TTL=128
```

pings a host once with one byte of data.

You should be aware that Ping works by sending ICMP echo packets, and some routers may filter these out, meaning Ping will not work.

17.19 How can I modify TCP retransmission timeout?

Service Pack 5 for Windows NT 4.0 adds a new Registry entry, InitialRtt, which allows the retransmission time to be modified. The range is 0–65535 milliseconds and can be set as follows:

1. Start the Registry editor (REGEDIT.EXE).
2. Move to HKEY_LOCAL_MACHINE\SYSTEM\CurrentControlSet\Services\Tcpip\Parameters.
3. From the Edit menu, select New > DWORD Value.
4. Enter a name of **InitialRtt** and press Enter.
5. Double-click the new value and set to the number of milliseconds for the timeout—for example, 5000 for 5 seconds (the old default was 3 seconds). Click OK.
6. Close the Registry editor.
7. Restart the machine for the change to take effect.

This parameter controls the initial retransmission timeout used by TCP on each new connection. It applies to the connection request (SYN) and to the first data segment(s) sent on each connection.

Care should be used when adjusting this value. Setting it to large values will dramatically increase the amount of time that it takes for a TCP connection attempt to fail, if the target IP address does not exist.

For instance, the default value is 3,000, or 3 seconds. By default, a connection request is retried two times. The total timeout is (3+6+12) seconds, or 21 seconds.

If this Registry value is set to 6,000 (6 seconds), the total timeout will be (6+12+24) seconds, or 42 seconds. During this time, an application can appear to stop responding (i.e., hang).

FAQ 17.20 How can I disable media-sense for TCP/IP?

Windows 2000 introduces media-sense, which a network interface card (NIC) can detect if it is connected to a network cable and if it is not connected, it disables protocols on that adapter (although the loopback address 127.0.0.1 and the local host name still works).

This may be very inconvenient especially on portables because you may have programs running that require the use of the machine's normal IP address so you can disable this media-sense for TCP/IP only (not the other protocols).

1. Start the Registry editor (REGEDIT.EXE).
2. Move to HKEY_LOCAL_MACHINE\SYSTEM\CurrentControlSet\Services\Tcpip\Parameters.
3. From the Edit menu, select New > DWORD Value.
4. Enter a name of **DisableDHCPMediaSense** and press Enter.
5. Double-click the new value and set to 1.
6. Click OK.
7. Reboot the computer.

FAQ 17.21 How can I check who owns subnet x?

The allocation of IP subnets is centrally controlled and maintained, and this central database can be queried to see who owns a certain subnet. It can also be queried to determine which companies own which subnets.

ARIN is a nonprofit organization that maintains this database and provides a Web-based whois program at http://www.arin.net/whois/.

You can type in a subnet—for example, 169.254—or a name—for example, Microsoft.

17.22 How can I disable APIPA?

APIPA (Automatic Private IP Addressing) is discussed in FAQ 19.18. APIPA is the mechanism in a small network that clients use to automatically allocate themselves an IP address in the range of 169.254.x.x when no DHCP server can be contacted.

It may be desirable to disable this mechanism. To do this, perform the following:

1. Start the Registry editor (REGEDIT.EXE).
2. Move to HKEY_LOCAL_MACHINE\SYSTEM\CurrentControlSet\Services\Tcpip\Parameters\Interfaces.
3. Select the required interface.
4. From the Edit menu, select New > DWORD Value.
5. Enter a name of **IPAutoconfigurationEnabled** and press Enter.
6. Double-click the new value and set to 0. Click OK.
7. Close the Registry editor.

If you have multiple adapters and wish to disable APIPA for all of them, just create and set HKEY_LOCAL_MACHINE\SYSTEM\CurrentControlSet\Services\Tcpip\Parameters\IPAutoconfigurationEnabled to 0.

17.23 What is Quality of Service (QoS)?

Quality of Service was first implemented in the 1970s over the X.25 network, which had limited Quality of Service built into it, allowing differentiation between various X.25 data streams, providing priority transmission for those packets deemed to be a priority. Other technologies since then have had QoS abilities, including the newest technologies such as ATM (Asynchronous Transfer Mode).

Quality of Service at present is not for use over the Internet because it requires end-to-end support. However, it has come from its primarily wide area network (WAN) usage to now be used over the whole network, mainly due to the extended use of networks such as voice over IP and so on. This is not to say QoS will not operate over the Internet; in the future, it will be important to the Internet. It is just not ready yet.

Quality of Service is an end-to-end concept. Every box, router, and bridge must support QoS. But what does it do? Basically you reserve an amount of bandwidth on the network; hence the need for it to be end to end. Suppose a router in the middle of the network did not support QoS. An amount of bandwidth would be reserved from your computer to the router. Suppose the target computer up to the router supported QoS. You would have a reserved pipe. But if the router did not support QoS and reserved no bandwidth, it would all have been wasted. Every component **has** to support QoS for it to work.

There is a second kind of QoS; one where bandwidth is not reserved but is given priority over other traffic. This is known as *differentiated service.*

For Quality of Service to work on a network, two things are required. The first is the reservation of resources, in this case bandwidth, on each component between the two ends of the link. This is done using the Resource Reservation Protocol or RSVP. The second is for the actual data to receive the bandwidth reserved, and while this sounds simple, it can be complicated in the real world.

Winsock 2.0, the Windows sockets implementation, provides full QoS support. However, until now there has never been an implementation method. With Windows 2000, applications can now have full Quality of Service support.

For more information see the following resources:

- http://www.microsoft.com/windows/server/Technical/networking/QoSOver.asp, which has some good information
- http://www.microsoft.com/windows/server/Technical/networking/enablingQOS.asp, which talks about enabling applications to use QoS
- http://support.microsoft.com/support/kb/articles/Q233/0/39.ASP, a Knowledge Base article on using QoS queuing techniques
- http://support.microsoft.com/support/kb/articles/Q228/8/30.ASP talks about SBM (Subnet Bandwidth Manager) used for QoS
- http://msdn.microsoft.com/library/backgrnd/html/msdn_qostech.htm, a MSDN QoS document

FAQ 17.24 How do I install QoS support in Windows 2000?

There are two parts to getting QoS support in Windows 2000.

The first component we have to install to implement QoS is the packet scheduler, which is installed as follows:

1. Right-click on Local Area Network under Network and Dial-Up connections Control Panel applet.
2. Click the install button.
3. Select Service and click Add.
4. Select QoS Packet Scheduler and click OK.
5. QoS will now be listed as an installed service. Click Close.

Although a reboot of the machine is not required after installing the QoS service, it does reset all TCP/IP connections, so make sure you are not doing anything important when installing the packet scheduler.

The next item is to install the QoS Admission Control Server (ACS) as follows:

1. Start the Add/Remove Software Control Panel applet (Start > Settings > Control Panel > Add/Remove Software).
2. Select Add/Remove Windows Components.
3. Select Network Services and click Details.
4. Select QoS Admission Control Service (see Figure 17-3) and click OK.
5. Click Next to the main component dialog.
6. A list of files to copy will be generated and the software installed. Click Finish.

The QoS packet scheduler is available on both Professional and Server Windows 2000 systems; however, the Access Control Service is only an option on Server. The QoS packet scheduler **has** to be installed on **all** clients that will be participating in QoS.

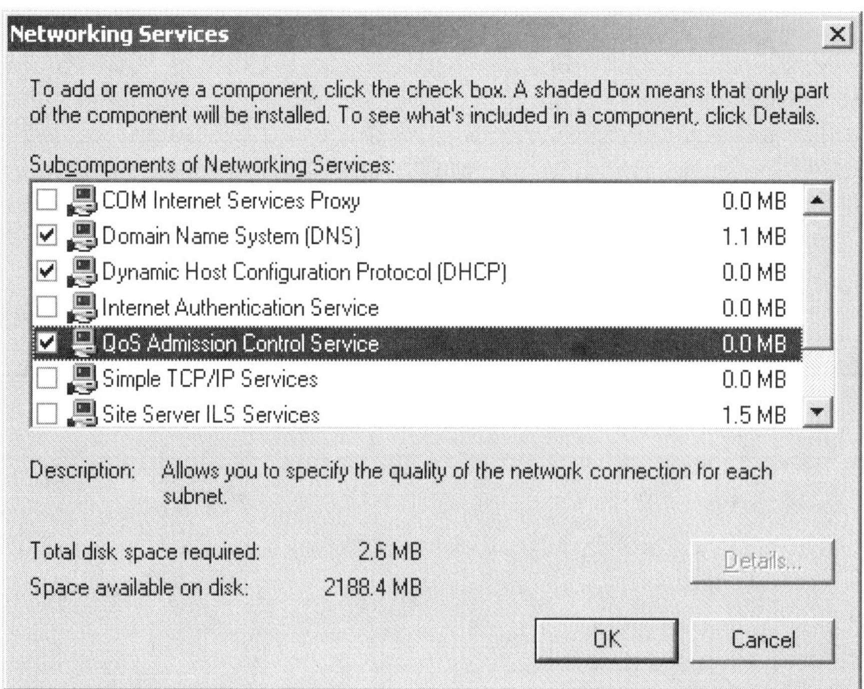

Figure 17-3 Installation of the QoS component

After installing the QoS ACS, a new item will be added to the Administrative menu, the QoS Admission Control MMC snap-in.

FAQ 17.25 How do I configure QoS in Windows 2000?

Installing QoS support is easy; the next task is to administer QoS, telling which users can reserve how much bandwidth and other tasks.

Policies are defined using the QoS Admission Control MMC snap-in (Start > Programs > Administrative Tools > QoS Admission Control), and policies can be defined for two areas, the entire enterprise or for individual subnets. These subnets are defined using the Active Directory Sites and Services MMC snap-in.

Within the various enterprise or subnet configurations are two types of policies, authenticated and unauthenticated users. An authenticated user is any user in a trusted domain who is requesting QoS from a Windows 2000 client; an unauthenticated user is anyone not fitting the former description. It is possible to add policies for a specific user or organizational unit also.

The actual configuration of the QoS policy is the same for an enterprise or a subnet. Thus we will just look at the configuration of a single policy:

1. Start the QoS Admission Control MMC.
2. Select the Enterprise Settings branch.
3. Right-click on Any Authenticated User and select Properties.

   Under the General property sheet, you will notice Any authenticated user is selected for the Identity. The direction is send and receive, and you will see the Service level is All. Other options for the service level are controller load, guaranteed service, and disabled.
4. Selecting the Flow limits tab allows the data rate (by default 500Kbps), the peak data rate, and the duration to be set for each data flow (see Figure 17-4).
5. Selecting the final tab, Aggregate limits, sets limits for **all** data flows combined and includes total combined data rate, combined peak data rate, and number of simultaneous data flows.

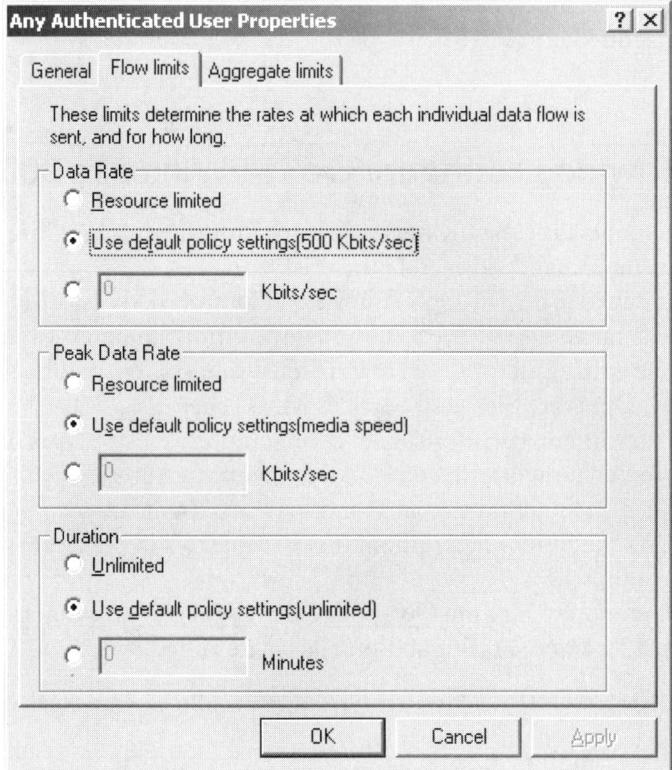

Figure 17-4 Selecting the default policy data rate option

FAQ 17.26 How can I change the account used for the QoS service?

By default the QoS service will run under the System account; however, you may prefer to create a special account for it and modify the service to use it:

1. Create a new account called "ACSService" (ACS for Access Control Service) and add it to the local Administrators group. When adding it, make sure you set the option "password never expires" and unselect the option "user much change password at next logon".
2. Start the Computer Management MMC snap-in (Start > Programs > Administrative Tools > Computer Management).
3. Select the Services and Applications branch.
4. Select Services.

5. Right-click on QoS Admission Control and select Properties.
6. Select the Log On tab.
7. Select the This account option and select the ACSService account; enter its password.
8. Click Apply, then OK (when clicking Apply, the account will be granted the "Log On As A Service" right).

FAQ 17.27 Is IP version 6 available for NT/Windows 2000/95/98?

IP version 6 was first discussed in FAQ 17.14.

Microsoft has provided a release of IP version 6 that can be downloaded from http://research.microsoft.com/msripv6/. It installs on Windows NT and Windows 2000 installations but not Windows 95 or 98. The stack does not replace the IP version 4 stack but sits beside it, allowing normal IP 4 connectivity to continue unaffected.

You can actually download the source and not just the images if you are interested.

FAQ 17.28 What is IPSec?

TCP/IP is widely used in most networks and, with Windows 2000, forms a compulsory part of your network; however, a number of problems with TCP/IP exist.

Data is not sent in an encrypted format over TCP/IP, which leaves it vulnerable to a number of attacks, including eavesdropping, which is when an attacker has access to the network and can therefore view all data sent.

Being able to view data sent over the network allows data such as passwords to be viewed when connecting to some services like FTP, which does not encrypt passwords sent over the network.

A solution was created in IPSec, an industry standard based on end-to-end security that only the transmitting and receiving computers need know about any encryption.

Windows 2000 provides an implementation of IPSec and Group Policy settings in which to define your environment's implementation of the IP add-on. This implementation was developed by Microsoft and Cisco.

One of the great things with IPSec is it operates at layer 3 so any application of IP and upper layer protocols such as TCP and UDP will gain the advantage of IPSec without any modifications being needed to the applications.

17.29 How do I enable IPSec on a machine?

IPSec in a Windows 2000 domain will normally be assigned using Group Policies; however, it can also be set on a computer basis.

1. Right-click on My Network Places and select Properties.
2. Right-click on Local Area Connection and select Properties.
3. Select Internet Protocol (TCP/IP) and click Properties.
4. Click the Advanced button.
5. Select the Options tab.
6. Select IP security and click Properties.
7. Check the Use this IP security policy and select a policy to use (see Figure 17-5):
   - Client (Respond Only)—It will use IPSec only if asked to by the other end of a session.
   - Secure Server (Require Security) —All IP traffic requires security using Kerberos trust.
   - Server (Request Security) —Use IP security if possible.
8. Click OK to all dialogs.

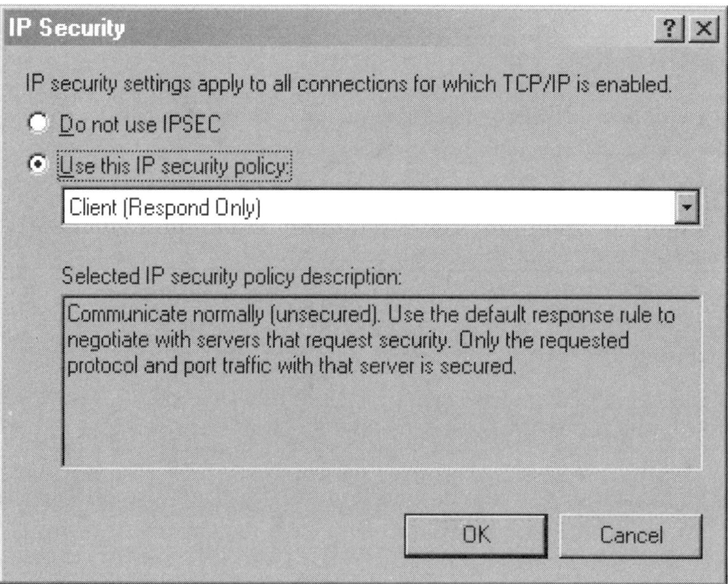

Figure 17-5 Selecting the client IP security policy

To set IPSec on a machine, you must be a member of the local Administrators group. Also if a domain IPSec policy has been defined, then you cannot override with a local policy; the options will be grayed out.

FAQ 17.30 How do I define IPSec policy for a Group Policy Object?

IPSec in a domain environment is defined using a Group Policy Object configured on a domain or organizational unit.

1. Start the Active Directory Users and Computers MMC snap-in (Start > Programs > Administrative Tools > Active Directory Users and Computers).
2. Right-click on the container that has the GPO and select Properties (e.g., the domain).
3. Select the Group Policy tab.
4. Select the Group Policy Object and select Edit.
5. Expand the Computer Configuration root.
6. Expand Windows Settings > Security Settings > IP Security Policies.
7. Right-click on the policy you wish to assign and select Assign from its context menu (see Figure 17-6).
8. You can only assign one; if you assign more than one, the previously assigned one will be unassigned.
9. Close the Group Policy editor.

If you wanted to remove the policy, you right-click on the assigned one and select Unassign from its context menu. Unlike other Group Policy settings, IPSec policies will remain even if the GPO is deleted so make sure you unassign them before deleting the GPO.

To force a GPO update on each client:

```
secedit /refreshpolicy machine_policy /enforce
```

```
Group policy propagation from the domain has been initiated for this
computer. It may take a few minutes for the propagation to complete
and the new policy to take effect. Please check Application Log for
errors, if any.
```

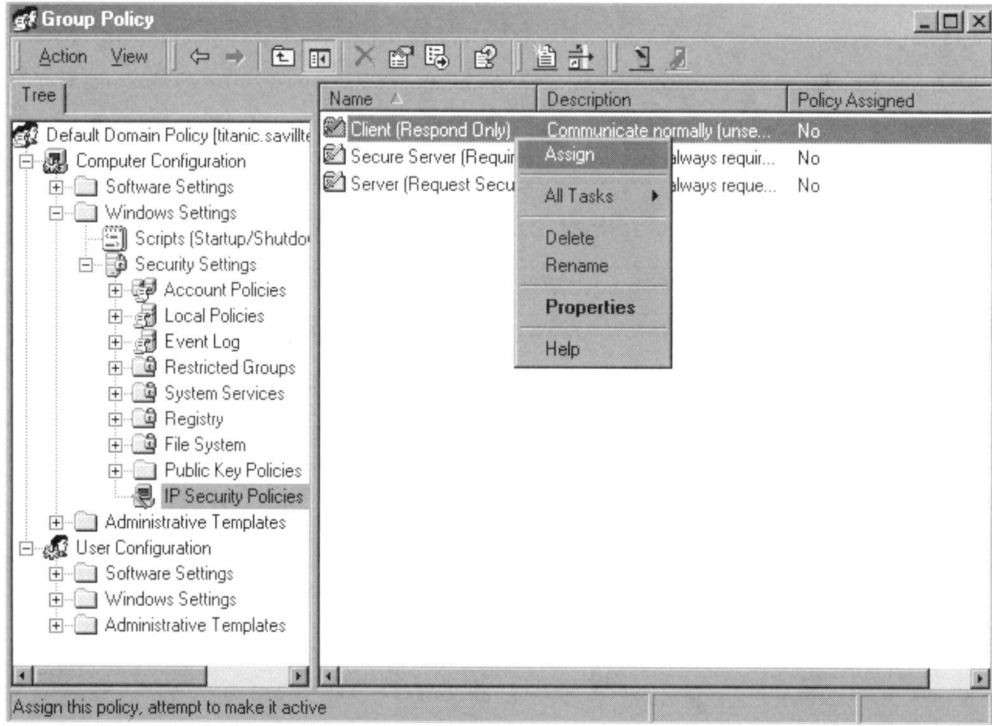

Figure 17-6 Assign a IP security policy content menu option

17.31 How do I enable IPSec traffic through a firewall?

IPSec is generally invisible to routers because it operates at layer 3 of the OSI layer, and all IP and upper-layer protocols are encrypted.

There is however a requirement for firewalls/gateways in the data path because the following IP protocols and UDP ports must be forwarded and not blocked for IPSec to correctly work.:

- IP Protocol ID 50—This is used for both inbound and outbound filters and is needed for Encapsulating Security Protocol (ESP) traffic to be forwarded.
- IP Protocol ID 51—As described for the previous bullet item but used for Authentication Header (AH) traffic.

- UDP Port 500—For both inbound and outbound filters and needs to allow ISAKMP (Internet Security Association and Key Management Protocol) traffic to be forwarded.

L2TP (layer 2 tunneling protocol)/IPSec traffic looks the same as just IPSec traffic on the wire, and you need to open IP Protocol ID 50 and UDP Port 500.

FAQ 17.32 How can I troubleshoot IPSec?

A number of tools are available to help you troubleshoot your IPSec configuration. The tools available are

- The IPSec snap-in for policy configuration
- The event log
- Group Policy snap-in to set IPSec policies for a GPO
- The file OAKLEY.LOG in the %systemroot%\debug directory

Here we will concentrate on two other tools, NETDIAG.EXE and IP Security Monitor (IPSECMON.EXE).

IP Security Monitor is part of standard Windows 2000, but NETDIAG.EXE is supplied as part of the Support Tools (<CD:>\Support\Tools) so you will need to install them.

IP Security Monitor is the simplest tool and shows current security associations for the hosts communicated with over IP and indicates whether IPSec is being used (and if it is, indicates what type of IPSec).

Clicking the Options button allows the update frequency to be changed. In Figure 17-7, one IPSec association is in place using Triple DES.

The meaning of each field is described in the following table:

Active Associations	The number of active security associations with the computer being monitored.
Confidential Bytes Sent	The total number of bytes sent with Confidentiality, indicating that the packets were sent using the Encapsulating Security Payload (ESP) security protocol (decimal ID 50).
Confidential Bytes Received	The total number of bytes received with Confidentiality, indicating that the packets were sent using the Encapsulating Security Payload (ESP) security protocol (decimal ID 50).

(continued)

Authenticated Bytes Sent	The total number of bytes sent with the authentication property enabled.
Authenticated Bytes Received	The total number of bytes received with the authentication property enabled.
Bad SPI Packets	The total number of packets for which the Security Parameters Index (SPI) was invalid. This probably indicates that the security association (SA) has expired or is no longer valid.
	The SPI is a unique identifying value in the SA that allows the receiving computer to select the SA under which a packet will be processed.
Packets Not Decrypted	The total number of packets the receiving IPSec driver was unable to decrypt. This may indicate that the security association (SA) has expired or is no longer valid, authentication did not succeed, or integrity checking did not succeed.
Packets Not Authenticated	The total number of packets that could not be successfully authenticated to the IPSec driver. This may indicate that the security association (SA) has expired or is no longer valid. The information in the security association is required for the IPSec driver to process the packets.
	It may also indicate that the two computers have incompatible authentication settings. Verify that the authentication method specified for each computer is the same.
Key Additions	The total number of keys that ISAKMP (the ISAKMP/Oakley mechanism) sent to the IPSec driver. This indicates that the ISAKMP Phase II security associations were successfully negotiated.
Oakley Main Modes	The total number of successful security associations established during ISAKMP Phase I. This indicates that the key information exchange was successful. Identities were authenticated, and common keying material was established.
Oakley Quick Modes	The total number of successful security associations established during ISAKMP Phase II. This indicates that the negotiation for protection services during the data transfer was successful.
Soft Associations	The total number of ISAKMP Phase II negotiations that resulted in the computers agreeing only to a clear-text data transfer (no encryption or signing of the packets).

Authentication Failures	The total number of times authentication of the computer identities did not succeed. Verify that the authentication method settings for each computer are compatible. This may also indicate that the security association has expired.

NETDIAG.EXE is a more generic tool that is used to troubleshoot network connectivity problems, but one of its options is to test IPSec as follows:

```
netdiag /test:ipsec /v /debug

Gathering IPX configuration information.
Opening \Device\NwlnkIpx failed
Querying status of the Netcard drivers... Passed
Testing Domain membership... Passed
Gathering NetBT configuration information.
Gathering IP Security information

Tests complete.
```

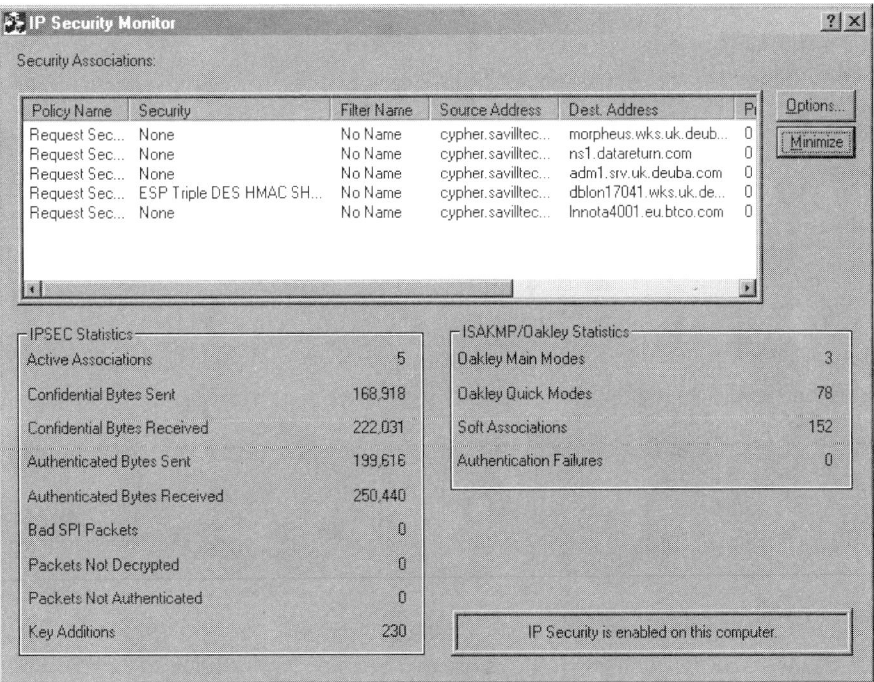

Figure 17-7 Using the IP Security Monitor

```
Computer Name: CYPHER
DNS Host Name: cypher.savilltech.com
DNS Domain Name: savilltech.com
System info : Windows 2000 Professional (Build 2195)
Processor : x86 Family 6 Model 5 Stepping 2, GenuineIntel
Hotfixes :
Installed? Name
..
..

IP Security test . . . . . . . . . : Passed
Directory IPSec Policy Active: 'Server (Request Security)'

IP Security Verbose Test . . . . . : Failed
Access is denied.

The command completed successfully
```

FAQ 17.33 How can I manage/create IP Security policies?

Windows 2000 supplies the IP Security Policies MMC snap-in, which can be used to modify and create IPSec policies. IPSec policies can then be assigned to computers and Group Policy Objects.

To open the snap-in, perform the following:

1. Start the MMC (Start > Run > MMC.EXE).
2. From the console menu, select Add/Remove Snap-in (or press Ctrl+M).
3. From the Standalone tab, click Add.
4. Select IP Security Policy Management snap-in and click Add.
5. Select either Local computer or the domain policy and click Finish. If it's for a domain, select Manage domain policy for this computer's domain. Click Finish.
6. Click Close to the dialog, then click OK.

Double-clicking the root will display the three built-in options.

- Client (Respond Only)
- Secure Server (Require Security)
- Server (Request Security)

If you right-click on the root, you can create a new policy by selecting Create IP Security Policy (see Figure 17-8). If you right-click on an existing policy and select Properties, you can modify its settings.

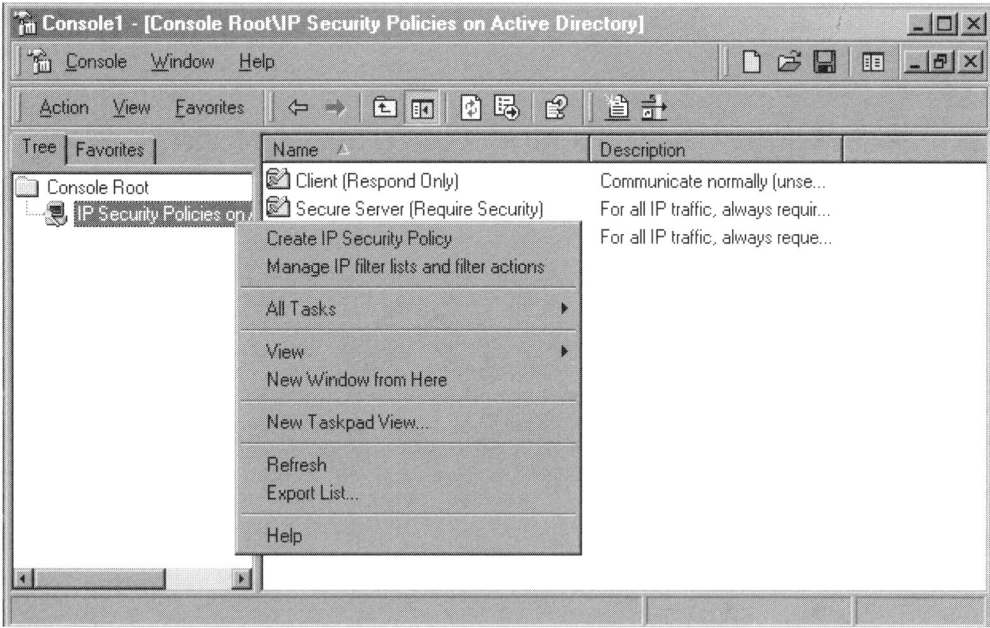

Figure 17-8 Creating a new IP Security Policy

FAQ 17.34 How can I change the authentication method used for IPSec by a policy?

By default IPSec will use Kerberos V5 protocol for its authentication method; however, there are other options:

- Use Windows 2000 Kerberos V5 protocol (the default)
- Use a certificate from a selected certificate authority
- Use a predefined string (a preshared key)

To modify an existing IPSec policy, start the IP Security Policy MMC snap-in as seen in the previous FAQ and perform the following:

1. Right-click on the policy and select Properties from the context menu.
2. Select one of the security rules you wish to change the authentication method for (see Figure 17-9) and click Edit.
3. Select the Authentication Methods tab. The current authentication method will be shown—for example, Kerberos by default. Select it and click Edit.

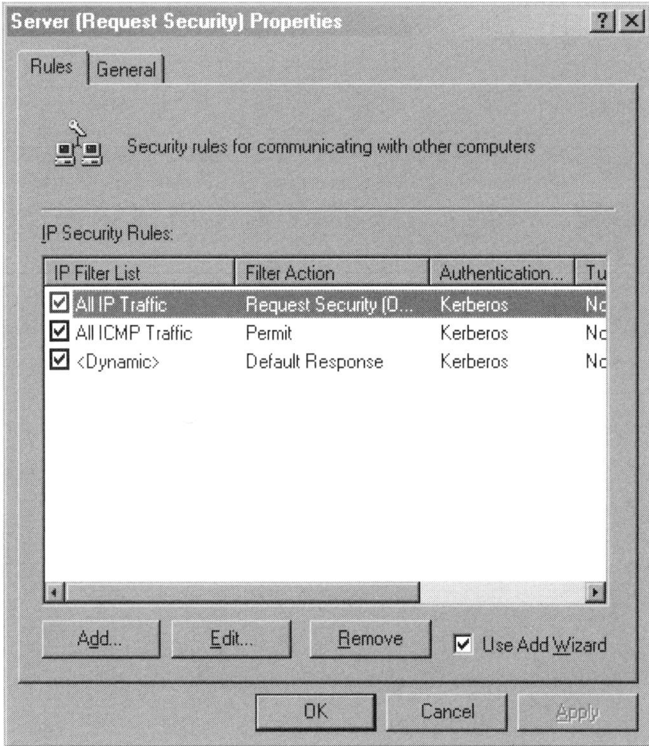

Figure 17-9 Options for securing traffic

4. Select the preferred authentication method.
5. Click Apply, then Close.
6. Close all dialogs.

If the change was made on a domain Group Policy Object to force the change to take effect, you would run the command:

```
secedit /refreshpolicy machine_policy
```

17.35 How can I install a certificate for use by IPSec?

If you wish to use certification for IPSec, then each machine has to have a client or server authentication certificate installed. These certificates can be obtained from a number of Certificate Authorities (including Microsoft for testing, which is what we will do here) and installed as follows:

1. Start Internet Explorer.
2. Move to http://sectestca2.rte.microsoft.com/certsrv.
3. Select Request a certificate and click Next.
4. In the request type screen, select Advanced request and click Next.
5. Under the advanced screen, select Submit a certificate request to this CA using a form and click Next.
6. Enter the details as follows (see Figure 17-10):
   - Name
   - Email

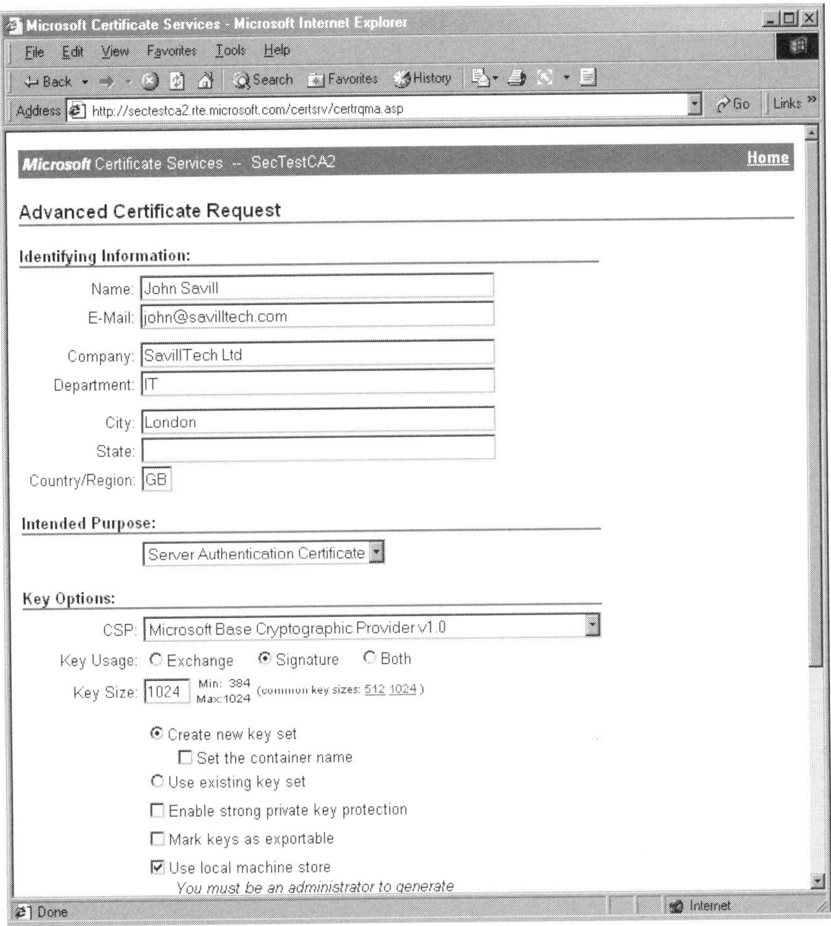

Figure 17-10 Requesting a certificate over the Web

- Select either Server Authentication Certificate or Client Authentication Certificate under Intended use
- For Key Options, set the CSP to Microsoft Base Cryptographic Provider v1.0
- Under Key Usage, select Signature and Key size of 1024
- Check Use local machine store

7. Click Submit. You will be informed to check back in a few days to receive your certificate.

FAQ 17.36 How can I restart the IPSec policy agent on a machine?

A. The policy agent is the component of Windows 2000 responsible for the negotiation between machines of the IPSec. If you experience problems and wish to restart to the policy agent, you can stop and restart its service as follows:

```
net stop policyagent
net start policyagent
```

FAQ 17.37 How do I enable debug logging for IPSec?

It's possible to enable logging for IPSec, which will result in logs being written to the %systemroot%\debug\oakley.log by performing the following Registry change:

1. Start the Registry editor (REGEDIT.EXE).
2. Move to HKEY_LOCAL_MACHINE\SYSTEM\CurrentControlSet\Services\PolicyAgent.
3. From the Edit menu, select New > Key.
4. Enter a name of **Oakley** and click OK.
5. Select the Oakley key and select New > DWORD Value from the Edit menu.
6. Enter a name of **EnableLogging**.
7. Double-click the new value and set to 1.
8. Close the Registry editor.

Restart the policy agent:

```
net stop policyagent
net start policyagent
```

FAQ 17.38 How can I disable "gratuitous ARP"?

When a Windows NT/2000 computer starts, a packet is broadcast on the network containing the computer's TCP/IP address to prevent the use of duplicate addresses on the same network. This is called a "gratuitous Address Resolution Protocol (ARP) packet."

For both performance and maintenance reasons, it is possible to disable this feature in Windows NT if you have Service Pack 5 installed or any version of Windows 2000.

1. Start the Registry editor (REGEDIT.EXE).
2. Move to HKEY_LOCAL_MACHINE\SYSTEM\CurrentControlSet\Services\Tcpip\Parameters.
3. Double-click the ArpRetryCount value, type **0**, and then click OK. If the value does not exist, create it of type REG_DWORD.
4. Close the Registry editor.
5. Reboot the machine.

FAQ 17.39 How do I enable IP forwarding in Windows 2000?

In Windows NT 4.0, you enable IP forwarding by checking Enable IP Routing in the Advanced TCP/IP configuration dialog box. However, to enable a multihomed Win2K box to act as an IP router, you must perform the following steps:

1. Start REGEDIT.EXE.
2. Go to HKEY_LOCAL_MACHINE\SYSTEM\CurrentControlSet\Services\Tcpip\Parameters.
3. Double-click IPEnableRouter.
4. Set the value to 1. Click OK.
5. Close Regedit.
6. Reboot the machine.

FAQ 17.40 How can I change the path used for the TCP/IP database path?

The TCP/IP Windows Sockets (Winsock) standard uses database files for certain information (e.g., host information and service information—stored in the services file). A Windows system typically stores these files in the %systemroot%\system32\drivers\etc folder, but if you want to move these files, perform the following steps to modify the path:

1. Start REGEDIT.EXE.
2. Go to HKEY_LOCAL_MACHINE\SYSTEM\CurrentControlSet\Services\Tcpip\Parameters.
3. Double-click DataBasePath and modify the value to reflect the new location.
4. Click OK.
5. Close Regedit.
6. Reboot the machine.

18 DNS

The Domain Name Service is used to convert host names into an IP address. You use DNS every day; when you open a Web site (e.g. http://www.savilltech.com), your Web browser performs a DNS lookup to your configured DNS servers, which communicate with other DNS servers and return the IP address of the destination server, allowing communications.

In this chapter, we look at installing DNS servers on our local intranets for local name resolution and also how to configure local DNS servers to forward external name resolution requests to other DNS servers.

FAQ 18.1 How do I install the DNS Service?

The DNS Service can only be installed on NT/2000 Server and is installed as follows under NT 4.0:

1. Start the Network Control Panel applet (Start > Settings > Control Panel > Network).
2. Click the Services tab and click Add.
3. Select Microsoft DNS Server and click OK.
4. The software will be installed, and the machine will then reboot.

For Windows 2000, perform the following (if you fail to install DNS and try to run DCPROMO to create a domain, it will offer to install DNS for you):

1. Start the Add/Remove Programs Control Panel applet (Start > Settings > Control Panel > Add/Remove Programs).
2. Click the Add/Remove Windows Components button.
3. Select Networking Services and click Details.
4. Check the Domain Name System (DNS) box and click OK.
5. Click Next to all other dialogs.

FAQ 18.2 How do I configure a domain on the DNS Server?

A new application has been added to the Administrative Tools group, DNS Manager. To configure the domain, follow these procedures for NT 4:

1. Start the DNS Manager (Start > Programs > Administrative Tools > DNS Manager).
2. From the DNS menu, select New Server, enter the IP address of the DNS Server—for example, 200.200.200.3, and click OK.

   The server will now be displayed with a CACHE subpart.
3. Next we want to add the domain (e.g., savilltech.com) from the DNS menu; select New Zone.
4. Select Primary and click Next.
5. Enter the name (e.g., savilltech.com) and then press Tab. It will fill in the Zone File Name. Click Next.
6. Click Finish.
7. Next a zone for reverse lookups has to be created, so select New Zone from the DNS menu.
8. Select Primary and click Next, enter the name of the first three parts of the domain IP plus "in-addr.arpa". For example, if the domain was 158.234.26, the entry would be "26.234.158.in-addr.arpa". In my example, it would be "200.200.200.in-addr.arpa". Click Tab for the filename to be filled and click Next, then click Finish.
9. Add a record for the DNS server, by right-clicking on the domain and select New Record.
10. Enter the name of the machine (e.g., BUGSBUNNY—I had a strange upbringing :-)), enter an IP address (e.g., 200.200.200.3), and click OK.
11. If you click F5 and examine the 200.200.200.in-addr.arpa, a record has been added for BUGSBUNNY there as well.

For Windows 2000, the procedure is similar but has a few changes:

1. Start the DNS MMC snap-in (Start > Programs > Administrative Tools > DNS).
2. Right-click on the DNS server and select Configure the server.
3. Click Next to the welcome screen.
4. Select Yes to create a forward lookup zone and click Next.

5. Select the type of zone. Active Directory integrated will be available only if the DNS server is also a domain controller. Select the type and click Next.
6. Enter the name for the zone (e.g. , savilltech.com) and click Next.
7. Select to create a new file and click Next.
8. Select Yes to create a reverse zone and click Next.
9. Again select the type, Active Directory integrated, standard, or secondary and click Next.
10. Enter the network ID (the first parts of your IP address) and click Next.
11. Select to create a new file and click Next.
12. Click Finish to create the zone.

FAQ 18.3 How do I add a record to the DNS?

To add a record—for example, TAZ with IP address 200.200.200.4—perform the following on NT 4.0:

1. Start the DNS Manager (Start > Programs > Administrative Tools > DNS Manager).
2. Double-click on the name of the DNS server to display the list of zones.
3. Right-click on the domain and select New Record.
4. Enter the name (e.g., TAZ) and enter the IP address. Select the record type. For adding a new host, accept the default, record type A.
5. If you have the Reverse Arpa zone configured and want the PTR record automatically added, make sure the Create Associated PTR record is checked
6. Click OK.

The procedure is basically the same on Windows 2000:

1. Start the DNS MMC snap-in (Start > Programs > Administrative Tools > DNS).
2. Expand Forward Lookup Zones and select the DNS domain you wish to add a record to.
3. Right-click on the DNS domain zone and select New Host from the context menu.
4. Enter the name and IP address for the record and if you want a reverse pointer to be created (see Figure 18-1).
5. Click Add Host.

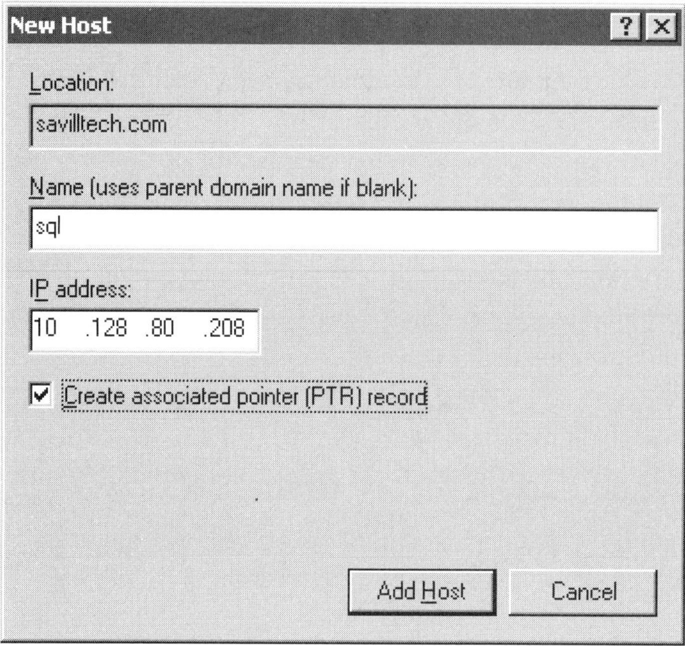

Figure 18-1 Adding a DNS host record with reverse pointer

FAQ 18.4 How do I configure a client to use the DNS?

Once you have DNS servers configured, the clients (and servers) need to be configured to contact them to resolve host names to IP addresses (and in some cases, IP addresses to host names).

If you are using DHCP, then DNS can be configured as part of the scope options for DHCP, and DNS does not need to be set at each client machine. Only if using static IP addresses, do you need to manually set DNS information.

For an NT machine (and Windows 95), perform the following:

1. Start the Network Control Panel applet (Start > Settings > Control Panel > Network).
2. Select the Protocols tab.
3. Select TCP/IP and select Properties.
4. Click the DNS tab.

5. Make sure the machine's name is entered in the first box and the domain name (e.g., savilltech.com) in the Domain box.
6. In the DNS Server part, click Add. In the dialog box, enter the IP address of the DNS Server and click Add.
7. In the Domain Suffix Search Order part, click Add, enter the domain (e.g.,savilltech.com), and then click Add.
8. Finally click OK.

For a Windows 2000 machine, perform the following:

1. Right-click on My Network Places and select Properties.
2. Right-click on Local Area Connection and select Properties.
3. Select Internet Protocol (TCP/IP) and click Properties.
4. Enter the DNS information (see Figure 18-2) and click OK.

To test, you can start a command prompt and enter

```
nslookup <host name>
```

For example, **nslookup taz**.

The IP address of Taz will be displayed. Also try the reverse translation by entering

```
nslookup <ipaddress>
```

For example, **nslookup 200.200.200.4**.

The name Taz will be displayed.

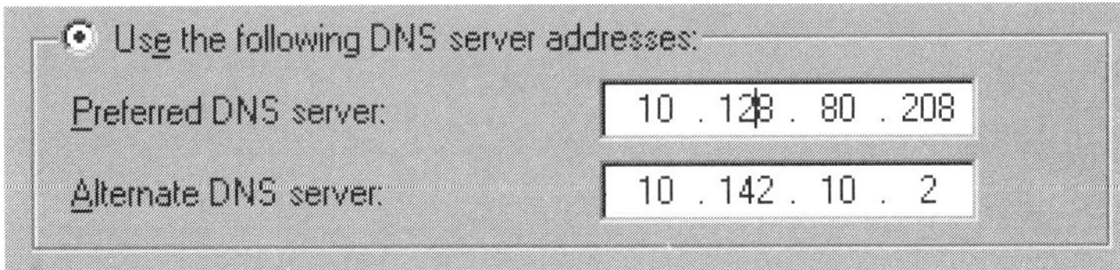

Figure 18-2 Selecting DNS servers for a client

FAQ 18.5 How do I change the IP address of a DNS server?

The following information assumes you have already changed the IP address of the machine (Start > Settings > Control Panel > Network > Protocols > TCP/IP > Properties) and have rebooted (there is no need to reboot for 2000/.NET). The following scenario assumes the old IP address was 200.200.200.3 and the new is 200.200.200.8.

1. We need to configure a second IP address for the network card (Start the Network Control Panel applet (Start > Settings > Control Panel > Network):
   - Click on the Protocol tab.
   - Select TCP/IP and click Properties.
   - Click Advanced and click Add.
   - Enter the old IP address (e.g., 200.200.200.3 and click Add.
   - Click OK until you are back at the Control Panel.
   - Reboot.
2. Start the DNS Manager (Start > Programs > Administrative Tools > DNS Manager):
   - Right-click the Server List and select New Server.
   - Enter the new IP address (e.g., 200.200.200.8) and click OK.
   - Select the old IP address (e.g., 200.200.200.3) and right-click.
   - Select Delete Server from the context menu and click Yes to confirm.
3. While in the DNS Manager, update the record for this server:
   - Select the IP address of the DNS server (e.g., 200.200.200.8) and select the domain name (e.g.,SAVILLTECH.COM).
   - Double-click the entry for the server and update the IP address (i.e., it would have had 200.200.200.3 to bugsbunny). Change to 200.200.200.8.
   - Click OK.
4. Now we will delete the secondary IP address we added:
   - Start the Network Control Panel Applet (Start > Settings > Control Panel > Network).
   - Click on the Protocol tab.
   - Select TCP/IP and click Properties.
   - Click Advanced and select the address (e.g., 200.200.200.3) and click Remove.
   - Click OK until back at Control Panel.

- You will need to reboot at some point to remove the 200.200.200.3 address from being active.

Update all the clients to use the new DNS server IP address.

The preceding procedure is the most complete way; however, it should still work if you only perform steps 2 and 3.

FAQ 18.6 How can I configure DNS to use a WINS server?

It is possible to configure the DNS to use a WINS server to resolve the host name of a Fully Qualified Domain Name (FQDN).

1. Start DNS Manager (Start > Programs > Administrative Tools > DNS Manager).
2. Right-click on the zone you wish to communicate with the WINS server and select Properties.
3. Click the WINS Lookup tab.
4. Select the Use WINS Resolution checkbox and then enter the WINS server IP address and click ADD.
5. Click OK when finished.

FAQ 18.7 Where in the Registry are the entries for the DNS servers located?

The entries for the DNS servers are stored in the Registry in the location HKEY_LOCAL_MACHINE\SYSTEM\CurrentControlSet\Services\Tcpip\Parameters under the NameServer value. Each entry should be separated by a space. Using the Resource Kit utility REG.EXE, the command to change is as follows:

```
reg update
HKLM\System\CurrentControlSet\Services\Tcpip\Parameters\NameServer="
158.234.8.70 158.234.8.100" \\<machine name>
```

where 158.234.8.70 and 158.234.8.100 are the addresses of the DNS servers you want to configure.

> **Note:** *The reg update command sets the value; it does not append. So be sure you enter the existing DNS servers as well as the new ones.*

The reg update command may be useful for granting users access to the Internet by remotely updating their Registry to know which DNS servers to use.

FAQ 18.8 I receive the error message "No More Endpoints." Why?

This error can be caused by installing DNS on a machine that has previous settings contained in the %systemroot%\system32\dns directory. To correct, perform the following:

1. Stop the Microsoft DNS server using the Services Control Panel applet (Start > Settings > Control Panel > Services). Select Microsoft DNS and select Stop.
2. Back up any zone files from the %systemroot%\system32\dns directory that you may want.
3. Remove the DNS server by right-clicking on Network Neighborhood and selecting Properties. Click the Services tab, select DNS, and click Remove.
4. Delete all files in the %systemroot%\system32\dns.
5. Reinstall the DNS server using the Services tab of the Network Control Panel applet.

FAQ 18.9 How do I configure DNS for a Windows 2000 domain?

Windows 2000 domains rely on DNS and require Dynamic DNS, which is an update to the basic DNS specification. Details about Dynamic DNS can be found in RFC 2136 that can be viewed at ftp://ftp.isi.edu/in-notes/rfc2136.txt.

Another major update in DNS 5.0 is the addition of service (SRV) records. These have already been seen as a mechanism for publishing the LDAP server, _ldap._tcp.<domain>. It is through these records that domains can be looked up through the DNS service.

You could configure DNS on a separate Windows 2000 machine. The domain controller and the DNS server will probably not be the same machine. The DNS server just has to exist before upgrading the server to a domain controller (unless you allow the DCPROMO process to configure DNS for you). To install DNS 5.0 on the server, perform the following:

1. Start the Install/Remove Programs Control Panel applet (Start > Settings > Control Panel > Add/Remove Programs).

2. Click the Configure Windows left pane.
3. Click the Components button that is displayed.
4. Select Networking Options and click Details.
5. Select Microsoft DNS Server and click OK.
6. Click Next.

Before actually configuring the DNS service, modify the TCP/IP properties of the machine to use itself as the DNS server:

1. Right-click on My Network Places and select Properties.
2. Right-click on the Local Area Connection and select Properties.
3. Select Internet Protocol (TCP/IP) and click Properties button.
4. Under the DNS section, select Use the following DNS server addresses and enter the machine's IP address.
5. You can also click Advanced, select the DNS tab, and ensure the DNS suffix for the connection is the DNS domain you are about to create. Click OK.
6. Click OK on all dialogs to close all windows.

Now check that the computer's primary suffix is set:

1. Right-click on My Computer and select Properties.
2. Select the Network Identification tab and click the Properties button.
3. Click the More button.
4. Ensure the primary DNS suffix of this computer is set to the DNS domain you are about to create (see Figure 18-3) and click OK.
5. Click OK to all dialogs to close all windows.
6. Click Yes to restart the computer.

If you don't do this first, your NS records for the zones will simply list the computer name, followed by a period (.), rather than the FQDN of your NS, which may cause problems. You can forgo this step, and the NS records will be updated after the machine becomes a DC, but I've heard of some problems with this approach.

You then need to configure the DNS service:

1. Start the DNS Management MMC snap-in (Start > Programs > Administrative Tools > DNS Management).
2. Right-click on the root and select Configure Server. This will start the configuration applet. Click Next.
3. It will detect there are no root servers so select This is the first DNS server on this network and click Next.

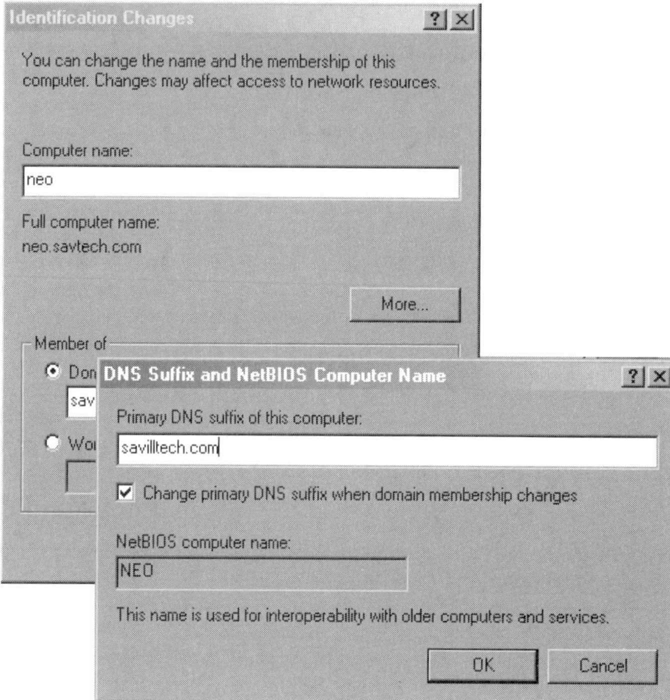

Figure 18-3 Setting the DNS suffix of a computer

4. Check Yes, add a forward lookup zone, and click Next. This zone is used for the storage of host name to IP addresses.
5. You should now select the zone type. Select Standard Primary and click Next. Active Directory Integrated stores the DNS database in the Active Directory; however, there is no Active Directory at this point. This option can be set later.
6. Enter the name of the zone (e.g.,savilltech.com) and click Next.
7. Select New File and click Next. If you had an existing .DNS file, you may import it.
8. Check Yes, add a reverse lookup zone, and click Next. The reverse lookup zone is used to find the host name from a IP address. When you create a host record, a PTR record can also be selected to be created, which adds a record in the reverse lookup zone.
9. Again select Standard Primary and click Next.
10. Enter the first parts of your subnet (e.g., 200.200.200.0—the subnet will be filled in for you). If your subnet mask was 255.255.0.0, you enter the first two parts of your IP address; if 255.255.255.0, you enter the first three. Click Next.

11. Again Check New File and click Next.
12. A summary will be displayed; click Finish to complete the installation.

The final stage is to configure the zones to be dynamic update enabled, which allows hosts to add records in the DNS server.

1. Start the DNS Management MMC snap-in (Start > Programs > Administrative Tools > DNS Management).
2. Expand the DNS server, expand the Forward Lookup Zones, select the domain (e.g., savilltech.com).
3. Right-click on the domain and select Properties from the context menu.
4. Select Yes from the Allow dynamic updates? drop-down box.
5. Click Apply, then OK.
6. Now expand the Reverse Lookup Zones and select the reverse lookup zone (e.g., 200.200.200.x Subnet).
7. Select the zone, right-click the zone, and select Properties from the context menu.
8. Again select Yes from the Allow dynamic updates? drop-down box.
9. Click Apply, then OK.

DNS is now configured for a domain, and you can create the domain.

To ensure all entries are correctly entered, enter the following command in a command window (CMD.EXE):

```
ipconfig /registerdns
```

FAQ 18.10 How do I configure Active Directory–integrated DNS?

It is possible to configure DNS servers that are also domain controllers to store the contents of the DNS database in the Active Directory, which will then be replicated to all domain controllers in the domain. The option to store the DNS database in the Active Directory is not available on DNS servers that are not domain controllers.

1. Start the DNS Management MMC snap-in (Start > Programs > Administrative Tools > DNS Management).
2. Expand the DNS server, expand the Forward Lookup Zones, select the domain (e.g., savilltech.com).
3. Right-click on the domain and select Properties from the context menu.
4. Under Type, click Change.

5. Select Active Directory-integrated and click OK.
6. Click OK to Are you sure you want this zone to become an Active Directory-integrated.
7. Click Apply, then OK.

NT4 ONLY

18.11 Why does setting a secondary DNS server as primary result in errors?

If you have a secondary DNS server configured to duplicate all entries from another DNS server, you may experience a problem. The problem arises when you try to set it as a primary DNS server, which results in the service not starting and an error to the effect of the data being wrong:

```
Event ID: 7023
The MS DNS Server service terminated with the following error:
The data is invalid.

Event ID: 130
DNS Server zone zone name has invalid or corrupted registry data.
Delete its registry data and recreate with DNSAdmin.

Event ID: 133 DNS
Server secondary zone zone name, had no master IP addresses in
registry.
Secondary zones require masters.
```

The DNS Manager forgets to set the correct value for the DNS Type in the Registry (secondary is remaining), but it is erasing the address of the primary DNS, where the data came from. To correct this problem, perform the following:

1. Start the Registry editor (REGEDIT.EXE).
2. Move to and locate the following key: HKEY_LOCAL_MACHINE\SYSTEM\CurrentControlSet\Services\Dns\Zones\< zonename >, where < zonename> is the domain (e.g., savilltech.com).
3. Double-click on the TYPE value and change from 2 to 1.
4. Close the Registry editor.

You should now be able to successfully start the DNS service.

```
net start dns
```

The TYPE value can have one of two values:

- 0x1—Specifies primary zone
- 0x2—Specifies secondary zone

This is fixed in Service Pack 4 for Windows NT 4.0.

FAQ 18.12 How do I turn off Dynamic DNS?

By default, the TCP/IP stack in Windows 2000 attempts to register its Host (A) record with its DNS server. This makes sense in an all Windows 2000 environments. But if you are using a static, legacy DNS server, the DNS guys might not like all the "errors" that show up on their server because the DNS servers will not understand these "updates."

You will get errors such as:

- `Dnsapi`
- `Failed to register network adapter with settings`
- `Sent update to server`

To make the clients stop attempting to publish their DNS names/addresses to the DNS server, perform the following:

1. Log on to each client as Administrator.
2. Start the Registry editor (REGEDIT.EXE).
3. Move to HKEY_LOCAL_MACHINE\SYSTEM\CurrentControlSet\Services\Tcpip\Parameters.
4. From the Edit menu, select New > DWORD Value.
5. Enter a name of **DisableDynamicUpdate** and press Enter.
6. Double-click on the new value and set to 1. Click OK.

If you have multiple adapters in the machine, you may not want to disable for all. So instead of setting HKEY_LOCAL_MACHINE\SYSTEM\CurrentControlSet\Services\Tcpip\Parameters\DisableDynamicUpdate to 1, set it as 0, and then move to the subkey Interfaces\<interface name>, create the DisableDynamicUpdate value there, and set it to 1.

If you needed to perform this on a large number of machines, you should create a REG script or set it from the logon script.

18.13 How do I configure a forwarder on Windows 2000 DNS?

If you create a DNS server on your network but it is not the main DNS server (i.e., your company has a central main DNS server), you will want to forward queries your DNS server cannot service to that DNS server.

This is because only certain servers in your network will have access to DNS servers outside your network (due to firewalls, etc.), and thus your (departmental?) DNS server cannot access the DNS servers higher up in the DNS hierarchy. To configure a forward, perform the following:

1. Start the DNS Management MMC snap-in (Start > Programs > Administrative Tools > DNS Management).
2. Right-click on the DNS server and select Properties.
3. Select the Forwarders tab.
4. Check the Enable forwarder(s) box.
5. Enter the IP address of the DNS server and click Add (see Figure 18-4).

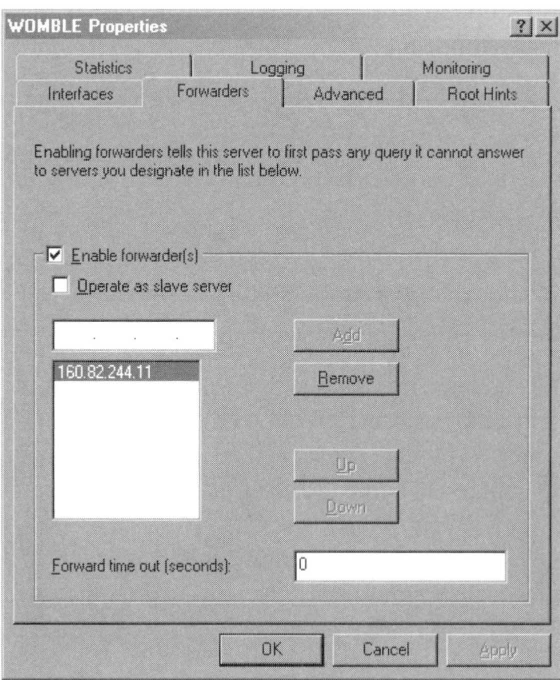

Figure 18-4 Enabling DNS forwarding on a DNS server

6. Click OK.
7. Close the DNS Management snap-in.

If you are missing the Forwarders tab or it's not available, see FAQ 18.14 following.

FAQ 18.14 I am missing the Forwarder and Root Hints tabs in DNS 5.0. What should I do?

This is caused if your server thinks it is the root server in the domain and will therefore have a "." zone. To enable the forwarder, you need to delete this zone from your server:

1. Start the DNS Management MMC snap-in (Start > Programs > Administrative Tools > DNS Management).
2. Expand the server, expand Forward Lookup Zones and select "." (see Figure 18-5).
3. Right-click and select Delete.
4. Click Yes to the confirmation.
5. Stop and start the DNS Manager, and the tabs are available.

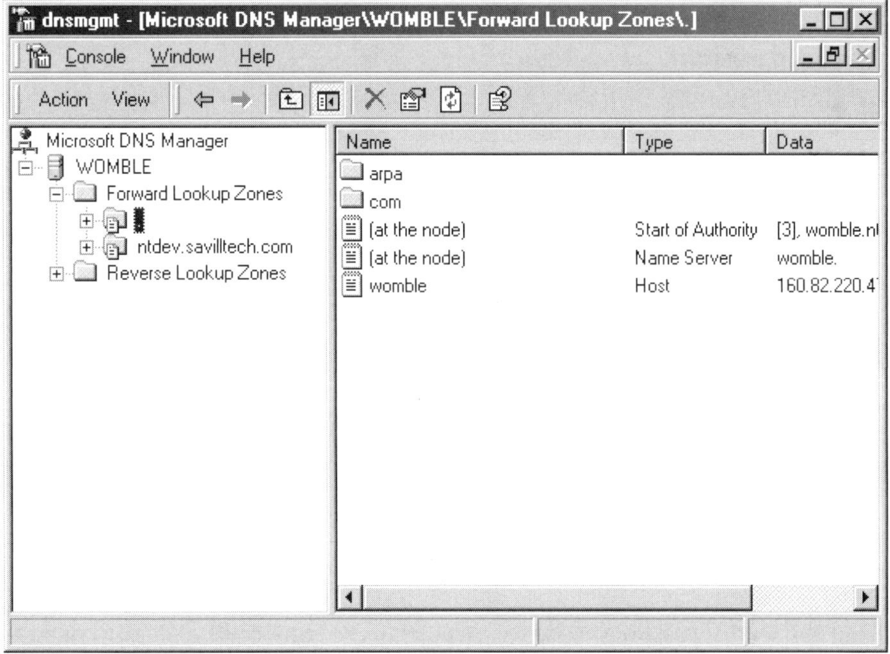

Figure 18-5 The "." DNS zone

This can also be done from the command line using

```
dnscmd /ZoneDelete . /DsDel
```

/DsDel is required if the zone is Active Directory integrated.

NT4.0 ONLY

FAQ 18.15 How do I enable DNS round robin resolution?

Recent Windows NT service packs introduced LocalNetPriority, which tries to return host resources that are local to the requestor instead of using round robin. However, round robin can be enabled as follows:

1. Start the Registry editor (REGEDIT.EXE).
2. Move to HKEY_LOCAL_MACHINE\SYSTEM\CurrentControlSet\Services\DNS\Parameters.
3. From the Edit menu, select New > DWORD Value.
4. Enter a name of LocalNetPriority and press Enter.
5. Double-click the new value and set to 0 to disable LocalNetPriority and reenable round robin. Click OK.
6. Close the Registry editor.
7. Stop and restart the DNS service.

FAQ 18.16 Why does DNS resolution of a valid domain fail on NT?

If you are running NT4 DNS with either SP4 or SP5 installed, you may find a domain that resolves on UNIX DNS servers several times out when you do an NSLOOKUP on NT. This is a known bug and is fixed in Service Pack 6a for Windows NT 4.0.

FAQ 18.17 How can I force a Windows 2000 domain controller to re-register its DNS entries?

To re-register the domain controller DNS entries, perform one of the following:

- Stop and start the netlogon service, which will re-register all SRV records in the NETLOGON.DNS file.

- Netdiag /fix will also do this.
- Ipconfig /registerdns.

FAQ 18.18 I'm getting DNS zone transfer messages in the event log. Is someone hacking me?

No, don't panic. It just means someone is listing the content of a zone, which is fine because you are making the information publicly available anyway.

If you want to prevent people from performing zone transfers, start the Microsoft DNS Manager, select the Zone, go into the Properties for the zone, and select the Notify tab. Check Only Allow Access for Secondaries included on the notify list. A typical event log is shown in Figure 18-6.

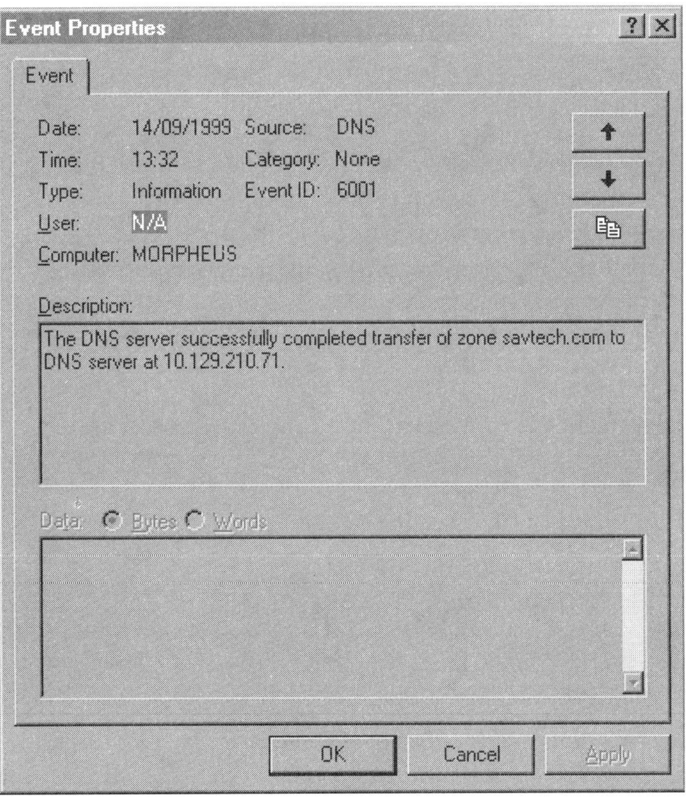

Figure 18-6 Performing a DNS zone transfer event log

18.19 How can I stop DNS cache pollution?

DNS cache pollution can occur if Domain Name Service (DNS) spoofing has been encountered. The term "spoofing" describes the sending of unsecure data in response to a DNS query. It can be used to redirect queries to a rogue DNS server and can be malicious in nature.

Windows NT DNS can be configured to filter responses to unsecured records by performing the following:

1. Start the Registry editor (REGEDIT.EXE).
2. Move to HKEY_LOCAL_MACHINE\System\CurrentControlSet\Services\DNS\Parameters.
3. From the edit menu, select New > DWORD Value.
4. Enter a name of **SecureResponses** and press Enter.
5. Double-click the new value and set to 1. Click OK.

The following is taken from Knowledge Base article Q198409, which helps us understand spoofing:

> Examples: DNS server makes MX query for domain.samples.microsoft.com to samples.microsoft.com's DNS server. The samples.microsoft.com DNS server responds but includes A record for A.ROOT-SERVERS.NET giving its own address. The rogue DNS server has then gotten itself set up as a root server in your DNS server's cache. Less malicious, but more common, are referral responses (or direct responses from BIND, see WriteAuthorityNs for discussion) that contain records for the DNS of an ISP: Authority section:
>
> new.samples.microsoft.com NS ns.new.samples.microsoft.com.
> new.samples.microsoft.com NS ns.isp.samples.microsoft.com.
>
> Additional section:
>
> ns.new.samples.microsoft.com. A 1.1.1.1
> ns.isp.samples.microsoft.com. A 2.2.2.2
>
> **Note:** *The address record for the ISP happens to be old\stale. If SecureResponses is on, records that are not in a subtree of the zone queried are eliminated. For example, in the example above, the samples.microsoft.com. DNS server was queried, so the all the samples.microsoft.com records are secure, but the ns.isp. microsoft.com. A record is not in the sample .microsoft.com. subtree, and is not cached or returned by the DNS server."*

18.20 How can I enable my Web site to be accessible as ntfaq.com instead of www.ntfaq.com?

We are all used to entering www.<domain> for a Web site, such as www.serverfaq.com; however, www is just a normal DNS host record. If you want your site to be accessible as just <domain> (e.g.,yahoo.com), just create a blank host record.

To create a blank host record for the domain in Windows 2000, perform the following:

1. Start the DNS MMC snap-in (Start > Programs > Administrative Tools > DNS).
2. Expand the server > Forward Lookup Zones > DNS domain.
3. Right-click on the domain and select New Host.
4. Leave the name blank and just enter the IP address (check the Create associated pointer record box—see Figure 18-7).
5. Click Add Host.

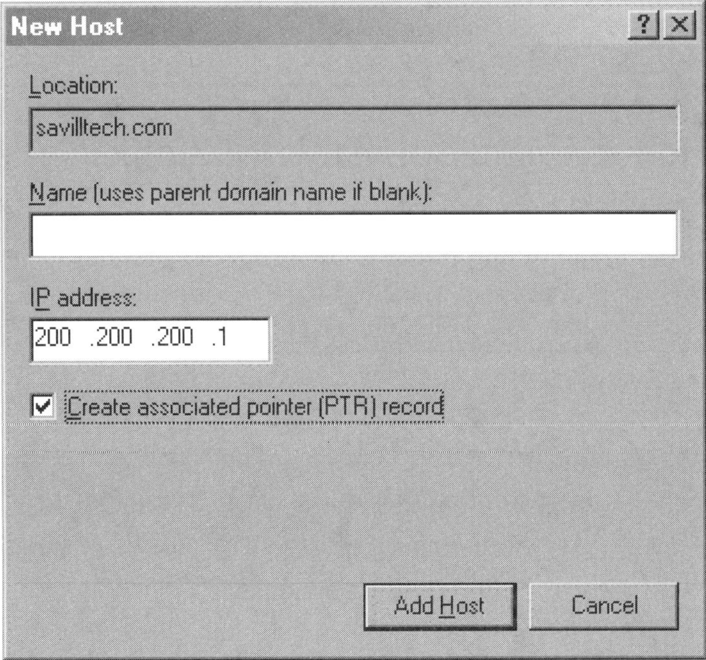

Figure 18-7 Creating a blank host record for a domain

A new host record will be listed of the form: (same as parent folder) Host <ip address>. To do this on NT 4.0 for the domain ntfaq.com at address W.X.Y.Z, complete the following steps:

1. Stop the DNS service:

```
net stop dns
```

2. Edit the file NTFAQ.COM.DNS (it can be found at %systemroot%\system32\dns*.dns).
3. Find a record that looks like:

```
www IN A W.X.Y.Z
```

4. Add the following record:

```
@ IN A W.X.Y.Z
```

5. Save the file.
6. Restart DNS Service:

```
net start DNS
```

FAQ 18.21 How can set the primary DNS suffix in Windows 2000?

In Windows NT 4.0, you set the primary DNS suffix using the domain field in the DNS tab of TCP/IP properties. In Windows 2000, this is performed as follows:

1. Right-click on My Computer and select Properties.
2. Select the Network tab.
3. Click the Properties button.
4. Click the More button.
5. Enter the Primary DNS suffix (see Figure 18-8) and click OK.
6. Click OK to the prompt informing you that you will need to reboot the computer.
7. Close all dialogs.
8. Reboot the computer.

This is very important on domain controllers before configuring DNS because without this configured, the created DNS records will not have the fully qualified host name.

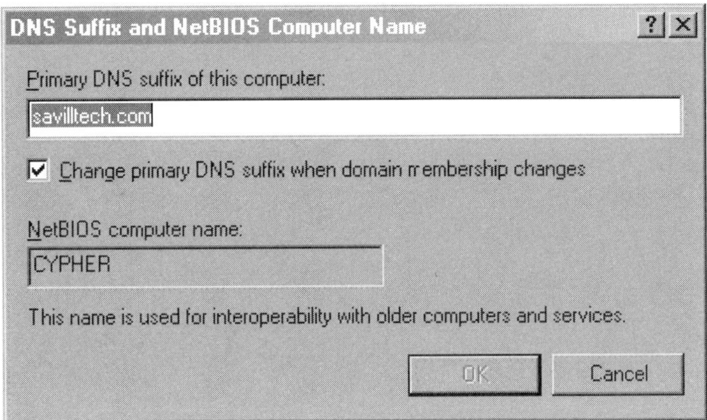

Figure 18-8 Modifying the DNS suffix with the ability to change if the domain membership changes

FAQ 18.22 How do I create a caching-only DNS server?

Normally a DNS server holds records about various DNS zones that are replicated between other DNS servers (via the Active Directory in a AD-integrated zone).

Caching-only DNS servers don't actually host any zones and are not authoritative for any domains, but rather just cache results from queries asked them by clients. If a client asks it to resolve www.savilltech.com, it will ask a zone holding DNS server to resolve it and cache the answer. If another client asks it to resolve the same record, it can answer from its cache. This is similar in a way to a proxy server that caches popular Web pages.

These are useful for sites connected via a WAN with a local caching-only DNS server saving on network traffic. To configure a caching-only DNS server, perform the following:

1. Ensure the machine has a static IP address.
2. Install the DNS service as per normal (Start > Settings > Control Panel > Add/Remove Software > Add/Remove Windows Components > Components > Networking Services > Details > Domain Name System (DNS) > OK > Next > Finish).
3. Start the DNS MMC (Start > Programs > Administrative Tools > DNS).
4. From the Action menu, select Connect To Computer.
5. In the Select Target Computer window, enable the option, "Connect to the specified computer now" and enter the name of a DNS server you want to cache (see Figure 18-9). Then click OK.

The machine will now start to gather a cache of host IP mappings.

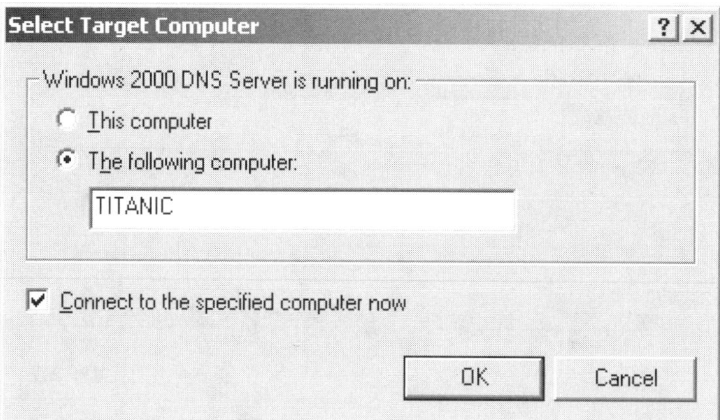

Figure 18-9 Selecting the target server

To clear the cache, right-click on the actual server name (not the server it is caching from) and select Clear Cache from the context menu.

18.23 How can I stop my Windows domain controllers from dynamically registering DNS names?

By default, the netlogon service on a domain controller (DC) registers dynamic DNS records to advertise Active Directory (AD) services. However, you can disable this feature with a Registry setting. Perform the following steps:

1. Start REGEDIT.EXE.
2. Go to HKEY_LOCAL_MACHINE\System\CurrentControlSet\Services\Netlogon\Parameters.
3. If the UseDynamicDns value exists, double-click it and set it to 0.
4. If the UseDynamicDns value doesn't exist, from the Edit menu, select New > DWORD Value.
5. Enter a name of **UseDynamicDns** and press Enter.
6. Double-click the new value and set it to 0.
7. Click OK.
8. Close Regedit.
9. Reboot the server.

If you disable dynamic DNS updates, you should manually create the needed records based on the %windir%\system32\config\netlogon.dns file.

FAQ 18.24 How can I tell which boot method my DNS service uses?

Windows can store DNS startup information in one of three possible locations. The OS records the location in the DNS BootMethod Registry subkey by using the following values:

- 1—In a BIND-style file (%SystemRoot%\System32\DNS\Boot); the system still checks the Registry for missing data in the file. Windows 2000 DNS doesn't support this option.
- 2—In the Registry.
- 3—In both the Registry and Active Directory (AD).

To check the BootMethod Registry subkey to see which location your DNS service uses, perform the following steps (don't modify the value):

1. Start REGEDIT.EXE.
2. Go to HKEY_LOCAL_MACHINE\SYSTEM\CurrentControlSet\Services\DNS.
3. View the BootMethod value and compare it to the three options listed previously.
4. Close Regedit.

Note that if you upgrade from Windows NT 4.0 to Win2K, you need to check this value after the upgrade. If you haven't applied Service Pack 4 (SP4) to NT 4.0, the system should use an alternate key, EnableRegistryBoot, until the DNS service populates the correct key.

FAQ 18.25 How do I use the DNSCMD application?

To configure DNS, you usually use the Microsoft Management Console (MMC) DNS snap-in; however, Microsoft supplies a new command-line tool, DNSCMD.EXE, as part of the Support Tools collection. You can either install all the Support Tools or simply extract DNSCMD.EXE as follows:

1. Insert the Windows 2000 CD-ROM.
2. Navigate to the \Support\Tools folder.

3. Right-click SUPPORT.CAB and select Explore from the context menu.
4. Locate DNSCMD.EXE, right-click it, and select Extract from the context menu.
5. Select a location to save the file to (somewhere within your PATH environment variable unless you want to type the full path every time you use the command).
6. After you install the tool, use the following syntax:

```
dnscmd [<target server>] <command> [<command options>]
```

FAQ 18.26 In a multi-DNS server environment, how do I configure the DNS servers to resolve both local and remote hosts?

Windows 2000, Windows NT, and Windows 9x let you identify multiple DNS servers. So, for example, you might have a local DNS server on your network and a remote DNS server if you connect to the Internet. In this situation, if you list your local DNS server first, you might not be able to resolve remote names, and if you list the remote DNS server first, you might not be able to resolve local names.

In a multiple DNS server environment, if a client queries the first DNS server and that server doesn't respond, the client will query the second DNS server. If the first DNS server (e.g., a local DNS server that doesn't know about a remote host) responds with an unknown host, then the client won't query other DNS servers. Instead, the client will resort to using other methods (e.g., LMHOSTS, WINS) to resolve the domain name.

To work around this problem, you need to configure your machines to forward DNS information, which typically means configuring local DNS server information on the clients and configuring the local DNS servers to forward unknown requests to the remote DNS servers.

19 DHCP

DHCP stands for Dynamic Host Configuration Protocol and is used to automatically configure a host during boot up on a TCP/IP network. DHCP is also used to change settings while the host is attached.

This means that you can store all the available IP addresses in a central database along with information such as the subnet mask, gateways, and DNS servers.

The basics behind DHCP are that the clients are configured to use DHCP instead of being given a static IP address. When the client boots up, it sends out a BOOTP request for an IP address (see Figure 19-1). A DHCP server then offers an IP address that has not been assigned from its database, which is then leased to the client for a predefined time period.

If the DHCP client is Windows 2000, no offer is made, and if IP auto configuration has not been disabled, the client will attempt to find and use an IP address not currently in use; otherwise, TCP/IP will be disabled.

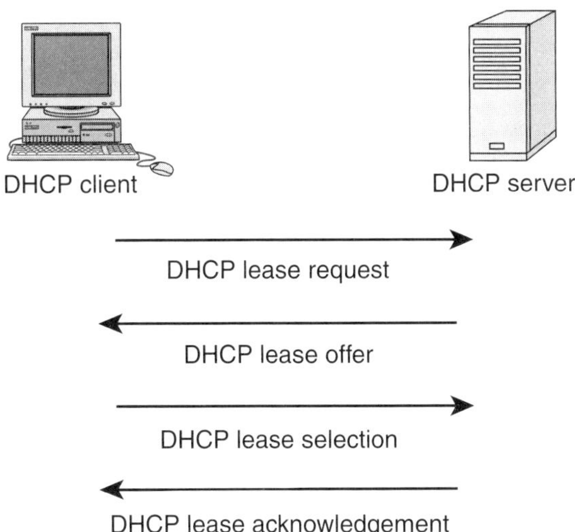

Figure 19-1 How DHCP works

FAQ 19.1 How do I install the DHCP Server service?

The DHCP Server service can only be installed on a NT Server.

1. Start the Network Control applet by clicking on Network from Control Panel (Start > Settings > Control Panel) or right-clicking on Network Neighborhood and selecting Properties.
2. Click on the Services tab and click Add.
3. Select Microsoft DHCP Server and click OK.
4. You will be prompted to insert the NT Server installation CD or say where the i386 directory is.
5. A warning that all local adapters must use a static IP address will be displayed, click OK.
6. Click Close and select Yes to reboot.

Under Windows 2000 to install, perform the following:

1. Start the Add/Remove Programs Control Panel applet (Start > Settings > Control Panel > Add/Remove Programs).
2. In the left pane, click Add/Remove Windows Components.
3. Click the Components button to start the Components Wizard.
4. Click Next.
5. Select Networking Services and click Details.
6. Check the Dynamic Host Configuration Protocol (DHCP) option and click OK.
7. Click Next, and the relevant files and services will be configured.
8. Click Finish when all operations have completed.
9. Click Close to the Add/Remove Programs dialog.

FAQ 19.2 How do I configure DHCP Server service?

The DHCP Server service is configured using DHCP Manager, which is installed after the installation of the DHCP Server service.

1. Start DHCP Manager (Start > Programs > Administrative Tools > DHCP Manager).
2. Double-click *Local Machine*.
3. From the Scope menu, select Create.

4. A dialog will be shown, and the following should be entered:
   - Start Address—for example, 200.200.200.10.
   - End Address—for example, 200.200.200.100. This means the address 200.200.200.10 to 200.200.200.100 is available.
   - Subnet Mask—for example, 255.255.255.0.
   - Exclusion, start and end—for example, 200.200.200.20 and 200.200.200.30—means available addresses are 200.200.200.10-200.200.200.20 and 200.200.200.30-200.200.200.100.
   - Exclusion, just entering the start value is a single address—for example, 200.200.200.56.
   - Set lease duration—by default three days; however, can be set to unlimited.
   - Name—this is the name of the scope—for example, subnet 200.200.200.
   - Comment—anything you want.
5. Click OK.
6. A message is displayed that the scope has been added but is not active. The message asks would you like it to be active; click Yes.

Items such as DNS servers, WINS server, etc. usually will be configured on a global scale, and this is also done using DHCP Manager:

1. Select the Scope and select Global from the DHCP Options menu.
2. Select 06 DNS Servers and click Add.
3. Click the Value button.
4. Click Edit Array at the bottom.
5. Enter the IP address and click ADD, continue adding until all DNS server addresses are added.
6. Click OK to close the Edit Array dialog.
7. Select 15 Domain name and click Add.
8. Select the domain name and edit the string at the bottom (e.g., savilltech.com).
9. Click OK to exit.

FAQ 19.3 How do I configure a client to use DHCP?

For NT workstation and Windows 95, follow these instructions:

1. Start the Network Control applet by clicking Network from Control Panel (Start > Settings > Control Panel) or right-click on Network Neighborhood and select Properties.

2. Click on the Protocol tab.
3. Select TCP/IP and click Properties.
4. Select "Obtain an IP address from a DHCP Service". DHCP settings will only override an IP address and subnet mask when they are locally configured. If you have configured DNS, WINS, etc. locally, then the DHCP configuration will not overwrite it.

For Windows 98:

1. Start the Network Control applet by clicking on Network from Control Panel (Start > Settings > Control Panel) or right-click on Network Neighborhood and select Properties.
2. Select TCP/IP > Adapter and click Properties.
3. Select the IP address tab.
4. Select Obtain an IP address automatically.

For a Windows 2000 machine, perform the following:

1. Right-click on My Network Places and select Properties.
2. Right-click on Local Area Connection and select Properties.
3. Select Internet Protocol (TCP/IP) and click Properties.
4. Select Obtain an IP address automatically (and repeat for DNS) and click OK.

FAQ 19.4 How can I compress my DHCP database?

NT Server ships with a utility called Jetpack (JETPACK.EXE), which can be used to compact DHCP and WINS databases. To compact your DHCP database, perform the following:

1. Start a command prompt (CMD.EXE).
2. Enter the following commands

```
cd %SystemRoot%\SYSTEM32\DHCP
```

For example, **cd d:\winnt\system32\dhcp**.

```
net stop DHCPSERVER
jetpack DHCP.MDB TMP.MDB
net start DHCPSERVER
```

Note: *While you stop the DHCP service, clients using DHCP to receive a TCP/IP address will not be able to start this protocol and may hang.*

Jetpack actually compacts DHCP.MDB into TMP.MDB, then deletes DHCP.MDB and copies TMP.MDB to DHCP.MDB! Simple :-)

For more information, see the Knowledge Base article Q145881 at http://support.microsoft.com/support/kb/articles/q145/8/81.asp.

FAQ 19.5 How can a DHCP client find its IP address?

Depending on the client:

- Windows NT/2000/XP machine—Type **ipconfig** from the command prompt.
- Windows 95/98/Me machine—Run **winipcfg.exe**

FAQ 19.6 How can I move a DHCP database from one server to another?

Perform the following steps on the server that currently hosts the DHCP Server service. Be warned that while doing this, no DHCP clients will be able to start TCP/IP. This should be done outside working hours.

1. Log on as an Administrator and stop DHCP (Start > Settings > Control Panel > Services > Microsoft DHCP server > Stop).
2. You also need to stop DHCP from starting again after a reboot so start the Services Control Panel applet, select Microsoft DHCP Server, and click Startup. From the startup, choose disabled and click OK.
3. Copy the DHCP directory tree %systemroot%\system32\DHCP to a temporary storage area for use later.
4. Start the Registry editor (REGEDT32.EXE).
5. Move to HKEY_LOCAL_MACHINE\SYSTEM\CurrentControlSet\Services\DHCPServer \Configuration.
6. From the Registry menu, click Save Key. Create a name for this key—for example, DHCPCFG.BCK.
7. Close the Registry editor.

Optionally if you want to remove DHCP from the source machine, totally delete the DHCP directory (%systemroot%\system32\dhcp) and then delete the

DHCP service (Start > Settings > Network > Services > Microsoft DHCP Server > Remove).

On the new DHCP server, perform the following:

1. Log on as an Administrator.
2. If the server does not have the DHCP Server service installed, install it (Start > Settings > Control Panel > Network > Services > Add > DHCP Server).
3. Stop the DHCP service (Start > Settings > Control Panel > Services > Microsoft DHCP server > Stop).
4. Delete the contents of %systemroot%\system32\dhcp.
5. Copy the backed up DHCP directory tree from the storage area to %systemroot%/system32/dhcp, but rename the file SYSTEM.MDB to SYSTEM.SRC. You may not have this file if you are using NT 4.0; if not, skip this step.
6. Start the Registry editor (REGEDT32.EXE).
7. Move to HKEY_LOCAL_MACHINE\SYSTEM\CurrentControlSet\Services\DHCPServer\Configuration and select it.
8. From the Registry menu, select restore.
9. Locate the file DHCPCGF.BCK you saved from the original machine and click open.
10. Click Yes to the warning.
11. Close the Registry editor.
12. Reboot the machine.

FAQ 19.7 How do I create a DHCP relay agent?

If you have routers separating some of your DHCP clients from the DHCP server, you may have problems if they are not RFC compliant. This can be solved by placing a DHCP relay agent on the local network area, which is not actually a DHCP server that communicates on behalf of the DHCP server. The DHCP relay agent must be a Windows NT Server computer.

1. On the NT Server, log on as an Administrator.
2. Start the Network Control Panel applet (Start > Settings > Control Panel > Network).
3. Click the Services tab and click Add.
4. Select DHCP Relay Agent and click OK.

5. Type the path of the files (e.g., d:\i386) and click OK.
6. You will be asked if you wish to add an IP address to the DHCP servers list; click Yes.
7. Click the DHCP relay tab and click Add.
8. In the DHCP Server field, enter the IP address of the DHCP server and click Add.
9. Click OK.
10. Restart the computer.

FAQ 19.8 How can I stop the DHCP relay agent?

All you have to do to stop the DHCP relay agent service is:

1. Log on as an Administrator.
2. Start the Services Control Panel applet (Start > Settings > Control Panel > Network).
3. Select DHCP Relay Agent.
4. Click the startup button.
5. Click disabled and click OK.
6. Close the Control Panel applet.
7. You can reboot or just stop the service.

FAQ 19.9 How can I back up the DHCP database?

The DHCP database backs itself up automatically every 60 minutes to the %SystemRoot%\System32\Dhcp\Backup\Jet directory. This interval can be changed:

1. Start the Registry editor.
2. Move to HKEY_LOCAL_MACHINE\SYSTEM\CurrentControlSet\Services\DHCPServer\Parameters\BackupInterval.
3. Double-click on BackupInterval and set to the number of minutes you want the backup to be performed. Click OK.
4. Close the Registry editor.
5. Stop and restart the DHCP Server service (Start > Settings > Control Panel > Services > DHCP Server > Start and Stop).

You could back up the %SystemRoot%\System32\Dhcp\Backup\Jet directory if you wish. DHCP database is also backed up as part of the system state for Windows 2000 and above.

FAQ 19.10 How can I restore the DHCP database?

Perform one of the following:

- When the DHCP Server service starts, if an error is detected in the database, it will automatically restore the backup version.
- Edit the Registry and set HKEY_LOCAL_MACHINE\SYSTEM\CurrentControlSet\Services\DHCPServer\Parameters\RestoreFlag to 1. Restart the DHCP Server service, which will restore the backed up version and set RestoreFlag back to the default 0.
- Stop the DHCP Server service; copy the files from %SystemRoot%\System32\Dhcp\Backup\Jet to %SystemRoot%\System32\Dhcp, and then start the DHCP Server service.

FAQ 19.11 How do I reserve a specific address for a particular machine?

Before performing this task, you will need to know the hardware address of the machine, which can be found by entering the command

```
ipconfig /all
```

Look for the line

```
Physical Address. . . . . . : 00-60-97-A4-20-86
```

Now at the DHCP server, perform the following

1. Log on as an Administrator.
2. Start the DHCP Server management software (Start > Programs > Administrative Tools > DHCP Manager).
3. Double-click on the DHCP server (e.g., *Local Machine*).
4. Select the light bulb and from the Scope menu, select Add Reservations.

5. In the Add Reserved Clients dialog box, you should enter the IP address you wish to reserve. In the Unique Identifier box, enter the hardware address of the client machine (obtained from ipconfig /all). Do **not** enter the hyphens—for example:

```
006097A42086
```

Also enter a name for the machine (and a comment if you wish) and click Add.
6. Click close when you have added all the reservations.

FAQ 19.12 What Registry settings control the DHCP log in Windows 2000?

DHCP has always had auditing abilities for DHCP; however, these abilities have been expanded in 2000 to reduce problems **caused** by the log files. These improvements will prevent log files from filling up and taking up whole partitions and causing system problems.

The following keys are all located under HKEY_LOCAL_MACHINE\SYSTEM\CurrentControlSet\Services\DHCPServer\Parameters:

Value Name	Type	Description
DhcpLogFilePath	REG_SZ	The partition and directory for the audit logs to be written to. Make sure you write the entire path.
DhcpLogMinSpaceOnDisk	REG_DWORD	If free space falls below this number (in megabytes), audit logging is stopped.
DhcpLogDiskSpaceCheckInterval	REG_DWORD	Number of times the audit log is written to before the monitor process checks for free disk space.
DhcpLogFileMaxSize	REG_DWORD	Maximum size in megabytes the logs can grow to. By default it is 7.

19.13 How do I authorize a DHCP server in Windows 2000?

Any user running Windows 2000 Server could install the DHCP Server service, causing potential problems. So Windows 2000 adds the concept of authorizing the servers with the Active Directory before they can service client requests. If the server, as part of a domain, is not authorized in the Active Directory, then the DHCP service will not be started.

To authorize a server, perform the following:

1. Log on as a member of the Enterprise Administrators group.
2. Start the DHCP MMC snap-in (Start > Programs > Administrative Tools > DHCP).
3. Select the DHCP root, right-click, and select Browse authorized servers.
4. A list of authorized DHCP servers will be displayed. Click Add.
5. Enter the name or IP address of the DHCP server and click OK.
6. Click Close.

The red arrow over the DHCP server should now change to a green one if you select refresh (it may take a few minutes).

19.14 How do I create a DHCP scope in Windows 2000?

A DHCP scope is a range of addresses that can be assigned to clients and can also optionally provide information about DNS servers, WINS, and other components.

DHCP scopes are configured using the DHCP MMC snap-in as follows:

1. Start the DHCP MMC snap-in (Start > Programs > Administrative Tools > DHCP).
2. Right-click on the server and select New > Scope from the context menu.
3. The Scope Creation Wizard will be started, click Next.
4. Enter a name and comment for the scope. Click Next.
5. Enter the address range to use (see Figure 19-2)—for example, from 200.200.200.1 to 200.200.200.15 (remember the host part cannot be 0). Also enter the subnet mask as either the number of bits used or the actual mask (e.g., 24 is the same as 255.255.255.0). Click Next.

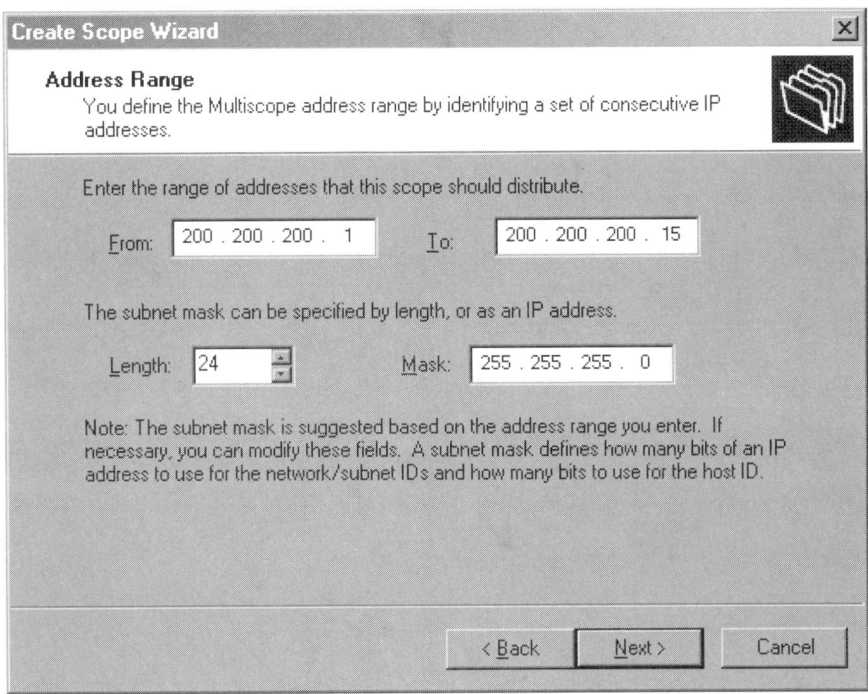

Figure 19-2 Adding a new DHCP scope

6. You can specify addresses to be excluded by range (e.g., 200.200.200.5 to 200.200.200.7) and click Add, or just enter a Start address and click Add (e.g., 200.200.200.12) to exclude a single address. Click Next.
7. You can now configure the lease time for the address. Setting it too large will mean you will lose the use of addresses if the client machine is inactive for long periods of time. If you set it too short, you will generate unnecessary traffic renewing the address. The default of eight days is fine. Click Next.
8. The wizard gives the option to configure the most common DHCP options. Select Yes and click Next.
9. Enter the address of the gateway and click Add. You can enter several. Click Next when all are entered.
10. Enter the DNS domain (e.g., savilltech.com) and the DNS server addresses (see Figure 19-3). Click Next.
11. Enter the WINS server addresses and click Add. Click Next.

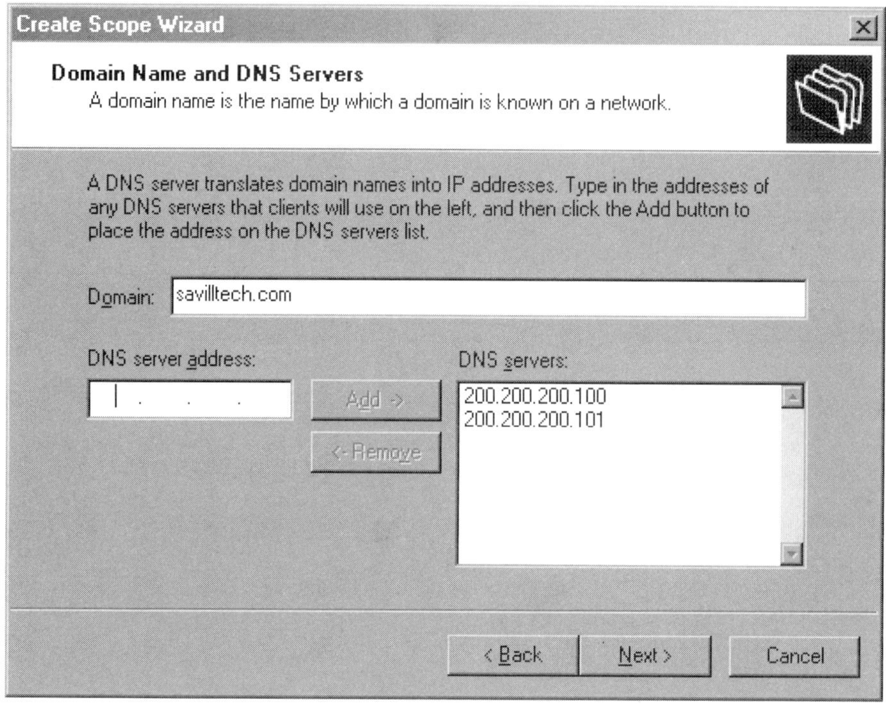

Figure 19-3 Setting optional DHCP values such as DNS servers

12. You will then be asked if you wish to activate the scope. Select your answer and click Next.
13. Click Finish to the wizard.

The new scope will now be listed, and the status as either Active or Inactive is displayed.

If you selected not to activate the scope, it can be manually activated by right-clicking on the scope, selecting All Tasks and then Activate, as shown in Figure 19-4. The activation is immediate. Likewise you can deactivate by selecting deactivate.

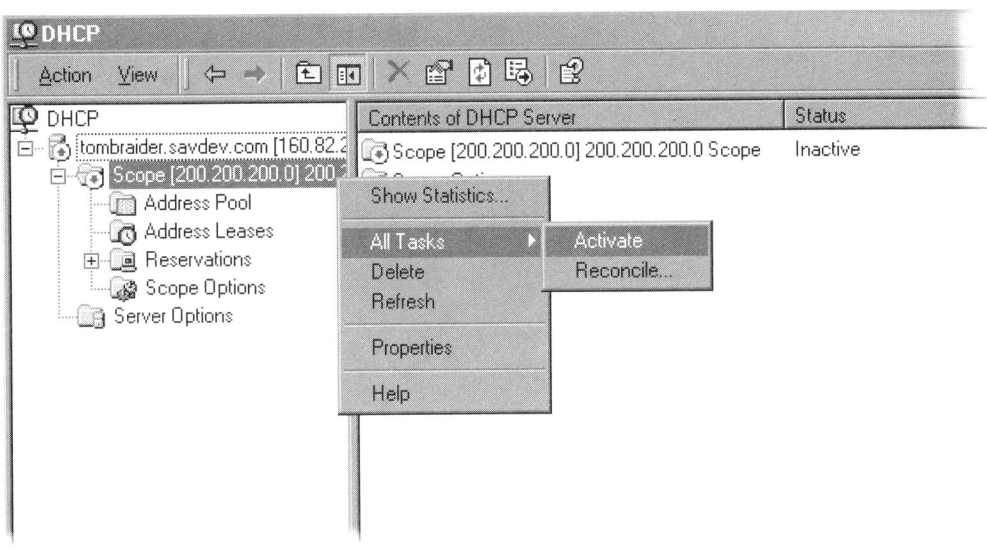

Figure 19-4 Activating a DHCP scope in a domain

19.15 How do I configure DHCP scope options in Windows 2000?

When you create a scope, the more common options such as DNS and WINS servers can be configured, but many more options are available.

1. Start the DHCP MMC snap-in (Start > Programs > Administrative Tools > DHCP).
2. Expand the server.
3. Expand the scope whose options you wish to modify.
4. Select the Scope Options branch, and in the right window, you will see the currently configured options.
5. Right-click on Scope Options and select Configure Options.
6. Select the Basic tab, and you can configure another option by checking its box and entering the details. For example, to configure a time server, check 004 Time Server, enter an IP address, and click Add (see Figure 19-5).
7. Click Apply. Click OK.

The new option(s) will now show in the right window. You can change existing options by performing the preceding, selecting an item already configured, and changing the details in the Data entry area.

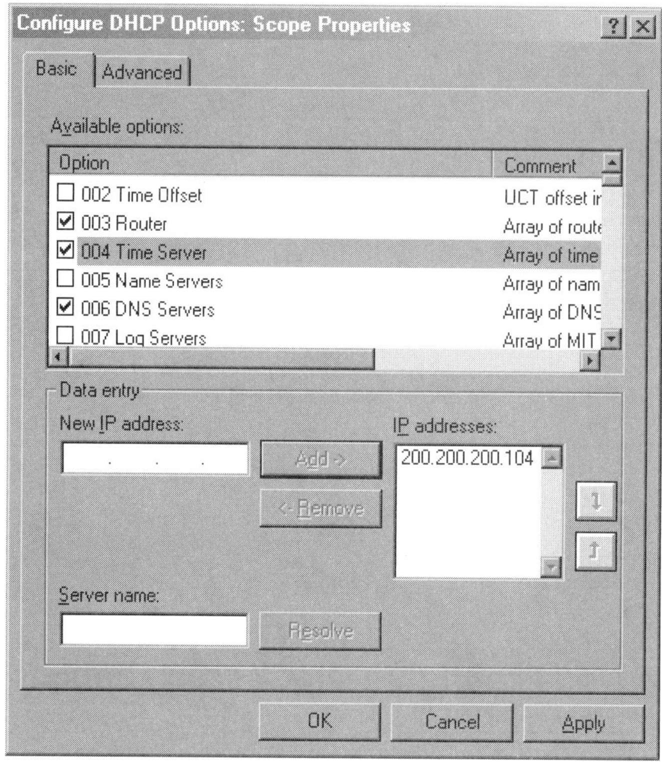

Figure 19-5 Setting optional DHCP options after scope creation

19.16 How can I view DHCP address leases in Windows 2000?

When a client is offered and accepts an IP address, a "lease" is created for x amount of days. To view current leases, perform the following:

1. Start the DHCP MMC snap-in (Start > Programs > Administrative Tools > DHCP).
2. Expand the server.
3. Expand the scope whose leases you wish to view.
4. Select the Address Leases branch, and in the right window, you will see the current lease details.

The window will give details of the IP address, client name, and the lease expiration date. Expired leases are also shown for approximately one day but have a dimmed icon.

This grace period protects a client lease in the event of the client and server being in different time zones, clocks not synched, or simply being offline.

FAQ 19.17 How do I change the DHCP address lease time in Windows 2000?

To modify the DHCP lease duration from the normal eight days, perform the following:

1. Start the DHCP MMC snap-in (Start > Programs > Administrative Tools > DHCP).
2. Expand the server.
3. Right-click the scope whose lease time you wish to change and select Properties.
4. Select the General tab.
5. At the bottom of the window, you can select lease duration—either unlimited or a finite time (see Figure 19-6).
6. Click Apply, then OK.

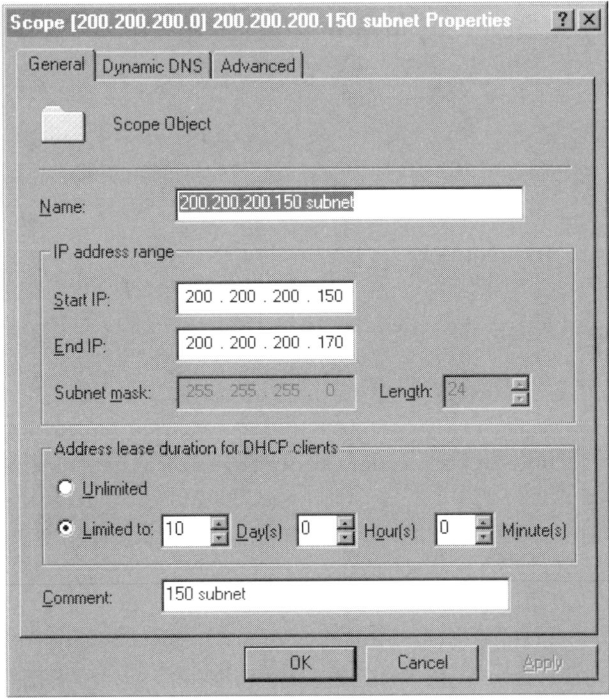

Figure 19-6 Setting the DHCP lease time

FAQ 19.18 My Windows 2000 DHCP client has an IP address not in any scopes. How did this happen?

Microsoft has tried to make Windows 2000 as easy to set up on a small network as possible, and by default machines installed are set up to use DHCP. On a very small network, you may not have a DHCP server, and rather than the machines failing to initialize TCP/IP, Microsoft has added code so that the machines will use an address not in use on the local network in the class B address range 169.254.x.x. This IP address range is reserved for internal use only and so should not clash with any "real" IP addresses on your network. The MacOS uses the same address range for its DHCP clients when a DHCP server cannot be contacted as does Windows 98 Second Edition.

This DHCP address allocation uses conflict detection via a NetBIOS naming broadcast over DHCP so each machine gets an IP address from the 169.254.x.x range, which is not in use. The actual address initially chosen at random.

If any of your machines have a 169.254.x.x address, it just means they could not contact a DHCP server, so check your network connectivity.

This automatic IP addressing is known as Automatic Private IP Addressing (APIPA).

FAQ 19.19 What is name hijacking?

Windows 2000 introduces support for Dynamic DNS, which allows clients to update/create DNS records. This is most commonly done via DHCP, but it introduces a potential problem where clients may incorrectly change DNS entries and "hijack" the record.

The solution is to use secure dynamic update, but this is available only on Active Directory-integrated zones so DNS service must be running on a domain controller. With secure dynamic update, the domain controllers group has full control over the zones. The problem is when DHCP is also installed on a domain controller, the DHCP Server service runs under the domain controller computer account, which has full control over the DNS zone even if secure update is configured. This situation would allow earlier DHCP clients or deliberate hacking code to overwrite DNS records of a legitimate computer and hijack its name. The solution to this situation is not to have DHCP installed on a domain controller, which is what Microsoft suggests.

FAQ 19.20 Why is my DHCP server not releasing client address leases?

A known problem exists with the Windows 2000 DHCP server that causes the server to ignore a lease release request from a client on another subnet because releasing the lease causes the DHCP server to use its own IP address instead of the client's. This problem occurs if you havent defined a scope for the DHCP servers primary interface's local subnet. To work around this problem, create a scope for the local subnet (you don't have to activate it).

You can also manually delete the leases. Perform the following steps:

1. Start the Microsoft Management Console (MMC) DHCP snap-in (Start > Programs > Administrative Tools > DHCP).
2. Select the Scope that contains the leases to be deleted.
3. Select the Address Leases container.
4. Right-click the lease to be deleted and select Delete.
5. Click OK to the confirmation.

FAQ 19.21 I used the DHCPEXIM tool to migrate a DHCP scope between machines. Why is the system not granting any new IP leases?

The DHCPEXIM tool (from the Windows 2000 Resource Kit, Supplement 1) lets you move scopes from one DHCP server to another. However, a bug causes the new scope not to grant IP leases. To resolve this problem, perform the following steps:

1. Start REGEDIT.EXE.
2. Go to HKEY_Local_Machine\Software\Microsoft\DhcpServer\Configuration\Subnets\[IP address subnet]\IpRanges\[IP address start].
3. Double-click RangeFlags.
4. Set RangeFlags to 1, 2, or 3 where
   - 1 = DHCP only
   - 2 = BootP only
   - 3 = Both (DHCP and BootP)
5. Click OK.
6. Close Regedit.

19.22 How do I enable DHCP server logging?

To enable enhanced DHCP logging, perform the following steps:

1. Start the DHCP administration tool (go to Start > Programs > Administrative Tools and click DHCP).
2. Right-click the DHCP server and select Properties from the context menu.
3. Select the General tab.
4. Select the Enable DHCP audit logging checkbox (see Figure 19-7).
5. Click OK.

Windows 2000 will now create a DHCP log file in the %systemroot%\system32\dhcp directory for each day using a DhcpSrvLog.XXX file format.

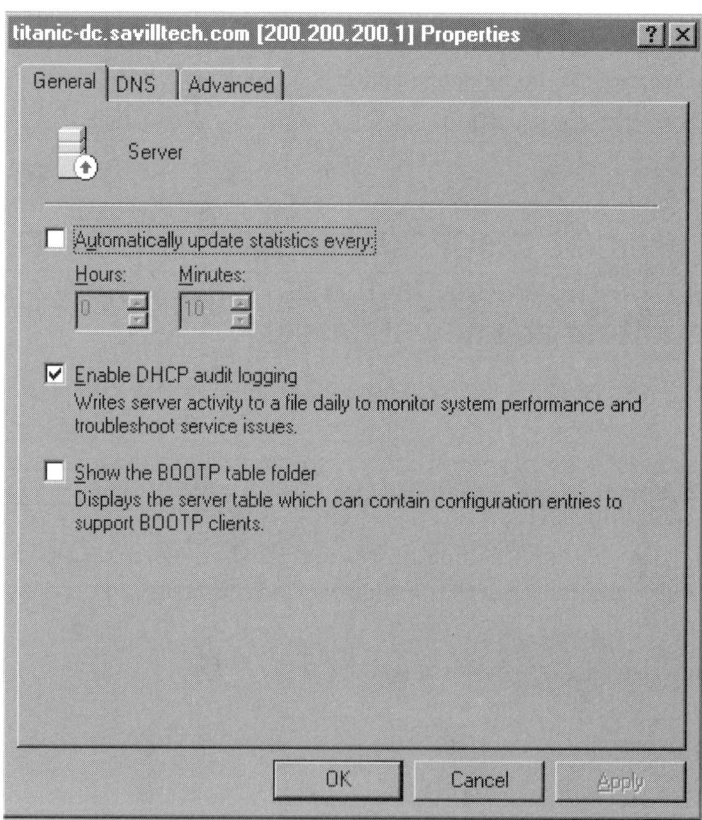

Figure 19-7 DHCP server options

Common audit codes that might appear in the log include

00—The log was started.
01—The log was stopped.
02—The log was temporarily paused due to low disk space.
10—A new IP address was leased to a client.
11—A lease was renewed by a client.
12—A lease was released by a client.
13—An IP address was found to be in use on the network.
14—A lease request could not be satisfied because the scopes address pool was exhausted.
15—A lease was denied.
16—A lease was deleted.
17—A lease was expired.
20—A BOOTP address was leased to a client.
21—A dynamic BOOTP address was leased to a client.
22—A BOOTP request could not be satisfied because the scopes address pool for BOOTP was exhausted.
23—A BOOTP IP address was deleted after verifying that it wasnt in use.

The DHCP Server uses codes above 50 for Rogue Server Detection information.

20 FILESYSTEMS

Windows NT supported a number of filesystems natively, File Allocation Table (FAT) and NT filesystem (NTFS); Windows 2000 added support for the Windows 9x filesystem FAT32 and also NTFS version 5.0. Windows XP does not add any new filesystems but extends the functionality of NTFS version 5.0.

FAT is supported for removable media and backwards compatibility and has none of the fault-tolerant security of NTFS, so should never be used on file servers of domain controllers.

It's important to understand the supportability of operating systems if dual booting—for example, Windows 9x cannot read NTFS; Windows NT 4.0 could not read FAT32—so you always need to use the lowest common filesystems when you need to access data from either operating system.

FAQ 20.1 How can a FAT partition be converted to an NTFS partition?

From the command line, enter **convert d: /fs:ntfs**. This command is one way only; you cannot convert an NTFS partition to FAT. If the FAT partition is the system partition, then the conversion will take place on the next reboot.

After the conversion, file permissions are set to Full Control for everyone (although this has been changed with Windows XP unless you use the /nosecurity switch), whereas if you install directly to NTFS, the permissions are set on a stricter basis.

FAQ 20.2 How can a NTFS partition be converted to a FAT partition?

A simple conversion is not possible, and the only course of action is to back up all the data on the drive, reformat the disk to FAT, and then restore your data backup.

Certain third-party products such as PartitionMagic by PowerQuest allow this conversion.

20.3 How do I compress a directory?

Follow these instructions (this procedure can be done only on an NTFS partition):

1. Using Explorer or My Computer, select a drive.
2. Right-click on a directory and choose Properties.
3. Select the Compress checkbox and click Apply.
4. You will be asked if you want to compress subdirectories, click OK.
5. Click OK to exit.

20.4 How do I uncompress a directory?

Follow the same procedure provided in the previous FAQ but uncheck the compress box.

20.5 Is there an NTFS defragmentation tool available?

A number are available for NT that I know of:

- Diskeeper—This tool is available from Executive Software, http://www.diskeeper.com. A free cut-down version, Diskeeper Lite, is available for download. An update to version 5 is available to enable it to run on Windows 2000.
- Norton Utilities for NT—This contains a disk defragmentation package, http://www.symantec.com.
- PerfectDisk 2000—From http://www.raxco.com, which has some new optimization that Diskeeper does not have and supports Windows 2000 out of the box.
- O&O Defragmentation—This tool works well, according to information I have been given. It can be purchased from http://www.oo-defrag.com/index-e.html.
- VoptNT—Available from Golden Bow Systems, http://www.goldenbow.com.

Windows 2000 has a limited built-in defragmentation tool that can be used as follows:

1. Start the MMC (Start > Run > MMC).
2. From the console menu, select Add/Remove Snap-in.
3. Click Add.

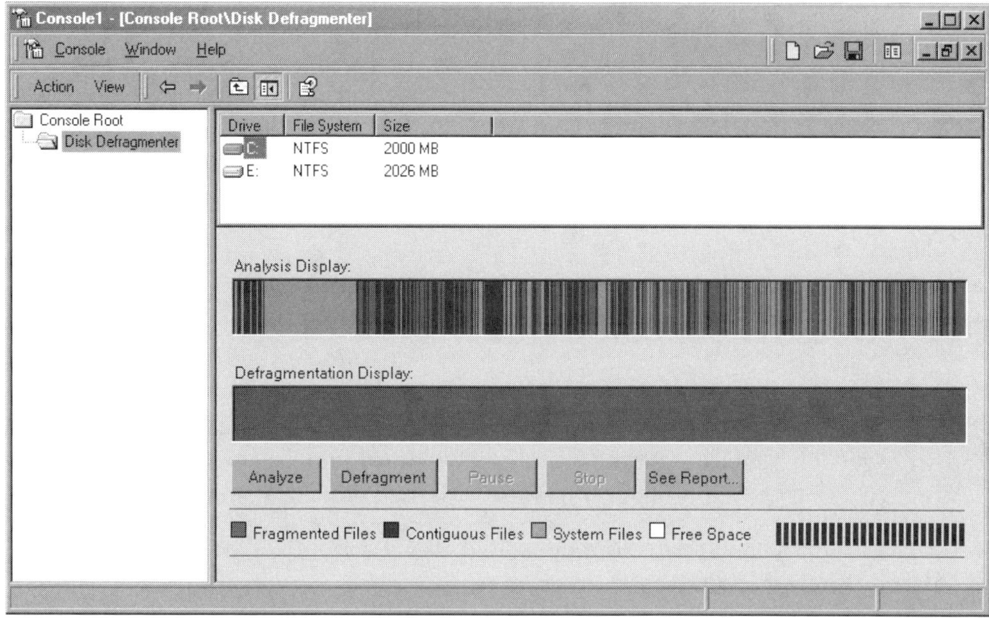

Figure 20-1 The disk defragmentation MMC snap-in

4. Select Disk Defragmenter and click Add. Click Close.
5. Click OK to the main Add/Remove dialog.
6. Select the Disk Defragmenter option from Console Root.
7. Select a partition, then Analyze and Defragment (see Figure 20-1).

FAQ 20.6 Can I undelete a file in NT?

It depends on the filesystem. NT has no undelete facility; however, if the filesystem was FAT, then boot into DOS and then use the DOS undelete utility. The NT Resource Kit includes a utility called DiskProbe that allows a user to view the data on a disk, which can then be copied to another file. It is possible to search sectors for data using DiskProbe.

If the files are deleted on an NTFS partition, booting using a DOS disk and using the UNDELETE.EXE program is not possible because DOS cannot read NTFS partitions. NTFS does not perform destructive deletes, which means the actual data is left intact on the disk (until another file is written in its place), and so a new application from Executive Software, Network Undelete, can be used to undelete files from NTFS partitions. A free 30-day version can be downloaded from http://www.networkundelete.com/.

Executive Software also has a free utility Emergency Undelete, which can undelete locally deleted files, http://www.execsoft.com.

Once any file is deleted, it is important that all activity on the machine is stopped to reduce the possibility of other files overwriting the data that you want to recover.

FAQ 20.7 Does NT support FAT32?

Native NT does not support FAT32. NT Internals has released a read-only FAT32 driver for Windows NT 4.0 from http://www.sysinternals.com/fat32.htm and a full read/write version can be purchased from http://www.winternals.com.

Windows 2000 has full FAT32(x) support with the following conditions:

- Preexisting FAT32(x) partitions up to 127GB will mount and be supported under Windows 2000.
- Windows 2000 will allow you to create new FAT32(x) volumes of only 32GB or less.

FAQ 20.8 Can you read an NTFS partition from DOS?

Not with standard DOS; however, a product called NTFSDos enables a user to read from an NTFS partition. The homepage for this utility is http://www.sysinternals.com.

FAQ 20.9 How do you delete a NTFS partition?

You can boot from the installation disks or the installation CD and follow these instructions:

1. Read the license agreement and press F8.
2. Select the NTFS partition you wish to delete.
3. Press L to confirm.
4. Press F3 twice to exit the NT setup.

Usually a NTFS partition can be deleted using FDISK (delete non-DOS partition); however, this will not work if the NTFS partition is in the extended partition.

You can delete an NTFS partition using Disk Administrator, by selecting the partition and pressing the Delete key (as long as it is not the system/boot partition).

The DELPART.EXE utility, which you can obtain from Microsoft, will delete a NTFS partition from a DOS bootup.

FAQ 20.10 What is the biggest disk NT can use?

The simple answer to this question is that NT can view a maximum partition size of 2 terabytes (or 2,199,023,255,552 bytes); however, there are limitations that restrict you well below this number.

FAT has internal limits of 4GB due to the fact it uses 16-bit fields to store file sizes; 2^16 is 65,536 with a cluster size of 64KB gives us the 4GB.

High Performance File System (HPFS) uses 32-bit fields and can therefore handle greater size disks, but the largest single file size is 4GB. HPFS allocates disk space in 512-byte sectors, which can cause problems in Asian markets where sector sizes are typically 1,024 bytes, which means HPFS cannot be used (although HPFS is not supported for Windows 2000 and above).

NTFS uses 64 bits for all sizes, leading to a max size of . . . 16 exabytes!!! (18,446,744,073,709,551,616 bytes); however, NT could not handle a volume this big.

For IDE drives, the maximum is 136.9GB; however, for a standard IDE drive, this size is constrained to 528MB. The new EIDE drives can access much larger sizes.

It is important to note that the system partition (holding NTLDR, BOOT.INI, etc.) **must** be entirely within the first 7.8GB of any disk (if this is the same as the boot partition, this limit applies). This is due to the BIOS (Basic Input/Output System) int 13H interface used by NTLDR to bootstrap up to the point where it can drive the native HDD IDE or SCSI. int 13H presents a 24-bit parameter for cylinder/head/sector for a drive. If, say, by defragmentation, the system boot area is moved beyond this point, you will not be able to boot the system.

The 7.8GB limit is true only on an IDE-type drive if the heads=255 and sectors=63. The real limit is the 1024-cylinder limit. If, for example, the heads=16 (as some IDE drives insist on), then the files mentioned must live within the first 504MB. This whole BIOS/big disk situation is getting worse and worse recently as manufacturers ghost images onto 20GB and 30GB single-partition volumes, and do it on machines without the BIOS INT13 support for a volume that size.

The boot process starts with your BIOS, not Windows NT. The BIOS locates the beginning of a partition by using three numbers, the starting side (or head), the starting cylinder, and the starting sector.

The end of a partition is identified by three similar numbers. The side value is 8 bits with a range from 0 to 255 (256 numbers); the cylinder is 10 bits and can range from

0 to 1023 (1024 numbers); the sector is 6 bits and can range from 1 to 63 (63 numbers). (Note that zero is not a valid sector number.) This means the maximum address on the disk is Side 255, Cylinder 1023, Sector 63. The number of sectors is 256 X 1023 X 63 or almost 16.5 million sectors. Standard sectors are 512 bytes, so hence the size of 7.87GB in which the system files must reside in.

Windows 2000 has no such limitation. These limits are imposed by the specific machine BIOS. Newer machines/BIOSes typically don't have this limitation.

FAQ 20.11 Can I disable 8.3 name creation on a NTFS?

From the key HKEY_LOCAL_MACHINE\SYSTEM\CurrentControlSet\Control\FileSystem, change the value NtfsDisable8dot3NameCreation from 0 to 1.

You may experience problems installing Office 97 if you disable 8.3 name creation and may have to reenable it during the installation of the software.

FAQ 20.12 How can I stop NT from generating LFNs (long filenames) on a FAT partition?

Using the Registry editor, change the value HKEY_LOCAL_MACHINE\SYSTEM\CurrentControlSet\Control\FileSystem\Win31FileSystem from 0 to 1, and only 8.3 filenames will be created.

The reason for not wanting the LFNs to be created is that some third-party disk utilities that directly manipulate FAT can destroy the LFNs. Utilities such as SCANDISK and DEFRAG that come with DOS 6.x and above do not harm LFNs.

FAQ 20.13 Why can't I create any files on the root of a FAT partition?

The root of a FAT drive has a coded limit of 512 entries, so if you have exceeded this limit, you will not be able to create any more files. I don't have this many! Remember long filenames (LFNs) take up more than one entry; see FAQ 20.14 for more information. If you have many LFNs on the root, it will drastically reduce the number of files you can have.

20.14 What is opportunist locking?

With Exclusive Oplock, if a file is opened in a nonexclusive (deny none) mode, the redirector requests an opportunistic lock of the entire file. As long as no other process has the file open, the server will grant this oplock, giving the redirector exclusive access to the specified file. This will allow the redirector to perform read-ahead, write-behind, and lock caching, as long as no other process tries to open the file.

When a second process attempts to open the file, the original owner will be asked to Break Oplock or Break to Level II Oplock. At that point, the redirector must invalidate cached data, flush writes and locks, release the oplock, or close the file.

Opportunistic Locking level II provides a method for granting read access to a file by more than one workstation, and these workstations can cache read data locally (read-ahead). As long as no station writes to the file, multiple stations can have the file open with level II oplock.

For more information, see http://support.microsoft.com/support/kb/articles/Q129/2/02.asp. This site has **loads** of information about tuning both the server and workstation.

20.15 How do LFNs work?

Long filenames (LFNs) are stored using a series of linked directory entries. A LFN will use one directory entry for its alias (the alias is the 8.3 name automatically generated), and a hidden secondary directory entry for every 13 characters in its name. Thus if you had a filename of 200 characters, it would use 17 entries!

The alias is generated using the first six characters of the LFN, then a ~ and a number for the first four versions of a file with the same first six characters—for example, for the file **john savills file.txt** the names generated would be johnsa~1.txt, johnsa~2, etc.

After the first four versions of a file, only the first two characters of the filename are used, and the last six are generated (e.g., jo0E38~1.txt).

20.16 How do I change access permissions on a directory?

You can set access permissions only on an NTFS volume. Follow these instructions:

1. Start Explorer (Start > Programs > Explorer).
2. Right-click on a directory and select Properties.

3. Click on the Security tab.
4. Click the Permissions button.
5. Enter the information required.
6. Click OK, and then click OK again to exit.

FAQ 20.17 How can I change access permissions from the command line?

A utility called CACLS.EXE comes standard with NT and can be used from the command prompt. Read the help text with the CACLS.EXE program (cacls /?). To give user john read access to a directory called files enter

```
CACLS files /e /p john:r
```

/e is used to edit the ACL instead of replacing it; therefore, other permissions on the directory will be kept. /p sets permission for user:<permission>.

FAQ 20.18 How can I stop a CHKDSK scheduled to start at the next reboot?

If the command chkdsk /f /r (find bad sectors, recover information from bad sectors, and fix errors on the disk) is run, on the next reboot, the check disk is scheduled. However, you may want to cancel this check disk. To do so, perform the following:

1. Run the Registry Editor (REGEDT32.EXE). You **must use REGEDT32 and not REGEDIT.EXE.**
2. Goto HKEY_LOCAL_MACHINE\SYSTEM\CurrentControlSet\Control\Session Manager.
3. Change the BootExecute value from:

   ```
   autocheck autochk * /r\DosDevice\<drive letter>:
   ```

   to:

   ```
   autocheck autochk *
   ```

FAQ 20.19 My NTFS drive is corrupt. How do I recover?

To restore an NTFS drive using the following information, it must have been created using Windows NT 4.0. If it was not created using NT 4.0, you should see Knowledge Base article Q121517.

To restore an NTFS partition, you must locate the spare copy of the boot sector and copy it to the correct position on the drive. You need the NTDiskedit utility, which is available from Microsoft Support Services. (You can also use DiskProbe that comes with the Resource Kit. Instructions for using DiskProbe can be found at http://support.microsoft.com/support/kb/articles/q153/9/73.asp.)

1. Using NTdiskedit for Windows NT 4.0, on the File menu, click Open.
2. Type the Volume Name as

   ```
   \\.\PhysicaldriveX
   ```

   where X=the ordinal of the disk that appears in Disk Administrator).
3. Click OK.
4. On the Read menu, click Sectors. Select 0 for Starting Sectors and select 1 for Run Length. Click OK.
5. On the View menu, click Partition Table. You should see a table that has four sections, Entry 0 through Entry 3. This refers to the order of partitions. If the partition in question is Partition 2 on the disk, you need the data in Entry 1. If the Partition in question is the Partition 1 on the disk, you need the data from Entry 0 and so on.
6. Write down the values of Starting Sector and Sectors.

   Note: *All of the values you see will be in hexadecimal format. Do not convert to decimal.*

7. Using a calculator that can add hexadecimal numbers (you can use the one from the Accessories group if it is available), add the values for Starting Sector and Sectors, and subtract 1 from the sum. For example:

   ```
   STARTING SECTOR=0x3F
   SECTORS=0x201c84 +
   ----------
   0x201CC3
   Less 1 0x1 -
   ```

```
----------
Copy of NTFS bootsector=0x201CC2
```

8. On the Read menu, click Sectors. In Starting Sectors, type the value from the equation in the previous step. Type **1** in Run Length. Click OK.
   You now should be at your copy of the NTFS boot sector. Visually inspect the boot sector for completeness, NTFS header at first line, text in the lower region (for example, "A kernel file is missing from the disk"), and so forth.
9. Click Relocate Sectors. This is the sector you use if you are going to write the boot sector. This will be the value of your Starting Sector with the Run Length of 1. Click OK.
10. Quit NTDiskedit. Use Disk Administrator to assign a drive letter if one is not already assigned. Restart the computer; the filesystem should be recognized as NTFS.

FAQ 20.20 How can I delete a file without it going to the Recycle Bin?

When you delete the file, hold down the Shift key.

FAQ 20.21 How can I change the serial number of a disk?

The serial number is located in the boot sector for a volume. For FAT drives, it's 4 bytes starting at offset 0x27; for NTFS drives, it's 8 bytes starting at offset 0x48. You'll need a sector-level editor to modify the number (like the Resource Kit's DiskProbe).

FAQ 20.22 How can I back up/restore the master boot record?

The master boot record on the hard disk used to start the computer (the system partition) is the most critical sector so make sure this is the sector you back up. The boot partition is also very important (where %systemroot% resides). You need the DiskProbe utility that comes with the Resource Kit.

1. Start DiskProbe
2. From Drives, click Physical Drive, and click on the drive that is the system partition (from the Open Physical Drive dialog).

3. The disk clicked will be displayed in the Handle 0 section. Click Set Active and then click Close.
4. From the sectors menu, click Read. Accept the default sectors of Starting Sector 0 and Number of Sectors 1.
5. From the File menu, click Save As and enter a filename.

To restore:

1. Start DiskProbe.
2. From File, click Open and select the file that the information was saved as.
3. From drives, click Physical Drive and click the disk you want to replace the boot partition on.
4. In the Handle 0 box, clear the Read Only box, and click Set Active. Then click Close.
5. From the Sectors menu, click write and set the starting sector to 0. Click Write it.
6. Verify and close DiskProbe.
7. Keep your fingers crossed ☺.

An alternative is the Windows NT Resource Kit utility DISKSAVE.EXE, which enables a binary image of the master boot record (MBR) or boot sector to be saved.

DISKSAVE has to be run from DOS, so you will need to create a bootable DOS disk and copy DISKSAVE.EXE to the disk. To create a DOS bootable disk, just use the following command from a DOS machine (not from a Windows NT command session):

```
format a: /s
```

Once you boot with the disk, you will have a number of options:

- **F2 Back up the Master Boot Record**—This function will prompt for a path and filename to save the MBR image to. The path and filename are limited to 64 characters. The resulting file will be a binary image of the sector and will be 512 bytes in size. The MBR is always located at Cylinder 0, Side 0, Sector 1 of the boot disk.
- **F3 Restore Master Boot Record**—This function will prompt for a path and filename for the previously save master boot record file. The only error checking is for the file size (must be 512 bytes). Copying an incorrect file to the MBR will permanently destroy the partition table information. In addition, the machine will not boot without a valid MBR. The path/filename is limited to 64 characters.
- **F4 Backup the Boot Sector**—This function will prompt for a path and filename to save the boot sector image to. The path and filename are limited to 64

characters. The resulting file will be a binary image of the sector and will be 512 bytes in size. The function opens the partition table, searches for an active partition, then jumps to the starting location of that partition. The sector at that location is then saved under the filename the user entered. There are no checks to determine if the sector is a valid boot sector.

- **F5 Restore Boot Sector**—This function will prompt for a path and filename for the previously save boot sector file. The only error checking is for the file size (must be 512 bytes). Copying an incorrect file to the boot sector will permanently destroy boot sector information. In addition, the machine will not boot without a valid boot sector. The path/filename is limited to 64 characters.
- **F6 Disable FT on the Boot Drive**—This function may be useful when Windows NT will not boot from a mirrored system drive. The function looks for the bootable (marked active) partition. It then checks to see if the SystemType byte has the high bit set. Windows NT sets the high bit of the SystemType byte if the partition is a member of a Fault Tolerant set. Disabling this bit has the same effect as breaking the mirror. There is no provision for reenabling the bit once it has be disabled.

FAQ 20.23 What CD-ROM filesystems can NT read?

NT's primary filesystem is Compact Disk File System (CDFS), a read-only filesystem; however, it can read any filesystem that is ISO9660 compliant.

FAQ 20.24 How do I disable 8.3 name creation on VFAT?

Start the Registry editor (REGEDIT.EXE) and set the value HKEY_LOCAL_MACHINE\SYSTEM\CurrentControlSet\Control\FileSystem\Win95TruncatedExtensions to 0.

FAQ 20.25 What is the maximum number of characters a filename can be?

This depends on whether the file is being created on a FAT or NTFS partition. The maximum filename length on a NTFS partition is 256 characters, and 11 characters on FAT (eight-character name.three-character extension). NTFS filenames keep their case, whereas FAT filenames have no concept of case (however, the case is ignored when performing a search, etc. on NTFS). The new Virtual File Application Table (VFAT) also has 256 character filenames.

NTFS filenames can contain any characters, including spaces, uppercase/lowercase, except for the following

```
" * : / \ ? < > |
```

These characters are reserved for NT; however, the filename must start with a letter or number.

VFAT filenames can also contain any characters except for the following

```
/ \ : | = ? " ; [ ] , ^
```

Once again the filename must start with a letter or number.

NTFS and VFAT also creates a 8.3 format filename. See FAQ 20.15 to learn more about LFNs.

FAQ 20.26 How can I stop chkdsk at boot time from checking volume x?

When NT boots, it performs a check on all volumes to see whether the dirty bit is set, and if it is, a full chkdsk /f is run. To stop NT performing this dirty bit check, you can exclude certain drives. You may want to do this for some type of removable drive (e.g., Iomega drives):

1. Run the Registry Editor (REGEDT32.EXE). You **must** use REGEDT32.EXE and not REGEDIT.EXE.
2. Goto HKEY_LOCAL_MACHINE\SYSTEM\CurrentControlSet\Control\Session Manager.
3. Change the BootExecute value from:

   ```
   autocheck autochk *
   ```

   to:

   ```
   autocheck autochk /k:x *
   ```

Where x is the drive letter (e.g., if you want to stop the check on drive F, you type **autocheck autochk /k:f** *). To stop the check on multiple volumes, just enter the drive names one after another (e.g., to stop the check on E and G. type **autocheck autochk /k:eg***; you do not retype the /k each time).

If you are using NT 4.0 with Service Pack 2 or above, you can also use the CHKNTFS.EXE command, which is also used to exclude drives from the check and updates the Registry for you. The usage to disable a drive is

```
chkntfs /x <drive letter>:
```

For example, chkntfs /x f: excludes the check of drive F. To set the system back to checking all drives just type

```
chkntfs /d
```

20.27 How can I compress files/directories from the command line?

A utility is supplied with the Resource Kit called COMPACT.EXE, which can be used to view and change the compression characteristics of a file/directory.

20.28 What protections can be set on files/directories on a NTFS partition?

When you right-click on a file in Explorer and select Properties (or select Properties from the File menu), you are presented with a dialog box providing information such as size and ownership. If the file/directory is on a NTFS partition, a Security tab is displayed with a Permissions button. When you press that button, you can grant access to users/groups on the resource at various levels.

There are six basic permissions:

- R—Read
- W—Write
- D—Delete
- X—Execute
- P—Change Permissions
- O—Take Ownership

These permissions can be assigned to a resource; however, they are grouped for ease of use.

- No Access—User has no access to the resource.
- List **R**—User can view directory and filenames in directory.
- Read **RX—**User can read files in directory and execute programs.
- Add **WX**—User can add files to the directory but cannot read or change the contents of the directory.
- Add & Read **RWX**—User has read and add permissions.
- Change **RWXD**—User has read, add, change contents, and delete files.
- All **RWXDPO**—User can do anything she wants!

The preceding permissions can all be set on a directory; however, this list is limited for a file. Permissions that can be set are only No Access, Read, Change, and Full Control.

Another permission exists called "Special Access." (On a directory there will be two:, one for files, one for directories.) From Special Access, you can set which of the basic permissions should be assigned.

20.29 How can I take ownership of files?

Sometimes you may want to take ownership of files/directories, usually as someone has removed all access on a resource and can't see it. You log on as the Administrator and take ownership. You **cannot** give ownership to someone else using standard NT functionality, only take ownership:

1. Log on as Administrator or as a member of the Admins group.
2. Start Explorer.
3. Right-click on the file/directory and select Properties.
4. Select the Security tab and click Ownership.
5. Click Take Ownership and then click Yes to the prompt.

For Windows 2000 and above, the procedure is similar; however, after selecting the Security tab, you then click Advanced, select the Owner tab, and select who should be the new owner.

20.30 How can I view from the command line the permissions a user has on a file?

The PERMS.EXE utility is supplied with the Resource Kit. This utility can be used to view permissions on files/directories. The usage is

```
perms <domain>\<user> <file>
```

For example, **perms savilltech\savillj d:\file\john\file.dat**.

You can add /s to also show details of subfiles/subdirectories. The permissions shown equate to

R	Read
W	Write
X	Execute
D	Delete
P	Change Permission
O	Take Ownership
A	All
None	No Access
*	User is the owner
#	A group the member is a member of owns the file
?	Permissions cannot be determined

To output to a file, just add > **filename.txt** at the end—for example:

```
perms <user> <file> > file.txt
```

FAQ 20.31 How can I tell the total amount of space used by a folder (including subfolders)?

There are at least two ways of doing this (there are more!), one using Explorer and one from the command line. Using Explorer:

1. Start Explorer (Win key+E or Start > Programs > Explorer).
2. Right-click on the required folder and select Properties.
3. Under the General tab, a size will be displayed, which is the total size of the folder, all subfolders, and their contents.

From the command line, you can just use the dir command with /s qualifier, which also lists all subdirectories. For example, the following lists all files/folders in the savilltechhomepage directory and, at the end, the total size:

```
dir/s d:\savilltechhomepage
```

FAQ 20.32 Files beginning with a dollar sign ($) are at the root of my NTFS drive. Can I delete them?

These files hold the information of your NTFS volume. Following is a table of all the files used by the filesystem:

$MFT	Master File Table (MFT)
$MFTMIRR	A copy of the first 16 records of the MFT
$LOGFILE	Log of changes made to the volume
$VOLUME	Information about the volume, serial number, creation time, dirty flag
$ATTRDEF	Attribute definitions
$BITMAP	Contains drive cluster map
$BOOT	Boot record of the drive
$BADCLUS	A list of bad clusters on the drive
$QUOTA	Quota information (used on NTFS 5.0)
$UPCASE	Maps lowercase characters to uppercase version

If you want to have a look at any of these files, use the command

```
dir /ah $mft
```

It's basically impossible to delete these files anyway because you can't remove the hidden flag, and if you can't remove the hidden flag, you can't delete them!

20.33 What filesystems do Iomega Zip disks use?

By default, the formatted Zip disks are FAT; however, you can format them with NTFS if you want. NTFS has a higher overhead than FAT on small volumes (an initial 2MB), which is why you don't have NTFS on 1.44 floppy disks.

20.34 What cluster size does a FAT or an NTFS partition use?

The default cluster size for a FAT partition is as follows:

Partition Size	Sectors per Cluster	Cluster Size
<32MB	1	512 bytes
<64MB	2	1KB
<128MB	4	2KB
<255MB	8	4KB
<511MB	16	8KB
<1023MB	32	16KB
<2047MB	64	32KB
<4095MB	128	64KB

This is why FAT volumes larger than 511MB are not recommended due to the amount of potentially wasted space due to the 16KB and above cluster size.

The default for NTFS is as follows:

Partition Size	Sectors per Cluster	Cluster Size
<512MB	1	512 bytes (or hardware sector size if greater than 512 bytes)
<1024MB	2	1KB
<2048MB	4	2KB
<4096MB	8	4KB

Partition Size	Sectors per Cluster	Cluster Size
<8192MB	16	8KB
<16384MB	32	16KB
<32768MB	64	32KB
<32768 MB	128	64KB

NTFS better balances the tradeoff between disk defragmentation due to smaller cluster size and wasted space due to a large cluster size.

When formatting a drive, you can change the cluster size using the **/a:<size> switch—for example:**

```
format d: /a:1024 /fs:ntfs
```

FAQ 20.35 How much free space do I need to convert a FAT partition to NTFS?

The following calculation can be used for disks of a standard 512 bytes per sector:

1. Take the size of the partition and divide by 100. If the result is less than 1,048,576, use 1,048,576; if greater than 4,194,304, use 4,194,304.
2. Add to the previously calculated number the size of the partition divided by 803.
3. Add to the number calculated the total number of files and directories multiplied by 1280. You can work out the total number of files and directories using the dir /s command at the base of the partition—for example:

   ```
   dir /s d:\
   ```

   Total files listed:

   3397 File(s) 300,860,372 bytes
4. Add to the result calculated previously 196096.

To summarize:

Free space needed = (<size of partition in bytes>/100) + (<size of partition in bytes>/803) + (<no of files & directories> * 1280) + 196096

For more information, see Knowledge Base article Q156560 at http://support.microsoft.com/support/kb/articles/q156/5/60.asp.

20.36 NT becomes unresponsive during an NTFS disk operation such as a dir. What should I do?

When you perform a large NTFS disk operation such as a dir/s *.* or a ntbackup :*.* NT can sometimes become unresponsive because NT updates NTFS files with a last access stamp. If viewing thousands of files, the NTFS log file can become full and waits to be flushed to the hard disk. This can cause NT to become unresponsive. To prevent NTFS from updating the last access stamp, perform the following:

1. Start the Registry editor (REGEDIT.EXE).
2. Move to HKEY_LOCAL_MACHINE\SYSTEM\CurrentControlSet\Control\FileSystem.
3. From the Edit menu, select New > DWORD value.
4. Enter a name of **NtfsDisableLastAccessUpdate** and click OK.
5. Double-click the new value and set to 1. Click OK.
6. Close the Registry editor.
7. Reboot the machine.

This should improve the performance of your NTFS partitions.

Following is an example or a .REG file that can be used to automate this process:

```
REGEDIT4
;
[HKEY_LOCAL_MACHINE\SYSTEM\CurrentControlSet\Control\FileSystem]
NtfsDisableLastAccessUpdate=dword:1
```

20.37 Why do I have missing space on my NTFS partitions (alternate data streams)?

It's possible to hide data from both Explorer and the dir command within an NTFS file that you cannot see unless you know its stream name. NTFS allows multiple streams to a file in the form of <filename>:<stream name>. You can try it:

1. Start a console window (CMD.EXE).
2. Run notepad NORMAL.TXT, enter some text, and save. **This has to be on an NTFS partition**.

3. Now edit the file again, but this time with a different stream notepad NORMAL.TXT:HIDDEN. You will be prompted to create a new file. Enter some text and save.
4. Perform a dir, and you still see only NORMAL.TXT with its original size.

You can have as many streams as you want. If you copy a file, it keeps the streams, so copying NORMAL.TXT to JOHN.TXT, JOHN.TXT:HIDDEN would exist. You cannot use streams from the command prompt as it does not allow a colon (:) in filenames except for drive letters.

Microsoft provides no way of detecting or deleting these streams. The two ways to delete them are

- Copy the file to a FAT partition and back again
- **ren <file> temp.exe**
  cat temp.exe > <file>
  del temp.exe

You can use Lizp, which is downloadable from http://www.lizp.com. I have not used it in earnest; however, what I have seen looks very good. The Lizp interface is shown in Figure 20-2.

```
Lizp Kernel Win32 - Lizp NT

Lizp Kernel Win32 16.960
Copyright (c) 1997-1998 Firma Stache. All rights reserved.

Operating system:  Windows NT version 4.0 build 1381 (Service Pack 4, RC 1.43)
User name:         savillj
Machine name:      WORKSTATION
SU speed index:    150%

*** LIZP KERNEL LOADED ***

(John Savill)
>(getaltstreams 'd:\temp\john.txt)
((:hidden.txt))
>(deletefile 'd:\temp\john.txt:hidden.txt)
d:\temp\john.txt:hidden.txt
>(getaltstreams 'd:\temp\john.txt)
nil
>_
```

Figure 20-2 Lizp interface

It's also possible to write a function to enumerate every altstream in every file matching c:\winnt*. To do this, let's define a function. We'll call it las, and it'll take one argument, the wild path. Then we could type the following and we'd get what we wanted:

```
(las 'c:\winnt\*)
```

Here's such a function definition:

```
(sequence
    (define
        (las Dir)
        (filter
            '(lambda
                (o)
                (cdr o) )
            (mapcar
                '(lambda
                    (FileInfo)
                    (if
                        (getfilesize
                            (car FileInfo) )
                        (cons
                            (car FileInfo)
                            (getaltstreams
                                (car FileInfo) ) )
                        (cons nil nil) ) )
                (dirlist Dir) ) ) )
    '(Enhanced with las) )
```

Even though you could type all this at the prompt, on one long line, it's easier to save this code to a file. Let's call the file LAS.LZP. Now, from the Lizp prompt, you could type

```
(eval (load 'las.lzp))
```

and voilà, you'll have a new function, las. Now try the thing previously described:

```
(las 'c:\winnt\*)
```

Suppose we think our Lizp should have this functionality always. Then type

```
(Compile (load 'las.lzp) 'Lizp_with_las.exe true)
```

and we'll have a new version of Lizp, called Lizp_with_las.exe.

Finally, suppose we wanted a GUI application that asked us for the wild path and then displayed the alternate streams in a window. Save the following lines to a file; let's call it LAS_GUI.LZP:

```
(local
    (Result)
    (setq Result
        (las
            (inputbox
                '((Wild path to check for Alt Streams)) ) ) )
    (messagebox
        (if Result Result
            '((No Alt Streams found in path.)) ) )
      (exit) )
```

Now, from Lizp_with_las' prompt, type

```
(Compile (load 'las_gui.lzp) 'Las.exe nil
```

and you'll have a new program, LAS.EXE, doing what we want. Note the last argument to the Compile function: The first time we compiled, we used true; this last time, we used nil. This is because the first time, we wanted the new program to create a console when run (because it was going to be our new Lizp interpreter). The second time we don't need a console.

Another way to delete these streams is to edit them in Notepad and delete all the text. When you quit Notepad, NT tells you that the file is empty and will be deleted, and you only have to confirm.

If you want to write your own programs to detect streams have a look at

- http://www.brilig.demon.co.uk/nt/streams.html
- http://www.mvps.org/win32/ntfs/streams.html

Basically the only reliable way of handling streams is to use the BackupRead() function. The only problem is that BackupRead() requires SeRestorePrivilege/ SeBackupPrivilege rights, which most users will not have.

BackupRead() actually does turn a file and its associated metadata (extended attributes, security data, alternate streams, links) into a stream of bytes. BackupWrite() converts it back.

20.38 How can I change the volume ID of a disk?

Windows NT provides functionality to change the volume name of a disk by using the command

```
label <drive>: <label name>
```

Windows NT does not provide built-in functionality to change volume IDs; however, NT Internals has produced a free utility, VolumeID, that can be downloaded from http://www.sysinternals.com/ntw2k/utilities.shtml. VolumeID can change the volume ID of a FAT or NTFS volume. To view a drive's current volume ID, you can just perform a dir <drive>: and the volume serial number is shown on the second line down—for example:

```
Volume in drive E is system
Volume Serial Number is BC09-8AE4
```

To change, enter the command

```
volumeid <drive letter>: xxxx-xxxx
```

20.39 How do I read NTFS 5.0 partitions from Windows NT 4.0?

Service Pack 4 includes a read/write driver for NTFS 5.0 volumes (an updated NTFS.SYS driver). This driver is installed by default when installing Service Pack 4; however, you do not have access to the more advanced features such as junction points and the Encrypted File System.

20.40 How do share and filesystem protections interact?

In general when you have protections on a share or on a file/directory, the privileges are added. For example, if user John was a member of two groups, one with read access and another with change, the user would have read and change access. The exception to this is when a group has no access, which means no matter what other group memberships there are, any user in that group will have no access.

The opposite is true when protections are set on the filesystem and on the share where the most restrictive policy is enforced. For example, if the file has full control set for a user and the share only has read, then the user will be limited to read-only privileges. Likewise, if the file had only read-only but the share had full, the user would still be limited to read-only.

Share protections are only used when the filesystem is accessed through a network connection; if the user is using the partition locally, then the share protections will be ignored.

FAQ 20.41 How do I convert an NTFS partition to NTFS 5.0?

Windows 2000 introduces NTFS 5.0, which enables a number of new features. By default when you install Windows 2000, it will automatically convert any NTFS 4.0 partitions to NTFS 5.0. **Any** and **all** NTFS volumes Windows 2000 sees—including removable media—are automatically converted to V5.0 on the fly when Windows 2000 mounts them.

Service Pack 4 has an updated NTFS.SYS that can read NTFS 5.0 partitions, so apply this to any systems that need to read Windows 2000 NTFS 5.0 partitions—and in a multiboot environment **before** installing Windows 2000.

By default (you can override it using the advanced option button) on server installations, the boot partition will be upgraded to NTFS if you're not in a dual-boot environment—yep, that's right, it automatically upgrades from FAT to NTFS.

FAQ 20.42 I cannot compress files on an NTFS partition. What can I do?

When you try to compress files on an NTFS partition using Explorer (right-click on a file/directory, select Properties, and check the compress box), if the option is not available. Or when you try from the command prompt using the following command:

```
compact /c ntfaq.txt /s
```

you get the error

```
The filesystem does not support compression.
```

The cause of this error is normally that the cluster size of the NTFS partition is greater than 4,096. To check the cluster size of your NTFS partition, use the CHKDSK command—for example:

```
chkdsk <disk>: /i /c
```

The /i /c are used to speed up chkdsk, and at the end of the display, it will tell you the bytes in each allocation unit:

```
2048 bytes in each allocation unit.
1012032 total allocation units on disk.
572750 allocation units available on disk.
```

If this number is greater than 4,096, you will need to back up all the data on the disk and then reformat the partition using any of the following methods:

- Start Explorer, make sure the partition is not being used, right-click on the partition, and select Format. Set the allocation unit size to 4,096 or less.
- Start Disk Administrator (Start > Programs > Administrative Tools > Disk Administrator), right-click on the partition, select Format and again set the unit size to 4,096 or less.
- Format from the command prompt

```
format <drive>: /fs:ntfs /a:4096
```

Once reformatted, you can then restore your backed up data.

To understand more about the 4,096 limit, read Knowledge Base article Q171892 at http://support.microsoft.com/support/kb/articles/q171/8/92.asp.

FAQ 20.43 How can I modify the CHKDSK timer?

Service Pack 4 introduces a new feature that, before performing a chkdsk, if a disk's dirty bit is set, a 30-second countdown timer is given, allowing you to cancel chkdsk from running.

If you want to modify this 30-second value, perform the following:

1. Start the Registry editor.
2. Move to HKEY_LOCAL_MACHINE\SYSTEM\CurrentControlSet\Control\Session Manager.
3. From the Edit menu, select New > DWORD Value. Enter a name of **AutoChkTimeOut** and press Enter.

4. Double-click this new value and set to 0 to disable the timer, or set it to the time in seconds you wish to be given to cancel chkdsk.
5. Close the Registry editor.

The change will take effect at the next reboot.

20.44 How can I view the current owner of a file?

The normal method would be to right-click on the file in Explorer, select Properties, click the Security tab, and click Ownership (or with 2000 and above, click Advanced from the Security tab, then select the Owner tab). This will then show the current owner and give the option to take ownership.

To view from the command line, you can use the SUBINACL.EXE utility that is shipped with the Windows NT Resource Kit Supplement 2. To view the current owner, use as follows:

```
subinacl /file <filename>
//++++
// D:\Documents\<filename>
//--
+ Owner = builtin\administrators
+ Primary Group= lnautd0001\domain users
+ System ACE count =0
+ Disc. ACE count =1
lnautd0001\saviljo ACCESS_ALLOWED_ACE_TYPE FILE_ALL_ACCESS
```

You could perform on *.* to list owners for all files in all subdirectories (no need for any /s switch).

20.45 How can I view/defrag pagefile fragmentation?

System Internals has released PageDefrag, a free utility that shows fragmentation in the pagefile and then offers the option of defragmentation at boot time. The utility can be downloaded from http://www.sysinternals.com/. Once you download it, just unzip the file and run PAGEDFRG.EXE. Figure 20-3 shows sample output.

Executive Software's Diskeeper 4.0 and above can also defragment pagefiles and works well (http://www.diskeeper.com).

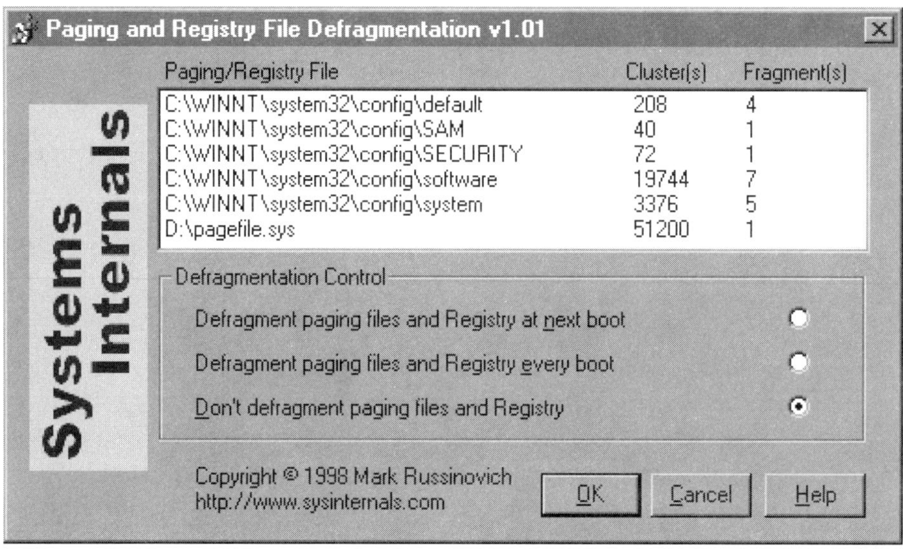

Figure 20-3 The System Internals paging and Registry defrag interface

20.46 Why do I get a disk maintenance message during setup?

If during setup, you get the following message:

```
Setup has performed maintenance on your hard disk(s) that
requires a reboot to take effect. You must reboot and restart
Setup to continue.
Press F3 to reboot.
```

This message is returned when the Autochk part of the installation was able to repair the partition, but the system will require a reboot.

For a FAT partition, these conditions could include corrupt extended attributes were fixed, a dirty bit was cleared, an orphaned long filename entry was fixed (or any other fixing of LFNs), directory entry fixed, crosslinked files fixed, nonunique filename uniqued, or any other structural issues at all fixed. Of course other specific fixing steps can cause this error for NTFS, or other nonfilesystem-specific structures can cause this error as well.

In short this is not a problem as long as the setup does not get stuck in a loop that keeps running this stage.

FAQ 20.47 Where is Disk Administrator in Windows 2000?

As with every other administration tool in Windows 2000, Disk Administrator has been replaced with a Microsoft Management Console (MMC) snap-in.

By default it is accessible via the Computer Management MMC snap-in:

1. Start the Computer Management MMC (Start > Programs > Administrative Tools > Computer Management).
2. Select the Storage branch.
3. Select Disk Management.
   It should look familiar (see Figure 20-4).

Alternatively you can create your own MMC console:

1. Start the MMC (Start > Run > MMC).
2. Select Add/Remove Snap-in from the Console menu.
3. Click Add.
4. Select Disk Management and click Add.
5. Select Local Computer and click Finish.

Figure 20-4 Disk Management MMC snap-in

6. Click Close.
7. Click OK to the main dialog.

You now have your own MMC with just the Disk Management. You could save by selecting Save As from the Console menu, enter **Disk Admin** as the name, and click Save. You will now see under the Programs menu a new folder, My Administrative Tools, with Disk Admin as a MMC snap-in.

FAQ 20.48 How do I convert a basic disk to dynamic?

Windows 2000 introduces the idea of a dynamic disk needed for fault-tolerant configurations. To convert, perform the following:

1. Start Computer Manager.
2. Expand Storage > Disk Management.
3. Right-click on the disk and select Upgrade to Dynamic Disk.
4. Select the disks to upgrade and click OK. A summary will be displayed.
5. Click Upgrade.
6. Click Yes to the confirmation.

Converting basic disks to dynamic disks don't require reboots (unless you are converting the disk containing the boot or system volume); however, any volumes contained on them after the conversion will generate a pop-up that basically says a reboot is necessary before the volumes can be used. I generally say—**No**, do not reboot, until all the volumes are identified and all the pop-ups go away; then perform a single reboot.

When you upgrade from basic to dynamic, any existing partitions become simple volumes. Any existing mirrored, striped, or spanned volumes sets created with NT 4.0 become dynamic mirrored, striped, or spanned volumes, respectively.

If you get a message that says you are out of space, then you may not have enough unallocated free space at the end of the disk for the private region database that dynamic disks use to keep volume information. To be dynamic, a disk needs about 1MB of this space; sometime the space is not visible to the user in the GUI, but it is still there.

You may not have the space if the partition(s) on the disk takes up the entire disk and was created with Setup, an earlier version of NT, or another OS. If partitions are created within Windows 2000, the space is reserved; partitions created with Setup will reserve the space in a later release.

To undo this conversion, run DMUNROOT.EXE, which will revert boot and system partitions back to basic, but all other volumes will be destroyed. Alternatively you should back up any data on the disk you wish to preserve; then delete all partitions—that should activate the menu choice Revert to Basic Disk. The entire disk **has** to be unallocated or free space. Dmunroot is an unsupported utility available from Microsoft.

FAQ 20.49 How do I delete a volume in Windows 2000?

To delete a volume, just perform the following. Be warned you will lose any data on these volumes.

1. Start the Computer Management MMC (Start > Programs > Administrative Tools > Computer Management).
2. Expand the Storage branch and select Disk Management.
3. Right-click on the volume to be deleted and select Delete Volume from the context menu shown.
4. Click Yes to the confirmation.

FAQ 20.50 How do I import a foreign volume in Windows 2000?

If you take a dynamic disk from another machine and place it in a Windows 2000 box, it will be shown as foreign, and its partitions are not available. However its volume information can be imported and volumes used. Any volumes that were part of a set will be deleted during the import phase unless the whole set of disks are imported.

1. Start the Computer Management MMC (Start > Programs > Administrative Tools > Computer Management).
2. Expand the Storage branch and select Disk Management.
3. Right-click on the volume to be imported and select Import Foreign Disks from the context menu shown (see Figure 20-5).
4. Click OK to the displayed dialog of the disk to import. If you import multiple disks, they will be grouped by the computer they were moved from and can be selected by clicking the Select Disk button. If the disks imported are not dynamic, they will all be imported regardless of your choices.
5. A dialog will be shown showing the volumes to import (see Figure 20-6). Click OK.

Notice the partition that was part of a RAID 5 set is not usable.

The data on the imported volumes will now be accessible (you have to refresh in Explorer to see them—press F5).

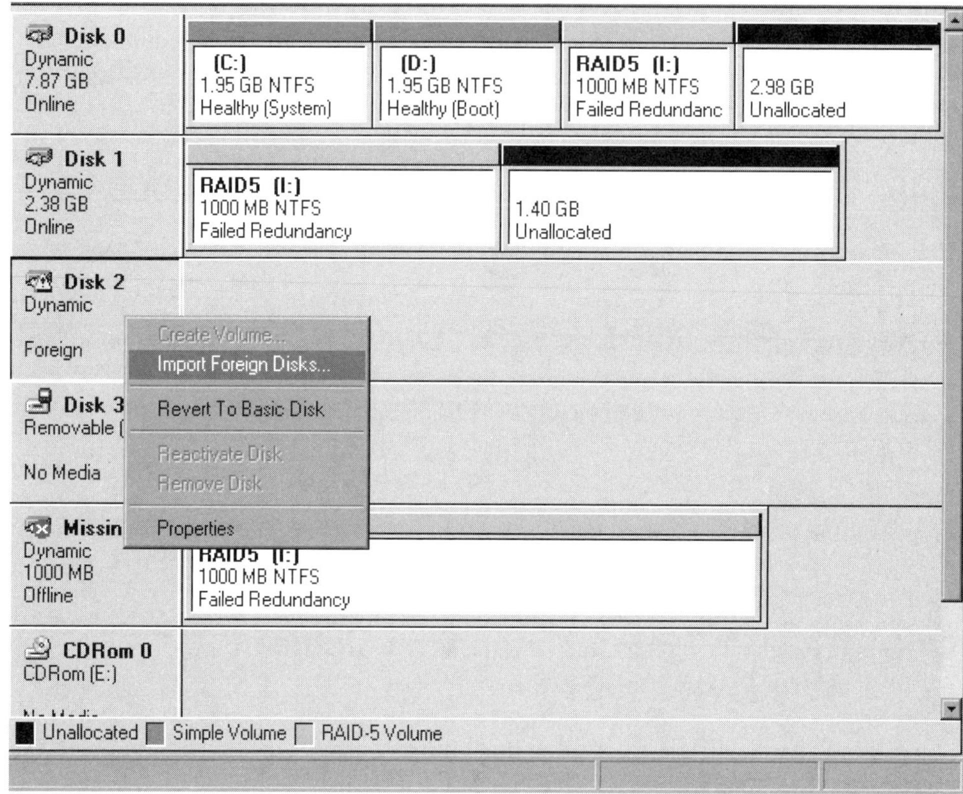

Figure 20-5 Importing a foreign dynamic disk

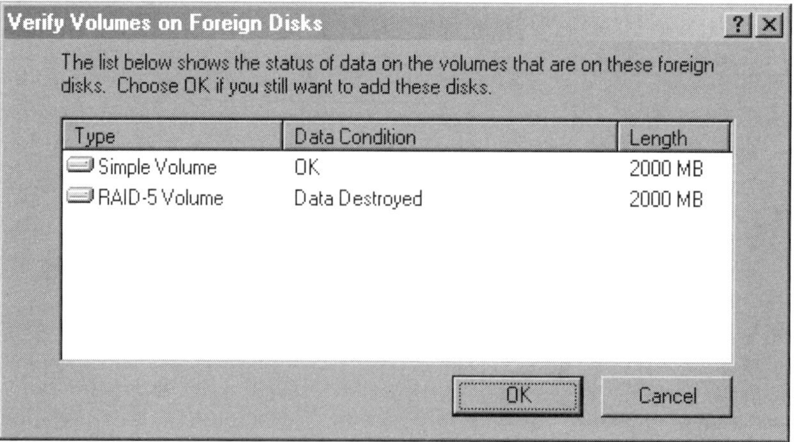

Figure 20-6 Checking volumes to import on a foreign disk

FAQ 20.51 How can I wipe the master boot record (MBR)?

The normal method is using the DOS FDISK command:

```
fdisk /mbr
```

However in some cases, this command does not work, and a more direct method may be needed.

A program called DEBUG.EXE is supplied with DOS, Windows 9x, and NT and can be used to run small assembly language programs. Just such a program can be used to wipe the MBR. Perform the following, but **be careful**; this **will** wipe your MBR, leaving your system unbootable and its data lost.

1. Boot to 9x or DOS (this cannot be done from NT because direct disk access is not allowed).
2. Start a command prompt.
3. Enter the following commands (in bold—see Figure 20-7):

```
debug
-F 9000:0 L 200 0
-a
0C5A:0100 Mov dx,9000
```

```
D:\WINNT\System32\cmd.exe - debug

D:\>debug
-f 9000:0 L 200 0
-a
0C5A:0100 Mov dx,9000
0C5A:0103 Mov es,dx
0C5A:0105 Xor bx,bx
0C5A:0107 Mov cx,0001
0C5A:010A Mov dx,0080
0C5A:010D Mov ax,0301
0C5A:0110 Int 13
0C5A:0112 Int 20
0C5A:0114
-u 100 L 12
0C5A:0100 BA0090        MOV     DX,9000
0C5A:0103 8EC2          MOV     ES,DX
0C5A:0105 31DB          XOR     BX,BX
0C5A:0107 B90100        MOV     CX,0001
0C5A:010A BA8000        MOV     DX,0080
0C5A:010D B80103        MOV     AX,0301
0C5A:0110 CD13          INT     13
-g

Program terminated normally
-
```

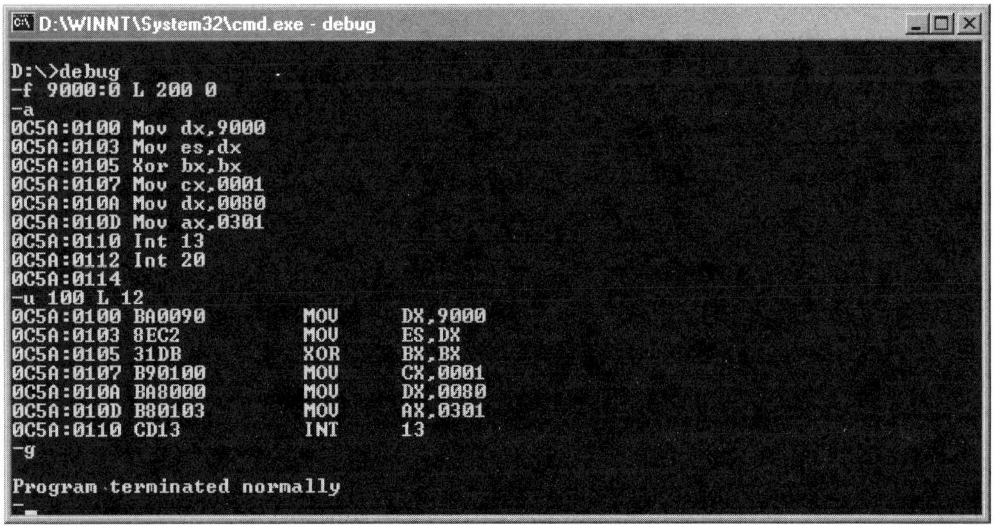

Figure 20-7 Wiping the master boot record

```
0C5A:0103 Mov es,dx
0C5A:0105 Xor bx,bx
0C5A:0107 Mov cx,0001
0C5A:0109 Mov dx,0080
0C5A:010A Mov ax,0301
0C5A:010D Int 13
0C5A:0110 Int 20
<press Enter twice>
-u 100 L 12   <check the code matches the above>
-g <executes>

Program terminated normally
-quit
```

You can now install a replacement MBR via a normal installation.

Thanks to Mark Minasi for giving permission to reproduce this assembler code. A full explanation can be found in *Windows NT Magazine*, Summer 1999.

Another method from David Lynch:

```
C:\> debug
-a
xxxx:0100 mov ax,0301
xxxx:01xx mov cx,1
xxxx:01xx mov dx,80
xxxx:01xx int 13
xxxx:01xx int 3
xxxx:01xx <CR>
-G
```

This method is much shorter. It has two theoretically possible failure cases:

- ES:BX accidentally and randomly points to a valid MBR, which is extremely unlikely and probably technically impossible. I ES:BX is initialized when debug starts. BX is normally the high part of the length of the file being debugged, and I think therefore 0 if there is no file, and I think ES is the same as DS, SS, CS by default.
- The 510th word pointed to by ES:BX is AA55. I do not know what the probability is here, but it is at least 1/64K. Further even if this is the case, it still may not fail, just subsequent attempts to format the drive will believe there is a valid, though maybe unusual, MBR.

There is nothing special about the process of filling the MBR with 0s. It just needs not to be valid. Any invalid MBR is the same as no MBR.

FAQ 20.52 How can I cancel a scheduled NTFS conversion?

If you have scheduled a NTFS conversion for the next reboot using the CONVERT command, it can be canceled as follows:

1. Start the Registry editor (REGEDT32.EXE **not** REGEDIT.EXE).
2. Move to HKEY_LOCAL_MACHINE\SYSTEM\CurrentControlSet\Control\Session Manager.
3. Double-click BootExecute.
4. Change from

   ```
   autoconv \DosDevices\x: /FS:NTFS
   ```

   to

   ```
   autocheck autochk *
   ```

5. Click OK.
6. Close the Registry editor.

FAQ 20.53 What is the Encrypted File System (EFS)?

New to Windows 2000 and the NTFS 5.0 filesystem is the Encrypted File System (EFS), which as the name suggests is used to encrypt files.

NTFS is a secure filesystem; however, with more and more people using portables and utilities such as NTFSDos from http://www.sysinternals.com/, which bypasses NTFS security, another layer of protection is needed.

EFS uses a public and private key encryption and the CryptoAPI architecture. EFS can use any symmetric encryption algorithm to encrypt files; however, the initial release only uses DES. Keys of 128 bits are used in North America and most other international sites, and 40 bits for everyone else.

No preparation is needed to encrypt files, and the first time a user encrypts a file, an encryption certificate for the user and a private key are automatically created.

If encrypted files are moved, they stay encrypted; if users add files to an encrypted folder, the new files are automatically encrypted. There is no need to decrypt a file before use; the operating system automatically handles this for you in a secure manner.

In the event of a user's private key being lost (either by reinstallation or new user creation), the EFS recovery agent can decrypt the files.

20.54 How do I encrypt/decrypt a file?

Encrypting and compressing a file/folder is mutually exclusive; you can encrypt a file or compress it, not both.

To decrypt a file, perform the following:

1. Start Explorer.
2. Right-click on the file/folder.
3. Select Properties.
4. Under the General tab, click Advanced.
5. Check the Encrypt contents to secure data (see Figure 20-8). Click OK.
6. Click Apply on the properties.
7. If you selected a file, Windows will ask if you want to encrypt the parent folder to prevent the file from becoming unencrypted during modification. Click OK if you selected a folder. Windows will ask if you want to encrypt subfolders and files also. Click OK.
8. Click OK to the main dialog.

To decrypt a file, repeat the preceding but unselect the box. If you decrypt a folder, Windows will ask if you also want to decrypt all child folders and files.

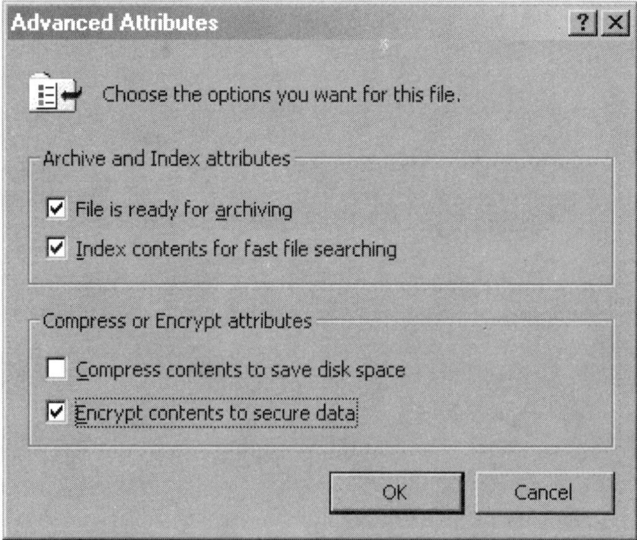

Figure 20-8 Encrypting a file via the GUI

A file cannot be both encrypted and compressed. There is a technical issue here. It is not because of a reparse point. Neither compression nor encryption use reparse points. The reason Microsoft does not support both is backup/restore. Microsoft provides a way for a backup operator to back up an encrypted file. The operator has no way to read the file in plain text. The NTFS compression result depends on the disk cluster. If the backup source and the restore destination have a different cluster size, NTFS cannot restore the encrypted data because NTFS does not know how to understand the data.

Encryption is compatible with sparse. In other words, you can encrypt a sparse file and still keep it a sparse file.

FAQ 20.55 How do I encrypt/decrypt a file from the command line?

A command-line utility, CIPHER.EXE, can be used to encrypt and decrypt files from the command line:

```
CIPHER [/E | /D] [/S:dir] [/I] [/F] [/Q] [dirname [...]]
```

- /E—Encrypts the specified directories. Directories will be marked so that files added afterward will be encrypted.
- /D—Decrypts the specified directories. Directories will be marked so that files added afterward will not be encrypted.
- /S—Performs the specified operation on directories in the given directory and all subdirectories.
- /I—Continues performing the specified operation even after errors have occurred. By default, CIPHER stops when an error is encountered.
- /F—Forces the encryption operation on all specified directories, even those that are already encrypted. Already encrypted directories are skipped by default.
- /Q—Reports only the most essential information.
- dirname—Specifies a pattern or directory.

Used without parameters, CIPHER displays the encryption state of the current directory and any files it contains. You may use multiple directory names and wildcards. You must put spaces between multiple parameters.

20.56 How can a user request an EFS recovery certificate?

To request a EFS certificate, you first need the domain to have a trusted list of Certificate Authorities, and the user needs to be a domain Administrator.

1. Start the MMC console (Start > Run > MMC.EXE).
2. From the Console menu, select Add/Remove Snap-in.
3. Click Add.
4. Select Certificates and click Add.
5. Select My user account and click Finish.
6. Click Close.
7. Click OK to the main dialog.
8. Expand the Certificates root and right-click on Personal.
9. Select Request New Certificate from the All Tasks menu.
10. Click Next to the Certificate Request Wizard.
11. Select EFS Recovery Agent and click Next.
12. Enter a friendly name and description. Click Next.
13. Click Finish the summary dialog.
14. Click Install Certificate. Click OK.

You will now have a File Recovery certificate under the Personal\Certificates folder.

20.57 How can I add a user as an EFS recovery agent for a domain?

Recovery agents are users who can recover encrypted files for a domain. To add new users as recovery agents, they must first have recovery certificates issued by the enterprise CA structure (a local certificate granted by the Administrator is of no use).

1. Start the Active Directory Users and Computers (Start > Programs > Administrative Programs > Active Directory Users and Computers).
2. Right-click on the domain and select Properties.
3. Select the Group Policy tab.
4. Select the Default Domain Policy and click Edit.

5. Expand Computer Configuration\Windows Settings\Security Settings\Public Key Policies\Encrypted Data Recovery Agents.
6. Right-click Encrypted Data Recovery Agents and select Add.
7. Click Next to the Add Recovery Agent Wizard.
8. Click Browse Directory. Locate the user and click OK.
9. Click Next to the agent dialog select wizard.
10. Click Finish to the confirmation.
11. Close the Group Policy editor.

Refresh the machine policy.

```
secedit /refreshpolicy machine_policy
```

The agent will be able to recover files encrypted only after the user was made an agent. If an encrypted file is unencrypted and then encrypted or even just opened, the new agent **will** be able to recover it because the file will "refresh" its recovery certificates (if the recovery policy has changed).

The local admin on a standalone PC or the first logon admin on a DC is the recovery agent by default. However this can be modified. You can remove the default recovery agent and assign anyone as the recovery agent. In other words, admin cannot read another person's encrypted file unless he is the recovery agent. The purpose of assigning the first logon admin as the recovery agent is to make life easier for most of our customers. The corporate user is recommended to modify the recovery agent.

FAQ 20.58 How do I delete an orphaned share?

When a share's shared directory is deleted, it is "orphaned." If you delete a directory in Explorer that is shared, any shares will automatically be removed. If you delete by a different method, such as from the command prompt, then the share will be left, and it may result in messages in the System event log of the form:

```
The server service was unable to recreate the share NTFAQ because
the directory D:\ntfaq files no longer exists.
```

You can manually update the Registry to remove these "rogue" shares.

1. Start the Registry editor (REGEDT32.EXE).
2. Move to HKEY_LOCAL_MACHINE\SYSTEM\CurrentControlSet\Services\lanmanserver\Shares. There is an entry for each share (see Figure 20-9).

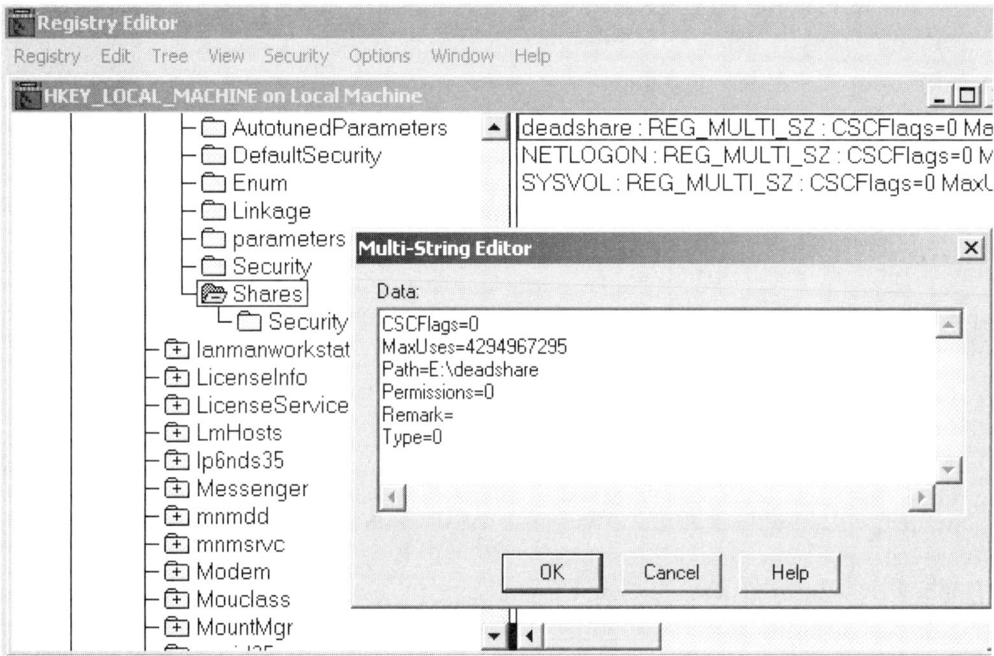

Figure 20-9 Share entry in the Registry

3. Select the entry for the share you wish to delete and select Delete from the Edit menu.
4. Click Yes to the confirmation.
5. If the share had special security set, it will also have an entry under the Security subkey, so move it to Security (under Shares), select the share value name, and delete it.

If you type **net share**, the share name will still be displayed until the Lanmanserver service is restarted. If you manually restart, the services interface will also stop the services, netlogon, computer browser, and Distributed File System.

Another method (if you have access) is to use Server Manager in NT 4.0. Connect to the machine, and orphaned shares are grayed out; you can then delete them. Windows 2000 Computer Manager does not display orphaned shares in a different color, making this approach impossible in Windows 2K.

FAQ 20.59 How can I check who last opened a file?

The only way I know of is to enable auditing on the file and then examine the Security event log for access (see Figure 20-10).

In order to do this, you will need the following:

1. Enable auditing for files and folders via User Manager (Policies > Audit > Audit These Events > File and Object Access). In Windows 2000, use the Group Policy editor and edit the local policy or another GPO (Computer Configuration > Windows Settings > Security Settings > Local Policies > Audit Policy).
2. Start Explorer.
3. Right-click on the files/folders and select Properties.
4. Select the Security tab.

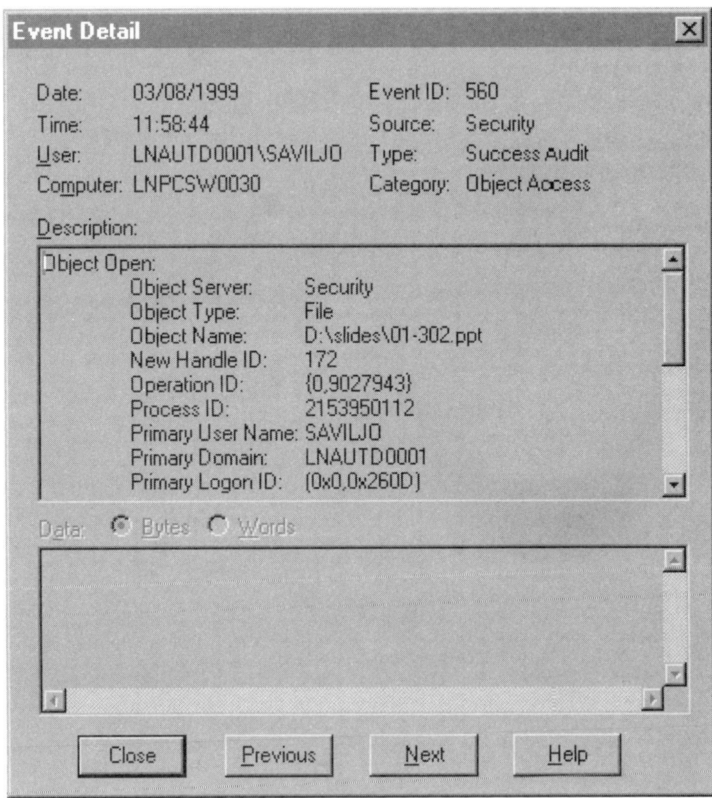

Figure 20-10 Event for a file access

5. Click the Advanced button.
6. Select the Audit tab.
7. Click Add.
8. Select Everyone.
9. Click OK.
10. Select the actions to audit such as List folder/read data.
11. Click OK.
12. Click OK to all dialogs.

FAQ 20.60 I've increased the size of a hardware RAID volume, but NT does not see the size increase. What can I do?

You need to reset the Disk Administrator configuration by performing the following:

1. Back up your disk configuration by starting Disk Administrator (Start > Programs > Administrative Tools > Disk Administrator or just run WINDISK.EXE).
2. Insert a floppy disk and from the Partition menu, select Configuration > Save. Your configuration will then be saved to the disk.
3. Close the Disk Administrator.
4. Start the Registry editor (REGEDIT.EXE).
5. Move to HKEY_LOCAL_MACHINE\SYSTEM\DISK.
6. Select the Disk key and press Delete.
7. Close the Registry editor.
8. Restart the Disk Administrator. Disk Administrator will say it's the first time it has been run, and it will update the disk configuration (see Figure 20-11).

Figure 20-11 Disk Administrator first run dialog

FAQ 20.61 Because I'm a member of a 4.0 domain, why am I unable to use the Encrypted File System under Windows 2000?

Because a machine in a domain uses the domain policy for recovery if the domain does not support EFS (such as a 3.51 or 4.0 domain), EFS is disabled. To get around this problem, perform the following:

1. Remove the Windows 2000 computer from the Windows NT 4.0 domain.
2. From the command prompt, type:

```
secedit /refreshpolicy machine_policy /enforce
```

3. Rejoin the Windows 2000 computer to the Windows NT 4.0 domain.

FAQ 20.62 How do I enable per-volume/user disk space quotas on NTFS 5.0?

Windows 2000 introduces limited quota support, which enables you to configure quota limits on a per-user/per-volume basis. You can't set a quota over multiple volumes.

Quotas are on file size, and even if files are compressed, you still only get the megabytes amount of the files. If you had a 5MB quota and compressed your 5MB of files using NTFS compression, you would have used all your quota.

Quota support is only available on NTFS 5.0 volumes and is enabled as follows:

1. Start Explorer.
2. Right-click on the volume and select Properties.
3. Check the Enable quota management box (see Figure 20-12).
4. You can set default options for new users and also set the actions to take if the quota is exceeded. Either deny disk space or allow the user to carry on. There are also various logging options, either when a user exceeds a warning level or when a user exceed an actual quota.
5. Click Apply.
6. A warning will be given. Click OK. The quota process will now check the volume and build a list of current disk usage.

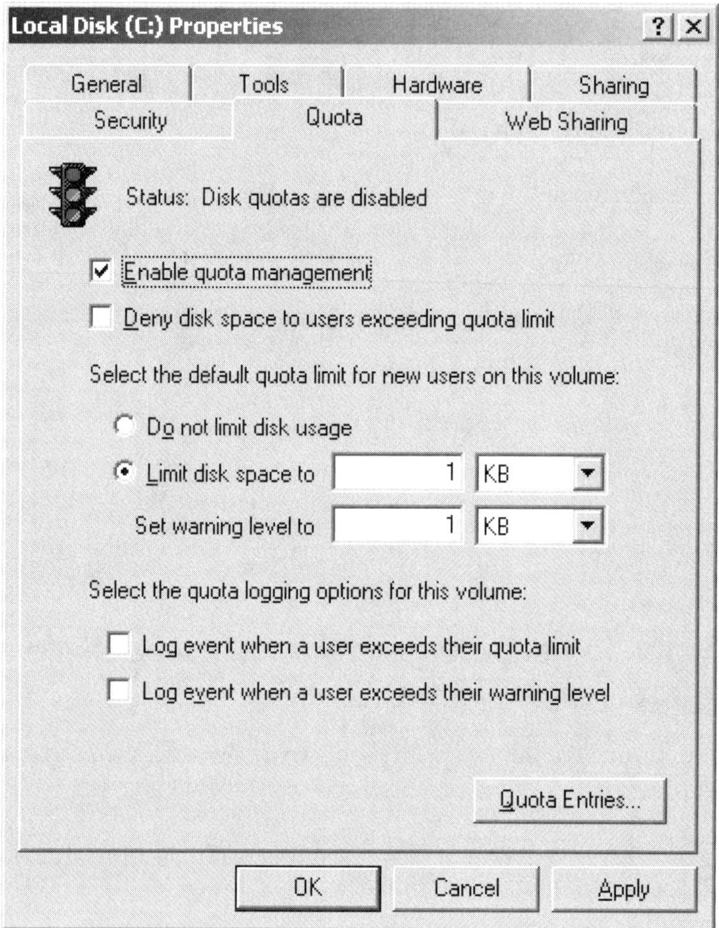

Figure 20-12 Enabling disk quotas

FAQ 20.63 How do I view current quota entries?

To view current quota usage on a volume, perform the following:

1. Start Explorer.
2. Right-click on the volume and select Properties.
3. Click the View Quota Entries button.
4. A list of quota entries and the amount used will be displayed as shown in Figure 20-13.

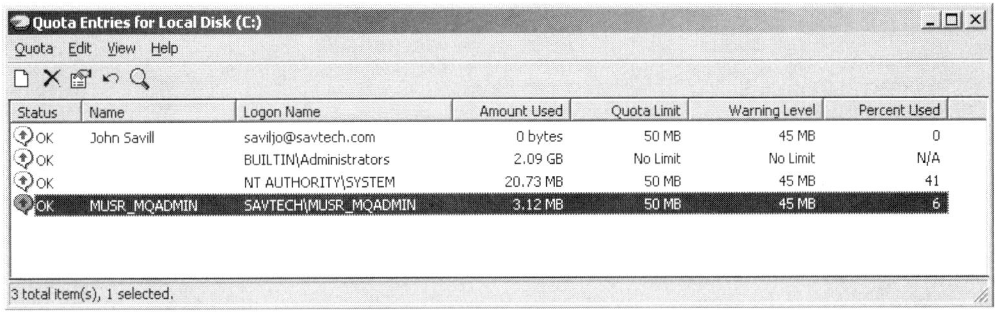

Figure 20-13 Viewing quota entries for a volume

20.64 How do I add a new user quota entry?

To add a new user quota entry, perform the following:

1. Start Explorer.
2. Right-click on the volume and select Properties.
3. Click the Quota Entries button.
4. A list of quota entries and the amount used will be displayed. From the Quota menu, select New quota entry or click the new document button.
5. Select the user(s) for the quota to be added. Click Add. When all are selected, click OK.
6. Set the warning level and final level for the user(s) as shown in Figure 20-14. Click OK.

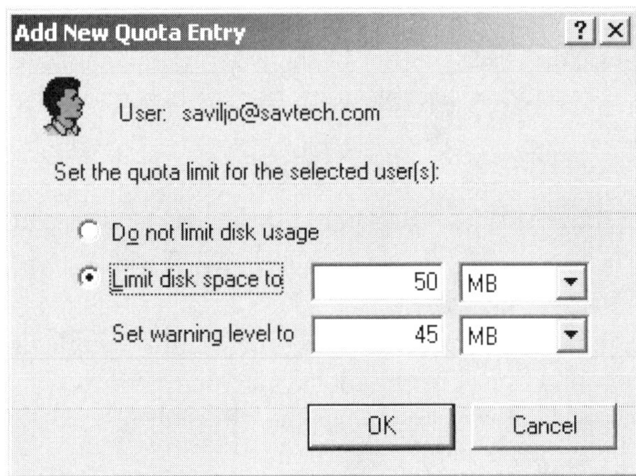

Figure 20-14 Setting the quota limits

If you select multiple users, they will **not** share the quota. It's just a quick way of adding lots of quota entries, all with the same properties.

20.65 What are reparse points?

Much of the new Windows 2000 filesystem enhancements are possible thanks to reparse points, which basically provide a hook into the filesystem and allow extensions to the storage subsystem without the need for proprietary code to be written.

Reparse points are actually special filesystem objects that have a special attribute that activate extra functionality in the storage subsystem. Any file or folder can have a reparse point, meaning a single path can trigger multiple portions of extended functionality.

20.66 What are directory junctions?

Directory junctions allow you to join folders together so you can map a directory to any local target directory. Imagine you had three folders, c:\folder1, c:\folder2, and c:\documents. It's possible to create a directory junction to c:\documents, appearing as a subdirectory of the other two folders, resulting in c:\folder1\documents and c:\folder2\documents.

Originally a utility, LINKD.EXE, was supplied that enabled the creation of these junction points; however, this utility is now removed from the product and is supplied with the Resource Kit. Directory junctions can also be created using the application programming interface (API), but you need to write a program.

On first view, directory junctions and the Distributed File System (Dfs) perform some of the same roles because they both give the appearance of a single directory tree, which actually consists of multiple, distributed folders; however, there are differences:

- Domain Dfs utilizes the Active Directory to store its information.
- Thanks to its Active Directory root Dfs can provide fault tolerance and load balancing; directory junctions cannot provide either of these (although in a local context, it's not so necessary).
- Dfs is more geared to merging network resources into a single namespace, whereas directory junctions only link local machine resources.
- Dfs can work using multiple filesystems, but directory junctions rely on NTFS 5.0.
- Dfs requires a client piece; directory junctions don't.

20.67 What are mount points?

Mount points are similar to junction points except that mount points allow only the root of a volume to be mounted as a folder. Mount points are created using reparse points, thus the NTFS 5.0 requirement.

Mount points are useful for increasing a drive's "size" without disturbing it. For instance, you could create a mount point to drive D as c:\documents, thus seeming to increase the size available on C.

20.68 How do I add a mount point?

Mount points are created using the Disk Administration MMC as follows:

1. Start the Computer Management MMC snap-in (Start > Programs > Administrative Tools > Computer Management).
2. Expand the Storage branch and select Disk Management.
3. Right-click on the volume you want to create as a mount point and select Change Drive Letter and Path.
4. Click Add.

Select a new folder for the folder to be mounted as (see Figure 20-15). If you click Browse, you will be shown only NTFS 5.0 volumes. Click OK.

If you then look in Explorer, the new mount point will have the icon of a disk but will have the full content of the disk.

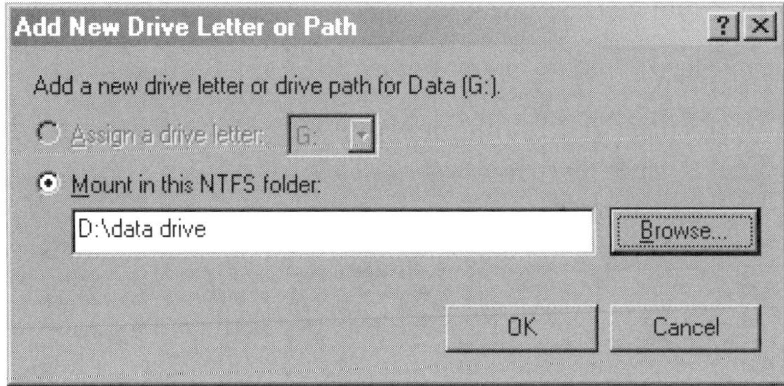

Figure 20-15 Adding a new mount point for a volume

20.69 How do I remove a mount point?

Mount points are removed using the Disk Administration MMC as follows:

1. Start the Computer Management MMC snap-in (Start > Programs > Administrative Tools > Computer Management).
2. Expand the Storage branch and select Disk Management.
3. Right-click on the volume you want to create as a mount point and select Change Drive Letter and Path.
4. Select the mount point to remove.
5. Click Remove.
6. Click Yes to the confirmation.

The process will leave the folder that was created so you need to manually remove it. In the example, the folder d:\data drive will be left as an empty folder.

20.70 How do I create a mount point from the command line?

In line with Microsoft's goal of everything being possible from the command line, Windows 2000 has a utility MOUNTVOL.EXE that can be used to create mount points from the command prompt.

Typing **MOUNTVOL** on its own will list all available volumes that can be mounted:

```
mountvol
```

Creates, deletes, or lists a volume mount point.

MOUNTVOL [drive:]path VolumeName
MOUNTVOL [drive:]path /D
MOUNTVOL [drive:]path /L

The elements on the preceding command line are

- path—Specifies the existing NTFS directory where the mount point will reside.
- VolumeName—Specifies the volume name that is the target of the mount point.
- /D—Removes the volume mount point from the specified directory.
- /L—Lists the mounted volume name for the specified directory.

Possible values for VolumeName along with current mount points are:

```
\\?\Volume{123504dc-643c-11d3-843d-806d6172696f}\
C:\
\\?\Volume{123504dd-643c-11d3-843d-806d6172696f}\
*** NO MOUNT POINTS ***

\\?\Volume{123504db-643c-11d3-843d-806d6172696f}\
D:\

\\?\Volume{123504da-643c-11d3-843d-806d6172696f}\
A:\
```

To create a mount point manually, create a new directory, then create the mount point using the volume ID listed from the MOUNTVOL command—for example:

1. Create a CD directory:

   ```
   md CD
   ```

2. Create a mount point to the CD-ROM drive:

   ```
   mountvol CD \\?\Volume{123504db-643c-11d3-843d-806d6172696f}\
   ```

That's it!

FAQ 20.71 What is Native Structured Storage?

Native Structured Storage or NSS was originally a new feature in Windows 2000; however, it has been withdrawn due to problems with other system components.

NSS was a method to transparently store ActiveX document files in a multistream format on NTFS volumes. Because NSS is no longer supported, ActiveX document files are now stored in the normal document file format.

Windows 2000 Beta 3 supplied a utility NSS2DOC.EXE (it is not supplied in newer beta releases), which converts NSS files to normal document file formats. This program is run automatically during upgrade, and any problems are logged in %systemroot%\setuperr.log.

You can also run it manually using:

```
NSS2DOC-ca
```

Normal causes for automatic conversion failure are:

- Files encrypted using the NTFS encrypted filesystem (because the account used at setup can not decrypt the files).
- Files that cannot be written due to their security settings (run NSS2DOC as the user who owns the files to get around this problem).

FAQ 20.72 How can I back up my local Encrypted File System recovery key?

When a machine is in a domain, the domain's EFS recovery agent is used to decrypt files for which the user has lost his or her private key.

In a workgroup or in a 4.0-based domain, the recovery agent is the local Administrator so it's vital to back up the Administrator's private key. To do this, perform the following:

1. Log on to the computer as the local Administrator account.
2. From the Start menu, select Run.
3. Enter the name **secpol.msc**.
4. Expand the Public Key Policies branch and select Encrypted Data Recovery Agents leaf. A certificate for Administrator with the role of File Recovery will be displayed.
5. Right-click on the certificate and select Export from the All Tasks context menu.
6. The Certificate Export Wizard will start. Click Next.
7. You have the option to also export the private key, select Yes. Click Next.
8. Make sure Enable strong protection is selected and click Next (you also have the option of removing the private key after it is backed up).
9. Enter a password for the exported key. Click Next.
10. Enter the name for the exported file. Click Next.
11. Click Finish.
12. Click OK when the export is complete.
13. If you choose to remove the private key after export, you should now restore the computer.

A 2KB file will now have been created in the target location containing the certificate. Make sure you keep it safe.

FAQ 20.73 How can I restore my local Encrypted File System recovery key?

If you backed up the local EFS recovery key, perform the following to restore it:

1. Log on to the computer as the local Administrator account.
2. Move to the directory containing the recovery key (it has a .PFX extension).
3. Right-click on the file and select Install PFX from the context menu.
4. The Certificate Import Wizard will start; click Next.
5. Click Next to confirm the file and folder.
6. Enter the password used and click Next.
7. Select Place all certificates in the following store and click Browse.
8. Select Personal and click OK.
9. Click Next and then select Finish.
10. Click OK to the confirmation box.

For other methods, see KB article Q242296 at http://support.microsoft.com/support/kb/articles/Q242/2/96.ASP.

FAQ 20.74 How can I perform a CHKDSK on an NTFS 5.0 partition from NT 4.0?

System Internals has released a utility, NTFSCHK from http://www.sysinternals.com/ntfschk.htm, which uses some of Windows 2000's core files and allows full CHKDSK functionality on NTFS 5.0 partitions from NT 4.0.

FAQ 20.75 Is there an alternative to the Linkd utility supplied with the Windows 2000 Resource Kit?

Linkd is used to create directory junctions, which are explained in FAQ 20.66. A utility to create directory junctions was supplied originally in the core product, but it has now been moved to the Resource Kit.

System Internals has written a clone of LINKD.EXE called junction, which can be downloaded from http://www.sysinternals.com/ and has some additional functions.

20.76 The Data in Remote Storage indicator is not correct. What can I do?

Windows 2000 has built-in support for removable media; however, the amount of data it thinks is offline can become inaccurate over time. Windows 2000 basically allows you to store data that is infrequently used to magnetic tape but allows it to be still accessible.

This inaccuracy happens because a Validate Files job is not run every time files are migrated to offline storage. When files are migrated to offline storage, the Data in Remote Storage value is increased to reflect the correct amount. However, when files in offline storage are deleted from the volume, this value is not decremented.

To fix this problem, you can force a Validate Files job to run:

1. Start the Remote Storage Administrators snap-in and then select Managed Volumes.
2. Right-click the RSS-managed volume you want to run the Validate Files job on.

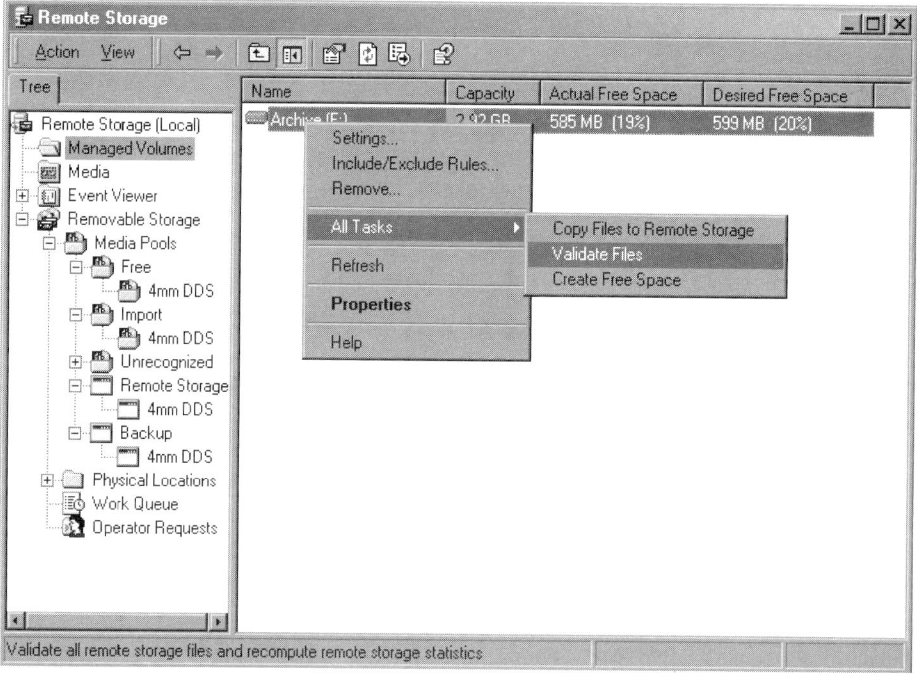

Figure 20-16 Validate Files context menu option

3. On the context menu, point to All Tasks and then click Validate Files (see Figure 20-16). You will receive notification that Remote Storage will create the task, and you can then view its progress using the Task Scheduler. Click OK.

If you view the Remote Storage properties for the volume, the Data In Remote Storage value has been reset to 0 and is slowly increasing while files are being validated.

FAQ 20.77 What is the Remote Storage System (RSS)?

The Remote Storage System is new to Windows 2000 and addresses the problem of limited disk space.

Prices of hard disks have fallen recently; however, tape is still much cheaper (at around $20 for 8GB) than hard drive space but is obviously slower to access. Windows 2000 introduces a hierarchical storage management facility (licensed from Seagate Software) that allows an NTFS 5 volume to be expanded by moving less-used files to tape while leaving a placeholder on the disk so users can still "see" the file. When the user tries to access one of these files that has been moved to tape, it is restored from the tape and opened in a read-only mode. The process is almost invisible to the user; all the user sees is a small dialog informing the user that the file is being restored from tape.

RSS is also known as Hierarchical Storage Management (HSM) because it allows two tiers of data storage: the first being the hard disk, the second the data moved to tape.

The file's original size will still be displayed; however, it will not be used when free space is calculated on the disk.

Programs need to be remote storage aware, especially backup and antivirus software, or Windows 2000 may attempt to fetch files from remote storage, causing long delays. Also you may **want** files to be fetched from remote storage for full backups. The Backup software package (NTBACKUP.EXE) supplied with Windows 2000 has full support for remote storage and can also back up files stored on remote storage if you require. Be especially careful of FindFast supplied with Office 97 and disable it!

You must have local Administrator rights to configure remote storage, and currently as of Windows 2000 first release, it supports 4mm/8mm DAT and DLT drives. The volumes must also be NTFS 5. In the future, media such as Zip or JAZ may be supported but not at present. Also the DAT/DLT drive should be on the HCL. However, I purchased a HP DAT8i for the test, and this DAT was not on HCL, and I had no problems. I'm not encouraging you to use hardware not on the Windows 2000 HCL; I'm just saying if it's a standard DAT/DLT type, it will probably be OK and worth a try. Non-DAT/DLT media will **not** work; I tried a Travan drive, which remote storage refused to use.

FAQ 20.78 How do I install the Remote Storage Subsystem?

Windows 2000 includes the Remote Storage Subsystem, which is used to copy the data in infrequently used files to remote storage media such as a tape, while leaving a file place holder still on the disk. When accessed, the data is fetched from the tape. It basically works by monitoring volumes, and when space dips below a defined level, files not accessed for a certain time are moved to a removable media.

The subsystem is supplied with all versions of Windows 2000 Server but **not** Professional. To install it, perform the following:

1. Start the Add/Remove Software Control Panel applet (Start > Settings > Control Panel > Add/Remove Software).
2. Select Add/Remove Windows Components.
3. Select Remote Storage (see Figure 20-17) and click Next.
4. The files will be copied, and you will have to reboot the server.

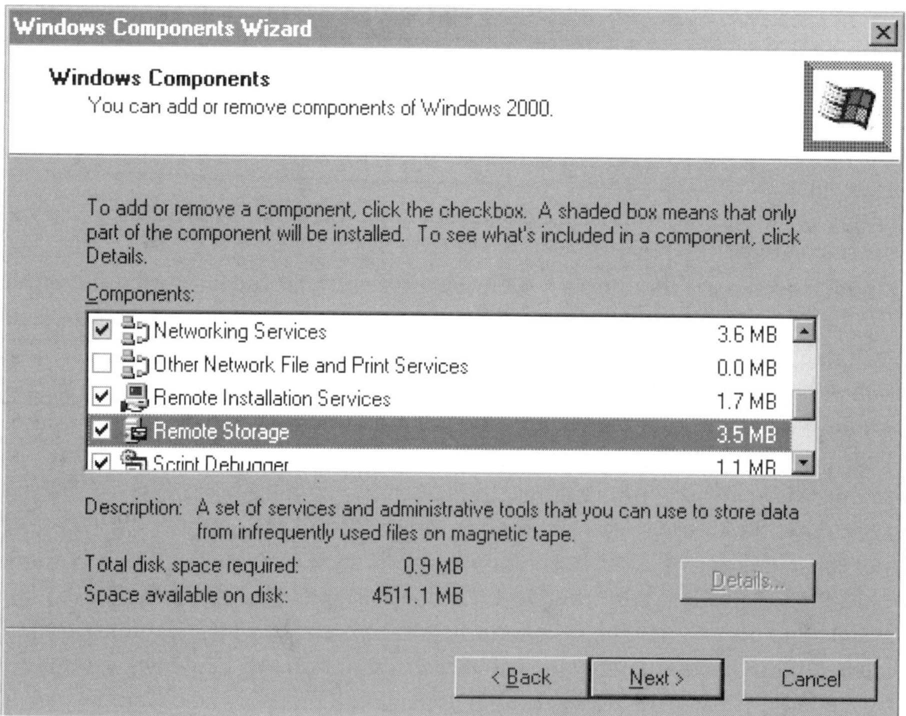

Figure 20-17 Installing the Remote Storage option

Once the reboot has completed, a new Remote Storage component will be added to Administrative Tools, and a number of new services configured.

FAQ 20.79 How do I configure the Remote Storage Subsystem?

When the Remote Storage MMC snap-in is run for the first time (from the Administrative Tools folder), a configuration wizard will run, which you can use to configure the basics. Before doing so, be sure you have a 4mm/8mm DAT or DLT drive, or the setup will not continue.

1. Click Next to the introduction.
2. The wizard will check for the correct local rights and a media device that matches the required specification. If it fails, but you have a DAT or DLT configured, click on Remote Storage under Removable Storage and ensure that you have a media pool of the required DAT/DLT type.
3. A list of drives that you can use with remote storage are displayed. Select the volumes (see Figure 20-18) and click Next.
4. Next set the percentage that the free space must dip below before files are moved to remote storage. Also select file sizes and how long since they have been accessed (see Figure 20-19). Click Next.
5. Select the media type you wish to have the files copied to (e.g., 4mm DDS). Click Next.
6. Next you can configure a schedule by which the check for files to be moved will be performed. Click the Change Schedule button to modify from the default of every day at 02:00. Click Next.
7. A summary will be displayed. Click Finish.

The information will now be displayed under the Managed Volumes branch and can be modified if required. A Remote Storage tab will also be added to Disk Properties from Explorer to enable easy configuration.

You can add more managed volumes by right-clicking on Managed Volumes and selecting New > Managed Volume(s).

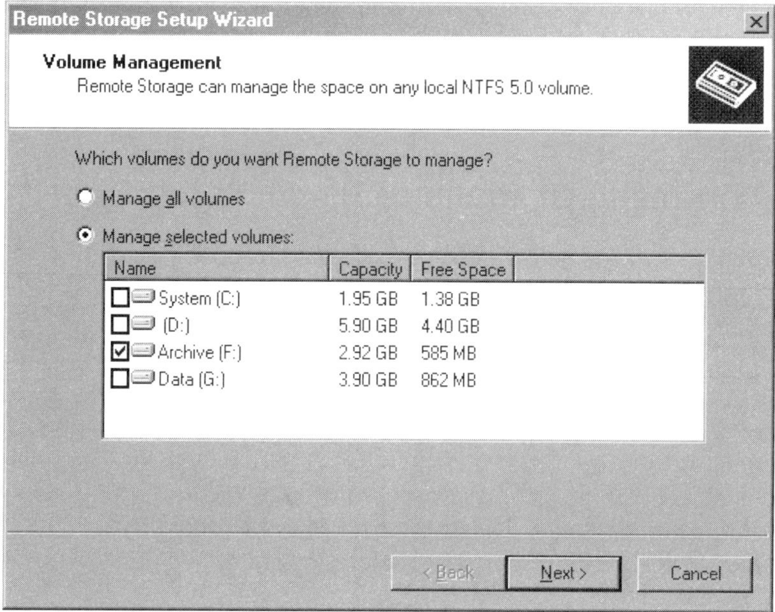

Figure 20-18 Selecting the volumes for remote storage

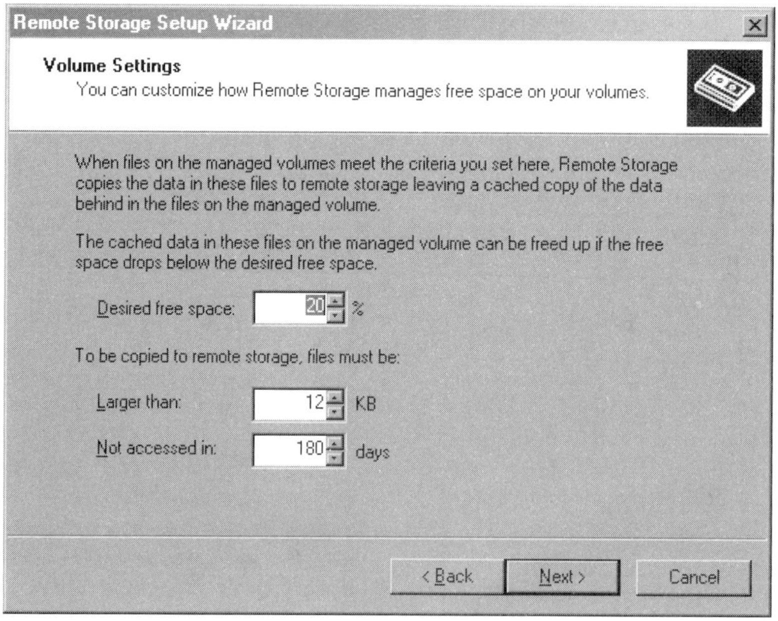

Figure 20-19 Setting the desired free space for remote storage implementation

FAQ 20.80 How do I force a remote storage scan?

Normally the remote storage scan is scheduled to run once a day; however, you can force it to run if you want.

1. Start the Remote Storage MMC (Start > Programs > Administrative Tools > Remote Storage).
2. Select Managed Volumes.
3. Right-click on the volume and from the context menu, select All Tasks > Copy Files to Remote Storage.
4. Click OK to start the check.

It may take some time to run, but you can monitor the progress using the Scheduled Tasks MMC snap-in (Start > Programs > Accessories > System Tools > Scheduled Tasks). When complete, the task can be removed from the list.

FAQ 20.81 How can I tell which files have been moved to remote storage?

Files that have been moved to remote storage have a small clock icon on them (see Figure 20-20), which means they have been moved to remote storage.

When you access the file, it will be fetched from remote storage, and a dialog will be displayed showing progress.

From the command prompt, you can tell because the file size is enclosed in parentheses—for example:

```
F:\NT FAQ Book>dir
Volume in drive F is Archive
Volume Serial Number is D44C-7669

Directory of F:\NT FAQ Book

30/06/1999 13:59 <DIR> .
30/06/1999 13:59 <DIR> ..
05/02/1999 16:58 1,618 2000only.tif
05/02/1999 16:57 1,758 4&5.tif
05/02/1999 16:58 1,638 40only.tif
04/01/1999 15:36 (281,088) appendixa.doc
04/01/1999 15:38 (310,272) appendixb.doc
09/02/1999 12:42 1,050,246 book cover.bmp
```

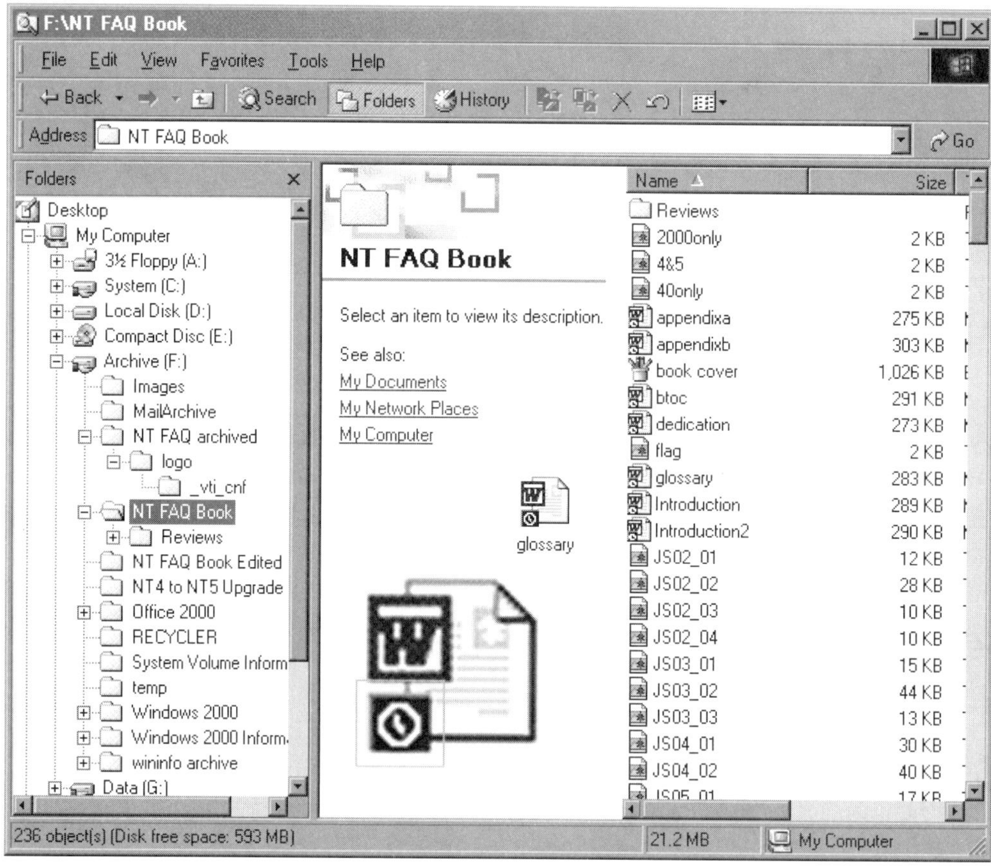

Figure 20-20 A file that has been moved to remote storage

```
23/02/1999 15:47 (297,472) btoc.doc
04/01/1999 15:35 (279,552) dedication.doc
```

20.82 How can I disable remote storage for a volume?

If you decide you want to disable the use of remote storage and instead just want normal file storage, you can disable it by using the following procedure. You must decide whether you wish to copy back any files that have been stored on remote storage or leave them on tape.

1. Start the Remote Storage MMC (Start > Programs > Administrative Tools > Remote Storage).
2. Select Managed Volumes.
3. Right-click on the volume you wish to disable remote storage for and select Remove.
4. Click Next to the Removal Wizard.
5. Select if you wish to move files stored on remote storage back to the disk or leave them on tape, but no new files will be moved. Select the recall option and click Next (see Figure 20-21).
6. Click Yes to the confirmation.
7. Click Finish to the final wizard screen.

A red cross will be displayed next to the volume while the files are recalled from tape. Once the files are fully restored, the volume will be removed from the window.

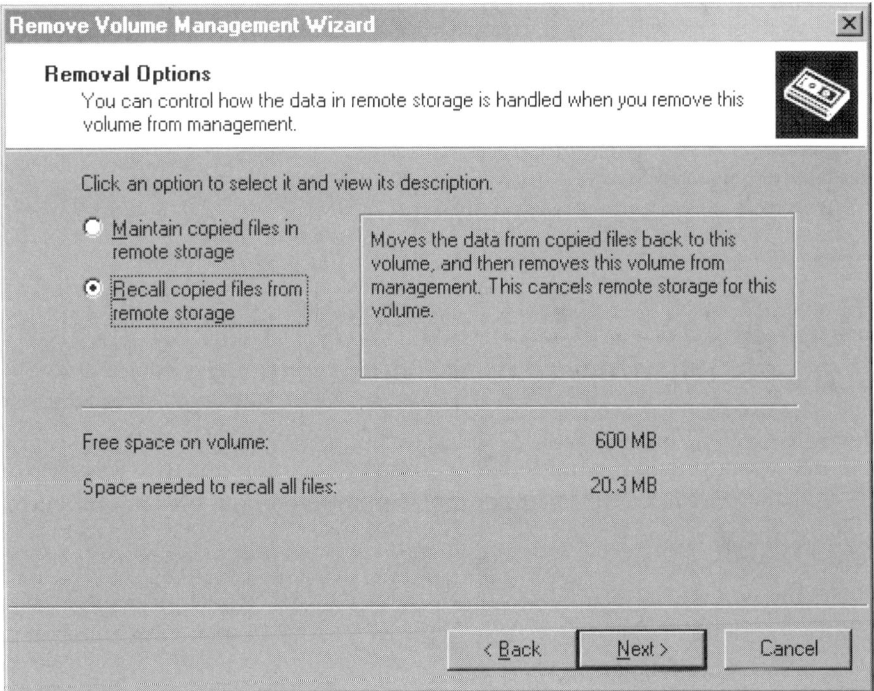

Figure 20-21 Removing remote storage to copy files back to the local disk

20.83 What does the File Replication Service *not* copy?

The File Replication Service (FRS) is Windows 2000's answer to the old LMREPL service from NT 3.x and 4.0 and is far more powerful in scope with its multimaster replication engine.

A replication cycle is triggered once the NTFS change log detects that a file in the Dfs or SYSVOL tree has been closed. Three seconds is given before the replication is started as an aging cache so that only the last iteration of a file being rapidly changed is copied.

The following files/folders are not replicated:

- Folders that are outside of FRS. FRS replicates files and folders in SYSVOL by default. The contents of Dfs fault-tolerant roots and child replica members are replicated when replication has been enabled in DFSGUI.MSC, and each level of the namespace is "backed" by more than one Windows 2000 server.
- Files with a .BAK or .TMP extension or files that begin with ~. Note that file and folder filters can be modified in Active Directory by using a suitable editor such as LDP.EXE (a Resource Kit utility) or ADSIEDIT.MSC.
- EFS-enabled files and folders. EFS-encrypted files are computer specific and are excluded from replication.
- Changes to a file's or folder's last access time.
- Changes to a file's or folder's archive bit.
- NTFS mount points.

20.84 Windows 2000 is incorrectly reporting a volume set size after creation. What can I do?

To correct this problem, you need to make a change via the Registry editor. This problem is caused when you do not immediately restart your computer after you create a volume set using the Disk Administrator tool, and the computer may not properly report the correct partition size.

1. Start the Registry editor (REGEDT32.EXE, not REGEDIT.EXE).
2. Move to HKEY_LOCAL_MACHINE\SYSTEM\CurrentControlSet\Control\Session Manager.
3. Double-click BootExecute.

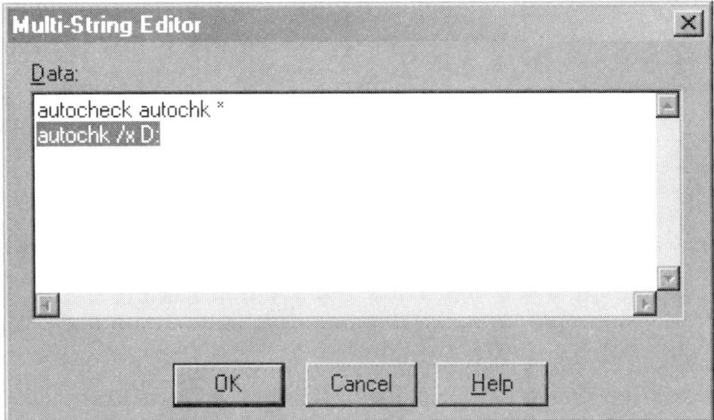

Figure 20-22 A scheduled disk check at next reboot

4. Add a new line (see Figure 20-22)

```
autochk /x D:
```

5. Click OK.
6. Close the Registry editor.
7. Reboot the machine

FAQ 20.85 Why don't I have the option to upgrade to dynamic disk on my laptop?

Windows 2000 introduced dynamic disk, which is required for the creation of its fault-tolerant volumes but isn't backwards compatible with non-Win2K OSs. By default, all disks are basic and can be upgraded using the Disk Management Microsoft Management Console (MMC) snap-in. You right-click the disk information and select Convert to dynamic disk.

However, on a portable, this option isn't available. The argument is that most portables have only one disk, so the advantages of a dynamic disk with fault tolerance aren't applicable. For users with docking stations with disks, a fault-tolerant volume causes problems when the portable isn't in the docking station. You can't work around this "feature."

20.86 Why has the NT File Replication System (NTFRS) stopped responding?

A typical cause for this problem is that the NTFRS's intermediate storage area, the staging area, is full. The staging area stores data as it travels between the network drive and the final local destination. Because data can move faster locally than across the network, this area's space fills quickly when you replicate large amounts of data. By default, the system allocates 660MB for the staging area, but you can increase this value if the staging area volume has sufficient free space.

Before you make the change, you must determine the hexadecimal value of the required size in kilobytes. For example, if you need a 1GB staging area (1,000,000KB), you would perform the following steps to calculate the hex value:

1. Start CALC.EXE.
2. From the View menu, select Scientific.
3. Set the type to Dec.
4. Enter the number in kilobytes (in this example, 1,000,000).
5. Set the type to Hex. The number will change to the hex equivalent (in this example, F4240).
6. Note the hex value.

To increase the staging area's size, perform the following steps:

1. Start REGEDIT.EXE.
2. Navigate to HKEY_LOCAL_MACHINE\SYSTEM\CurrentControlSet\Services\NtFrs\Parameters.
3. Double-click the Staging Space Limit in KB value.
4. Change the base to hex and enter the value (in this example, F4240).
5. Click OK.
6. Close Regedit.

20.87 Why can't I eject an NTFS-formatted Zip disk?

An NTFS-formatted Zip disk is lock mounted because NTFS is a fixed-disk filesystem. Because the disk is lock mounted, you can't eject it using the eject button on the Zip drive. To eject the disk, log on as a member of the local Administrators group. Close all programs that might be accessing the Zip disk, right-click the Iomega icon on the desktop or My Computer and select Eject.

I've experienced problems using this approach with the newer Iomega drivers. The Eject option is grayed out, and the only way I've found to eject the Zip disk is to reboot the machine or protect the disk using a password. The best option is to format the Zip disk in FAT or FAT32 format, which doesn't have the eject problem.

FAQ 20.88 How do I enable Windows 98 compressed folders in Windows 2000?

Win98 includes as part of its Plus! kit a Zip package that lets you browse ZIP files from Explorer. Windows 2000 does not include this feature. However, you can enable this functionality in Win2K by performing the following steps:

1. Insert your Win98 Plus! CD-ROM.
2. From PLUS98.CAB, extract all the ZIP-related files (i.e., *ZIP*.*):
   - DUNZIP.DLL
   - DUNZIP32.DLL
   - DZIP.DLL
   - DZIP32.DLL
   - ZIPFLDR.DLL
3. Copy these files to your system32 directory (e.g., c:\winnt\system32).
4. Run the following command:

   ```
   regsvr32.exe c:\winnt\system32\zipfldr.dll
   ```

5. You will receive the following message:

   ```
   DllRegisterServer in [path]\zipfldr.dll succeeded.
   ```

You don't need to restart the machine or your Explorer session. Compressed folders will now have a small Zip icon with them. To open a compressed folder, double-click it or right-click it and select Explore. To extract files from the compressed folder, perform the following steps:

1. Right-click the compressed folder and select Extract from the context menu.
2. The Extract Wizard will start (see Figure 20-23).
3. Select your destination folder. (If the ZIP file has a password, click Password, and type the password.) Click Next.
4. The system will extract the files and display a results dialog box that shows the end status and provides the option of showing the extracted files. Click Finish.

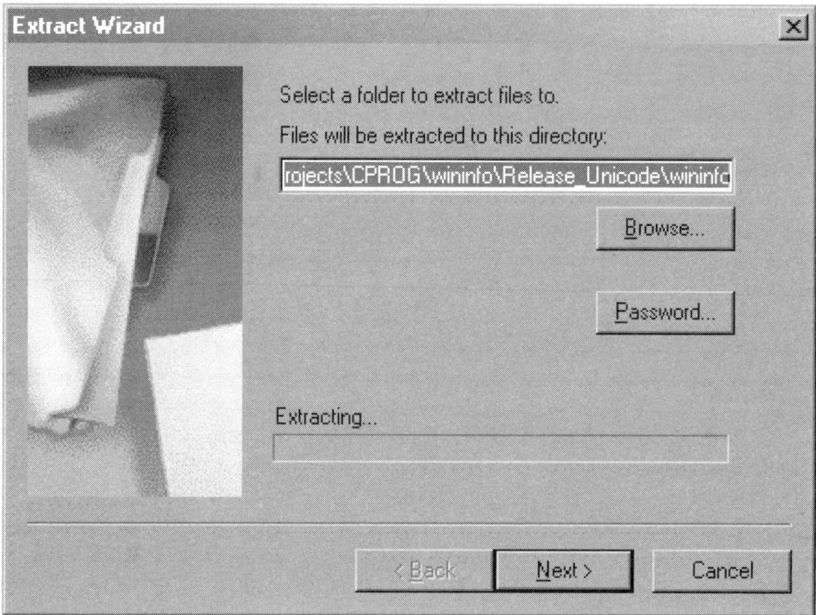

Figure 20-23 Extract Wizard

To compress a file, right-click the file and, from the context menu, select Send to. Then select Compressed Folder. The system creates a compressed folder with the same name as the original file but with the .ZIP extension. If you select multiple files to compress, the folder name will be the first file's name (alphabetically and numbers come at the end of the alphabet). For example, let's say you select three files to compress: WININFO.EXE, DELOLD.EXE, and L365.TXT. The folder name will be DELOLD.ZIP.

FAQ 20.89 How can I schedule disk defragmentation in Windows 2000?

Win2K includes a disk defragmentation program that you access via its Microsoft Management Console (MMC) front-end interface. However, you can't schedule a disk defrag with the Scheduler service because the defrag program has no command-line interface.

Winternals has released Defrag Commander 2000, a bolt-on to the Win2K disk defrag program that lets you schedule defrags. It doesn't replace the Win2K defrag program; it simply lets you schedule its execution.

Winternals has also released Defrag Commander NE, which lets you schedule defrags on remote computers (Win2K machines require no extra software; Windows Millennium Edition—Windows Me—and Windows 98 require a small client installation). Defrag Commander NE works not only with the Win2K built-in defrag program but also with Diskeeper Professional.

See http://www.winternals.com for more information.

FAQ 20.90 Why can't I copy a compressed file/folder to another drive when the system says enough free space is available?

When you copy a compressed file, the system first uncompresses it, copies it, then compresses it on the destination drive. Consequently, if the destination drive doesn't have enough space to accommodate the uncompressed file, the copy operation fails. To resolve this problem, free up more space on the destination drive.

FAQ 20.91 How can I check the name of my dynamic disk group?

If you have upgraded to dynamic disks to take advantage of their increased functionality (e.g., RAID), the system has assigned a name to your dynamic disk group, which is usually the machine name with a suffix of "Dg0". To check the name, perform the following steps:

1. Start REGEDIT.EXE.
2. Go to HKEY_LOCAL_MACHINE\SYSTEM\CurrentControlSet\Services\dmio\Boot Info\Primary Disk Group.
3. The Name value is the dynamic disk group name.
4. Close Regedit.

Microsoft advises against changing this name.

FAQ 20.92 Will my disk configuration let me multiboot OSs?

With Windows NT 4.0 and 3.51, Microsoft recommends that you install a small (200MB) FAT partition at the beginning of your hard disk to assist in troubleshooting your NT installation (if the installation is on FAT). Thus, you have a dual-boot scenario for DOS and NT. These days, the system doesn't require (and Microsoft doesn't recommend) the DOS installation—thanks to Windows 2000 support for safe boot (F8) and the Recovery Console (RC). However, you might still want more than one OS on your machine for beta testing, software requirements, or hardware support. (With the Win2K and Windows 9x convergence in Windows XP, the difference in application and hardware support should disappear, but you might still want a multiboot system in certain circumstances.)

Win2K introduces the dynamic disk, which removes the primary and extended partitions. However, dynamic disks introduce some compatibility issues. The following table summarizes the possibilities and supported OSs for the various disk types:

Disk Configuration	What's Possible	Supported OSs
Basic disk(s)	With basic disks, the system supports all OSs. Each OS instance should be on a separate partition/logical drive.	XP/.NET Win2K, NT 4.0/ NT 3.51, Windows Me, Windows 9x, Win98SE, and DOS
Single dynamic disk	With one dynamic disk, you can install one OS per partition if the partition has an underlying partition entry.	XP/.NET, and Win2K
Multiple dynamic disks	With multiple dynamic disks, you can install one OS per physical dynamic disk if the volume has an underlying partition.	XP/.NET, and Win2K

If you have a mixture of disk types, each disk-type rule applies; thus, if you have one basic disk and one dynamic disk, you can install one OS per partition on the basic disk and one OS on the dynamic disk.

If you want to install XP and Win2K on one disk, it must be a basic disk.

FAQ 20.93 Why do I receive an access-denied error when I try to access the Microsoft Management Console (MMC) Disk Management snap-in?

When you try to access the Disk Management MMC snap-in (by going to the Storage branch in the MMC under Start > Programs > Administrative Tools > Computer Management), you might receive the following error (see Figure 20-24):

```
Access to Disk Manager on XXX is denied.
You don't have access rights to the service.
```

You must be logged on as an Administrator to resolve this problem. A common cause is that the Distributed COM (DCOM) configuration for authentication might have been changed from Connect to Default. To resolve this situation, perform the following steps:

1. Start the DCOM Configuration utility (go to Start > Run and type **dcomcnfg.exe**).
2. Select the Default Properties tab.
3. Change the Default Authentication Level from Default to Connect (see Figure 20-25) and click OK.
4. Restart the machine.

Figure 20-24 Unable to access the Disk Manager component

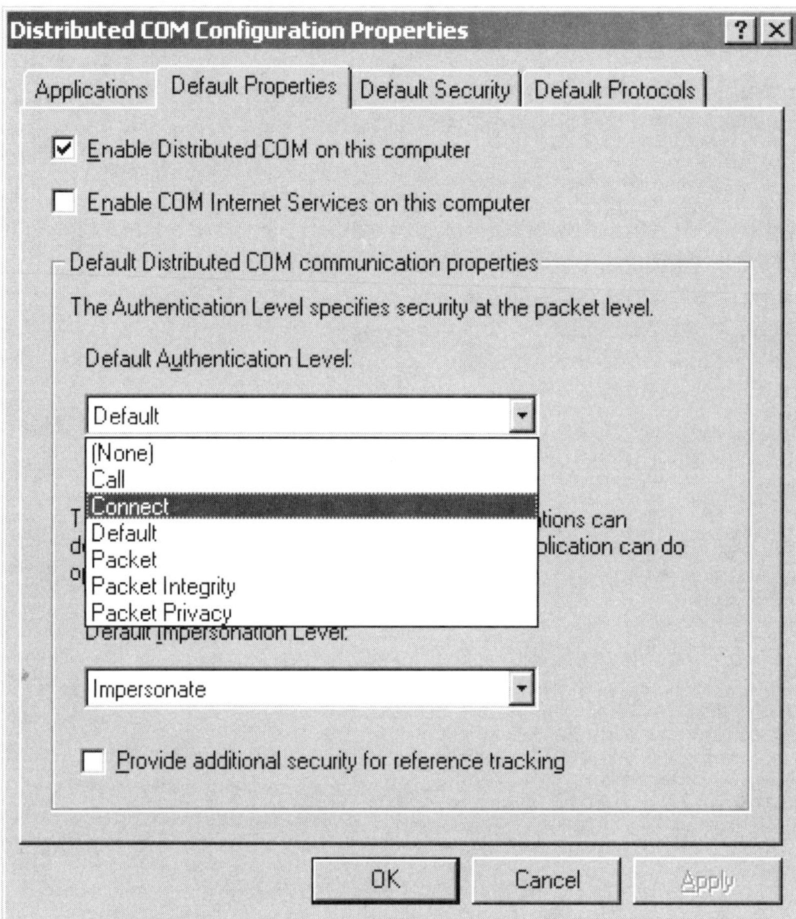

Figure 20-25 DCOM properties

20.94 How can I determine whether I've enabled boot defragment in Windows XP?

Windows XP includes an option to perform a boot defragment, which places all files required for booting next to each other on disk to provide a faster boot time. The OS enables this option by default, but you can check the status and enable this option by performing the following steps:

1. Start the Registry editor (REGEDIT.EXE).
2. Navigate to HKEY_LOCAL_MACHINE\SOFTWARE\Microsoft\Dfrg\BootOptimizeFunction.
3. If Enable isn't set to Y, double-click Enable and set the value to Y.
4. Click OK.
5. Close the Registry editor.
6. Reboot the machine.

If you want to disable boot defragment, set Enable to N.

FAQ 20.95 Why does my computer tell me I can't open a file that I know I should be able to access?

Windows XP and Windows 2000 both include the Encrypted File System (EFS). If you have NTFS permissions to a file that another user has encrypted, you will receive an "access is denied" error.

To determine whether a file is encrypted, perform the following steps to enable the view attributes option in Windows Explorer:

1. Start Windows Explorer.
2. From the View menu, select Details.
3. Select the Attributes option and click OK.

If a file has an E attribute, that file is encrypted. Only the user who encrypted the file or the recovery agent user can decrypt the file.

FAQ 20.96 How do I perform Scandisk in Windows XP or Windows 2000?

XP and Win2K don't include the DOS SCANDISK utility. However, you can perform the same task using XP's and Win2K's Error Checking feature. To access this feature, perform the following steps:

1. Open Windows Explorer.
2. Right-click the drive you want to check and select Properties from the context menu.
3. Select the Tools tab.

4. Under Error Checking, click Check Now.
5. If you want the scan to automatically attempt to make repairs or check the disk for bad sectors, select those options and click Start.
6. Close Windows Explorer.

FAQ 20.97 What is DEFRAG.EXE?

One of the problems with the welcome addition of the disk defragmenter in Windows 2000 is that it has no command-prompt equivalent. As a result, you can't easily schedule the defragmenter to run. To address this problem, Microsoft included DEFRAG.EXE in Windows XP for command-level disk defragmentation.

An example analysis execution shows

```
C:\>defrag d: -a

   Windows Disk Defragmenter
   Copyright (c) 2001 Microsoft Corp. and Executive Software
   International, Inc.

   Analysis Report
   6.91 GB Total, 6.73 GB (97%) Free, 2% Fragmented (5% file
   fragmentation)
```

The command format is

```
defrag <volume> [-a] [-f] [-v] [-?]
volume drive letter or mount point (d: or d:\vol\mountpoint)
-a Analyze only
-f Force defragmentation, even if free space is low
-v Verbose output
-? Display this help text
```

FAQ 20.98 How can I view the information displayed when running a boot time chkdsk?

When a CHKDSK runs, information is displayed to screen. This information is also written to the event log in the Application section if CHKDSK is run with the /f (fix) and/or /r (recover bad sectors) options:

```
Event Type: Information
Event Source: Winlogon
Event Category: None
Event ID: 1001
Date: 03/12/2001
Time: 12:47:52
User: N/A
Computer: DBLON20344
Description:
Checking file system on G:
The type of the file system is NTFS.
Volume label is DBWXP.

A disk check has been scheduled.
Windows will now check the disk.
Cleaning up minor inconsistencies on the drive.
Cleaning up 30 unused index entries from index $SII of file 0x9.
Cleaning up 30 unused index entries from index $SDH of file 0x9.
Cleaning up 30 unused security descriptors.

14333728 KB total disk space.
3961616 KB in 45629 files.
13040 KB in 4297 indexes.
0 KB in bad sectors.
116436 KB in use by the system.
65536 KB occupied by the log file.
10242636 KB available on disk.

4096 bytes in each allocation unit.
3583432 total allocation units on disk.
2560659 allocation units available on disk.

Internal Info:
47 c3 00 00 11 c3 00 00 e4 fb 00 00 00 00 00 00 G...............
ba 00 00 00 00 00 00 00 c7 00 00 00 00 00 00 00 ................
70 bf cc 03 00 00 00 00 36 cd 4d 09 00 00 00 00 p.......6.M.....
7e e6 d3 03 00 00 00 00 00 00 00 00 00 00 00 00 ~...............
00 00 00 00 00 00 00 00 74 2a c1 18 00 00 00 00 ........t*......
a0 ad 7e 33 00 00 00 00 3d b2 00 00 00 00 00 00 ..~3....=.......
00 40 cc f1 00 00 00 00 c9 10 00 00 00 00 00 00 .@..............

Windows has finished checking your disk.
Please wait while your computer restarts.
For more information, see Help and Support Center at
http://go.microsoft.com/fwlink/events.asp.
```

21 DFS

Distributed File System (Dfs) was a new tool for NT Server that was not completed in time for inclusion as part of NT 4.0 but is available for download (see FAQ 21.1). It basically allows administrators to simulate a single server share environment that actually exists over several servers—basically a link to a share on another server that looks like a subdirectory of the main server.

Dfs allows a single view for all of the shares on your network, which can simplify your backup procedures because you can simply back up the root share, and Dfs will take care of actually gathering all the information from the other servers across the network.

You do not **have** to have a single tree (Dfs directory structures are called *trees*) but rather can have a separate tree for different purposes (i.e., one for each department). Each tree can have exactly the same structure (sales, info., etc.).

FAQ 21.1 Where can I get Dfs?

Dfs is available for download from Microsoft (http://www.microsoft.com/ntserver/nts/downloads/winfeatures/NTSDistrFile/default.asp) for Windows NT 4.0 but is standard in Windows 2000 and above. (Windows 2000 has Dfs built in as a core component.) Follow the instructions at the site and fill in the form about your site. The file you want for the i386 platform is Dfs-V41-I386.EXE.

Once you've downloaded the file, just double-click it and agree to the license. It will then install files to your drive, which you need to install.

FAQ 21.2 How do I install Dfs?

Follow these instructions. You must have first downloaded and expanded the file Dfs-V40-I386.EXE:

1. Right-click on Network Neighborhood and select Properties (or double-click Network in the Control Panel).

2. Click the Services tab and click Add.
3. Click the Have disk button and when asked where, enter %systemroot%/system32/dfs. Do not actually type "%systemroot%", but rather what it points to (i.e., d:\winnt), so the full path would be d:\winnt\system32\dfs.
4. Click Enter and press OK for Dfs installation.
5. A dialog box will be shown. Click New Share, type the name of the required root (e.g., c:\dfsroot), and click Yes to create the directory.
6. Select Shared As, fill in required information, and click OK.
7. Close the dialogs and reboot the machine.

Windows 2000 does not require you to install Dfs; it is built into the operating system. Only configuration is required.

21.3 How do I create a new folder as part of the Dfs?

Once Dfs is installed, a new application, the Dfs Administrator, is created in the Administrative Tools folder. This app should be used to manage Dfs. To add a new area as part of the Dfs tree, follow this procedure:

1. Start the Dfs Administrator application (Start > Programs > Administrative Tools > Dfs Administrator).
2. Select Add to Dfs from the Dfs menu.
3. Enter the name of folder you want an existing share to be known as.
4. Next select what it should point to. You can either type the path or use Browse.
5. Click Add.
6. Close the Dfs Administrator.

21.4 How do I uninstall Dfs?

Follow this procedure:

1. Start the Network Control Panel applet or right-click on Network Neighborhood and select Properties.
2. Click the Services tab.
3. Select Distributed File System and click Remove.
4. You will be prompted to continue, click Yes.
5. A reboot will then be required.

FAQ 21.5 How do I create a Dfs root volume in Windows 2000?

Windows 2000 currently supports one Dfs root per server; however, this will be expanded in future versions of the operating system/service packs.

The Distributed File System has its own Distributed File System MMC snap-in, which has a shortcut on the Administrative Tools folder. To create a new Dfs root, perform the following:

1. Start the Distributed File System MMC snap-in (Start > Programs > Administrative Tools > Distributed File System).
2. Right-click on the Distributed File System root and select New Dfs Root (see Figure 21-1).
3. The Dfs Root Creation Wizard will be started. Click Next to the introduction screen.
4. The next screen gives the option of a fault-tolerant Dfs root, which uses the Active Directory to store the information or a standalone Dfs root if the Active Directory is not available or not wanted. Select Create a domain Dfs root (see Figure 21-2) and click Next.
5. Select a domain to use. A list of available domains will be displayed and the current domain will be selected as the current choice. Click Next. This screen is not displayed if you are not creating a fault-tolerant Dfs root.
6. You will need to select a server to host the Dfs root (a domain member if fault tolerant), and the server must be running the Dfs service. The current server will

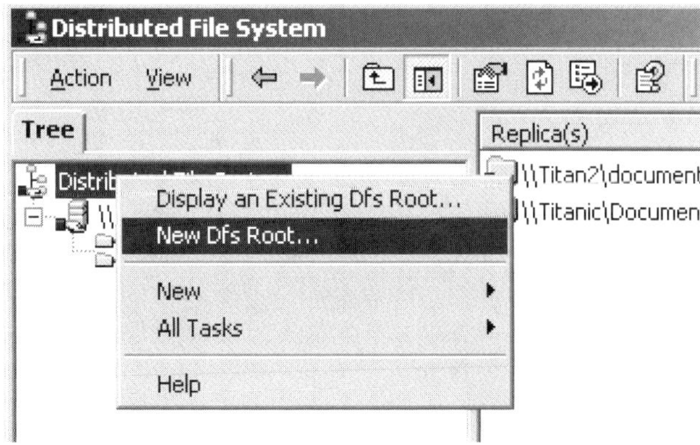

Figure 21-1 Creating a New Dfs root

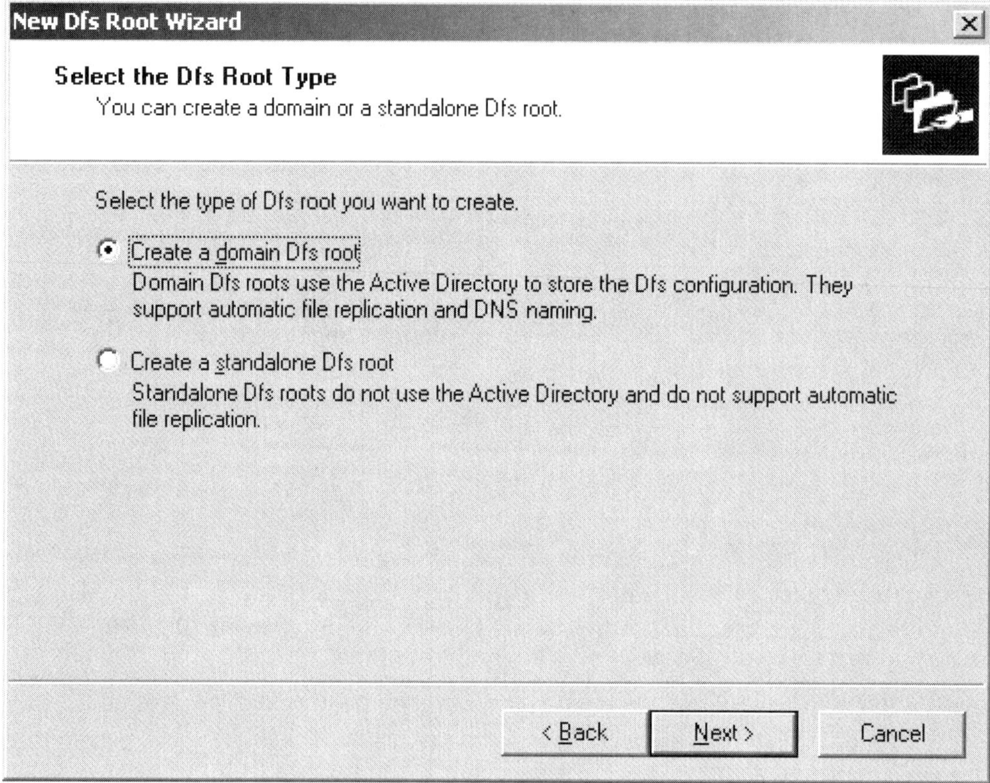

Figure 21-2 Specifying the type of Dfs root

be selected but can be changed by typing a domain name or by clicking Browse. Click Next.

7. The next stage is to select a share to act as the Dfs root. A list of existing shares will be displayed, or you can select to create a new share by entering a share name and location. Click Next.
8. Each Dfs root requires a unique name and will, by default, be the name of the share although you can change this. You can also select to add the new Dfs root to the current console. Click Next.
9. A summary screen will be displayed showing the domain, server, share, and Dfs root name. Click Finish to create the Dfs root.
10. Once complete, a success message will be displayed. Click OK.

FAQ 21.6 How can I add a replica Dfs root volume in Windows 2000?

If your Dfs root was created as a fault-tolerant Dfs root, you may add other Dfs servers as part of the Dfs root replica set. To add a new Dfs root replica member, perform the following:

1. Start the Distributed File System MMC snap-in (Start > Programs > Administrative Tools > Distributed File System).
2. Right-click on the root you wish to add a replica to and select New Root Replica.
3. You will be asked for a server that will host a copy of the Dfs root. Click Next.
4. As when creating the original, you need to either select an existing share or create a new folder and share. Click Finish.
5. Click OK to the success confirmation.

These root replicas will all contain the Dfs root information by utilizing and replicating via the Active Directory. You can actually see the Dfs information using the Active Directory Users and Computers snap-in. Select Advanced Features view > System > Dfs.

FAQ 21.7 How can I add a child node to Dfs in Windows 2000?

Once your Dfs root is created, the next step is to populate it with child nodes/leaves, which actually link to information.

To add a new Dfs child node or Dfs link, as it's now called, perform the following:

1. Start the Distributed File System MMC snap-in (Start > Programs > Administrative Tools > Distributed File System).
2. Right-click on the root you wish to add a replica to and select New Dfs Link.
3. You will need to enter a location and name for the child node, a UNC for the destination, and a comment (see Figure 21-3). You can also select the amount of time clients cache the request. Then click OK.

Any subdirectories of the child leaf will also be published to the Dfs with the parent directory. For example, if a share, ntfaq, was added as a child node to Dfs, any subdirectories of that share would be viewable on the Dfs tree as children of the document's Dfs entry.

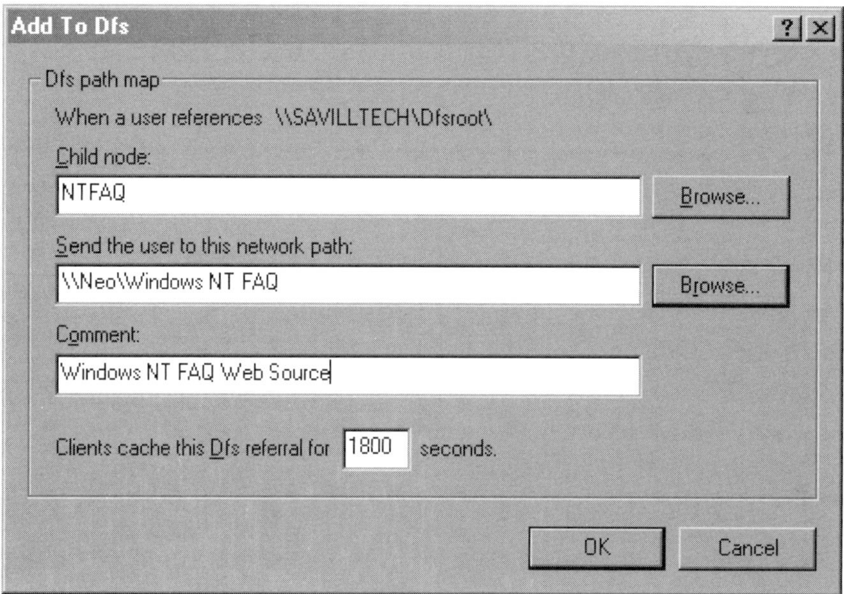

Figure 21-3 Adding a branch to a Dfs tree

21.8 How can I add a replica child node to Dfs in Windows 2000?

The Windows 2000 version of Dfs allows child replica sets to be created in which a single Dfs leaf points to multiple shares on different servers. The File Replication Service (FRS) will keep the contents of all shares in sync. This allows fault tolerance **and** load balancing.

Members of a node replica set must

- All be members of the domain.
- Use NTFS 5.0.
- Must be on different servers. You cannot replicate between shares on the same server.

To add a new Dfs child replica member, perform the following:

1. Ensure an up-to-date copy of the resource to which a new replica member is to be added is placed in the new share that will join the set.
2. Start the Distributed File System MMC snap-in (Start > Programs > Administrative Tools > Distributed File System).

3. Right-click on the child node you wish to add a replica to and select New Replica.
4. You will need to enter the UNC of the new share, and you have the option for

   - Manual replication
   - Automatic replication

   Manual replication is useful if the contents are read-only documents that do not often change. Joint replication will replicate the contents of the shares with all members in the replica set. Click OK.
5. The replication set topology dialog will be shown. Check replication has been enabled. Click OK.

Multimaster replication is used except on the first replication path where the contents of the primary server are copied to the other members. Any content currently in the other shares is moved to a NtFrs-PreExisting subdirectory (but a checksum is performed, and if the files match with the primary server's share, they are moved back into the main directory to save network bandwidth in copying them from the primary server).

Replication is every 15 minutes by default.

22 RAID

Redundant Array of Inexpensive Disks provides a high level of availability and redundancy by using a number of inexpensive disks changed together logically.

Hardware RAID solutions are invisible to Windows; however, software RAID is also possible. Software RAID is controlled by the operating system, and in Windows, RAID levels 0, 1, and 5 are supported.

An exception to RAID is SLED (Single Large Expensive Disk), and large disks are recently no longer very expensive. But you won't gain the same fault tolerance.

FAQ 22.1 What RAID levels does Windows Server support?

Windows Server supports RAID 1 (disk mirroring) and RAID 5 (stripe sets with parity check). Windows also supports RAID 0, which is striping without parity; however, RAID 0 doesn't offer data redundancy.

FAQ 22.2 How do I create a RAID 5 set in Windows 2000?

Windows 2000 introduces dynamic disks, and all members of a RAID volume set must be on a dynamic disk. (If you upgrade RAID sets from Windows NT 4.0, the RAID sets will still be on basic disks; however, there are problems if you upgrade NT 4.0 to XP/.NET. See Microsoft Knowledge Base article Q303246 for more information.) To convert a disk from basic to dynamic, see FAQ 20.48.

To create a RAID 5 set, perform the following steps:

1. From the Start menu, select Programs > Administrative Tools, then the Computer Management Microsoft Management Console (MMC) snap-in.
2. Expand the Storage branch and select Disk Management.
3. Right-click an area of unallocated space and select Create Volume from the context menu (see Figure 22-1).

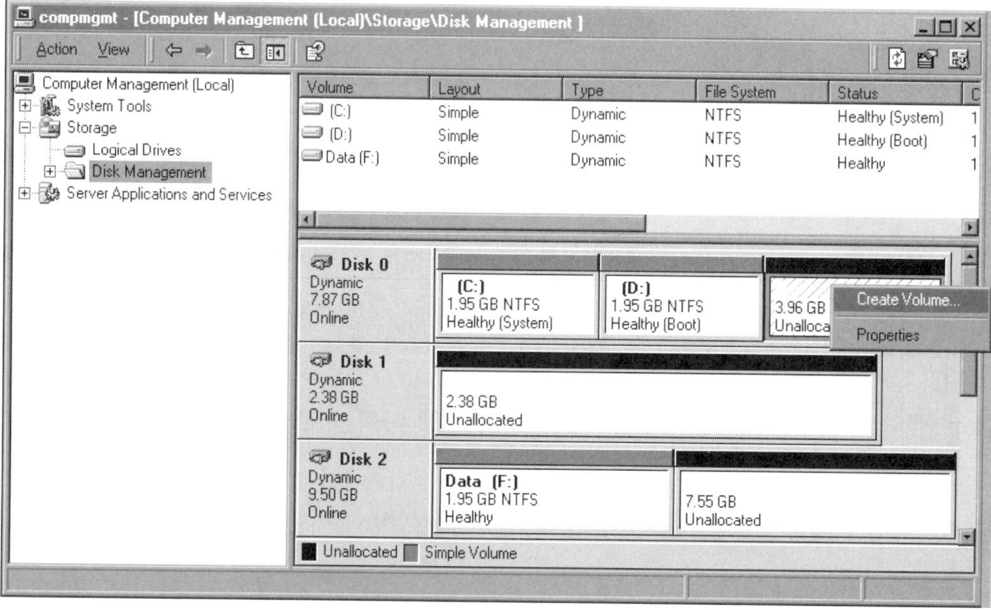

Figure 22-1 Creating a new volume in unused space

4. Click Next to the Create Volume Wizard.
5. Select a RAID 5 volume type (see Figure 22-2) and click Next.
6. In the left pane, select the disks you want to use (at least three in total) and click Add.
7. Select the size to use from each disk. The size must be equal for each disk, so the largest space you can use is the smallest free space on any disk. After you select the size, click Next. If you select 1,000MB from each disk, the total size would be only 2,000MB because parity information uses a third of the space.
8. Select a drive letter to use and click Next.
9. Select the filesystem to use and the label. You might also select whether to enable file and folder compression. Click Next.
10. The program displays a summary screen. Click Finish.

Win2K shows the disk areas as RAID 5 and in a regenerating mode.

You might receive the message "The operation did not complete because the partition/volume is not enabled. Please reboot the computer to enable the partition/volume" from the Logical Disk Manager. Click OK to this message but don't reboot until the regeneration is complete and Win2K shows the volume as healthy. Otherwise, you'll

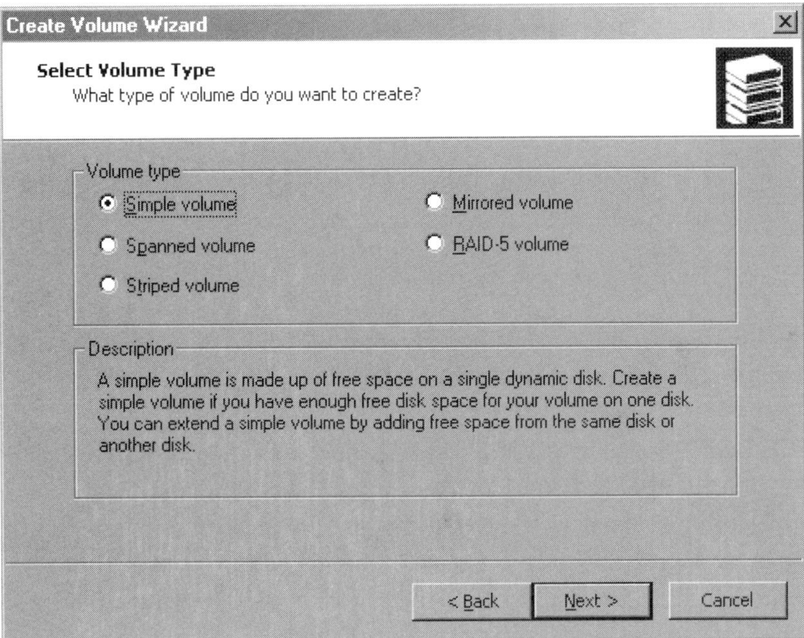

Figure 22-2 Selecting the type of volume to create

need to reformat the partition upon reboot completion. You might still need to reformat the volume if you experience issues.

FAQ 22.3 How do I delete a RAID 5 set in Windows 2000?

When you delete a RAID 5 set in Windows 2000, you lose all the data that the set contains. Therefore, make sure you first back up your data. To delete a RAID 5 set, perform the following steps:

1. From the Start menu, select Programs > Administrative Tools, then the Computer Management Microsoft Management Console (MMC) snap-in.
2. Expand the Storage branch and select Disk Management.
3. Right-click an element of the RAID 5 volume and select Delete Volume from the context menu.
4. Click Yes to the confirmation.

Win2K will now list the space that the RAID 5 volume used as unpartitioned.

FAQ 22.4 How do I regenerate a RAID 5 set in Windows 2000?

In Windows 2000, if you replace one hard disk of a RAID 5 set as a result of faulty hardware, the volume won't lose any data because of the stored parity information. However, you must replace the broken disk to reenable the RAID 5 set's fault-tolerant ability.

After you replace the bad disk, complete the following steps:

1. From the Start menu, select Programs > Administrative Tools, then the Computer Management Microsoft Management Console (MMC) snap-in.
2. Expand the Storage branch and select Disk Management. Win2K still shows the removed disk as Missing.
3. Right-click an element of the RAID 5 volume and select Repair Volume from the context menu.
4. From the list, select a disk to use as the bad disk's replacement and click OK. Win2K will show the set as regenerating.

Your RAID 5 set is now fault tolerant again, but you need to remove the RAID5 partition from the missing disk.

If you had other partitions on the disk that you removed, you can right-click the partitions and select Delete Volume to remove them. You should now right-click the Missing text and select Remove Disk from the context menu (see Figure 22-3).

If you ever reuse the original disk, Win2K displays the disk as Foreign. To learn how to read this disk, see FAQ 20.50.

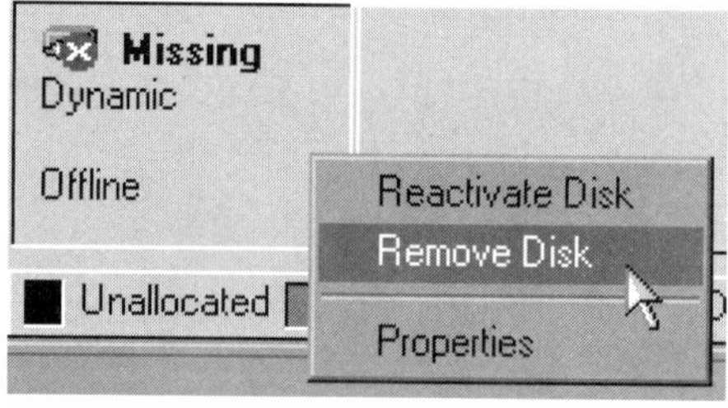

Figure 22-3 Removing a no longer available disk from view

FAQ 22.5 How do I create a mirror set (RAID 1) in Windows 2000?

All members of a RAID 1 volume set must be on a dynamic disk. To convert a disk from basic to dynamic, see FAQ 20.48.

To create a RAID 1 set in Windows 2000, complete the following steps:

1. From the Start menu, select Programs > Administrative Tools, then the Computer Management Microsoft Management Console (MMC) snap-in.
2. Expand the Storage branch and select Disk Management.
3. Right-click the partition you want to mirror and select Add Mirror from the context menu.
4. Select the disk that will host the mirror and click Add Mirror.
5. If you mirror the boot partition, a dialog box details the changes that the program will make to BOOT.INI to enable mirror booting (see Figure 22-4). Click OK.

Windows shows the mirror set in a regenerating mode.

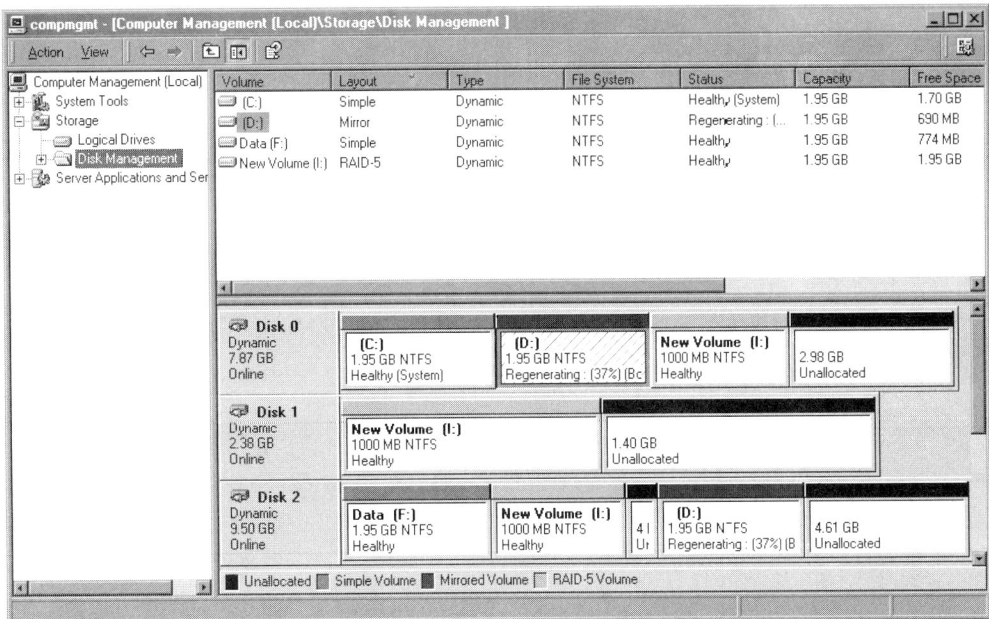

Figure 22-4 Disk with RAID 5 and mirrored volumes

FAQ 22.6 How do I break a mirror set (RAID 1) in Windows 2000?

Breaking a mirror set won't result in data loss but will give you two volumes with duplicate data. To break a RAID 1 set in Windows 2000, perform the following steps:

1. From the Start menu, select Programs > Administrative Tools, then the Computer Management Microsoft Management Console (MMC) snap-in.
2. Expand the Storage branch and select Disk Management.
3. Right-click the mirror volume you want to remove and select Break Mirror from the context menu. (In this step, you can also select Delete Mirror to remove both volumes that make up the mirror, but you lose the data on it.)
4. To confirm your selection, click Yes.
5. Another dialog might warn you about possible data loss on the broken mirror. Click Yes to continue.

You will now have two volumes, so you might want to delete the unwanted mirror to avoid confusion.

23 TERMINAL SERVICES

Modern day PC users are used to having a system with large amounts of memory, disk, and CPU power to run their applications. This is very different for UNIX and VMS environments where servers have all the memory, disks, and CPU, and users have "dumb" terminals that just send keystrokes to the server, which in turn sends back screen updates.

The UNIX/VMS approach has a number of advantages. Most desktop computers are idle for most of the time with the CPU only 10 percent busy normally and a significant amount of memory spare, which is a waste of resources. A central server approach distributes resources to sessions as needed, minimizing waste and ensuring resources are available when needed.

Installing applications and maintaining them on each desktop is very time consuming. A central server-based install simplifies this significantly and lowers the Total Cost of Ownership (TCO).

Windows NT Server Terminal Server Edition and Windows 2000 address this issue with client software for Windows 9x/NT and Windows for Workgroups machines that allows a window to be created that enables all processing and execution to be carried out on the server. The only task the local machine does is to pass back keyboard and mouse actions. The terminal server does all the computation and storage and passes back screen updates to the client.

In Figure 23-1, you can see an example terminal server session in its own windows, with its own Start menu and taskbar. All applications in this window are being run on the terminal server. The information shown in Explorer is the server's drives, not the local machine's drives.

Obviously Windows NT and Windows 95 are operating systems of their own, and it may seem pointless running terminal server clients on these machines. However, they could be used for application management. Install Office 97 on the terminal server, and all clients use Office via the terminal server connection. Imagine running Office XP on a Windows for Workgroups machine!

Communication is via RDP (Remote Desktop Protocol), which was designed by Microsoft.

Windows Terminal Server (TS) is based on Citrix's WinFrame product, and Citrix provides a bolt-on MetaFrame, which adds functionality to Terminal Server, including support for DOS, OS/2, UNIX, Java, and much more. (See http://www.citrix.com.)

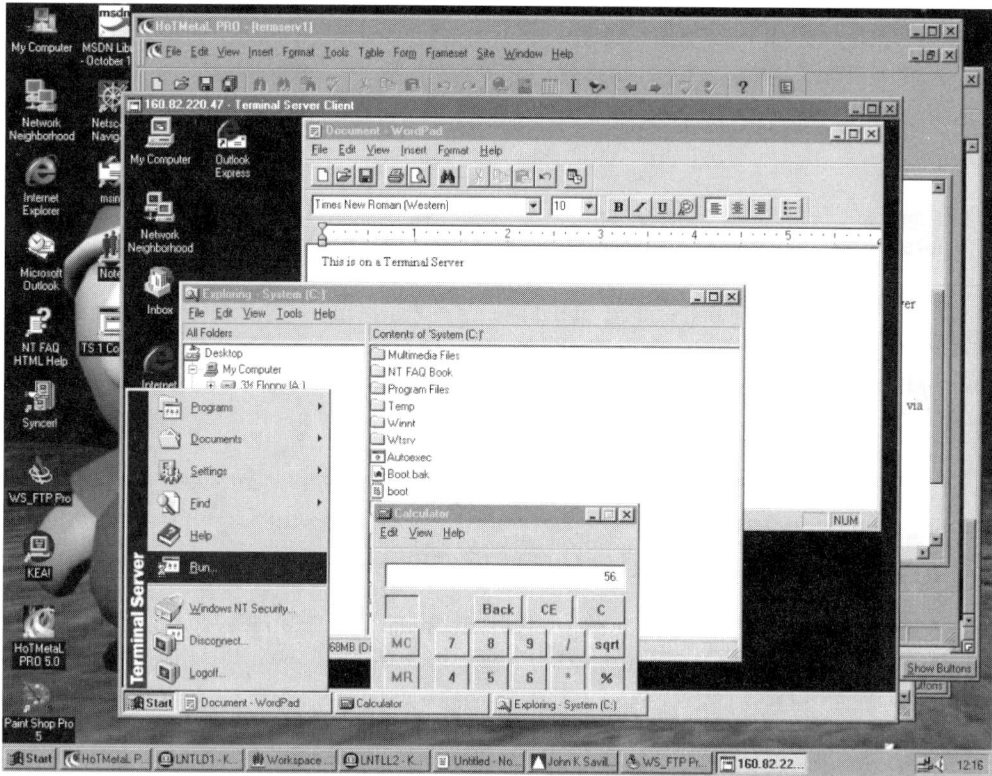

Figure 23-1 Terminal Services in action

23.1 How do I enable Terminal Server under Windows 2000?

Windows 2000 has Terminal Services components built into the operating system, and they can be installed at installation time or at a later time. To install the components, perform the following:

1. Start Control Panel (Start > Settings > Control Panel).
2. Select Add/Remove Programs.
3. Select Configure Windows in the left pane.
4. Click the Components button.
5. Click Next at the wizard.

6. Check the Terminal Services and Terminal Services Licensing components. Click Next.
7. Warnings may be given about installed components, click Next.
8. You can select to install printer drivers. Click Next.
9. Files will be copied to the server.
10. Click Finish.
11. The machine will reboot.

Once reboot is complete, four new programs will be under the Administrative Tools branch of the Start menu:

- Terminal Server Administration
- Terminal Server Client Creator
- Terminal Server Connection Configuration
- Terminal Server License Manager

FAQ 23.2 How do I install Windows NT/9x-based clients?

Terminal Server has built-in client versions for the following clients:

- Windows 95
- Windows 98
- Windows NT
- Windows 2000
- Windows for Workgroups

The first four all share a common piece of software, and Terminal Server (both NT 4.0 and Windows 2000) ships with a utility to create this software on a single floppy disk:

1. Log on to the Terminal Server machine.
2. Select Terminal Server Client Creator from the Administrative tools branch (Start > Programs > Administrative Tools > Terminal Server Client Creator).
3. You will be shown a dialog box (see Figure 23-2), listing options for
    - Terminal Server Client for WFW
    - Terminal Server Client for Windows 95/NT Intel
    - Terminal Server Client for Windows 95/NT Alpha

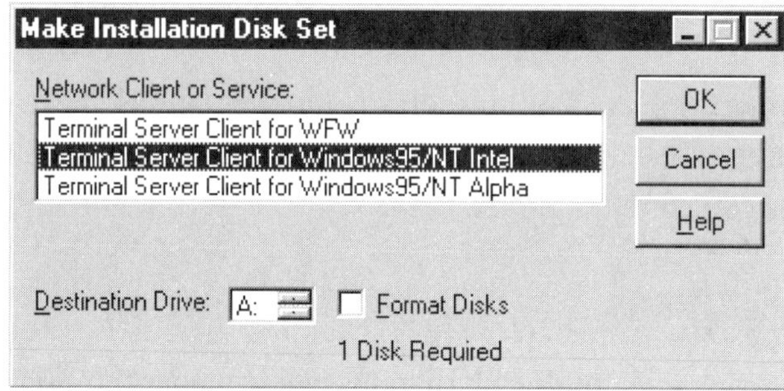

Figure 23-2 Creating a Terminal Service client disk

4. Select the client (Terminal Server Client for Windows 95/NT Intel) and the destination drive (you can only select a floppy) and click OK.
5. You will be asked to insert a disk. Click OK. The required files will then be copied to the disk.
6. Click OK once complete.
7. Close the dialog box.

All the preceding does is copy the contents of %systemroot%\system32\clients\tsclient\win32\disks\disk1 to disk so you could directly copy or share this directory. A net subdirectory of tsclient also contains the clients with each client in its own subdirectory without the disk1, etc. folders, so you could share out this folder to allow access to all client installations. Sharing the net folder is the preferred method.

To install the client, perform the following:

1. Either insert the disk created previously or connect to a share containing its files.
2. Execute SETUP.EXE.
3. The Terminal Server client execution program will start. Click Continue to the license agreement.
4. Enter username and company. Click OK. Click OK again to the confirmation.
5. Click I agree to the license agreement.
6. Click the large Setup button (you can change the installation folder at this point).
7. You will be asked how you want the application installed, either for all users to have the same initial settings or just for you. Click Yes.
8. Files will be copied and a success message shown. Click OK.

A new folder Terminal Server Client has been added with two utilities and an uninstall option.

FAQ 23.3 How do I install Windows for Workgroups-based Terminal Server clients?

Terminal Server (TS) has built-in support for Windows for Workgroups, but the Windows for Workgroups installation must have TCP/IP 32b installed (which can be downloaded from Microsoft at http://support.microsoft.com/support/kb/articles/q111/6/82.asp). I found this out the hard way! TCP/IP can be installed using the Network setup icon in WFW. You may want to run MEMMAKER after installation of TCP/IP to "tidy" your memory—I had to—just choose Express.

To create floppy disks for Windows for Workgroups TS client installation, perform the following:

1. Log on to the Terminal Server machine.
2. Select Terminal Server Client Creator from the Administrative tools branch (Start > Programs > Administrative Tools > Terminal Server Client Creator).
3. You will be shown a dialog box giving options for
    - Terminal Server Client for WFW
    - Terminal Server Client for Windows 95/NT Intel
    - Terminal Server Client for Windows 95/NT Alpha
4. Select the client (Terminal Server Client for WFW) and the destination drive (you can only select a floppy) and click OK.
5. You will be asked to insert a number of disks. Click OK.
6. The required files will then be copied to the disk.
7. Click OK once complete.
8. Close the dialog box.

All the preceding does is copy the contents of %systemroot%\system32\clients\tsclient\win32\disks\disk1 to disk so you could directly copy or share this directory. A net subdirectory of tsclient also contains the clients with each client in its own subdirectory without the disk1, etc. folders, so you could share out this folder to allow access to all client installations. Sharing the net folder is the preferred method.

To install the client, perform the following:

1. Either insert the disk created previously or connect to a share containing its files.
2. Execute SETUP.EXE.

3. The Terminal Server client execution program will start. Click OK to the dialog.
4. Enter username and company. Click OK. Click OK again to the confirmation.
5. Click I agree to the license agreement.
6. Click the large Setup button (you can change the installation folder at this point).
7. You will be asked how you want the application installed, either for all users to have the same initial settings or just for you. Click Yes.
8. Files will be copied and a success message shown. Click OK.

A new program group Terminal Server Client has been added with two utilities and an uninstall option.

Figure 23-3 shows Windows 2000 3D Pinball on Windows for Workgroups 3.11—impressive ☺.

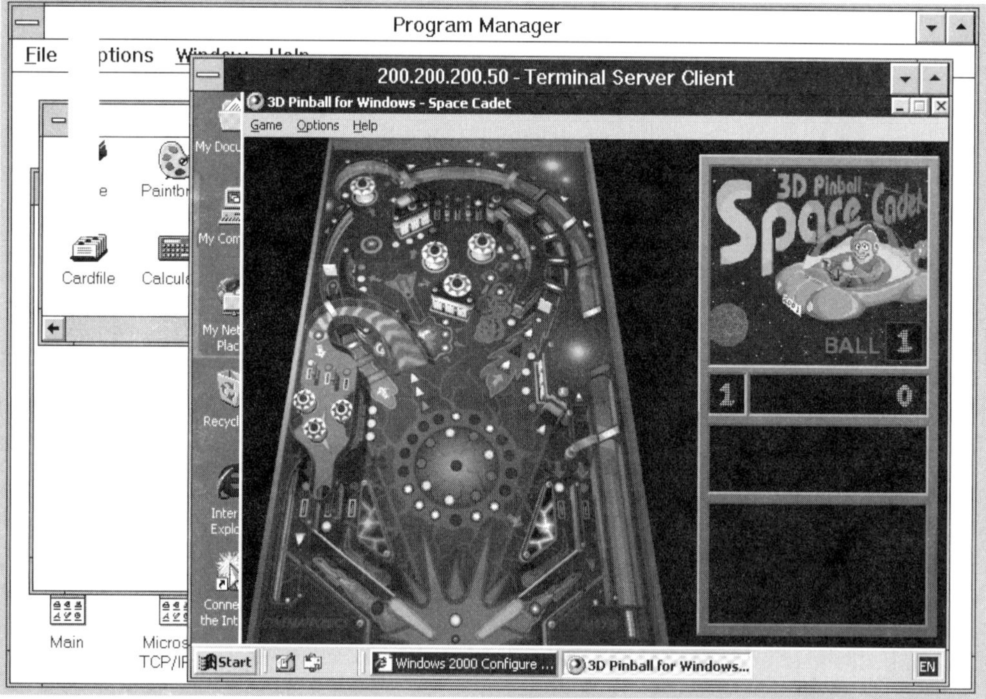

Figure 23-3 Terminal Services from a Windows for Workgroups machine

FAQ 23.4 How do I connect to a Terminal Server from 9x/NT/2000?

The first action is to install the client, which is explained in FAQ 23.2. Once the client is installed, you can use one of two methods to connect to a terminal server. The first is a very manual method and, while simple, may not be ideal for many normal users.

1. Select Terminal Server Client from the Terminal Server Client programs folder.
2. From the dialog, select the server (or enter a different server name or IP address) and select a screen resolution. (The WFW version is slightly different in look but functionally the same).
3. Click Connect.
4. You will then have a window displayed with a logon screen. Log on, and you are now running a terminal server session!

You should be aware that pressing Ctrl+Alt+Del will bring up the local security menu and not the remote. To bring up the remote security menu, select Windows NT Security from the Start menu. You will notice you don't have a shutdown button (unless you are an Administrator) because it would shut down the terminal server machine.

An alternative is to set up a shortcut to connections, and you can accomplish this using the Client Connection Manager.

1. Start Client Connection Manager (CCM) by selecting it from the Terminal Server Client programs branch of the Start menu.
2. From the File menu, select New Connection.
3. Enter a description and the server name or IP address of the terminal server. Click Next.
4. You may select Automatic logon by checking the autologon box and entering username, password, and domain details. Click Next.
5. Select settings such as desktop size and speed settings. Click Next.
6. The next screen gives the option of either running a full desktop or a specific application. If you select a program, you must enter the executable's name and location and a working directory. Click Next.
7. You should now select an icon for the connection by clicking the Change Icon button and the program group to house the shortcut (Terminal Server Client by default). Click Next.
8. A summary will be displayed, click Finish.
9. A new icon will now be displayed in CCM.

You may create a shortcut to this icon on the desktop by right-clicking on it and selecting Create shortcut on desktop. This shortcut actually calls the normal Terminal Server client with a parameter of the configuration name—for example:

```
"C:\Program Files\Terminal Server Client\MSTSC.EXE" "TS 1 Connect"
```

This may be useful for you to build into batch menus, etc. The actual connection details are stored in the Registry under the HKEY_CURRENT_USER\Software\Microsoft\Terminal Server Client key. You could therefore dump out this Registry key and import it into other machines, automating the shortcut installations. The only item not read in is the password if autologon was selected.

To dump out to a file, just select the Registry key in REGEDIT.EXE (e.g., TS 1 Connect) and select Export Registry File from the File menu. Enter a filename and click OK. You can then copy this .REG file to any machine and execute using

```
regedit /s <file>.reg
```

23.5 How do I close a Terminal Server connection?

If you click Start from a Terminal Server session, you will see two options when connected to a Windows NT 4.0 box, as shown in Figure 23-4:

- Logoff
- Disconnect

There is a major difference between the two options. If you select Logoff, your session is logged off, and your connection to the Terminal Server is closed. The connection slot you were using may be used by someone else.

If you select Disconnect, you are not logged off; rather the session window is closed, but if you restart and log on as the same person, the Terminal Server will remember all

Figure 23-4 Disconnect Start menu option from a Terminal Services session

applications and their state. This may seem the ideal option, but remember a Terminal Server has a finite number of allowed connections, and a disconnected session constantly uses a connection, stopping someone else from connecting.

A disconnected session remains active until one of the following:

- You log back on as the same user, then log off.
- The idle timeout is reached, and the session is automatically logged off.
- An Administrator forces you to log off using the Terminal Server Administration tool.

If you connect to a Windows 2000 box, you will see Disconnect and Shutdown; selecting Shutdown gives the option of logging off.

FAQ 23.6 How do I install applications for use with Terminal Server?

Installing applications on a terminal server has to be done in a special way to ensure the application is usable by all users of the Terminal Server.

Terminal Server has two modes, Execute and Install. By default all users are logged on in Execute mode, which means they can run programs, etc. When you want to install an application for use by everyone, the Administrator should change to Install mode.

The best way to install software is to use the Add/Remove programs Control Panel applet because this will automatically set the mode to Install during the installation and then back to Execute at the end. Alternatively, you can manually change your mode to Install by typing

```
change user /install
```

To change back to Execute, use

```
change user /execute
```

And to check you current mode, use

```
change user /query
```

In this example, we will use Add/Remove to install Winzip on a Terminal Server.

1. Start the Add/Remove programs Control Panel applet (Start > Settings > Control Panel > Add/Remove Programs).

2. Select the Install/Uninstall tab and click Install.
3. You will be told to insert the setup media; click Next.
4. The installation wizard will look for SETUP.EXE on the CD or disk. It won't find it. Select an alternate by clicking the Browse button and select the WINZIP.EXE file. Click Next.
5. You will now be given the option to change your mode so all users can use the application. Select All users begin with common application settings and click Next.
6. The installation of the application will begin, and you will notice your mode has been changed to Install if you typed change user/query.
7. Proceed to install the application as normal.
8. Once setup is complete, click Next to the install dialog, then click Finish.

All Terminal Server users will now have Winzip. An alternative would be to manually set the mode to Install, install the software, and set the mode back to Execute.

FAQ 23.7 Why can't I install Office 97 SR2 on Terminal Server?

When you try to install Office 97 SR2 on a Terminal Server via the Add/Remove Programs Control Panel applet, you get the error:

```
Setup cannot register MSJET35.dll in the system Registry because an
older version is in use. Close all applications and try again.
```

You receive this error because the Terminal Server License Service is using the file. To work around this problem, stop the licensing service:

```
net stop "terminal server licensing"
```

Click Retry on the error dialog, and installation will continue. Once installation is complete, restart the service:

```
net start "terminal server licensing"
```

Office 97 has now been installed for use by all your Terminal Server clients.

23.8 How do I send a message to a Terminal Server client?

Terminal Server supports two methods of communicating with a Terminal Server client process. The first is via the GUI:

1. Start the Terminal Services Manager MMC snap-in (Start > Programs > Administrative Tools > Terminal Services Manager).
2. Expand the domain > Server, and a list of connected processes will be shown.
3. Right-click on the process and select Send Message from the context menu (see Figure 23-5).
4. You can then enter a title for the message and message text. Click OK.

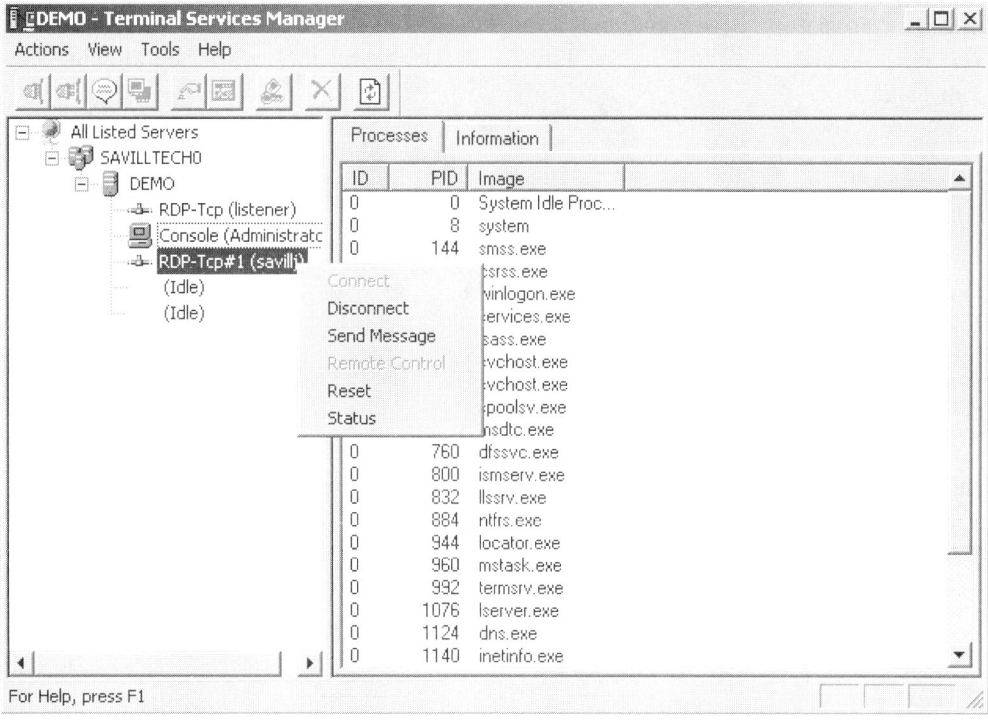

Figure 23-5 Context menu options for a Terminal Services session from the control console

To send from the command line, use the MSG command:

```
msg <user> [/time:<seconds>] [/w] [/server:<server name>] <message>
```

For example:

```
msg savillj /w Get off that computer John!
```

The /w switch forces the Administrator's session to pause until the user has clicked OK to the message.

FAQ 23.9 How do I locate machines that are running Terminal Server?

Starting the Terminal Services Manager MMC snap-in (Start > Programs > Administrative Tools > Terminal Services Manager) will list machines running the Terminal Services by expanding the domain. It can also be done with the following command:

```
qappsrv [/address] [/domain:<domain name>] [/continue]
```

For example:

```
qappsrv /address
Known Terminal servers Network Node Address
----------- ---- ------
DEMO [ A024E34948]*
```

The /domain is optional unless you wish to query a domain other than the machine's membership, and /continue does not pause after each screen of information.

FAQ 23.10 How can I check whether a user is logged on via Terminal Server?

Starting the Terminal Services Manager MMC snap-in (Start > Programs > Administrative Tools > Terminal Services Manager) will list user processes by machine, but this may be cumbersome if a large number of Terminal Servers are running. It can also be done with the following command:

```
query user [<user name>] [/server:<server name>]
```

For example

```
query user
USERNAME    SESSIONNAME     ID  STATE    IDLE    TIME    LOGON TIME
>administrator  console     0   Active             . 09/05/99 18:19
savillj         rdp-tcp#1 1   Active            10 09/05/99 14:23
```

The preceding lists all users.

You can also check what the user is running with the QPROCESS command:

```
qprocess <user name>
```

To check who is running a certain program (e.g., WINWORD.EXE):

```
qprocess <process>
```

The preceding command will list all users running the passed program.

FAQ 23.11 Why is mouse movement jerky in Terminal Server sessions?

By default the Terminal Server client sends updates to the Terminal Server every 100 milliseconds; however, you can change this as follows:

1. Log on to the client.
2. Start the Registry editor (REGEDIT.EXE).
3. Move to HKEY_CURRENT_USER\Software\Microsoft\Terminal Server Client.
4. From the Edit menu, select New > DWORD Value.
5. Enter a name of **Min Send Interval** and press Enter.
6. Double-click the new value and set to the number of milliseconds between each update. The lower you set it the more bandwidth will be used. Click OK.
7. Close the Registry editor.
8. Restart the Terminal Server Client software.

FAQ 23.12 Does MetaFrame run on Windows 2000?

The normal MetaFrame 1.8a runs on Windows 2000 and can be purchased from the Citrix Web site, http://www.citrix.com/.

FAQ 23.13 How can I switch a session between a window and full screen?

Normally Terminal Server client sessions are in a window; however, you can switch to full-screen mode so you can't tell you are in a session. To toggle between window and full-screen mode press Ctrl+Alt+Break.

You can always tell a Terminal Server session because the Start menu text says "Windows 2000 Terminal" instead of "Windows 2000 Professional" or "Server."

FAQ 23.14 How can I remote-control another Terminal Server session in Windows 2000?

Users and Administrators may be familiar with the software that allows an Administrator to take control of a user's desktop in order, for example, to install software or fix a problem. The Citrix Metaframe add-on for 4.0 TSE enabled Administrators to take control or view user's sessions without the need for third-party software.

The new Windows 2000 Terminal Server component allows session shadowing without the need for the MetaFrame add-on, but now this facility is called *remote control.*

A condition that controls the console must have a resolution equal or greater than that of the session that will be shadowed.

By default Administrators have the ability to shadow other users' sessions providing the users agree to have their sessions controlled/viewed. By default the ability to remote-control a user's session is defined on the user object on the Remote Control tab. The default is to enable remote control, providing that the user gives permission.

It's possible to override these user settings by editing the configuration of the RDP connection using the Terminal Services Configuration MMC snap-in—yes, as with everything else in Windows 2000, all of the Terminal Server tools are MMC snap-ins (but more on them later).

Under the connections branch, right-click on the RDP-Tcp connection and select Properties. Select the Remote Control tab, and by default, the dialog will say to use the user's settings. However, selecting one of the other options allows you to set the remote control to whatever you wish.

In order to remote-control a session, you must be logged on as a Terminal Server session; you can't remote-control from the console (but MetaFrame allows you to do this).

Once you have logged on as an Administrator to remote-control a session, just

1. Start the Terminal Services Manager.
2. Right-click on the remote user's session and select Remote Control.
3. You will be asked for a key sequence that will allow you to stop controlling a session and return to your own Terminal Server session.
4. The user to be controlled is asked if he agrees, and if so, click yes. Then you have control of his session. The session does not display in a window; rather your session "switches" to his.
5. To end remote control, press the key sequence you defined earlier.

FAQ 23.15 What user environment extensions does the Windows 2000 Terminal Server component add?

A new built-in group, Terminal Services Users, has been added in 2000. Terminal Services Users works in a similar way to the Interactive Users Group. When a user logs on via Terminal Services, she is part of this group.

The Terminal Services Users group security identifier (SID) can then be applied to files, folders, or anything with an access control list (ACL) and allow access to only people logged on via Terminal Services. You could also test for this group membership during logon script, etc. to perform different actions.

On top of the Remote Control tab for users, three extra tabs are added. As shown in Figure 23-6, Terminal Services Profile allows settings for session timeouts as well as an alternative profile and local path to be specified when connecting via Terminal Server via the Terminal Services Profile tab.

The Environment tab allows you to specify a program to automatically run when you log on via Terminal Services and provides options to connect to client drives and printers.

Finally, the Sessions tab allows times to be set before active and idle sessions are disconnected and enables you to specify how long after a session is disconnected before it is totally closed.

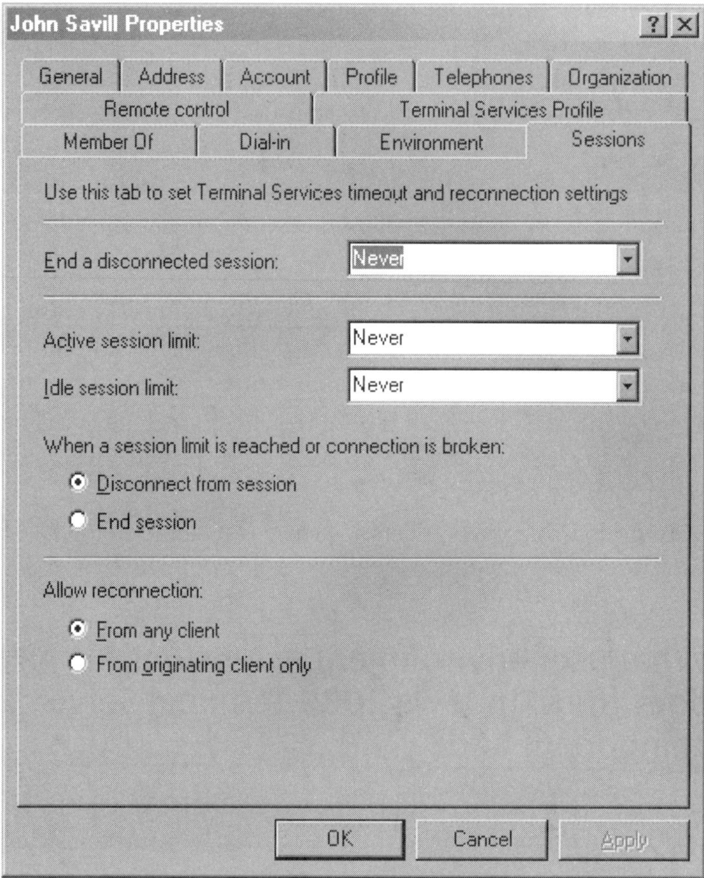

Figure 23-6 Configuring Terminal Service Session Attributes

FAQ 23.16 How do I enable client computers to log on to Windows 2000 Terminal Server?

To log on successfully to Windows 2000 Terminal Server, follow these steps:

1. Log on to the Terminal Server as an Administrator.
2. Start the Computer Management MMC snap-in (Start > Programs > Administrative Tools > Computer Management).

3. To expand the branches, click the plus symbol (+) next to System Tools, click the plus symbol next to Local Users and Groups, and then click the plus symbol next to Users.
4. Double-click the user that you want to be able to log on as a Windows NT Terminal Server client.
5. On the Profile tab, click to select the Allow to log on to Terminal Server checkbox and then click OK.
6. Close Computer Management.
7. Start the Terminal Services Configuration MMC snap-in (Start > Programs > Administrative Tools > Terminal Services Configuration).
8. Open the Connections folder and then click Rdp-Tcp.
9. On the Actions menu, click Properties.
10. On the Permissions tab, add the users or groups that you want to have permissions to this Windows Terminal Server.

FAQ 23.17 How do I install the Windows 2000 Terminal Services Web interface?

The Windows 2000 Service Pack 1 and above CD supplies an add-on to Terminal Services (the Terminal Services Advanced Client), which allows a Terminal Services session to be imbedded into a Web page using a supplied ActiveX control. This add-on can also be downloaded from http://www.microsoft.com/WINDOWS2000/downloads/recommended/TSAC/tsac.asp.

The add-on does not have to be installed on a Windows 2000 Terminal Services server but does require NT Server 4.0 or above with IIS 4.0 or above installed.

To install, perform the following:

1. Log on as Administrator to the IIS server machine.
2. Insert the Windows 2000 Service Pack x CD.
3. Move to the VALUEADD\ECP folder.
4. Double-click TSWEBSETUP.EXE.
5. Click Yes to install the Terminal Services Web Client package.
6. Click Yes to the license agreement.
7. You will be asked for the location to install the sample pages (e.g., d:\Inetpub\wwwroot\TSWeb). Click OK.

8. You may be prompted that software is trying to be installed with a certificate. Accept it.
9. You will be asked if you wish to read the release notes, click No.
10. Click OK to the install completion message.

The ActiveX Client Control setup program creates a Tsweb directory under the WWWRoot directory of the target computer and copies the following files into it:

MSTSCAX.CAB
DEFAULT.HTM
CONNECT.ASP
MANYSERVERS.HTM

Once the Windows 2000 Terminal Services Web interface is installed, you will be able to connect to http://<server>/TSWeb, where you can enter a server name and connect (see Figure 23-7). You can also choose to have full screen or a specific size.

Once connected, you will be asked for a username/password/domain, unless you click "Send logon information for this connection", which enables you to send authentication information as part of the connection request. Another file,

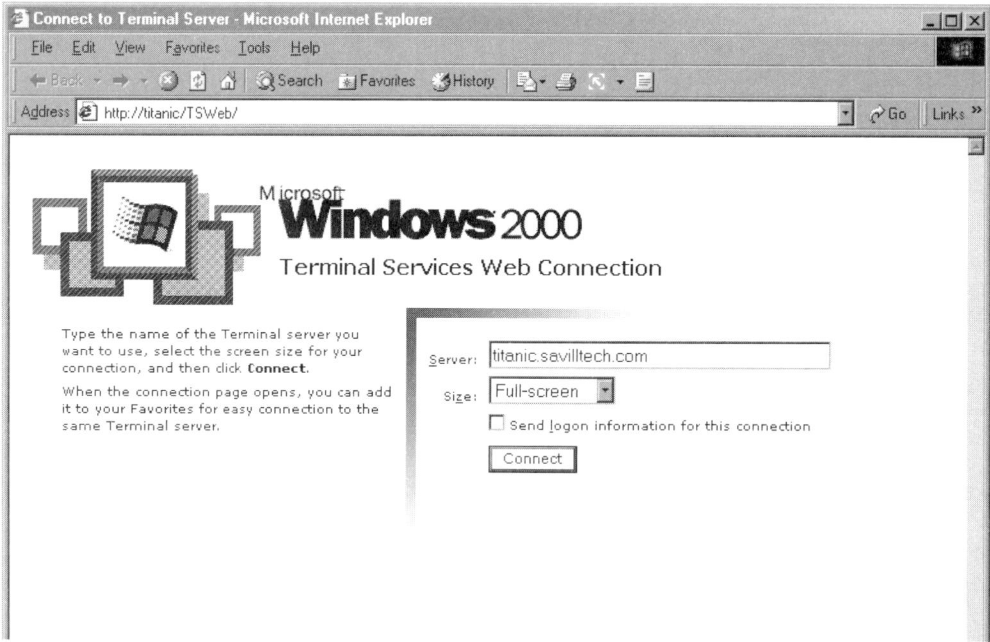

Figure 23-7 Terminal Services connection from the Web

MANYSERVERS.HTM, is supplied, which allows multiple connections on a single page.

23.18 How do I install the Windows 2000 Terminal Services MMC interface?

The Windows 2000 Service Pack 1 and above CD supplies an add-on to Terminal Services, which allows Terminal Services sessions to be managed via an MMC interface, making it easy to navigate between them. To install the add-on, perform the following:

1. Insert the Windows 2000 Service Pack x CD.
2. Start Explorer.
3. Move to the VALUEADD\ECP folder.
4. Double-click TSMMCSETEUP.EXE.
5. Click Yes to install the Terminal Services Connections package.
6. Click Yes to the license agreement.
7. Select an install location, %ProgramFiles%\Terminal Services MMC Snap-in and click OK.
8. You will be asked if you wish to read the release notes, click No.
9. Click OK to the install completion message.
10. You may need to reboot.

Once you've complete the preceding steps, perform the following to use the Windows 2000 Terminal Services MMC interface:

1. Start the MMC (Start > Run > MMC.EXE).
2. From the Console menu, select Add/Remove snap-in.
3. Click Add.
4. Select Terminal Services Connections and click Add.
5. Click Close.
6. Click OK.

You can now right-click on the root of Terminal Services Connections and select Add New Connect to create a connection to a Terminal Services server. You will access the dialog shown in Figure 23-8.

Select a connection to switch between them, right-click, and click Disconnect to close.

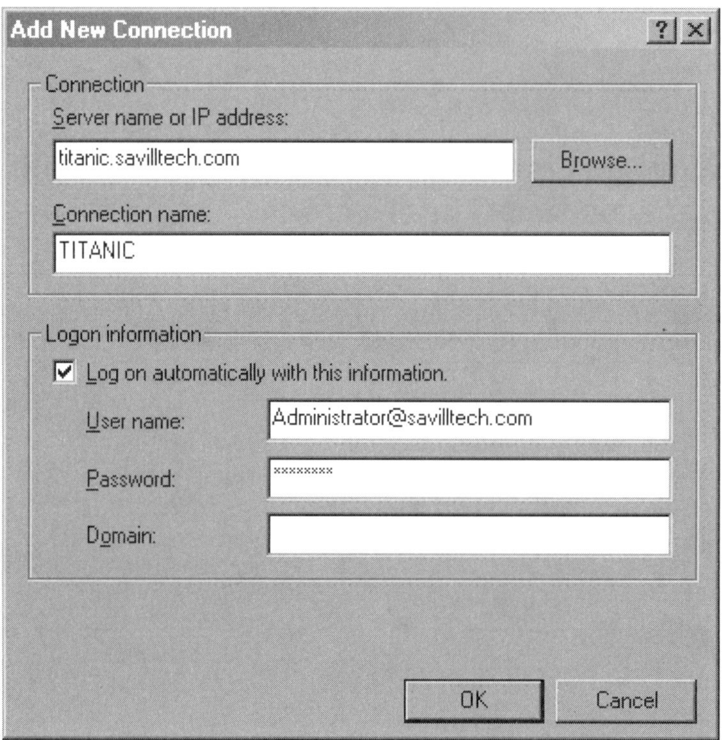

Figure 23-8 Enabling automatic logon for a Terminal Services configuration

FAQ 23.19 How do I install Office 2000 on a Terminal Services machine?

Due to Terminal Services architecture (be it NT 4.0 Terminal Services Edition or Windows 2000 with Terminal Services enabled), some software cannot be installed in the normal way as is the case for Office 2000.

If you attempt to install Office 2000 on a Terminal Services machine, you will receive the following error:

```
Some default settings in Microsoft Office 2000 setup do not work
properly on a Windows Terminal Server. To install Office on Terminal
Server, you must use the instructions and tools available in your
Office 2000 Resource Kit or at http://www.microsoft.com/office/ork/.
```

To install successfully, you must use the Resource Kit TRANSFORM.MST file as follows:

1. Copy TERMSRVR.MST from the Resource Kit or from the download file at http://www.microsoft.com/office/ork/2000/download/ORKTools.exe to a folder on your machine.
2. Start the Add/Remove Programs Control Panel applet (Start> Settings > Control Panel > Add/Remove programs).
3. Click Install for NT 4.0 or click Add New Programs. Then click CD or Floppy if using Windows 2000.
4. Click Next.
5. Click the Browse button, select SETUP.EXE in the root of the Office 2000 CD, and click OK (Open in 2000).
6. On the command line for installation program box, append the following parameter after SETUP.EXE, separated by a space:

   ```
   TRANSFORMS="<path>\TermSrvr.mst"
   ```

   where path is the location of the .MST file. This command identifies the Terminal Server transform to use during installation.
7. Click Next.
8. In the Change User Options dialog box, select All users begin with common application settings and then click Next to run Office Setup.

FAQ 23.20 How do I remove the additional privileges granted to Terminal Services users?

To allow older programs to work with Terminal Services, additional privileges are granted; however, it's possible to remove these additional permissions.

Windows 2000 provides two additional security templates: NOTSSID.INFO and DEFLTSV.INF. NOTSSID.INFO removes the additional permissions, and DEFLTSV.INF sets them back to the default. To disable:

1. Start the command prompt session (CMD.EXE).
2. Move to %systemroot%\security\templates folder:

   ```
   cd /d %systemroot%\security\templates
   ```

3. Implement the NOTSSID.INF information file:

```
secedit /configure /db notssid.sb /cfg notssid.inf /verbose
```

To set it back to the default:

1. Start the command prompt session (CMD.EXE):
2. Move to the %systemroot%\inf folder:

```
cd /d %systemroot%\inf
```

3. Implement the DEFLTSV.INF information file:

```
secedit /configure /cfg defltsv.inf /db defltsv.sb /log
defltsv.log /verbose
```

You can also directly edit the Registry to prevent users from being a member of a dynamic group TERMINAL SERVER USER when connecting via Terminal Services. This will prevent them from getting the extra permissions:

1. Start the Registry editor (REGEDIT.EXE).
2. Move to HKEY_LOCAL_MACHINE\SYSTEM\CurrentControlSet\Control\Terminal Server.
3. Double-click TSUserEnabled.
4. Set to 1 so that all users logging on via Terminal Services are made members of the Terminal Server User group or set to 0 so they are not.
5. Click OK.

FAQ 23.21 How do I transfer a Windows 2000 Terminal Services CAL to another computer?

Windows 2000 clients come with a built-in TS CAL (Client Access License), and hence they do not receive a CAL from the TS server. The TS CAL is a per-seat license that allows for a one-time transfer to another client.

To transfer the licenses:

1. Run the Terminal Services Licensing program on your Windows 2000 server (Start > Programs > Administrative Tools > Terminal Services Licensing).
2. Press Properties on the View menu.

3. On the Connection Method tab, press Telephone and select your country.
4. Press OK.
5. Use the Action menu to press Install Licenses. This starts the Licensing Wizard and returns a phone number.
6. Call the Customer Service Center (CSC) and describe your need to reissue licenses. The Customer Service Representative (CSR) will direct you how to continue.

If you wish to remove the TS CAL from the original client device, use the Registry editor.

1. Start the Registry editor (REGEDIT.EXE).
2. Move to HKEY_LOCAL_MACHINE\Software\Microsoft\MSLicensing\Store\LICENSE00x.
3. Delete the LICENSE000 or LICENSE00x key. (There may be two keys, one for the Windows 2000 or Windows NT computer and one for the TS CAL).
4. Close the Registry editor.

FAQ 23.22 How do I enable users to log on successfully to Windows 2000 Server Terminal Services?

To ensure that a user can connect via Terminal Services, perform the following steps:

1. Start the Active Directory Users and Computers Microsoft Management Console (MMC) snap-in (Start > Programs > Administrative Tools > Active Directory Users and Computers).

   Note: *If the user is in a domain or if the Computer Management MMC is a local account, use Start > Programs > Administrative Tools > Computer Management.*

2. Expand the Users folder (if you are using Computer Management System Tools—Local > Users and Groups).
3. Right-click the user to whom you want to grant permission and select Properties.
4. If this account is a domain account, select the Terminal Services Profile tab, then check Allow logon to Terminal Server. If this account is a local account, on the Profile tab, select Allow logon to Terminal Server.
5. Click Apply.

Next, ensure that the user/group has access:

1. Start the Terminal Services Configuration MMC (Start > Programs > Administrative Tools > Terminal Services Configuration).
2. Open the Connections folder, then click Rdp-Tcp.
3. On the Actions menu, click Properties.
4. On the Permissions tab, add the users or groups that you want to have permissions to Win2K Terminal Services.

FAQ 23.23 How can I secure communications between client and server using Terminal Server?

Windows 2000 Server Terminal Services supports three levels of encryption: low, medium, and high. The default encryption is medium, which should be fine for most networks. Nevertheless, let's review all the levels:

Low	This level secures the user logon information and data sent to the server but not the data sent from the server to the client. Microsoft recommends that you use this encryption level when the network is secure (e.g., an intranet).
Medium	This level encrypts the data transmission in both directions. Microsoft recommends that you use this encryption level when the network isn't secure and resides outside of North America (because of 128-bit export restrictions). Note: If you connect to a Win2K server running Terminal Services set for Low or Medium encryption levels and use version 4.0 of the Terminal Services client, your data is encrypted using a 40-bit key. If you are using version 5.0 of the Terminal Services client, your data is encrypted with a 56-bit key.
High	This level encrypts the data transmission in both directions using a 128-bit key. Microsoft recommends that you use this encryption level when the network isn't secure and resides within North America.

To modify the encryption setting, perform the following steps:

1. Start the Terminal Services Configuration MMC snap-in (Start > Programs > Administrative Tools > Terminal Services Configuration).
2. Select the Connections branch and double-click the connection whose encryption level you want to change.

3. Select the General tab.
4. Select the appropriate encryption level from the Encryption level drop-down list (see Figure 23-9).
5. Click OK.

The new encryption level takes effect the next time a user logs on. If you need multiple levels of encryption running on one server, install multiple network adapters and configure each one separately.

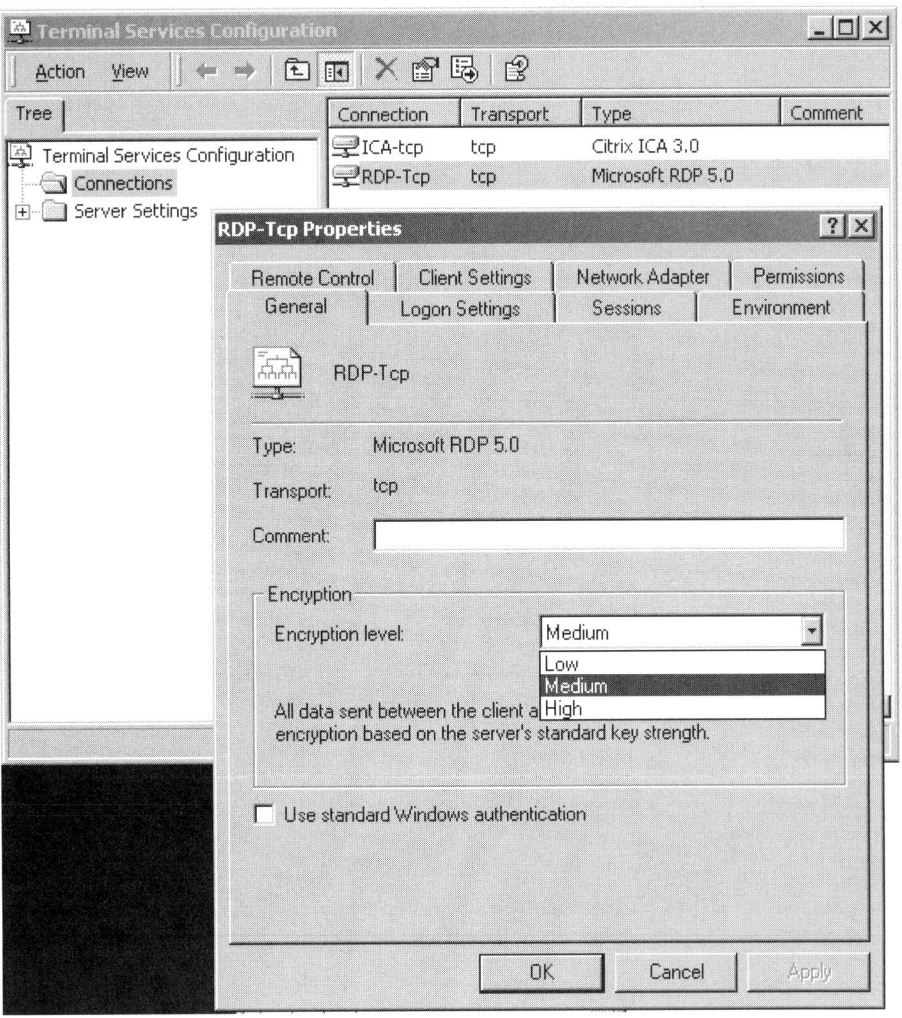

Figure 23-9 Setting the encryption used over Terminal Services

FAQ 23.24 Why are my Terminal Services clients with roaming profiles being lost?

If you use the same roaming profile for a Windows client and a Windows 2000 Server Terminal Services client, the profile may be corrupted because changes made to the profile from the Windows client overwrite the Terminal Services profile changes if the Windows client logs off last, and vice versa. The same is true for multiple Terminal Services client sessions that use the same roaming profile concurrently.

Roaming profiles are useful when all desktops in the workplace have the same applications and settings. However, a Terminal Services server has a different configuration from your desktops, so Microsoft doesn't advise sharing a profile among Terminal Services clients and standard sessions. You should disable this option by performing the following steps:

1. Start the Active Directory Users and Computers snap-in (Start > Programs > Administrative Tools > Active Directory Users and Computers).
2. Select the Users branch.
3. Right-click the user whose profile you want to change and select Properties.
4. Select the Terminal Services Profile tab.
5. Remove the User Profile: string.
6. Click OK.

FAQ 23.25 What keyboard shortcuts can I use in a Windows 2000 Server Terminal Services session?

The typical shortcuts, such as Ctrl+Alt+Del for the Security window, don't work in a Terminal Services session and affect only your local session. The following table lists alternatives that work with a Terminal Services session:

Local Combination	Terminal Services Session Equivalent	Description
Ctrl+Alt+Del	Ctrl+Alt+End	Brings up the Security dialog box
Alt+Tab	Alt+PgUp	Displays application selector and moves selection to the right

Local Combination	Terminal Services Session Equivalent	Description
Alt+Shift+Tab	Alt+PgDn	The same as Alt+Tab but moves the selection to the left
Alt+Esc	Alt+Insert	Swaps among running applications
Ctrl+Esc	Alt+Home	Opens the Start menu
Alt+Spacebar	Alt+Del	Right-clicks the active application's icon button
	Ctrl+Alt+Break	Toggles between window and full-screen mode
PrtScn	Ctrl+Alt+Plus sign on numeric keypad	Snapshot of full Terminal Services screen
Alt+PrtScn	Ctrl+Alt+Minus sign	Snapshot of current window in session on numeric keypad

FAQ 23.26 I've entered a password for a Terminal Services client connection. Why does the system continue to prompt me?

By default, a Windows 2000 Server Terminal Services connection always prompts for a password, even if you've configured one in the connection logon information. To disable this option, perform the following steps:

1. Start the Microsoft Management Console (MMC) Terminal Services Configuration snap-in (Start > Programs > Administrative Tools > Terminal Services Configuration).
2. Right-click the configuration for which you want to disable the default password setting and select Properties from the context menu.
3. Select the Logon Settings tab.
4. Clear the Always prompt for password checkbox. Click Apply, then click OK.
5. Close the dialog box. Future connections will no longer force a password entry, which will facilitate automatic logon.

23.27 How can I initiate remote control of a session from the command line in Windows 2000 Server Terminal Services?

You can use the SHADOW command-line utility to initiate remote control of a session. Before you use this utility, you must ascertain the name of the session you want to control. You can obtain the session name with the QINSTA command. (Remember that you can only remotely control a session from within another Terminal Services session, so don't try any of the following commands except from within a session.)

```
G:\>qwinsta
SESSIONNAME USERNAME ID STATE TYPE DEVICE
console Administrator 0 Active wdcon
rdp-tcp 65536 Listen rdpwd
>rdp-tcp#10 Administrator 1 Active rdpwd
rdp-tcp#11 Administrator 2 Active rdpwd
The session prefixed with a right angle bracket (>) is the current
session.
```

To shadow a session, use the following syntax:

```
SHADOW [session name]
```

For example, to shadow the rdp-tcp#11 session, you type the following command and see the following system messages:

```
G:\>shadow rdp-tcp#11
Your session may appear frozen while the remote control approval is
being negotiated.
Please wait...

To stop the remote control, press the default escape sequence Ctrl +
the * key on the numeric keypad.
```

FAQ 23.28 How can I stop users from performing Clipboard and printer redirection from the Windows 2000 Server Terminal Services client?

Many people consider Clipboard and printer redirection a security risk. Clipboard redirection lets users cut and paste data from their Terminal Services sessions to their local sessions. Printer redirection makes users' local printers accessible from their Terminal Services sessions. You can add two Registry values on your users' local machines to disable Clipboard and printer redirection.

1. Start REGEDIT.EXE.
2. Go to HKEY_LOCAL_MACHINE\SOFTWARE\Microsoft. If a Terminal Server Client key doesn't exist, you need to create it.
3. From the Edit menu, select New > Key.
4. Enter a name of **Terminal Server Client** and press Enter.
5. Select the new key.
6. From the Edit menu, select New > DWORD Value.
7. Enter a name of **DisableClipRedirection** to disable Clipboard redirection or **DisablePrinterRedirection** to disable printer redirection. Press Enter.
8. Double-click the new value and set it to 1. Click OK.
9. Close REGEDIT.EXE.

You don't need to reboot the machine. Clipboard/printer redirection will no longer work from the normal or advanced Terminal Services client.

You can also stop Clipboard/printer redirection on the server side from the Terminal Services Configuration > Connect > Client Settings tab.

FAQ 23.29 How do I use the Terminal Services Microsoft Installer (MSI) Client?

Part of the Windows 2000 Server Terminal Services Advanced Client is the new MSI Client. This client is very similar to the existing Terminal Services client except that Microsoft has packaged it in the new Win2K Windows Installer format (i.e., as an .MSI file).

This client is located in the %systemDrive%\Program Files\Terminal Services Client MSI folder. To install it, right-click it and select Install from the context menu. The best feature of the MSI format is that you can deploy it as part of a Group Policy.

When you do and you experience a file/Registry corruption problem, the installation will self-heal.

FAQ 23.30 How can I configure a preferred Terminal Services license server?

Windows 2000 Server Terminal Services usually uses a license server in the local domain; however, you might want to have a central license server for audit purposes or use a server in another domain. Perform the following steps to designate the license server you want a Terminal Services server to use:

1. Start REGEDIT.EXE.
2. Go to HKEY_LOCAL_MACHINE\SYSTEM\CurrentControlSet\ServicesTermService\Parameters.
3. From the Edit menu, select New > String value.
4. Enter a name of **DefaultLicenseServer** and press Enter.
5. Double-click the new value and set it to the name of the license server you want to use.
6. Click OK.
7. Close REGEDIT.EXE.
8. For the change to take effect, use the following commands to stop and restart the license logging service:

```
net stop "license logging service"
net start "license logging service"
```

If the preferred license server isn't available, a Terminal Services server uses the next available license server in the domain.

FAQ 23.31 Why do my Terminal Services clients disconnect upon connection?

When your Windows 2000 Server Terminal Services clients try to connect to a server, you might receive the following error message:

```
Terminal Services Client Disconnected. The Terminal server has ended
the connection.
```

A server without a valid Terminal Services license causes this error. When you install Terminal Services in Application mode, you have a 90-day temporary license. After the 90 days expire, clients won't be able to connect. The only solution is to purchase a valid license.

FAQ 23.32 How do I use the Terminal Services File Copy extension?

Windows 2000 Server Terminal Services sessions let you copy, cut, and paste text and graphics between client and server sessions. File Copy is an extension to Terminal Services that lets you also use copy, cut, and paste to transfer files and folders between client and server sessions. Using File Copy, you can

- Copy, cut, and paste multiple files and directories
- Copy, cut, and paste on Windows 32-bit or 16-bit clients

To use File Copy, perform the following steps on the server:

1. Install the Microsoft Windows 2000 Resource Kit.
2. Go to http://www.microsoft.com/windows2000/library/resources/reskit/tools/hotfixes/rdpclip-o.asp and click Download this tool to download file RDPCLIP_HOTFIX.EXE.
3. Start REGEDT32.EXE.
4. Go to HKEY_LOCAL_MACHINE\SYSTEM\CurrentControlSet\Control\Terminal Server\AddIns\Clip Redirector.
5. Double-click the Name value.
6. Change the RDPCLIP entry to FXRDPCLP.
7. Go to HKEY_LOCAL_MACHINE\SYSTEM\CurrentControlSet\Control\Terminal Server\Wds\rdpwd.
8. Double-click the Startup Programs value.
9. Change the RDPCLIP entry to **FXRDPCLP** (if you have installed Drive Share, change the entry to **FXRDPCLP,DRMAPSRV**).
10. Rename the new RDPCLIP.EXE file (located in the Resource Kit folder) to FXRDPCLP.EXE and then copy the file to the %systemroot%\System32 folder.
11. Copy the FXFR.DLL file (located in the Resource Kit folder) to the %systemroot%\System32 folder.
12. Restart the computer.

On the clients, perform the following steps:

1. Copy the 32-bit FXFR.DLL file to the Program Files\Terminal Services Client folder.
2. Rename the RDPDR.DLL file in the Program Files\Terminal Services Client folder to **RDPDR.PSS**.
3. Copy the 32-bit RDPDR.DLL file to the Program Files\Terminal Services Client folder.

To use File Copy, simply select the desired file or files on the client or Terminal Services session, press Ctrl+C, then paste into the Terminal Services or client session.

FAQ 23.33 How do I enable Remote Desktop in Windows XP?

XP includes the ability to host a single Terminal Services session, which lets you access applications and files on your machine from a remote machine. To enable remote access, perform the following steps:

1. Right-click My Computer and select Properties.
2. Select the Remote tab.
3. Select Allow users to connect remotely to this computer (see Figure 23-10).
4. Click Select Remote Users if you want to add a non-Administrator user.
5. Click Add.
6. Select the users and click OK.
7. Click OK to close the Remote Desktop Users dialog box.
8. Click OK to close the main dialog box.

You can use this session only when your computer is locked or nobody is logged on. When you log on to the machine remotely, you see all the applications that were running when you were logged onto the local computer.

To log onto the session, use the Terminal Services client, or if you're logging on from an XP machine, use the built-in Remote Desktop Connection application, MSTSC.EXE.

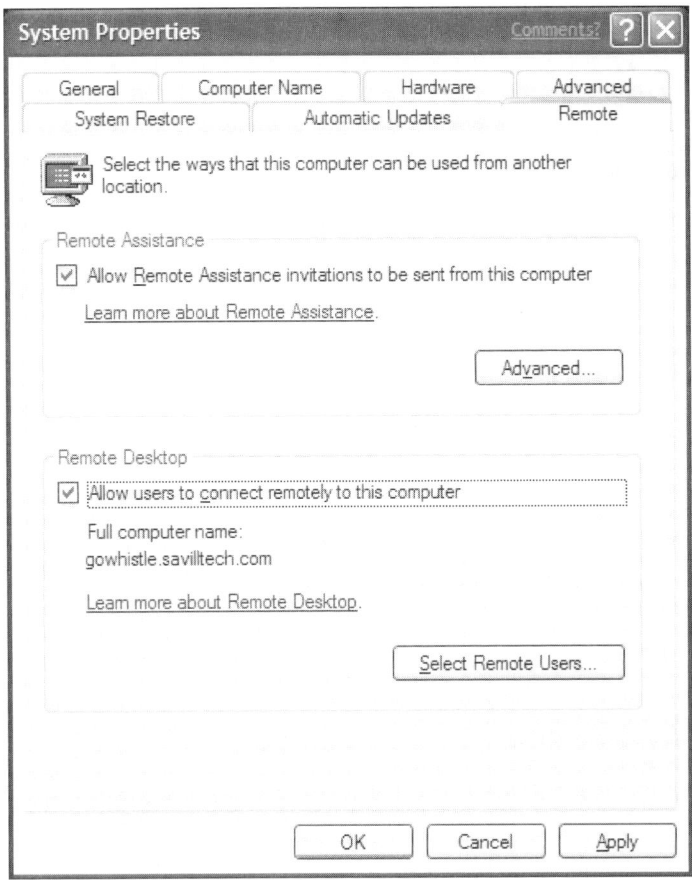

Figure 23-10 Enabling Remote Desktop on a XP machine

FAQ 23.34 How do I use the Windows XP Remote Desktop Connection application?

XP has a built-in Terminal Services client (MSTSC.EXE) that you can use to connect to XP Remote Desktop sessions and regular Terminal Services servers. To use the Remote Desktop Connection, perform the following steps:

1. Start the Remote Desktop Connection application (Start > Programs > Accessories> Communications > Remote Desktop Connection).
2. By default, the system displays a cut-down version that requires only a computer name (see Figure 23-11).

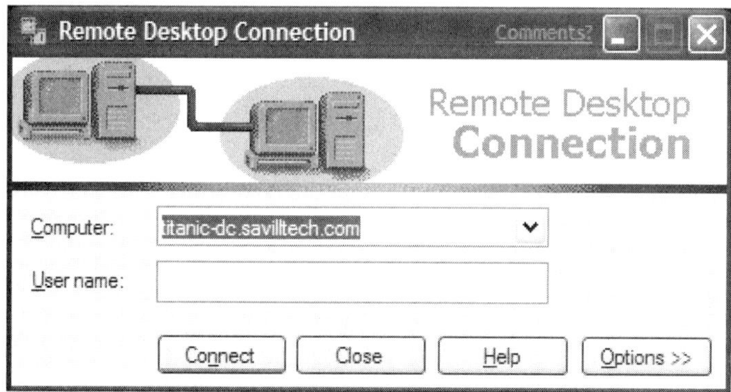

Figure 23-11 The Remote Desktop client

3. Click Connect to start a session in full-screen mode. Or click Options to first configure screen resolution, sound and keyboard options, local devices, bitmap caching, and compression.

FAQ 23.35 What is Remote Assistance?

In previous FAQs, we've seen that Windows XP permits a single Terminal Services-style session (known as "Remote Desktop"). Remote Assistance builds on this feature to offer a Help desk/troubleshooting feature that lets authorized personnel view a user's desktop session and, with permission, take control. Whereas Remote Desktop lets you connect via a Terminal Services client on any platform, Remote Assistance requires that both computers be running XP.

If a user has a computer problem, he or she sends an invitation for assistance to someone via e-mail or Windows Messenger or as a file. The assistant receives a message with a file attachment. Executing the attachment opens the Remote Assistance application, which sends a request to the user for permission to connect. When the user grants permission, the assistant can assist the user.

FAQ 23.36 How do I enable Remote Assistance?

By default, Remote Assistance is enabled. However, to double-check that it's enabled or to reenable it, perform the following steps:

1. Start the System Control Panel applet (Start > Settings > Performance and Maintenance > System).
2. Select the Remote tab.
3. Ensure that the Allow Remote Assistance invitations to be sent from this computer checkbox is checked.
4. Click Advanced to set the maximum length of time for which invitations are valid (30 days, usually). You can also indicate whether the assistant can take control of your machine.
5. Click OK.

You can also use the Registry to enable Remote Assistance:

1. Start REGEDIT.EXE.
2. Go to HKEY_LOCAL_MACHINE\SYSTEM\CurrentControlSet\ ControlTerminal Server.
3. Double-click fAllowToGetHelp (or create this entry of type DWORD if it doesn't exist).
4. Set fAllowToGetHelp to 1 to enable connections or 0 to deny.
5. Click OK.
6. Close Regedit.

Remote Assistance is enabled immediately; you don't need to reboot.

FAQ 23.37 How do I send a Remote Assistance request?

The best way to send a Remote Assistance request is via XP's Help and Support component:

1. Click Start, then select Help and Support.
2. Select Invite a friend to connect to your computer with Remote Assistance, as shown in Figure 23-12.
3. The system will display a dialog box with options to create a new invitation or view current open invitations. Click Invite someone to help you.
4. The system will offer three options for sending the invitation: Windows Messenger, e-mail, or as a file (see Figure 23-13).
5. If you select either Windows Messenger or e-mail, you can enter a message that explains why you want help.

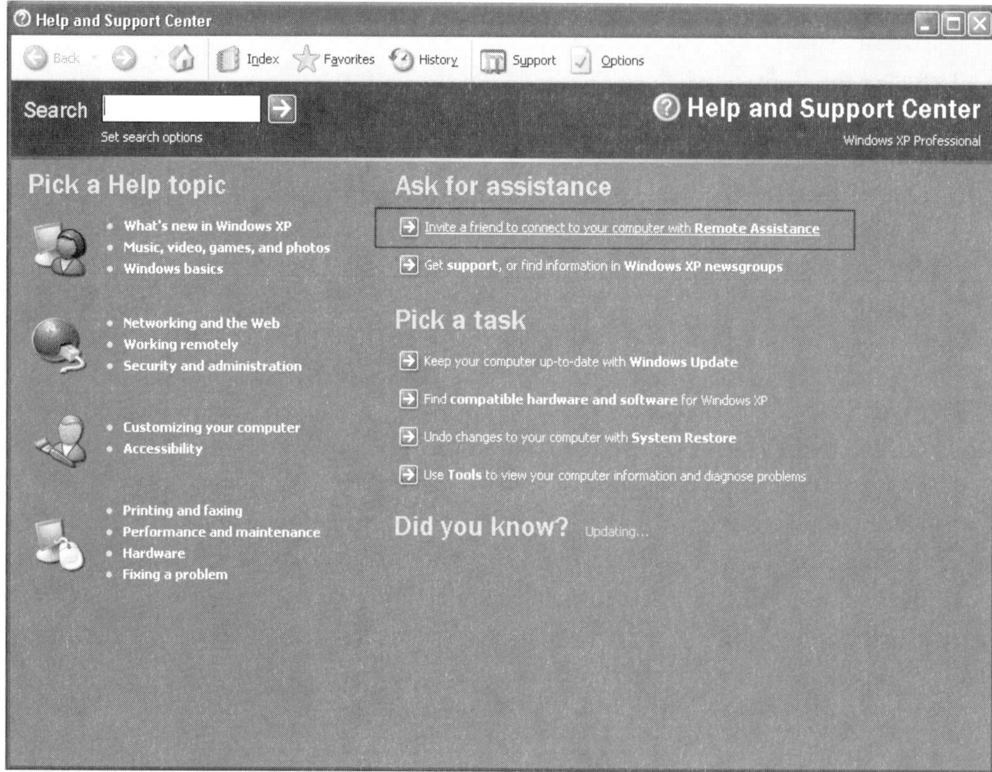

Figure 23-12 The Help and Support center, which hosts the ability to ask a friend to provide Remote Assistance

6. You can also enter a password the assistant must know (you need to communicate the password via phone or in person).
7. When you've completed all the details, click Send Invitation.

The system creates a file with an MsRcIncident extension (the default filename is RAINVITATION.MSRCINCIDENT). If you selected the Windows Messenger or email option, the system attaches the file to a message and sends the message to the assistant. If you chose the file option, you can manually deliver the file. The file is an XML package that looks something like the following:

```
<?xml version="1.0" encoding="Unicode" ?>
<UPLOADINFO TYPE="Escalated">
<UPLOADDATA USERNAME="savillj"
```

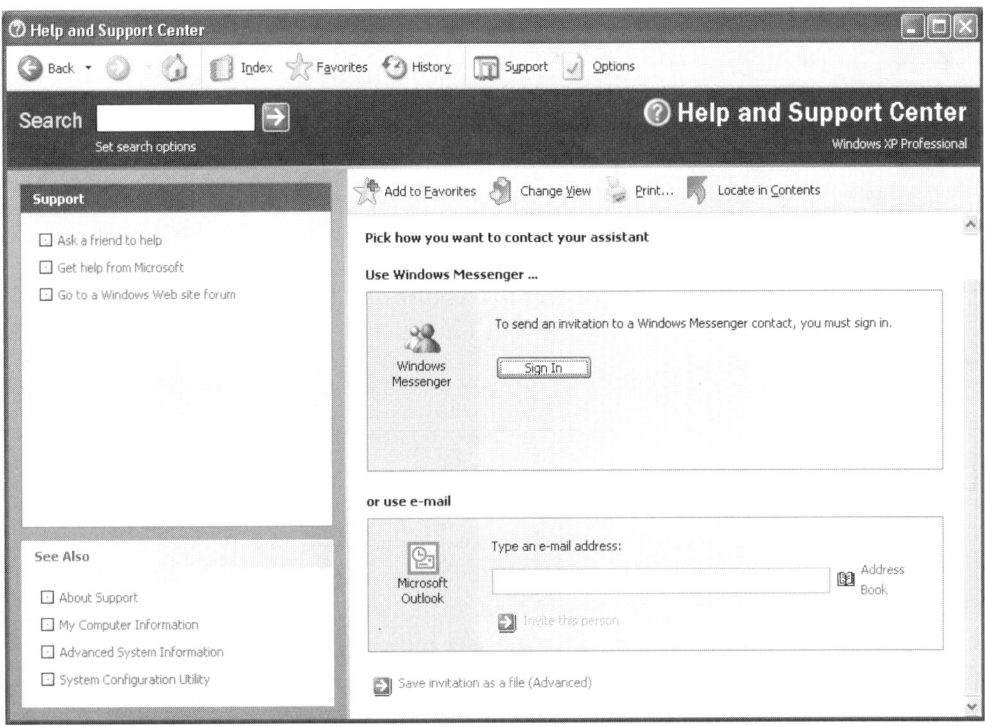

Figure 23-13 Page with options for requesting help

```
RCTICKET="65538,1,10.128.62.201:3389;chicago.savilltech.com:3389,7Klph/
EQOTcQhojZPew=,pbyDuQJnoIoi7qzc5IxaXnJaHZg+bQXy/uD0OUS/IVQ=,Solicited
Help,7otj4PASdDx8h5ejesUyTkqLnosaAT+1ue6i/E//9mjmuh005JvDcA==,iq5lV681t
DMjvRtY3PXcnPtf4Pc=" RCTICKETENCRYPTED="1" DtStart="992591553"
DtLength="120" PassStub="51$0Wtlw98MTP_" L="0" />
</UPLOADINFO>
```

Notice that the file contains the IP address of the machine that's requesting help. If the requester uses DHCP and the address changes after the requester sends the invitation, when Remote Assistance sends a request to the user for permission to connect, the request won't go through.

FAQ 23.38 How do I accept a Remote Assistance request and what can I do?

When you receive an invitation, you must execute the .MSRCINCIDENT file that's attached to a Windows Messenger or e-mail message or that the requesting user gives you manually. If the user set a password, you must enter the password and then click Yes to connect to the user's computer (see Figure 23-14).

The computer you're trying to connect to will display a dialog box that lets the user know that you've accepted the invitation and asks whether she wants to let you view the session and chat with the user.

When the user clicks Yes, the user's session appears in a window on your monitor, and you can see all activity. The user has a dialog box that lets him communicate with you.

If you need to take control, click Take Control, and the system will ask the user whether it's OK for you to do so. If the user accepts, both you and the user will be able to move the mouse, type, etc. To end control, either you or the user can press the Esc key (or any key combination that uses Escape, so be careful).

To end the help session, either you or the user can click Disconnect. If you want to assist the user again, you can reuse the original invitation as long as it hasn't expired or the user hasn't deleted it.

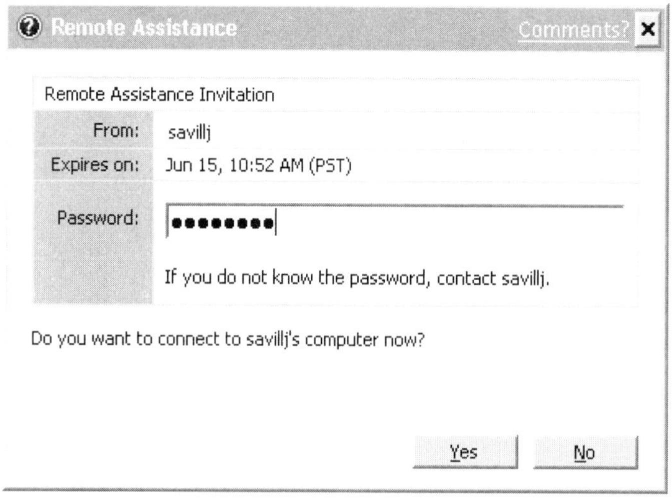

Figure 23-14 To accept an invitation, you need to know the password

FAQ 23.39 How do I enable unsolicited Remote Assistance?

Usually, with Remote Assistance, a user must request help. However, via a Group Policy setting, you can configure machines not to have to send an invitation to be assisted. On each machine on which you want to enable unsolicited Remote Assistance, perform the following steps:

1. Start the Microsoft Management Console (MMC) (Start > Run > MMC).
2. From the File menu, select Add/Remove Snap-in.
3. On the Standalone tab, click Add.
4. Select Group Policy and click Add.
5. Accept the default of Local Computer and click Finish.
6. Click Close, then click OK.
7. Expand Local Computer Policy > Computer Configuration > Administrative Templates > System > Remote Assistance.
8. Set the policy to Enabled and click Apply.
9. Close the MMC.

This policy setting is also available through Group Policy if you're in a Windows .NET domain.

FAQ 23.40 How do I initiate an unsolicited Remote Assistance connection?

If a computer has unsolicited Remote Assistance enabled, use the following URL (from a Windows XP machine) to initiate a connection: hcp://CN=Microsoft%20Corporation,L=Redmond,S=Washington,C=US/Remote%20Assistance/Escalation/unsolicited/unsolicitedrcui.htm

The program displays a dialog box in which you can insert the IP address of the machine you want to connect to. Click Start Remote Assistance. Follow the same procedure you would if a user had invited you to assist as seen previously in FAQ 23.38.

FAQ 23.41 How do I disable the automatic assignment of Allow Logon to Terminal Server?

To modify the default state, perform the following steps:

1. Start REGEDIT.EXE.
2. Go to HKEY_LOCAL_MACHINE\SYSTEM\CurrentControlSet\Control Terminal Server\DefaultUserConfiguration.
3. Double-click fLogonDisabled and set it to 1.
4. Click OK.
5. Close Regedit.

FAQ 23.42 Do I have to call Microsoft if I've lost my Windows 2000 Server Terminal Services license tokens?

With Terminal Services licenses, you must contact Microsoft to enable Client Access Tokens on the server. If you rebuild a Terminal Services license server, you typically must contact Microsoft to reenable the licenses.

Microsoft has released a hotfix at its Web site at http://support.microsoft.com/support/kb/articles/Q287/6/87.asp that lets you recover any future Client Access Licenses (CALs) that you apply. You must be running Win2K Service Pack 1 (SP1) or newer to apply this fix. Be aware, however, that you'll still need to contact Microsoft to recover any CALs that you install before applying the hotfix if you have no backup of the license database.

FAQ 23.43 Why can't I get Windows 2000's Clipboard redirection feature to work?

Clipboard redirection lets you cut and paste between remote and local sessions. If you encounter problems using this feature, the virtual channel might be absent. The virtual channel lets Win2K Server Terminal Services work but without the advanced features. To determine whether the virtual channel is available, perform the following steps:

1. Start the Microsoft Management Console (MMC) Terminal Services Configuration snap-in (go to Start > Programs > Administrative Tools > and click Terminal Services Configuration).

2. Select the Connections branch.
3. Right-click RDP-Tcp and select Properties.
4. Select the Permissions tab.
5. Click Advanced.
6. Select the Users checkbox and click View/Edit.
7. Ensure that Virtual Channels is set to Allow and not to Deny.
8. Click OK to close all dialog boxes.

FAQ 23.44 How do I use the Registry to enable and disable Windows XP's Remote Desktop feature?

In FAQ 23.33, I described how to enable XP's Remote Desktop setting. You can also use the Registry to configure this setting by performing the following steps:

1. Start the Registry editor (e.g., REGEDIT.EXE).
2. Navigate to HKEY_LOCAL_MACHINE\SYSTEM\CurrentControlSet\Control\Terminal Server.
3. Double-click fDenyTSConnections.
4. Change the value of this setting to 0 to enable Remote Desktop or 1 to disable it and click OK.
5. Close the Registry editor and reboot the computer for the change to take effect.

24 INTERNET EXPLORER

There has been much legal wrangling about whether Internet Explorer (IE) is part of the operating system; however, none of that concerns us. We can just concentrate on getting the most out of this experienced and sophisticated browser.

As operating systems have evolved, the Web has become more important, and so the browser has become more integrated into the operating system. Now it's no longer possible to remove it, but why would we want to? ☺

FAQ 24.1 How can I remove the Active Desktop?

You can turn off the Active Desktop without removing it by performing the following:

1. Right-click on the desktop.
2. Select Active Desktop.
3. Unselect View as Web Page (by clicking it).

To actually remove Active Desktop completely while leaving the browser intact:

1. Start the Add/Remove Programs Control Panel applet (Start > Settings > Control Panel > Add/Remove Programs).
2. Select Microsoft Internet Explorer 4.0 and click the Add/Remove button.
3. Click the Remove the Windows Desktop Update component but keep the Internet Explorer 4.0 Web browser option and click OK.
4. A dialog box explaining the change will be shown, and you should click the Restart Windows button.

Once restarted, the Active Desktop will have been removed.

24.2 How can I get past the Active Desktop Recovery page?

This can usually be fixed by deleting the DESKTOP.HTT file:

1. Start Explorer.
2. Move to %systemroot%\Profiles\<your username>\Application Data\Microsoft\Internet Explorer.
3. Select DESKTOP.HTT and delete it (it is a hidden file so you will need to change the view first—View > Folder Options > View).
4. Close Explorer.
5. Right-click on the desktop and choose Refresh.

24.3 What keyboard commands can I use with Internet Explorer 4.0 and above?

Following is a list of common keyboard commands:

Alt+Left Arrow (or backspace)	Go Back
Alt+Right Arrow	Go Forward
Tab	Move to next hyperlink
Shift+Tab	Move to previous hyperlink
Enter	Move to page referenced by hyperlink
Down Arrow	Scroll down
PgDn	Scroll down in greater jump
End	Move to bottom of document
Up Arrow	Scroll up
PgUp	Scroll up in greater jump
Home	Move to top of document
F5	Refresh

Ctrl+F5	Refresh not from cache
Esc	Stop download
F11	Full screen/normal toggle

FAQ 24.4 How can I create a keyboard shortcut to a Web site?

It is possible to create your own keyboard shortcuts with a Ctrl+Alt+<letter> combination as follows:

1. Start Internet Explorer.
2. Select Organize Favorites from the Favorites menu.
3. Right-click on the link and choose Properties.
4. In the Shortcut key dialog box, type the combination, any combination of Ctrl, Shift, Alt, and a key that is not used.
5. Click OK.

You can also use the preceding to create a keyboard shortcut to a desktop item by right-clicking on the shortcut and choosing Properties.

NT4.0 ONLY

FAQ 24.5 How can I customize folders with Web view enabled?

If you have installed the Windows Desktop Update and have View as Web page enabled (View > As Web page), you can customize the folder (View > Customize this folder) and then select the type (background picture or a whole HTML file), or you can change the default, which is stored in a hidden HTML file (%systemroot%\web\folder.htt). You can then edit this file and change it accordingly.

A line in FOLDER.HTT, "HERE'S A GOOD PLACE TO ADD A FEW LINES OF YOUR OWN", is where you can add your own links that will then appear on all folders.

There are four other templates you can edit:

- CONTROLP.HTT—Control Panel
- PRINTERS.HTT—Printers
- MYCOMP.HTT—My Computer
- SAFEMODE.HTT—Safe mode

As I said, these files are hidden, so you will either need to remove the hidden attribute (**attrib <file> -h**) or just enter the name specifically in the edit utility you use to change these files.

Warning: *Make a backup of these files before you break them* ☺.

FAQ 24.6 How can I change the icons in the QuickLaunch toolbar?

The icons on the QuickLaunch toolbar (Internet Explorer, Outlook Express, Show Desktop, and Channels by default) are all stored in %systemroot%/profiles/<user>/Application Data/Microsoft/Internet Explorer/Quick Launch. To add or remove them, just add and remove the files from this directory using Explorer.

You can copy any shortcut to this directory, and the update will be done straight away; there's no need to logoff and reboot. You can add a shortcut by simply copying the shortcut to the QuickLaunch directory—easy. An alternative method is to just drag a shortcut over the QuickLaunch bar, and it will add the shortcut for you.

All the files in this folder are shortcuts except for Show Desktop and View Channels. See the next FAQ for their contents.

FAQ 24.7 Why have I have lost Show Desktop/View Channels from the QuickLaunch bar?

As was discussed in the previous FAQ, these icons are just files in the %systemroot%/profiles/<user>/Application Data/Microsoft/Internet Explorer/Quick Launch directory. To get the Show Desktop/View Channels icons back, create the following files in the QuickLaunch directory (or copy from another user).

For Show Desktop, create Show Desktop.SCF with the following content:

```
[Shell]
Command=2
IconFile=explorer.exe,3

[Taskbar]
Command=ToggleDesktop
```

For View Channels, create View Channels.SCF with the following content:

```
[Shell]
Command=3
IconFile=shdocvw.dll,-118

[IE]
Command=Channels
```

FAQ 24.8 How do I change the default search engine for IE 4.0?

The URL for the search engine used with the Go > Search the Web is stored in the Registry so this can easily be changed:

1. Start the Registry editor (REGEDIT.EXE).
2. Move to HKEY_CURRENT_USER\Software\Microsoft\Internet Explorer\Main.
3. Double-click on Search Page.
4. Change to the search page you want (e.g., http://www.altavista.digital.com) and click OK.
5. Close the Registry editor.

Now when you select search, you will be taken to this URL. If you want to change back to the default, enter **http://www.msn.com/access/allinone.htm**.

FAQ 24.9 How do I remove the Internet Explorer icon from the desktop?

This can be done from the Advanced options of Internet Explorer. For Internet Explorer 4.0:

1. Start Internet Explorer.
2. From the View menu, select Internet Options.
3. Click the Advanced tab.
4. Deselect Show Internet Explorer on Desktop.
5. Click OK.
6. Restart the machine.

If you are using Internet Explorer 5.0 or above, select Internet Options from the Tools menu.

24.10 How can I browse offline?

As you may be aware, when you connect to a site, the information you view is cached locally to speed up future visits to the site (the cache size can be set via View > Internet Options > General > Temporary Internet files > Settings). It's actually possible to view the Web using only the cache when not connected; obviously you can only view sites that are stored in the cache. To work offline:

1. Start Internet Explorer.
2. From the file menu, select Work Offline.

You can then enter URLs and link as normal but will receive an error if you attempt to link to a site that is not cached. To stop working offline, just deselect Work Offline.

24.11 How can I reclaim wasted space by Microsoft's Internet e-mail readers?

Microsoft's Internet e-mail clients (both Internet Mail under IE3 and Outlook Express under IE4 and above) waste a large amount of disk space due to the method used to store mail. The reason behind this is to improve performance; however, if you want to reclaim some of the lost space, perform the following:

1. Select one of the folders (e.g., Inbox, Outbox, Sent Items).
2. Select Folder from the File menu and select Compact all Folders.

Also set up Outlook to automatically delete the Deleted Items folder contents:

1. Select Options from the Tools menu.
2. Select the General tab.
3. Check the Empty messages from the Deleted Items folder on exit and click OK.

FAQ 24.12 Why can't I specify a download directory when I download a file?

When you download a file, you are asked what you want to do, "Open this file from its current location" or "Save this file to disk". If you take the latter option, you are asked for a storage location, and you then click Save. Also on the selection screen is "Always ask before opening this type of file". If you clear this check in the future, any downloads of this type will be downloaded to the Temporary Internet Files folder and opened by the program associated with the file type. To undo this, perform the following:

1. Double-click on My Computer.
2. From the View menu, select Folder Options.
3. Select the File Types tab.
4. Select the file type you have the problem with in the Registered File Types box and click Edit.
5. In the bottom-right corner is Confirm open after Download. Check the box so there is a tick in it and click OK.
6. Click OK again to close the Folder Options dialog box.
7. Close My Computer.

FAQ 24.13 Why does Internet Explorer open .EXE files instead of downloading them?

As explained in the previous FAQ, if you unselect "Always ask before opening this type of file" for an executable, it updates the Registry so you are not asked. However, this can be fixed:

1. Start the Registry editor (REGEDT32.EXE).
2. Move to HKEY_CLASSES_ROOT\exefile.
3. Double-click on EditFlags.
4. Change the third pair of numbers from 01 to 00 (e.g., D8070100 to D8070000).
5. Close the Registry editor.

For files such as WAV, MOV, and AVI (ActiveMovie files), you modify the entry HKEY_CLASSES_ROOT\AMOVIE.ActiveMovieControl.2\EditFlags to 00000000.

FAQ 24.14 How can I change the default start page?

When you first start Internet Explorer, it loads a page—by default, a Microsoft page (http://home.microsoft.com). However, this default page can be changed:

1. Start Internet Explorer.
2. Select Internet Options from the View menu.
3. Select the General tab.
4. In the first section Home page, enter the page you wish to be displayed when you start Internet Explorer and click Apply, then OK. If you just want a blank page, click the Use Blank button; again click Apply, then OK.
5. Close Internet Explorer.

The preceding just updates Registry entry HKEY_CURRENT_USER\Software\Microsoft\Internet Explorer\Main\Start Page. You could create a Registry script that updates a machine's Registry to set your page up as the client's homepage. The REG script would have the following:

```
REGEDIT4

[HKEY_CURRENT_USER\Software\Microsoft\Internet Explorer\Main]
"Start Page"="http://www.ntfaq.com/"

[HKEY_LOCAL_MACHINE\Software\Microsoft\Internet Explorer\Main]
"Default_Page_URL"="http://www.ntfaq.com/"
```

You would then set up a link on your page to the script, and people would select Open from current location.

If Netscape Navigator is your browser, use the following to change your default homepage:

1. Start Netscape.
2. From the Edit menu, select Preferences.
3. Select the Navigator category.
4. Enter the required start page in the Home Page box and click OK.

Netscape Navigator does not store the start page location in the Registry; rather in a Javascript file PREFS.JS, which is located in the Program Files\Netscape\Users\ directory. The line in the file is

```
user_pref("browser.startup.homepage", "http://www.ntfaq.com/");
```

However, you should not edit this file.

24.15 I have forgotten the content advisor password. What can I do?

The password for the content advisor is stored in an encrypted form, and decrypting it, while possible, is too complicated for our purposes. Instead, we will just "reset" the password as if it had never been set:

1. Start the Registry editor (REGEDIT.EXE).
2. Move to HKEY_LOCAL_MACHINE\SOFTWARE\Microsoft\Windows\CurrentVersion\Policies\Ratings\.
3. If this is a Key value, select it and press Delete. Click OK to the confirmation. A FileName0 value may also be deleted, and you may also delete the file it points to.
4. If there was not a value but was instead a subkey ".default", move to this folder and delete the Key value.
5. Restart IE, and you should be able to set the password with Internet Options > Content.

24.16 Where can I download IE 5.0 and above?

IE 5.0 and above can be downloaded from http://www.microsoft.com/windows/ie/default.htm. Internet Explorer 5.0 does not ship with the Active Desktop, so if you want Active Desktop, you will need to have installed IE 4.0 Service Pack 2 with Active Desktop and then upgrade to IE 5.0.

24.17 How do I clear Internet Explorer's history?

Internet Explorer keeps a history of the sites you visit. You can view this history by clicking the History button on the toolbar. If you wish to clear this history, perform the following. For IE 4:

1. Select Internet Options from the View menu.
2. In the History section, click Clear History. (You can also set the number of days to keep history for.)
3. Click Yes to the confirmation.
4. Click OK to close the Internet Options dialog box.

For IE 5, use the same steps as the preceding except Internet Options is under the Tools menu.

The history files are actually stored under the directory %systemroot%\Profiles\<user name>\History\History; however, the permissions on the files are complex, so deleting them manually is not advised.

24.18 How can I modify IE's toolbar background?

The picture behind the IE toolbar buttons can be set to any bitmap you wish. To do this, perform the following:

1. Start the Registry editor (REGEDIT.EXE).
2. Move to HKEY_CURRENT_USER\Software\Microsoft\Internet Explorer\Toolbar.

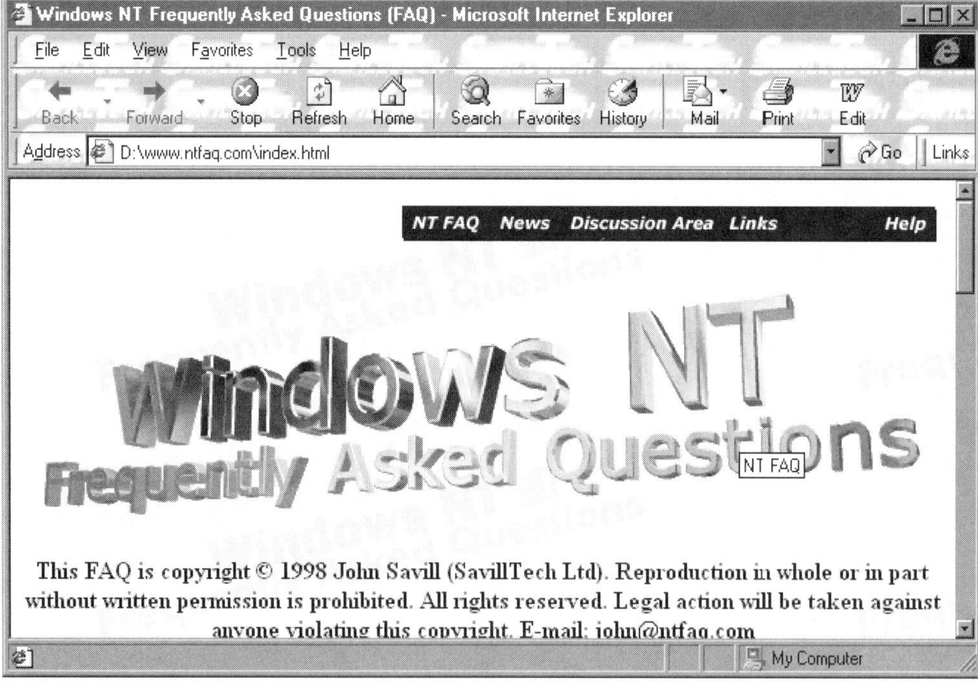

Figure 24-1 A modified main Internet Explorer title bar (and a very old version of NTFAQ.COM!)

3. From the Edit menu, select New > String Value.
4. Enter a name of BackBitmap and press Enter.
5. Double-click the new value and set to the name and location (e.g., c:\images\savtech.bmp).
6. Close the Registry editor.
7. Restart IE.

Figure 24-1 provides an example.

FAQ 24.19 How can I restore the IE animated logo?

Using the Internet Explorer Admin K, it is possible to modify the small E logo in the top-right corner of Internet Explorer (ISPs such as MSN do this). To restore to the default, perform the following:

1. Start the Registry editor (REGEDIT.EXE).
2. Move to HKEY_CURRENT_USER\Software\Microsoft\Internet Explorer\Toolbar.
3. Select BrandBitmap and click Delete. Confirm.
4. Select SmBrandBitmap and click Delete. Confirm.
5. Close the Registry editor.
6. Restart the computer.

FAQ 24.20 Are there any Easter Eggs in Internet Explorer 5.0?

There are two Easter Eggs I know of for IE 5.0.

Easter Egg 1

1. Open Notepad.
2. Type

```
<!-- introducing the Trident team -->
```

3. Save the file as **"TEST.HTM"** (make sure you add the quotes or .txt will be added to the end).
4. Open up TEST.HTMtest.htm in IE5. IE5 Easter Egg 1 is shown.

(Actually this Easter Egg also runs on IE4.01.)

Easter Egg 2

1. Start IE5.
2. From the Tools menu, select Internet Options.
3. Select the General tab.
4. Click the Languages button.
5. Click Add.
6. Type **ie-ee** and click OK.
7. Move User Defined [ie-ee] to the **top** of the list. Click OK.
8. Click OK to the main dialog.
9. Click on the Search icon (to pull up the side search menu) and notice the new Search options ☺.
10. Select Previous Searches.

To remove ie-ee, just start the Languages dialog again, select ie-ee, and click Remove.

FAQ 24.21 How can I prevent users from accessing local drives via Internet Explorer?

If you type **C:** (or any other drive) in the Microsoft Internet Explorer address box, you will be shown the contents, and if proper NTFS file permissions are not in place, users will be able to delete, rename, and read any files on the disk. This is usually a problem if you have a locked-down environment where users do not normally have access to Explorer, etc. (such as an Internet Cafe).

To prevent the ability to view local drives from Internet Explorer, perform the following:

1. Start the Registry editor (REGEDIT.EXE).
2. Move to HKEY_CURRENT_USER\Software\Microsoft\Windows\CurrentVersion\Policies\Explorer.

3. From the Edit menu, select New > DWORD Value.
4. Enter a name of NoRun and press Enter.
5. Double-click the new value and set to 1. Click OK to close the value Edit dialog.
6. From the Edit menu, select New > DWORD Value.
7. Enter a name of **NoDrives** and press Enter.
8. Double-click the new value and set to a number representing the drives you wish to hide (explained following this procedure). Click OK to close the value edit dialog.
9. For IE 4.01 SP1 and above, perform the following steps:
   1. From the Edit menu, select New > DWORD Value.
   2. Enter a name of **NoFileUrl** and press Enter.
   3. Double-click the new value and set to 1. Click OK to close the value edit dialog.
10. Close the Registry editor.

The NoRun setting disables viewing local files by typing a file address or URL (for example, file://d:\) in the Address box and also disables the Run command on the Start menu.

The NoDrives setting disables the selected drives. It is explained in FAQ 7.6. Basically drive A is 1, B is 2, C is 4, D is 8, and so on, and you add the values together. So to hide drive C and D, you add 4 and 8, which is 12 or C in hexadecimal and set NoDrives to C (selecting Hex mode).

FAQ 24.22 How can I configure proxy settings in Internet Explorer 5.0?

To configure LAN proxy settings in Internet Explorer 5.0, perform the following:

1. Start Internet Explorer.
2. From the Tools menu, select Internet Options.
3. Select the Connections tab.
4. Click the LAN Settings button.
5. By default the Automatically detect settings option will be selected. You can also configure the location of a configuration script.

6. To manually configure, check the Use a proxy server and enter the DNS or IP address of the server and the port it uses.
7. Click OK.
8. Click OK to the main dialog.

If you select Automatically detect settings, the discovery cycle will typically involve one DHCP request or DNS request. Further, a discovery cycle happens quite infrequently.

When you install IE5, the first time it runs, it will perform a discovery cycle only if you are on a LAN and not a dial-up connection. (discovery is disabled by default for dial-up).

If this initial discovery fails, then auto discovery is disabled until a user reenables it. If the discovery succeeds, then discovery is performed only when the downloaded configuration file expires according to HTTP semantics. If no expiry information is supplied, then the default is discovery once every seven days. Again, this is only if it initially succeeds.

The following Registry entries can be directly updated instead:

- HKEY_CURRENT_USER\Software\Microsoft\Windows\CurrentVersion\Internet Settings\ProxyEnable—Set to 1.
- HKEY_CURRENT_USER\Software\Microsoft\Windows\CurrentVersion\Internet Settings\ProxyServer—Set to <proxy server>:port (e.g., proxy:80).
- HKEY_CURRENT_USER\Software\Microsoft\Windows\CurrentVersion\Internet Settings\ProxyOverride—When not to use the proxy server. For local, set to "<local>" (don't type the quotes but do type the angle brackets—< and >).

FAQ 24.23 How can I install Internet Explorer 4.0 without adding the IE icon to the desktop?

Install using the following command to prevent IE from adding an icon on the desktop or from becoming the default browser. (This will not work if you have installed the Windows Desktop Updated.)

```
IE4SETUP.EXE /C:"ie4wzd" /S:""#e"" /X /R:N /Q:A /m:0"
```

FAQ 24.24 How do I use the Internet Explorer 5.0 Repair tool?

The Internet Explorer Repair tool can be used to diagnose and possibly fix problems with Internet Explorer 5. This tool has the following features:

- It is used to identify problems with Internet Explorer caused by the presence of files that are out-of-date.
- It is used to fix problems caused by the incorrect or incomplete registration of Internet Explorer files.
- It is used to restore or repair the desktop or Start menu shortcuts for Internet Explorer that have been deleted or do not function properly.

To start the Repair tool, perform the following:

1. From the Start menu, select Settings > Control Panel.
2. Double-click the Add/Remove Software Control Panel applet.
3. Select Microsoft Internet Explorer 5 and Internet Tools.
4. Click the Add/Remove button.
5. Select Repair Internet Explorer and click OK.
6. Click Yes to the repair confirmation.

If you don't have the option in the Add/Remove Software Control Panel applet, it can be run from the command line:

```
rundll32 setupwbv.dll,IE5Maintenance "C:\Program Files\Internet
Explorer\Setup\SETUP.EXE" /g "C:\WINDOWS\IE Uninstall Log.Txt"
```

FAQ 24.25 I have forgotten the content advisor password under Windows 9x/IE 5.0. What can I do?

The password for the content advisor is stored in an encrypted form, and decrypting it, while possible, is too complicated for our purposes. Instead, we will just "reset" the password as if it had never been set:

1. Start the Registry editor (REGEDIT.EXE).
2. Move to HKEY_LOCAL_MACHINE\SOFTWARE\Microsoft\Windows\CurrentVersion\Policies\.

3. Select Ratings and delete (press the Delete key). Click OK to the confirmation.
4. Delete the RATINGS.POL file (it is hidden) out of the \WINDOWS\SYSTEM directory.
5. Restart IE, and you should be able to set the password with Internet Options > Content.

FAQ 24.26 The Tab key does not select the right pane in an IE5 Help search. Is there a substitute for this functionality?

This is a known problem. Press F6 to toggle between left and right panes instead. It works in the Microsoft Developer Network (MSDN) library as well.

FAQ 24.27 How do I turn off Internet Explorer AutoComplete?

IE has the neat ability to automatically complete a URL as you type it. This can, however, be annoying, and you may want to turn it off. It can be accomplished by performing the following:

1. Start Internet Explorer.
2. From the Tools menu, select Internet Options.
3. Select the Content tab.
4. Click AutoComplete under the Personal Information section.
5. Unselect Web addresses (see Figure 24-2) and click OK.
6. Click OK to the main dialog.

You can also accomplish this by setting HKEY_CURRENT_USER\Software\Microsoft\Windows\CurrentVersion\Explorer\AutoComplete\AutoSuggest to **no** in the Registry.

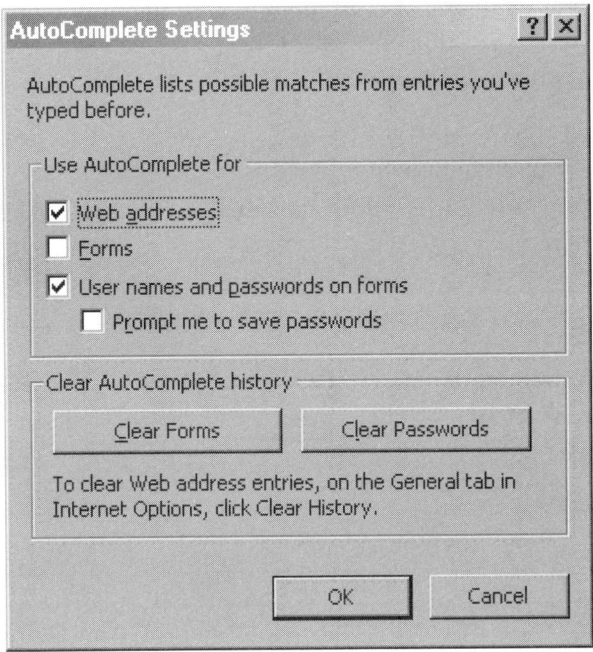

Figure 24-2 AutoComplete option page

FAQ 24.28 Why do I get an error when I try to install Internet Explorer 4.0 using Active Setup?

A bug exists in the Internet Explorer 4.0 setup process that can cause problems when installing, resulting in a number of possible errors:

```
Internet Explorer 4.0 Active Setup
Internet Explorer 4.0 was not successfully installed.

Setup was unable to download all the required components. The
Internet is likely busy. Please try Setup again later and select
Smart Recovery to continue downloading.
```

Knowledge Base article Q171714 (at http://support.microsoft.com/support/kb/articles/Q171/7/14.ASP) explains fixes to this problem; however, to fix under Windows NT 4.0, perform the following:

1. Start Explorer.
2. Move to %systemroot%\system32.
3. Rename the file WINTRUST.DLL to WINTRUST.OLD.
4. Start the IE 4.0 installation (I did not have to reboot).

FAQ 24.29 How do I set an Internet Explorer favorite icon for my Web site?

Internet Explorer 5 allows the setting of an icon for favorites, which you can easily enable for your Web site.

When you create a favorite in IE 5.0 and above, it checks the root of the Web site for FAVICON.ICO, which should be a 16x16 icon. Or it may be ignored (in Windows 2000 version, it handled a 32x32 icon fine). Create the icon with any icon editor such as the one supplied with Visual Studio.

You can also manually specify an icon with a different name with the following code snippet:

```
<HEAD>
<LINK REL="SHORTCUT ICON" HREF="http://www.mydomain.com/myicon.ico">
<TITLE>NT FAQ</TITLE>
</HEAD>
```

Obviously your header section of the HTML will be different from mine but the important part is the LINK REL section (see Figure 24-3).

This icon is used only for favorites and will not be checked and read in until the site is added as a favorite.

Figure 24-3 Shortcut with modified page icon

FAQ 24.30 How can I detect whether Windows Update is installed on a machine?

Windows 2000 includes Windows Update as a core component, but it was also supplied with Internet Explorer 4.0 for NT 4.0 as an option. A number of methods can be used to check whether it's installed:

1. Right-click on the taskbar, and if a toolbar option is present, then Windows Update is installed.
2. Right-click an item in the Start menu's Programs area, and if a menu is shown, then Windows Update is installed.

To tell from a script, check for the following key HKEY_LOCAL_MACHINE\SOFTWARE\Microsoft\Active Setup\Installed Components\{89820200-ECBD-11cf-8B85-00AA005B4340},and if its IsInstalled value is 1, then Windows Update is installed.

You could use the Resource Kit REG.EXE utility with the /query switch to perform this check.

FAQ 24.31 The Internet Explorer Admin Kit version of IE 5.0 replaces the 128-bit encryption on Windows 2000. What does this mean?

If you install a version of IE 5.0 on Windows 2000 created by the Internet Explorer Admin Kit with 128-bit encryption (IE5DOM.EXE), you may receive the following error:

```
System cannot log you on because domain <Computer name> is not
available.
```

This error is caused by the RSAENH.DLL and SCHANNEL.DLL files in Windows 2000 being replaced by the earlier IE 5 versions (but only RSAENH.DLL matters).

Basically you should not install IE 5.0 on Windows 2000; it already has 5.01 as part of the core product.

If you do want to distribute a newer version of IE in the future, make sure you have the new encryption pack and create a separate build of Internet Explorer that includes the latest 128-bit encryption update for Windows 2000 (ENCPACK.EXE). If this pack is not available and you use the IE5DOM.EXE component to create a separate build of IE for Win2K, do not include the /n:v switch.

To resolve the issue, download ENCPACK.EXE and run (or run from the supplied floppy disk if you're located in the United States).

If you can't log onto the machine, then you need to use the Recovery Console to replace RSAENH.DLL with the high encryption pack version (or use an alternate NT installation):

1. Start Recovery Console.
2. Change to the system32 directory

   ```
   cd system32
   ```

3. Check the RSAENH.DLL file

   ```
   dir rsaenh.dll
   ```

4. Rename the existing RSAENH.DLL file

   ```
   ren rsaenh.dll rsaenh.old
   ```

5. Insert the floppy disk that contains the high encryption pack files into the floppy drive.
6. Copy the file RSAENH.DLL to RSAENG.DLL.

   ```
   copy a:\rsaenhs.dll rsaenh.dll
   ```

7. Type **exit** and then press Enter to restart the computer normally. Remove the floppy disk from the floppy drive.

FAQ 24.32 How can I start Internet Explorer without the toolbars?

Internet Explorer has a Kiosk mode that fills the entire screen with no toolbars. You can access this mode using

```
iexplore -k
```

This may not be exactly what you want though, so you could write a Windows Scripting Host program that starts an IE object with the toolbar disabled:

```
Dim objIE
Set objIE = WScript.CreateObject ("InternetExplorer.Application")
ObjIE.Toolbar = false
objIE.Navigate "http://www.savilltech.com"
objIE.Visible = true
```

If you save the file as IENOBAR.VBS and then execute with the following, IE will be started with no toolbars:

```
cscript ienobar.vbs
```

FAQ 24.33 Why is my default printer wrong in IE5.5 and Outlook Express?

Internet Explorer 5.5 and Outlook Express remember the last printer used and set it as the default next time you run the application instead of using the system default. This is a known bug, and the only work around is to make sure you set the printer to the system before closing the application.

FAQ 24.34 Why am I unable to connect to a secure Web page using Internet Explorer?

When you connect to a secure Web page, you may receive the following error messages. In Internet Explorer 4:

```
An error occurred in the secure channel support.
```

In Internet Explorer 5:

```
The page cannot be displayed. Cannot find server or DNS Error.
```

These errors are caused when one of the following authentication methods is not enabled:

- PCT (Private Communications Technology) 1.0
- SSL (Secure Socket Layer) 2.0
- SSL 3.0

To resolve this issue, perform the following:

1. Start Internet Explorer.
2. From the Tools menu, select Internet Options.
3. Select the Advanced tab.
4. Check either PCT 1.2, SSL 2.0, or SSL 3.0.
5. Click Apply, then OK.

Another cause for receiving these errors could be if you are connecting through a firewall. In that case, you have not configured the proxy for HTTPS (Hypertext Transfer Protocol over Secure Socket Layer).

1. Start Internet Explorer.
2. From the Tools menu, select Internet Options.
3. Select the Connections tab.
4. Click Lan Settings.
5. Under the Proxy area, click Advanced.
6. Make sure under Secure, you have a valid host and port (check with the Admin if you're unsure). See Figure 24-4.
7. Click OK to all dialogs.

If this looks OK, but you still have problems, try reapplying the latest service pack.

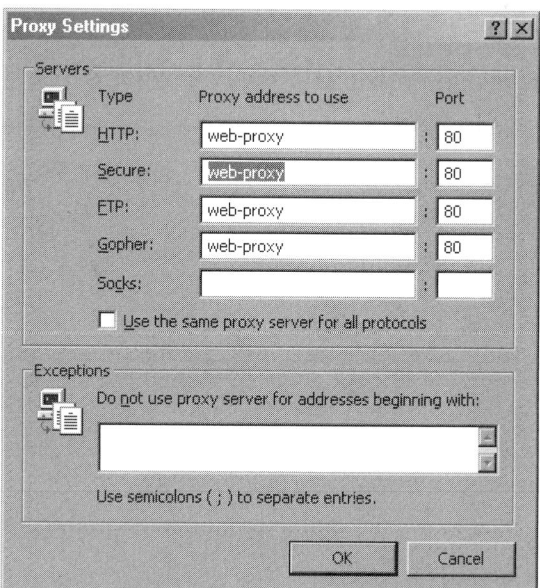

Figure 24-4 Setting proxy information on Internet Explorer

FAQ 24.35 Why does IE under Windows 2000 only show two digits of the days to keep pages in history?

This is caused by a sizing issue in Windows 2000. The full number (from 0 to 999) is still kept, but only two digits are displayed (see Figure 24-5).

1. Start Internet Explorer.
2. Select Internet Options from the Tools menu.
3. Select the General tab.
4. At the bottom of the dialog is the History section with the Days to keep pages in history.

If you want all three digits displayed, you can change the size used by the scrollbar, but this will affect all windows:

1. Start the Display Control Panel applet (Start > Settings > Control Panel > Display).
2. On the Appearance tab, click Scrollbar in the Item box.

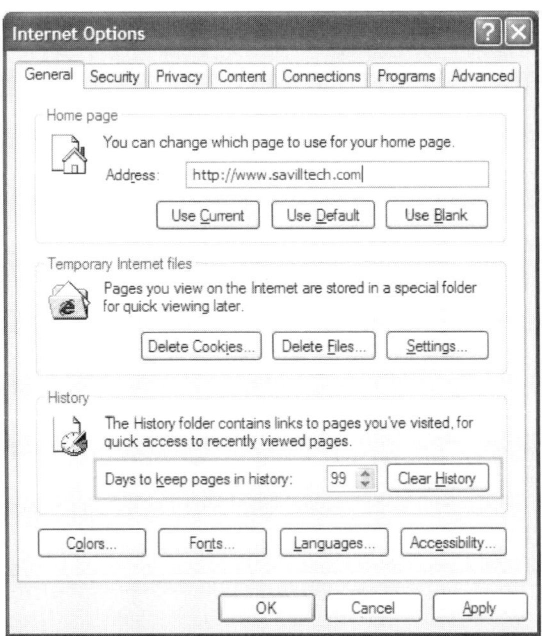

Figure 24-5 The number of days showing history information

3. In the Size box next to Item, decrease the size to a smaller value. For example, if it is set to 13 (the default), change it to 10.
4. Click OK.

All days will now be displayed.

The actual value is stored in HKEY_CURRENT_USER\Software\Microsoft\Windows\CurrentVersion\Internet Settings\Url History\DaysToKeep.

FAQ 24.36 How can I force IE 4 to use a particular search engine?

By default Internet Explorer 4 will use a random search engine when you click the Search button; however, it is possible to force it to a particular search engine by editing the Registry:

1. Start the Registry editor (REGEDIT.EXE).
2. Move to HKEY_CURRENT_USER\Software\Microsoft\Internet Explorer\SearchUrl.
3. Double-click the (Default) value.
4. Set to one of the values in the following table and click OK.
5. Close the Registry editor.

Altavista	http://www.altavista.com/cgi-bin/query?q=%s
Ask Jeeves	http://askjeeves.com/AskJeeves.asp=%s
Excite	http://search.excite.com/search.gw?search=%s
Goto.com	http://www.goto.com/d/search/?type=topbar&Keywords=%s
HotBot	http://hotbot.com/?MT=%s
Infoseek	http://www.infoseek.com/Titles?qt=%s
Lycos	http://www.lycos.com/cgi-bin/pursuit?query=%s
Magellan	http://www.mckinley.com/searcher.cgi?query=%s
Metacrawler	http://www.metacrawler.com/crawler?general=%s
Yahoo	http://search.yahoo.com/bin/search?p=%s

FAQ 24.37 Why am I unable to perform a download only of IE 5.5 in Windows 2000?

Due to the Windows 2000 file protection feature, a download only of IE 5.5 will not work. To work around this, perform the following:

1. Go to http://www.msdn.microsoft.com/downloads/webtechnology/ie/iepreview.asp.
2. Click your language download (e.g., English).
3. Select Save this program to disk and click OK.
4. Select a download location and click Save.
5. Once the download has finished (around 500KB), start a command session (CMD.EXE) and move to the directory the file was download to.
6. Type the following:

   ```
   ie5setup /c:"ie5wzd.exe /d /s:""#E"""
   ```

7. Download away.

Optionally for step 6, you can add /q to perform a quiet download, which will download the files for the current operating system. You can optionally change the /d to /d:1, which downloads files for **all** operating systems; you can't download a specific OS installation set though.

FAQ 24.38 Internet Explorer 5 is leaking large amounts of memory. How can I reclaim it?

When you use the default download behavior to download and parse Extensible Markup Language (XML) data (for example, by using Digital Dashboard), the memory used by Internet Explorer may grow quickly. This memory is reclaimed by clicking the Refresh button. However, if you leave Digital Dashboard running for many hours or days, the computer may slow down because of a memory shortage because IE is not correctly performing garbage collection.

To avoid having to manually click Refresh every x minutes, you can write a script that does this automatically for you in VBScript (or you could use another scripting language). You can add the following to your Web page:

```
<script language="vbscript">
sub Refresh()
top.History.go 0
end sub
</script>
```

And then have a call to call it every x seconds:

```
SetInterval("Refresh()",10000)
```

The SetInterval sets a timer for the Refresh() calls, and 10,000 is the number of milliseconds between each call.

FAQ 24.39 Why after upgrading to Windows 2000 has my Internet Explorer 5.5 installation been downgraded to IE 5.0?

This is by design. Windows 2000 ships with Internet Explorer 5.0, and if you have manually installed 5.5 before upgrading, the Windows 2000 Upgrade Exception pack that is included with Internet Explorer 5.5 downgrades Internet Explorer to version 5.0 for compatibility with Windows 2000.

Once you have upgraded to Windows 2000, you can then install the IE 5.5 product for Windows 2000.

FAQ 24.40 How can I check my previous version of Internet Explorer?

When you install Internet Explorer 4 or 5, it stores the previous version of Internet Explorer in HKEY_LOCAL_MACHINE\SOFTWARE\Microsoft\IE Setup\Setup\PreviousIESysFile for IE 5.0 installations or HKEY_LOCAL_MACHINE\SOFTWARE\Microsoft\IE4\Setup\PreviousIESysFile for IE 4.0 installations.

The possible values are listed in the following table:

Value	Version
4.70.0.1155	3.0
4.70.0.1158	3.0
4.70.0.1215	3.01
4.70.0.1300	3.02
4.72.3110.3	Windows 98 Internet Explorer

FAQ 24.41 How can I create a fifth security zone in Internet Explorer?

By default Internet Explorer has four security zones; however, it's possible to add a fifth by directly editing the Registry. If you copy the following into 5TH.REG and then double-click, the fifth zone will be created:

```
REGEDIT4

[HKEY_CURRENT_USER\Software\Microsoft\Windows\CurrentVersion\
Internet Settings\Zones\5]
@=""
"DisplayName"="Internet with Cookies"
"Description"="This zone contains all Web sites you haven't placed
in other zones"
"Icon"="inetcpl.cpl#001313"
"CurrentLevel"=dword:00000000
"MinLevel"=dword:00011000
"RecommendedLevel"=dword:00011000
"Flags"=dword:00000003
"1001"=dword:00000001
"1004"=dword:00000003
"1200"=dword:00000000
"1201"=dword:00000003
"1400"=dword:00000000
"1402"=dword:00000000
"1405"=dword:00000000
```

```
"1406"=dword:00000001
"1407"=dword:00000000
"1601"=dword:00000101
"1604"=dword:00000000
"1605"=dword:00000000
"1606"=dword:00000000
"1607"=dword:00000000
"1800"=dword:00000001
"1802"=dword:00000000
"1803"=dword:00000000
"1804"=dword:00000001
"1805"=dword:00000001
"1A00"=dword:00020000
"1A02"=dword:00000000
"1A03"=dword:00000000
"1C00"=dword:00010000
"1E05"=dword:00020000
```

If you now restart Internet Explorer, a new option will be available under Tools > Internet Options > Security, which you can select (see Figure 24-6).

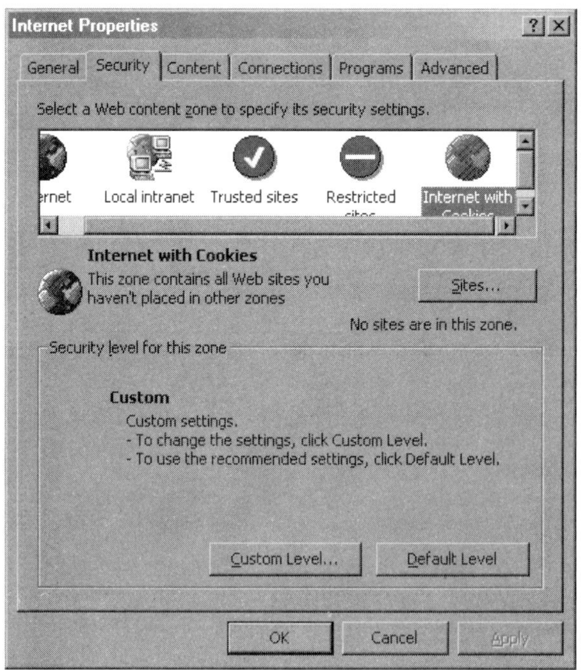

Figure 24-6 Setting a security zone

FAQ 24.42 Why does Office 2000 not work after I've installed IE 5 Service Pack 1?

This is an amazing fault and questions the testing performed. Basically after you installed Service Pack 1 for Internet Explorer 5, you receive an error:

```
Help requires Microsoft Internet Explorer 3.0 or greater. You can
install the latest version of IE from www.Microsoft.com.
```

The problem is that IE 5 SP1 sets the build in the Registry of Windows 2000 using an incorrect format for the build number. So Office thinks IE is a **very** old build.

To correct, perform the following:

1. Start the Registry editor (REGEDIT.EXE).
2. Move to HKEY_LOCAL_MACHINE\SOFTWARE\Microsoft\Internet Explorer.
3. Double-click Build.
4. It will be 5.00.3103.1000. This is the wrong format; normal Internet Explorer 5 is 52920, so change the value of build to 52920.
5. Click OK.

Office 2000 Help is now OK. This is also fixed with Internet Explorer 5.5, which sets the value to 54134.0600.

FAQ 24.43 How can I change the "- Microsoft Internet Explorer" text appended to the title of all Microsoft Internet Explorer windows?

Perform the following steps to change the IE title:

1. Start REGEDIT.EXE.
2. Navigate to HKEY_CURRENT_USER\SOFTWARE\Microsoft\Internet Explorer\Main.
3. From the Edit menu, select New, String value.
4. Type a new value name of **Window Title** and press Enter.
5. Double-click the new value, type the title you'd like to appear in place of the IE title (e.g., SavillTech Web), and click OK.
6. Close REGEDIT.EXE.

Figure 24-7 A modified Internet Explorer title bar

The change takes effect immediately (see Figure 24-7). To remove your new title, simply delete the Windows Title value you created in step 4.

FAQ 24.44 How do I toggle IE to show or hide images on Web pages?

In the early days of the Web, images didn't appear automatically in browser windows because of bandwidth limitations. Instead, just a placeholder appeared. Today, you can configure IE to show or hide images.

1. Start IE.
2. From the Tools menu, select Internet Options.
3. Select the Advanced tab and scroll down to the Multimedia section.
4. Select or clear the Show pictures checkbox.
5. Click Apply, then click OK. The change will take effect the next time you view a Web page.

FAQ 24.45 How can I keep the Internet Connection Wizard from running and still let my users access the Internet?

Although a policy template exists that lets you disable the Internet Connection Wizard (ICW), restricted users can't run IE until they have run the ICW at least once. If you are using Windows 2000, follow the steps that Microsoft article Q250380 presents, making sure you can view all hidden and system folders so the Default User profile shows up. This approach works well on Win2K but doesn't apply under Windows NT. What follows is one way to create a system that lets any new user create a profile at the first logon and not be forced to run the ICW when attempting to start IE. This fix was designed for single systems that have multiple users with unique logons.

To suppress the ICW when a new user logs on under Win2K or NT, perform the following steps:

1. Start REGEDIT.EXE.
2. Go to HKEY_USERS\.DEFAULT\Software\Microsoft.
3. From the Edit menu, select New > Key.
4. For the new key, enter a name of **Internet Connection Wizard** and press Enter.
5. Go to the new key.
6. From the Edit menu, select New > DWORD value.
7. For the new value, enter a name of **DesktopChanged** and press Enter.
8. Double-click the DesktopChanged value and set it to 1. Click OK.
9. From the Edit menu, select New > Binary value.
10. For the new binary value, enter a name of **Completed** and press Enter.
11. Double-click the Completed binary value and set it to 01 00 00 00. Click OK.
12. Close Regedit.

The system will no longer prompt new users to run the ICW.

FAQ 24.46 What restrictions are available with Internet Explorer 5.01 Service Pack 1 and above?

With Internet Explorer 5.x, you have many options for limiting the actions that users can perform (see the following table for a complete list). You can apply these restrictions either to one user by setting the HKEY_CURRENT_USER\SOFTWARE\Policies\Microsoft\Internet Explorer\Restrictions Registry key or to all users by setting the HKEY_LOCAL_MACHINE\SOFTWARE\Policies\Microsoft\Internet Explorer\Restrictions Registry key. If you set a restriction at both the user and the machine level, the machine level setting takes precedence. A value of 1 enables the restriction; a value of 0 disables the restriction.

To add a restriction, perform the following steps:

1. Start REGEDIT.EXE.
2. Go to either HKEY_CURRENT_USER\SOFTWARE\Policies\Microsoft\Internet Explorer\Restrictions (for a user) or HKEY_LOCAL_

MACHINE\SOFTWARE\Policies\Microsoft\Internet Explorer\Restrictions (for all users).

3. From the Edit menu, select New > DWORD Value.
4. In the table that follows this procedure, find the desired value, enter it for the Value name, and press Enter.
5. Double-click the new value and set it to 1 to enable the restriction. Click OK.
6. Close Regedit.

Value	Description
NoToolbarCustomize	Customize the toolbar.
NoBandCustomize	Customize the band.
SmallIcons	Force small icons.
LockIconSize	Change the icon size.
SpecifyDefaultButtons	Must be set to 1 if you are going to disable any of the default buttons, such as the Back button (Btn_Back).
Btn_Back	Back button and menu item.
Btn_Forward	Forward button and menu item.
Btn_Stop	Stop button and menu item.
Btn_Refresh	Refresh button and menu item.
Btn_Home	Home button and menu item.
Btn_Search	Search button and menu item.
Btn_History	History button and menu item.
Btn_Favorites	Favorites button and menu item.
Btn_Folders	Folders Options command on the View menu.
Btn_Fullscreen	Full Screen command on the Edit menu.
Btn_Tools	Tools button and menu item.
Btn_MailNews	Mail and News button and menu item.
Btn_Size	Edit text size menu item.

Value	Description
Btn_Print	Print button and menu item.
Btn_Edit	Edit menu item.
Btn_Discussions	Discussion button and menu item.
Btn_Cut	Edit/Cut menu item.
Btn_Copy	Edit/Copy menu item.
Btn_Paste	Edit/Paste menu item.
Btn_Encoding	View/Encoding menu item.
NoWindowsUpdate	Removes Windows Update from the Tools menu.
NoExpandedNewMenu	Expand new menus.
NoFileUrl	Run link to local file URL.
NoChannelUI	Channels user interface.
NoAddingChannels	Add channels.
NoEditingChannels	Edit channels.
NoRemovingChannels	Remove channels.
NoAddingSubscriptions	Add subscriptions.
NoEditingSubscriptions	Edit subscriptions.
NoRemovingSubscriptions	Remove subscriptions.
NoChannelLogging	Channel logging.
NoManualUpdates	Manual updates.
NoScheduledUpdates	Update schedules.
NoUnattendedDialing	Unattended dialing.
NoChannelContent	Channel Channel Definition Formats (CDFs) will be delivered but without content. Overrides the per-channel settings.

(*continued*)

Value	Description
NoSubscriptionContent	Subscriptions will be monitored for changes, but content will not be downloaded.
NoEditingScheduleGroups	Edit schedule groups and create new ones.
MaxChannelSize	Maximum size in KB of channel elements in the cache. Overrides channel maximums the user sets.
MaxSubscriptionSize	Maximum size in KB of subscription elements in the cache. Overrides subscription maximums the user sets.
MaxChannelCount	User can't add more than n channels. Not applied retroactively. Administrators can push more than n. N may not be zero.
MaxSubscriptionCount	User can't add more than n subscriptions. Not applied retroactively. Administrators can push more than n. N may not be zero.
MinUpdateInterval	Channels and subscriptions can't be updated more often than this number of minutes.
UpdateExcludeBegin	Number of minutes from midnight where schedule changes are excluded. Zero is not valid.
UpdateExcludeEnd	End of a range in which to exclude schedule updates. May be lower than UpdateExcludeBegin.
UpdateInNewProcess	Subscriptions will be updated in a separate process, making the system more stable but slightly slower.
MaxWebcrawlLevels	Site subscriptions will be limited to MaxWebcrawlLevels—1. Zero disables the restriction.
MaxChannelLevels	Channel subscriptions that contain LEVEL tags will be limited to MaxChannelLevels—1.Zero disables the restriction.
NoSubscriptionPasswords	Prevents the entering and caching of passwords.
NoBrowserSaveWebComplete	Only save as .HTML, .HTM, or .TXT.
NoSearchCustomization	Customize search.
NoSplash	Startup splash screen.
NoFileOpen	File/Open menu item (IE only).

Value	Description
NoFileNew	File/New menu item (IE only).
NoBrowserSaveAs	File/Save as menu item (IE only).
NoBrowserOptions	Tools/Internet options menu item (IE only).
NoFavorites	Favorites menu item (IE only).
NoSelectDownloadDir	Select download directory (IE only).
NoBrowserContextMenu	Browser context menu (IE only).
NoBrowserClose	Close browser (IE only).
NoOpeninNewWnd	New browser window (IE only).
NoTheaterMode	Theater mode (IE only).
NoFindFiles	Find files dialog (IE only).
NoViewSource	Edit/View source menu item (IE only).
RestGoMenu	View/Go to menu item (IE only).
NoToolbarOptions	Toolbar options (IE only).
AlwaysPromptWhenDownload	Always prompts when downloading (IE only).
NoHelpItemTipOfTheDay	Tip of the day (IE only).
NoHelpItemNetscapeHelp	Netscape help (IE only).
NoHelpItemTutorial	Tutorial (IE only).
NoHelpItemSendFeedback	Send feedback (IE only).
NoNavButtons	Navigation buttons (IE only).
NoHelpMenu	Help menu item (IE only). (There is a known problem with this not working with IE 5.01 SP1, and a fix is available.)
NoBrowserBars	Browser bars (IE only).
NoToolBar	Toolbar (IE only).
NoAddressBar	Address bar (IE only).
NoLinksBar	Links bar (IE only).

NoFindFiles and NoTheaterMode are created by default during the installation of Service Pack 2 but are of type BINARY due to limitations of .INF files. You can, if you wish, delete and recreate these values as DWORD values.

FAQ 24.47 How can I set Advanced Internet Explorer settings using Group Policy?

The Internet Explorer Maintenance portion of the Group Policy (User Configuration > Windows Settings) has a hidden option. To access this option, perform the following steps:

1. Open the Group Policy you want to modify.
2. Expand User Configuration > Windows Settings.
3. Right-click Internet Explorer Maintenance.
4. Select Preference Mode from the context menu.
5. The system will add a new Advanced branch with two groups, Corporate and Internet Settings. Double-click one of them.

   The system will open a dialog box with various settings that you can change as desired. (The Advanced Settings option under the Internet Settings is **very** useful—see Figure 24-8.)
6. Click OK.

If you want to remove the Advanced object, you must select Reset Browser Settings, which loses all your other settings but removes the Advanced object. Likewise, if a Group Policy is already applied, you need to reset it and then enable the Preference mode.

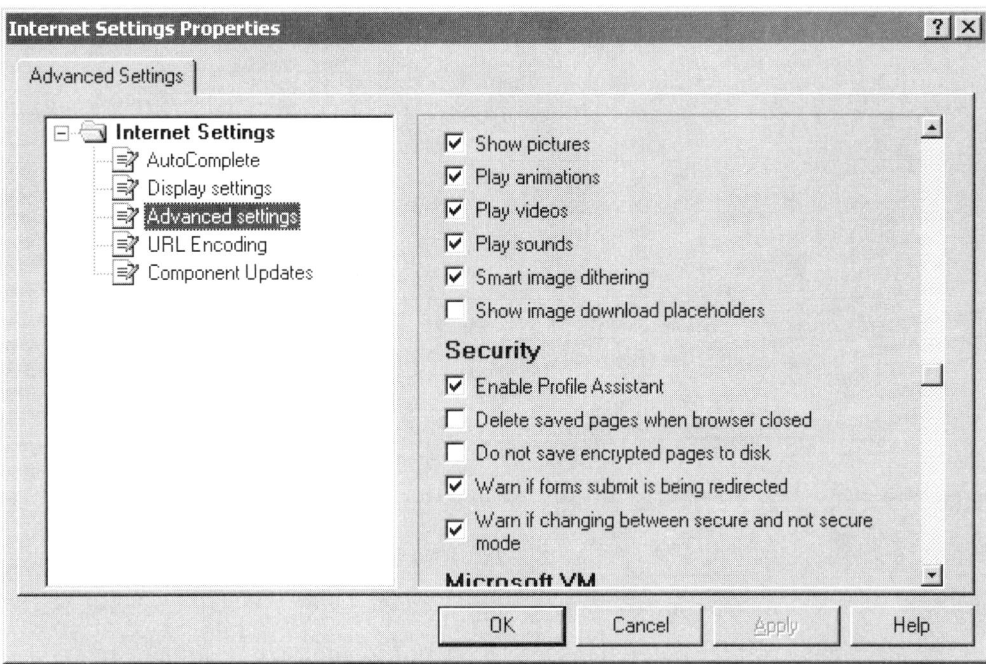

Figure 24-8 Configuring advanced Internet settings

FAQ 24.48 How can I clear saved passwords/form information from within Internet Explorer?

IE has a neat feature—AutoComplete—that remembers previous answers to password prompts/forms and automatically fills them in on subsequent visits. If you want to clear this information, perform the following steps:

1. Start IE.
2. From the Tools menu, select Internet Options.
3. Select the Content tab.
4. Click Autocomplete.
5. Click Clear Forms if you want to remove all information except passwords. Click Clear Passwords to clear only passwords.
6. Click OK to the confirmation.
7. Close all dialog boxes.

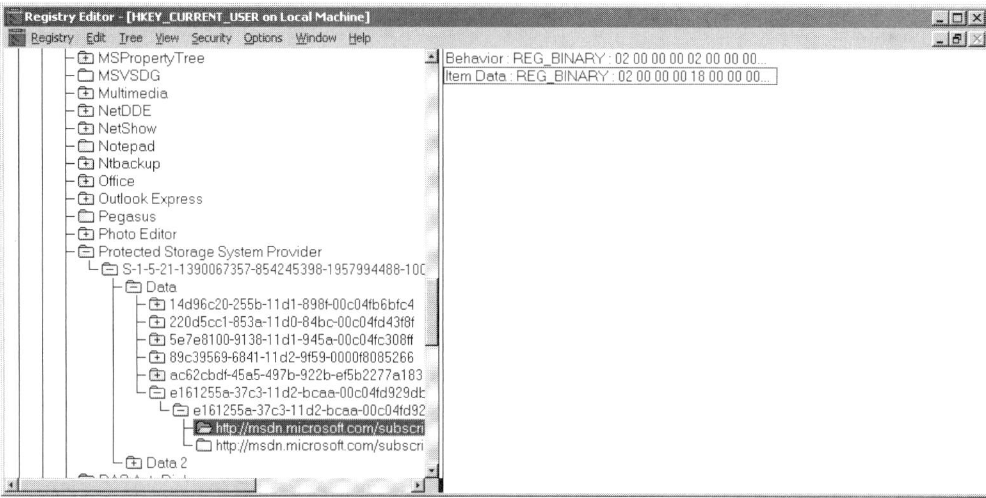

Figure 24-9 My encrypted MSDN password (well, some of it ☺)

The actual information is stored in a protected portion of the Registry under HKEY_CURRENT_USER\SOFTWARE\Microsoft\Protected Storage System Provider\[SID of the user]\Data. However, a user can't view the information (although as you're an Administrator, you can change the access control list—ACL—via REGEDT32.EXE to have a look). For example, in Figure 24-9, you can see my (encrypted!) password to the MSDN download area.

24.49 How do I use Internet Explorer in Kiosk mode?

IE has a full-screen mode that you access by pressing F11; however, the screen still shows boxes to minimize, resize, or close the window. The Kiosk mode, on the other hand, hides all buttons. To start IE in Kiosk mode, from the Run prompt (Start > Run), start IE with the following command:

```
iexplore -k [site]
```

where [site] is

- Blank—Uses your default start page
- A URL (e.g., http://www.savilltech.com)—Uses the page the URL specifies

- A local Web page (e.g., c:\folder\page.htm)—Uses the specified local page
- A remote Web page (e.g., \\server\share\folder\page.htm)—Uses the remote page

For example, to start IE in Kiosk mode with the Windows 2000 FAQ site as the start page, type the following command:

```
iexplore -k http://www.windows2000faq.com
```

Within Kiosk mode, you can use the commands in the following table:

Ctrl+A	Select all (editing)
Ctrl+B	Organize favorites
Ctrl+C	Copy (editing)
Ctrl+F	Find (on current page)
Ctrl+H	View History folder
Ctrl+L	Open Location dialog box (same as Ctrl+O)
Ctrl+N	New window (opens in non-Kiosk mode)
Ctrl+O	Open Location dialog box (same as Ctrl+L)
Ctrl+P	Print
Ctrl+R	Refresh
Ctrl+S	Save
Ctrl+V	Paste (editing)
Ctrl+W	Close (same as Alt+F4)
Ctrl+X	Cut (editing)
Alt+F4	Close (same as Ctrl+W)
Alt+Left Arrow	Back
Alt+Right Arrow	Forward
Esc	Stop
F5	Refresh

24.50 How can I remove the Task Scheduler from Internet Explorer 5.0 if the Add/Remove Programs option isn't available?

When the Add/Remove Programs option isn't available, you need to remove IE 5.0's Task Scheduler the old fashioned way (i.e., edit the Registry).

1. Start REGEDIT.EXE.
2. Go to HKEY_LOCAL_MACHINE\SOFTWARE\Microsoft\Windows\CurrentVersion\Uninstall\SchedulingAgent.
3. Double-click the UninstallString value.
4. Copy the value data and click OK.
5. Close Regedit.
6. In the Run dialog box (Start > Run), paste the content from the UninstallString and click OK.

The system will remove the Task Scheduler.

24.51 How can I back up the Internet Explorer AutoComplete URLs?

When you type a URL in Internet Explorer, the system automatically completes known entries, which are located in the Registry key HKEY_CURRENT_USER\SOFTWARE\Microsoft\Internet Explorer\TypedURLs. To back up this key, perform the following steps:

1. Start REGEDIT.EXE.
2. Go to HKEY_CURRENT_USER\Software\Microsoft\Internet Explorer.
3. Select TypedURLs.
4. From the Registry menu, select Export Registry File.
5. In the Save In box, select the location where you want to save the key, give the key a name, and click Save.

To restore the key, perform the same steps, but in step 4, select Import Registry File, and select the file you created in step 5.

FAQ 24.52 How can I enable/disable style sheets in Internet Explorer?

In Web pages, style sheets make the content look better. However, at times, you might want to restrict their use. To do so, perform the following steps:

1. Start REGEDIT.EXE.
2. Go to HKEY_CURRENT_USER\SOFTWARE\Microsoft\Internet Explorer\Main.
3. Double-click Use StyleSheets (or create this value of type String if it doesn't exist).
4. To allow style sheets, set StyleSheets to Yes; to disallow, set it to No.
5. Click OK.
6. Close Regedit.
7. Restart Internet Explorer.

FAQ 24.53 How can I enable or disable the QuickLaunch icons?

You can remove the QuickLaunch icons by setting the following Registry entry to 0: HKEY_CURRENT_USER\Software\Microsoft\Windows\CurrentVersion\Policies\Explorer\ClassicShell

If the icons are missing and you want them, simply delete the preceding value.

FAQ 24.54 MSN Messenger Service starts each time I log on, but it isn't in a Startup group. How do I stop it?

The MSN Messenger Service places itself in the run portion of the Registry as %systemdrive%:\Program Files\Messenger\msmsgs.exe /background. If you want to remove MSN Messenger Service entirely, use the Add/Remove programs Control Panel applet. However, if you simply want to stop the Messenger Service from starting, perform the following steps:

1. Start REGEDIT.EXE.
2. Go to HKEY_CURRENT_USER\Software\Microsoft\Windows\CurrentVersion\Run.

3. Right-click the MSMSGS entry and select Delete.
4. Click Yes to the confirmation.

24.55 I've upgraded to Internet Explorer 5.0. Why don't I have the option to enable Active Desktop?

When you upgrade to IE 5.0 from an earlier version that doesn't have Active Desktop, Active Desktop won't be installed. To resolve this problem, you must remove IE 5.0, reinstall your original IE version adding the Active Desktop option, then reinstall IE 5.0.

24.56 When I try to install Internet Explorer 5.0, why do I get an error message?

When you try to install IE 5.0, you might receive the following error message:

```
Windows Update Setup

A previous program installation was never completed. You need to
restart your computer to complete that installation before running
Internet Explorer Setup. Setup will now close.
```

You receive this error message because a previous program installation still has pending file-rename operations. IE won't install until all the rename operations complete. If you reboot your computer, you should be able to proceed with the IE installation. If you receive the same error message, you need to remove the pending operations. Perform the following steps:

1. Start REGEDIT.EXE.
2. Go to HKEY_LOCAL_MACHINE\SYSTEM\CurrentControlSet\Control\Session Manager.
3. Double-click PendingFileRenameOperations and remove any entries. Click OK.
4. Also check the following locations for any rename operations:
   - HKEY_LOCAL_MACHINE\Software\Microsoft\Windows\CurrentVersion\RunOnce
   - HKEY_LOCAL_MACHINE\Software\Microsoft\Windows\CurrentVersion\RunOnceEx

- HKEY_LOCAL_MACHINE\Software\Microsoft\Windows\CurrentVersion\RunServicesOnce
- HKEY_CURRENT_USER\Software\Microsoft\Windows\CurrentVersion\RunOnce

5. Close Regedit.

FAQ 24.57 Why does Internet Explorer hang when it accesses Temporary Internet files (disk cache)?

IE can enter a state where it almost immediately hangs and starts to use 100% of CPU time. In particular, trying to delete Temporary Internet files via Tools > Internet Options triggers this behavior. Also, all attempts to delete files or folders from %systemdrive%\Documents and Settings\%username%\Local Settings\Temporary Internet Files (or wherever the Temporary Internet files folder is located) causes Windows Explorer to hang. This behavior occurs because the Temporary Internet files database is corrupt.

The Temporary Internet files aren't really files but entries in %systemdrive%\Documents and Settings\%username%\Local Settings\Temporary Internet Files\Content.IE5\index.dat. Deleting that file solves the problem.

1. Exit IE and Windows Explorer (IEXPLORE.EXE and EXPLORER.EXE, respectively, in Task Manager).
2. Use the following command from a command prompt to delete the file:

```
del "%systemdrive%\Documents and Settings\%username%\Local
Settings\Temporary Internet Files\Content.IE5\index.dat"
```

3. Restart IE and Windows Explorer.

FAQ 24.58 How do I disable or enable the flashing toolbar that IE 6 installs?

IE 6 displays a new four-button toolbar, as shown in Figure 24-10, when the mouse hovers over a Web image.

The four tools let you save the image to disk, print it, or send it in an e-mail message, or open the My Pictures folder. To disable or enable the toolbar, perform the following steps:

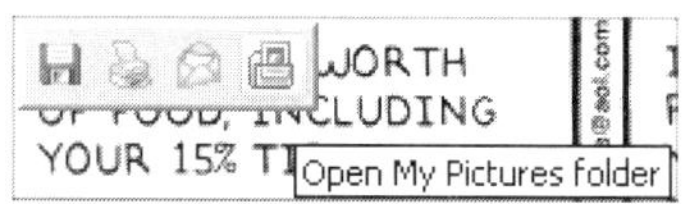

Figure 24-10 The four-button picture dialog

1. Start IE.
2. From the Tools menu, select Internet Options.
3. Select the Advanced tab.
4. Scroll down to Multimedia.
5. Select (to enable) or clear (to disable) the Enable Image Toolbar (requires restart) checkbox (see Figure 24-11).
6. Click OK.
7. Close IE and any other applications and restart your computer.

Figure 24-11 Configuring the Image Toolbar via Internet options

FAQ 24.59 How do I install the Windows Desktop Update component directly from the Internet Explorer 5.0 setup process?

You usually must first install IE 4.0 with the Windows Desktop Update component, then upgrade to IE 5.0 or higher. However, you can perform the following steps to directly install the component from the IE 5.0 setup process:

1. Run IE 5.0's setup file (IE5SETUP.EXE).
2. When IE 5.0's license dialog box appears, find IESETUP.CIF in one of the subdirectories of the Windows Temp directory.
3. Open IESETUP.CIF with Notepad and locate in [IE4Shell_Win] (for Windows 98/95) or [IE4Shell_NTx86] (for Windows NT) DisplayName= %MSIE4Shell%. Change UIVISIBLE=0 to UIVISIBLE=1 and save the file.
4. Accept the license, then click CustomInstall.
5. You can see the Windows Desktop Update component in the components list. Select it and any other components you need. Then click Continue.

FAQ 24.60 Why do I receive the error "The procedure entry point PrivacyGetZonePreferenceW could not be located in the dynamic link library WININET.dll." when I try to use the Internet Explorer Administration Kit (IEAK) 6?

This error indicates that you've tried to use IEAK 6 without first installing Microsoft Internet Explorer 6, which the IEAK requires to access the updated WININET.DLL file. To fix the problem, simply install IE 6.

FAQ 24.61 What is the Internet Explorer 6 unsafe-file list?

IE 6 contains a hard-coded list of unsafe files in the SHDOCVW.DLL file. IE 6 uses the unsafe-file list to prevent you from accidentally opening a file type that might cause problems on your computer.

The complete list of unsafe extensions is

.AD	.ASP	.BAT	.CMD
.ADP	.BAS	.CHM	.COM

.CPL	.JSE	.PIF	.VBS
.CRT	.LNK	.REG	.VSD
.EXE	.MDB	.SCR	.VSS
.HLP	.MDE	.SCT	.VST
.HTA	.MSC	.SHB	.VSW
.INF	.MSI	.SHS	.WS
.INS	.MSP	.URL	.WSC
.ISP	.MST	.VB	.WSF
.JS	.PCD	.VBE	.WSH

To add file extensions to the unsafe-file list, perform the following steps:

1. Start the Registry editor (REGEDIT.EXE).
2. Navigate to HKEY_LOCAL_MACHINE\SOFTWARE\Microsoft\Internet Explorer\UnsafeFiles\Include (if this Registry value doesn't exist, you'll need to create it).
3. From the Edit menu, select New > Key.
4. Enter a name of the extension you want to add (e.g., enter .txt as HKEY_LOCAL_MACHINE\SOFTWARE\Microsoft\Internet Explorer\UnsafeFiles\Include\.txt).
5. Close the Registry editor.

To establish exceptions to the core product's unsafe-file list, perform the following steps:

1. Start the Registry editor (REGEDIT.EXE).
2. Navigate to HKEY_LOCAL_MACHINE\SOFTWARE\Microsoft\Internet Explorer\UnsafeFiles\Exclude (if this Registry value doesn't exist, you'll need to create it).
3. From the Edit menu, select New > Key.
4. Enter the name of the extension you want to exclude (e.g., enter .exe as HKEY_LOCAL_MACHINE\SOFTWARE\Microsoft\Internet Explorer\UnsafeFiles\Exclude\.exe).
5. Close the Registry editor.

If you remove the Registry entries, Windows will restore the IE 6 unsafe-file list to its default values.

FAQ 24.62 Why do I receive Microsoft Passport-related errors when I visit some Web sites?

I recently encountered this problem in the Microsoft Developer Network (MSDN) subscriber download area. I could connect to several Microsoft Passport-related Web sites, but I was unable to use my Microsoft Passport to connect to the MSDN site.

To remedy this situation, I had to delete my MSDN Microsoft Passport cookie. Your Web browser stores cookies on your computer in the Cookies subfolder of your user profile using the following format:

```
<username>@<site name>
```

If you're running IE 5.5 or IE 6.0, you can choose to delete all cookies simultaneously. However, if you remove all your cookies, you'll lose any information contained within your Web site profiles. To remove all cookies in IE 5.5 or IE 6.0, perform the following steps:

1. Start IE.
2. From the Tools menu, select Internet Options.
3. In the Temporary Internet files section of the General tab, click Delete Cookies.
4. Click OK.
5. Close IE.

FAQ 24.63 Why does IE save pictures from the Web in bitmap format even though the pictures exist in another format?

This problem in IE will manifest when you attempt to save a picture to disk. Your only option is to save the picture as a .BMP file instead of as a native .GIF or .JPG file. Because several situations can lead to this problem, I've listed them along with a suggested solution.

- Your Temporary Internet files cache is full—Delete the temporary Internet files by selecting Tools > Internet Options, General tab, then clicking Delete Files.
- You selected Do not save encrypted pages to disk under Tools > Internet Options, Advanced tab and are loading the page over a secure connection

(i.e., HTTP over Secure Sockets Layer—HTTPS)—Uncheck the Do not save encrypted pages to disk option and select View > Refresh to reload the page.

- You connect to a Web site using an address that contains a username and password (e.g., http://<username:password@site>/default.htm instead of http://<site>/default.htm)—To remedy this problem, perform the following steps:
  1. Open the Temporary Internet Files directory and locate the image that you attempted to save.
  2. Right-click the image and click Open.
  3. When the image loads into IE, right-click the image and click Save Picture As. The file type and name should be correct.

FAQ 24.64 How do I disable IntelliMenus (i.e, personalized menus) in Internet Explorer Favorites?

To disable the Internet Explorer personalized menus, perform the following:

1. Select Options from the Tools menu.
2. Select the Advanced tab.
3. Uncheck Enable Personalized Favorites Menu and click OK.

This can also be set via the Registry:

1. Start the Registry editor (REGEDIT.EXE).
2. Move to HKEY_CURRENT_USER\Software\Microsoft\Internet Explorer\Main.
3. Set FavIntelliMenus to no (if it does not exist, create it of type String).
4. Close the Registry editor.

FAQ 24.65 How do I disable the HTML Source Editor check in Internet Explorer?

When you open files in Internet Explorer, it checks the creator meta tags and modifies the Edit option under File accordingly from the default (e.g., if it was created in Word, IE will say "Edit with Microsoft Word"; if the file was created in FrontPage, IE will say "Edit with Microsoft FrontPage"). If you would prefer to use your default editor, perform the following:

1. Start the Registry editor (REGEDIT.EXE).
2. Move to HKEY_CURRENT_USER\Software\Microsoft\Internet Explorer\Main.
3. From the Edit menu, select New > String value.
4. Enter a name of **CheckDocumentForProgID** and press Enter.
5. Double-click the new value and set to No. Click OK.
6. Close the Registry editor.

25 PERFORMANCE

With great power comes great responsibility. Windows' power has increased substantially, but with that power, the tuning we can perform gives even greater improvements.

There will always be a bottleneck in a system; otherwise, tasks would finish instantly. Our goal is to have our systems perform the requirements in an acceptable (and realistic) time frame. The term "bottleneck" comes from visualizing a bottle when you're pouring water. The pouring of the liquid is slowed by the neck of the bottle, which is limiting the amount of liquid that can drain out of the bottle.

Physicist Werner Heisenberg's uncertainty principle states that measuring the exact position and exact momentum of a particle at the same time is physically impossible—the act of observing interferes with the observation. This principle also applies to performance monitoring. When you monitor performance, you use additional CPU time; if you enable disk monitoring, you will experience slower disk access. However, the resource use is negligible and rarely affects your results significantly.

FAQ 25.1 How do I move my pagefile?

Follow this procedures:

1. Start Control Panel and double-click the System icon.
2. Click Performance and Virtual Memory Change. (Under 2000 and above, select the Advanced tab and select Settings under Performance; select the Advanced tab on the new dialog and under Virtual Memory, click Change.)
3. Select the current pagefile disk, change the initial size to 0, and click Set.
4. Select a different disk, change initial size and max size, and click Set.
5. Click OK and then close.
6. Reboot machine.

FAQ 25.2 How big and where should my pagefile be?

Following are things to consider:

- Do not have two pagefiles on the same physical disk.
- The pagefile should be size of memory +11MB (or 2.5 times the size of the Security Access Manager—SAM—file, whichever is larger).
- If possible, have multiple pagefiles on separate physical disks.
- Some performance gains are to be had by placing a pagefile on a stripe set; however, not as much as on separate disks.
- Defragment the disk the pagefile is on.
- Try to make the drive NTFS.
- Minimum pagefile size is 2MB.

To enhance performance, one can create a second pagefile on another physical disk. **Moving**, however, is never advised, because it disables the option to create a memory dump file at a crash (System Properties > Startup tab). In order to be able to dump the RAM content to the pagefile (saved, for example, as MEMORY.DMP), the pagefile **must** be located (as well) on the boot partition.

FAQ 25.3 Users complain that the server response is slow, but when I use the server everything is fine. Why is the server response slow?

It could be the server screensaver! The Open GL screensavers (especially the pipes) can use every CPU cycle off the server. In general, you should always use the blank screen-saver on a server.

FAQ 25.4 How can I tell if I need a faster CPU?

You use Performance Monitor (Start > Programs > Administrative Tools > Performance Monitor) to see how much time the computer is waiting to use the CPU:

1. Start Performance.
2. Click the plus (+) button (if you cannot see a title bar, press Ctlr+T).
3. From the drop-down Object box, select System.
4. Select Processor Queue Length from the counters.

5. Monitor the system for a typical day of work, and if the counter exceeds 2, then you should consider a faster processor.

FAQ 25.5 I need to run a number of 16-bit applications. What is the best way to do this?

The best way is to create a shortcut to the 16-bit application, then right-click on the shortcut, and select Properties. Click on the shortcut tab and check the Run in a separate memory space box, which will make the app run in its own VDM (Virtual DOS Machine) with its own memory space. This improves performance and system stability because one 16-bit app can no longer affect another's.

An application can also be forced to run in its own memory space using

```
start /separate <application name>
```

FAQ 25.6 How can I run an application at a higher priority?

It is possible to start an application at a priority other than normal; however, if you run applications at high priority, they may slow performance. Priorities range from 0 to 31. Priorities 0–15 are used by dynamic applications, such as user applications and most of the operating system parts. Priorities 16–31 are used by real-time applications like the kernel, which cannot be written to the pagefile. Normal priority is level 8 (NT 3.51 normal was 7). The full list is

- Realtime priority 24
- High priority 13
- Normal priority 8
- Low priority 4
- Above normal 10 (Windows 2000 only)
- Below normal 6 (Windows 2000 only)

To start an application at a priority other than the default, use the start command—for example:

```
start /<priority> <application>
```

For example: **start /high winword**

To do the same thing from a shortcut, just use:

```
cmd /c start /<priority> <application>
```

Be warned that running applications at high priority may slow performance because other applications get less I/O time. To use the /realtime option, you have to be logged on as a user with Administrator privileges.

To modify the privilege of a currently running application, use Task Manager:

1. Start Task Manager (right-click on the Start bar and select Task Manager).
2. Click on the Processes tab.
3. Right-click on the required process and select Set Priority.
4. You can then select a different priority.
5. Close Task Manager.

It is also possible to increase the priority of whichever application is currently in the foreground, as opposed to the background processes.

1. Start the System Control Panel applet (Start > Settings > Control Panel > System).
2. Click the Performance tab.
3. In the Application Performance tab, move the arrow

None—The foreground application runs the same as background applications (quantum value of 6).
Middle—The foreground application has its priority increased to a quantum value of 12; background applications stay the same.
Maximum—The foreground application has its priority increased to 18; background applications stay the same.

25.7 How can I monitor processes that start after I start the Performance Monitor?

If you are running Performance Monitor in Log mode, after the log is closed and you wish to view certain processes in the drop-down list, you will only see processes that were running at the time you started the log. This is not true ☺.

1. Start Performance Monitor (Start > Programs > Administrative Tools > Performance Monitor).
2. Select Log View (View > Log or Ctrl+L).

3. Add to the log the objects you wish to monitor (Edit > Add to Log), including Process. When finished, click Done.
4. From the Options menu, select Log and enter a filename and a period of time. Click Start Log.
5. When you have logged enough, switch to Performance Monitor, and from Options menu, select Log and then select Stop Log.
6. Move to Chart view (View > Chart or Ctrl+C).
7. Load in the log you created by selecting Options > Data From , and selecting the file and click OK.
8. From the Edit menu, select Add and add the counters you wish to see. You will notice that under Processes, the instances are only those running when you started—don't worry.
9. There will probably be an area you wish to investigate, such as a spike in CPU use, disk I/O. Alter the time window to start from the peak:
   1. From the Edit menu, select Time Window
   2. Move the left bar until the left line is in the correct place on the chart (i.e., the spike). Click OK.
10. Now from the Edit menu, select Add. Under processes, there will now be processes that were running at **this** point, allowing you to diagnose the problem process. You can also put the time window back to normal, and this process will still show.

What this means is the instances shown are only those running at the start of the time window, so to add other processes running at other times, you may need to continue moving the start of the time window.

NT ONLY

FAQ 25.8 How can I stop Windows NT system code and drivers being paged?

Normally user-mode and kernel-mode drivers and kernel-mode system code is written to either pageable or nonpageable memory. It is possible to configure NT never to page out drivers and system code to the pagefiles that are in the pageable memory area. However, this should be done only on systems with large amounts of RAM, or severe performance problems could develop.

1. Start the Registry editor.
2. Move to HKEY_LOCAL_MACHINE\SYSTEM\CurrentControlSet\Control\Session Manager\Memory Management.

3. Double-click on DisablePagingExecutive and set to 1. Click OK (it is of type DWORD so create it, if it does not exist).
4. Reboot the machine.

25.9 How can I change the size of the pagefile?

We have previously discussed moving the pagefile (see FAQ 25.1). You may just need to modify the size of an existing pagefile or add a new one as an addition to your existing one. Remember the more disk heads, the better the performance, so moving your pagefile to a RAID 0 disk arrangement would give excellent performance (RAID 0 is a stripe set without parity), while writing to a RAID 5 disk may adversely affect performance due to the extra parity information that needs to be written (RAID 5 is a stripe set with parity). There is little point in adding a second pagefile to another partition if it is on the same physical disk; it would be better to just increase the size of the existing file. However, two smaller pagefiles on different physical disks will give better results.

1. Start the System Control panel applet (Start > Settings > Control Panel > System).
2. Click the Performance tab (under 2000 and above, select the Advanced tab and select Settings under Performance; select the Advanced tab on the new dialog and under Virtual Memory, click Change).
3. Under the Virtual Memory section, the currently configured amount is displayed. Click Change.
4. A list of all partitions and the size of any pagefiles that exist will be listed next to them. To modify the size of an existing pagefile, select the drive (e.g., C) and in Paging File Size for Selected Drive, enter a new initial and maximum size. Click Set when you have changed the values. The minimum size is 2MB, but the total size of all pagefiles should be at least the size of memory, +11MB.
5. If you want to add an additional pagefile, select a drive that does not currently have a pagefile (e.g., D), enter an initial and maximum (see Figure 25-1), and then click Set.
6. Once you have completed all changes, click OK.
7. Click OK to the System Control Panel applet.
8. You will have to reboot the machine for the change to take effect.

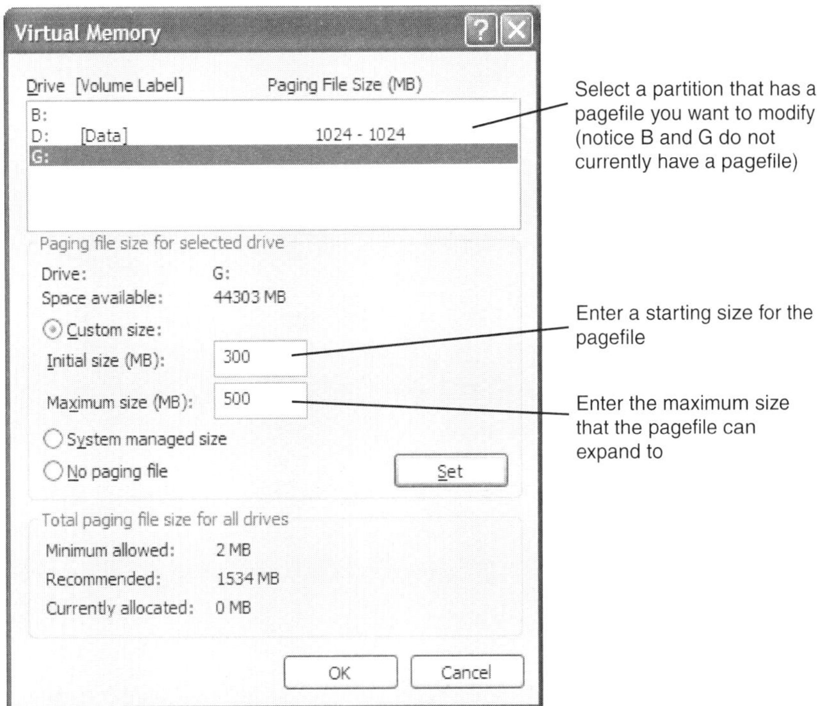

Figure 25-1 Pagefile information

FAQ 25.10 How can I remotely change the size of a pagefile?

Pagefile information is stored in the Registry as a multi_string (so you **have** to use REGEDT32.EXE) to change it locally as follows:

1. Start the Registry editor (REGEDT32.EXE).
2. Move to HKEY_LOCAL_MACHINE\SYSTEM\CurrentControlSet\Control\Session Manager\Memory Management.
3. Double-click PagingFiles.
4. There is one line for each page file with the format (see Figure 25-2)

```
<location> <initial size> <maximum size>
```

For example:

```
C:\pagefile.sys 120 140
```

Click OK.

5. Close the Registry editor.
6. Reboot the machine.

To change it on another machine, you should use the Resource Kit REG.EXE utility, but the following command will replace the current page file and will **not** check whether you have enough disk space. So you may want to create a script that does check. Make sure the machine is rebooted after the change.

```
C:\> reg update
"HKEY_LOCAL_MACHINE\SYSTEM\CurrentControlSet\Control\Session
Manager\Memory Management\PagingFiles"="<location> <initial size>
<max size>" \\<remote machine>
```

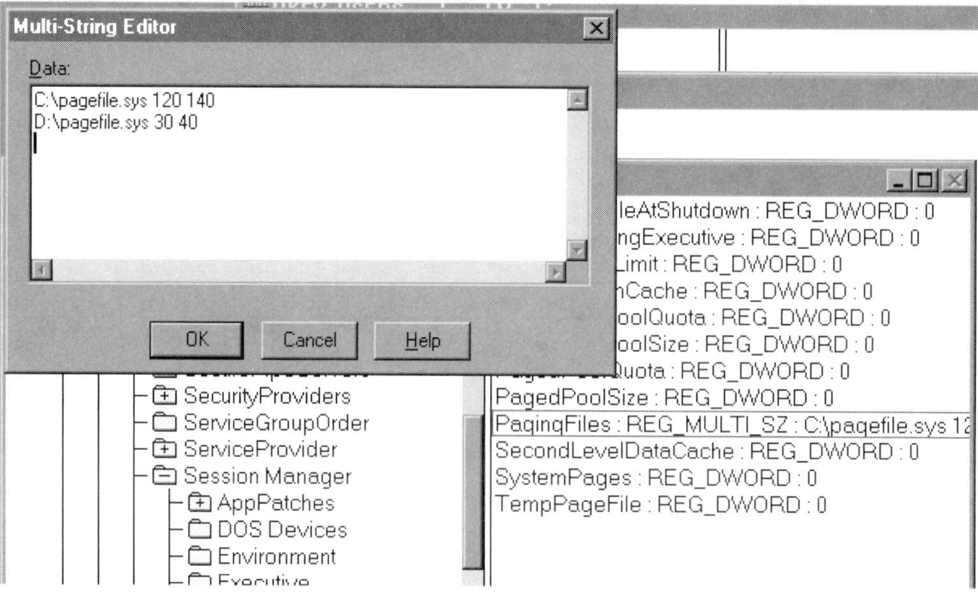

Figure 25-2 Changing pagefile values via the Registry

For example:

```
C:\> reg update
"HKEY_LOCAL_MACHINE\SYSTEM\CurrentControlSet\Control\Session
Manager\Memory Management\PagingFiles"="C:\pagefile.sys 120 140"
\\titanic.savilltech.com
```

Make sure you test this script before trying to use it on live machines.

FAQ 25.11 Why is Performance Monitor not listing all possible objects and counters?

When trying to add a counter and the list of objects and counters is incomplete or blank, the problem could be the data files that hold the list have become corrupted.

Under the Registry key HKEY_LOCAL_MACHINE\SOFTWARE\Microsoft\Windows NT\CurrentVersion\Perflib is a key identifying the language of the system (e.g., 009 for U.S. English). Performance Monitor will only list the counters for the selected language ID (this can be changed via Control Panel).

To resolve the problem, restore the files PERFC<country code>.DAT and PERFH<country code>.DAT (e.g., PERFC009.DAT and PERFH009.DAT for U.S. English) from the installation CD to the %systemroot%\system32 directory.

FAQ 25.12 How do I enable disk counters in Performance Monitor?

In Windows NT 4.0, all disk counters are disabled by default, but the situation is slightly different in Windows 2000. In Windows 2000, the physical disk object is turned **on** by default, and the logical disk object is turned **off** by default.

To enable the logical disk objects, enter the command

```
diskperf -yv
Both Logical and Physical Disk Performance counters on this system
are now set to start at boot.
```

To disable all disk counters, use the following command:

```
diskperf -n
```

The full options are

```
DISKPERF [-Y[D|V] | -N[D|V]] [\\computername]
```

- -Y—Sets the system to start all disk performance counters when you restart the computer.
- -YD—Enables the disk performance counters for physical drives when you restart the computer.
- -YV—Enables the disk performance counters for logical drives or storage volumes when you restart the computer.
- -N—Sets the system to disable all disk performance counters when you restart the computer.
- -ND—Disables the disk performance counters for physical drives.
- -NV—Disables the disk performance counters for logical drives.

FAQ 25.13 How can I configure a program to run interactively in response to a performance alert?

To configure an alert to trigger an application, perform the following steps:

1. Start the Microsoft Management Console (MMC) Performance snap-in (Start > Programs > Administrative Tools > Performance).
2. Expand Performance Logs and Alerts and select Alerts.
3. Right-click in the right pane and select New Alert Settings.
4. Enter a name for the setting that reflects what the alert will monitor and click OK.
5. On the General tab, add the counter the alert will monitor and specify the values that will trigger the action.
6. On the Action tab, select the Run this Program checkbox.
7. Click the Browse button and select the name of the application you want to run.
8. Click OK.

You have just configured an application to run in response to an alert. Unfortunately, because the program doesn't interact with the desktop, it runs in the background, visible only in Task Manager. To enable the program to run interactively, perform the following steps:

1. Start the MMC Services snap-in (Start > Programs > Administrative Tools > Services).
2. Right-click Performance Logs and Alerts and select Properties.
3. On the Log On tab, specify the Local System account and select the Allow service to interact with desktop checkbox as shown in Figure 25-3.

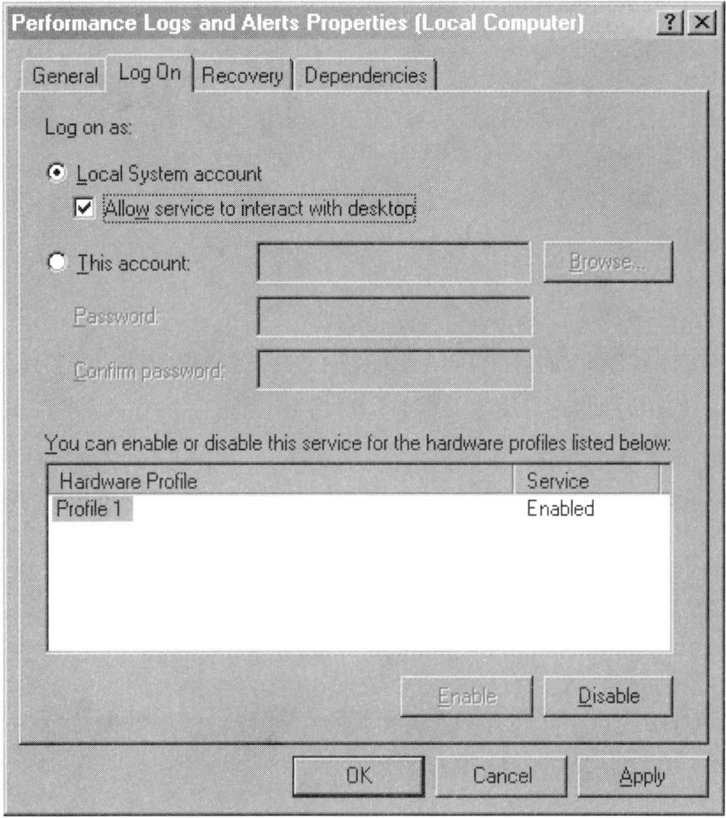

Figure 25-3 Enabling a service to interact with the desktop

4. Click OK.
5. Restart the service, and the change will take effect.

FAQ 25.14 Why is viewing Windows Me or Windows 98 shares from a Windows 2000 machine so slow?

When Win2K attempts to browse shares on a Windows Me or Win9x machine, it also checks for scheduled tasks that are enabled on the machine. Disabling this check speeds browsing. Perform the following steps:

1. Start REGEDIT.EXE.
2. Go to HKEY_LOCAL_MACHINE\SOFTWARE\Microsoft\Windows\CurrentVersion\Explorer\RemoteComputer\NameSpace.
3. Right-click {D6277990-4C6A-11CF-8D87-00AA0060F5BF} and select Delete.
4. Click Yes to the confirmation.
5. Close Regedit.

FAQ 25.15 What is Windows Datacenter Server Limited Edition (Datacenter LE)?

Datacenter LE is a new server product in the Windows product line that Microsoft targets at customers who require high scalability and fast performance on systems that have 16 or more processors. Datacenter LE builds on Windows 2000 Datacenter Server and was available exclusively through the Windows Datacenter Program in the first or second quarter of 2002 for Intel's 64-bit Itanium chipset only.

FAQ 25.16 Why does Windows XP slow down when I enable fast user switching?

When you use an XP system in a workgroup, the fast user switching feature lets multiple users log on to the same computer without requiring the current user to close his or her programs. So, the programs that the first user was running when the next user logged on are still running and using system resources. As a result, the machine will tend to slow down just as the machine would slow down if you were running those same applications in the current session.

This drain on performance isn't a bug, and users need to be aware that the computer is still running the programs in the switched session. To improve performance, you must log on to the other session and close some of the programs. If logging on and closing down some of these other programs isn't an option, you can restart the computer to close the other sessions and free resources. If you are an administrator, you can run Task Manager and terminate other users' processes.

26 PRINTING

We should be living in a paperless society now; everything can be shared via wireless networks to our PDA and stored on tiny media storage devices. Obviously we won't totally turn away from paper because hopefully you may be trying to make up your mind at a bookstore whether to purchase this book. So paper is good, and to encourage the use of paper, we look at the best ways of printing from Windows.

FAQ 26.1 How do I create a queue to a network printer?

If you have a printer that has its own network card and IP address, you can create a queue to the device by following these instructions:

1. Log on as a member of the Administrators group.
2. Start Control Panel (Start > Settings > Control Panel).
3. Double-click Network and select the Services tab.
4. Click Add and select Microsoft TCP/IP printing.
5. Click OK and then Close.
6. Click Yes to the reboot.
7. After the machine has booted up, double-click My Computer (or what you have named it to—you have renamed it!).
8. Double-click Printers and select Add Printer.
9. Select the Printer is a local printer and then continue.
10. Click Add Port and select LPR port.
11. Click New Port. Fill in the IP address of the printer in the top box and a name in the bottom box.
12. Click OK and ignore the error about not being able to communicate.
13. Click Next and then select the printer driver.
14. Click Next and select if you want to share it. Then click Finish.
15. Print and be happy.

26.2 How do I delete a network port (for example, LPT3)?

Network ports are defined in the Registry at HKEY_LOCAL_MACHINE\SOFTWARE\Microsoft\Windows NT\CurrentVersion\Ports. Select the port you wish to delete and from the Edit menu, select Delete.

You can also delete it from the command line

```
net use lpt3: /del
```

26.3 How do I configure my print jobs to wait to print until after work hours?

If you have large print jobs that you would rather run after work hours, it is possible to configure usage hours on a print queue:

1. Select My Computer.
2. Select Printers.
3. Right-click on your printer and select Properties.
4. Click the Scheduling tab and, at the top in the Available section, enter a From and a To time (e.g., 18:00–08:30).
5. Click OK to save your changes.

Jobs submitted to this print queue will now be printed only between the hours specified. If you want some jobs to be printed straight away, you should define two printers, one for overnight, one for all hours.

26.4 How can I disable the printer pop-up message?

Start the Registry editor, change KHEY_LOCAL_MACHINE\SYSTEM\CurrentControlSet\Control\Print\Providers, and set the entry NetPopup to 0. You should then reboot Windows (however, stopping and restarting the print spooler will suffice). If the printer is on an NT Server, then this setting needs to be set on the server that controls the print queue.

This change can also be done from the Printer Control Panel applet:

1. Start the Printer Control Panel applet (Start > Settings > Printers).
2. From the File menu, select Server Properties.

3. Select the Advanced tab.
4. Uncheck the Notify when remote documents are printing.
5. Click OK.
6. Reboot the computer.

FAQ 26.5 How do I change the print spool location?

Using the Registry editor, change the value HKEY_LOCAL_MACHINE\SYSTEM\CurrentControlSet\Control\Print\Printers\DefaultSpoolDirectory by double-clicking on it and setting it to the required area. This will change the print spool area for all printers; to change the print spool for only one printer, move down to a printer key and create a value of type REG_SZ called SpoolDirectory, and set this to where the spool files should be.

In Windows 2000/XP, this change can be done in Printers/File/Server Properties/Advanced/Spool folder.

FAQ 26.6 How do I enable Print Auditing?

If you need to check what is being printed, then you can enable Print Auditing:

1. Double-click on My Computer, then double-click Printers.
2. Right-click on the desired printer and select Properties.
3. Click on the Security tab.
4. Select Auditing and click the Add button; you will be prompted with an Add Users and Groups dialog box.
5. Select the users/groups that you want to audit for the printer and click Add.
6. Once finished, click the OK button, and in the Printer Auditing main dialog, select the events to audit (i.e., Print, Delete).

Print events will now be sent to the Security log, which can be read from the Event Viewer (Start > Programs > Administrative Tools).

If you experience problems with events not being audited, try enabling File and Object Access as well.

FAQ 26.7 How do I enable drag-and-drop printing?

To enable drag-and-drop printing, all you have to do is create a shortcut to the printer on your desktop:

1. Double-click on My Computer.
2. Double-click Printers.
3. Right-click on the printer and drag to the desktop. Release and select create shortcut here.

You can then just drag files over the printer, and they will be printed (providing they are registered file types that NT knows how to print).

FAQ 26.8 How do I configure a print separator page?

A printer separator page is configured by creating a text file using a number of special control codes. The basic format of the separator page is as follows:

- $—This can be any character and must be the first character on the first line. Choose a character not normally used to be the control character; in this case, a dollar sign ($).
- $LUser Name $N—$L is used to display normal test until another code is found; $N displays the username.
- $L, Job Number $I—$I displays the job number.
- $E—$E means end of page.

Other characters you can use are the following:

- BS—Turn on block character printing.
- $D—Data job printer.
- $F<filename>—A file to print.
- $H—Printer-specific control code.
- $x—Where x is a number of blank lines to print.
- $T—Time job was printed.
- $U—Turns off block character printing.
- $Wxx—Width of the separator page.

To configure the printer to use the separator file:

1. Start the Printer Control Panel applet (Start > Settings > Printers).
2. Right-click on a printer and select Properties.

3. Click the Separator Page button.
4. Enter the path and filename of the separator page file and click OK.
5. Click OK again to exit the Printer Setup.

FAQ 26.9 How can I restrict which users can install local printer drivers?

It is possible to restrict print driver installation so that only Administrators and Print operators (on a server) or Power Users (on a workstation) can install local printer drivers.

1. Start the Registry editor (REGEDIT.EXE).
2. Move to HKEY_LOCAL_MACHINE\SYSTEM\CurrentControlSet\Control\Print\Providers\LanMan Print Services\Servers.
3. From the Edit menu, select New > DWORD Value. Enter a name of **AddPrinterDrivers** and click OK.
4. Double-click on the value and set to 1. Click OK.
5. Close the Registry editor.
6. Reboot the machine.

FAQ 26.10 How can I print to an ASCII text file?

A print driver Generic/Text only can be used with the file output ability as its default.

1. Start the Printer Control Panel applet (Start > Settings > Printers).
2. Start the Add Printer Wizard (click Add Printer).
3. Select My Computer and click Next.
4. Under Ports check File and click Next.
5. Under Manufacturers, select Generic and select Generic / Text Only as the Printer. Click Next.
6. Enter a printer name and specify whether or not you want it as the default printer. Click Next.
7. Select Not shared and click Next.
8. Select No to print a test page; click Finish.
9. Insert your NT installation CD-ROM and click OK.

To use the ASCII print driver, go into your application and print. Select the Generic/Text Only printer and click OK. A dialog will be displayed. Enter the filename you want to output to and click OK. You will now be able to view the file using Notepad or the like.

FAQ 26.11 How do I set security on a printer?

You can set various levels of security on a printer:

- No Access—User may not print to the device.
- Print—User may print to the device and pause, resume, and delete their own jobs.
- Manage Documents—Enables the user to change the status of **any** print job submitted by any user. The user may not change the status of the printer.
- Full—Enables complete access and administrative control of the printer.

By default all users have Print access (the Everyone group), and also the Creator Owner name has Manage Documents access. Creator Owner is the user that printed the document, which means users have the ability to delete their own entries on the print queue.

To change print permissions, perform the following:

1. Double-click on My Computer.
2. Double-click on Printers.
3. Right-click the printer whose permissions you wish to change and select Properties.
4. Select the Security tab.
5. Click the Permissions tab.

You can now set permissions for users.

FAQ 26.12 Where in the Registry is the default printer set?

The default printer is set on a per-user basis and so is part of the HKEY_USERS hive. To view the default printer for the currently logged on user, view the following value:

HKEY_CURRENT_USER\Software\Microsoft\Windows NT\
CurrentVersion\Windows\Device

It is of the format "\\LN014\LN.S651.CSP001.HPLJ5,winspool,Ne01:", where the first part is the actual printer share, then the spooler, and finally the connection (e.g., network or parallel port).

To view a different user or view remotely, you view HKEY_USERS\<SID of user>\Software\Microsoft\Windows NT\CurrentVersion\Windows\Device. To check which user has which SID, see FAQ 7.14.

If no default printer is manually defined, then the first printer alphabetically will be set as the default.

FAQ 26.13 When I try to print to a parallel device (LPT1),why do I receive the error: "System could not find the file"?

This error is usually caused by the parallel service not running. To check/fix, perform the following:

1. Start the Registry editor (REGEDIT.EXE).
2. Move to HKEY_LOCAL_MACHINE\SYSTEM\CurrentControlSet\Services\Parallel.
3. Double-click on Start.
4. If the value is 0, it means the service will start too early in the boot-up, so change this value to 2 and click OK.
5. Close the Registry editor.
6. Reboot the machine.

If you still have problems, check the Parport and ParVdm services under HKEY_LOCAL_MACHINE\SYSTEM\CurrentControlSet\Services\ because these services are also needed for parallel printing.

Another cause for this error is that LPT1 is sometimes disabled via the system BIOS, so you should also check this.

FAQ 26.14 How can I allow members of the Printer Operators group to add printers?

While members of the Printer Operators group can stop and restart the print spooler, modify jobs, and other admin functions, they cannot add or modify the actual printers. This can be changed by performing the following:

1. Start the Registry editor (REGEDT32.EXE, **not** REGEDIT.EXE).
2. Move to HKEY_LOCAL_MACHINE\SYSTEM\CurrentControlSet\Control\Print\Monitors.

3. From the Security menu, select Permissions.
4. Click the Add button.
5. Select Printer Operators and give them Full Control access. Click OK.
6. Close the Registry editor.

Stop and start the machine for the change to take effect. Alternatively just stop and start the Print Spool service:

```
net stop spooler
net start spooler
```

NT ONLY

26.15 How can I audit the number of pages printed by any particular user on an NT network?

If you need only basic information for NT-based workstations, you can extract this information from the print server's event log. The event log will record each job, including the page count. However, the page count is always 0 for Win98, Win95, Win3.x, and non-Windows workstations, as well as for print jobs from the console or MS-DOS applications—and it does not take into account the number of copies requested by the user.

To enable the auditing of prints, perform the following:

1. Start the printer's Start menu options (Start > Settings > Printers and Faxes).
2. From the File menu, select Server Properties.
3. Click the Advanced tab.
4. Check the Log spooler information events box and click OK.
5. You will need to restart the server for the auditing to start (or stop and start the Print Spool service).

Once auditing is enabled, the audits can be viewed using the Event Viewer application, System Log. To view only print logs, select Filter Events from the View menu and set the Source to Print. Each print job will be logged with its size in bytes and number of pages.

If you need to have accurate page counts, you must purchase a third-party package for monitoring and managing the printing activities. One such package is Printer Accounting Server from Software Metrics (http://www.metrics.com/); it works with a wide variety of printer types and network connections to accurately track printing.

FAQ 26.16 How do I create a custom page size for a printer?

Custom size pages can be useful in a number of scenarios, and the following information helps you to create a custom page size.

1. Start the Printer Control Panel applet (Start > Settings > Printer).
2. Select Add Printer—click only once, not double-click. (You don't add printer, only activate the icon. Also you need Administrator rights.)
3. From the File menu, select Server Properties (Print server properties).
4. Select the Forms tab
5. Click Create a New Form and add information that you want.
6. Click OK.

FAQ 26.17 How can I prevent print jobs from writing to the System log?

By default, Windows NT and Windows NT Advanced Server log every print job processed by the server in the System log. To stop this, perform the following:

1. Select Printers from the Settings Start menu folder (Start > Settings > Printers).
2. From the File menu, select Server Properties.
3. Select the Advanced tab.
4. You can then select the events to log:
   - Log spooler error events
   - Log spooler warning events
   - Log spooler information events
5. You have to restart the computer for the change to take effect.

Setting these values actually updates the Registry entry HKEY_LOCAL_MACHINE\SYSTEM\CurrentControlSet\Control\Print\Providers\EventLog, which is a DWORD value. Each option has a value:

- Log spooler error events is 1.
- Log spooler warning events is 2.
- Log spooler information events is 4.

You then add these numbers for the combination you want—for example:

- A value of 7 means log information, error, and warning events.
- A value of 3 means only log error and warning events.

You have probably noticed the 1, 2, and 4 are because the numbers are just setting the relevant bit in the DWORD, so bit 1 is error, bit 2 warning, and bit 3 is information.

FAQ 26.18 How do I create a queue to a network printer in Windows 2000?

If you have a printer that has its own network card and IP address such as a HP JetDirect card, you can create a queue to the device by following these instructions:

1. Log on as a member of the Administrators Group.
2. From the Start menu, select Settings > Printers.
3. Double-click Add Printer.
4. Click Next to the Add Printer Wizard introduction screen.
5. Select Local printer and uncheck Automatically detect my printer. Click Next.
6. The next screen asks for the port. Select Create a new port and select Standard TCP/IP Port. Click Next.
7. The TCP/IP Printer Wizard will be started. Click Next.
8. Enter the IP address or DNS name of the printer (by default the port name will be IP_<IP/DNS name>). Click Next.
9. Click Finish to the port creation.
10. You will have to select the printer make and model. Click Next.
11. Enter a name for the printer (a default name will be displayed). Click Next.
12. Select to share the printer and a name for the share. Click Next.
13. Enter a location for the printer and a comment (this is useful for people searching for printers using the Active Directory). Click Next.
14. Select to print a test page and whether you want to install additional drivers for other clients (such as Windows 98). Click Next.
15. A summary will be shown. Click Finish.

If the port on the printer is incorrect (e.g., for a JetDirect card, it will use 9100, but the actual port is 9099 for an internal card), perform the following:

1. Select Settings > Printers from the Start menu.
2. Right-click on the network printer and select Properties.

3. Select the Ports tab.
4. Select the IP port and click Configure Port.
5. Under the Raw Settings section, you can change the port number. Click OK.
6. Click Close to the main Properties dialog.

FAQ 26.19 How can I view print jobs from the command line?

Windows NT provides built-in ability to monitor print queues from the command line using the NET PRINT command. To view the current print queue, use the following syntax

```
net print \\<server>\<print share>
```

For example:

```
net print \\LNPSPA0001\LNPRTP0017
Printers at \\LNPSPA0001
Name Job # Size Status

---------------------------------------------------------------------
LNPRTP0017 Queue 1 jobs *Printer Active*
saviljo 247 120 Printing
The command completed successfully.
```

Notice the single print job by user saviljo that is being printed.

FAQ 26.20 How can I delete a print job from the command line?

You can delete a print job using the NET PRINT command, but you must first know its job ID, which can be ascertained by typing

```
net print \\<server>\<print share>
<user> <job id> <size> <status>
```

Once you know the job ID to delete, just type

```
net print \\<server> <job number> /delete (or /del)
```

FAQ 26.21 How can I add a printer to the Send To context option?

To add a printer to the Send To context option, perform the following:

1. Start Explorer.
2. Move to your SendTo folder of your profile (e.g., %systemroot%\Profiles\<user>\SendTo).
3. Open the printer's folder (Start > Settings > Printers).
4. Right-click on the printer, drag to the SendTo directory, and select Create shortcut here.
5. Rename the shortcut to a shorter name by pressing F2.

You will now be able to right-click on a document and send it to the printer, as shown in Figure 26-1—cool!

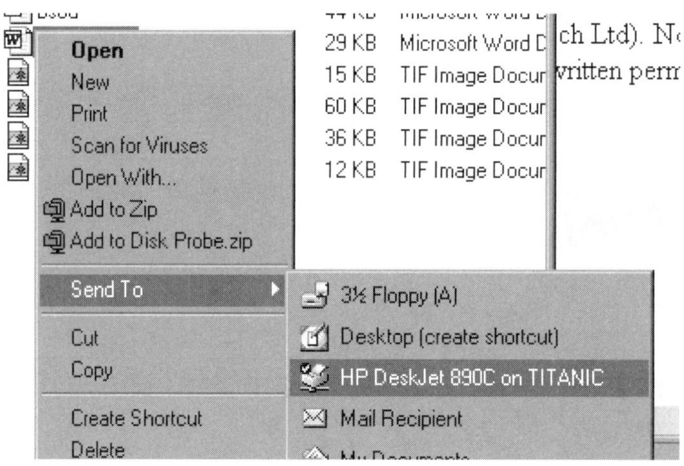

Figure 26-1 Sending a document to a printer from the context menu

FAQ 26.22 How can I add a printer from the command line?

Microsoft has a utility that can add printers from the command line, but it's available only to OEM suppliers. Another option is by directly manipulating the PRINTUI.DLL dynamic link library.

```
rundll32 printui.dll,PrintUIEntry [options]
```

For example, to add a HP DeskJet 970Cxi on LPT1 on Windows 2000, use the following:

```
rundll32 printui.dll,PrintUIEntry /if /b "HP DeskJet 970Cxi" /f
%windir%\inf\ntprint.inf /r "lpt1: " /m "HP DeskJet 970Cxi"
```

Other options are:

```
/a[file] binary file name
/b[name] base printer name
/c[name] unc machine name if the action is on a remote machine
/dl delete local printer
/dn delete network printer connection
/dd delete printer driver
/e display printing preferences
/f[file] either inf file or output file
/ga add per machine printer connections
/ge enum per machine printer connections
/gd delete per machine printer connections
/h[arch] driver architecture one of the following, Alpha | Intel |
Mips | PowerPC
/ia install printer driver using inf file
/id install printer driver using add printer driver wizard
/if install printer using inf file
/ii install printer using add printer wizard with an inf file
/il install printer using add printer wizard
/in add network printer connection
/j[provider] print provider name
/k print test page to specified printer, cannot be combined with
command when installing a printer
/l[path] printer driver source path
/m[model] printer driver model name
/n[name] printer name
```

```
/o display printer queue view
/p display printer properties
/q quiet mode, do not display error messages
/r[port] port name
/s display server properties
/Ss Store printer settings in a file
/Sr Restore printer settings from a file
Store or restore printer settings option flags that must be placed
at the end of command:
2 PRINTER_INFO_2
7 PRINTER_INFO_7
c Color Profile
d PrinterData
s Security descriptor
g Global DevMode
m Minimal settings
u User DevMode
r Resolve name conflicts
f Force name
p Resolve port
/u use the existing printer driver if it's already installed
/t[#] zero based index page to start on
/v[version] driver version one of the following, Windows 95 or 98 |
Windows NT 3.1 | Windows NT 3.5 or 3.51 | Windows NT 3.51 | Windows
NT 4.0 | Windows NT 4.0 or 2000 | Windows 2000
/w prompt the user for a driver if specified driver is not found in
the inf
/y set printer as the default
/Xg get printer settings
/Xs set printer settings
/z do not auto share this printer
/Z share this printer, can only be used with the /if option
/? help this message
@[file] command line argument file
```

The following are examples:

```
Run server properties:
rundll32 printui.dll,PrintUIEntry /s /t1 /n\\machine
Run printer properties:
rundll32 printui.dll,PrintUIEntry /p /n\\machine\printer
Run add printer wizard localy:
rundll32 printui.dll,PrintUIEntry /il
```

```
Run add printer wizard on \\machine:
rundll32 printui.dll,PrintUIEntry /il /c\\machine
Run queue view:
rundll32 printui.dll,PrintUIEntry /o /n\\machine\printer
Run inf install:
rundll32 printui.dll,PrintUIEntry /if /b "Test Printer" /f
%windir%\inf\ntprint.inf /r "lpt1: " /m "AGFA-AccuSet v52.3"
Run add printer wizard using inf:
rundll32 printui.dll,PrintUIEntry /ii /f %windir%\inf\ntprint.inf
Add per machine printer connection:
rundll32 printui.dll,PrintUIEntry /ga /c\\machine
/n\\machine\printer /j"LanMan Print Services"
Delete per machine printer connection:
rundll32 printui.dll,PrintUIEntry /gd /c\\machine
/n\\machine\printer
Enumerate per machine printer connections:
rundll32 printui.dll,PrintUIEntry /ge /c\\machine
Add printer driver using inf:
rundll32 printui.dll,PrintUIEntry /ia /c\\machine /m "AGFA-AccuSet
v52.3" /h "Intel" /v "Windows 2000" /f %windir%\inf\ntprint.inf
Remove printer driver:
rundll32 printui.dll,PrintUIEntry /dd /c\\machine /m AGFA-AccuSet
v52.3" /h "Intel" /v "Windows 2000"
Set printer as default:
rundll32 printui.dll,PrintUIEntry /y /n "printer"
Set printer comment:
rundll32 printui.dll,PrintUIEntry /Xs /n "printer" comment "My Cool
Printer"
Get printer settings:
rundll32 printui.dll,PrintUIEntry /Xg /n "printer"
Get printer settings saving results in a file:
rundll32 printui.dll,PrintUIEntry /f "results.txt" /Xg /n "printer"
Set printer settings command usage:
rundll32 printui.dll,PrintUIEntry /Xs /n "printer" ?
Store all printer settings into a file:
rundll32 printui.dll,PrintUIEntry /Ss /n "printer" /a "file.dat"
Restore all printer settings from a file:
rundll32 printui.dll,PrintUI /Sr /n "printer" /a "file.dat"
Store printer information on level 2 into a file :
rundll32 printui.dll,PrintUIEntry /Ss /n "printer" /a "file.dat" 2
Restore from a file printer security descriptor:
rundll32 printui.dll,PrintUIEntry /Sr /n "printer" /a "file.dat" s
Restore from a file printer global devmode and printer data:
rundll32 printui.dll,PrintUIEntry /Sr /n "printer" /a "file.dat" g d
```

```
Restore from a file minimum settings and resolve port name:
rundll32 printui.dll,PrintUIEntry /Sr /n "printer" /a "file.dat" m p
```

Also see Knowledge Base article Q189105 (http://support.microsoft.com/support/kb/articles/Q189/1/05.ASP).

Another option is to use the START command:

```
start \\print_server\print_name
```

The first time the system asks whether you want to install the new printer to your system. This means no wizards and no questions to answer; the driver is directly downloaded from the printer server.

FAQ 26.23 How can a printer be listed in the Active Directory?

When you share a printer, you have the option to list it in the Active Directory, which will enable users to search for it and find printers nearest to their location.

To share a printer in the Active Directory, perform the following:

1. Right-click on the printer you wish to list in the Active Directory and select Properties.
2. Select the Sharing tab.
3. Check the List in the Directory checkbox (see Figure 26-2).
4. You can also select the General tab and enter details of location for the printer.
5. Click Apply, then OK.

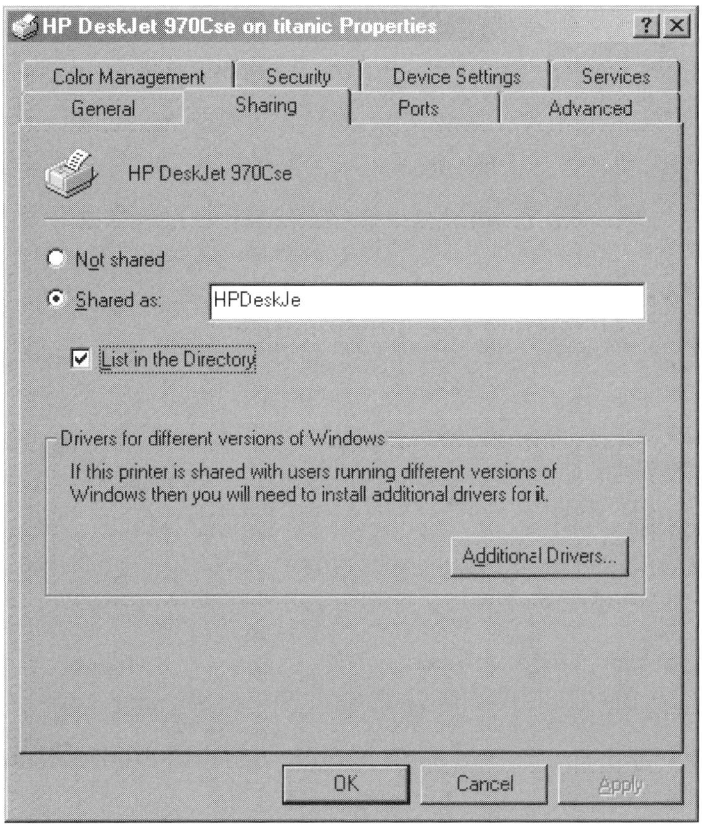

Figure 26-2 Allow a printer to be listed in the Active Directory

26.24 How can I print from the command window or use LPT1?

There are really two questions here. If you know a server and a printer share and you just need to print a file, it can be done by copying to the print share, for example:

```
copy readme.1st \\morpheus\HPLaserJ
```

If copying binary file, the /b switch should be also used. You may, however, need to actually use a device such as LPT1, and for this, we can use the net use command:

```
net use lpt1 \\10.129.210.71\HPLaserJ [/p:n]
```

The /p:n makes the connection nonpersistent.

If the preceding command fails, check that LPT1 is not already in use:

```
net use lpt1
Local name LPT1
Remote name \\10.129.210.71\HPLaserJ
Resource type Print
Status OK
# Opens 0
# Connections 1
The command completed successfully.
```

And if you want to delete the existing connection, perform the following:

```
net use lpt1 /d
lpt1 was deleted successfully.
```

You can then use LPT1 as if it's a local port for command-based programs.

The Windows 2000 Resource Kit also supplies CON2PRT, which can be used to connect to a printer—for example:

```
con2prt /c \\morpheus\HPLaserJ
Connected to printer: \\morpheus\HPLaserJ
```

which actually adds the printer as a normal printer under the Printers Control Panel applet. Using /cd sets it to the machine's default printer.

FAQ 24.25 How can I check/replace incompatible Windows 2000 printer drivers?

On the Windows 2000 CD is a folder \Printers\Fixprnsv that contains a utility FIX-PRNSV.EXE, which can be used to either replace NT 4.0 printer drivers with the Windows 2000 equivalent, or replace NT 4.0 drivers that are known to have problems.

If you run FIXPRNSV.EXE with the /fix switch on an NT 4.0 machine, Windows 2000 drivers will be installed, allowing Windows 2000 clients to connect and use the print server. If you run it on a Windows 2000 server, it will replace all non-NT 4-compatible printer drivers with compatible ones, allowing NT 4 client access.

Running the utility with the /diag switch just checks for incompatible drivers but does not replace any.

For full instructions, see Knowledge Base article http://support.microsoft.com/support/kb/articles/Q247/1/96.ASP.

FAQ 26.26 How can I administer printers via the Web?

Windows 2000 adds a virtual directory Printers (which points to %systemroot%\web\printers) to the IIS service, which allows remote managing of printers on a server. Just connect to http://<server>/Printers. It will display a list of all printers (see Figure 26-3), and clicking on a printer enables viewing documents' properties as well as managing documents.

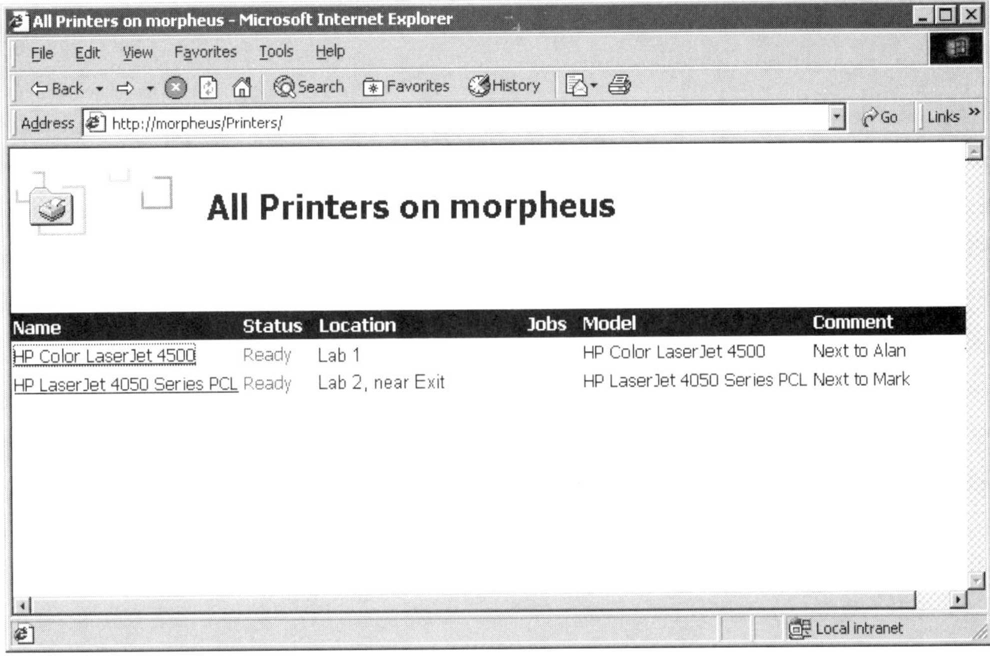

Figure 26-3 Viewing printer information via the Web

FAQ 26.27 How do I enable printer location tracking?

Printer location tracking, when enabled, allows Windows 2000 to calculate a location based on the user's subnet and fills in the Location field.

When a user searches for a printer, Windows 2000 uses the specified location (and other search criteria) to find a printer nearby. You can also use this policy to direct users to a particular printer or group of printers that you want them to use.

If you disable this policy, or do not configure it, and the user does not enter a location as a search criterion, Windows 2000 searches for a nearby printer based on the IP address and subnet mask of the user's computer.

To use printer location tracking, you must have the following:

- Active Directory must be installed on the network.
- You must have more than one site and subnet.
- The IP addressing scheme must match the network physical layout within reason.
- Client computers must be able to query via LDAP 2 or later.
- Each site must be on a separate subnet.
- Each subnet must have its own subnet object in the Active Directory.

To enable, perform the following:

1. Start the Active Directory Users and Computers MMC snap-in (Start > Programs > Administrative Tools > Active Directory Users and Computers).
2. Right-click on the domain and select Properties.
3. Select the Group Policy tab.
4. Select the Default Domain Policy object and click Edit.
5. Expand Computer Configuration > Administrative Templates > Printers.
6. Double-click Pre-populate printer search location text.
7. Select Enable and click Apply, then OK.
8. Close the Group Policy and the MMC snap-in.

You then need to set a location for each printer:

1. Select properties for the printer.
2. Enter a location.
3. Click Apply, then OK.

To test, try to find a printer, and a new browse button will be available. Your location is found!

FAQ 26.28 How do I enable/disable printers to be listed in the Active Directory?

Active Directory allows printers to be listed in the directory; however, it's possible to control whether or not printers can be listed for domains, OUs, etc. via a Group Policy setting:

1. Start the Active Directory Users and Computers MMC snap-in (Start > Programs > Administrative Tools > Active Directory Users and Computers).

2. Right-click on the domain and select Properties.
3. Select the Group Policy tab.
4. Select the Default Domain Policy object and click Edit.
5. Expand Computer Configuration > Administrative Templates > Printers.
6. Double-click Allow printers to be published.
7. Select Enable or Disable and click Apply, then OK.
8. Close the Group Policy and the MMC snap-in.

If this is not set, then by default, users will be able to list printers in the Active Directory.

The policy Automatically publish new printers in Active Directory if set to enabled or if not configured will result in all shared printers being listed automatically. If set to disabled, then printers are not automatically published.

FAQ 26.29 How can I prevent published printers from being removed from the Active Directory?

If a computer that has published printers fails to respond, by default its printers are removed from the Active Directory. This check happens every eight hours, and contact is tried twice. The next time the computer restarts, the printers are republished again.

It's possible to stop printers being pruned in the case of temporary disconnection as follows:

1. Start the Active Directory Users and Computers MMC snap-in (Start > Programs > Administrative Tools > Active Directory Users and Computers).
2. Right-click on the domain and select Properties.
3. Select the Group Policy tab.
4. Select the Default Domain Policy object and click Edit.
5. Expand Computer Configuration > Administrative Templates > Printers.
6. Double-click Prune printers that are not automatically republished.
7. Select Disable and click Apply, then OK.
8. Close the Group Policy and the MMC snap-in.

Other options are to change the length between checks and the number of retries:

- Directory pruning interval—Change from eight hours to Immediately up to Never.
- Directory pruning retry—Change from the default of two to 0–6.
- Directory pruning priority—Change from normal priority for the thread running the check.

FAQ 26.30 How can I change the link in the left pane of the printer's pane?

By default the printer's panel has a link to Microsoft support, but you may wish to change this to something more local:

1. Start the Active Directory Users and Computers MMC snap-in (Start > Programs > Administrative Tools > Active Directory Users and Computers).
2. Right-click on the domain and select Properties.
3. Select the Group Policy tab.
4. Select the Default Domain Policy object and click Edit.
5. Expand Computer Configuration > Administrative Templates > Printers.
6. Double-click Custom support URL in the Printer folder's left pane.
7. Select Enable and set the URL Title and URL (see Figure 26-4). Click Apply, then OK.
8. Close the Group Policy and the MMC snap-in.

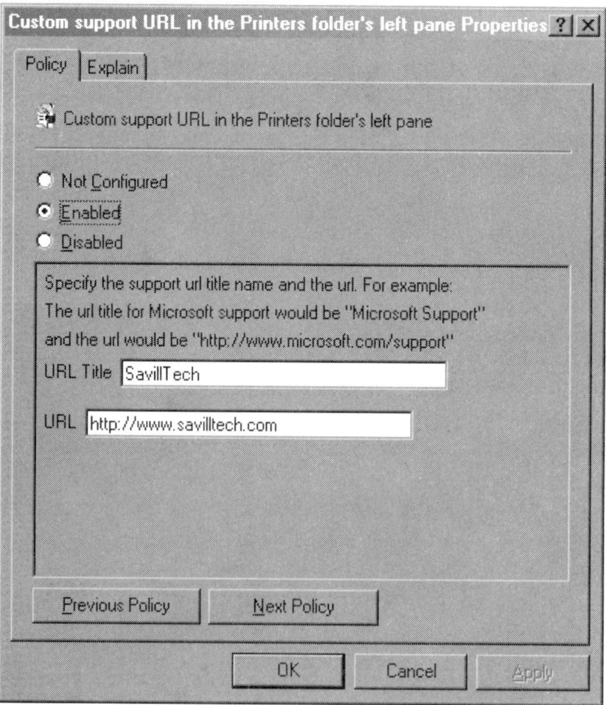

Figure 26-4 Setting a helpful support site

The Printers panel will now show your link. This can also be set by directly editing the Registry at HKEY_LOCAL_MACHINE\SOFTWARE\Policies\Microsoft\Windows NT\Printers:

- SupportLink—The URL link (e.g., http://www.savilltech.com)
- SupportLinkName—The link title

FAQ 26.31 How can I prevent printers on NT Line Print Remote (LPR) queues from pausing between print jobs on high-volume print servers?

By default, Windows NT 4.0 uses only the 11 ports between 721 and 731. This means you can have only 11 simultaneous connections from the print server to printers. See Microsoft article Q179156 at http://support.microsoft.com/support/kb/articles/Q179/1/56.asp for more details.

To improve performance on systems running NT 4.0 Service Pack 3 (SP3) and above, you can modify the Registry for Line Print Remote (LPR) to use other ports:

1. Start REGEDT32.EXE.
2. Go to HKEY_LOCAL_MACHINE\SOFTWARE\Microsoft\LPDSVC\lpr.
3. On the Registry menu, click Save Key and type a filename to save the current key values.
4. Delete the lpr key to remove all of the individual IP address entries.
5. Select the LPDSVC key.
6. On the Edit menu, click Add Key and then, in the Key Name box, type

   ```
   lpr
   ```

7. Select the newly created lpr key.
8. On the Edit menu, click Add Value and then type the following information:

   Value Name: **UseNonRFCSourcePorts**
   Data Type: **REG_DWORD**

   Value: **0** (to use ports 721 through 731—the default) or **1** (to use any port above 1024)

FAQ 26.32 Why do some MS-DOS applications print incomplete pages in Windows XP, Windows 2000, and Windows NT?

MS-DOS applications use the NT spooler to print. The spooler waits for a timeout period (15 seconds, by default) to expire before sending data to the printer. If the print job takes longer to generate than the timeout period, the spooler sends the generated data to the printer, causing the print job to split over multiple pages.

To work around this problem, perform the following steps to increase the timeout value:

1. Start the Registry editor (REGEDIT.EXE).
2. Navigate to HKEY_LOCAL_MACHINE\SYSTEM\CurrentControlSet\Control\WOW.
3. Double-click LPT_timeout.
4. Set the LPT_timeout value to a longer time (e.g., 30 seconds).
5. Click OK.
6. Close the Registry editor.

FAQ 26.33 How do I install a printer over the Web under Windows 2000/XP?

Windows 2000 and XP machines host a page at http://<server>/printers that displays a list of available printers. If you're running XP, you can add a printer to your client systems by selecting the printer from this Web page and clicking Connect. The client will install the driver and list the printer as a regular network device. The printer detail screen can be seen in Figure 26-5.

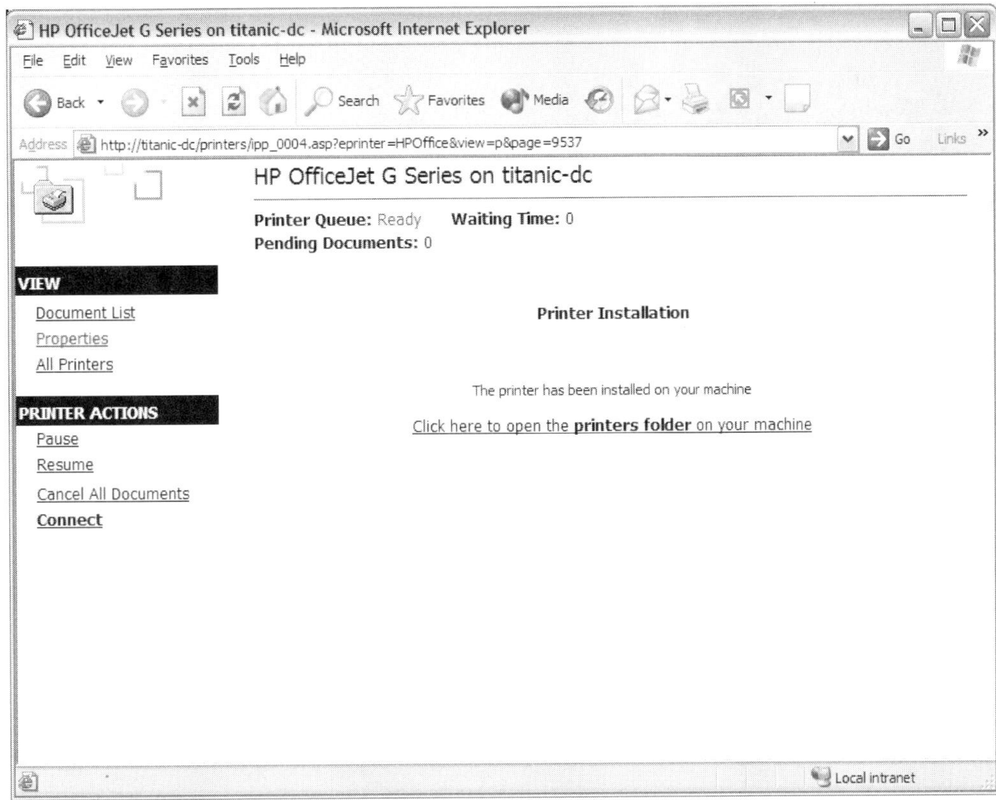

Figure 26-5 Controlling a specific printer via the Web

FAQ 26.34 Why do I receive an exception error when I run the Add Printer Wizard?

You might experience an exception error when you try to add a new printer if the Installation Sources value at HKEY_LOCAL_MACHINE\SOFTWARE\Microsoft\Windows\CurrentVersion\Setup is of type REG_SZ (String) instead of the correct REG_MULTI_SZ (Multi-line String). To correct this problem, perform the following steps:

1. Start the Registry editor (REGEDIT.EXE or REGEDT32.EXE if you're using Windows 2000 or Windows NT).
2. Navigate to HKEY_LOCAL_MACHINE\SOFTWARE\Microsoft\Windows\CurrentVersion\Setup.

3. Check the value type for the Installation Sources value. If this value is of type REG_SZ, make a note of its content, delete the value, and continue to the next step; otherwise, if the value is of type REG_MULTI_SZ, the problem lies elsewhere, and you will need to diagnose further.
4. From the Edit menu, select New > Multi-String Value in Regedit or REG MULTI SZ in Regedt32.
5. Enter a name of **Installation Sources**.
6. Double-click the value name and populate it with the original content that you deleted in step 3 with each value on a new line.
7. Click OK.
8. Close the Registry editor.

FAQ 26.35 How do I allow non-Administrator users to redirect LPT1?

In Windows XP Pro/2000, nonadministrative users are not permitted to redirect LPT1 (for example, using the command **net use lpt1 \\server\printer /yes**).

If you have legacy apps that require users to print to a redirected LPT1 port, there's a work around. Disable LPT1 in Device Manager, and users can now redirect it because it's no longer a physical port.

1. Start Device Manager (Start > Programs > Administrative Tools > Computer Management > Device Manager).
2. Expand Ports (COM & LPT).
3. Right-click on LPT1 and select Properties.
4. Under Device usage, select Do not use this device (disable).
5. Click OK.

Now LPT1 is just a logical port, like LPT2 and LPT3.

27 MULTIMEDIA

Because the merging of Windows 9x and NT, Windows XP now has great multimedia capabilities with its Media Player, Movie Maker, and CD-writing abilities. In this chapter, we look at MP3 (MPEG-1 Audio Layer-3) issues, DVD movies, and many other great tips related to multimedia.

27.1 How do I disable CD AutoPlay?

You can use the TweakUI utility and go to the Paranoia tab or edit the Registry HKEY_LOCAL_MACHINE\SYSTEM\CurrentControlSet\Services\Cdrom by changing Autorun 0x1 to 0x0 to disable autorun. If you use TweakUI, your actions will affect only the current user, whereas the Registry entry will set the change for all users. To edit the Registry so that your actions affect only the current user, perform the following:

1. Start the Registry editor (REGEDIT.EXE).
2. Move to HKEY_CURRENT_USER\Software\Microsoft\Windows\CurrentVersion\Policies\Explorer.
3. Double-click NoDriveTypeAutoRun.
4. Modify 0x95 to 0xff and click OK.
5. Close the Registry editor.

27.2 Why have I lost the speaker icon from my taskbar?

You can easily recreate the speaker icon by running SYSTRAY.EXE. To ensure that you have the speaker icon every time you start Windows, you can place it in your Startup group:

- Verify that the SystemTray value name at HKEY_LOCAL_MACHINE\Software\Microsoft\Windows\CurrentVersion\Run has a text string of SYSTRAY.EXE.
- Alternatively, start the Multimedia Control Panel applet (Start > Settings > Control Panel > Multimedia) and check that Show volume control on the taskbar is checked.

FAQ 27.3 How can I get my PCI-based sound card to work under Windows 2000?

There are currently problems in 2000 with PCI-based sound cards, including the Creative PCI 64 and Creative PCI 128. However, it is possible to use the NT 4.0 drivers after making a small change to your system.

The problem is that Windows 2000 uses Interrupt Request Line (IRQ) steering by default. PCI bus IRQ steering gives Windows 2000 the flexibility to reprogram PCI interrupts when rebalancing plug-and-play PCI and ISA resources around non-plug-and-play ISA devices.

Without IRQ steering, Windows 2000 cannot rebalance PCI and ISA IRQs for plug-and-play devices around non-plug-and-play ISA devices to solve resource conflicts. For example, if your computer's BIOS is unaware of non-plug-and-play ISA cards, if the operating system does not have PCI bus IRQ steering, and if the BIOS has set a PCI device to IRQ 10, you may have a resource conflict when you add a non-plug-and-play ISA device that is configured for IRQ 10. However, with PCI bus IRQ steering, the operating system can resolve this IRQ resource conflict. To do so, the operating system:

1. Disables the PCI device.
2. Reprograms a free IRQ to a PCI IRQ—for example, IRQ 11.
3. Assigns an IRQ holder to IRQ 11.
4. Moves the PCI device to IRQ 11.
5. Reprograms IRQ 10 to be an ISA IRQ.
6. Removes the IRQ holder for IRQ 10.

To disable IRQ steering, perform the following:

1. Start the Computer Management MMC snap-in (Start > Programs > Administrative Tools > Computer Management).
2. Expand the System Tools branch.
3. Select Device Manager.
4. In the right pane, expand Computer and right-click on Standard PC.
5. Select Properties from the context menu.
6. Select the IRQ Steering tab.
7. Uncheck the Use IRQ Steering checkbox (see Figure 27-1).
8. Click OK.
9. Reboot the machine.

Once the machine has restarted, you should be able to install your NT 4.0 PCI sound drivers. (Make sure you get the new drivers from the sound card maker's Web site.)

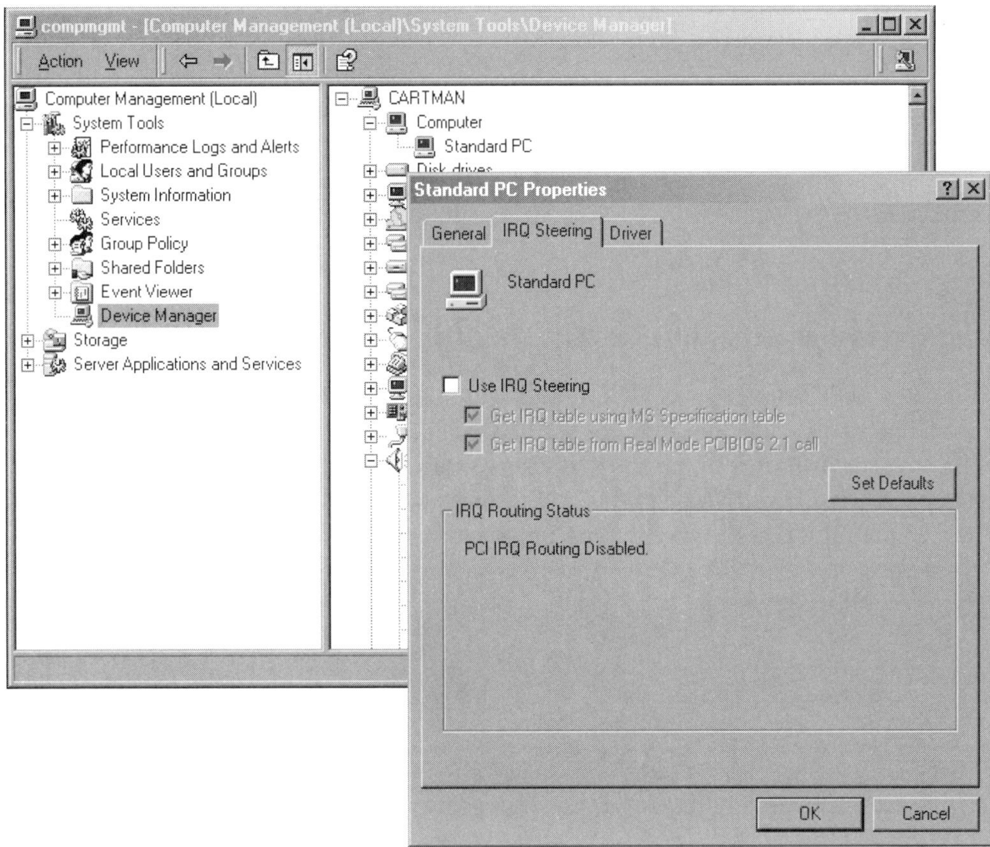

Figure 27-1 IRQ Steering options

If you do not have a standard PC, you must disable ACPI BIOS detection as follows:

1. Modify the file TXTSETUP.SIF in the Windows 2000 Setup folder.
2. Change the line

```
ACPIEnable=2
```

to

```
ACPIEnable=0
```

3. Reinstall Windows 2000.

An alternative to the reinstall is to open the Device Manager (right-click on My Computer, select Properties, and select Device Manager), open the Computer, double-click on the system type shown (for example, MPS PC), go to the Driver tab, and click on update driver. Choose display a list of drivers, choose Show all hardware of this device class, and choose Standard PC.

Now you can change the IRQ steering option. Reboot and install the proper sound card driver.

27.4 How can I check my machine's DirectX support?

Windows 2000 includes a tool DXDIAG.EXE (see Figure 27-2) that can check DirectX compatibility on a machine including DirectSound, DirectDraw, and DirectPlay.

Many screens have test buttons that test the various components of DirectX—for example, testing DirectMusic plays various tunes to check whether you have the relevant required resources correctly configured (and it's a cool tune) ☺.

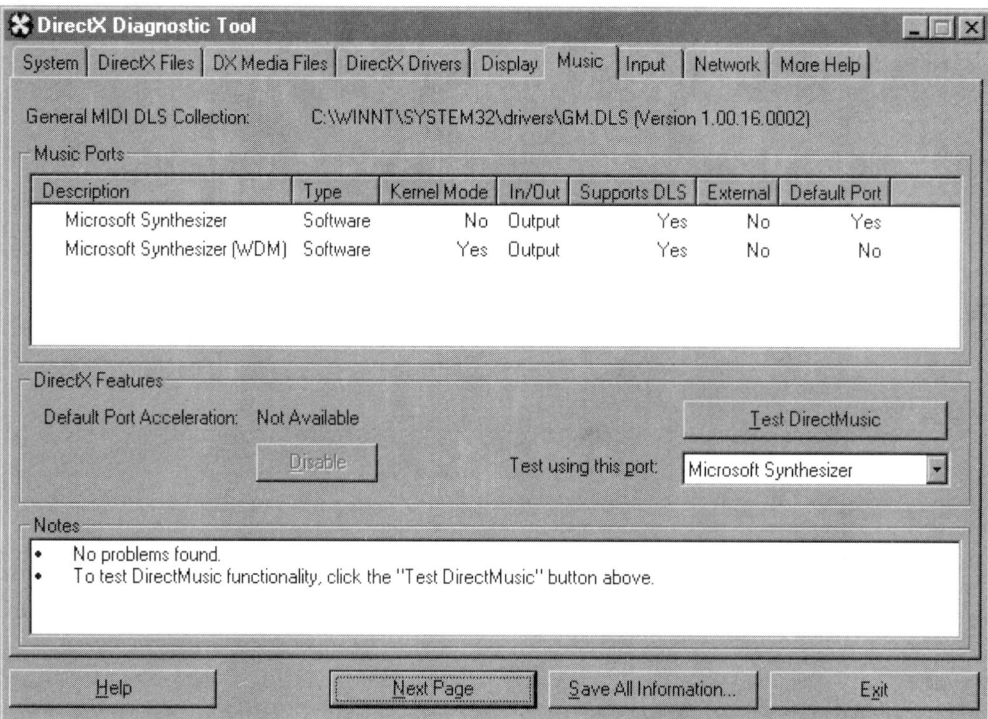

Figure 27-2 DirectX diagnostic tool

FAQ 27.5 Does Windows 2000 support FireWire?

FireWire lets you connect digital camcorders and disks to your computer. It provides a data transfer rate of up to 400Mbps (i.e., 50MB per second) and is very useful for capturing digital video (DV). Win2K has built-in support for most FireWire cards. After you install the card, you should see it under the "IEEE 1394 Bus host controllers" section of the Device Manager. Once you've installed your card, you can plug in your device, and the system will automatically recognize it.

FAQ 27.6 How can I enable Windows Media Player (WMP) to play DVDs?

If your computer has the hardware-based support for playing DVDs, you can make the following Registry change to enable WMP to play DVDs:

1. Start REGEDIT.EXE.
2. Go to HKEY_CURRENT_USER\SOFTWARE\Microsoft\MediaPlayer\Player\Settings.
3. From the Edit menu, select New > String value.
4. Enter a name of **EnableDVDUI** for the new string value, then press Enter.
5. Double-click the new value and set it to Yes. Click OK.
6. Close Regedit.

To start playing DVDs, select File > Open > DVD, then click Play.

FAQ 27.7 Why do I receive a WMPLAYER.EXE error when I start Windows Media Player 7 or later versions?

If you receive the following error when you start Windows Media Player, you might have a bad play list, or you might not have the appropriate user rights:

```
wmplayer.exe has generated errors and will be closed by Windows.
You will need to restart the program.

An error log is being created.
```

The problem might be the result of a play list (a .ASX file) that contains invalid STARTMARKER or ENDMARKER tags. To resolve this error, you can either delete and recreate the play list or open the .ASX file in Notepad and correct the STARTMARKER and ENDMARKER tags (correcting these tags is more complicated than simply recreating the play list). The correct format is

```
<STARTMARKER NUMBER = "1" />
```

or

```
<STARTMARKER NAME = "Marker_StartHere" />
```

and

```
<ENDMARKER NUMBER = "20" />
```

or

```
<ENDMARKER NAME = "Marker_StopHere" />
```

If you are unsure of what the values should be, simply back up the file and try deleting the <STARTMARKER> and <ENDMARKER> statements.

You will also receive the previously shown error message when a user without administration rights logs on and tries to play a CD-ROM while Start player in Media Guide is enabled. To resolve this error so that users with regular permission rights can use WMP, perform the following steps:

1. Log on as an Administrator.
2. Start WMP.
3. From the Tools menu, select Options.
4. Select the Player tab, clear the Start player in Media Guide checkbox and click OK.

FAQ 27.8 How do I manually add music art to my MP3 files?

If you create MP3 files from CD from Media Player, it will not only download the album information, if available, but also will download the album cover as two images and store them in the MP3 folder for the album. These images can then be read in by the MP3 player and displayed in its visualization window. The two images stored are:

- FOLDER.JPG—A 200x197 image
- ALBUMARTSMALL.JPG—A 75x74 image used for small windows

If you have already ripped your MP3 files to disk and wish to add this information, you can manually download these images and save them in the album folder as the previously listed filenames. The images can be downloaded from http://windowsmedia.com/mg/home.asp by searching for your album/artist name.

If you downloaded the Windows Media XP bonus pack, one of the tools, Media Library Management Wizard, will automatically download album art if available.

27.9 What is the Windows Media XP bonus pack?

The Windows Media XP bonus pack can be downloaded from http://www.microsoft.com/windows/windowsmedia/download/bonuspack.asp and contains the following utilities:

- A cut-down version of the Plus! pack MP3-to-WMA conversion utility
- Media Player PowerToys
- New visualizations
- New skins
- Movie Maker creativity kit

27.10 How can I make a program auto-start when inserting a CD?

When a CD is inserted, Windows looks for the file AUTORUN.INF at the root of the media. If it exists, then the file is checked, and the program you wish to be executed should be listed in the OPEN option:

```
[autorun]
OPEN=DELOLD.EXE
```

An option is to also specify an icon for the CD:

```
ICON=DELOLD.ICO
```

27.11 How do I use Phone Dialer?

If you have a modem, a sound card, speakers, and a microphone, you can use your computer as a phone and connect to people; however, another great feature is the ability to connect to people on the Internet. If they are running Phone Dialer, they can receive your calls and communicate with you via voice without any calls being placed.

To start Phone Dialer, just select from the Communications folder of the Accessories group (see Figure 27-3). You can also start it by directly running DIALER.EXE.

Once Phone Dialer is running on a remote computer, to make a call to that machine, perform the following:

1. Start Dialer on your machine.
2. Click the Dial button (or select Dial from the Phone menu).
3. Select Internet Call and enter the IP address or host name of the recipient computer.
4. Click Place Call.
5. On the remote machine, a window will be displayed with a Take Call button (see Figure 27-4). Click Take Call.
6. Any voice will now be transmitted; to hang up, just click Disconnect on either system.

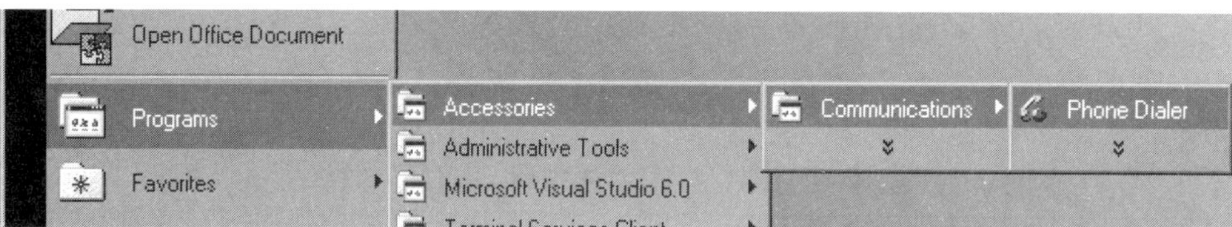

Figure 27-3 Finding the Phone Dialer

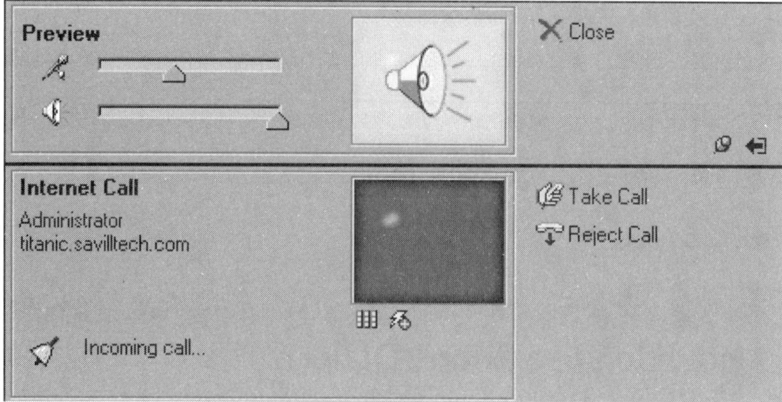

Figure 27-4 An incoming call from the Administrator—better take it!

27.12 How can I view a log of Phone Dialer calls?

The previous 30 days of calls (both incoming and outgoing) are logged to file %userprofile%\Local Settings\Application Data\Microsoft\Dialer\<username>_call_log.txt. Phone Dialer calls can also be viewed by Call Log from the View menu. The following is an example of an outgoing and incoming log:

```
"Outgoing","6/7/2000","20:01","1:19","","titanic"
"Incoming","6/7/2000","20:03","0:39","Administrator;titanic.
savilltech.com",""
```

27.13 Why has my computer started to randomly play classical (and not so classical) music?

Computers with BIOSes developed by Award/Unicore since 1997 have a feature whereby the BIOS sends to the PC speaker either "Für Elise" or "It's a Small World" as an indication that either the CPU fan is failing or has failed or that the power supply voltages have drifted out of tolerance. Visit the DFI Web site at http://www.dfiusa.com/support/music.htm for more information.

27.14 How do I use Windows XP's CD-burning feature?

XP has built-in, easy-to-use, CD-Recordable (CD-R) disc-burning support for most CD writers. Before you use the feature, you should check your CD-burning options:

1. Start Windows Explorer (Win key+E).
2. Right-click your CD-R drive and select Properties.
3. Select the Recording tab (if this tab isn't available, your device doesn't support CD burning).
4. You can then set the following options:
    - Whether to enable CD recording (see Figure 27-5).
    - The drive to hold the staging files. (Before the system burns a CD-R disc, the system writes the files to be recorded to an intermediary area known as the *staging area*. This area must have enough free space to hold an entire CD's content.)

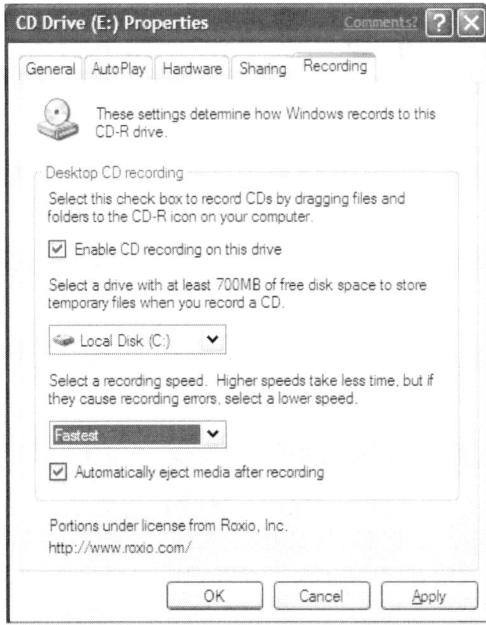

Figure 27-5 Enabling XP's built-in CD-writing ability

- The CD recording speed (Fastest, 4X, 2X, and 1X).
- Whether to eject the media after recording.

5. Set your options and click OK.

Then, to use the CD-burning feature, perform the following steps:

1. Insert a blank CD-R disc into your CD burner (you don't need the blank CD-R disc until step 4, but it's a good idea to insert it when you begin).
2. Drag the appropriate files/folders to the CD-R drive, or select the files/folders and from the context menu, select Send To >Writable CD.
3. After you copy all the files, select the CD-R drive, and you'll see the waiting files as "Files to add to the CD."
4. Right-click the CD-R drive and select Write to CD (if this option isn't available, you don't have a blank CD-R disc in the drive).
5. Enter a name for the CD-R disc and click Next.
   The system will write the files to the CD-R disc. After the system writes all the files, it will eject the CD-R disc (if you chose that option previously).
6. Click Finish.

FAQ 27.15 How can I clear files that are currently waiting to be written to CD?

To clear the waiting files, select the folders/files from the Files to add to the CD area and press Delete. However, if you want to clear all the files, right-click the CD-Recordable (CD-R) drive and select Clear staging area from the context menu.

You can also manually delete the files, which are stored in the %USERPROFILE%\Local Settings\Application Data\Microsoft\CD Burning folder. You can change this location by modifying the Registry value HKEY_CURRENT_USER\Software\Microsoft\Windows\CurrentVersion\ExplorerShell Folders\CD Burning.

FAQ 27.16 How can I erase files from a CD?

If your CD is a CD-Rewritable (CD-RW) disc, perform the following steps to erase files:

1. Start Windows Explorer.
2. On the CD-RW disc, select the files/folders that you want to erase.
3. From the CD burning tasks, select Erase files on CD-RW (if your CD isn't erasable, this option isn't available).
4. The system displays the Erase dialog box and deletes the files.
5. After the system deletes all the files, it writes a notification to the notification area (the right part of the taskbar, where the time appears).

28 SECURITY

With operating systems coming under more and more attacks from hackers, security is at the top of most peoples' concerns, and in this chapter, we look at some of the major issues.

28.1 How do I view/clear the Security event log?

Log on as the Administrator (or a member of the Administrators group) and perform the following:

1. From the Start menu > Programs > Administrative Tools and start Event Viewer.
2. From the Log menu, select Security.
3. Double-click any entry for more information.
4. Close the individual event information window.
5. To clear, select Log and clear all events. A dialog will ask if you want to save the info, click No.
6. It will prompt again if you are sure, click Yes.
7. Close Event Viewer.

In Windows 2000, start the Event Viewer MMC snap-in (Start > Programs > Administrative Tools > Event Viewer, or via Computer Manager). Right-click on the Security log, and you can clear it from the context menu.

28.2 Where can I get information on NT security problems?

Various sites provide this information:

- http://www.ntsecurity.com
- http://www.ntsecurity.net
- http://www.microsoft.com/security

28.3 How can I restore the default permissions to the NT structure?

Follow this procedure:

1. Log on as Administrator.
2. The built-in SYSTEM account needs access to the Windows NT default directories and subdirectories. To get this access, do the following:
    1. In File Manager, use Security/Permissions to grant the SYSTEM account FULL CONTROL to the root directory of the NTFS volume that contains Windows NT.
    2. Next, select the option to Replace Permissions on Subdirectories, which gives SYSTEM access to the entire volume.
3. Start the Registry editor (REGEDIT.EXE).
4. Go to HKEY_LOCAL_MACHINE\System\CurrentControlSet\Control\SessionManager.
5. Double-click the value BootExecute.
6. Under BootExecute, you may find a few entries, such as:

```
autocheck autochk *
```

After any entries, add on a separate line:

```
setacl /a
\DosDevices\<systemdrive>:\<winnt_root>\System32\winperms.txt
\DosDevices\<systemdrive>:
```

Here <systemdrive> is the drive that Windows NT is installed on, and <winnt_root> is the Windows NT root directory on that drive.

7. Save changes by clicking OK.
8. Exit the Registry editor and restart the computer.
9. On restart, the system will set security on the system files to the norm.

The preceding procedure will work only on an NT 3.51 system. To perform the preceding on an NT 4.0 system, you require the Windows NT Resource Kit Supplement 2:

1. Log on as an account that has the Backup files and folders privilege.
2. Run the FIXACLS.EXE utility (Start > Run > fixacls).

3. Click the Continue button.
4. Click OK when completed.

FIXACLS in NT 4.0 sets the permissions to the values defined in %SYSTEMROOT%\INF\PERMS.INF. Therefore, access to this file is also required to run FIXACLS.

For Windows 2000, you should perform the following:

1. Start MMC.EXE.
2. From the Console menu, select Add/Remove snap-in.
3. Add the Security Configuration and Analysis snap-in.
4. Click Close, then OK.
5. Right-click on the Security Configuration and Analysis root and select Open database.
6. Enter a new database name and click OK.
7. Select the basicwk.infBASICWK.INF template and click OK.
8. Right-click on the node again and select Configure Computer now.

FAQ 28.4 How can I copy files and keep their security and permissions?

By default when you copy files from one NTFS partition to another, the files inherit their protections from the parent directory. It is possible to copy the files and keep their settings using the **SCOPY** program that comes with the NT Resource Kit. SCOPY can copy owner and security audit information:

```
SCOPY c:\savilltech\secure.dat d:\temp\ /o /a
```

The preceding copies owner and auditing information. You can also use /s to copy information in subdirectories.

The restriction for this command is that both the origin and target drives **must** be NTFS, or the command will fail.

NT 4.0 ONLY

28.5 How do I enable auditing on certain files/directories?

Auditing is only available on NTFS volumes. Follow these instructions:

1. Start Explorer.
2. Right-click on the file/directory you want to audit, and from the context menu, select Properties.
3. Select the Security tab and click Auditing.
4. If you have selected a directory, check replace auditing on subdirectories.
5. Click the Add button and add the user(s) who you wish to audit by selecting and clicking Add. When finished adding users, click OK.
6. Select the events you wish to audit and then click OK.

You must ensure that File access auditing is enabled (Start > Programs > Administrative Tools > User Manager > Policies > Audit).

These events can then be viewed using the Event Viewer (Start > Programs > Administrative Tools > Event Viewer > Log > Security).

28.6 How do I use the System Key functionality of Service Pack 3 and above?

Windows NT 4.0 Service Pack 3 introduced a new feature in NT with the ability of increasing security on the Security Access Manager (SAM) database. This is performed by introducing a new key in one of three modes.

- A secure key generated by the system. The key is used to encrypt the SAM and is stored on the local hard disk.
- A secure key generated by the system. The key is stored on a floppy disk, which has to be placed in the computer at boot-up.
- A password given by the user is used to encrypt the SAM and has to be entered on boot-up.

To generate the system key, you use SYSKEY.EXE; however, be warned, once you activate the encryption, you cannot turn it off without performing a system recovery using an Emergency Recovery Disk (ERD) produced before syskey was enabled. To enable encryption, perform the following:

1. Make sure Service Pack 3 is installed.
2. Log on to the system as a member of the Administrators group (only Administrators can run SYSKEY.EXE).

3. Create a new ERD (**rdisk /s**), store it somewhere safe, and label the disk "Pre System Key ERD."
4. Run the System Key generation utility (Start > Run > syskey.exe).
5. A dialog box will be displayed with encryption disabled. Select Encryption enabled and click OK.
6. Click OK to the warning dialog box.
7. Select which of the three encryption modes you require. If password is selected, enter a password and then enter it again for verification. If you chose to store the secure key on a floppy disk, you will be prompted to insert a disk and then click OK.
8. Click OK, and a success message will be displayed; click OK
9. You now need to reboot the machine.
10. Once rebooted you should create a new ERD (**rdisk /s**).

After you reboot the system, if you choose a password and after the GUI phase of NT starts, a dialog box will be displayed, and you should enter the password you gave and click OK. After that, you may log on as normal. If you choose floppy disk, you will be prompted to insert the disk and then click OK.

Although you cannot remove the system key, you can change the mode by running SYSKEY.EXE and click Update. You will be asked to either enter the existing password or insert the system key floppy if changing from one of these modes.

For more information see Q143475 at http://support.microsoft.com/support/kb/articles/q143/4/75.asp.

FAQ 28.7 How do I remove the System Key functionality of Service Pack 3 and above?

As stated previously in FAQ 28.6, no simple remove function is available; however, if you restore the SAM from an ERD that was taken before the system key was enabled, the restoration process will remove this feature from the system.

1. Boot off of the NT installation disks.
2. After disk 2, press R for repair.
3. Deselect everything except "Inspect Registry files" and select Continue.
4. Continue as per normal, inserting disk 3 and then the ERD (the one created before syskey was run).
5. Once completed, reboot, and the system key should no longer be in use.

28.8 How can I configure the system to stop when the Security log is full?

To avoid Security logs being lost, you can configure the system to halt if the Security log becomes full so that only Administrators can log on. They can then archive the log and purge.

1. Start the Registry editor (REGEDIT.EXE).
2. Move to HKEY_LOCAL_MACHINE\SYSTEM\CurrentControlSet\Control\Lsa.
3. If CrashOnAuditFail exists, then skip to step 4; if not, from the Edit menu, select New > DWORD Value and enter a name of **CrashOnAuditFail**. Click OK.
4. Double-click on CrashOnAuditFail and set to either:
   - 1—Stop if the audit log is full.
   - 2—Only the Administrator can log on. This is set by the operating system just before the system crashes due to a full audit log.
5. Close the Registry editor.

When this happens, the OS will display a BSOD.

28.9 How can I clear the pagefile at shutdown?

As you will be aware, the pagefile contains areas of memory that were swapped out to disk, such as in a secure environment. You want this pagefile cleared when the machine is shut down because parts of memory containing passwords/sensitive information may have been mapped out to the pagefile.

1. Start the Registry editor (REGEDIT.EXE).
2. Move to HKEY_LOCAL_MACHINE\SYSTEM\CurrentControlSet\Control\Session Manager\Memory Management.
3. If the value ClearPageFileAtShutdown does not exist, from the Edit menu, select New > DWORD Value and enter a name of **ClearPageFileAtShutdown**.
4. Double-click on ClearPageFileAtShutdown and set to 1.
5. Reboot the machine, and the next time you shut down, the pagefile will be cleared.

FAQ 28.10 How do I set what happens during a crash?

By default a crash dump file will be produced, but two other items can be configured.

The first option is to enter a log entry in the System log, which can be set using the Startup/Shutdown tab of the System Control Panel applet in NT 4.0 and the Startup and Recovery button under the Advanced tab of the System Control Panel applet in Windows 2000 and XP by checking Write an event to the system log.

This can also be achieved by setting the Registry key HKEY_LOCAL_MACHINE\SYSTEM\CurrentControlSet\Control\CrashControl\LogEvent to 1.

The other option is to send an Administrative alert (you need the Alerter service to be running to enable this option). Again using the same dialog as before, check Send an administrative alert.

This can also be achieved by setting the Registry key HKEY_LOCAL_MACHINE\SYSTEM\CurrentControlSet\Control\CrashControl\SendAlert to 1.

FAQ 28.11 How can I configure the system to automatically reboot in the event of a crash?

This can be set using the Startup/Shutdown tab of the System Control Panel applet in NT 4.0 and the Startup and Recovery button under the Advanced tab of the System Control Panel applet in Windows 2000 and XP by checking Automatically reboot.

This can also be achieved by setting the Registry key HKEY_LOCAL_MACHINE\SYSTEM\CurrentControlSet\Control\CrashControl\AutoReboot to 1.

FAQ 28.12 How do I disable LanManager challenge/response in NT?

Windows NT servers with Service Pack 4 and above support three authentication types:

- LanManager (LM) challenge/response
- Windows NT challenge/response (also known as NTLM challenge/response)
- Windows NT challenge/response version 2.0 (also known as NTLM2)

By default when a client connects to a server, both LM and NTLM are used in case the server does not support NTLM; however, LM is far weaker than NTLM so you may wish to disable LM for security reasons.

Editing the Registry key as follows enables the client to select which authentication will be used. If you select NTLM2, make sure that SP4 is applied to all servers. The following setting is required on the clients and servers so you may wish to automate this via a logon script or policy.

1. Start the Registry editor.
2. Move to HKEY_LOCAL_MACHINE\SYSTEM\CurrentControlSet\Control\Lsa.
3. From the Edit menu, select New > DWORD Value.
4. Enter a name of **LMCompatibilityLevel** and press Enter.
5. Double-click the new value and set to one of the following
   - 0—Send LM response and NTLM response; never use NTLMv2 session security.
   - 1—Use NTLMv2 session security if negotiated.
   - 2—Send NTLM response only.
   - 3—Send NTLMv2 response only.
   - 4—DC refuses LM responses.
   - 5—DC refuses LM and NTLM responses (accepts only NTLMv2).
6. Close the Registry editor.
7. Reboot the machine.

For more information on deploying, see http://support.microsoft.com/support/kb/articles/q147/7/06.asp.

FAQ 28.13 How can I restrict guest access to event logs?

By default guests and anonymous can view an event log, but because an event log may reveal important information, anonymous/guest access can be disabled as follows:

1. Start the Registry editor (REGEDIT.EXE).
2. Move to HKEY_LOCAL_MACHINE\SYSTEM\CurrentControlSet\Services\EventLog.
3. Move to the subkey Application.
4. From the Edit menu, select New > DWORD Value. Enter a name of **RestrictGuestAccess**. Click OK.
5. Double-click the new value and set to 1.
6. Repeat steps 4 and 5 for the Security and System subkeys also.

In fact this is also governed by the Registry rights on the corresponding eventlog parameters (HKEY_LOCAL_MACHINE\SYSTEM\CurrentControlSet\Services\EventLog—application and system). You can even remove Administrator rights to read the files by using the Registry rights. Use REGEDT32.EXE to change these rights.

FAQ 28.14 How can I enable auditing of base objects?

To enable auditing of base objects, perform the following:

1. Start the Registry editor (REGEDIT.EXE).
2. Move to HKEY_LOCAL_MACHINE\SYSTEM\CurrentControlSet\Control\Lsa.
3. From the Edit menu, select New > DWORD Value. Enter a name of **AuditBaseObjects**. Click OK.
4. Double-click the new value and set to 1.

You can also turn on full privilege auditing (but this will fill your event log):

1. Start the Registry editor (REGEDIT.EXE).
2. Move to HKEY_LOCAL_MACHINE\SYSTEM\CurrentControlSet\Control\Lsa.
3. From the Edit menu, select New > DWORD Value. Enter a name of **FullPrivilegeAuditing**. Click OK.
4. Double-click the new value and set to 1.

FAQ 28.15 How can I enforce an Internet access control policy?

If you wish to ensure that Web browsing during company time is strictly for business use, you have to install a product that can enforce this policy. There are two ways of doing this:

- Installing a proxy server with content control feature
- Installing a network monitor/scanner with content control feature.

If you use the first alternative, you will need to reconfigure all your users' browsers. Additionally, you could suffer a performance penalty. If you already use a proxy server such as Microsoft Proxy Server, you do not need to reconfigure though, and you can purchase add-on modules that do content checking.

The second option requires no network reconfiguration and can block all types of Internet traffic. Examples of such products are

- Languard (http://www.languard.com)
- Surfcontrol (http://www.surfcontrol.com)
- Littlebrother (http://www.littlebrother.com)

FAQ 28.16 What is a SID (security ID)?

SID stands for security identifier and is used within NT/2000/XP as a value to uniquely identify an object such as a user or a group. The SID assigned to a user becomes part of the access token, which is then attached to any action attempted or process executed by that user or group. If a duplicate SID did exist, then all users with this SID would authenticate as what would be seen as the same user. It is possible for cloned machines to have the same SID, which would be seen by the authentication mechanism as the same machine. The SID under normal operation will be unique and will identify an individual object such as a user, group or a machine.

A SID contains:

- User and group security descriptors
- 48-bit ID authority
- Revision level
- Variable subauthority values

For example: S-1-5-21-917267712-1342860078-1792151419-500.

Following is a list of the values for SIDs on a default NT 4 installation (notice the unique value 500 for Administrator and 501 for Guest):

- Built-in users
  DOMAINNAME\ADMINISTRATOR
  S-1-5-21-917267712-1342860078-1792151419-500 (=0x1F4)
  DOMAINNAME\GUEST
  S-1-5-21-917267712-1342860078-1792151419-501 (=0x1F5)
- Built-in global groups
  DOMAINNAME\DOMAIN ADMINS
  S-1-5-21-917267712-1342860078-1792151419-512 (=0x200)
  DOMAINNAME\DOMAIN USERS
  S-1-5-21-917267712-1342860078-1792151419-513 (=0x201)
  DOMAINNAME\DOMAIN GUESTS
  S-1-5-21-917267712-1342860078-1792151419-514 (=0x202)

- Built-in local groups
  BUILTIN\ADMINISTRATORS S-1-5-32-544 (=0x220)
  BUILTIN\USERS S-1-5-32-545 (=0x221)
  BUILTIN\GUESTS S-1-5-32-546 (=0x222)
  BUILTIN\ACCOUNT OPERATORS S-1-5-32-548 (=0x224)
  BUILTIN\SERVER OPERATORS S-1-5-32-549 (=0x225)
  BUILTIN\PRINT OPERATORS S-1-5-32-550 (=0x226)
  BUILTIN\BACKUP OPERATORS S-1-5-32-551 (=0x227)
  BUILTIN\REPLICATOR S-1-5-32-552 (=0x228)
- Special groups
  \CREATOR OWNER S-1-3-0
  \EVERYONE S-1-1-0
  NT AUTHORITY\NETWORK S-1-5-2
  NT AUTHORITY\INTERACTIVE S-1-5-4
  NT AUTHORITY\SYSTEM S-1-5-18
  NT AUTHORITY\authenticated users S-1-5-11 (for Windows NT 4.0 Service Pack 3 and later only)

These values can be displayed by using the utility GETSID.EXE from the Windows NT Resource Kit:

```
getsid \\MACHINE ACCOUNT \\MACHINE ACCOUNT
```

The SID for account MACHINE\ ACCOUNT matches account MACHINE\ ACCOUNT. The SID for account MACHINE\ ACCOUNT is

```
S-1-5-21-1271857391-537538043-240200450-4294967295
```

The SID for account MACHINE\ ACCOUNT is

```
S-1-5-21-1271857391-537538043-240200450-4294967295
```

For more information, see FAQ 7.14 and FAQ 6.108. For Web-based resources, see http://support.microsoft.com/support/kb/articles/Q163/8/46.asp.

For information on extracting a SID from an access control entry (ACE), see http://support.microsoft.com/support/kb/articles/q102/1/01.asp. For information on how to associate a username with a SID, see http://support.microsoft.com/support/kb/articles/Q154/5/99.asp.

The answer to this FAQ was contributed by Nathan House.

FAQ 28.17 What security mailing lists exist for keeping up-to-date?

Mailing lists will help keep you up-to-date with all the latest bugs, exploits, and information on security. Hackers like to keep up-to-date with this information so maybe you should too. If you have an interest and a need for security, I personally do recommend joining mailing lists, but do be prepared for the amount of mail you will receive. Digest versions of mailing lists are also available, which send only the general highlights from a given period of time. Following are two of the most popular mailing lists for NT security:

- NTBugtraq
  NTBugtraq is a mailing list for the discussion of security exploits and security bugs in Windows NT and its related applications. To join, send e-mail to listserv@listserv.ntbugtraq.com and, in the text of your message (not the subject line), write

  ```
  subscribe ntbugtraq
  ```

  To remove, send e-mail to listserv@listserv.ntbugtraq.com and, in the text of your message (not the subject line), write:

  ```
  unsubscribe ntbugtraq
  ```

- NT Security
  To join, send e-mail to majordomo@iss.net and, in the text of your message (not the subject line), write:

  ```
  subscribe ntsecurity
  ```

  To remove, send e-mail to majordomo@iss.net and, in the text of your message (not the subject line), write:

  ```
  unsubscribe ntsecurity
  ```

NT Security Mailing List is a moderated mailing list discussing Windows NT security as well as security issues related to Windows 95 and Windows for Workgroups—everything at the host- and application-level security as well as at the network level.

Following is a list of some of the other well-known and popular security-related mailing lists:

General Security Mailing Lists
Alert
Best of Security
Bugtraq
COAST Security Archive
Computer Privacy Digest (CPD)
Computer Underground Digest (CuD)
Cypherpunks
Cypherpunks-Announce
European Firewalls
Firewalls
Intruder Detection Systems Infsec-L
NTBugtraq
NT Security
Phrack
PRIVACY Forum
Risks
SAS (French Speaking Firewalls)
S-HTTP
Sneakers
Secure Socket Layer—Talk
UNINFSEC—University Info Security Forum
Virus
Virus Alert
WWW Security
Security Products
SOS Freestone Firewall package
Tiger
TIS Firewallk Toolkit
Vendors and Organizations
CERT
CIAC
HP
Sun

See http://xforce.iss.net/maillists/ for more information on security mailing lists and how to join them. Also see http://www.sans.org, which has information and a mailing list.

The answer to this FAQ was contributed by Nathan House.

28.18 How can I protect against password hackers that use sniffers like l0pht?

Nowadays, NT administrators face a tough task in ensuring network security, because of password sniffers such as l0pht, which can sniff an NT password easily. To protect against this sniffer, one can use a network sniffer that can detect such password sniffers. The network sniffer can log a user running a password sniffer and also issue an alert. An example of such a network sniffer is LANguard at http://www.languard.com.

The user password never leaves the local machine with Windows 2000 using Kerberos security. It is never exposed to the network so it should not be able to be sniffed.

28.19 How can I detect that users have cracked a password?

To detect this, you either have to review the security logs regularly or use a network sniffer to monitor users accessing shares in real time. A combination of the two is the most prudent. Security logging can be switched on from the Event Viewer.

A network sniffer can be used to log IPs and users accessing particular servers or shares. In real time, an administrator can see which users are accessing which shares. An example of such a sniffer is LANguard at http://www.languard.com or Sessionwall at http://www.sessionwall.com.

28.20 How do I use the Security Configuration and Analysis snap-in?

The Security Configuration and Analysis snap-in has two important abilities. First, it can load in a security template and then compare your system to it, highlighting any possible problems. Second, it can then apply those changes to bring your system to meet the requirements of the template.

To use this snap-in, perform the following:

1. Start the MMC snap-in (MMC.EXE).
2. Add the Security Configuration and Analysis snap-in (Console > Add/Remove Snap-in > Add > Security Configuration and Analysis > Add > Close > OK).
3. Right-click on the Security Configuration and Analysis route and select Open database.

4. Enter a new name and click Open (e.g., TITANIC.SDB).
5. Select a template to use (e.g., SECUREDC.INF) and click Open.
6. Right-click on the root and select Analyze Computer Now.
7. Select a location for the log and click OK.
8. After the analysis, if you select a branch, entries will have one of three options (see Figure 28-1):
   - A green tick means it meets the template's required value.
   - A red cross means it does not meet the template's required value.
   - A generic icon means the value is not defined in the template.
9. To apply the changes, right-click on the root and select Configure Computer Now.

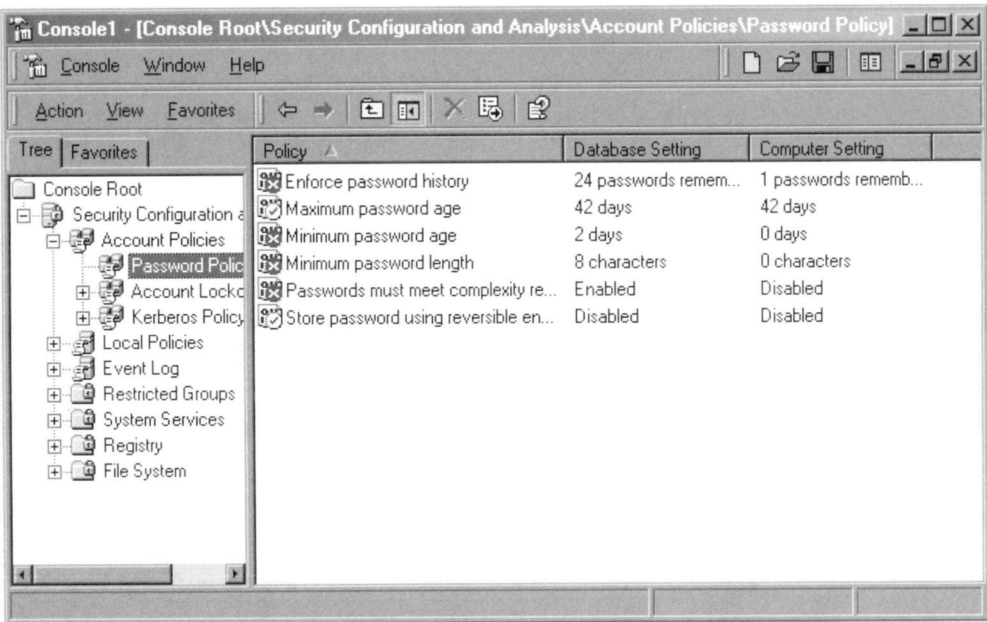

Figure 28-1 Viewing the results of the password policy check

FAQ 28.21 What is Kerberos?

Kerberos is new to Windows 2000 and is

> The hound of Hell. A three-headed Dog with a Snake for a tail, guarding the entrance to the kingdom of Hades, the Underworld.

Kerberos replaces the Microsoft NTLM native communication for Windows 2000 computers, but NTLM is still supported for compatibility with older NT 4, Windows 9x clients (as a side note NTLM version 2 is not supported in Windows 2000).

The idea is if two people know a secret, they can communicate by encrypting a message with the secret. If they both know the secret, they know the other person is who she says she is. The problem is the "secret" can't be sent as just text over the network because anyone with a network sniffer could find the "secret."

The Kerberos protocol solves this problem with secret key cryptography. Rather than sharing a password, communication partners share a cryptographic key that is symmetric in nature, which means the single key can both encrypt and decrypt.

To communicate, one side sends the other an encrypted message containing its name and local time; the other machine then decrypts the packet with the symmetric key, and if the time is close to its time, then the match is OK.

Figure 28-2 shows this where K_{JB} is the symmetric key shared by **J**ohn and **B**ob. The fact that time is part of the encryption technology is why Windows 2000 machines need to be time-synchronized with a Simple Network Time Protocol (SNTP) service.

But how is the shared key distributed if it can't be sent over the network? See FAQ 28.22 following.

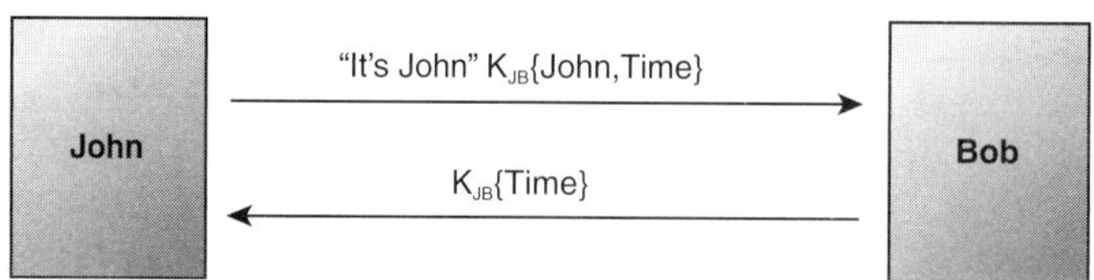

Figure 28-2 How Kerberos sends encrypted message information

28.22 How is the shared key used by Kerberos distributed?

The previous FAQ explained that two machines (a client and a server) can communicate via a shared symmetric key used to encrypt data. However, the problem is how can they distribute that shared key between them.

This is where the Key Distribution Center (KDC—see Figure 28-3) is used. It consists of a service that runs on all Windows 2000 domain controllers, generates the shared key for the client and server, and sends it in an encrypted form to the client.

The KDC responds to the client's request to talk to a server by sending both copies of the session key to the client (one for the client, one for the server—the same key, just packaged differently). The client's copy of the session key is encrypted with the key that the KDC shares with the client. The server's copy of the session key is embedded, along with authorization data for the client, in a data structure called a *session ticket*. The entire structure is then encrypted with the key that the KDC shares with the server. The session ticket—with the server's copy of the session key safely inside—becomes the client's responsibility to manage until it contacts the server.

The client extracts the session key using its key shared with the KDC. It extracts the server's session ticket (it can't decrypt it because it does not know the key shared between the server and the KDC). This information is stored in a secure cache on the client in memory (it's never written to disk). When it wants to communicate, it sends its name and time encrypted in the shared key (which is extracted) to the server along with the server's session ticket. The server then decrypts the session ticket using the key shared with the KDC, extracts the session key, and decrypts the client authenticator replying back with the workstation's time encrypted with the session key.

All of this means the server does not have to store session keys for clients; it's the client's responsibility to send the server's session ticket to the server as part of communication.

In addition, session tickets are good for a defined amount of time based on the Kerberos policy. This period of time is normally eight hours (a normal logon time) so the KDC is not contacted every time the client wants to talk to a server; it has the session ticket cached, which is good for the day.

What about the server-KDC and client-KDC long-term key—how is that distributed? See the next FAQ!

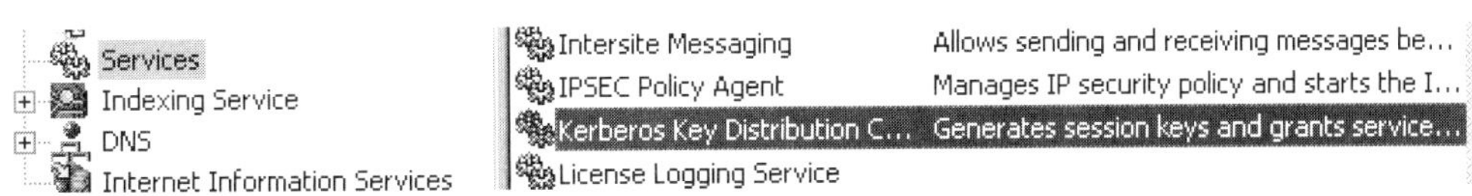

Figure 28-3 The Key Distribution Center (KDC)

28.23 How is the long-term key between a client and the KDC distributed?

The final stage in the Kerberos key exchange is the key used between a client (or server) and the KDC for distributing the session key used to encrypt information between a client and a server.

For this, the client and the KDC share a long-term key, and this long-term key is just a hashed version of the client user's password.

The password is never sent over the network. When John logs on, the Kerberos client on the workstation runs the password through the one-way hash algorithm, producing a cryptographic key. This key is sent to the KDC, where it extracts this hash from its record and checks that they match. This happens only on initial logon to the network.

At initial logon, the Kerberos client asks the KDC for a session key and ticket it can use for further KDC communication during the logon session, which avoids the need for the hashed password to be constantly generated and checked.

The KDC replies with a copy of the session key it has generated for communication between the client and itself. The copy of the session key is encrypted with the client's long-term key (i.e., a hashed password). The client can decrypt it using its cached long-term key.

The KDC also sends a copy of the session key encrypted with the KDC's own long-term key, which is known as the ticket-granting ticket (TGT), and the client will send this in the future to the KDC for communication in the same way the client-server session ticket worked. Only the KDC can decrypt the TGT because only the KDC has the long-term key, which the session key was encrypted with.

The TGT is valid only for the logon and discarded on logoff; hence, it's also called a "logon session key." In future KDC communication, the client sends the normal requests encrypted with its session key shared with the KDC and the KDC's TGT from which it can extract the session key needed to talk to the client. This means the KDC does not have to maintain a list of session keys for each client.

28.24 How can I change the ticket lifetime used by Kerberos?

The default lifetime for a Kerberos ticket is defined by the Group Policy for the domain, which is ten hours by default. It can be changed as follows, but ten hours will normally suffice (unless people work very long days):

1. Start the Active Directory Users and Computers MMC snap-in (Start > Programs > Administrative Tools > Active Directory Users and Computers).
2. Right-click on the domain and select Properties from the context menu.
3. Select the Group Policy tab.
4. Select the domain Group Policy Object and click Edit.
5. Expand the Computer Configuration root, then Windows Settings > Security Settings > Kerberos Policy.
6. Double-click the time you wish to change (see Figure 28-4), modify it, and click OK.
7. Close the Group Policy editor.

To force the GPO change to take effect, you can run

```
secedit /refreshpolicy machine_policy /enforce
```

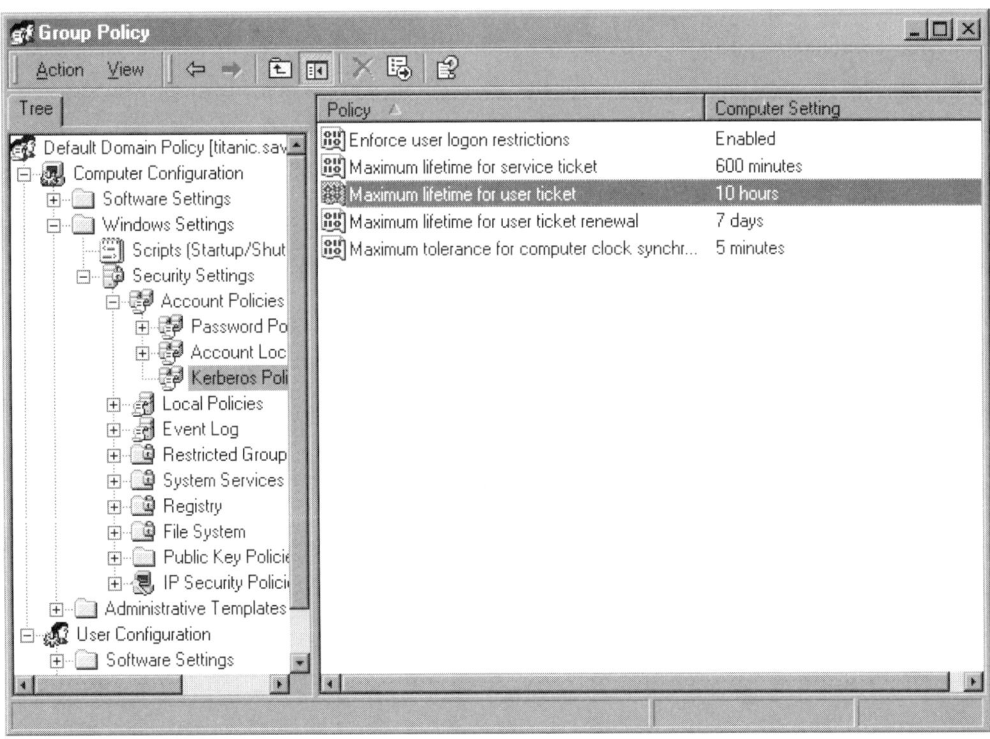

Figure 28-4 Setting the lifetime for a user ticket

28.25 What is PKI?

PKI stands for Public Key Infrastructure, which over recent years has been gaining momentum. PKI basically consists of two keys, a public and a private key.

Previous encryption methods we have looked at use a symmetric key, which means the same key is used to both encrypt and decrypt. Public key encryption is different; here there are the two keys, and if something is encrypted with the private key, only the public key can decrypt it. If something is encrypted with the public key, only the private key can decrypt it. See Figure 28-5.

As the names suggest, the private key is known only by the owner, but the public key is known by all. This means you have to keep the private key very private!

X.509 certificates are used for the distribution of the public key, which means Certificate Authorities (CA) are needed and must be configured as trusted for the domains.

If a user wants to send a message in private to another user, the sender encrypts the message using the recipient's public key. This means only the owner of the private key (the recipient) can decrypt it.

The problem with public key encryption however is that it is slow, and so public key encryption is more commonly used to distribute a faster symmetric key, which is then used to encrypt actual data.

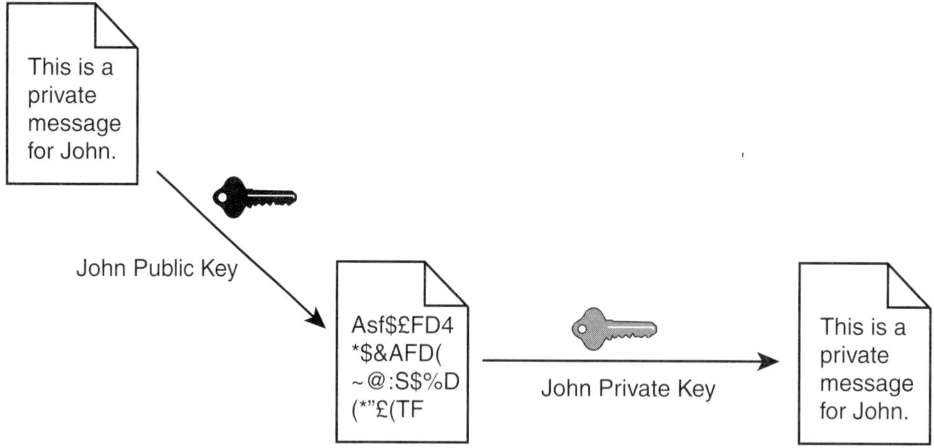

Figure 28-5 Illustration of how public and private key encryption works

FAQ 28.26 What is a digital signature and how does it work?

As we saw in the previous FAQ 28.25, public-private keys are used to pass sensitive information. Keys can also be used to provide authentication that a sender is who they say they are. A key does not protect the contents of the message; it only proves it is from who it says its from.

It provides authentication and integrity but does not provide confidentiality; data is sent as normal but acts like a normal signature we use on a letter.

A digital signature works by creating a message digest, which ranges from between a 128-bit and a 256-bit number that is generated by running the entire message through a hash algorithm. If the message was slightly different, the digest will be totally different. This generated number is then encrypted with the sender's private key and added to the end of the message.

When the recipient receives the message, he or she runs the message through the same hash algorithm and generates the message digest number. The recipient then decrypts the signature using the sender's public key, and providing the two numbers match, they know the message is from who it says its from, **and** that is has not been modified.

FAQ 28.27 What are secret keys?

We have seen that public key encryption is slow compared to symmetric key encryption and that public key encryption is useful for distributing a key between two parties. The public key can then be used for symmetric encryption. The exact workings for this process are as follows:

1. Each side generates half of the key.
2. They encrypt the half they generated with the other person's public key.
3. Each side then sends its half to the other.
4. As each side receives the other half, it decrypts with its private key so both parties now have both parts of the key and can now use symmetric key encryption.

While it would be possible for one side to generate the whole key, this doubles the security because even if someone knew one party's private key, he or she would have only half the key.

FAQ 28.28 How can I prevent a Windows 2000 upgrade from overwriting special security settings?

When an NT installation is upgraded to Windows 2000, security is defined in one of the following templates:

- DWUP.INF for Windows 2000 Professional upgrades
- DSUP.INF for Windows 2000 Server upgrades

To prevent these files from overwriting your custom security settings, you need to edit the files, which means you need the files on a central/local writable form for the upgrade:

1. Copy the appropriate template file (DWUP.INF for Professional or DSUP.INF for Server) from your Windows 2000 distribution share into the %WinDir%\Security\Templates folder on your local computer. It may be in unexpanded form in the i386 folder so you may need to expand it:

```
D:\I386>expand dwup.in_ dwup.inf
Microsoft (R) File Expansion Utility Version 5.00.2134.1
Copyright (C) Microsoft Corp 1990-1999. All rights reserved.

Expanding dwup.in_ to dwup.inf.
dwup.in_: 17285 bytes expanded to 252850 bytes, 1362% increase.

D:\I386>copy dwup.inf %windir%\security\templates
1 file(s) copied.
```

2. Start Microsoft Management Console (Start > Run > MMC).
3. From the Console menu, select Add/Remove Snap-in, click Add, click Security Templates, click Add, click Close, and then click OK.
4. Expand the Security Templates root, then the templates folder. You will see your copied template (e.g., DWUP.INF).
5. Click the security area that you want to modify (Registry or File System).
6. In the result pane, a list of all of the Registry keys or filesystem objects configured by the default upgrade template is displayed. Determine whether or not the object you want the upgrade to ignore is explicitly configured by the template, and then use one of the following methods.

Method 1

If the object you want the upgrade to ignore is not explicitly configured by the upgrade template, you must add it using the following steps:

1. Right-click Registry or File System, and then click Add Key or Add File.
2. Browse the dialog box to select the key or filesystem object you want to protect (for example, Machine\Software\DelOld). If the key, folder, or file does not exist on your computer, you can type the path to the object in the available box.
3. Click OK to start the access control list (ACL) editor.
4. Click OK again to accept the default security provided by the ACL editor.
5. Click Do not allow permissions on this key\file to be replaced.
6. Click OK to add the object to the template and then go to step 3 in method 2.

Method 2

If the object you want the upgrade to ignore is already explicitly configured in the upgrade template, modify it using the following steps:

1. In the result pane, double-click the object you want to protect.
2. Click Do not allow permissions on this key\file to be replaced, click OK.
3. In the result pane, the object you want the upgrade to ignore should now be listed with the Ignore property listed under both the permission and audit columns. Right-click the name of the template and then click Save.
4. Copy the modified template back to the distribution share. If you had to uncompress the file, recompact the file before copying it back to the distribution share:

```
F:\WINNT\security\templates>compress dwup.inf dwup.in_
Microsoft (R) File Compression Utility Version 5.00.2134.1
Copyright (C) Microsoft Corp. 1990-1999. All rights reserved.

Compressing dwup.inf to dwup.in_.
dwup.inf: 251177 bytes compressed to 46002 bytes, 82% savings.
```

FAQ 28.29 Where are the security event IDs listed?

They are defined in Knowledge Base article Q174074 at http://www.microsoft.com/technet/support/searchkb.asp. The following table makes them easier to view.

Event ID	Type	Description
512	Success Audit	Windows NT is starting up.
513	Success Audit	Windows NT is shutting down. All logon sessions will be terminated by this shutdown.
514	Success Audit	An authentication package has been loaded by the Local Security Authority. This authentication package will be used to authenticate logon attempts.
515	Success Audit	A trusted logon process has registered with the Local Security Authority. This logon process will be trusted to submit logon requests.
516	Success Audit	Internal resources allocated for the queuing of audit messages have been exhausted, leading to the loss of some audits.
517	Success Audit	The audit log was cleared.
518	Success Audit	A notification package has been loaded by the Security Account Manager. This package will be notified of any account or password changes.
528	Success Audit	Successful logon.
529	Failure Audit	Logon Failure: Reason: Unknown user name or bad password.
530	Failure Audit	Logon Failure: Reason: Account logon time restriction violation.
531	Failure Audit	Logon Failure: Reason: Account currently disabled.
532	Failure Audit	Logon Failure: Reason: The specified user account has expired.
533	Failure Audit	Logon Failure: Reason: User not allowed to logon at this computer.
534	Failure Audit	Logon Failure: Reason: The user has not been granted the requested logon.
535	Failure Audit	Logon Failure: Reason: The specified account's password has expired.

Event ID	Type	Description
536	Failure Audit	Logon Failure: Reason: The NetLogon component is not active.
537	Failure Audit	Logon Failure: Reason: The NetLogon component is not active.
538	Success Audit	User logoff.
539	Failure Audit	Logon Failure: Reason: Account locked out.
560	Success Audit	Object open.
561	Success Audit	Handle allocated.
562	Success Audit	Handle closed.
563	Success Audit	Object open for delete.
564	Success Audit	Object deleted.
576	Success Audit	Special privileges assigned to new logon.
577	Success Audit	Privileged service called.
578	Success Audit	Privileged object operation.
592	Success Audit	A new process has been created.
593	Success Audit	A process has exited.
594	Success Audit	A handle to an object has been duplicated.
595	Success Audit	Indirect access to an object has been obtained.
608	Success Audit	User right assigned.
609	Success Audit	User right removed.
610	Success Audit	New trusted domain.
611	Success Audit	Removing trusted domain.
612	Success Audit	Audit policy change.
624	Success Audit	User account created.
625	Success Audit	User account type change.

(*continued*)

Event ID	Type	Description
626	Success Audit	User account enabled.
627	Success Audit	Change password attempt.
628	Success Audit	User account password set.
629	Success Audit	User account disabled.
630	Success Audit	User account deleted.
631	Success Audit	Global group created.
632	Success Audit	Global group member added.
633	Success Audit	Global group member removed.
634	Success Audit	Global group deleted.
635	Success Audit	Local group created.
636	Success Audit	Local group member added.
637	Success Audit	Local group member removed.
638	Success Audit	Local group deleted.
639	Success Audit	Local group changed.
640	Success Audit	General account database change.
641	Success Audit	Global group changed.
642	Success Audit	User account changed.
643	Success Audit	Domain policy changed.
644	Success Audit	User account locked out.

FAQ 28.30 How can users change their passwords from the command line?

Only Administrators can change their passwords from the command line. The following DOS screen shows how to do it with the net user command:

```
C:\>net user Administrator *
```

```
Type a password for the user:
Retype the password to confirm:
The command completed successfully.
```

An Administrator can also use the following variation of the net user command:

```
net user Administrator newpassword
```

This variation eliminates the need to type the password twice, and you can use it from a batch file. If users who aren't Administrators try to change their passwords with this command, they receive the following error message:

```
System error 5 has occurred. Access is denied
```

FAQ 28.31 Why doesn't my computer prompt me for a password when it returns from hibernation?

For your computer to prompt you for a password when it returns from hibernation, you must select the Prompt for password when computer goes off standby checkbox on the Power Options Advanced tab:

1. Start the Power Options Control Panel applet (Start > Settings > Control Panel > Power Options).
2. Select the Advanced tab.
3. Check the Prompt for password when computer goes off standby checkbox.
4. Click OK.

FAQ 28.32 How can I enable users to set the Administrator password during a Remote Installation Services installation?

When you use Microsoft Remote Installation Services (RIS), by default the Administrator password is set to NULL (blank) during the installation. You can, however, let the user set a password during the final GUI portion of installation. Perform the following steps:

1. On the RIS server, open the .SIF file of the installation you want to modify. By default, this file is in the RemoteInstall\Setup\[language]\Images\[folder name]\I386\Templates folder with a name of RISTNDRD.SIF.

2. Go to the [GuiUnattended] section of the .SIF file and find the following line:

```
AdminPassword = *
```

3. Change this line to read as follows:

```
AdminPassword = ""
```

4. Save the change.

During installation, the system will prompt the user to type an Administrator password. You should test this change to ensure that it works correctly.

As a side note, instead of "" you could type a password (e.g., **AdminPassword = "fred"**), which sets the Administrator password to the password you specify and doesn't prompt the user. However, this password travels as clear text, so I don't recommend this approach.

The Windows 2000 Resource Kit describes another option (although not well!). You can use a Custom Installation Wizard (CIW), and let the user type in a password. However, this approach is quite complex.

FAQ 28.33 How can I prevent users from changing their passwords except when Windows 2000 prompts them to?

You can configure your domain via a Group Policy so that users can change their passwords only when the system prompts them:

1. Start the Microsoft Management Console (MMC) Active Directory Users and Computers snap-in (Start > Programs > Administrative Tools > Active Directory Users and Computers).
2. Right-click the container (site/domain or organizational unit—OU) you want to enforce the policy on and select Properties.
3. Select the Group Policy tab.
4. Select the policy and click Edit.
5. Expand User Configuration > Administrative Templates > System > Logon/Logoff.
6. Double-click Disable Change Password, and on the Policy tab, select Enabled.
7. Click Apply, then OK.
8. Close all dialog boxes.

9. Refresh the policy on all clients with the following command:

```
secedit /refreshpolicy user_policy
```

You can also configure this feature on a per-user basis. Perform the following steps:

1. Start REGEDIT.EXE.
2. Go to HKEY_CURRENT_USER\Software\Microsoft\Windows\CurrentVersion\Policies.
3. If the System key exists, select it. Otherwise create it (Edit > New > Key > System).
4. Under System, create a new value of type DWORD (Edit > New > DWORD Value).
5. Type a name of **DisableChangePassword** and press Enter.
6. Double-click the new value and set it to 1. Click OK.
7. Close Regedit.

You don't need to log off; the change takes effect immediately.

FAQ 28.34 Do any Web sites exist for checking a machine's security?

The Microsoft Personal Security Advisor (MPSA) is a Web application that uses an ActiveX plug-in to perform security checks on Windows 2000 and Windows NT 4.0 systems. The MPSA is available at http://www.microsoft.com/technet/mpsa/start.asp. MPSA checks include the following:

- Account password strength
- Password length
- Automatic logon
- Anonymous access
- Auditing
- Service packs
- Shares
- Filesystems
- Services
- Microsoft Internet Explorer (IE) and Microsoft Outlook zones
- Microsoft Office macro settings

The MPSA provides a solution and detailed implementation instructions for any problems the tool finds. Although Microsoft designed the MPSA for Win2K and NT machines, the application also works with Windows XP.

FAQ 28.35 Why do I receive an error message in Win2K that says my password must be at least 18,770 characters?

This error occurs when you're running Windows 2000 Service Pack 1 (SP1), you connect to an MIT realm, and select Change Password from the Security dialog box (Ctrl+Alt+Del). (An MIT realm is a Kerberos realm used for authentication in the same way that Win2K uses Kerberos 5 for authentication.) The full error you'll receive is

```
Your password must be at least 18770 characters and cannot repeat
any of your previous 30689 passwords. Please type a different
password. Type a password that meets these requirements in both
text boxes.
```

To correct this problem, contact Microsoft Support Services and request an updated MSGINA.DLL file (version 5.0.2195.3351 or later).

29 RAS AND RRAS

Remote Access Server (RAS) and Routing and Remote Access Server (RRAS) enable users to dial into a Windows server via the RAS client to gain access to resources. With the Internet and more broadband connections, when wanting access to work resources, we may now use technologies such as PPTP (Point to Point Tunneling Protocol), which allows secure access over the Internet.

29.1 Is it possible to dial an Internet service provider (ISP) using the command line?

Yes, use **RASPHONE -d <entry>** or RASDIAL <entry>. To disconnect, you can type **RASPHONE -h <entry> or** RASDIAL /disconnect.

29.2 How can I prevent the RAS connections from closing when I log off?

Perform the following:

1. Start the Registry editor (REGEDT32.EXE, **not** REGEDIT.EXE).
2. Move to HKEY_LOCAL_MACHINE\SOFTWARE\Microsoft\Windows NT\CurrentVersion\Winlogon.
3. Create a new value called **KeepRasConnections** of type REG_SZ.
4. Set the new value to have a value of 1.

FAQ 29.3 How can I create a RAS connection script?

It is possible to write a script that will run when you connect during a RAS connection to automate actions such as entering your username and password. To specify a script, perform the following:

1. Double-click on My Computer and start up the Dial-up Networking applet.
2. Select the phonebook entry and click More.
3. From the More menu, select Edit entry and modem properties.
4. Click the Script tab and select Run this script.
5. Click the Edit script button, and the SWITCH.INF file will be opened.
6. Go to the bottom of the file and create a new connection section and then select Exit.
7. Answer Yes to save changes.
8. Click the Refresh List button, and the new entry will now be displayed.
9. Select the new entry you created and click OK.

Here's an example addition to the SWITCH.INF:

```
; the phonebook entry
[Savill1]
; send initial carriage return
COMMAND=<cr>
; wait for : (after username, may be different at your site)
```

Omit the U as it may be capitals. You could just have :

```
OK=<match>"sername:"
LOOP=<ignore>
; send username as entered in the connection dialog box. Alternately
you could just enter the username—for example:

savillj<cr>
COMMAND=<username><cr>
; wait for : (after password this time, may be different at your
site)
OK=<match>"password:"
LOOP=<ignore>
; send the password entered in the connection dialog box, again you
could just manually enter the password, e.g. password<cr>
```

```
COMMAND=<password><cr>
NoResponse
; send the "start ppp" command
COMMAND=ppp default<cr>
OK=<ignore>
```

In depth information on all of the commands can be found in the SWITCH.INF file, which is located in %systemroot%\system32\ras.

FAQ 29.4 How can I debug the RAS connection script?

It is possible to create a log file of the connection by performing the following steps:

1. Start the Registry editor (REGEDIT.EXE).
2. Move to HKEY_LOCAL_MACHINE\SYSTEM\CurrentControlSet\Services\RasMan\Parameters.
3. Double-click on Logging.
4. Change the value data to 1 and click OK.
5. Close the Registry editor.
6. Restart the computer.

Each dial-up session will now be appended to the file %systemroot%/system32/RAS/device.log. To stop logging, perform the preceding steps but set the value back to 0.

FAQ 29.5 How do I configure RAS to connect to a leased line?

The method will vary depending on your system's current setup; however, assuming you have RAS already installed, following are the actions needed to configure your leased line. It is assumed the modems (at both ends) are configured correctly for leased line usage (&D0 for DTR override).

1. Start the Modem Control Panel applet (Start > Settings > Control Panel > Modems).
2. Click Add.
3. Check the Don't detect my modem, I will select it from a list and click Next.
4. In the Manufacturers box, select Standard Modem Types, and in the Models area, select Dial-Up Networking Serial Cable between 2 PCs. Click Next.
5. Select the port (e.g., COM1) and click Next. You now have a modem setup ready for leased line use.

You should now configure the RAS connection (server/client) in the normal way (use the RAS service properties).

1. Right-click on Network and select Properties. Click the Services tab and select RAS. Click Properties.
2. Select the COM port and click Configure.
3. Select the connection type dial-in/dial-out/both and click OK. Click Continue.
4. You will be asked about NetBEUI client access; select the desired option and click OK.
5. If you selected server, you will be prompted for TCP/IP access and also which IP addresses should be given, either by Dynamic Host Configuration Protocol (DHCP—if configured) or from a given pool of addresses. You can also check the box to allow a client to request a specific IP address.
6. Click Close in the Network dialog box. The bindings of the machine will be updated, and you will be asked if you want to reboot. Click Yes.

Once this has been done, you may also want a phonebook entry for outgoing use as you would normally except under the Dialing section, check the Persistent connection box.

FAQ 29.6 RAS tries to dial out even on local resources. What should I do?

Perform the following:

1. Start the Registry editor (REGEDIT.EXE).
2. Move to HKEY_CURRENT_USER\Software\Microsoft\RAS Autodial\Addresses (a better way to view these is to type **rasautou -s** from the command prompt).
3. In the subkeys, look from the local address (and name). If you find it, select the key and select Delete from the Edit menu.
4. Close the Registry editor.

You may also wish to add addresses to the disabled list:

1. Start the Registry editor (REGEDT32.EXE **not** REGEDIT.EXE).
2. Move to HKEY_CURRENT_USER\Software\Microsoft\RAS Autodial\Control.

3. Double-click on DisabledAddresses and add the address on a new line. Click OK when finished.
4. Close the Registry editor.

You will need to reboot the machine in both of the preceding cases.

FAQ 29.7 I have connected via RAS to a server; however, I can see resources only on the machine I connect to. Why?

When you configure the RAS server, you set for each protocol the scope of the connection, the server, or the whole network. To change this, perform the following:

1. Start the Network Control Panel applet (right-click on Network and select Properties).
2. Select the Service tab, select the Remote Access Service, and click Properties.
3. Select the COM port and click the Network button.
4. Click the Configure button next to the protocol you wish to change access (e.g., TCP/IP).
5. At the top, check the Entire network button.
6. Click OK.

Clients should now be able to view the entire network.

FAQ 29.8 How do I force the Logon Using Dialup Networking option to be checked by default on the logon screen?

This can be accomplished with a Registry change on each client machine.

1. Start the Registry editor (REGEDIT.EXE).
2. Move to HKEY_LOCAL_MACHINE\SOFTWARE\Microsoft\Windows NT\CurrentVersion\Winlogon.
3. From the Edit menu, select New > String Value (REG_SZ type).
4. Enter a name of **RASForce**.

5. Double-click the new value and set to 1.
6. Close the Registry editor.
7. Reboot the machine.

FAQ 29.9 Where are the RAS phonebook entries and settings stored?

The actual phonebook entries are stored in the file %systemroot%/system32/ras/rasphone.pbk (pbk—**p**hone**b**oo**k**). You could therefore copy this file to another machine to copy the phonebook entries.

Another important file is %systemroot%/system32/ras/switch.inf, which is used to create terminal logon scripts (as discussed earlier in this chapter), and phonebook entries may refer to an entry in this file at the end of the entry:

```
DEVICE=switch
Type=Terminal
```

In this case, Type=Terminal means bring up a terminal window after connection so it does not use SWITCH.INF.

```
DEVICE=switch
Type=Pipex
```

causes the script Pipex (which is in SWITCH.INF) to be run once a connection has been made. If these two lines are missing, don't worry; it just means you don't need a terminal window once you have connected (it probably means you are connecting to a Windows NT box). If you connect to a non-NT machine, you usually have to send it a username and password, along with the connection type (i.e., protocol), which is usually Point to Point Protocol (PPP) on most modern systems (Serial Line Internet Protocol—SLIP—is an older option).

RAS information relating to phone book entries and outbound connections in the Registry is actually stored under HKEY_CURRENT_USER\Software\Microsoft\RAS Phonebook and contains details about redial attempts, display settings, and other settings. Again you export this section of the Registry to a REG file (using REGEDIT.EXE) and import into another machine to copy the machine-specific settings.

FAQ 29.10 How can I change the number of rings that a RAS server waits before answering?

The normal method is to edit the file %systemroot%\system32\ras\modem.inf. In the file, find the sections relating to your modem, and find the line

```
COMMAND_LISTEN=ATS0=1<cr>
```

Change the numeric value to the number of rings to answer after—for example:

```
COMMAND_LISTEN=ATS0=10<cr>
```

would answer after ten rings (you must really hate your users, don't we all ☺). You must restart Windows NT for this change to take effect.

The preceding does not work if RAS is using any TAPI (Telephony Application Programming Interface)/Unimodem-based devices. If this is the case, perform the following:

1. Start the Registry editor (REGEDIT.EXE).
2. Move to HKEY_LOCAL_MACHINE\SYSTEM\CurrentControlSet\Services\RasMan\Parameters.
3. From the Edit menu, select New > DWORD Value.
4. Enter a name of **NumberOfRings** and press Enter.
5. Double-click on this new value and set to the number of rings you want the RAS server to wait before answering the phone (1–20). If you enter any number greater than 20, the default value of 1 is used. Click OK.
6. Close the Registry editor.

FAQ 29.11 How can I configure how long a RAS server waits before calling back a user when callback is enabled?

By default the RAS server will wait 12 seconds before calling back a RAS client; however, this can be changed by editing the Registry.

1. Start the Registry editor (REGEDIT.EXE).
2. Move to HKEY_LOCAL_MACHINE\SYSTEM\CurrentControlSet\Services\RasMan\PPP.

3. From the Edit menu, select New > DWORD Value.
4. Enter a name of **DefaultCallbackDelay** and press Enter.
5. Double-click on this new value and set to the number of seconds you want the RAS Server to wait before dialing the client (1–255). Click OK.
6. Close the Registry editor.

FAQ 29.12 Whenever I connect via RAS, I cannot connect to local machines on my LAN. What should I do?

To enable Web and FTP browsing when you connect via RAS, you enable the use default gateway on remote network option of the RAS options. Thereafter, when the connection is made, a new route is added to the route list, superseding the existing LAN routes, so any traffic destined for a node outside your local subnet will attempt to be sent using the RAS route. This is because a metric is used to identify the number of hops needed, and once connected to RAS, it will have a metric 1, and existing routes will be bumped out to a metric of 2.

To solve this, a persistent route can be manually added for your LAN's subnet and the associated subnet gateway. While not connected via RAS, you can examine your route information using the ROUTE PRINT command.

If your network was 160.82.0.0 (i.e., your company has a class B address) and the gateway was 160.82.220.1 for your local subnet, you could add a route for the LAN only, and all addresses outside of 160.82.0.0 would be routed using the RAS gateway.

```
route -p add <ip network> mask <subnet mask> <local gateway for the
route>
```

For example, **route -p add 160.82.0.0 mask 255.255.0.0 160.82.220.1**. This would mean all addresses from 160.82.1.1 to 160.82.254.254 would be routed via 160.82.220.1 and anything else via the RAS gateway.

If you wanted to add a route for a single host (maybe your Internet firewall, which is on another subnet), use the following:

```
route -p add 192.168.248.8 mask 255.255.255.254 160.82.220.1
```

Notice the subnet mask of 255.255.255.254, which means only for this single host.

When connected via RAS, you will still be able to access resources outside of your local subnet on the LAN with no problems.

FAQ 29.13 How can I disable the Save Password option in dial-up networking?

When you connect via RAS, you can cache the password. If you feel this is a security problem, then you can disable the option to enable the password to be saved.

1. Start the Registry editor (REGEDIT.EXE).
2. Move to HKEY_LOCAL_MACHINE\System\CurrentControlSet\Services\RasMan\Parameters.
3. From the Edit menu, select New > DWORD Value.
4. Enter a name of **DisableSavePassword** and press Enter.
5. Double-click the new value and set to 1.

If you disable the save password option, make sure redial on link failure is not activated as one redial attempt because it does not save user information. It will attempt to connect as Administrator, which will not work (unless the ISP has very poor security ☺).

FAQ 29.14 How can I set the number of authentication retries for dial-up connections?

By default after two unsuccessful authentication attempts, the dial-up networking (DUN) component will hang up the line. This can be changed to between 0 and 10: 0 means the line will be hung up after the first attempt, 1 will allow one retry, and so on.

1. Start the Registry editor (REGEDIT.EXE).
2. Move to HKEY_LOCAL_MACHINE\SYSTEM\CurrentControlSet\Services\RemoteAccess\Parameters.
3. Double-click on AuthenticateRetries and set to the required value. Click OK.
4. Close the Registry editor.
5. Reboot the machine for the change to take effect (or stop and restart the RAS services).

29.15 How can I set the authentication timeout for dial-up connections?

As well as changing the number of authentication retries that are allowed, you can also configure the amount of time between each attempt. After that time has elapsed, the authentication attempt will count as a logon failure. The amount of time between each attempt can be configured to be between 20 and 600 seconds.

1. Start the Registry editor.
2. Move to HKEY_LOCAL_MACHINE\SYSTEM\CurrentControlSet\Services\RemoteAccess\Parameters.
3. Double-click on AuthenticateTime and set to the required value. Click OK.
4. Close the Registry editor.
5. Reboot the machine for the change to take effect (or stop and restart the RAS services).

29.16 Why does my RAS client have the wrong subnet mask, and so forth?

The only parameter from DHCP that the RAS client uses is the IP address. Other parameters are discussed in the following paragraphs.

The subnet mask is that used by the network interface card (NIC) in the workstation, if fitted. IPCONFIG shows the mask as being the default mask for the class of IP address in use, but this is irrelevant. MS used to display it as 0.0.0.0, which is clearly wrong, but the default is more subtly wrong. If there is no NIC in the client, then the subnet mask is irrelevant because all traffic is passed through the dial-up connection.

The default router is displayed as the same as the address of the client RAS interface. What is actually used as default router is the RAS server itself.

WINS server addresses and DNS server addresses for use by the client similarly do not come from the parameters set on the DHCP server but instead are those used by the RAS server itself.

Node type is not taken from the DHCP parameters but can change on the RAS client depending on WINS information. If the RAS server has no WINS servers defined locally, a b-node Windows NT RAS client will remain a b-node client. If the RAS server has WINS servers defined locally, a b-node Windows NT RAS client will switch to h-node for the duration of the connection.

More information can be found in Knowledge Base article Q160699 at http://support.microsoft.com/support/kb/articles/q160/6/99.asp.

29.17 How can I disable the modem speaker when dialing?

It's possible to disable the modem speaker in a number of ways. The easiest method is to use the RAS properties:

1. Double-click My Computer.
2. Double-click Dial-Up Networking.
3. Select the dial-up connection, click More, and select Edit entry and modem Properties.
4. Select the Basic tab and, at the bottom, next to Dial using, click Configure.
5. At the bottom of the Modem Configuration dialog is a Disable modem speaker checkbox (see Figure 29-1). Check it and click OK.
6. Click OK to the main dialog and close all other dialogs.

An alternative (and you may try this if the preceding fails to work) is to edit the dial string and add the control sequence for your modem to disable the speaker (it's normally M0; however, it can vary).

Figure 29-1 Disabling the modem speaker

1. Start the Modem Control Panel applet (Start > Settings > Modems).
2. Select the modem and click Properties.
3. Select the Connection tab.
4. Click the Advanced button at the bottom of the dialog.
5. In the Extra settings box, enter the command string to disable the speaker—for example:

   ```
   M0
   ```

6. Click OK to the dialogs.

FAQ 29.18 How can I limit RAS callers to see only the machine they connect to rather than the whole network?

When you configure the RAS server, you set for each protocol the scope of the connection: the server or the whole network. To change this, perform the following:

1. Start the Network Control Panel applet (right-click on Network and select Properties).
2. Select the Service tab and the Remote Access Service and click Properties.
3. Select the COM port and click the Network button.
4. Click the Configure button next to the protocol you wish to change access (e.g., TCP/IP).
5. At the top, check the This computer only option.
6. Click OK.

Clients should now be able to view only local RAS server connections.

FAQ 29.19 How can I remove the dial-up networking icon from My Computer?

The dial-up networking icon can be removed by editing the Registry as follows:

1. Start the Registry editor (REGEDIT.EXE).
2. Move to HKEY_LOCAL_MACHINE\SOFTWARE\Microsoft\Windows\CurrentVersion\Explorer\MyComputer\NameSpace.

3. Select {a4d92740-67cd-11cf-96f2-00aa00a11dd9}.
4. This step is optional. From the Registry menu, select Export Registry File. Enter a name for the REG file that will be created. This file will allow you to automatically undo this procedure if you wish.
5. Press the Delete key to delete the key.
6. Click Yes to the deletion confirmation dialog.

Dial-up networking will no longer be visible from My Computer. To restore it using your REG file, just double-click on the REG file from Explorer, and dial-up networking will be restored.

FAQ 29.20 I've connected two computers using two 56Kbps modems, but I never connect at more than 33Kbps. Why?

The problem is that your modems cannot send faster than 33.6Kbps. The 56Kbps technologies, such as X2, K56flex, and the V.90 standard are asymmetric—56Kbps from a service such as an ISP to you, and 33.6Kbps (maximum negotiated rate, may be less) from you to an ISP.

Having one of your V.90 modems call the other won't create a connection faster than 33.6Kbps because neither side can transmit faster than 33.6Kbps. The 56Kbps is possible because the line from your house to the telephone company switching office is analog, and the rest of the path from the company switching office (CO) to the service (ISP) is 100 percent digital. At the service end, they specifically install digital modems designed to operate as the service end of V.90/X2/K56flex connection.

This means you need one of the boxes of the same kind of modem that an ISP buys. You may find, however, that you can't get one of those without also having the digital phone circuit to connect it to.

If you need 56Kbps, look at ISDN. The easiest way to set up a system that can accept 56Kbps V.90 incoming connections is to get an ISDN2 or home highway and a 3COM Courier-I modem. The Courier-I can act as a standard and ISDN modem. It will also act in V.90 mode as a server if it detects an incoming analog call across the ISDN.

FAQ 29.21 DEVICE.LOG does not capture modem commands. What can I do?

When you use a Unimodem, the DEVICE.LOG no longer captures the command. However, you can create an alternate log file to capture the modem commands:

1. Start the Modems Control Panel applet (Start > Settings > Control Panel > Modems).
2. Select the modem for which a log file should be created.
3. Click Properties.
4. Click the Connection tab.
5. Click Advanced.
6. Select the Record a Log File checkbox. There is no need to restart the computer.

The log file will be created in the %systemroot% directory with name MODEMLOG_<modem>.TXT.

FAQ 29.22 How do I create a dial-up connection in Windows 2000?

Windows 2000 has removed the segregation between LAN and dial-up connections; they are all just connections now.

To create a dial-up connection to an ISP or your work, you need to create a new connection using a modem as the connection medium:

1. From the Start menu, select Network and Dial-up Connection.
2. Double-click Make New Connection.
3. Click Next to the Introduction Wizard.
4. Select Dial-up to the Internet (see Figure 29-2) and click Next.
5. Select I want to set up my Internet connection manually and click Next.
6. Select I connect through a phone line and a modem (if you are using ISDN, you would select local area network). Click Next.
7. Make sure your modem is connected and turned on; check the Don't detect my modem box is not selected and click Next.
8. If it can't find your modem, click Next, and you can choose it from a list.
9. Enter the phone details of the ISP. Click Next.
10. Enter your username and password and click Next.

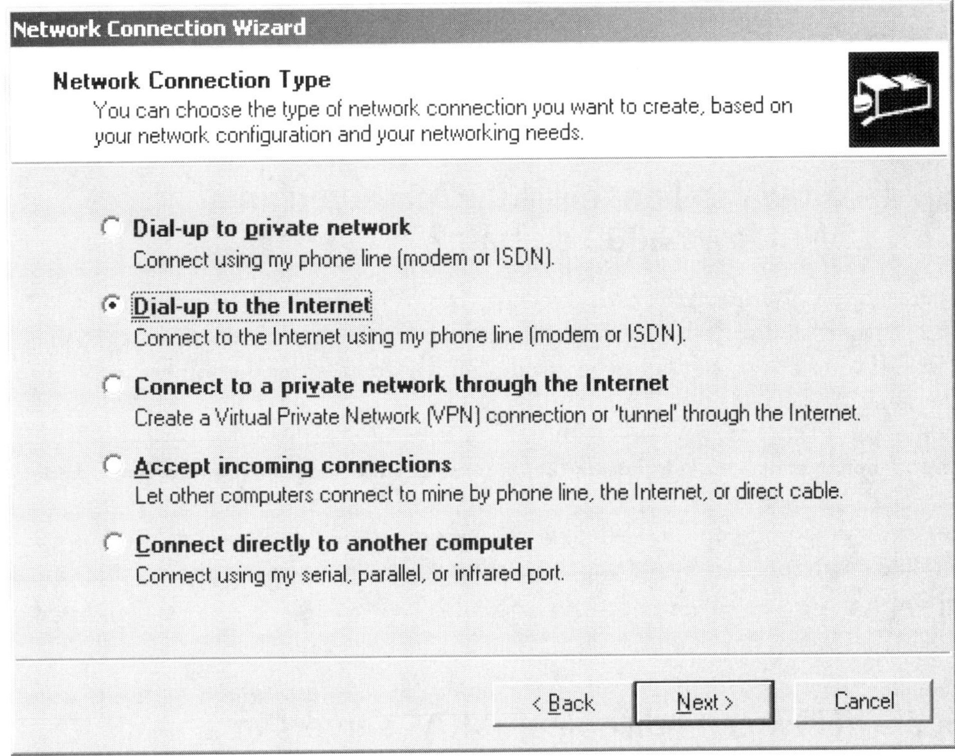

Figure 29-2 Creating a new network connection

11. Finally give it a name—for example, Connection to UUnet. Click Next.
12. You will be asked if you wish to set up mail. Make your choice and click Next.
13. Click Finish.

Your new connection will now be visible from Network and Dial-up Connections. To change its properties, right-click on the connection and select Properties.

FAQ 29.23 When loading a program, why do I get the error message RASMAN.DLL failed to load?

This can happen if you have uninstalled RAS. The official way to detect whether or not RAS is installed is to check for a certain file. Unfortunately that file doesn't get deleted when RAS is uninstalled, so the program thinks that RAS is still installed.

If you delete the WINNT\SYSTEM32\RASAPI32.DLL file manually, the program will realize that RAS has been uninstalled, and it will not try to initialize RASMAN.DLL

29.24 How can I enable 4.0 RAS servers in a Windows 2000 domain?

When you run DCPROMO.EXE to create your Windows 2000 domain, one of the stages asks if you wish to weaken security to enable 4.0 servers to act as RAS servers. If you said No, but later you decide you require it, enter the following command:

```
net localgroup "Pre-Windows 2000 Compatible Access" everyone /add
```

This creates a local group Pre-Windows 2000 Compatible Access and adds the everyone group to it. After entering the command, you must restart the domain controller.

29.25 How can I disable 4.0 RAS servers in a Windows 2000 domain?

When you run DCPROMO.EXE to create your Windows 2000 domain, one of the stages asks if you wish to weaken security to enable 4.0 servers to act as RAS servers. If you said Yes, but later you decide you don't require it, enter the following command:

```
net localgroup "Pre-Windows 2000 Compatible Access" everyone
/delete
```

This removes everyone from the local group Pre-Windows 2000 Compatible Access. After entering the command, you must restart the domain controller.

Security may be compromised when enabled because Pre-Windows 2000 Compatible Access allows anonymous users to read information in this domain. When Windows NT 4.0 RAS servers no longer exist in the domain, you can remove legacy access to Active Directory by using the previously shown command.

FAQ 29.26 How can I get the dial-up networking information in Windows 2000?

If you select Properties for a live connection in Windows NT 4.0, you get details such as connected speed, bytes in, bytes out, duration, and so on.

If you right-click on the connection and select Status in Windows 2000, you get less information (although it's presented better). You can still get the old NT 4.0 connection information by running

```
rasphone -s
```

This will start the Dial-Up Networking Monitor and display NT 4.0 format connection information as shown in Figure 29-3.

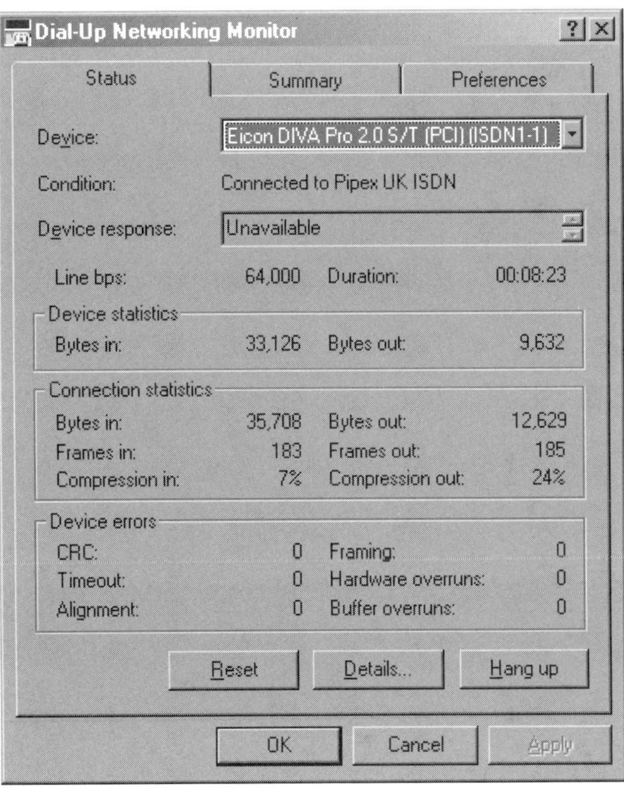

Figure 29-3 Viewing information about a network connection

29.27 How do I create an incoming connection in Windows 2000?

In Windows NT 4.0 you could configure connections to be dial-in/dial-out or both. In Windows 2000 you can also create an incoming connection that allows people to dial into the machine via Public Switch Telephone Network (PSTN)/ISDN and even parallel ports.

To configure an incoming connection, perform the following:

1. Select Make new connection from Start > Settings > Network and dial-up connections.
2. Click Next to the wizard.
3. Select Accept incoming connections. Click Next.
4. Select the device that you wish to accept incoming connections on and click Next.
5. Select if you wish to allow Virtual Private Connections and click Next.
6. Select the users who will be able to dial into the connection and click Next.
7. Select the networking components to be enabled for the connection. If you select TCP/IP, click Properties. You can then choose if the connector can talk to the local network and if the address is assigned by DHCP—one from a list or let the caller set his or her own address (see Figure 29-4).

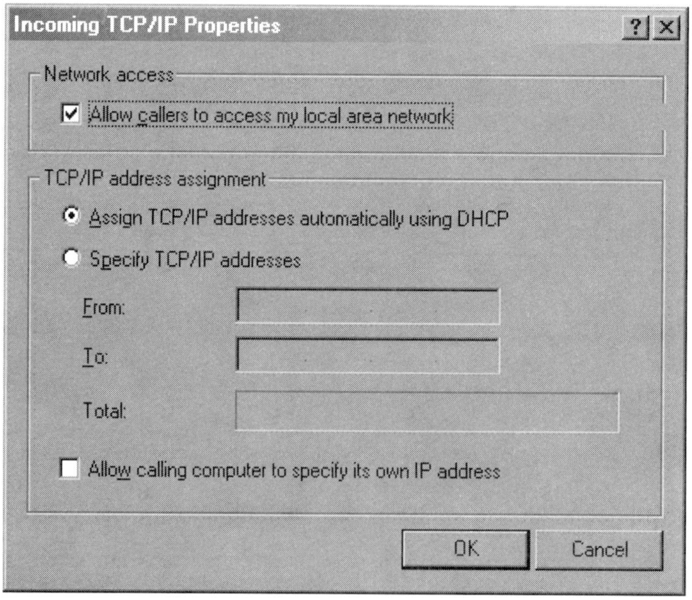

Figure 29-4 Selecting options for an incoming TCP connection

8. Click OK.
9. Click Next, give the connection a name, and click Finish.

To modify the connection in the future, just select from Start > Settings > Network and Dial-up connections where you can modify the adapters users can connect on, users who can connect, and so on.

FAQ 29.28 How do I stop a Windows 2000 incoming connection from answering?

Rather than delete the Incoming Connection object every time you want to stop it from answering, another method is to disassociate it from all connection equipment such as PSTN/ISDN. To do this, perform the following:

1. Select the Incoming Connection object (Start > Settings > Network and Dial-up Connections > Incoming connection).
2. Select the General tab.
3. Uncheck all devices (or a specific one you wish to currently suspend).
4. Click OK.

When you wish to reenable, perform the preceding but check the devices instead of unchecking them.

FAQ 29.29 How do I disable operator/assisted dial on my RAS connections?

If when you try to connect to your ISP via RAS, you receive the following:

```
Operator or Assisted Dial
Pick up the handset and dial (or ask the operator to dial).
Press OK after dialing, then replace the handset.
```

To resolve, perform the following:

1. Right-click My Network Places.
2. Select Properties.
3. Select the Advanced menu.
4. Uncheck Operated-Assisted Dialing.

FAQ 29.30 How do I enable PPP logging in Windows 2000?

It you are using PPP and wish to debug, it's possible to enable logging. To enable logging on a server box:

1. Start the Routing and Remote Access Services (RRAS) tool in Microsoft Management Console (MMC).
2. In the left pane, right-click the RRAS server for which you want to enable logging and then click Properties.
3. Click the Event Logging tab.
4. Click to select the Enable Point-to-Point Protocol (PPP) logging checkbox.

On a Windows 2000 Professional machine:

1. Open a command prompt window on the RRAS server for which you want to enable logging.
2. Type the following command, pressing Enter after each command:

   ```
   netsh
   ras
   set tracing PPP enable
   ```

   All PPP activity will be logged to the PPP log file in the %systemroot%\tracing\ folder. This uses quite a lot of resources so make sure you disable it once you have logged the required data.
3. Open a command prompt window on the RRAS server for which you want to disable logging.
4. Type the following command, pressing Enter after each command:

   ```
   netsh
   ras
   set tracing PPP disabled
   ```

This can also be set via the Registry:

1. Start the Registry editor (REGEDIT.EXE).
2. Move to HKEY_LOCAL_MACHINE\SOFTWARE\Microsoft\Tracing\PPP.
3. Set EnableConsoleTracing (for Win2k Server) or EnableFileTracing (for Win2k Prof) to 1.
4. Close the Registry editor.

FAQ 29.31 Why aren't the dial-up options available on my Windows 2000 domain?

If you go to the Active Directory Users and Computers Microsoft Management Console (MMC) snap-in, select User properties and then the Dial-in tab, you might find that the following options aren't available:

- Control access through remote access policy
- Verify caller ID
- Assign a static IP address
- Apply static routes
- Static routes

These options aren't available when your domain is mixed mode instead of native mode because other non-Win2K domain controllers don't support the options. If you don't have any non-Win2K domain controllers, you can upgrade to native mode to enable the options.

I **have** noticed a bug in the Win2K Administration tools for Win2K Professional. If you have a mixed-mode domain, these options **appear** to be available, but when you try to select one of them, the system returns an error.

FAQ 29.32 How can I speed up my Asymmetric Digital Subscriber Line (ADSL) line connection?

Because TCP/IP is packet based, each time a packet is sent, it must be acknowledged via an acknowledgment packet, which slows down the system. To keep the sender from having to wait for every packet to be acknowledged before sending another one, you can increase the window size (TcpWindowSize) value on the receiver end. Then, the sender can send packets until that value is reached before the receiver needs to send an acknowledgment. To tweak the TCP/IP parameters to increase the window size, you need to manually update the Registry:

1. Start REGEDIT.EXE.
2. Go to HKEY_LOCAL_MACHINE\SYSTEM\CurrentControlSet\Services\Tcpip\Parameters.
3. From the Edit menu, select New > DWORD Value.
4. Enter a name of **TcpWindowSize** and press Enter.

5. Double-click the new value, change the Base value to decimal, and enter a value of 32767. Click OK.
6. Close Regedit.
7. Reboot the machine.

In step 5, you can actually specify a higher value (up to 256000). However, on slow networks, this larger window size means that more data will need to be retransmitted.

If you're interested in a great site that helps you test your DSL connection speed and configuration, check out http://www.dslreports.com.

FAQ 29.33 Why does RRAS ignore my dial-on-demand settings?

A problem exists with RRAS that requires that you restart RRAS before changes to DNS server settings take effect. To restart RRAS, perform the following steps:

1. Start the Microsoft Management Console (MMC) Routing and Remote Access snap-in (Start > Programs > Administrative Tools > Routing and Remote Access).
2. Right-click the server, and from the All Tasks context menu, select Restart.
3. Close the MMC snap-in.

You can also restart RRAS from the command line:

```
net stop remoteaccess
net start remoteaccess
```

FAQ 29.34 What is Internet Connection Sharing?

In a small office/home office (SOHO) environment with two or more networked computers, Internet Connection Sharing (ICS) is a great addition to Windows XP and Windows 2000. ICS lets all machines on your network use one machine's RAS connection (e.g., modem, ADSL, cable modem, ISDN) for Internet access without additional software. ICS is available on XP and Win2K Professional systems as well as on Win2K Server products.

When you enable ICS, the machine becomes a cut-down DHCP server with the nonroutable IP address 192.168.0.1. The ICS machine gives out addresses in the 192.168.0.x range to the other machines in the network (which you must configure to use DHCP). Because of the IP address change, you shouldn't enable ICS on a domain controller, DNS server, DHCP server, or any other machine that offers a static service. When you enable ICS, you lose any current TCP/IP connections, and you have to reconnect them.

You can't modify the network configuration ICS uses (e.g., changing the range of private IP addresses it hands out, enabling or disabling DNS, configuring a range of public IP addresses, or configuring inbound mappings); this is possible in full NAT implementation (which is also included in Windows 2000 and can be administered through RRAS). In addition, some services can't run on the same box as ICS. ICS uses Network Address Translation (NAT), and only one service per box can run NAT. So if, for example, you also have RRAS's NAT capability enabled, ICS won't start. To resolve this problem, you have to remove NAT from the IP routing section of the RRAS administrative menu. The same is true for such products as Proxy Server or Internet Security and Acceleration (ISA) Server 2000—which are both superior to ICS anyway.

Other computers on the network don't have to run XP or Win2K to access the Internet through ICS. They can run Windows NT, Windows Me, or Windows 9x. Because the ICS machine must use IP address 192.168.0.1, you can't have more than one machine on the network running ICS.

FAQ 29.35 How do I enable Internet Connection Sharing?

To enable ICS, you must be an Administrator for the machine. Ensure that the machine has at least one RAS connection configured and has a network connection to the rest of your computers. Then perform the following steps:

1. Click Start > Settings > Control Panel > Network and Dial-up Connections > [RAS connection].
2. Click Properties.
3. Select the Sharing tab.
4. Select Enable Internet Connection Sharing for this connection (see Figure 29-5).
5. If the connection is a dial-up connection and you want it to automatically dial out when another machine makes a connection request, also select Enable on-demand dialing.
6. Click OK.
7. You will see a confirmation dialog box that explains that the IP address will change to 192.168.0.1. Click Yes to confirm.
8. Close the RAS Properties dialog box.

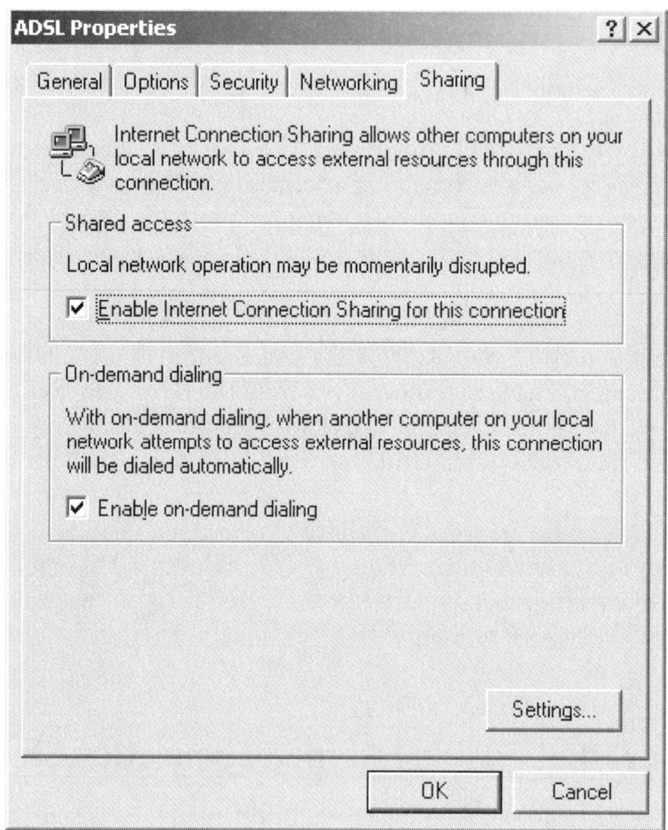

Figure 29-5 Enabling Internet Connection Sharing

FAQ 29.36 How do I enable machines to use a computer with Internet Connection Sharing?

You enable machines to use ICS the same way you enable them to use DHCP and a proxy server. To enable DHCP, perform the following steps:

1. Right-click My Network Places or start the Control Panel Network applet (Start > Settings > Control Panel > Network).
2. Right-click the LAN connection (e.g., Local Area Connection) and select Properties.

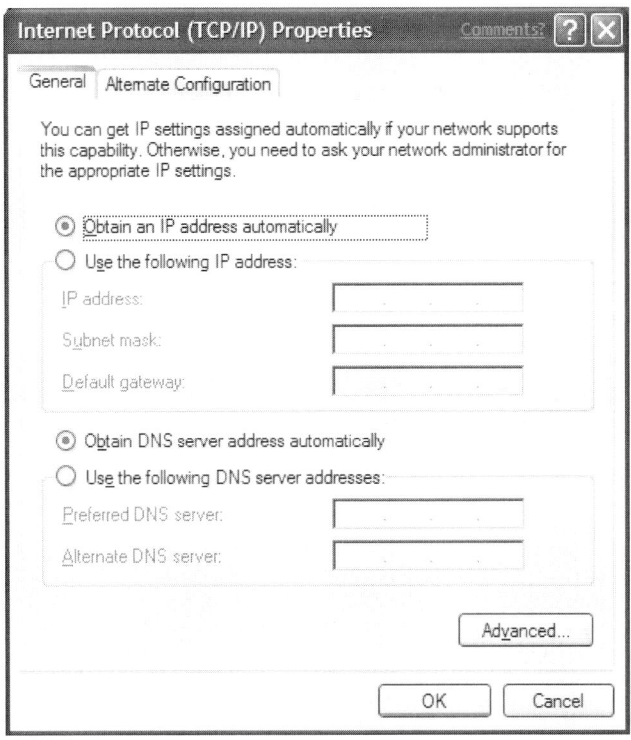

Figure 29-6 Options needed for clients of Internet Connection Sharing

3. Select Internet Protocol (TCP/IP) and click Properties.
4. On the General tab, select Obtain an IP address automatically (see Figure 29-6). Then click OK.

To enable a proxy server (for Internet Explorer), perform the following steps:

1. Start IE.
2. From the Tools menu, select Internet Options.
3. Select the Connections tab.
4. Click LAN Settings.
5. Select Automatically detect settings and click OK.
6. Click OK to close the main dialog box.

You should now be able to use ICS from this machine.

FAQ 29.37 How do I configure the services that Internet Connection Sharing provides?

With ICS, you can offer services (e.g., FTP and Telnet) to remote networks from clients on your network. To enable services, perform the following steps:

1. Click Start > Settings > Control Panel > Network and Dial-up Connections > [RAS connection]).
2. Select Properties.
3. Select the Sharing tab.
4. Click Settings.
5. Select the Services tab.
6. Select the services you want to enable:
   - FTP Server
   - Internet Mail Access Protocol Version 3 (IMAP3)
   - Internet Mail Access Protocol Version 4 (IMAP4)
   - Internet Mail Server (SMTP)
   - Post Office Protocol Version 3 (POP3)
   - Telnet Server
7. When you select a service, you need to enter the DNS name and IP address of the machine on the local network.
8. Click OK.
9. Click OK to close the main dialog box.

To add a service, on the Services tab, click Add and enter a name for the service, the port number to use, whether it's TCP or UDP, and the DNS name or IP address of the machine on the local network offering the service.

FAQ 29.38 How can I obtain a list of all user accounts that have permission to dial in to the network?

The Windows NT Server Resource Kit includes the Rasusers command. To get a list of user accounts that have dial-in permission to a domain or server, type one of the following commands:

```
rasusers MYDOMAIN
```

or

```
rasusers MYSERVER
```

30 UTILITIES

In this chapter, we look at other tools: some of which are part of the operating system, some are from Microsoft, and some are from third parties—all of which add to our overall Windows day-to-day experience.

30.1 What is TweakUI?

TweakUI is part of the PowerToys set originally released for Windows 95. Many incarnations of TweakUI that were designed for Windows NT4/2000/XP can be downloaded from http://www.microsoft.com (the exact URL changes).

TweakUI allows users to easily change advanced settings of the machine that otherwise require editing the Registry.

30.2 Where is File Manager?

It is still shipped with NT 4; just run WINFILE.EXE. However it is not available under Windows 2000 or above.

If you upgraded a 4.0 machine to Windows 2000, then File Manager is not deleted and will still be available. Also you may copy WINFILE.EXE from a 4.0 machine to Windows 2000. Under Windows 2000, you may also use the File Management MMC snap-in.

I would say that by now you should be using Explorer and not File Manager anyway to take advantage of the advanced feature set provided by Explorer.

30.3 How can I fix/replace/copy files on an NTFS partition from outside Windows NT?

NT Internals has released ERD Commander, which allows you to perform read and write operations on NTFS/FAT and CDFS partitions. ERD Commander can be purchased from http://www.winternals.com/products/erdcommander.shtml and a free read-only version can be obtained from http://www.sysinternals.com/erdcmndr.htm.

Once you've downloaded ERD Commander, just run the executable ERDCMNDR.EXE, and it will self-install to a directory of your choosing. It will also create a program group ERD Commander. Once installed, it will ask if you want to create ERD Commander disks. ERD Commander works by altering a set of NT installation disks with its own special versions of certain files, so instead of installing NT, it brings up a DOS-like command prompt. You can either modify an existing set of installation disks or let ERD Commander create a new set (you will need to insert your NT installation CD-ROM). The following instructions are for creating the disks:

1. Run ERD Commander setup32 (Start > Programs > ERD Commander). This instruction assumes you are booted in NT; if you are running a 16-bit OS, you can run ERD Commander setup16.
2. Click Next and then Next again to confirm the license agreement.
3. If you have a set of NT installation disks you want to modify, check I already have NT setup floppies; if you don't and want the installation to create them, leave the box unchecked. Click Next.
4. Insert your NT installation CD-ROM and click Next.
5. Click Next at the next screen and then in the dialog box, enter the location of your installation files, **<CD-ROM>:\i386**.
6. You will then be prompted to insert three blank, formatted disks, and you should follow the onscreen instructions. You put the disks in reverse order, so disk 3 first, then disk 2, and disk 1 last. This order is because if you are installing, you can just leave disk 1 in the machine once created and reboot—clever ☺.
7. Once the disks are created, make sure disk 1 is in the disk drive and click Next on the ERD Commander window; it will alter the disk and then ask you to put in disk 2 and again alter a number of files. You do not have to put in disk 3 (this disk just contains drivers).

When the creation has completed, you can insert disk 1 and reboot the machine to boot into ERD Commander. You will then be prompted to insert disk 2, then disk 3, and then finally disk 2 again.

There is a pause of about 30 seconds when it first displays "Microsoft Windows NT"; don't worry, this is normal. You will then be shown a list of all the drives. Pay attention to the drive letters; they may not match your usual drive assignments. This is because Windows NT grants letters on active partitions of each disk first, whereas ERD Commander assigns them as it comes across them from floppy disk 0, hard disk 0, and then CD-ROM 0 onward. For example, if you had two hard disks, hard disk 0 and hard disk 1, with hard disk 0 having two partitions, Windows NT would assign the letters as

```
Hard disk 0, partition 1 c:
Hard disk 1, partition 1 d:
Hard disk 0, partition 2 e:
```

This is because active partitions are assigned drive letters first. ERD Commander would label the partitions as

```
Hard disk 0, partition 1 c:
Hard disk 0, partition 2 d:
Hard disk 1, partition 1 e:
```

This is not a problem; just be aware of it. Don't panic that your files have disappeared ☺.

You can now enter normal commands like dir, rename, copy, and so on. When you are finished, Ctrl+Alt+Del does not work. Just remove the ERD Commander disk and type **exit**.

FAQ 30.4 What is the Microsoft Management Console (MMC)?

Microsoft Management Console (MMC), previously known by the code name "Slate," is Microsoft's new interface for machine and application management and allows the user to create a custom console with snap-ins loaded. MMC provides a shell with no functionality; a snap-in provides the functionality, such as DNS management, and while a number of default console configurations will be supplied with certain snap-ins preloaded, you will be able to create your own console with one or more snap-ins loaded. A custom console with the Group Policy editor, Services, and Disk Management snap-in loaded can be seen in Figure 30-1.

The main MMC window has the Console menu, which is used to add and remove snap-ins to the console and to also save the configuration to enable you to reload any useful snap-in combinations. In Figure 30-2, the main MMC components are labeled.

Newer Microsoft applications, such as Exchange 2000, will use MMC snap-ins instead of normal applications, and other software providers will follow suit with snap-ins for most application management interfaces.

The MMC is core in Windows 2000 and was first seen in NT 4.0 with Option Pack 4, Internet Information Server 4.0, and Service Pack 4's Security Configuration editor.

The latest version of the MMC for Windows NT 4.0 can be downloaded from http://support.microsoft.com/default.aspx?PR=MMC.

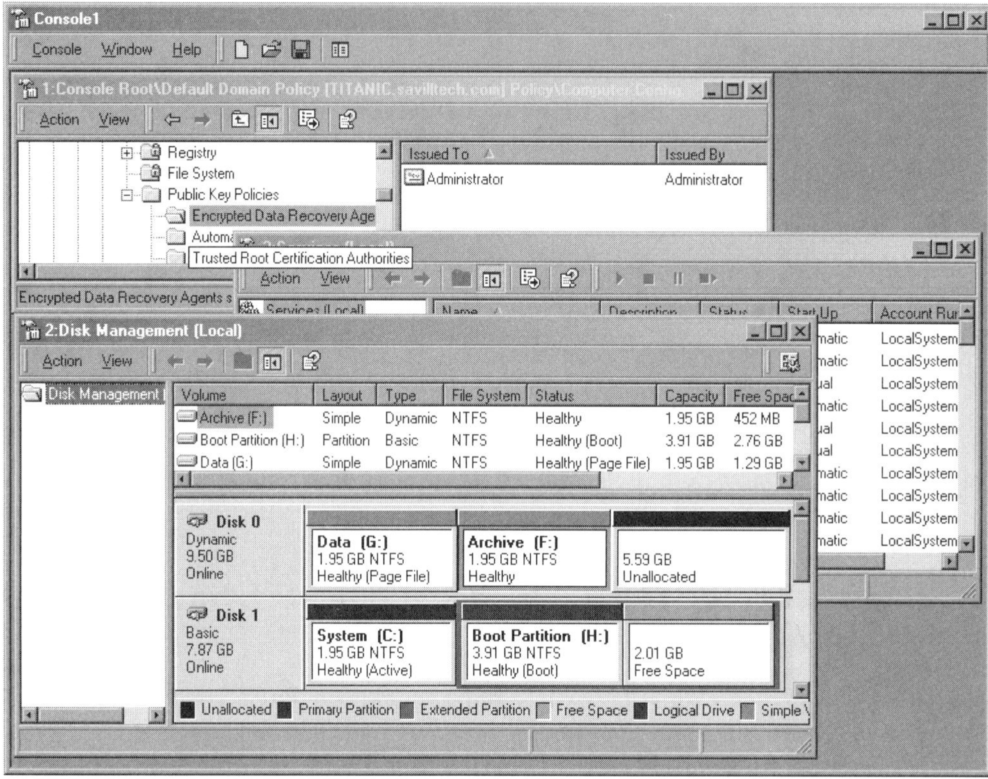

Figure 30-1 Our own console view

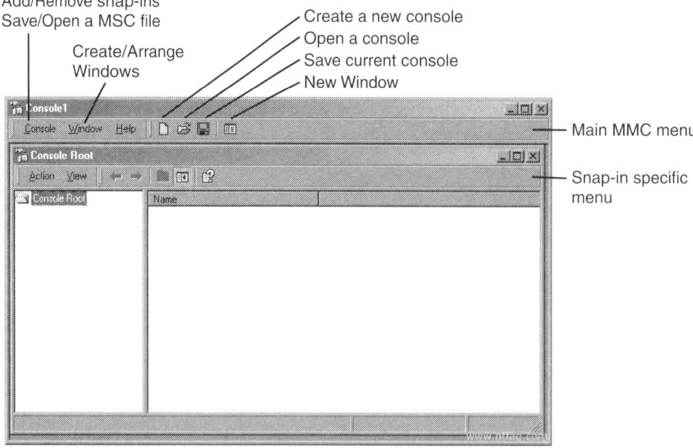

Figure 30-2 MMC components

30.5 How do I create a custom MMC configuration?

One of MMC's great features is that it's flexible. Let's take a quick look at this flexibility by creating our own custom console. The first step is to start the MMC shell, select Start > Run and type **MMC.EXE**. MMC will be started with no snap-ins loaded and with no functionality.

The next step is to add a snap-in:

1. From the main MMC menu, select Console > Add/Remove Snap-in.
2. The Add/Remove dialog will be shown, and no snap-ins will be listed. Click Add.
3. A list of all known snap-ins will be displayed. Select a snap-in (e.g., Disk Management—see Figure 30-3) and click Add.
4. Depending on the snap-in added, other options may be displayed. For example, on Disk Management, you can choose the local computer or a remote computer. Click Finish.
5. You may add other snap-ins (e.g., DNS). When finished adding snap-ins, click Close.
6. The dialog will show the snap-ins added. Click OK.

Figure 30-3 Adding a snap-in to a console

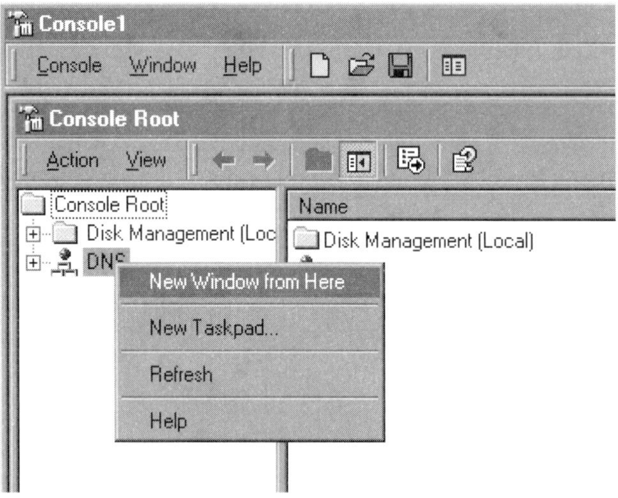

Figure 30-4 Moving a branch into its own window

The main console will now show the snap-ins added at the root. It's possible for each snap-in to be in its own window within the MMC rather than to be depicted as a single tree by right-clicking on the snap-in and selecting New Windows from Here from the context menu (see Figure 30-4). If you did this for all snap-ins loaded, you could close the main tree window.

Once your console is laid out to your liking, you can save it as follows:

1. Select Save As from the Console menu.
2. Select a location to save the configuration as and enter a name. It will have a .MSC extension.
3. Click Save.

If you save to your profile area (e.g., d:\Documents and Settings\Administrator\Start Menu\Programs\Administrative Tools), the new MMC configuration will be displayed on the Start menu.

30.6 Where is X from NT 4.0 in Windows 2000?

Windows NT 4.0 had a large number of applications for domain and system management that have been replaced in Windows 2000 as, or part of, an MMC snap-in. The following table shows mappings of 4.0 applications to MMC snap-ins.

4.0 Application	Windows 2000 Snap-in	Notes
Backup (NTBACKUP.EXE)	NTBACUP.EXE	New utility but same name. Does not use MMC because it may be called from command prompt as part of automated procedure. Based on Seagate technology.
Disk Administrator (WINDISK.EXE)	Disk Management	By default in Computer Manager MSC file, Start > Programs > Administrative Tools > Computer Management > Storage > Disk Management.
Event Viewer (EVENTVWR.EXE)	Event Viewer	By default in Computer Manager MSC file, Start > Programs > Administrative Tools > Computer Management > System Tools > Event Viewer.
License Manager (LLSMGR.EXE)	LLSMGR.EXE	Start > Programs > Administrative Tools > Licensing.
Migration Tool to NetWare (NWCONV.EXE)		
Network Client Administrator (NCADMIN.EXE)	Remote Install Service	Start > Programs > Administrative Tools > Active Directory Users and Computers > Select computer > Remote Install tab.
Performance Monitor (PERFMON.EXE)	Performance Logs and Alerts	By default in Computer Manager MSC file, Start > Programs > Administrative Tools > Computer Management > System Tools > Performance Logs and Alerts.
Remote Access Admin (RASADMIN.EXE)	Routing and Remote Access	By default in Computer Manager MSC file, Start > Programs > Administrative Tools > Computer Management > Server Applications and Services > Routing and Remote Access.

(*continued*)

4.0 Application	Windows 2000 Snap-in	Notes
Server Manager (SRVMGR.EXE)	Active Directory Users and Computers	Start > Programs > Administrative Tools > Active Directory Users and Computers > Select Domain > Computers branch Promotion of a machine to a domain controller is via DCPROMO.EXE utility.
System Policy editor (POLEDIT.EXE)	Group Policy editor	Right-click on a container, select Properties and select Group Policy tab.
User Manager for Domains (USRMGR.EXE)	Active Directory Users and Computers	Start > Programs > Administrative Tools > Active Directory Users and Computers > Select Domain > Users branch.
User Manager for Domains (USRMGR.EXE)—Trusts	Active Directory Domains and Trusts	Start > Programs > Administrative Tools > Active Directory Domains and Trusts. Right-click domain > Select Properties > Select Trusts tab.
User Manager for Domains (USRMGR.EXE)—Account Policies	Group Policy	Start > Programs > Administrative Tools > Active Directory Users and Computers. Right-click on Domain > Select Properties > Select Group Policy. Select Domain Policy and click Edit > Computer Configuration > Windows Settings > Account Policies.
User Manager for Domains (USRMGR.EXE)—User Rights	Group Policy	Start > Programs > Administrative Tools > Active Directory Users and Computers. Right-click on Domain, select Properties, select Group Policy select Domain Policy (or a container) and click Edit > Computer Configuration > Windows Settings > Local Policies > User Rights Assignment.

4.0 Application	Windows 2000 Snap-in	Notes
User Manager for Domains (USRMGR.EXE)—Audit	Group Policy	Start > Programs > Administrative Tools > Active Directory Users and Computers. Right-click on Domain. Select Properties, select Group Policy, select Domain Policy (or a container) and click Edit > Computer Configuration > Windows Settings > Local Policies > Audit Policy.
Windows Diagnostics (WINMSD.EXE)	System Information	By default in Computer Manager MSC file, Start > Programs > Administrative Tools > Computer Management > System Tools > System Information.
Domain Network Services (DNS)	DNS	Start > Programs > Administrative Tools > DNS.
Dynamic Host Configuration Protocol (DHCP)	DHCP	Start > Programs > Administrative Tools > DHCP.
WINS	WINS	Start > Programs > Administrative Tools > WINS.

In many situations the 2000 application has its own snap-in but is usually called from a larger group snap-in (e.g., Computer Management MMC snap-in, which contains many other snap-ins).

FAQ 30.7 What is MSINFO32.EXE?

MSINFO32.EXE was first introduced with Office 97 and provides detailed information about your computer. In Windows 2000, MSINFO32.EXE has replaced WINMSD.EXE, and if you try to start WINMSD, MSINFO32 will be started.

MSINFO32 not only gives information about your hardware, it can give full information about currently running processes, programs configured to start when the system starts, and much more (see Figure 30-5).

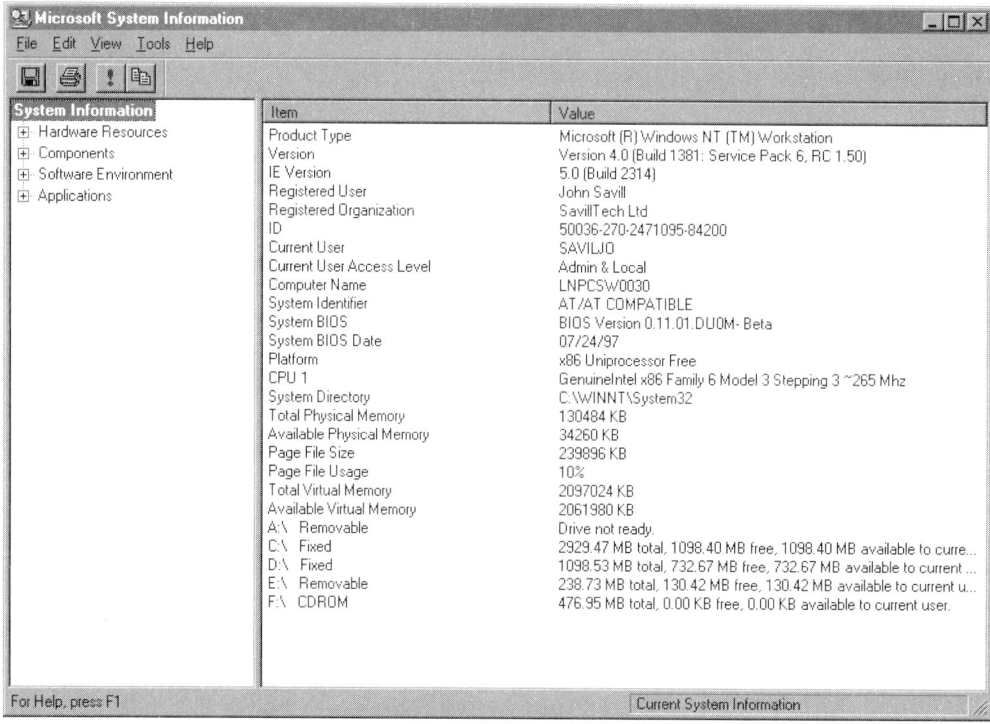

Figure 30-5 Viewing a system's information

30.8 How can I run a program as another user in Windows 2000?

Windows 2000 includes the utility RUNAS.EXE, which allows you to run a program as another user without having to log off, which is most useful for Administrators who may need to run a single command as an Administrator. The basic usage is

```
runas /user:Administrator@savtech.com regedit.exe
```

or

```
runas /user:savtech\Administrator regedit.exe
```

Both the Windows 2000 naming methods can be used—the 4.0-style domain\user or the Windows 2000 User Principal Name (UPN), user@<domain>. Full help can be found by typing **runas /?**.

After entering the runas command, you will be prompted for the password of the specified account—for example:

```
runas /user:Administrator@savtech.com regedit.exe
Enter password for Administrator@savtech.com:
Attempting to start "regedit.exe" as user
"Administrator@savtech.com"...
```

Another option is to install the Telnet service on the machine to then telnet back into the machine as the other user and run the command without having to log off the main user.

You can also Shift+right-click on an item and choose Run As from either Explorer, Desktop to bring up the Run As Other User dialog (see Figure 30-6), which allows you to specify a user/password.

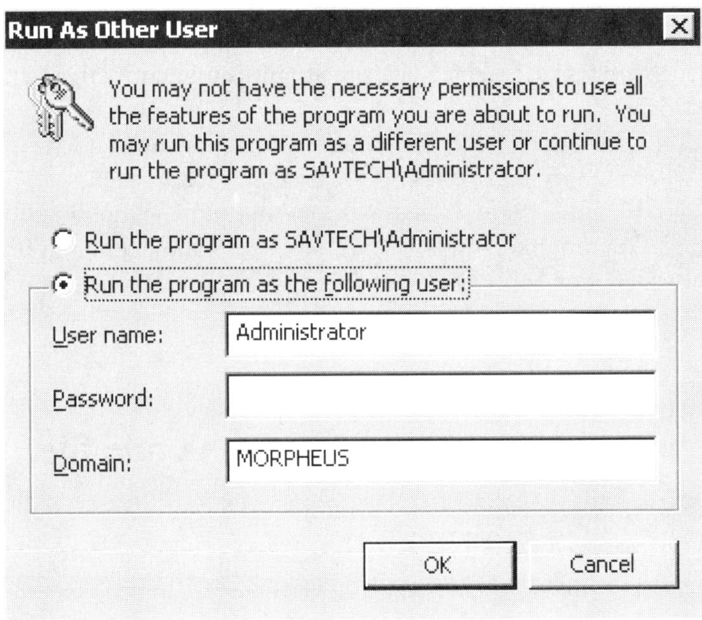

Figure 30-6 The Run As Other User dialog

30.9 Where is SCOPY in Windows 2000?

Scopy was a useful NT 4.0 Resource Kit utility that enabled files/folders to be copied with their ACLs and audit settings kept intact. SCOPY is not supplied in the Windows 2000 Resource Kit, but its functionality has instead been packaged into the XCOPY utility:

- /X copies the audit settings (as /a in SCOPY)
- /O copies ACL information (same as SCOPY)
- /S copies subdirectories (same as SCOPY)

30.10 Does Regclean work on Windows 2000?

Regclean is a Microsoft utility that is used to tidy up the Registry of a computer. When you install and remove programs, sometimes Registry keys/associations get left behind, which wastes space, and Regclean attempts to identify these and remove them from the system.

REGCLEAN.EXE can be downloaded from http://download.microsoft.com/download/win98SE/Utility/4.1a/W9XNT4/EN-US/regclean.exe.

Version 4.1a of Regclean build 7364.1 is compatible with Windows 2000. There are some issues running it on NT 4 Service pack 4 and below, but if you're using Windows 2000, none of these issues apply, and Regclean should work as documented.

30.11 I'm unable to run the Regclean undo file.

This is not actually a Regclean problem but rather just an association problem between .REG files and REGEDIT.EXE. Use the following steps to correct this problem:

1. Start Explorer.
2. From the Tools menu, select Folder Options.
3. Select the File Types tab.
4. Find REG Registration Entries and select it.
5. Click Advanced.

6. Under Actions, select open and click Edit.
7. Change to:

   ```
   regedit.exe "%1"
   ```

   and click OK.
8. Click OK to all dialogs.

You should now be able to run the undo file by double-clicking on it.

FAQ 30.12 Where is REGEDT32.EXE in Windows XP?

Microsoft removed REGEDT32.EXE from XP. REGEDIT.EXE's functionality has been merged with REGEDT32.EXE's, so REGEDIT.EXE now supports all the extra data types (e.g., multistring, security). If you start REGEDT32.EXE, the system runs REGEDIT.EXE.

FAQ 30.13 How can I interpret trace logs from the command line?

The Windows 2000 Resource Kit provides TRACEDMP.EXE, which you can use to either process trace log data or poll the trace log in real time and convert the information to a Comma Separated Value (CSV) file. To enable/disable tracing, use the Resource Kit TRACELOG.EXE program. The syntax is as follows (see the Resource Kit Help file for more details):

```
Usage: tracedmp [options]
          | [-h | -? | -help]
         -o                   Output CSV file
         -guid                MOF definition file
         -rt [LoggerName]     Realtime tracedmp from the logger
                              [LoggerName]
         -summary             Summary.txt only
         -h
         -help
         -?                   Display usage information
```

30.14 Is a Plus! pack available for Windows XP?

Microsoft has released a Plus! add-on pack for XP similar to the Plus! 98 pack that the company released for Windows 98. The XP Plus! pack contains several extra utilities and features, including

- Plus! speaker enhancement for greater sound clarity through desktop speakers
- Plus! Personal DJ for playlist generation
- Plus! Voice Command for Windows Media Player
- Plus! CD Label Maker
- Windows Media Player (WMP) skins
- MP3-to-Windows Media Audio (WMA) converter
- Games
- Screensavers, including one with a virtual fish tank

30.15 Does Windows XP include a compressed folders feature?

Yes, XP includes a compressed folders feature similar to the compressed folders feature in Windows Me and in the Plus! 98 pack for Windows 98. XP's compressed folders feature lets you manipulate .ZIP files; however, this feature can be slow with large numbers of files. I'm glad that Microsoft is including this functionality in XP, but I still recommend using a third-party compression program.

30.16 Where is TLIST.EXE in Windows XP?

Microsoft has replaced TLIST.EXE with TASKLIST.EXE in XP. TLIST.EXE lets you list all the processes running on your machine and the associated task name and memory usage. TASKLIST.EXE replicates all the functionality of the original utility. For information about TASKLIST.EXE, type the following at the XP command prompt:

```
tasklist /?
```

FAQ 30.17 Which administrator pack should I use for Windows .NET and Windows XP?

In FAQ 30.17, I looked at the administrator packs for XP and Windows 2000. It's imperative that you don't install the Win2K ADMINPAK.MSI on XP machines. However, you should use the Windows .NET Server ADMINPAK.MSI with XP. You can access these files from the installation CD-ROMs or from the Microsoft Web site.

As a side note, if you wish to install the Exchange 2000 Administration tools, they don't currently understand the .Net administration tools and so will not install. To install all of the required tools, you will need to perform the following:

1. Install Windows 2000 admin tools from Win 2000 Server CD.
2. Install Exchange 2000 admin tools from the Exchange 2000 CD.
3. Uninstall the Windows 2000 admin tools.
4. Install the Windows XP/.Net admin tools.

31 MISCELLANEOUS

This chapter looks at all those tips that I couldn't think of where to put ☺. You'll also find out what that symbol I just printed means and other really useful titbits HHOJ.

31.1 What does abbreviation/acronym x stand for?

See the table that follows.

ACL	access control list	A list that controls the access to an object.
API	application programming interface	An API is an interface through which programs interact with each other, normally through DLL calls.
BDC	Backup Domain Controller	An NT Server machine that receives a copy of the master user-database from the PDC and can validate logons.
COLD	Computer Output to Laser Disk	
DAP	Directory Access Protocol	Used to access a directory service.
DHCP	Dynamic Host Configuration Protocol	A service that automatically assigns IP-addresses to clients from a given range (scope).
DLC	Data Link Control	International standard protocol IEEE 802.2. Used with mainframe gateways to control printers with a JetDirect card.
DSA	Directory System Agent	The name of a domain controller (e.g., titanic).
DSA	UUID DSA Universally Unique ID	The 128-bit number used to identify objects stored in the directory.

(continued)

FAT	File Allocation Table	The DOS way of organizing a hard disk, which is responsible for lots of wasted space on large disks. FAT provides little file security.
GUID	globally unique identifier	A 64-bit number that is statistically unique.
HPFS	High Performance File System	The OS/2 way of organizing a hard disk. Available in NT 4.0 but not in Windows 2000 and above.
ICMP	Internet Control Message Protocol	A maintenance protocol specified in RFC 792 that is normally considered to be part of the IP layer. ICMP messages are encapsulated within IP datagrams, so they can be routed throughout an internetwork. ICMP is used by Windows NT to: Build and maintain route tables. Assist in Path Maximum Transfer Unit (PMTU) discovery. Diagnose problems (using the utilities Ping and Tracert). Adjust flow control to prevent link or router saturation.
IPX/SPX	Internetwork Packet Exchange/Sequenced Packet Exchange	Novell NetWare protocol that is based on the Xerox protocol XNS (Xerox Networking Services).
LDAP	Lightweight Directory Access Protocol	Protocol used to query a directory service.
MAC-addresses	Media Access Control layer addresses	A 48-bit address that is hard-wired into the netcard. DHCP, among others, use this address to identify a machine requesting a certain IP address within its lease duration.
NBT	NetBIOS over TCP/IP	NetBIOS built on top of the TCP/IP suite.
NDIS	Network Driver Interface Specification	Microsoft binding standard (interface between netcard driver and protocol). Can load into high memory on DOS systems.
NetBEUI	NetBIOS Extended User Interface	The actual NetBIOS transport protocol.

NetBIOS	Network Basic Input/ Output System	An API of 18 networking-related commands.
NIC	network interface card	Such as an Ethernet card. InterNIC, the organization that assigns domain names and IP addresses to Internet hosts, is accessible at http://www.internic.net.
NTFS	NT File System	The NT way of organizing a hard disk that provides efficient storage and a high level of security.
ODI	Open Datalink Interface	Novell binding standard (i.e., an interface between netcard driver and protocol). Cannot load into high memory on DOS systems.
PDC	Primary Domain Controller	The NT Server machine that stores the master (writable) user-database in a domain.
RAID	Redundant Array of Inexpensive Disks	A number of disks with data distributed all over them to allow for faster access. Can also provide data-recoverability. NT supports RAID levels 0, 1, and 5.
RIP	Routing Information Protocol	The protocol that takes care of routing on the Internet.
SID	number security identification number	Every object in a domain has a SID number. Reinstalling a machine will not give the same SID number.
SPS	standby power supply	Device that is installed between the wall outlet and the computer inlet. The power goes directly into the computer with a branch to the batteries. When the power fails, the batteries take over but with a delay. The delay should be 4ms or better for proper operation.
TCP/IP	Transmission Control Protocol/Internet Protocol	The protocol used for Internet and intranet communications.
UDP	User Datagram Protocol	A basic alternative to TCP for IP communication. Among other things, UDP is used for communicating with DHCP servers.

(continued)

UPS	uninterruptible power supply	Device that is installed between the wall outlet and the computer inlet. The power is directed through the batteries, thus stabilizing the variance of the power from the outlet. Because of this, the switch delay is 0ms.
WINS	Windows Internet	Naming Service A dynamic IP-to-name database.

FAQ 31.2 What are the shortcuts available with the Win key?

See the following table:

Win+R	Display the Run dialog
Win+M	Minimize all windows
Win+Shift+M	Undo minimize all windows
Win+F1	Help
Win+E	Explorer
Win+F	Find files
Ctrl +Win+F	Find computer
Win+TAB	Cycle through minimized taskbar icons
Win+BREAK	Systems properties

FAQ 31.3 What keyboard shortcuts are available?

See the table that follows:

F1	Help
F2	Rename
F3	Find

F4	Display combo box in Explorer
F5	Refresh
F6	Switch panes in Explorer
F10	Menu mode
Alt+Enter	Properties
Ctrl+Draga file	Copy
Ctrl+G	Go to
Ctrl+Z	Undo
Ctrl+A	Select all
Ctrl+Esc	Start menu
Ctrl+Shift+Esc	Task Manager

FAQ 31.4 I have 95 and NT installed. How can I configure the applications to run on both?

While it is possible to add the Windows 95 system directory to the NT path (which would mean you would find any DLLs, etc. associated with applications), many applications write a large amount of information to the Registry, which would be missing. The best approach, and one I have tested, is to just install the application twice to the same directory, once when you are booted into NT, and once when you are booted into 95. This has the effect of only having one set of EXEs but duplicates both DLLs and Registry settings to both machines. Obviously, the applications cannot be on an NTFS or a FAT32 partition.

FAQ 31.5 What is USER.DMP?

USER.DMP is created by Dr. Watson when a program crashes and it is there to help you fix the problem. It can be examined using \support\debug\i386\dumpexam.exe (for Windows NT 4) or using windbg -z user.dmp. You can delete this file without any worries. The syntax for DUMPEXAM.EXE is

```
dumpexam -y <symbol file location> <dumpfile name and location>
```

For example:

```
dumpexan -y d:\winnt\symbols d:\winnt\memory.dmp
```

The output from dumpexam will be placed at %SystemRoot%\MEMORY.TXT.

To prevent this file from being created, execute DRWTSN32.EXE and unselect the option Create Crash Dump File.

FAQ 31.6 How can I save a file in Notepad without the .TXT extension?

When you save the file, just put the filename in double quotes. For example, "JOHNS.BAT" saves the file as johns.bat with **no** .TXT extension.

FAQ 31.7 How can I delete files that are over x days old?

The DelOld utility can be downloaded from http://www.savilltech.com. The Web site contains full instructions for its use.

FAQ 31.8 How can I install a font from the command line/batch file?

When you install a font, all it does is copy the .TTF file to %systemroot%\fonts and add an entry in HKEY_LOCAL_MACHINE\SOFTWARE\Microsoft\Windows NT\CurrentVersion\Fonts. This can be automated with a batch file as follows

```
Rem fontinst.bat
copy akbar.ttf %systemroot%\fonts
regedit /s font.reg
```

FONT.REG contains the following:

```
REGEDIT4

[HKEY_LOCAL_MACHINE\SOFTWARE\Microsoft\Windows NT\CurrentVersion\
Fonts]
"Akbar Plain (TrueType)"="akbar.ttf"
```

In this example, FONT.REG copies AKBAR.TTF, which is called "Akbar Plain (TrueType)" (yes, it's the Simpsons font ;-)). The REG scipt actually creates a value called Akbar Plain (TrueType) under HKEY_LOCAL_MACHINE\SOFTWARE\Microsoft\Windows NT\CurrentVersion\Fonts with its contents AKBAR.TTF. The new font is visible once the machine has been rebooted.

If you have some older 16-bit applications, you may want to add the font to WIN.INI as well in the [fonts] section. This could be accomplished using a .INF file—for example:

```
[UpdateInis]
"E:\WINNT\WIN.INI","Fonts",,"Akbar Plain (TrueType)=akbar.ttf"
```

FAQ 31.9 What are the ErrorControl, Start, and Type values under the Services subkeys?

Descriptions of each of the main three values and their contents follow.

- ErrorControl
  This is used if the service fails to start up upon boot.

Value	Meaning
0x00	If this driver can't be loaded or started, ignore the problem and display no error.
0x01	If the driver fails, produce a warning but let boot-up continue.
0x02	Panic. If the current config is the last known good, continue; if not, switch to last known good.
0x03	Record the current startup as a failure. If this is last known good, run diagnostic; if not, switch to last known good and reboot.

- Start
  This defines when in the boot sequence the service should be started. You can also set these by using the Services Control Panel applet.

Value	Start Type	Meaning
0x00	Boot	The kernel loaded will load this driver first because it's needed to use the boot volume device.
0x01	System	This is loaded by the I/O subsystem.
0x02	Autoload	The service is always loaded and run.
0x03	Manual	This service does not start automatically and must be manually started by the user.
0x04	Disabled	The service is disabled and should not be started.

- Type
  This defines the kind of service or driver. They are loaded in the following order down the list.

Value	Meaning
0x01	Kernel-mode device driver
0x02	Kernel-mode device driver that implements the filesystem
0x04	Information used by the network adapter
0x10	A Win32 service that should be run as a standalone process
0x20	A Win32 service that can share address space with other services of the same type

FAQ 31.10 How do I type the Euro (€) symbol?

For Euro support, you must be running windows NT4.0 Service Pack 4 (or Service Pack 3 with the Euro hotix) or Windows 2000 or above. If you see something else, you need to install either of the aforementioned fixes, or you are not using Internet Explorer. Netscape does not seem to understand the Euro symbol. Also the fix also applies to True Type fonts and not PostScript.

Once you've installed the required fix, just press Ctrl+Alt+4 at the same time to type the Euro symbol. The keys may be different in other European countries. For example, it's Ctrl+Alt+5 on a Swedish keyboard (so I'm informed) or Alt+Gr+E.

For NT4 Terminal Server edition, with only Service Pack 3 installed, one could download from Microsoft a patch EUROFIXI.EXE, which is included in Service Pack 4 for the Terminal Server Edition.

Under the Terminal Server/Citrix Environment, you could use also Alt 0128 for the € sign (U.S. keyboard layout and settings).

More information can be found at

- http://www.microsoft.com/typography/faq/faq12.htm
- http://www.eu.microsoft.com/technet/euro/
- http://www.eu.microsoft.com/windows/euro.asp

FAQ 31.11 How can I check if a virus warning is real or a hoax?

More and more warnings are being sent to people from misinformed people trying to help regarding viruses that don't actually exist. The originators of these messages just try to see how many people their messages can be distributed to in order to cause panic.

Some of the best known hoaxes include

- The "Returned Mail" virus, which essentially tells you not to read any e-mail that was returned because the mailing system was "Unable to deliver" it. (If you can't read it, you may never find out why it wasn't delivered!) In fact, viruses can't be communicated very well with e-mail (except in certain file attachments).
- The "Penpal Greetings" virus
- The "Good Times" virus, one of the oldest
- Budweiser Screensaver (obviously started by someone who likes Beck's)

A number of sources list these hoaxes so if you receive a message always check these sources before forwarding a message to others (otherwise, you just make the situation worse). If you find it is a hoax message, reply to the sender informing him or her of the fact to avoid future distribution.

- http://www.nai.com/asp_set/anti_virus/library/hoaxes.asp
- http://vil.mcafee.com/villib/hoax.asp
- http://www.europe.datafellows.com/news/hoax.htm
- http://www.av.ibm.com/BreakingNews/HypeAlert/
- http://www.irisav.com/lab/hoax.htm
- http://www.icsa.net/services/consortia/anti-virus/alerthoax.shtml
- http://www.kumite.com/myths/myths/#a2z
- http://www.uk.sophos.com/virusinfo/scares/
- http://www.stiller.com/hoaxes.htm
- http://www.symantec.com/avcenter/hoax.html
- http://afcert.kelly.af.mil/hoaxes.html
- http://ciac.llnl.gov/ciac/CIACHoaxes.html
- http://www.cybec.com.au/html/vvcc/anti-virus/hoaxes/index.html

31.12 What DO those smileys mean :-)?

In newsgroups and other online media, you will often see smileys, which are used to portray various moods of the author. Following are their meanings.

<table>
<tr><td>:-||</td><td>Angry</td></tr>
<tr><td>:-)</td><td>Basic happy</td></tr>
<tr><td>:-(</td><td>Basic sad</td></tr>
<tr><td>(:-)</td><td>Bald</td></tr>
<tr><td>:-)></td><td>Bearded</td></tr>
<tr><td>%+(</td><td>Beaten up</td></tr>
<tr><td>R^)</td><td>Broken glasses</td></tr>
<tr><td>:^)</td><td>Broken nose</td></tr>
<tr><td>|:-)</td><td>Bushy eyebrows</td></tr>
<tr><td>X-)</td><td>Cross-eyed</td></tr>
<tr><td>:-e</td><td>Disappointed</td></tr>
<tr><td>:-)'</td><td>Drooling</td></tr>
<tr><td>{:V</td><td>Duck</td></tr>
<tr><td>>:-)</td><td>Evil grin</td></tr>
<tr><td>:'''-(</td><td>Floods of tears</td></tr>
<tr><td>8)</td><td>Frog</td></tr>
<tr><td>8:)</td><td>Gorilla</td></tr>
<tr><td>:-')</td><td>Has a cold</td></tr>
<tr><td>:-|</td><td>Hmmmph!</td></tr>
<tr><td>:-C</td><td>Jaw hitting the floor</td></tr>
<tr><td>.-)</td><td>Keeping an eye out</td></tr>
<tr><td>:-#</td><td>Kiss</td></tr>
</table>

<table>
<tr><td>:+)</td><td>Large nose</td></tr>
<tr><td>:-D</td><td>Laughing out loud</td></tr>
<tr><td>:-}</td><td>Leering</td></tr>
<tr><td>(-:</td><td>Left-handed</td></tr>
<tr><td>:-9</td><td>Licking lips</td></tr>
<tr><td>:- |</td><td>Monkey</td></tr>
<tr><td>(-)</td><td>Needs haircut</td></tr>
<tr><td>:8)</td><td>Pig</td></tr>
<tr><td>=:-)</td><td>Punk</td></tr>
<tr><td>O:-)</td><td>Saint</td></tr>
<tr><td>:-@</td><td>Screaming</td></tr>
<tr><td>:-O</td><td>Shocked</td></tr>
<tr><td>:-V</td><td>Shouting</td></tr>
<tr><td>|-)</td><td>Sleeping</td></tr>
<tr><td>:-p</td><td>Tongue-in-cheek</td></tr>
<tr><td>:-&t</td><td>Tongue-tied</td></tr>
<tr><td>:-/</td><td>Undecided</td></tr>
<tr><td>:-[</td><td>Vampire</td></tr>
<tr><td>:-))</td><td>Very happy</td></tr>
<tr><td>:-((</td><td>Very sad</td></tr>
<tr><td>:-(#)</td><td>Wears teeth braces</td></tr>
<tr><td>;-)</td><td>Winking</td></tr>
<tr><td>|-O</td><td>Yawning</td></tr>
</table>

31.13 What DO those acronyms and abbreviations, such as NIFOC and HHOJ, mean in mail messages?

In newsgroups and other online media, you often see acronyms and abbreviations, which can be puzzling. Let's remove the mystery.

AFAIK	As Far As I Know	NRN	No Reply Necessary
BRB	Be Right Back	OBTW	Oh, By The Way
BTDT	Been There Done That	OMG	Oh My God
BTW	By The Way	OTOH	On The Other Hand
GAL	Get A Life	OTT	Over The Top
HHOJ	Ha Ha, Only Joking	PITA	Pain In The Arse
MOTOS	Member Of The Opposite Sex	POD	Piece Of Data
IMHO	In My Humble Opinion	ROFL	Rolls On Floor Laughing
IWBNI	It Would Be Nice If	RTFM	Read The Flipping (there are other F words here ☺) Manual
JAM	Just A Minute	RUOK	Are You OK
NIFOC	Nude In Front Of Computer	TIA	Thanks In Advance
STFW	Search The Flipping Web		

31.14 How can I move a dialog/window by using just the keyboard?

Sometimes due to a video or other problem, it's useful to be able to move a dialog using the keyboard because the outside of the dialog may be off the screen.

To move a dialog by using just the keyboard:

1. Hold down the Alt key.
2. Press the Spacebar.
3. Press M (Move).

4. When a four-headed arrow appears, use your arrow keys to move the outline of the window.
5. When you are happy with its position, press Enter.

FAQ 31.15 How can I extract files from a CAB file?

The new method of packaging files is to store them in a CAB file, which is a non-proprietary format based on Lempel-Ziv compression. Both DriveSpace and DoubleSpace also use Lempel Ziv-based compression algorithms.

A common way of extracting files is to use a tool such as Winzip, which supports extraction of CAB files. New to the Windows NT Resource Kit (as of supplement 4) is EXTRACT.EXE, which can also extract files from a CAB file. Windows 2000 and XP includes the command prompt utility EXTRACT.EXE, which could be used for extracting such files. Windows XP has built-in GUI compressed file extraction.

FAQ 31.16 What are the Event Viewer logon codes?

In the event log, you sometimes see logon codes for certain events. Their meaning follows:

LogonTypes:
0 and 1 are not valid.
2 = Interactive
3 = Network
4 = Batch
5 = Service
6 = Proxy

FAQ 31.17 How can I convert a binary number to hexadecimal?

In some Windows NT operations, you must provide a hexadecimal value rather than a binary or decimal value—for example, setting which drives should be excluded from a user's view (see FAQ 7.6).

The easiest way to convert a binary number to hexadecimal is to use the Calculator application in Scientific mode:

1. Start Calculator (CALC.EXE).
2. From the View menu, select Scientific.
3. Select Bin and set the data type to Dword (Dword is 4 bytes—32 bits—the biggest possible in Calculator).
4. Enter your binary string.
5. Select Hex, and your binary number is converted to hexadecimal (see Figure 31-1).

Hexadecimal is base 16, and each digit can therefore be between 0 and 15 (0–9, A–F). Binary is base 2, and each digit can therefore be 0 or 1.

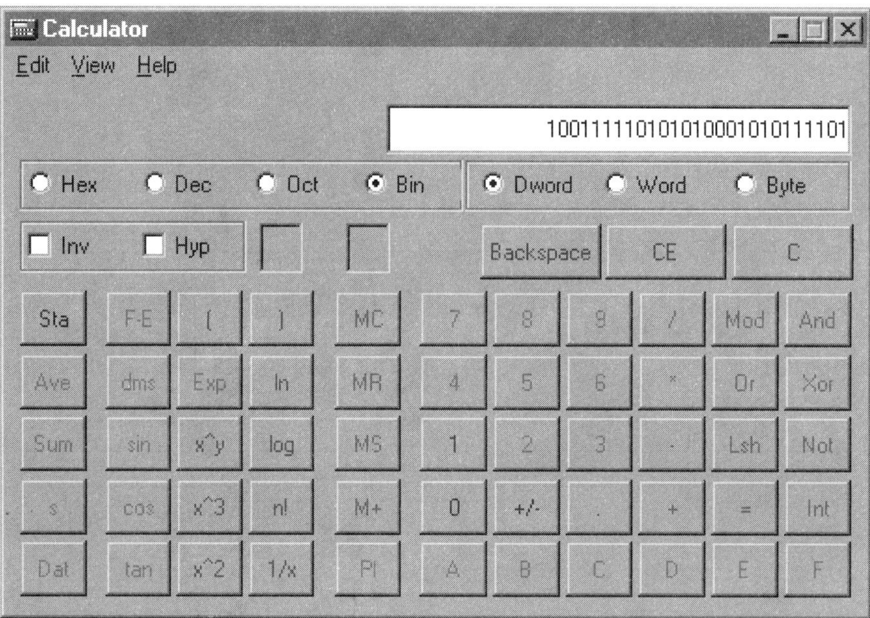

Figure 31-1 Calculator showing a binary value in Scientific mode

FAQ 31.18 What switches can be used with EXPLORER.EXE?

In FAQ 6.31, we saw how to configure Explorer to start with a specific drive. Following is a list of **all** its switches:

```
Explorer [/n][/e][,/root,(object)][[,/select],(sub object)]
```

- /n opens a new single-paned window.
- /e opens Explorer in the standard view at the current folder.
- /root,(object) opens at the specified root level.
- /Select, folder tells Explorer which folder gets the focus.
- /select, (filename) tells Explorer which file gets the focus.

To Start Explorer in desktop view mode use the command:

```
explorer /e,/root,
```

FAQ 31.19 Where are files in the Recycle Bin actually stored?

When you delete a file and the Recycle Bin is enabled, the file is not actually deleted but just moved to the Recycle Bin.

A hidden folder named Recycled is created on each volume that has the Recycle Bin enabled. Any deleted files are moved to this folder and renamed to

```
D<original drive letter><number file deleted>.<original extension>
```

The original full name and path stored in a mapping file Info (Info2 in Windows 98). For example, the filename D:\www.ntfaq.com\index.html becomes Dd1.html (if it was the first file deleted on the partition).

FAQ 31.20 My Recycle Bin is corrupt. What should I do?

The Info file in the Recycler folder sometimes gets corrupted and thus shows an empty Recycle Bin, even though plenty of files are in the Recycler folder. Windows will automatically recreate the Info file if it's missing, so the easiest way to repair it is to delete the Info file:

1. Start a command prompt (CMD.EXE).
2. Move to the Recycler folder.
3. Enter the command

   ```
   attrib -h info*.*
   ```

   Delete the file

   ```
   del info
   ```

4. Restart the computer.

If the Recycler folder has actually become corrupted, you may need to delete it by removing the system and hidden attributes (by entering **attrib -h -s c:\recycler** at the command line) and then deleting it.

FAQ 31.21 What is the OEM version of NT/2000?

We talk about OEM versions of NT, but what is OEM? OEM stands for "original equipment manufacturer." OEMs are basically the large computer companies like Compaq and Dell who get special versions of operating systems and applications that are potentially tailored for their machine hardware. For example, special versions of NT exist for OEMs, which can support more than the standard four processors.

OEMs have access to special tools like the OEM Preinstallation Wizard (OPKWIZ.EXE) for Windows 9x to help define installations, applications. I wish I had OEM status ☺.

FAQ 31.22 How can I check DLL versions on my system?

Windows NT has problems with "DLL Hell" where many applications may replace core DLLs, which may cause incompatibilities between applications.

Windows 2000 takes steps to elevate the problem by protecting core DLLs from being replaced, but in the mean time, a good Web site is available that helps to track DLL versions, etc: File Version Information Center from Microsoft, http://support.microsoft.com/servicedesks/fileversion/default.asp?vartarget=msdn.

FAQ 31.23 How do I fly in Excel 97?

No, this is not a performance improvement but actually flying ☺. Excel has a neat Easter Egg, which is really old, but I've only just found it. I thought it was better than work.

1. Start Excel 97 (it does not work on Excel 2000).
2. Open a new spreadsheet.
3. Press F5 (the goto command).
4. Enter

```
X97:L97
```

5. Click OK.
6. Press the Tab key once to move to M97.
7. Press and hold the Ctrl and Shift key while left-clicking the chart icon on the toolbar.
8. Cool! Use the mouse to steer, and left and right mouse buttons to control speed.

FAQ 31.24 How do I drive in Excel 2000?

Yep, another Easter Egg, but this one is even cooler than the Excel 97. If anyone remembers the old Spectrum Spy Hunter game, then you will love this. If you have DirectX, the spy hunter game will start with all the coder's names! If you don't have DirectX, it won't work so don't try the following procedure.

1. Start Excel 2000.
2. From the File menu, select Save as Web Page.
3. Select Save: Selection: Sheet.
4. Check the Add interactivity box and click Save.
5. Close Excel.
6. Load the saved HTML in Internet Explorer.
7. Scroll to row 2000, column WC.
8. Select row 2000 (makes the whole line active) and click Tab until WC is selected again.

9. Hold down Shift+Ctrl+Alt and click the Office logo in the upper left.
10. Use the arrow keys to steer, the spacebar to fire, O to drop oil, and H for headlights—it's very cool!

You can download it from http://www.ntfaq.com/ntfaq/misc/page.htm if you fancy a shortcut!

FAQ 31.25 How do I delete the FrontPage Express Recent File List?

Microsoft FrontPage Express doesn't have an option to clear the Recent File List; however, you can clear it using the Registry editor:

1. Start REGEDIT.EXE.
2. Go to HKEY_CURRENT_USER\SOFTWARE\Microsoft\FrontPad\FrontPage Editor\Recent File List.
3. Delete the Recent File List key.
4. Close Regedit.

The next time you start FrontPage Express, the system will recreate the Recent File List key that you deleted.

FAQ 31.26 Why doesn't my Windows 2000 laptop with two batteries sound the low/critical power alarms?

The algorithm Win2K uses to calculate the amount of remaining time if you have two batteries is incorrect. The algorithm **should** be

```
Remaining time = (RemainingCapacity1 + RemainingCapacity2) /
(PresentRate1 + PresentRate2)
```

This algorithm simply says that the amount of time left is the total capacity left of both batteries divided by the rate at which they are being used.

The **actual** algorithm Win2K uses is

```
Remaining time = (RemainingCapacity1 + RemainingCapacity2) /
(PresentRate1)
```

The system calculates remaining time based on the use rate for one battery, so the system thinks you have much longer left than you actually have. To work around this bug, set your alarms at a higher power percentage level.

FAQ 31.27 How can I remove individual cookies from my computer?

Web sites use cookies to hold certain information about your activity so the sites can track your use and tailor their content to meet your needs. Cookies are stored in the %USERPROFILE%\Local Settings\Temporary Internet Files folder (this is the default location, but it can be changed). To remove a cookie, you can simply select the appropriate file and delete it. The preferred (long-winded) approach is as follows:

1. Start Internet Explorer (IE).
2. From the Tools menu, select Internet Options.
3. Select the General tab.
4. Under Temporary Internet Files, click Settings.
5. Click View Files to get into the Temporary Internet Files folder.
6. Select the cookie to delete (it will be of the form name@domain.com).
7. Click Del.
8. Click OK to the confirmation.
9. Close the IE dialog box.
10. Close all dialog boxes.

FAQ 31.28 How can I automate Emergency Repair Disk (ERD) creation?

The old RDISK /-s silent switch no longer works because NTBACKUP.EXE is now used to create the ERD. In Windows XP, it is replaced with the new ASR functionality. However, using Windows Script Host (WSH), you can emulate this option by including the following text in file RDISK.JS. After you add the text, simply double-click RDISK.JS, insert a diskette, and the script will create the ERD.

```
var shell = new ActiveXObject("WScript.Shell");
shell.Popup("Please insert blank floppy disk in the drive A:", 15);
```

```
shell.Run("ntbackup.exe");
WScript.Sleep("500");

shell.Sendkeys("%m"); //selects the Emergency repair, % is Alt

shell.Sendkeys("~"); //presses Enter (could have used {Enter}
instead of ~)

WScript.Sleep("15000"); //pauses for 15 seconds so as to not Enter
the Cancel!!! You may need to change this.

shell.Sendkeys("%{F4}"); //tries to close but fails and selects the
OK button.

shell.Sendkeys("~"); //presses Enter (could have used {Enter}
instead of ~) after it has completed

shell.Sendkeys("%{F4}"); //closes NTBACKUP

WScript.Quit();
```

FAQ 31.29 When I access a certain Web site, why does it seem to be a Microsoft site when it isn't?

Generally, you read a Web URL from left to right. Thus, http://www.microsoft.com@support@www.windows2000faq.com seems to be a page on Microsoft's site although it's the Windows 2000 FAQ home page. The browser actually reads from right to left up to the first at symbol (@) it encounters, so the only part of the URL the browser uses is www.windows2000faq.com! Keep an eye on the URLs you access because some sites use this technique to mislead you.

FAQ 31.30 How can I create a shortcut that includes a space character?

A space in a shortcut isn't a valid target and results in the system not finding the target. For example, if a link is to http://www.savilltech.com/delold help.htm, when you use the link, it points only to http://www.savilltech.com/delold. To work around this problem, use the %20 sequence (which is the standard HTML sequence for a space in a URL) instead of the space.

This approach works for any protocol, including HTTP, HTTPS, FTP, MAILTO, File, NNTP, Telnet, News, Outlook, and UNC Naming. See the following examples:

- HTTP example: http://someserver.com/Some%20Link.htm
- FTP example: ftp://someserver.com/Some%20File.zip
- MAILTO example: mailto:some%20user@someserver.com
- UNC example: \\someserver\Some%20Share\Some%20Filename%20with %20spaces.zip

The other official method is to place the shortcut in double quotes with the spaces as normal characters.

FAQ 31.31 How do I migrate Open Database Connectivity (ODBC) data sources from one server to another?

To migrate ODBC data sources, perform the following steps:

1. Start REGEDIT.EXE.
2. Go to HKEY_LOCAL_MACHINE\SOFTWARE\ODBC\ODBC.INI and highlight the ODBC.INI key in the left pane.
3. From the Registry menu, select Export Registry File.
4. Select ODBC.REG and save it to a network share.
5. Go to your target machine and browse to the same key in the Registry. Right-click ODBC.INI and choose Rename. As a backup, rename ODBC.INI as ODBC.INI.OLD.
6. Highlight ODBC.INI's parent Registry key (ODBC).
7. From the Registry menu, select Import Registry File and browse to the network share where you saved ODBC.REG. Double-click ODBC.REG to import it.
8. Test your applications that use the data sources to verify that the import worked properly.

Remember, you can always roll back by renaming ODBC.INI.OLD to ODBC.INI.

FAQ 31.32 Can I open multiple items from the Start menu without having to reopen the menu each time?

Typically, after you select an item from the Start menu, the Start menu closes. To open another item from the same location without having to reopen the Start menu, hold down the Shift key when you select the first menu item. This feature applies only to Windows 2000 and later Windows OSs.

32 COMMAND PROMPT

The Windows operating system has a graphical interface; however, even Windows 3.1, which was a bolt-on to DOS, had a command window element. With Windows 2000, Microsoft made the decision to improve the support for command windows with the goal of making all actions that could be completed via the GUI also possible via the command prompt. This new goal enables us to quickly perform actions interactively and by writing script files. If you are interested in script files, you should ensure you also read Chapters 33 and 34.

FAQ 32.1 What is the difference between CMD.EXE and COMMAND.COM?

Windows NT/2000/XP supply CMD.EXE and COMMAND.EXE. CMD.EXE is the Windows NT command-line interface; it's **not** a DOS window. COMMAND.COM is a 16-bit DOS application that is used for older DOS compatibility and actually runs inside the NTVDM (NT Virtual DOS Machine) due to its 16-bit nature.

You may be surprised that COMMAND.COM and CMD.EXE have almost identical features, which is because any command entered in COMMAND.COM is packaged and sent to CMD.EXE for execution. Thanks to this, COMMAND.COM can take advantage of all the functions and facilities of CMD.EXE. This is possible because the version of COMMAND.COM shipped with NT **is** a special NT version designed to pass all execution to CMD.EXE.

If you had Task Manager running, you would actually see a CMD.EXE process started when executing commands in COMMAND.COM.

32.2 Why do international versions of NT behave strangely in command prompt sessions?

The cause may be that the commands require a U.S. set of characters. Try starting your command prompt session with

```
CHCP 437
```

This will hopefully help. It just sets the active code page to English (MS-DOS Latin US).

32.3 How can I configure a scrollbar on my command window?

It is possible to increase the line buffer for the command windows above the normal 25. To change the history, perform the following:

1. Start a command session (CMD.EXE).
2. Right-click on the title bar and select Properties.
3. Click the Layout tab.
4. In the Screen Buffer Size section, increase the Height value.
5. Click OK.
6. You will be asked Apply properties to current windows only or Save properties for future windows with same title. Select the latter and click OK.

You will now see a scrollbar on side of your command window. You also will see that under Properties, you can change the default starting location for command windows. The preceding actually creates HKEY_CURRENT_USER\Console\E:_WINNT_System32_cmd.exe key with a value ScreenBufferSize where the first part is the buffer height in hexadecimal.

32.4 How can I configure the command prompt?

When you are in a CMD.EXE session, it is possible to change the prompt to display other information, such as time, date, OS version, and so on. To change the prompt, just use

```
prompt <text>
```

For example, **prompt johns prompt**.

While basic text will work, it is not very helpful. Following is a list of all the codes you can use:

$A	& Ampersand
$B	| Pipe
$C	(Open parenthesis
$D	Current date
$E	Escape code (ASCII code 27)
$F	) Close parenthesis
$G	> Greater-than sign
$H	Backspace (erases previous character)
$L	< Less-than sign
$N	Current drive
$P	Current drive with path
$Q	= Equal sign
$S	Space
$T	Current time
$V	Windows NT version number
$_	Carriage return and linefeed
$$	$ Sign

If you have command extensions, you can also use the following:

- $+—Zero or more + characters depending on the depth of the PUSHD directory stack
- $M—Displays the remote name associated with the current drive letter

FAQ 32.5 How can I configure the command prompt to output to files in Unicode/ANSI?

Windows NT/2000 include full Unicode support, and it's possible to configure a CMD.EXE session to output in Unicode or ANSI (ANSI being the default). To set this when starting the CMD.EXE session, just add

- /A—Output to files or pipes will be in ANSI.
- /U—Output to files or pipes will be in Unicode.

For example, the following starts a session in Unicode output mode:

```
cmd.exe /u
```

FAQ 32.6 What commands can be used to configure the command window?

The following commands may be useful:

- **mode con lines=n**—Where n is the number of lines to keep (if n is larger than can fit on the screen, a scrollbar will be added).
- **mode con cols=n**—Where n is the number of columns to show (again a scrollbar will be added).

FAQ 32.7 How do I enable/disable command extensions?

When you use CMD.EXE, various extensions are enabled by default. To enable/disable these extensions, perform the following

1. Start the Registry editor (REGEDIT.EXE).
2. Move to HKEY_CURRENT_USER\Software\Microsoft\Command Processor.
3. Double-click on EnableExtensions.
4. Set to 1 for them to be enabled or set to 0 for extensions to be disabled.
5. Click OK.

You can also enable/disable them for a specific command session by using the appropriate qualifier to CMD.EXE. The following disables command extensions for this command session:

```
cmd /y
```

The following enables command extensions for this command session:

```
cmd /x
```

FAQ 32.8 What keyboard actions can I take to navigate the command line?

Rather than just using the left and right arrows to move one character at a time through the command, you can also use the following

Home	Start of the line
End	End of the line
Ctrl+Left Arrow	Move back one word
Ctrl+Right Arrow	Move forward one word
Insert	Toggle between insert and overstrike mode
Esc	Delete current line

You can also use the Tab key to complete filenames for you as described in FAQ 32.12.

If you enable QuickEdit on command windows (right-click on the title bar, select Properties > Options > QuickEdit Mode), you can select an area of text with the left mouse button. Right-click on it to copy it to the Clipboard and then click the right mouse button again to paste it the current cursor location (reminds me of the good old VT keyboards with the hold key ;-)).

32.9 How can I open a command prompt at my current directory in Explorer?

It may be a normal situation: You are browsing directories in Explorer and want to open a command prompt at the current location without having to type a long cd . . . to get to the correct directory. It is possible to add a context menu option to folders to bring up a "Command prompt here" option, which opens a command prompt at your current Explorer location.

A PowerToy, Command Prompt Here, can be downloaded from Microsoft (and is also included with the Resource Kit, CMDHERE.INF); however, all it does is update a couple of Registry entries, which can be accomplished manually allowing greater flexibility:

1. Start the Registry Editor (REGEDIT.EXE).
2. Move to HKEY_CLASSES_ROOT\Folder\shell (you could use HKEY_CLASSES_ROOT\Directory\shell, but it would then not apply to folders, whereas Folder does both).
3. From the Edit menu, select New > Key and enter a name of **CmdHere** (or anything else).
4. Under the new key, select New > Key and enter a name of the command in lowercase letters.
5. Under the key (CmdHere), double-click on (Default), and enter a name that will be displayed when you right-click on the directory (e.g., "Command Prompt Here." As an extra, if you add an ampersand (&) to the front of a character, it will cause it to be underlined (e.g., &John Prompt here produces John Prompt here).
6. Move to the command key and again double-click on (Default) and enter

   ```
   \System32\cmd.exe /k cd "%1"
   ```

   For example, **c:\winnt\System32\cmd.exe /k cd "%1"**. You can use "%l" instead of "%1", which will support long filenames.
7. Close the Registry editor.

There is no need to reboot the machine, and the new option will be available when you right-click on a folder (see Figure 32-1).

Applying this change in Windows 2000 also results in a command prompt for drives and not just folders.

Figure 32-1 Our new command prompt context menu item

32.10 How can I force the output of a program into an environment variable?

Some programs return values to the command line. You may want these values in a variable so they can be viewed/queried by other processes. The easiest way to put the result into an environment variable is to trap it in a FOR statement:

```
For /f "Tokens=*" %i in ('command') do set variable="%i"
```

For example:

```
For /f "Tokens=*" %i in ('ver') do set NTVersion="%i"

set NTVersion="Windows NT Version 4.0 "

echo %NTVersion%
"Windows NT Version 4.0 "
```

If you place the command in a batch file, you require two percent signs (%) in front of i. For example:

```
For /f "Tokens=*" %%i in ('ver') do set NTVersion="%%i"
```

FAQ 32.11 How can I change the title of the CMD window?

By default the title display name is the location of CMD.EXE; however, this title can be changed using two methods depending on the situation. If you currently have a command session and you wish to change its title, use the title command:

```
title <title>
```

For example, **title John Savill's Command Window**.

Alternatively, if you want to start a new command session from an existing command prompt, use the start command:

```
start "<title>"
```

For example, **start "John Savill's Command Window"**.

FAQ 32.12 How do I enable the Tab key to complete filenames?

NT has this functionality built in; however, by default it is disabled. To enable, perform the following:

1. Start the Registry editor (REGEDIT.EXE).
2. Move to HKEY_CURRENT_USER\Software\Microsoft\Command Processor.
3. Double-click on the value CompletionChar.
4. The base can be either hexadecimal or decimal. Set the value to 9 and click OK. (If you were using a character higher than 10, make sure you pick the correct hex/dec option for the value you type.)
5. Close the Registry editor.
6. Start a new CMD.EXE session, and the change will have taken effect.

This can also be enabled using the TweakUI tool for Windows 2000 and above:

1. Start TweakUI (either from Control Panel or from the PowerToys' programs folder if you're using XP).
2. Select Command Prompt or Cmd.
3. Under Filename completion, select the required character from the list as shown in Figure 32-2.
4. Click OK.

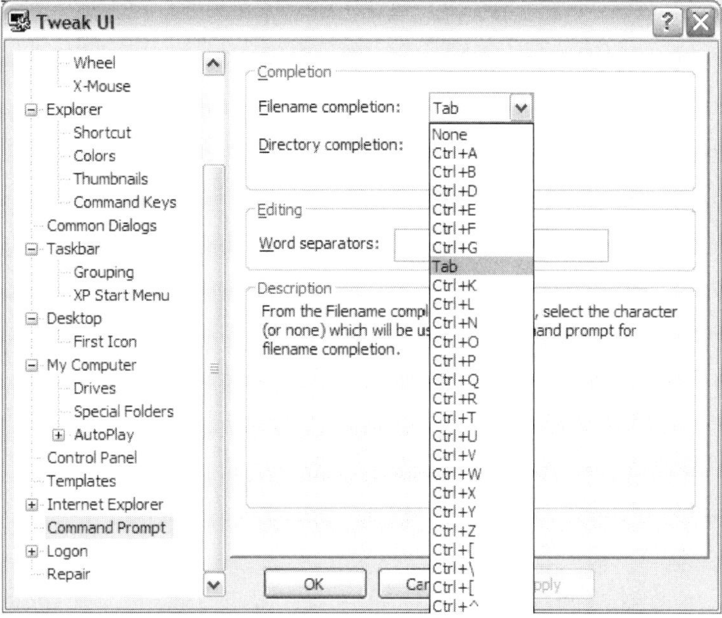

Figure 32-2 Setting the completion combination via TweakUI

FAQ 32.13 Why am I missing mouse support for programs using COMMAND.COM?

Windows NT 4.0 programs running under COMMAND.COM enjoyed mouse capabilities; however, under Windows 2000, the same programs may no longer respond to mouse events. This is caused by QuickEdit mode being enabled by default in the PIF for COMMAND.COM. To resolve this situation, perform the following:

1. Start your MS-DOS program.
2. Right-click the title bar.
3. Press Properties.
4. Select the Options tab.
5. Clear the QuickEdit Mode box.
6. Press OK.
7. Press Save Properties for future use.
8. Press OK.
9. Close all the windows that the program opened and restart the application.

32.14 How do I create a shortcut from the command prompt?

The SHORTCUT.EXE utility supplied with the Windows NT Server Resource Kit Version 4.0 Supplement One (phew) can be used to create .LNK files. The utility is quite powerful and allows you to specify not only the resource to link to but also an icon, etc. An example follows:

```
shortcut -t "d:\program files\johnsapp\test.exe" -n "Johns App.lnk"
-i "d:\program files\johnicon\icon1.ico" -x 0 -d "e:\johns\data"
```

What does it mean?

- -t—The location of the resource to be linked to
- -n—The name of the link file to be created
- -i—The icon file
- -x—The icon index to use in the icon file
- -d—The starting directory for the application once started

You can copy SHORTCUT.EXE off the CD with the Resource Kit, and it is located in <processor>\desktop (e.g., i386\desktop). No other files are needed, just SHORTCUT.EXE.

32.15 How can I switch my command window to full-screen mode?

Normally your command prompt (CMD.EXE) is displayed in a window; however, it can be configured to be displayed full screen.

1. Right-click on the title of the command window and select Properties.
2. Select the Options tab. Click OK.
3. You have the option to make the change either for the current session or for all future sessions. Make your choice and click OK.

An alternative (which allows you to switch from full screen to window) is to press Alt+Enter, which toggles between window and full-screen mode.

FAQ 32.16 How can I get a list of commands I have entered in a command session?

You can press the Up and Down arrow keys when in a command session to display your old commands (same as the old DOSKEY software); however, if you press the F7 key, a list of all the commands entered will be displayed as shown in Figure 32-3. You can then select the command and press Enter to run it.

You can configure the history by right-clicking on the title bar and selecting the Options tab. Update the Command History section. Other keys you can use are as follows:

F2	Searches for a character in the previous command and will display up to that character
F3	Recalls the last command issued
F8	Moves backwards through the command history
F9	Lets you return to a command but its number is given by F

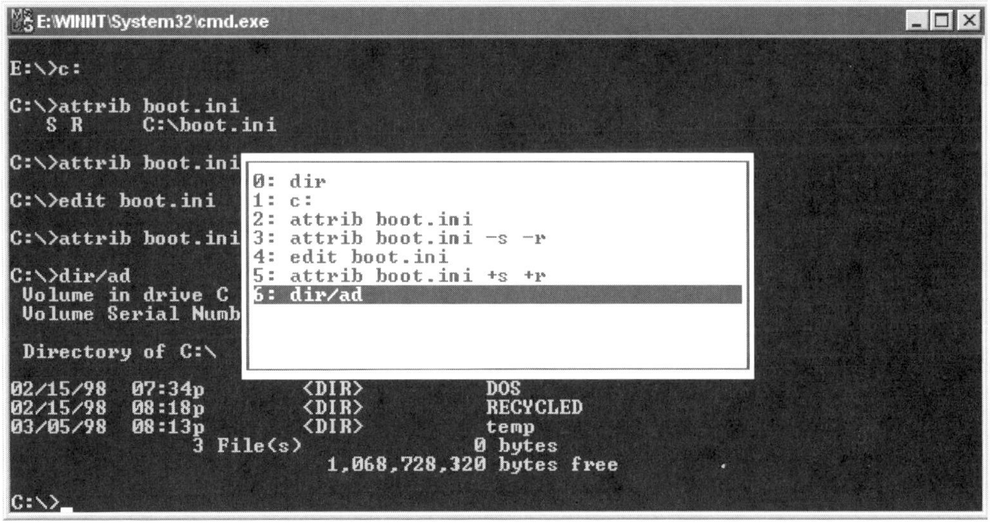

```
E:\WINNT\System32\cmd.exe

E:\>c:

C:\>attrib boot.ini
  S R     C:\boot.ini

C:\>attrib boot.ini   0: dir
                      1: c:
C:\>edit boot.ini     2: attrib boot.ini
                      3: attrib boot.ini -s -r
C:\>attrib boot.ini   4: edit boot.ini
                      5: attrib boot.ini +s +r
C:\>dir/ad            6: dir/ad
 Volume in drive C
 Volume Serial Numb

 Directory of C:\

02/15/98  07:34p        <DIR>          DOS
02/15/98  08:18p        <DIR>          RECYCLED
03/05/98  08:13p        <DIR>          temp
               3 File(s)              0 bytes
                          1,068,728,320 bytes free

C:\>_
```

Figure 32-3 The F7 window in action

32.17 How do I cut/paste information in a command window?

To copy the entire contents of a command window, you can maximize the window (Alt+Enter) and press the Print Scrn button. Alternatively:

1. Right-click the title bar.
2. Select Mark from the Edit menu.
3. Click the left mouse button at the start of the text you wish to copy and drag until the end of the selection.
4. Press Enter to copy the selection, or right-click the menu again, and select Copy from the Edit menu.
5. To paste, right-click the menu bar and select Paste from the Edit menu.

Alternatively you can enable QuickEdit mode by right-clicking on the title bar and selecting Properties. Select the Options tab and check the QuickEdit Mode box. Now you can select text with the left mouse button and just press Enter to copy it into the Clipboard.

When QuickEdit is turned on, you also can paste text into the command window by right-clicking with the mouse.

In either mode you can paste by pressing Alt+Enter, then E, then P.

32.18 How can I start Explorer from the command prompt?

Enter the following command to start Explorer in your current directory:

```
explorer /e
```

Or to bring up the single-pane version of Explorer, enter the following:

```
explorer .
```

FAQ 32.19 How can I redirect the output from a command to a file?

The most basic use is as follows:

```
<command> ><filename>
```

For example, **dir/s >list.txt**.

However, with this errors still get output to the screen. To rectify this, use the 2> for the errors.For example:

```
<command> ><filename> 2><error file>
```

For example, **dir/s >list.txt 2>error.txt**.

If you want the errors and output to go to the same file, use the following:

```
<command> ><filename> 2>&1
```

FAQ 32.20 How can I change the default dir output format?

The DIR command has many switches, and you can configure your own default behavior for the command instead of the normal format. For example, you may want to view the output one page at a time (/p), in lowercase (/l), with the files' times as their creation rather that last write (/tc), and sorted by extension then name (/oen). Normally you would type

```
dir /p /l /tc /oen
```

However, this is slightly tedious, so to set it as your default, perform the following:

1. Start the system Control Panel applet (Start > Settings > Control Panel > System).
2. Select the Environment tab.
3. Create the variable dircmd and set the value to your qualifiers (e.g., /p /l /tc /oen) and click Set (see Figure 32-4).
4. Click Applet, then click OK.

Any new command session will now use the new dir output format.

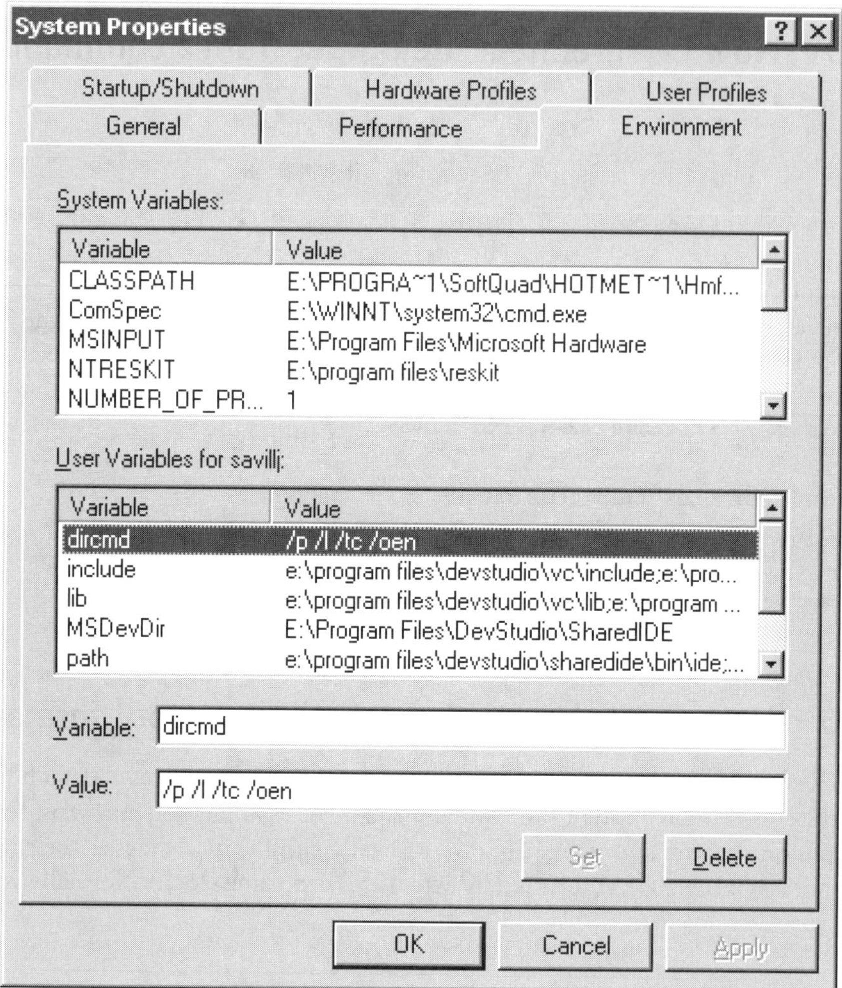

Figure 32-4 Setting the default dir options

32.21 How do I pause output from a command to one screen at a time?

Just add |**more** to the end of the command. For example, the following displays the help one screen at a time:

```
findstr /? |more
```

32.22 How do I get ANSI support on the command line?

To get ANSI support, perform the following steps:

1. Create a shortcut to COMMAND.COM.
2. Create a file called ANSI.NT.
3. Include the following lines in the ANSI.NT file:

```
dosonly
device=%systemroot%\system32\ansi.sys
device=%SystemRoot%\system32\himem.sys
files=40
dos=high,umb
```

4. Under Properties for the COMMAND.COM shortcut, go to the Programs tab. In the Config Path field, enter the path to ANSI.NT.

Now when you open the shortcut, any DOS applications you run will have ANSI support.

32.23 How can I increase the environment space for a single command session?

You can update CONFIG.NT with a larger shell to effect all command sessions, to set the environment space just for a single session, and call the command with the /e switch. For example:

```
COMMAND /E:2048 MYAPP.EXE
```

where /e:nnnnn is sets the initial environment size to nnnnn bytes.

32.24 How can I redirect the output from a command to the end of a file?

In FAQ 32.19, we saw how to redirect a command's output to a file using a single right angle bracket (>). However, this method replaces the file's existing content with the command's output.

To append the command's output to a file, you use double right angle brackets (>>). For example, the following results in the output being appended to file DIRLIST.TXT.

```
dir d:\temp\*.* >> dirlist.txt
```

FAQ 32.25 How can I stop a process from the command line?

To stop a process, you usually start Task Manager, select the Processes tab, select the process, and click End Process. However, you can also accomplish the same from the command prompt using two Resource Kit utilities.

First, you need to get a list of all processes on the system, which is accomplished using the TLIST.EXE utility:

```
tlist

0 System Process
2 System
20 smss.exe
26 csrss.exe
34 WINLOGON.EXE
42 SERVICES.EXE
45 LSASS.EXE
72 SPOOLSS.EXE
91 Nettime.exe
64 navapsvc.exe
...
198 notepad.exe Untitled - Notepad
214 TLIST.EXE
```

The first part, the number, is the process ID. For example, 198 is the process ID of the NOTEPAD.EXE process that is running. Once we know the process ID (or PID), we can stop it using the KILL.EXE utility:

```
kill 198
process #198 killed
```

You can optionally use the -f switch, which forces the process kill.

You may, if you wish, kill a process on its name instead—for example, the following will also work:

```
kill notepad.exe
```

FAQ 32.26 How can I append the date and time to a file?

You can use the following batch file that will rename a file to filename_YYYYMMDDHHMM:

```
@Echo OFF
TITLE DateName
REM DateName.CMD
REM takes a filename as %1 and renames as %1_YYMMDDHHMM
REM
REM -----------------------------------------------------------
IF %1.==. GoTo USAGE
Set CURRDATE=%TEMP%\CURRDATE.TMP
Set CURRTIME=%TEMP%\CURRTIME.TMP

DATE /T > %CURRDATE%
TIME /T > %CURRTIME%

Set PARSEARG="eol=; tokens=1,2,3,4* delims=/, "
For /F %PARSEARG% %%i in (%CURRDATE%) Do SET YYYYMMDD=%%l%%k%%j

Set PARSEARG="eol=; tokens=1,2,3* delims=:, "
For /F %PARSEARG% %%i in (%CURRTIME%) Do Set HHMM=%%i%%j%%k

Echo RENAME %1 %1_%YYYYMMDD%%HHMM%
RENAME %1 %1_%YYYYMMDD%%HHMM%
GoTo END

:USAGE
Echo Usage: DateName filename
Echo Renames filename to filename_YYYYMMDDHHMM
GoTo END

:END
REM
TITLE Command Prompt
```

For example:

```
D:\Exchange> datetype logfile.log
RENAME logfile.log logfile.log_199809281630
```

Another method is as follows without temporary files (a leading zero is inserted for hour values below 10):

```
for /f "tokens=1,2" %%u in ('date /t') do set d=%%v
for /f "tokens=1" %%u in ('time /t') do set t=%%u
if "%t:~1,1%"==":" set t=0%t%
set timestr=%d:~6,4%%d:~3,2%%d:~0,2%%t:~0,2%%t:~3,2%
echo %timestr%
```

Other date options include LOGTIME.EXE, which enables you to specify a string and then writes the time followed by the string to the file LOGTIME.LOG at the current default directory. The other option is NOW.EXE, which just replaces itself with the date and time—for example:

```
D:\temp>now Batch complete
Mon Sep 28 15:54:19 1998 -- Batch complete
```

Both LOGTIME.EXE and NOW.EXE are part of the Resource Kit.

Another way is by using the following FOR command—a log file can be created using real dates.

```
rem created unique log filename, e.g. Wed0804
FOR /F "tokens=1-4 delims=/" %%i in ('date/t') do set file=%%i%%j%%k
Set LOG=drive:\directory\filename-%file%.log
```

The result is a file named FILENAME-DATE.LOG. This method is easier and works great!

You could also use the following, which also adds the time to the bottom of a file (but also has a success message so one of the other methods is better):

```
net time >> file.txt
```

You can also use

```
Echo | more | time | find "current">>file.txt
```

FAQ 32.27 How can I change the editor used to edit batch/command files?

If you right-click on a .BAT or .CMD file and select Edit, the file will be opened in Notepad; however, you may want to use a different editor as the default. This can be accomplished by making two small Registry modifications:

1. Start the Registry editor (REGEDIT.EXE).
2. We will first change the editor used for .BAT files. Move to HKEY_CLASSES_ROOT\batfile\shell\edit\command.
3. Double-click on the (Default) value and change to the executable you want to use to edit the batch files (e.g., C:\Program Files\DevStudio\SharedIDE\BIN\msdev.exe "%1" if you wanted to use Microsoft Development editor). Click OK.
4. We shall now perform the same for .CMD files. Move to HKEY_CLASSES_ROOT\cmdfile\shell\edit\command.
5. Double-click on the (Default) value and again change to the editor to use. Click OK.

No reboot is required, and any changes take immediate effect.

You could also perform the preceding via a GUI front end by selecting View > Folder options > File Types from Explorer. You could then select the file type (e.g., MS-DOS Batch file) and click Edit. The context menu options available are listed, and you can modify them. All this does is update the Registry values we have looked at.

If you wanted to leave the existing option and add a new Edit option (e.g., Edit with MSDEV), perform the following (in this example we will update only a .BAT file with a second edit option, but the same could be performed on a .CMD file):

1. Start the Registry editor (REGEDIT.EXE).
2. Move to HKEY_CLASSES_ROOT\batfile\shell.
3. From the Edit menu, select New > Key and enter a name of **editms**.
4. Double-click on the (Default) value under editms and set the name to be displayed on the context menu (e.g., Edit with MSDEV), click OK.
5. Select editms, select New > Key from the Edit menu, and enter a name of **command**.
6. Double-click the (Default) under command and set to the required value (e.g., C:\Program Files\DevStudio\SharedIDE\BIN\msdev.exe "%1" for msdev). Click OK.
7. Close the Registry editor.

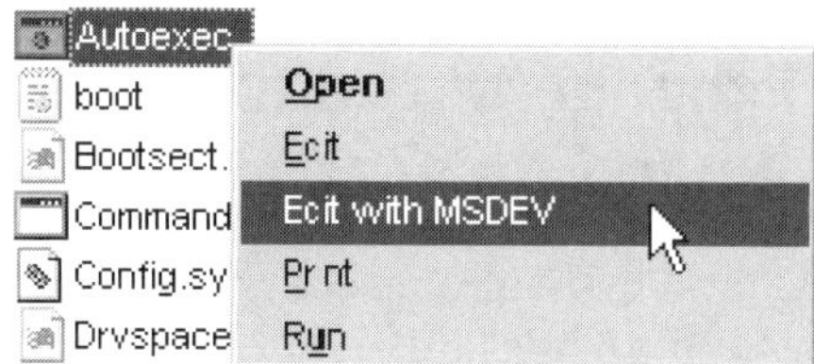

Figure 32-5 A new Edit with option

You will now have two options when you right-click on a batch file: Edit and Edit with MSDEV (see Figure 32-5).

You can use this on any type of file (e.g., .TXT files by editing HKEY_CLASSES_ROOT\txtfile\shell\open\command). Just look through HKEY_CLASSES_ROOT\xxxfile where xxx is the extension. (Actually to find the correct file type, use the assoc command—ASSOC.TXT. It will then return the file type.)

32.28 How can I configure the command-line history, DOSKEY?

In olden DOS days, a utility was available, DOSKEY.EXE, which enabled the user to cycle through previous commands. In NT this functionality is enabled by default, and you can cycle through old commands; however, DOSKEY has other abilities.

To clear the current command-line history, use the command

```
doskey /reinstall
```

You can also optionally tell DOSKEY how many old commands to keep with the /listsize parameter. The following keeps 50 old commands:

```
doskey /reinstall /listsize=50
```

It's also possible to create macros that allow you to assign a complex command to a single word—for example, the following creates a macro dird that lists only directories:

```
doskey dird=dir /ad
```

It's also possible to assign a macro to a specific command-level application using the /exename switch—for example:

```
doskey /exename=nslookup.exe sets=server 10.129.210.71
```

Entering sets in NSLOOKUP would now set the server to 10.129.210.71. To view current macros for an image, use

```
doskey /exename=<exe name> /macros
```

For example:

```
doskey /exename=nslookup.exe /macros
sets=server 10.129.210.71
```

FAQ 32.29 Why does the AT command work differently under NT 4.0 than under NT 3.51?

To better support long filenames, the parsing algorithm was changed in NT 4.0 so that only the target file should be surrounded by quotes. For example, under Windows NT 3.51:

```
at 20:00 "notepad d:\documents\bonde\maxfactor.txt"
```

Whereas under Windows NT 4.0:

```
at 20:00 notepad "d:\documents\bonde\maxfactor.txt"
```

The preceding causes a problem as if you surround the whole command in double quotes—for example, a batch file—it will not run correctly.

Support for a Registry key has been improved in Windows NT 4.0 Service Pack 4, which allows you to force the parse of the AT command to behave in the same manner as 3.51. To achieve this, perform the following:

1. Start the Registry editor (REGEDIT.EXE).
2. Move to HKEY_LOCAL_MACHINE\SYSTEM\CurrentControlSet\Services\Schedule.
3. From the Edit menu, select New > Key and enter a name of **Parameters** and press Enter.

4. Move to this new parameters key and from the Edit menu, select New > DWORD Value. Enter a name of **UseOldParsing** and press Enter.
5. Double-click on the new value and set to 1.
6. Reboot the machine.

FAQ 32.30 How can I open a command prompt at my current drive in Explorer?

Here we add a command prompt for a base drive (which has a separate context menu):

1. Start the Registry Editor (REGEDIT.EXE).
2. Move to HKEY_CLASSES_ROOT\Drive\shell.
3. From the Edit menu, select New > Key and enter a name of **CmdHere** (or anything else).
4. Under the new key, select New > Key and enter a name of **command** (lowercase).
5. Under the key (CmdHere), double-click on (Default) and enter a name that will be displayed when you right-click on the directory (e.g., Command Prompt Here). As an extra, adding an ampersand (&) to the front of a character causes it to be underlined (e.g., &John Prompt here produces John Prompt here).
6. Move to the command key and again double-click on (Default) and enter

   ```
   <system dir>\System32\cmd.exe /k cd "%1"
   ```

   For example, **c:\winnt\System32\cmd.exe /k cd "%1"**.
7. Close the Registry editor.

Following is an INF file that incorporates the creation of the Command Here for drives and directories if you don't have CMDHERE.INF that comes with the Resource Kit. Save it with an .INF extension and then right-click on it and select install.

```
; Command Here
[Version]
Signature = "$Windows NT$"
Provider=%Provider%

[Strings]
Provider="SavillTech Ltd"
```

```
[DefaultInstall]
AddReg = AddReg

[AddReg]
HKCR,Directory\Shell\CmdHere,,,"Command Here"
HKCR,Directory\Shell\CmdHere\command,,,"%11%\cmd.exe /k cd ""%1"""
HKCR,Drive\Shell\CmdHere,,,"Command Here"
HKCR,Drive\Shell\CmdHere\command,,,"%11%\cmd.exe /k cd ""%1"""
```

33 BATCH FILES

A batch file is a text file with a .BAT or .CMD extension. A batch file adheres to syntax and a set of valid commands or instructions. To run a batch file, enter the filename. You don't need to enter the .CMD or .BAT extension. To write a basic batch file, perform the following steps.

1. Open Notepad.
2. Enter the command **@echo hello world**.
3. Text that follows the echo command will output to the screen. The @ symbol suppresses the command from printing to the screen. To prevent commands from displaying for an entire batch file, enter **@echo off** at the top of the batch file.
4. Select Save As from the File menu.
5. Enter the batch file's name as **"<name>.cmd"**. Be sure to enter the name in quotes, or Notepad will add ".txt" to the end.
6. Run CMD.EXE to start a command session.
7. Enter the batch file's name, without the extension.

FAQ 33.1 What commands can I use in a batch file?

Windows NT 4.0 introduced several extensions to CMD.EXE. Use these extensions to ensure that the HKEY_CURRENT_USER\Software\Microsoft\Command Processor\EnableExtensions Registry entry is set to 1. The following table lists the most commonly used commands:

call <batch file>	Calls one batch file from inside another. The current batch file's execution is suspended until the called batch file completes.
exit	Stops a batch file from running. If one batch file calls another, exit stops both batch files.

(continued)

findstr <string> <filename(s)>	Finds a string in a file. This powerful command has several parameters.
for	Standard for loop. The command for /L %n IN (1,1,10) DO @ECHO %n prints 1 to 10.

goto <label>	Causes a program's execution to skip to a given point. A colon must precede the label name. For example,
	`goto label1`
	`...`
	`:label1`
	`...`

if <condition> ..	The if statement has a lot of functionality. Common uses include the if /i <string1> <compare> <string2> <command> The /i parameter makes the comparison case-insensitive. The comparison can be one of the following. EQU—equal NEQ—not equal LSS—less than LEQ—less than or equal GTR—greater than GEQ—greater than or equal if errorlevel if exist <filename>
rem <string>	A comment.
start <window title> <command>	Starts a new command session and runs a given command. Unlike with the call command, the current batch file's execution continues.

The Microsoft Windows NT Resource Kit includes some additional utilities that you might find useful.

FAQ 33.2 Why don't batch files that I've executed using the Scheduler service work?

Diagnosing batch files that work on their own but that don't execute correctly under the Scheduler service is difficult. However, in most cases, the problem involves granting the appropriate permissions. When you run a batch file, you're executing it under your user context, with all your rights and permissions. When you use the Scheduler service to run the same batch file, you're executing the batch file under the System account, which likely has different permissions. To determine whether your batch files will work running under the System account, use the Scheduler service to start a command session and try to run your batch file:

```
at <time in the near future> /inter cmd.exe /k
```

The /k switch tells the command window not to close after the command completes. At the time specified, a command window will open under the System account, and you can use it to test your commands in the same environment as scheduled tasks run.

FAQ 33.3 How do I include freehand comments in a batch file without using REM statements?

When Windows NT batch file processing encounters the goto command, the process ignores lines in the batch file until it finds the appropriate goto label.

```
@echo off
goto Begin

John Savill
Put in all comments required

:Begin
<...>

:End
```

Another method, which works on Windows NT 4.0 and Windows 95, is to use a double colon, as follows.

```
@echo off
echo Hello
echo.
:: This is equivalent to rem at the beginning of a line
rem This is an equivalent statement to the line above
:: This looks and reads better than rem
:: That's all
echo Bye!
```

FAQ 33.4 How do I call a subroutine in a batch file?

An easy solution is to have the batch file call itself recursively and pass itself a couple of parameters, as the following example illustrates:

```
@echo off
if (%1)==(Recurse) goto Recurse
goto Begin

:Begin
echo Batch file begins.
call %0 Recurse test
goto End

:Recurse
echo This is a recursive call.
echo The parameters received were "%1" and "%2".
goto Clean-End

:End
echo Finished.

:Clean-End
```

Be careful using this method, because recursive batch files can be dangerous if your subroutine fires off another program. The following example illustrates an alternative method:

```
:Begin
echo start subroutine
call :Subroutine
echo finished subroutine
```

```
goto End
:Subroutine
echo In subroutine
goto :EOF
:End
```

The following example illustrates yet another method, which you can use on Windows NT .CMD files. Note the syntax for calling subroutines (with parameters) and the special construction for returning (i.e., goto :eof).

```
@echo off
call :Begin
echo Finished.
goto :eof
:Begin
echo Batch file begins.
call :recurse Recurse test
goto :eof
:Recurse
echo This is a recursive call.
echo The parameters received were "%1" and "%2".
goto :eof
```

FAQ 33.5 How do I change the command prompt window's color within a batch file?

You can use the Windows NT Workstation 4.0 color command to set the command prompt window's colors. The first number sets the background color; the second number sets the foreground color. For example, the following command sets the window's color to yellow on black:

```
color 06
```

The following table lists the color options.

0	Black
1	Blue

(*continued*)

2	Green
3	Aqua
4	Red
5	Purple
6	Yellow
7	White
8	Gray
9	Light Blue
A	Light Green
B	Light Aqua
C	Light Red
D	Light Purple
E	Light Yellow
F	Bright White

FAQ

33.6 How do I perform an operation on every machine running on the network?

Normally, you can use a logon script. However, if you want to run a command or copy a file to every machine, you can use the following command.

```
net view > list.txt
```

This command outputs a list of current machines to the file LIST.TXT. You can then parse that file to perform an operation (e.g., to copy files).

```
FOR /F " tokens=1 " %i in (list.txt) do copy quaropts.dat
"%i\C$\program files\navnt"
```

If you placed this command in a file, you would need to use two percent signs (i.e., %%), as follows:

```
FOR /F " tokens=1 " %%i in (list.txt) do copy quaropts.dat
"%%i\C$\program files\navnt"
```

You could change the for command as follows to avoid using a temporary file:

```
FOR /F " tokens=1 " %i in ('net view') do copy quaropts.dat
"%i\C$\program files\navnt"
```

FAQ 33.7 Environment settings that a batch file sets aren't working. What should I do?

When you run a batch file (or any DOS command without a program information file—PIF—setting), the system uses the _DEFAULT.PIF file in the %systemroot% directory. If the Close on exit setting is enabled, the batch process will close. To fix the problem, perform the following steps:

1. Start Windows Explorer.
2. Go to the %systemroot% directory (e.g., d:\winnt).
3. Right-click _DEFAULT.PIF.
4. Select the Program tab.
5. Clear the Close on exit checkbox.
6. Click Apply, OK.

FAQ 33.8 How do I search files for a batch file or command-line string?

The find command lets you search one file at a time for a string, but the findstr command is more versatile. This command has the following switches:

```
findstr [/b] [/e] [/l] [/r] [/s] [/i] [/x] [/v] [/n] [/m] [/o]
[/f:file] [/c:string] [/g:file] [strings] [[drive:][path]filename[
...]]
```

The following table explains each parameter.

Parameters	Meaning
/b	Matches pattern if at the start of a line
/e	Matches pattern if at the end of a line

(*continued*)

Parameters	Meaning
/l	Searches literally
/r	Uses text as a regular expression (default)
/s	Searches current directory and all subdirectories
/i	Ignores case
/x	Selects lines that are an exact match
/v	Selects lines that don't match
/n	Displays the line number before the matched line
/m	Displays only the matching filenames
/o	Displays the offset of the match before the matched line
/g:<file>	Gets the search string from the specified file (e.g., /g:argument.txt)
/c:"<string>"	Uses text as a literal (e.g., /c:"string")
/f:<file>	Gets the file list from the specified file (e.g., /f:filelist.txt)
strings	Denotes the search string (in double quotes if multiple words)
files	Shows the files to search

Use spaces to separate multiple search strings unless you use /c.

The following command searches for Windows, NT, or FAQ in NTFAQ.HTML:

```
findstr "Windows NT FAQ" ntfaq.html
```

The following command searches for Windows NT FAQ in NTFAQ.HTM:

```
findstr /c:"Windows NT FAQ" ntfaq.html
```

33.9 How do I fix .BAT files that have lost their associations?

Fixing .BAT files that have lost their associations is simple. Enter the following commands:

```
ftype batfile="%1" %*
assoc .bat=batfile
```

FAQ 33.10 How do I call a batch file from within another batch file?

Simply entering a batch file's name within another batch file will run the batch file you want to call. However, after the called batch file completes, it won't pass control back to the calling batch file. Thus, the calling batch file will be incomplete. To call a batch file and have the file return to the calling batch file after the called file completes, use the call command.

FAQ 33.11 How do I stop a batch file from outputting a command to the screen as the file runs the command?

To stop this action, enter the following command at the beginning of the batch file:

```
@echo off
```

To prevent just one command from outputting to the screen, enter @ in front of the command.

FAQ 33.12 How can I convert a Unicode file to text?

Windows 2000 is Unicode based, meaning that two bytes are used for each character. However, certain text utilities may not understand Unicode, so if you want to create a one-byte-per-character version, type the following command:

```
type [unicode filename] > [text filename]
```

For example, you can type the following command to convert file UNICODE.TXT to a standard text file FILE.TXT:

```
type unicode.txt > file.txt
```

The type command performs the conversion. It is useful if you're dumping out Registry keys from REGEDIT.EXE, which writes out in Unicode format.

FAQ 33.13 How do I perform an action that depends on a file's arrival?

Users on hosts often transfer a file over an FTP link from another host and need to perform an action on the file when the file arrives. The following batch file, which requires the Microsoft Windows NT Resource Kit, lets you check for a file and run the file when it arrives:

```
:filecheck
if exist e:\upload\file.txt goto actionfile
sleep 100
goto filecheck
:actionfile
...
```

This batch file checks for the file FILE.TXT every 100 seconds. You might run into problems if the file is large and is still under construction when the batch file looks for it (e.g., if the file is transferring over an FTP link and is still writing). To solve this problem, rename the file to itself, as the following command shows:

```
RENAME e:\upload\file.txt file.txt
if not errorlevel 0 goto actionfile
```

The rename command generates an error message if the file doesn't exist or isn't available to write to (e.g., because it is still being written to). The errorlevel is the same, but the error message changes, in case you want to distinguish between the two in the .BAT file.

FAQ 33.14 How do I automate a response when I enter a command that asks for input?

Most commands have a switch to confirm an action. For commands that require a response (e.g., a logon that asks you to enter a password), try the following command:

```
echo <password> | logon savillj
```

This command runs the command logon savillj. When the logon command asks for a password, the echo command echos the password with a return, thus entering your password.

You can also use the following code to echo a return:

```
echo.|cmd.exe
```

FAQ 33.15 How do I obtain the currently running batch file's PID?

If you've installed the Microsoft Windows NT Resource Kit, you can use the following batch file to obtain the currently running batch file's process identifier (PID). To use this script at the command line, change the double percent sign to a single character (i.e., %).

```
for /f "Tokens=*" %%I in ('f:\tlist ^| grep %0 ^| grep CMD ^| awk "{
print $1 }"') do call :SETPID %%I
:next
.......
:SETPID
set MASTER_PID=%1
goto :next
.......
```

The following alternative uses the Resource Kit's Tlist utility:

```
for /f "Tokens=1 Delims= " %I in ('c:\tlist ^| find "%0"') do goto
:SETPID %I
:next
.......
:SETPID
set MASTER_PID=%1
goto :next
.......
```

Use the command tlist rather than pulist, because pulist doesn't give enough information. You need the batch file's name, which tlist provides. Because the shell uses the pipe character (i.e., |), you must use the caret character (i.e., ^) to escape the pipe.

You can compile the tlist alternative on one line, as follows:

```
for /f "Tokens=1 Delims= " %I in ('c:\tlist ^| find "%0"') do set
MASTER_PID=%1
```

33.16 How do I send a program's output to a NULL device?

If you want to suppress a program's output, you can use the NULL device (as you would use UNIX's /dev/null command). To make a program output to the NULL device instead of the screen, enter the following command:

```
program.exe > nul
```

You can also use the nul command if you want to blank a file, as the following example shows:

```
copy nul file.name
```

33.17 How do I send a message from a batch file?

To send a message from a batch file, use the Net Send command, as follows:

```
net send <machine> "<message>"
```

33.18 How do I access files on other machines?

To access files on other machines, you can use the Uniform Naming Convention (UNC—e.g., \\server name\share name\dir\file). Alternatively, you can map the drive, use a drive letter to access the file, then unmap the drive. To use this method, enter the following commands:

```
net use g: \\savilltech\<filetosee>
... g:\dir\file.txt
net use g: /d
```

33.19 The %logonserver% variable isn't available after I log on. What should I do?

When you log on, the logon process creates several volatile environment variables. These variables remove after the logon process completes, as the user's environment unloads.

One of these variables is %logonserver%, which shows the domain controller (DC) that validated the user logon. This variable is useful in logon scripts and for other tasks after logon. In Windows NT 4.0, the %logonserver% variable removes after logon. To view this variable, use the following command:

```
echo %logonserver%
\\TITANIC
```

If you want to use the %logonserver% variable after logon, you can use the Microsoft Windows NT Resource Kit's Setx utility to manually set the variable into another environment variable. Enter the following command:

```
setx MyLogonServer %logonserver%
```

FAQ 33.20 How do I pass parameters to a batch file?

When you call a batch file, you can enter data after the command that the batch file refers to as %1, %2, etc. For example, in the batch file HELLO.BAT, the following command

```
@echo hello %1 boy
```

would output

```
hello john boy
```

if you called it as

```
hello john
```

The following table outlines how you can modify the passed parameter.

Parameter	Description
%1	The normal parameter.
%~f1	Expands %1 to a fully qualified pathname. If you passed only a filename from the current directory, this parameter would also expand to the drive or directory.

(continued)

Parameter	Description
%~d1	Extracts the drive letter from %1.
%~p1	Extracts the path from %1.
%~n1	Extracts the filename from %1, without the extension.
%~x1	Extracts the file extension from %1.
%~s1	Changes the *n* and *x* options' meanings to reference the short name. You would therefore use %~sn1 for the short filename and %~sx1 for the short extension.

The following table shows how you can combine some of the parameters.

Parameter	Description
%~dp1	Expands %1 to a drive letter and path only.
%~sp1	For short path.
%~nx1	Expands %1 to a filename and extension only.

To see all the parameters in action, put them into the batch file TESTING.BAT, as follows:

```
@echo off
echo fully qualified name %~f1
echo drive %~d1
echo path %~p1
echo filename %~n1
echo file extension %~x1
echo short filename %~sn1
echo short file extension %~sx1
echo drive and directory %~dp1
echo filename and extension %~nx1
```

Then, run the file with a long filename. For example, the batch file run on the file c:\temp\longfilename.long would produce the following output:

```
fully qualified name c:\TEMP\longfilename.long
drive c:
path \TEMP\
```

```
filename longfilename
file extension .long
short filename LONGFI~1
short file extension .LON
drive and directory c:\TEMP\
filename and extension longfilename.long
```

This method also works on the second and subsequent parameters. You simply substitute the parameter for 1 (e.g., %~f2 for the second parameter's fully qualified path name).

The %0 parameter in a batch file holds information about the file when it runs and indicates which command extensions you can use with the file (e.g., %~dp0 gives the batch file's drive and path).

34 WINDOWS SCRIPTING HOST

The Windows Scripting Host (WSH) is a tool that will allow you to run Visual Basic Scripting Edition and JScript by default, but it's extensible, allowing support for other languages to be added within the base operating system, either on Windows 95 or Windows NT 4.0. Using the scripting languages you already know, you can now write scripts to automate common tasks and to create powerful macros and logon scripts.

Windows 2000 and XP natively support the Windows Scripting Host.

34.1 Where can I get the Windows Scripting Host?

The Windows Scripting Host software can be downloaded from http://msdn.microsoft.com/scripting/ along with a large amount of help files/samples.

The JScript and VScript engines you need are supplied with Internet Explorer 3.01 and above; however, the latest versions are supplied with the latest versions of Internet Explorer. These engines can be downloaded separately from the same address as the WSH.

34.2 How do I install the Windows Scripting Host software?

When the software is downloaded from the URL provided previously (http://msdn.microsoft.com/scripting/), a single file is fetched, WSH.EXE. Switches for WSH.EXE are

- /Q—Quiet mode
- /T:<full path>—Specifies temporary working folder
- /C—Extract files only to the folder when used also with /T
- /C:<CMD>—Override Install command defined by script's author

To install perform the following:

1. Start WSH.EXE either by running or clicking in Explorer.
2. Click Yes to the installation confirmation.

3. Click Yes to the license agreement.
4. Click OK to the install success message.

If you wanted to install as part of a logon script or the like, you would use

```
wsh /q
```

Which then asks no questions and gives no confirmations. You could check to see if WSH is installed and only install if not found—for example:

```
if not exist %systemroot%\system32\wscript.exe
\\<server>\<share>\wsh.exe /q
```

Where \\<server>\<share> is a share that holds the WSH.EXE image.

FAQ 34.3 Where can I get more information on WSH?

A number of sites provide information:

- http://msdn.microsoft.com/scripting/
- http://msdn.microsoft.com/scripting/windowshost/docs/reference/whitepaper.htm
- http://msdn.microsoft.com/scripting/windowshost/docs/reference/objectmodel.htm
- http://communities.msn.com/windowsscript
- http://www.winscripter.com

For more information on ADSI, see http://www.15seconds.com/focus/ADSI.htm.

FAQ 34.4 How do I create a new user in NT using Active Directory Scripting Interface (ADSI)?

Use the following ADSI script:

```
On Error Resume Next
strUser="UserID"
Set oDomain=GetObject("WinNT://YourDomain")
Set oUser=oDomain.Create ("user", strUser)
If (err.number=0) Then 'If not 0 then user ID already exists
oUser.SetInfo
```

```
oUser.SetPassword "mypassword"
oUser.SetInfo
End If
```

To update other elements of information you can use

```
set user=GetObject("WinNT://domain/user")
 User.FullName=FirstNameVar
 User.HomeDirectory=UserHome
 User.Profile="\\Server\Share\user"
 User.LoginScript=LogonScript
 User.Description="Description"
User.setinfo
```

FAQ 34.5 How do I run a Windows script from the command line?

Normally, when you run a WSH file such as a Visual Basic or Javascript file from Explorer, WSCRIPT.EXE is executed and runs the script using the necessary script plug-in.

To run from the command line, use CSCRIPT.EXE, which has a number of optional parameters as follows:

- **//B**—Batch mode: Suppresses script errors and prompts from displaying.
- **//D**—Enable Active Debugging.
- **//E:engine**—Uses engine for executing script.
- **//H:CScript**—Changes the default scripting host to CSCRIPT.EXE.
- **//H:WScript**—Changes the default scripting host to WSSCRIPT.EXE (default).
- **//I**—Interactive mode (default, opposite of //B).
- **//Job:xxxx**—Executes a WSC job.
- **//Logo**—Displays logo (default).
- **//Nologo**—Prevents logo display; no banner will be shown at execution time.
- **//S**—Saves current command-line options for this user.
- **//T:nn**—Displays timeout in seconds; maximum time a script is permitted to run.
- **//X**—Executes script in debugger when Active Debugging is enabled.

Yes, you need to type a forward slash (/) twice. Suppose you had the following HELLO.VBS file:

```
Wscript.Echo "Hello"
Wscript.Quit 0
```

You would run it with the command

```
cscipt hello.vbs
```

which would print Hello to the command window. Typing the following brings up Hello in a window:

```
wscript hello.vbs
```

34.6 How do I run a DOS command in WSH?

It's possible to run a DOS command from inside a WSH program using the following:

```
DIM objShell
set objShell = wscript.createObject("wscript.shell")
iReturn = objShell.Run("cmd.exe /C set var=hello", 1, TRUE)
```

You could use %Comspec% variable instead of CMD.EXE if you wish. The /C closes the command window after the command is completed. The actual command set var=hello just creates an environment variable var set to hello.

34.7 How do I rename a file using WSH?

Using the MoveFile method on a FileSystem object will result in a file being renamed:

```
Dim fso
Set fso = CreateObject("Scripting.FileSystemObject")
fso.MoveFile "file1.txt", "file2.txt"
```

34.8 How do I set the default scripting engine in Windows 2000?

By default, when you run a script, it executes in the WScript shell, and the system displays all interaction with the user in pop-up windows. You can modify the default script engine to be CScript so that the system displays all output in a command window.

To change the default scripting engine from WScript to CScript, type the following command at a system prompt:

```
cscript //h:cscript //s
```

To switch back to WScript as the default, use the following command:

```
cscript //h:wscript //s
```

35 HARDWARE

One of the biggest reasons people chose Windows 9x over Windows NT was Windows NT's very strict hardware requirement and limited compatibility; however, with Windows 2000, this has all changed. With Windows XP, there is now a single product line: Windows XP Professional from Windows 2000, Windows XP Home from Windows 9x.

This chapter contains some of the usual hardware-related questions.

FAQ 35.1 How do I change the letter associated with a drive?

From the Start menu, select Administrative Tools and Disk Administrator. Right-click on the partition and choose Assign Drive Letter; then just select the drive letter you wish to use. It is a good idea to recreate the Emergency Repair Disk after changing any drive information.

Under Windows 2000 and above, this is accomplished as follows:

1. Start the Computer Management MMC snap-in (Start > Programs > Administrative Tools > Computer Management).
2. Expand Storage and select Disk Management.
3. Right-click the partition or drive and select Change Drive Letter and Paths.
4. Select the current letter and click Edit.
5. Select the new letter and click OK to all dialog boxes.
6. Close the snap-in.

FAQ 35.2 How do I install dual screens?

Both Windows 2000 and Windows XP support multiple display adapters without any special drivers. This functionality is enabled by simply using the Display Control Panel applet and enabling the extra screens by selecting to "extend desktop on this monitor".

FAQ 35.3 How much memory can NT support?

NT is a 32-bit operating system, which means it can support 2^32 amount of memory (4GB).

Windows 2000 Advanced Server supports up to 8GB of physical memory, and Datacenter supports even 64GB of physical memory.

FAQ 35.4 What are the interrupt requests (IRQs) used for?

An interrupt allows the piece of hardware to get the CPU's attention. For something like a network card, this is important because the card has limited buffer space, so unless the CPU does not move the data out of the buffer, it will get lost. Following is a table of the common IRQ uses.

IRQ Level	Common Use	Comments
0	Timer.	Hard-wired on motherboard.
1	Keyboard.	Hard-wired on motherboard.
2	Cascade from IRQ 9.	May be available depending on motherboard.
3	COM2 or COM4.	
4	COM1 or COM3.	
5	LPT2.	This is usually free because not many people have two parallel ports. Sound blaster cards usually use this.
6	Floppy disk controller.	
7	LPT1.	Sound blaster cards can use this.
8	Real-time clock.	Hard-wired on motherboard.
9	Cascade to IRQ 2.	Wired directly to IRQ 2; sometimes it is possible to tell the software to use IRQ 9 when actually meaning IRQ 2.
10	Unused.	This is usually used by network cards, many of them not allowing it to be changed.

IRQ Level	Common Use	Comments
11	Unused.	Usually used by SCSI controllers.
12	PS/2, bus mouse.	If you are not using a PS/2 or bus mouse, this can usually be used by another device.
13	Math coprocessor.	Used to signal errors.
14	Hard disk controller.	If you are not using an IDE hard disk, you may use this for another device.
15	Some computers use this for the secondary IDE controller.	If you do not use the secondary IDE controller, you may use this for another device.

Note: *About attempting to free IRQs used by unused motherboard devices: If your BIOS lets you disable the device manually and doesn't get reset by any plug-and-play software you have (e.g., Windows 95), you are probably OK. Otherwise, you'll just have to experiment to determine whether you can really use the IRQ occupied by the unused motherboard device.*

FAQ 35.5 How Many CPUs does NT support?

NT Workstation can support 2 CPUs. NT Server supports 4 CPUs; however, the OEM version of NT Server can support up to 32 CPUs.

In Windows 2000 as follows:

- Windows 2000 Professional—2
- Windows 2000 Server—4
- Windows 2000 Advanced Server—8
- Windows 2000 Datacenter Server—32

FAQ 35.6 Is there a list of hardware NT supports?

Microsoft has a NT Hardware Compatibility List at http://www.microsoft.com/hcl/, which covers NT, Windows 2000, Windows XP, and so on.

35.7 How do I disable mouse detection on a COM port (for UPS usage)?

Follow these steps after first removing the UPS from the computer:

1. Start a command prompt (Start > Run > Command).
2. Move to the boot partition

```
c:
cd\
```

3. Change the attributes of BOOT.INI. so it can be edited

```
attrib boot.ini -r -s
```

4. Edit the file (**edit boot.ini**) and for each line with multi(x) (for IDE) and scsi(x) (for SCSI) drives, add at the end

```
/noserialmice=comx
```

   where x is the com port number.

5. Exit edit.
6. Set the permissions back on BOOT.INI

```
attrib boot.ini +r +s
```

7. Shut down NT and power off.
8. Attach the UPS.
9. Boot the machine and start NT. NTDETECT will no longer try to search for a mouse on that COM port.

The /NoSerialMice switch only disables the Microsoft Serial Mouse device driver. If you have installed any third-party mouse drivers, go into Control Panel > Devices and disable their serial mouse drivers as well. For example, if you installed the Logitech Mouseware V8.0 for a Trackman Marble, you must also disable the Logitech Serial Mouse device, called "lsermous" (note that the Arial lowercase l looks like a capital i).

FAQ 35.8 How can I view which resource devices are using under NT?

The easiest way to view resource usage by devices is to use the built-in WINMSD.EXE utility supplied with Windows NT:

1. Start the WINMSD.EXE utility (Start > Run > winmsd).
2. Click on the Resources tab.
3. You can then view any of the following by clicking the appropriate button:
   - IRQ
   - I/O Port
   - DMA
   - Memory
   - Devices
4. When finished, click OK to close WINMSD.

You could also use the WINMSDP.EXE utility that is supplied with the Resource Kit. The following command outputs the IRQ usage information to the file MSDRPT.TXT:

```
winmsdp /i
```

For Windows 2000 and above. use the new MSINFO32.EXE utility. Under Hardware Resources are areas for DMA, IRQ, I/O, memory, and so on.

FAQ 35.9 Does Windows NT/2000 support USB?

Universal Serial Bus is the new external bus standard for the connection of PC peripherals. The idea behind USB is that the devices attached via the technology will be plug-and-play, and as devices are connected they will automatically be detected and installed.

Windows NT 4.0 does not provide built-in USB support, but Windows 2000 and above have full support.

35.10 How can I check the amount of physical RAM in my machine?

Loads of methods are available to get this information:

- Right-click on My Computer and select Properties. The General tab shows the amount of memory.
- Run WINMSD.EXE and select the Memory tab.

From the command line, you can use

- PSTAT.EXE (part of the Resource Kit). The first line shows the amount of RAM.
- Download MEMORY.EXE from http://www.savilltech.com/download/memory.zip, which just displays the physical memory and nothing else. (You can use the /s switch, and it will show only the number, no other text. This is useful for information gathering.) For example:

```
memory /s
66506752
```

35.11 How can I safely disable a device?

When you disable a device, you may have to reboot. When we reboot, many of us have experienced, the Blue Screen of Death, and then we are stuck. Following is a method to allow you to test the system without the device:

1. Right-click My Computer and choose Properties.
2. Select the Hardware Profiles tab.
3. Click Copy and give the profile a name (e.g., Device Test).
4. Click OK, go back to Control Panel/Devices, and disable the device you want to test using the Device Test profile.
5. Restart your system and when the Hardware Profile/Configuration Recovery screen comes up, choose Device Test Profile and let it continue to boot (see Figure 35-1).

If you don't see a Blue Screen of Death, this configuration is probably safe. If you get the blue screen, shut the computer off. When it comes back up, choose Original Configuration, and let your computer continue to boot. You can then go back into Control Panel and enable that device again.

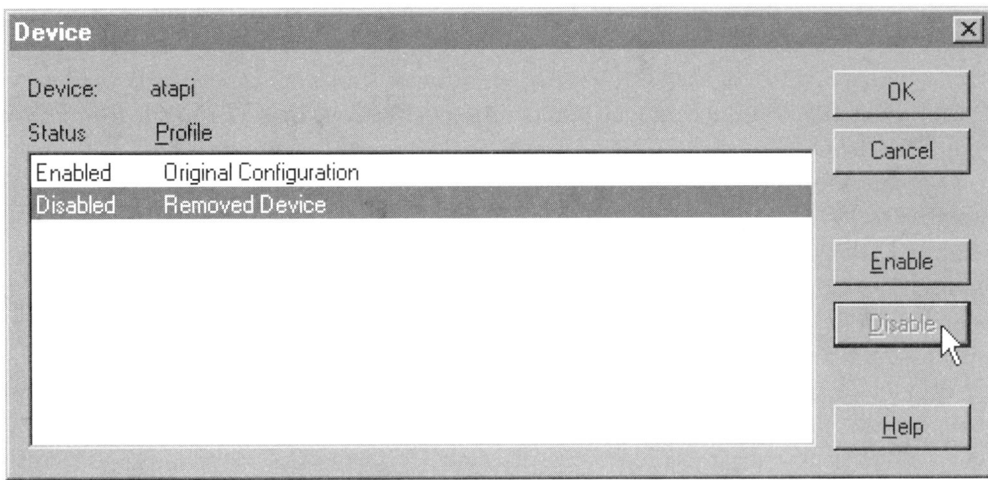

Figure 35-1 Selecting hardware configuration device status

35.12 How can I make NT see more than eight units on SCSI?

By default Windows NT 4.0 will detect only the first eight logical units on a SCSI device. This has been fixed in Service Pack 5 with the following action:

1. Start the Registry editor (REGEDIT.EXE).
2. Move to HKEY_LOCAL_MACHINE\SYSTEM\CurrentControlSet\Services\<Driver Service Name>\Parameters\Device<N>.
3. From the Edit menu, select Add > DWORD Value.
4. Enter a name of **LargeLuns** and press Enter.
5. Double-click the new value and set to 1. Click OK.
6. Close the Registry editor.
7. Restart the machine.

NT will now support up to 255 SCSI units.

35.13 Does Windows support the Promise Ultra ATA/66?

The Promise Ultra ATA/66 is an IDE interface card, which with newer hard disks, you can have 66Mbps transfer times.

Promise has produced drivers for Windows NT 4.0, which can be downloaded from http://www.promise.com. A special version for Windows 2000 is now available; however, a built-in driver for the Ultra ATA/66 is supplied and works great. If you move from IDE to the Promise card, you will need to change your BOOT.INI file from the multi() to the scsi() syntax.

If you perform an in-place upgrade of NT 4.0 with the Promise Ultra card/driver installed to Windows 2000 (2031) Pro, it works absolutely perfectly with the Promise card. In Device Manager, the Ultra 66 card is listed correctly under SCSI devices, and under Driver Details, you will get "c:\winnt\system32\drivers\ultra66.sys" with a file version of 1.42 (build 0218), by Promise Technology. To be on the safe side, you should update to the new Windows 2000 driver once installation has completed.

Windows 2000 supports the Ultra ATA/66 out of the box, and Windows XP/.Net supports the Ultra ATA/100 out of the box.

FAQ 35.14 How do I enable hibernate on my machine?

Like Windows 9x, Windows 2000 has full support for APM (Advanced Power Management), which basically allows the operating system to instruct the computer to go into a suspended state or actually switch off. It does this through a special ACPI (Advanced Configuration and Power Interface) HAL (Hardware Abstraction Layer), which it uses if it detects the BIOS supports ACPI.

ACPI is the foundation for the OnNow industry initiative that allows system manufacturers to deliver computers that will start at the touch of a key on a keyboard. ACPI design is essential to take full advantage of power management and plug-and-play in Windows 2000.

Hibernate allows the machine to save its current state to disk and then power off. When you power the machine back on, it will reload its old state, meaning any applications/files that were open will still be running, and you will lose nothing.

Hibernate basically dumps out the contents of memory to a file, c:\hiberfil.sys (which is slightly bigger than the amount of memory in the machine). To enable hibernate support, perform the following:

1. Start the Power Options Control Panel applet (Start > Settings > Control Panel > Power Options).
2. Select the Hibernate tab.
3. Check the Enable hibernate support box (see Figure 35-2).
4. Click Apply, then click OK.

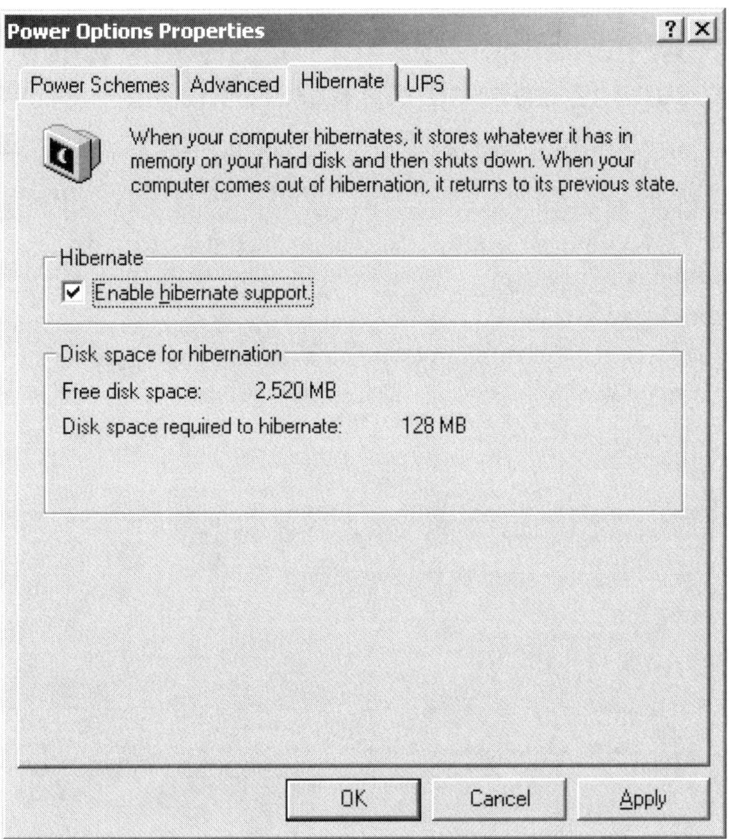

Figure 35-2 Enabling hibernation

The dialog shows the exact amount of memory that will be used for the hibernate file (HIBERFIL.SYS).

Once hibernate is enabled and you select Shutdown, an addition option is displayed (by holding down the Shift key in XP) of Hibernate, which will write out the memory to disk and power off the machine. When you turn it back on, you will see a Resuming Windows message, and (by default) it will ask for the password of the user who locked it (or an Administrator account and password).

You should make sure that your laptop has been updated to the most recent manufacturer's BIOS before attempting to set hibernate options on Win2K. If this isn't done, then hibernate may work correctly, or it may not depending on how up-to-date your BIOS is. Each manufacturer's BIOS details should be available on that manufacturer's Web site.

35.15 How do I enable/disable passwords when resuming from hibernate/standby?

In FAQ 35.14, we saw how to enable hibernate. I stated that by default upon restarting your computer, you need to enter a password; however, this can be changed as follows:

1. Start the Power Options Control Panel applet (Start > Settings > Control Panel > Power Options).
2. Select the Advanced tab.
3. Check/uncheck the Prompt for password when computer goes off standby checkbox (see Figure 35-3).
4. Click Apply, then OK.

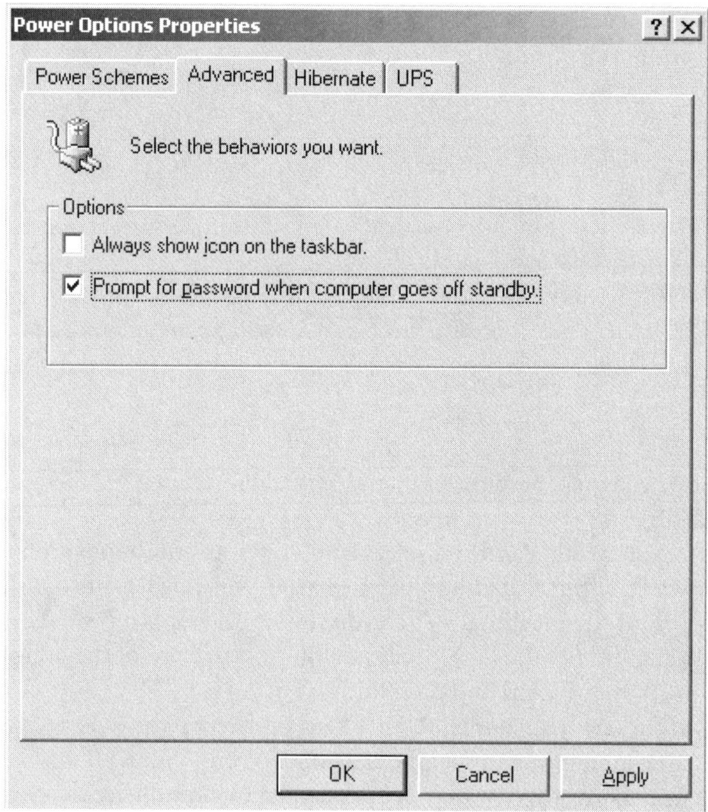

Figure 35-3 Setting password options when a computer is resumed from standby

FAQ 35.16 How can I put my machine in standby mode?

Portable computers that support APM (Advanced Power Management) and/or ACPI will have the ability to go into standby mode.

While on standby, your entire computer switches to a low power state, when devices such as the monitor and hard disks turn off and your computer uses less power. When you want to use the computer again, it comes out of standby quickly, and your desktop is restored exactly as you left it. Standby is particularly useful for conserving battery power in portable computers. Because standby does not save your desktop state to disk, a power failure while on standby can cause you to lose unsaved information so its best to save any open documents before going into standby.

A small amount of power is still used because the machine is not totally turned off. The computer isn't completely turned off because it has to maintain the memory state so any programs running when put in standby will still be active.

To put your machine in standby mode manually, select Stand by from the shutdown menu. Some portables will also support tapping the power button, which will also put the portable in suspend mode rather than powering it off—but check the manual.

You can also configure the machine to automatically go into standby or hibernate after x minutes using the Power Options Control Panel applet.

FAQ 35.17 Does the new Microsoft IntelliPoint 3.0 software install on NT/2000?

The new Microsoft mice use IntelliPoint 3.0 software, which runs under Windows NT with Service Pack 3 installed. The software is not currently supported under Windows 2000; however, you can install with the following command:

```
<CD ROM>:\setup\setup setup win2000
```

For example:

```
d:\setup\setup setup win2000
```

A Windows 2000 version of the IntelliPoint software is also available.

You cannot use the USB connection in Windows NT 4.0, but it works fine in Windows 2000.

BTW: The new Microsoft IntelliMouse Explorer is very cool ☺. An update that runs on Windows 2000 is now available from http://www.microsoft.com/products/hardware/mouse/driver/drivers_pc.htm.

FAQ 35.18 Does the new Microsoft IntelliType Pro software install on NT/Windows 2000?

The new Microsoft keyboards with the IE extra buttons use IntelliType software, which runs under Windows 2000 and Windows NT with Service Pack 3 installed. When used with Windows 2000, you do not get the onscreen display when pressing the keys such as Volume Up, but the keys still work, all except for the Computer and Calculator keys, which do not currently function.

You cannot use the USB connection in Windows NT 4.0, but it works fine in Windows 2000. As a side note, if you are using Windows 2000 and the keyboard in the USB hub, you may need to enable legacy USB support in the BIOS to allow it to "see" a USB keyboard during bootup.

IntelliType 1.1 and above runs on Windows 2000 and more information can be found at http://www.microsoft.com/products/hardware/keyboard/download/pc/download_PC.htm.

FAQ 35.19 How do I enable bus mastering (Direct Memory Access—DMA) in Windows 2000?

DMA support is included in Windows 2000; however, it is not enabled for the devices by default and so requires configuration. Enabling DMA if supported will result in performance gains.

1. Right-click on My Computer and select Properties.
2. Select the Hardware tab and select Device Manager.
3. Expand IDE ATA/ATAPI controllers.
4. Right-click on Primary IDE Channel (and secondary if available).
5. Select Advanced Settings.
6. For Device 0 and Device 1 under Transfer Mode, select DMA if available (see Figure 35-4).
7. Click OK.
8. Click OK to the main system properties.
9. Click OK to reboot the computer.

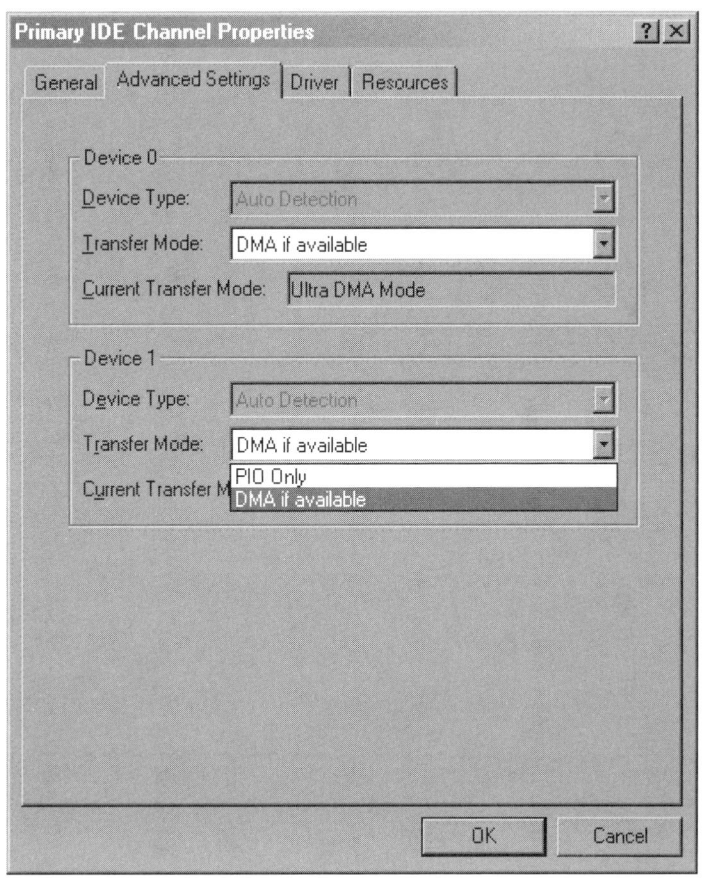

Figure 35-4 Device transfer mode

FAQ 35.20 How do I set the DVD region in Windows 2000?

Windows 2000 provides built-in DVD support and will keep track of the DVD region. However, it initially needs to be set as explained in this FAQ. After setting it, you are allowed to change it once more using the same method.

1. Start Device Manager (right-click on My Computer > Properties > Hardware tab > Device Manager).
2. Expand DVD/CD-ROM drives.
3. Right-click on the DVD drive and select Properties.
4. Select the Advanced Settings tab.
5. Select your region (see Figure 35-5) and click OK.

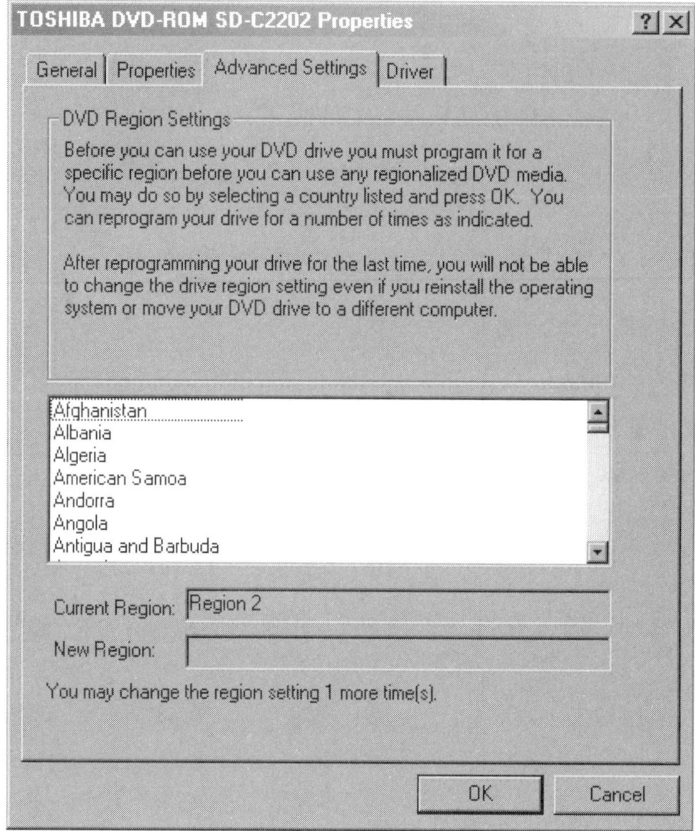

Figure 35-5 Selecting DVD region

6. Click OK to the confirmation.
7. Click OK to all other dialogs.

If you have other drivers for hardware/software that track regions, then they also need to be set.

FAQ 35.21 How do I reset the DVD region count?

Windows 2000 keeps track of the DVD region, and after its initial setting, you are allowed to change it only once more. It's possible to reset the counter by performing the following Registry change:

1. Start the Registry editor (REGEDIT.EXE).
2. Move to HKEY_LOCAL_MACHINE\SOFTWARE\Microsoft.
   There will be a subkey (the first) of a strange format (e.g., ;t-z% with a single REG_QWORD value).
3. Select the key and delete it (Figure 35-6).
4. Restart the computer.

Upon restarting your computer, you should be able to modify the region again.

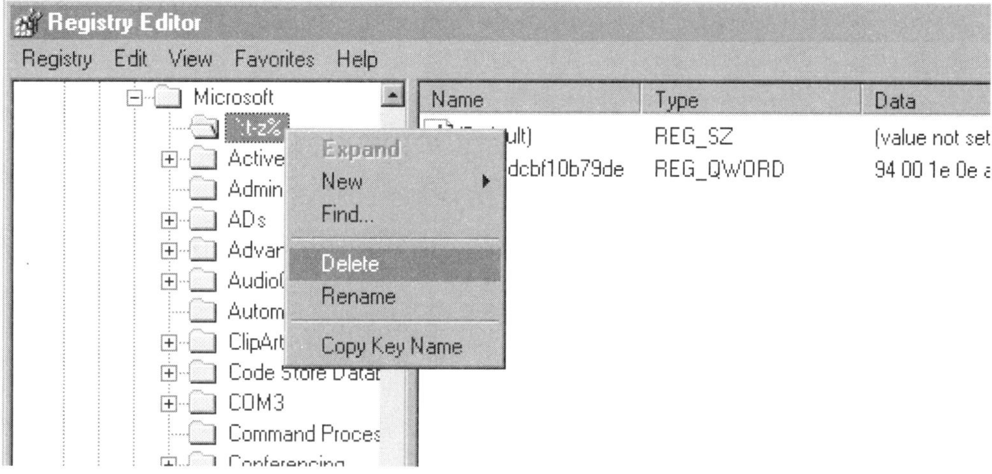

Figure 35-6 Resetting our region count

FAQ 35.22 How do I disable bus mastering on the 3COM 3C590 card?

It's possible to disable bus mastering on the 3C590 to alleviate any possible bus master contention. To disable, perform the following:

1. Start the Registry editor (REGEDIT.EXE).
2. Move to HKEY_LOCAL_MACHINE\SYSTEM\CurrentControlSet\Services\EL59X1 (if you have multiple adapters, you will also have EL59X2, etc.).
3. Select the Parameters key (if the key does not exist, create it).
4. From the Edit menu, select New > String value.

5. Enter a name of **Busmaster** and press Enter.
6. Double-click the new value and set to No.
7. Click OK.
8. Restart the computer.

Upon restarting your computer, there should now be a system event:

```
Busmaster support has been turned off for slot XX.
```

A newer version of the driver can be found at http://support.3com.com/infodeli/tools/nic/3C590.htm#ship.

FAQ 35.23 How do I allow PS2 keyboard hot plugging in Windows 2000?

If you attach a keyboard via the PS/2 port after the Windows 2000 installation has booted, the keyboard will not work.

Service Pack 1 introduces a fix to I8042PRT.SYS (which can also be obtained from Microsoft) that introduces hot-plugging ability, assuming the BIOS supports this functionality. To enable, perform the following:

1. Start the Registry editor (REGEDIT.EXE).
2. Move to HKEY_LOCAL_MACHINE\SYSTEM\CurrentControlSet\Services\i8042prt\Parameters.
3. Double-click Headless (or create it of type DWORD).
4. Set to 1.
5. Click OK.
6. Close the Registry editor.
7. Restart the machine.

FAQ 35.24 My computer has full ACPI/APM support, but I still can't hibernate or standby using a VGA adapter. Why?

To use hibernate or standby, the components of the system need to support power management, which custom video drivers provide. The built-in VGA driver is a bare-bones VGA-only driver with no power management. If you want hibernate/standby options in the Power Options Control Panel applet, then install the correct driver for your video card.

FAQ 35.25 When I connect a USB device to a USB hub, why do I receive an error message about available power?

When you connect a USB device to a USB hub, you might receive the following error message:

```
The hub doesn't have enough power available to operate the [device]
USB Device. Would you like assistance in solving this problem?
```

As this error message indicates, not enough power is available to operate the device correctly. You should use the AC adapter that came with the device to resolve the power distribution problem.

FAQ 35.26 When I upgraded to Windows 2000, I lost my Windows 98 multimonitor configuration. How do I restore it?

Both Win2K and Win98 support multiple monitors. However, Win2K uses a different architecture than Win98. When Win2K installs new video adapters, you lose any Win98 configurations. You need to configure your Win2K multimonitor support from scratch using the Display applet in Control Panel.

FAQ 35.27 I have a large number of devices sharing an interrupt request. Is this OK?

It's OK to have a large number of devices sharing an interrupt request (IRQ) if you're not experiencing any problems. You can use the Device Manager to view resource usage (see Figure 35-7). Right-click My Computer, select Properties, and on the Hardware tab, click Device Manager. From the View menu, select Resources by type. Expand IRQ to display the device usage.

In Windows 2000, PCI devices can share IRQs by design. Per the plug-and-play capability that the PCI specification defines, the computer's BIOS configures adapters,

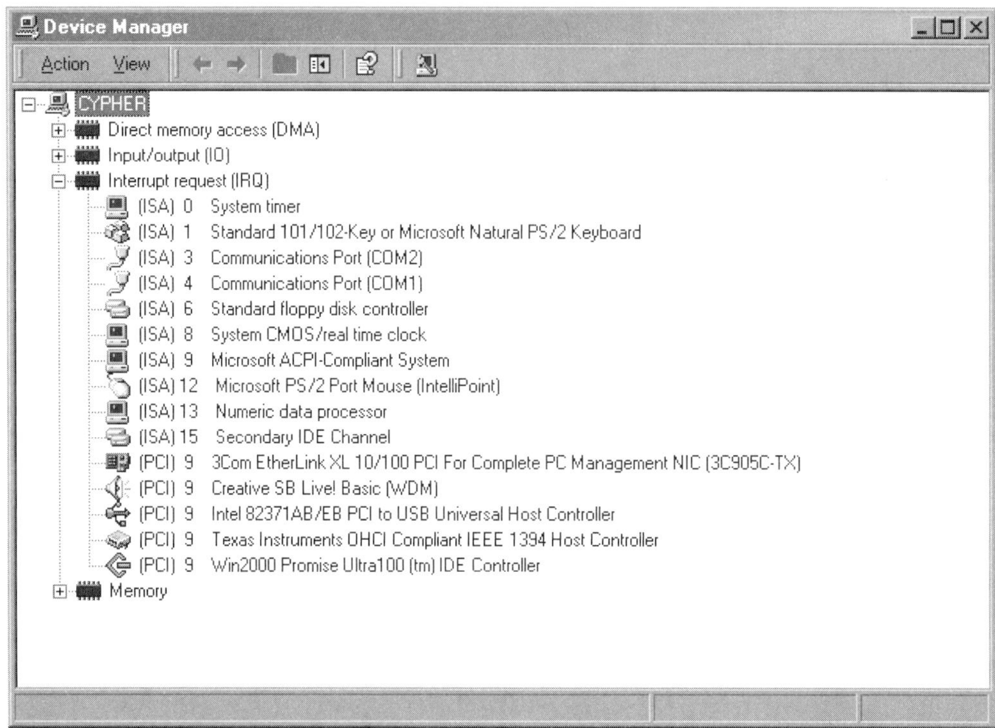

Figure 35-7 IRQ view using Device Manager

which the OS then examines and changes if necessary. PCI devices typically share IRQs, especially on Advanced Configuration and Power Interface computers with Win2K ACPI support enabled.

The PCI slot that's in use can sometimes cause problems. In the event of a freeze, try moving something (e.g., the sound card) to a different PCI slot.

35.28 How can I keep my ACPI-enabled PC from restarting instead of shutting down?

First, make sure your Advanced Configuration and Power Interface (ACPI)-enabled computer has an AT extension (ATX) case. You can usually tell this by looking at the back of your computer on the power supply. If the power supply has only one plug and a small switch on it, the case is probably an ATX case. If you don't have an ATX case, you'll have to find out how to remove automatic shutdown (which turns off power on ATX computers).

Second, download and install Windows 2000 Service Pack 1 (SP1) or newer, which includes an updated version of HAL.DLL, the culprit file in the shutdown issue. You can get SP1 from the Microsoft Web site.

After you download and install SP1, the computer will attempt to restart. If this fails, wait until the computer presents a black screen and you see no evidence of hard disk activity. Then, press the reset button on the computer (or switch the power to it off and on). When Win2K starts up again, all should be well!

Thanks goes to Erik Tomlinson for this tip.

FAQ 35.29 How do I enable Intel Physical Address Extensions?

Windows 2000 Advanced Server and Windows 2000 Datacenter can both address more than 4GB (8GB and 64GB, respectively). You enable this feature with the /PAE switch. Perform the following steps:

1. Use the following command to remove the system and read-only BOOT.INI attributes:

   ```
   attrib c:\boot.ini -s -r
   ```

2. Use the following command to open BOOT.INI in Notepad:

   ```
   notepad c:\boot.ini
   ```

3. Add the /PAE switch to the end of the OS you use. For example:

   ```
   multi(0)disk(0)rdisk(0)partition(1)\WINNT="Microsoft Windows 2000
   Advanced Server" /fastdetect /pae
   ```

4. Save the change.
5. Use the following command to reset the system and read-only attributes:

   ```
   attrib c:\boot.ini +s +r
   ```

The 4GB limitation for each program still exists; however, the OS can address more memory, so the programs won't encounter physical memory limitations and the system will experience less paging.

35.30 How can I force my machine to use only the first processor?

If you want to use only one processor of a multiprocessor machine, you can use the numproc BOOT.INI switch (see FAQ 6.48 for more information about numproc and other BOOT.INI switches).

1. Start a command session (Start > Run > cmd.exe).
2. Go to the root of the C drive.
3. Use the following command to modify the BOOT.INI file so it is not a system file, not hidden, and not read-only:

```
attrib boot.ini -r -s -h
```

4. Open the file in Notepad:

```
notepad boot.ini
```

5. Locate the entry that starts the OS and add **/numproc=1** to the end. For example,

```
multi(0)disk(0)rdisk(0)partition(1)\WINNT="Microsoft Windows 2000
Professional" /fastdetect /numproc=1
```

6. Save the change and exit Notepad.
7. Use the following command to reset the BOOT.INI attributes:

```
attrib boot.ini +r +s +h
```

35.31 How do I enable network adapter task offloading?

Some network cards have an onboard processor that you can use instead of the main CPU for certain functions. If your NIC driver supports this onboard processor, you can enable it as follows:

1. Start REGEDIT.EXE.
2. Go to HKEY_LOCAL_MACHINE\SYSTEM\CurrentControlSet\Services\Tcpip\Parameters.
3. From the Edit menu, select New > DWORD Value.

4. Enter a value name of **DisableTaskOffload** and press Enter.
5. Double-click the new value and ensure that it's set to 0. Click OK.
6. Close Regedit.
7. Reboot the machine.

FAQ 35.32 Does Windows 2000 work with a 64-bit processor?

All current versions of Windows 2000 and Windows NT are 32-bit OSs (although Microsoft has made some enhancements to let Win2K and NT access more than 4GB of memory when used with an Intel Xeon processor, providing access to 64GB of memory).

Windows XP Professional and Windows .NET server family will be the first Windows version to support a true 64-bit processor, such as the Intel Itanium. Even if the OS fully supports a 64-bit processor, the applications will also need to be written to use the new abilities (e.g., 64GB of memory), so the move to 64-bit will be a major step.

FAQ 35.33 When I install a scanner card, what do I do when the system prompts me for the file SCMAPPER.SYS?

When you try to install a scanner, Windows 2000 might prompt you for the file SCMAPPER.SYS. If you receive this prompt, open a text editor and create a file with absolutely nothing in it. Save the file as SCSIMAP.SYS (note the difference in name from what Win2K prompted for) in %systemroot%\system32.

FAQ 35.34 How can I confirm how many processors my version of Windows supports?

You can check the Registry value HKEY_LOCAL_MACHINE\SYSTEM\CurrentControlSet\Control\Session Manager\RegisteredProcessors to see how many processors your version of Windows supports. This Registry key value is informational only. In other words, changing the value to 128 won't enable your version of Windows to support 128 processors!

35.35 Why won't my computer boot after I installed the drivers for my Creative Labs Live!Ware sound card?

If you installed Live!Ware drivers for Windows NT or earlier versions, your Windows 2000 machine might not boot and might display the following error:

```
STOP: 0x0000001E KMODE_EXCEPTION_NOT_HANDLED error
```

To work around this problem, perform the following steps:

1. Press F8 when you boot the machine to display the Options menu.
2. Select Safe mode with command prompt.
3. Move to the %systemroot%\system32 folder.
4. Rename the CTMM32.DLL file, changing the extension to .OLD (i.e., CTMM32.OLD).
5. Reboot the machine in Normal mode.
6. Download and install the latest Windows 2000 drivers.

35.36 After I updated my keyboard driver to the new Microsoft Natural Keyboard Pro driver, why did my keyboard and mouse stop working?

The latest Natural Keyboard Pro driver supports only the keyboard's USB socket (even though the keyboard also has a PS/2 connection). When installing the new driver, the setup program disables the i8042 port and enables Human Interface Device (HID) support. The i8042 service must be running for a PS/2 keyboard and mouse to function.

Unless you can log on (which, unless you have enabled autologon, might be impossible), try booting into the last known good configuration by pressing F8 at the boot menu to undo the change. If the last known good configuration doesn't resolve the problem, you can change the following Registry values remotely or by using third-party tools:

1. Change HKEY_LOCAL_MACHINE\SYSTEM\CurrentControlSet\Services\i8042prt\Start to 1
2. Change HKEY_LOCAL_MACHINE\SYSTEM\CurrentControlSet\Services\kbdhid\Start to 4

If you can't edit these Registry settings, you need to use the Recovery Console (RC) by performing the following steps:

1. Boot the computer from the Windows installation media and press F10 when you see the Welcome to Setup screen to start the RC.
2. Type the following command to navigate to the system32\drivers folder:

   ```
   cd \system32\drivers
   ```

3. Type the following command to back up the current enhanced keyboard driver:

   ```
   ren kbdhid.sys kbdhid.org
   ```

4. Type the following command to copy the i8042 port driver over the enhanced keyboard driver:

   ```
   copy i8042prt.sys kbdhid.sys
   ```

5. Type **exit** to quit the RC. This step will cause the system to reboot.
6. Log on as an administrator and reinstall the Standard 101/102-Key or Microsoft Natural PS/2 Keyboard drivers by clicking the Keyboard applet in Control Panel, selecting the Hardware tab, clicking Properties, selecting the Driver tab, and starting the Update Driver Wizard. Your mouse will not function until you perform this step.
7. Install the full Microsoft IntelliType Pro 1.1 update or later drivers for Windows 2000 that support the Microsoft Natural Keyboard Pro.

FAQ 35.37 How can I control the modem speaker volume?

Normally you can configure the modem speaker on or off via the properties of the modem; however, you can also set this via a user initialization string:

1. Start the Phone and Modem Control Panel applet (Start > Settings > Control Panel > Phone and Modem).
2. Select the Modems tab.
3. Select the modem and click Properties.
4. Select the Advanced tab.
5. Add to the initialization string one of the options in the following table and click OK.
6. Close the Control Panel applet.

Setting	Effect
L0	Selects the lowest speaker volume.
L1	Selects a low speaker volume.
L2	Selects medium speaker volume.
L3	Selects high speaker volume.
M0	The speaker is always off.
M1	Enables the speaker during call establishment, but off after the carrier is detected.
M2	The speaker is always on.
M3	Disables the speaker during the dialing period and receiving carrier, but on during answering.

FAQ 35.38 I'm unable to enter a modem initialization string over 40 characters. What can I do?

If when trying to enter a modem initialization string you are limited to 40 characters, a fix can be obtained by Microsoft Support quoting Knowledge Base article Q311941. If you cannot wait for this fix, you can work around this by directly editing the Registry:

1. Start the Registry editor (REGEDIT.EXE).
2. Move to HKEY_LOCAL_MACHINE\SYSTEM\CurrentControlSet\Control\Class\{4D36E96D-E325-11CE-BFC1-08002BE10318}\<modemnumber>.
3. From the Edit menu, select New > String value.
4. Enter a name of **UserInit** and press Enter.
5. Double-click the value, set to the required modem initialization, and click OK.

36 COMPATIBILITY ISSUES

In a pure Microsoft world where they made all software and hardware, we would have no compatibility issues. However, we do have to contend with multiple vendors and hardware components, which can lead to support issues. In this chapter, we look at some common compatibility problems.

FAQ 36.1 In what order should I install OSs if I want to multiboot?

The rule is to install the oldest OS first and work forward. For example, if you want to install DOS, Windows Me, and Windows 2000, you should install them in that order. Following, I've listed the requirements for each OS when you plan a multiboot environment:

- MS-DOS—Requires a FAT partition on a basic disk, and if you don't install DOS on the system partition, the system partition must also be FAT.
- Windows 95—Requires a FAT partition on a basic disk, and if you don't install Win95 on the system partition, the system partition must also be FAT. Windows XP and Win2K won't be able to see any volumes compressed with DriveSpace or DoubleSpace.
- Windows Me, Windows 98, Windows 95 OEM Service Release 2 (OSR2)—Requires a FAT/FAT32 partition on a basic disk, and if you don't install the OS on the system partition, the system partition must also be FAT/FAT32. Windows XP and Win2K won't be able to see any volumes compressed with DriveSpace or DoubleSpace.
- Windows NT 4.0—Requires a FAT/NTFS partition on a basic disk, and if you don't install NT 4.0 on the system partition, the system partition must not be FAT32 or NTFS 5.0 (NTFS5). Any NTFS-formatted volumes won't be available to any Windows Me or Win9x OSs.
- XP, Win2K—Requires a FAT/FAT32/NTFS or NTFS5 partition on a basic or dynamic disk. Any NTFS-formatted volumes won't available to any Windows Me or

Win9x OSs. Any NTFS5-formatted volumes will be available to NT 4.0 machines only if you've installed Service Pack 4 (SP4) or newer.

FAQ 36.2 Does game x work with NT 4.0/ Windows 2000/XP?

See http://www.ntcompatible.com for an extensive lists of games that work with the various versions of Windows. This site also contains tips to make them work.

FAQ 36.3 What services are available to talk to UNIX?

Microsoft released Services for UNIX 2.0, which provides the following main components:

- Client for NFS
- Server for NFS
- Gateway for NFS
- Server for PCNFS
- Many UNIX programs, as well as the ability to run UNIX scripts within Windows
- Network Information Service (NIS) compatibility

The NIS compatibility is useful for account matching and provides the following:

- NIS-to-Active Directory (AD) Migration Wizard—Consolidates account management by moving UNIX source files, such as password and host files, from NIS domains into AD
- Server for NIS—Enables a Win2K domain controller (DC) to act as the primary NIS server, integrating NIS domains with Win2K domains, letting administrators manage an NIS domain from AD
- Two-way password synchronization—Provides the ability to synchronize passwords from both platforms, making it easier for users to maintain one password for both Windows and UNIX
- User name mapping—Associates Windows and UNIX usernames, letting users connect to NFS network resources seamlessly

For more information, visit the Microsoft Web site at http://www.microsoft.com/windows2000/sfu/default.asp.

36.4 Why do I receive an error when I attempt to run a 16-bit program under Windows NT?

When you attempt to run a 16-bit application under NT, you might receive the following message:

```
Application popup: 16-bit Windows Subsystem : An application has
attempted to directly access the hard disk, which cannot be
supported. This may cause the application to function incorrectly.
Choose 'Close' to terminate the application.
```

This error is typically the result of an invalid entry in the COMMAND.COM, AUTOEXEC.NT, or CONFIG.NT files, which NT maintains for compatibility with 16-bit applications. To resolve this error, restore the default versions of these files from the NT installation CD-ROM by performing the following steps:

1. Run CMD.EXE (go to Start > Run, and type **cmd.exe**).
2. Navigate to the %systemroot%\system32 folder by typing

   ```
   cd %systemroot%\system32
   ```

3. Rename the current COMMAND.COM, AUTOEXEC.NT, and CONFIG.NT files and append the word old to the filenames by typing

   ```
   rename command.com command.comold
   rename autoexec.nt autoexec.ntold
   rename config.nt config.ntold
   ```

4. Navigate to the i386 structure of your Windows installation path (e.g., d:\i386) by typing

   ```
   cd /d d:\i386
   ```

   The /d lets you change the drive and path at the same time.
5. Expand the original files from the NT installation CD-ROM by typing

   ```
   expand command.co_ %systemroot%\system32\command.com
   expand autoexec.nt_ %systemroot%\system32\autoexec.nt
   expand config.nt_ %systemroot%\system32\config.nt
   ```

6. Restart your computer, and run your 16-bit application again.

FAQ 36.5 Does NT run 16-bit applications?

There is no definitive answer. NT does not allow an application to directly access hardware, so any application that directly tries to access hardware would cause a violation. Also private device drivers are not supported (such as a VXD). A VXD is usually a .386 file.

Besides direct hardware access, some 16-bit apps will not run under NT because they use a 16-bit API function call that either has no 32-bit equivalent, or the 32-bit equivalent has a completely different function call (different number/types of arguments) and NT can't convert the 16-bit version to the 32-bit version. If either of these things occur, NT will halt execution of the 16-bit app and throw some sort of error similar to the one it throws when direct hardware access occurs. This doesn't happen very often, but it seems that NT 4.0 has more problems with 16-bit code than NT 3.51 due to the 16-bit to 32-bit conversion process.

As a side note: This conversion of 16-bit code to 32-bit code is one of the reasons that NT will run 16-bit code slower than Win95 given all other things are equal. This has nothing to do with the Pentium Pro's problem with 16-bit code; it is an NT problem.

The NT Virtual DOS Machine (NTVDM) simulates MS-DOS environment for MS-DOS-based applications. Applications that run in user mode do not have direct access to hardware. The Virtual Device Drivers (VDD) intercept the application's h/w calls and interact with the Windows NT 32-bit device driver. This process is transparent to the application.

FAQ 36.6 If I have a multiboot scenario on my machine, can each instance of an OS have the same computer name?

If each instance of an OS participates in the same Windows .NET/XP/2000 domain, each OS instance must have a different machine name because the system uses the machine name to create the domain account. If the OSs are in a workgroup or in different domains, they can have the same machine name.

Sharing a static IP address isn't an issue because no more than one OS can run on the machine at any given time.

36.7 How do I enable compatibility mode with Windows 2000 Service Pack 2 and later?

Win2K machines with SP2 or later include a compatibility mode that lets programs run as if they were on a Windows NT 4.0 SP5 or Windows 95 box. To enable this interface, perform the following steps:

1. Start a Run box (Start > Run).
2. Enter the following command:

```
regsvr32 %systemroot%\apppatch\slayerui.dll
```

3. Click OK.
4. Click OK to the confirmation.

If you right-click a shortcut and select Properties, you'll see a Compatibility tab that lets you select whether the program target should run under an NT 4.0 SP5 or a Win95 compatibility layer (see Figure 36-1).

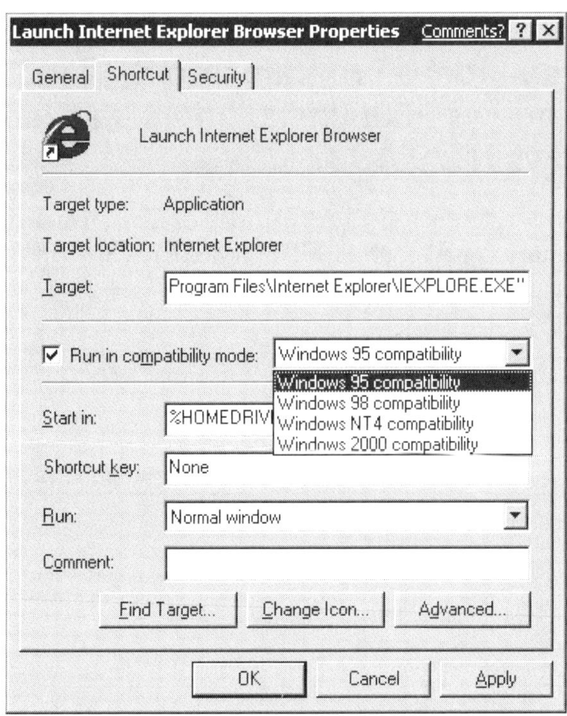

Figure 36-1 Selecting the application compatibility mode for an application

With Windows XP, the compatibility option is located on the General tab in its own compatibility section.

36.8 How do I disable compatibility mode with Windows 2000 Service Pack 2 and later?

To disable the compatibility mode, perform the following steps:

1. Start a Run box (Start > Run).
2. Enter the following command:

```
regsvr32 /u %systemroot%\apppatch\slayerui.dll
```

3. Click OK.
4. Click OK to the confirmation.

The Compatibility tab will no longer appear.

36.9 How can I fool a program into thinking my Windows 2000 installation is actually Windows NT/95/98?

Windows 2000 provides a utility called APCOMPAT.EXE, which can fool a program into thinking it is running on Windows NT (Service Pack 3, 4, or 5), Windows 95, or Windows 98. The syntax of the command is as follows:

```
apcompat [-?] [-v version name] [-x program path] [-d] [-t] [-g] [-k]
```

The following table lists the parameters:

-?	Displays the syntax for the command-line parameters.	
-v <version name>	Specifies the name of the operating system you want to return to the specified program.	
	1	Returns the version Windows NT4 SP3.
	2	Returns the version Windows NT4 SP4.

	3 Returns the version Windows NT4 SP5.
	4 Returns the version Windows 98.
	5 Returns the version Windows 95.
-x <program path>	Specifies the path and name of the executable (.EXE) file for the program you want to run.
-d	Disables the Heap Manager for the portion of memory reserved for the specified program.
-t	Uses \Temp for the Temp folder when running the specified program.
-g	Corrects disk space detection.
-k	Stores the specified Application Compatibility settings.

The tool is part of the Windows 2000 Support Tools and is documented in the W2RKSUPP.CHM HTML Help file. You can run APCOMPAT.EXE with no qualifiers, which will launch a GUI version allowing you to make choices onscreen (see Figure 36-2). It can be found in SUPPORT.CAB in the support\tools folder of your CD.

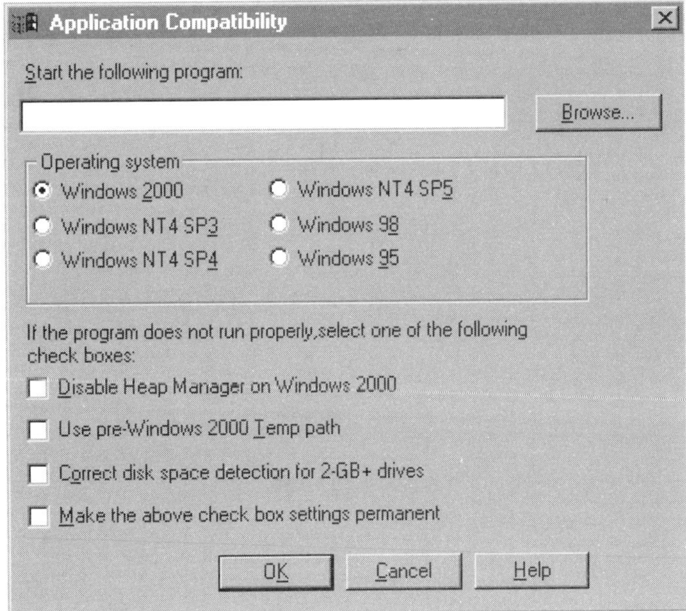

Figure 36-2 Application Compatibility program main window

FAQ 36.10 What software DVD players work with Windows 2000?

A number of hardware solutions for DVD decoding are available; however, with faster processors, software decoding is fine is most situations, and less configuration is required. Not all software players work on Windows 2000.

The one I personally use is PowerDVD from CyberLink, but others work on Windows 2000:

- DVD Express—http://www.mediamatics.com/ (you get this with the IBM portables).
- PowerDVD 2.55 and above—http://www.gocyberlink.com/.
- Win DVD—http://www.intervideoinc.com/.

Be aware that to use these, you do need a good processor, at least a PII 400, but they work best with a PIII.

37 PROBLEM SOLVING

Many FAQs in other chapters deal with resolving "features" of the operating system. This chapter deals with general issues such as deleting reserved filenames, fixing the Scheduler service, and what's in the dreaded Blue Screen of Death.

37.1 Why can't I delete AUX.BAT or COM1 files?

A file of which the name (or a part of it) is equal to a DOS device's (NUL, COMx, AUX, LPTx, PRN . . .) cannot be deleted with Explorer or the usual DEL syntax. Use DEL \\.\drive:\path\AUX.BAT instead (replace "drive" and "path" with the appropriate values). (The files may be the remains of a failed installation; you can create them—e.g., with COPY—some existing file \\.\drive:\path\COM1).

37.2 Why does the AT command not work?

A sine qua non to using AT is running the Scheduler service. To start it, type **net start schedule** on the command line or use Control Panel/Services (if you want to use it regularly, set the Startup Type to Automatic).

A common problem is that people try to use the example given in the online Help: AT <time> CMD /C DIR > TEST.OUT. Unfortunately, in NT 4.0, this does not work anymore. You must use AT sometime CMD /C \"DIR > TEST.OUT\" instead.

> **Note:** *You must now include an escaped quote before the command and after the filename you are redirecting the output to.*

The execution of the command starts by default in %systemroot%\system32, as can be seen from the output of the preceding example. You should specify the complete path if the command is in a different directory (e.g., AT sometime C:\TEMP\TEST.BAT). A further problem is that the command is executed in the security context of the LOCAL SYSTEM account, not the caller. However, the SYSTEM account does not have access to network resources you may have mapped under your account, so your program cannot reside or access files on mapped drives (even if they are mapped from the local machine!). Also, environment variables (e.g., PATH) may be set differently. You can test the environment interactively with AT sometime /INTERACTIVE CMD.

The AT command in NT runs under the SYSTEM account and therefore has no privileges to the network resources (i.e., can't write or read a file from the network). But if you go into Control Panel > Services > Scheduler and change Log On As to a user who has the appropriate permissions (a user with access to the network), then an AT command that runs can actually use the network. This may be useful if you find submitted jobs are failing at certain network operations.

FAQ 37.3 Why does my desktop disappear after a crash?

When Explorer crashes, it automatically restarts by default, but this may have been corrupted or changed. Using the Registry editor, change the value HKEY_LOCAL_MACHINE\SOFTWARE\Microsoft\Windows NT\CurrentVersion\Winlogon\AutoRestartShell to 1.

FAQ 37.4 Why does an application keep starting every time I start Windows?

Applications can be started from a number of places:

- In the Startup folder for the current user and all user groups
- In the Registry:
  HKEY_LOCAL_MACHINE\Software\Microsoft\Windows\CurrentVersion\Run
  HKEY_LOCAL_MACHINE\Software\Microsoft\Windows\CurrentVersion\RunOnce
  HKEY_LOCAL_MACHINE\Software\Microsoft\Windows\CurrentVersion\RunServices
  HKEY_LOCAL_MACHINE\Software\Microsoft\Windows\CurrentVersion\RunServicesOnce
  HKEY_LOCAL_MACHINE\Software\Microsoft\Windows NT\CurrentVersion\Winlogon\Userinit
  HKEY_CURRENT_USER\Software\Microsoft\Windows\CurrentVersion\Run

HKEY_CURRENT_USER\Software\Microsoft\Windows\CurrentVersion\Run Once
HKEY_CURRENT_USER\Software\Microsoft\Windows\CurrentVersion\Run Services
HKEY_CURRENT_USER\Software\Microsoft\Windows\CurrentVersion\Run ServicesOnce
HKEY_CURRENT_USER\Software\Microsoft\Windows NT\CurrentVersion\Windows, run and Load keys

- In %systemroot%\win.ini

The easiest way to resolve this problem is to search the Registry using Regedit on the application name.

FAQ 37.5 Sometimes when I run a program or Control Panel applet, Windows says no disk in drive A. Why?

It is possible the NT path statement has an "a:" included. Check the following:

- Registry entry HKEY_LOCAL_MACHINE\SYSTEM\Setup\WinntPath
- Registry entry HKEY_LOCAL_MACHINE\SYSTEM\CurrentControlSet\Control\Session Manager\Environment\Path
- Control Panel > System > Environment > the global and user path statements
- AUTOEXEC.BAT
- %systemroot%/system32/Autoexec.nt

FAQ 37.6 When I try to create an Emergency Repair Disk, I get an error: "One or more configuration files missing." How can I fix this?

Run RDISK /S a few times, and this error will fix itself.

FAQ 37.7 Why does Explorer start showing the system32 directory every time I start NT?

This is caused by an incorrect program call at startup. Search the areas a program can be started from for an incorrect entry. Such entries are listed at "An Application keeps starting every time I start NT."

One example is as follows:

1. Start the Registry Editor (REGEDIT.EXE).
2. Open this Registry key HKEY_CURRENT_USER\SOFTWARE\Microsoft\Windows\CurrentVersion\Run and HKEY_LOCAL_MACHINE\SOFTWARE\Microsoft\Windows\CurrentVersion\Run.
3. Verify that all the values in these keys do not contain any incorrect, incomplete, or NULL entries (such as "").
4. If the (Default) Name variable has a value of "" (an empty string), delete the Name variable. After the deletion, the value for (Default) should be "(value not set)".

This procedure should resolve the problem. Obviously the preceding is only one possible solution, and so all entries should be checked.

FAQ 37.8 What information is shown in the Blue Screen of Death (BSOD) ?

The NT operating system has two basic layers, the user mode and kernel mode. The user mode cannot directly access hardware, is limited to an assigned address space, and operates at Ring 3 (lower priority). If a user mode program has an error, then NT just halts the program's process and generates an Operation error. Because the application runs in its own virtual address, it cannot affect any other program. Common components that run in user mode are

- Logon process
- Security subsystem
- Win32 application and subsystem
- OS/2 application and subsystem
- POSIX application and subsystem

NT 4.0 introduced a change in the NT architecture because kernel mode processes run much faster (Ring 0). Video and printer drivers were moved from user mode to kernel mode. Kernel mode is a privileged processor mode, allowing direct access to the memory and hardware. Kernel mode errors are not usually recoverable, and a reboot of the system will be required. The BSOD is a built-in error-trapping mechanism that is used to halt any further processing to avoid system/data corruption. This means a faulty graphics/print driver could crash NT. Components in kernel mode are

- Various managers, handling IO, objects, security, IPC (interprocess communication), graphics, windows, and virtual memory

- Microkernel that provides the basic operating system functionality
- Hardware Abstraction Layer
- Device drivers

But what does the BSOD (or STOP message screen) show? Following is the basic structure of the BSOD; however, what you see will differ, and you may not have some of the sections that I describe following the listing of the BSOD structure.

```
Section 1: Debug Port Status Indicators
DSR CTS SND
--------------------------------------------------
Section 2: BugCheck Information
*** STOP: 0x0000000A (0x00000002,0x00000000,0xDB30442D)
IRQL_NOT_LESS_OR_EQUAL *** Address db30442d has base at db300000 -
matrxmil.SYS
CPUID: GenuineIntel 5.2.4 irql:1f SYSVER 0xF0000565
--------------------------------------------------
Section 3: Driver Information
Dll Base DateStmp - Name Dll Base DateStmp - Name
80100000 2cd348a4 - ntoskrnl.exe 80400000 2cd348b2 - hal.dll
80010000 2cd348b5 - ncrc810.sys 80013000 2cda574d - SCSIPORT.SYS
etc..
--------------------------------------------------
Section 4: Kernel Build and Stack Dump
Address dword dump Build [1381] -Name
xxxxxxxx xxxxxxxx xxxxxxxx xxxxxxxx xxxxxxxx xxxxxxxx xxxxxxxx -
matrxmil.SYS
xxxxxxxx xxxxxxxx xxxxxxxx xxxxxxxx xxxxxxxx xxxxxxxx xxxxxxxx -
ntoskrnl.exe
xxxxxxxx xxxxxxxx xxxxxxxx xxxxxxxx xxxxxxxx xxxxxxxx xxxxxxxx -
ntoskrnl.exe
etc..
-------------------------
Section 5: Debug Port Information
Restart and set the recovery options in the system control panel
or the /CRASHDEBUG system start option if this message reappears,
contact your system administrator or technical support group
```

Or if your system is started with /debug or /crashdebug

```
Kernel Debugger Using : Com2 (Port 0x2f8, Baud Rate 9600)
Beginning Dump of physical memory
Physical memory dump complete. Contact your system administrator or
technical support group
```

Section 1

This section will be shown **only** if the system was started with /debug or /crashdebug. To tell whether your system is debugger enabled, just look at the boot menu when you start the machine, and the words "[debugger enabled]" will be shown next to the Windows NT menu choice. To enable /debug, follow these instructions:

1. Modify BOOT.INI to be editable:

   ```
   attrib c:\boot.ini -r -s
   ```

2. Edit the file and the Windows NT start line to include /debug (to tell the system to load the kernel debugger into memory at boot-up) or /crashdebug (to tell the system to load the kernel debugger but swap it out to the pagefile). Other options are /Debugport to tell which COM port to use (by default COM2) and /Baudrate for the speed (by default 19200, but it's better to be 9600). For example:.

   ```
   [operating systems]
   multi(0)disk(0)rdisk(0)partition(0)\WINDOWS="Windows NT" /debug
   /debugport=com3 /baudrate=9600
   ```

3. Save the file.
4. Set BOOT.INI attributes back

   ```
   attrib c:\boot.ini +r +s
   ```

The three-letter words are signals (e.g., RTS is Ready to Send, DSR Data Send Ready, CTS Clear to Send, and SND means data is being sent to the COM port).

Section 2

This section contains the error (or BugCheck) code with up to four developer-defined parameters (defined in the KeBugCheckEx() function call). In this case, the BugCheck was 0x0000000A IRQL_NOT_LESS_OR_EQUAL, which means a process attempted to access pageable memory at a process level that was too high and is usually caused by a device driver.

For example, a BugCheck of 0x00000077 or 0x0000007A means the pagefile could not be loaded into memory. The second hexadecimal value will help you diagnose the causes, which are listed in the following table.

0xC000009A	STATUS_INSUFFICIENT_RESOURCES, caused by lack of nonpaged pool.
0xC000009C	STATUS_DEVICE_DATA_ERROR, generally due to bad block on the drive.
0xC000009D	STATUS_DEVICE_NOT_CONNECTED, bad or loose cabling, termination, or controller not seeing drive.
0xC000016A	STATUS_DISK_OPERATION_FAILED, also caused by bad block on the drive.
0xC0000185	STATUS_IO_DEVICE_ERROR, caused by improper termination or bad cabling on SCSI devices.

Section 3

This lists all drivers that were loaded at the time of the crash. It is split into two sides, with three columns to each side. The first column is the link time stamp (in seconds since the year 1970) and can be converted into real time using the CVTIME.EXE application (f$cvtime on VMS ☺).

Section 4

This shows the build number of the operating system and a stack dump that shows the addresses that were used by the failed module. The top lines may show the offending code/driver but not always because kernel trap handlers may execute last to preserve error information.

Section 5

This will depend on whether you have the /debug setup, but it basically just shows the communication settings and whether a .DMP file has been created.

FAQ 37.9 I have created my own application service; however, when the user logs off the application stops. Why?

When a user logs off, a number of messages are sent. For graphical applications, the messages WM_QUERYENDSESSION and WM_ENDSESSION are sent, and to console (character mode) applications, the message CTRL_LOGOFF_EVENT is sent. If your application responds to these messages, then it may cause it to stop. You will need to modify your program to either ignore or handle the messages differently. More information about this topic is in the Resource Kit.

FAQ 37.10 Why can't I install any software?

Sometimes the file CONFIG.NT can become corrupted—specifically files= line—therefore:

1. Start Notepad (Start > Programs > Accessories > Notepad).
2. Open %systemroot%/system32/config.nt (e.g., d:/winnt/system32/config.nt.
3. Check at the bottom the line

   ```
   files=40
   ```

   If the file is something like

   ```
   files=20$%THY
   ```

   it has been corrupted, and you should change it to show only a number after the equals sign.
4. Save the file.
5. Reboot.

FAQ 39.11 Why do I get an error "This application is not supported by Windows NT"?

This error can sometimes be caused by the following files not having everyone:full access protection if the boot partition is NTFS.

- %SystemRoot%\system32\config.nt
- %SystemRoot%\system32\autoexec.nt

To check/change this protection:

1. Start Explorer (Start > Programs > Explorer).
2. Move to %SystemRoot%\system32 (e.g., d:\winnt\system32).
3. Right-click on the file (config.nt/autoexec.nt) and select Properties.

4. Click the Security tab and click Permissions.
5. You can then change/view the protection.
6. Click OK when finished.

Incorrect or missing entries in either file can also cause problems. For example, removing the FILES=nnn line from CONFIG.NT will result in problems. Compare your files to another working computer. It can also be caused by a missing or damaged .DLL file.

Expand the following files from the original Windows NT compact disc or you latest service pack/hot fix to the %Systemroot%\System32 directory:

- COMPOBJ.DLL
- DDEML.DLL
- OLE2.DLL
- OLE2DISP.DLL
- STORAGE.DLL
- CTL3DV2.DLL
- OLE2NLS.DLL
- STDOLE.TLB
- TYPELIB.DLL
- VER.DLL

> **Note:** *The VER.DLL file is located in the %SystemRoot%\System folder and the %SystemRoot%\System32 folder, and both versions have the same file size and date.*

I had this exact problem a short time ago, and it was because a Windows 98 version of VER.DLL had replaced the NT one.

FAQ 37.12 I have installed IE 4.0; now my shortcut icons are corrupt. How can I correct this?

Windows keeps a cache of icons, which can become corrupted. One method of correcting this problem is to try to delete the hidden file %SystemRoot%\ShellIconCache and to restart Windows NT. The "correct" desktop icons will be recreated when you log on.

```
attrib %systemroot%\shelliconcache -h
del %systemroot%\shelliconcache
```

If the icons are still corrupt, delete the file again and reboot. I have seen many occasions where two reboots are necessary.

This problem can also be caused by an incompatibility between Internet Explorer 4.0 and TweakUI. To fix this, you will need to uninstall TweakUI.

1. Start the Add/Remove Control Panel Applet (Start > Settings > Add/Remove Programs).
2. Select TweakUI and click Add/Remove.

If you get an error saying TweakUI couldn't be removed, you can manually remove it by entering the following command:

```
rundll32 syssetup.dll,SetupInfObjectInstallAction DefaultUninstall 4
e:\winnt\inf\tweakui.inf
```

You should then reboot the computer. If you find after the reboot the icons are still corrupt, install TweakUI again and then remove it.

FAQ 37.13 I have lost access to the root of the boot partition; now I can't log on. How can I fix this problem?

If you set the root of the boot partition to no access, then you will be unable to log on. To get around this, perform the following:

1. Log on to the NT machine as Administrator.
2. When you get the blue screen and "Path too Long," press the OK button.
3. Press Ctrl+Alt+Del, and the Windows NT Security dialog box will be shown.
4. Press the Task Manager button, and the Task Manager will be shown.
5. Select the Applications tab and click the New Task button.
6. Enter the path %systemroot%\system32\cmd.exe.
7. Enter the command

   ```
   CACLS d:\ /e /g everyone:F
   ```

   where d is the boot partition.
8. Select Task Manager again and click New Task. Enter the following, after which the desktop should appear

   ```
   %systemroot%\explorer.exe
   ```

9. Log out and log on again to confirm everything is OK.

You should now set the permissions on the root, see Q155315 at http://support.microsoft.com/support/kb/articles/q155/3/15.asp for more information.

FAQ 37.14 I receive the error "WNetEnumCachedPasswords could not be located in MPR.DLL." What should I do?

This problem is caused by the file MAPI32.DLL being replaced by an application installation, usually with the Windows 95 version. To correct the problem, reinstall the MAPI32.DLL file from the NT installation CD-ROM.

1. Insert the NT installation CD-ROM.
2. Back up your current MAPI32.DLL

```
copy %systemroot%\system32\mapi32.dll
%systemroot%\system32\mapi32.old
```

3. Move to your processor type on the CD-ROM—for example:

```
cd i386
```

4. Enter the command

```
expand -r mapi32.dl_ %systemroot%\system32
```

Be aware that if you have applied service packs, MAP32.DLL was redelivered in some of the service packs, so you should take the file from the service pack delivery (expand the service pack and then copy the file over).

FAQ 37.15 How can I perform a kernel debug?

To perform a kernel debug, the computer should be connected via a NULL modem cable or a modem connection for dial-in purposes. The computers will be referred to as "Host" for the machine that will perform the debug, and "Target" for the machine that has the problem and is being debugged.

The computers should both be running the same version of Windows NT, and the symbol files for the Target machine should be installed on the Host computer. The symbol files are supplied on the Windows NT installation CD-ROM in the Support\Debug directory.

The Target computer's BOOT.INI entry needs to be modified to allow debugging as follows:

1. Modify BOOT.INI to be editable

```
attrib c:\boot.ini -r -s
```

2. Edit the file and the Windows NT start line to include /debug (to tell the system to load the kernel debugger into memory at boot-up). Other options are /Debugport to tell which COM port to use (by default COM2) and /Baudrate for the speed (by default 19200; it's better to be 9600)—for example:

```
[operating systems]
multi(0)disk(0)rdisk(0)partition(0)\WINDOWS="Windows NT Debug"
/debug /debugport=com2 /baudrate=9600
```

3. Save the file.
4. Set BOOT.INI attributes back

```
attrib c:\boot.ini +r +s
```

In the preceding example, the Target machine will allow debug connection using COM2 at a speed of 9600bps.

The Host computer must be configured with the information it needs to perform the debug and the installation of the symbol files. To install the symbol files, move to the \support\debug directory on the CD-ROM and enter the command

```
expndsym <CD-ROM>: <target drive and directory>
```

For example, **expndsym f: d:\symbols**.

This may take some time. Remember if you have installed service packs on the target machine, the symbol files for these will also need to be installed on the host computer. The symbol files for service packs must be downloaded from Microsoft separately.

The next stage is to configure the environment variables needed for the debugging, such as the symbol file location, etc. Descriptions of these variables follow:

_NT_DEBUG_PORT	COM port to be used (e.g., COM2).
_NT_DEBUG_BAUD_RATE	Speed for the connection (e.g., 9600). Make sure this matches the /baudrate specified on the target machine.
_NT_SYMBOL_PATH	Location of the symbols files (where you expanded them to using the expndsym utility).
_NT_LOG_FILE_OPEN	Name of the file used for the log of the debug session (optional).

It may be worth putting the definition of the preceding into a command file to avoid having to type the commands every time—for example:

```
echo off
set _nt_debug_port=com2
set _nt_debug_baud_rate=9600
set _nt_symbol_path=d:\symbols\i386
set _nt_log_file_open=d:\debug\logs\debug.log
```

Next you should copy over the kernel debug software, which is located in the support\debug\<processor> directory on the NT installation CD-ROM (e.g., support\debug\I386). It is easier just to copy over the entire directory because it is not very large (around 2.5MB). The actual debugger for the i386 platform is I386KD.EXE, and you would just enter **I386KD** to start the debugger. To enter a command, press Ctrl+C and wait for the **kd**> prompt.

FAQ 37.16 Why do I get the error "Not enough server storage is available to process this command"?

This problem may be due to the machine having a nonzero PagedPoolSize in the Registry. This can be set by performing the following:

1. Log onto the server as an Administrator.
2. Start the Registry editor (REGEDIT.EXE).
3. Move to HKEY_LOCAL_MACHINE\SYSTEM\CurrentControlSet\Control\Session Manager\Memory Management.
4. Double-click on PagedPoolSize and set to 0.
5. Click OK.
6. Close the Registry editor.
7. Reboot the machine.

If PagedPoolSize is 0, it allows NT to dynamically allocate memory. The installation of software such as ARCServe is known to cause this problem.

This problem can also be caused when accessing a Windows NT Server share from a Windows NT client if IRPstackSize is too small. To correct it, try the following:

1. Log onto the server as Administrator.
2. Start the Registry editor (REGEDIT.EXE).
3. Move to HKEY_LOCAL_MACHINE\SYSTEM\CurrentControlSet\Services\LanmanServer\Parameters.

4. Double-click on IRPstackSize.
5. Increase the value. Valid ranges are between 1 and 12. Click OK.
6. Reboot the machine.

You may find once setting this, other connections, such as those to NetWare volumes, gain a performance boost.

Another cause for this error is if you installed Service Pack 3 onwards before installing any network components. If this is the case, then reapply Service Pack 3 and any subsequent hotfixes. It is good practice to reapply a service pack whenever you modify/add components to the system.

37.17 Why can't I delete a directory called con, prn?

Con is a reserved name, so to delete it, you must use the universal naming convention (UNC) of the file:

```
rd \\.\<drive letter>:\<dir>
```

For example, rd \\.\c:\john\con.

This can also apply to the prn directory. At boot time, prn is internally configured to direct any communication with the prn device to LPT1 (just some background ☺).

37.18 I get an error when I try to export a profile other than Administrator. What can I do?

This is usually due to insufficient privilege on the Protected Storage System Provider\<SID> key. To be able to export **your** profile, perform the following:

1. Log on as yourself.
2. Start the Registry editor (REGEDT32.EXE).
3. Select the HKEY_CURRENT_USER on Local Machine window.
4. Move to Software\Microsoft\Protected Storage System Provider\<SID>.
5. Select Permissions from the Security menu.
6. Click Add.
7. Select Domain Admins (or whatever you want), access type READ, and click Add. When finished, click OK.

You should now be able to export this profile. To be able to export someone **else's** profile, perform the following:

1. Log on as an Administrator.
2. Start the Registry editor (REGEDT32.EXE).
3. Select the HKEY_USERS on Local Machine window.
4. From the Registry menu, select Load hive.
5. Move to the person's profile area in the %systemroot%\Profiles\<name> (e.g., d:\winnt\Profiles\batman).
6. Select the NTUSER.DAT file and click OPEN.
7. When asked for a key name, enter the user's name (e.g., John) and click OK.
8. Now move to <user name>\Software\Microsoft\Protected Storage System Provider\<SID>.
9. Select Permissions from the Security menu.
10. Click Add.
11. Select Domain Admins (or whatever you want), access type READ, and click Add. When finished, click OK.
12. Select Unload Hive from the Registry menu.
13. Close the Registry editor.

You will now be able to export this user's profile.

FAQ 37.19 I have chosen a screen resolution that has corrupted the display and now I can't change it back. What can I do?

When you try to change screen resolution, Windows NT asks you to test it. If you ignore this request and set the display to a resolution that causes a problem, your only course of action to boot in VGA mode. Once in VGA mode, set the resolution back to something you know works.

1. Reboot the machine.
2. Select the following option:
   Windows NT Workstation Version 4.00 [VGA mode]
3. If you find you don't have this option, edit BOOT.INI and add a line similar to your normal NT Workstation startup with the /basevideo /sos—for example:

```
multi(0)disk(0)rdisk(0)partition(2)\WINNT="Windows NT Workstation
Version 4.00 [VGA mode]" /basevideo /sos
```

The machine will boot in base 16-color VGA mode.

4. Select the Display Control Panel applet (Start > Settings > Control Panel > Display).
5. Click the Settings tab and change to a resolution you know works (use test).
6. Click OK.

FAQ 37.20 Why do I get the error "Boot record signature AA55 not found (1079 found)"?

If Windows NT is installed on a logical drive in an extended partition (the fourth partition is usually the extended start), after you select the OS choice and NTDETECT runs, this error message will appear:

```
OS Loader 4.0 Boot record Signature AA55 Not Found, xxyy Found.

Windows NT could not start because of a computer disk hardware
configuration problem.

Could not read from the selected boot disk. Check boot path and disk
hardware.

Please check the Windows NT Documentation about hardware disk
Configuration and your hardware reference manuals for additional
information.
```

The master boot record (MBR) consists of boot code that is used by the system BIOS to read the partition table. From data contained in the partition table, the MBR can determine which partition is set to be bootable (active) and also the starting sector of that partition. Once that location is determined , the BIOS jumps to that sector and begins the next phase of the boot process by executing additional code that is operating system specific.

If you have files required for boot located above 1024 cyl, the boot process will fail. If you're running a SCSI disk-based system, there's a chance you can get around it by using the SCSI driver as NTBOOTDD.SYS. If you're on IDE, you're out of luck.

Windows 2000 gets round the boot failure if any files needed for boot-up are above cylinder 1024 with an updated NTLDR. This file can be copied to a Windows NT 4.0 installation on the active partition without any ill effects; just make sure you have Service Pack 4 or above applied to the system before copying the Windows 2000 NTLDR.

If the only thing wrong with sector zero is that the last two bytes are not 55AA, it can be fixed with a disk editor such as Norton Diskedit. However, this message is usually indicative of something overwriting or destroying the entire boot sector (sector zero) including the partition table entries.

When you install Windows NT on a logical drive in an extended partition, OSLOADER needs to "walk the extended partition table" through BIOS calls in order to get to the partition you have Windows NT installed in. Each of these logical drives is addressed in a daisy chain of partition tables. Each sector that contains a partition table entry **must** end with a 55AA as the last two bytes in the sector.

The best way to determine how to recover is to use a disk editor to see if the partition table entries are still intact. Each sector occupies 512 bytes. The first 446 bytes of sector zero contain the MBR boot code followed by the partition table entries and ends with 55AA. If the partition table entries are still intact at offsets 1BE through 1FD, manually record their values, then write 55AA starting at offset 1FE. Once the signature 55AA is written, the MBR boot code can be regenerated by using the FDISK.EXE program from MS-DOS version 5.0 or later.

```
FDISK /MBR
```

> **Warning:** *This process will repair the bootstrap code and the 55AA signature by rewriting sector zero but will also overwrite the partition table entries with all zeros, rendering your logical drives useless (unless, that is, the 55AA signature is manually entered using a disk editor prior to your performing the FDISK /MBR).*

If the partition table entries are not intact or were overwritten with unreadable characters, the problem is more involved and entails locating the master boot sector (MBS) for each partition and manually rebuilding the partition table entries. A discussion of this process is beyond the scope of this FAQ.

To speed recovery from future MBR corruption, use the Windows NT 4.0 Resource Kit utility DISKSAVE.EXE to save a copy of the MBR to a floppy disk. This can be used if needed at some future date to restore the MBR using DISKSAVE.EXE.

In the case where Windows NT is installed on a logical drive in an extended partition, you will need a disk-editing utility like Norton Diskedit to examine each sector containing an extended partition logical drive entry to make sure it ends with a 55AA. A discussion of this process is beyond the scope of this FAQ.

A virus in your boot sector may also cause this problem so run an antivirus program on your boot sector if in doubt.

Most of this information is from Knowledge Base article Q149877.

37.21 When I boot up NT, why does it pause for about 30 seconds on the blue screen?

Each dot is part of the boot-time chkdsk (AUTOCHK.EXE), and each three dots represent one drive so there should be 3*<number of drives> dots. If something is wrong with that drive, the startup sometimes will be delayed. However there is a known problem with NT: If your computer has one or more IDE disks **and** one or more SCSI disks, it results in a pause of around 30 seconds. The problem is due to the detection code used by NT.

37.22 I receive a RDISK error—"disk is full". What can I do?

When you run RDISK.EXE, it updates the directory %systemroot%\repair with the following files:

File	Registry Hive
AUTOEXEC.NT	This is not a Registry hive but rather a copy of the AUTOEXEC.NT file located in the %systemroot%\system32 directory.
CONFIG.NT	As in the preceding entry.
DEFAULT._	HKEY_USERS\.Default.
NTUSER.DA_	New user profile.
SAM._	Parts of HKEY_LOCAL_MACHINE\Security.
SECURITY._	HKEY_LOCAL_MACHINE\Security.
SETUP.LOG	Details of the location of system and application files along with cyclic redundancy check information for use with a repair.
software._	HKEY_LOCAL_MACHINE\Software.
system._	HKEY_LOCAL_MACHINE\System.

As the system is used, the files SETUP.LOG, SAM._, and SECURITY._ will grow. The SAM._ and SECURITY._ files are updated only if RDISK.EXE is run with /s qualifier (e.g., rdisk /s).

If the contents of the %systemroot%\repair directory exceeds 1.44MB, then you will receive the error "The Emergency Repair disk is full. The configuration files were saved in your hard disk". You should look at the contents of the repair directory and ascertain which file is the problem (i.e., SETUP.LOG is 1MB!). If SETUP.LOG is the problem, then you can perform the following:

1. Create a copy of SETUP.LOG in the repair directory

```
copy %systemroot%\repair\setup.log
%systemroot%\repair\setup.backup
```

2. Edit the SETUP.BACKUP file using dNotepad.
3. Move to the [Files.WinNt] section and remove all entries except those starting with %systemroot%\system32 (or whatever %systemroot% equates to—e.g., winnt).
4. Save the modified file.
5. Run RDISK.EXE.
6. When completed, delete the SETUP.LOG that was created.

```
del %systemroot%\repair\setup.log
```

7. And copy the backup version back

```
copy %systemroot%\repair\setup.backup
%systemroot%\repair\setup.log
```

If the problem is not SETUP.LOG and it's that the SAM._ and SECURITY._ files are too large, then too many accounts are on the system. You need to delete some of your user accounts ☺. Only joking!

What you can do is locate an ERD that was created early in the computer's life where the SAM.._ and SECURITY._ files are small and copy them to the %systemroot%\repair directory. In the future do **not** run RDISK.EXE with the /s option. This does mean that account information will not be recoverable. You will need to know what the Administrator password was when the original ERD was created (as if the repair disk was used the account passwords would be set back to the disks' values).

Obviously, you will still want to be able to restore accounts in the event of a disaster so I would suggest one of the following:

- Use NTBACKUP.EXE with the option of backing up the local Registry
- Use REGBACK.EXE and REGREST.EXE that come with the Resource Kit to back up the entire Registry to file and then restore it—for example

```
REGBACK d:\Registry.bku
```

For more information, see Knowledge Base article Q130029 at http://support.microsoft.com/support/kb/articles/q130/0/29.asp.

FAQ 37.23 Why are drive mappings being created by themselves?

One known cause of this behavior is the FINDFAST.EXE application that is supplied with Office 97. If either set of the following conditions are **both** true, then drive mappings may be created automatically.

Condition set 1

- You perform a search in either the Open dialog box or the Advanced Find dialog box in any Microsoft Office 97 program.
- The drive you search contains shortcuts that specify a target location that uses a network drive letter instead of a universal naming convention (UNC) path (for example, \\<Server>\<Share>).

Condition set 2

- Find Fast is installed in your Startup group.
- You index a drive that contains shortcuts that specify a target location that uses a network drive letter instead of a UNC path.

A number of resolutions can solve this problem.

- Install Service Pack 3.
- Avoid searching folders that contain shortcuts (.LNK files).
- Change shortcut target locations to UNC paths (e.g., d:\folder\john.txt to \\<server>\<folder>\john.txt).
- Disable Find Fast.

My experience with Find Fast is that is uses up a great deal of system resources and is not worth the resource usage for what it does. Hence, disabling Find Fast may be your best bet.

See Knowledge Base article Q150604 (http://support.microsoft.com/support/kb/articles/q150/6/04.asp) for more information.

37.24 Why can't I create a partition over 1GB on an Adaptec 2940 SCSI controller?

As you boot up, you should be able to do a Alt+A, which takes you into the SCSI BIOS; under Advanced Host Adaptor Settings. "Extended BIOS Translation for DOS Drives >1Gb" must be enabled.

37.25 Why do I get a STOP 0x00000078 error?

This error can be caused by a bug in Windows NT where the error is produced if the NonPagedPoolSize is greater than 7/8 of your physical memory. To correct this, perform the following:

1. Start the Registry Editor (REGEDIT.EXE).
2. Move to HKEY_LOCAL_MACHINE\SYSTEM\CurrentControlSet\Control\Session Manager\Memory Management.
3. Double-click on NonPagedPoolSize.
4. Change this to less than 7/8 of your physical memory (or set it to 0 to let NT dynamically set it). Click OK.
5. Close the Registry editor.
6. Reboot the computer.

37.26 Why is a file TESTDIR.TMP left on my drive?

When a file/folder is copied to a shared NTFS volume, a file TESTDIR.TMP is created and then automatically deleted. Sometimes the user performing the copy does not have delete permission on the shared NTFS volume. The file is not deleted and has to be manually deleted by someone who has the Delete privilege.

To fix this, give the Delete permission to the user or group who perform the copies.

1. Log on to the machine that hosts the NTFS volume as an Administrator.
2. Start Explorer (Win+E).
3. Right-click on the NTFS volume and select Properties from the context menu.
4. Select the Security tab and click the Permissions button.
5. Click the Add button and select the user or group required.

6. Click OK.
7. In the main Permissions dialog box, select the new user and in the Type of access box, select Special File Access.
8. Check the Delete box and click OK.
9. Click OK to close the Permissions dialog box and OK again to close the drive properties dialog box.

FAQ 37.27 How can I replace an in-use NT system file?

You can set a Registry entry to perform a boot-time file move:

1. Start the Registry editor (REGEDT32.EXE **not** REGEDIT.EXE).
2. Move to HKEY_LOCAL_MACHINE\SYSTEM\CurrentControlSet\Control\Session Manager.
3. Double-click on PendingFileRenameOperations (or create of type mutli_str if it does not exist).

   On the first line is the name of the file that will be replacing the current file with \??\ in front—for example:

   ```
   \??\d:\time\ntfs.sys
   ```

   On the second line is the file to replaced with !\??\ in front—for example:

   ```
   !\??\d:\winnt\system32\drivers\ntfs.sys
   ```

4. Click OK.

Figure 37-1 is an example value for PendingFileRenameOperations.

Once the reboot is complete and the file replaced, the PendingFileRename Operations value will be deleted from the Registry.

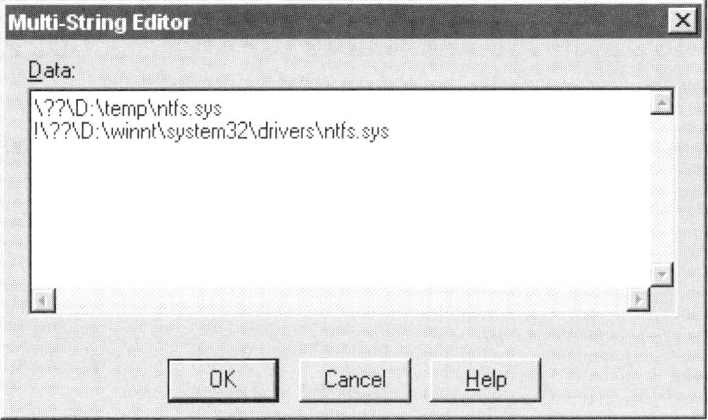

Figure 37-1 Replacing an in-use file via the Registry

FAQ 37.28 I removed my folder association and cannot open any folders. What can I do?

This can be fixed with two simple commands, which should be run from a command session (CMD.EXE):

1. From the Start menu—select Programs and then Command Prompt (or select Run and enter **CMD.EXE**).
2. Enter the following commands:

```
ftype folder=%SystemRoot%\Explorer.exe /idlist,%I,%L
assoc folder=folder
```

3. Close the command session.

The first command creates a new file type, folder, and the action associated with it. The second command creates the association between the "extension" and its file type.

37.29 The batch file I schedule to run does not work with the /every switch. Why?

You may find that if you submit a batch file without the /every switch, it works fine—for example:

```
at 22:00 /interactive command.bat
```

However, if you try the following, it fails:

```
at 23:00 /interactive /every:M,T,W,Th,F command.bat
```

To correct this problem, add **cmd /c** "". For example:

```
at 23:00 /interactive /every: M,T,W,Th,F cmd /c "command.bat"
```

37.30 Why am I unable to use Start from the command line with files with spaces in them?

The Windows NT Start command allows the user to create a separate window/process to run a specified program. If you try to run something that consists of a long filename with a space in quotes, it fails and just brings up an empty CMD.EXE window—for example:

```
start "d:\documents\ntfaq book\contents.doc"
```

In order to make it work, only the part that has the long name should be in quotes—for example, the following works:

```
start d:\documents\"ntfaq book"\contents.doc
```

This applies to anything such as a server, share, and so on. For example,

```
start \\"<server with space>"\"<share with space>"\"<dir with
space>"\"<file with space>"
start \\"johns server"\"docs share"\"ntfaq dir"\"table of
contents.doc"
```

This is basically due to the fact that the first item in quotes should be the title of the window, and so a better way to work around the problem is to use the following. It works, and there can be as many spaces as you want in any part.

```
start "" "d:\documents\ntfaq book\contents.doc"
```

37.31 Why am I not offered the option to install from an INF context menu?

The options given from a context menu are derived from its file type entry under HKEY_CLASSES_ROOT\inffile. The first item to check is that .INF is associated with inffile, which can be checked with

```
assoc .inf
.inf=inffile
```

If you do not get the preceding response, enter the command

```
assoc .inf=inffile
```

The next step is to check that the context menu item install exists for inffile:

1. Start the Registry editor (REGEDT32.EXE).
2. Move to HKEY_CLASSES_ROOT\inffile\shell.
3. Check for a subkey Install; if it does not exist, select Add Key from the Edit menu and enter a name of **Install**.
4. The default entry from Install (called <No Name>) should be &Install. If it does not exist, select Add Value from the Edit menu; do **not** enter any name, select type REG_SZ, and click OK. It will then ask for a string that should be "&Install" (don't actually enter the quotes). Click OK.
5. Under the Install key should be another key, command. If this does not exist, again create it, using "Add Key" from the Edit menu.
6. Under the command key should be a default value (called <No Name>), which should have the data %SystemRoot%\System32\rundll32.exe setupapi,InstallHinf-Section DefaultInstall 132 %1 in it. If the default key is missing, select Add Value from the Edit menu; do **not** enter any name. Select type REG_EXPAND_SZ and click OK. The Registry editor will then ask for a string, which should be

%SystemRoot%\System32\rundll32.exe setupapi,InstallHinfSection DefaultInstall 132 %1. Click OK.

7. Close the Registry editor.

You should now have an install option for .INF files.

FAQ 37.32 How can I deallocate corrupt memory?

If you often get the blue screen or Dr. Watson, your memory may be corrupt, or you may have mixed the memory.

To test this FAQ, I mixed two EDO-SIMMs (2x16MB) with two normal SIMMs (2x16MB) on a ASUS-Board P55 TP4-XE (this board can use mixed memory). After doing this, I often received Dr. Watson errors.

You should use the MAXMEM-Switch in BOOT.INI to deactivate the corrupt memory bank until such time as mixed memory is no longer in the motherboard. The MAXMEM switch will always use the lowest physical memory addresses, and therefore always uses bank0+. During the NT boot process, NT probes the memory hard to make sure that it is really there and working, generating a blue screen if any memory tests fail. The following procedure provides an example of using the /maxmem parameter.

1. Set the attributes on BOOT.INI so you can edit it:

   ```
   attrib c:\boot.ini -r -s -h
   ```

2. Edit BOOT.INI and add the switch (e.g., /MAXMEM=32) to the end of your Windows NT option—for example:

   ```
   multi(0)disk(0)rdisk(0)partition(1)\WINNT="Windows NT Workstation
   Version 4.00" /maxmem=32
   ```

3. Save the file and reset the attributes:

   ```
   attrib c:\boot.ini +r +s +h
   ```

4. Reboot.

Windows NT uses this switch, limits the whole memory from 64 to 32MB, and chooses only the good memory bank. You can also use this switch to observe the swapping process if limiting the whole memory.

FAQ 37.33 Why am I unable to run certain 16-bit applications?

Certain 16-bit applications won't run under Windows NT—for example, if they try to directly access hardware. If you are receiving any of the following errors, then you may be able to do something about it:

- `Cannot run 16-bit Windows program. This program requires a newer version of Windows.`
- `Cannot run the 16-bit program. The application is not supported by Windows NT.`
- `Can't run 16-bit Windows program. One of the library files needed to run <program> is damaged. Please reinstall this application.`

A possible cause for these errors is if any of the following dynamic link libraries are missing, corrupt, or simply the wrong version:

- COMPOBJ.DLL
- DDEML.DLL
- OLE2.DLL
- OLE2DISP.DLL
- STORAGE.DLL
- CTL3DV2.DLL
- OLE2NLS.DLL
- STDOLE.TLB
- TYPELIB.DLL
- VER.DLL
- COMMDLG.DLL

To fix this problem, expand, or copy the files from the latest service pack or hotfix you have applied. If you can't find these files in the latest service pack, locate them in your Windows NT installation CD-ROM.

Another cause may be that the file NTVDM.EXE has been deleted from your %systemroot%\system32 directory, so check this.

FAQ 37.34 I have a service stopping NT from booting. What can I do?

Normally, you can modify the startup of services using the Services Control Panel applet or Computer Management MMC snap-in—System Tools > Services in Windows 2000. Modifying the startup of a service actually changes a value, Start, under the

Services Registry key, HKEY_LOCAL_MACHINE\SYSTEM\CurrentControlSet\Services.

When Windows NT boots, select Last Known Good configuration. If this does not work, you can use one of the solutions discussed in the text that follows.

The start value of a service can have a number of values as defined in FAQ 31.9. In order to modify the startup state of a service from outside of NT, you must install a second copy of Windows NT on the machine (or if you can get the System file from the machine onto another machine using a tool like ERD Commander—from http://www.winternals.com—the extra copy is not necessary). In Windows 2000/XP, the Recovery Console can be used for this.

1. Install a second copy of NT (minimal) to a different partition.
2. Boot into the second copy of NT.
3. Start REGEDT32.EXE.
4. Select the HKEY_LOCAL_MACHINE window.
5. From the Registry menu, select Load Hive.
6. Move to your **original** NT installation partition and folder and then to system32\config (e.g., c:\winnt\system32\config).
7. Select System file and click Open.
8. Enter a name for this temporary hive open (e.g., OrigSystemHive).
9. Select the new hive (e.g., OrigSystemHive) and select the Select key.
10. Check the value of Default; this value is usually 1. This number is x (you'll see what I mean).
11. Now move to OrigSystemHive\ControlSet00x (e.g., OrigSystemHive\ControlSet001).
12. Now under this key, select Services, find your problem service, and select it.
13. Double-click its Start value and modify: 4 disables the service, 2 sets it to auto start. If you have a more complex problem, changing the Type value may be necessary to alter when the service attempts to load.
14. Move back to the base (e.g., OrigSystemHive) and select Unload Hive from the Registry menu. Click Yes to the warning box.
15. Reboot into your original NT installation, and your service problem should be resolved.

You can now deleted your second copy of NT if you wish; however, it is always useful and takes up a minimal amount of space.

Another solution is to use ERD Professional, which allows you to specify startup options for services/drivers from outside of NT; have a look at http://www.winternals.com.

FAQ 37.35 If I run winfile d:, it starts Explorer. Why?

If you try to pass WINFILE.EXE (the old File Manager pre 4.0) a drive, expecting it to start by default on that drive, you will find that WINFILE starts as normal and then an Explorer view of the drive specified is opened. For example, the following command starts a File Manager session and an Explorer session that point to D:

```
winfile d:
```

This behavior is not a bug and is caused by a misunderstanding of the parameters expected by WINFILE.EXE. Any parameters passed to WINFILE.EXE are interpreted that it should run as a program. For example, the following starts a File Manager session and a Notepad session, editing FILE.TXT:

```
winfile notepad c:\file.txt
```

The reason Explorer starts if you specify a drive letter is that under NT and 95/98, any directory listings are executed by Explorer. Try typing **C:** from Run, and it will start Explorer pointing to C.

NT4 ONLY

FAQ 37.36 Why do I get the error "Your password must be at least 0 characters long"?

If you have enabled the strong password but your domain account policy has no password restrictions and allows blank passwords, then you will get the following error:

```
Your password must be at least 0 characters long. Your new password
cannot be the same as any of your previous 0 passwords. Also, your
site may require passwords that must be a combination of upper case,
lower case, numbers, and non-alphanumeric characters. Type a
password which meets these requirements in both text boxes.
```

To resolve this problem, you will need to turn off the secure password filter:

1. Start the Registry editor (REGEDT32.EXE).
2. Move to HKEY_LOCAL_MACHINE\SYSTEM\CurrentControlSet\Control\Lsa.
3. Double-click on Notification Packages.
4. Remove the value PASSFILT.

5. Click OK.
6. Close the Registry editor.
7. Reboot the machine.

Alternatively turn off the ability to have blank passwords:

1. Start User Manager.
2. Select Account from the Policies menu.
3. Set the minimum password length to 6 or above.
4. Click OK.

FAQ 37.37 When I try to edit the default domain controller policy from Directory Management MMC, the local policy is shown. Why?

To edit the default domain controller policy, you normally do the following:

1. Start the Directory Management MMC (Start > Programs > Administrative Tools > Directory Management).
2. Select the domain, right-click on Domain Controllers, and select Properties.
3. Select the Group Policy tab.
4. The policies in effect will be shown, normally Default Domain Controllers Policy. If you select this policy and click Edit, the Group Policy editor MMC should start with Default Domain Controllers Policy as its root. You can then make changes.

When Group Policy Editor starts, if you instead have Local Policy at the root, the likely cause is that the MMC start setting has been corrupted. This is usually caused by the installation of Office 2000. To repair this problem, perform the following:

1. Start the Registry editor (REGEDIT.EXE).
2. Move to HKEY_CLASSES_ROOT\MSCFile\Shell\Open\Command.
3. Double-click on (Default).
4. If the line reads (your NT installation location may be different)

   ```
   D:\WINNT\System32\MMC.EXE "%1"
   ```

   Add **%*** to the end—for example:

   ```
   D:\WINNT\System32\MMC.EXE "%1" %*
   ```

5. Click OK.

The policy editing should now work as expected. The basic problem is that MMC was not being passed all the parameters and thus opening the default Local policy.

FAQ 37.38 My desktop icons are corrupt. What can I do?

To speed up desktop refresh and its creation, the desktop icons are cached. Sometimes this file can become corrupted and will lead to the icons on the desktop being blank or incorrect.

To resolve this, you can delete the icon cache file, %SystemRoot%\ShellIconCache. Before doing so, you must stop Explorer (right-click on the taskbar and stop all instances of EXPLORER.EXE):

```
attrib %systemroot%\shelliconcache -h
del %systemroot%\shelliconcache
```

Restart the computer. This can also be accomplished using the Repair tab of the TweakUI utility.

FAQ 37.39 How can I kill an orphaned process?

When a service terminates abnormally, it can sometimes leave an "orphaned" child process behind.

If you have the Resource Kit, you can use the following to view a list of all processes and their relationships to one another:

```
tlist -t
```

To then kill a process, use

```
kill <process name or id>
```

For Windows XP, tlist has been replaced with tasklist and kill replaced with taskkill. If this fails, add -F to force the kill (e.g., **kill -F <process name or id>**). If this still fails, you could try submitting the kill command because it will then run under the computer's built-in System account:

```
AT <time> /INTERACTIVE CMD /C KILL -F <process name or id>
```

(The Schedule service must be running for this to work—net start schedule.)

If this still fails, one last approach is possible using the Resource Kit PVIEW.EXE utility:

1. Start PVIEW.EXE (Start > Run > PVIEW).
2. Select the process you wish to kill from the drop-down list.
3. Click the Process button in the Security section.
4. Grant the Administrators All Access to the process. Click OK.
5. Repeat for Thread and P.Token.
6. Close PLIST.
7. Use KILL.EXE to terminate the process.

If none of the preceding works you will have to reboot.

FAQ 37.40 I have lost my executable association. What can I do?

If your computer configuration has been corrupted and executable files no longer behave correctly, enter the following from the command prompt (CMD.EXE):

```
assoc .exe=exefile
ftype exefile="%1" %*
```

Executables should now work as normal.

FAQ 37.41 How can I save the BSOD information?

System Internals has a utility called BlueSave, which can be downloaded from http://www.sysinternals.com. BlueSave will save up to three BSODs before expiring, and at that point, you should purchase the commercial version from http://wininternals.com.

Once you've installed BlueSave, the BSOD will be saved in file %systemroot%\BLUESCRN.TXT to help you diagnose problems.

FAQ 37.42 Why do I get the message "Initialization of USER32.DLL" or "KERNEL32.DLL failed"?

Every desktop object on the system has a desktop heap associated with it. The desktop object uses the heap to store menus, hooks, strings, and windows.

There is soft limit on the desktop heap size (128KB). This size can be expanded by changing a parameter in the Registry as follows:

1. Start the Registry editor (REGEDT32.EXE).
2. Move to HKEY_LOCAL_MACHINE\SYSTEM\CurrentControlSet\Control\Session Manager\SubSystems.
3. Double-click on the Windows value.

   The data will be of the format:

```
%SystemRoot%\system32\csrss.exe ObjectDirectory=\Windows
SharedSection=1024,3072 Windows=On SubSystemType=Windows
ServerDll=basesrv,1
ServerDll=winsrv:UserServerDllInitialization,3
ServerDll=winsrv:ConServerDllInitialization,2
ProfileControl=Off MaxRequestThreads=16
```

4. Find the SharedSection value and add **,512** or **,1024** after the second number, for example:

```
%SystemRoot%\system32\csrss.exe ObjectDirectory=\Windows
SharedSection=1024,3072,1024 Windows=On SubSystemType=Windows
ServerDll=basesrv,1
ServerDll=winsrv:UserServerDllInitialization,3
ServerDll=winsrv:ConServerDllInitialization,2
ProfileControl=Off MaxRequestThreads=16
```

   Setting to ,512 will set the desktop heap to 512KB for each desktop associated with noninteractive window stations. Setting to ,1024 sets it to 1MB.

5. Close the Registry editor.
6. Reboot the machine.

If you try to set the value to anything less than 128, a default of 128 will be used by the system, ignoring your value.

FAQ 37.43 How can I use path names longer than 255 characters?

Windows NT has a maximum path size defined as MAX_PATH, which is 255 characters. It is possible to use more characters by calling the wide (W) version of CreateFile and prefixing \\?\ to the path. The \\?\ tells the function to turn off path parsing, which lets you use paths that are nearly 32,000 Unicode characters long. You must use fully qualified paths with this technique. This also works with UNC names.

The \\?\ is ignored as part of the path. For example, \\?\D:\documents\faq.txt is seen as D:\documents\faq.txt.

Programs expecting to find legal file lengths may crash, attempting to open a file with a long path—if, for example, the buffer they are putting the path into expects a legal file length.

FAQ 37.44 Why do I get the error "Setup was unable to copy the following file CDROM.SYS"?

This problem can be caused if you are loading the ATAPI real mode CD-ROM driver in CONFIG.SYS.

1. Edit the CONFIG.SYS file from the command prompt (CMD.EXE):

   ```
   edit c:\config.sys
   ```

2. Find the Device= line that contains the ATAPI Real Mode CD-ROM driver. Edit the line so the /D: switch does not contain the word value cdrom—for example:

   ```
   Device=<driver> /d:cdrom
   ```

   to

   ```
   Device=<driver> /d:testa
   ```

3. Save the file.

FAQ 37.45 Why are my logon scripts hanging and looping?

A known problem exists as reported in Microsoft KB article 234049, which can result in logon scripts hanging or looping if a file called NET.BAT or NET.CMD exists in the netlogon folder of the domain controller.

This problem is caused by any client attempting net commands such as net use or net time, which incorrectly uses the .BAT file in the netlogon share rather than the correct NET.EXE on the client.

To resolve, remove the NET.BAT or NET.CMD from the netlogon share.

FAQ 37.46 The NTVDM and WOW subsystems cannot start correctly. What can I do?

The NT Virtual DOS Machine and the Windows On Windows subsystem are used to run older 16-bit software applications. Following are some troubleshooting steps:

1. Check AUTOEXEC.NT and CONFIG.NT for anything unusual or anything that can be commented out (in the %systemroot%\system32 directory).
2. Rename AUTOEXEC.BAT (e.g., c:\AUTOEXEC.BAT).
3. Check for changes in WIN.INI or SYSTEM.INI, or replace by expanding the original files off of the installation media (%systemroot% directory).
4. Rename all other *.INI files if possible.
5. In the CONFIG.NT file, allow only:

```
dos=high, umb
device=%SystemRoot%\system32\himem.sys
files=60
shell=%SystemRoot%\system32\command.com /e:4096
```

If you still have problems, check out Knowledge Base article http://support.microsoft.com/support/kb/articles/q196/4/53.asp, which has more information.

These files are also on the Emergency Repair Disk so you could just copy the versions from the disk over your existing ones, which may fix the problem.

This problem can also be caused by a virus—for example, "NYB" in the boot sector of the machine. (PC has a bootable DOS and a bootable NT partition.)

FAQ 37.47 When I double-click on a MSI file, it has no association. What can I do?

MSI files are Microsoft's new software installation package format and will allow applications to be published to a domain, site, or group in Windows 2000. MSI files also allow the application to self-repair.

If when double-clicking a MSI file, it asks for an application to run under, its default association has been lost. Perform the following to fix this problem:

1. Start a command prompt (Start > Run > CMD.EXE).
2. Type the command:

   ```
   ftype Msi.Package
   ```

3. If the response is

   ```
   Msi.Package="%SystemRoot%\System32\msiexec.exe" /i "%1"
   ```

   then continue to the next step. If it is not found, type

   ```
   ftype Msi.Package="%SystemRoot%\System32\msiexec.exe" /i "%1"
   ```

   Continue to the next step.
4. Type the command:

   ```
   assoc .msi
   ```

   If the response is

   ```
   .msi=Msi.Package
   ```

5. then check the %systemroot%\system32 folder for the MSIEXEC.EXE file and replace it if it is missing.
6. If there is no association (the most usual problem), type

   ```
   assoc .msi=Msi.Package
   ```

7. Close the command prompt.
8. Retry double-clicking on a MSI file.

FAQ 37.48 I am unable to stop a process from Task Manager even though I'm an Administrator. What can I do?

I recently had this exact problem with some antivirus processes I could not kill. Windows said I had insufficient access so all I did was start a Task Manager session under the System process by submitting with the AT command—for example:

```
at <time one minute in the future> /inter taskmgr.exe
```

When Task Manager starts, you should be able to stop anything (but be **careful**!).

An alternative to AT would be the SOON Resource Kit command. The syntax is

```
soon 30 /interactive taskmgr
```

Another option is to use the PVIEW Resource Kit utility to change the security on the process and then stop as normal.

Another way is to use the kill -f command, but you would need to be a local Administrator of the machine. You could use the Resource Kit PULIST.EXE program to view the processes.

FAQ 37.49 I am unable to run CHKDSK; it cannot lock or open a volume for direct access. Why?

When you run CheckDisk (CHKDSK) or AutoChk on a partition on which NT is installed, you may receive one of the following messages:

- `Cannot lock volume for direct access`
- `Cannot open volume for direct access`

This can be caused by a third-party application locking the partition such as a virus checker or disk monitor tool. To correct, disable any third-party services or devices that may be locking the partition.

1. Start the Services Control Panel applet (Start > Settings > Control Panel > Services).
2. Select the service and click Startup.
3. Set the startup type to Manual and click OK.

4. Repeat for any other services.
5. Start the Devices Control Panel applet (Start > Settings > Control Panel > Devices).
6. Set the startup type to disabled for any third-party devices who you think might be causing the lock problem but **be careful**. If you are unsure whether the device you are disabling may stop system startup, create a second hardware profile and test it (see FAQ 35.11).
7. Restart the machine; the drive should no longer be locked.

FAQ 37.50 I get the Blue Screen of Death during setup. What can I do?

If after you remove the third setup disk from the machine and reboot, the blue screen is displayed.

```
Setup has encountered a fatal error that prevents it from
continuing. Contact your software representative for help.
Status code (-x4, 0, 0, 0)
```

This error indicates a virus in the master boot record of the disk (which affects NTFS as well as FAT). Use an antivirus product to clear the MBR and proceed with installation.

FAQ 37.51 After uninstalling Windows 98, why am I unable to boot NT?

When you uninstall Windows 98 from a dual-boot machine with 95 and NT, its setup program may delete the Windows NT BOOT.INI file, which is needed by NTLDR to start Windows NT.

To resolve, either manually copy a backup of BOOT.INI to the active partition (C) or use the Emergency Repair Disk to restore it.

FAQ 37.52 I've installed a Promise Ultra IDE card, but NT/2000 will no longer work. Why?

Although the Promise card is an IDE card, Windows NT/2000 treats it as a SCSI card. Hence the BOOT.INI file ARC path needs to be changed from the multi().../signature() format to scsi().

> **Note:** *The new signature() format is used in Windows 2000 for IDE devices. An example line is*

```
signature(a1bb)disk(0)rdisk(0)partition(2)\WINNT="Windows NT
Workstation Version 4.00"
```

For example, if I had BOOT.INI file:

```
[boot loader]
timeout=30
default=multi(0)disk(0)rdisk(0)partition(1)\WINNT
[operating systems]
multi(0)disk(0)rdisk(0)partition(1)\WINNT="Windows NT Workstation
Version 4.00"
multi(0)disk(0)rdisk(0)partition(1)\WINNT="Windows NT Workstation
Version 4.00 [VGA mode]" /basevideo /sos
```

and then installed the Promise card (and installed the driver before moving the IDE cable from the motherboard to the card), I would change BOOT.INI to:

```
[boot loader]
timeout=30
default=scsi(0)disk(0)rdisk(0)partition(1)\WINNT
[operating systems]
scsi(0)disk(0)rdisk(0)partition(1)\WINNT="Windows NT Workstation
Version 4.00"
scsi(0)disk(0)rdisk(0)partition(1)\WINNT="Windows NT Workstation
Version 4.00 [VGA mode]" /basevideo /sos
```

Make sure you also change the "default=" part. Obviously, make sure you have loaded the Promise driver before trying to boot (Windows 2000 as of build 2114 has built-in support).

FAQ 37.53 Why are some entries missing from the Add/Remove programs Control Panel applet?

The Add/Remove Control Panel applet Remove tab builds its list by searching HKEY_LOCAL_MACHINE\SOFTWARE\Microsoft\Windows\CurrentVersion\Uninstall for any entries with a DisplayName value. A bug causes entries with a text string of >64 characters to be ignored, so you may want to check the DisplayName values and shorten them where appropriate.

FAQ 37.54 Why is the default source path for my Windows 2000 installation not correct?

If you install Windows 2000 from a local hard disk, it defaults to the first installed CD-ROM drive letter when you make any changes to your installation that require files from the installation source. This does not occur if installation was completed using a network share. This means whenever it wants to add a component, you have to correct the installation location.

For example, if you install Windows 2000 from D:\2128\I386 (a local hard disk), Windows 2000 will default to **E**:\2128\I386 when the source files are needed (where **E** is the first CD-ROM drive letter).

To fix the problem, perform the following:

1. Start the Registry editor (REGEDIT.EXE).
2. Move to HKEY_LOCAL_MACHINE\SOFTWARE\Microsoft\Windows\CurrentVersion\Setup.
3. Double-click on SourcePath and change to the correct location. Click OK.
4. Now move to HKEY_LOCAL_MACHINE\SOFTWARE\Microsoft\Windows NT\CurrentVersion.
5. Double-click on SourcePath and change to the correct location. Click OK. Move to HKEY_LOCAL_MACHINE\SOFTWARE\Microsoft\Windows\CurrentVersion\Setup.
6. Double-click on SourctPath and change to the correct drive letter (e.g., C—it must have a i386 structure).
7. Close the Registry editor.

It should now use the correct location when adding/fixing components.

FAQ 37.55 What keys are available to troubleshoot during startup of Windows 2000?

Windows 2000 inherits some of the Windows 98 features including the ability to press F8 to bring up a menu allowing various “safe” startup options.

- Safe Mode
- Safe Mode with Networking
- Safe Mode with Command Prompt
- Enable boot logging
- Enable VGA mode
- Enable Last Known Good configuration
- Directory Services Restore Mode
- Debugging Mode
- Boot Normally

Other startup keys are available, some of which are not documented:

- F5—If during installation at the “Setup is inspecting your computer”, the system hangs, press F5, and a list of PC types will be listed. Select Standard PC, which should resolve your problem.
- F6—Displayed early in setup and allows third-party drivers to be loaded.
- F7—Load the normal PC HAL instead of the ACPI HAL.
- F8—As shown previously.
- <Shift+F10>—Open command prompt during GUI phase of installation.

FAQ 37.56 The installation of Windows 2000 hangs at the “Setup is inspecting your computer.” What can I do?

This is normally caused by Setup attempting to detect settings such as ACPI. You can override this and tell Setup to use a standard PC type by pressing F5 while it’s hung and select Standard PC.

FAQ 37.57 What logs are available to troubleshoot Windows 2000 installation problems?

Following are a list of useful log files:

- WINNT32.LOG/WINNT.LOG—Created during installation
- SETUPLOG.TXT—Text mode logging of installation
- SETUPERR.LOG—Log of errors during installation
- SETUPACT.LOG—GUI mode logging of setup
- BOOTLOG.TXT—Drivers loaded during setup
- NTBTLOG.TXT—Boot logging from Safe Mode option

FAQ 37.58 Why are my AT and SOON commands not working properly?

When you install IE5 on NT, IE replaces the Scheduler service with its own Task Scheduler, which messes with the AT and SOON commands. (For example, see http://support.microsoft.com/support/kb/articles/Q237/8/40.ASP, http://support.microsoft.com/support/kb/articles/Q214/4/20.ASP, and other KB articles.) Microsoft's documentation on this problem (and especially how to fix it) is confusing and contradictory. The only article that explains how to revert to the Scheduler service in a way that worked on my machine is http://support.microsoft.com/support/kb/articles/Q226/3/70.ASP, but note that if MSTASK.INF does not exist, you can specify MSTASK.PNF. The "uninstall" then will work. The basics are as follows.

Internet Explorer 4.x

To uninstall the Internet Explorer 4.x Task Scheduler:

1. Click Start, point to Settings, click Control Panel, and then double-click Add/Remove Programs.
2. Click the Install/Uninstall tab and click Task Scheduler 1.0 (Remove Only).
3. Click Add/Remove and then click Yes when you are prompted to remove Task Scheduler.
4. Click Yes when you are prompted to restart your computer.

Internet Explorer 5

To uninstall the Internet Explorer 5 Task Scheduler:

1. Click Start and then click Run.
2. In the Open box, type the following command and then press Enter:

```
RunDll32 advpack.dll,LaunchINFSectionEx
%systemroot%\INF\mstask.inf,,,256
```

3. Restart your computer.

FAQ 37.59 Why do I get an event log "Crash Dump is Disabled"?

The following event log:

```
Event ID 43

Description: Crash dump is disabled! NT failed to initialize the
boot partition paging file for crash dump. This may be because the
system has more than 3.8 gigabytes of physical memory.
```

is caused if the pagefile size is set to smaller than that of the actual physical RAM in the machine. To correct this problem, increase the pagefile size:

1. In Control Panel, double-click System.
2. On the Performance tab, click Change and then change the minimum size of the pagefile on the system partition to a value at least the size of physical RAM plus 1MB.
3. Restart the computer.

FAQ 37.60 Why am I getting a BSOD at startup with error C0000135?

There are various flavors of this Blue Screen of Death, but all have the text:

```
Stop: c0000135 {Unable to Locate DLL}
The dynamic link library <file name> could not be found in the
specified path Default Load Path."
```

The <filename> could be a number of different DLL files—a common one is WINSRV.DLL. There are a number of causes for this error:

- FILE_NAME.DLL is missing from the %SystemRoot%\system32 directory.
- Your laptop is loading the SERMOUSE.SYS file.
- If <filename>.DLL does exists, the software hive may be corrupted, and therefore, cannot load.

If your Windows NT installation is FAT, you can just boot from a floppy disk and change it so that the DLL it is listing as the error cause exists on the filesystem. If in doubt, replace it with the latest service pack version. If your NT installation is NTFS, you can either use something like ERD Commander (http://www.winternals.com) to access the NTFS drive or install a parallel copy of Windows NT.

If after checking the DLL you still have problems, it is likely a Registry hive corruption and if WINSRV.DLL is listed as the missing DLL, it is always the software hive. The way to test this is to again use a parallel copy of Windows NT and try to load each hive from your original NT installation:

1. Start REGEDT32.EXE.
2. Select the HKEY_LOCAL_MACHINE on Local Machine window.
3. Select the HKEY_LOCAL_MACHINE key in the left pane of the window.
4. On the menu bar, click Registry and then click Load Hive.
5. Browse to %SystemRoot%\System32\config, where %SystemRoot% is the original installation of Windows NT that you want to check.
6. Click the file software. This will be the software file with the generic Windows icon next to it, not the file with the Notepad icon.
7. The system will prompt for a key-name to use in loading the hive. You can type whatever you prefer in the dialog box—for example, probsoft. The hive is corrupted if you receive the following error message:

```
Registry Editor could not load the key. The file is not a valid
Registry file.
```

The only course of action now is to replace the problem Registry hive with the most recent backup, which is your Emergency Repair Disk:

1. Start the system with the Windows NT Setup disks.
2. At the first screen, press R for repair.
3. Use the arrow keys to move the cursor to Inspect Registry Files and then press Enter to select that option. Next, move the cursor to Continue (Perform Selected Tasks) and press Enter.

4. Let Windows NT perform the mass storage detection. When prompted, select S to specify additional drivers if your computer requires OEM drivers.
5. When prompted to do so, insert the Emergency Repair Disk that was originally created for this computer, or press Esc to let Windows NT search for repair information.
6. Setup will then ask which Registry files should be replaced. Using the arrow keys, move the cursor to Software (Software Information) and press Enter. Next, move the cursor to Continue (Perform Selected Tasks) and press Enter.
7. When finished, restart your computer when Setup prompts you to do so.

FAQ 37.61 I'm unable to install Outlook 98 and IE 5.0. I get an error about log file command line. What can I do?

If when you try to install IE 5.0 and Outlook, you get the error:

```
The log file command line option (/G) must have a valid filename as
an argument
```

This may be caused by the fact you have disabled long filenames. To fix, perform the following:

1. Start the Registry editor (REGEDIT.EXE).
2. Move to HKEY_LOCAL_MACHINE\SYSTEM\CurrentControlSet\Control\FileSystem.
3. Double-click Win31FileSystem.
4. Set to 0.
5. Click OK.
6. Restart the computer.

After reboot, the install should work OK.

FAQ 37.62 Why is the SUBST command not working correctly in Windows 2000?

A bug exists in Windows 2000, which will not be fixed before its Release To Manufacturing. Normally you can substitute a drive letter for a folder, be it local or remote. If you substitute a drive letter for a remote folder—for example,

```
subst h: \\titanic\home\savillj
```

When you try to access H you get error:

```
The filename, directory name, or volume label syntax is incorrect.
```

To work around the problem, use net use instead—for example:

```
net use h: \\titanic\home\savillj
```

A Knowledge Base article Q218740 is available for more information.

37.63 Why am I unable to install the Recovery Console on a mirror in Windows 2000?

As we saw in FAQ 4.51, the Recovery Console can be used to boot into a special console that allows us to repair an inoperable Windows 2000 installation.

Like a normal Windows installation, we cannot install the Recovery Console on a mirrored partition (be it a basic or dynamic mirror set). If the system partition is part of a mirror (the partition with Ntldr, NTDETECT.COM, etc.), you need to break the mirror, install the Recovery Console, and then recreate the mirror:

1. Start the Computer Manager MMC snap-in (Start > Programs > Administrative Tools > Computer Management).
2. Select the Storage branch.
3. Select the Disk Management leaf.
4. Break the mirror.
5. Install the Recovery Console as normal (WINNT32 /CMDCONS).
6. Recreate the mirror.

> **Note:** *In Windows 2000, you can only create mirrors on dynamic disks, although older mirror sets are supported from an upgrade to 4.0 to Windows 2000 on a basic disk. But if you broke the mirror, you would have to upgrade to dynamic disks to recreate.*

37.64 Why am I receiving Event ID 3013?

The message for Event ID 3013:

```
The redirector has timed out to <server name>
```

It usually means the server is one of the following:

- It is either busy and cannot respond before the rdr timeout.
- The network could be busy.
- There is a bottleneck in the network.

To resolve this problem, it's possible to modify the timeout so as to increase the redirector timeout. To modify, perform the following:

1. Start the Registry editor (REGEDIT.EXE).
2. Move to HKEY_LOCAL_MACHINE\SYSTEM\CurrentControlSet\Services\LanmanWorkstation\Parameters.
3. From the Edit menu, select New > DWORD Value.
4. Enter a name of **SESSTIMEOUT** and press Enter.
5. Double-click the new value and set in the range of 10–65535 seconds (45 seconds is the default). Click OK.
6. Close the Registry editor.
7. Reboot the machine.

FAQ 37.65 Why do I get an error event 1501 when trying to start the Event Log service?

If when you try to start the Event Log service, you get error 1501, "unable to open Event log files", it is usually caused by one of two things:

- The Event log files are missing.
- The Event log files have read only set on them.

The Event log files are stored in the %systemroot%\system32\config and are named APPEVENT.EVT, SECEVENT.EVT, and SYSEVENT.EVT. If any files are missing, try copying the missing file from another machine. If the read-only attribute is set, remove it via Explorer.

It is possible to move the Event log files, and to check that you are looking in the correct place, check the Registry entries:

- HKEY_LOCAL_MACHINE\SYSTEM\CurrentControlSet\Services\EventLog\Application\File
- HKEY_LOCAL_MACHINE\SYSTEM\CurrentControlSet\Services\EventLog\Security\File
- HKEY_LOCAL_MACHINE\SYSTEM\CurrentControlSet\Services\EventLog\System\File

37.66 How can I configure a service to automatically restart if it stops?

Under Windows 2000, the built-in support for service recovery has been greatly enhanced. Using the Computer Management MMC, Services and Applications > Services under the Recovery tab for each service are a number of definable actions to take in the event of the service stopping (see Figure 37-2):

- Take no action
- Restart the service
- Run a user-defined file
- Reboot the machine

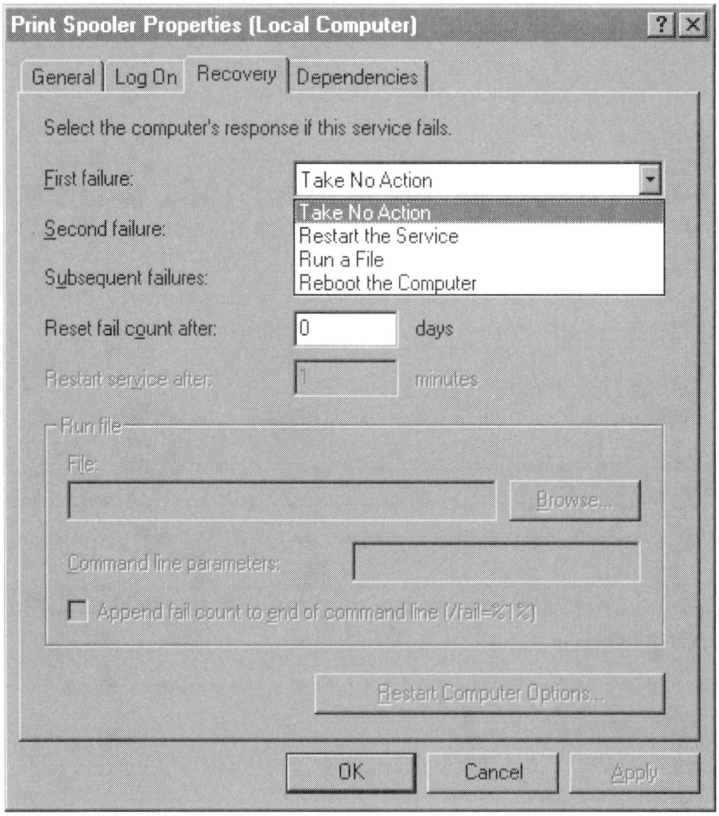

Figure 37-2 Selecting service failure actions

Service failure options are not possible under Windows NT 4.0; however, by writing a custom script that runs continuously, you could achieve a similar effect using a batch file. For example, in the following, I use the SC.EXE and SLEEP.EXE Resource Kit utilities:

```
:start
sc query spooler > state.txt
find "STOPPED" state.txt
if %errorlevel% EQU 0 goto error
sleep 300
goto start

:error
sc start spooler
sleep 5
goto start
```

You could add a server name (e.g., sc \\server query, etc.) if you want to check a remote system. Basically, the preceding checks every five minutes, but you can change it and check multiple services if you like.

FAQ 37.67 I've disabled ACPI in my BIOS; now Windows 2000 will not boot. What can I do?

During installation if Advanced Configuration and Power Interface (ACPI) is detected, specific changes are made to the configuration in the form of Registry entries and system files.

If you then disable ACPI in the BIOS, the OS will fail to boot with a BSOD:

```
0x00000079 (0x00000004, 0x0000AC31, 0x00000000, 0x00000000)
```

This is because a separate HAL is used for ACPI, non-ACPI systems. If you no longer want ACPI, you will need to reinstall Windows 2000.

FAQ 37.68 How do I upgrade/downgrade to a multiprocessor system in Windows 2000?

To upgrade to a multiprocessor system in Windows 2000, you just need to change the computer's driver as follows:

1. Right-click on My Computer and select Properties.
2. Select the Hardware tab.
3. Click Device Manager.
4. Expand the Computer branch and right-click on the computer (e.g., MPS Uniprocessor PC).
5. Select the Driver tab and click Update Driver (see Figure 37-3).
6. Click Next to the Hardware Wizard.
7. Select Display a list of known drivers and click Next.

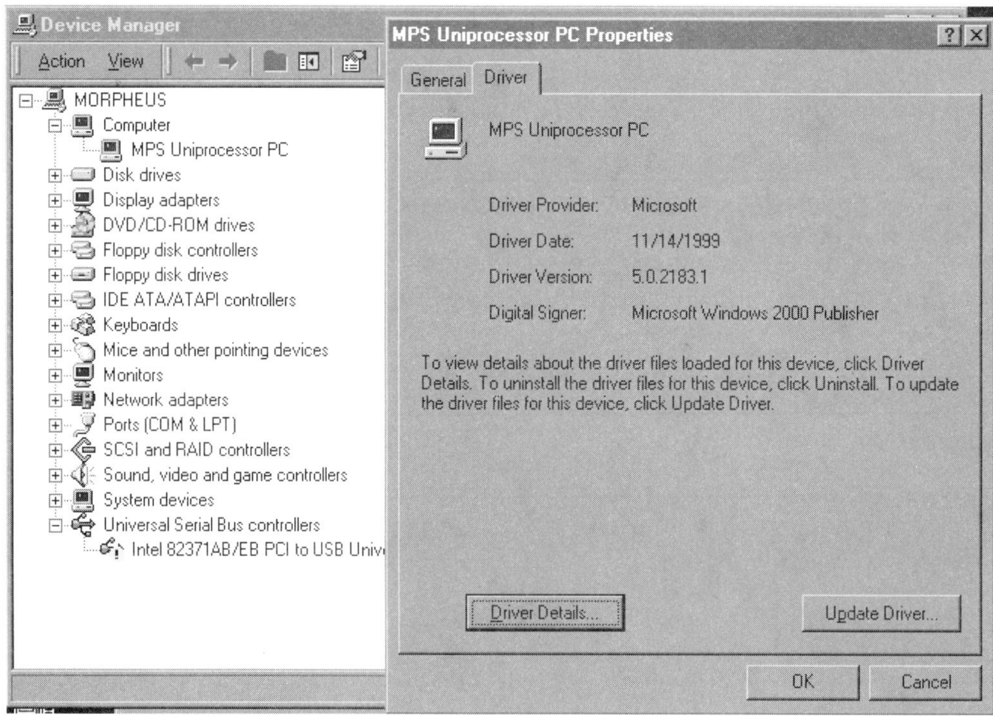

Figure 37-3 Changing the computer processor driver

8. Select the multiprocessor system and click Next.
9. Click Next to the confirmation.
10. The device driver will be updated. Click Finish to close the wizard.
11. Click Yes to restart the computer.

If you wish to switch from multiprocessor to uniprocessor, follow the same procedure.

FAQ 37.69 My machine BSODs whenever I try to watch a DVD. What can I do?

More and more DVD hardware now works under Windows NT. This DVD hardware includes the Creative Labs Encore bundle, which I recently installed in my NT machine, but it crashed every time I tried to watch a DVD. After much digging, I discovered the problem was because Direct Memory Access (DMA) was enabled. After disabling DMA, it worked fine, and I can now happily watch *The Matrix* while I'm supposed to be working ☺. This is not to say you all should disable DMA, because it's a good thing, but if the hardware does not correctly support it, problems can occur.

For information on setting DMA options, see FAQ 35.19.

FAQ 37.70 Where are the Dr. Watson logs in Windows 2000?

Windows 2000 includes version 5 of Dr. Watson (DRWTSN32.EXE), which has relocated the log and user dump location to %systemdrive%\Documents and Settings\All Users\Documents\DrWatson (see Figure 37-4). This location can be changed by starting DRWTSN32.EXE and modifying the locations.

These locations can also be changed by directly editing the Registry:

1. Start the Registry editor (REGEDIT.EXE).
2. Move to HKEY_LOCAL_MACHINE\SOFTWARE\Microsoft\DrWatson.
3. From the Edit menu, select New > String Value.
4. Enter a name of **CrashDumpFile** if you want to set the crash dump filename and location or **LogFilePath** to set the location of the log file. Press Enter.
5. Double-click the new value and set to the required location/filename. Click OK.
6. Close the Registry editor.

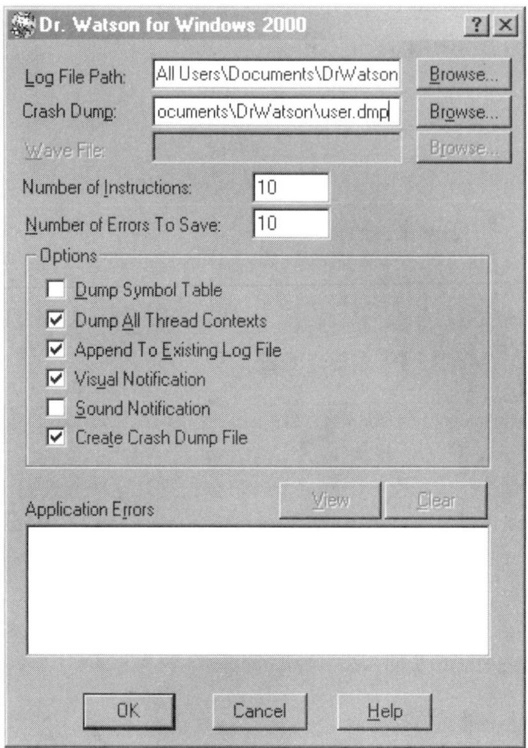

Figure 37-4 Dr. Watson options

FAQ 37.71 Why do I get a BSOD, "SYSTEM_LICENSE_VIOLATION"?

Stop hacking! I've seen this when I was experimenting and tried to modify the HKEY_LOCAL_MACHINE\SYSTEM\CurrentControlSet\Control\ProductOptions\ProductSuite value to test a program I was writing. My experimenting just crashed the OS!

I think the operating system could have just displayed a warning, but Microsoft decided to teach us a lesson ☺.

If you are not changing keys and still get this crash, check any programs you might have running, which may be trying to modify keys that the program should not!

FAQ 37.72 Why can't I install Office 2000 on Windows 2000?

Office 2000 requires 131MB of free disk space on the boot drive (where %systemroot% resides) for installation to complete successfully.

To be on the safe side, make sure you have more than 131MB because other programs/processes, such as dynamic pagefile growth, may use up disk space, giving you less than the needed 131MB.

FAQ 37.73 Why am I missing the Windows 2000 Advanced menu option on startup?

If you have Windows 2000 dual-booted with NT 4.0 and reinstall/repair NT 4.0, it will remove some of the 2000 boot options because the NT 4.0 repair process is unaware of the extra functionality of 2000 and replaces the startup files.

To restore the Windows 2000 F8 Advanced startup menu and logo screen, etc., perform the following:

1. Boot to another operating system (NT4, Recovery Console).
2. Copy the NTLDR and NTDETECT.COM files from the i386 directory of Windows 2000 to the C drive.
3. If you have a protection problem, enter the following commands:

```
attrib c:\ntdetect.com -r -s -h
attrib c:\ntldr -r -s -h
```

4. Upon the next reboot, the Windows 2000 Advanced menu will be available.

FAQ 37.74 Why can't I access the information in MEMORY.DMP as a normal user?

As of Windows NT Service Pack 4 for Windows NT 4.0 and all versions of Windows 2000, MEMORY.DMP is now created with an ACL of

- Administrators—Full Control
- System—Full Control

Other users may not access the file. Before Service Pack 4, the file was created with the same permissions as the parent directory, but the memory dump may have sensitive information, so its access has now been restricted. If you wish to access the file, log on as an Administrator.

37.75 Why can't I delete a file named CON or NUL?

The syntax \\.\ does not work with a file named CON or NUL. In fact, no Win32 tool may delete these files. A solution is to use non-Win32 tools.

For instance, the Resource Kit contains POSIX utilities such as RM.EXE, which allows you to delete these files:

```
NTReskit\posix\rm con
```

> **Note:** *The files may have been created with a tool such as Notepad, using the streams notation. For instance, type* ***notepad con:foo*** *on an NTFS partition, or* ***more < any_file > nul:bar****.*

There is an easier way, without using reskit and non-native subsystems, which is to rename the file, then just delete:

```
ren \\.\c:\nul. file
del file
```

37.76 I get an IRPStackSize event log every time I start Windows 2000. What can I do?

I've seen this on all my Windows 2000 installations. It's caused when the Registry key HKEY_LOCAL_MACHINE\SYSTEM\CurrentControlSet\Services\lanmanserver\parameters\IRPStackSize is less than 11 (see Figure 37-5).

To correct the problem, perform the following:

1. Start the Registry editor (REGEDIT.EXE).
2. Move to HKEY_LOCAL_MACHINE\SYSTEM\CurrentControlSet\Services\lanmanserver\parameters.
3. Double-click on IRPStackSize.
4. Set the type to decimal and enter **11**. Click OK.
5. Close the Registry editor.

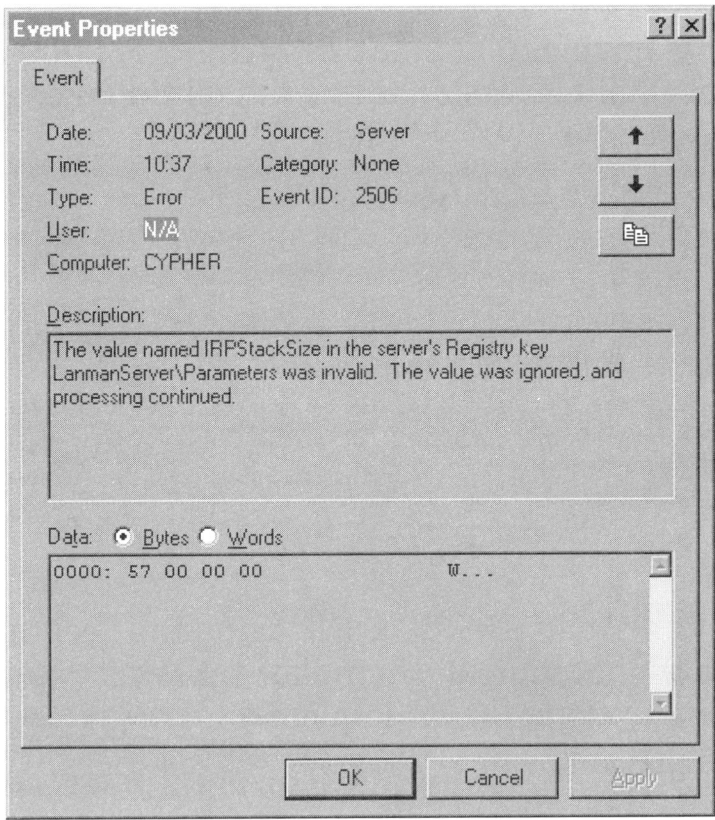

Figure 37-5 Event log for invalid IRPStackSize

You can also run the REG file at http://www.ntfaq.com/misc/fixirpstacksize.reg to fix it for you.

It is my understanding that Norton Antivirus is guilty of changing this value to an invalid one.

FAQ 37.77 Why does GLOBAL.EXE not work with DNS domain names?

GLOBAL.EXE is used to display members of global groups on remote servers or domains; however, it does not support the Windows 2000 DNS domain name. You must use the alternate NetBIOS domain name.

FAQ 37.78 I'm unable to upgrade my Windows 2000 evaluation version to the full edition using a Windows 2000 upgrade CD. Why?

The Windows 2000 upgrade CD cannot be used to "upgrade" an existing Windows 2000 installation (a similar problem with NT 4.0 existed), and so you cannot use the Windows 2000 upgrade CD to upgrade Windows 2000 evaluation edition to the full version.

Microsoft has responded to customer feedback and released a wizard at http://www.microsoft.com/WINDOWS2000/downloads/tools/evalupg/, which can be used to upgrade the evaluation version to a full one using a Windows 2000 upgraded CD, providing you also have a valid qualifying CD such as Windows 98 or NT 4.0.

If you have the full Windows 2000 CD, then you don't need the evaluation upgrade wizard.

FAQ 37.79 I can't load BASICDC.INF using the Security Configuration and Template editor, or I get errors in the event log if I implement it. What can I do?

If you try to load the BASICDC.INF file using the Security Configuration and Template MMC snap-in, you get an error. You also get errors in Event Viewer if you try to import it into a default domain controllers Group Policy Object. This is basically caused by an error in the .INF file that is trying to reference the following environment variables:

- SYSVOL
- DSDIT
- DSLOG

The problem is they only exist during the DCPROMO process. To resolve this situation, you need to manually add them to the machine's environment space.

You should first make a note of what the values should be. To find SYSVOL, enter the following:

```
net share sysvol
Share name SYSVOL
Path C:\WINNT\SYSVOL\sysvol
Remark Logon server share
```

```
Maximum users No limit
Users
The command completed successfully.
```

Make a note of the path name.

To find the DSDIT and DSLOG values, check the Registry at HKEY_LOCAL_MACHINE\SYSTEM\CurrentControlSet\Services\NTDS\Parameters (see Figure 37-6). DSDIT is equal to DSA Working Directory, and DSLOG is equal to the Database log files path.

The next step is to create the environment variables:

1. Right-click on My Computer and select Properties.
2. Select the Advanced tab and click Environment Variables.
3. Under the System variables area and click New.
4. Enter a name of **SYSVOL** and the value equal to your net share sysvol value (e.g., C:\WINNT\SYSVOL\sysvol).

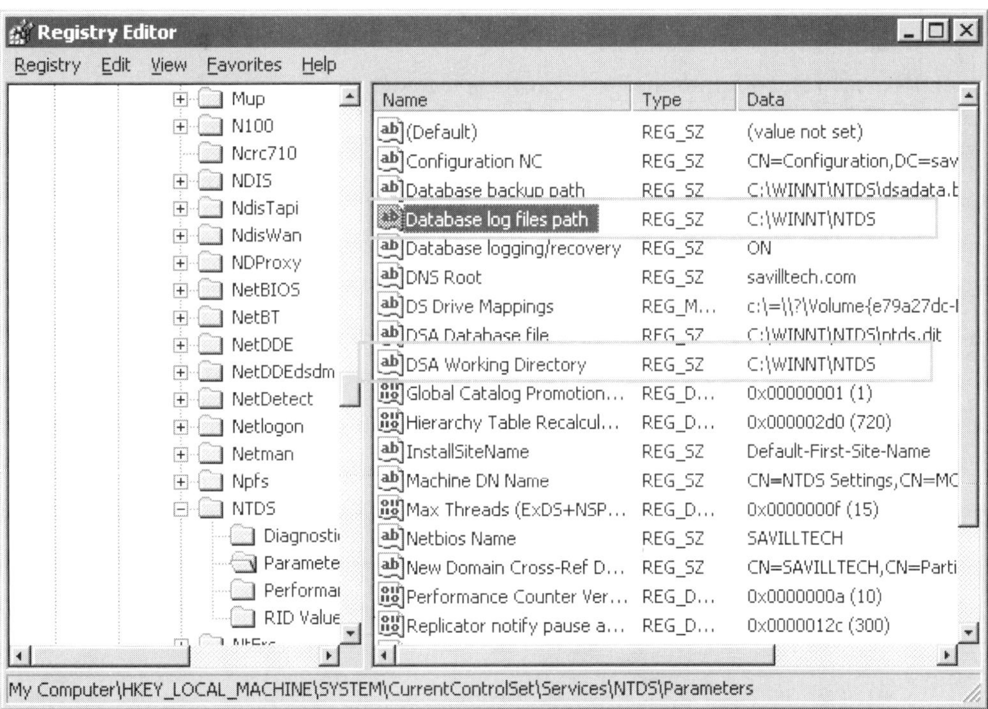

Figure 37-6 Registry values for NTDS path information

5. Click OK.
6. Repeat steps 3 through 5 for DSDIT and DSLOG also.
7. Click OK to all dialogs.
8. Go to the command prompt and enter:

```
secedit /refreshpolicy machine_policy /enforce
```

You should now be able to load the template with no problems. This will solve any event log errors.

37.80 Why am I unable to view/delete PAGEFILE.SYS using the Recovery Console?

A bug exists in Windows 2000 Recovery Console that does not display or let you delete PAGEFILE.SYS. The workaround is to copy another file to be PAGEFILE.SYS, which will then expose the true file allowing it to be deleted:

1. Boot into Recovery Console.
2. Because you boot into the %SystemRoot% folder (most commonly the C:\Winnt folder), type the following command:

```
cd \
```

3. Type the following command to overwrite the existing PAGEFILE.SYS file with BOOT.INI:

```
copy c:\boot.ini pagefile.sys
```

4. Type the following command:

```
del pagefile.sys
```

5. After you copy BOOT.INI over to PAGEFILE.SYS, PAGEFILE.SYS appears in the directory listing.

FAQ 37.81 I get error messages when I try to eject/format/label a removable disk. What can I do?

There is a known issue in Windows 2000 that non-Administrators have problems with removable disks. A workaround is as follows:

1. Log onto the computer using a local Administrator account or an account that has Administrator privileges.
2. Click Start, click Run, type **mmc.exe**, and then click OK.
3. In Microsoft Management Console (MMC), click Add/Remove Snap-in on the Console menu.
4. Click Add.
5. Click Group Policy and then click Add.
6. Verify that Local Computer is in the Group Policy Object box and then click Finish.
7. Click Close and then click OK.
8. Under Local Computer Policy, browse to the following branch: Computer Configuration\Windows Settings\Security Settings\Local Policies\Security Options
9. Right-click Allowed to eject removable NTFS media policy (see Figure 37-7) and then click Security.
10. In the Local policy setting box, click the group you want and then click OK. Your choices are:
    - Administrators—Only administrators can eject removable media.
    - Administrators and Power Users—Administrators and power users can eject removable media.
    - Administrators and Interactive Users—Administrators and interactive (standard users) can eject removable media.
11. Quit MMC, type the following command at a command prompt, and then press Enter:

```
secedit /refreshpolicy machine_policy
```

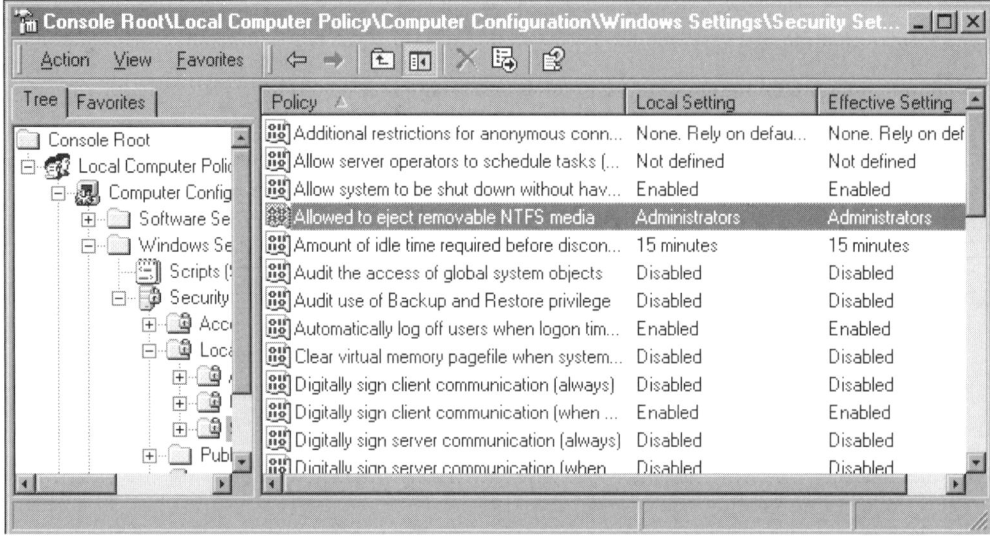

Figure 37-7 Allowing NTFS removable media ejection via policy

37.82 Why am I missing the Computers Near Me My Network Places group?

If the Computers Near Me group is deleted, it is not automatically recreated. If you wish it to be created again, perform one of the following options:

- Change the computer to a different workgroup, which should cause the Computers Near Me group to be recreated. Then, change the workgroup back to the original workgroup.
- The second method is to directly edit the Registry to force the group to be recreated:

12. Start the Registry editor (REGEDIT.EXE).
13. Move to HKEY_CURRENT_USER\Software\Microsoft\Windows\CurrentVersion\Explorer.
14. From the Edit menu, select New > String value if Last Domain does not exist. Enter a name of **Last Domain**.
15. Double-click the value and set to **0,0,Unknown**.
16. Click OK.
17. Close the Registry editor.

You don't need to reboot the computer, and the next time you go into My Network Places, the Computers Near Me will be recreated.

Be aware it can also be removed using a domain policy, so if the preceding does not work, check with the Administrators.

FAQ 37.83 Why do I get an error running Windows 2000 Setup that Setup cannot detect the version?

If you try to run Setup from within Windows 95/98 or Windows NT 4.0, you may get the following error:

```
Windows 2000 Setup could not detect the version of Windows you are
currently running. Setup cannot continue.
```

This error is caused by the Setup program not being able to detect the current installation's product ID, which may be caused by using disk duplication to install. To resolve this situation, perform the following:

1. Start the Registry editor (REGEDIT.EXE).
2. Set the value to your product ID; if using Windows NT:
   HKEY_LOCAL_MACHINE/Software/Microsoft/WindowsNT/CurrentVersion/ProductID

   Or, if using Windows 9x:

   HKEY_LOCAL_MACHINE/Software/Microsoft/Windows/CurrentVersion/ProductID
3. Close the Registry editor.

FAQ 37.84 Why do I get an "Access is denied" error when trying to browse my domain?

When trying to add users from a Windows 2000 domain to an access control list or a group on a Windows NT 4.0 machine, you may receive error:

```
Unable to browse the selected domain because the following error
occurred: Access is denied.
```

This error is caused by incompatible permission settings on the Windows 2000 domain, which were configured when running the DCPROMO command to create the domain.

When running DCPROMO, a page asked which permissions you wanted. If you selected "Permissions compatible only with Windows 2000 servers", then you will experience this problem. To remedy it, add the Everyone group to the Pre-Windows 2000 Compatible Access group and reboot the domain controller. This can be done with the command:

```
net localgroup "Pre-Windows 2000 Compatible Access" everyone /add
```

FAQ 37.85 Why is the Standby option missing on my portable?

If your portable has full Advanced Power Management (APM) but does not have a battery in it, then standby will not be available. Options to hibernate and power-off will still be available, however. This is by design and is caused by the standby vector in NTAPM.SYS being disabled on any computer that does not have a battery.

If you do have a battery and you don't have the option, it may be your computer is not APM compliant or is not correctly configured. Check with the computer manufacturer.

FAQ 37.86 Why do I get a MaxMpxCt event log every time I start Windows 2000?

This is caused when the Registry key HKEY_LOCAL_MACHINE\SYSTEM\CurrentControlSet\Services\lanmanserver\parameters\MaxMpxCt is less than 50. Following is the event log that will be received:

```
---Systemprotocol---

Eventtype: Error
Eventsource: Server
Eventcategory: None
EventID: 2506
Description:
The value "MaxMpxCt" in registry key "LanmanServer\Parameters" is
not valid.
The value will be ignored and server operation will continue.
```

To correct the problem, perform the following:

1. Start the Registry editor (REGEDIT.EXE).
2. Move to HKEY_LOCAL_MACHINE\SYSTEM\CurrentControlSet\Services\lanmanserver\parameters.
3. Double-click on MaxMpxCt.
4. Set the type to decimal and enter **50**. Click OK.
5. Close the Registry editor.

It is my understanding that Norton Antivirus is guilty of changing this value to an invalid one.

FAQ 37.87 I can't view any Web pages with Norton Internet Securities 2000 installed. What can I do?

This known issue is caused by bugs in Norton Internet Securities 2000. To resolve the problem, you will need to perform the following:

1. Uninstall Norton Internet Securities 2000.
2. Reinstall Norton Internet Securities 2000 again to reset values to default.
3. Uninstall Norton Internet Securities 2000 to totally remove the product.

FAQ 37.88 Why do I receive File Replication Service errors in the event log?

A known problem exists that if a domain controller, which is a File Replication Service (FRS) partner of a server, cannot be contacted due to a network problem or is rebooted within a single polling interval (five minutes), then the server will be unable to resolve the SID of the FRS partner because the binding handle will be invalid.

The actual event log received will be:

```
Event ID:13526

The file replication service cannot replicate c:\winnt\sysvol\domain
with the computer TITANIC because the computer SID cannot be deter-
mined from the distinguished name "cn=dc1,ou=domain controller,
dc=savilltech,dc=com". The file Replication Service will try later.
SYSVOL and DFS content is not being replicated.
```

This problem will stop information from being replicated. To resolve it, restart the FRS service on the machine logging the 13526 events:

```
net stop "file replication service"
The File Replication Service service is stopping.....
The File Replication Service service was stopped successfully.

net start "file replication service"
The File Replication Service service is starting.
The File Replication Service service was started successfully.
```

FAQ 37.89 Why is my dual monitor installation running out of system page table entries?

This is a known issue with Windows 2000 and is caused as page table entries (PTEs) are required to map the frame buffer, and with multiple graphics adapters, more PTEs are used, causing a shortage.

To correct this, the number of system pages should be increased as follows:

1. Start the Registry editor (REGEDIT.EXE).
2. Move to HKEY_LOCAL_MACHINE\SYSTEM\CurrentControlSet\Control\Session Manager\Memory Management.
3. Double-click SystemPages.
4. Set to decimal and set to value 36000.
5. Click OK.
6. Close the Registry editor.
7. Reboot the machine.

FAQ 37.90 The Find tab of Windows Help does not work. What can I do?

When selecting the Find tab of Windows help, you may receive the error:

```
Unable to display the find tab.(177)
```

This error is caused by an OEM installation. To remedy it, perform the following:

1. Start Explorer.
2. Move to %systemroot%\Help.

3. Rename the SUPP_ED.CNT and SUPP_ED.HLP files (to a name without .CNT or .HLP as an extension).

If the problem persists, rename the UPDATE.CNT file in the %systemroot%\Help folder (again to a name without a .CNT extension) and delete the hidden WINDOWS.GID file (which will be recreated automatically).

FAQ 37.91 I receive an error "NGINA.DLL cannot be found" and am unable to log on to my machine. How can I resolve this?

When you log on, a GINA, by default MSGINA.DLL, is used for the purpose of the logon. However, it can be changed. Recently I installed Lotus Notes, rebooted, and could not log on because of an error, "NGINA.DLL could not be found".

After some research, I found NGINA.DLL was the Lotus GINA, which somehow had been set to be used but not installed! To remedy the situation, I booted with the Recovery Console, went to system32, and copied MSGINA.DLL to NGINA.DLL and rebooted.

Once I rebooted and could log on, I changed the GINA the logon process was trying to use as follows:

1. Start the Registry editor (REGEDIT.EXE).
2. Move to HKEY_LOCAL_MACHINE\SOFTWARE\Microsoft\Windows NT\CurrentVersion\Winlogon.
3. Double-click GinaDLL and set to MSGINA.DLL.
4. Close the Registry editor.

Another approach would be to install a second copy of Windows NT/2000 on the machine and perform the following:

1. Start Registry Editor (REGEDT32.EXE).
2. Go to the HKEY_LOCAL_MACHINE window.
3. Select the HKEY_LOCAL_MACHINE key entry.
4. From the Registry menu, click Load Hive.
5. Browse and select the failed Windows NT installation path—for example, Winnt.
6. Go to the System32\Config directory and select the Software file.

Note: *The software file with no extension is the correct one.*

7. Click OK and type a key name of **test**.
8. Double-click the new test key and follow this path: Microsoft\Windows NT\Current Version\Winlogon
9. Modify the entry Ginadll:REG_SZ:MSGINA.DLL.
10. From the Registry menu, click Unload Hive.
11. Restart into the original Windows NT installation.

FAQ 37.92 I'm unable to run the Group Policy editor for the domain even though I'm a domain Administrator. What can I do?

Perhaps you are unable to run the Group Policy editor or other tools under the Administrative Tools folder and receive the following error:

```
The snapin below, referenced in this document has been restricted by
policy. Contact your administrator for details.
```

This error can be caused by a number of configuration settings on your domain.

It's possible to restrict users to a set of snap-ins and/or administrative tools using a Group Policy. To check, perform the following:

1. Start Active Directory Users and Computers snap-in (Start > Programs > Administrative Tools > Active Directory Users and Computers).
2. Right-click on the domain and select Properties.
3. Select the Group Policies tab.
4. Select the default domain policy and click Edit.
5. Move to User Configuration\Administrative Templates\Windows Components\Microsoft Management Console.
6. Double-click Restrict Users to the explicitly permitted list of snap-ins (see Figure 37-8).
7. Set to Not configured.

You can drill down further to Restricted/Permitted snap-ins\Group Policy and set the Group Policy snap-in to enabled and Administrative Templates (User) to enabled or not configured.

This can also be done on a local computer by directly editing the Registry:

1. Start Registry editor (REGEDIT.EXE).
2. Move to HKEY_CURRENT_USER\Software\Policies\Microsoft\MMC.

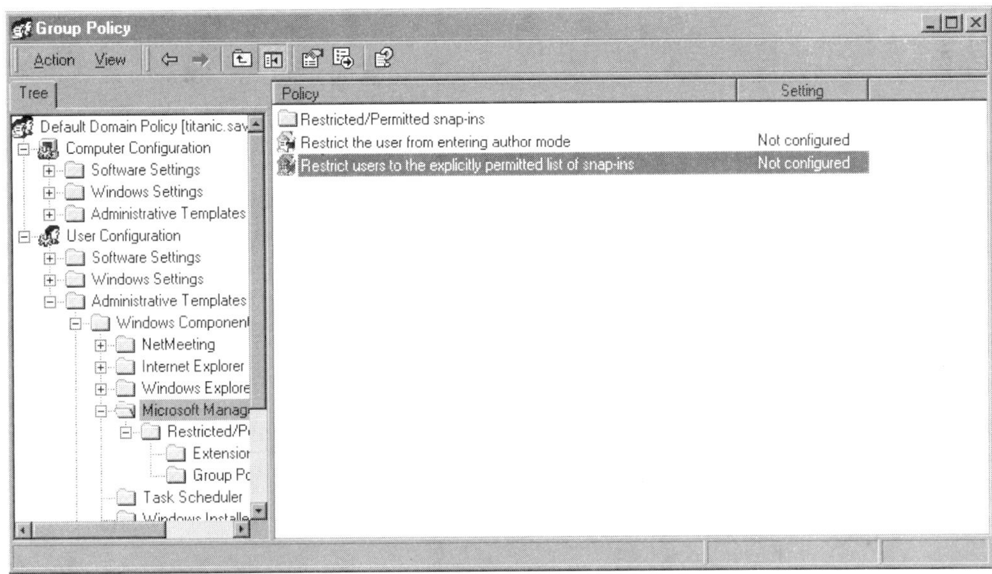

Figure 37-8 Restricting the use of snap-ins

3. Double-click RestrictToPermittedSnapins.
4. Set to 0 and click OK.
5. Close the Registry editor.

If you are still unable to start the Group Policy snap in, perform the following additional actions:

1. Start Registry editor (REGEDIT.EXE).
2. Move to HKEY_CURRENT_USER\Software\Policies\Microsoft\MMC.
3. Change the Restrict_Run value to 0 in the following keys if they exist:
    - {8FC0B734-A0E1-11D1-A7D3-0000F87571E3}—This is the restriction for Group Policy snap-in.
    - {0F6B957E-509E-11D1-A7CC-0000F87571E3}—This is the restriction for the Administrative templates.
4. Close the Registry editor.

If you still can't run the Group Policy snap in, contact Microsoft ☺.

FAQ 37.93 I've installed Internet Explorer 5.01 International version with high encryption. Why can't I now install SP6a?

If you attempt to install the standard-encryption version of Windows NT 4.0 Service Pack 6a (SP6a) on a Windows NT 4.0-based computer that already has Microsoft Internet Explorer High Encryption Pack installed, you may receive the following error message:

```
You have chosen to install a version of the Service Pack with
Standard Encryption onto a system with High Encryption. This is not
supported. To successfully install this version of the Service Pack,
you must install the High Encryption version. Press Help for more
information about obtaining the High Encryption Version of this
Service Pack. Service Pack Setup will now exit.
```

This happens because the SCHANNEL.DLL file that is installed by Internet Explorer High Encryption Pack cannot be overwritten by the service pack installation program.

To work around this, perform the following:

1. Start a text editor (such as Notepad).
2. Open the UPDATE.INF file in the Service Pack 6a folder.
3. Remove the reference to the SCHANNEL.DLL file from the [CheckSecurity.System32.files] section.
4. Save the file.
5. Now install SP6a!

An alternative method that you may find quicker is:

1. Take a copy of SCHANNEL.DLL from another NT4 machine without high encryption.
2. Rename SCHANNEL.DLL on the machine with high encryption to SCHANNEL.DLL_HIGH.
3. Place your low encryption SCHANNEL.DLL into your system32 folder.
4. Install SP6a.
5. Reboot your machine.
6. Now you can remove SCHANNELL.DLL safely and replace with the saved SCHANNEL.DLL_HIGH.

FAQ 37.94 Help! I installed the Win2K High Encryption Pack and failed to restart before installing SP1. What can I do?

When you install the High Encryption Pack, you must reboot the computer, or you might experience problems. Because you didn't reboot the computer before you installed Service Pack 1 (SP1), you need to perform the following steps:

1. Go to the i386 folder of the service pack CD-ROM or the i386 folder of the expanded SP1NETWORK.EXE (use sp1network.exe /x). Insert a blank disk in the disk drive, then type the following command to copy LSARSV.DLL to the disk:

   ```
   expand -r \i386\lsasrv.dl_ a:\
   ```

2. Go to the problem computer and boot from the Win2K installation media. When you see "Welcome to Setup", press F10 to start the Recovery Console (or if you have the Recovery Console installed, simply boot into that option).
3. Copy LSARV.DLL from the disk to %SystemRoot%\System32. Press Yes to overwrite.
4. Type **exit** to restart your computer.
5. Reinstall the High Encryption Pack.
6. Restart you computer.

Note: *You **don't** need to reinstall SP1 after performing the preceding.*

FAQ 37.95 Why doesn't Windows 2000 retain my pagefile settings?

When you change your pagefile settings in Win2K, sometimes they aren't restored (this happened to me today!). The correct way to set the pagefile size is to use Start > Settings > Control Panel > System > Advanced > Performance Options > Change. Select the drive whose settings you want to modify and enter values in the Initial Size and Maximum Size boxes. Click Set, then click OK three times.

To avoid pagefile fragmentation as a page grows, you should set the Initial Size and Maximum Size values to the same value. A minimum value of your RAM x 1.5 is recommended. If you don't set these values to the same value, as a page grows and shrinks, it becomes scattered all over the hard disk.

Even when you set the values properly, some systems don't retain your settings. If this happens, perform the following steps:

1. Start REGEDT32.EXE (not REGEDIT.EXE).
2. Go to HKEY_LOCAL_MACHINE\SYSTEM\CurrentControlSet\ControlSession Manager\Memory Management.
3. Double-click PagingFiles. The entry will appear as

   ```
   D:\pagefile.sys 700 700
   ```

   The first value is the location; the second is the minimum size; and the third is the maximum size.
4. Ensure the values are correct and click OK.
5. Reboot the machine.

FAQ 37.96 Why do the offline folders that I've compressed on NTFS keep losing their compression?

Manually compressing the offline files cache (the %SystemRoot%\CSC folder) isn't supported. The files you compress will be compressed, but new files will **not** be compressed, and existing compressed files will lose their compression after synchronization.

To ensure that a deadlock doesn't occur, Windows 2000 writes files in uncompressed format even when the folder is marked for compression. Marking the Client Side Caching (CSC) folder for compression and leaving it that way can cause a variety of complications, ranging from caching update problems to Win2K not responding (hanging) while you attempt to access files residing within the cache. The upshot is that you shouldn't compress the offline files cache (the CSC folder).

FAQ 37.97 When I add the AD Schema Manager snap-in to the MMC, why doesn't the snap-in connect to the Operations Master?

If the Active Directory (AD) Schema Manager snap-in doesn't connect to the Operations Master when you attempt to view the schema's permissions, you may receive the following error message:

```
Could not connect to the current schema master server. The server
may not be available, or you may have insufficient privileges to
manage the schema.
```

If you attempt to view or change the Operations Master, you may receive the following error message:

```
The server is currently offline.
```

To resolve this problem, first click the plus sign (+) to expand the hive and then connect the snap-in to the Operations Master. After the hive has expanded, you can connect to the Operations Master.

FAQ 37.98 Why am I receiving a large number of Event ID 13507, 13552, and 13555 messages on the domain controller?

This problem occurs on domain controllers that have the Windows 2000 Server Terminal Services component installed in application server mode and also have the Citrix MetaFrame 1.8 add-on installed. All three event IDs refer to the File Replication System (FRS). MetaFrame has a neat option to remap the servers' drive letters (e.g., C becomes M) to let Citrix clients continue to see local drives as C, D, etc. The problem is that when the drive is remapped, FRS doesn't work because it's looking for the old drive letters, which no longer exist.

To resolve this problem, perform the following steps (you'll need another machine to temporarily make a domain controller):

1. Install another Win2K Server-based computer as an additional domain controller (to save any created user accounts or permissions).
2. Run the DCPROMO.EXE file to demote the domain controller that has Citrix MetaFrame installed to a member server on the domain.
3. Run the DCPROMO.EXE file again to promote the member server back to a replica domain controller on the domain. Doing so allows the NTDS.DIT file, the System Volume (SYSVOL) folder, and log files to be created on the drive that Citrix MetaFrame has remapped as N.
4. Stop NetLogon and FRS on the domain controller.
5. Delete the NTFRS.JDB file in the %Windir%\Ntfrs\Jet folder.
6. Delete the EDB.TXT file in the %Windir%\Ntfrs\Jet\Sys folder.

7. Delete the EDB.TXT, RES1.TXT, and RES2.TXT files in the %Windir%\Ntfrs\Jet\Log folder.
8. Restart the domain controller.

The system should now start and run properly.

FAQ 37.99 When Windows 2000 users try to change their passwords, why do they get the error message "The password cannot be changed at this time"?

This behavior, a known issue, occurs when you haven't defined a minimum password age for the users' Group Policy. To resolve this issue, configure a minimum password age of 0 instead of none.

1. Start the Active Directory Users and Computers Microsoft Management Console (MMC) snap-in (Start > Programs > Administrative Tools > Active Directory Users and Computers).
2. Right-click the domain or organizational unit (OU) that contains the users (and has a Group Policy defined).
3. Select Properties from the context menu.
4. Select the Group Policy tab.
5. Select the appropriate Group Policy (e.g., Default Domain Policy) and click Edit.
6. Expand Computer Configuration > Windows Settings > Security Settings > Account Policies > Password Policy.
7. Double-click Minimum password age.
8. Select Define this policy setting and set it to 0 (see Figure 37-9).
9. Click OK.
10. Close the Group Policy windows and the Active Directory Users and Computers MMC snap-in.
11. On the domain controller, run the following command to force the policy change to take effect:

```
secedit /refreshpolicy machine_policy /enforce
```

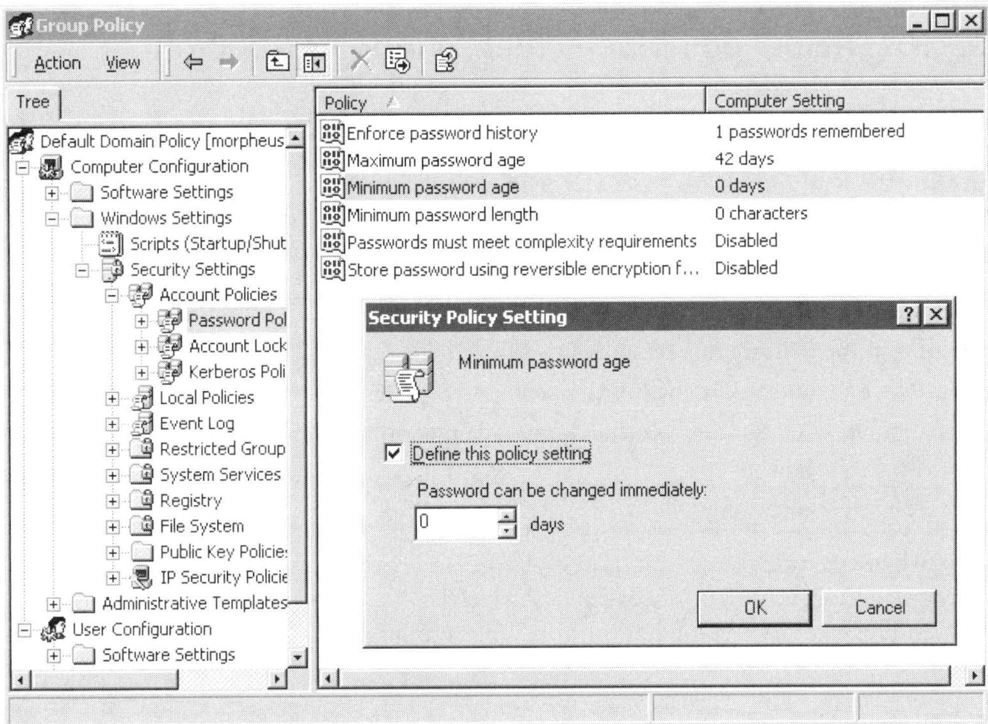

Figure 37-9 Enabling the minimum password age policy

FAQ 37.100 I have a program called Explorer on the root of my C drive. When I boot, why does this program replace my shell?

When you start your computer, the system first checks the C drive, so if you place a program called EXPLORER.EXE on the root of C, the system uses that program rather than the one in %systemroot% (e.g., c:\winnt). This behavior occurs because the shell value (under HKEY_LOCAL_MACHINE\SOFTWARE\Microsoft\Windows NT\CurrentVersion\Winlogon) simply says "explorer.exe." If you edit the Registry to make this value c:\winnt\explorer.exe, this behavior won't occur because you've specified the search path in the value.

Microsoft has provided a fix for this problem in Windows 2000 Service Pack 2 (SP2). In addition, check out Microsoft article Q269049 for a Windows NT fix.

FAQ 37.101 How do I blue-screen Windows 2000 on demand?

Win2K includes a feature that lets you crash the OS by holding the right Ctrl key and pressing the Scroll Lock key twice. To enable this feature, perform the following steps:

1. Start REGEDIT.EXE.
2. Go to HKEY_LOCAL_MACHINE\SYSTEM\CurrentControlSet\Services\i8042prt\ Parameters.
3. From the Edit menu, select New > DWORD.
4. Enter a name of **CrashOnCtrlScroll** and press Enter.
5. Double-click the new value and set it to any nonzero value (e.g., 1). Click OK.
6. Close Regedit.
7. Reboot your system.

Now, when you hold the right Ctrl key and press the Scroll Lock key twice, the system will crash and display a bug check code of MANUALLY_INITIATED_CRASH (0xE2). This keystroke combination works in some situations where Ctrl+Alt+Del has no effect.

FAQ 37.102 Is there a Windows 2000 equivalent to running RDISK /s-?

Because Microsoft moved RDISK into NTBACKUP, you no longer have the quick option of updating your repair information with the RDISK /s- command. However, Andrej Budja has written a neat script that basically types the keystrokes necessary to run RDISK under Win2K. Save the following script to a file called RDISKS.JS. Then, to run the script, double-click the RDISKS.JS file.

```
var shell = new ActiveXObject("WScript.Shell");
shell.Popup("Please insert blank floppy disk in the drive A:\n\n (C)
2000 Andrej Budja.\n Feel free to distribute\n\n", 6);

shell.Run("ntbackup.exe");
WScript.Sleep("500");

shell.Sendkeys("{ENTER}");
WScript.Sleep("200");
```

```
shell.AppActivate("Backup");
shell.Sendkeys("{TAB}");
WScript.Sleep("50");
shell.Sendkeys("{TAB}");
WScript.Sleep("50");
shell.Sendkeys("{TAB}");
WScript.Sleep("50");

shell.Sendkeys("{ENTER}");
WScript.Sleep("200");

shell.AppActivate("Emergency Repair Diskette");
shell.Sendkeys("{ }");
WScript.Sleep("200");

shell.Sendkeys("{ENTER}");
WScript.Sleep("12000");

shell.AppActivate("Emergency Repair Diskette");
shell.Sendkeys("%{F4}");
WScript.Sleep("200");

shell.Sendkeys("{ENTER}");
WScript.Sleep("200");

shell.AppActivate("Backup");
shell.Sendkeys("%{F4}");

WScript.Quit();
```

FAQ 37.103 How do I perform an emergency shutdown in Windows 2000?

We are all familiar with the Ctrl+Alt+Del keystroke combination that lets us shut down a system. However, sometimes the system hangs, and this approach doesn't work. If you hold down the Ctrl key and click Shutdown, you receive the following message:

```
If you continue, your machine will reboot and any unsaved data will
be lost. Use this only as a last resort.
```

Clicking OK should result in a shutdown, but—as the message warns—you'll lose all unsaved work.

FAQ 37.104 Why does Windows 2000 halt with a 0x0000001E exception error on install?

If your computer has a mainboard with a VIA MVP3 chipset and an ATA/100 hard disk, Win2K might halt with the exception error you mention. Generally, these mainboards don't support the UDMA 100 rate that the ATA/100-compliant disk requires (these systems usually support UDMA 33 or UDMA 33/66). Apparently the drives don't report backward compatibility properly, and because the Win2K install process is so hardware intensive, the system hangs at this point.

The solution seems to be one of the following:

- Upgrade your BIOS if doing so will give you the ATA/100 (UDMA 100) support.
- Make the following changes to your BIOS:
  1. Go into your BIOS and disable UDMA on the IDE channel that holds your hard drive.
  2. Still in the BIOS, set your programmed input/output (PIO) to Mode 4 instead of auto.
  3. Install Win2K. The installation should proceed with no problems.
  4. Restore the two BIOS changes from steps 1 and 2 to what they were before and see whether Win2K is still stable.
  5. If Win2K isn't stable, you'll probably need to keep the two BIOS changes as long as you use that drive.
- Use the drive on a board that is ATA/100-compliant.

FAQ 37.105 Why can't I find my BOOT.INI file?

When your computer starts up, it uses the BOOT.INI file to find the instances of Windows 2000 or Windows NT (and other OSs, such as Windows Millennium Edition—Window Me—and Windows 98). It also specifies the amount of time to pause before the system automatically executes the default choice.

The BOOT.INI file is on the system partition at the root of the drive, usually C:\BOOT.INI. However, it's a hidden file, which is probably why you can't see it. Perform the following steps to find the file:

1. Start a Command session (Start > Run > CMD.EXE).
2. Type the following command (ah stands for attribute hidden):

```
dir c:\boot.ini /ah
```

3. You should see the BOOT.INI file. If you can't find the file on the root of the C drive, you might have some boot software installed or the C drive isn't the active partition. Check the root of each drive with the dir /ah command.

To remove the hidden attribute from the BOOT.INI file, type the following command from a command session:

```
attrib c:\boot.ini -s -h -r
```

This command removes the system (s), hidden (h), and read-only (r) flags. You must remove the system attribute to remove the hidden attribute. Now, you can modify the file. After you've modified it, you should reset the attributes:

```
attrib c:\boot.ini +s +h +r
```

FAQ 37.106 When I run the NBTSTAT -c command, why do some lines have a period (.) in the name column?

An incorrect entry in the LMHOSTS file causes this problem. Here's sample output indicating a problem:

```
C:\>nbtstat -c

Local Area Connection:
Node IpAddress: [200.200.200.1] Scope Id: []

NetBIOS Remote Cache Name Table

Name Type Host Address Life [sec]
------------------------------------------------------------
savilltech2 UNIQUE 200.200.200.2 -1
SAVILLTECH . UNIQUE 200.200.200.1 -1
SAVILLTECH . UNIQUE 200.200.200.1 -1
SAVILLTECH . UNIQUE 200.200.200.1 -1

The LMHOSTS entry must have the following format:

[IP address][tab]"[15-character domain name]\0x1b" [tab] #PRE
```

For example,

```
200.200.200.1 "savilltech \0x1b" #PRE
```

Notice the five spaces after savilltech to make the domain name 15 characters. If the domain name isn't the full 15 characters (padded with space characters), the period appears in the Name column. To correct the problem, edit your LMHOSTS file (in the %systemroot%\system32\drivers\etc folder) and ensure that all domains defined in this format are padded with spaces to make them 15 characters.

FAQ 37.107 Why can't my Windows 98 clients log on to the Windows 2000 domain?

This problem occurs when you upgrade a Windows NT 4.0-based domain to Win2K, and in the process the SAM becomes corrupt. The Win98 clients receive the following message:

```
This device does not exist on the network.
The domain password you supplied is incorrect or access to your
logon server has been denied.
```

Currently, a fix to this problem doesn't exist. The only way around it is to back up the users, remove Active Directory (AD), recreate AD, and import the users. Perform the following steps:

1. Back up the users and groups to a text file using the ADDUSERS.EXE utility (in the Win2K Resource Kit):

   ```
   addusers /d users.txt
   ```

2. Remove AD using the DCPROMO.EXE utility.
3. Reinstall AD using the DCPROMO.EXE utility.
4. Use the ADDUSERS.EXE utility to import the users and groups contained in the text file, thus recreating the accounts:

   ```
   addusers /c users.txt
   ```

Obviously, in a large environment, this solution might be difficult, but it does stress the importance of making sure you test your whole range of clients when you upgrade to Win2K.

FAQ 37.108 What causes a STOP screen with the error DRIVER_POWER_STATE_FAILURE?

This error occurs when you try to put the system in standby mode. The cause is a third-party driver that doesn't comply with the Advanced Configuration and Power Interface (ACPI) standard for power management. When the system goes into standby mode, it tells all drivers that the system is changing power state. If a driver doesn't respond correctly, the system displays a blue screen. Almost any kind of driver (e.g., CD-ROM drivers, network drivers, keyboard filter drivers) can cause this problem.

The easiest way to fix it is to perform the following steps:

1. Create a hardware profile and boot into it.
2. Go to the device manager (My Computer > Manage > Device Manager), select View > Show hidden devices > and disable all suspect devices (i.e., non-Microsoft devices) for the current hardware profile. (You disable a device on the General tab of the device's property sheet.)
3. Reboot using the same hardware profile and try to reproduce the problem. If you can't, start reenabling drivers and rebooting until the problem reappears. Then delete or update the offending driver.
4. If the problem persists, disable all unnecessary drivers, update the necessary ones, and try again.

See Microsoft article Q246243 for more information.

FAQ 37.109 How do I use the Recovery Console SET command?

The Recovery Console (RC) lets you access the Windows filesystem from outside Windows 2000 to perform recovery actions. Four variables make this environment more user friendly:

- allowwildcards—Lets you use wildcards with some commands (e.g., del *.tmp)
- allowallpaths—Lets you change directories (the cd command) to include all folders on all drives
- allowremovablemedia—Lets you copy files from the hard disk to a diskette or other recognized removable media
- nocopyprompt—Lets you copy files without being prompted to continue when you overwrite an existing file

By default these variables are set to false. Use the following syntax to set these variables to true:

```
set [set variable] = true
```

For example, set nocopyprompt = true removes the copy prompt when you overwrite a file.

Before you can use these variables, you must use one of the following methods to enable them:

- Domain Controller Security Policy in Administrative Tools
- Domain Security Policy in Administrative Tools
- Local Security Policy in Administrative Tools

After you open a policy, expand the Computer Configuration branch, then expand Windows Settings, Local Policies, Security Options. Double-click Recovery Console: Allow floppy copy and access to all drives and all folders, and set it to Enabled.

Use the following command to refresh the policy:

```
secedit /refreshpolicy machine_policy
```

For a full list of all available commands, see Microsoft article Q229716.

FAQ 37.110 When I start the Recovery Console, why doesn't the system prompt me for a password?

When you start the RC, the system usually prompts you for the password for the selected Windows 2000 installation. If the RC can't find a valid Win2K installation, it doesn't ask you for a password, and you can perform only basic functions—such as the fixmbr, fixboot, manage, and format partitions commands—but you can't access any folder other than the root of the hard disk.

FAQ 37.111 Why does Windows 2000 reboot and display an event log-related error message?

An event log corruption usually causes this behavior. To resolve the problem, boot the Recovery Console (RC), and rename the event log files %systemroot%\system32\config\AppEvent.Evt, %systemroot%\system32\config\SecEvent.Evt, and %systemroot%\system32\config\SysEvent.Evt to .OLDEVT. Then reboot the system, and it should behave correctly.

FAQ 37.112 I've configured the Terminal Services Manager to start in minimized mode. Why can't I restore it to normal or maximized mode?

A problem exists with the Terminal Services Manager: If you configure it to start in minimized mode, when you try to restore it to normal or maximized mode, it stays minimized—rendering it useless. The only solution is to modify it to start in normal or maximized mode as described in FAQ 6.188.

FAQ 37.113 Why doesn't WordPerfect 8 open for Windows 2000 users?

After you install a program as an Administrator, a user with restricted or even elevated rights can't always access some elements of the Registry, which can prevent a program from running correctly. To resolve this situation, grant your WordPerfect 8 users Full Control over the Corel software key:

1. Start a Registry editor (REGEDT32.EXE for Win2K, REGEDIT.EXE for Windows XP).
2. Go to HKEY_LOCAL_MACHINE\SOFTWARE\Corel.
3. From the Security menu, select Permissions.
4. Select Users, and then select Full Control.
5. Click OK.
6. Close the Registry editor.

FAQ 37.114 What does Event ID 41 in the System event log mean?

Event ID 41 appears on systems with multiple CPUs if the CPUs have different stepping levels. The text in the Event log will be:

```
The CPUs in this multiprocessor system are not all the same revision
level. To use all processors, the operating system restricts itself
to the features of the least capable processor in the system. Should
problems occur with this system, contact the CPU manufacturer to see
if this mix of processors is supported.
```

Contact your system supplier to ensure that your particular machine will work with Windows 2000 and Windows NT without any problems. For example, if the first CPU supports features A, B, and C, and the second CPU supports feature A, the machine will use only feature A on both CPUs. Also, for these two CPUs to work together, you might need to disable features B and C on the first CPU.

37.115 Why do I receive a 0x0000001E error when I start my computer?

0x0000001E is a common bug code. To resolve this error, you should typically contact Microsoft support with all the information from the failure. However, if you receive this error after you perform a new installation, look for the following culprits:

- Lack of disk space for installation
- Third-party video drivers (and the Windows 2000 or Windows NT WIN32K.SYS driver)
- System BIOS incompatibilities

To help resolve these problems

- Ensure that you have plenty of disk space
- Remove the third-party video driver
- Upgrade to the newest BIOS version, and ensure that it's on the Microsoft Hardware Compatibility List (HCL)

37.116 Why won't the CD and CHDIR commands work in Windows 2000's Recovery Console?

The CD and CHDIR commands let you change the current directory at the command prompt. However, in the Recovery Console, the following commands don't work:

Changing drive and path

```
cd/d <drive>:\<path>
chdir/d <drive>:\<path>
```

Move to parent folder

```
cd..
chdir..
```

Move to the root of the drive

```
cd\
chdir\
```

To work around this problem, you must add a space between cd or chdir and the parameters (e.g., cd .. won't work in the Recovery Console but cd .. will). Just remember, this space isn't required at the Windows command prompt but is mandatory when you're working from the Recovery Console.

FAQ 37.117 How should I address the error message "Windows could not start because the following file is missing or corrupt: \Winnt\System32\Config\System.ced"?

Although this error message suggests that the System Registry hive is missing or corrupt, this message typically results from the System Registry hive being too large for the OS to load. For Intel-based systems, the initial stage of the boot process is limited to 16MB of available memory. During this phase of the boot process, the system must load the following items:

- Loader
- Kernel
- The hardware abstraction layer (HAL)
- Boot drivers
- System Registry hive

If the System Registry hive exceeds 13MB, an error can occur, resulting in the preceding error message. The System Registry hive is meant to store only information that the OS needs to start the machine.

To resolve this error, you must replace the existing System Registry hive with a smaller backup version:

1. Boot your system to the Recovery Console using the Windows 2000 installation CD-ROM, selecting R for Repair and C for the Console.
2. Select the installation to repair and enter its associated recovery/administrator password.
3. Navigate to the System32\Config folder by typing the command

   ```
   cd system32\config
   ```

4. Rename the current system files by typing the commands

```
ren system system.old
ren system.alt systemalt.old
```

5. Run the Emergency Repair Disk Wizard from Win2K Backup and Recovery tools and copy the backup System Registry hive from the %systemroot%\repair folder or the %systemroot%\repair\regback folder to the current folder by typing the command

```
copy %systemroot%\repair\system %systemroot%\system32\config
```

6. Exit the Recovery Console by typing the command

```
exit
```

After you replace the System Registry hive, any extra services or drivers that you installed since you created the backup hive might not work correctly, so you might need to reinstall them.

FAQ 37.118 How do I use the new Microsoft troubleshooting Web site?

Microsoft has an improved Web site at http://support.microsoft.com/Directory/search_wizard/searchwizard.asp?ln=en-us for finding answers to problems relating to

- Internet Explorer 5.0 and later
- Outlook 98 and later (including Outlook Express)
- Exchange 2000 Server
- SQL Server 2000
- Windows 98 and Win98 SE
- Windows NT Server 4.0 and NT Workstation 4.0
- Windows XP
- Windows Media Player
- NetMeeting

The Web site prompts you to select a product and describe your problem. Using the information you provide, the Web site presents you with several Help sections. You can then refine your search to find the best matches. This site is a great troubleshooting tool.

FAQ 37.119 How do I make the Domain Users group a member of the Pre-Windows 2000 Compatible Access group?

Win2K includes a Pre-Windows 2000 Compatible Access group that lets you authenticate users who connect to your network through Windows NT 4.0 RAS servers. If the Domain Users group isn't a member of the Pre-Windows 2000 Compatible Access group, perform the following steps:

1. Start the Microsoft Management Console (MMC) Active Directory Users and Computers snap-in (go to Start > Programs > Administrative Tools > Active Directory Users and Computers).
2. Select the required server and select the BUILTIN folder.
3. In the Details pane, right-click the Pre-Windows 2000 Compatible Access group and select Properties from the context menu.
4. On the Members tab, click Add (from here, you can also determine whether the Domain Users group is a member of the Pre-Windows 2000 Compatible Access Group).
5. In the Select Users > Contacts > Computers or Groups dialog box, click the Domain Users group, click Add, and click OK.
6. Verify that the Domain Users group has been added and click OK.
7. Close the Active Directory Users and Computers snap-in.

You can also enter the following command at the command line to add the Domain Users group (or another group):

```
net localgroup "Pre-Windows 2000 Compatible Access" "Domain Users"
/add
```

FAQ 37.120 Why do I receive memory or storage space errors after I install new software?

Windows XP, Windows 2000, and Windows NT all have an IRPStackSize value that controls how much physical storage space and RAM are available to new applications, and some new software installations incorrectly set this value. This value ranges from 11 to 20 for XP and from 11 to 15 for Win2K and NT. If you set this value to less than 11, you'll receive an error message indicating that the system doesn't have enough server storage. As a result, clients won't be able to access network shares, and Event ID 2011 will appear in the System log.

To set the IRPStackSize back to the default (15 for XP, 11 for NT), perform the following steps:

1. Start the Registry editor (e.g., REGEDIT.EXE).
2. Navigate to HKEY_LOCAL_MACHINE\SYSTEM\CurrentControlSet\Services\lanmanserver\parameters.
3. Double-click IRPStackSize (or if this Registry setting doesn't exist, create it of type DWORD and ensure the case is correct).
4. Change the base to decimal, set the value to 11 for Win2K or NT or 15 for XP, and click OK.
5. Reboot the computer.

FAQ 37.121 Why does my system crash and display error 0x00000054 on a blue screen?

You might receive this error message when you assign a drive letter to an unformatted drive partition. However, depending on your configuration, your machine might automatically reboot before you can diagnose the problem. Regardless of whether your machine reboots, you can view the error in the event log, which will contain the following information:

```
Event Type: Information
Event Source: Save Dump
Event Category: None
Event ID: 1001
Description: The computer has rebooted from a bugcheck.
The bugcheck was: 0x00000054 (0x003612ca, 0xf2688d00, 0x00000000,
0x00000000).
```

To resolve this error, perform one of the following actions:

- Use the Disk Management component of Windows 2000's Computer Management Microsoft Management Console (MMC) snap-in to delete the unformatted partition.
- Use the Disk Management component of Win2K's Computer Management MMC snap-in to format the partition.
- Use the Disk Management component of Win2K's Computer Management MMC snap-in to remove the drive letter.

FAQ 37.122 How can I submit a Windows crash online?

Microsoft has a site at http://oca.microsoft.com/welcome.asp, which allows you to submit details from a crash or BSOD to Microsoft and track its progress.

FAQ 37.123 Why do I get a "Failed to expand domain list" message when trying to map a network drive?

You may get a message that says "Failed to expand domain . . ." when you attempt to map a network drive using the Map Network Drive icon of Explorer under Windows NT 4.0. After displaying the message, the drive does get mapped. If you navigate through Network Neighborhood, right-click map a drive, you get no error message, and the mapping is successful.

This can be caused by Registry permissions being too tight. To correct, perform the following:

1. Start the Registry editor (REGEDT32.EXE—you need to use this editor because we are modifying permissions).
2. Move to and select HKEY_LOCAL_MACHINE\SOFTWARE\Microsoft\Windows NT\CurrentVersion\Network\World Full Access Shared Parameters.
3. Click on Security, then Permissions. Make sure Everyone (or Authenticated Users) has at least Change permission to this key and values.
4. Close the Registry editor.

38 ISA

Internet Security and Acceleration (ISA) 2000 is Microsoft's latest offering for the proxy server solution but much more, which at last offers real firewall functionality. More information can be found at http://www.microsoft.com/ISAServer.

The principals of ISA are the same as any other firewall/proxy server, but the software integrates very tightly with Windows 2000, in particular Windows 2000 security, directory, virtual private networking (VPN), and bandwidth control with Quality of Service (QoS). ISA requires either Windows 2000 Server or Windows 2000 Advanced Server. The Active Directory is not required unless you wish to implement the cache array feature that allows multiple ISA servers to be chained together.

Also new to ISA is a software development kit (SDK) that allows other third-party vendors to develop applications that can hook into ISA to perform other value-adding tasks such as virus detection and site blocking/categorization at a firewall level.

The following lists ISA features at a glance:

Multilayer firewall	Maximizes security with packet-level, circuit-level, and application-level traffic screening.
High-performance Web cache	Provides users with accelerated Web access and saves network bandwidth.
Windows 2000 integration	Manages ISA Server users, configuration, and rules with Windows 2000 Active Directory service. Authentication, management tools, and bandwidth control extend Windows 2000 technologies.
Stateful inspection	Examines data crossing the firewall in the context of its protocol and the state of the connection.
Scalability	Adds servers to scale up your cache easily and efficiently with dynamic load balancing and the Cache Array Routing Protocol (CARP). Maximizes network availability and efficient bandwidth use with distributed and hierarchical caching.

(continued)

Virtual private networking	Provides standards-based secure remote access with the integrated virtual private networking services of Windows 2000.
Detailed rules for managing traffic and enforcing policy	Controls network and Internet access by user, group, application, content type, schedule, and destination.
Broad application support	Integrates with major Internet applications using dozens of predefined protocols.
Transparency for all clients	Offers compatibility with clients and application servers on all platforms, with no client software required.
Smart application filters	Controls application-specific traffic, such as e-mail and streaming media, with data-aware filters that block only certain types of content.
Smart caching	Ensures the freshest content for each user through proactive caching of popular objects, and preloads the cache with entire Web sites on a defined schedule.
Rich administration tools	Takes advantage of powerful remote management capability, detailed logging, customizable alerts, and graphical task pads to simplify security and cache management.
Dynamic packet filtering	Reduces the risk of external attacks by opening ports only when needed.
Distributed and hierarchical caching	Maximizes availability and saves bandwidth for efficient network utilization, with multiple and backup routes.
Integrated bandwidth control	Prioritizes bandwidth allocation by group, application, site, or content type.
Secure publishing	Protects Web servers and e-commerce applications from external attacks.
Efficient content distribution	Distributes and caches Web sites and e-commerce applications, bringing Web content closer to users, improving response times and cutting bandwidth costs.
Integrated intrusion detection	Identifies common denial-of-service attacks such as port scanning, "WinNuke," and "Ping of Death."
Built-in reporting	Runs scheduled standard reports on Web usage, application usage, network traffic patterns, and security.
System hardening	Secures the operating system with multiple levels of lockdown.
Streaming media support	Saves bandwidth by splitting live media streams on the firewall.

38.1 How do I install Internet Security and Acceleration Server 2000?

To install, perform the following:

1. Either run SETUP.EXE from the ISA folder, or to run from the main dialog, run SITAUTORUN.EXE and select Install ISA Server.
2. Click Continue.
3. Enter the CD key NNN-NNNNNNN and click OK.
4. The product ID will be shown, click OK.
5. Click I Agree to the license.
6. The next screen allows you to specify the installation directory (by default, %systemDrive%\Program Files\Microsoft ISA Server) and the installation type: Full, which will install all the components and optional extras, and Custom, which enables you to select the exact components that will be installed.
7. If you selected Custom, then a list of options will be displayed. Make your selections and click Continue.
8. If you did not run the Schema update to the Active Directory, which adds the information needed for arrays, then you will be warned you cannot join an array. You will be asked whether you want to continue. Click Yes.
9. You can now select the type of ISA being installed (see Figure 38-1). Make your choice and click Continue.

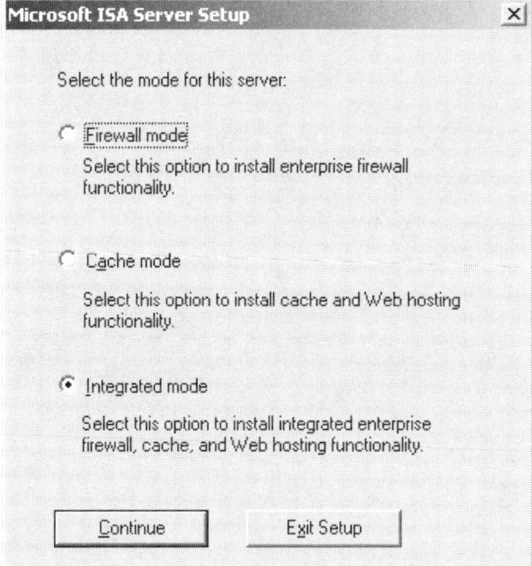

Figure 38-1 Selecting the installation mode

10. If IIS is running (which uses port 80), it will be stopped as ISA captures ports 80 and 8080. You are advised after setup to change the port the Web Publishing Service uses. Click OK.
11. If you selected Cache or Integrated mode, then you will be asked for the location of the cache. All NTFS volumes will be shown, and you should select the volume to hold the cache. Click OK.
12. You now need to enter the IP addresses that make up your internal network. Enter the From and To numbers and click Add, or you can click Table and let the service work out your table for you (make sure you select the adapter from your machine) if your network is simple. Click OK. (Notice the wizard adds the standard sets of IP addresses that are defined as internal only.) (See Figure 38-2).

    The files will now be copied over.
13. Once completed, you will be asked if you wish to start the Getting Started tutorial. Click OK.
14. Click OK to confirm the completion of the install.

You are now ready to configure ISA for use.

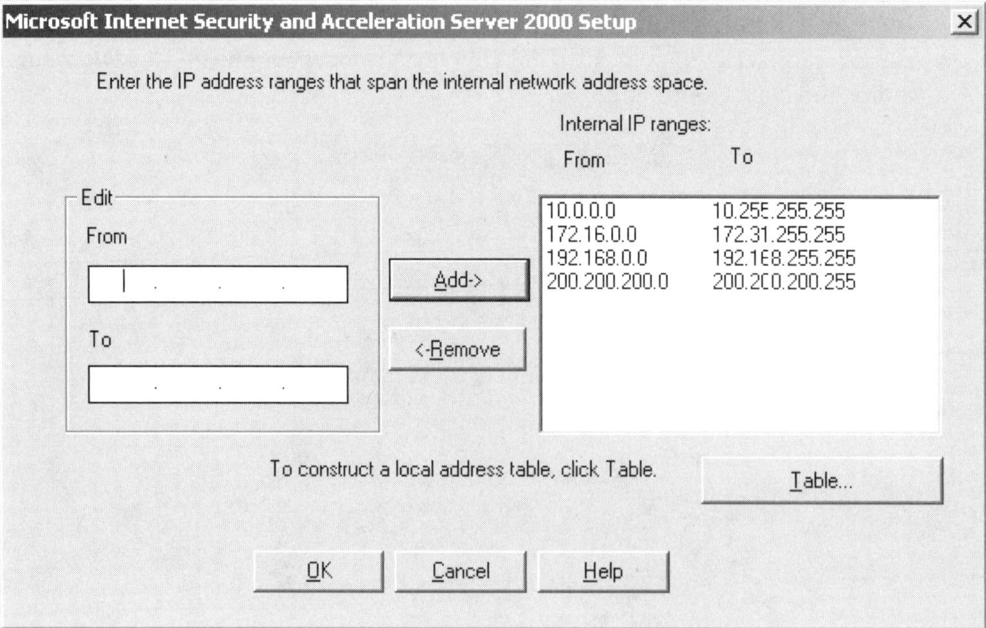

Figure 38-2 Selecting the internal IP addresses

FAQ 38.2 How do I uninstall Internet Security and Acceleration Server 2000?

As with most new Windows 2000 applications, to uninstall Internet Security and Acceleration Server 2000, you can just remove the Add/Remove Programs Control Panel applet:

1. Add/Remove Programs.
2. Select Microsoft ISA Server.
3. Click Remove.
4. Click Yes to the Are you sure you want to uninstall Microsoft Internet Security and Acceleration Server dialog.
5. The Uninstall Wizard will start.
6. Click Yes to remove the cache content, logs, and configuration backup files.
7. Click OK to confirm the uninstall completed dialog.

FAQ 38.3 After I've installed ISA, why does my Internet Connection Sharing no longer work?

You cannot have Internet Connection Sharing enabled on the same machine that ISA is installed on. If you want to use ISA, you will need to disable ICS and configure your clients to use ISA. ISA and Internet Connection Sharing are mutually exclusive.

FAQ 38.4 How do I enable outbound HTTP requests via ISA?

After installing ISA, you will find you can no longer read in pages from a remote Web site even after configuring the Web client with the proxy details. This is because you require a filter to allow requests to port 80 (HTTP):

1. Start the ISA Admin tool (Start > Programs > Microsoft ISA Server > ISA Administration Tool).
2. Expand the Arrays, the specific array, Access Policy.
3. Select IP Packet Filters.
4. Right-click New and select Filter.
5. Enter a filter name (e.g., HTTP) and click Next.

6. Select if this filter will apply to just the local server or all in the array. Click Next. The filter options—Allow packet transmission and Block packet transmission—are displayed. Select Allow and click Next.
7. Select the Custom filter type and click Next.
8. Now you must select the Filter details (see Figure 38-3):
   - IP Protocol : TCP
   - Direction: Both
   - Local Port: Dynamic (1025-5000)
   - Remote Port: Fixed port, Port number 80
9. Click Next.
10. Under the applicable section, select Default external IP address and click Next.
11. Select All remote hosts for the remote computers and click Next.
12. Check the settings and click Finish.

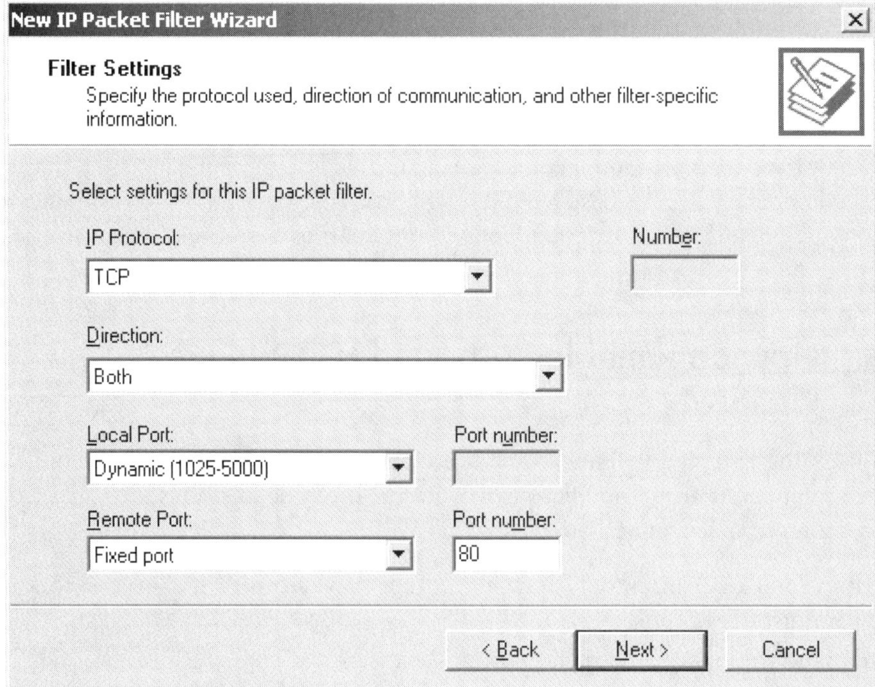

Figure 38-3 Adding a custom packet filter

FAQ 38.5 How do I enable outbound HTTP SSL requests via ISA?

This is exactly the same as the previous FAQ on enabling outbound HTTP requests except the Remote Port is 443 instead of port 80. In addition, provide the name of HTTP SSL.

FAQ 38.6 How do I disable packet filters for ISA?

This is not advisable; you should define filters for all the traffic you wish to allow. However, if you want to try something quickly, you can just disable the filter as follows:

1. Start the ISA Admin tool (Start > Programs > Microsoft ISA Server > ISA Administration Tool).
2. Expand the Arrays, the specific array, Access Policy.
3. Right-click IP Packet Filters.
4. Select Properties.
5. Unselect Enable packet filtering.
6. Click OK.

To enable again, perform the preceding, but in step 5, you select rather than unselect.

FAQ 38.7 How do I configure ISA to automatically dial out via Remote Access Service (RAS)?

If you expand your ISA array, expand Network Configuration and select Routing, you will see "Default rule". If you right-click on the default rule, select Properties, and select the Action tab, you will see "Automatically dial out," but none of your entries are shown.

You first need to run a VBS script, ADD_DOD.VBS, which is in the \sdk\samples\admin\scripts folder of the ISA CD. However, you will need to edit it first.

```
''''''''''''''''''''''''''''''''''''''''''''''''''''''''''''''''''''''''''''
'''''''''
'
' Copyright (c) 2000 Microsoft Corporation. All rights reserved.
'
```

```
''''''''''''''''''''''''''''''''''''''''''''''''''''''''''''''''''''''''
'''''''''
''''''''''''''''''''''''''''''''''''''''''''''''''''''''''''''''''''''''
'''''''''
' This script will add new Dialup Entry and set the Dialup Entry
Credentials.
' After that the script will set one Routing rule to use the new
Dialup Entry
''''''''''''''''''''''''''''''''''''''''''''''''''''''''''''''''''''''''
'''''''''

Sub SetDialupEntry()
Set ISA = CreateObject("FPC.Root")
ISA.Refresh
Set Arrays = ISA.Arrays

arrayname = InputBox("Please enter the array name, or for the first
array:")

If arrayname = "" Then
Set arr = Arrays(1)
Else
' Look for the specified array
On Error Resume Next
Set arr = Arrays(arrayname)

If Err.Number <> 0 Then
MsgBox "The array specified array was not found"
Exit Sub
End If
End If

'Add Dialup Entry
Set objDialupEntry = Arr.PolicyElements.DialupEntries.Add
("ISA_DISPLAY", "RAS_ENTRY")
'Set the Dialup entry credentials
objDialupEntry.Credentials.UserName = "UserName" 'Enter here your
username
objDialupEntry.Credentials.Password = "Password" 'Enter here your
password
objDialupEntry.AuthenticationEnabled = True
Arr.Save
```

```
Arr.Refresh

'Select routing rule and set the Autodial to the added Dialup Entry
Set objRoutingRule= arr.NetworkConfiguration.RoutingRules(1)
objRoutingRule.PrimaryRoute.AutoDialOut.SetAutoDial True,
"ISA_DISPLAY" objRoutingRule.Save

MsgBox "Done"
End Sub

SetDialupEntry
```

You need to change the underlined items. The first, ISA_DISPLAY, should be the display name as it should be displayed in ISA; the next is the actual RAS entry name. Set the correct connection username and password. Finally, set the autodialout to the dialout entry name.

Now double-click the VBS file; you will be asked for the array (just press Enter). Once done, the dial-up entry should be selected under the Default Rule.

If you have any problems and want to remove the dial-up entries, run REMOVE_UNUSED_DIALUPENTRIES.VBS script in the same directory and try again!

FAQ 38.8 How do I install the ISA client?

When you install the Internet Security and Acceleration (ISA) Server software, it includes a firewall client that is located in the %systemdrive%\Program Files\Microsoft ISA Server\clients directory and shares the folder as mspclnt.

To install this client, perform the following steps:

1. Connect to the mspclnt share on the ISA server.
2. Run SETUP.EXE.
3. Click Continue.
4. Click Install Microsoft Firewall Client.
5. Click OK.

All IP connectivity will now be routed via the ISA Server. To configure the client, use the Firewall Client Control Panel applet, which lets you select the ISA Server.

FAQ 38.9 How do I enable NNTP/POP/SMTP for the ISA Server?

To enable clients to access news servers (Network News Transfer Protocol—NNTP), POP3, and SMTP, you need to create custom filters with the following details:

- NNTP—Custom, Both, Local Fixed Port 119, Remote Fixed Port 119
- POP3—Custom, Both, Local Fixed Port 110, Remote Fixed Port 110
- SMTP—Custom, Both, Local Fixed Port 25, Remote Fixed Port 25

For example, to create an NNTP filter, perform the following steps:

1. Start the ISA Server administration tool (Start > Programs > Microsoft ISA Server > ISA Administration Tool).
2. Expand Array > Server > Access Policy > IP Packet Filters.
3. Click Create Packet Filter.
4. Enter a packet filter name (e.g., NNTP Filter) and click Next.
5. Select the server and click Next.
6. Select Allow packet transmission and click Next.
7. Select a type of Custom and click Next.
8. Select the following options:
    - IP protocol—TCP
    - Direction—Both
    - Local fixed port—119
    - Remote fixed port—119
9. Click Next.
10. Select the IP address to apply the filter to and click Next.
11. Select All remote computers for IP packet filter to apply to and click Next.
12. Click Finish.

The preceding method is manually creating an IP packet filter to cater for the protocols; however, ISA can also dynamically create them if you instead create a protocol rule:

1. Start the Internet Security and Acceleration Server administration tool (Start > Programs > Microsoft ISA Server > ISA Administration Tool).
2. Expand the Array > Server > Access Policy > Protocol Rules.
3. Create a new protocol rule or open an existing one.

4. Select the Protocol tab.
5. Select the SMTP (client), NNTP, and POP3 protocols.
6. Click OK.

This would be the preferred method and is easier. If you're running one of those services directly on your ISA server, then IP Packet Filters may have to be defined.

FAQ 38.10 I have just installed the ISA Server. When I try to use my Web browser from one of my client computers, I get the message "502 Proxy Error", and the client computer can't view any Web pages. What causes this?

First, check that the system isn't filtering the packets. If the system isn't filtering packets, you need to create a protocol rule. (You do this by selecting the array, then going to Access Policy, Protocol Rules.) To get your clients up and running quickly, you can create a blanket protocol rule:

1. Right-click Protocol Rules and select New > Rule.
2. Enter a name for your rule (e.g., Default).
3. Select Allow responses to client requests.
4. Select Apply this rule to All IP Traffic.
5. Select Use this schedule Always.
6. Select Apply this rule to requests from any user, group, or client computer.
7. Click Finish to save your rule.

Note: *You should use this blanket rule only as a quick method of giving access to client computers for testing purposes. By following the preceding steps, you are letting **any** client access **any** IP port. After you complete the testing, you should create a more restrictive rule.*

FAQ 38.11 How do I uninstall the ISA Server client?

First, be aware that removing the ISA client application prevents client computers from accessing external IP addresses that they can access via ISA. To remove the ISA client application, perform the following steps:

1. Start the Add/Remove Programs Control Panel applet (Start > Settings > Control Panel > Add/Remove Programs).
2. Select Microsoft Firewall Client.
3. Click Remove.
4. Click Yes to the confirmation.

The Firewall Client uninstall program will run and then ask you to reboot the computer.

FAQ 38.12 Why won't ISA Server let me input the whole username for my dial-up entry?

The ISA Server 2000 GUI doesn't let you enter a username longer than 20 characters (Arrays > Array name > Policy Elements > Dial-up Entries). It also doesn't let you specify a name with more than 20 characters via VBScript. Thus, you have to enter a shorter name, and when you try to connect to a Web site from another computer, ISA returns an error that the dial-up failed, and you then must connect manually.

To work around the problem, you must manually enter your username in the Registry. However, be aware that if you subsequently attempt to view the information in the ISA GUI, the GUI will report that the data is too long or contains an invalid character. Take the following steps to enter the username in the Registry:

1. Start REGEDIT.EXE.
2. Go to HKEY_LOCAL_MACHINE\SOFTWARE\Microsoft\Fpc\Arrays\[your array GUID]\PolicyElements\DialupEntries\[entry GUID]\Credentials.
3. Double-click msFPCUserName.
4. Set the value to the correct name and click OK.
5. Close Regedit.

Note: *"GUID" in the previously shown Registry key stands for "globally unique ID." If you have multiple arrays and aren't sure of the GUID, open each array GUID in turn and change the msFPCUserName. Then for the dial-up entry, select each GUID in turn and change the msFPCUserName.*

FAQ 38.13 Can I install the ISA firewall client on the ISA Server?

No, ISA Server 2000 doesn't support this configuration (although I've seen it work). Granted, this approach seems like the logical solution to the problem that all the ISA clients can see the Internet resources via the ISA Server but the ISA Server itself can't view anything. However, you shouldn't install the client on the server.

Instead, to grant the ISA Server access to resources, you must configure packet filters. For example, if you want to allow outbound Web server access, create a packet filter that allows outbound requests to TCP 80.

FAQ 38.14 Why is my ISA Server using 50 percent of available memory for the RAM proxy cache?

By default, ISA Server 2000 uses 50 percent of the available memory for a RAM-based proxy cache. To modify the amount ISA Server uses, perform the following steps:

1. Start the Microsoft Management Console (MMC) ISA Server Admin snap-in (Start > Programs > Microsoft ISA Server > ISA Management).
2. Right-click the Cache Configuration branch and select Properties.
3. Select the Advanced tab.
4. For Percentage of free memory to use for caching, change the number from 50 (the default) to the value you want (e.g., 5—see Figure 38-4).
5. Click OK. When the system prompts you, choose to either save changes but not restart the service or save changes and restart the service. Click OK.

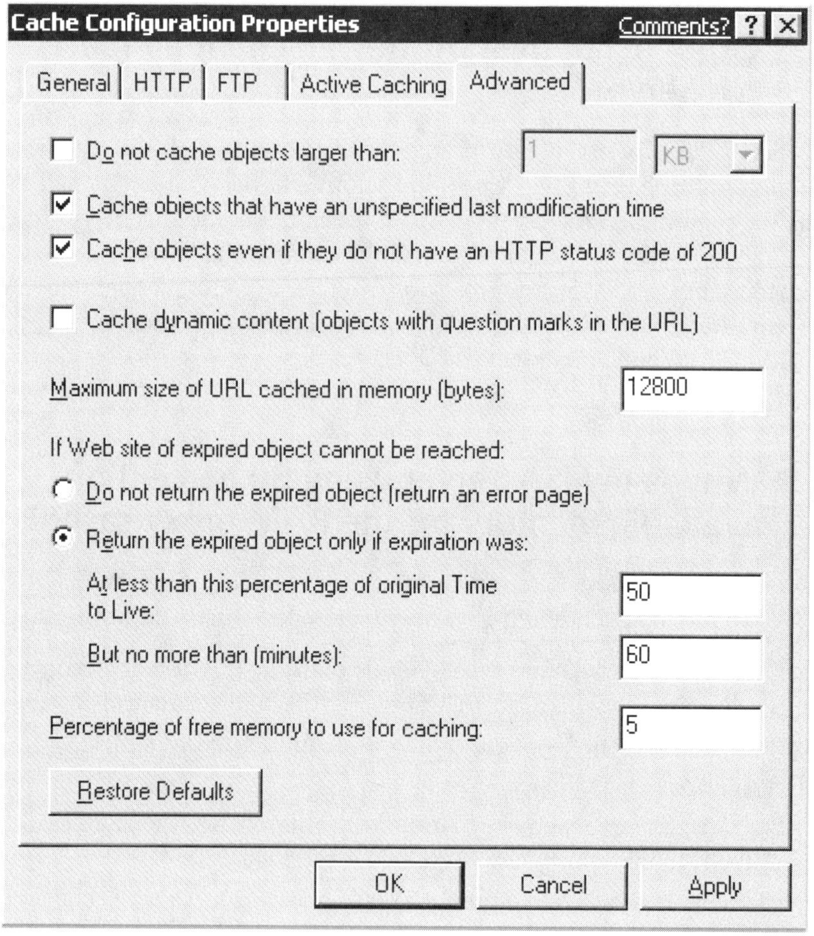

Cache Configuration Properties
Comments? ? ×

General | HTTP | FTP | Active Caching | Advanced

☐ Do not cache objects larger than: 1 KB

☑ Cache objects that have an unspecified last modification time

☑ Cache objects even if they do not have an HTTP status code of 200

☐ Cache dynamic content (objects with question marks in the URL)

Maximum size of URL cached in memory (bytes): 12800

If Web site of expired object cannot be reached:

○ Do not return the expired object (return an error page)

◉ Return the expired object only if expiration was:

At less than this percentage of original Time to Live: 50

But no more than (minutes): 60

Percentage of free memory to use for caching: 5

Restore Defaults

OK Cancel Apply

Figure 38-4 Setting cache options

INDEX

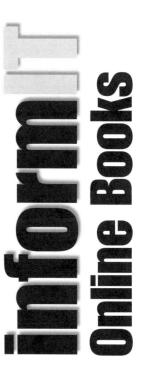